Routledge International Handbook of Consumer Psychology

This unique handbook maps the growing field of consumer psychology in its increasingly global context. With contributions from over 70 scholars across four continents, the book reflects the cross-cultural and multidisciplinary character of the field. Chapters relate the key consumer concepts to the progressive globalization of markets in which consumers act and consumption takes place.

The book is divided into seven sections, offering a truly comprehensive reference work that covers:

- The historical foundations of the discipline and the rise of globalization
- The role of cognition and multisensory perception in consumers' judgements
- The social self, identity and well-being, including their relation to advertising
- Social and cultural influences on consumption, including politics and religion
- Decision making, attitudes and behaviourally based research
- Sustainable consumption and the role of branding
- The particularities of online settings in framing and affecting behaviour

The *Routledge International Handbook of Consumer Psychology* will be essential reading for anyone interested in how the perceptions, feelings and values of consumers interact with the decisions they make in relation to products and services in a global context. It will also be key reading for students and researchers across psychology and marketing, as well as professionals interested in a deeper understanding of the field.

Cathrine V. Jansson-Boyd is a reader in consumer psychology at Anglia Ruskin University, Cambridge, UK. Her areas of research include tactile perception, aesthetics and sustainability. She has conducted research for many large organizations to further the understanding of various aspects of consumer perception. Her work has been published in both books and journals.

Magdalena J. Zawisza is a senior lecturer in psychology at Anglia Ruskin University, Cambridge, UK. She obtained her PhD from Royal Holloway, University of London, UK and MSc from Gdansk University, Poland. Her main research interests include consumer, gender and social psychology. She employs quantitative methodology in her research and consultancy.

The Routledge International Handbook Series

For further information and the full range of titles, see www.routledge.com/series/RIHAND

The Routledge International Handbook of Psychosocial Resilience
Edited by Updesh Kumar

The Routledge International Handbook of Intercultural Arts Research
Edited by Pamela Burnard, Elizabeth MacKinlay and Kimberly Powell

The Routledge International Handbook of Philosophies and Theories of Early Childhood Education and Care
Edited by Tricia David, Kathy Goouch and Sacha Powell

The Routledge International Handbook of Early Childhood Education
Edited by Tony Bertram, John Bennett, Philip Gammage and Christine Pascal

Routledge International Handbook of Educational Effectiveness
Edited by Christopher Chapman, Daniel Muijs, David Reynolds, Pam Sammons and Charles Teddlie

The Routledge International Handbook of Research on Teaching Thinking
Edited by Rupert Wegerif, James Kaufman and Li Li

The Routledge International Handbook of Social Psychology of the Classroom
Edited by Christine Rubie-Davies, Jason Stephens and Penelope Watson

International Handbook of E-learning, Volume 2: Implementation and Case Studies
Edited by Mohamed Ally and Badrul H. Khan

International Handbook of E-learning, Volume 1: Theoretical Perspectives and Research
Edited by Badrul H. Khan and Mohamed Ally

The Routledge International Handbook of the Arts and Education
Edited by Mike Fleming, John O'Toole and Loira Bresler

The Routledge International Handbook of Dyscalculia and Mathematical Learning Difficulties
Edited by Steve Chinn

The Routledge International Handbook of Young Children's Thinking and Understanding
Edited by Sue Robson and Suzanne Flannery Quinn

Routledge International Handbook of Consumer Psychology

Edited by
Cathrine V. Jansson-Boyd
Magdalena J. Zawisza

Routledge
Taylor & Francis Group
LONDON AND NEW YORK

First published 2017
by Routledge
4 Park Square, Milton Park, Abingdon, Oxon OX14 4RN
605 Third Avenue, New York, NY 10017

First issued in paperback 2022

Routledge is an imprint of the Taylor & Francis Group, an informa business

Publisher's Note
The publisher has gone to great lengths to ensure the quality of this reprint but points out that some imperfections in the original copies may be apparent.

British Library Cataloguing in Publication Data
A catalogue record for this book is available from the British Library

Library of Congress Cataloging-in-Publication Data
Names: Jansson-Boyd, Cathrine V., editor. | Zawisza, Magdalena J., editor.
Title: Routledge international handbook of consumer psychology/edited by Cathrine V. Jansson-Boyd, Magdalena J. Zawisza.
Other titles: Handbook of consumer psychology.
Description: First Edition. | New York: Routledge, 2017. |
Series: Routledge international handbooks | Includes bibliographical references and index.
Identifiers: LCCN 2016019225 | ISBN 9781138846494 (hardback: alk. paper) | ISBN 9781315727448 (ebk)
Subjects: LCSH: Consumer behavior–Psychological aspects. | Consumers–Psychology. | Marketing–Psychological aspects.
Classification: LCC HF5415.32 .R688 2017 | DDC 658.8/342–dc23
LC record available at https://lccn.loc.gov/2016019225

ISBN 13: 978-1-138-84649-4 (hbk)
ISBN 13: 978-1-03-247708-4 (pbk)
ISBN 13: 978-1-315-72744-8 (ebk)

DOI: 10.4324/9781315727448

Typeset in Bembo
by Deanta Global Publishing Services, Chennai, India

Contents

Figures

Tables

Preface

Consumer psychology has enjoyed a continuous increasing interest. In particular, there has been a growth in the number of researchers engaging in this scholarly field in Europe, Asia and Australasia. Hence, what used to be a field dominated by researchers from North America, has become more of an international subject area. This is reflective of the fact that people these days are avid travellers and many emigrate and settle in different countries. This global mobility poses new challenges to marketers when establishing who their target audiences are. Thus, it seemed timely to publish the first *International handbook of consumer psychology*. The aim of this book is to provide, for the first time, an outline of the current state of research on a wide range of areas within consumer psychology in its increasingly global context.

We invited 71 authors to contribute to this handbook. Not coincidentally, these authors are based in 11 different countries on four continents: Canada, Germany, Spain, USA, China, Poland, the United Kingdom, Austria, Sweden, Australia and Korea. Many of the contributors are originally from a different country than the one they currently reside in. Where suitable, the authors have emphasized cross-culturally relevant research to emphasize the international aspect of this book. This book is written by authors with an extensive knowledge of their respective fields, who come from a range of different cultural backgrounds. Hence, it presents consumer psychology in a comprehensive manner that should appeal to an international audience.

This handbook is divided into seven sections, each focusing on a different consumer-related theme. The first section includes a historical perspective of the rise of consumerism and an outline of some of the early researchers that laid the foundation for consumer psychology. Additionally, the first section includes two chapters specifically exploring cross-culturally based consumer issues. One of the chapters offers a review of research conducted within cross-cultural consumption contexts and its focal point is the meaning of consumption. The other chapter focuses on the globalization of consumption. It explores aspects such as how brands may have different cultural meanings and how this may influence consumer behaviour.

In the second section, the focus turns to consumer cognition and perception. Different modalities are looked at and, in particular, visual attention and tactile input are emphasized. Judgement and decision making is another sub-theme and it is explored in terms of procedural knowledge. This is mainly done within a cognitively based framework. Finally, this section also deals with how consumers are affected by unconsciousness and how it may be measured.

The third section looks at aspects linked to social perception, the self in consumption, identity and general well-being. The chapters explore the relationships between perception of the self, others and different brands, as well as how consumers compare themselves to those advertising products and services. Questions are asked about the reciprocal relation between the self and consumption, the role of self-congruity in consumer behaviour and whether the universal dimensions of social perception apply to consumer context. This section also tackles the importance of body imagery and aspects of healthy food intake. The negative effects of the media on body image on one side and the obesity crisis on the other are discussed alongside preventative interventions and policy recommendations.

In the fourth section, the authors delve into different aspects of social and cultural influences. Here the discussion centres on politics, religion, the role of money in consumption and the vulnerability of young consumers. Similarities and differences between political and mainstream marketing are explored and followed by a discussion of the economic and social consequences of money. Next, this section turns to an examination of the role of religious and non-religious beliefs in consumer behaviour and to questions of the extent to which children are vulnerable to commercials and advergames.

Section five looks at decision making, attitudes and behaviourally based research. It provides insight into how consumer decisions are affected by the way in which information is framed, as well as how their attitudes can be altered. The role of implementation intentions at various stages of consumer behaviour is explored alongside classic topics regarding persuasion processes, mental cost–benefit trade-offs, consumers' naïve theories involved in decisions and self-control dilemmas in pursuit of long-term consumption goals. Further, examples are provided with regards to how intentions, sex drive and the age of a consumer influence thought processes and behaviours. Other aspects of exploration in this section include links between consumer processing, motivations and emotions.

Products, branding preferences and sustainability are the themes of the sixth section. Psychological theories and research relevant to understanding sustainable consumption are reviewed followed by a consideration of the case of public transport. Other areas of research covered include the underlying value of the forms that products take. Examples include an overview of the concept of branding with its complex relations to functional, symbolic and experiential brand benefits as well as the discussion of the antecedents, underlying mechanism and consequences of aesthetics and brand anthropomorphism in consumer context.

In the final seventh section, the focus turns to the Internet and electronic media including computer games. The discussion features the particularities of social influence in the online vs. offline settings, a consideration of individual differences both in terms of the media user as well as the representations made through these mediums and the concept of "customized advertising" in the digital world of e-commerce.

We are hoping that scholars, researchers, practitioners and students around the globe will enjoy this book. Even though this handbook is aimed at those interested in a particular area of consumer psychology, we believe that it is also of value to all those who work in any closely related disciplines such as marketing or behavioural economics. Let us take you on the international journey of consumer psychology. We direct our thanks to all the contributing authors without whom this fascinating journey would not be possible.

Cathrine V. Jansson-Boyd
Magdalena J. Zawisza

Contributors

Pankaj Aggarwal, Department of Management, University of Toronto, Canada

Russell Belk, Schulich School of Business, York University, Canada

Maik Bieleke, Department of Psychology, University of Konstanz, Germany, and Graduate School of Decision Sciences, University of Konstanz, Germany

Pablo Briñol, Department of Psychology, Universidad Autónoma de Madrid, Spain

C. Clark Cao, Department of Marketing, Eller College of Management, University of Arizona, USA

Stephanie M. Carpenter, Department of Marketing, Ross School of Business and Department of Psychology, University of Michigan, USA

Rui Chen, Advertising Department, School of Journalism and Communication, Xiamen University, China

Maria L. Cronley, Farmer School of Business, Miami University, USA

Wojciech Cwalina, Department of Psychology, University of Social Sciences and Humanities, Warsaw, Poland

Hélène Deval, Rowe School of Business, Dalhousie University, Canada

Phillippa C. Diedrichs, Centre for Appearance Research, University of the West of England, UK

Karen E. Dill-Shackleford, School of Psychology, Fielding Graduate University, USA

Claudiu V. Dimofte, Department of Marketing, San Diego State University, USA

Helga Dittmar, School of Psychology, University of Sussex, UK

Andrzej Falkowski, Department of Marketing Psychology, University of Social Sciences and Humanities, Warsaw, Poland

Arnd Florack, Department of Psychology, University of Vienna, Austria

Susan Forquer Gupta, Department of Marketing and International Business, Monmouth University, USA

Margareta Friman, Department of Psychology, Karlstad University, Sweden

Agata Gasiorowska, Faculty in Wroclaw, SWPS University of Social Sciences and Humanities, Poland

Tommy Gärling, Department of Psychology, University of Gothenburg, Göteborg, and Karlstad University, Sweden

Peter M. Gollwitzer, Department of Psychology, New York University, USA, and Department of Psychology, University of Konstanz, Germany

Aiden Gregg, Department of Psychology, University of Southampton, UK

Eda Gurel-Atay, Independent Researcher, USA

Emma Halliwell, Centre for Appearance Research, University of the West of England, UK

Michael Häfner, Department of Psychology, Berlin University of the Arts, Germany

Megan Hurst, School of Applied Social Sciences, University of Brighton, UK

J. Wesley Hutchinson, Department of Marketing, Wharton School, University of Pennsylvania, USA

Cathrine V. Jansson-Boyd, Department of Psychology, Anglia Ruskin University, Cambridge, UK

Lynn R. Kahle, Lundquist College of Business, University of Oregon, USA

Bernadette Kamleitner, Department of Marketing, Vienna University of Economics and Business, Austria

Frank R. Kardes, Lindner College of Business, University of Cincinnati, USA

Tobias Krüger, Department of Psychology, University of Heidelberg, Germany

Aparna A. Labroo, Kellogg School of Management, Northwestern University, USA

Claire Lambert, School of Business, Edith Cowan University, Australia

Cait Lamberton, Katz Graduate School of Business, University of Pittsburgh, USA

Alvin Lee, BL Deakin Business School, Deakin University, Australia

Dong-Jin Lee, School of Business, Yonsei University, Korea

Maggie Wenjing Liu, School of Economics and Management, Tsinghua University, China

Joy Lu, Department of Marketing, The Wharton School, University of Pennsylvania, USA

Dominika Maison, Department of Psychology, University of Warsaw, Poland

Nigel Marlow, Innovation Bubble, UK

Sandra Matz, The Psychometrics Centre, University of Cambridge, UK

Ann L. McGill, Booth School of Business, University of Chicago, USA

Elizabeth A. Minton, Department of Marketing, University of Wyoming, USA

Dick Mizerski, Marketing Department, University of Western Australia

Bruce I. Newman, Driehaus College of Business, DePaul University, Chicago, USA

Johanna Palcu, Department of Psychology, University of Vienna, Austria

Richard E. Petty, Department of Psychology, Ohio State University, USA

Anastasiya Pocheptsova, Moore School of Business, University of South Carolina, USA

Susan Powell Mantel, Department of Marketing, Ball State University, USA

Martin Reimann, Department of Marketing, University of Arizona, USA

María Rodas, Carlson School of Management, University of Minnesota, USA

Ruta Ruzeviciute, Institute for Marketing and Consumer Research, Vienna University of Economics and Business, Austria

Paschal Sheeran, Department of Psychology, University of North Carolina at Chapel Hill, USA

M. Joseph Sirgy, Department of Marketing, Virginia Polytechnic Institute & State University, USA

Lara Spiteri-Cornish, School of Marketing and Management, University of Coventry, UK

Melody A. Stotler, Media Psychology Department, Fielding Graduate University, USA

Jacob Teeny, Department of Psychology, Ohio State University, USA

Carlos J. Torelli, Department of Business Administration, University of Illinois at Urbana-Champaign, USA

Tobias Vogel, Department of Psychology, University of Mannheim, Germany

Rebecca Walker Reczek, Fisher College of Business, The Ohio State University, USA

Shasha Wang, Business School, University of Western Australia

Michaela Wänke, Department of Psychology, University of Mannheim, Germany

Evan Weingarten, Department of Marketing, The Wharton School, University of Pennsylvania, USA

Robert S. Wyer, Jr., CUHK Business School, The Chinese University of Hong Kong, China

Carolyn Yoon, Department of Marketing, Ross School of Business, Institute for Social Research, University of Michigan, USA

Grace B. Yu, Department of Business Administration, Duksung Women's University, Korea

Tomasz Zaleskiewicz, SWPS University of Social Sciences and Humanities, Faculty in Wroclaw, Poland

Magdalena J. Zawisza, Department of Psychology, Anglia Ruskin University, Cambridge, UK

Abbreviations

AIDA	Attention, Interest, Desire, Action
ANGELO	Analysis Grid for Environments Linked to Obesity
ANT	autotelic need for touch
APA	American Psychological Association
ASA	Advertising Standards Authority
AT&T	American telecommunications company (acronym defunct)
BBC	British Broadcasting Company
BIAF	Brands as Intentional Agents Framework
BIAS	Behaviours form Intergroup Affect and Stereotypes
BIAT	Brief Implicit Association Test
BMI	body mass index
BSE	breast self-examination
CBS	Columbia Broadcasting System
CSI	consumer style index
DIA	Double Interest Account
EAST	Extrinsic Affective Simon Task
EES	Emotional Eating Scale
fMRI	functional magnetic resonance imaging
FTC	Federal Trade Commission
GNAT	Go No-Go Association Test
HMM	hidden Markov model
IAT	Implicit Association Test
IAT-RF	Recoding Free Implicit Association Test
INT	instrumental need for touch
IRAP	Implicit Relational Assessment Procedure
ITC	inferotemporal cortex
ITV	Independent Television
KDKA	Pennsylvanian broadcaster
LIPC	left inferior prefrontal cortex
MNC	multinational corporation
mPFC	medial prefrontal cortex
NBC	National Broadcasting Company
NES	National Election Studies
NFC	need for cognition
NFT	need for touch
PI	purchase intent

PPC	posterior parietal cortex
PSA	public service announcement
RT	reaction time
SAT	Simple Association Test
SB-IAT	Single-Block Implicit Association Test
SC-IAT	Single-Category IAT
SCM	Stereotype Content Model
SEM	structural equation modelling
SPF	Sorted Paired Features Task
TRA	theory of reasoned action
vmPFC	ventromedial prefrontal cortex
VNS	Voter News Service

Part I

Introduction and cross-cultural research

1

The history of consumer psychology

Cathrine V. Jansson-Boyd and Nigel Marlow

> There is no escaping the fact that modern day humans live in a culture of consumption.
>
> *Kasser & Kanner, 2002, p. 3*

It is astounding how much people consume. For example, in 2014, the American toy market grew to a value of $18.1 billion (Toy Association, 2015). In 2013, the coffee shop industry in the United Kingdom was worth £5.8 billion, and over 74 million units of LCD TVs were sold in Asia. Moreover, in 2015, 74 million automobiles were sold worldwide (Statista, 2015). With figures such as the aforementioned, it is hardly surprising that what people consume plays a key part in their lives. Consumerism is hardly a new concept. At first glance, historically it appears that people have been interested in consuming for as long as they have existed. From a survival point of view, this is almost obvious, because early humans would have to have been interested in feeding and clothing themselves, providing shelter etc. in order to survive. These processes would have involved what might be termed "natural consumption". By *natural*, we are implying that the consumption came from readily available resources. Food was provided for by hunting and gathering; shelter was fashioned from resources already existing in the ecosystem, for example cave-dwellings or huts built from branches and woven reeds. This "natural consumption" provided the minimum for survival. It was literally living "hand-to-mouth". The step-change, of course, was the development of farming.

Agriculture was also a step-change in the relationship that humans had with nature. It represents intervention and *control* over nature. This control allowed nomadic people to settle; life became much more predictable, and importantly, the nascent farming communities could for the first time produce *more than they needed to survive*. This excess then became available for stockpiling and, more importantly, exchange and trading. The exchange and trading of produce also involved non-agricultural goods, and it can be readily imagined how this process developed into trading systems involving a variety of craft-manufactured goods, which included, for example, pottery, jewellery, fine fabric and perfumes. Note how the "things" being consumed changed in nature. Paradoxically, consumption changed from being "natural" (that which is found in nature) to a mixture of natural and manufactured. Note also how the benefits to the consumer subtly changed. We can see how agricultural products benefit the *survival* of the consumer, but what benefits do jewellery, fine fabric or perfume bestow? The answer to this question is the key to today's consumption patterns; the benefits of such products are mainly *psychological*. Jewellery and perfume are not *functional* in any great practical sense; their value lies in the realms of "love and belonging" and "self-esteem". These are psychological concepts and exist only as ethereal constructs in the minds of people. Hence, a change can be identified in *what* is being consumed in the societies developing out of the early agricultural economies. Perhaps we should say that the change is in *why* it is being consumed. There is a shift in emphasis from the consumption of the *functional* towards the consumption of the *psychological*.

The historical "journey" of consumption is truly fascinating. Alongside this journey, there has been a scientific interest in understanding the relationship between consumption and humans. Gradually, we have seen the discipline of consumer psychology emerge, and it is centred on the study of human responses to products, service-related information and experiences. Effectively, consumer psychology "is about understanding why and how individuals and groups engage in consumer activities, as well as how they are affected by them" (Jansson-Boyd, 2010, p. 1). It is beyond the scope of this chapter to outline all that is related to the history of consumer psychology. Hence, we here attempt to present a global "snapshot" of the history of consumption and the research conducted since the mid-1800s. It seems logical to start from this time period, as this is when the Industrial Revolution spread throughout Europe and North America. Fuelled by industrial developments, it made consumption accessible to a mass audience. That is not to say that we are dismissive of any consumer-related developments prior to this time, but simply that we are focusing on the outlined time period in order to be able to fit the information into this chapter.

Rapid development of consumerism

In 1712, Thomas Newcomen installed a new type of water pump at a mine in the United Kingdom that could effectively remove floodwater from mines. It was the first commercially successful steam engine and marked the onset of the Industrial Revolution. Additionally, it was also the early beginnings of people becoming consumers of the railways. Newcomen's engine was developed further by James Watt and Matthew Boulton during the 1770s. Thereafter, technology developed swiftly. One example of newly developed technology was put on show in 1804, when the world saw the first steam-driven railway journey in Wales. However, it was not until 1830 that the first public railway opened in the United Kingdom, and travelling by rail became a common mode of transport.

During the seventeenth century, cotton fabric became popular as it was easier to wash. To start with, cotton clothing was imported from India. However, this changed when James Hargreaves invented the Spinning Jenny (a multi-spindle spinning frame) and Richard Arkwright created the Water Frame (a water-powered spinning frame) during the 1760s. By the 1790s, Britain was producing over a million cotton garments a year, making clothing more readily accessible to consumers. There was also a gradual change in how food was produced. With an increasing population, it was clear that new ideas about farming were required. New technologies meant that more food could be produced from the same area of land. Large areas of land were also made usable through drainage and deforestation. This was also the onset of producing more food than was needed. The fact that there was an overall increase in the production of different types of goods meant that the way they were sold also changed.

The retail revolution

Small shops were common during the 1700s and 1800s. Many were of a specialist nature, e.g., bakeries, butchers and so on. However, during 1796 a development that would change the retail structure took place: the opening of Harding, Howell & Co. in London (BBC, 2014). This was the forerunner to the department store concept and the onset of a shift away from small shops. Harding, Howell & Co. catered for the fashion-conscious women of the time. For unknown reasons, it closed in 1820, even though it is said to have been a success (Stories of London, 2015). It was not until over 30 years later that the world saw the first proper department store, when Le Bon Marché opened in Paris in 1852. Soon others followed: Macy's opened in New York in 1878, the current Harrods store in London was built between 1894 and 1905 and thereafter the world gradually became accustomed to large retail spaces that offered a wide range of products.

The retail landscape was to change once more during the 1920s, when mail-order catalogues became popular (Boorstin, 1973), meaning that people could shop from the comfort of their own homes. It was also during this time period that drive-in restaurants popped up all over the United States (Green, 1992), perhaps a natural development as the automobile was becoming the favoured mode of transport for consumers.

The development of radio

In 1893, early work on wireless radio communication by Nikolai Tesla (a Serbian-born inventor who had immigrated to America) marked the very early beginnings of creating radio. However, he was not the only person researching wireless communication. A German professor of physics at the Karlsruhe Polytechnic, by the name of Heinrich Rudolf Hertz, was hard at work in his laboratory between 1885 and 1889. Hertz established beyond doubt that light and heat are electromagnetic radiations. The waves were called Hertzian at first, and later on radio waves (Britannica, 2015a). In 1894, an Italian by the name of Guiglielmo Marconi became interested in Hertz's work and used his "invisible waves" to build wave-generating equipment that could send signals to locations further afield (History, 2015). Marconi took his idea to England in 1896. He was backed by the British Post Office to further his development, and in 1899 his signals crossed the English Channel.

Commercial radio broadcasting in the United States started in 1920 with the first officially government-licensed radio station, KDKA. Not long after, there were thousands of radio stations that reached people who had bought or built their own receivers. The government did not want people to be able to simply build their own radios, and therefore the Radio Corporation Agreements was formed to manage patents for the radio technology used, giving AT&T the monopoly over toll broadcasting. The control also paved the way for radio advertising. However, the fact that AT&T had control over radio advertising caused conflict with other radio stations owned by businesses that wished to advertise their own products. National Broadcasting Company (NBC) and Columbia Broadcasting System (CBS), two broadcasting companies, were created as a solution to break the monopoly in the late 1920s.This meant that radio listeners were exposed to a wider range of advertising and consequently were encouraged to buy more.

Marconi's technology also helped the British Broadcasting Company (BBC) in the United Kingdom, which began transmitting in 1922. In the United Kingdom, the newspaper industry was a fierce rival to the radio. This, however, changed in 1926, when newspapers in England went on strike and it was up to the radio to supply the public with information. Soon the radio was introduced elsewhere, and broadcasting started in Japan in 1925 (Japan Radio, 2015). Radio continued to grow globally with the introduction of different types of radio programmes and stations. For example, in 1926, there were over 20 million listeners in the United States. However, broadcasters had a limited understanding of their audiences. This is why the NBC asked Professor Daniel Starch to conduct a study of their audience. In 1929 he concluded his report, and one of the findings was that one-third of the 30 million homes in the United States had radio access (Spalding, 1963). The radio continued to increase in popularity, and in particular, it became the source of information during the world wars.

The development of mass production

Approximately at the same time as the radio was being developed, other technological advancements were made. One piece of technology in particular, the creation of the assembly line, contributed significantly to a dramatic increase in consumption.

Henry Ford had the dream of ensuring that every person in America had a car. He was continuously searching for ways to make the car manufacturing process quicker and more efficient. Ford was looking for solutions to do so from continuous-flow productions used by breweries and flour mills. The result was that in 1913 he started using the first moving assembly line to produce his automobiles (History, 2014). This new idea reduced the time it took to build a car by a factor of four, and also allowed the replacement of skilled craftsmen by unskilled machine operators. Consequently, Ford cars were soon cheaper and more numerous than the competition. The advantages of Ford's assembly line were quickly spotted by other industries, and manufacturers adapted and adopted the main tenets of mass production. The characteristics of "Fordism" can be seen throughout the world today in all areas of the manufacturing and service industries.

The assembly line was undoubtedly the first big step towards mass production and mass consumption, and it decreased the prices of goods sold. The result was a clear increase in consumption. However, mass production was slowed down by the two world wars, even though it soon picked up again afterwards. Hence, it was only in the 1950s that mass production became truly commonplace.

Advertising

The Industrial Revolution and the techniques of mass manufacturing that emerged thereafter made the role of advertising essential in order to fuel sales. Without it, people would not be aware of the existence of goods and services; hence, sales would dwindle and in turn slow down manufacturing. Consequently, it was advertisers' job to ensure that they created a "want" for the produced goods and services so that manufacturers could supply the products that would satisfy consumers' wants (Kotler, 1997). In this process, the importance of "brands" became apparent. Consequently, this moulded the advertising industry, in that it became important to assign unique labels and advantages to products, and so the Unique Selling Proposition was born (Fennis & Stroebe, 2010).

It was James Gordon Bennett, publisher of the *New York Herald* from 1835 to 1867, who came up with the idea of raising the cost of advertisements to lower the cost of newspapers, something that is still common practice today. He also changed how frequently the ads were published. Long into the nineteenth century, it was normal to repeat the same ads from issue to issue. Bennett changed it so that ads only ran on one single day, forcing people to read the ads more carefully, as they would otherwise miss out on the opportunity to see them.

To start with, advertising demanded no particular prior skills, and there were no restrictions or ethics that needed to be applied. When one of the first advertising agents, Volney Palmer, opened his business in America in 1843, he was more of an agent for the media rather than the advertisers (Fox, 1984). Soon other advertising agencies emerged, and during the 1860s and

1870s, companies such as N. W. Ayer in Philadelphia and J. Walter Thompson in New York were established. The latter became the first American agency to open an office in the United Kingdom in 1899 (West, 1987). It has since become common for advertising agencies to have offices in different countries, something that has contributed to similar advertising strategies being used worldwide.

The small screen becomes part of people's lives

John Logie Baird, a Scottish man, used already existing technology to create prototype video systems. In 1925, in London, he gave the first demonstration of televised silhouette images in motion (*Nature*, 1925). Not long after this, in 1928, the first American broadcast was made, which was shortly followed by a broadcast in the United Kingdom in 1929. In the same year, Bernard Natan also set up France's first television company, but it was not until 1931 that the first transmission took place. Countries such as Germany, Italy and Russia also introduced their people to television around this time, while others, such as the former Czechoslovakia and Canada, started television broadcasting in the early 1950s.

It was also Baird who demonstrated the first colour transmission in 1928 and who made the world's first colour broadcast from his studios in London in 1938. All-electronic colour was introduced in 1953 in the United States. However, it took until the mid-1960s for colour television sets to become commonplace. The uptake of colour television took a little longer in Europe, and frequent colour broadcasts did not start until the late 1960s.

It was during the 1940s and 1950s that television viewers were introduced to advertising. The first paid advertising to appear on American television was for watches, in 1941, while the first television advert in the United Kingdom was aired in 1955 and was for a brand of toothpaste. This was also the year when the first commercial television station, ITV, was set up in the United Kingdom, and many other countries soon followed suit, meaning that advertising became a key feature of television.

This concludes the history of consumption. The next part of the chapter will take you on another historical journey, one that reviews how the research of consumer psychology has developed as a discipline.

The early researchers

Consumer psychology is often thought of as a relatively new area of psychology, and as a discipline in its own right, such an assumption may be correct. However, as a general research field, nothing could be further from the truth. Consumer psychology today has clearly been shaped by the work of many early psychologists, both applied and more theoretically or experimentally driven. Without the work that was conducted many years ago, the discipline would not have the solid theoretical underpinnings that it has today. The list of early researchers who could be included here is rather long, and it is debatable which may be the most appropriate to include in a chapter about the history of consumer psychology. We decided to include those who, we felt, have made a particularly important contribution to taking us to where we are today as a discipline. However, we fully appreciate that there may be differences in opinion in regard to the choices made. Unfortunately, not only did we have to choose whom we included, but we also had to be selective in what we wrote about the researchers included. Consequently, we think of this part of the chapter as a "snapshot" of some forefathers to consumer psychology. Clearly, consumer psychology has emerged alongside the evolvement of psychology as a discipline in general. Even though psychology research today is segregated into different schools of thought, consumer psychology is different in that it has embraced different strands of thinking. This is important, as it enables researchers to present a more comprehensive picture that truly enables us to understand consumer behaviour. Therefore, it is not surprising that our roots take us on a journey that provides evidence for how consumer psychologists have been influenced by the early mentalist approach and the behaviourist school of thought, as well as dynamic approaches.

Wundt and his disciples

Experimental psychology developed during the late 1800s. It was during this time that a "new type" of psychology emerged, which consisted of less philosophical characteristics than before. This was to be known as structuralism (Hothersall, 2004). One of its supporters was Willhelm Wundt, a German, who believed that a key aspect of psychology should be to focus on immediate conscious experience. He was the first to set up a laboratory, in 1879, focusing specifically on using experimental methods (Mandler, 2007) and hence many consider him to be the father of experimental psychology. Wundt expressed that it was important for psychologists to work towards their discipline becoming a pure science. He was particularly interested in attention, as he believed that this was the part of perception that mirrors what humans are consciously aware of. Some of his students, including Harlow Gale, James Cattell (who early on challenged the idea that introspection was the most valid method to use when studying psychology) and E.B. Titchener went on to become notable psychologists (Hothersall, 2004).

James Cattell was an American psychologist who advocated the use of objective experimental methods for the application of psychology to the field of advertising in the United States. He studied under Wundt for less than two years after his graduation from Lafayette College in 1880. He then went back to America, just to return to work with Wundt once more as his assistant. Upon receiving his PhD from Leipzig in 1886, he moved to the United Kingdom, where he worked with Sir Francis Galton. Two years thereafter, he took up a professorship in psychology at the University of Pennsylvania. However, he did not stay long, as he moved to Columbia University in 1891. During his career, he had several noteworthy achievements. For example, he established a journal titled *Popular Science Monthly*, which he continued to edit until 1943. He was the president of the American Psychological Association (APA) in 1895 as well as the editor of *Science* for almost 50 years (Thorne & Henley, 2001). In 1921, he also founded the Psychological Corporation in order to make applied psychology-based research more accessible to businesses. Cattell was particularly interested in individual differences, an area that lent itself well to application to business (Pillsbury, 1947). In his work on individual differences, he published nine different articles between 1883 and 1886. Galton, in particular, made a significant contribution to consumer psychology in that his work on measuring intelligence is the underpinning for factor analytic work. Factor analysis, in turn, is also an essential component of structural equations modelling, a tool that is very important to consumer psychology researchers (Iacobucci, 2009).

Edward Bradford Titchener was a British-born psychologist who became a prominent figure in establishing experimental psychology in the United States. He is best known for introducing structuralism, as he described the structure of the mind. Titchener studied under Wundt at the University of Leipzig between 1890 and 1892. Similarly to Wundt, he believed that psychology as a discipline should focus on systematic and experimental studies of the normal adult mind. Such studies should be undertaken using the method of introspection. However, his idea of introspection differed somewhat from Wundt's, as he believed that strict guidelines were required when employing the method. His approach to structuralism also differed from

Wundt's in that the former focused on the relationship between elements of consciousness, while Titchener was more interested in identifying the basic elements themselves (Schacter, Gilbert, & Wegner, 2010).

Titchener suggested that when identifying an object, people put together memories of sensations in order to infer what the object is. Together with numerous colleagues, he collected data that created a mapping table of what the disparate elements of sensations were. The table consisted of over 40,000 sensory elements, such as hues and affective dispositions. It was thought that different combinations of the elements included in the table would make up perception. Titchener (1909a, 1909b) has also been credited with introducing the word *empathy* into the English dictionary. The meaning has perhaps changed a little since, but is today commonly used by consumer researchers and now refers to an individual's "capacity to feel within or in another person's feelings" (Langfeld, [1920] 1967, p. 138).

Essentially, Titchener continued Wundt's ideas about the mentalistic approach to attention while based at Cornell in America, where he later became a professor of psychology (Britannica, 2015b). During his time in America, he translated 11 German works linked to the Wundt movement in Germany. Titchener himself wrote eight books, of which the most important were *Experimental Psychology*, published in 1901, and *A Textbook of Psychology*, published in 1910. In 1904, he founded the Society of Experimental Psychology. The interest in Titchener's idea about structuralism started to fade soon after his demise. Some say that his ideas and methods were simply too narrow to keep the idea alive (Hothersall, 2004).

Harlow Gale (by some considered to be the founder of the psychology of advertising) conducted experiments on the effects of advertising during the late 1800s (Kuna, 1976; Eighmey & Sar, 2007). Just like Wundt (under whom he had studied), he showed an interest in attention. In particular, he conducted a series of experiments to test the effects of advertising on attention and memory (Eighmey & Sar, 2007). He moved from Germany to the United States in 1895 to become a lecturer at University of Minnesota, where he ran one of the first experimental psychology laboratories on that side of the Atlantic.

Walter Dill Scott was also critical in psychology's participation in advertising. He wrote a dissertation under Wilhelm Wundt on psychological research into actuating impulses. However, his interests shifted from theorizing to a more practical application of psychology. He had an interest in non-rational aspects of human action and motivation (Von Mayrhauser, 1989). Scott published a book in 1903 titled *The Theory and Practice of Advertising*, in which he suggested that even though people can be reasonable, they are generally suggestible and obedient (Benjamin & Baker, 2004). In particular, he suggested that sentimentality, emotions and sympathy made consumers open to suggestions made by advertisers (Scott, 1903). He tried to encourage advertisers to appeal to consumers' desires for sensuous enjoyment. This, he proposed, would make them more open to suggestions. He questioned: "How many advertisers describe a piano so vividly that the reader can *hear* it?" If the advertiser was persuasive enough, he could make the consumer respond without thought or hesitation (Scott, 1903). He believed that the main purpose of advertising was to capture people's attention (Schultz & Schultz, 2004). Scott lacked empirical backing for his ideas, but still became popular with advertisers (Benjamin & Baker, 2004). Most likely the focus on attention was, just as with Gale, a consequence of having worked under Wundt. His ideas and interest in advertising also paved the way for other psychologists who were to enter the field, such as Hollingworth and Watson.

The two major revolts against Wundtian introspective atomism were the Gestalt approaches and Pavlov's behaviourist approach. In the United States, Titchener was followed by the objectivist tradition of behaviourism, while in Europe, Wundt's ideas were followed by the holistic and experiential psychologies of the Gestalt psychologists.

Functional psychology

William James was an American psychologist who originally trained in medicine and philosophy. He is at times referred to as the father of American psychology (Pajares, 2002), and was one of the main spokespersons for functional psychology. Functionalism's main concern was with the function of mental processes, including consciousness. James and the functionalist school opposed the structuralist focus on introspection. Rather than approving of breaking down mental events into small elements, James advocated the importance of taking the wholeness of an event into account.

For most of his academic career, he worked at Harvard University, where he was first appointed as an instructor in anatomy and physiology in 1873. In 1876, he became an assistant professor in psychology, and continued to work within either psychology or philosophy. He taught his first class in experimental psychology at Harvard in 1875 (Schultz & Schultz, 2004). Similarly to Wundt, he felt that psychology needed to evolve. James's early career in medicine made him particularly sensitive to the natural experiment. He continuously applied his psychology and readily offered advice for training the will, memory, attention and self-perceptions. James supported a mentalistic perspective and defined psychology as the "science of mental life, both of its phenomena and their conditions" (James, 1950 [1890]). Specifically, he was interested in how consciousness helps individuals to adapt to their environment, something that became the underpinning for industrial psychology. James recognized that how we are is affected by multiple aspects, including material possessions. This was evident when, in 1890, he said that the self is affected by "all that he can call his, not only his body and psychic powers, but his clothes and his house ..." (p. 291). It was ideas such as this that paved the way for the application of psychology.

It appeared that James was not convinced about psychology being a discipline in its own right. In 1892, he wrote that "This is no science; it is only the hope of a science" (p. 335). It may, therefore, seem a paradox that he is today one of psychology's most historically famous people. James and Wundt had both managed to initiate a new school of psychology that moved away from the idea that psychological knowledge could be derived from self-observation by looking at the psychology of the subject. This is particularly interesting, as neither James nor Wundt had a solid base upon which to build – there was no genuine empirical underpinning for their ideas.

The Gestalt school of psychology

The Gestalt movement effectively came about as a protest against the reductionist theories that were prominent within the psychology field at that time. Gestalt is a German word that loosely translates into meaning "whole", and essentially represents the idea of perceptual constancy. Gestalt ideas ranged far beyond their concerns with perception: They were deployed in Wolfgang Köhler's work on problem solving with primates, Kurt Koffka's concerns with development, and Max Wertheimer's contributions to human problem solving (Luchins & Luchins, 1997). However, their ideas about perception are of particular importance to consumer psychology, as they are still used as the underpinnings to investigate different areas such as aesthetic preference of product design and congruent brand communication in advertising (e.g., Kirmani & Shiv, 1998; Veryzer & Hutchinson, 1998).

Koffka was born in Berlin. Between 1904 and 1905, he studied at the University of Edinburgh in Scotland. He conducted his PhD at the University of Berlin and then went to the University of Frankfurt, where he met Köhler and Wertheimer (the other two of the trio that established

Gestalt psychology). In 1927, he moved to America, where he became a spokesperson for Gestalt psychology. In 1935, Koffka published the *Principles of Gestalt Psychology*, in which he stated that the behavioural environment cannot sufficiently account for the totality of our behaviour (Luchins & Luchins, 1997). The book essentially put together a huge amount of work conducted by the Gestalt group and their students. Koffka was engaged in many different kinds of experimental studies. History tends to remember him for his systematic application of Gestalt principles to numerous types of enquiries. In 1921, he wrote "*Die Grundlagen der psychischen Entwicklung*", in which he argued that infants experience organized "wholes", even though they have very little life experience (Britannica, 2015c).

Wolfgang Köhler was born in Estonia and moved to Germany at a young age. He studied for his PhD in Berlin and thereafter joined the University of Frankfurt. After a few years, he moved to the Canary Island Anthropoid Station in Spain, where he pursued his perceptional ideas and researched them on chimpanzees. He observed the apes' problem-solving skills and concluded that they solved problems through insight rather than, as previously suggested by Thorndike, through trial and error. He returned to Germany in 1920 to become a professor at the University of Berlin. While there, he co-founded a journal about perceptual psychology and wrote a book titled *Gestalt Psychology*. Apart from his colleagues with a particular interest in Gestalt psychology, he also crossed paths with Kurt Lewin, who was at the university until 1933. In 1935, he fled to America due to unsettling circumstances linked to pre-war ideologies. Later on, in 1959, he became the president of the APA. Köhler once said that "The whole is different from the sum of its parts", demonstrating the core concept of Gestalt psychology, in that it suggests that when something is perceived in its entirety, it can be seen very differently.

Max Wertheimer was a Czech psychologist who started his academic career at the University of Frankfurt. He left in 1916 to become a lecturer at the Friedrich-Wilhelm University in Berlin. In 1921, he co-founded a journal titled *Psychological Research*, which was to become a key part in promoting the Gestalt school of thought. He returned to Frankfurt in 1929 to become a professor in psychology, but left again in 1933, when he emigrated to the United States. In New York, he worked at the New School for Social Research, where he stayed for a decade. Towards the end of his academic career, he also became interested in social ethics. Wertheimer was interested in the way in which humans thought, organized and grouped information together. His interest in perception started after observing how flashing lights created the illusion of movement. He established the concept of Pragnanz, which highlights his belief that the truth was determined by the entirety of a structure rather than by individual sensations. Koffka, Köhler and Wertheimer worked closely together for many years. World War II interrupted the work on Gestalt ideas, but it was resumed shortly afterwards.

Gestalt theory advocated that the real subject matter of psychology is to be found at the level of experience itself, something that had not previously been emphasized. Many ideas of understanding human perception came from the Gestalt school: Not only the idea of perceptual constancy (the inclusiveness and perpetuation of an object's parts in a perceptual experience, but also different aspects of perceptual organization principles of proximity, similarity, closure, simplicity, continuity and figure/ground [Schultz & Schultz, 2004]). The contribution of the Gestalt school to consumer psychology today mainly stems from the combined works of those establishing the approach. Aspects such as proximity (whereby objects that are close together are perceived as a single stimulus) and closure (an automatic process whereby humans fill in gaps to perceive an object as complete) are often used in advertising. The various elements combined into effective package design are often underpinned by the works of Koffka (1922) and Wertheimer (1925) in an attempt to achieve a holistic design that creates a specific sensory effect (e.g. Orth & Malkewitz, 2008).

The influence of behaviourism

The founder of behaviourism, John B. Watson, can be viewed as the first psychologist to apply empirically based psychology to advertising. He received his PhD in 1903 from the University of Chicago, where he remained until 1908, when he became a professor of psychology at Johns Hopkins University. His keen interest in behavioural science led him to advocate that prediction and control were the basis of any science. Watson (1913) said that the study of behaviour was not only to be free from the domination of consciousness but was to take entire possession of the field of psychology. He had experimented with Ivan Pavlov's classical conditioning technique, most notably in the Little Albert experiment (Watson & Rayner, 1920). Watson (1924) believed that by using the systematic application of the principles of classical conditioning, it would be possible to create any kind of human being. He famously said: "Give me a dozen healthy infants, well-formed, and my own specified world to bring them up in, and I'll guarantee to take any one at random and train him to become any type of specialist I might select – doctor, lawyer, artist, merchant-chief and yes, even beggarman and thief – regardless of his talents, penchants, tendencies, abilities, vocations, and race of his ancestors" (Watson, 1924, p. 104). The idea that any person or behaviour could be changed by using behaviourally based techniques appealed to the advertising industry.

There had been a continued interest in psychology by advertisers ever since the publication of Walter Dill Scott's book (which was by then in its third edition). Perhaps, therefore, it was inevitable that when Watson left academia in 1920, the biggest advertising agency in the United States, J. Walter Thompson, took him in. While working in advertising, his main message was that psychology could be used to predict and control consumer behaviour. Making use of his earlier work, he proposed that at birth, infants possessed a register of only three basic emotional responses: love, fear and rage. In particular, he believed that indirect testimonials were effective because they appealed to these basic human emotions. This had important implications for advertising, as the structure proposed by Watson suggested that advertising stimuli would produce the same reactions in all people. Watson helped develop techniques such as usage of fear, which is today commonly incorporated into advertisements. Only four years after he was hired by J. Walter Thompson, he became the vice president of the company. While there, he worked on accounts such as Johnson and Johnson Baby Powder and Baker's Chocolate (Cohen, 1979).

The emerging applied psychologists (early 1900s)

Throughout the history of psychology, there is (apart from some of the aforementioned) an emerging pattern of an interest in applied psychology. One person who had a particularly keen interest in applied psychology was the Harvard-based Hugo Münsterberg. He is considered to have been the first industrial psychologist. Münsterberg was a strong voice in favour of having an applied psychology department at Harvard (Münsterberg, 1909). His ideas about needs, wants and desires have been picked up by many consumer researchers, and he is still often cited in journal articles. Even though his work was not directly linked to consumer-related aspects, his championing of applied research in business settings was important in furthering a willingness to conduct research outside the more traditional psychology areas.

In 1911, Coca-Cola were preparing for a trial: The company was being prosecuted by the US government for selling a drink containing caffeine, which was deemed to be a harmful ingredient. Coca-Cola realized that they lacked evidence for the effect of caffeine on behaviour. Hence, they asked Harry Hollingworth (who had been Cattell's student) to research the effects of caffeine on sensory, cognitive and motor functioning in humans. He conducted this research together with his wife Leta. The results showed that caffeine had no negative effects on behavioural or cognitive performance. This was found to be the case even when people consumed substantial amounts of caffeine (Benjamin, Rogers, & Rosenbaum, 1991). Consequently, Coca-Cola won the trial, but later lost in a court of appeal. Hollingworth continued to conduct applied research, such as investigating how advertisements influence purchasing behaviour. He also wrote a book in 1913 that looked at the links between advertising and responses to it. The book was titled *Advertising and Selling: Principles of Appeals and Responses*. Hollingworth was not the only psychologist to be interested in advertising around that time. So, also, was the man who had conducted an extensive investigation into radio audiences for NBC in 1929, Daniel Starch. He worked at the University of Wisconsin and Harvard while employed as an academic. Starch was the author of a book that was to be read by many people who worked within the American advertising industry: *Advertising: Its Principles, Practice and Technique* (Starch, 1914). It was pioneering in that it highlighted the links between attention and response. The book included Walter Dill Scott's ideas about attention and an outline of how primacy and recency effects can affect whether or not attention is paid to advertisements. However, even though the book included the "psychology of advertising", it also outlined non-psychology-based topics such as "advertising strategy". One aspect sketched out in the book was techniques that could be employed to stimulate consumer interest. Starch suggested that "interest" was effectively an extension to attention, in that it ensured that consumers would focus longer on an advertisement. He left academia to set up his own business, which focused on measuring the effectiveness of advertising (Borden, 1957). His first book was followed by a second, *Principles of Advertising*, in which he discussed the rapid expansion of advertising (Starch, 1923).

Albert T. Poffenberger had also been one of Cattell's mentees. He, too, had a keen interest in applied psychology. In 1915, he was appointed secretary of the APA's New York branch. Poffenberger wrote three books, which were all closely linked to the areas of applied psychology. Hollingworth co-authored the first one, *The Psychology of Taste and Applied Psychology* (Hollingworth & Poffenberger, 1917; Wenzel, 1979). The other two books focused solely on advertising; *Psychology in Advertising* (1925) and *Applied Psychology: Its Principles and Methods* (1927). Poffenberger was also the vice-chairman of the Division of Anthropology and the chairman of the Psychology Division of the National Research Council from 1931 to 1933. Some of his other achievements included being the APA president in 1934 (Wenzel, 1979).

H.K. Nixon was another researcher who focused on advertising. He was based at the School of Business at Columbia University in America. He had a particular interest in attention, and can be credited with conducting the first studies on tracking eye movements. Nixon (1924) was trying to establish which parts of advertisements people looked at. His techniques were constrained to crudely observing eye movements. Nixon concluded from his experimental work that when pictures are used in advertisements, they can guide people's attention to the relevant text (Nixon, 1924, 1926). The fact that he worked for a business school and published widely in both marketing and psychology journals makes him a true "forefather" of consumer psychology.

The latter part of the 1900s

World War II broadened the horizon for some researchers. Increasingly, it became evident that the application of psychology was essential in order to truly demonstrate why people engage in certain behaviours. Here, we will take a brief look at Kurt Lewin, George Katona and Ernest Dichter, as they all brought psychology into new territories. Lewin was born in Prussia. He was a social psychologist who had studied in Berlin. During World War I, he served in the German Army, but decided to go back to academia once the war was over. He was then appointed to the Psychological Institute, which brought him together with Gestalt psychologists such as Koehler and Wertheimer (Patnoe, 1988). In 1930, he became a visiting lecturer at Stanford University, and thereafter settled in America (Hothersall, 2004). He believed that the social environment was a dynamic field that influenced the human consciousness. Lewin thought that situations (or fields) are important in studying group behaviour because individual human behaviour is derived from, and likely to change due to, the individual's perception of current situations based on their past cultural orientation, status and experience. He was well known for practical use of his theories and ideas in studying group dynamics and solving social problems. Unlike some of the Gestalt psychologists (e.g., Wertheimer, Koffka and Köhler), who started with perception and then moved to behaviour, Lewin first considered behaviour and what caused it before he moved on to how people perceived their own and others' behaviour.

Lewin made a valuable contribution to understanding consumers during World War II, when he was asked by the American Department of Agriculture to help persuade people to eat offal. The American government was worried about food shortage, and eating all edible parts of animals was deemed important in maintaining food supplies and the health of the nation, as hearts and livers are high-protein foods. He used scientifically based ideas to test how people could be encouraged to eat offal. His findings showed that when groups of people were encouraged to discuss food-related issues themselves, and could make their own decisions, they were more likely to change their habits than if they had just been provided with information, recipes and advice.

Just like Lewin, Katona left Europe behind to settle in the United States. He was born in Hungary in 1901. Katona originally trained in psychology, but then shifted his interests towards economics. He co-founded the Survey Research Center at the University of Michigan, where he worked between 1946 and 1972. During this time, he pioneered methods of applying survey research to consumer buying. He researched consumers' expectations of financial issues, summarized in the "Index of Consumer Sentiment", which has since been used in many studies. The index showed whether consumers are optimistic or pessimistic about their financial future (Wärneryd, 1999). Katona used the index to demonstrate that when consumers felt confident, they were more likely to enter into new credit agreements (Lea, 1999). This meant that the index could be used as a forecasting tool with regard to predicting consumer behaviour. Katona published many journal papers and books during his career. The books that most clearly make him deserving of a mention in the context of consumer psychology are *The Powerful Consumer*, published in 1960, and *The Mass Consumption Psychology*, published in 1964.

Finally, there is Dichter, who is sometimes considered the founding father of motivational research. He introduced Freudian ideas into the American advertising industry. Dichter was interested in the unconscious mind and believed that consumer purchases were driven by unconscious desires. He used in-depth interviews and projective techniques to tap into people's unconscious, which, he believed, guided behaviour. Dichter was born in Vienna, but in 1937 went to live in the United States, where he set up the Institute for Motivational Research. His ideas became very well known when, in 1957, Vance Packard published a book about what he thought were "hidden persuaders". The book revealed how psychologists had developed selling techniques of which consumers were unaware. Some big US-based firms were keen to work with him, including Procter & Gamble. However, not everyone agreed with Dichter's ideas of understanding consumer behaviour. Some of his critics included his own mentor, Paul Lazerfeld, and Wroe Alderson – a well-respected marketer and, according to some, the father of modern marketing (Ferber & Wales, 1958; Kassarjian, 1994).

New beginnings

There is no doubt that modern psychology began with the adoption of experimental methods. Consumer psychologists today largely employ such methods, and this is a tradition that started with Wundt in the late 1800s. At the same time, the application of psychology to real life began with James, who recognized the importance of material possessions to the self. It was not long until a wide range of different papers relating to consumer psychological areas began to appear. Many focused on advertising (e.g., advertising and recall; Brutt & Crockett, 1928; De Wick, 1935; Guest & Brown, 1939), but there was also an interest in other aspects, such as whether people had preferences for different kinds of glass containers (Hovde, 1931). From then on, research within the area of consumer psychology developed relatively quickly, and in 1961 Joseph M. Kamen (who was also the president of the Consumer Psychology Division in 1971–2) and Howard Schultz suggested that the APA should allow Division 23 to be set up: The Society for Consumer Psychology. Division 23 is today one of 54 APA divisions and has around 650 members. Since the division was established, many well-known consumer-related psychologists have acted as its president, including George Katona, Curtis P. Haugtvedt, Paul M. Herr, John Cacioppo, Frank R. Kardes and Laura A. Peracchio, to mention a few. Along the way, we have also seen a string of journals being set up that have helped further the understanding of consumer-related aspects including the *Journal of Consumer Psychology*, *Journal of Marketing*, and *Journal of Consumer Research*.

References

BBC. (2014). Retrieved May 5, 2015 from www.bbc.com/culture/bespoke/story/20150326-a-history-of-the-department-store/index.html

Benjamin, L. T., & Baker, D. B. (2004). *From séance to science: A history of the profession of psychology in America*. Belmont, CA: Wadsworth/Thomson Learning.

Benjamin, L. T., & Baker, D. B. (2004). Industrial-organizational psychology: The new psychology and the business of advertising. In *From séance to science: A history of the profession of psychology in America* (pp. 118 121). California: Wadsworth/Thomson Learning.

Benjamin, L. T., Rogers, A. M., & Rosenbaum, A. (1991). Coca-Cola, caffeine, and mental deficiency: Harry Hollingworth and the Chattanooga trial of 1911. *Journal of the History of the Behavioural Sciences*, *27*(1), 42–55.

Boorstin, D. J. (1973). *The Americans: The democratic experience*. New York, NY: Vintage Books.

Borden, N. H. (1957). Daniel Starch, *The Journal of Marketing*, *3*, 265–267.

Britannica. (2015a). Retrieved June 3, 2015 from www.britannica.com/biography/Heinrich-Hertz

Britannica. (2015b). Retrieved June 8, 2015 from www.britannica.com/biography/Edward-Bradford-Titchener

Britannica. (2015c). Retrieved July 10, 2015 from www.britannica.com/biography/Kurt-Koffka

Brutt, H., & Crockett, T. (1928). A technique for psychological study of poster board advertising and some preliminary results. *Journal of Applied Psychology*, *12*, 43–55.

Cohen, D. (1979). *JB Watson, the founder of behaviourism: A biography*. London: Routledge Kegan & Paul.

De Wick, H. (1935). The relative effectiveness of visual and auditory presentations of advertising material. *Journal of Applied Psychology*, *19*, 245–264.

Eighmey, J., & Sar, S. (2007). Harlow Gale and the origins of the psychology of advertising. *Journal of Advertising*, *36*(4), 147–158.

Fennis, B. M., & Stroebe, W. (2010). *The psychology of advertising*. New York, NY: Psychology Press.

Ferber, R., & Wales, H. G. (Eds.) (1958). *Motivation and market behaviour*. Homewood, IL: RD Irwin.

Fox, S. R. (1984). *The mirror makers: A history of American advertising and its creators*. New York, NY: University of Illinois Press.

Green, H. (1992). *The uncertainty of everyday life, 1915–1945*. New York, NY: HarperCollins.

Guest, L. P., & Brown, R. H. (1939). A study of the recall of radio advertising material. *Journal of Psychology*, *89*, 381–387.

History. (2014). Retrieved from www.history.com/this-day-in-history/fords-assembly-line-starts-rolling
History. (2015). Retrieved July 5, 2015 from www.history.com/topics/inventions/guglielmo-marconi
Hollingworth, H. L., & Poffenberger, A. T. (1917). *The sense of taste*. Moffat, NY: Yard.
Hothersall, D. (2004). *History of psychology*. New York, NY: McGraw-Hill.
Hovde, H. T. (1931). Consumer preferences for small glass containers. *Journal of Applied Psychology*, *15*, 346–357.
Iacobucci, D. (2010). Structural equations modeling: Fit indices, sample size, and advanced topics. *Journal of Consumer Psychology*, *20*(1), 90–98.
James, W. (1950 [1890]). *The principles of psychology*. New York, NY: Holt.
Jansson-Boyd, C. V. (2010). *Consumer psychology*. Basingstoke: Open University Press.
Japan Radio (2015). Retrieved August 9, 2015 from www.japanradiomuseum.jp/index-e.html
Kassarjian, H. H. (1994). Scholarly traditions and European roots of American consumer research. In G. Laurent, G. L. Lilien & B. Pras (Eds.), *Research traditions in marketing* (pp. 265–279). Boston, MA: Kluwer.
Kirmani, A., & Shiv, B. (1998). Effects of source congruity on brand attitudes and beliefs: The moderating role of issue-relevant elaboration. *Journal of Consumer Psychology*, 7(1), 25–47.
Koffka, K. (1922). Perception: An introduction to the Gestalt-theorie. *Psychological Bulletin*, *19*, 531–585.
Koffka, K. (1935). *Principles of gestalt psychology*, International Library of Psychology, Philosophy and Scientific Method.
Kotler, P. (1997). *Marketing management: Analysis, planning and control* (9th ed). Englewood Cliffs, NJ: Prentice Hall.
Kuna, D. P. (1976). The concept of suggestion in the early history of advertising psychology. *Journal of the History of the Behavioural Sciences*, *12*(4), 347–353.
Langfeld, H. S. ([1920] 1967). *The aesthetic attitude*. Port Washington, NY: Kennikat.
Lea, S. E. G. (1999). Credit, debt and problem debt. In P. E. Earl & S. Kemp (Eds.), *The Elgar companion to consumer research and economic psychology*. Cheltenham: Edward Elgar.
Luchins, A. S., & Luchins, E. H. (1997). A sampling of Gestalt psychologists' remarks on psychoanalysis. *Gestalt Theory*, *19*, 128–139.
Mandler, G. (2007). *A history of modern experimental psychology: From James and Wundt to cognitive science*. Cambridge, MA: MIT Press.
Münsterberg, H. (1909). *Psychology and the teacher*. New York, NY: D. Appleton.
Nature. (1925). Current topics and events, *Nature*, *115*, 505–506.
Nixon, H. K. (1924). *Attention and interest in advertising* (Unpublished doctoral dissertation). New York, NY: Columbia University.
Nixon, H. K. (1926). *An investigation of attention to advertisements*. New York: Columbia University Press.
Orth, U. R., & Malkewitz, K. (2008). Holistic package design and consumer brand impressions. *Journal of Marketing*, *72*(3), 64–81.
Pajares, F. (2002). Biography, chronology, and photographs of William James. Retrieved April 4, 2005 from www.emory.edu.
Patnoe, S. (1988). *A narrative history of experimental social psychology*. New York, NY: Springer Science & Business Media.
Pillsbury, W. B. (1947). Biographical memoir of James McKeen Cattell 1860–1944. *National Academy of Sciences Biographical Memoirs*, *25*, 3.
Schacter, D. L., Gilbert, D. T., & Wegner, D. M. (2010). *Psychology* (p. 600). New York, NY: Worth.
Schultz, D. P., & Schultz, E. S. (2004). *A history of modern psychology* (8th ed.). Belmont, CA: Wadsworth/Thomson.
Scott, W. D. (1903). *The theory of advertising*. Boston, MA: Small, Maynard & Co.
Spalding, J. W. (1963 [1928]). Radio becomes a mass advertising medium. *Journal of Broadcasting & Electronic Media*, *8*(1), 31–44.
Starch, D. (1914). *Advertising: Its principles, practice, and technique*. Scott, Foresman.
Starch, D. (1923). *Principles of advertising*. New York, NY: McGraw-Hill.
Statista. (2015). Retrieved July 13, 2015 from www.statista.com/statistics/200002/international-car-sales-since-1990/
Stories of London. (2015). Retrieved June 14, 2015 from http://stories-of-london.org/history-department-store
Thorne, B. M., & Henley, T. (2001). *Connections in the history and systems of psychology*. Boston: Houghton Mifflin.

Titchener, E. (1909a). *Elementary psychology of the thought processes*. New York, NY: Macmillan.
Titchener, E. B. (1909b). *Lectures on the experimental psychology of the thought-processes*. New York, NY: Macmillan.
Toy Association. (2015). Retrieved August 12, 2015 from www.toyassociation.org/tia/industry_facts/salesdata/industryfacts/sales_data/sales_data.aspx?hkey=6381a73a-ce46-4caf-8bc1-72b99567df1e
Veryzer, R. W., & Hutchinson, J. W. (1998). The influence of unity and prototypicality on aesthetic responses to new product designs. *Journal of Consumer Research*, *24*(4), 374–393.
Von Mayrhauser, R. T. (1989). Making intelligence functional: Walter Dill Scott and applied psychological testing in World War I. *Journal of the History of the Behavioural Sciences*, *25*, 60–72.
Wärneryd, K. E. (1999). *The psychology of saving: A study on economic psychology*. Cheltenham: Edward Elgar.
Watson, J. B. (1913). Psychology as a behaviourist views it. *Psychological Review*, *20*(2), 158–177.
Watson, J. B. (1924). *Behaviourism*. New York, NY: Norton.
Watson, J. B., & Rayner, R. (1920). Conditioned emotional reactions. *Journal of Experimental Psychology*, *3*(1), 1.
Wenzel, B. M. (1979). Obituary: Albert Theodore Poffenberger (1885–1977). *American Psychologist*, *34*, 88–90.
Wertheimer, M. (1925). "Untersuchungen zur Lehre von der Gestalt: II," *Psychologische Forschung*, *4*(2), 301–350.
West, D. C. (1987). From T-Square to T-Plan: The London office of the J. Walter Thompson advertising agency 1919–70. *Business History*, *29*(2), 199–217.

2

Cross-cultural consumption

Susan Forquer Gupta

Theodore Levitt's 1983 article "The globalization of markets" is used frequently as a beginning in the shift of the multinational corporation (MNC) market strategy from international to global market segments. The emphasis was now focused on building the global brand to take advantage of the similarities across national borders and the economies of scale that result from serving large global markets with a single brand identity. Only recently has the pendulum begun to swing back to a position where both global and local brand identity are important players in the market, where competition and choice exist to serve unique cultural groups or market segments. Throughout the decades, research attention on how culture defines meaning in consumption and experiences has swung with the pendulum, providing evidence for similarities across cultures or significant differences between cultures based on the context where the consumption occurs and on what overall theory was driving the research. Cultural meaning and perceptions, along with economic conditions and availability of choice, combine into contextual consumption of products and services with unique meanings for the consumers. The importance of a product (or brand) to a consumer lies in the meaning associated with the product as well as the associated products, beliefs and uses. The study of this contextual web of meaning ascribed to products and the meaning in consumption is the focus of the chapter. Cross-cultural consumption is a fragmented and woefully underdeveloped area, where researchers occasionally either take their primary line of inquiry "across the border" in a comparative study or delve into a deeply descriptive single population study that replicates earlier work on the majority population and results in a cross-cultural extension of their work. As a result, there has been no focused development of theory unique to this area but a collection of studies that enlighten our understanding of how the cultural context of consumption is critical in understanding the meaning ascribed to consumption practices. Research methods and measures have morphed as well – a change primarily driven by advances in technology allowing more complicated approaches to data. New techniques have been developed that span attributes and interviews across multiple national samples while controlling for differences inherent to cross-cultural research, such as response bias, measurement equivalence and translation errors.

Cross-cultural research is a unique approach to any topical inquiry whereby the constructs to be measured, or the models to be developed, must be relevant in two or multiple cultural contexts, and those contexts are compared to provide evidence that the culture is at the root of the similarities or differences between respondent pools. In order to show that the difference is due to culture, many controls have to be in place and the data have to be collected under similar conditions as well as on similar samples. The time and monetary costs of conducting cross-cultural research are exponentially more than for single-culture research. It is also high risk for researchers to pursue cross-cultural research, as it is more difficult to publish, given the number of ways such research can be questioned regarding the appropriateness of the samples, as well as the methods and analysis of the results. Due to the time and connections it takes to collect data across multiple cultures, there have been an increasing number of immigrant or single-country cross-cultural studies in the literature. "Immigrant" cross-cultural studies are those that use a sample of an immigrant population in their home country and compare them directly with the majority culture of the home country; for example, a sample consisting of American consumers is compared with a sample consisting of immigrant Mexican consumers and then conclusions are drawn regarding the cultural differences. Single-country studies, on the other hand, choose a sample from a single country and then compare it indirectly against the results of previous research from a different country. These are interesting studies on assimilation and acculturation via the consumed products and utilize a manageable and accessible population for research purposes, at the risk of validity and reliability of the comparisons. But these studies are many times presented as proxies for measuring the cultural differences of the originating nation using the immigrant sample, although, by virtue of immigrating to a foreign land, the respondents are less representative of the home culture. Immigrants are a unique group of individuals who are willing to uproot themselves from their families and communities and put down roots in a new country, and may not be representative of their originating nation's consumers. Difficulties aside, cross-cultural consumption research provides a window into the true meaning of what is important in the lives of individuals around the world and has shown at times that fairly common drivers of human emotion, decisions, motivations and success underlie the differing product choices and usages.

This chapter is a brief review of cross-cultural consumption research. Articles chosen for inclusion in this discussion focus on the meaning of consumption instead of economic counts or trends in consumption, and provide a comparative discussion between at least two cultures. Sixty-five articles were chosen across the decades from peer-reviewed academic journals in marketing and are listed, along with the main findings and cultures investigated, in a table arranged by year of publication (see Table 2.1). This chapter will discuss the developments in cross-cultural consumption research chronologically, beginning with the years prior to Levitt's (1983) article and going forward approximately in decades as we see changes in topical focus and methodology defining the discussions in the field. Due to the lack of any dominant psychological construct or theory and the great variety of constructs utilized in these cross-cultural consumption studies, this chapter will focus on the overarching themes or trends defining points of change in cross-cultural consumption research as a whole, and direct the reader to subsequent chapters that dedicate in-depth discussion to specific psychological constructs and theory.

The early years of cross-cultural consumption research

Early work in cross-cultural consumption consisted of a few researchers testing existing measures in a country other than where the measures were originally developed and validated, or of theoretical discussions of differences between cultures that impact the success of advertising or market growth into foreign lands. In fact, as early as 1959, A.C. Neilson Jr (president of AC Neilson Inc.) warned of the dangers of standardized advertising strategies for products

Table 2.1 Chronological summary of peer-reviewed academic journals in marketing pertaining to cross-cultural consumption research

Year	*Authors*	*Journal*	*Population/sample*	*Topic*	*Method*	*Constructs/ measures*	*Contribution*
1959	Neilsen	*Journal of Marketing*		Cross-cultural selling	Theoretical paper		15-point discussion of marketing hazards in foreign countries.
1974	Belcher & Crader	*Social Forces*	Puerto Rico	Fertility and consumption in Puerto Rico	Survey research Factor analysis	Four factors, consumption levels and lifestyle, and used Hollingshead SOL	Fertility decreased with the consumption of goods, and consumption patterns or lifestyle were better indicators of fertility than Hollingshead social position measures. Lifestyle measured by consumption and male dominance are important variables in understanding patterns of fertility in low-income households.
1974	Goldman	*Journal of Marketing*	Developing nations (Brazil, Bolivia)	Food retailing, pricing and shopping behaviour	Theoretical paper	Theoretical constructs developed to capture low income shopping behaviour	Guidelines for large retail stores to follow to capture low-income shoppers in developing nations, including overcoming spatial, social cultural and informational barriers.
1975	Green, Cunningham, & Cunningham	*Journal of Advertising*	United States, France, India and Brazil	Product attributes of soda and toothpaste rated in four cultures	Survey, F ratios comparing countries	Product attributes	Found significant differences in importance of advertising attributes by country to support the need to recognize that standardized advertising may not work for products where consumers place differing importance on various attributes.

1977	Anderson & Engledow	*Journal of Consumer Research*	United States and Germany	Consumer information seeking	Survey data, factor analysis	Information type and relevance	Identified factors from consumer data regarding information used in purchase decisions.
1978	Arndt	*Advances in Consumer Research*		Cross-cultural consumer research	Review		Called attention to the issues faced in cross-cultural research and the need for large collaborative teams.
1978	Hoover, Green, & Saegert	*Journal of Marketing*	Mexico and United States	Perceived risk and brand loyalty	Comparative survey	Perceived risk and brand loyalty	Showed differences between Mexican and American consumers for four products.
1981	Jolibert & Baumgartner	*Journal of Consumer Research*	France	Consumerists	Survey and scale validation	Berkowitz and Luttman social responsibility scale	Invalid on French sample – some findings at the variable level.
1983	Green, Leonardi, Chandon, Cunningham, Verhage, & Strazzieri	*Journal of Consumer Research*	United States, West Germany, Belgium, Finland, Denmark, France and Japan	Family purchasing roles	Survey Six country study	Rodman's ideal society typology and decision making on several products	Used corresponding analysis, showed differences by country on marital decision making across multiple product categories.
1983	Wallendorf & Reilly	*Journal of Consumer Research*	Mexico, United States	Assimilation of Mexicans into Anglo culture Immigrants	Garbology	Assimilation, product categories	Not a linear relationship; each sample had unique product consumption and was not a linear progression as hypothesized.
1986	McCullough, Chin Tiong, & Wong	*Advances in Consumer Research*	Singapore Chinese, Chinese Americans and Americans	Ethnicity measures	Theoretical paper	Chineseness	Value belief items to measure Chineseness does not discriminate between groups.

(*Continued*)

Table 2.1 (Continued)

Year	*Authors*	*Journal*	*Population/sample*	*Topic*	*Method*	*Constructs/ measures*	*Contribution*
1986	Lindman & Lang	*International Journal of Psychology*	Finland and United States	Beliefs or attitude towards types of alcohol and behaviour they produce	Survey	Likert scale items	Similar categorization of expected behaviour that differed for the four types of alcohol (wine, beer, spirits and mixed drinks), yet both samples had similar conceptualizations of the differing behaviour.
1987	Tan, McCullough, & Teoh	*Advances in Consumer Research*	Singapore	Individual analysis of buying behaviour	Multi-attribute attitude model – individual-level analysis to show differences in decision processes	Choice attributes across 130 products	Showed differences in decision making within a single cultural population, and that relying on cultural-level data may be misleading.
1988	Tso, Wong, & Chin Tiong	*Advances in Consumer Research*	Japan, Hong Kong, Singapore, South Korea and Taiwan	Product attributes across five Asian samples	Factor analysis of survey data	Product attributes, factor structures that differed by sample	There are substantial differences between the populations on how they make consumption decisions.
1988	Lutz	*Journal of Consumer Research*		Editorial change to the journal			Stated a focus shift that included more focus on consumption rather than purchase decisions and cross cultural.
1989	Penaloza	*Advances in Consumer Research*	Taiwan	Acculturation	Theoretical paper	Consumer acculturation model	Model.
1989	McCarty	*Advances in Consumer Research*		Cross-cultural construct and model development in consumer	Theoretical paper	Built on Strobeck and Triantis	Calls for pan-cultural development of models and constructs.

1989	Tso, Belk, & Zhou	*Journal of Consumer Research*	PRC, Hong Kong and Taiwan	Consumption values	Content analysis of print ads	Identified differing sets of consumption values	Hedonism, utilitarianism etc. are shown to differ in the three samples.
1990	Tansey, Hyman, & Zinkhan	*Journal of Advertising*	Brazil and United States	Themes in advertising questioning standardization	Content analysis of print ads	themes	Found differences between Brazilian and American ads' themes.
1993	Ger, Belk, & Lascu	*Advances in Consumer Research*	Romania and Turkey	Descriptive consumption	Observation and interview	Case, description	Romanian and Turkish consumption after free market goods flood the markets – consumer desire, consumption frenzy and consumer confusion.
1993	Durvasula & Lysonski	*Journal of Consumer Affairs*	United States and New Zealand	Cross-cultural validation of CSI scale	Structural equation modelling	CSI	General support of the CSI (consumer style index) can be generalized to the New Zealand consumer and may have cross-cultural validity.
1993	Englis, Solomon, & Olofsson	*Journal of Advertising*	Sweden and United States	Music video and consumption imagery	Content analysis, MANOVA, ANOVA	Types of music, types of consumption imagery	Swedish and US music videos differed in amount and type of consumption imagery even when controlling for type of music.
1994	Brewer Doran	*Advances in Consumer Research*	Chinese and Canadians	Chinese immigrant buying/ consumption decision making	Etic snowball interview process	Information search, purchase decisions	Chinese immigrants have different consumer decision process than Canadians but assimilate over time. Trust in personal network, need for quality etc.

(*Continued*)

Table 2.1 (Continued)

Year	*Authors*	*Journal*	*Population/sample*	*Topic*	*Method*	*Constructs/ measures*	*Contribution*
1994	Wells	*Journal of Advertising*	Russian/Soviet Union and "Western" markets	Advertising in Russia	Interview	Interviews concerning the meaning of ad content and advertising	Identified large perceptual differences in advertising from the perspective of the Russian consumer as compared with mature markets.
1994	Penaloza	*Journal of Consumer Research*	Mexican immigrants to United States	Acculturation	Ethnographic study	Agents, processes, outcomes	Model developed.
1994	Arnould & Wallendorf	*Journal of Marketing*		Market ethnography	Detailed instructions	Ethnography via interviews, photos and video	Provides evidence of the strengths of using ethnographic approaches in marketing.
1995	Brunsø & Grunert	*Advances in Consumer Research*	Copenhagen, London, Paris and Germany	Food lifestyle measurement development	Survey, factor analysis, creation of construct	Food-related lifestyle	Five-factor model tested across four countries.
1995	Gilly	*Advances in Consumer Research*	American women living in Spain	Expats	Interview	Changes in consumption	Process of acculturation.
1996	Houston & Venkatesh	*Advances in Consumer Research*	Vietnamese immigrants to the United States	Health-care consumption patterns	Interview	Grounded theory	Descriptive of Vietnamese health-care consumption.
1997	Eastman, Fredenberger, Campbell, & Calvert	*Journal of Marketing Theory and Practice*	United States, PRC, Mexico	Materialism and status consumption	Questionnaire	Materialism, status	No difference in consuming for status; materialism had differences.
1997	Ganesh	*Journal of Consumer Marketing*	Tamil Indian immigrants in the United States	Purchase decision and assimilation	Survey	Spousal Influence	Cultural assimilation of the Indian immigrant, in terms of relative spousal influence by product and stage of purchase.

1998	Wong & Ahuvia	*Psychology and Marketing*	SE Asia and "West"	Theoretical model	Theoretical Paper	Luxury consumption	Model.
1999	Askegaard, Jensen, & Holt	*Advances in Consumer Research*	Denmark and United States	Post-structuralist	Qualitative	Concepts of fat and fat-related food choices	Differences were found between Danish and US respondents.
1999	Rose	*Journal of Marketing*	Japan and the United States	Child consumer socialization	Survey	Age of child and advertising and purchase beliefs	Differences were found between Japanese and US respondents.
1999	Oswald	*Journal of Consumer Research*	Haiti and United States	Symbolism, qualitative	Descriptive, interviews	Culture is mutable	How individuals may swap out products as they strive to maintain a cultural identity when migrant.
1999	Smith, Solgaard, & Beckmann	*Journal of Consumer Studies and Home Economics*	15 countries in EU	Alcohol consumption	Trends in alcohol consumption across EU	Time and consumption	Changes that can be explained due to taxation, age, culture.
2000	Bagozzi, Wong, Abe, & Bergami	*Journal of Consumer Psychology*	Japan, United States, China and Italy	Theory of reasoned action	Survey of students, structural equation model	TRA held for all cultures, Japan, United States, China and Italy with difference in frequency of eating fast food	Strong evidence for generalizability of TRA across cultures.
2000	Viswanathan, Childers, & Moore	*Journal of the Academy of Marketing Science*	United States and Thailand	Development of the IGEN scale	Survey of two cultures	Parent influence on child	Evidence of scale validity.
2001	Squires, Juric, & Cornwell	*Journal of Consumer Marketing*	Denmark and New Zealand	Organic food consumption attitudes	Factor analysis of survey data	Model	Factors were developed regarding views towards organic consumption.

(*Continued*)

Table 2.1 (Continued)

Year	*Authors*	*Journal*	*Population/sample*	*Topic*	*Method*	*Constructs/ measures*	*Contribution*
2001	Martin & McCracken	*Journal of Consumer Marketing*	United Kingdom and New Zealand	Music video and consumption imagery		Content analysis, MANOVA, ANOVA	Builds on the Englis article.
2001	Aaker, Benet-Martínez, & Garolera	*Journal of Personality and Social Psychology*	United States, Japan and Spain	Brand personality constructs	Survey – view ads and rate on set of terms	Found some consistent constructs across three cultures	Three constructs were validated across three cultures; each culture also had unique constructs.
2001	Kragh & Djursaa	*European Journal of Marketing*	Denmark and United Kingdom	Product syntax	Data	Product syntax	Comparison of Danish and British perceptions regarding furniture.
2002	de Mooij & Hofstede	*Journal of Retailing*	Europe	Hofstede measures and product across Europe	Secondary data		Made assumptions regarding Hofstede rankings and product purchases.
2002	Clarke & Micken	*Journal of International Consumer Marketing*	Australia, France, Mexico, United States	Materialism	Survey		Differences in the internal and external values associated with high and low materialism between countries.
2003	Belk, Ger, & Askegaard	*Journal of Consumer Research*	United States, Turkey and Denmark	Desire and consumer behaviour			Phenomenological research into "desire" and how it is global.
2004	Luomala, Kumar, Worm, & Singh	*Journal of International Consumer Marketing*		Mood states		Perceived ease of initiating, and emotional outcomes of, mood-regulatory activities	Mood-regulatory activities are less consumption oriented, have more socially based emotional consequences, and are more easily pursued and more effective in collectivistic cultures as opposed to individualistic cultures.

2005	Chen, Ng, & Rao	*Journal of Marketing Research*	United States and Singapore	Impatience	Experimental design, students	Impatience in waiting for product, promotion and delay	Found there to be a difference in America primed and Singaporean primed respondent in the type of impatience.
2007	Juan Li & Chenting	*International journal of Market Research*	United States and China	Face and consumption	Survey	Rating statements regarding consumption	Constructs of face consumption.
2007	Hung, Li, & Belk	*Journal of International Business Studies*	China	Image of Asian women in advertising	Experimental design	Images	Four distinct Asian women types in advertising.
2008	Chui & Kwok	*Journal of International Business Studies*	41 countries	National culture and life insurance		Hofstede dimensions	The findings show that individualism indeed has a significant, positive effect on life insurance consumption, whereas power distance and masculinity/femininity have significant, negative effects.
2008	Ruvio, Shoham, & Maja	*International Marketing Review*	Israel, Palestine and Slovenia		Survey	CNFU	Data support the within-group validation and the cross-national equivalency of the new CNFU-S scale through SEM models, a powerful and rigorous test of within- and between-group validation. The reduced scale also exhibited the same nomological validity as the original.

(*Continued*)

Table 2.1 (Continued)

Year	*Authors*	*Journal*	*Population/sample*	*Topic*	*Method*	*Constructs/ measures*	*Contribution*
2008	Mathur, Guiry, & Tikoo	*Journal of International Consumer Marketing*	Asian Indians in United States and Asian Indians in New Delhi	Consumption of culture-specific products		Culture-specific consumption	Difference were found.
2008	Saba, Messina, Turrini, Lumbers, & Raats	*International Journal of Consumer Studies*	Senior citizens of eight European countries	Attitudes via survey	Repertory grid method	Perceptions, preferences and attitudes towards convenience of vegetable soups	Overall, vegetable-related foods with convenience in preparation were perceived in similar ways across the countries.
2008	Lim & Ang	*Journal of Business Research*	Shanghai, Singapore	Advertisement	Hedonistic vs. utilitarian	Cultural conditioning, product type and benefit claim type on attitudes and brand personality perceptions among consumers	Consumers in Shanghai preferred ads promoting utilitarian rather than hedonic products, and rated brands of utilitarian products as more sophisticated, competent, exciting and sincere. Singaporean consumers preferred hedonic over utilitarian products but did not perceive them as being different from utilitarian products in terms of brand personality.
2008	d'Astous, Zannie, Colbert, Carù, Caldwell, & Courvoisier	*International Marketing Review*	Australia, Canada, Italy, Switzerland and United States	COO and art/theatre	Comparison of 16 countries' products, and four countries of respondents	Nine cultural arts	The results indicate that product-country images in the arts are affected by country and product familiarity as well as consumers' openness to foreign cultures and home country bias.
2009	Cleveland, Laroche, & Papadopoulos	*Journal of International Marketing*	Eight-country comparison	Survey research		CET MAT and COS	Structural equation model to develop the constructs.

2010	Sutton-Brady, Davis, & Jung	*Journal of Consumer Behaviour*	Korean Australian	Food	Interview	Acculturation	Acculturation on food and media consumption patterns of Korean migrant families in Australia. Findings of the study demonstrate the conflicted and negotiated construction of consumption around the dual cultural identities.
2010	Palan, Gentina, & Muratore	*Journal of Business Research*	France and United States	Adolescent consumer autonomy	In-depth interviews	Consumption autonomy	Four dimensions of adolescent consumption autonomy are identified, including attitudinal, emotional, functional and financial.
2011	Flight, Allaway, Wan-Min, & D'Souza	*Journal of Marketing Theory and Practice*	South Korea and United States	Innovation diffusion of technology-based durables	Survey	Individualism and Confucianism	Significant cultural effects exist between consumers from an individualism-centred and a Confucian/collectivism-centred country.
2012	Demangeot & Sankaran	*Journal of Marketing Management*	11 COO for individuals living in UAE	Interview and survey research	Grounded theory, decision-making roles	Cultural pluralism	Conceptualization of cultural pluralism, its main antecedents and consequences.
2012	Shukla	*International Marketing Review*	United States, United Kingdom, Malaysia, India	Luxury goods	Questionnaire. structural equation modelling	Social personal and functional perceptions	The study highlights the importance of understanding the homogeneity and heterogeneity in consumer consumption decisions and provides managers with a basis to adapt their strategic responses.

(*Continued*)

Table 2.1 (Continued)

Year	*Authors*	*Journal*	*Population/sample*	*Topic*	*Method*	*Constructs/ measures*	*Contribution*
2013	Guo	*Journal of International Marketing*	China and India	Attitudes via survey	Structural EQUATION MODELS	Global orientation, including global consumption orientation and global identity	Studies in China show that consumers' global orientation positively influences global brands of developed-country origin. Ethnocentrism negatively influences attitudes towards brands, Indian consumers yield a similar pattern to Chinese consumers with regard to the global orientation effect.
2014	Cross & Gilly	*Journal of Marketing*	United States, India, China, Japan, Taiwan, Philippines, Belarus, Mexico	Interview and survey research	Grounded theory, decision-making roles	Cultural competency	A model of cultural competence and cultural compensatory mechanisms in bi-national homes.
2014	Yim, Sauer, Williams, Lee, & Macrury	*International Marketing Review*	United Kingdom and Taiwan	Survey research	Multi-group structural equation modelling	Attitude towards luxury brands SNII, LUX and BCO	Horizontal individualism, vertical individualism, horizontal collectivism and vertical collectivism are antecedent to consumer SNII and the endogenous part of the model in which consumer SNII affects LUX through the mediating role of BCO.
2014	Xu, Chen, Burman, & Zhao	*International Journal of Consumer Studies*	United States and China	Second-hand clothing consumption		Past purchase experience, perceived values and concerns, perceived subjective norm and future purchase intention	Significant differences in young consumers' second-hand clothing consumption behaviour between the two countries.

across international borders in his *Journal of Marketing* article titled "Do's and don'ts in selling abroad", where he called for a research approach to foreign markets and presented a 15-point list of "Rules and warnings" that included such sage advice as "Adapt the product to the market" and "Gauge the impact of culture and tradition". The tone of the article suggests that there were large failures by companies who approached foreign markets from a view that their product and marketing strategy were superior and would win over the existing products and competition without acknowledging the deep differences in market development, cultural meaning and individual preferences. This suggests that the prevailing marketing strategy was domination over the market and customer. This approach does have some success in developing nations with product scarcity and monopolized markets where real choice does not exist for the consumer, i.e., many African nations, where they may purchase products regardless of the relevance of the brand messaging, price point or suitability for the purpose due to lack of any realistic alternative.

Several studies published in the mid-1970s provide evidence that measures developed and validated in one country, as well as market assumptions or strategies proven successful there, may not hold any validity in another culture. Belcher and Crader (1974) attempted to validate Hollingshead's four-factor index of social position in Puerto Rico. Hollingshead's index is a widely accepted index used in the social sciences to control for social position based on the respondents' occupation, education and type of housing. Belcher and Crader found that the index did not hold any explanatory power in fertility rates in Puerto Rico, but controlling for consumption patterns did. This recognition that the consumption environment played a powerful role in family planning, and the discrediting of a measure of social position developed in a mature, stable market-driven economy, provided strong evidence that the economic structure and culture of a market must be taken into consideration and brought into question the generalizability of measures across culture lines. Furthermore, Goldman's (1974) article gave a descriptive account of just how different market environments can function and how mature market food retailing strategies fail in developing markets. For example, consumers were paying significantly more for food goods in developing economies due to lack of transportation and refrigeration – issues that cannot be readily addressed by food retailers. Similarly, the market strategy of the large supermarkets that provide lower-cost price points but are located and built on models that expect shoppers to stop in once a week to load their carts and vehicles with food goods fails in markets where most shoppers have no ability to store fresh food or transport more than one or two bags at a time.

One of the earliest cross-cultural research papers is the article by Green, Cunningham and Cunningham (1975) that surveyed consumers in the United States, France, India and Brazil on their ratings of product attributes of soda and toothpaste. This empirical work found that the four groups placed differing importance on the various product attributes, making it untenable to develop standardized advertising to serve all four markets. Anderson and Engledow's (1977) article used factor analysis to create a model of consumer decision making and compared the factor structures between German and American respondents. They found evidence that the same factor structures existed for both samples, showing that the decision processes were quite similar, but also found that American consumers were more impulsive or impatient in purchasing, as they ranked product availability more highly than their German counterparts, and that German consumers were more information driven.

Similar research was published for the remainder of the 1970s and early 1980s, with multi-county validation of existing constructs or factor-analysed survey data to create new constructs across culture groups, either revealing similarities or shedding light on the differences. The topics range from perceived risk and brand loyalty (Hoover, Green, & Saegert, 1978) to social responsibility (Jolibert & Baumgartner, 1981) to family purchasing roles (Green et al., 1983). These studies are useful in that they build a reference library of similarities and differences, but fall short in discussing why the differences exist. Wallendorf and Reilly's (1983) article detailing a study utilizing "garbology" as the method of inquiry aids the field in turning the corner. The study focused on Mexican immigrants in the United States but included data from Mexicans in Mexico as well as non-Mexican Americans to set comparative points for acculturation via product usage as evidence in the waste disposed of by each respondent's home. This approach removes the response error that occurs when asking individuals about past or intended behaviour, when they may not remember, or may change the information to project a different image of themselves than what exists in reality. Instead, it focuses on the evidence. The study found that the assimilation models used to create hypotheses for the study assumed a linear assimilation from one culture to another, with those "in-between" expected to be "in-between" the two cultures in product consumption. However, the result of this study highlighted that the immigrant group was not following a linear path of assimilation, but had created an entirely different consumption culture that did not mirror either the home country (Mexico) or the new host country (United States) population's consumption of products.

The decades of increased globalization and the growth of the multinational

While early cross-cultural consumption research through the 1970s was defined by the theoretical papers cautioning companies against making assumptions that foreign markets were similar (Neilsen 1959; Goldman 1974) as well as by large comparative surveys providing evidence that difference did exist, there was a growing recognition that large teams of researchers would be needed to conduct cross-cultural research (Arndt, 1978). The 1980s and 1990s by comparison were decades that were dominated by growth of the MNCs and the power of standardization, globalization and profits driven by economies of scale. The pendulum had swung. Advances in logistics and supply chain management, dropping of trade barriers and the birth of computers streamlined international business. There was increased interest in locating global similarities. Theodore Levitt's 1983 article is often cited as the beginning of globalization in its modern strategic form. Levitt called for standardization and growth via global markets, global segments and global brands. The cross-cultural consumption literature witnessed an increase in the publication of articles that showed similarities in markets, for example ethnicity measures that did not show differences between intended groups (McCullough, Chin Tiong, & Wong, 1986) or differences in beliefs and attitudes in alcohol consumption and behaviour (Lindman & Lang, 1986). However, research continued to document the differences and provide evidence that culture was a determining factor along with market conditions. Tse, Wong and Chin Tiong (1988) provided a factor analysis that showed substantial difference in how five Asian samples (Japan, Hong Kong, Singapore, South Korea and Taiwan) viewed product attributes. This brought into question whether a product strategy could be standardized across Asian countries. Adding evidence towards the need for adaptive strategies, Tse, Belk and Zhou (1989) content analysed print ads and found that consumption values of hedonism and utilitarianism differed significantly across the People's Republic of China, Hong Kong and Taiwan. In a similar vein, markets under centralized governmental control had created consumption constrictions that had broad effects on the consumer and the consumption experience. As government controls over markets loosened, allowing increased free market competition across Eastern European countries, research showed that consumption patterns could change dramatically depending upon the prevailing market environment. This sheds light on how control over product availability and information can dramatically impact consumption meaning. Ger, Belk and Lascu (1993) found that Romanian and Turkish consumers faced consumption frenzy and confusion in the market change that occurred as barriers to international imports fell and the markets became flooded with goods, providing confusing amounts of choice to consumers nearly overnight. This confusion was created not only by a sudden increase in choice and information on new products, but also due to the consumers' need to somehow decide which product to buy when they previously had only been able to purchase what was available. They had to learn how to make choices and what to base their choices on while protecting themselves in the process.

Cross-cultural consumption research experienced a dual channel of research invigoration in the 1990s. Lutz in 1988, as the editor of the *Journal of Consumer Research*, announced a change in the focus of the journal towards articles on consumption rather than purchase decisions. This invitation to produce work on consumption created a strong surge in ethnographic and qualitative, deep description-focused consumption research. Ethnographic research methods are particularly well suited for cross-cultural consumption research (Luna & Gupta, 2001), and yet are time intensive and uniquely problematic in that they require either research partners or bilingual capability to collect quality data across language barriers. As a result of this shift in research focus and methodology, information on how differences manifest between cultural groups became central in the discussion of results. Examples include a study of Russian consumers that found respondents had large perceptual differences in advertising compared with consumers in mature markets (Wells, 1994) due to their historical disregard for print and advertising information and lack of control and choice in consumer products. Interviews provided the basis for Penaloza (1994) to create an acculturation model of Mexican immigrants to the United States. And in a peak of interest in the field regarding ethnographic methods, the *Journal of Marketing* published Arnould and Wallendorf's (1994) paper detailing the process of conducting a "market ethnography". The domination of consumption research by ethnographic or qualitative methodology continues to this day.

Parallel to the shift in focus of cross-cultural consumption research towards increased attention to and importance of ethnography is the utilization of structural equation modelling (SEM), which became the method of preference for large-sample empirical quantitative work. SEM research surged with the advent of computing power, and is well suited for cross-cultural empirical research due to its ability to control multiple variables and discriminate between groups. Durvasula and Lysonski (1993) published one of the earliest papers utilizing SEM, in which they found general support for the consumer style index (CSI) using respondents from the United States and New Zealand. Bagozzi, Wong, Abe and Bergami (2000) found strong evidence for generalizability of the theory of reasoned action (TRA) across Japanese, American, Chinese and Italian consumers.

This split between large-sample multi-country/culture comparative research and small-sample two-country in-depth ethnographic comparisons was likely due to the differing advantages and disadvantages as well as time constraints that exist between quantitative research (usually survey data) and qualitative/ethnographic research. We also can note a reliance on immigrant, expatriate or displaced groups in qualitative research, as the investigators have to solve the issue of access to individual respondents. Both streams of research have provided valuable findings and advanced our understanding of cross-cultural consumption.

Into the new millennium

The most recent decade has seen an increased sophistication of methods and constructs along with an increasing focus on Asian cultures as we attempt to unravel consumption differences between Western and Asian cultures or to understand the fine differences between Asian cultures. The increased attention paid to Asia and, in particular, to China is not surprising, since research has always followed the markets, as evidenced by increased discussion of post-soviet countries and communist markets as they opened their borders for trade. But the discoveries found in the course of researching Asian culture have provided evidence that our Western theoretical models are myopic in their ignorance of Asian cultural and mental constructs – these discoveries include, for example, Confucian consumerism (Flight, Allaway, Wan-Min, & D'Souza, 2011); concepts of "face" consumption (Juan Li & Chenting, 2007); and four types of Asian women in advertising (Hung, Li, & Belk, 2007).

There are an increasing number of studies in cross-cultural consumption research that test theory first developed in domestic consumer research in order to provide evidence of generalizability across cultures. For example, research into the concept of materialism (Clarke & Micken, 2002), desire (Belk, Ger, & Askegaard, 2003) and mood states (Luomala, Kumar, Worm, & Singh, 2004) is occurring in cross-cultural comparative studies, in addition to the documentation of assimilation, acculturation and consumption meaning across cultures. Each began with the development of constructs and measures by testing the validity and reliability in a single culture and then was later tested in additional cultures in order to ascertain whether there was any evidence to support validity and reliability across cultures.

Even with the decades of cross-cultural consumption research that has been produced, it is still in its early stages. Currently, we have convincing evidence that there are considerable differences in consumption practices and meanings of products across cultures, and that these meanings can readily change given shifts in the consumption environment. We have a growing body of studies documenting meaning structures in cultures. These meaning structures are strongly highlighted when directly compared with another differing culture. What began as near voyeurism into the lives of consumers in other nations has become a necessity for profitable growth as strong competition has emerged from new growth economies. Cemex (Mexico), Tata, Infosys, Reliant (India) and Alibaba (China) are currently dominant global players. Western dominance of products and services is now seriously in question. Local players provide strong competition in once underserved markets, and provide culturally appropriate product choices for local consumers. Cross-cultural consumption research has grown in sophistication over the preceding decades, and now, due to the changes in the global markets, is being recognized as an essential part of international business growth.

Implications for future cross-cultural consumption research

Research in cross-cultural consumption has not only established that meaningful differences exist across cultural divides in product meaning, consumer motivations and use of information, but has also shown that many of our measures and the models employing them are myopic and need to be adjusted or completely re-envisioned if the goal is to create a global measure or model of consumption. We are seeing rapid changes in consumer access to information as well as consumer access to like-minded groups, which will add new dimensions to how we define cultures, sub-cultures, consumption groups and market segments. Major drivers in research will come from technology, connectivity and strengthening cultural confidence of the consumer.

Technology

Technology and innovation are global in their consumption and rapid innovation to meet the needs of the consumer. The importance of particular technology and the preferences of the consumers will remain culturally dependent on the meaning ascribed to technology by the culture group. Cell phone technology leads in emerging markets due to the desperate need for information and communication. Cell phones aid farmers in India with access to market pricing and information on weather and pests (Beyond voice, 2009). They are able to sign up for information on crop prices and weather as well as information regarding crop damage and advice via services by Reuters or Tata consulting services. Similar plans are available in China and Africa, as cell phones are now owned by even the poorest villagers due to the premium placed on access to information and communication. Not only have cell phones in Africa aided farmers, but in some economically torn countries, such as Zimbabwe, cell phone credits have become a dominant currency since the Zimbabwean currency has no value (Airtime is money, 2013). Credits can be exchanged in exact amounts instead of having to barter goods. The use and meaning of the technology differ due to local economic conditions and where cell phones can provide communication and information to a population that does not have regular access to the Internet or other communication technology.

Technology is allowing markets to develop customized products, as they can be sold to individuals anywhere in the world via the Internet and home delivery services. It is not uncommon to purchase and consume products directly from a foreign provider without reliance on physical stores or local distributors. This allows savvy customers to find what they believe is the product that perfectly fits their consumption needs. How will manufacturing, customization and logistics respond to the increasing demands for the right product by consumers wishing to build a personal empire of consumption meaning via Internet/smartphone access to the world of product choice? Search engines allow consumers to locate manufacturers and product retailers with little to no effort or cost on their part other than a few minutes of search. Manufacturers and retailers can provide information and customization via web access for consumers at a lower cost than if they had to rely upon conventional marketing methods.

Advances in technology will provide researchers with a whole new set of tools that increase access to data about the consumer, advance our ability to interpret the data through new statistical software, and reduce the difficulty in accessing consumer respondents. Timelines of data collection will also dramatically improve, as methods that automatically collect consumer data will provide up-to-date detailed data via web tracking of information search, social media feeds regarding expressed attitudes, video content regarding consumer product usage, Twitter feedback tracking consumer reactions to company actions and media stories, and Facebook or other personal life-tracking websites that provide insight into very personal family events. "Big Data" is a current topic for corporate discussion regarding how it can harness web information and consumer search and purchasing data to find complex patterns that would aid company strategy.

Connectivity

Information at your fingertips creates influence and isolation. The customer's ability to access consumption information from around the globe can change the meaning of their own consumption practices. At the very same time, consumers can choose to dramatically narrow the influences on their lives by limiting their information to only sources that reinforce their current belief system. Consumers can decide what to view and what to ignore. Even though world events and sensational news items dominate the information channels and have never before seen such far-reaching effects on consumers around the globe, individual consumers can tune this out and replace that information with alternate information sources that reinforce their personal beliefs. One outcome from this increase in the access and ability to filter information could be an increase in the confidence of culture groups in maintaining traditions out of respect, comfort or pride in their culture. How does the 24/7 access to customized information change consumption meaning and choice of products to consume? Increasing concerns about sustainability, global warming, energy, food safety, organics, health care and access to clean water dominate the conversations and resonate in consumption choices and meanings in the lives of those concerned. As a result of the power consumer opinion holds over organizations, companies have quickened their response to any potentially harmful incident. For example, when the head of FIFA's executive committee was accused of misuse of funds and corruption, several major corporate sponsors announced that they were pulling their sponsorships within days of the news stories, as consumer reaction has become immediate and is often fuelled by viral discussions.

Increased choice

With the ability not only to purchase and consume product that is available in a local retail store, but also to purchase online from a multitude of retailers, the consumer can be particular about the products they purchase. In some cases, it is less expensive in time and money to purchase online, and the consumer can get the exact product attributes they prefer. This increased choice at the fingertips of consumers has created a much more particular consumer with higher expectations. In order to compete, one must provide something of value to the consumer. This forces companies to need to know much more about their customers and how the customers view their products and services. In mature markets (the United States, Europe and Japan), the customer has a wide array of product competing for their interest even in the average retail store. "Category killers" (Kotler, 2014) such as Toys R Us, Best Buy or Staples provide every brand in a particular product category with the implicit promise that the customer will find the toy, electronic item or office supply they need if they come to their store. The customer then must choose from a wide array of goods that satisfy the same base needs. Supermarkets, malls and department stores have provided the same large selection to consumers for decades. We are now seeing this same highly competitive choice-rich environment develop in India, China and other previously restricted market environments. Finally, with the increased competition from quality-driven home-grown companies in India and China, global brands are facing tough competition from local brands that have a better fit with the needs of the local consumer. This all leads to an increased importance in understanding what the consumer really wants in the product, as well as during the decision process, and final use of the product. Cross-cultural consumption research has become a necessity for survival in this rapidly localizing competitive environment for goods and services.

Conclusions

Cross-cultural consumption research needs to continue to investigate and catalogue the meaning ascribed to products, consumption practices and experiences, as we have still a long way to go in understanding the meaning of consumption. Incorporation of technology into the research methods and documenting of consumption would greatly benefit new techniques. Innovation is rapidly paced and there is little evidence that high-tech approaches to gathering interview or experiential data is occurring in the field.

Models need to be developed that capture the entire global variation of consumer decision making, motivations and consumption meaning to replace the myopic models used in the past. This is difficult, time-consuming work that is best accomplished through multicultural team research. Working in large multicultural teams is challenging as there are competing research backgrounds and expectations, so careful selection of research partners and strong organizational skills are important to the success of the team.

Much of the cross-cultural research published is focused on the "culture of the day". Editors of journals need to consider the value of the research as part of a larger need to document and catalogue consumption meaning and practices. It is a reality of the publishing world that there is concern over increasing the visibility of the journal via "hot topics", but while Asia and India are receiving much needed increased attention, Africa is non-existent, and various Eastern European and South American cultures are only of interest if they are bundled in multi-country studies with more "important" cultures. That being said, China and India are significant markets of importance for future consumption and little is known about the consumers in those countries. It is interesting to note the lack of studies looking at the cultures within those two massive countries. Both share the common misperception that they are single cultures, but locals know there are vast cultural differences within each country as significant as the differences between cultures in Europe. India, for example, has distinctive cultural groups, hundreds of languages and subdialects. Treating India as a single market or culture is a weak strategy for any company. China is similarly complex. We are only scratching the surface of understanding consumption in these markets.

Researchers publishing cross-cultural consumption research need to be very aware that even with the recognition that has been generated from the work of a handful of well-respected researchers, the field can easily damage itself by publishing methodologically weak studies. Cross-cultural research in any topical area is one of the most challenging research pursuits given the metric and measurement equivalency issues, including translations, interpretation and difficulties in gathering data in more than one country while trying to keep the conditions identical. It is not a research agenda for the faint hearted. There will be a longer timeline to publication. But it is possibly one of the most important areas for contribution currently in business and consumer research. The preceding decades of work have provided a solid foundation for the future and convinced many naysayers that the work is critically important. That given, there is still much work to be done.

References

Aaker, J. L., Benet-Martínez, V., & Garolera, J. (2001). Consumption symbols as carriers of culture: A study of Japanese and Spanish brand personality constructs. *Journal of Personality & Social Psychology, 81*(3), 492–508.

Airtime is money; the other type of mobile money. (2013, January 19). *The Economist, 406*, 72–74.

Anderson, R., & Engledow, J. (1977). A factor analytic comparison of U.S. and German information seekers. *Journal of Consumer Research, 3*(4), 185–196.

Arndt, J. (1978). Comments on cross-cultural consumer research. *Advances in Consumer Research, 5*(1), 705.

Arnould, E. J., & Wallendorf, M. (1994). Market-oriented ethnography: Interpretation building and marketing strategy formulation. *Journal of Marketing Research (JMR), 31*(4), 484–504.

Askegaard, S., Jensen, A. F., & Holt, D. B. (1999). Lipophobia: A transatlantic concept? *Advances in Consumer Research, 26*(1), 331–336.

Bagozzi, R. P., Wong, N., Abe, S., & Bergami, M. (2000). Cultural and situational contingencies and the theory of reasoned action: Application to fast food restaurant consumption. *Journal of Consumer Psychology, 9*(2), 97–106.

Belcher, J. C., & Crader, K. W. (1974). Social class, style of life and fertility in Puerto Rico. *Social Forces, 52*(4), 488–495.

Belk, R. W., Ger, G., & Askegaard, S. (2003). The fire of desire: A multisited inquiry into consumer passion. *Journal of Consumer Research, 30*(3), 326–351.

Beyond voice. (2009, September 26). *The Economist, 392*, 15-S.18.

Brewer Doran, K. (1994). Exploring cultural differences in consumer decision making: Chinese consumers in Montréal. *Advances in Consumer Research, 21*(1), 318–322.

Brunsø, K., & Grunert, K. G. (1995). Development and testing of a cross-culturally valid instrument: Food-related life style. *Advances in Consumer Research, 22*(1), 475–480.

Chen, H., Ng, S., & Rao, A. R. (2005). Cultural differences in consumer impatience. *Journal of Marketing Research, 42*(3), 291–301.

Chui, A. W., & Kwok, C. Y. (2008). National culture and life insurance consumption. *Journal of International Business Studies, 39*(1), 88–101.

Clarke III, I., & Micken, K. S. (2002). An exploratory cross-cultural analysis of the values of materialism. *Journal of International Consumer Marketing, 14*(4), 65.

Cleveland, M., Laroche, M., & Papadopoulos, N. (2009). Cosmopolitanism, consumer ethnocentrism, and materialism: An eight-country study of antecedents and outcomes. *Journal of International Marketing, 17*(1), 116–146.

Cross, S. N., & Gilly, M. C. (2014). Cultural competence and cultural compensatory mechanisms in binational households. *Journal of Marketing, 78*(3), 121–139.

d'Astous, A., Zannie, G. V., Colbert, F., Carù, A., Caldwell, M., & Courvoisier, F. (2008). Product-country images in the arts: A multi-country study. *International Marketing Review, 25*(4), 379–403.

de Mooij, M., & Hofstede, G. (2002). Convergence and divergence in consumer behaviour: Implications for international retailing. *Journal of Retailing, 78*(1), 61–69.

Demangeot, C., & Sankaran, K. (2012). Cultural pluralism: Uncovering consumption patterns in a multicultural environment. *Journal of Marketing Management, 28*(7/8), 760–783.

Durvasula, S., & Lysonski, S. (1993). Cross-cultural generalizability of a scale for profiling consumers' decision-making styles. *Journal of Consumer Affairs, 27*(1), 55–65.

Eastman, J. K., Fredenberger, B., Campbell, D., & Calvert, S. (1997). The relationship between status consumption and materialism: A cross-cultural comparison of Chinese, Mexican, and American students. *Journal of Marketing Theory & Practice, 5*(1), 52.

Englis, B. G., Solomon, M. R., & Olofsson, A. (1993). Consumption imagery in music television: A bi-cultural perspective. *Journal of Advertising, 22*(4), 21–33.

Flight, R. L., Allaway, A. W., Wan-Min, K., & D'Souza, G. (2011). A study of perceived innovation characteristics across cultures and stages of diffusion. *Journal of Marketing Theory & Practice, 19*(1), 109–126.

Ganesh, G. (1997). Spousal influence in consumer decisions: A study of cultural assimilation. *The Journal of Consumer Marketing, 14*(2), 132–155.

Ger, G., Belk, R. W., & Lascu, D. (1993). The development of consumer desire in marketizing and developing economies: The cases of Romania and Turkey. *Advances in Consumer Research, 20*(1), 102–107.

Gilly, M. C. (1995). The consumer acculturation of expatriate Americans. *Advances in Consumer Research, 22*(1), 506–510.

Goldman, A. (1974). Outreach of consumers and the modernization of urban food retailing in developing countries. *Journal of Marketing, 38*(4), 8–16.

Green, R. T., Cunningham, W. H., & Cunningham, I. C. (1975). The effectiveness of standardized global advertising. *Journal of Advertising, 4*(3), 25–29.

Green, R. T., Leonardi, J., Chandon, J., Cunningham, I. M., Verhage, B., & Strazzieri, A. (1983). Societal development and family purchasing roles: A cross-national study. *Journal of Consumer Research, 9*(4), 436–442.

Guo, X. (2013). Living in a global world: Influence of consumer global orientation on attitudes toward global brands from developed versus emerging countries. *Journal of International Marketing, 21*(1), 1–22.

Hoover, R. J., Green, R. T., & Saegert, J. (1978). A cross-national study of perceived risk. *Journal of Marketing, 42*(3), 102–108.

Houston, H. R., & Venkatesh, A. (1996). The health care consumption patterns of Asian immigrants: Grounded theory implications for consumer acculturation theory. *Advances in Consumer Research, 23*(1), 418–423.

Hung, K. H., Li, S. Y., & Belk, R. W. (2007). Glocal understandings: Female readers' perceptions of the new woman in Chinese advertising. *Journal of International Business Studies, 38*(6), 1034–1051.

Jolibert, A. J., & Baumgartner, G. (1981). Toward a definition of the consumerist segment in France. *Journal of Consumer Research, 8*(1), 114–117.

Juan Li, J., & Chenting, S. (2007). How face influences consumption. *International Journal of Market Research, 49*(2), 237–256.

Katz-Gerro, T. (1999). Cultural consumption and social stratification: Leisure activities, musical tastes, and social location. *Sociological Perspectives, 42*(4), 627–647.

Kotler, P., & Keller, K. L. (2014). *Marketing Management*. New York: Prentice Hall.

Kragh, S. U., & Djursaa, M. (2001). Product syntax and cross-cultural marketing strategies. *European Journal of Marketing*, *35*(11), 1301–1310.

Levitt, T. (1983). The globalization of markets. *Harvard Business Review*, *61*(3), 92–102.

Lim, E. C., & Ang, S. H. (2008). Hedonic vs. utilitarian consumption: A cross-cultural perspective based on cultural conditioning. *Journal of Business Research*, *61*(3), 225–232.

Lindman, R., & Lang, A. R. (1986). Anticipated effects of alcohol consumption as a function of beverage type: A cross-cultural replication. *International Journal of Psychology*, *21*(1–4), 671–678.

Luna, D., & Gupta, S. F. (2001). An integrative framework for cross-cultural consumer behaviour. *International Marketing Review*, *18*(1), 45.

Luomala, H. T., Kumar, R., Worm, V., & Singh, J. D. (2004). Cross-cultural differences in mood-regulation: An empirical comparison of individualistic and collectivistic cultures. *Journal of International Consumer Marketing*, *16*(4), 39–62.

Lutz, R. J. (1988, December). Editorial. *Journal of Consumer Research*, 288.

Martin, B. A. S., & McCracken, C. A. (2001). Music marketing: Music consumption imagery in the UK and New Zealand. *Journal of Consumer Marketing*, *18*(4), 426–436.

Mathur, S., Guiry, M., & Tikoo, S. (2008). Intergenerational culture-specific consumption differences between Asian Indian immigrants in the U.S. and Indians residing in an Indian metropolis. *Journal of International Consumer Marketing*, *20*(3/4), 69–80.

McCarty, J. A. (1989). Current theory and research on cross-cultural factors in consumer behaviour. *Advances in Consumer Research*, *16*(1), 127–129.

McCullough, J., Chin Tiong, T., & Wong, J. (1986). Effects of stereotyping in cross cultural research: Are the Chinese really Chinese? *Advances in Consumer Research*, *13*(1), 576–578.

Nielsen Jr, A. C. (1959). Do's and don'ts in selling abroad. *Journal of Marketing*, *23*(4), 405–411.

Oswald, L. R. (1999). Culture swapping: Consumption and the ethnogenesis of middle-class Haitian immigrants. *Journal of Consumer Research*, *25*(4), 303–318.

Palan, K. M., Gentina, E., & Muratore, I. (2010). Adolescent consumption autonomy: A cross-cultural examination. *Journal of Business Research*, *63*(12), 1342–1348.

Penaloza, L. N. (1989). Immigrant consumer acculturation. *Advances in Consumer Research*, *16*(1), 110–118.

Penaloza, L. (1994). Atravesando fronteras/border crossings: A critical ethnographic exploration of the consumer acculturation of Mexican immigrants. *Journal of Consumer Research*, *21*(1), 32–54.

Rose, G. M. (1999). Consumer socialization, parental style, and development timetables in the United States and Japan. *Journal of Marketing*, *63*(3), 105–119.

Ruvio, A., Shoham, A., & Maja, M. B. (2008). Consumers' need for uniqueness: Short-form scale development and cross-cultural validation. *International Marketing Review*, *25*(1), 33–53.

Saba, A., Messina, F., Turrini, A., Lumbers, M., & Raats, M. M. (2008). Older people and convenience in meal preparation: A European study on understanding their perception towards vegetable soup preparation. *International Journal of Consumer Studies*, *32*(2), 147–156.

Shukla, P. (2012). The influence of value perceptions on luxury purchase intentions in developed and emerging markets. *International Marketing Review*, *29*(6), 574–596.

Smith, D. E., Solgaard, H. S., & Beckmann, S. C. (1999). Changes and trends in alcohol consumption patterns in Europe. *Journal of Consumer Studies & Home Economics*, *23*(4), 247–260.

Squires, L., Juric, B., & Cornwell, T. B. (2001). Level of market development and intensity of organic food consumption: Cross-cultural study of Danish and New Zealand consumers. *The Journal of Consumer Marketing*, *18*(4), 392–409.

Sutton-Brady, C., Davis, T., & Jung, M. (2010). Perceived cultural spaces and cultural in-betweens: Consumption among Korean Australians. *Journal of Consumer Behaviour*, *9*(5), 349–363.

Tan, C. T., McCollough, J., & Teoh, J. (1987). An individual analysis approach to cross cultural research. *Advances in Consumer Research*, *14*(1), 394–397.

Tansey, R., Hyman, M. R., & Zinkhan, G. M. (1990). Cultural themes in Brazilian and U.S. auto ads: A cross-cultural comparison. *Journal of Advertising*, *19*(2), 30–39.

Tse, D. K., Belk, R. W., & Zhou, N. (1989). Becoming a consumer society: A longitudinal and cross-cultural content analysis of print ads from Hong Kong, the People's Republic of China, and Taiwan. *Journal of Consumer Research*, *15*(4), 457–472.

Tse, D. K., Wong, J. K., & Chin Tiong, T. (1988). Towards some standardized cross-cultural consumption values. *Advances in Consumer Research*, *15*(1), 387–395.

Viswanathan, M., Childers, T. L., & Moore, E. S. (2000). The measurement of intergenerational communication and influence on consumption: Development, validation, and cross-cultural comparison of the IGEN scale. *Journal of the Academy of Marketing Science*, *28*(3), 406.

Wallendorf, M., & Reilly, M. D. (1983). Ethnic migration, assimilation, and consumption. *Journal of Consumer Research*, *10*(3), 292–302.

Wong, N. Y., & Ahuvia, A. C. (1998). Personal taste and family face: Luxury consumption in Confucian and western societies. *Psychology & Marketing*, *15*(5), 423–441.

Xu, Y., Chen, Y., Burman, R., & Zhao, H. (2014). Second-hand clothing consumption: A cross-cultural comparison between American and Chinese young consumers. *International Journal of Consumer Studies*, *38*(6), 670–677.

Yim, M. Y., Sauer, P. L., Williams, J., Lee, S., & Macrury, I. (2014). Drivers of attitudes toward luxury brands: A cross-national investigation into the roles of interpersonal influence and brand consciousness. *International Marketing Review*, *31*(4), 363–389.

3

Globalization, branding and multicultural consumer behaviour

Carlos J. Torelli and María Rodas

With globalization on the rise, the world is shrinking and people can more easily move across physical and virtual borders, rapidly intensifying the interaction and integration among consumers and companies of different countries. These global interactions have facilitated the emergence of a consciousness of the world as a whole (Robertson, 1992) and have increased the cultural diversity of the marketplace, making it more complex and challenging for marketers. Increased cultural diversity due to globalization has brought dramatic changes to both the demand (i.e., consumers' values and desires) and supply (i.e., brands that are offered) sides of markets.

The need for marketers to better understand how these globalization forces on both the demand and supply side impact the marketplace and consumer behaviour has never been more important (Shavitt, Lee, & Torelli, 2008). Doing so will help them identify the drivers of success for building global brands and thrive in this increasingly multicultural marketplace. In the pages that follow, we review the market trends towards multiculturalism and discuss the impact that these globalization forces have on consumer behaviour. This chapter will shed light on the cultural factors that shape consumers' responses in the marketplace, the ways in which multicultural consumers react to the cultural meanings in brands and the psychological processes underlying these responses. We start by describing the globalization forces on the demand and supply sides, followed by defining culture and identifying the key cultural dimensions used to predict consumer behaviour. This discussion is followed by an exploration of cultural meanings in global brands and the implications for consumer behaviour. Finally, the chapter discusses how marketers can leverage their cultural understanding for building stronger brands and identifies knowledge gaps for guiding a future research agenda.

Globalization forces

Globalization forces on the demand side

Increased cultural diversity of the demand side of the market is fuelled by two main forces: growing multiculturalism and increased connectivity and co-creation. Multiculturalism is on the rise, driven by the emergence of a robust middle class in emerging economies (such as those of China, Russia, Brazil and India), the immigration patterns changing the cultural landscape of developed markets (e.g., the growth of Hispanics in the United States or that of Muslim populations in Europe), and the increased cultural curiosity of worldwide consumers thanks to Internet connectivity, social media platforms and global travel (e.g., in the last 10 years Chinese travellers have become the top source of tourism cash in the world; UNWTO, 2012).

Technology has also enabled a highly interconnected world, with developed countries almost reaching complete penetration of Internet access and developing countries rapidly catching up. This interconnectivity has allowed consumers to voice their opinions and be active players in the co-creation of meaning in the marketplace. For example, Dove's Campaign for Real Beauty was a huge success, mainly due to consumers sharing the content with each other, and their input shaped future extensions of the campaigns (www.dove.us/Our-Mission/Real-Beauty/default.aspx). Consumers' increased influence due to increased connectivity has also gone beyond impacting marketing campaigns (e.g., Arab Spring's Twitter revolution).

Globalization forces on the supply side

On the supply side of the market, two main forces are increasing the cultural diversity of the global marketplace: competition from every corner of the world and cultural mixing. While major American brand names such as Coke and Nike have traditionally enjoyed sustained growth in emerging economies, including China, India and Brazil, the last decade has witnessed a tremendous growth in the number of new American and European brands successfully establishing a global presence in emerging markets. For instance, one may consider the American brand Jack Daniel's success in China and Europe, which has helped the company to sell more whiskey abroad than in the United States (Kiley, 2007), or the high-stake expansion of Spanish phone company Telefónica into Latin America, which has been instrumental in helping the company become the largest telecommunications company in Europe (O'Brien, 2012). More importantly, brands from emerging markets have also recently emerged as global challengers. Consider, for example, the leadership position achieved in recent years by Chinese Lenovo Group in the personal computer industry, overtaking competitors Hewlett-Packard and Dell in worldwide sales (Hachman, 2014), or the recent entry of Indian's Tata Group into the luxury cars segment via the acquisition of the Jaguar and Land Rover brands, or the growth of Brazilian's Embraer in the Western-dominated aerospace industry.

Not only does globalization enable the proliferation of global brands; it also results in cultural mixing, whereby symbols of different cultural traditions are often found in the same location or product. Some examples of this phenomenon are the presence of Starbucks in Beijing's Forbidden City, the ownership of Budweiser, an American icon, by ABInBev, a Belgian company, and Apple products with a "Designed by Apple in California Assembled in China" label. Globalization has also increased the tension between accepting foreign cultural influence and preserving the heritage culture (Fu & Chiu, 2007). Such tension is evident in the marketplace, where contrastive cultural meanings and messages of global and local brands interact to jointly influence consumer perceptions (Robertson, 1995).

Understanding multicultural consumers

What is culture?

Culture is defined here as shared elements that provide the standards for perceiving, believing, evaluating, communicating and acting among those who share a language, a historical period and a geographic location (Triandis, 1989, 1996). Two important aspects of this definition deserve careful attention. First, as a collective phenomenon, culture consists of shared meanings that provide a common frame of reference for a human group to make sense of reality, coordinate their activities and adapt to their environment (Shore, 2002). Culture is the lens through which individuals see and provide meanings to the phenomenal world. A group of individuals who share the same standards form a cultural category or group, and such a cultural group can reside within a single country, extend across several country boundaries or coexist within the same nation as other cultural groups. In other words, cultural groups and nations are not necessarily the same thing. However, for historical and geographical reasons, nations and cultures can often overlap. Second, culture is a time-bound concept. The shared meanings that provide a frame of reference for a social group are dynamic and fluid, so American culture in the 1950s is quite different from that of the twenty-first century. Thus, cultural elements are moving targets that are not always easy to classify into discrete categories.

As a collective phenomenon, culture exists in different forms. Culture is subtly reflected in thinking styles, ideas, beliefs and values that are shared by members of a social group. At the individual level, culture can exist in two related, yet different, forms. First, culture can be present as values and beliefs that are endorsed by individuals, such as individualist versus collectivist cultural orientations (Triandis, 1989). Second, culture can exist in the form of intersubjective perceptions of culture – beliefs and values that members of a social group perceive to be widespread in their society (often referred to as intersubjective culture) (Chiu, Gelfand, Yamagishi, Shteynberg, & Wan, 2010). In other words, culture can be evident in a distinctive pattern of beliefs, thinking styles and values that are endorsed by individuals in a given group, as well as in the shared understanding that group members have about how widespread these beliefs, thinking styles and values are.

Culture exists both as a mental representation "in the head" of individuals – values and beliefs shared by a cultural group – as well as an external reality represented in material objects, social practices and social institutions (Kitayama, Duffy, & Uchida, 2007). For instance, Japanese culture is represented in beliefs about the importance of modesty and humility (Markus & Kitayama, 1991) and in the endorsement of collectivistic values of harmony and appreciating the beauty of nature (Howard, Shudo, & Umeshima, 1983). These values and beliefs are also represented externally in the Japanese tea ceremony, which embodies the recognition of harmony and the beauty of nature and life that characterizes Japanese culture (Watanabe, 1974). Similarly, Indian culture exists in the collective endorsement by its members of values of parental control, ancestral lineage and sense of kinship. These values are also externally represented in the matchmaker (or *nayan*) – the individual who serves as a broker for families trying to arrange a marriage for their marriageable-age children (Rao & Rao, 1982).

How to study culture?

The previous discussion highlights how complex it is to study culture and how cross-cultural research can be conducted at multiple levels of analyses. A first dichotomy in the study of culture is whether it should be studied inside the person (i.e., focusing on beliefs, values and interpretive frameworks for making sense of reality) or outside the person (i.e., analyzing practices, objects or institutions shared by a group) (Triandis, 2007). A second issue when studying culture is deciding the social level of analysis: across nations, across ethnic groups within nations, across individuals within nations (focusing on cultural orientation) and even across situations within individuals through the priming of cultural frames.

Regardless of how culture is studied, differences emerge in relation to the standards, behaviours and practices adopted by cultural groups throughout the world. Cross-cultural psychologists who study these differences attempt to identify the constructs underlying these cultural variations in psychological functioning (i.e., cultural syndromes; Triandis, 1996). Understanding these cultural distinctions has been demonstrated to have important implications for advertising content, persuasiveness of appeals, consumer motivation, consumer judgement processes and consumer response styles. We turn to these issues next.

Cultural effects on consumer behaviour

Research in the last three decades has demonstrated how culture impacts basic psychological domains such as self-definition, perception, knowledge organization, self-presentation, motivation and self-regulation (Shavitt, Lalwani, Zhang, & Torelli, 2006; Shavitt, Torelli, & Riemer, 2010; Triandis, 1995). A great deal has also been learned in recent years about the role of culture in consumer psychology (see Briley, Wyer, & Li, 2014; Shavitt et al., 2008, for reviews). For instance, in the persuasion domain, extensive research has clearly established that the content of and responses to advertising appeals are culturally influenced. Some cultures are more likely to use certain kinds of ad appeals than are other cultures (e.g., Alden, Hoyer, & Lee, 1993; Han & Shavitt, 1994; Kim & Markus, 1999). Culturally matched ad appeals are more likely to be effective than mismatched appeals (e.g., Aaker & Maheswaran, 1997; Han & Shavitt, 1994). A consumer's culture or cultural orientation also influences the nature of information processing that accompanies a message (Aaker & Maheswaran, 1997; Aaker & Sengupta, 2000), the role of affect in that processing (Aaker & Williams, 1998) and the types of goals that motivate consumers (Aaker & Lee, 2001).

Although most of the cross-cultural research in consumer behaviour has focused on culture as an aspect of consumers, recent research has started to acknowledge that culture is also present in products and brands. As such, consumers respond to the cultural meanings in brands and form bonds with these brands due to their ability to fulfil cultural identity goals (see Torelli, 2013; Torelli & Cheng, 2015, for reviews). Considering culture as an aspect of products and brands adds to the traditional view of culture as an aspect of consumers and highlights the fact that culture exists both "in the head" and "in the world", and as such should be incorporated in models of consumer behaviour.

Cultural dimensions driving consumer behaviour

Individualism–collectivism classification

The majority of the cross-cultural research has involved the individualism (IND) and collectivism (COL) cultural classifications (Shavitt et al., 2008). This classification was originally introduced by Hofstede (1980), and it refers to the different ways in which individuals construe their self and where they place the emphasis on the attainment of goals. In individualistic cultures, people prefer to define themselves independently of others and place the attainment of their personal goals above the goals of their in-group. In contrast, in collectivistic cultures, people prefer to define themselves interdependently with others and place the goals of their in-group above their personal goals.

National cultures that celebrate the values of independence, as in the United States, Canada, Germany and Denmark, are typically categorized as individualistic societies in which an independent self-construal is common. In contrast, cultures that nurture the values of fulfilling one's obligations and responsibilities over one's own personal wishes or desires, including most East

Asian and Latin American countries, such as China, Korea, Japan and Mexico, are categorized as collectivistic societies in which an interdependent self-construal is common (Hofstede, 1980; Triandis, 1989).

Vertical–horizontal distinction

While the IND–COL classification is the most widely used for comparison across cultures (Gudykunst & Ting-Toomey, 1988), it is too broad, resulting in potential limitations (Shavitt et al., 2006). Describing a delineation of different "species" of individualism and collectivism, Triandis and his colleagues noted that, nested within individualism and collectivism categories, some societies are horizontal (valuing equality), whereas others are vertical (emphasizing hierarchy) (Singelis, Triandis, Bhawuk, & Gelfand, 1995; Triandis & Gelfand, 1998). The vertical–horizontal distinction emerges from the observation that American or British individualism differs from, say, Australian or Norwegian individualism in much the same way that Chinese or Japanese collectivism differs from the collectivism of the Israeli kibbutz. Whereas individuals in horizontal societies value equality and view the self as having the same status as others in society, individuals in vertical societies view the self as differing from others along a hierarchy and accept inequality (Triandis, 1995). Thus, combining the horizontal–vertical distinction with the individualism–collectivism classifications produces four cultural orientations: horizontal individualist, vertical individualist, horizontal collectivist and vertical collectivist.

In vertical individualist societies (VI; e.g., the United States and the United Kingdom), people tend to be motivated by self-enhancement values of power and achievement – standing out, displaying success and status. On the other hand, in horizontal individualist societies (HI; e.g., Australia and Scandinavia), people tend to consider themselves equal to others in terms of status and instead are motivated by stimulation and self-direction – modestly expressing uniqueness and being self-reliant. In vertical collectivist societies (VC; e.g., Singapore and Mexico), people are motivated by maintaining in-group status and traditions – prioritizing collective goals over their personal goals and believing in the importance of existing hierarchies. Finally, in horizontal collectivist societies (HC; e.g., the Israeli kibbutz), people are motivated by the welfare of others – focusing on sociability and cooperation (Shavitt, et al., 2006).

The horizontal–vertical distinction resembles the power distance (PDI) continuum at the national level (Hofstede, 1980, 2001). However, there are important conceptual and structural differences between the horizontal–vertical distinction and power distance. From a conceptual standpoint, the horizontal–vertical distinction refers to differences in the acceptance of hierarchies as being valid or important in one's society. Power distance reflects the degree to which the less powerful members of organizations and institutions in a society perceive and accept inequalities in power (Hofstede, 2001). From a structural standpoint, power distance is conceptualized as a single dimension (from high to low PDI; Hofstede, 1980, 2001). The horizontal–vertical classification represents distinct categories that are conceptualized as nested within collectivism and individualism classifications and that have divergent validity (Triandis & Gelfand, 1998). Although Hofstede (1980) conceptualized IND and power distance as distinct dimensions, data do not appear to support the independence of these dimensions at the national level. The high correlation between power distance and IND, before controlling for country wealth, obtained with his operationalization suggests that there may be overlap between these two constructs (e.g., Earley & Gibson, 1998), leading to an association of high-PDI societies with VC and low-PDI societies with HI (Singelis et al., 1995).

Cultural meanings in global brands

Brands as cultural symbols

Culture not only exists in the values, beliefs and thinking styles of individuals, but also manifests itself in objects such as brands and products. Brand meanings originate in the culturally constituted world and move into brands through several instruments, such as advertising, the fashion system and reference groups (McCracken, 1986). Thus, brands can acquire cultural meanings (Aaker, Benet-Martínez, & Garolera, 2001) and become associated with the abstract characteristics that define a cultural group. There is evidence that consumers attribute cultural significance to certain commercial brands (Aaker et al., 2001). For example, some brands in the United States are associated with ruggedness (e.g., Harley-Davidson associations with strength, masculinity and toughness) and some brands in Japan are associated with peacefulness, and ruggedness and peacefulness are abstract dimensions characteristic of American and East Asian cultures, respectively. Brands that acquire cultural meanings can reach the level of a cultural symbol. This happens when the brand is consensually perceived to symbolize the abstract image that characterizes a certain cultural group (Torelli, Keh, & Chiu, 2010). To the extent that these brands are associated with knowledge about the culture, they can reach an iconic status and act as cultural reminders (see Betsky, 1997). Encountering such iconic brands can serve as subtle cultural primes that can lead to culturally patterned responses (Torelli & Cheng, 2011).

The dynamic constructivist view of culture

The notion that brands can bring to mind their attendant cultural knowledge is consistent with the dynamic constructivist view of culture. According to the dynamic constructivist theory of culture (Chiu & Hong, 2007; Hong, Morris, Chiu, & Benet-Martínez, 2000), culture is stored in memory as an associative network of knowledge. It is internalized in the form of a loose network of domain-specific knowledge structures consisting of a central concept (e.g., American culture) and its associated categories (e.g., individualist values of freedom and self-reliance), implicit theories (e.g., an individual's behaviour originates in internal dispositions) and cultural icons (e.g., the statue of liberty or the American flag) (Hong et al., 2000; Torelli & Ahluwalia, 2012; Torelli & Cheng, 2011). These knowledge structures guide cognition and behaviour only when they come to the fore in an individual's mind – because they are either chronically accessible or activated by environmental stimuli (Hong et al., 2000).

A culturally symbolic brand, which belongs to the cultural knowledge network, connects to the central cultural concept (e.g., Harley-Davidson's symbolism of American culture) as well as to the values, beliefs, ideas and other shared elements that form part of the culture (e.g., American cultural values of freedom and independence; Torelli & Cheng, 2011). Like other cultural icons, a culturally symbolic brand can activate its associated cultural knowledge and lead to culturally appropriate behaviours (Chiu, Mallorie, Keh, & Law, 2009; Torelli & Ahluwalia, 2012; Torelli, Chiu, Keh, & Amaral, 2009). For instance, after encountering American iconic brands such as Coke or Levi's (vs. non-iconic brands such as Dasani or New Balance), American participants feel more comfortable and are more successful explaining to others what it means to be an American (Torelli et al., 2009).

Consumer behaviour in a global village

Global brands and the fulfilment of cultural identity goals

Consumers often buy brands as a way of signalling to the self and others those aspects of their personality that are self-defining (Levy, 1959). For instance, a consumer might buy a

Harley motorcycle as a way of signalling the importance of being free and independent (core associations with Harley-Davidson brand) in his self-definition. However, another consumer might buy the same product due to its meanings for American culture (because of the consensual belief that Harley-Davidson is an American icon). In the latter case, the consumer uses the brand to symbolize to the self and others a cultural identity (Swaminathan, Page, & Gürhan-Canli, 2007; Torelli, 2013). A cultural identity relates to the membership in a particular cultural, or subcultural, group that is clearly distinguishable from other cultural groups (Chiu & Hong, 2006). Culturally symbolic brands are public expressions of the abstract meanings of a cultural group and, because such brands symbolize culturally important beliefs, ideas and values, consumers with a heightened need to symbolize a cultural identity will judge culturally symbolic brands as highly instrumental for fulfilling such needs (Torelli, 2013). By consuming a culturally symbolic brand, one can emphasize the possession of the cultural identity and the alignment with and adherence to the culture (Escalas & Bettman, 2005).

Making salient a cultural identity triggers favourable attitudes towards objects that are identity-congruent. For instance, when making an ethnic identity salient (e.g., Asian), consumers evaluate more favourably advertisements that are targeted to the ethnic in-group (e.g., by means of the copy or the images in the ad) (Forehand, Deshpandé, & Reed, 2002) or that include a spokesperson from the ethnic in-group (Forehand & Deshpandé, 2001) than when the identity is not made salient. Because commitment to a cultural identity makes the identity more likely to be salient in different contexts, highly identified consumers are especially motivated to favour culturally symbolic brands (over non-symbolic ones) to fulfil their salient cultural identity needs (Torelli et al., 2009; Torelli, Chiu, Keh, & Amaral, 2010; Torelli, Keh, et al., 2010).

A salient cultural identity increases the desirability of brands that symbolize it, which causes consumers to evaluate more favourably and to be willing to pay more for culturally symbolic brands (Torelli, Chiu, et al., 2010). Furthermore, because a salient social identity brings to mind identity-consistent decisions that do not require further reflection, the higher valuation of culturally symbolic brands occurs rather automatically and without conscious deliberation. In other words, consumers process information about a culturally symbolic brand easily and feel that it is right to favour the brand. In turn, this feeling results in a pleasing processing experience and an accompanying enhanced brand valuation (Torelli & Ahluwalia, 2012).

Consumer relationships with culturally symbolic brands

Over time, continued reliance on culturally symbolic brands for fulfilling salient cultural identity needs can result in the development of strong self-brand relationships (Torelli, Chiu et al., 2010). This is particularly true among consumers with a chronic need to identify with a cultural identity – or who are highly identified with the culture. Because chronic identification with a cultural identity increases the likelihood that the identity is salient when evaluating a brand, highly identified consumers establish stronger bonds with culturally symbolic brands. Recent research illustrates this phenomenon (Torelli, Chiu, & Keh, 2010). In one study, American and Chinese participants were prompted to spontaneously elicit their favourite brand and assessed the extent to which they were likely to elicit a brand that was high (vs. low) in cultural symbolism, as well as rating the brand in terms of their self–brand connections. In addition, participants indicated their level of identification with their American or Chinese identity. Results showed that participants with a chronically salient cultural identity (i.e., those highly identified with their cultural group) (a) were more likely to spontaneously list a brand that was strongly associated with their salient cultural identity and (b) reported a higher level of self–brand connection for brands that were high in cultural symbolism for their corresponding cultural group. No such relationships emerged for participants low in identification with the cultural identity. In a second study, upon heightening the level of cultural symbolism of an American brand (Sprite) by telling participants that most Americans believe that Sprite is associated with other American icons such as the Statue of Liberty and the Super Bowl, American participants reported a stronger level of self-brand connection with Sprite to the extent that the brand was perceived to be higher in cultural symbolism. This effect was absent in a neutral condition in which the brand's associations with American culture were not made salient.

The results just described illustrate how a brand's cultural symbolism impacts the strength of the relationship that consumers establish with the brand. Stronger bonds with culturally symbolic brands are more likely to emerge when cultural identities are chronically or temporarily salient. This occurs because identity salience heightens the valuation of culturally symbolic brands. Furthermore, forming a strong bond with a culturally symbolic brand, due to its cultural identity meaning, can also shield the brand against negative publicity when cultural identity needs are salient (Swaminathan et al., 2007).

Culture mixing and its consequences

In globalized markets, symbols of different cultures often occupy the same space at the same time. Unlike the situation investigated in most monoculture priming research (e.g., Hong et al., 2000), exposure to symbols of multiple cultures or culture mixing, activates not only one, but two or more, cultural representations at the same time. Recent research has found some distinctive effects of culture mixing that are different from the effects of typical cultural priming (i.e., single-culture priming). Specifically, culture mixing draws attention to cultural differences, resulting in the expectation that cultures are discrete entities with relatively impermeable boundaries. For instance, compared with showing American participants culture-neutral products that carried prototypic British brand names (monocultural priming), showing them iconic Mexican products that carry British brand names (culture-mixed product) activates representations of Mexican and British cultures at the same time and increases perceived differences between cultures (Torelli, Chiu, Tam, Au, & Keh, 2011). This effect emerges not only for the target cultures (e.g., Mexican and British), but also for other cultures (e.g., Puerto Rican and Canadian). Culture-mixed products can also trigger negative consumer reactions. For instance, American participants evaluate less favourably a culture-mixed product (Sony cappuccino machines – the Sony brand is iconic of Japan whereas cappuccino machines are iconic of Italy) than a monocultural product (Sony toaster oven – only the Japanese Sony is culturally symbolic), in spite of the similar levels of moderate fit of the two products with the Sony brand (Torelli & Ahluwalia, 2012). This unfavourable evaluation is driven by the subjective experience of disfluency triggered by the simultaneous activation of two different cultural schemas.

Recent studies (Cheng, 2010; Cheng et al., 2011; Chiu & Cheng, 2007; Torelli & Ahluwalia, 2012; Torelli et al., 2011) have uncovered two factors that foster negative reactions towards culture mixing: salience of intercultural competition and culture defence mindset. First, salient intercultural competition highlights the in-group–out-group boundary and heightens a sense of distrust of out-groups (Turner, Hogg, Oakes, Reicher, & Wetherell, 1987). This should result in more unfavourable attitudes towards potential cultural mixing and exclusionary reactions towards other cultures. Cheng et al. (2011) investigated this notion with Chinese consumers during the 2008 Beijing Olympics. Mainland Chinese participants evaluated brands that symbolize either Chinese (e.g., LiNing) or American cultures (e.g., Nike) before and after the Beijing Olympics. Before the Olympics, only respondents who were highly identified with Chinese culture showed favouritism for Chinese- (over American-) symbolic brands. However, as the Olympics progressed, presumably because of the salient rivalry between the United States and China, participants who were both high and low in their identification with Chinese culture exhibited favouritism for Chinese- (over American-) symbolic brands. This finding suggests that, in the face of salient intercultural competition, people shifted their preferences in favour of brands that symbolize the local culture over brands that symbolize a competing foreign culture.

Second, resistance to culture mixing can be fostered by a culture defence mindset, such as that triggered by thoughts of one's own death (Torelli et al., 2011). When reminded of their mortality, people adhere to and defend their cultural worldview as a way to achieve symbolic immortality (Greenberg, Porteus, Simon, & Pyszczynski, 1995). This in turn encourages aggression against those who violate the cultural worldview (McGregor et al., 1998) and evokes intolerance of using cultural icons in an inappropriate way (e.g., using the crucifix as a hammer; Greenberg et al., 1995). Extending this notion to culture-mixed situations, Torelli and colleagues (2011) show that people are particularly intolerant of contamination of brands that symbolize their culture when they are under the joint influence of culture mixing and mortality salience. Upon inducing (vs. not) mortality salience, American participants were asked to evaluate a marketing plan of Nike (an American icon), which involved some questionable actions to increase its competitiveness in a foreign market (e.g., eliminating the "Swoosh" symbol and replacing the Nike brand name with the Arabic word for "Sportsmanship" to penetrate the Middle East market). Results showed that, only upon making mortality salient, participants evaluated the marketing plan less favourably after evaluating culture-mixed products (e.g., a Chinese brand of breakfast cereal) than after evaluating monocultural products (e.g., an American brand of breakfast cereal).

However, there are also instances in which culture mixing in brands can be favourably received by consumers. This is particularly likely among young biculturated consumers (i.e., knowledgeable about two cultures) who tend to be proficient in foreign languages and are familiar with foreign and domestic brands alike. This kind of multicultural exposure is associated with appreciation of the complementary strengths of dissimilar cultures, which in turn promotes integrating the two mixed cultures and recognizing the value of such cultural integration (Leung & Chiu, 2010; Leung, Maddux, Galinsky, & Chiu, 2008). Furthermore, younger (vs. older) biculturated consumers are also more likely to value autonomy, independence and individualism (Zhang, 2009), and endorsement of autonomy values is positively correlated with openness to experience (Roccas, Sagiv, Schwartz, & Knafo, 2002), a personality variable that also promotes integrating dissimilar cultures (Leung et al., 2008). Thus, because of their multiculturalism and openness to experience, younger biculturated consumers can evaluate more favourably culture mixing in the marketplace.

Recent research with younger, educated Chinese consumers illustrates how these highly biculturated consumers respond favourably to culture mixing in brand name translations (Keh, Torelli, Hao, & Chiu, 2011). Translation of Western brand names into Chinese represents a complex case of name translation, as it involves translation from a phonographic system into a logographic system (Zhang & Schmitt, 2001). There are three common ways of translating brand names into Chinese: by sound (phonetic translation), by meaning (semantic translation) and by sound plus meaning (phonosemantic translation). Because this latter approach mixes a Western-sounding name with the meaning of the name in Chinese language, phonosemantic translations result in a culture-mixed brand name. In contrast, phonetic and semantic translations include only symbols of a single culture (via sound or meaning only). Studies conducted by Keh and colleagues (2011) demonstrate that young, educated Chinese consumers evaluate more favourably culture mixing in phonosemantic translations than they do in monocultural phonetic or semantic ones. This occurs because young, educated Chinese consumers integrate the autonomy values associated with a phonosemantic brand translation (due to its Western-sounding name) with inferences about the cultural sensitivity of the marketer (due to the brand meaning in Chinese language), which in turn leads them to evaluate more favourably culture-mixed phonosemantic (vs. monocultural semantic or phonetic) brand name translations. Furthermore, such favourable attitudes towards culture mixing are more likely to emerge among individuals with a higher (vs. lower) endorsement of autonomy values, as well as for products higher (vs. lower) in value-expressiveness – which are more easily able to communicate things about their users.

Regional cultural identities and social identity needs

Several cultures can coexist within the same region, and the geographic borders that delineate a cultural region might or might not coincide with country boundaries (Triandis, 1995). Furthermore, it is often the case that different cultures that coexist within a common region compete with each other, collaborate with each other or interact with each other within a hierarchical arrangement of social groups. For instance, people in the United States share the same American culture. However, we can easily identify subgroups of individuals within the United States that share distinctive cultural elements on the basis of ethnic background (e.g., White Americans, Black Americans, Latinos or Native Americans) or regional history (e.g., Southerners or Upper Midwesterners). We refer to the patterns of cultural meanings shared by these subgroups as sub-cultures within the superordinate American culture. These sub-cultures often compete with each other for the allocation of economic resources, but also cooperate with each other in shaping a common American identity.

National groups with different country-level identities (e.g., Americans or Canadians) can also develop a sense of belongingness to a superordinate regional identity (e.g., North American identity; Resnick, 2012). For instance, researchers often consider that East Asians share common cultural meanings rooted in Confucianism (Nisbett, 2003; Triandis, 1995), or deliberate about the emergence of an overarching European identity (Checkel & Katzenstein, 2009). Nevertheless, Chinese, Korean and Japanese cultures have their distinct cultural elements (e.g., the notion of *amae* in Japan (Doi, 1973) or that of *chong* in Korea (U. Kim & Choi, 1994)) in the same way that Spanish and Danish cultures share unique cultural scripts (e.g., the *Janteloven* in Denmark (Nelson & Shavitt, 2002) or the cultural script of *simpatía* in Spain (Triandis, Marín, Lisansky, & Betancourt, 1984)).

Because people can define themselves in terms of either subgroup or superordinate regional identities depending on the context, consumers can factor in their sense of belongingness to a superordinate cultural group when interacting with brands that symbolize an out-group. Specifically, when members of different subgroups (e.g., Koreans and Japanese) are induced to think of themselves as a single superordinate group (e.g., recategorization as East Asians) rather than two separate groups, attitudes towards former out-group members (i.e., Koreans' views of Japanese) can become more positive (i.e., pro-in-group bias; Gaertner, Dovidio, Anastasio, Bachman, & Rust, 1993).

Because symbolic markers of identities are potential substitutes for one another (Braun & Wicklund, 1989), when the need to symbolize a cultural identity is heightened (e.g., being a Minnesotan), encountering a brand associated with a subgroup (e.g., Wisconsinite) nested within a superordinate regional identity (e.g., Upper Midwesterner) can trigger recategorization at this superordinate level, which in turn results in more favourable brand evaluations, or pro-in-group bias. Recent research (Torelli, Ahluwalia, Stoner, & Cheng, forthcoming) investigated the factors and psychological processes that impact people's reactions towards brands that symbolize out-group cultures that are nested within the same superordinate regional identity. Specifically, this research shows that salient cultural identity needs induce recategorization processes, which in turn result in preference for products associated with a subgroup nested within a common superordinate social identity (i.e., pro-in-group bias towards a former out-group). For instance, one study shows that Mexican immigrants living in the United States – a minority group that commonly exhibits higher levels of cultural identity salience (Forehand et al., 2002) – prefer more Argentine products compared with Mexican consumers living in Mexico (for whom cultural identity needs are less salient). Furthermore, this higher preference for Argentine products is mediated by the inclusion of the nested subgroup (i.e., Argentines) within participants' social group.

However, this recategorization effect is more likely to occur when in-group–out-group rivalries are not salient. Because aggregate regional identities consist of subgroups that can compete for resources, supremacy or cultural dominance, the salience of intergroup rivalries can interfere with recategorization (Torelli et al., forthcoming). When recategorization at a superordinate regional identity becomes a threat to positivity and distinctiveness, as when negative aspects of a rival subgroup are made salient, such recategorization processes can backfire and increase intergroup bias (Crisp, Stone, & Hall, 2006). In the face of antagonism or when strong rivalries between subgroups are situationally salient (e.g., during sports competitions; Cheng et al., 2011), recategorization at the superordinate social identity level does not occur and people are even more likely to devalue what can be perceived as a rival out-group brand. This effect is illustrated in a study conducted during the 2014 Sochi Winter Olympics (Torelli et al., forthcoming). American participants were interviewed the day before the women's curling final between Canada (nested subgroup in the regional North American identity) and Sweden (non-nested subgroup), just a few hours before the highly publicized gold medal final between the American women's hockey team and its archrival Canadian team (a loss for the US women's team). It is important to note that throughout the Winter Olympics, the American media focused heavily on the Canada vs. United States rivalry in the medal count and particularly on the flagship hockey games between Canada and the United States (both men and women). Participants were asked about their support for Canada or Sweden in the curling final. Results showed that a heightened need to express their cultural identity led Americans to support the Canadian (Swedish) team less (more). This effect occurred because the recategorization process was interrupted due to the salient intergroup rivalry, and instead, it triggered an alternative process for expressing the salient cultural identity – denigrating the rival.

Leveraging global brands

Given the above review on the positive and negative reactions to global brands that have cultural symbolism attached to them, how does a brand's status as a cultural symbol influence its ability to leverage its brand equity through product extensions? Prior research on this topic suggests that for well-known brands, country or culture associations play only a nominal role in attitudes and choices (Balabanis & Diamantopoulos, 2008). However, the discussion in the previous pages suggests that, depending on the context, a culturally symbolic status might be an asset or a liability when leveraging brand equity.

Exposure to a culturally symbolic brand activates its associated cultural schema. Previous research suggests that cueing of a schema, via the process of spreading activation, can create expectancies by activating other concepts strongly related to it (Whittlesea, 1993). The increased activation of these associated concepts facilitates their identification (Biederman, 1995), making their processing easier or more fluent (i.e., rendering them conceptually fluent; Shapiro, 1999).

Conceptual fluency, or the ease with which a target stimuli is processed when primed by an associated concept, is known to enhance stimuli evaluations (Lee & Labroo, 2004; Whittlesea, 1993). Fluency effects are typically driven by the perceiver attributing "ease of processing" to better quality of the target (Avnet & Higgins, 2003). It stands to reason that when a product extension is associated with the cultural schema activated by the brand (i.e., the brand and extension product category are culturally congruent) the extension is likely to be processed fluently, generating a feeling of ease and leading to a more favourable evaluation of the extension. Importantly, if the context involves lower involvement or motivation conditions, such as those typically prevalent in the marketplace, people are even more likely to rely on this fluency experience for their evaluations (Fang, Singh, & Ahluwalia, 2007).

In a series of studies using familiar culturally symbolic brands from a variety of cultures (Italian, American, British, Mexican or Japanese), Torelli and Ahluwalia (2012) demonstrate the advantage in terms of favourable evaluations enjoyed by culturally symbolic brands when extending into culturally congruent products, beyond what one might expect given the brand–product fit. These advantages emerged relative to extensions into culturally neutral products with similar levels of fit with the parent brand, as well as relative to product extensions introduced by brands low in cultural symbolism. For instance, in one study (Torelli & Ahluwalia, 2012), participants evaluated more favourably an extension by Sony (a Japanese icon) into the culturally congruent sushi serving set product (a product symbolic of Japan) compared with an extension into the culturally neutral food serving set. This effect emerged in spite of the similar levels of low fit between the Sony brand and the two product extensions (food-related products are incompatible with Sony's image) and after controlling for participants' prior attitudes towards both Sony and the extension product. In another study (Torelli & Ahluwalia, 2009), participants also evaluated more favourably a Sony sushi serving set compared with a similar product extension introduced by Panasonic – a brand that, although associated with Japan, is relatively neutral in terms of its cultural symbolism. Attesting to the generalizability of the cultural congruity effect, Torelli and Ahluwalia (2012) demonstrate that this effect emerges for both moderate and low-fit brand extensions, as well as for narrow and broad brands. Furthermore, empirical evidence confirmed that the effect was driven by the processing fluency generated by the simultaneous activation of the same cultural schema by the product and the brand.

What if the brand and the product category activate incongruent or different cultural schemas? As indicated earlier, the simultaneous activation of two different cultural schemas can increase perceptions of cultural contamination. When two contrasting cultural schemas are activated, their incongruency is also likely to result in a decreased fluency or ease in processing the new product. This sense of unease or disfluency generated by the incongruency is likely to make consumers less receptive to the extension, overriding the effects of conscious elaboration on the potential fit between the brand and the extension product. In support of this prediction, Torelli and Ahluwalia (2012) demonstrated that people exhibit more unfavourable evaluations of culturally incongruent brand extensions (e.g., Sony cappuccino makers or Budweiser tequila) compared with culturally neutral ones (e.g., Sony toaster oven or Budweiser brandy) with similar levels of brand–product fit. However, the effects only emerged when both the brand and the product were culturally symbolic, likely to automatically activate a cultural schema; they did not emerge for brands low in cultural symbolism (e.g., for Coors tequila – where Coors, although clearly an American brand, is rated relatively low in American culture symbolism). Furthermore, the effects were driven by the processing disfluency generated by the simultaneous activation of different cultural schemas by the product and the brand.

In summary, the findings reviewed in this section show that a brand's cultural symbolism can be a liability or an asset, and to harness it profitably, a manager needs to understand the cultural symbolism of the potential extension categories under consideration. Culturally symbolic brands may successfully extend into culturally congruent products regardless of fit, and may backfire in culturally incongruent categories despite their perceived fit. Cultural associations, however, are not likely to be of concern for managers of brands that are neutral or low in cultural symbolism, as these associations are unlikely to drive people's judgements.

Conclusions and future directions

Marketing efforts are becoming increasingly globalized, so it is imperative for marketers to understand how the multiculturalism triggered by globalization forces impact consumer behaviour. Our discussion above sheds light on the cultural factors that shape consumers' responses in a global marketplace, as well as providing marketers with a theoretical framework for deepening consumer–brand bonds in multicultural markets. However, many questions still remain unanswered. What other cultural dimensions beyond the ones discussed in this chapter have the greatest potential to further refine our predictions of consumer behaviour? How is knowledge about different cultures acquired and organized in consumers' minds? Would the way in which people organize cultural knowledge in memory influence their consumption behaviour? How do iconic cultural brands emerge? How are meanings for different cultural groups appropriated by consumers to build their identities?

In trying to uncover the cultural dimensions that would provide a more nuanced understanding of consumer behaviour, researchers should consider the distinction between cultures that are "tight" – having strong norms and a low tolerance of deviant behaviour – and those that are "loose" – having weak norms and a high tolerance of deviant behaviour (Gelfand et al., 2011). This distinction has important implications for a variety of psychological domains. For instance, individuals in tight (vs. loose) cultures are more prevention-focused (i.e., concerned with avoiding mistakes) and have higher self-regulatory strength (i.e., higher impulse control) (Gelfand et al., 2011). Research linking the cultural dimensions of tightness and looseness with consumer behaviour aligned with these culturally distinctive self-regulatory tendencies offers great potential.

This chapter discussed how the coexistence of two or more cultures within a consumer or within a market offering can impact consumer behaviour. One fruitful avenue to further advance this domain of inquiry is to investigate the cognitive and motivational principles governing activation and application of cultural knowledge. Recent research suggests that making a cultural identity salient triggers a motivational pull towards identity-congruent judgements and behaviours (i.e., identity-based motivation; Oyserman, 2009; Oyserman, Fryberg, & Yoder, 2007). When situations cue an identity, the cued identity triggers a general readiness to make sense of the world in identity-congruent terms, including the norms and goals associated with that identity. Furthermore, research also suggests that the way in which cultural frames are organized in memory can impact the motivations triggered by exposure to cultural primes (Mok & Morris, 2013). Thus, research should further investigate the differential effect on behaviour of cultural knowledge acquired by a substantial cultural immersion (e.g., growing up in a culture and developing a cultural identity) or by more superficial encounters via international travel and indirect cultural contacts. In general, cultural knowledge acquired through substantial cultural immersion seems more likely to be identity relevant. Thus, activation and application of this knowledge might have not only cognitive consequences (as is also the case for cultural knowledge acquired through briefer encounters) but also motivational consequences.

Due to the rise in globalization, people are increasingly recognizing the commonalities rather than dissimilarities among people around the world and are also more interested in global events. The emergence of a global culture, characterized by cosmopolitanism and a zest for wide international experience, is evident in the growing number of individuals who identify themselves with people from around the world (Arnett, 2002). These individuals seem to develop a bicultural identity that can foster the integration of the meanings from different cultural traditions and appreciate the cultural mixing in brands (Keh et al., 2011). However, because the values of a global culture are closer to those of the Western world, it seems plausible that a global mindset might be more easily embraced by individuals with different cultural backgrounds. For a Westerner, a global identity might be more similar to the local identity than for an Easterner. If so, Westerners (vs. Easterners) might find it easier to integrate a global and a local identity. Future research should investigate these issues by trying to uncover the psychological processes underlying the fulfilment of global identity goals among consumers of different cultures, as well as to more clearly delineate the psychological characteristics of a global mindset as manifested in different cultures.

Research has just started to investigate how brands that symbolize regional identities consisting of subgroups in close geographical proximity can help consumers fulfil their salient cultural identity needs. These subgroups are likely to share common resources (e.g., waterways and ecosystems) and to have common historical and cultural roots, which should help in developing the sense of a shared regional cultural identity. However, shared identities could also emerge from colonization processes in which a dominant power spreads its cultural influence across diverse geographies. Consider for instance the Commonwealth, a group of 53 country-states spread throughout the world that were mostly territories of the former British Empire. Although many of these countries are not in close proximity to one another, they are united by language, history and culture (thecommonwealth.org, 2015). Indeed, the Commonwealth can play a role in providing a sense of cultural identity to the people in some of these countries (Merchant & Rich, 2004), or even infuse their identity with a level of Britishness (Meaney, 2001). Further research should investigate the more complex identity processes associated with regional identities emerging from colonization processes.

Little is known about how brands emerge as cultural symbols. Unlike some cultural icons such as the American national flag that are created to symbolize a nation, brands and products are originally created for commercial purposes. Yet, some brands or products gradually become widely regarded as cultural icons. Torelli and colleagues (Torelli, 2013; Torelli, Keh et al., 2010; Torelli & Stoner, 2015) identify some of the factors that contribute to a brand's cultural symbolism (or its cultural equity). They propose that country (or region) of origin associations, global-ness associations (i.e., perceiving the brand as being global), embodiment of abstract cultural characteristics, and cultural authority are four building blocks of cultural symbolism. This chapter discussed how both translating a brand name into a foreign language and developing a communication campaign in a foreign market can help the brand to shape its cultural meanings. However, little is known about the sociological or psychological processes that determine how these different actions are integrated into a consensual view of brands as symbols of a culture. Although marketers might spend time and resources in positioning brands as cultural symbols, not all attempts will succeed. It seems important, then, to study the psychological conditions that would facilitate, or hinder, the emergence of cultural symbols within a group.

References

Aaker, J. L., Benet-Martínez, V., & Garolera, J. (2001). Consumption symbols as carriers of culture: A study of Japanese and Spanish brand personality constructs. *Journal of Personality and Social Psychology*, *81*, 492–508.

Aaker, J. L., & Lee, A. Y. (2001). "I" seek pleasures and "we" avoid pains: The role of self-regulatory goals in information processing and persuasion. *Journal of Consumer Research, 28*, 33–49.
Aaker, J. L., & Maheswaran, D. (1997). The effect of cultural orientation on persuasion. *Journal of Consumer Research, 24*, 315–328.
Aaker, J. L., & Sengupta, J. (2000). Addivity versus attenuation: The role of culture in the resolution of information incongruity. *Journal of Consumer Psychology, 9*, 67–82.
Aaker, J. L., & Williams, P. (1998). Empathy versus pride: The influence of emotional appeals across cultures. *Journal of Consumer Research, 25*, 241–261.
Alden, D. L., Hoyer, W. D., & Lee, C. (1993). Identifying global and culture-specific dimensions of humor in advertising: A multinational analysis. *Journal of Marketing, 57*, 64–75.
Arnett, J. J. (2002). The psychology of globalization. *American Psychologist, 57*, 774–783.
Avnet, T., & Higgins, T. E. (2003). Locomotion, assessment, and regulatory fit: Value transfer from "how" to "what". *Journal of Experimental Social Psychology, 39*, 525–530.
Balabanis, G., & Diamantopoulos, A. (2008). Brand origin identification by consumers: A classification perspective. *Journal of International Marketing, 16*, 39–71.
Betsky, A. (1997). *Icons: Magnets of meaning*. San Francisco, CA: Chronicle Books.
Biederman, I. (1995). Visual object recognition. In S. M. Kosslyn & D. N. Osherson (Eds.), *Visual cognition: An invitation to cognitive science* (pp. 121–166). Cambridge, MA: The MIT Press.
Braun, O. L., & Wicklund, R. A. (1989). Psychological antecedents of conspicuous consumption. *Journal of Economic Psychology, 10*, 161–187.
Briley, D. A., Wyer Jr, R. S., & Li, E. (2014). A dynamic view of cultural influence: A review. *Journal of Consumer Psychology, 24*(4), 557–571.
Checkel, J. T., & Katzenstein, P. J. (2009). *European identity*. Cambridge: Cambridge University Press.
Cheng, S. Y.-y. (2010). *Social psychology of globalization: Joint activation of cultures and reactions to foreign cultural influence* (Unpublished dissertation). University of Illinois at Urbana-Champaign.
Cheng, S. Y. Y., Rosner, J. L., Chao, M. M., Peng, S., Chen, X., Li, Y., ... & Chiu, C.-Y. (2011). One world, one dream? Intergroup consequences of the 2008 Beijing Olympics. *International Journal of Intercultural Relations, 35*, 296–306.
Chiu, C.-Y., & Cheng, S. Y.-y. (2007). Toward a social psychology of culture and globalization: Some social cognitive consequences of activating two cultures simultaneously. *Social and Personality Psychology Compass, 1*, 84–100.
Chiu, C.-Y., Gelfand, M. J., Yamagishi, T., Shteynberg, G., & Wan, C. (2010). Intersubjective culture: The role of intersubjective perceptions in cross-cultural research. *Perspectives on Psychological Science, 5*, 482–493.
Chiu, C.-Y., & Hong, Y.-Y. (2006). *Social psychology of culture*. New York, NY: Psychology Press.
Chiu, C.-Y., & Hong, Y.-Y. (2007). Cultural processes: Basic principles. In T. E. Higgins & A. W. Kruglanski (Eds.), *Social psychology: Handbook of basic principles* (pp. 785–806). New York, NY: Guilford.
Chiu, C.-Y., Mallorie, L., Keh, H. T., & Law, W. (2009). Perceptions of culture in multicultural space: Joint presentation of images from two cultures increases in-group attribution of culture-typical characteristics. *Journal of Cross-Cultural Psychology, 40*, 282–300.
Crisp, R. J., Stone, C. H., & Hall, N. R. (2006). Recategorization and subgroup identification: Predicting and preventing threats from common ingroups. *Personality and Social Psychology Bulletin, 32*, 230–243.
Doi, T. (1973). *The anatomy of dependence*. Tokyo: Kodansha International.
Earley, P. C., & Gibson, C. B. (1998). Taking stock in our progress on individualism-collectivism: 100 years of solidarity and community. *Journal of Management, 24*, 265–304.
Escalas, J. E., & Bettman, J. R. (2005). Self-construal, reference groups, and brand meaning. *Journal of Consumer Research, 32*, 378–389.
Fang, X., Singh, S., & Ahluwalia, R. (2007). An examination of different explanations for the mere exposure effect. *Journal of Consumer Research, 34*, 97–103.
Forehand, M. R., & Deshpandé, R. (2001). What we see makes us who we are: Priming ethnic self-awareness and advertising response. *Journal of Marketing Research, 38*, 336–348.
Forehand, M. R., Deshpandé, R., & Reed, A. (2002). Identity salience and the influence of differential activation of the social self-schema on advertising response. *Journal of Applied Psychology, 87*, 1086–1099.
Fu, H.-y., & Chiu, C.-Y. (2007). Local culture's responses to globalization: Exemplary persons and their attendant values. *Journal of Cross-Cultural Psychology, 38*, 636–653.

Gaertner, S. L., Dovidio, J. F., Anastasio, P. A., Bachman, B. A., & Rust, M. C. (1993). The common ingroup identity model: Recategorization and the reduction of intergroup bias. *European Review of Social Psychology*, *4*, 1–26.

Gelfand, M. J., Raver, J. L., Nishii, L., Leslie, L. M., Lun, J., Lim, B. C., … & Yamaguchi, S. (2011). Differences between tight and loose cultures: A 33-nation study. *Science*, *332*, 1100–1104.

Greenberg, J., Porteus, J., Simon, L., & Pyszczynski, T. (1995). Evidence of a terror management function of cultural icons: The effects of mortality salience on the inappropriate use of cherished cultural symbols. *Personality and Social Psychology Bulletin*, *21*, 1221–1228.

Gudykunst, W. B., & Ting-Toomey, S. (1988). *Culture and interpersonal communication*. Newbury Park, CA: Sage.

Hachman, M. (2014). Lenovo widens lead as PC market decline slows. *pcworld.com*. Retrieved September 3, 2014 from www.pcworld.com/article/2086561/lenovo-widens-lead-as-pc-market-decline-slows.html

Han, S.-p., & Shavitt, S. (1994). Persuasion and culture: Advertising appeals in individualistic and collectivistic societies. *Journal of Experimental Social Psychology*, *30*, 326–350.

Hofstede, G. H. (1980). *Culture's consequences: International differences in work-related values*. Newbury Park, CA: Sage.

Hofstede, G. H. (2001). *Culture's consequences: Comparing values, behaviours, institutions and organizations across nations*. Thousand Oaks, CA: Sage.

Hong, Y.-Y., Morris, M. W., Chiu, C.-Y., & Benet-Martínez, V. (2000). Multicultural minds: A dynamic constructivist approach to culture and cognition. *American Psychologist*, *55*, 709–720.

Howard, A., Shudo, K., & Umeshima, M. (1983). Motivation and values among Japanese and American managers. *Personnel Psychology*, *36*, 883–898.

Keh, H. T., Torelli, C. J., Hao, J., & Chiu, C.-y. (2011). The effects of brand translations and their cultural symbolism on brand evaluations among young Chinese consumers. In R. Ahluwalia, T. L. Chartrand & R. K. Ratner (Eds.), *Advances in Consumer Research* (Vol. 39, pp. 70–71). Duluth, MN: Association for Consumer Research.

Kiley, D. (2007). Jack Daniel's international appeal. *businessweek.com*. Retrieved September 3, 2014 from www.bloomberg.com/news/articles/2007-10-10/jack-daniels-international-appealbusinessweek-business-news-stock-market-and-financial-advice

Kim, H. S., & Markus, H. R. (1999). Deviance or uniqueness, harmony or conformity? A cultural analysis. *Journal of Personality and Social Psychology*, *77*, 785–800.

Kim, U., & Choi, S.-H. (1994). Individualism, collectivism, and child development: A Korean perspective. In P. M. Greenfield & R. R. Cocking (Eds.), *Crosscultural roots of minority child development* (pp. 227–257). Hillsdale, NJ: Lawrence Erlbaum Associates.

Kitayama, S., Duffy, S., & Uchida, Y. (2007). Self as cultural mode of being. In D. Cohen & S. Kitayama (Eds.), *Handbook of cultural psychology* (pp. 136–174). New York, NY: Guilford.

Lee, A. Y., & Labroo, A. A. (2004). The effect of conceptual and perceptual fluency on brand evaluation. *Journal of Marketing Research*, *41*, 151–165.

Leung, A. K.-y., & Chiu, C.-y. (2010). Multicultural experience, idea receptiveness, and creativity. *Journal of Cross-Cultural Psychology*, *41*, 723–741.

Leung, A. K.-y., Maddux, W. W., Galinsky, A. D., & Chiu, C.-Y. (2008). Multicultural experience enhances creativity: The when and how. *American Psychologist*, *63*, 169–181.

Levy, S. J. (1959). Symbols for sale. *Harvard Business Review*, *37*, 117–124.

Markus, H. R., & Kitayama, S. (1991). Culture and the self: Implications for cognition, emotion, and motivation. *Psychological Review*, *98*, 224–253.

McCracken, G. (1986). Culture and consumption: A theoretical account of the structure and movement of the cultural meaning of consumer goods. *Journal of Consumer Research*, *13*, 71–84.

McGregor, H. A., Lieberman, J. D., Greenberg, J., Solomon, S., Arndt, J., Simon, L., & Pyszczynski, T. (1998). Terror management and aggression: Evidence that mortality salience motivates aggression against worldview-threatening others. *Journal of Personality and Social Psychology*, *74*, 590–605.

Meaney, N. (2001). Britishness and Australian identity: The problem of nationalism in Australian history and historiography. *Australian Historical Studies*, *32*, 76–90.

Merchant, D., & Rich, P. (2004). Canada and the Commonwealth: Does the Commonwealth have a future as well as a past? *American Behavioural Scientist*, *47*, 1319–1328.

Mok, A., & Morris, M. W. (2013). Bicultural self-defense in consumer contexts: Self-protection motives are the basis for contrast versus assimilation to cultural cues. *Journal of Consumer Psychology*, *23*, 175–188.

Nelson, M. R., & Shavitt, S. (2002). Horizontal and vertical individualism and achievement values: A multimethod examination of Denmark and the United States. *Journal of Cross-Cultural Psychology, 33*, 439–458.

Nisbett, R. E. (2003). *The geography of thought: How Asians and Westerners think differently … and why.* New York, NY: Free Press.

O'Brien, K. J. (2012). Telefónica's 20-year gamble pays off. *nytimes.com*. Retrieved September 3, 2014, www.nytimes.com/2012/02/27/business/global/telefonicas-20-year-gamble-pays-off.html

Oyserman, D. (2009). Identity-based motivation: Implications for action-readiness, procedural-readiness, and consumer behaviour. *Journal of Consumer Psychology, 19*, 250–260.

Oyserman, D., Fryberg, S. A., & Yoder, N. (2007). Identity-based motivation and health. *Journal of Personality and Social Psychology, 93*, 1011–1027.

Rao, P., & Rao, N. (1982). *Marriage, the family and women in India*. New Delhi: South Asia Books.

Realbeautysketches.dove.us. (2015). Dove real beauty sketches. Retrieved January 16, 2015.

Resnick, P. (2012). *The labyrinth of North American identities*. Ontario, Canada: University of Toronto Press.

Robertson, R. (1992). *Globalization: Social theory and global culture*. London: Sage.

Robertson, R. (1995). Glocalization: Time-space and homogeneity-heterogeneity. In M. Featherstone, S. Lash & R. Robertson (Eds.), *Global modernities* (pp. 25–44). London: Sage.

Roccas, S., Sagiv, L., Schwartz, S. H., & Knafo, A. (2002). The big five personality factors and personal values. *Personality and Social Psychology Bulletin, 28*, 789–801.

Shapiro, S. (1999). When an ad's influence is beyond our conscious control: Perceptual and conceptual fluency effects caused by incidental ad exposure. *Journal of Consumer Research, 26*, 16–36.

Shavitt, S., Lalwani, A. K., Zhang, J., & Torelli, C. J. (2006). The horizontal/vertical distinction in cross-cultural consumer research. *Journal of Consumer Psychology, 16*, 325–356.

Shavitt, S., Lee, A. Y., & Torelli, C. J. (2008). Cross-cultural issues in consumer behaviour. In M. Wanke (Ed.), *Social psychology of consumer behaviour* (pp. 227–250). New York, NY: Psychology Press.

Shavitt, S., Torelli, C. J., & Riemer, H. (2010). Horizontal and vertical individualism and collectivism: Implications for understanding psychological processes. In M. J. Gelfand, C.-Y. Chiu & Y.-y. Hong (Eds.), *Advances in culture and psychology* (Vol. 1). New York, NY: Oxford University Press.

Shore, B. (2002). Taking culture seriously. *Human Development, 45*, 226–228.

Singelis, T. M., Triandis, H. C., Bhawuk, D., & Gelfand, M. J. (1995). Horizontal and vertical dimensions of individualism and collectivism: A theoretical and measurement refinement. *Cross-Cultural Research: The Journal of Comparative Social Science, 29*, 240–275.

Swaminathan, V., Page, K. L., & Gürhan-Canli, Z. (2007). "My" brand or "our" brand: The effects of brand relationship dimensions and self-construal on brand evaluations. *Journal of Consumer Research, 34*, 248–259. thecommonwealth.org. (2015). About us. *thecommonwealth.org*. Retrieved May 19, 2015 from http://thecommonwealth.org/about-us

Torelli, C. J. (2013). *Globalization, culture, and branding: How to leverage cultural equity for building iconic brands in the era of globalization*. New York, NY: Palgrave Macmillan.

Torelli, C. J., & Ahluwalia, R. (2009). Cultural symbolism of brands: Effects on the evaluation of brand extensions. *Paper presented at the Society for Consumer Psychology Winter Conference, San Diego, CA.*

Torelli, C. J., & Ahluwalia, R. (2012). Extending culturally symbolic brands: A blessing or a curse? *Journal of Consumer Research, 38*, 933–947.

Torelli, C. J., Ahluwalia, R., Stoner, J. L., & Cheng, S. Y. Y. (2014). Superordinate regional identities and the salience of intergroup rivalry: Effects of spontaneous recategorization on brand attitudes. *Advances in Consumer Research, 42*, 709–710.

Torelli, C. J., & Cheng, S. Y.-Y. (2011). Cultural meanings of brands and consumption: A window into the cultural psychology of globalization. *Social and Personality Psychology Compass, 5*, 251–262.

Torelli, C. J., & Cheng, S. Y.-Y. (2015). Culture and brand iconicity. In S. Ng & A. Y. Lee (Eds.), *Handbook of culture and consumer behaviour* (pp. 274–296). New York, NY: Oxford University Press.

Torelli, C. J., Chiu, C.-Y., & Keh, H. T. (2010). Cultural symbolism of brands in globalized economy. *Paper presented at the Global Brand Management Conference, Istanbul-Turkey.*

Torelli, C. J., Chiu, C.-Y., Keh, H. T., & Amaral, N. (2009). Brand iconicity: A shared reality perspective. *Advances in Consumer Research, 36*, 108–111.

Torelli, C. J., Chiu, C.-Y., Keh, H. T., & Amaral, N. (2010). American = men? Gender and cultural dynamics in the marketing of male-symbolic brands to women. In D. W. Dahl, G. V. Johar & S. M. J. van Osselaer (Eds.), *NA - Advances in consumer research* (Vol. 38, pp. 91). Duluth, MN: Association for Consumer Research.

Torelli, C. J., Chiu, C.-Y., Tam, K.-p., Au, A. K. C., & Keh, H. T. (2011). Exclusionary reactions to foreign cultures: Effects of simultaneous exposure to cultures in globalized space. *Journal of Social Issues, 67*, 716–742.

Torelli, C. J., Keh, H. T., & Chiu, C.-Y. (2010). Cultural symbolism of brands. In B. Loken, R. Ahluwalia & M. J. Houston (Eds.), *Brands and brand management: Contemporary research perspectives* (pp. 113–132). New York, NY: Routledge.

Torelli, C. J., & Stoner, J. L. (2015). Managing cultural equity: A theoretical framework for building iconic brands in globalized markets. *Review of Marketing Research (Brand Meaning Management), 12*, 83–120.

Triandis, H. C. (1989). The self and social behaviour in differing cultural contexts. *Psychological Review, 96*, 506–520.

Triandis, H. C. (1995). *Individualism and collectivism.* Boulder, CO: Westview Press.

Triandis, H. C. (1996). The psychological measurement of cultural syndromes. *American Psychologist, 51*, 407–415.

Triandis, H. C. (2007). Culture and psychology: A history of the study of their relationship. In S. Kitayama & D. Cohen (Eds.), *Handbook of cultural psychology* (pp. 59–76). New York, NY: Guilford Press.

Triandis, H. C., & Gelfand, M. J. (1998). Converging measurement of horizontal and vertical individualism and collectivism. *Journal of Personality and Social Psychology, 74*, 118–128.

Triandis, H. C., Marín, G., Lisansky, J., & Betancourt, H. (1984). Simpatía as a cultural script of Hispanics. *Journal of Personality and Social Psychology, 47*, 1363–1375.

Turner, J. C., Hogg, M. A., Oakes, P. J., Reicher, S. D., & Wetherell, M. S. (1987). *Rediscovering the social group: A self-categorization theory.* Oxford: Blackwell.

UNWTO (2012). UNWTO Annual Report 2012. Madrid: UNWTO. Retrieved from www.unwto.org

Watanabe, M. (1974). The conception of nature in Japanese culture. *Science, 183*, 279–282.

Whittlesea, B. W. (1993). Illusions of familiarity. *Journal of Experimental Psychology: Learning, Memory, and Cognition, 19*, 1235–1253.

Zhang, J. (2009). The effect of advertising appeals in activating self-construals: A case of bicultural Chinese generation X consumers. *Journal of Advertising, 38*, 63–82.

Zhang, S., & Schmitt, B. H. (2001). Creating local brands in multilingual international markets. *Journal of Marketing Research, 38*, 313–325.

Part II
Consumer cognition and perception

4

Visual attention in consumer settings

J. Wesley Hutchinson, Joy Lu and Evan Weingarten

In order to understand the role of visual attention in consumer behaviour, it is important to understand the various time scales of human behaviours and the multilevel cognitive processes that support these behaviours. We will use grocery shopping as an example. The broadest time scale is the lifespan. Small children ride in shopping carts, begging for the treats that catch their eye, such as the colourful Lucky Charms cereal boxes, toys and the oh-so-close candy in the oh-so-slow checkout line. Teenagers do occasional supplementary shopping for items not found in the pantry or refrigerator, and most adults shop frequently for themselves and their families. Thus, we all have extensive knowledge structures, decision strategies and visuomotor programs for supporting this essential activity of modern life, and these have been acquired gradually over time from experience mainly outside the classrooms of formal education.

The next time scale is that of planning and executing ordinary purchases, which can be extensive (e.g., several months spent shopping for a new car) or brief (e.g., 30 minutes spent shopping for dinner tonight). This is the time scale of the classic "purchase funnel" models of consumer choice (e.g., Attention, Interest, Desire, Action (AIDA); Hierarchy or Effects: Awareness, Knowledge, Liking, Preference, Conviction, Purchase; see Barry, 1987). These models adopt a single purchase decision as the focal event to be explained and describe a series of other activities that surround this decision. These activities typically last from a few hours (e.g., test driving a car) to a few seconds (e.g., noticing an end-aisle display in the grocery store).

Intuitively, it might seem that we have reached the final level of time resolution for consumer behaviour. However, from the perspective of cognitive neuroscience, the next level down is the most important. It is comprised of psychological events that last from 0.2 seconds (e.g., noting a posted price) to 1 or 2 seconds (e.g., assessing the acceptability of that noted price). This micro-level of information processing is the critical level for understanding the role of visual attention in supporting all of the broader levels we have described. In a nutshell, attention is the mechanism through which information in the environment is selected for further processing. Without micro-level attention, information in the environment has no effect on behaviours at any other time scale. Attention is the gatekeeper for everything that enters our experienced world.

Attention, perception, cognition and behaviour

There is a broad consensus in psychology and neuroscience about the general flow of information in the environment into and throughout the brain, and how new information is combined with previously processed information (at all time scales) to create our perceived world, guide our actions and achieve our goals (e.g., Gazzaniga, Ivry, & Mangun, 2013; Purves et al., 2013). Of course, there are many unanswered questions and controversies, but it is useful at the outset to place attention within the broader framework of human information processing. Figure 4.1 provides a schematic diagram of this consensus model of human information processing.

The environment provides us with a constantly changing assortment of objects and patterns of energy. We have several types of sensory receptors that transduce different types of energy into neurally coded information. Visual information from the eye projects to several subcortical areas and to the visual cortex in the occipital lobe (located at the back of the brain). This information is immediately divided into two pathways: the ventral "what" pathway that connects the occipital to the temporal lobes (which are located at the sides of the brain) and the dorsal "where" pathway that connects the occipital to the parietal lobes (which are located at the top of the brain). The ventral pathway is non-spatial and primarily supports object recognition. The dorsal pathway is retinotopic (i.e. it reflects the spatial organization of the visual field that is projected onto the retina of the eyes) and primarily supports object location. Working memory and the selection and control of behaviours are generally ascribed to the frontal lobe of the brain (although the "location" of working memory is somewhat controversial).

Controlled behaviours are designed to achieve specific goals based on perceptions of the current environment and expectations based on knowledge about the world that is maintained in long-term memory (e.g., Gabrieli, 1998; Gluck, Mercado, & Myers, 2008; LaBar & Cabeza, 2006). Goal-directed attention prevents most information in the environment and in long-term memory from becoming active in working memory. It allows only the most immediately goal-relevant information to be selected for guiding controlled behaviour. In addition to controlled behaviours, many behaviours have become automatic and occur without conscious awareness whenever environmental or memorial information triggers them. Table 4.1 summarizes the information-processing functions of the main brain structures that support visual attention, learning and memory (also see Gazzaniga, Ivry, & Mangun, 2013 and Purves et al., 2013, especially chapters 6 and 7 in both texts).

Overview of the chapter

In this chapter, we first discuss the relationship between visual attention and eye movements. Then, we examine the psychological and consumer literatures in three, increasingly complex, problem domains in visual attention: visual search, scene perception and spatial navigation. In addition to reviewing the empirical findings across these three domains, we also review quantitative models of visual attention. Finally, we conclude with a few thoughts about the most important directions for future research.

Visual attention and eye movements

Earlier, we said "Attention is the gatekeeper for everything that enters our experienced world". Eye-tracking data is a "gold standard" measure of visual attention (for reviews see Duchowski, 2002; Holmqvist et al., 2011; Rayner, 1998). Historically, this technology provided measurement methods and data that yielded major breakthroughs in our understanding of reading, which continues today. It has also been a critical source of information in the areas of visual

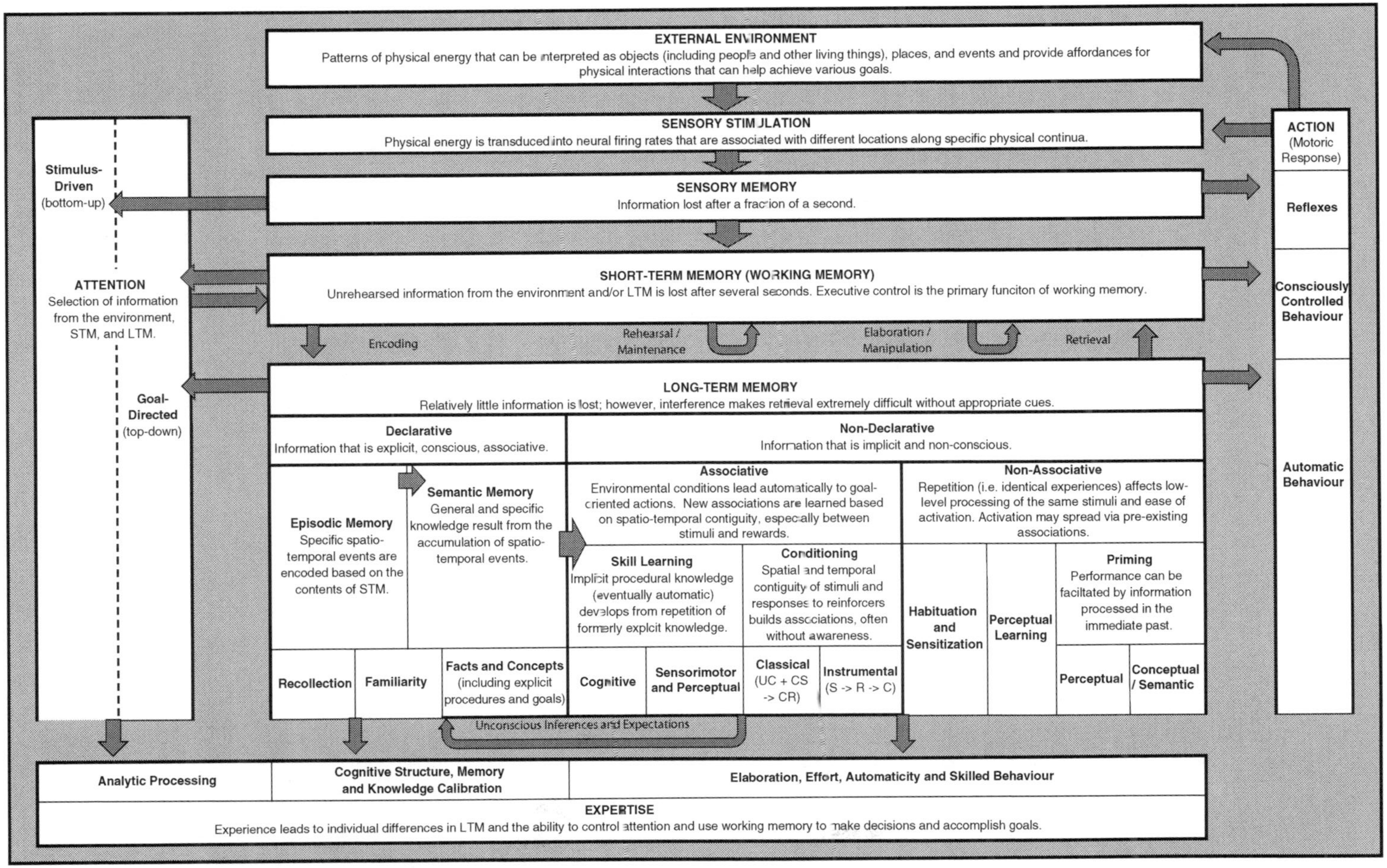

Figure 4.1 A "consensus" model of attention, perception, cognition and behaviour.

Table 4.1 Critical brain structures for attention, learning and memory

Information-processing functions	*Brain structures*
Representation of low-level visual features	Occipital cortex (V1–V4)
Object location ("Where?")	Dorsal occipitoparietal pathway (especially PPC)
Object recognition ("What?")	Ventral occipitotemporal pathway (especially ITC)
Working memory, goal selection and executive control	Prefrontal cortex
Goal monitoring and executive monitoring	Medial frontal cortex (especially ACC)
Goal-directed (endogenous) attention	Dorsal frontoparietal pathway (especially FEF and IPS)
Stimulus-driven (exogenous) attention	Ventral parietofrontal pathway (especially RTPJ and RVFC)
Reflexive attention	Subcortical (especially SC)
Navigation and scene processing	Parahippocampal place area
Declarative memory (episodic and semantic)	Medial temporal cortex (especially H), middle diencephalon (especially AT), neocortex (especially MPFC)
Skill learning	Basal ganglia
Classical conditioning	Dopamine system, cerebellum

Notes
These general correspondences neglect many details and system interconnections. They reflect common summaries in cognitive neuroscience texts (Ganzzaniga, Ivry, & Mangun, 2013; Purves et al., 2012; also see Glimcher & Fehr, 2014).

ACC: anterior cingulate cortex; AT: anterior thalamus; FEF: frontal eye field; H: hippocampus; IPS: intraparietal sulcus; ITC: inferotemporal cortex; MPFC: medial prefrontal cortex; PPC: posterior parietal cortex; RTPJ: right temporoparietal junction; RVFC: right ventral frontal cortex; SC: superior colliculus; V1–V4: primary visual cortex.

search, scene perception and spatial navigation in psychology and in the areas of advertising, package design, retail display and software/website usability in marketing research.

The eye does not work like a camera. Unlike film and digital image sensors that have uniform resolution, the retina at the back of the human eye has a very small, central area of high-resolution colour sensitivity called the fovea (about 2 degrees of visual angle or eight letters at reading distance). Resolution drops rapidly with distance from the fovea. Large shapes, motion and the "gist" of a scene are apprehended rapidly everywhere in the visual field. However, high-resolution information requires the eye to *fixate* that information on the fovea (although covert attentional shifts can improve peripheral vision; see below). Because of our need for high-resolution colour information, the eye moves three to six times per second, gathering the information that the brain determines to be to most important, where importance is based on (1) previously fixated information, prior knowledge, expectations and current goals and (2) the inherent salience of environmental stimuli (see next section). High-resolution information includes the internal details of objects (e.g., facial features) and text (e.g., letters and numbers). Thus, the coherent world we "see" is computationally constructed by the brain from this ongoing, fragmented stream of low-level information.

Goal-directed and stimulus-driven attention

The contents of working memory are heavily influenced by goal-directed attention processes (which are sometimes called endogenous or top-down); however, stimulus-driven attention processes (which are sometimes called exogenous or bottom-up) can sometimes capture or reorient attention (Corbetta & Shulman, 2002; Corbetta, Patel, & Shulman, 2008; also see Carrasco, 2011; Egeth & Yantis, 1997; Theeuwes, 2010). Some stimulus-driven processes are reflexive and capture attention through subcortical, automatic mechanisms (e.g., the orienting reflex towards especially intense or novel stimuli). However, there is also a cortical stimulus-driven system that interacts with a cortical goal-directed system (see Table 4.1). Corbetta et al. (2008) summarize these systems as follows: "A dorsal frontoparietal (or dorsal attention) network enables the selection of sensory stimuli based on internal goals or expectations (goal-directed attention) and links them to appropriate motor responses. A ventral frontoparietal (or ventral attention) network detects salient and behaviourally relevant stimuli in the environment, especially when unattended (stimulus-driven attention). These systems dynamically interact during normal perception to determine where and what we attend to". The key characteristic of the ventral stimulus-driven system is that it monitors salient information that is currently being filtered out by the dorsal goal-directed system, and it interrupts and reorients the goal-directed system when it detects task-relevant information that is currently outside conscious awareness.

For example, a shopper might be examining the various sizes and prices of Extra-Strength Tylenol on a store shelf immediately in front of him. The ventral system might be activated by a large "SALE" in-aisle display and reorient attention to it because saving money is always important, even if it is for some other product. Also, the ventral system is sensitive to "irrelevant" objects that are similar to target objects. Thus, the ventral stimulus-driven system might detect the red store brand products displayed next to Tylenol (a common retail practice) and reorient attention to the adjacent store brand. The shopper would then consciously decide whether or not the store brand was worth further consideration based on information provided by the reoriented dorsal goal-directed system.

The Tylenol example represents a major connecting point of psychological and consumer research on visual attention. In both retailing and advertising, an important goal of marketing actions is to capture attention in the face of competition from external visual clutter and internal consumer goals and expectations. Thus, the distinction between goal-directed and stimulus-driven attention is a major theme in our review.

Covert attention, overt attention and eye movements

In order to connect eye movements to visual attention, it is important to understand covert and overt changes in the location of attention. Even when stimuli are presented so briefly that an eye movement is not possible, people are able to move their attention covertly to different locations in the presented display. The methods through which this result has been demonstrated are beyond the scope of this review (see Carrasco, 2011; Theeuwes, 2010). However, the picture that emerges is that a very rapid, low-level system can scan all locations (possibly in parallel) for certain types of low-resolution information in a stimulus-driven manner. Then, without the eye moving, attention can be covertly reallocated spatially via goal-directed processes to improve resolution in specific locations. Although the improvement for peripheral locations is not as great as with foveal fixation, it is enough to rapidly guide where that next fixation should be. Eye fixations are overt, sequential reallocations of attention that are relatively slow but still occur three to six times every second. Subsequent perceptual and cognitive processes that operate at broader time scales are constructed from these low-level attention-based building blocks.

Visual search

One of the simplest functions of visual attention is to guide a search for a specific target object. A moment's reflection reveals that visual search is ubiquitous in our everyday lives. We search for food in our refrigerators, doorways and steps as we walk through rooms, keys and wallets as we prepare to leave home, street names and traffic patterns as we drive, products when we shop, characters within the scenes we view on television; the list is unending. In this section we review the basic findings from research on visual search in psychology and consumer behaviour.

Visual search in psychology

Classic visual search paradigms in psychology use brief presentations of a set of items that include a target item to be found among some number of distractor items. Presentation is so brief that eye movement is not possible, and search must rely upon covert attention. Success in visual search tasks requires both object recognition (i.e., the ventral "what" pathway) and object location (i.e., the dorsal "where" pathway). In a seminal paper, Treisman and Gelade (1980) reported several critical findings about visual search and proposed Feature Integration Theory to explain those findings. Their paradigm used stimuli that had two visual features: colour (e.g., green vs. brown) and shape (e.g., T vs. L). Two tasks are of particular interest. The first task was conjunctive search (e.g., Is a "green T" present?). Feature conjunction is a simplified version of one of the central problems of human vision, called the "binding problem". Given the very low-level, fragmented information that is available in the environment, the viewer must know how to bind specific perceptual features together as coming from a single coherent object. The second task used by Treisman and Gelade was feature-based search (e.g., Is a "T" present?). For the conjunctive task, decision times ranged from under a second to over 3 seconds. Importantly, times increased linearly with the number of distractors (which varied from 1 to over 30), and the slope for positive trials when the target was present was about half the slope for negative trials when the target was absent (about 0.03 vs. 0.07 seconds per item). This is exactly what would be expected if people sequentially search through items by shifting their attention from location to location. That is, on average, the target should be found after about half of the items have been examined for positive trials, but only after all items have been examined for negative trials. For feature-based search, decision times were very fast (about 0.4 seconds) and unaffected by the number of distractors (i.e., slopes were close to zero). The rapid detection of single features is often called a "pop-out" effect, as the target seems to appear quickly and without cognitive effort.

Feature Integration Theory explains these classic results by proposing that features are detected early in the search process by rapid parallel processing that is independent of location. In the feature-based task, this is all that is required. In the conjunction task, focal attention is required so that specific locations can be sequentially examined for the presence of both features. Treisman and Gelade noted, however, that their results depended on the objects being novel and confusable with the distractors. They hypothesized that for familiar objects in familiar contexts, prior experience would lead to goal-directed expectations that would greatly speed up the search process and allow fairly accurate object recognition without sequential search.

Although both the empirical findings and the theoretical explanations have become more complicated over time, this general idea of sequential, location-specific visual search remains. The overt attention created by eye movements has been found to be very similar to sequential covert attention, and overt attention is more effective than covert attention because eye movements focus the high resolution of the fovea on specific locations (see Carrasco, 2011;

Rayner, 1998). Most researchers now believe that sequential visual search (whether overt or covert) is not random, but is guided by the salience of objects, which is determined by a combination of goal-directed and stimulus-driven factors (Corbetta et al., 2008; Theeuwes, 2010; Wolfe, 1994).

Visual search in consumer behaviour

Pure visual search tasks are not common in consumer research. In fact, we know of only one paper in which the task was simply to find a pre-specified target presented among distractors (i.e., van der Lans, Pieters, & Wedel, 2008). Instead, a choice task is often used in which the "target" is the product that the subject would most likely purchase from an offered set of products that are visually displayed. In most cases, the display is a grid format of some sort because such product grids are common in store displays, mail catalogues and online shopping sites. Thus, the target criteria are personally determined, are heterogeneous across subjects and require more complex decision processes than object recognition. In some paradigms, there is no explicit search task of any sort and subjects are simply asked to view the display as they normally would (e.g., browse a catalogue or read a newspaper). Despite these procedural differences, visual attention should guide the ways in which information is acquired from the displays in much the same way as is the case for the visual search paradigms used in psychology, thereby providing a test of external validity for those paradigms. In particular, we will highlight the findings in consumer research that extend our understanding of goal-directed and stimulus-driven visual information processing.

Brand search paradigms

van der Lans et al. (2008) presented subjects with a realistic store display of laundry detergents (16 images and 6 different brands that varied in location, number of images, colour and package design). On each trial, subjects were asked to locate a specific brand, and eye movements were tracked. Response latencies and accuracy were modelled as a function of fixations during search, and fixations were modelled using a hidden Markov model (HMM) based on Wolfe's work on saliency maps (1994; Wolfe & Horowitz, 2004; see also Liechty, Pieters, & Wedel, 2003, which is discussed in the Quantitative Models section). The HMM has two states: an identification state, which determines whether the currently fixated brand is the target brand (local information search), and a localization state that is influenced by stimulus-driven factors (i.e., main effects of colour and search strategy) and goal-directed factors (i.e., the interaction of colour with brand). Based on these definitions, stimulus-driven factors were found to have twice the effect size compared with goal-directed factors. It is not clear that the stimulus-driven factors meet the same criteria as those used in the psychological literature. However, the modelling is admirable in its ability to link a variety of attention-related variables via a theory-based stochastic process and thereby estimate the contributions of different components of the process.

Choice paradigms

Choice paradigms have been used by Chandon, Hutchinson, Bradlow and Young (2007, 2009), Mandel and Johnson (2002) and Townsend and Kahn (2014). Chandon et al. (2009) used a complicated, fractional factorial design to construct 12 realistic store displays that manipulated area (i.e., number of facings), brands (11 familiar brands and 1 novel brand), location (top vs.

bottom and left vs. right) and price. The search task was either choice of a single brand or selection of a set of brands worthy of further consideration. Stimulus-driven factors (especially number of facings) were found to exert a strong influence on number of fixations, but only modest effects on recall, consideration and choice. Goal-directed factors (especially prior brand usage) exhibited the opposite pattern: a modest influence on number of fixations, but strong effects on recall, consideration and choice. They also showed that whether or not visual attention affected choice depended on which stimulus-driven factor enhanced attention. In particular, number of facings, left vs. right location, and top vs. bottom location affected choice, but having a central location had no effect on choice (despite having a very large effect on number of fixations). Overall, goal-directed factors exerted a much larger effect on choice than did stimulus-driven factors, which replicated earlier work (Chandon et al., 2007) that used quantitative modelling of a similar task to estimate relative contributions to choice. However, small short-term effects can result in larger long-term changes in behaviour. The small stimulus-driven changes created by in-store marketing on one trip may result in purchase, or at least increased brand familiarity based on in-store consideration. Thus, these changes increase the impact of goal-driven factors for the brand on the next trip, and repeating the purchase cycle can "ratchet up" the small effects into enduring brand loyalty.

These results, combined with those of van der Lans et al. (2008), suggest that stimulus-driven factors strongly affect consumer attention, but these large effects on attention translate into only slight "nudges" in purchase behaviour. Because purchase is mainly goal directed, long-term effects will only be achieved when stimulus-driven factors affect goal-driven factors (e.g., a trial purchase evolves into repeated purchases).

Mandel and Johnson (2002) used the images that formed the "wallpaper" of a simulated online store as a stimulus-driven priming manipulation for product choice (i.e., images were related to either price or quality), and attention was measured using clickstream data (i.e., the time stamps on clicks for information of a given type – price vs. quality – for a specific product). Novice consumers exhibited priming effects for both looking times and choice frequencies; however, expert consumers exhibited only the choice effect (presumably because they were more efficient at visual information processing).

Using a choice task, Townsend and Kahn (2014) manipulated the number of products in a display (e.g., 8 vs. 27 items in the "assortment") and whether item information was verbal or visual. Similarly to the classic results in visual search, total decision time increased with assortment size. However, time per item (as measured by eye-tracking analyses) was less for large assortments than for small assortments during an initial viewing, and this effect reversed during the choice phase. Perhaps there are efficiency gains from even small amounts of prior experience searching in a display. This efficiency explanation is speculative at this point, and the interactions in the results from these two experiments (i.e., interactions with expertise for Mandel & Johnson and interactions with initial vs. final decision phases in Townsend & Kahn) pose interesting questions about visual attention in paradigms that embed visual search within a more complex task (such as product choice).

Natural viewing paradigms

Natural viewing paradigms have been used by Janiszewski (1998) for catalogue browsing and Pieters, Wedel and Zhang (2007) for newspaper reading. In this paradigm, subjects are instructed only to read materials as they normally would. Both papers used eye-tracking data and found effects of stimulus-driven factors on incidental attention. In particular, the area given to target information had a positive effect on attention and the amount of competitive "clutter" had a negative effect. Janiszewski also reported evidence from actual product sales consistent with the hypothesis that attention to catalogue items affected consumer purchases.

Scene perception

Although a fundamental task, most research on visual search has used rather unnatural displays. Even commercial consumer research has mainly used isolated shelf displays and advertisements devoid of their normal environmental context. In this section we review research on the perception of natural scenes in psychology and consumer behaviour.

Scene perception in psychology

In daily life, individuals devote a lot of time to natural scene perception and can quickly learn the gist of scenes comprised of both high-level semantic knowledge and low-level statistics (Henderson, 1992, 2003, 2007; Larson et al., 2014; Oliva, 2005; Oliva & Torralba, 2006; Potter, 1976). Individuals can readily identify scenes presented as briefly as 250 ms based on semantic meaning alone (Henderson, 2007, 2013; Henderson & Hollingworth, 1999; Potter, 1976), although this may be impaired by the presence of other tasks that also demand visual attention (Cohen, Alvarez, & Nakayama, 2011; Freedman, Ringer, & Loschsky, 2014).

How individuals process natural scenes has been the subject of much research in psychology and neuroscience. For example, in psychology, scene perception research has examined the processing of both coarse (low-resolution) and fine (high-resolution) information (Oliva & Schyns, 1997, 2000; Schyns & Oliva, 1994). Neuroscience studies using functional magnetic resonance imaging (fMRI) have identified the parahippocampal place area as being critical for identification and habituation to changing viewpoints during scene processing (Epstein, 2005, 2008; Epstein, Graham, & Downing, 2003; Epstein, Higgins, & Thompson-Schill, 2005).

Natural scene perception may be influenced by goal-directed factors as well as stimulus-driven factors. These factors contribute to how individuals attend to different areas of scenes and identify objects within scenes.

Goal-directed influences underlying scene perception

Early research in scene perception focused on how the goal-directed semantics or "informativeness" of scenes can influence visual attention. It was speculated that visual attention to works of art, for example, may depend on prior experience, and that individuals may look at parts of a scene strategically based on interest or pattern (Buswell, 1935). This was empirically verified in studies that measured and manipulated the informativeness of art pieces, which was correlated with people's eye movements while they viewed the art. People tend to look longer, more often and earlier at more informative regions of scenes, and also exhibit longer-amplitude saccades (Antes, 1974; Loftus & Mackworth, 1978). However, we note that work following these investigations was unable to replicate many of these results (De Graef, Christiaens, & d'Ydewalle, 1990; Henderson & Hollingworth, 1999; Hollingworth & Henderson, 1998), so the role of informativeness in scene perception is still open to further research.

People's accuracy and speed when identifying objects in scenes can be decreased by knowledge-driven semantic and structural violations. Such violations may include scene jumbles as well as unusual sizes or spatial arrangements of objects (Biederman, 1972; Biederman, Mezzanotte, & Rabinowitz, 1982; Henderson, 1992). Research on the effects of these violations lend support to the schema hypothesis, in which a scene's meaning activates relevant knowledge about what exists in a scene, which in turn influences object identification (Biederman et al., 1982; Henderson, 1992). However, more recent work has failed to replicate the results supporting the schema model (Vo & Henderson, 2009), and researchers have suggested alternative explanations, such as a priming model in which scene knowledge can change individual sensitivity for judging an object's presence and a model in which scene knowledge and object identification do not interact (Henderson & Hollingworth, 1999).

Researchers have also investigated the effects of goal-directed factors such as prior exposure and task demands on visual attention (Hayhoe & Ballard, 2005; Land & Hayhoe, 2001). Even brief exposure to a scene, such as a prime of the spatial layout, may inform judgements and speed up response times (Sanocki & Epstein, 1997). Where people look also depends on task goals. For example, individuals look at clothing and furniture when asked to remember the clothing in a painting, but they look at faces when asked to estimate ages of the people in a painting (Yarbus, 1967). While performing everyday activities, such as making a sandwich, people tend to fixate on the relevant task objects at each step of the task, and fixations precede actions, with frequent look-ahead fixations (Land & Hayhoe, 2001; Land, Mennie, & Rusted, 1999). Task instructions can also modulate where people look and for how long (Sullivan, Johnson, Rothkopf, Ballard, & Hayhoe, 2012; Torralba, Oliva, Castelhano, & Henderson, 2006). For example, drivers in a virtual environment will fixate longer and more often on either the leader car or the speedometer when asked to follow the leader or maintain a specific speed, respectively (Sullivan et al., 2012). Pedestrians fixate more on people who are on a collision course with them, suggesting that individuals learn where in the scene it is valuable to look and allocate attention based on these demands (Jovancevic-Misic & Hayhoe, 2009).

Stimulus-driven influences on scene perception

Different research streams have argued for the importance of stimulus-driven features in scene perception. One approach in particular is to model natural scene statistics such as colour and spatial orientation (Oliva, 2005; Torralba & Oliva, 2003), which are thought to be relevant to perceptual tasks such as image representation, object identification and estimating spatial distances (Geisler, 2008). "Visual crowding" or failure to properly detect a target among distractors may be due to saccades interrupting the process of acquiring scene statistics (Nandy & Tjan, 2012). Faster saccades seem to be correlated with attention to incorrect distractors and are thought to be stimulus-driven, while slower saccades are more accurate and seem to be goal-directed (Van Zoest, Donk, & Theeuwes, 2004). Natural scene statistics can also be used to determine depth based on convexity and concavity (Burge, Fowlkes, & Banks, 2010) as well as to predict saliency (Tkacik, Prentice, Victor, & Balasubramanian, 2010).

Researchers have developed models to predict where people look based on the comparison of different regions within a scene. For example, one model incorporates saliency maps within the environment based on how feature maps of objects in scenes differ from neighbouring areas (Itti & Koch, 2001; Itti, Koch, & Niebur, 1998). This setup relies on a centre-surround system akin to that of the earliest stages of vision in the retina and primary visual cortex (Purves et al., 2013). The contextual guidance model incorporates both goal-directed and stimulus-driven factors, with scenes processed by a local pathway of low-level scene elements that form a saliency map (Koch & Ullman, 1985; Rosenholtz, 1999), as well as a global pathway based on priors or more holistic assessments (Torralba et al., 2006).

Finally, we review how specific scene characteristics such as colour, luminance, clarity and number of objects can affect scene identification. Colouration can enhance scene identification relative to greyscale, while abnormal coloration may slow identification (Oliva & Schyns, 2000). However, the benefit from colour cues may be limited to specific scenes such as seascapes, as opposed to urban scenes, for example (Rousselet, Joubert, & Fabre-Thorpe, 2005). Researchers have also suggested that colour may illusorily bolster confidence during target image identification (Yao & Einhauser, 2008). Studies in which subjects viewed scenes of varying luminance showed that fixation length increases as luminance drops (Henderson, Nuthmann, & Luke, 2013). Factors such as image clarity and blurring can also affect where people look and for how long, depending on the visual task (Enns & MacDonald, 2013). Studies have also shown that increasing the number of objects in a scene results in decreased fixation duration and saccade length (Unema, Pannasch, Joos, & Velichkovsky, 2005).

Scene perception in consumer behaviour

In this section we examine a few particular types of scenes within consumer behaviour, namely advertisements and shopping assortments, both of which have received considerable attention in the consumer behaviour and eye-tracking literatures. Research findings regarding visual attention to advertisements and assortments have been consistent with the general scene perception literature from psychology. Individuals are able to categorize ads even with exposures as low as 100 ms, and may rely on coarse details and colour during ad recognition (Pieters & Wedel, 2012; Wedel & Pieters, 2014). Researchers have used eye tracking to examine visual attention to product assortments. Eye fixations during a grocery trip may be broken down into multiple stages, including orientation, evaluation and product verification (Russo & Leclerc, 1994). More recent work has examined how consumers view product-by-attribute matrices (Shi, Wedel, & Pieters, 2013) and choice-based conjoint cards (Yang, Toubia, & de Jong, 2015). We separate the remaining consumer behaviour literature on scene perception into research about the goal-directed factors that influence how people browse and evaluate advertisements and assortments, and the stimulus-driven factors that affect these processes.

Goal-directed factors underlying consumer scene perception

We examine attention to goal-directed factors and how they shift attention, starting with task goals. Similarly to how task-based consumption goals may shift attention to specific elements of a scene (Land & Hayhoe, 2001; Land et al., 1999; Hayhoe & Ballard, 2005; Sullivan et al., 2012), goals and expectations for advertisements and assortments can affect where and how people look. Different goals such as ad memorization or product learning and evaluation may influence gaze duration on different parts of ads (Pieters & Wedel, 2007), as well as how consumers switch between local and global processing, defined by long vs. short saccadic amplitudes and short vs. long fixations, respectively (Wedel, Pieters, & Liechty, 2008). Out-of-store marketing factors such as prior product experience, product market share, shopper education and age have been shown to influence product evaluation and whether a product is noticed when shoppers view product assortments within a grocery store (Chandon et al., 2009).

Just as in the psychology literature, violations of prior expectations about an assortment can influence people's perceptions. For example, cutting highly preferred or expected items can diminish perceptions of assortment variety and even lead to decline in sales (Boatwright & Nunes, 2001; Borle, Boatwright, Kadane, Nunez, & Shmueli, 2005; Broniarczyk, Hoyer, & McAlister, 1998). In general, consumers seem to form expectations about assortment sizes and product organization, which can vary by past experience and individual-level product familiarity and expertise. This can help or hurt consumer satisfaction depending on whether or not expectations are met or product arrangements are congruent with consumer goals (Diehl & Poynor, 2010; Morales, Kahn, McAlister, & Broniarczyk, 2005; Poynor & Wood, 2010).

Even certain positions within assortments can receive different amounts of attention. Shelf position and number of facings influence what products people notice (Chandon et al., 2009). Much work in retailing supports the notion that central positions receive more visual attention during browsing and are desirable for sales (Atalay, Bodur, & Rasolofoarison, 2012; Dreze, Hoch, & Purk, 1994). Central gaze and selection bias may be due to a mixture of goal-directed and stimulus-driven effects. For example, people could possess priors about where to attend to in a scene (i.e., believing centre options to be more popular), which could lead to visual preference for centre areas (Hutchinson & Turk-Browne, 2012; Torralba et al., 2006; Valenzuela & Raghubir, 2009).

Stimulus-driven factors underlying consumer scene perception

Similar to research on saliency maps (Itti & Koch, 2001; Torralba et al., 2006), it has been shown that stimulus-driven factors can create large variation in where consumers look while shopping. Assortment size and presentation style can influence what consumers see and how they judge assortments. For example, in specific contexts, perceived variety increases when assortments are organized (e.g., flavours of jellybeans are separated by colour), but not when they are disorganized (Kahn & Wansink, 2004). In other contexts, organized assortments are perceived to have more variety only when shoppers are also engaging in a choice-based task (Hoch, Bradlow, & Wansink, 1999). Visual (as opposed to verbal) presentation of assortments may increase perceived variety but also increase perceived complexity (Townsend & Kahn, 2014). Thus, there may be contributions to perceived variety from both contextual modulation and stimulus-driven factors (Torralba et al., 2006).

Colour organization of an assortment may also shape how much time individuals spend on different parts of the assortment. In a mobile eye-tracking study, shoppers looked at more SKUs (stock keeping unit) in regions that had sharper colour blocks (Weingarten, Kahn, & Hutchinson, in preparation). This result may emerge due to two additive mechanisms. First, the enhanced visual contrast of sharper colour blocks may promote greater figure–ground separation (Pinna, 2010; Pinna, Brelstaff, & Spillman, 2001; Pinna & Tanca, 2008; Pinna, Werner, & Spillman, 2003; Von der Heydt & Pierson, 2006). Since each section is more clearly distinct from its neighbour, consumers may attend to the regions that have heightened salience (Atalay et al., 2012; Chandon et al., 2009). Second, colour blocking may make it easier for consumers to locate target items among distractors (Bauer, Jolicoeur, & Cowan, 1996; D'Zmura, 1991; Dhar, 1997). These results point to simple, actionable strategies for arranging assortments to increase perceived variety and visual attention (Geisler, 2008; Shevell & Kingdom, 2008; Weingarten, Kahn, & Hutchinson, in preparation).

Spatial navigation

Arguably, the most complex area of visual attention is spatial navigation, because it embeds search tasks in natural environments with concurrent, dynamic processes for navigating in those environments. However, this is the area of greatest evolutionary value. Hunting and gathering are not possible without seeing and walking. In this section, we review the basic findings from research on spatial navigation in psychology and consumer behaviour.

Spatial navigation in psychology

Contrary to the position of early behavioural theorists, spatial navigation is not simply a result of stimulus–response learning. The results of Tolman's (1948) rat studies, in addition to subsequent work with humans, suggest that they may possess a cognitive map or spatial representations of their environment that grows from travel experience (Lew, 2011; Moar & Carleton, 1982; O'Keefe & Nadel, 1978; Tolman, 1948; Wolbers & Hegarty, 2010). Results from studies in which human participants physically navigate routes suggest that people can represent multiple target destinations and routes simultaneously (Levine, Jankovic, & Palij, 1982).

Landmarks and spatial navigation

Some research in spatial navigation examines how individuals use landmark cues (Chan, Baumann, Bellgrove, & Mattingley, 2012; Epstein & Vass, 2014) and may rely heavily on landmarks during navigation without actually having a geometric representation of the world (Foo, Warren, Duchon, & Tarr, 2005). Individuals attend to and use landmarks at decision points, such as at the end of a hallway, more than landmarks that occur between decision points (Hamid, Stankiewicz, & Hayhoe, 2010). Similar results are found for perceptually salient landmarks (Miller & Carlson, 2011). These results are supported by fMRI evidence that suggests increased parahippocampal place area activation for decision-point landmarks compared with non-decision-point landmarks (Schinazi & Epstein, 2010).

Landmarks vary in usefulness based on whether they provide orientation information or precise position information (Ruddle, Volkova, Mohler, & Bulthoff, 2011; Steck & Mallot, 2000) and whether they serve as beacons or associative cues (Chan et al., 2012; Ruddle et al., 2011; Waller & Lippa, 2007). Studies in which participants navigate virtual environments show that beacon landmarks facilitate faster learning of route information than associative cue landmarks (Waller & Lippa, 2007). In addition, landmarks may not always be useful if street information is vivid enough (Tom & Tversky, 2012).

Motion and spatial navigation

Both visual and motion-based cues can contribute to cognitive maps and spatial navigation. Research has shown that studying maps improves people's ability to judge Euclidean distances to rooms in a building, while physical navigation and movement experience result in better route distance estimates and fewer errors when orienting to target locations (Klatsky, Loomis, Beall, Chance, & Golledge, 1998; Thorndyke & Hayes-Roth, 1982). These results suggest that motion may be important in determining position. In studies where participants browsed real or virtual reality environments, it was found that motion may be a sufficient cue for navigation with degraded visual information (Ruddle & Lessels, 2006) and can contribute to cognitive maps even when visual cues go completely dark (Tcheang, Bulthoff, & Burgess, 2011).

Spatial navigation in consumer behaviour

Recent experimental work within the consumer behaviour literature investigates how consumers navigate their shopping environment, and how navigation influences purchase decisions. Park, Iyer, & Smith (1989) found that low store familiarity and time pressure decreased shopping success for planned purchases, and low familiarity increased unplanned purchases when time pressure was low. It is important to note that planned purchases necessarily depend heavily on goal-directed attention, while in-store marketing designed to increase unplanned purchases depends heavily on stimulus-driven attention.

Some research suggests that while the store environment is not optimally travelled, consumers are not too far off in some respects. Using the shopping cart data from Sorensen (2003), Hui et al. (2009a) computed the shortest path that shoppers could have taken in the store, given their purchases, and found large deviations (69 per cent) from optimal paths calculated using algorithms for the travelling salesman problem (Lawler, 1985). Despite these deviations, the order in which consumers browsed items based on what they bought was actually close to optimal (under 20 per cent deviation), implying that while shoppers do not use perfect navigation, their behaviour is much closer to optimal than to random navigation.

Researchers have used RFID (radio frequency identification) markers to test other hypotheses regarding in-store navigation. Data from a sample of a few hundred shoppers at a grocery store show that more unplanned movements in a store are associated with more unplanned purchases. Counterfactual simulation of repositioning product categories revealed a potential benefit to creating more travelled distance and unplanned purchases (Huang et al., 2013).

Researchers have also analysed data from videos of shopping trips to provide descriptive results about in-store shopping behaviour in relation to shelf display distances, product locations and number of displays. Smaller distance from displays results in more unplanned purchases, categories closer to planned purchase categories receive more unplanned purchases, and fewer displays examined by the shopper lead to more unplanned purchases (Hui et al., 2013a).

Quantitative models of visual attention and decision making

A recent trend in consumer research has been to model visual attention quantitatively. In this section, we focus mainly on the consumer literature, but also identify areas of overlap with psychology, economics and artificial intelligence.

Models of information acquisition during choice

Rational models of choice assume that consumers are complete-information utility maximizers (Guadagni & Little, 1983). However, MouseLab[1] and eye-tracking studies that measure attention have demonstrated that people don't always look at all available information before making a choice (Bettman & Kakkar, 1977; Reutskaja, Nagel, Camerer, & Rangel, 2011). Information acquisition imposes a degree of cognitive load or "cost of thinking", and it is unrealistic to assume that decision makers have unlimited cognitive capacity (Payne, Bettman, & Johnson, 1993; Shugan, 1980). Alternative models of "bounded rationality" have been proposed to explain how people may use simplified choice rules or heuristics when making decisions (Gilbride & Allenby, 2004; Payne et al., 1993; Simon, 1955; von Neumann & Morgenstern, 1947). For example, the satisficing choice rule assumes that consumers sequentially evaluate choices until one is found to be satisfactory on all attributes, and accounts for the observation that even in eye-tracking lab studies that present relatively small numbers of options, people do not always consider all options (Reutskaja et al., 2011; Stüttgen, Boatwright, & Monroe, 2012).

Visual attention is not evenly distributed among choices (as a rational model would predict when prior knowledge is low). It has been shown that manipulating visual attention can influence preferences, and vice versa. Gaze cascade is the phenomenon in which eye fixations gradually shift towards the alternative that is ultimately chosen as the decision time approaches. Conversely, preferences can be biased by showing one of the alternatives for longer durations. People have demonstrated gaze cascade and duration bias while choosing between attractive faces (Shimojo, Simion, Shimojo, & Scheier, 2003), as well as snack foods and posters (Armel, Beaumel, & Rangel, 2008). However, duration bias was not replicated in an eight-alternative choice task between random black and white photos (Glaholt & Reingold, 2009), suggesting that more complicated processes may occur for more complex tasks. In marketing research, gaze cascade was demonstrated in an eye-tracking study in which subjects paid increasing attention to the chosen option among different brands in a grid display (Atalay et al., 2012).

Although the precise direction of causality in the relationship between preferences and visual attention remains unclear, these findings lend validity to several alternative models of choice that take information processing into account. More extensive reviews of the models we discuss here can be found in previous work (Bogacz, Brown, Moehlis, Holmes, & Cohen, 2006; Orquin & Loose, 2013; Otter et al., 2008; Ratcliff & McKoon, 2008; Ratcliff & Smith, 2004). These models fall under the umbrella category of sequential sampling models, which are based on the assumption that the decision maker accumulates bits of information through sequential sampling over the course of the decision-making process, with a choice being made once enough evidence has been accumulated in favour of one of the alternatives (Townsend & Ashby, 1983). The sequential sampling process has a natural fit with information acquisition through visual attention, and has been applied by many researchers in psychology and consumer neuroscience.

One subset of sequential sampling models is the race model (or Poisson counting model), which borrows much of its conceptualization from the study of neural networks. Race models were first applied to perceptual identification and recognition memory tasks in order to account for the psychological processes that result in different reaction times and accuracy (Townsend & Ashby, 1983; Smith & Van Zandt, 2000; Van Zandt, 2000). The model has been shown to outperform traditional thought-listing methods in predicting attitudes towards ads in a belief verification task, using choices, reaction times and confidence ratings as dependent variables (Huang & Hutchinson, 2008). Race models can also be extended to incorporate inhibitory competition between alternatives and memory decay or "leaky" accumulation. The leaky accumulator model was used for a visual perception task in which subjects identified whether a tilted rectangle was longer on the upper left or upper right-hand side (Usher & McClelland, 2001).

Decision field theory (Busemeyer & Townsend, 1993) gives us a closely related model in which evidence accumulation is modelled as a continuous random walk process rather than a discrete Poisson process. The continuous model can incorporate the time it takes to sample and process each piece of incoming evidence, determined by the alternative's relative valence. Decision field theory has been used to explain violations in assumptions of rational decision making, including preference reversals and decision times during gambles. A multi-alternative extension has been used to account for the similarity, attraction and compromise effects (Roe, Busemeyer, & Townsend, 2001).

Another class of sequential sampling models are drift diffusion models, which were first applied in psychology to model memory retrieval during object recognition tasks (Ratcliff, 1978). Drift diffusion models involve a single accumulator and are generally limited to binary choices due to computational complexity (Ratcliff et al., 1999; Ratcliff & Rounder, 1998; Ratcliff & Smith, 2004). A consumer's relative preference for the two options drifts constantly towards the preferred option until it reaches a decision threshold. Drift diffusion models have been applied to binary visual perception tasks such as brightness and colour classification (Ratcliff & Rounder, 1998). The attentional extension of the model specifies drift rate as dependent on the difference in the inherent preferences of alternatives, with the sign of the drift rate determined by which alternative the decision maker was actually looking at. The model can account for accuracy and reaction times of binary choices between snack foods (Krajbich,

Armel, & Rangel, 2010), decisions under high and low time pressure (Mormann, Malmaud, Huth, Koch, & Rangel, 2010), buy–no-buy decisions (Krajbich, Camerer, & Rangel, 2012) and trinary choices (Krabjbich & Rangel, 2011). However, it is computationally difficult to extend the model further to more options, for which the same processes may also not apply.

Although there is debate over how visual attention is related to alternative value processing, some evidence comes from findings in neuroscience. In one study, subjects in an fMRI scanner chose between pairs of snacks, and visual attention was exogenously manipulated by asking subjects to alternate their attention between the options (Lim, O'Doherty, & Rangel, 2011). Inherent preference for the fixated option was positively correlated with activity in the ventromedial prefrontal cortex (vmPFC) and striatum – areas of the brain established to be involved in choice value computation (Gold & Shadlen, 2007). Further evidence that evaluations are being made at the visual fixation level comes from studies demonstrating the speed of visual saccades and evaluations during choice (Milosavljevic, Madsen, Koch, & Rangel, 2011; Mormann, Koch, & Rangel, 2011). Finally, a recent eye-tracking study demonstrates that during gambling choices, early fixations are guided towards areas with new information that may reduce uncertainty about value, while later visual attention is guided by the expected value of the options (Manohar & Husain, 2013). Furthermore, preference reversals between different contexts of risky choice (i.e., choosing between two gambles vs. bidding on a single gamble) have been shown to be accompanied by changes in attention to different attributes of the choices (Kim, Seligman, & Kable, 2012).

Models of dynamic information search

The models discussed thus far assume a random process of sampling information. However, for more complex tasks, it is less realistic to assume that information sampling is random. There may be systematic patterns that vary across individuals and across consumption goals. In the marketing literature, it has been shown that consumers tend to process attribute information in the earlier stages of decision making, and then brand information later on (Bettman & Park, 1980). Earlier, we described the results of Russo and Leclerc (1994) for supermarket shopping. Eye fixations follow a three-stage pattern: orientation, evaluation and verification. Consumers also exhibit systematic eye-fixation patterns when viewing print ads. Fixations move from large print to small print to pictures (Rayner, 2009), and certain brand elements tend to transfer attention more to other elements (Pieters & Wedel, 2004). Similarly, Gilchrist and Harvey (2006) found that regular grid-like displays (compared with random displays) generated more horizontal saccades than vertical saccades, but even when the display was disrupted, scan paths exhibited a systematic component.

Other work has modelled how previous fixations influence subsequent fixations in a probabilistic way. Research on natural scene viewing supports the existence of alternating local and global search periods, with statistical dependencies between successive eye movements (Tatler & Vincent, 2008). This work is supported by findings from neuroscience that suggest different brain areas control global and local attention. The posterior parietal cortex (PPC) globally directs visual attention towards regions of interest in a scene, while the inferotemporal cortex (ITC) is involved in local exploration, recognition and identification of objects (consistently with the "where" and "what" pathways discussed earlier; Itti & Koch, 2001). The transitions between local and global search states have been explicitly captured using HMMs (Liechty, Pieters, & Wedel, 2003). A recent eye-tracking study modelled search among products in a shelf display as a satisficing choice process, with local (within-brand) and global (across-brand) search states in an HMM (Stüttgen et al., 2012). Other eye-tracking work has used

HMMs to capture transitions between different search strategies within product-by-attribute matrices (Shi et al., 2013) and to model local and global transitions within scan paths of search engine results (Shi & Trusov, under review).

As discussed earlier, work in neuroscience has also identified that goal-directed attention is controlled by the dorsal frontoparietal network. This can be overridden by the ventral frontoparietal network, which is specialized for stimulus-driven attention and detecting salient and unexpected – but still behaviourally relevant – stimuli (Corbetta & Shulman, 2002; Corbetta et al., 2008). Goal-directed and stimulus-driven attention can be exogenously manipulated using search task instructions, resulting in different search patterns among consumers, as measured via eye tracking for online and in-store shopping (Lu & Hutchinson, in preparation). This research modelled landing page information search as a two-stage process in which the consumer first decides whether or not to exit the page by clicking on a link, and then, if exit is not chosen (i.e., visual search continues), the next fixation location on the page is chosen. As such, it closely follows the models of optimal search developed in economics (see also Yang et al., 2015). The manipulation of interest was whether the shopping instructions encouraged a strict focus on the stated goal (utilitarian instructions) or encouraged reorientation (hedonic instructions). The results revealed eye fixations and choice behaviour consistent with the predicted levels of goal-directed and stimulus-driven attention, and estimated model parameters showed that the search was more product focused (vs. exiting to a new, goal-related page) and hedonic attributes were more important in the hedonic condition. Moreover, the price coefficient was positive in the hedonic condition (indicating price-quality inference) and negative in the utilitarian condition (indicating a value-for-the-money orientation).

Directions for future research

Our review reveals that the research literatures in psychology and marketing have been surprisingly independent, despite the fact that they purport to investigate essentially the same phenomena. Thus, we believe that the greatest opportunities exist in three areas. First, much consumer research on visual attention has been rather descriptive and focused on important applied problems (e.g., the extent to which in-store marketing or advertising can capture attention, reorient attention and affect consumer choice). This research will benefit from more careful attention to the more theory-based models being developed in cognitive neuroscience. Second, although many (arguably most) areas of psychological vision research have developed important quantitative models, consumer research appears to be leading the way in developing quantitative models that combine attention and decision making. We believe both fields are poised for an era of productive "cross-fertilization". Finally, eye-tracking technologies have advanced tremendously in recent years and at the same time decreased in cost. Right now, this may be the area of greatest overlap between psychology and consumer research. Field research using eye-tracking glasses to examine real-world shopping behaviour (which combines visual search, scene perception and navigation) seems to be the area in which the interests of the two fields are most aligned.

Note

1 Before the development and widespread use of eye-tracking in consumer behaviour research, techniques such as MouseLab (Johnson, Payne, Bettman, & Schkade, 1989) and information booklets (Bettman & Kakkar, 1977) were used to trace consumer search and information acquisition during purchase decisions. MouseLab is a classic method that measures attention by having individuals click on product information cards on a computer screen to reveal information about the products (Johnson et al., 1989). MouseLab has been used by researchers to study choice strategies, such as adaptive decision making according to the effort-accuracy framework (Bettman, Johnson, Luce, & Payne, 1993).

References

Antes, J. R. (1974). The time course of picture viewing. *Journal of Experimental Psychology, 103*(1), 62–70.

Armel, K. C., Beaumel, A., & Rangel, A. (2008). Biasing simple choices by manipulating relative visual attention. *Judgment and Decision Making, 3*(5), 396–403.

Atalay, A. S., Bodur, H. O., & Rasolofoarison, D. (2012). Shining in the center: Central gaze cascade effect on product choice. *Journal of Consumer Research, 39*(4), 848–866.

Barry, T. E. (1987). The development of the hierarchy of effects: An historical perspective. *Current Issues & Research in Advertising, 10*(2), 251–295.

Bauer, B., Jolicoeaur, P., & Cowan, W. B. (1996). Visual search for colour targets that are or are not linearly-separable from distractors. *Vision Research, 36*, 1439–1466.

Bettman, J. R., & Kakkar, P. (1977). Effects of information presentation format on consumer information acquisition strategies. *Journal of Consumer Research, 3*(4), 233–240.

Bettman, J. R., & Park, C. W. (1980). Effects of prior knowledge and experience and phase of the choice process on consumer decision processes: A protocol analysis. *Journal of Consumer Research*, 7(3), 234–248.

Bettman, J. R., Johnson, E. J., Luce, M. F., & Payne, J. W. (1993). Correlation, conflict, and choice. *Journal of Experimental Psychology: Learning, Memory, and Cognition, 19*(4), 931.

Biederman, I. (1972). Perceiving real-world scenes. *Science, 177*, 77–80.

Biederman, I., Mezzanotte, R. J., & Rabinowitz, J. C. (1982). Scene perception: Detecting and judging objects undergoing relational violations. *Cognitive Psychology, 14*, 143–177.

Boatwright, P., & Nunes, J. C. (2001). Reducing assortment: An attribute-based approach. *Journal of Marketing, 65*(3), 50–63.

Bogacz, R., Brown, E., Moehlis, J., Holmes, P., & Cohen, J. D. (2006). The physics of optimal decision making: A formal analysis of models of performance in two-alternative forced-choice tasks. *Psychological Review, 113*(4), 700.

Borle, S., Boatwright, P., Kadane, J. B., Nunez, J. C., & Shmueli, G. (2005). The effect of product assortment changes on customer retention. *Marketing Science, 24*(4), 616–622.

Broniarczyk, S. M., Hoyer, W. D., & McAlister, L. (1998). Consumers' perceptions of the assortment offered in a grocery category: The impact of item reduction. *Journal of Marketing Research, 35*, 166–176.

Burge, J., Fowlkes, C. C., & Banks, M. S. (2010). Natural-scene statistics predict how the figure-ground cue of convexity affects human depth perception. *The Journal of Neuroscience, 30*(21), 7269–7280.

Busemeyer, J. R., & Townsend, J. T. (1993). Decision field theory: A dynamic-cognitive approach to decision making in an uncertain environment. *Psychological Review, 100*(3), 432.

Buswell, G. T. (1935). *How people look at pictures: A study of the psychology of perception in art*. Chicago, IL: University of Chicago Press.

Carrasco, M. (2011). Visual attention: The past 25 years. *Vision Research, 51*, 1484–1525.

Chan, E., Baumann, O., Bellgrove, M. A., & Mattingley, J. B. (2012). From objects to landmarks: The function of visual location information in spatial navigation. *Frontiers in Psychology, 3*, 1–11.

Chandon, P., Hutchinson, J. W., Bradlow, E., & Young, S. H. (2007). Measuring value of point-of-purchase marketing with commercial eye-tracking data. In M. Wedel and R. Peters (Eds.), *Visual marketing: From attention to action* (pp. 225–258). Mahwah, NJ: Lawrence Erlbaum Associates.

Chandon, P., Hutchinson, J. W., Bradlow, E. T., & Young, S. H. (2009). Does in-store marketing work? Effects of the number and position of shelf facings on brand attention and evaluation at the point of purchase. *Journal of Marketing, 73*, 1–17.

Cohen, M. A., Alvarez, G. A., & Nakayama, K. (2011). Natural-scene perception requires attention. *Psychological Science, 22*(9), 1165–1172.

Corbetta, M., & Shulman, G. L. (2002). Control of goal-directed and stimulus-driven attention in the brain. *Nature Reviews Neuroscience, 3*(3), 201–215.

Corbetta, M., Patel, G., & Shulman, G. L. (2008). The reorienting system of the human brain: From environment to theory of mind. *Neuron, 58*(3), 306–324.

De Graef, P., Christiaens, D., & d'Ydewalle, G. (1990). Perceptual effects of scene context on object identification. *Psychological Research, 52*, 317–329.

Dhar, R. (1997). Consumer preference for a no-choice option. *Journal of Consumer Research, 24*(2), 215–231.

Diehl, K., & Poynor, C. (2010). Great Expectations?! Assortment size, expectations, and satisfaction. *Journal of Marketing Research, 47*(2), 312–322.

Dreze, X., Hoch, S. J., & Purk, M. E. (1994). Shelf management and space elasticity. *Journal of Retailing, 70*(4), 301–326.
Duchowski, A. T. (2002). A breadth-first survey of eye-tracking applications. *Behaviour Research Methods, Instruments, & Computers, 3*(4), 455–470.
D'Zmura, M. (1991). Color in Visual Search. *Vision Research, 31*(6), 951–966.
Egeth, H. E., & Yantis, S. (1997). Visual attention: Control, representation, and time course. *Annual Review of Psychology, 48*, 269–297.
Enns, J. T., & MacDonald, S. C. (2013). The role of clarity and blur in guiding visual attention in photographs. *Journal of Experimental Psychology: Human Perception and Performance, 39*(2), 568–578.
Epstein, R. A. (2005). The cortical basis of visual scene processing. *Visual Cognition, 12*(6), 954–978.
Epstein, R. A. (2008). Parahippocampal and retrosplenial contributions to human spatial navigation. *Trends in Cognitive Sciences, 12*(10), 388–396.
Epstein, R. A., & Vass, L. K. (2014). Neural systems for landmark-based wayfinding in humans. *Philosophical Transactions of the Royal Society London B, 369*(1635), 20120533.
Epstein, R., Graham, K. S., & Downing, P. E. (2003). Viewpoint-specific scene representations in human parahippocampal cortex. *Neuron, 37*, 865–876.
Epstein, R. A., Higgins, S., & Thompson-Schill, S. L. (2005). Learning places from views: Variation in scene processing as a function of experience and navigational ability. *Journal of Cognitive Neuroscience, 17*(1), 73–83.
Foo, P., Warren, W. H., Duchon, A., & Tarr, M. J. (2005). Do humans integrate routes into a cognitive map? Map- versus landmark-based navigation of novel shortcuts. *Journal of Experimental Psychology: Learning, Memory, and Cognition, 31*(2), 195–215.
Gabrieli, J. D. E. (1998). Cognitive neuroscience of human memory. *Annual Review of Psychology, 49*, 87–115.
Gazzaniga, M. S., Ivry, R., & Mangun, G. R. (2013). *Cognitive neuroscience: The biology of mind* (4th ed.). New York, NY: W.W. Norton.
Geisler, W. S. (2008). Visual perception and the statistical properties of natural scenes. *Annual Review of Psychology, 59*, 167–192.
Gilbride, T. J., & Allenby, G. M. (2004). A choice model with conjunctive, disjunctive, and compensatory screening rules. *Marketing Science, 23*(3), 391–406.
Gilchrist, I. D., & Harvey, M. (2006). Evidence for a systematic component within scan paths in visual search. *Visual Cognition, 14*(4–8), 704–715.
Glaholt, M. G., & Reingold, E. M. (2009). Stimulus exposure and gaze bias: A further test of the gaze cascade model. *Attention, Perception, & Psychophysics, 71*(3), 445–450.
Glimcher, P. W. & Fehr, E. (2014). *Neuroeconomics: Decision making and the brain* (2nd ed.). New York, NY: Academic Press.
Gluck, M., Mercado, E., & Myers, C. (2008). *Learning and memory: From brain to behaviour.* New York, NY: Worth.
Gold, J. I., & Shadlen, M. N. (2007). The neural basis of decision making. *Annual Review of Neuroscience, 30*, 535–574.
Guadagni, P. M., & Little, J. D. (1983). A logit model of brand choice calibrated on scanner data. *Marketing Science, 2*(3), 203–238.
Hamid, S. N., Stankiewicz, B., & Hayhoe, M. (2010). Gaze patterns in navigation: Encoding information in large-scale environments. *Journal of Vision, 10*(12), 28.
Hayhoe, M., & Ballard, D. (2005). Eye movements in natural behaviour. *Trends in Cognitive Sciences, 9*(4), 188–194.
Henderson, J. M. (1992). Object identification in context: The visual processing of natural scenes. *Canadian Journal of Psychology, 46*(3), 319–341.
Henderson, J. M. (2003). Human gaze control during real-world scene perception. *Trends in Cognitive Sciences*, 7(11), 498–504.
Henderson, J. M. (2007). Regarding scenes. *Current Directions in Psychological Science, 16*(4), 219–222.
Henderson, J. M. (2011). Eye movements and scene perception. In I. D. Gilchrist & S. Liversedge (Eds.), *Oxford handbook of eye movements.* Oxford: Oxford University Press.
Henderson, J. M., & Hollingworth, A. (1999). High-level scene perception. *Annual Review of Psychology, 50*, 243–271.
Henderson, J. M., Nuthmann, A., & Luke, S. G. (2013). Eye movement control during scene viewing: Immediate effects of scene luminance on fixation durations. *Journal of Experimental Psychology: Human Perception and Performance, 39*(2), 318–322.

Hoch, S. J., Bradlow, E. T., & Wansink, B. (1999). The variety of an assortment. *Marketing Science, 18*(4), 527–546.

Hollingworth, A., & Henderson, J. M. (1998). Does consistent scene context facilitate object perception? *Journal of Experimental Psychology: General, 127*, 398–415.

Holmqvist, K., Nystrom, M., Andersson, R., Dewhurst, R., Jarodzka, H., & van de Weijer, J. (2011). *Eye tracking: A comprehensive guide to methods and measures.* Oxford: Oxford University Press.

Huang, Y., & Hutchinson, J. W. (2008). Counting every thought: Implicit measures of cognitive responses to advertising. *Journal of Consumer Research, 35*(1), 98–118.

Huang, Y., et al. (2013). Estimating the effect of in-store travel distance on unplanned spending: Applications to store layout and mobile promotion strategies. *Journal of Marketing,77*, 1–16.

Hui, S., Fader, P., & Bradlow, E. T. (2009a). Path data in marketing: An integrative framework and prospectus for model-building. *Marketing Science, 28*(2), 320–335.

Hui, S., Bradlow, E. T., & Fader, P. (2009b). Testing behavioural hypotheses using an integrated model of grocery store shopping paths. *Journal of Consumer Research, 36*(3), 478–493.

Hui, S. K., Huang, Y., Suher, J., & Inman, J. J. (2013a). Deconstructing the "first moment of truth": Understanding unplanned consideration and purchase conversion using in-store video tracking. *Journal of Marketing Research, 50*(4), 445–462.

Hui, S. K., Huang, Y., Inman, J. J., & Suher, J. (2013b). The effect of in-store travel distance on unplanned spending: Applications to mobile promotion strategies. *Journal of Marketing*, 77(2), 1–16.

Hutchinson, J. B., & Turk-Browne, N. B. (2012). Memory-guided attention: Control from multiple memory systems. *Trends in Cognitive Sciences, 16*(12), 576–579.

Itti, L., & Koch, C. (2001). Computational modelling of visual attention. *Nature Reviews Neuroscience, 2*, 194–203.

Itti, L., Koch, C., & Niebur, E. (1998). A model of saliency-based visual attention for rapid scene analysis. *IEE Transactions on Pattern Analysis and Machine Intelligence, 20*(11), 1254–1259.

Janiszewski, C. (1998). The influence of display characteristics on visual exploratory search behaviour. *Journal of Consumer Research, 25*, 290–301.

Johnson, E. J., Payne, J. W., Bettman, J. R., & Schkade, D. A. (1989). *Monitoring information processing and decisions: The mouselab system* (No. TR-89-4-ONR). Durham, NC: Duke University Center for Decision Studies.

Jovancevic-Misic, J., & Hayhoe, M. (2009). Adaptive gaze control in natural environments. *Journal of Neuroscience, 29*(19), 6234–6238.

Kim, B. E., Seligman, D., & Kable, J. W. (2012). Preference reversals in decision making under risk are accompanied by changes in attention to different attributes. *Frontiers in Neuroscience, 6*, 1–10.

Klatzky, R. L., Loomis, J. M., Beall, A. C., Chance, S. S., & Golledge, R. G. (1998). Spatial updating of self-position and orientation during real, imagined, and virtual locomotion. *Psychological Science, 9*(4), 293–298.

Koch, C., & Ullman, S. (1985). Shifts in selective visual attention: Towards the underlying neural circuitry. *Human Neurobiology, 4*, 219–227.

Krajbich, I., & Antonio, R. (2001). Multialternative drift-diffusion model predicts the relationship between visual fixations and choice in value-based decisions. *Proceedings of the National Academy of Sciences*, 108(33), 13852–13857.

Krajbich, I., Armel, C., & Rangel, A. (2010). Visual fixations and the computation and comparison of value in simple choice. *Nature Neuroscience, 13*(10), 1292–1298.

Krajbich, I., Lu, D., Camerer, C., & Rangel, A. (2012). The attentional drift-diffusion model extends to simple purchasing decisions. *Frontiers in Psychology, 3*, 1–18.

LaBar, K. S., & Cabeza, R. (2006). Cognitive neuroscience of emotional memory. *Nature Review of Neuroscience, 7*, 54–64.

Land, M., Mennie, N., & Rusted, J. (1999). The roles of vision and eye movements in the control of activities of daily living. *Perception, 28*, 1311–1328.

Land, M. F., & Hayhoe, M. (2001). In what ways do eye movements contribute to everyday activities? *Vision Research, 41*, 3559–3565.

Larson, A. M., Freeman, T. E., Ringer, R. V., & Loschky, L. C. (2014). The spatiotemporal dynamics of scene gist recognition. *Journal of Experimental Psychology: Human Perception and Performance, 40*(2), 471–487.

Lawler, E. L., Lenstra, J. K., Rinnooy Kan, A. H. G., & Shmoys, D. B., (Eds.) (1985). *The traveling salesman problem.* Chichester, UK: John Wiley.

Levine, M., Jankovic, I. N., & Palij, M. (1982). Principles of spatial problem solving. *Journal of Experimental Psychology: General, 111*(2), 157–175.

Lew, A. R. (2011). Looking beyond the boundaries: Time to put landmarks back on the cognitive map? *Psychological Bulletin, 137*(3), 484–507.

Liechty, J., Pieters, R., & Wedel, M. (2003). Global and local covert visual attention: Evidence from a Bayesian hidden Markov model. *Psychometrika, 68*(4), 519–541.

Lim, S. L., O'Doherty, J. P., & Rangel, A. (2011). The decision value computations in the vmPFC and striatum use a relative value code that is guided by visual attention. *The Journal of Neuroscience, 31*(37), 13214–13223.

Loftus, G. R., & Mackworth, N. H. (1978). Cognitive determinants of fixation location during picture viewing. *Journal of Experimental Psychology: Human Perception and Performance, 4*, 565–572.

Lu, J. & Hutchinson, J. W. (2016). Information search during online and in-store shopping: Comparison of boundedly rational models of split-second decision making. Working Paper, University of Pennsylvania.

Mandel, N. and Johnson, E. J. (2002). When web pages influence choice: Effects of visual primes on experts and novices. *Journal of Consumer Research, 29*, 235–245.

Manohar, S. G., & Husain, M. (2013). Attention as foraging for information and value. *Frontiers in Human Neuroscience*, 7, 1–16.

Miller, J., & Carlson, L. (2011). Selecting landmarks in novel environments. *Psychonomic Bulletin & Review, 18*, 184–191.

Milosavljevic, M., Madsen, E., Koch, C., & Rangel, A. (2011). Fast saccades toward numbers: Simple number comparisons can be made in as little as 230 ms. *Journal of Vision, 11*(4), 4.

Moar, I., & Carleton, L. R. (1982). Memory for routes. *Quarterly Journal of Experimental Psychology, 34A*, 381–394.

Morales, A., Kahn, B. E., McAlister, L., & Broniarczyk, S. M. (2005). Perceptions of assortment variety: The effects of congruency between consumers' internal and retailers' external organization. *Journal of Retailing, 81*, 159–169.

Mormann, M. M., Koch, C., & Rangel, A. (2011). Consumers can make decisions in as little as a third of a second. *Judgment and Decision Making, 6*(6), 520–530.

Mormann, M. M., Malmaud, J., Huth, A., Koch, C., & Rangel, A. (2010). The drift diffusion model can account for the accuracy and reaction time of value-based choices under high and low time pressure. *Judgment and Decision Making, 5*(6), 437–449.

Nandy, A. S., & Tjan, B. S. (2012). Saccade-confounded image statistics explain visual crowding. *Nature Neuroscience, 15*, 463–469.

von Neumann, J., & Morgenstern, O. (2007). *Theory of games and economic behaviour* (60th Anniversary Commemorative Edition). Princeton, NJ: Princeton University Press.

O'Keefe, J., & Nadel, L. (1978). The hippocampus as a cognitive map.

Oliva, A. (2005). Gist of the scene. In L. Itti, G. Rees & J. K. Tsotsos (Eds.), *Neurobiology of attention* (pp. 251–256). San Diego, CA: Elsevier.

Oliva, A., & Schyns, P. G. (1997). Coarse blobs or fine edges? Evidence that information diagnosticity changes the perception of complex visual stimuli. *Cognitive Psychology, 34*, 72–107.

Oliva, A., & Schyns, P. G. (2000). Diagnostic colors mediate scene recognition. *Cognitive Psychology, 41*, 176–210.

Oliva, A., & Torralba, A. (2006). Building the gist of a scene: The role of global image features in recognition. *Progress in Brain Research, 155*, 23–36.

Orquin, J. L., & Loose, S. M. (2013). Attention and choice: A review on eye movements in decision making. *Acta Psychologica, 144*(1), 190–206.

Otter, T., Johnson, J., Rieskamp, J., Allenby, G. M., Brazell, J. D., Diederich, A., ... & Townsend, J. (2008). Sequential sampling models of choice: Some recent advances. *Marketing Letters, 19*(3–4), 255–267.

Park, C. W., Iyer, E. S., & Smith, D. C. (1989). The effects of situational factors on in-store grocery shopping behaviour: The role of store environment and time available for shopping. *Journal of Consumer Research, 15*(4), 422–433.

Payne, J. W., Bettman, J. R., & Johnson, E. J. (1993). *The adaptive decision-maker.* Cambridge: Cambridge University Press.

Pieters, R., Rosbergen, E., & Wedel, M. (1999). Visual attention to repeated print advertising: A test of scanpath theory. *Journal of Marketing Research, 36*(4), 424–438.

Pieters, R., & Wedel, M. (2004). Attention capture and transfer in advertising: Brand, pictorial, and text-size effects. *Journal of Marketing, 68*(2), 36–50.
Pieters, R., & Wedel, M. (2007). Goal control of attention: The Yarbus implication. *Journal of Consumer Research, 34*, 224.
Pieters, R., & Wedel, M. (2012). Ad gist: Ad communication in a single eye fixation. *Marketing Science, 31*(1), 59–73.
Pieters, R., Wedel, M., & Zhang, J. (2007). Optimal feature advertising design under competitive clutter. *Management Science, 53*(11), 1815–1828.
Pinna, B. (2010). New Gestalt principles of perceptual organization: An extension from grouping to shape and meaning? *Gestalt Theory, 32*(1), 11–78.
Pinna, B., & Tanca, M. (2008). Perceptual organization reconsidered in the light of the watercolor illusion: The problem of perception of holes and the object-hole effect. *Journal of Vision, 8*(7), 1–15.
Pinna, B., Brelstaff, G., & Spillmann, L. (2001). Surface color from boundaries: A new "watercolor" illusion. *Vision Research, 41*(20), 2669–2676.
Pinna, B., Werner, J. S., & Spillmann, L. (2003). The watercolor effect: A new principle of grouping figure-ground organization. *Vision Research, 43*(1), 43–52.
Potter, M. C. (1976). Short-term conceptual memory for pictures. *Journal of Experimental Psychology: Human Learning and Memory, 2*(5), 509–522.
Poynor, C., & Wood, S. (2010). Smart subcategories: How assortment formats influence consumer learning and satisfaction. *Journal of Consumer Research, 37*(1), 159–175.
Purves, D., Brannon, E. M., Cabeza, R., Huettel, S. A., LaBar, K. S., Platt, M. L., & Woldorff, M. G. (2013). *Principles of cognitive neuroscience* (2nd ed.). Sunderland, MA: Sinauer Associates, Inc.
Ratcliff, R. (1978). A theory of memory retrieval. *Psychological Review, 85*(2), 59–108.
Ratcliff, R. (1998). Modeling response times for two-choice decisions. *Psychological Science, 9*(5), 347–356.
Ratcliff, R., & McKoon, G. (2008). The diffusion decision model: Theory and data for two-choice decision tasks. *Neural Computation, 20*(4), 873–922.
Ratcliff, R., & Smith, P. L. (2004). A comparison of sequential sampling models for two-choice reaction time. *Psychological Review, 111*(2), 333.
Ratcliff, R., Van Zandt, T., & McKoon, G. (1999). Connectionist and diffusion models of reaction time. *Psychological Review, 106*, 261–300.
Rayner, K. (1998). Eye movement in reading and information processing: 20 years of research. *Psychological Bulletin, 124*(3), 372–422.
Rayner, K. (2009). Eye movements and attention in reading, scene perception, and visual search. *Quarterly Journal of Experimental Psychology, 62*(8), 1457–1506.
Reutskaja, E., Nagel, R., Camerer, C. F., & Rangel, A. (2011). Search dynamics in consumer choice under time pressure: An eye-tracking study. *The American Economic Review, 101*(2), 900–926.
Roe, R. M., Busemeyer, J. R., & Townsend, J. T. (2001). Multialternative decision field theory: A dynamic connectionist model of decision making. *Psychological Review, 108*(2), 370–392.
Rosenholtz, R. (1999). A simple saliency model predicts a number of motion popout phenomena. *Vision Research, 39*, 3157–3163.
Rousselet, G. A., Joubert, O. R., & Fabre-Thorpe, M. (2005). How long to get the "gist" of real-world natural scenes? *Visual Cognition, 12*(6), 852–877.
Ruddle, R. A., & Lessels, S. (2006). For efficient navigational search, humans require full physical movement, but not a rich visual scene. *Psychological Science, 17*(6), 460–465.
Ruddle, R. A., Volkova, E., Mohler, B., & Bulthoff, H. H. (2011). The effect of landmark and body-based sensory information on route knowledge. *Memory & Cognition, 39*, 686–699.
Russo, J. E., & Leclerc, F. (1994). An eye-fixation analysis of choice processes for consumer nondurables. *Journal of Consumer Research, 21*, 274–290.
Sanocki, T., & Epstein, W. (1997). Priming spatial layout of scenes. *Psychological Science, 8*(5), 374–378.
Schinazi, V. R., & Epstein, R. A. (2010). Neural correlates of real-world route learning. *NeuroImage, 53*, 725–735.
Schyns, P. G., & Oliva, A. (1994). From blobs to boundary edges: Evidence for time- and spatial-scale-dependent scene recognition. *Psychological Science, 5*(4), 195–200.
Shevell, S. K., & Kingdom, F. A. A. (2008). Color in complex scenes. *Annual Review of Psychology, 59*, 143–166.
Shi, S. W., & Trusov, M. The path to click: Are you on it? Working Paper, Santa Clara University.

Shi, S. W., Wedel, M., & Pieters, R. (2013). Information acquisition during online decision making: A model-based exploration using eye-tracking data. *Management Science, 59*(5), 1009–1026.
Shimojo, S., Simion, C., Shimojo, E., & Scheier, C. (2003). Gaze bias both reflects and influences preference. *Nature Neuroscience, 6*(12), 1317–1322.
Shugan, S. M. (1980). The cost of thinking. *Journal of Consumer Research*, 7(2), 99–111.
Simon, H. A. (1955). A behavioural model of rational choice. *The Quarterly Journal of Economics, 69*(1), 99–118.
Smith, P. L., & Van Zandt, T. (2000). Time-dependent Poisson counter models of response latency in simple judgment. *British Journal of Mathematical and Statistical Psychology, 53*(2), 293–315.
Sorensen, H. (2003). The Science of shopping. *Marketing Research, 15*(3), 30–35.
Steck, S. D., & Mallot, H. A. (2000). The role of global and local landmarks in virtual environment navigation. *Presence, 9*(1), 69–83.
Stüttgen, P., Boatwright, P., & Monroe, R. T. (2012). A satisficing choice model. *Marketing Science, 31*(6), 878–899.
Sullivan, B. T., Johnson, L., Rothkopf, C. A., Ballard, D., & Hayhoe, M. (2012). The role of uncertainty and reward on eye movements in a virtual driving task. *Journal of Vision, 12*(13), 1–17.
Tatler, B. W., & Vincent, B. T. (2008). Systematic tendencies in scene viewing. *Journal of Eye Movement Research, 2*(2), 1–18.
Tcheang, L., Bulthoff, H. H., & Burgess, N. (2011). Visual influence on path integration in darkness indicates a multimodal representation of large-scale space. *Proceedings of the National Academy of Sciences of the United States of America, 108*(3), 1152–1157.
Theeuwes, J. (2010). Top–down and bottom–up control of visual selection. *Acta Psychologica, 135*(2), 77–99.
Thorndyke, P. W., & Hayes-Roth, B. (1982). Differences in spatial knowledge acquired from maps and navigation. *Cognitive Psychology, 14*, 560–589.
Tkacık, G., Prentice, J. S., Victor, J. D., & Balasubramanian, V. (2010). Local statistics in natural scenes predict the saliency of synthetic textures. *Proceedings of the National Academy of Sciences of the United States of America, 107*(42), 18149–18154.
Tolman, E. C. (1948). Cognitive maps in rats and men. *Psychological Review, 55*(4), 189–208.
Tom, A. C., & Tversky, B. (2012). Remembering routes: Streets and landmarks. *Applied Cognitive Psychology, 26*, 182–193.
Torralba, A., & Oliva, A. (2003). Statistics of natural image categories. *Network: Computation in Neural Systems, 14*, 391–412.
Torralba, A., Oliva, A., Castelhano, M. S., & Henderson, J. M. (2006). Contextual guidance of eye movements and attention in real-world scenes: The role of global features in object search. *Psychological Review, 113*(4), 766–786.
Townsend, C., & Kahn, B. E. (2014). The "visual preference heuristic": The influence of visual versus verbal depiction on assortment processing, perceived variety, and choice overload. *Journal of Consumer Research, 40*(5), 993–1015.
Townsend, J. T., & Ashby, F. G. (1983). *Stochastic modeling of elementary psychological processes*. Cambridge, MA: Cambridge University Press.
Treisman, A. M., & Gelade, G. (1980). A feature-integration theory of attention. *Cognitive Psychology, 12*(1), 97–136.
Unema, P. J. A., Pannasch, S., Joos, M., & Velichkovsky, B. M. (2005). Time course of information processing during scene perception: The relationship between saccade amplitude and fixation duration. *Visual Cognition, 12*(3), 473–494.
Usher, M., & McClelland, J. L. (2001). The time course of perceptual choice: The leaky, competing accumulator model. *Psychological Review, 108*(3), 550.
Valenzuela, A., & Raghubir, P. (2009). Position-based beliefs: The center-stage effect. *Journal of Consumer Psychology, 19*, 185–196.
Van der Lans, R., Pieters, R., & Wedel, M. (2008). Eye-movement analysis of search effectiveness. *Journal of the American Statistical Association, 103*(482), 452–461.
Van Zandt, T. (2000). ROC curves and confidence judgments in recognition memory. *Journal of Experimental Psychology: Learning, Memory, and Cognition, 26*(3), 582.
Van Zoest, W., Donk, M., & Theeuwes, J. (2004). The role of stimulus-driven and goal-driven control in saccadic visual selection. *Journal of Experimental Psychology: Human Perception and Performance, 30*(4), 746–759.

Vo, M. L. H., & Henderson, J. M. (2009). Does gravity matter? Effects of semantic and syntactic inconsistencies on the allocation of attention during scene perception. *Journal of Vision*, *9*(3), 1–15.

Von der Heydt, R., & Pierson, R. (2006). Dissociation of color and figure-ground effects in the watercolor illusion. *Spatial Vision*, *19*(2–4), 323–340.

Waller, D., & Lippa, Y. (2007). Landmarks as beacons and associative cues: Their role in route learning. *Memory & Cognition*, *35*(5), 910–924.

Wedel, M., & Pieters, R. (2014). The buffer effect: The role of color when advertising exposures are brief and blurred. *Marketing Science*, *34*(1) 132–143.

Wedel, M., Pieters, R., & Liechty, J. (2008). Attention switching during scene perception: How goals influence the time course of eye movements across advertisements. *Journal of Experimental Psychology: Applied*, *14*(2), 129–138.

Weingarten, E., Kahn, B. E., & Hutchinson, J. W. (2016). Color-blocking in retailing. Work in progress, University of Pennsylvania.

Wolbers, T., & Hegarty, M. (2010). What determines our navigational abilities? *Trends in Cognitive Sciences*, *14*(3), 138–145.

Wolfe, J. M. (1994). Guided search 2.0: A revised model of visual search. *Psychonomic Bulletin & Review*, *1*, 202–238.

Wolfe, J. M., & Horowitz, T. S. (2004). What attributes guide the deployment of visual attention and how do they do it? *Nature Reviews Neuroscience*, *5*(6), 495–501.

Yang, L., Toubia, O., & de Jong, M. G. (2015). A bounded rationality model of information search and choice in preference measurement. *Journal of Marketing Research*, *52*, 166–183.

Yao, A. Y. J., & Einhauser, W. (2008). Color aids late but not early stages of rapid natural scene recognition. *Journal of Vision*, *8*(16), 1–13.

Yarbus, A. L. (1967). *Eye movements and vision*. New York, NY: Plenum Press.

5

Perception and consumption

Touch, multisensory integration and congruency

Cathrine V. Jansson-Boyd

> Equipped with his five senses, man explores the universe around him and calls the adventure Science.
>
> *Edwin Powell Hubble, 1929, p. 732*

People's sensory input guides their daily experiences. That in itself is perhaps not too surprising, as our perception has to draw information from the different senses to understand and perceive the world around us. However, what is interesting is the way in which our different senses affect our perception. It is also noteworthy that different types of stimuli can be used to alter an individual's perception of stimuli. The vast field of visual perception has shown that visual input generally dominates human perception, as it allows people to rapidly recognize environmental obstacles, colours, shapes etc. (Heller & Clark, 2008; Schifferstein, 2006). However, in the last couple of decades researchers have increasingly found that other senses can at times dominate our perception and subsequently make vision a secondary source of input (e.g., Jansson-Boyd, 2011, Spence & Gallace, 2011). From a consumer perspective, this is important as it opens up multiple new possibilities concerning how marketers, product designers and manufacturers can communicate with consumers as well as affect how stimuli are perceived. Increasingly, there is emerging evidence for how the different senses (vision, touch, smell, hearing and taste) all independently make valid contributions to consumer perception. It is also evident from the current research literature that our senses are very much connected and that one often affects the others in terms of evaluation of consumer products, environments and services (e.g., Spence & Gallace, 2011). Consequently, it is important to understand not only how the senses work in isolation but also what the role of multisensory perception in consumption is. In most consumer settings our perception will be exposed to multiple sensory stimuli, such as music (auditory) and fragrance (smell), often in addition to visual input. So if we truly wish to comprehend how consumers perceive products and consumer environments, it needs to be understood how the senses interact, as it is not possible to segregate one from another in real-life settings. However, before senses are looked at in unison, in order to produce ecologically valid findings similar to those of a genuine consumer experience, it is important to appreciate how they affect perception individually.

It is beyond the scope of this chapter to explore how all the senses function individually. Nor is it possible to present an in-depth picture of how they function when combined with other senses. Hence, this chapter focuses mainly on one sense, touch and presents findings from other modalities in parallel to broaden the understanding of sensory research. Compared with other senses, i.e., vision and hearing, touch is relatively under researched, and it is only in the last decade or so that consumer researchers have realized the importance of touch. This is the reason why touch is the focal point of this chapter. First, the chapter will present an overview of tactile research and how it is applicable to consumer behaviour and environments. The chapter will then go on to discuss the importance of investigating the tactile sense in combination with other senses in order to create an ecologically valid picture. This will be followed by a discussion about congruency, and finally some directions for future research will be provided. Even though it is not possible here to go into any great depth into what the outcomes are when combining sensory input, it is important to at least recognize that simultaneous exposure to more than one sense will affect the way in which stimuli are perceived. Equally, it is imperative to recognize that congruency has a role to play when consumers are exposed to multimodal input.

The importance of touch in consumption

Touch can refer to different types of stimulation on our skin (Stevens & Green, 1996). However, the focus here will mostly be on tactile information received through our hands, as this is the most common way through which consumers gather information about products. Hence, throughout this chapter the word *touch* or *haptics* will be used to describe the system involved when our hands pick up sensory information (Gibson, 1966).

It has become clear that touch has an important role to play when it comes to understanding consumer perception. One explanation as to why touch affects consumers is because of its connection to emotion. When people touch something that is pleasant or unpleasant, regions of the orbitofrontal cortex are activated and parts of the cingulate cortex are involved (Rolls et al., 2003). The cingulate cortex is an integral part of the limbic system that is involved with formation of emotions and processing (Hadland, Rushworth, Gaffan, & Passingham, 2003). This demonstrates that touch and emotion are closely connected. It is therefore not surprising that people can read and signal different types of emotions through touch. This was shown by Hertenstein, Keltner, App, Bulleit, & Jaskolka (2006), who found that people can identify specific emotions when touched on the arm by a stranger without actually seeing them. This connection appears to be a cross-cultural phenomenon, as participants from both Spain and the United States were capable of decoding emotions such as anger, disgust and sympathy through interpersonal touch.

The fact that emotion and touch are closely connected suggests that when consumers touch something pleasant or unpleasant, it triggers an emotional response that drives the evaluation of a product. Therefore, when people touch a product they can become emotionally (dis)connected and consequently feel more or less closely linked to the stimulus they are touching. The connection between touch and emotion can explain two relatively well-investigated aspects of touch: 1) the endowment effect and 2) that consumers appear to be subconsciously influenced by touch (both points are discussed further on in this chapter).

However, there is another interesting point to consider when it comes to the relationship between emotion and touch: the possibility that a "positive" emotion may have the capacity to reduce or even eliminate the importance of touch. It has been suggested that consumers with a high need for touch can become frustrated when deprived of tactile input (Peck & Childers, 2003a). However, this is not the case for those who lack a need for tactile input. Since frustration is linked to strong negative emotions, especially in the light of failed achievements (e.g., Colman, 2006; Shorkey & Crocker, 1981), it would appear feasible to assume that the negative impact of being unable to engage in touch could be weakened by the experience of a positive emotion. This idea was tested by Yazdanparast and Spears (2013) when they looked at online purchase decisions made when touch was not possible. They hypothesized that those with a high need for touch would not be affected by the lack of tactile input in a positive mood condition but would be negatively influenced in a negative mood condition. Their results confirmed their hypotheses. Both purchase intentions and confidence in product judgement in a positive mood condition were similar for those with a high and low need for touch. However, there was a significant difference between the two groups when they were exposed to a negative mood condition. Yazdanparast and Spears' study shows that positive emotions can "compensate" for the lack of tactile input, and this raises the possibility that positive valence may be used as a "substitute" for tactile input. In order to clarify to what extent emotion may cancel out touch, it could be tested on a concept such as the endowment effect, where touch is known to be an influencing factor.

The endowment effect

The endowment effect is a well-known concept in economics. It shows that people value objects more if they think of them as their own (Franciosi, Kajual, Mitchelitsch, Smith, & Deng, 1996; Kahneman, Knetsch, & Thaler, 1990). However, what causes people to feel that something belongs to them is not always clear-cut. For example, it has been found that feelings of ownership can be established within a consumer simply by touching an item (Peck & Shu, 2009; Shu & Peck, 2011). Even the thought of simply touching an object can generate the endowment effect (Peck, Barger, & Webb, 2013). Thus, feelings of ownership can be created without actually owning an object, and this shows that the notion of touch has an important role to play in such perceived ownership.

Reb and Connolly (2007) demonstrated the relative contribution of touch to the endowment effect when they manipulated factual ownership and tactile interaction with an object. Participants in the study were shown a coffee mug, but only half of them were handed the mug to keep on their desk. Half of the participants were also told that they could keep the mug, while the other half were told that they had a choice between the coffee mug and a sum of money. The design meant that they had four groups of participants: 1) those who owned a mug and had it with them ("possessed it"), 2) those who owned it but did not possess it, 3) those who did not own it but possessed it and 4) those who neither owned nor possessed a mug. All were also given the opportunity to exchange the mug for a small amount of money. Their findings showed that ownership did not lead to greater differences in value, but possession did. The participants who had the coffee mug in their possession valued it more highly ($3.84) than the participants who did not have it in their possession ($3.00). Those who had possessed the coffee mug also had stronger feelings of ownership than those who did not have one in their possession. This shows that physical touch is linked to feelings of ownership, rather than ownership alone. Even though Reb and Connolly demonstrate that physical touch is a mediator in generating the endowment effect, their study did not take actual physical properties into account. It could have been that the coffee mugs used were pleasant to touch and therefore more likely to create stronger feelings of ownership.

But what happens if the sensory feedback is unpleasant to touch? Does it still generate the endowment effect? Peck and Shu (2009) realized that there is a possibility that negative sensory feedback may generate different perceptions. They explored whether there is a relationship between "negative" tactile input and perceived ownership and subsequent valuation. In their study they used playfoam sculpting beads (deemed unpleasant to touch) and divided their participants into buyers (non-owners) and sellers (owners). Half the participants were asked to touch the playfoam sculpting beads, while the other half did not get the opportunity to touch them. Peck and Shu found that touching the stimuli increased perceived ownership for both buyers and sellers, but did not lead to increase in valuation. This shows that it may be the perceived pleasantness of touch that influences perceived value and that touch itself is what affects perceived ownership. However, there is a possibility that there are different levels of perceived unpleasantness, which consequently may impact differently on the perceived value – an area that could be explored in future studies.

Since the aforementioned studies, several researchers have confirmed that there is a relationship between touch and the endowment effect. More recently, this was also explored in regard to touch technologies. Brasel and Gips (2014) investigated how touchscreen interfaces can increase perceived ownership and the likelihood of an endowment effect taking place. They found that touch interfaces interacted with the importance of product haptics and actual interface ownership in their effects on perceived product ownership. There were also stronger effects for products for which tactile input is important and interfaces that were owned. Effectively, this means that the interface used while conducting online shopping influences the value given to products. The use of tablets (which are touch-based devices) increased the value of a product compared with when participants used traditional computers. Brasel and Gips therefore demonstrated that it is important to recognize how touch-based "shopping tools" impact on evaluation and perceived ownership, as the touch-based interface effectively becomes a filter between the consumer's perception and online products. Consequently, it appears that the role of touch, even though not directly linked to a particular aspect of consumption, subconsciously guides the consumer.

Subconscious influences

It appears that on many occasions tactile input influences people on a subconscious level. For example, Williams and Bargh (2008) found that people's perceptions of others were altered depending on whether they held a hot or a cold drink in their hands. Participants were asked to rate a person, but were seemingly unaware of the fact that their ratings were guided by whether the tactile input was hot or cold. Unconscious tactile influences are also evident from the ergonomic design that is used by fast-food restaurants. A commonly used technique in the fast-food industry is to make use of uncomfortable seating in their restaurants, as it encourages customers to leave more rapidly. That way, the restaurants can ensure a higher turnover of customers and increase the overall profits, as it means more paying customers can get a seat in any one day (Chow, 2015). Basically, the tactile sensory system sends "uncomfortable" signals from our bottoms to our brains saying we need to leave. So why is it that people keep going back to such restaurants and at times even say they like them? Well, one explanation can be found in the length of the neural paths that send signals to our brain. In 1963, Von Békésy discovered that the length of the neural paths can affect our awareness of tactile stimulation. If you touch your lip with your index finger, you feel the sensation in the lip. If you then touch your ankle with the same finger, most people report that they feel the sensation in their finger. The reason is that the neural path from the tactile receptors in the lip to the brain is shorter than that from the finger to the brain, which again is shorter than that from the ankle to the brain. Hence, the length of the neural path can affect our awareness of tactile stimulation. So, in the case of the fast-food restaurant, when people sit down and eat they are much more aware of the tactile input that comes through their lips (i.e., it tastes great) and the feeling they experience through their hands (i.e., holding a burger feels nice) than they are of the tactile input coming through their bottom (i.e., the seat is not very comfortable). The fact that seating material can affect perception also highlights how the physical properties of an object have a role to play in guiding our sensory modalities.

Physical properties of touch

Researchers within the area of cognitive psychology have identified that objects can be rapidly and correctly recognized through the use of touch (e.g., Klatzky, Lederman, & Metzger, 1985; Norman, Norman, Clayton, Lianekhammy, & Zielke, 2004). Furthermore, it has been found that touch can also be helpful in assessing features of stimuli such as texture and weight (Klatzky & Lederman, 1992, 1993; Lederman & Klatzky, 1987) – the latter in particular has an important role to play in product evaluation.

The influence of texture upon aesthetic evaluation is evident from research conducted on DVD boxes (Jansson-Boyd & Marlow, 2007). Altering the surface texture of a DVD box can alter the overall appreciation for the box. Furthermore, the tactile input (depending on the texture) can influence the perception more than the visual input. However, it is still not known in what specific circumstances tactile properties have a greater weighting than visual input. Nor is it known whether this is product specific, even though it appears that tactile properties are likely to mould most types of evaluations, as there are similar research findings in support of this. For example, Ackerman, Nocera and Bargh (2010) asked participants to evaluate people based on fictitious curricula vitae (CVs). In their study, participants were handed one of two types of clipboard that varied in weight with a CV attached. The evaluations made by those who had been handed a heavier clipboard were higher than those made by the group handed the lighter clipboard, again suggesting that participants were subconsciously affected by the weight of an unrelated object.

The physical properties of products also influence the way in which their content is evaluated. Krishna and Morrin (2008) showed that the hardness of a bottle influenced the evaluation of mineral water. Similar findings have also been reported when researching other food-related products. For example, Piqueras-Fiszman, Harrar, Alcaide and Spence (2011) observed that when yoghurt was consumed from heavier bowls, people rated the yoghurt to be denser, more likeable and of better quality. This was also confirmed in a follow-on study (Piqueras-Fiszman & Spence, 2012) in which they explored whether the weight of a container in which food was kept could affect the satiety-inducing aspects of the food. This was looked at prior to and after consumption. Their findings show that when food was presented in a heavier container, it was perceived to be more satiating both prior to and after consumption. This demonstrated that in addition to influencing product quality and likeability, weight also affects satiety.

A broader influence of touch

In the context of retailing, it is useful to know that it is not only tactile properties that can mould perception of consumers but also physical touch by others, something referred to as the "Midas Touch" (e.g., Crusco & Wetzel, 1984). The role of "interpersonal" touch has been explored within psychology for several decades, and the research output has repeatedly found that it can be useful in influencing some kind of "compliance". In an early study on interpersonal touch, it was found that students who had their hand touched by a library clerk while checking out books rated the library clerk as more personable (Fisher, Rytting, & Heslin, 1976). A decade later, Crusco and Wetzel (1984) also demonstrated that interpersonal touch can be used to increase the value of the tip given to a waitress in a restaurant. When the waitress briefly touches the customer on the arm, the tip increases, but the services are usually not reported to be any better. The increase in tips may stem from the fact that customers view the waitress as more likeable as a consequence of having been briefly touched. Other researchers have also found that interpersonal touch increases the willingness to take part in on-the-spot interviews in retail settings (Hornik & Ellis, 1988) and to taste snacks in supermarkets (Hornik, 1992).

The idea of positive effect upon touch-induced compliance has also been applied to health settings. In a study conducted by Guéguen, Meineri, & Charles-Sire (2010), six general practitioners were asked to touch (or not) patients who had mild pharyngitis on the arm for a couple of seconds. At the end of the consultation session the practitioners asked the patients to promise to take the antibiotic medication as prescribed. A week later, patients were contacted and asked whether they had taken the medication and what they thought of the practitioner they had met. The findings showed that patients who had been touched were more likely to have taken the medication as prescribed. However, the likelihood was higher for male patients. Furthermore, it was also found that patients viewed the practitioner as more concerned and competent in the touch condition.

The aforementioned outlined what happens when interpersonal touch is intentional. However, it appears that unintentional interpersonal touch also has a role to play in consumer settings. For example, Martin (2012) investigated accidental interpersonal touch in retail settings in a field experiment. She found that when consumers had been touched by another consumer while examining products it resulted in more negative brand evaluations and product beliefs. It was also found that they spent less time within the store compared with consumers who had not been touched. Presumably such findings are likely to be linked to perception of general politeness and personal space-related issues. However, this may be something that store designers may wish to be aware of if they want to ensure that small retail spaces are cleverly designed in order to avoid accidental tactile interaction. What the findings show is that haptically acquired information exerts a rather broad influence over perception and behaviour, and such influence most likely happens with little or no awareness (Jansson-Boyd & Marlow, 2007).

Explanations for interpersonal touch

So why does intentional interpersonal touch lead to favourable perceptions and compliance while unintentional touch leads to less positive evaluations? In regard to the latter, the previous suggestion that it is linked to personal space and perception of how polite others are (as it is not usually deemed polite to bump into someone) seems feasible, even though this is just speculation, as there is currently no research evidence to support this. However, there are other suggestions, both substantiated and unsubstantiated, in regard to why intentional interpersonal touch leads to positive outcomes. First, it has been suggested that the underlying explanation may be found in oxytocin levels (Morhenn, Park, Piper, & Zak, 2008). Oxytocin levels have been found to lead to a higher level of generosity towards strangers, and Morhenn et al. have shown that oxytocin also increases after touch, but only when it is followed by an intentional act of trust. The aforementioned will not entirely explain the positive influence of intentional touch but may shed some light on findings such as those produced by Guéguen et al. (2010) whereby the practitioners who had touched the patients had a better success rate in getting the patients to take their medication.

Another explanation may be found in a study conducted by Levav and Argo (2010). They found that a brief touch can increase the likelihood of taking a financial risk. In their study, students were asked to play an investment game, and participants were patted (or not) on the back. When they were patted briefly on the back the participants were more likely to take bigger financial risks. This was particularly so when patted by a female confederate. Because the female touch was more influential (this has also been found in other studies, e.g., Guéguen 2002) in generating risk taking, Levav and Argo speculated that it may be linked to motherly instincts. Perhaps people are "conditioned" from a very early age into feeling that the touch of a mother is more comforting and makes them feel safe, which is why people later in life find that being touched by a female has a comforting effect.

Individual differences

People do not respond to tactile input in the same way, as it is linked to whether or not people have a need to touch (Peck & Childers, 2003b). It has been established that people's need for touch (NFT) varies, and it has been proposed that some are high or low on instrumental need for touch (INT) while other are high or low on autotelic need for touch (ANT) (e.g., Peck & Childers, 2003b). This particular differentiation of NFT is coupled to consumers' need for tactile interaction. However, it is not unfeasible to assume that different levels of NFT will (at least indirectly) play a role in all kinds of tactile interaction.

INT-oriented individuals can be defined as those who use tactile properties for the purpose of goal-driven evaluative outcomes. Peck and Childers (2003a) proposed that judgements would be based on tactile properties that reflect a product's texture, such as hardness or weight. A consumer high in INT is more likely to consciously explore tactile properties for evaluative purposes. For example, a consumer out shopping for a mobile phone may simultaneously hold two in order to compare weight and how they fit in the hand.

People who are driven by ANT differ from individuals high on INT in that they are not utilizing tactile input for a particular purpose. Rather than using touch to evaluate specific properties, they use touch for their own enjoyment. This kind of touch is hedonically oriented in that the consumer touches for pleasure and for the sake of experiencing sensory stimulation. Those high in ANT find it difficult not to engage in tactile interaction, and the continuous exposure to tactile input is less likely to be consciously processed (Peck & Wiggins 2006).

Those high in ANT have been found to be less influenced by haptic input when they are faced with "irrelevant" tactile information, while those low in ANT are more affected by haptic input (Krishna & Morrin, 2008). Consequently, low autotelics evaluate products lower when faced with a low-quality input that is irrelevant than when facing higher-quality irrelevant cues. Level of involvement also appears to play a part in how persuaded people are, depending on level of ANT. The relationship is not entirely straightforward, but it appears that those high in ANT are more easily persuaded by information when a haptic element is present, regardless of whether they feel some level of involvement with the information (Peck & Wiggins Johnson, 2011).

NFT also impacts on what happens when consumers are deprived of tactile interaction. The judgement decisions that consumers make are clearly affected by NFT (Peck, 1999; Peck & Childers, 2003b). The higher the NFT, the more likely it is that individuals will experience a sense of frustration (Peck, 1999; Peck and Childers, 2003b). Furthermore, such consumers also tend to be "less confident in their judgements" (Peck, 1999, p. 191) due to the fact that they cannot draw upon their tactile experiences, and hence the consumer decision-making process can be affected.

Touch in later life

Less confident tactile judgements can be the consequence of becoming older. With age, people naturally lose their grip strength, and this can impact upon the effective use of devices, as the motion of wrist and grip strength is linked to them being used effectively. Hence, the question is how it may impact on elderly users' perception of electronic devices such as touch screens and mobile phones (Biswas, Robinson, & Langdon, 2012; Biswas & Robinson, 2013). So, similarly to what was found in Brasel and Gips' study, that touch-based interfaces impact on the evaluation of an online product, it is likely that users' decreased physical performance will negatively impact on tasks such as online shopping or use of technology as it becomes a mediating variable.

Due to the fact that some sensory cortices are affected more by aging (Raz, 2000), it is possible that touch simply will not be as effective in guiding and aiding elderly consumers' perceptions of products. However, there is currently no research that has effectively tackled this topic, and more research is needed to show how tactile input may or may not affect the elderly consumer. Even though movement and perception are affected by age, it is still possible that touch may be a factor to be reckoned with. It needs to be remembered that our tactile perception is not the only sense that is affected by age, and it raises the possibility that touch can perhaps be used as a persuasive input in favour of a particular product (Spence & Gallace, 2010).

In the absence of touch

The Internet is of great interest when talking about touch as it means that no tactile input is required. We have already touched on the fact that the types of electronic devices used for online shopping act as a mediator for how online products are perceived (Brasel & Gips, 2014). However, so far we have not discussed the exact role of "lack of touch" while Internet shopping. This is important, as e-commerce sales now account for a big part of retail sales. In 2014, sales in the United Kingdom, Germany, France, Sweden, the Netherlands, Italy, Poland and Spain were £132.05 billion (Retail Research, 2015). It has also been proposed that return rates for items bought online that are often important to touch, such as clothing, are high. In Canada approximately 27 per cent of all purchased clothing is returned (ELC, 2008). Tactile input may not be a barrier for all kinds of shopping online, but may very well be product specific. For example, McCabe and Nowlis (2003) found that products with material properties such as clothes or carpets are more likely to be purchased in retail environments where consumers can physically inspect the products.

So how do individual tactile differences affect consumers when they cannot touch the products? This was explored by Peck and Childers (2003a) when they asked their participants to evaluate a mobile phone and a sweater. Half of the participants were allowed to touch the products, while the other half could only see them but were not allowed to touch them. Their findings showed that when people had a high NFT, they were more confident in their evaluations when they were allowed to touch the products, while no significant difference was found for those low in NFT. The study found that one way of decreasing the frustration felt by those high in NFT when deprived of tactile input was by using descriptions of how the products felt. This was done with more success for mobile phones, as concrete aspects such as weight could be described, but less successful for the sweater, where more subjective concepts such as softness were used. Hence, the lack of tactile input for online shopping may be overcome (at least for some products) by good descriptions of the products' physical properties. Another "future" possibility of how to overcome the problem of lack of tactile input may eventually be found in the use of three-dimensional virtual touch systems. For example, Jin (2011) investigated three-dimensional virtual touch created by Novint Falcon haptic interfaces and how it affected consumer behaviour in the interactive marketing of automobiles. Novint Falcon provides consumers with a sense of touch within computer-generated environments and makes the stimulus seem real and tangible. Jin found that when her participants were good at gathering information through touch (using Novint Falcon) they evaluated the products more positively and enjoyed the test-driving experience more. The Novint Falcon (or similar) technology is not currently sophisticated enough to be used as an Internet touch substitute, but it may be indicative of where the future lies in terms of experiencing online tactile interaction.

Integrative sensory research: Creating a holistic perspective of consumer perception

So far the focus of this chapter has been on the sensory input of touch. However, it is important to understand the role of multisensory perception in consumption, as consumers are rarely exposed to only one sense at a time. In most consumer settings our perception will be exposed to multiple sensory stimuli such as music (auditory), a fragrance (smell) and visual input. So if we truly wish to appreciate how consumers perceive products and consumer environments, we need to understand how the senses interact, as it is not possible to segregate one from another in real-life settings. Within the consumer research domain, most researchers focus on five senses (vision, touch, smell, hearing and taste). At times, the senses are researched in isolation from other senses, and clearly this is useful in that it furthers our knowledge of the individual senses. However, it is evident from the current research literature that our senses are very much connected and that one often affects the others in terms of evaluation of consumer products, environments and services. Findings are also suggesting that there is often a dominant sense that "regulates" the sensory input (e.g., Jansson & Haggard, 2006; Jansson-Boyd & Marlow, 2007). For example, if a product is perceived via one modality (such as vision) it may "guide" a consumer's perceptual intake from another modality (such as touch) and consequently align their tactile perception with their visual input.

Different theories have been suggested in regard to why multisensory integration happens. Examples include that it is more likely to occur when stimuli in different modalities are presented closely in time (e.g., Jones & Jarick, 2006; van Wassenhove, Grant, & Poeppel, 2007) and that spatial coincidence may enable multisensory integration (e.g., Frens, Van Opstal, & Van der Willigen, 1995; Slutsky & Recanzone, 2001). The idea that different sensory input is presented in close time proximity should be of particular interest to marketers, as they often attempt to stimulate more than one sense at the time. If the time proximity theory is correct, then marketers should be careful in introducing different sensory inputs simultaneously. This is because the inputs linked to the different senses are likely to be integrated, and hence the consumer's perception will be based on how the combined factors are interpreted rather than how they may be perceived in isolation. A particularly good example of explaining this is by looking at the McGurk effect (McGurk & MacDonald, 1976). The McGurk effect shows that there is a "fusion effect" when different sensory input is perceived simultaneously. For example, a voice is dubbed saying "ba, ba, ba", but you see a face articulating "ga, ga, ga". In such instances your mind tries to reconcile them so that what you are hearing is more in line with the visual input, and hence you perceive the sound as "da, da, da". Even though this provides clear evidence that a "fusion effect" can take place on the back of multisensory integration, it is worth noting that the fused perception can be dependent on the clarity of the components involved (e.g., Saalasti et al., 2012; Tiippana, 2014). Hence, this suggests that when marketing stimuli aimed at different senses are kept clear and distinctive, consumers will be less likely to perceive them in a fused fashion. Obviously, the McGurk effect shows that different modality input can lead to an "unexpected" perception of stimuli. Furthermore, it also demonstrates that different modality input is processed together so that one factor affects the other, even if they are not fused. What is also interesting is that it has been found that people cannot ignore the input from one modality even though they have been instructed to focus and respond to another (e.g., Spence, Ranson, & Driver, 2000).

Research such as the aforementioned has undoubtedly helped the consumer sciences take an interest in different aspects of sensory stimulation. It is only in the past two decades that we have seen a number of consumer psychologists and marketers show an interest in multisensory input (touch, smell, hearing, taste and sight), even though it has been known for quite some time that it forms the basis for human cognition (Neisser, 1976).

Why do we need to be aware of congruency?

Since the different senses mould consumers' perceptions, it is important to understand how different types of input may "complement" (or not, as the case may be) one another to generate a strong, coherent picture of a stimulus. In some instances such as when consuming food, modalities (i.e., taste and smell) are virtually inseparable (Prescott, 2015). This highlights the significance of comprehending how the senses influence one another.

Even though consumer-based practitioners (e.g., marketers, product designers and advertisers) would most likely want to be presented with an exact formula of how different "pairs" of stimuli can be matched to create a positive consumer perception, the reality looks a little different. There is now a plethora of research demonstrating that when different sensory inputs are congruent or incongruent, it may lead to more or less favourable perception of consumer goods. However, researchers are still a long way off from being able to provide practitioners with an exact guide on "how to match sensory input effectively". That is not to say that one should give up on the idea that product features can be used to create desired sensory expectations, but simply that at this point in time current research findings can only act as guidance to how this may be achieved. (In)congruent sensory input is applicable to all the senses, regardless of combinations. However, it is worth noting that (in)congruency between a sensory input and the actual stimulus or environment is also important.

Before looking at some of the effects identified when exploring multisensory input, let's first take a look at a couple of examples as to why one needs to be careful about ensuring that sensory input is congruent with the "target" stimulus. Even though this is slightly different from looking at what happens when consumers are exposed to two different sensory inputs simultaneously, it is still perhaps just as important. If sensory input is not congruent with the stimulus itself, it is likely to lead to a negative perception of some sort. For example, researchers have found that the sensory input itself needs to be congruent with the "message" or product. Peck and Wiggins (2006) demonstrated this when they found that donations for an arboretum increased when the donation appeal brochure contained congruent tactile material (e.g., bark of a tree) rather than incongruent tactile material (e.g., steel) for those with a high NFT. Other studies demonstrating that the sensory input needs to be congruent with the "stimulus" include one conducted by Cirrincione, Estes and Carù (2014). They explored the possibility that using ambient scent could enhance the experience of visiting an art exhibition. Their study specifically looked at how scents impact on the perception and memory of art. It was found that a pleasant scent decreased the way in which artworks were evaluated and decreased likelihood of recall, especially when the two were incongruent. However, presumably there is some difficulty in matching a scent with a suitable artwork. Hence, art museums should be cautious in using ambient scents, as they may be a hindrance to spreading knowledge of the art exhibited (Cirrincione et al., 2014). Both the aforementioned studies demonstrate that it is not only multisensory input that needs to be congruent; also, the sensory input needs to be congruent with the product.

Multisensory (in)congruency

Food is a good example for demonstrating how different sensory input can mould the way in which it is perceived. As already mentioned, odour and taste are usually perceived together for food products (Prescott, 2015). The integration of the senses means that the "pleasurable" properties of taste are closely linked to the smell (e.g., Yeomans, Mobini, Elliman, Walker, & Stevenson, 2006; Zellner, Rozin, Aron, & Kulish, 1983) and this most likely stems from repeated exposure to both, resulting in evaluative conditioning taking place (De Houwer, Thomas, & Baeyens, 2001). Hence, it is not too surprising that when odour and taste are incongruent, it has a negative impact upon the evaluation of a food product. Somewhat more surprising is that the auditory sense can affect the perception of foods. For example, it has been found that the impressions consumers form about food can be influenced by the product name itself. Yorkston and Menon (2004) found that the vowels used in a name can influence the perceived qualities of ice cream. When an ice cream was named Frosch, participants in their study thought it would taste creamier and smoother than when it was called Frisch. Hence, it would seem that people have associations between a sound and the way in which it may taste, suggesting that there is cross-modal correspondence (Spence, 2011). It is worth noting that the participants in Yorkston and Menon's study did not actually test the ice creams; they only read descriptions of the products. However, in a study by Ngo, Misra and Spence (2011), participants were allowed to taste the products tested, and in this scenario support for cross-modal correspondences was also found. Their findings showed that more milky-based chocolates were more closely associated with softer-sounding words, while chocolates containing high levels of cocoa were associated with sharper-sounding words. This demonstrates that speech sounds can form the basis for how products are perceived. This may have implications for the brand names given to products, as manufacturers should ensure that the name chosen represents the actual product. Even though the name may be a contributing factor to the success of a product, it is worth noting that other factors come into play, such as how memorable, attention grabbing and easy to process the factors are (e.g., Ewald & Moskowitz, 2007; Keller, Hecker, & Houston, 1998; Labroo, Dhar, & Schwartz, 2008; Lowrey, Shrum, & Dubitsky, 2003; Robertson, 1989; Vanden Bergh, Collins, Schultz, & Adler, 1987).

Clearly, other senses and products are also influenced by multisensory input. This was nicely demonstrated by Krishna and her colleagues (Krishna, Elder, & Caldara, 2010) when they researched how touch is affected by smell. They explored whether multisensory semantic congruence between olfactory and tactile properties (temperature and texture) could heighten tactile perception and, in turn, product evaluation. It was hypothesized that the effect of smell on tactile perception would be driven by the semantic congruence across the sensory inputs. They confirmed this when they found that scent-infused products have a role to play in how the tactile perception is affected and that the effect is stronger when the scent is semantically congruent with the tactile perception.

There is also the possibility that touch (just like some other senses) is influenced by previous experiences, hence indicating that repeated previous exposure together with other stimuli results in evaluative conditioning taking place. This could explain why unexpected tactile input results in less desirable evaluations of products (Jansson-Boyd & Marlow, 2007).

As a final note, it is worth mentioning that congruency does not only need to be applied to a product in order to ensure a more favourable perception. It is also applicable to in-store environments – something that was found by Spangenberg, Grohmann, & Sprott (2005) when they looked at the interactive effects of scent and music during the festive Christmas period.

Advantages and demerits of using multiple sensory input

There are clear advantages for advertisers and marketers in making use of features that target processing from different sensory modalities, as they do not compete for available cognitive resources (e.g., Olsen, 1997; Tavassoli & Lee, 2003). Hence, if markets want to try to ensure that consumers process as much of the provided information as possible, it is best to try to communicate through different sensory channels. However, in order to generate a preferable perception of stimuli, it is important that the senses are stimulated in a congruent manner, as otherwise the end result may not be the intended outcome. Another advantage of ensuring that sensory input is congruent is that people recognize the stimuli more rapidly (Laurienti et al., 2002). This should be of interest to product designers, who can make use of it to ensure quick recognition and hence reduce the risk of consumers looking at competitors' products.

Finally, it is worth considering that incongruent sensory input may attract attention and enhance memory. Designing something that feels totally different from the way it looks may be one way of doing so (Schifferstein & Spence, 2008) and may provide a highly memorable experience (Spence & Gallace, 2011). However, using incongruent multisensory input should be done with caution (Ludden & Schifferstein, 2007, Ludden, Schifferstein, & Hekkert, 2007; Schifferstein & Spence, 2008) for two reasons in particular. One reason is that there is the possibility of cognitive overload (Morrin & Chebat, 2005), and if the incongruency is not perceived as intended, e.g., to capture attention with an element of surprise, the perception may instead become negative in nature when the consumer simply interprets it as an unfortunate design. The second reason is linked to the consumption of food. In the case of food, people do not like to be surprised; they prefer to have the culinary experience that they expect. When food items are not congruent with expectations, people perceive them in a more negative manner (e.g., Cardello, 1994; Deliza & MacFie, 1997; Deliza, MacFie, & Hedderley, 2003), and this can be a lingering impression, meaning that people will not attempt to consume the items again.

There are also other potential drawbacks. This can be noted when looking at ambient scents. On their own, they have the capacity to increase cognitive elaboration (Bone & Ellen, 1999) and enhance both attention (Morrin & Ratneshwar, 2000) and product evaluation (Spangenberg, Crowley, & Henderson 1996), which are all clearly positive outcomes. However, couple a relaxing fragrance together with loud music within a retail setting, and all of a sudden it has a negative impact on consumer perception (Morrin & Chebat, 2005). Ambient scents can influence consumers who are more reflective in their shopping style, in that they consciously deliberate upon product information (Morrin & Chebat, 2005). Retailers should therefore be cautious when introducing sensory input into a consumer environment. If they are using incongruent sensory information to communicate a particular message (e.g., a pleasant ambient scent with loud music), they may find that more careful elaboration of the information provided will decrease the overall evaluation of a retail environment or a product.

What drives cross-modal congruency?

So far it is not entirely clear why consumers have preconceived ideas about what types of sensory inputs are congruent. In some instances it is clearly learned. This was evident from a study conducted by Piqueras-Fiszman and Spence (2011). They investigated associations held between the colour of a crisp (chips) packet and the flavour. They found that their participants took longer to pair colours with flavours they considered to be incongruent. Furthermore, they also found that the participants made more mistakes in the incongruent conditions. Piqueras-Fiszman and Spence suggested that the time delay and errors made were due to participants being more familiar with a brand of crisps that were associated with a particular colour. Hence, the results show that consumers learn congruency and incongruency through repeated exposure.

However, what happens when consumers are not familiar with a product? What if the product is new on the market? This is an area that has not really been explored. However, studies by Jansson and Haggard (2006) in which they investigated how people would aesthetically evaluate unfamiliar stimuli shed some light on the matter. They found that when their participants used both visual and tactile input during the evaluation process, congruency between the visual and tactile design was not essential for a higher aesthetic rating. Instead, they suggested that visual attractiveness released haptic aesthetic evaluation. Nevertheless, they did find that there seemed to be some pre-established haptic stimuli preference – something that has also been supported by other researchers (e.g., Essick et al. 2010).

The aforementioned shows that the underlying factors in regard to what consumers perceive to be congruent or incongruent will depend on whether a stimulus is familiar or unfamiliar. In the case of familiar products, it appears to be learned from previous experiences, while if the product is unfamiliar, people use one sense to guide them in their evaluations and congruency seems to take a different form in that they are trying to identify sensory input based on preference rather than congruency. In the light of this, it would seem that product designers in particular may wish to be cautious with regard to changing existing product design/packaging so that they are in line with perceived congruency, though designing a new product may give designers greater freedom with regard to what textures, fragrances etc. can be used, as consumers will have no "pre-established" perception of what is congruent.

Future research perspectives

There are still many different aspects that could be investigated in the area of sensory perception and consumption, some of which have been highlighted throughout the chapter. One particular angle that could be interesting to research further is Williams and Bargh's (2008) findings that that people's perception of a person changed depending on whether the "judger" held a cup of hot or chilled ice coffee. It is worth pointing out that this has been refuted by Lynott et al. (2014). The latter makes the original study very interesting. Williams and Bargh's study seems to suggest that "tactile" input can be incorrectly attributed to a stimulus that happens to be present at the point of experiencing tactile interaction. This may be partially explained by findings suggesting that it is difficult for people to shift their attention away from tactile input, much more so than it is for other modalities such as vision and hearing (e.g., Spence, Nicholls, & Driver 2001; Spence, Shore, & Klein 2001; Turatto, Galfano, Bridgeman, & Umiltà, 2004). So in the case of Williams and Bargh's study, it may be possible that "touching" significantly different temperatures generates a "focal point", and when someone is subsequently asked to "evaluate" a person, the hot or cold "focal point" is used to guide their judgement about the person. However, the question is whether the hot and cold temperatures would become a "focal point" if the tactile input was presented after the evaluation had started. It is possible that if a person is *already* engaged in an evaluation of another person they become fully focused on it. Therefore, a subsequent introduction of cold or warm tactile input may fail to influence the evaluative outcome. It is also feasible to assume that those more sensitive to tactile input may be more receptive to such manipulations – something that could also be the underlying reason for the differences found between Lynott et al.'s and Williams and Bargh's studies. Furthermore, their studies also seem to propose that we are unaware of tactile influences. This is feasible, as we have previously pointed out that tactile input seems at times to affect us subconsciously. However, it would be interesting to find out further *how*, *why* and *when* we may make "misattributions" based on subconscious tactile input and to what extent this is linked to positive and negative valence rather than to touch itself.

On a final note, it would also be nice to see a larger number of cross-cultural studies conducted in this area. Even though many of the aforementioned studies are likely to be just as applicable to different nations and cultures, there are also aspects of touch that may vary depending on where it is tested. In particular, the fact that touch affects perception is not likely to vary across cultures. However, the way in which physical properties are perceived may vary in different cultures.

References

Ackerman, J. M., Nocera, C. C., & Bargh, J. A. (2010). Incidental haptic sensations influence social judgments and decisions. *Science, 328*(5986), 1712–1715.

Biswas, P., & Robinson, P. (2013). A survey on technology exposure and range of abilities of elderly and disabled users in India. In *Proceedings of the 15th International conference on Human Computer Interaction*, Las Vegas.

Biswas, P., Robinson, P., & Langdon, P. M. (2012). Designing inclusive interfaces through user modelling and simulation. *International Journal of Human Computer Interaction, 28*(1), 1–33.

Bone, P. F., & Ellen, P. S. (1999). Scents in the marketplace: Explaining a fraction of olfaction. *Journal of Retailing, 75*(2), 243–262.

Brasel, S. A., & Gips, J. (2014). Tablets, touchscreens, and touchpads: How varying touch interfaces trigger psychological ownership and endowment. *Journal of Consumer Psychology, 24*(2), 226–233.

Cardello, A. V. (1994). Consumer expectations and their role in food acceptance. In H. J. H. MacFie & D. M. H. Thomson (Eds.), *Measurement of food preferences* (pp. 253–297). London: Blackie Academic & Professional.

Cirrincione, A., Estes, Z., & Carù, A. (2014). The effect of ambient scent on the experience of art: Not as good as it smells. *Psychology & Marketing, 31*(8), 615–627.

Chow. (2015). Retrieved from www.chow.com/food-news/53699/eat-and-get-out/

Colman, A. M. (2006). *A dictionary of psychology*. Oxford, NY: Oxford University Press.

Crusco, A. H., & Wetzel, C. G. (1984). The Midas Touch: The effects of interpersonal touch on restaurant tipping. *Personality and Social Psychology Bulletin, 10*(4), 512–517.

De Houwer, J., Thomas, S., & Baeyens, F. (2001). Association learning of likes and dislikes: A review of 25 years of research on human evaluative conditioning. *Psychological Bulletin, 127*(6), 853.

Deliza, R., & MacFie, H. J. H. (1997). The generation of sensory expectation by external cues and its effect on sensory perception and hedonic ratings: A review. *Journal of Sensory Studies, 2*, 103–128.

Deliza, R., MacFie, H., & Hedderley, D. (2003). Use of computer-generated images and conjoint analysis to investigate sensory expectations. *Journal of Sensory Studies, 18*, 465–486.

ELC. (2008). The business link: E-commerce returns. Retrieved from www.elcnetwork.ca/ebusiness/efc_e-c_returns.pdf

Essick, G. K., McGlone, F., Dancer, C., Fabricant, D., Ragin, Y., Phillips, N., & Guest, S. (2010). Quantitative assessment of pleasant touch. *Neuroscience & Biobehavioural Reviews, 34*(2), 192–203.

Ewald, J., & Moskowitz, H. (2007). The push–pull of marketing and advertising and the algebra of the consumer's mind. *Journal of Sensory Studies, 22*, 126–175.

Fisher, J. D., Rytting, M., & Heslin, R. (1976). Hands touching hands: Affective and evaluative effects of an interpersonal touch. *Sociometry, 39*, 416–421.

Franciosi, R., Kujal, P., Michelitsch, R., Smith, V., & Deng, G. (1996). Experimental tests of the endowment effect. *Journal of Economic Behaviour and Organization, 30*, 215–226.

Frens, M. A., Van Opstal, A. J., & Van der Willigen, R. F. (1995). Spatial and temporal factors determine auditory-visual interactions in human saccadic eye movements. *Perception & Psychophysics, 57*(6), 802–816.

Gibson, J. J. (1966). *The senses considered as perceptual systems*. Boston, MA: Houghton Mifflin.

Guéguen, N. (2002). Touch, awareness of touch, and compliance with a request. *Perceptual and Motor Skills, 95*, 355–360.

Guéguen, N., Meineri, S., & Charles-Sire, V. (2010). Improving medication adherence by using practitioner nonverbal techniques: A field experiment on the effect of touch. *Journal of Behavioural Medicine, 33*(6), 466–473.

Hadland, K. A., Rushworth, M. F. S., Gaffan, D., & Passingham, R. E. (2003). The effect of cingulate lesions on social behaviour and emotion. *Neuropsychologia, 41*(8), 919–931.

Heller, M. A., & Clark, A. (2008). Touch as a "reality sense". In J. J. Rieser, D. H. Ashmead, F. Ebner & A. L. Corn (Eds.), *Blindness and brain plasticity in navigation and object perception* (pp. 259–280). Mahwah, NJ: Erlbaum.

Hertenstein, M. J., Keltner, D., App, B., Bulleit, B. A., & Jaskolka, A. R. (2006). Touch communicates distinct emotions. *Emotion, 6*(3), 528.

Hornik, J. (1992). Tactile stimulation and consumer response. *Journal of Consumer Research, 19*, 449–458.

Hornik, J., & Ellis, S. (1988). Strategies to secure compliance for a mall intercept interview. *Public Opinion Quarterly, 52*(4), 539–551.

Hubble, E. (May 1929). The exploration of space. *Harper's Magazine, 158*, 732.

Jansson, C. V., & Haggard, P. (2006). *Visual and tactile influences upon aesthetic preference*. Poster presented at the Birmingham Meeting of the Experimental Psychology Society, UK.

Jansson-Boyd, C. V. (2011). Touch matters: Exploring the relationship between consumption and tactile interaction. *Social Semiotics, 21*(4), 531–546.

Jansson-Boyd, C. V., & Marlow, N. (2007). Not only in the eye of the beholder: Tactile information can affect aesthetic evaluation. *Psychology of Aesthetics, Creativity, and the Arts, 1*(3), 170.

Jin, S. A. A. (2011). The impact of 3D virtual haptics in marketing. *Psychology & Marketing, 28*(3), 240–255.

Jones, J. A., & Jarick, M. (2006). Multisensory integration of speech signals: The relationship between space and time. *Experimental Brain Research, 174*(3), 588–594.

Kahneman, D., Knetsch, J. L., & Thaler, R. H. (1990). Experimental tests of the endowment effect and the Coase theorem. *Journal of Political Economy, 98*, 1325–1348.

Keller, K. L., Heckler, S. E., & Houston, M. J. (1998). The effects of brand name suggestiveness on advertising recall. *Journal of Marketing, 62*(January), 48–57.

Klatzky, R. L., & Lederman, S. J. (1992). Stages of manual exploration in haptic object identification. *Perception & Psychophysics, 52*(6), 661–670.

Klatzky, R. L., & Lederman, S. J. (1993). Toward a computational model of constraint-driven exploration and haptic object identification. *Perception, 22*, 597–621.

Klatzky, R. L., Lederman, S. J., & Metzger, V. A. (1985). Identifying objects by touch: An "expert system". *Perception & Psychophysics, 37*(4), 299–302.

Krishna, A., Elder, R., & Caldara, C. (2010). Feminine to smell but masculine to touch? Multisensory congruence and its effect on the aesthetic experience. *Journal of Consumer Psychology, 20*, 410–418.

Krishna, A., & Morrin, M. (2008). Does touch affect taste? The perceptual transfer of product container haptic cues. *Journal of Consumer Research, 34*(6), 807–818.

Labroo, A. A., Dhar, R., & Schwartz, N. (2008). Of frog wines and frowning watches: Semantic priming, perceptual fluency, and brand evaluation. *Journal of Consumer Research, 34*, 819–831.

Laurienti, P. J., Burdette, J. H., Wallace, M. T., Yen, Y. F., Field, A. S., & Stein, B. E. (2002). Deactivation of sensory-specific cortex by cross-modal stimuli. *Journal of Cognitive Neuroscience, 14*(3), 420–429.

Lederman, S. J., & Klatzky, R. L. (1987). Hand movements: A window into haptic object recognition. *Cognitive Psychology, 19*, 342–368.

Levav, J., & Argo, J. J. (2010). Physical contact and financial risk taking. *Psychological Science, 21*, 804–810.

Lowrey, T. M., Shrum, L. J., & Dubitsky, T. M. (2003). The relation between brand-name linguistic characteristics and brand-name memory. *Journal of Advertising, 32*(3), 7–17.

Ludden, G. D., & Schifferstein, H. N. (2007). Effects of visual-auditory incongruity on product expression and surprise. *International Journal of Design, 1*(3), 29–39.

Ludden, G. D., Schifferstein, H. N., & Hekkert, P. N. (2007). Surprising the senses. *The Senses and Society, 2*(3), 353–362.

Lynott, D., Corker, K. S., Wortman, J., Connell, L., Donnellan, M. B., Lucas, R. E., & O'Brien, K. (2014). Replication of "Experiencing physical warmth promotes interpersonal warmth" by Williams and Bargh (2008). *Social Psychology, 45*(3), 216–222.

Martin, B. A. (2012). A stranger's touch: Effects of accidental interpersonal touch on consumer evaluations and shopping time. *Journal of Consumer Research, 39*(1), 174–184.

McCabe, D. B, & Nowlis, S. M. (2003). The effect of examining actual products or product descriptions on consumer preference. *Journal of Consumer Psychology, 13*, 431–439.

McGurk, H., & MacDonald, J. (1976). Hearing lips and seeing voices. *Nature, 264*, 746–748.

Morhenn, V. B., Park, J. W., Piper, E., & Zak, P. J. (2008). Monetary sacrifice among strangers is mediated by endogenous oxytocin release after physical contact. *Evolution and Human Behaviour, 29*(6), 375–383.

Morrin, M., & Chebat, J. C. (2005). Person-place congruency: The interactive effects of shopper style and atmospherics on consumer expenditures. *Journal of Service Research, 8*(2), 181–191.

Morrin, M., & Ratneshwar, S. (2000). The impact of ambient scent on evaluation, attention, and memory for familiar and unfamiliar brands. *Journal of Business Research, 49*(2), 157–165.

Neisser, U. (1976). *Cognition and reality: Principles and implications of cognitive psychology*. San Francisco, CA: Freeman.

Ngo, M. K., Misra, R., & Spence, C. (2011). Assessing the shapes and speech sounds that people associate with chocolate samples varying in cocoa content. *Food Quality and Preference, 22*(6), 567–572.

Norman, J. F., Norman, H. F., Clayton, A. M., Lianekhammy, J., & Zielke, G. (2004). The visual and haptic perception of natural object shape. *Perception & Psychophysics, 66*(2), 342–351.

Olsen, G. D. (1997). The impact of interstimulus interval and background silence on recall. *Journal of Consumer Research, 23*, 295–303.

Peck, J. (1999). *Extraction of haptic properties: Individual characteristics and stimulus characteristics* (Unpublished doctoral dissertation). University of Minnesota.

Peck, J., & Childers, T. L. (2003a). To have and to hold: The influence of haptic information on product judgments. *Journal of Marketing, 67*(2), 35–48.

Peck, J., & Childers, T. L. (2003b). Individual differences in haptic information processing: The "need for touch" scale. *Journal of Consumer Research, 30*(3), 430–442.

Peck, J., & Shu, S. B. (2009). The effect of mere touch on perceived ownership. *Journal of Consumer Research, 36*(3), 434–447.

Peck, J., & Wiggins, J. (2006). It just feels good: Customers' affective response to touch and its influence on persuasion. *Journal of Marketing, 70*(4), 56–69.

Peck, J., & Wiggins Johnson, J. (2011). Autotelic need for touch, haptics, and persuasion: The role of involvement. *Psychology & Marketing, 28*(3), 222–239.

Peck, J., Barger, V. A., & Webb, A. (2013). In search of a surrogate for touch: The effect of haptic imagery on perceived ownership. *Journal of Consumer Psychology, 23*(2), 189–196.

Piqueras-Fiszman, B., & Spence, C. (2011). Crossmodal correspondences in product packaging. Assessing color–flavor correspondences for potato chips (crisps). *Appetite, 57*(3), 753–757.

Piqueras-Fiszman, B., & Spence, C. (2012). The weight of the container influences expected satiety, perceived density, and subsequent expected fullness. *Appetite, 58*(2), 559–562.

Piqueras-Fiszman, B., Harrar, V., Alcaide, J., & Spence, C. (2011). Does the weight of the dish influence our perception of food? *Food Quality and Preference, 22*, 753–756.

Prescott, J. (2015). Multisensory processes in flavour perception and their influence on food choice. *Current Opinion in Food Science, 3*, 47–52.

Raz, N. (2000). Aging of the brain and its impact on cognitive performance: Integration of structural and functional findings. In F. I. M. Craik & T. A. Salthouse (Eds.), *The handbook of aging and cognition* (2nd ed., pp. 1–90). Mahwah, NJ: Erlbaum.

Reb, J., & Connolly, T. (2007). Possession, feelings of ownership, and the endowment effect. *Judgment and Decision Making, 2*(2), 107–114.

Retail Research (2015). Retrieved August 28, 2015, from www.retailresearch.org/online retailing.php

Robertson, K. (1989). Strategically desirable brand name characteristics. *Journal of Consumer Marketing, 6*(4), 61–71.

Rolls, E. T., O'Doherty, J., Kringelbach, M. L., Francis, S., Bowtell, R., & McGlone, F. (2003). Representations of pleasant and painful touch in the human orbitofrontal and cingulate cortices. *Cerebral Cortex, 13*(3), 308–317.

Saalasti, S., Kätsyri, J., Tiippana, K., Laine-Hernandez, M., von Wendt, L., & Sams, M. (2012). Audiovisual speech perception and eye gaze behaviour of adults with Asperger syndrome. *Journal of Autism and Developmental Disorders, 42*(8), 1606–1615.

Schifferstein, H. N. J. (2006). The perceived importance of sensory modalities in product usage: A study of self-reports. *Acta Psychologica, 121*, 41–64.

Schifferstein, H. N. J., & Spence, C. (2008). Multisensory product experience. In H. N. J. Schifferstein & P. Hekkert (Eds.), *Product experience* (pp. 133–161). Amsterdam: Elsevier.

Shorkey, C. T., & Crocker, S. B. (1981). Frustration theory: A source of unifying concepts for generalist practice. *Social Work, 26*(5), 374–379.

Shu, S. B., & Peck, J. (2011). Psychological ownership and affective reaction: Emotional attachment process variables and the endowment effect. *Journal of Consumer Psychology, 21*(4), 439–452.

Slutsky, D. A., & Recanzone, G. H. (2001). Temporal and spatial dependency of the ventriloquism effect. *Neuroreport, 12*(1), 7–10.

Spangenberg, E. R., Crowley, A. E., & Henderson, P. W. (1996). Improving the store environment: Do olfactory cues affect evaluations and behaviours? *The Journal of Marketing, 60*, 67–80.

Spangenberg, E. R., Grohmann, B., & Sprott, D. E. (2005). It's beginning to smell (and sound) a lot like Christmas: The interactive effects of ambient scent and music in a retail setting. *Journal of Business Research, 58*(11), 1583–1589.

Spence, C. (2011). Crossmodal correspondences: A tutorial review. *Attention, Perception, & Psychophysics, 73*(4), 971–995.

Spence, C., & Gallace, A. (2011). Multisensory design: Reaching out to touch the consumer. *Psychology & Marketing, 28*(3), 267–308.

Spence, C., Nicholls, M. E., & Driver, J. (2001). The cost of expecting events in the wrong sensory modality. *Perception & Psychophysics, 63*(2), 330–336.

Spence, C, Ranson, J., & Driver, J. (2000). Crossmodal selective attention: On the difficulty of ignoring sounds at the locus of visual attention. *Perception & Psychophysics, 62*, 410–424.

Spence, C., Shore, D. I., & Klein, R. M. (2001). Multisensory prior entry. *Journal of Experimental Psychology: General, 130*(4), 799–832.

Stevens, J. C., & Green, B. G. (1996). *History of research on touch. Pain and touch.* San Diego, CA: Academic Press.

Tavassoli, N. T., & Lee, Y. H. (2003) The differential interaction of auditory and visual advertising elements with Chinese and English. *Journal of Marketing Research, 40*(4), 468–480.

Tiippana, K. (2014). What is the McGurk effect? *Frontiers in Psychology, 5*.

Turatto, M., Galfano, G., Bridgeman, B., & Umiltà, C. (2004). Space-independent modality-driven attentional capture in auditory, tactile and visual systems. *Experimental Brain Research, 155*(3), 301–310.

Vanden Bergh, B. G., Collins, J., Schultz, M., & Adler, K. (1984). Sound advice on brand names. *Journalism Quarterly, 61*, 835–840.

van Wassenhove, V., Grant, K. W., & Poeppel, D. (2007). Temporal window of integration in auditory-visual speech perception. *Neuropsychologia, 45*(3), 598–607

Von Békésy, G. (1963). Interaction of paired sensory stimuli and conduction in peripheral nerves. *Journal of Applied Physiology, 18*(6), 1276–1284.

Williams, L. E., & Bargh, J. A. (2008). Experiencing physical warmth promotes interpersonal warmth. *Science, 322*(5901), 606–607.

Yazdanparast, A., & Spears, N. (2013). Can consumers forgo the need to touch products? An investigation of nonhaptic situational factors in an online context. *Psychology & Marketing, 30*(1), 46–61.

Yeomans, M. R., Mobini, S., Elliman, T. D., Walker, H. C., & Stevenson, R. J. (2006). Hedonic and sensory characteristics of odors conditioned by pairing with tastants in humans. *Journal of Experimental Psychology: Animal Behaviour Processes, 32*(3), 215–228.

Yorkston, E., & Menon, G. (2004). A sound idea: Phonetic effects of brand names on consumer judgments. *Journal of Consumer Research, 31*(1), 43–51.

Zellner, D. A., Rozin, P., Aron, M., & Kulish, C. (1983). Conditioned enhancement of human's liking for flavor by pairing with sweetness. *Learning and Motivation, 14*(3), 338–350.

6

The role of procedural knowledge in consumer judgement and decision making

Robert S. Wyer, Jr.

When consumers receive information about a product or service, they usually construe its implications with reference to their previously acquired knowledge about the type of stimulus to which it refers. The cognitive operations they perform in doing so can depend on not only the nature of the information itself but also the purpose for which the information is to be used. However, they can also be influenced by situational and individual difference factors that are independent of the information content – for example, the way the information is presented, the amount of time and effort that recipients are willing and able to spend thinking about it and the mood they happen to be in. Moreover, recent experiences that are objectively unrelated to the information presented or the object to which it refers can influence the cognitive processes that underlie recipients' construal of its implications and, therefore, the judgement or decision they make on the basis of it.

This chapter reviews a number of these processes. In doing so, I distinguish between the *content* of cognition (that is, the concepts and previously acquired knowledge that consumers bring to bear on their interpretation of judgement-relevant information) and the *procedures* that they apply to this content in comprehending it and making inferences on the basis of it (Smith, 1990, 1994). These procedures can be of two types (Wyer, Shen, & Xu, 2013; Wyer, Xu & Shen, 2012). On one hand, the sequence of steps involved in attaining an objective can be stored in memory as part of declarative knowledge. These sequences can be consciously retrieved and used as a basis for decisions about what to do in order to attain a goal to which they pertain, much as one might consult a recipe for making a cake. These procedures may be represented in memory as scripts (Schank & Abelson, 1977; Graesser, 1981) or plan-goal schemas (Kruglanski et al., 2002).

Although these procedures specify the actions that people decide to perform in order to attain a goal, they do not govern the specific cognitive and motor behaviours that are required in order to implement these decisions. These behaviours can be elicited automatically by a set of cognitions with which they have become associated through learning and are performed with little if any conscious monitoring. Thus, a person who is driving to the supermarket might consciously decide to turn right at a particular intersection, but the motor actions involved in doing so (such as activating the turn signal) could occur spontaneously without awareness. As a more obvious example, we may consciously decide to communicate an idea to another person without consciousness of the particular words we use in doing so, and we might not remember exactly what we said even seconds after speaking. These procedures, which have the form of *productions* (Anderson, 1983; see also Smith, 1990, 1994), are conceptually equivalent to complex conditioned responses that are acquired through learning and are governed by processes that differ from those that govern deliberative goal-directed processing.

These two types of procedural knowledge and their use in judgement and decision making were distinguished in a general formulation of social information processing proposed by Wyer and Srull (1989) and have since become the focus of several "dual processing" models of behaviour (e.g.,, Strack & Deutsch, 2004; for other examples, see Chaiken & Trope, 1999). The way in which deliberative and automatic processes combine to influence behaviour has been discussed in some detail elsewhere (Wyer, Xu, & Shen, 2012; Wyer, Shen, & Xu, 2013; see also Janiszewski & Wyer, 2014). Both types of procedural knowledge are important. In this chapter, however, I focus on procedures that govern conscious goal-directed processing.

General considerations

A procedure can be conceptualized as a goal concept along with a series of concepts that specify the steps to be followed in attaining it. In combination, these concepts compose a plan-goal schema of the sort postulated by Kruglanski et al. (2002; see also Wyer & Srull, 1989). In effect, each of the concepts that compose a plan denotes a subgoal that is itself attained through a series of actions at a higher level of specificity. For example, a plan for buying groceries might include subgoals pertaining to making a list, driving to the store, buying food and paying. "Making a list", in turn, may be a subgoal that involves checking the refrigerator to see what one already has, deciding what one would like to eat over the next few days, etc.

Three implications of this conceptualization are important. First, a particular subgoal concept may be part of more than one schema. Thus, "deciding which option to choose" could be contained in both a schema that is activated in the course of shopping for ice cream and a schema that governs the choice of where to submit a journal article for publication. Second, more than one plan can be associated with the attainment of a particular goal. Thus, a book might be obtained by either ordering it on the Internet or getting it from the library. Third, a goal concept and the subgoals that facilitate its attainment may exist at different levels of abstractness. Thus, "buying *Les Miserables*" exemplifies "buying a book", which, in turn, is an example of "making a purchase".

The cognitive processes that govern the identification and use of a plan-goal schema can be conceptualized in terms of general theories of knowledge accessibility (Förster & Liberman, 2007; Higgins, 1996; Wyer, 2008). Although specific conceptualizations of these processes differ in detail (Higgins, Bargh, & Lombardi, 1985; Ratcliff, 1978; Wyer & Carlston, 1979; Wyer & Srull, 1989), they converge on at least two general principles:

1. Individuals do not perform any more extensive cognitive processing than is necessary to attain the goal they happen to be pursuing at the time (Taylor & Fiske, 1978). Thus, when concepts and knowledge are required for use in attaining a particular objective, those concepts that are most easily accessible in memory, and thus that come to mind most easily, are likely to be applied.
2. The accessibility of concepts and knowledge in memory is a positive function of both the frequency and the recency with which they have been activated and used in the past (Higgins et al., 1985; Srull & Wyer, 1979).

In the present context, these assumptions imply that when several alternative procedures can be used to attain a particular goal or subgoal, the procedure that is selected is likely to be one whose components have been activated and used most frequently or recently in the past. Moreover, this selection may be made without consciousness of the reason for doing so. The effect of performing goal-directed behaviour in one situation on the strategy used to attain a quite different goal in a later, unrelated situation can be conceptualized as a *behavioural mindset* (Wyer & Xu, 2010). These mindsets, which can operate at many stages of processing, are discussed in later sections of this chapter. I will first review a representative subset of the procedures involved in comprehension and inference and will then discuss procedures used in decision making.

Comprehension and inference processes

The information that people receive about an object or event can be conveyed in different forms and in different sense modalities. It can come from an external source or can be generated internally. Thus, it can be either verbal or visual and may include both thoughts and feelings that are spontaneously elicited by the object or event under consideration. Individuals can use many different procedures in extracting meaning from such information and construing its implications. When they have a particular objective in mind, they presumably identify a procedure that will attain this objective. At other times, they may simply comprehend the information with no specific purpose in mind at all. In most cases, however, more than one procedure could be used to extract meaning from the information.

Advertisements and television commercials, for example, consist of both pictures of a product or service and verbal descriptions of its features. When people receive this information, they may first encode it in the modality in which it is received (Wyer & Radvansky, 1999). That is, they may interpret verbal information in terms of semantic concepts and form visual images on the basis of the pictures. Then, if their goal is to make a judgement or evaluation of the information's referent, recipients could apply several strategies to accomplish this:

1. They might recode features of the picture semantically and combine the evaluative implications of these features with those described in the verbal information to form an evaluation of the product in the manner suggested by Fishbein (1963) or Anderson (1981).
2. They might form visual images of the verbally described features of a product and combine them with features of the pictures, using them to construct a more complete non-verbal representation of the referent as a whole.
3. They might imagine themselves using the object or having the experience implied by the information and construct a mental sequence of the events that compose such an experience.
4. They might assess their affective reactions to the information's referent, based on the information about it, and use these feelings as a basis for evaluating it.

When are these alternative strategies employed and what are the implications of using them? Research in several areas has attempted to answer these questions.

Visual and verbal processing strategies

Wyer and Radvansky (1999) postulate that individuals construct visual images spontaneously in the course of comprehending verbal descriptions of events that are temporally and situationally constrained (that occur at a particular time and place). Several studies of verbal information processing suggest that this is so (Black, Turner, & Bower, 1979; Bransford & Johnson, 1982; Garnham, 1981; Glenberg, Meyer, & Lindem, 1987). On the other hand, chronic differences may exist in the disposition to process information either visually or verbally (Childers, Houston, & Heckler, 1985). Moreover, the use of these processing strategies can be influenced by recent experiences in which individuals have processed information either visually or verbally in an unrelated task, thus inducing a behavioural mindset that influences processing in other situations as well.

Effects of familiarity on visual information processing

In a series of studies by Jiang, Steinhart and Wyer (2011; see Wyer, Hung, & Jiang, 2008), participants evaluated a computer mouse on the basis of verbal descriptions of its features. The descriptions were the same in all cases. However, the product was described as either a standard mouse, with which participants were quite familiar, or an optical mouse, about which they had little knowledge. In one study, participants' disposition to process information either visually or verbally was assessed on the basis of Childers et al.'s (1985) styles-of-processing scale. In a second study, however, these dispositions were situationally induced by asking participants before receiving the product information to perform a task that required either visual processing (a hidden figures task) or verbal processing (a hidden words task). In both experiments, participants with a disposition to process information verbally (*verbalizers*) construed the semantic implications of the product's features and evaluated the product similarly regardless of its familiarity. In contrast, participants with a disposition to form visual images (*visualizers*) attempted to organize representations of the product's features around a visual image of what the product looked like. They found this easy to do when the product was familiar but found it difficult when it was unfamiliar. Consequently, they evaluated the product less favourably in the latter case than in the former. On the other hand, providing a picture of the product increased visualizers' evaluations to a level equal to that of the familiar mouse. These effects were very similar regardless of whether the dispositions to process information verbally or visually were chronic or situationally induced.

Effects of goals on visual information processing

The effect of visual images can depend on the particular goal that recipients have in mind. In a later study by Jiang and his colleagues (Jiang, Adaval, Steinhart, & Wyer, 2014), participants received pictures of a resort hotel that were taken from either the inside of the hotel or the outside. Some participants were told to acquire as much information about the hotel as possible. When participants had this objective, which did not require the integration of the pictures into a single representation, they evaluated the hotel more favourably when successive pictures were taken from different perspectives and, therefore, were perceived as more informative. Other participants, however, were asked to form an impression of the experience they might have if they stayed at the hotel. These participants tried to imagine the sequence of activities they might experience and found it more difficult to construct this image when successive pictures were taken from different perspectives than when they were taken from the same perspective. Consequently, they evaluated the hotel less favourably in the former case than in the latter. Thus, both groups of participants formed visual images. However, they used different procedures to construe the implications of these images when they had different goals in mind, and these procedures affected the judgements they made.

The impact of self-referent processing and self-focused attention

A contingency in Jiang et al.'s (2014) findings is important. That is, the detrimental effects of shifts in perspective on participants' judgements were only evident when they attempted to construct an image-based representation of *themselves* experiencing the events at the hotel. When participants were told to construct a more general representation of a person's experience at the hotel without thinking about it with reference to themselves, the effects of perspective shift were not evident. Thus, individuals only had difficulty integrating the information when they imagined themselves personally experiencing the sequence of events conveyed by the pictures and subjectively had to "move" from one location to the next. When they imagined the events from the perspective of an outside observer, this difficulty was not evident.

The different procedures that people employ when they focus their attention on themselves were also evident in a study by Hung and Wyer (2011). Participants evaluated a list of products, some of which were typically used in social situations (e.g., popcorn) and others of which were more often used in non-social situations (e.g., herbal tea). While making these ratings, they listened to incidental background music that was associated with either social situations (jazz) or non-social ones (classical). In control conditions, participants based their evaluations on their prior knowledge of the products' individual features, and music had no impact on these evaluations. In other conditions, however, participants made their ratings in front of a mirror that had ostensibly been left on the table as part of another experiment, thereby drawing their attention to themselves (Duval & Wicklund, 1972). In these conditions, participants imagined themselves using the product they were judging and the incidental background music activated concepts of the type of situation in which they might use it. Consequently, they evaluated social products more favourably when social music was playing, and evaluated non-social products more favourably when non-social music was playing, than they did when the music activated concepts of a situation in which the products were not typically used.

A later study by Hung and Wyer (2014) identified further effects of self-focused attention. Participants saw an ad for a tennis racquet containing a picture of a player whose similarity to them varied in both sex and status (Roger Federer and Maria Sharapova vs. a peer). When participants' self-focused attention was not activated, their similarity to the protagonist had little impact on the ad's effectiveness. However, inducing self-focused attention increased the effect of the ad when participants were similar to the protagonist in both sex and status but decreased its effect when they were dissimilar to the protagonist in one of these respects.

A distinction should be made between the effect of self-focused attention and the effect of imagining oneself in the situation described in a message without thinking of oneself. Self-referential processing strategies are often induced by advertisements that use second-person pronouns ("you") and encourage participants to imagine themselves being in a situation in which the advertised product is used (e.g. "Imagine yourself driving down the highway …"). Although this strategy can often increase the impact of a communication (Escalas, 2007; Sujan, Bettman, & Baumgartner, 1993), its effects can be independent of the effects of self-focused attention (Hung & Wyer, 2014).

Moreover, self-referential strategies can sometimes backfire. In another study by Hung and Wyer (2009), participants read a donation appeal for money to help victims of child trafficking. In some conditions, the appeal was self-referential, stimulating readers to think about the situation from the perspective of the victims. When participants were not asked to donate money until after reading the appeal, self-referencing increased the amount of money they gave. When participants were asked whether they would donate money at the outset, however, they were stimulated to take a donor's perspective. This perspective conflicted with the victims' perspective that was activated by the self-referential appeal, making the appeal difficult for recipients to process and decreasing its effectiveness.

A quite different area of research that bears on the impact of self-referencing was stimulated by Green and Brock's (2000) analysis of the conditions in which recipients of a communication become "transported" into the situation it describes, thus vicariously experiencing thoughts and feelings similar to those of the protagonists. Escalas (2004, 2007; Escalas & Luce, 2004) has applied this notion in investigating the impact of marketing communications. That is, individuals who become transported into the situation described in a message are unlikely to counterargue its implications, and so the message has an impact regardless of the quality of the arguments it contains.

An interesting application of this conceptualization with implications for the effects of television commercials was reported by Wang and Calder (2006). They found that commercials that are conveyed at the end of an episode had a positive influence when viewers had become transported into the episode. However, ads that were inserted into the middle of the episode were disruptive and had a negative impact on evaluations of the product being promoted.

Narrative-based processing strategies

The aforementioned research calls attention to the role of narrative-based processing strategies in judgements and decisions. That is, people who receive information about temporally related events might often construct a narrative, or story describing the sequence in which the events occur, and use the implications of this narrative as a basis for judgement. On the other hand, they might also consider each event separately and combine the implications of each event individually without considering their relatedness.

The different effects of using these strategies were first identified in a series of studies of jury decision making by Pennington and Hastie (1988, 1992). In one study, participants received a transcript of the testimony provided by witnesses in a murder trial. However, the way in which the prosecution and defence testimonies were presented was independently varied. In *witness-order* conditions, the testimony was organized according to the witness who provided it, as in the original trial. In *story-order* conditions, however, it was conveyed in the order in which the events to which it pertained were relevant. That is, events leading up to the crime were conveyed first, followed by events surrounding the crime and then its aftermath. When testimony for one side was conveyed in story order and the other was conveyed in witness order, recipients' verdicts typically favoured the side whose testimony was conveyed in story order. When testimony for both sides was conveyed in the same way, participants were equally likely to favour each side. However, they were more confident of their judgements when the testimonies were both in story order.

In Pennington and Hastie's research, the construction of a narrative-based representation was particularly relevant to participants' objective of deciding what had actually happened. In other situations, however, an evaluation of the individual features of a sequence might be equally applicable, and the impact of the two processing strategies can be hard to predict. In a study by Adaval, Isbell and Wyer (2007), participants received either favourable or unfavourable information about events in the life of a political candidate. The information was either presented in the order in which the events occurred or conveyed in an unordered list. In these conditions, participants evaluated the politician more extremely (more favourably or more unfavourably, depending on the information's implications) when the information was listed than when it was in narrative form. However, accompanying the information by a picture of the candidate increased the extremity of judgements based on a narrative but decreased the extremity of judgements based on a list. Consequently, the relative effects of the two processing strategies were reversed. When the information was conveyed in temporal order, pictures apparently provided cognitive "glue" that increased the coherence of the narrative representation that was formed and led it to have greater impact. When the information was listed and individuals computed their judgements by integrating the implications of the individual items, pictures were irrelevant to this integration process. In fact, they interfered with the process and consequently decreased the information's effectiveness. Similar effects occurred when individuals evaluated a vacation described by information in analogous formats (Adaval & Wyer, 1998).

The use of affect in information processing

When individuals are experiencing positive or negative affect at the time they receive information, and when the type of judgement they intend to make is typically based on feelings, they are likely to use these feelings as a basis for judgement. This is true even when the source of the affect is objectively irrelevant to the stimulus being judged (Schwarz & Clore, 1983, 1996, 2007; Wyer, Clore & Isbell, 1999). This may sometimes be used at the expense of other information that is objectively more relevant (Pham, 1998). This depends in part on whether the object being judged is *typically* evaluated on the basis of feelings (Adaval, 2001; Yeung & Wyer, 2004).

However, people may use the incidental affect they are experiencing to infer not only their feelings about an external stimulus but also their feelings about the situation in which the stimulus occurs and the appropriateness of a particular procedure for evaluating it. Schwarz, Bless and Bohner (1991a) hypothesized that when people are feeling happy at the time they are confronted with a judgement or decision, they use these feelings as an indication that the situation is "benign" and that they do not need to think much about the judgement or decision they wish to make. When they are feeling sad, however, they may use these feelings as an indication that they think the situation is problematic and that they should consider its implications carefully. Thus, affect may influence the strategy they employ in processing the information they receive.

In support of this hypothesis, Bless, Bohner, Schwarz and Strack (1990) found that happy individuals were less sensitive to the quality of arguments contained in a persuasive message than unhappy individuals were, and therefore were persuaded by the message regardless of whether the arguments were strong or weak. In a similar vein, Bodenhausen (1993) found that happy individuals were more likely than unhappy individuals to base their judgements of the defendant in a court case on an ethnic stereotype rather than on the content of the defendant's case file. In the marketing domain, this suggests that consumers who experience positive affect at the time they receive product information are likely to use simplistic processing strategies and thus to base their judgements on global criteria (e.g., the product's brand name) rather than analyzing more detailed, item-specific criteria (the product's attributes).

The influence of affect on goal evaluations

The affect that people experience could influence their information processing in yet another way. Martin and his colleagues (Martin, Ward, Achee, & Wyer, 1993) proposed that when people engage in goal-directed processing, they implicitly ask themselves whether they feel they have attained their objective and use the affect they are experiencing as a basis for answering this question. Therefore, if they have the goal of making a good judgement or decision, they implicitly ask themselves whether they feel they have done enough to attain this goal.

Consequently, they stop working sooner, and think less extensively about the judgement or decision they wish to make, if they feel happy than if they feel unhappy. If their goal is to enjoy themselves, however, they implicitly ask themselves whether they feel they are attaining this objective. In this case, happy persons should be more likely to infer that they are attaining this objective and should continue working *longer* than unhappy persons do. Martin et al. (1993) confirmed this conclusion. Thus, the impact of affect on the extensiveness of their information processing depends on the goal they have in mind.

This difference could account for the findings by Bodenhausen (1993) and Bless et al. (1990). In these studies, in which participants had an achievement goal (i.e., to make a good judgement), participants processed information less extensively if they were happy than if they were sad. In a study by Wegener, Petty and Smith (1995), however, participants in some conditions received a message with which they agreed and were led to believe they would enjoy reading it. In this case, participants processed the information more extensively, and were more sensitive to the quality of the arguments contained in it, if they were happy than if they were not.

Martin et al.'s conceptualization has obvious implications for consumer behaviour outside the laboratory. If consumers are shopping for a particular product, they are likely to spend less time, and consider fewer choice alternatives, when they feel happy than when they do not. If they are simply browsing and have no more specific goal in mind, they may shop longer and consider more alternatives when they are happy. In a simulated Internet search situation, Chen, Wyer and Shen (2015) found that participants with the objective of buying a product for a friend reviewed fewer items if they were happy than if they were sad, whereas those who were surfing the net for enjoyment reviewed more items in the former condition. Moreover, males, who are inclined to shop with a particular purchase objective in mind, spend less time searching for products when they are happy, whereas females, who are relatively more disposed to shop for enjoyment (Campbell, 1997), spend more time searching for products when they are happy. These findings suggest that situational factors that put shoppers in a good mood (e.g., pleasant background music) could have either beneficial or detrimental effects, depending on consumers' goal at the time.

The affect that individuals experience can potentially influence their evaluations of not only the amount of processing they perform in order to attain the goal they are pursuing but also the *quality* of this processing. In another study by Wegener et al. (1995), happy and sad participants read a communication that contained either strong or weak arguments against a proposition. Participants used the affect they were experiencing to evaluate the quality of their cognitive responses to the message rather than the message itself. Thus, when the arguments were strong and participants elaborated their implications, happy participants judged their elaborations to be more valid and were more persuaded than sad participants were. When the arguments were weak and participants typically counterargued, happy participants judged these counterarguments to be more valid and were *less* persuaded than sad participants were.

Motivational influences of affect

The preceding studies suggest that the affect people happen to be experiencing can influence both their interpretation of a stimulus they are judging and the strategy they use to process information about it. However, affect can also have a motivational influence. Individuals who feel unhappy are typically motivated to engage in behaviour that will help them to eliminate this unpleasant emotional state (Isen, 1987). Or, if they are experiencing positive affect, they may attempt to maintain these feelings by avoiding behaviour that might bring them down.

The impact of these motives can differ from the informational influence of affect (Andrade, 2005; Cohen, Pham, & Andrade, 2008).

Individuals could use at least two strategies in an attempt to eliminate their negative feelings. On the one hand, they might distract themselves from thinking about the source of their mood by doing things that are enjoyable. For example, they might see a movie or indulge themselves by eating an appealing but unhealthy dessert. These strategies may only succeed in the short run. On the other hand, a more permanently effective strategy would be to eliminate the source of the feelings. Shen and Wyer (2008) found that when individuals were induced to feel unhappy by exposing them to pictures showing examples of bad health, their first inclination was to watch happy movies. When the source of their unhappiness was unobtrusively called to their attention, however, they chose to participate in a relatively unpleasant exercise course and took fewer candies as a reward upon leaving the experiment.

Effects of other subjective reactions

Although the preceding discussion focused on the influence of affect, other types of subjective feelings can also have an impact on judgements. Stepper and Strack (1993), for example, found that participants judged themselves to be more assertive when they reported their self-descriptions in a questionnaire that was located on a high stand, requiring them to stand erect, than when they reported their descriptions on a low table that required them to bend over. Inducing subjective feelings of processing difficulty while recalling features of a stimulus can lead people to infer that the stimulus does not have the characteristic implied by these features and thus decrease their judgements of this characteristic (Jiang, Shen, & Adaval, 2013; Schwarz et al., 1991b; Wänke, Bohner, & Jurkowitz, 1997; for reviews, see Schwarz, 1998, 2004).

Subjective feelings can also have indirect effects on judgements. Research on embodied cognition (Barsalou, 2008; Landau, Meier, & Keefer, 2010; Niedenthal, Barsalou, Winkielman, Krauth-Gruber, & Ric, 2005) provides substantial evidence that subjective reactions that are metaphorically related to concepts that are relevant to judging a stimulus in an unrelated situation can increase the likelihood of applying these concepts. To give but a few examples, carrying a heavy shopping bag can influence participants of the importance (weight) of a social issue (Zhang & Li, 2012), and holding a warm cup can increase judgements of an experimenter's personality (Williams & Bargh, 2008). Warm ambient temperatures can increase individuals' feelings of social closeness (IJzerman & Semin, 2010) and this, in turn, can increase individuals' adoption of others' opinions in an unrelated situation (e.g., the likelihood of betting on the favourite at the races; see Huang, Zhang, Hui, & Wyer, 2014). Moreover, inducing negative feelings can stimulate behaviour that symbolically eliminates these feelings. Thus, telling a lie by email increases individuals' preference for hand-soap that will "wash away" their feelings of guilt, whereas telling a lie orally increases their preference for mouthwash (Lee & Schwarz, 2010). Analogously, feelings of embarrassment can increase preferences for sunglasses or facial cream that symbolically allow them to hide their face or save their face, respectively (Dong, Huang, & Wyer, 2013).

Pragmatic comprehension processes

The processes reviewed in previous sections govern the comprehension of the literal meaning of information and experiences. However, there is often a discrepancy between the literal meaning of a message and the meaning that the communicator intends to convey. Many communications, for example, are intended to be ironic or sarcastic. Others may be intended to convey an attitude rather than matters of fact.

The processes that underlie the recognition of the intended meaning of a communication were identified by Grice (1975; see also Green, 1989). In the absence of situational factors that suggest otherwise, recipients of a message may typically assume that a communication is intended to be informative and to convey the truth as the communicator sees it, and they may spontaneously construe its literal meaning on the basis of this normative principle. If, however, a message's literal meaning violates this assumption, they may question whether the literal meaning of the message is, in fact, the meaning that the communicator intends to convey, and may reinterpret it in a manner that is more consistent with the principle that is violated.

The factors that underlie the identification of a communication's pragmatic meaning have been discussed elsewhere (Higgins, 1981; Wyer & Gruenfeld, 1995; Wyer & Shrum, in press; for an application to humour elicitation, see Wyer & Collins, 1992). An understanding of these factors is particularly important when the information is conveyed in a consumer context. Advertisers and salespeople are primarily motivated to persuade consumers to purchase the products they are promoting. To attain this objective, they may often provide accurate information about the product's desirable features. However, this is not always the case. A common advertising strategy is to describe a product in terms that purport to be informative but are actually meaningless. Most consumers, of course, are aware of the persuasive intentions of advertisers and that their claims for the product are likely to be exaggerated. (For a detailed discussion of persuasion knowledge, see Campbell & Kirmani, 2008.) Hung and Wyer (2008) found that if a message requires cognitive effort in order to be understood, recipients may accept its implications without devoting additional cognitive resources to an assessment of its validity. If the communication can be interpreted without much effort, however, individuals are more likely to counterargue its implications and so it may have less effect (see also Anand & Sternthal, 1989). These considerations imply that difficulty in comprehending an advertisement can actually increase its effectiveness.

Several examples of deceptive or misleading advertising can be conceptualized in this manner. For example, individuals who read that "Brand X contains strocacium" may have no idea what strocacium is. To interpret the message in a way that conforms to the informativeness principle, however, they may infer that (a) strocacium is a desirable attribute and (b) other products do not have it. By the same token, they might interpret the assertion that "Brand X contains no strocacium" as implying that strocacium is undesirable but other products *do* have it.

In a related vein, individuals who read that "Brand X is better" may mentally complete the claim in a way that is informative and relevant ("better than other brands") rather than in other ways that may in fact be more accurate ("better than it used to be", "better than the most inferior brands on the market"). Somewhat ironically, these claims are more likely to be effective when participants are highly motivated to evaluate the product at the time they receive the information about it (Johar, 1995). That is, less involved participants do not expend the cognitive effort required to make the claim informative, and so the claim has little effect. For other evidence that involved consumers are more likely to make inferences about the implications of an advertisement in the absence of explicit conclusions about its implications, see Kardes (1988) and Sawyer & Howard (1991).

Consumers' a priori knowledge about the product being advertised can also influence the interpretation of deceptive advertising claims. Xu and Wyer (2010) found that although an ad's descriptions of a product are objectively meaningless, consumers who have little knowledge about the product infer that these descriptions would be informative to persons who know more about the product than they do. As a result, the descriptions increase their evaluations of the product. If consumers perceive that they know as much or more about the product as persons to whom the ad is directed, however, they infer that descriptions they can't understand would not be understood by anyone and are intended only to persuade. Consequently, they react negatively to the descriptions. Xu and Wyer (2010) found that when either (a) individuals received an advertisement about a product they knew little about or (b) the ad appeared in a magazine that was read only by experts in the area to which the product was relevant, objectively meaningless information in the ad increased product evaluations. However, when the ad appeared in a popular magazine and participants believed they knew as much or more about the product as consumers in the general population, inserting meaningless information into the ad decreased its effectiveness.

Effects of behavioural mindsets on comprehension and inference

The procedure that individuals use to comprehend and construe the implications of information clearly depends on the goal they happen to be pursuing. When several alternative procedures can be used to attain a goal, however, the selection of one procedure over another can be rather arbitrary. In this case, the behaviour that individuals happen to have performed shortly before they pursue this goal can influence the procedure they decide to apply.

The cognitive processes that underlie these effects are described by Wyer and Xu (2010; Wyer et al., 2012) in their conceptualization of *behavioural mindsets*. Briefly, engaging in goal-directed behaviour in one situation can activate more general concepts that the behaviour exemplifies. Once these general concepts are accessible in memory, they can increase the likelihood that other behaviours that exemplify the concepts will be identified and applied in the pursuit of other, quite different goals to which they are applicable. In the study by Jiang et al. (2011) mentioned earlier, for example, performing a hidden figures task increased participants' disposition to form visual images of a product on the basis of verbal information about it and to base their judgements on the implications of these images. Other examples of relevance to consumer judgement are also worth noting.

Global processing mindsets

Consumers who receive information about a product or service might sometimes construe its implications in terms of abstract concepts that refer to the stimulus as a whole. At other times, however, they might focus their attention on specific features of the stimulus and base their evaluations on these criteria instead. These dispositions could often result from the performance of a prior task that required them. Numerous studies by Jens Förster and his colleagues provide evidence of this (for a review, see Förster & Dannenberg, 2010). In these studies, participants initially performed a task that required attention either to a stimulus as a whole or to its detailed features. In some cases, for example, they were given pictures of a large letter composed of a number of small ones of a different type (e.g.,, a large H that is formed from an array of small Ts) and asked to identify either the large letter or the small ones. Once these global or local processes are activated, they can influence the processing of information in a number of quite different situations in which they are applicable. For example, inducing a global processing mindset leads individuals to focus on similarities between stimuli rather than dissimilarities in a comparative judgement situation (Förster, 2009). Moreover, it leads people to judge themselves as more similar to a target person, whereas a local processing mindset leads to contrast effects (Förster, Liberman, & Kuschel, 2008).

The disposition to process information globally or locally can have a more indirect effect on judgements. According to construal level theory (Trope & Liberman, 2010), the disposition to apply abstract concepts in construing the implications of information is associated with greater psychological distance. To this extent, a disposition to process information globally should lead individuals to estimate psychological distances to be greater than they otherwise would. Consistently with this hypothesis, Liberman and Förster (2009) found that inducing a global processing mindset led individuals (a) to estimate a longer period of time before engaging in a target activity, (b) to estimate a greater physical distance between themselves and a target location, (c) to decrease estimates of their social closeness to their family doctor and (d) to decrease their estimate of the likelihood that they would become well known during their lifetime.

A global or local mindset may be induced in other ways, of course. If positive affect leads individuals to use more global concepts in processing information (Bless, 2001), for example, it could have similar effects. A global processing mindset can also be induced by aspects of the judgement task itself. In a study by Wyer et al. (1991), for example, participants first saw a videotaped speech of a political candidate's testimonial to another public figure. The speech conveyed either a favourable or an unfavourable impression of the candidate but contained no information relevant to his political ideology. Either immediately or a day later, however, participants heard an audiotaped radio programme that enumerated the candidate's stands on several issues that conveyed either a liberal or a conservative orientation. When the candidate's speech was not salient at the time of judgement, participants based their evaluation of the candidate on their agreement with his stands on specific issues. When the speech was salient, however, it stimulated participants to use more global criteria for evaluating the candidate, and thus to base their evaluation of him on the general ideology conveyed by the candidate's issue positions independently of their agreement with these positions.

A study by Adaval et al. (2007) provides a quite different example. That is, when participants had received information about a politician in the form of a narrative rather than an unordered list, they processed this information more globally in construing its implications. Later, as part of an unrelated experiment, they received information about a product's brand name along with a set of individual features. Participants who had received narrative information in the first task were more likely to base their judgements on brand name than those who had received the same information in a list.

Elaboration and counterarguing mindsets

The effects of global and local processing primarily occur when information is first received and comprehended. Once the information is understood, however, recipients may either elaborate its implications or counterargue them, depending on their perceptions of its persuasiveness. The effects of these cognitive responses, which have been investigated extensively in research on communication and persuasion (Petty & Cacioppo, 1986; Petty, Priester, & Wegener, 1994), can often depend on recipients' a priori attitude towards the position being advocated. However, individuals are often indifferent to the information they receive about a commercial product. In this case, elaborating or refuting information in an unrelated task might induce an elaboration or counterarguing mindset, respectively, and this mindset, once activated, could influence their responses to product information that they encounter later.

Xu and Wyer (2012) obtained evidence of this influence. Participants first reported their thoughts in response to a series of propositions with which they either agreed on a priori grounds (e.g., "reading is good for the mind") or disagreed ("reading is bad for the mind"). Thus, the responses constituted elaborations in the first case but counterarguments in the second. After responding to these propositions, participants as part of an ostensibly unrelated study received an ad for a commercial product. Participants evaluated the product more favourably if they had elaborated in response to the earlier propositions than if they had counterargued.

In a second study, participants during the 2008 presidential election campaign listened to a videotaped speech on the economy by either John McCain or Barack Obama. Then, in an ostensibly unrelated experiment, they heard a speech by the chief executive of Toyota that extolled the virtues of the company and its products. Participants who had heard a speech by the candidate they favoured on a priori grounds (that is, Republicans who had heard McCain's speech and Democrats who had heard Obama's) were positively influenced by the speech on Toyota. When participants had heard a speech by the candidate they opposed, however, they decreased their evaluations of Toyota.

Counterfactual reasoning mindset

When individuals' actions turn out to have negative consequences, they are likely to think about how they could have avoided these consequences. This counterfactual thinking can induce a mindset that increases the likelihood of considering alternative outcomes in a later situation. As a result, it might decrease their confidence in their predictions of what might actually occur. Hirt, Kardes and Markman (2004) found that after participants had generated alternative hypotheses concerning which TV sitcom would win a "best programme" award, they reported less strong beliefs that a favoured basketball team would win the NBA championship. Analogously, Kray and Galinsky (2003) found that inducing a counterfactual thinking mindset led participants to consider the disadvantages of pursuing a very attractive goal rather than considering only its advantages.

Note that the mindsets described in this section pertain only to judgements of single stimuli. Mindsets also can influence comparative judgements, as will be noted presently.

Comparative judgement procedures

Many consumer judgements are comparative; that is, individuals base a purchase decision on their relative preference for the alternatives available. The cognitive procedures involved in making these judgements can often be quite different from those involved in making absolute judgements of the sort we considered in the previous section.

For example, suppose consumers decide between two alternatives, each of which is described along a set of attribute dimensions. They could make a choice by computing an evaluation of each alternative separately and comparing the magnitudes of these overall evaluations. However, they could also perform a dimension-by-dimension comparison of the alternatives along the dimensions they have in common and choose the alternative that is superior along the greater number of these dimensions. If the attributes of the alternatives are alignable, the second strategy is typically easier than the first.

The different effects of these strategies are evident in research on "decoy" effects, that is, the impact of adding a third alterative on preferences for the other two (Huber, Payne, & Puto, 1982; Simonson, 1989). For simplicity, consider the alternatives, T and C, shown in Table 6.1. If the dimensions along which they are evaluated are equally important, these alternatives should be equal in attractiveness. However, suppose the alternative D1 is added to the set. Although this alternative is not itself a viable candidate, its addition to the choice set increases preferences for T. Why is this so?

Table 6.1 Hypothetical utilities of two choice alternatives, A and B, a standard decoy (D1) and an inferior decoy (D2) along two attribute dimensions

	A	*B*	*Standard decoy (D1)*	*Inferior decoy (D2)*
Dimension 1	4	2	4	2
Dimension 2	2	4	1	1

Both of the decision strategies described earlier could potentially account for this effect. First, suppose individuals perform a dimension-by-dimension comparison. Simonson (1989; Shafir, Simonson & Tversky, 1993) assumes that individuals attempt to justify their choice, even if their justification is not particularly rational. In the present case, T is superior to D1 but C is not. This may provide a sufficient basis for choosing T and increase the likelihood of doing so.

However, suppose instead that individuals evaluate each alternative independently and then compare their overall evaluations. This strategy could also account for the effect. Because D1 has a lower value along dimension 2 than does either T or C, it expands the range of subjective values that are assigned to the stimuli along this dimension. This leads T and C to appear more similar to one another along the dimension, decreasing the weight attached to this difference and correspondingly increasing the impact of T's superiority to C along dimension 1.

Thus, either strategy could account for the effect. However, the strategies could be distinguished by introducing a decoy, D2, that is clearly inferior to both T and C (see Table 6.1). In this case, if a dimension-by-dimension comparison is made, this decoy should not affect the preference for T. However, D2, like D1, expands the range of values along dimension 2. Therefore, if an absolute judgement strategy is used, the introduction of this decoy could increase preferences for T just as introducing D1 does.

This difference provides a way of distinguishing between the use of the two strategies and when they are invoked. Park and Kim (2005) assumed that a dimension-by-dimension comparison strategy was easier to use than an absolute judgement strategy. However, they further assumed that if participants had already computed separate judgements of the alternatives at the time they reported a preference, the absolute judgement strategy would be easier. Consistent with these assumptions, they found that introducing the clearly inferior decoy, D2, had no effect when absolute judgements had not already been made. When participants had made absolute judgements before computing a preference, however, D2 increased their preference for T in much the same way that D1 did.

Compromise effects on affect-based preferences

Justification processes can influence a quite different type of decision situation. Consumers are often confronted with a choice between an intrinsically attractive option that would be immediately gratifying but detrimental to long-term goal attainment and a less appealing alternative that is consistent with long-term objectives. A prototypic example of this conflict is a choice between a hedonically appealing but unhealthy food and a less attractive but healthy alternative. Because the hedonic alternative spontaneously elicits affect, people's initial inclination in such a situation is usually to indulge themselves. After cognitive deliberation, however, they may forego this temptation. Thus, Shiv and Fedorikhin (1999) found that when participants had the opportunity to think about whether they would choose a fruit salad or a chocolate cake, they typically chose the salad. However, preventing participants from thinking about their decision led them to choose the cake instead.

The manner in which individuals resolve conflicts between immediate gratification and long-term goal attainment has been studied extensively (Dhar & Simonson, 1999; Hoch & Loewenstein, 1991; Metcalfe & Mischel, 1999). This research suggests that individuals in these situations are likely to give in to temptation if they can justify doing so, even if the basis for this justification is not completely rational (Shafir et al., 1993). Thus, they are more likely to choose an appealing but unhealthy dessert if they have eaten a healthy main course (Dhar & Simonson, 1999) or have previously engaged in a virtuous act of a different sort (Khan & Dhar, 2006). People apparently believe that exerting self-control in one situation gives them licence to indulge in a later situation. Thus, when individuals are confronted with two unhealthy but appealing alternatives, they choose the option that they consider less attractive or that they have to exert effort in order to attain (but see Li, Gao, & Wyer, 2015 for another interpretation).

Cancellation and direction of comparison

Additional effects of comparative judgement strategies are suggested by research on cancellation and direction-of-comparison effects (Brunner & Wänke, 2006; Dhar & Sherman, 1996; Houston & Sherman, 1995; Houston, Sherman, & Baker, 1989). This research indicates that when individuals compare one product with another, they consider features of the second product that the first product does not have, but ignore features of the second product that the first does not have. Thus, if the second product has unique positive features, people prefer this product to the first one. If the second has unique negative features, however, they prefer the first product instead.

Moreover, when the products being compared have attributes in common, these attributes tend to be ignored. Moreover, these attributes, having been ignored in the course of making comparative judgements, are *also* ignored when participants later make overall evaluations of each alternative separately. Thus, for example, suppose the two products have unique desirable attributes and similar undesirable ones. In computing a preference, consumers are likely to ignore the unfavourable attributes and base their preferences on the favourable ones. If they later evaluate each alternative separately, they should evaluate both the chosen and the rejected alternative more favourably than they would if the comparative judgement had not been made. Correspondingly, if persons have compared alternatives that have common favourable features but unique unfavourable features, they should later evaluate the alternatives less favourably than they would otherwise. In short, the process that individuals employ in the comparative judgement task can activate a "cancellation" mindset that generalizes to the absolute evaluations that participants perform later.

If this is so, however, the effect of this mindset should generalize to evaluations of other choice alternatives that were not involved in the initial task. Wang and Wyer (2002) confirmed this prediction. Participants who had compared choice alternatives in the conditions described above made more favourable evaluations of the alternatives when the alternatives had unique positive features and common negative ones than when they had unique negative features and common positive ones. Then, after either a short delay or a delay of 24 hours, participants recalled the product they had chosen earlier and compared it with a *new* product whose attributes differed from those of the products they had considered earlier. Participants evaluated this product more favourably if the products they had considered earlier had unique positive (and common negative) features than if they had unique negative (and common positive) features. In short, participants' cancellation of favourable or unfavourable features when comparing products in the first task disposed them to weight similarly valenced features less heavily in evaluating an unrelated product they encountered later, and this disposition persisted over a period of 24 hours.

The effects of behavioural mindsets in decision making

Implemental mindsets and shopping momentum

A purchase decision may involve three steps. First, individuals may decide whether they want to buy anything at all. If they decide affirmatively, they may then decide which of the available alternatives to purchase. Finally, they may decide how to implement their purchase. The procedure involved in making each decision is different. This means that the effect of making a decision in one situation on the strategy employed in a later situation depends on which stages of decision making were employed.

Gollwitzer and his colleagues (Gollwitzer & Bayer, 1999; Gollwitzer, Heckhausen, & Steller, 1990; Henderson, de Liver, & Gollwitzer, 2008) confirmed this possibility. In a study by Henderson et al. (2008), for example, participants were first asked either to consider *whether* they might pursue a particular objective or, alternatively, to plan *how* they would do so. Deciding whether to engage in an action typically involves a consideration of both positive and negative consequences of the action being contemplated. Consequently, it is likely to create some ambivalence. In contrast, considering how to pursue a goal presupposes that a decision to pursue it has already been made. In this case, ambivalence should be less. Thus, suppose some participants have previously considered whether to engage in an activity and others have considered how to do so. These considerations could activate a *deliberative* and an *implemental* mindset, respectively. If these mindsets generalize to objectively unrelated situations the individuals encounter later, their effects may be reflected in their ambivalence about the judgements they make in these situations.

Henderson et al. confirmed these predictions. Participants after performing the first task considered a series of objects and reported how ambivalent they felt about their reaction to each. As expected, participants reported feeling generally greater ambivalence in the second task if they had considered whether to pursue the goal they had contemplated earlier than if they had considered how they would do so. The effects of these mindsets on participants' report of their attitude towards a social issue (i.e., whether a list of convicted sex offenders should be made available to the general public) were analogous.

A phenomenon with more direct implications for consumer behaviour was identified by Dhar, Huber and Khan (2007). They noted that performing the implemental stage of a decision sequence (deciding how to undertake an action) presumes that the first, deliberative stage (deciding whether to do so) has already been completed. Therefore, if people have performed actions associated with an implemental stage of processing in an earlier situation, concepts activated by this procedure may be particularly salient if participants are called upon to make a different decision later, leading them to apply the procedure without performing the first, deliberative stage.

Dhar et al. (2007) confirmed this possibility. Participants at the start of an experiment were given an opportunity to purchase a pen for either a low price or a high one. They typically accepted the opportunity in the first case but rejected it in the second. Later, they were given a chance to buy a moderately expensive key chain. Participants were more likely to purchase the key chain if they had decided to make a purchase earlier than if they had declined.

Which-to-choose mindsets

In Dhar et al.'s studies, participants were given only one option and could either choose it or not. However, similar effects can occur when individuals are given a choice of alternatives and must decide which option to take. In this case, comparing alternatives in one situation might activate more general concepts associated with this comparison process, and this could increase the likelihood of applying the process in a later situation. To this extent, it might increase individuals' likelihood of making a choice between alternatives without performing the first stage of decision making, that is, without considering whether they want to choose anything at all.

Xu and Wyer (2007, 2008) confirmed this possibility. They found, for example, that expressing a preference for one of two computers in one situation increased participants' reported willingness to choose one of two vacation packages in a later situation without considering the possibility of choosing nothing (Xu & Wyer, 2007).

A which-to-choose mindset can be activated by making comparative judgements in a situation that is totally unrelated to the choices made in a later one (Xu & Wyer, 2008). For example, choosing which of two wild animals they preferred, or deciding which of two animals had more of a particular attribute (e.g., "which is large, a lion or a rhinoceros?") not only increased participants' willingness to purchase one of two products they considered in a later situation but also increased their likelihood of purchasing a snack that was on sale after the study.

Variety-seeking mindsets

Consumers often choose a number of products to use over a period of time. For example, they may choose the vegetables they will eat for dinner during the week ahead, the types of tea they will drink or the books they will buy to read on vacation. In such cases, they might either choose the same type of option for use each time or choose a variety of options. The strategy they use depends in part on the type of product. For example, people are likely to choose the same brand of bottled water to use on each occasion but to choose different vegetables to eat over a series of meals. On the other hand, the disposition to choose the same or a variety of alternatives can also be the result of a variety-seeking mindset that has been activated by performing an unrelated task.

In a study by Shen and Wyer (2010), for example, participants first answered a series of questions about four animals (a dog, a tiger, a chicken and a pig). In *different-choice* priming conditions, the answer to each question differed ("Which animal is largest?", "Which animal is most loyal?" etc.). In *same-choice* priming conditions, the answer to each question was the same ("Which animal is largest?", "Which animal is most ferocious?" etc.). After completing this task, participants as part of an ostensibly different experiment were told to assume that they were shopping for herbal tea and to indicate which of four brands they would choose to drink on each of the next four days. The number of different teas they chose was significantly greater when their answers to the questions in the first task had differed than when their answers had been the same.

Prevention and promotion mindsets

Many actions that individuals contemplate have both positive and negative consequences. In deciding whether to undertake such an action, they may weight these consequences differently. Some people may make the choice that provides the greatest benefits without thinking about the costs of doing so. Others may choose an option that minimizes the negative consequences of their decision without regard to the benefits that might also occur.

Numerous factors can influence these dispositions, as Higgins (1997, 1998) postulated in his conceptualization of promotion and prevention focus. For example, calling individuals' attention to a discrepancy between their actual self and their ideal self can induce a promotion orientation, whereas calling their attention to a difference between their actual self and what others think they ought to be can induce a prevention focus. Many other factors can have similar effects (Lee & Semin, 2009). For example, characterizing possible outcomes in terms of gains (or non-gains) can induce a promotion mindset, whereas describing them in terms of losses (or non-losses) stimulates a prevention mindset (Aaker & Lee, 2001).

These mindsets can also be induced by leading people to think of themselves either as individuals or as part of a group. For example, people who think of themselves as independent can induce a promotion orientation, whereas leading them to think of themselves in relation to others can induce a prevention orientation (Lee, Aaker, & Gardner, 2000). In an empirical demonstration of these effects (Briley & Wyer, 2002), participants performed an initial task either as individuals or as part of a group. Then, in an unrelated situation, they chose between an alternative whose attributes were extremely favourable and extremely unfavourable (e.g., +3 and −3) and an alternative whose attributes were moderately favourable and unfavourable (+1 and −1). Participants who were disposed to think of themselves as individuals preferred the option with the most favourable attributes without regard to the unfavourableness of the attributes that accompanied them. In contrast, participants who had been primed to think of themselves as part of a group preferred the option with the least unfavourable attributes regardless of the favourableness of the attributes it had.

Chronic differences in the disposition to think of oneself as independent or interdependent can have similar effects. Westerners typically have independent self-construals, whereas Asians are more inclined to think of themselves as part of a group (Markus & Kitayama, 1991; Triandis, 1995). Thus, they may have chronic promotion and prevention orientations. Briley and Wyer (2002) found that making Western and Asian participants aware of their cultural identity by exposing them to cultural symbols affected their choice behaviour in much the same way as inducing differences in group membership. Moreover, Briley, Morris and Simonson (2005) found that bicultural Chinese preferred the option that maximized gain when the experiment was conducted in English but the option that minimized loss when the study was conducted in Chinese.

However, these orientations have an effect only if individuals are conscious of their cultural identity, thus making culture-related norms and values accessible in memory. Thus, Briley, Morris and Simonson (2000) found evidence of a cultural difference in choices only when participants were asked to give a reason for their choice, thus leading them to activate and use culture-related criteria for making a decision. In the absence of this priming, cultural differences in choice behaviour were not evident.

Concluding remarks

This chapter has reviewed the procedures that consumers are likely to apply to information in extracting its implications and making a judgement, independently of the content of the information itself. Although the chapter has covered a lot of ground, many processes that govern consumer judgements and decisions have not been discussed. For example, the processes governed by cognitive productions, which are applied automatically and govern overt behaviour (Wyer et al., 2012, 2013), have not been addressed. The procedures that underlie the use of subjective reactions in judgement (Schwarz, 2004) and the impact of bodily sensations (Barsalou, 2008; Niedenthal et al., 2005) have also received little attention. Despite these limitations, however, the review hopefully makes salient the importance of procedural knowledge in consumer behaviour, thereby stimulating further research on the nature of this knowledge and how it comes into play.

Acknowledgements

This preparation of this chapter and some of the research described therein were supported in part by Grants GRF 453110 and GRF 640011 from the Research Grants Council, Hong Kong.

References

Aaker, J. L., & Lee, A. Y. (2001). I seek pleasures, we avoid pains: The role of self-regulatory goals in information processing and persuasion. *Journal of Consumer Research, 27*, 33–49.

Adaval, R. (2001). Sometimes it just feels right: The differential weighting of affect-consistent and affect-inconsistent product information. *Journal of Consumer Research*, 7, 207–245.

Adaval, R., & Wyer, R. S. (1998). The role of narratives in consumer information processing. *Journal of Consumer Psychology*, 7, 207–245.

Adaval, R., Isbell, L. M., & Wyer, R. S. (2007). The impact of pictures on narrative-based impression formation: A process interference model. *Journal of Experimental Social Psychology, 43*, 352–364.

Anand, P., & Sternthal, B. (1989). Strategies for designing persuasive messages: Deductions from the resource matching hypothesis. In P. Cafferata & A. M. Tybout (Eds.), *Cognitive and affective responses to advertising* (pp. 135–159). Lexington, MA: Lexington Books.

Anderson, J. R. (1983). *The architecture of cognition*. Cambridge, MA: Harvard University Press.

Anderson, N. H. (1981). *Foundations of information integration theory*. New York, NY Academic Press.

Andrade, E. B. (2005). Behavioural consequence of affect: Combining evaluative and regulatory mechanisms. *Journal of Consumer Research, 32*, 355–362.

Barsalou, L. W. (2008). Grounded cognition. *Annual Review of Psychology, 59*, 617–645.

Black, J. B., Turner, T., & Bower, G. H. (1979). Point of view in narrative comprehension, memory, and production. *Journal of Verbal Learning and Verbal Behaviour, 11*, 717–726.

Bless, H. (2001). Mood and the use of general knowledge structures. In L. L. Martin & G. L. Clore (Eds.), *Theories of mood and cognition: A user's guidebook* (pp. 9–26). Mahwah, NJ: Erlbaum.

Bless, H., Bohner, G., Schwarz, H., & Strack, F. (1990). Mood and persuasion: A cognitive response analysis. *Personality and Social Psychology Bulletin, 16*, 331–345.

Bodenhausen, G. V. (1993). Emotions, arousal, and stereotypic judgments: A heuristic model of affect and stereotyping. In D. M. Mackie & D. L. Hamilton (Eds.), *Affect, cognition, and stereotyping: Interactive processes in group perception* (pp. 13–37). San Diego, CA: Academic Press.

Bransford, J. D., & Johnson, M. K. (1972). Contextual prerequisites for understanding: Some investigations of comprehension and recall. *Journal of Verbal Learning and Verbal Behaviour, 11*, 717–726.

Briley, D. A., & Wyer, R. S. (2002). The effect of group membership salience on the avoidance of negative outcomes: Implications for social and consumer decisions. *Journal of Consumer Research, 29*, 400–415.

Briley, D. A., Morris, M., & Simonson, I. (2000). Reasons as carriers of culture: Dynamic versus dispositional models of cultural influence on decision making. *Journal of Consumer Research, 27*, 157–178.

Briley, D. A., Morris, M., & Simonson, I. (2005). Language triggers cultural frames: In bicultural Hong Kong consumers, English versus Chinese communication evokes divergent cultural patterns of decision making. *Journal of Consumer Psychology, 15*.

Brunner, T. A., & Wänke, M. (2006). The reduced and enhanced impact of shared features on individual brand evaluations. *Journal of Consumer Psychology, 16*, 101–111.

Campbell, C. (1997). Shopping, pleasure and the sex war. In F. Pasi & C. Campbell (Eds.), *The shopping experience* (pp. 166–176). London: Sage.

Campbell, M. C., & Kirmani, A. (2008). I know what you're doing and why you're doing it: The use of the persuasion knowledge model in consumer research. In C. P. Haugtvedt, P. M. Herr & F. R. Kardes (Eds.), *Handbook of consumer psychology* (pp. 549–573). New York, NY: LEA/Psychology Press.

Chaiken, S., & Trope, Y. (Eds.) (1999). *Dual-process theories in social psychology*. New York, NY: Guilford Press.

Chen, F., Wyer, R. S., & Shen, H. (2015). *The interactive effects of affect and task focus on information search and product evaluations* (Unpublished manuscript). Hong Kong University of Science and Technology.

Childers, T. L., Houston, M. J., & Heckler, S. E. (1985). Measurement of individual differences in visual versus verbal information processing. *Journal of Consumer Research, 12*, 125–134.

Cohen, J. B., Pham, M. T., & Andrade, E. B. (2008). The nature and role of affect in consumer behaviour. In C. P. Haugtvedt, P. M. Herr & F. R. Kardes (Eds.), *Handbook of consumer psychology* (pp. 297–348). New York, NY: Lawrence Erlbaum Associates.

Dhar, R., & Sherman, S. J. (1996). The effect of common and unique features in consumer choice. *Journal of Consumer Research, 23*, 193–203.

Dhar, R., & Simonson, I. (1999). Making complementary choices in consumption episodes: Highlighting versus balancing. *Journal of Marketing Research, 36*, 20–44.

Dhar, R., Huber, J., & Khan, U. (2007). The shopping momentum effect. *Journal of Marketing Research, 44*, 370–378.

Dong, P., Huang, X., & Wyer, R. S. (2013). The illusion of saving face: How people symbolically cope with embarrassment. *Psychological Science, 24*, 2005–2012.

Duval, S. T., & Wicklund, R. A. (1972). *A theory of objective self awareness*. Oxford: Academic Press.

Escalas, J. E. (2004). Narrative processing: Building consumer connections to brands. *Journal of Consumer Psychology, 14*, 105–113.

Escalas, J. E. (2007). Self-referencing and persuasion: Narrative transportation versus analytical elaboration. *Journal of Consumer Research, 33*, 421–429.

Escalas, J. E., & Luce, M. F. (2004). Understanding the effects of process-focused versus outcome-focused thought in response to advertising. *Journal of Consumer Research, 31*, 274–285.

Fishbein, M. (1963). An investigation of the relationships between beliefs about an object and attitude toward that object. *Human Relations, 16*, 233–239.

Förster, J. (2009). Relations between perceptual and conceptual scope: How global versus local processing fits a focus on similarity versus dissimilarity. *Journal of Experimental Psychology: General, 138*, 88–111.

Förster, J., & Dannenberg, L. (2010). GLOMO^{sys}: A systems account of global versus local processing. *Psychological Inquiry, 21*, 175–197.

Förster, J., & Liberman, N. (2007). Knowledge activation. In A. Kruglanski & E. T. Higgins (Eds.), *Social psychology: Handbook of basic principles* (2nd ed., pp. 201–231). New York, NY: Guilford Press.

Förster, J., Liberman, N., & Kuschel, S. (2008). The effect of global versus local processing styles on assimilation versus contrast in social judgment. *Journal of Personality and Social Psychology, 94*, 579–599.

Garnham, A. (1981). Mental models as representations of text. *Memory & Cognition, 9*, 560–565.

Glenberg, A. M., Meyer, M., & Lindem, K. (1987). Mental models contribute to foregrounding during text comprehension. *Journal of Memory and Language, 26*, 69–83.

Gollwitzer, P. M., & Bayer, U. (1999). Deliberative versus implemental mindsets in the control of action. In S. Chaiken & Y. Trope (Eds.), *Dual-process theories in social psychology* (pp. 403–422). New York, NY: Guilford Press.

Gollwitzer, P. M., Heckhausen, H., & Steller, B. (1990). Deliberative and implemental mind-sets: Cognitive tuning toward congruous thoughts and information. *Journal of Personality and Social Psychology, 59*, 1119–1127.

Graesser, A. C. (1981). *Prose comprehension beyond the word*. New York, NY: Springer.

Green, G. M. (1989). *Pragmatics and natural language understanding*. Hillsdale, NJ: Erlbaum.

Green, M. C., & Brock, T. C. (2000). The role of transportation in the persuasiveness of public narratives. *Journal of Personality and Social Psychology, 79*, 701–721.

Grice, H. P. (1975). Logic and conversation. In P. Cole & J. L. Morgan (Eds.), *Syntax and semantics: Speech acts* (pp. 41–58). New York, NY: Academic Press.

Henderson, M. D., de Liver, Y., & Gollwitzer, P. M. (2008). The effects of an implemental mind-set on attitude strength. *Journal of Personality and Social Psychology, 94*, 396–411.

Higgins, E. T. (1981). The "communication game": Implications for social cognition and persuasion. In E. T. Higgins, C. P. Herman & M. P. Zanna (Eds.), *Social cognition: The Ontario Symposium* (Vol. 1, pp. 342–392). Hillsdale, NJ: Erlbaum.

Higgins, E. T. (1996). Knowledge activation: Accessibility, applicability, and salience. In E. T. Higgins & A. Kruglanski (Eds.), *Social psychology: Handbook of basic principles* (pp. 133–168). New York, NY: Guilford Press.

Higgins, E. T. (1997). Beyond pleasure and pain. *American Psychologist, 55*, 1217–1233.

Higgins, E. T. (1998). Promotion and prevention: Regulatory focus as a motivational principle. In M. P. Zanna (Ed.), *Advances in experimental social psychology* (Vol. 30, pp. 1–46). San Diego, CA: Academic Press.

Higgins, E. T., Bargh, J. A., & Lombardi, W. (1985). The nature of priming effects on categorization. *Journal of Experimental Psychology: Learning, Memory, and Cognition, 11*, 59–69.

Hirt, E. R., Kardes, F. R., & Markman, K. D. (2004). Activating a mental simulation mind-set through generation of alternatives: Implications for debiasing in related and unrelated domains. *Journal of Experimental Social Psychology, 40*, 374–383.

Hoch, S. J., & Loewenstein, G. F. (1991). Time-inconsistent preferences and consumer self-control. *Journal of Consumer Research, 17*, 492–507.

Houston, D. A., & Sherman, S. J. (1995). Cancelation and focus: The role of shared and unique features in the choice process. *Journal of Experimental Social Psychology, 31*, 357–378.

Houston, D. A., Sherman, S. J., & Baker, S. M. (1989). The influence of unique features and direction of comparison on preferences. *Journal of Experimental Social Psychology, 25*, 121–141.

Huang, X., Zhang, M., Hui, M. K., & Wyer, R. S. (2014). Warmth and conformity: The effect of ambient temperature on product preferences and financial decisions. *Journal of Consumer Psychology, 24*, 241–250.

Huber, J., Payne, J. W., & Puto, C. (1982). Adding asymmetrically dominated alternatives: Violations of regularity and the similarity hypothesis. *Journal of Consumer Research, 9*, 90–98.

Hung, I. W. P., & Wyer, R. S. (2008). The role of implicit theories in the impact of problem-solving print advertisements. *Journal of Consumer Psychology, 18*, 223–235.

Hung, I. W., & Wyer, R. S. (2009). Differences in perspective and the influence of charitable appeals: When imagining oneself as the victim is not always beneficial. *Journal of Marketing Research, 46*, 421–434.

Hung, I. W., & Wyer, R. S. (2011). Shaping the content of consumers' imaginations: The role of self-focused attention in product evaluations. *Journal of Marketing Research, 48*, 381–392.

Hung, I. W., & Wyer, R. S. (2014). Effects of self-relevant perspective-taking on the impact of persuasive appeals. *Personality and Social Psychology Bulletin, 40*, 402–414.

IJzerman, H., & Semin, G. R. (2010). Temperature perceptions as a ground for social proximity. *Journal of Experimental Social Psychology, 46*, 867–873.

Isen, A. M. (1987). Positive affect, cognitive processes, and social behaviour. In L. Berkowitz (Ed.), *Advances in experimental social psychology* (Vol. 20, pp. 203–253). New York, NY: Academic Press.

Janiszewski, C. A., & Wyer, R. S. (2014). Content and process priming: A review. *Journal of Consumer Psychology, 24*, 96–118.

Jiang, Y., Adaval, R., Steinhart, Y., & Wyer, R. S. (2014). Imagining yourself in the scene: The interactive effects of self-imagery goals and visual perspectives on consumer behaviour. *Journal of Consumer Research, 41*, 418–435.

Jiang, Y., Steinhart, Y., & Wyer, R. S. (2011). *The role of visual and semantic processing strategies in consumer information processing* (Unpublished manuscript). Hong Kong University of Science and Technology.

Johar, G. V. (1995). Consumer involvement and deception from implied advertising claims. *Journal of Marketing Research, 32*, 267–279.

Kardes, F. R. (1988). Spontaneous inference processes in advertising: The effects of conclusion omission and involvement on persuasion. *Journal of Consumer Research, 15*, 225–233.

Khan, U., & Dhar, R. (2006). Licensing effect in consumer choice. *Journal of Marketing Research, 43*, 259–266.

Kray, L. J., & Galinsky, A. D. (2003). The debiasing effect of counterfactual mind-sets: Increasing the search for disconfirmatory information in group decisions. *Organizational Behaviour and Human Decision Processes, 91*, 69–81.

Kruglanski, A. W., Shah, J. Y., Fishbach, A., Friedman, R., Chun, W. Y., & Sleeth-Keppler, D. (2002). A theory of goal systems. In M. P. Zanna (Ed.), *Advances in experimental social psychology* (Vol. 34, pp. 331–378). San Diego, CA: Academic Press.

Landau, M. J., Meier, B. P., & Keefer, L. A. (2010). A metaphor-enriched social cognition. *Psychological Bulletin, 136*, 1045–1067.

Lee, A. Y., Aaker, J. L., & Gardner, W. L. (2000). The pleasures and pains of distinct self-construals: The role of interdependence in regulatory focus. *Journal of Personality and Social Psychology, 78*, 1122–1134.

Lee, A. Y., & Semin, G. (2009). Culture through the lens of self-regulatory orientations. In R. S. Wyer, C.-y. Chiu & Y.-y Hong (Eds.), *Understanding culture: Theory, research and application* (pp. 299–310). New York, NY: Psychology Press.

Lee, S. W. S., & Schwarz, N. (2010). Dirty hands and dirty mouths: Embodiment of the moral-purity metaphor is specific to the motor modality involved in moral transgression. *Psychological Science, 21*, 1423–1425.

Li, Y., Gao, L., & Wyer, R. S. (2015). *Choosing between two evils: An attention-avoidance model of spontaneous self-control* (Unpublished manuscript). Chinese University of Hong Kong.

Liberman, N., & Förster, J. (2009). The effect of psychological distance on perceptual level of construal. *Cognitive Science, 33*, 1330–1341.

Markus, H. R., & Kitayama, S. (1991). Culture and the self: Implications for cognition, emotion and motivation. *Psychological Review, 98*, 224–253.

Martin, L. L., Ward, D. W., Achee, J. W., & Wyer, R. S. (1993). Mood as input: People have to interpret the motivational implications of their moods. *Journal of Personality and Social Psychology, 64*, 317–326.

Metcalfe, J., & Mischel, W. (1999). A hot/cool-system analysis of delay of gratification: Dynamics of willpower. *Psychological Review, 106*, 3–19.

Niedenthal, P. M., Barsalou, L. W., Winkielman, P., Krauth-Gruber, S., & Ric, F. (2005). Embodiment in attitudes, social perception, and emotion. *Personality and Social Psychology Bulletin, 9*, 184–211.

Park, J. W. & Kim, J. K. (2005). The effects of decoys on preference shifts: The role of attractiveness and providing justification. *Journal of Consumer Psychology, 15*, 94–107.

Pennington, N., & Hastie, R. (1988). Explanation-based decision making: Effects of memory structure on judgment. *Journal of Experimental Psychology: Learning, Memory and Cognition, 14*, 521–533.

Pennington, N., & Hastie, R. (1992). Explaining the evidence: Tests of the story model for juror decision making. *Journal of Personality and Social Psychology, 62*, 189–206.

Petty, R. E., & Cacioppo, J. T. (1986). *Communication and persuasion: Central and peripheral routes to attitude change*. New York, NY: Springer.

Petty, R. E., Priester, J. R., & Wegener, D. T. (1994). Cognitive processes in attitude change. In R. S. Wyer & T. K. Srull (Eds.), *Handbook of social cognition* (2nd ed., Vol. 2, pp. 69–142). Hillsdale, NJ: Erlbaum.

Pham, M. T. (1998). Representativeness, relevance and the use of feelings in decision making. *Journal of Consumer Research, 25*, 144–159.

Ratcliff, R. (1978). A theory of memory retrieval. *Psychological Review, 85*, 59–108.

Sawyer, A. G., & Howard, D. J. (1991). Effects of omitting conclusions in advertisements to involved and uninvolved audiences. *Journal of Marketing Research, 28*, 467–474.

Schank, R. C., & Abelson, R. P. (1977). *Scripts, plans, goals and understanding*. Hillsdale, NJ: Erlbaum.

Schwarz, N. (1998). Accessible content and accessibility experiences: The interplay of declarative and experiential information in judgment. *Personality and Social Psychology Review, 2*, 87–99.

Schwarz, N. (2004). Metacognitive experiences in consumer judgment and decision making. *Journal of Consumer Psychology, 14*, 332–348.

Schwarz, N., & Clore, G. L. (1983). Mood, misattribution, and judgments of well-being: Informative and directive functions of affective states. *Journal of Personality and Social Psychology, 45*, 513–523.

Schwarz, N., Bless, H., & Bohner, G. (1991a). Mood and persuasion: Affective states influence the processing of persuasive communications. In M. P. Zanna (Ed.), *Advances in experimental social psychology* (Vol. 24, pp. 161–199). San Diego, CA: Academic Press.

Schwarz, N., Bless, H., Strack, F., Klumpp, G., Rittenauer-Schatka, H., & Simons, A. (1991b). Ease of retrieval as information: Another look at the availability heuristic. *Journal of Personality and Social Psychology, 61*, 195–201.

Schwarz, N., & Clore, G. L. (1996). Feelings and phenomenal experiences. In E. T. Higgins & A. W. Kruglanski (Eds.), *Social psychology: Handbook of basic principles* (pp. 433– 465). New York, NY: Guilford Press.

Schwarz, N., & Clore, G. L. (2007). Feelings and phenomenal experiences. In A. W. Kruglanski & E. T. Higgins (Eds.), *Social psychology: Handbook of basic principles* (2nd ed., pp. 385–407). New York, NY: Guilford Press.

Shafir, E., Simonson, I., & Tversky, A. (1993). Reason-based choice. *Cognition, 49*, 11–36.

Shen, H., & Wyer, R. S. (2008). The impact of negative affect on responses to affect-regulating experiences. *Journal of Consumer Psychology, 18*, 39–48.

Shen, H., & Wyer, R. S. (2010). The effect of past behaviour on variety seeking. Automatic and deliberative processes. *Journal of Consumer Psychology, 20*, 33–42.

Shiv, B., & Fedorikhin, A. (1999). Heart and mind in conflict: The interplay of affect and cognition in consumer decision making. *Journal of Consumer Research, 26*, 278–292.

Simonson, I. (1989). Choice based on reasons: The case of attraction and compromise effects. *Journal of Consumer Research, 16*, 158–174.

Smith, E. R. (1990). Content and process specificity in the effects of prior experiences. In T. K. Srull & R. S. Wyer (Eds.), *Advances in social cognition* (Vol. 3, pp. 1–59). Hillsdale, NJ: Erlbaum.

Smith, E. R. (1994). Procedural knowledge and processing strategies in social cognition. In R. S. Wyer & T. K. Srull (Eds.), *Handbook of social cognition* (2nd ed., Vol. 1, pp. 101–151). Hillsdale, NJ: Erlbaum.

Srull, T. K., & Wyer, R. S. (1979). The role of category accessibility in the interpretation of information about persons: Some determinants and implications. *Journal of Personality and Social Psychology, 37*, 1660–1672.

Stepper, S., & Strack, F. (1993). Proprioceptive determinants of emotional and nonemotional feelings. *Journal of Personality and Social Psychology, 64*, 211–220.

Strack, F., & Deutsch, R. (2004). Reflective and impulsive determinants of social behaviour. *Personality and Social Psychology Review*, 8, 220–247.

Sujan, M., Bettman, J. R., & Baumgartner, H. (1993). Influencing consumers' judgments using autobiographical memories: A self-referencing perspective. *Journal of Marketing Research, 30*, 422–436.

Taylor, S. E., & Fiske, S. T. (1978). Salience, attention and attribution: Top of the head phenomena. In L. Berkowitz (Ed.), *Advances in experimental social psychology* (Vol. 11, pp. 249–288). New York, NY: Academic Press.

Triandis, H. C. (Ed.) (1995). *Individualism and collectivism*. Boulder, CO: Westview Press.

Trope, Y., & Liberman, N. (2010). Construal-level theory of psychological distance. *Psychological Review, 117*, 440–463.

Wang, J., & Calder, B. J. (2006). Media transportation and advertising. *Journal of Consumer Research, 33*, 151–162.

Wang, J., & Wyer, R. S. (2002). Comparative judgment processes: The effects of task objectives and time delay on product evaluations. *Journal of Consumer Psychology, 12*, 327–340.

Wänke, M., Bohner, G., & Jurkowitsch, A. (1997). There are many reasons to drive a BMW: Does imagined ease of argument generation influence attitudes? *Journal of Consumer Research, 24*, 170–177.

Wegener, D. T., Petty, R. E., & Smith, S. M. (1995). Positive mood can increase or decrease message scrutiny: The hedonic contingency view of mood and message processing. *Journal of Personality and Social Psychology, 69*, 5–15.

Williams, L. E., & Bargh, J. A. (2008). Experiencing physical warmth promotes interpersonal warmth. *Science, 322*, 606–607.

Wyer, R. S. (2004). *Social comprehension and judgment: The role of situation models, narratives, and implicit theories*. Mahwah, NJ: Erlbaum.

Wyer, R. S. (2008). The role of knowledge accessibility in cognition and behaviour: Implications for consumer information processing. In C. P. Haugtvedt, P. M. Herr & F. R. Kardes (Eds.), *Handbook of consumer psychology* (pp. 31–76). New York, NY: LEA/Psychology Press.

Wyer, R. S., & Carlston, D. E. (1979). *Social cognition, inference and attribution*. Hillsdale, NJ: Erlbaum.

Wyer, R. S., & Collins, J. E. (1992). A theory of humor elicitation. *Psychological Review, 99*, 663–688.

Wyer, R. S., & Gruenfeld, D. H. (1995). Pragmatic information processing in social contexts: Implications for social memory and judgment. In M. Zanna (Ed.), *Advances in experimental social psychology* (Vol. 27, pp. 49–92). San Diego, CA: Academic Press.

Wyer, R. S., & Radvansky, G. A. (1999). The comprehension and validation of social information. *Psychological Review, 106*, 89–118.

Wyer, R. S., & Shrum, L. J. (2015). The role of comprehension processes in communication and persuasion. *Media Psychology, 18*, 163–195.

Wyer, R. S. & Srull, T. K. (1989). *Memory and cognition in its social context*. Hillsdale, NJ: Erlbaum.

Wyer, R. S., & Xu, A. J. (2010). The role of behavioural mindsets in goal-directed activity: Conceptual underpinnings and empirical evidence. *Journal of Consumer Psychology, 20*, 107–125.

Wyer, R. S., Hung, I. W., & Jiang, Y. (2008). Visual and verbal processing strategies in comprehension and judgment. *Journal of Consumer Psychology, 18*, 244–257.

Wyer, R. S., Shen, H., & Xu, A. J. (2013). The role of procedural knowledge in the generalization of social behaviour. In D. Carlston (Ed.), *Oxford handbook of social cognition* (pp. 257–281). New York, NY: Oxford University Press.

Wyer, R. S., Clore, G. L., & Isbell, L. M. (1999). Affect and information processing. In M. P. Zanna (Ed.), *Advances in experimental social psychology* (Vol. 31, pp. 1–77). San Diego, CA: Academic Press.

Wyer, R. S., Xu, A. J., & Shen, H. (2012). The effects of past behaviour on future goal-directed activity. In M. P. Zanna & J. Olson (Eds.), *Advances in experimental social psychology* (Vol. 46, pp. 237–284). San Diego, CA: Academic Press.

Wyer, R. S., Budesheim, T. L., Shavitt, S., Riggle, E. J., Melton, J., & Kuklinski, J. H. (1991). Image, issues and ideology: The processing of information about political candidates. *Journal of Personality and Social Psychology, 61*, 533–545.

Xu, A. J., & Wyer, R. S. (2007). The effect of mindsets on consumer decision strategies. *Journal of Consumer Research, 34*, 556–566.

Xu, A. J., & Wyer, R. S. (2008). The comparative mindset: From animal comparisons to increased purchase intentions. *Psychological Science, 19*, 859–864.

Xu, A. J., & Wyer, R. S. (2010). Puffery in advertisements: The effects of media context, communication norms, and consumer knowledge. *Journal of Consumer Research, 37*, 329–343.

Xu, A. J., & Wyer, R. S. (2012). The role of bolstering and counterarguing mindsets in persuasion. *Journal of Consumer Research, 38*, 920–932.

Yeung, C. W. M., & Wyer, R. S. (2004). Affect, appraisal and consumer judgment. *Journal of Consumer Research, 31*, 412–424.

Zhang, M., & Li, X. (2012). From physical weight to psychological significance: The contribution of semantic activations underlying the effects of carrying weight on the judgment of importance. *Journal of Consumer Research, 38*, 1063–1075.

7

Unconscious cognition effects in consumer research

Claudiu V. Dimofte

This chapter focuses on research findings that demonstrate the operation of unconscious factors driving individuals' responses to social (including marketplace) stimuli and contexts, and highlights the importance of understanding these factors from both theoretical and practical perspectives. Whereas this issue is clearly related to the measurement of unconscious or implicit effects, this chapter will not provide an in-depth review of implicit measures and will instead be limited to discussing research findings that document the unconscious effects of interest (details on measuring implicit effects are provided elsewhere – e.g., Chapter 8 of this book or Dimofte, 2010). For the purposes of this review, the terms *unconscious*, *automatic* and *implicit* will be used interchangeably to refer to cognitive processes that are not accessible to individuals' awareness or introspection (see Bargh & Morsella, 2008; Kihlstrom, 1999).

The appeal that the topic of unconscious cognition presents to both academic researchers and the general public resides in the basic premise that underlies it. Unlike the historical reliance on the rational consumer model (see Lancaster, 1966), which argues that individuals have set preferences that they purposefully and efficiently pursue within the constraints of the market, the contrasting unconscious or automatic processing model is at once simpler in its requirements and more complex in its implications. It proposes that environmental inputs can routinely trigger automatic processes that require no individual control or even attention and that are largely unaffected by processing capacity constraints (Schneider & Shiffrin, 1977). Naturally, the implications of this model for understanding and influencing the behaviour of individuals in the marketplace elicited interest. The earliest association of unconscious cognition and consumer behaviour in the American media occurred outside academia around the middle of the twentieth century and was marred by controversy. It involved the claim of a market researcher (James Vicary) that consumer responses can be influenced by subliminally presented stimuli through what thenceforth would become known as *subliminal advertising*. Vicary cited his field experimental data arguing that imperceptibly flashing the messages "Eat Popcorn" and "Drink Coke" on a movie theatre screen every five seconds for 30 milliseconds each time throughout a feature film had boosted popcorn sales by 58 per cent and Coke sales by 18 per cent (Packard, 1957). Despite the fact that this finding could not be replicated and Vicary did not actually have any data (he eventually admitted to fabricating the entire story), the notion that subliminal communication could impact people's thinking and behaviour held significant appeal for both the popular press and academic researchers. A large amount of literature in cognitive psychology has since demonstrated that subliminal priming is in fact a bona fide, reliable phenomenon (at least in the laboratory), in particular in the contexts of action priming and emotional response. In fact, even Vicary was partly exonerated, half a century later, by consumer research showing that his priming effects are possible: Karremans, Stroebe and Claus (2006) found that the subliminal priming of a soft drink brand name produced enhanced preference for the primed brand, though only for thirsty participants.

Despite the fact that psychological research began to award increasingly more attention to the topic of unconscious cognition, consumer research was initially slow to follow suit – perhaps due to the stigma that the Vicary scandal seemed to have placed on the marketing field in general. In fact, in a review piece published three decades later, Pratkanis and Greenwald (1988) attributed the lack of reliable related findings in consumer psychology research to poor methods and limited theoretical accounts of the unconscious. In further suggesting that sensationalism-driven research focused on subliminal effects was misguided (see Theus, 1994 for a review), the authors encouraged the field to place more emphasis on understanding the way consumers may process information outside awareness and under what conditions marketer tactics may ethically engage that type of unconscious processing (Pratkanis & Greenwald, 1988). The appeal did not go unheeded. In the intervening decades, the field has followed this advice and has largely kept pace with, and built on, theoretical developments on the topic established in the broader field of psychology. In addressing the various streams of research on the unconscious nature of consumer thought and behaviour, the structure of this chapter will largely follow a sequential path reminiscent of the simple, classic hierarchy of effects model in cognitive and consumer research (e.g.,, Lavidge & Steiner, 1961): stimulus exposure – attitude formation – behaviour. In the process, the next section will review both classic and more recent accounts from cognitive and consumer psychology addressing the exposure to and the processing of information in the absence of awareness.

Unconscious information processing

Some of the earliest psychology work on the topic involved the *mere exposure* phenomenon, which argued that exposing individuals repeatedly to the same stimulus will produce more positive affect toward it (Zajonc, 1968). Subsequent research demonstrated the emergence of the mere exposure effect with unattended stimuli (e.g., Kunst-Wilson & Zajonc, 1980; Wilson, 1979) and in the process showed that explicit accounts of information processing were inadequate to explain the fact that stimulus recognition was independent of affective judgements (Pratkanis & Greenwald, 1988). Consumer research contributed the idea of *preattentive mere exposure* effects (Janiszewski, 1993) to this line of work, by showing how unintentional exposure to brand names or packaging leads to more favourable brand attitudes even when consumers do not pay attention to or have any recall for the initial exposure to the marketing stimulus (Janiszewski, 1993). The often-used product placement strategy in movies or TV shows is banking on precisely this effect, and marketers are willing to pay for the consumer favour that it brings (e.g., over $100 million worth of placements were featured in 1999's *The World Is Not Enough* movie for brands including BMW, Heineken, Motorola, Omega and Smirnoff).

Although perception without attention and perception in the absence of awareness may be theoretically distinct (Lamme, 2003), they operate in a similar manner and produce qualitatively equivalent results (Merikle & Joordens, 1997). This is important because many of the actions that consumers engage in during marketplace interactions involve patently low levels of attention, due to either habituation to the focal marketing stimuli (e.g., routine, repeated purchases in the daily basket) or apparent disinterest towards them (e.g., indifference to or even avoidance of advertising messages; see Greenwald & Leavitt, 1984). Indeed, a significant amount of consumer research on the topic has demonstrated that processing occurs even when consumers do not explicitly allocate attentional resources to incoming marketing stimuli and that attitude formation can occur in the absence of conscious thought (Janiszewski, 1988). The related construct of *incidental exposure* was addressed in several consumer research articles (e.g., Ferraro, Bettman, & Chartrand, 2009; Shapiro, 1999; Shapiro, MacInnis, & Heckler, 1997) and showed the influence that marketing stimuli can have even when consumers lack explicit memory for them. In the incidental exposure paradigm, research participants are asked to attend to a focal stimulus that requires most of their processing resources, while minimal attention is allocated to a product advertisement (Shapiro et al., 1997). This superficial level of ad processing is nonetheless sufficient to activate related concepts for the exposed consumer and create both perceptual and conceptual fluency. This fluency can make advertising elements more likely to be included in a subsequent purchase consideration set (Shapiro, 1999) or brands subtly placed in unrelated photos of people in everyday situations more desirable (Ferraro et al., 2009), despite no explicit awareness or memory for any of these processes and stimuli.

The more recent development of various cognitive psychology measures of implicit processing (see Dimofte, 2010) has allowed consumer researchers to quantify the ways in which individuals acquire marketing information and are influenced by it without awareness. An important framework for these efforts was provided by the *associative model* of knowledge representation and memory (Anderson, 1983), which suggests that the stimulus-driven activation of specific nodes may spread to neighbouring ones in ways that bypass conscious control. This is an example of the *mere association effect* introduced by Dimofte and Yalch (2011), which argues for the automatic activation of associative relationships across networks of interconnected nodes. Importantly, these associations need not make logical (i.e., semantic) sense in order to be subject to this activation. For example, in that research the authors found that an American university is more likely to be deemed "sexy" if its sports mascot shares a name with a sexually related product (in that case, "Trojan" – a leading brand of condoms) and, relatedly, sell more football team jerseys if they feature the number 69 (Dimofte & Yalch, 2011). In a less risqué domain, the same research found that merely reading about a river delta and its fast waters impacted individuals' subsequent perceptions of the speed of beverage service on Delta Airlines flights (Dimofte & Yalch, 2011).

The mere association effect also operates on visual rather than lexical cues. In another study, participants were shown two wine bottles that were alike in every way except for the pictures on their labels (Dimofte & Yalch, 2011). One bottle had the image of a frog on its label and the other had a label that featured the image of a boy stomping grapes. Subsets of participants were then exposed, respectively, to a neutral word (*airplane*), a word affiliated with the label image (*boy* or *frog*), or a word associated with frogs – one positively (*Kermit*) and one negatively (*warts*). Participants were then asked to make their wine choice between the two bottles. Those exposed to the unrelated word *airplane* split their choice (as random choice would suggest), while most of the participants exposed to the words *frog* or *boy* expectedly chose the wines with labels representing those respective images. However, those exposed to the word *warts* perceived the wine with the frog label as "bad" and avoided it, while those exposed to the word *Kermit* made a positive association instead and favoured it. Clearly, participants' previous knowledge of frog-associated words of specific valence unconsciously impacted their attitudes towards the product

(Dimofte & Yalch, 2011). In short, it seems that consumers automatically recognize and process brand names and related images, and that during this information processing mental associations are spontaneous, uncontrolled and prompted by unexpected sources.

Another research area illustrative of the unconscious nature of consumer information processing is that of language comprehension and semantic meaning extraction. For example, Dimofte and Yalch (2007a) looked at how consumers make sense of polysemous (i.e., multiple-meaning) brand slogans. In addressing the issue, they assessed whether some individuals may access more information from such slogans than they can explicitly report and found that to be indeed the case. In one study, they exposed consumers to an advertisement for a new luxury vehicle that featured the slogan "No One Comes Close". Although explicit participant responses to this message focused on the technology and quality advantage enjoyed by the brand, strong implicit associations between the brand and attributes related to out-of-reach perceptions (e.g., *unattainable, unapproachable*, etc.) were shown via many participants' scores on the Implicit Association Test (IAT: Greenwald, McGhee, & Schwartz, 1998). This was not the case when the ad featured a comparable, single-meaning slogan ("Unlike Any Other"). The effects were particularly apparent for consumers of high working memory capacity (who were able to quickly access and maintain multiple meanings active in working memory; Dimofte & Yalch, 2007b). These findings are important and interesting because they display an apparent dissociation between the explicit and implicit responses that the consumers exhibited towards the same stimuli. In the same manner, related polysemy-driven implicit effects were responsible for consumers developing positive automatic associations between an orange juice brand and *fresh* when its slogan was "The Natural Choice" (but not when the slogan was "The Obvious Choice"). Conversely, negative automatic associations between a winter skiing resort and *bad* emerged when its slogan was "Going Downhill Fast" (but not when it was "Going Fast"; Dimofte & Yalch, 2007b). These associations were more predictive of consumer attitudes than self-reported perceptions, attesting to the relevance of studying and measuring consumers' implicit associations.

An instantiation of the mere association effect (Dimofte & Yalch, 2011) in the lexical domain is that of *homophone priming*, recently illustrated in the consumer research literature by Davis and Herr (2014). Homophones are words with shared phonology but different spelling (e.g., *bye* and *buy*) that come with their own, unrelated networks of cognitive associations. These authors found that individuals who are exposed to and process such words often fail to suppress the irrelevant associations that the corresponding homophone brings about, and this produces priming across a variety of unrelated marketing stimuli (Davis & Herr, 2014). In one study, embedding the word *goodbye* in the text of a restaurant advertisement produced enhanced perceptions of value and higher willingness-to-pay levels for its service (due to the "good buy" homophone) than when the advertisement used the semantically identical salutation "so long" (Davis & Herr, 2014).

The topic of unconscious information processing has also been recently addressed in the context of Internet media, where much of the marketing effort (and spending) is being routed these days. Despite consumer habituation to and presumed disregarding of web advertisements, research shows that online ads work: consumers develop more favourable attitudes towards promoted brands while not being able to recall seeing their Internet ads (Yoo, 2008). Recent functional magnetic resonance imaging (fMRI) work also supports the early findings on the incidental exposure paradigm, in even more conservative contexts. For example, Tusche, Bode and Haynes (2010) had a group of participants focus their attention on a black square placed centrally on a white screen and hit a specific button depending on which side of the square (left or right) opened up after 800 milliseconds. In between these tasks, irrelevant images of cars were briefly shown outside the focus of attention while the fixation task continued. A second group of participants simply evaluated the attractiveness of the same set of cars. Neural responses of the two sets of participants were similar and predictive, in each case, of car preference, suggesting that distraction and lack of conscious processing produced the same choice as explicit, deliberative thought (Tusche et al., 2010). These results attest to the power of unconscious information processing for consumer decision making: Even in non-marketing contexts or when consciously avoiding marketing stimuli, consumers cannot escape absorbing associated information and being influenced.

Finally, unconscious processing can impact consumer response to marketing stimuli depending on the type of scale employed to measure that response. For example, Dimofte and Johansson (2009) built on the psychology findings of Biernat, Manis and Nelson (1991) by uncovering the existence of a *shifting standards effect* in marketing with respect to consumer brand evaluations. The shifting standards model argues that individuals routinely adjust their subjective (but not objective) judgement standards as they evaluate members of stereotyped social groups (e.g., women are stereotypically expected to earn less than men if judged in "objective" annualized dollar amounts, but they are at the same time seen to be more financially successful than men on "subjective" (i.e., word-based) semantic differential success scales; Biernat et al., 1991). In marketing contexts, it seems that, in the case of inferior brands that engender strong (and low) expectations, consumers unconsciously lower their evaluative standards and "cut them slack" on word-based, subjective scales (but not on number-based, objective scales). Thus, a 1500 dpi screen resolution for a Chinese-made DVD player is objectively unimpressive, but in subjective terms (i.e., on a scale anchored by "very poor" and "very good resolution"), a dpi rating at that level sounds pretty good *for a Chinese DVD player.* The automatic nature of this adjustment was captured via the IAT and was further demonstrated by the fact that consumers did not feel that they had engaged in the evaluative shift when informed about it during debriefing (Dimofte & Johansson, 2009).

The various lines of research presented here attest to the fact that much of the information processing that individuals in general, and consumers in particular, engage in on a routine basis is pursued in the absence of conscious awareness. The related acquisition and development of valenced perceptions about encountered stimuli (i.e., implicit attitudes) are discussed next.

Unconscious attitude formation and change

Attitudes consist of associations between objects and valenced thoughts (i.e., evaluations) that emerge upon personal experience (direct or indirect) with the respective objects (Greenwald & Banaji, 1995). Their importance resides in the fact that they commonly impact individuals' responses, ranging from perception to behaviour (Nosek & Hansen, 2008). One of the basic ways in which such associations emerge is classical conditioning (Olson & Fazio, 2001), which over time produces implicit attitudes within what has been termed an individual's *culturally bound experience* (Nosek & Hansen, 2008). Indeed, Gibson (2008) demonstrated that, for consumers without strong prior brand attitudes, evaluative conditioning managed to change implicit attitudes towards the leading soft drink brands. Earlier research on the formation of consumer attitudes had shown that it may occur even in the absence of conscious thought (e.g., Janiszewski, 1988), and a more recent review piece addressing the evaluative conditioning phenomenon argues that empirical evidence increasingly supports the view that awareness is not required for attitude formation (Sweldens, Corneille, & Yzerbyt, 2014).

Two more conceptual points deserve attention before turning to some consumer research work employing the implicit attitude construct. First, there has been some debate within the broader psychology field about the origin and "ownership" of implicit attitudes, in particular as measured by arguably the most popular measure thereof – the IAT (Greenwald et al., 1998). One side of the debate argues that implicit attitudes (captured via automatic associations) reflect not only personal, but also extrapersonal, associations (Olson & Fazio, 2004) that emerge from cultural knowledge and norms and could cloud individual responses to the IAT by prompting and activating irrelevant information that is associated with the focal attitude object (Olson & Fazio, 2004). The other side of the argument claims that the endorsement of these associations is not required for them to be deemed personal, since the source of the information is not important as long as the information produces or impacts cognitive and behavioural response (Nosek & Hansen, 2008). This issue is closely related to the second conceptual point to address: the predictive validity of implicit attitudes (as measured by the IAT or otherwise). To the extent that implicit attitudes (a) do not predict behaviour or (b) do not diverge from explicit attitudes, their treatment is superfluous and their incremental contribution to understanding individuals' thought and action is nil. However, a significant body of psychology research argues for the fact that neither is the case, and in fact implicit attitudes can be dissociated from their explicit analogues while occasionally having superior predictive power when it comes to behaviour (see Friese, Hofmann and Wäncke, 2008; Greenwald, Poehlman, Uhlmann, & Banaji, 2009; Maison, Greenwald, & Bruin, 2004; Perugini, 2005). The following consumer research articles contribute to that body of work.

One of the interesting but challenging issues in brand management entails consumer response to brand rumours. The difficulty in addressing these rumours is that consumers report universally low belief in them and claim that their brand attitudes are unchanged by these messages. However, the post-exposure behaviour exhibited by most consumers demonstrates a clear avoidance of the affected brand (e.g.,, Tybout, Calder, & Sternthal, 1981) and is in line with rumour acceptance, despite explicit disbelief. Indeed, Ozubko and Fugelsang's (2011) research suggests that rumours, even though not believed to be true when initially received by individuals, might affect judgements when recalled at the time a brand is being evaluated, via an implicit route. At the same time, the explicit processing of brand rumours is likely to involve truth verification consistent with the Spinozan view of information processing as researched by Gilbert and colleagues (e.g.,, Gilbert, Krull, & Malone, 1990; Gilbert, Tafarodi, & Malone, 1993). In this view, individuals' default mode of explicit information processing involves a two-step process: de facto acceptance followed by truth verification. However, if consumers lack the motivation or resources to consciously evaluate the truthfulness of incoming marketplace information, they will not reject dubious information. For implicit associations, motivation and cognitive resources are less likely to matter, as the rumour information is automatically associated with the brand knowledge structure (Dimofte & Yalch, 2014). Importantly, the commonly used refutation strategy that most affected brands tend to employ does little to address the problem; in fact, it has been argued that refuting the rumour is the least effective way to quell it (Tybout et al., 1981), largely due to the fact that it mainly rehearses the initial rumour and creates stronger automatic associations between the brand and the rumour-related negative contaminant (e.g., a rumour about a fast-food brand having worms in its burgers will produce an automatic association between the brand name and worms). However, a quelling strategy that involves exposing consumers to novel information cues about the negative contaminant (e.g., worms are used in high-end French cuisine) was shown to work via an unconscious route by Dimofte and Yalch (2014). The authors employed the IAT to demonstrate that the brand name–negative contaminant automatic association is quick to emerge and cannot be suppressed, but the positive nature of the new information about the contaminant manages to significantly improve implicit attitudes towards it and by extension recover brand attitudes (thus, worms are somehow not that bad after all and therefore the rumour is less damaging to the brand).

Other consumer research demonstrating the occasional dissociation of explicit and implicit attitudes includes work by Forehand and Perkins (2005), who employed both self-report and the IAT to assess consumer response to advertising using celebrity voices. Liking a celebrity produced positive responses to advertising featuring the celebrity's voice if consumers did not recognize the celebrity. This was not the case if the celebrity was recognized or if consumers were motivated to eliminate irrelevant influences on their advertising response. The latter case involved an explicit correction for the perceived influence of the celebrity (i.e., resetting because of its actual irrelevance) via a conscious evaluation that the IAT did not allow for, leading to dissociation between the explicit and implicit attitudinal results (Forehand & Perkins, 2005). A similar dissociation was found by Priluck and Till (2009) in terms of consumer explicit and implicit attitudes towards comparable marketplace brands: Whereas explicit brand measurement scales found the brands to be indistinguishable, implicit responses via the IAT demonstrated an implicit preference for pioneering brands (Priluck & Till, 2009).

The consumer response to global brands in the US marketplace was the focus of research by Dimofte, Johansson and Ronkainen (2008). In explicit self-reports, American consumers reported no particular value associated with global brands (be they domestic or foreign based), in contrast to the typical perceptions of developing nations' consumers, who like global brands due to their aspirational nature. However, US consumers' responses to an indirect explicit measure showed that an individual described along several attributes was liked better if described as a global (vs. local) beer drinker, while an IAT uncovered their clear implicit associations favouring global over local brands (Dimofte, Johansson, & Ronkainen, 2008). The research demonstrates that despite explicit claims to the contrary, American consumers prefer global brands (i.e., they harbour positive implicit attitudes towards them). Importantly, the superior market performance of global brands in the US is in line with the implicit preference results, reinforcing the argument that implicit attitudes can be better predictors of actual behaviour than explicit attitudes (Dimofte, 2010).

In a different domain, Dimofte, Goodstein and Brumbaugh (2015) looked at aspirational brand advertising and the threats it may present to consumers' self-esteem. Marketers often promote their products through ads featuring individuals with desirable qualities that the target consumers seek (e.g., strong athletes of great stamina – provided by an energy drink), with the idea of presenting consumers with social out-groups that are desirable and potentially accessible via the purchase of the promoted product. In highlighting the difference between a consumer's inferior current in-group (e.g., casual runner) and superior potential out-group (e.g., professional athlete), it is expected that the resulting need gap motivates the consumer to gain access into the desired out-group via product purchase. However, the ad-implied gap between the consumer's current in-group and the desirable out-group prompts a social comparison process that puts the consumer's in-group at a disadvantage (Dimofte et al., 2015) and can be threatening to one's self-esteem. In several studies the authors find that these comparisons can lead to negative attitudinal responses and lower purchase intentions. Although in self-reports consumers do not (like to) admit that something as mundane as a product advertisement is threatening, results suggest that their implicit collective self-esteem (i.e., the self-esteem automatically associated with their in-group) is lowered without their conscious awareness. This, in turn, leads to less positive perceptions of the featured brand and reduced purchase intentions (Dimofte et al., 2015).

Whereas the role of the unconscious in the formation of consumer attitudes appears largely uncontroversial, a more complex proposition is that even higher-order processes (e.g., the setting and pursuit of specific consumer goals) could occur in the absence of purposeful, conscious thought. The next section addresses this possibility.

Unconscious goal setting and goal pursuit

Similarly to attitudes, goals can become automatically activated by contextual cues even in the absence of conscious intent (Gollwitzer & Bargh, 2005). The underlying auto-motive model (Bargh, 1990) essentially posits the existence and operation of unconscious motivation as a common cognitive driver of thought and behaviour, in a manner qualitatively no different (in terms of its outcomes) from that associated with conscious goal pursuit. Thus, Bargh, Gollwitzer, Lee-Chai, Barndollar, & Trötschel (2001) argue that once the goal concept is activated without one's awareness, it operates over time in the absence of purposeful monitoring to guide progress towards the goal. In one study, these authors had participants engage in a word-search task wherein they had to find as many words as possible among a set of letter tiles from the Scrabble board game. This activity was interrupted early on, with participants being given the option of resuming the relatively challenging Scrabble task or switching instead to a more enjoyable alternative task of rating cartoons. Participants who had been primed at the beginning of the study with words related to high performance (i.e., had an activated, albeit unconscious, high-performance goal) were significantly more likely to return to the tedious Scrabble task than participants in a neutral prime control condition (Bargh et al., 2001). Thus, interrupting unconscious goals produced more task persistence in the face of obstacles (Bargh et al., 2001), despite individuals' lack of awareness of their goal progress.

However, such unconscious effects seem most likely in the case of goal pursuit associated with routine, well-established and rehearsed or primed behaviours (Bargh, 1990; Bagozzi & Dholakia, 1999) and it is not apparent that spontaneous goal activation and unconscious pursuit thereof can also apply to unrehearsed, novel actions. The related distinction between goal setting and goal pursuit is therefore important: Whereas the activation and salience of specific goals commonly occur unconsciously, the subsequent efforts to reach them (i.e., planning, implementation and controls) are typically consciously pursued (see Bagozzi & Dholakia, 1999). That said, more recent consumer research on the topic (e.g., Chartrand, Huber, Shiv, & Tanner, 2008; Fitzsimons et al., 2002) argues for the possibility that the entire process (i.e., both goal activation and goal pursuit) can occur in the absence of awareness, with marketplace brands often as contributing factors to the process. For example, in one study Chartrand et al. (2008) exposed participants subliminally to either prestige brands (i.e., Nordstrom, Tiffany, Neiman Marcus) or thrift brands (i.e., Wal-Mart, Dollar Store, K-Mart). In a subsequent task, these participants were asked to make two product choices in two product categories (socks and microwave ovens). In both categories, those primed with the thrift brands preferred the thrift option more compared with those primed with the prestige brands. Importantly, no experimental participant suspected that the prior subliminal brand exposure was responsible for the effect (Chartrand et al., 2008).

Among the rehearsed and established behaviours that lend themselves to unconscious goal pursuit are those related to individuals in one's immediate social circle (i.e., personal relationships). In this context, Fitzsimons and Bargh (2003) showed that interpersonal goals can become activated by the mere psychological presence of relationship partners and then unconsciously guide thought and action. As critical components of an individual's social life, significant others have powerful influence on our motivations, even when physically absent. In one study, participants whose mental representations of their mothers were activated during a priming task worked harder on a verbal task than in the absence of that representation if they had reported having the goal of making their mother proud (Fitzsimons & Bargh, 2003). This finding is reminiscent of previous social psychology research on automatic stereotype activation and the self-fulfilling behavioural confirmation response it can produce (e.g., Chen & Bargh, 1999). Both lines of work are supportive of the idea that environmentally triggered goal pursuit (Bargh & Ferguson, 2000) occurs and its influence on individual action can be equally profound whether it takes a conscious or an unconscious form (e.g., Williams, Nocera, Gray, & Bargh, 2009). Clearly consumption behaviours associated with significant others can therefore be influenced by activating consumption-related goals. For example, if a mother always pushed her child to make thrifty product choices, when this child becomes an adult his mere wearing of a bracelet that is reminiscent of the respective parent will have the potential to induce choices such as lodging at a two-star rather than a three-star hotel when travelling.

Indeed, individuals often pursue and reach goals as well as experience their consequences without awareness (Fitzsimons et al., 2002). Various moderators have been addressed in this context, for example involving the affective consequences of goal pursuit. Oettingen, Grant, Smith, Skinner, & Gollwitzer (2006) compared self-reported affect after unconscious and conscious goal pursuit that either conformed to or violated prevailing social norms. When goal-directed behaviour conformed to norms, affective experiences did not differ after unconscious and conscious goal pursuit. On the other hand, when this behaviour violated norms, unconscious goal pursuit induced more negative affect, as the unconscious goal did not provide an explicit, self-apparent reason for one's norm-violating behaviour (Oettingen et al., 2006). The different limitations associated with conscious and unconscious processes and the effects they may have on the self-regulation of emotion were addressed by Williams et al. (2009). In one study, they had participants engage in an anxiety-eliciting task. Those primed with a reappraisal emotion control goal that operated unconsciously exhibited identical physiological reactivity reductions as those explicitly instructed to reappraise, suggesting that unconscious self-regulatory processes are useful during instances of emotion regulation (Williams et al., 2009). These findings are relevant in the contexts of consumption behaviours that may be attractive but anxiety producing (e.g., flying on commercial aircraft, watching certain movies or going on a rollercoaster ride). Subtle contextual messages placed in airport environments, for example, could lessen the anxiety some fliers experience even if they cannot consciously recall attending to the respective messages.

On the consumer research side, Chartrand et al. (2008) followed a procedure similar to that of Bargh et al. (2001) to show that, as described above, when primed with thrift versus prestige goals consumers preferred more expensive Nike socks and cheaper Hanes ones, respectively. The research also demonstrated that the impact of unconsciously activated goal pursuit is stronger over time and that attenuating the goal-priming effect requires real, as opposed to hypothetical, goal satiation (Chartrand et al., 2008). Finally, the same authors found that brands can serve as subliminal primes for unconscious purchasing goals (Chartrand et al., 2008), attesting to the power that brands hold over consumer behaviour and choice.

Unconscious behavioural responses

Some of the most striking research findings in cognitive and social psychology in the past couple of decades refer to the unconscious effects that various environmental stimuli can have on human behaviour. Whereas the previously discussed work on unconscious influences on perception, attitudes and goal setting may have hinted at the fact that downstream behaviour would be just as susceptible to unconscious effects, it is nonetheless both exciting and unsettling to observe the multitude of instances wherein behaviour is altered while individuals deny ever lacking full conscious control over their actions. In a classic study on behavioural priming, Bargh, Chen and Burrows (1996), for example, found that experimental participants for whom an elderly stereotype was primed walked more slowly away from the experimental location than did control participants, in apparent conceptual alignment with the activated stereotype but without any awareness of its influence.

In the social psychology literature in particular, the activation of implicit stereotypes is an important topic because of the nefarious unconscious impact that it can have on behaviour. Although many of these stereotypes emerge from cultural knowledge acquired in social contexts (Olson & Fazio, 2004), they may not be consciously subscribed to, or their associated biases endorsed, by the individuals who hold them (many such contexts are relevant to marketers, for example involving how consumers and salespeople interact during shopping encounters). To the extent that through explicit responses towards the stereotyped objects these individuals can ignore or inhibit their dissociated implicit stereotypes, merely holding these stereotypes should not be a major problem (in other words, one's implicit preference for Whites vs. Blacks in a racial bias IAT need not convey that the person is prejudiced; in fact, most people who take that specific IAT exhibit an implicit preference for Whites over Blacks – see Nosek, Banaji, & Greenwald, 2002). However, making conscious adjustments to the various implicit biases that we hold (e.g., young over old, males as more science inclined than females, etc.) is, research suggests, an overly optimistic expectation. Thus, our behaviour is oftentimes unduly influenced by stereotypes that we implicitly hold about specific social objects; we are typically unable to notice their influence and rarely consciously correct for it. A classic illustration of this claim comes from research on the effects of implicit racial bias on hiring managers' decisions. In one field study, Bertrand and Mullainathan (2004) assembled fictitious personal resumes for presumed applicants to newspaper job ads in two large US cities and randomly assigned White- or Black-sounding names to these resumes. Interview callbacks favoured applicants of White-sounding names (e.g., Emily Walsh) over those of Black-sounding names (e.g., Lakisha Washington) by a 3:2 ratio, demonstrating that implicit labour discrimination (Bertrand, Chugh, & Mullainathan, 2005) is something we need to account for. The insidious effect of implicit bias is more prevalent perhaps than thought, as subsequent organizational behaviour research has found similar effects underlying interviewers' response to job applicants speaking with an accent (e.g., Segrest Purkiss, Perrewé, Gillespie, Mayes, & Ferris, 2006). It is not difficult to imagine that salespeople or service providers may treat their customers differently (and the reverse is clearly possible as well) depending on their name, race or accent despite not being aware of engaging in this biased behaviour.

The effects of implicit stereotypes on behaviour are unfortunate because the prejudiced behaviour they induce diverges from the behavioural intent of the stereotype holders (i.e., the hiring managers in the discrimination studies were likely not looking to explicitly favour one ethnic group over another). However, another situation that can produce dissociation between behavioural intent responses and actual behaviour is when individuals consciously alter the truthfulness of their behavioural intent responses, for various self-presentation reasons: providing answers that are more socially acceptable, that are more in line with popular belief, that put the respondent in a better light or that the respondent thinks the surveyor wants to hear. In these cases, the value of implicit measures is that they do not allow for conscious adjustments and the individuals' true (i.e., actually held) implicit associations will determine eventual behaviour (see Dimofte, 2010). For example, empirical work by Greenwald, Smith, Sriram, Bar-Anan and Nosek (2009) found excellent predictive power for voters' implicit candidate preferences (as captured by the IAT) in the 2008 US presidential elections, beyond what polled self-reports predicted. In a similar vein, consumers generally report positive explicit attitudes towards "green behaviour" (e.g., recycling) but display behaviour that is largely inconsistent with these self-reports. However, their implicit attitudes were shown to be more predictive of their actual (i.e., limited) green behaviour (Vantomme, 2004).

An interesting area where some of the unconscious behaviour effects have been uncovered is mimicry (see Chartrand, 2005). In one of the earliest studies on the topic, Johnston (2002) had study participants engage in an ice cream taste test, trying the product in the presence of another person who was in fact a confederate of the experimenter. The unsuspecting subject mimicked the ice cream consumption of the confederate (in terms of volume), although not when the latter was obese and therefore socially stigmatized in terms of the focal behaviour (Johnston, 2002). The finding is important as it demonstrates the unconscious activation *and* inhibition of behaviour mimicry as well as their operation in consumption contexts. Other social psychology work has built on this theme and found that unconscious behavioural mimicry is context specific and can operate as a coping mechanism of sorts: for example, Lakin, Chartrand and Arking (2008) argued that mimicking others can benefit individuals who have experienced social exclusion by restoring their belongingness needs. In one study, the authors had participants play an online game with two presumed other players that entailed ball tossing; in fact, the co-players were computer controlled and manipulated to offer the ball to the subjects either as often as to the others or much less so (the latter scenario thus provided the social exclusion condition). A subsequent task had participants interact with a confederate who kept moving her foot, and the extent to which the participants replicated this foot movement was recorded. Results suggest that unconscious behavioural mimicry was deployed strategically, such that socially excluded individuals displayed more of it in their pursuit of post-exclusion affiliation (Lakin et al., 2008). Clearly, this strategic behaviour can be used to one's advantage during marketplace interactions.

Indeed, in a consumer context, Tanner, Ferraro, Chartrand, Bettman, & Van Baaren (2008) addressed the issue from both a mimicker (i.e., self) and mimicked (i.e., other) behaviour perspective. They built on Johnston (2002) to argue that automatic behavioural mimicry of others is a common marketplace occurrence in the context of consumption and choice, but go on to propose that being mimicked has automatic behavioural consequences as well (Tanner et al., 2008). Thus, when someone is mimicked by another (via body posture and movement), pro-social emotions (e.g., building rapport and personal liking) are elicited, which in turn have the capacity to produce enhanced liking for a product that the mimicker introduces (e.g., a new sports drink; Tanner et al., 2008). This suggests the distinct possibility that individuals who are aware of the power of mimicry to induce behaviour change in others can use this knowledge strategically, to their advantage. Indeed, research confirms that mimicry can be, and often is, used strategically: Van Baaren, Holland, Steenaert and van Knippenberg (2003) found that verbal mimicry (repeating someone's words ad litteram) has strong effects on behavioural outcomes associated with the others. In one study, a restaurant server who merely repeated the patrons' orders as they were being made obtained significantly larger tips at check time than if the orders were confirmed but not repeated (Van Baaren et al., 2003). While it could be argued that in this case one party in the mimicry dyad obtained gains at the expense of the other (i.e., higher server tips mean more spending for the patron), other research finds that mimicry can produce superior outcomes for both parties. In a negotiation context, Maddux, Mullen and Galinsky (2008) showed that individuals engaged in mimicking the other party managed to produce superior outcomes for themselves but also for the other party during negotiations compared with the identical scenario that lacked mimicry (i.e., the negotiated solution produced more value for the dyad and not all of it was appropriated by the mimicker).

This line of research is reminiscent of early psychological research on the unconscious effect that one's own bodily feedback can have on individual preferences and choices (see Wilson, 2002 on various perspectives addressing the related topic of embodied cognition). In a seminal study, Wells and Petty (1980) asked experimental participants to test headphone sets by listening to radio broadcasts while moving their heads horizontally or vertically. These head movements, automatically associated with disagreement and agreement responses, respectively, induced correspondingly less or more positive attitudes towards the editorial radio content, in the absence of any participant awareness of the effect (Wells & Petty, 1980).

Finally, another interesting context in which unconscious influences on behaviour emerge is that involving the use of behavioural intent questions. A significant body of work by Morwitz, Fitzsimons and colleagues (largely in a consumer research context) has documented the impact that exposing individuals to these types of questions has on their eventual related behaviour. This *mere measurement effect* was demonstrated by Morwitz, Johnson and Schmittlein (1993) through large field studies with personal computer and car buyers exposed to up to six waves of purchase intent surveys mailed to their homes over three years. Results suggested that asking consumers about their intent to buy was more likely to lead to purchase than not asking the respective intent question (although if this intent was low initially, repeated questions tended to produce less purchase – Morwitz et al., 1993; also see Chandon, Smith, Morwitz, Spangenberg, & Sprott, 2011). Subsequent work detailed these effects at the brand level: For example, it has been shown that product category novices award their post-measurement purchases to the dominant market brands, whereas non-novices tend to repurchase their initial brands upon the mere measurement of their purchase intent (Fitzsimons & Morwitz, 1996). In demonstrating that the underlying process for these effects is consumer recourse to the most accessible and positively valenced options, further work reinforced the automatic nature of the mere measurement effect (e.g., Fitzsimons & Williams, 2000; Morwitz & Fitzsimons, 2004). And in a closely related vein, Fitzsimons and Shiv (2001) proposed and demonstrated similar unconscious behavioural effects following the asking of hypothetical questions. For example, in one particular study individuals were either exposed to political marketing information according to which one candidate had either been convicted of fraud or asked how they would feel if that candidate were to be accused and convicted of fraud (Fitzsimons & Shiv, 2001). Compared with a control condition, both factual and hypothetical framings were equally damaging in significantly lowering the percentage of voters selecting the respective candidate (Fitzsimons & Shiv, 2001). This finding and its unconscious processing explanation are largely similar to the previously discussed brand rumour research by Dimofte and Yalch (2014): In both cases, irrelevant information of a negative nature cannot be suppressed once it is activated and becomes implicitly associated with the object of the rumoured or hypothetical story.

Future research directions in unconscious consumer cognition

The research reviewed here offers some exciting examples of the impact that the unconscious can have on people's perceptions of and responses to contextual stimuli, and these effects naturally and frequently occur in marketplace scenarios as well. The importance of understanding these effects stems from the downstream consequences they have the potential to produce, in a virtually stealth mode (i.e., in the absence of consumer awareness): For example, they may create biased product performance perceptions given the automatic shifts in evaluation standards that subjective scales induce (Dimofte & Johansson, 2009); they can lead to misplaced avoidance of relevant products in categories socially associated with unfavourable user stereotypes (Dimofte et al., 2015); they can prompt undesirable brand name associations from patently irrelevant contextual cues (Dimofte & Yalch, 2011); they may produce unplanned actions when others mimic one's behaviour (Van Baaren et al., 2003); and they can change one's behaviour by merely responding to a predictive or hypothetical question (Fitzsimons & Shiv, 2001; Morwitz & Fitzsimons, 2004). Yet at the same time these effects can produce favourable outcomes: They can push one towards reaching relevant goals (Fitzsimons et al., 2002); they allow self-regulatory processes during instances of emotion regulation (Williams et al., 2009); and they can be strategically used via unconscious behavioural mimicry to satisfy affiliation needs after social exclusion (Lakin et al., 2008) with clear consumer applications as described above. In general, it is encouraging that the amount of consumer research on the topic has been increasing at a relatively fast pace. Pinning down the processing mechanism behind these effects and understanding how they impact consumers and brands should produce an improved body of knowledge that leaves both consumers and companies better off.

To this end, there are several consumer research areas wherein the assessment of unconscious cognition effects deserves perhaps more careful scrutiny. One of these involves the *mere association effect* (Dimofte & Yalch, 2011) and its operation during advertising information processing. In these situations, the interplay of the ad copy elements themselves (visual or lexical) may produce ad hoc contextual cues that interact in ways that could be detrimental to the brands, if not carefully assessed. For example, a current campaign by McDonald's is banking on the brand's ubiquitous slogan ("I'm lovin' it") by repeatedly using the visual of a heart symbol while simultaneously featuring detailed depictions of its burger patties and fries. Unlike some McDonald's meals, it is very likely that this association is not a happy one: These foods prime implicit thoughts of grease, oil and cholesterol, which, when paired with the heart visual, will have negative connotations and will likely produce less favourable consumer response.

Research on unconscious brand attitude formation could also benefit, for example, from a more careful examination of the way related cultural knowledge gets accumulated and appropriated via one's implicit associations. To this end, it could be argued that high-equity brands are not simply those that are well positioned in the marketplace and have established strong customer relationships, but instead (or perhaps also) those that are adept at creating buzz, chatter and social conversation. Novel metrics for social media buzz are now available in the marketplace, and it would be interesting to assess the extent to which the frequent mentioning of a brand in these channels is sufficient to lead to consumer choice in the absence of consciously held positive attitudes towards the brand. Given the generally low involvement that consumers display when it comes to marketing information processing and the ever-growing importance of social affiliation (and, relatedly, conspicuous consumption), there is a distinct possibility that consumers acquire and display products and brands for which they have implicit preferences but little explicit understanding.

There is also a need for more consumer research on unconscious goal setting and goal pursuit. With the exception of Chartrand et al. (2008), not much work has been done in the area since the review by Fitzsimons et al. (2002). This context, as well as the behavioural mimicry topic, may benefit from a closer look at the buyer–seller marketplace dyad in a personal selling scenario in particular, which seems ripe with possibilities. For example, consumer interactions with salespeople could be addressed along the lines of Fitzsimons and Bargh (2003) as a particular type of relationship that activates specific goals for each party (i.e., perhaps avoidance-related for consumers and approach-related for salespeople). At the same time, extending the negotiations findings on unconscious behavioural mimicry (Maddux et al., 2008) would suggest that training salespeople in the art of body mimicry may in fact be conducive to better deals for both the company and the client.

Conclusions

In line with the review piece by Dijksterhuis, Smith, Van Baaren and Wigboldus (2005) on the unconscious consumer and the role that automatic processes play in the daily functioning of individuals in the marketplace, this chapter paints an optimistic picture of the relevance that the exciting topic of unconscious cognition has for the consumer research field. In briefly outlining several of the past, current and future relevant research topics, the focus here has admittedly been exclusively on findings that identify and explain these unconscious processes. However, it is not meant to suggest that conscious awareness does not enter into consumers' decision making, despite their generally low level of involvement with marketing and during consumption-related interactions (see Dijksterhuis & Smith, 2005; Simonson, 2005). In fact, it is likely the case that when marketplace decisions truly matter (i.e., they have significant financial implications), consumers become observant, careful processors whose perceptions are keen, attitudes are well defended, goals are pursued via meticulous implementation plans, and behaviours are rational and fully justifiable. However, the vast majority of consumer decisions are of relatively low importance (though not trivial, to be sure) and accordingly individuals' need to function as efficient information processors will render their usual scrutiny of contextual marketing cues less than rigorous. It is under these conditions that the unconscious effects discussed in this chapter have major importance.

References

Anderson, J. R. (1983). A spreading activation theory of memory. *Journal of Verbal Learning and Verbal Behaviour, 22*(3), 261–295.

Bagozzi, R. P., & Dholakia, U. (1999). Goal setting and goal striving in consumer behaviour. *Journal of Marketing, 63*, 19–32.

Bargh, J. A. (1990). Auto-motives: Preconscious determinants of social interaction. In E. T. Higgins & R. M. Sorrentino (Eds.), *Handbook of motivation and cognition: Foundations of social behaviour* (pp. 93–130). New York, NY: Guilford Press.

Bargh, J. A., & Ferguson, M. J. (2000). Beyond behaviourism: On the automaticity of higher mental processes. *Psychological Bulletin, 126*(6), 925–945.

Bargh, J. A., & Morsella, E. (2008). The unconscious mind. *Perspectives on Psychological Science, 3*(1), 73–79.

Bargh, J. A., Chen, M., & Burrows, L. (1996). Automaticity of social behaviour: Direct effects of trait construct and stereotype activation on action. *Journal of Personality and Social Psychology, 71*(2), 230–244.

Bargh, J. A., Gollwitzer, P. M., Lee-Chai, A., Barndollar, K., & Trötschel, R. (2001). The automated will: Nonconscious activation and pursuit of behavioural goals. *Journal of Personality and Social Psychology, 81*(6), 1014–1027.

Bertrand, M., & Mullainathan, S. (2004). Are Emily and Greg more employable than Lakisha and Jamal? *American Economic Review, 94*(4), 991–1013.

Bertrand, M., Chugh, D., & Mullainathan, S. (2005). Implicit discrimination. *American Economic Review, 95*(2), 9–98.

Biernat, M., Manis, M., & Nelson, T. E. (1991). Stereotypes and standards of judgment. *Journal of Personality and Social Psychology, 60*(4), 485–499.

Chandon, P., Smith, R. J., Morwitz, V. G., Spangenberg, E. R., & Sprott, D. E. (2011). When does the past repeat itself? The interplay of behaviour prediction and personal norms. *Journal of Consumer Research, 38*(3), 420–430.

Chartrand, T. L. (2005). The role of conscious awareness in consumer behaviour. *Journal of Consumer Psychology, 15*(3), 203–210.

Chartrand, T. L., Huber, J., Shiv, B., & Tanner, R. J. (2008). Nonconscious goals and consumer choice. *Journal of Consumer Research, 35*(2), 189–201.

Chen, M., & Bargh, J. A. (1999). Consequences of automatic evaluation: Immediate behavioural predispositions to approach or avoid the stimulus. *Personality and Social Psychology Bulletin, 25*(2), 215–224.

Davis, D. F., & Herr, P. M. (2014). From bye to buy: Homophones as a phonological route to priming. *Journal of Consumer Research, 40*(6), 1063–1077.

Dijksterhuis, A., & Smith, P. K. (2005). What do we do unconsciously? And how? *Journal of Consumer Psychology, 15*(3), 225–229.

Dijksterhuis, A., Smith, P. K., Van Baaren, R. B., & Wigboldus, D. H. (2005). The unconscious consumer: Effects of environment on consumer behaviour. *Journal of Consumer Psychology, 15*(3), 193–202.

Dimofte, C. V. (2010). Implicit measures of consumer cognition: A review. *Psychology & Marketing, 27*(10), 921–937.

Dimofte, C. V., & Johansson, J. K. (2009). Scale-dependent automatic shifts in brand evaluation standards. *Journal of Consumer Psychology, 19*(2), 158–170.

Dimofte, C. V., & Yalch, R. F. (2007a). Consumer response to polysemous brand slogans. *Journal of Consumer Research, 33*(4), 515–522.

Dimofte, C. V., & Yalch, R. F. (2007b). The SMAART Scale: A measure of individuals' automatic access to secondary meanings in polysemous statements. *Journal of Consumer Psychology, 17*(1), 49–58.

Dimofte, C. V., & Yalch, R. F. (2011). The mere association effect and brand evaluations. *Journal of Consumer Psychology, 21*(1), 24–37.

Dimofte, C. V., & Yalch, R. F. (2014). *Developing effective counter messages to negative brand rumors* (Unpublished manuscript). San Diego State University, San Diego CA.

Dimofte, C. V., Goodstein, R. C., & Brumbaugh, A. M. (2015). A social identity perspective on aspirational advertising: Implicit threats to self-esteem and strategies to overcome them. *Journal of Consumer Psychology, 3*(25), 416–430.

Dimofte, C. V., Johansson, J. K., & Ronkainen, I. A. (2008). Cognitive and affective reactions of U.S. consumers to global brands. *Journal of International Marketing, 16*(4), 113–135.

Ferraro, R., Bettman, J. R., & Chartrand, T. L. (2009). The power of strangers: The effect of incidental consumer brand encounters on brand choice. *Journal of Consumer Research, 35*(5), 729–741.

Fitzsimons, G. J., Hutchinson, J. W., Williams, P., Alba, J. W., Chartrand, T. L., Huber, J., & Tavassoli, N. T. (2002). Non-conscious influences on consumer choice. *Marketing Letters, 13*(3), 269–279.

Fitzsimons, G. J., & Morwitz, V. G. (1996). The effect of measuring intent on brand-level purchase behaviour. *Journal of Consumer Research, 23*(1), 1–11.

Fitzsimons, G. J., & Shiv, B. (2001). Nonconscious and contaminative effects of hypothetical questions on decision making. *Journal of Consumer Research, 28*(2), 224–238.

Fitzsimons, G. J., & Williams, P. (2000). Asking questions can change choice behaviour: Does it do so automatically or effortfully? *Journal of Experimental Psychology: Applied, 6*(3), 195–206.

Fitzsimons, G. M., & Bargh, J. A. (2003). Thinking of you: Nonconscious pursuit of interpersonal goals associated with relationship partners. *Journal of Personality and Social Psychology, 84*(1), 148–164.

Forehand, M. R., & Perkins, A. (2005). Implicit assimilation and explicit contrast: A set/reset model of response to celebrity voice-overs. *Journal of Consumer Research, 32*(3), 435–441.

Friese, M., Hofmann, W., & Wänke, M. (2008). When impulses take over: Moderated predictive validity of explicit and implicit attitude measures in predicting food choice and consumption behaviour. *British Journal of Social Psychology, 47*(3), 397–419.

Gibson, B. (2008). Can evaluative conditioning change attitudes toward mature brands? New evidence from the Implicit Association Test. *Journal of Consumer Research, 35*(1), 178–188.

Gilbert, D. T., Krull, D. S., & Malone, P. S. (1990). Unbelieving the unbelievable: Some problems in the rejection of false information. *Journal of Personality and Social Psychology, 59*(4), 601–613.

Gilbert, D. T., Tafarodi, R. W., & Malone, P. S. (1993). You can't not believe everything you read. *Journal of Personality and Social Psychology, 65*(2), 221–233.

Gollwitzer, P. M., & Bargh, J. A. (2005). Automaticity in goal pursuit. In A. J. Elliot & C. S. Dweck (Eds.), *Handbook of competence and motivation* (pp. 624–646). New York, NY: Guilford Press.

Greenwald, A. G., & Banaji, M. R. (1995). Implicit social cognition: Attitudes, self-esteem, and stereotypes. *Psychological Review, 102*(1), 4–27.

Greenwald, A. G., & Leavitt, C. (1984). Audience involvement in advertising: Four levels. *Journal of Consumer Research, 11*(1), 581–592.

Greenwald, A. G., McGhee, D. E., & Schwartz, J. L. (1998). Measuring individual differences in implicit cognition: The implicit association test. *Journal of Personality and Social Psychology, 74*(6), 1464–1480.

Greenwald, A. G., Poehlman, T. A., Uhlmann, E. L., & Banaji, M. R. (2009). Understanding and using the Implicit Association Test: III. Meta-analysis of predictive validity. *Journal of Personality and Social Psychology, 97*(1), 17–41.

Greenwald, A. G., Smith, C. T., Sriram, N., Bar-Anan, Y., & Nosek, B. A. (2009). Implicit race attitudes predicted vote in the 2008 U.S. presidential election. *Analyses of Social Issues and Public Policy, 9*(1), 241–253.

Janiszewski, C. (1988). Preconscious processing effects: The independence of attitude formation and conscious thought. *Journal of Consumer Research, 15*(2), 199–209.

Janiszewski, C. (1993). Preattentive mere exposure effects. *Journal of Consumer Research, 20*(3), 376–392.

Johnston, L. (2002). Behavioural mimicry and stigmatization. *Social Cognition, 20*(1), 18–35.

Karremans, J. C., Stroebe, W., & Claus, J. (2006). Beyond Vicary's fantasies: The impact of subliminal priming and brand choice. *Journal of Experimental Social Psychology, 42*(6), 792–798.

Kihlstrom, J. F. (1999). The psychological unconscious. *Handbook of personality: Theory and Research, 2*, 424–442.

Kunst-Wilson, W. R., & Zajonc, R. B. (1980). Affective discrimination of stimuli that cannot be recognized. *Science, 207*(4430), 557–558.

Lakin, J. L., Chartrand, T. L., & Arkin, R. M. (2008). I am too just like you: Nonconscious mimicry as an automatic behavioural response to social exclusion. *Psychological Science, 19*(8), 816–822.

Lamme, V. A. (2003). Why visual attention and awareness are different. *Trends in Cognitive Sciences, 7*(1), 12–18.

Lancaster, K. J. (1966). A new approach to consumer theory. *The journal of political economy, 74*(2), 132–157.

Lavidge, R. J., & Steiner, G. A. (1961). A model for predictive measurements of advertising effectiveness. *Journal of Marketing, 25*(1), 59–62.

Maddux, W. W., Mullen, E., & Galinsky, A. D. (2008). Chameleons bake bigger pies and take bigger pieces: Strategic behavioural mimicry facilitates negotiation outcomes. *Journal of Experimental Social Psychology, 44*(2), 461–468.

Maison, D., Greenwald, A. G., & Bruin, R. H. (2004). Predictive validity of the Implicit Association Test in studies of brands, consumer attitudes, and behaviour. *Journal of Consumer Psychology, 14*(4), 405–415.

Merikle, P. M., & Joordens, S. (1997). Parallels between perception without attention and perception without awareness. *Consciousness and Cognition, 6*(2), 219–236.

Morwitz, V. G., & Fitzsimons, G. J. (2004). The mere-measurement effect: Why does measuring intentions change actual behaviour? *Journal of Consumer Psychology, 14*(1), 64–74.

Morwitz, V. G., Johnson, E., & Schmittlein, D. (1993). Does measuring intent change behaviour? *Journal of Consumer Research, 20*(1), 46–61.

Nosek, B. A., Banaji, M., & Greenwald, A. G. (2002). Harvesting implicit group attitudes and beliefs from a demonstration web site. *Group Dynamics: Theory, Research, and Practice, 6*(1), 101–115.

Nosek, B. A., & Hansen, J. J. (2008). The associations in our heads belong to us: Searching for attitudes and knowledge in implicit evaluation. *Cognition & Emotion, 22*(4), 553–594.

Oettingen, G., Grant, H., Smith, P. K., Skinner, M., & Gollwitzer, P. M. (2006). Nonconscious goal pursuit: Acting in an explanatory vacuum. *Journal of Experimental Social Psychology, 42*(5), 668–675.

Olson, M. A., & Fazio, R. H. (2001). Implicit attitude formation through classical conditioning. *Psychological Science, 12*(5), 413–417.

Olson, M. A., & Fazio, R. H. (2004). Reducing the influence of extrapersonal associations on the Implicit Association Test: Personalizing the IAT. *Journal of Personality and Social Psychology, 86*(5), 653–667.

Ozubko, J., & Fugelsang, J. 2011. Remembering makes evidence compelling: Retrieval from memory can give rise to the illusion of truth. *Journal of Experimental Psychology: Learning, Memory, and Cognition, 37*(1), 270–276.

Packard, V. (1957). *The hidden persuaders*. New York, NY: David McKay Company.

Perugini, M. (2005). Predictive models of implicit and explicit attitudes. *British Journal of Social Psychology, 44*(1), 29–45.

Pratkanis, A. R., & Greenwald, A. G. (1988). Recent perspectives on unconscious processing: Still no marketing applications. *Psychology & Marketing, 5*(4), 337–353.

Priluck, R., & Till, B. D. (2010). Comparing a customer-based brand equity scale with the Implicit Association Test in examining consumer responses to brands. *Journal of Brand Management, 17*(6), 413–428.

Schneider, W., & Shiffrin, R. M. (1977). Controlled and automatic human information processing: I – Detection, search, and attention. *Psychological Review, 84*(1), 1–66.

Segrest Purkiss, S. L., Perrewé, P. L., Gillespie, T. L., Mayes, B. T., & Ferris, G. R. (2006). Implicit sources of bias in employment interview judgments and decisions. *Organizational Behaviour and Human Decision Processes, 101*(2), 152–167.

Shapiro, S. (1999). When an ad's influence is beyond our conscious control: Perceptual and conceptual fluency effects caused by incidental ad exposure. *Journal of Consumer Research, 26*(1), 16–36.

Shapiro, S., MacInnis, D. J., & Heckler, S. E. (1997). The effects of incidental ad exposure on the formation of consideration sets. *Journal of Consumer Research, 24*(1), 94–104.

Simonson, I. (2005). In defense of consciousness: The role of conscious and unconscious inputs in consumer choice. *Journal of Consumer Psychology, 15*(3), 211–217.

Sweldens, S., Corneille, O., & Yzerbyt, V. (2014). The role of awareness in attitude formation through evaluative conditioning. *Personality and Social Psychology Review, 18*(2), 187–209.

Tanner, R. J., Ferraro, R., Chartrand, T. L., Bettman, J. R., & Van Baaren, R. (2008). Of chameleons and consumption: The impact of mimicry on choice and preferences. *Journal of Consumer Research, 34*(6), 754–766.

Theus, K. T. (1994). Subliminal advertising and the psychology of processing unconscious stimuli: A review of research. *Psychology & Marketing, 11*(3), 271–290.

Tusche, A., Bode, S., & Haynes, J. D. (2010). Neural responses to unattended products predict later consumer choices. *Journal of Neuroscience, 30*(23), 8024–8031.

Tybout, A. M., Calder, B. J., & Sternthal, B. (1981). Using information processing theory to design marketing strategies. *Journal of Marketing Research, 23*(1), 73–79.

Van Baaren, R. B., Holland, R. W., Steenaert, B., & van Knippenberg, A. (2003). Mimicry for money: Behavioural consequences of imitation. *Journal of Experimental Social Psychology, 39*(4), 393–398.

Vantomme, D. (2004). *Implicit attitudes toward green consumer behaviour* (Doctoral dissertation). Ghent: Ghent University.

Wells, G. L., & Petty, R. E. (1980). The effects of overt head movements on persuasion: Compatibility and incompatibility of responses. *Basic and Applied Social Psychology, 1*(3), 219–230.

Williams, L. W., Nocera, C. C., Gray, J. R., & Bargh, J. A. (2009). The unconscious regulation of emotion: Nonconscious reappraisal goals modulate emotional reactivity. *Emotion, 9*(6), 847–854.

Wilson, M. (2002). Six views of embodied cognition. *Psychonomic Bulletin & Review, 9*(4), 625–636.

Wilson, W. R. (1979). Feeling more than we can know: Exposure effects without learning. *Journal of Personality and Social Psychology, 37*(6), 811–821.

Yoo, C. Y. (2008). Unconscious processing of Web advertising: Effects on implicit memory, attitude toward the brand, and consideration set. *Journal of Interactive Marketing, 22*(2), 2–18.

Zajonc, R. B. (1968). Attitudinal effects of mere exposure. *Journal of Personality and Social Psychology, 9*(2p2), 1–27.

8

Capturing the consumer's unconscious

Applying the implicit association test in consumer research

Dominika Maison and Aiden Gregg

Lauren is taking part in a study on "consumer preferences". On the surface, the study seems straightforward. Lauren is given 12 different pairs of teas to smell. Each time, she must say which tea she prefers. A few times, Lauren is given back the tea she said she preferred. After smelling it once again, she is then asked to explain why she preferred it. The experimenter, Sam, makes a note of which tea Lauren picks on each trial, and the reasons she gives for preferring some over others.

It looks like a typical blind test in marketing research. However, all is not as it seems. Sam – the person conducting the study – is not merely a market researcher but a consumer psychologist. On some trials where she invites Lauren to provide reasons for her preference, Sam engages in a sneaky switcheroo. Instead of giving Lauren back the tea she said she preferred, she gives her back the *other* tea.

One might think that, when this happened, Lauren would notice that something is amiss, and register an objection. However – like the majority of people on the majority of such trials – she does not (Hall, Johansson, Tärning, Sikström, & Deutgen, 2010). Despite having just smelled two teas, and having just picked the one she preferred, she blithely accepts the tea returned to her. What is more, Lauren goes on to provide, without batting an eyelid, reasons for picking the tea she did not actually prefer – reasons that cannot be valid. In so doing, Lauren exhibits the recently established phenomenon of *choice blindness* (Johansson, Hall, Sikström, & Olsson, 2005).

For researchers interested in what makes consumers tick – who frequently rely on self-reports of existing preferences, as well as reasons for these preferences – the phenomenon of choice blindness has troubling implications. It serves as an empirical warning that people might not really know their own minds – even when it comes to the simplest of stimuli, such as the scents of alternative teas, which they were only a moment ago fully aware of. People seem to have difficulty knowing both *what* they prefer and *why* they prefer it. In choice blindness studies, participants frequently confuse what they do prefer with what they do not; and they then conveniently come up with false rationalizations for why they prefer what they do not. The phenomenon of choice blindness shows that self-reporting is not always a valid source of knowledge about consumers.

Even though most consumers think they know *why* they like the products and brands they choose, very often they do not. Despite being intimately familiar with the contents of their consciousness, people do not automatically qualify as experts on the *origins* of those contents, any more than patients, despite being intimately familiar with the symptoms of their physical disease, automatically become authorities on its pathogenesis (Nisbett & Wilson, 1977; Pronin, 2009). In other words, people are often *not consciously aware* of the real reasons why they think and feel as they do. They do not even realize that they are limited in this regard; therefore they dutifully produce on demand credible accounts of the origin of their thoughts and feelings.

Consumers have limited access to their inner processes, and this presents a challenge for practitioners who want to know, for example, the impact of branding on consumer product choice (Blackston, 1993). In many cases, consumers have fully conscious and easily verbalized thoughts and feelings about features of the product itself (e.g., in the case of cars, the spaciousness of the interior, or the power of the engine), as well as explicit associations with brand image (e.g., Volvo = safety; Jaguar = prestige; Land Rover = adventure; Fiat = family). These will obviously shape their product choices. Alongside these conscious thoughts and feelings, however, consumers may harbour unconscious or hard-to-articulate thoughts and feelings about the product and brand, which may also subtly shape their product choices (Hansen & Christensen, 2007). Accordingly, producers may sometimes wonder why, in spite of the superiority that one product has over another, and in spite of the fact that consumers say it has the features they prefer, those consumers will sometimes choose an objectively inferior product that seems to be less suited to them. Unconscious attitudes towards the brand or product are often responsible for this (Cohen & Areni, 1991; Zaltman, 2003).

Perhaps the most remarkable examples of the role of unconscious consumer processes are to be found in the polished but questionable reasons consumers give to explain their choice or rejection of a product (e.g., why did they purchase one branded product over an alternative, or over an unbranded product?). Answers typically fulfil the consumer's positive self-image as a rational person, and cite functional or utilitarian explanations when instructed to do so (e.g., "because it is the best product", "because it has the right technical parameters"). However, their choice or rejection of a product may be the result of positive or negative associations with the brand that they may not easily bring to mind and describe verbally (Maison, 2014; Zaltman & Zaltman, 2008).

What follows is an example of how an unconscious attitude shaped consumer behaviour, despite initially being masked by false self-reporting. It has to do with the launch of the first cake mix powders in the United States in the 1950s (Morgan, 1998). At first, this product sold very poorly, despite having the objectively desirable feature that it made cakes more convenient to make. During marketing research, the consumers, mainly housewives, explicitly noted the product's advantages (it made cake preparation faster and simpler), but they also pointed out its fatal disadvantage: the "artificial" taste that it imparted to the cakes made from it, which made them disinclined to purchase it. However, when housewives tasted alternative cakes without knowing whether they had been made from the powder mix (i.e., in a blind test), they could not correctly identify them. This surprising finding suggested that the consumers' aversion to the product derived from other sources (albeit unconscious and non-verbalized). Qualitative projection techniques revealed the real reasons for rejecting the products (Branthwaite & Lunn, 1985; Zaltman, 2003). The housewives were reluctant to adopt cake mix for an entirely different reason: their unacknowledged belief that making something as special as a cake for their family required more, rather than less, effort. Accordingly, the "artificial taste" explanation for not buying cake mix turned out to be a post hoc rationalization for their overall negative (and to some extent unconscious) attitude towards the product.

So, let us summarize the situation, psychologically speaking. First, consumers had a conscious belief about the product that was correct ("cake mix powder makes baking easier"). Second, they had a conscious belief about the product that was incorrect ("cake mix powder imparts an artificial flavour"). And third, they had an unconscious belief about the product that was the real reason for their reluctance to buy ("when I bake using a cake mix, I am a bad housewife").

Unconscious consumer processes: Proofs from psychological research

Nowadays not many consumer researchers, whether scientists or practitioners, doubt that many consumer processes are unconscious (Neale & Kyle, 2011). However, for a very long time, consumer choices were explained in terms of overt factors relating to economics or the market, such as income or demographics on the part of the consumer, or features and price on the part of the product (Modigliani & Brumberg, 1954). This approach assumed that consumers make rational and conscious decisions. It implied two things. First, consumers with fewer financial resources would buy cheaper products, whereas those with greater financial resources would purchase ones that are more expensive. Second, products of objectively higher quality would sell better than those of objectively lower quality. Nowadays, however, there is no question that many key consumer choices are made without a conscious and careful analysis of product information. Rather, they are often made unconsciously and automatically (Allen, Fournier, & Miller, 2008; Vargas, 2008).

Research in psychology over the past 20 years has yielded many proofs of the existence and importance of unconscious mental processes (Bargh, 2002; Greenwald & Banaji, 1995; Zajonc, 1980). For example, the human mind can receive and process stimuli that do not register on a conscious level (Zajonc, 2001). Murphy and Zajonc (1993) showed that affective primes (e.g., faces expressing positive or negative emotion) presented so briefly as to be subliminal (≈ 4 ms) can nonetheless influence the evaluation of targets that follow immediately afterwards (e.g., "meaningless" Chinese ideograms) in a valence-consistent direction. The brevity of the presentation, and the virtual synchrony of the prime–target pairing, rules out the possibility that conscious visual perception is necessary for creating the effect. Similar influences on evaluations have been observed in the context of stimuli of which one is only peripherally or incidentally aware (Ohme, 2001). For example, people with bigger pupils are perceived to be more attractive than those with smaller ones, although the perceivers are not able to single out this feature of the face as being the reason why (Niedenthal & Showers, 1991). Neuropsychological studies provide strong support for the theory that conscious and unconscious processes are realized in independent substrates of the brain (so-called "high road" vs. "low-road", mediated by the amygdala) and that affective reactions to stimuli might occur prior to cognitive processing and via separate neural pathways (LeDoux, 1998).

Other studies show that non-conscious priming (whether subliminal or peripheral) can activate goals and facilitate goal pursuit, all in the absence of conscious awareness (Bargh, Gollwitzer, Lee-Chai, Barndollar, & Trötschel, 2001; Dijksterhuis & Aarts, 2010). Most pertinently, Winkielman, Berridge and Wilbarger (2005) showed that subliminally presented emotional expressions could influence people's actual consumption behaviour. Happy expressions, relative to angry expressions, caused participants to pour more into their own cups, and to drink more of what they poured. Importantly, participants reported no conscious awareness of any change in their subjective state (i.e., feeling more pleasant or aroused) after having been shown happy versus angry expressions subliminally. This shows that affective states inaccessible to the conscious mind can drive consumption.

Another set of evidence about unconscious human processes came from studies on attitudes. Weak correlations between different attitudinal components (cognitive, affective and behavioural; see Kraus, 1995) prompted psychologists to revise their traditional way of understanding this concept. They subsequently introduced new concepts to describe attitudes, such as "dual attitudes" (Chaiken & Trope, 1999) and "implicit attitudes" (Greenwald & Banaji, 1995), which captured this unconscious element. The dual attitudes approach assumed that the same person can at the same time have two different attitudes towards an object, a conscious one and an unconscious one, which might not be correlated (Chaiken & Trope, 1999). Implicit attitude, in contrast to explicit attitude, was defined as the "introspectively unidentified (or inaccurately identified) traces of past experience" that can influence reactions, even if the experience is no longer remembered (Greenwald & Banaji, 1995). Psychologists have since tended to adopt the technical term "implicit" in preference to the more everyday term "unconscious" in order to designate phenomena beyond the reach of normal consciousness.

Social psychologists have therefore sought reliable and valid ways of assessing this unconscious realm. How have they gone about it? Well, a fundamental feature of all *direct measures*, which involve self-reports that can be either open-ended or close-ended, is that they require respondents to *declare*, with the help of symbols (language, numbers, scales), what they think or feel. However, by definition, what is "introspectively unidentified" cannot be captured by such declarations, for they only reflect what is *explicit* in the mind of the respondent. Hence, social psychologists have developed *indirect measures* that instead rely on *non-declarative* features of people's responses. The handiest non-declarative feature to capitalize upon turned out to be *reaction time* (RT; Fazio, 1990; Jensen, 2006). This is an entirely objective and, with the advent of widespread computer technology, precisely quantifiable feature of all responses to all stimuli. Ultimately, two classes of indirect measure based on RT have emerged. These might be labelled *adjunctive* and *standalone* instruments (Gregg & Klymowsky, 2013).

While adjunctive RT instruments still have respondents answer questions, albeit often of a simplified sort, the *speed* with which they answer those questions is now treated as an additional property of the response (Bassili, 1996; Mayerl, 2013). In general, faster RTs indicate, for the response to which they are attached, greater psychological relevance (Markus, 1977), attitude strength (Fazio, 2001) or truthfulness (Walczyk, Mahoney, Doverspike, & Griffith-Ross, 2009) – all of which promise to enhance attitude–behaviour consistency. Fazio and Williams (1986) notably found that the speed with which respondents answered questions in a telephone survey about political candidates predicted whether they voted in accordance with the answers they gave. Similarly, higher levels of attitude–behaviour consistency are observed for consumer products that are more rapidly evaluated (Kokkinaki & Lunt, 1997).

In contrast, standalone RT instruments feature specialized tasks for which faster or slower RTs take on an instrument-specific meaning (Nosek, Hawkins, & Frazier, 2011; Wittenbrink & Schwarz, 2007). There are different examples of such methods based on standalone RT, for example the Extrinsic Affective Simon Task (EAST; DeHouwer, 2003), the Implicit Relational Assessment Procedure (IRAP; Barnes-Holmes, Barnes-Holmes, Stewart, & Boles, 2010), as well as various lexical decision tasks in which primes and targets are sequentially presented (Klauer & Musch, 2003; Wittenbrink, Judd, & Park, 1997). In all cases, the goal is to detect the presence and quantify the strength of semantic or evaluative associations between objects and attributes. Here, we focus on one standalone RT instrument, which is probably the best known, the Implicit Association Test (IAT; Greenwald, McGhee, & Schwartz, 1998; Nosek, Greenwald, & Banaji, 2007), and its application in consumer psychology.

An outline of the IAT

Early IAT research focused on characterizing subtle racial prejudice (Greenwald et al., 1998), gender stereotypes (Rudman, Greenwald, & McGhee, 2001) and self-esteem (Greenwald & Farnham, 2000). Since then, however, IAT research has diversified substantially (Nosek et al., 2007). Nowadays, the IAT is also used as a method to research consumer attitudes, both in an academic research context and in a practical context (Gregg & Klymowsky, 2013; Maison, Bruin, & Greenwald, 2001; Perkins, Forehand, Greenwald, & Maison, 2008).

Consider an IAT designed to assess implicit consumer attitudes towards two well-known global brands, such as Coke and Pepsi, or more precisely, people's *implicit preferences* for one of these brands versus the other. Respondents sort words or pictures into one of four possible categories by pressing either of two computer keys on the left or right of the keyboard. Two categories, represented by labels also on different sides of the screen, pertain to the *target* brands, such as Coke and Pepsi. Two other categories, likewise positioned, pertain to the brand *attributes*, such as Positive and Negative. The items sorted are themselves either pictures (e.g., of Coke and Pepsi products) or words (e.g., generic adjectives of contrasting valence, such as *great* and *awful*), with at least three items per category. Ultimately, the IAT assesses whether and to what extent the bipolar dimensions respectively implied by the target and attribute categories map on to one another, either as [*Coke* ↔ *Pepsi* ≡ *Positive* ↔ *Negative*] or as [*Coke* ↔ *Pepsi* ≡ *Negative* ↔ *Positive*]. This cashes out as an overall implicit preference for one of the two target brands of a particular strength (i.e., Coke being more liked and less disliked than Pepsi, or vice versa, to some degree).

The IAT as standard comprises five blocks: three practice and two critical. In the practice blocks (which may be sacrificed for the sake of brevity), items are classified into only two categories, either target (Coke, Pepsi), or attribute (Positive, Negative; Negative, Positive). In both critical blocks, all four categories appear, with their labels configured differently. In one critical block, respondents sort Coke and Positive items with one key and Pepsi and Negative items with the other; in the other critical block, they sort Coke and Negative items with one key and Pepsi and Positive items with the other. Respondents then frequently sort more quickly under one configuration than under the other. The block they sort more quickly is called *compatible*; the block they sort more slowly, *incompatible*. A difference in average RT between the blocks (or some derivative algorithm controlling for idiosyncratic difference in response speed; Greenwald, Nosek, & Banaji, 2003) reflects the difference in compatibility between the blocks, and accordingly, in the direction and magnitude of the implicit preference for Coke over Pepsi, or vice versa.

One common misunderstanding should immediately be pre-empted. The IAT is designed to assess implicit associations *between pairs of categories*; it is *not* designed to assess implicit associations *towards the individual items* sorted. Some research finds that item content does not moderate IAT effects (De Houwer, 2001), and other research that it does (Govan & Williams, 2004), but any impact is likely due to the items shaping interpretation of the categories. It is ultimately the different configuration of the categories, in the compatible and incompatible blocks, that determines the ease or difficulty of sorting all items, not the isolated characteristics of the items themselves. All items should be duly representative of their categories, so that there is no ambiguity about which one they belong to.

Although IAT is limited in the above respect, it still exhibits some versatility in terms of what it can assess. In particular, the IAT can detect more than just implicit preferences – which involve evaluative associations. It can also detect implicit *beliefs* – which involve *semantic* associations (e.g., Gattol, Sääksjärvi, & Carbon, 2011). For example, an IAT designed to assess the implicitly perceived "youthfulness" versus "oldness" of Coke and Pepsi would test the relative compatibility of the mappings [*Coke* ↔ *Pepsi* ≡ *Old* ↔ *New*] and [*Coke* ↔ *Pepsi* ≡ *New* ↔ *Old*]. This enables researchers to fill out the picture of how products and brands might be unconsciously construed. Moreover, given that liking is not quite the same as wanting (Tindell, Smith, Berridge, & Aldridge, 2009), IATs can also be engineered to tap into implicit *inclinations*, using stimuli that evoke ideas of attraction and repulsion (Palfai & Ostafin, 2003). For example, an IAT designed to assess implicit motivations to opt for Coke versus Pepsi would test the relative compatibility of the mappings [*Coke* ↔ *Pepsi* ≡ *Approach* ↔ *Avoid*] and [*Coke* ↔ *Pepsi* ≡ *Avoid* ↔ *Approach*].

The top half of Figure 8.1 illustrates the layout of its two critical blocks. The bottom half of Figure 8.1 illustrates the stimuli that can be used to assess implicit preferences, beliefs and inclinations.

In a moment, research bearing on the reliability, validity and utility of the IAT in consumer psychology will be discussed. However, in order to evaluate that research properly, it helps to

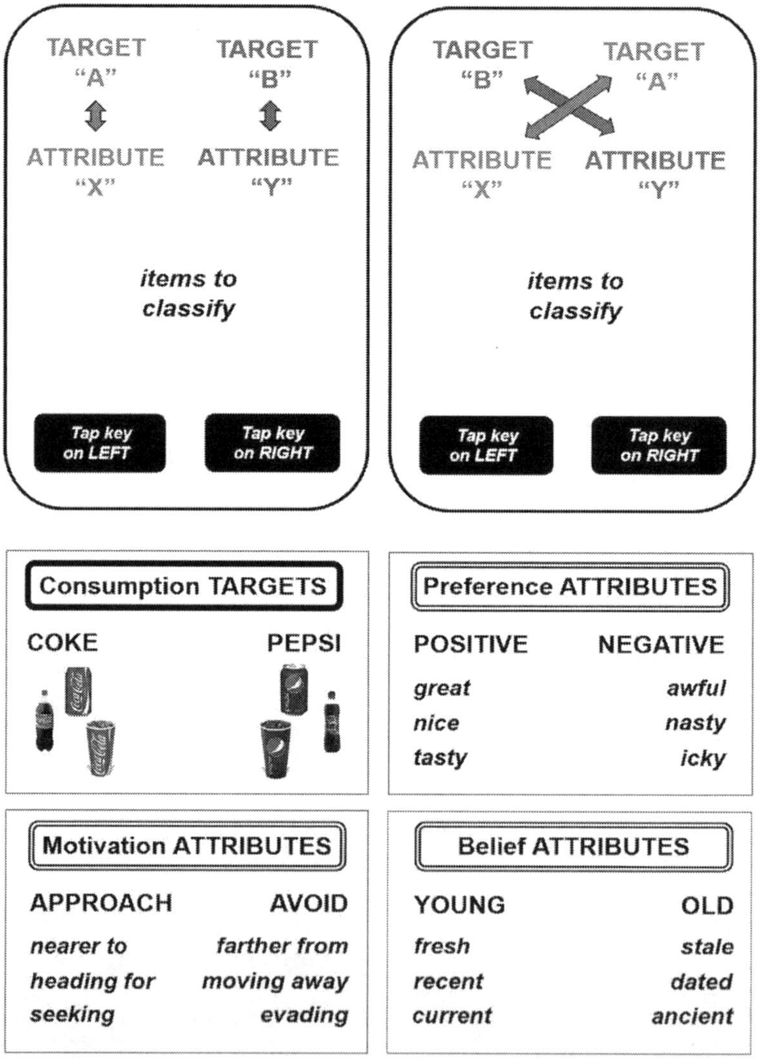

Figure 8.1 IAT layout and stimuli.

understand how implicit and explicit cognition might, in principle or in practice, relate to the direct and indirect measures designed to assess them. That is, to get to grips with the unconscious mind and its assessment with indirect instruments (compared with the conscious mind and its assessment with self-report instruments), a general map of the terrain is needed.

Mapping the conscious and unconscious mind

For several reasons, mapping the unconscious mind is a challenge. For one thing, the subject matter itself is far from simple. What defines the explicit–implicit distinction? How, precisely, does this distinction apply to content versus processes, to phenomena versus causes, and to constructs versus measurements? (For many useful and technical clarifications here, see De Houwer, Teige-Mocigemba, Spruyt, & Moors, 2009; Gawronski, Hofmann, & Wilbur, 2006.) Making matters more confusing, the relevant research literature exhibits a profusion of technical terms with similar but not quite identical meanings. One makeshift remedy is to characterize the explicit–implicit distinction as broadly as possible. So, for present purposes, "explicit" can be taken as encompassing those foreground features of the mind that are relatively *conscious, slow, deliberate, controlled, intentional, propositional* or *reflective*. In contrast, "implicit" can be taken as encompassing those background features of the mind that are relatively *unconscious, fast, spontaneous, automatic, unintended, associative* or *impulsive* (Bargh & Morsella, 2008; Chaiken & Trope, 1999; Gawronski & Bodenhausen, 2006; Greenwald & Banaji, 1995; Gregg & Klymowsky, 2013; Kahneman, 2011; Searle, 1992; Strack & Deutsch, 2004).

What follows is a practical framework for understanding this explicit/implicit distinction with respect to direct/indirect assessment instruments. The framework will be demonstrated with the use of topological diagrams (see Figure 8.2, Diagrams A through O). This broad framework is also applicable to consumer cognition, where it sharpens appreciation of whether and to what extent indirect instruments such as the IAT (as well as "neuroscientific" techniques) might prove most or least informative, comparatively speaking.

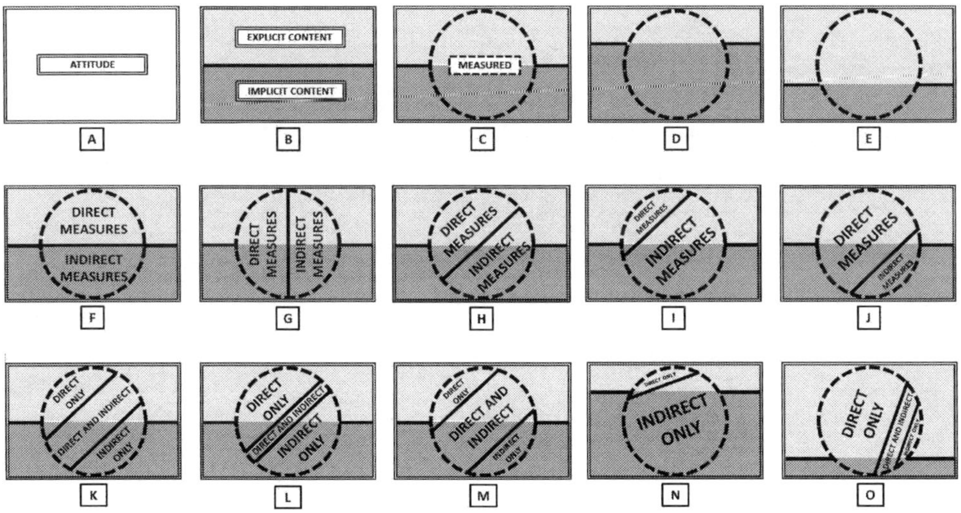

Figure 8.2 Measurement scenarios.

First, of course, there is the attitude to be assessed (represented by the rectangle in Diagram A). This comprises both explicit content and implicit content to some degree (the lighter and darker shaded areas in Diagram B, respectively). This categorical division already implies that the human mind is at least *partly opaque*. For, if it were instead *fully transparent*, the attitude would consist solely of explicit content (i.e., the entire rectangle would have a lighter shade). In that case, self-report, via introspective reflection, would in principle suffice to capture everything about an attitude.

However, the assessment of attitude content will always be partial, because the measuring instruments used, whether they assess explicit or implicit content, will always be imperfectly calibrated or methodologically confounded, resulting in at least some systematic or random measurement error. Accordingly, the totality of an attitude will never be assessed, only some subset of it (represented by the circular area in Diagram C).

Now, it could be that implicit content predominates (Diagram D). If so, then the human mind, either in general across cases, or specifically in some case, is mostly opaque (as the Freudians have long suggested, invoking an iceberg metaphor). Alternatively, explicit content could predominate (Diagram E). To the extent that the truth resembles Diagram D rather than Diagram E, however, there will be *more implicit consumer cognition to capture*, and indirect measures like the IAT will be potentially more useful. As previously mentioned (see also Dimofte, Chapter 7, this volume), there is ample evidence that implicit cognition plays a non-trivial role in human psychology. Accordingly, the darker shaded area should be substantial, although its exact extent may be hard to determine.

How might assessment instruments capture this attitude content? We must reaffirm the crucial distinction between the instruments doing the assessing and the content they seek to assess. The content is either explicit or implicit, in some relative proportion; and direct instruments such as self-report are designed to capture explicit content, whereas indirect instruments like the IAT are designed to capture implicit content. However, it would be wrong to identify explicit and implicit content with what such instruments are designed to assess; for what they happen to assess might not perfectly correspond to it. Whether and to what extent any correspondence exists is ultimately an empirical question. Hence it is sensible to characterize such assessment instruments, not in terms of their presumptive validity, but in terms of how they work. To reiterate: Direct measures seek to assess explicit content from what respondents openly declare, whereas indirect measures seek to assess implicit content from inferences based on non-declarative features of people's responses.

The various empirical possibilities are illustrated in additional diagrams. Diagram F represents the optimistic possibility that direct measures only ever capture explicit content, and indirect measures only ever capture implicit content. Accordingly, the diameter of the measurement circle is parallel to the dividing line between explicit and implicit cognition. Diagram G represents the pessimistic possibility that neither type of measure is better suited to measuring either type of content. Accordingly, the diameter of measurement circle is orthogonal to the dividing line. Diagram H represents the more realistic intermediate possibility. It features a diagonal diameter, indicating that direct measures are relatively more sensitive to explicit content, and indirect measures to implicit content. The degree of *differential sensitivity* – and the corresponding angle of the diagonal – will depend on the precise type of indirect measure used (De Houwer et al., 2009). All else being equal, the more the diagonal approaches the horizontal, the more suited indirect measures, like the IAT, will be to uniquely reflect the implicit aspects of consumer cognition (and direct measures, such as self-report, will be to its explicit aspects).

Naturally, there are predictive implications. To the extent that indirect and direct measures tap into distinct cognitive realms, and to the extent that these realms prompt distinct types of behaviour (e.g., impulsive versus reflective (Strack & Deutsch, 2004); spontaneous versus controlled (Fazio, 1990)), those measures could in principle predict those distinct types of behaviour. Part of the appeal of indirect measures like the IAT to consumer psychology is that consumption and purchasing decisions can often be emotionally rash (Vohs & Faber, 2004) or habitually thoughtless (Neal, Wood, Wu, & Kurlander, 2011), and the IAT may be better able to predict them.

Another mundane issue to consider is the *absolute sensitivity* of direct and indirect measures of attitudinal content. In Diagram I, indirect measures, covering a larger area of the measurement circle, are more absolutely sensitive, whereas in Diagram J, indirect measures are. Importantly, even if direct and indirect measures captured unique aspects of consumer cognition (i.e., had differential sensitivity), they would still need, in order to exhibit adequate predictive validity, to capture those aspects adequately well (have absolute sensitivity).

All diagrams so far have one drawback: They depict direct and indirect measures as capturing different types of content to different degrees, but never the *same* content. However, direct and indirect measures typically overlap in what they assess, with the extent of that overlap empirically reflected in the size of their correlation, something that varies markedly across domains (Nosek, 2007). Hence, an additional "intermediate" area must be added to the hatched circle, reflecting what is assessed by both direct and indirect measures (Diagram K). The overlap could be sometimes small (Diagram L) or sometimes large (Diagram M), but its extent matters in that it puts a ceiling on the *incremental predictive validity* that indirect measures like the IAT are capable of achieving, and by extension their unique diagnostic value in domains such as consumer psychology.

Now consider all the different dimensions simultaneously. What might represent the "best case" scenario and the "worst case" scenario in terms of what indirect measures such as the IAT have to offer? Consider attitudes towards products or brands of interest. In Diagram N, most attitude content is implicit (the darker shade predominates); indirect measures alone are well geared for assessing implicit content (the diagonal is nearly horizontal); indirect measures are relatively more sensitive overall (take up most of the circle); and indirect measures capture entirely distinct content (there is no intermediate area). Here, by assessing that implicit content with indirect measures – either independently or alongside assessing explicit content with direct measures – a consumer psychologist would be liable to gather much potentially predictive accurate information about attitudes towards a product or brand. In contrast, in Diagram O, most attitude content is explicit (the lighter shade predominates); direct measures are also quite well geared for assessing any implicit content (the diagonal is nearly vertical); indirect measures are less sensitive overall (take up little of the circle); and indirect measures capture hardly any distinct content (there is a large intermediate area). Accordingly, indirect measures would be liable to provide little in the way of added predictive value.

The diagrams illustrate the complexities of whether, to what extent, under what circumstances, and when indirect measures like the IAT might prove informative. Yet the diagrams still oversimplify the reality! First, the boundary between the explicit and implicit realms may not be neat and discrete; rather, one shades into the other. In this vein, some researchers (Winkielman & Schooler, 2011) have empirically established intermediate levels of conscious cognition, such that you can be vaguely aware of attitudinal content (*consciousness* – say, of liking a brand) without also knowing *that* you are aware of it and being able to articulate that knowledge (*meta-consciousness* – say, of what you like about it, and why). Regardless, the explicit–implicit continuum is fundamentally about the degree to which content is *known*, whether that content is evaluative, semantic or conative in character. Second, degrees of knowledge may vary, not only continuously, but along any of the *multiple subdimensions* mentioned earlier (e.g., conscious–unconscious, controlled–automatic), and not necessarily in lockstep.

For example, one might be aware of craving pizza (= consciousness), but unable to repress the thoughts that involuntarily come to mind (= control). In more than one way, the division between explicit and implicit cognition is not hard and fast. Nonetheless, the diagrams still offer a helpful graphical guide to represent the various possibilities that exist for how direct and indirect measures might map on to implicit and explicit cognition.

Given that the domain of interest here is consumer psychology, it is worth stating that respondents are usually more forthcoming when it comes to expressing what they are thinking compared with other areas of psychology, where topics may be of a more sensitive nature (Greenwald & Banaji, 1995). Accordingly, any defects in self-report are likely to be *largely or purely cognitive* in character (Wilson, 2002). Still, in cases where motivational bias does also undermine the validity of self-report (e.g., in response to questions about desiring or consuming illegal drugs), the impact will depend on underlying level of content knowledge. *Lying* (Vrij, 2008), an act of deliberately falsifying communicated content, requires that one be aware of the content lied about. In contrast, *self-deception* (Gregg & Mahadevan, 2014) requires one to be neither wholly aware, nor wholly unaware, of the content being denied: awareness should be sufficient to recognize the troubling nature of the content to be suppressed, but insufficient to recognize that content as the reason for suppressing it (Greenwald, 1997). Finally, *self-presentation bias* (Steenkamp, de Jong, & Baumgartner, 2010) is probably something in between: It falls short of outright lying, being a form of implicit social tuning, but also lacks the suppression of content seen in self-deception.

The ultimate question is whether and to what extent indirect measures of consumer attitudes, such as the IAT, can capture implicit content, and in ways that illuminate consumer psychology or predict consumer behaviour. In particular, how sensitive is the IAT to implicit content, both absolutely and relative to direct measures such as self-report? And to what extent is it capable of delivering unique predictive validity, by virtue of tapping into content that direct measures such as self-report miss?

Does the IAT capture implicit content relevant to consumer cognition and behaviour?

What precisely is it about the IAT that gears it towards assessing implicit content? In requiring participants to sort items *as quickly and accurately as they can*, and in being at least *somewhat obscure* about what it measures, it tends to reflect relatively automatic and unconscious cognition. But the automatic component is arguably primary: The differential ease with which compatible and incompatible blocks can be completed often becomes subjectively apparent to respondents, especially on repeated administration; but this only attests to how stubbornly the IAT resists attempts at conscious control. Experimental research on the fakeability of the IAT duly indicates that, although IAT effects can sometimes be intentionally modified to some degree (Czellar, 2006; Fiedler & Bluemke, 2005), this does not usually happen spontaneously, but only when respondents are permitted to practise (Röhner, Schröder-Abé, & Schütz, 2011) or issued with specific instructions (Kim, 2003). Accordingly, what the IAT assesses as an indirect measure is liable to be more implicit than explicit, at least relative to what self-report assesses as a direct measure. That is, there is a good a priori argument for differential sensitivity. Graphically, the diameters or chords of the hatched circles in Figure 8.2 should be substantially less than vertical. That said, they should not be quite horizontal either: The IAT does register the impact of recent pairings that have merely been consciously imagined (De Houwer, Beckers, & Moors, 2007), and self-report does register the impact of repeated unconscious presentations that have augmented familiarity (Bornstein & D'Agostino, 1992).

But how sensitive is the IAT as an attitude index in general compared with self-report? Its internal consistency – which would put a ceiling on its validity – works out at a respectable $\alpha = 0.79$, both generally (Hofmann, Gawronski, Gschwendner, Le, & Schmitt, 2005) and in consumer psychology studies (Gattol et al., 2011), which is comparatively high for indirect measures (Bar-Anan & Nosek, 2014), and comparable to many explicit measures (Anastasi, 1988). However, although the IAT sidesteps some of the biases that undermine the validity of self-report instruments, this does not insulate it against validity-undermining biases of its own (Fiedler, Messner, & Bluemke, 2006). Several have been alleged, including that the IAT assesses not privately held associations, but publicly acknowledged ones (Han, Czellar, Olson, & Fazio, 2010), and that the IAT reflects not underlying associations, but only superficial overlaps in category salience (Rothermund & Wentura, 2004). The relevant literatures are complex and contentious. However, two assertions can be made without undue controversy: (a) no confound wholly invalidates the IAT; and (b) remedial measures are available that attenuate their impact (for further discussion of IAT confounds, see Gregg & Klymowsky, 2013). Accordingly, although such confounds and issues may blunt the sensitivity of the IAT overall, they fall far short of eliminating its construct validity. Hence, the IAT has at least a reasonable degree of absolute sensitivity. Graphically, the "INDIRECT" area of the hatched circles in Figure 8.2 should be non-trivial in size.

The first positive sign of the IAT's distinctive validity – of its affording preferential access to a meaningful implicit realm – would be a *divergence* between the effects it yields and the effects yielded by self-report instruments. Such divergences are plentiful. Considering brands, Friese, Wänke and Plessner (2006) found that, although respondents showed no preference for branded versus unbranded products on self-report, the great majority showed a preference for branded products on the IAT. Similarly, Priluck and Till (2010) found that, although respondents showed preferences for high-equity versus low-equity brands on both the IAT and self-report, only the IAT showed preferences within high-equity brands (Coke versus Pepsi), or between brands lacking or possessing a sexual connotation (Kodak versus Trojan) – the latter possibly due to motivational distortions undermining self-report.

Such divergences also occur for brands, depending on their national or international reach. For example, one study (Perkins et al., 2008) found that Polish respondents, despite generally reporting an explicit preference for foreign brands (e.g., Marlboro cigarettes), nonetheless showed an implicit preference for domestic ones (e.g., Sobieski cigarettes). This finding suggests a type of consumer ethnocentrism, albeit only at an unconscious or automatic level. Interestingly, the study also found that actual experience with foreign cigarettes (which were of objectively superior quality at that time) reduced the size of this implicit ethnocentric preference. Dimofte, Johansson and Ronkainen (2008) found another type of divergence among US respondents: They showed an implicit preference for global brands, regardless of whether they self-reported having a "pro-global" or "anti-global" attitude towards brands in general. Although the findings from these studies conflict somewhat (i.e., in the Polish study the implicit preference was for local brands, whereas in the US study it was for global brands), direct and indirect measures gave different results in both cases.

Other mean-level divergences have been found. For example, young women showed preferences for low-calorie products on the IAT, despite providing more ambivalent self-reports (Maison, Greenwald, & Bruin, 2001). Another study found that respondents showed preferences for ads featuring White spokespersons on the IAT, while self-reporting no preference (Brunel, Tietje, & Greenwald, 2004). In addition, individual-level correlations between IAT scores and self-reports in the consumer domain, although positive as standard and hence indicative of convergent validity, still leave plenty of room for divergence. For example,

Maison et al. (2001) obtained values ranging between $r = 0.10$ to $r = 0.44$ across a primary IAT and various self-report measures, and Maison, Greenwald and Bruin (2004) obtained values between $r = 0.44$ and $r = 0.47$. Finally, divergences between self-reported and IAT-assessed preferences can be identified at source. Research on both social attitudes (Gregg, Seibt, & Banaji, 2006), and consumer brands (Ratliff, Swinkels, Klerx, & Nosek, 2012) finds that, although preferences can be induced at both explicit and implicit level, they subsequently resist change at an implicit level more than at an explicit level, suggesting that the IAT may serve as an index of residual brand loyalty. All such findings provide *empirical* evidence for the differential sensitivity of self-report and the IAT.

That IAT effects are not idle curiosities, and rise above any potential confounds, is attested to by their predictive validity, not only in classic IAT domains such as prejudice and discrimination (Greenwald, Poehlman, Uhlmann, & Banaji, 2009), but equally in the consumer psychology domain. For example, Maison et al. (2004) showed that the proof of the pudding was in the consumption – quite literally. In three studies, they identified users of one brand versus another (yogurts: Danone versus Bakoma; fast food: McDonald's versus Milk Bar; colas: Coke versus Pepsi), and showed that IAT-assessed preferences reflected actual behaviour. Moreover, they reflected behaviour above and beyond self-reports, with partial coefficients in the range of $r_p = 0.30$, which is crucial evidence for the independent values of indirect measures of implicit cognition in the consumer domain. One particularly noteworthy finding was that implicit preferences for Coke versus Pepsi predicted not only product usage, but also brand recognition in a blind taste test. That is, respondents who could tell one cola from the other without seeing it had at the same time a stronger implicit preference towards their favourite brand.

Similarly, when it comes to deciding between healthy and unhealthy foods, Richetin, Perugini, Prestwich and O'Gorman (2007) found that IAT scores predicted the experimental choice of fruits versus snacks above and beyond self-reported liking for both. However, other studies of predictive validity have scored both hits and misses. For example, whereas Prestwich, Hurling and Baker (2011) found that only IAT scores, and not self-report, predicted the purchase of fruit versus chocolate in an online shopping paradigm, Ayres, Conner, Prestwich and Smith (2012) found that, although IAT scores predicted the consumption of fruit versus chocolate, they did not do so above and beyond self-reported measures of their relative tastiness. More subtly, Ellis, Kiviniemi and Cook-Cottone (2014) found that IAT-assessed preferences for fruit predicted the choice of fruit only among respondents with fewer symptoms of eating disorder, whereas self-reported preferences predicted the choice of fruit regardless. Finally, Kraus and Scholderer (2015) reported that the consumption of different types of chewable candy (liquorice versus gummy bears) was successfully predicted, at least some of the time, by two different types of IAT, one assessing implicit preferences, the other implicit inclinations.

Research in areas thematically similar to consumer psychology also underscores the potential of the IAT to achieve incremental predictive validity. For example, Chassota, Klöcknerb, & Wüstenhagen (in press) reported that, among professional investors, IAT-assessed preferences (using the category labels *Risk* versus *Return*) for renewable over non-renewable energy sources (such as *Solar Energy* versus *Natural Gas*) predicted how much of their portfolio they had allocated to one or the other. Moreover, it did so better than self-reported preferences, and regardless of other predictive background variables, such as investor type. Another study found that IAT-assessed inclinations towards alcohol versus water predict binge drinking episodes (though not total alcohol consumption) above and beyond standard self-report scales (Ostafin et al., 2003). However, related research found that *implicit identification* with alcohol versus water – measured by including categories *Me* and *Not-Me* in the IAT as attributes – predicted future alcohol consumption, even controlling for past consumption (Gray, LaPlante, Bannon,

Ambady, & Shaffer, 2011) and for self-report measures of consumption (Lindgren et al., 2013). Given the centrality of self and identity to consumer psychology (e.g., Lee, Gregg, & Park, 2013; see also Belk, Chapter 13, Sirgy, Chapter 14, and Veer, Chapter 15, this volume), similar IATs might be profitably deployed there in future (none have been so far, to our knowledge). For now, a defensible summary of the predictive power of the IAT would be the following: The IAT sometimes, though not always, uniquely assists in the prediction of consumer behaviour, and may do so potentially in complex ways.

Note that the predictive results outlined above were general, pitting the IAT against self-report overall. However, if implicit cognition is more elementary and explicit cognition is more sophisticated, then one might expect the IAT's predictivity to be greatest under conditions where consumer choices are made more mechanically or mindlessly. Some studies show results consistent with this expectation. For example, Hofmann, Rauch and Gawronski (2007) experimentally manipulated the capacity of some participants to control their appetite, by wearing out their willpower in advance using a difficult unrelated task. They subsequently found that, although self-reported dietary standards, but not IAT scores, predicted candy consumption under normal conditions, IAT scores became a superior predictor among participants whose willpower had previously been depleted (apparently, there is conventional wisdom in positioning snacks at supermarket checkouts, to take advantage of worn-out shoppers!). In a slightly more complex result, Friese et al. (2006) found that, although respondents' self-reported preferences predicted both hurried and leisurely product choice when they matched their IAT preferences, when they *mis*matched their IAT preferences, they failed to predict hurried product choice.

Finally, if the IAT taps into implicit cognition, then one might expect it to correlate with other indirect measures, including those of a radically different sort. Recently, Maison and Ohme (2012) – building on other work showing a link between IAT scores and neurophysiological indictors (Thomas, Hartmann, & Killgore, 2013; Williams & Themanson, 2011) – investigated whether implicit attitudes towards brands measured by the IAT could predict EEG activity in an advertising context. Participants watched a Coke commercial while their EEG was recorded live. A signature pattern known to be indicative of positive emotional reactions towards advertising was then found to correlate more closely with IAT-assessed attitudes towards the brand than with self-reported attitudes towards the brand.

Cumulatively, such findings indicate that, at least some of the time, the IAT has incremental predictive power in consumer domains, by virtue of tapping otherwise overlooked aspects of consumers' attitudes. The situation may not be quite as favourable to the IAT as that depicted in Diagram N of Figure 8.2; however, it is certainly much more favourable than that depicted in Diagram O.

The IAT: From consumer psychology principles to market research practice

Over a decade of research in consumer psychology indicates that the IAT can shed useful light on the contents of what has traditionally been called the unconscious mind. Although this realm of the implicit may not be as all-determining as Freudians once asserted, it nonetheless is real and relevant, and in need of rigorous assessment. As an indirect measure of consumer attitude, the IAT can reveal something of what people think and feel about a product or brand even when they do not know themselves. This is evident not only from the fact that the IAT yields results at odds with self-report, but also because the IAT frequently predicts consumer behaviour and decision making independently of self-report, including under conditions when it would theoretically be expected to do so. Otherwise put, the IAT is an indirect measure of implicit content in the consumer domain, which although hardly infallible, is still reasonably sensitive, frequently predictive and meaningfully distinctive. Accordingly, it has its place in academic consumer psychology, either in its own right or as an adjunct to self-report.

One question that now naturally arises is whether and to what extent the IAT has a role to play in the applied discipline of *marketing research*. The distinction between marketing research and consumer research should perhaps be noted here. Marketing research consists of studies conducted by practitioners with the goal of identifying opportunities to sell products or promote brands. Based on data collected mostly from consumers, such studies should give direct and practical answers to questions such as whether or not to launch a new product, which version of an advertisement to place in media, which of several possible brand strategies to adopt or which of several consumer insights to prioritize (Grover & Vriens, 2006; Weiers, 1988). In contrast, consumer research is an academic field, where scientists, especially psychologists, conduct the relevant studies. The goal here is to establish general knowledge about mechanisms underlying consumers' attitudes, decisions and behaviours. Both marketing research and consumer research focus on the consumer, but each addresses different questions and often uses different tools.

However, the question of the applicability of the IAT to marketing research is not only worth considering because marketing research should borrow promising assessment instruments from consumer psychology. It is also worth considering because it serves to highlight some of the practical limitations and potential pitfalls of the IAT, which consumer psychologists themselves would do well to bear in mind (see Gregg & Klymowsky, 2013, for a full discussion).

The first point to note is that the IAT yields large effects – so large, indeed, that it becomes not only possible to detect effects in very small sample sizes, but tempting to interpret the results for individual respondents. With the possible exception of the IRAP, which also reliably exhibits large effect sizes (e.g., Barnes-Holmes et al., 2010), no other indirect measure quite matches the IAT in this respect.

That said, such large effects are achieved at a cost. The IAT is far less efficient to administer than a regular self-report measure (though perhaps still more efficient than some "neuroscience" approaches, such as functional magnetic resonance imaging (fMRI)). Whereas it takes mere moments to gauge, via direct self-report, whether people explicitly prefer Coke to Pepsi, it takes many minutes to gauge, via an indirect IAT, whether people implicitly prefer the same. That is, the information yielded per unit time from any one IAT is relatively low, pertaining only to category pairs, not to individual items.

A further drawback of the IAT is that the categorical associations it reveals are necessarily comparative. The IAT does not quantify whether and to what extent category C is linked to attribute A, but whether and to what extent one bipolar pair of categories, $C1 \leftrightarrow C2$, maps on to another bipolar pair of categories, $A1 \leftrightarrow A2$. Hence, it cannot reveal whether some product or brand is linked to some attribute per se, but only whether some brand or product, relative to a plausible rival, is linked to some attribute, relative to some natural contrast (usually an antonym, as in Positive versus Negative). Such specificity, although suitable for head-to-head comparisons, is highly limiting. When only a single product or brand is of interest, the researcher is essentially forced to add a rival to get the IAT to "work". This comparative straightjacket makes it even more challenging to fit an IAT to a natural question of interest to a market researcher. The results obtained will, moreover, vary depending on the rival chosen (cf. Pinter & Greenwald, 2005). Hence, the IAT never indicates what "the" implicit attitudes towards some product or brand are. For example, suppose a market researcher wanted to assess implicit consumer attitudes towards the car brand Lexus itself. He or she could assess implicit preferences for Lexus versus BMW, or Lexus versus Audi, or Lexus versus Mercedes. However, the result would also be relative to some other brand. The lack of a "single answer" could make it more difficult to draw general conclusions and make general practical decisions about a product or brand.

The other drawback – anticipated earlier – is that the IAT does not permit associations towards individual items to be assessed, only associations towards categories. This makes it unwieldy to assess how a brand like Coke (even relative to some other brand like Pepsi) is linked to a whole set of attributes, such as tasty, cheap or healthy. Hence, if a researcher wishes to characterize some product or brand in terms of multiple attributes, several IATs must be run back-to-back (e.g., Gattol et al., 2011). As well as being a logistical challenge, doing so introduces the possibility of order effects (due to familiarity or fatigue) and carry-over effects (due to practice or priming). Indeed, the IAT itself has the same problem internally: The researcher has to decide which of the two critical blocks to present first. Which one is given priority sometimes, but not always, moderates the magnitude of the effects obtained (Nosek, Greenwald, & Banaji, 2005). Such methodological confounds can be alleviated by counterbalancing, but their existence means that any individual results need to be interpreted more cautiously. Ultimately, marketing researchers are typically interested in characterizing associations towards brands on a variety of dimensions rather than on only one or two specific dimensions. Hence, the fact that the IAT only permits a handful of associations to be investigated is perhaps the greatest practical obstacle to its widespread applied adoption.

Interpreting the magnitude and direction of IAT effects presents additional challenges. By what criterion should IAT effects be considered real, and if real, then small, moderate or large in size? Statistical significance, and Cohen's *d*s, may suffice for research studies in consumer psychology. But in market research, some index of practical significance is required. The basic IAT score – the average difference in RT between critical blocks – is easy to comprehend and compute; however, its underlying metric remains poorly defined, as is the case for many psychological measures (Blanton & Jaccard, 2006). For example, what IAT denotes a maximal effect for most purposes? Yet, despite much large-scale data collection (e.g., Nosek, Banaji, & Greenwald, 2002), there are few guidelines here.

Furthermore, spurious IAT effects can be inadvertently generated. Most notably, category pairs may be construed as connected merely by virtue of being jointly salient (Rothermund & Wentura, 2004). For example, if a novel brand, being unfamiliar, stands out relative to an established brand (e.g., Nova-Cola > Coca-Cola), and if bad things, being rarer, stand out relative to good things (e.g., Negative > Positive), then an artefactual IAT effect may emerge linking a novel brand to bad things, thereby serving to exaggerate an underlying implicit preference for an established brand, or to obscure an underlying implicit preference for a novel brand.

However, IAT researchers have duly acknowledged and technically addressed many of these problems. For example, various attempts have been made to devise modified IATs that assess the links between two categories more specifically. These include the Simple Association Test (SAT; Blanton, Jaccard, Gonzales, & Christie, 2006), the Single-Category IAT (SC-IAT; Karpinski & Steinman, 2006) and the Go No-Go Association Test (GNAT; Nosek & Banaji, 2001). Other variants attempt to shorten the IAT, such as the Brief Implicit Association Test (BIAT; Sriram & Greenwald, 2009), or permit implicit associations between a variety of items to be assessed, such as the EAST (De Houwer, 2003), the Sorted Paired Features Task (SPF) (Bar-Anan, Nosek, & Vianello, 2009) and the IRAP (Barnes-Holmes et al., 2010). Yet others dispense with discrete consecutive blocks in favour of alternating trial types, such as the Single-Block Implicit Association Test (SB-IAT; Teige-Mocigemba, Klauer, & Rothermund, 2008) and the Recoding Free Implicit Association Test (IAT-RF; Rothermund, Teige-Mocigemba,

Gast, & Wentura, 2009). Although such variants can yield smaller and less predictive effects than the IAT (e.g., De Houwer & De Bruycker, 2007), they often fare adequately and sometimes even better (e.g., Hofmann, Rauch, & Gawronski, 2007; Kraus & Scholderer, 2015). Practically speaking, these IAT variants should be of great interest to marketing researchers who wish to apply indirect measures practically, because they at least start to solve two key problems with the original IAT. The first is the *relativity* of the assessment (as these IAT variants now permit attitudes to be assessed towards *individual* products or brands). The second is *small number* of possible assessments (as these IAT variants now permit implicit attitudes to be assessed towards *multiple* products or brands).

As for interpreting the practical significance of IAT effects, here is one strategy that a market researcher, or a consumer psychologist, might employ: alongside some focal IAT, administer a suitably matched *baseline* IAT. For example, suppose one wanted to determine whether and to what extent respondents implicitly liked the novel Nova-Cola relative to the iconic Coca-Cola. Here, instead of contrasting one brand against the other (using attribute categories such as Positive and Negative), one could contrast *both* brands against something else, such as the mundane beverage Water. Here, the baseline IAT – representing an implicit preference already known to be practically significant – would feature Coca-Cola. In contrast, the focal IAT – representing an implicit preference of as yet unknown practical significance – would feature Nova-Cola. Now, suppose one compared the results of these two IATs (adjusting for any order effects in their administration). In particular, suppose one found that, in an amply large sample, the control IAT yielded a difference score of 500 milliseconds, whereas the focal IAT yielded a difference score of 50 milliseconds. Assuming rough linearity in IAT's underlying metric, one might then reasonably infer that implicit liking for Nova-Cola stood at about 10 per cent of liking for Coca-Cola – a discouraging result. However, if the focal IAT had instead yielded a difference score of 450 milliseconds, one might have then reasonably inferred that implicit liking *for Nova-Cola stood at about 90 per cent of liking for Coca-Cola* – an encouraging result. Intermediate results would warrant more nuanced inferences.

Thus, with a little care and ingenuity, the IAT can be successfully deployed, by consumer psychologists and market researchers alike, to unmask the realm of the implicit.

References

Allen, C. T., Fournier, S., & Miller, F. (2008). Brands and their meaning makers. In C. P. Haugtvedt, P. Herr & F. R. Kardes (Eds.), *Handbook of consumer psychology* (pp. 781–822). New York, NY: Taylor & Francis.

Anastasi, A. (1988). *Psychological testing* (6th ed.). New York, NY: Macmillan.

Ayres, K., Conner, M. T., Prestwich, A., & Smith, P. (2012). Do implicit measures of attitudes incrementally predict snacking behaviour over explicit affect-related measures? *Appetite*, *58*, 835–841.

Bar-Anan, Y., & Nosek, B. A. (2014). A comparative investigation of seven implicit measures of social cognition. *Behaviour Research Methods*, *46*, 668–688.

Bar-Anan, Y., Nosek, B. A., & Vianello, M. (2009). The Sorting Paired Features Task: A measure of association strengths. *Experimental Psychology*, *56*, 329–343.

Bargh, J. A. (2002). Losing consciousness: Automatic influences and consumer judgment, behaviour, and motivation. *Journal of Consumer Research*, *29*, 280–285.

Bargh, J. A., & Morsella, E. (2008). The unconscious mind. *Perspectives on Psychological Science*, *3*, 73–79.

Bargh, J. A., Gollwitzer, P. M., Lee-Chai, A., Barndollar, K., & Trötschel, R. (2001). The automated will: Nonconscious activation and pursuit of behavioural goals. *Journal of Personality and Social Psychology*, *81*, 1014–1127.

Barnes-Holmes, D., Barnes-Holmes, Y., Stewart, I., & Boles, S. (2010). A sketch of the Implicit Relational Assessment Procedure (IRAP) and the Relational Elaboration and Coherence (REC) model. *The Psychological Record*, *60*, 527–542.

Bassili, J. N. (1996). Meta-judgmental versus operative indices of psychological properties: The case of measures of attitude strength. *Journal of Personality and Social Psychology*, *71*, 637–653.
Blackston, M. (1993). Beyond brand personality. Building brand relationship. In D. A. Aaker & A. L. Biel (Eds.), *Brand equity & advertising* (pp. 113–124). Hillsdale, NJ: Erlbaum.
Blanton, H., & Jaccard, J. (2006). Arbitrary metrics in psychology. *American Psychologist*, *61*, 27–41.
Blanton, H., Jaccard, J., Gonzales, P., & Christie, C. (2006). Decoding the Implicit Association Test: Implications for criterion prediction. *Journal of Experimental Social Psychology*, *42*, 192–212.
Bornstein, R. F., & D'Agostino, P. R. (1992). Stimulus recognition and the mere exposure effect. *Journal of Personality and Social Psychology*, *63*, 545–552.
Branthwaite, A., & Lunn, T. (1985). Projective techniques in social and market research. In R. Walker (Ed.), *Applied Qualitative Research*. Aldershot, VT: Gower.
Brunel, F. F., Tietje, B. C., & Greenwald, A. G. (2004). Is the Implicit Association Test a valid and valuable measure of implicit consumer social cognition? *Journal of Consumer Psychology*, *14*, 385–404.
Chaiken, S., & Trope, Y. (1999). *Dual process theories in social psychology*. New York, NY: Guilford Press.
Chassota, S., Klöcknerb, C. A., & Wüstenhagen, R. (in press). Can implicit cognition predict the behaviour of professional energy investors? An explorative application of the Implicit Association Test (IAT). *Journal of Applied Research in Memory and Cognition*.
Cohen, J. B., & Areni, C. S. (1991). Affect and consumer behaviour. In T. S. Robertson & H. H. Kassarjian (Eds.), *Handbook of consumer behaviour* (pp. 188–240). Englewood Cliffs, NJ: Prentice Hall.
Czellar, S. (2006). Self-presentational effects in the Implicit Association Test. *Journal of Consumer Psychology*, *16*, 92–100.
De Houwer, J. (2001). A structural and process analysis of the Implicit Association Test. *Journal of Experimental Social Psychology*, *37*, 443–451.
De Houwer, J. (2003). The extrinsic affective Simon task. *Experimental Psychology*, *50*, 77–85.
De Houwer, J., & De Bruycker, E. (2007). The implicit association test outperforms the extrinsic affective Simon task as an implicit measure of inter-individual differences in attitudes. *British Journal of Social Psychology*, *46*, 401–421.
De Houwer, J., Beckers, T., & Moors, A. (2007). Novel attitudes can be faked on the Implicit Association Test. *Journal of Experimental Social Psychology*, *43*, 972–978.
De Houwer, J., Teige-Mocigemba, S., Spruyt, A., & Moors, A. (2009). Implicit measures: A normative analysis and review. *Psychological Bulletin*, *135*, 347–368.
Dijksterhuis, A., & Aarts, H. (2010). Goals, attention, and (un)consciousness. *Annual Review of Psychology*, *61*, 467–490.
Dimofte, C. V., Johansson, J. K., & Ronkainen, I. A. (2008). Spanning the globe: Win over the anti-globals. *Marketing Management*, *17*, 40–43.
Ellis, E. M., Kiviniemi, M. T., & Cook-Cottone, C. M. (2014). Implicit affective associations predict snack choice for those with low, but not high levels of eating disorder symptomatology. *Appetite*, *77*, 122–130.
Fazio, R. H. (1990). A practical guide to the use of response latency in social psychological research. In W. C. Hendrick & M. S. Clark (Eds.), *Research methods in personality and social psychology* (pp. 74–97). London: Sage.
Fazio, R. H. (2001). On the automatic activation of associated evaluations: An overview. *Cognition and Emotion*, *15*, 115–141.
Fazio, R. H., & Williams, C. J. (1986). Attitude accessibility as a moderator of the attitude-perception and attitude-behaviour relations: An investigation of the 1984 presidential election. *Journal of Personality and Social Psychology*, *5*, 505–514.
Fiedler, K., & Bluemke, M. (2005). Faking the IAT: Aided and unaided response control on the implicit association tests. *Basic and Applied Social Psychology*, *27*, 307–316.
Fiedler, K., Messner, C., & Bluemke, M. (2006). Unresolved problems with the "I", the "A", and the "T": A logical and psychometric critique of the Implicit Association Test (IAT). *European Review of Social Psychology*, *17*, 74–147.
Friese, M., Wänke, M., & Plessner, H. (2006). Implicit consumer preferences and their influence on product choice. *Psychology & Marketing*, *23*, 727–740.
Gattol, V., Sääksjärvi. M., & Carbon, C.-C. (2011). Extending the Implicit Association Test (IAT): Assessing consumer attitudes based on multi-dimensional implicit associations. *PLoS ONE*, *6*, e15849.

Gawronski, B., & Bodenhausen, G. V. (2006). Associative and propositional processes in evaluation: An integrative review of implicit and explicit attitude change. *Psychological Bulletin, 132*, 692–731.

Gawronski, B., Hofmann, W, & Wilbur, C. J. (2006). Are "implicit" attitudes unconscious? *Consciousness and Cognition, 15*, 485–499.

Govan, C. L., & Williams, K. D. (2004). Changing the affective valence of the stimulus items influences the IAT by re-defining the category labels. *Journal of Experimental Social Psychology, 40*, 357–365.

Gray, H. M., LaPlante, D. A., Bannon, B. L., Ambady, N., & Shaffer, H. J. (2011). Development and validation of the Alcohol Identity Implicit Associations Test (AI-IAT). *Addictive Behaviours, 36*, 919–926.

Greenwald, A. G. (1997). Self-knowledge and self-deception: Further consideration. In M. S. Myslobodsky (Ed.), *The mythomanias: An inquiry into the nature of deception and self-deception*. Mahwah, NJ: Erlbaum.

Greenwald, A. G., & Banaji, M. R. (1995). Implicit social cognition: Attitudes, self-esteem, and stereotypes. *Psychological Review, 102*, 4–27.

Greenwald, A. G., & Farnham, S. D. (2000). Using the Implicit Association Test to measure self-esteem and self-concept. *Journal of Personality and Social Psychology, 79*, 1022–1038.

Greenwald, A. G., McGhee, D. E., & Schwartz, J. K. L. (1998). Measuring individual differences in implicit cognition: The Implicit Association Test. *Journal of Personality and Social Psychology, 74*, 1464–1480.

Greenwald, A. G., Nosek, B. A., & Banaji, M. R. (2003). Understanding and using the Implicit Association Test: I. An improved scoring algorithm. *Journal of Personality and Social Psychology, 85*, 197–216.

Greenwald, A. G., Poehlman, T. A., Uhlmann, E., & Banaji, M. R. (2009). Understanding and using the Implicit Association Test: III. Meta-analysis of predictive validity. *Journal of Personality and Social Psychology, 97*, 17–41.

Gregg, A. P., & Klymowsky, J. (2013). The Implicit Association Test in market research: Potentials and pitfalls. *Psychology & Marketing, 30*, 588–601.

Gregg, A. P., & Mahadevan, N. (2014). Self-deception. In *Encyclopedia of lying and deception*. London: Sage.

Gregg, A. P., Seibt, B., & Banaji, M. A. (2006). Easier done than undone: Asymmetry in the malleability of automatic preferences. *Journal of Personality and Social Psychology, 90*, 1–20.

Grover, R., & Vriens, M. (2008). *The handbook of marketing research. Uses, misuses, and future advances*. Thousand Oaks, CA: Sage.

Hall, L., Johansson, P., Tärning, B., Sikström, S., & Deutgen, T. (2010). Magic at the marketplace: Choice blindness for the taste of jam and the smell of tea. *Cognition*, 117, 54–61.

Han, H. A., Czellar, S., Olson, M. A., & Fazio, R. H. (2010). Malleability of attitudes or malleability of the IAT? *Journal of Experimental Social Psychology, 46*, 286–298.

Hansen, F., & Christensen, S. R. (2007). *Emotions, advertising and consumer choice*. Copenhagen: Copenhagen Business School Press.

Hofmann, W., Gawronski, B., Gschwendner, T., Le, H., & Schmitt, M. (2005). A meta-analysis on the correlation between the Implicit Association Test and explicit self-report measures. *Personality and Social Psychology Bulletin, 31*, 1369–1385.

Hofmann, W., Rauch, W., & Gawronski, B. (2007). And deplete us not into temptation: Automatic attitudes, dietary restraint, and self-regulatory resources as determinants of eating behaviour. *Journal of Experimental Social Psychology, 43*, 497–504.

Jensen, A. R. (2006). *Clocking the mind: Mental chronometry and individual differences*. Amsterdam: Elsevier.

Johansson, P., Hall, L., Sikström, S., & Olsson, A. (2005). Failure to detect mismatches between intention and outcome in a simple decision task. *Science, 310*, 116–119.

Kahneman, D. (2011). *Thinking, fast and slow*. New York, NY: Farrar, Strauss, Giroux.

Karpinski, A., & Steinman, R. B. (2006). The single category Implicit Association Test as a measure of implicit social cognition. *Journal of Personality and Social Psychology, 91*, 16–32.

Kim, D. (2003). Voluntary controllability of the Implicit Association Test (IAT). *Social Psychology Quarterly, 66*, 83–96.

Klauer, K. C., & Musch, J. (2003). Affective priming: findings and theories. In J. Musch & K. C. Klauer (Eds.), *The psychology of evaluation* (pp. 7–36). Mahwah, NJ: Erlbaum.

Kokkinaki, F., & Lunt, P. (1997). Attitude accessibility as a function of involvement with the attitude object: Moderators of the attitude-behaviour relationship. *British Journal of Social Psychology, 36*, 497–409.

Kraus, A. A., & Scholderer, J. (2015). Indirect measurement of motivation: Developing and testing a motivational recoding-free implicit association test (m-iat-rf). *Social Psychology*, 43, 142–156.

Kraus, S. J. (1995). Attitudes and the prediction of behaviour: A meta-analysis of the empirical literature. *Personality and Social Psychology Bulletin, 21*, 58–75.

LeDoux, J. (1998). *The emotional brain: The mysterious underpinnings of emotional life*. New York: Simon & Schuster.

Lee, S., Gregg, A. P., & Park, S. (2013). The person in the purchase: Narcissistic consumers prefer products that distinguish them. *Journal of Personality and Social Psychology, 105*, 335–352.

Lindgren, K. P., Neighbors, C., Teachman, B. A., Wiers, R., Westgate, E., & Greenwald, A. G. (2013). I drink therefore I am: Validating alcohol-related implicit association tests. *Psychology of Addictive Behaviours, 27*, 1–13.

Maison, D. (2014). Values and lifestyle segmentation of Poles 55+ and its implications for consumers' attitude and behaviour. *Management and Business Administration in Central Europe, 22*, 3–19.

Maison, D., Greenwald, A. G., & Bruin, R. (2001). The Implicit Association Test as measure of implicit consumer attitudes. *Polish Psychological Bulletin, 32*, 61–70.

Maison, D., Greenwald, A. G., & Bruin, R. H. (2004). Predictive validity of the Implicit Association Test in studies of brands, consumer attitudes, and behaviour. *Journal of Consumer Psychology, 14*, 405–415.

Maison, D., & Ohme, R. (2012). Validation of biometric methods as a tool for advertising pre-testing. How explicit and implicit attitude toward brand influences the biometric reaction to the TV commercial. Presentation in *Global Marketing Conference*, Seoul, Korea, 19–22 July 2012.

Markus, H. R. (1977). Self-schemata and processing information about the self. *Journal of Personality and Social Psychology, 35*, 63–78.

Mayerl, J. (2013). Response latency measurement in surveys: Detecting strong attitudes and response effects. *Survey Methods: Insights from the Field*. Retrieved from http://surveyinsights.org/?p=1063

Modigliani, E., & Brumberg, R. (1954). Utility analysis and the consumption function: An interpretation of cross-section data. In K. K. Kurihara (Ed.), *Post-Keynesian economics* (pp. 388–436). New Brunswick, NJ: Rutgers University Press.

Morgan, D. L. (1998). *The focus group guidebook. Focus Group Kit 1*. Thousand Oaks, CA: Sage.

Murphy, S. T., & Zajonc, R. B. (1993). Affect, cognition, and awareness: Affective priming with optimal and suboptimal stimulus exposures. *Journal of Personality & Social Psychology, 64*, 723–739.

Neal, D., Wood, W., Wu, M., & Kurlander, D. (2011). The pull of the past: When do habits persist despite conflict with motives? *Personality and Social Psychology Bulletin, 37*, 1428–1437.

Neale, M., & Kyle, M. (2011). Unconscious mental processes in consumer choice: Toward a new model of consumer behaviour. *Journal of Brand Management, 18*, 483–505. doi:10.1057/bm.2011.10

Niedenthal, P., & Showers, C. (1991). The perception and processing of affective information. In J. P. Forgas (Ed.), *Emotion and social judgement*. Oxford: Pergamon Press.

Nisbett, R. E., & Wilson, T. D. (1977). Telling more than we can know: Verbal reports on mental processes. *Psychological Review, 84*, 231–259.

Nosek, B. A. (2007). Implicit-explicit relations. *Current Directions in Psychological Science, 16*, 65–69.

Nosek, B. A., & Banaji, M. R. (2001). The Go/No-Go Association Task. *Social Cognition, 6*, 625–664.

Nosek, B. A., Banaji, M. R., & Greenwald, A. G. (2002). Harvesting implicit group attitudes and beliefs from a demonstration website. *Group Dynamics, 6*, 101–115.

Nosek, B. A., Greenwald, A. G., & Banaji, M. R. (2005). Understanding and using the Implicit Association Test: II. Method variables and construct validity. *Personality and Social Psychology Bulletin, 31*, 166–180.

Nosek, B. A., Greenwald, A. G., & Banaji, M. R. (2007). The Implicit Association Test at age 7: A methodological and conceptual review. In J. A. Bargh (Ed.), *Social psychology and the unconscious: The automaticity of higher mental processes* (pp. 265–292). New York, NY: Psychology Press.

Nosek, B. A., Hawkins, C. B., & Frazier, R. S. (2011). Implicit social cognition: From measures to mechanisms. *Trends in Cognitive Sciences, 15*, 152–159.

Ohme, R. K. (2001). The implicit conditioning of consumer attitudes: Logo substitution effect. *Polish Psychological Bulletin, 32*, 71–78.

Palfai, T. P., & Ostafin, B. D. (2003). Alcohol-related motivational tendencies in hazardous drinkers: Assessing implicit response tendencies using the modified-IAT. *Behaviour Research and Therapy, 41*, 1149–1162.

Perkins, A., Forehand, M., Greenwald, A. G., & Maison, D. (2008). The influence of implicit social cognition on consumer behaviour: Measuring the non-conscious. In C. Haugtvedt, P. Herr & F. Kardes (Eds.), *Handbook of consumer psychology*. Hillsdale, NJ: Erlbaum.

Pinter, B., & Greenwald, A. G. (2005). Clarifying the role of the "other" category in the self-esteem IAT. *Experimental Psychology, 52*, 74–79.

Prestwich, A., Hurling, R., & Baker, S. (2011). Implicit shopping: Attitudinal determinants of the purchasing of healthy and unhealthy foods. *Psychology and Health, 26*, 875–885.

Priluck, R., & Till, B. D. (2010). Comparing a customer-based brand equity scale with the Implicit Association Test in examining consumer responses to brands. *Journal of Product Brand Management, 17*, 413–428.

Pronin, E. (2009). The introspection illusion. In M. P. Zanna (Ed.), *Advances in experimental social psychology* (Vol. 41, pp. 52–53). Burlington, MA: Academic Press.

Ratliff, K. A., Swinkels, B. A. P., Klerx, K., & Nosek, B. A. (2012). Does one bad apple (juice) spoil the bunch? Implicit attitudes toward one product transfer to other products by the same brand. *Psychology & Marketing, 29*, 531–540.

Richetin, J., Perugini, M., Prestwich, A., & O'Gorman, R. (2007). The IAT as a predictor of spontaneous food choice: The case of fruits versus snacks. *International Journal of Psychology, 42*, 166–173.

Röhner, J., Schröder-Abé, & Schütz, A. (2011). Exaggeration is harder than understatement, but practice makes perfect! Faking success in the IAT. *Experimental Psychology, 58*, 464–472.

Rothermund, K., Teige-Mocigemba, S., Gast, A., & Wentura, D. (2009). Minimizing the influence of recoding in the Implicit Association Test: The Recoding-Free Implicit Association Test (IAT-RF). *Quarterly Journal of Experimental Psychology, 62*, 84–98.

Rothermund, K., & Wentura, D. (2004). Underlying processes in the Implicit Association Test (IAT): Dissociating salience from associations. *Journal of Experimental Psychology: General, 133*, 139–165.

Rudman, L. A., Greenwald, A. G., & McGhee, D. E. (2001). Implicit self-concept and evaluative implicit gender stereotypes: Self and ingroup share desirable traits. *Personality and Social Psychology Bulletin, 27*, 1164–1178.

Searle, J. (1992). *The rediscovery of the mind*. Cambridge, MA: MIT Press.

Sriram, N., & Greenwald, A. G. (2009). The Brief Implicit Association Test. *Experimental Psychology, 56*, 283–294.

Steenkamp, J.-B. E. M., de Jong, M. G., & Baumgartner, H. (2010). Socially desirable response tendencies in survey research. *Journal of Marketing Research, 47*, 199–214.

Strack, F., & Deutsch, R. (2004). Reflective and impulsive determinants of social behaviour. *Personality and Social Psychology Review, 8*, 220–247.

Teige-Mocigemba, S., Klauer, K. C., & Rothermund, K. (2008). Minimizing method-specific variance in the IAT: A Single Block IAT. *European Journal of Psychological Assessment, 24*, 237–245.

Thomas, J. J., Hartmann, A. S., & Killgore, W. D. (2013). Non-fat-phobic eating disorders: Why we need to investigate implicit associations and neural correlates. *International Journal of Eating Disorders, 46*, 416–419.

Tindell, A. J., Smith, K. S., Berridge, K. C., & Aldridge, J. W. (2009). Dynamic computation of incentive salience: "Wanting" what was never "liked". *Journal of Neuroscience, 29*, 12220–12228.

Vargas, P. T. (2008). Implicit consumer cognition. In F. Kardes, C. Haugdtvedt & P. Herr (Eds.), *Handbook of consumer psychology*. Mahwah, NJ: Erlbaum.

Vohs, K. D., & Faber, R. J. (2004). Spent resources: Self-regulatory resource availability affects impulse buying. *Journal of Consumer Research, 33*, 537–547

Vrij, A. (2008). *Detecting lies and deceit: Pitfalls and opportunities* (2nd ed.). Chichester: Wiley.

Walczyk, J. J., Mahoney, K. T., Doverspike, D., & Griffith-Ross, D. A. (2009). Cognitive lie detection: Response time and consistency of answers as cues to deception. *Journal of Business & Psychology, 24*, 33–49.

Weiers, R. M. (1988). *Marketing research*. Englewood Cliffs, NJ: Prentice-Hall International.

Williams, J. K., & Themanson, J. R. (2011). Neural correlates of the implicit association test: Evidence for semantic and emotional processing. *Social Cognitive and Affective Neuroscience, 6*, 468–476.

Wilson, T. D. (2002). *Strangers to ourselves: Discovering the adaptive unconscious*. Cambridge, MA: Harvard University Press.

Winkielman, P., Berridge, K. C., & Wilbarger, J. L. (2005). Unconscious affective reactions to masked happy versus angry faces influence consumption behaviour and judgments of value. *Personality and Social Psychology Bulletin, 1*, 121–135.

Winkielman, P., & Schooler, J. (2011). Splitting consciousness: Unconscious, conscious, and metaconscious processes in social cognition. *European Review of Social Psychology, 22*, 1–35.

Wittenbrink, B., & Schwarz, N. (2007). An introduction to the assessment of attitudes with implicit measures. In B. Wittenbrink & N. Schwartz (Eds.), *Implicit measures of attitudes* (pp. 1-13). New York: Guilford Press.

Wittenbrink, B., Judd, C. M., & Park, B. (1997). Evidence for racial prejudice at the implicit level and its relationship with questionnaire measures. *Journal of Personality and Social Psychology, 72*, 262–274.
Zajonc, R. B. (1980). Feeling and thinking: Preferences need no inferences. *American Psychologist, 35*, 151–175.
Zajonc, R. B. (2001). Mere exposure: A gateway to the subliminal. *Current Directions in Psychological Science, 10*, 224–228.
Zaltman, G. (2003). *How customers think*. Boston, MA: Harvard Business Press.
Zaltman, G., & Zaltman, L. H. (2008). *Marketing metaphoria: What deep metaphors reveal of consumers*. Boston, MA: Harvard Business Press.

Part III

Social perception, self, identity and well-being

9

The self in consumption

Russell Belk

At least since William James and Thorstein Veblen in the late nineteenth century, we have realized that the self is intimately implicated in our consumption and that consumption is intimately implicated in the self. In this chapter I review research in support of these relationships and consider the ways in which the role of possessions in self-definition may change when these possessions are virtual and digital rather than tangible. In so doing I reconsider Charles Cooley's notion of the looking glass self in an Internet age when others increasingly help to co-construct our sense of self and to influence our consumption in new ways. I conclude with a brief discussion of future research questions. This includes calling for more work on cultural differences in consumption and the self, as relatively little has been done in this area.

The self

The idea that there is an individual self is a relatively new one. Self-prefixes such as self-esteem did not appear in English until the rise of individualistic Puritanism in the seventeenth century (Kirmani, 2009). Tuan (1982) notes further signs of the rise of the individual in approximately the same time frame. These signs include the increasing frequency of autobiographies, family and self-portraits and mirrors, as well as a shift in Europe from benches and shared trenchers to chairs and individual dinner plates, the rise of psychoanalysis, the growing importance of childhood, the rise of more introspective drama and literature, and the growth of increasingly private and specialized rooms in the house. The individual self is also not a cultural universal. In India, if a villager is asked who they are they might begin by identifying their village, ancestry and father before getting to their individual name. While people are aware of themselves as individual experiencing persons, in many societies concern with the group and the aggregate "we" dominates the individual "I", if it even exists (Doob, 1960). Many traditional languages lack a first person singular "I" (Belk, 1984) or use it with lower frequency (Kitayama & Park, 2013; Markus & Kitayama, 1991). In Japanese, for example, rather than "I see the book on the table", an expression like "On the table the book is seen" would be used. Brewer and Gardner (1996) have expanded Markus and Kitayama's (1991) distinction between independent and interdependent sense of self into three components: the personal, relational and collective dimensions of self-construal (Wong & Hogg, 2013). Besides differing culturally, self-construal can also differ by gender, with women showing more interdependence and men showing more independence (Wang, Bristol, Mowen, & Chakraborty, 2000). And where there is greater interdependent self-construal there is also more likely to be a sense of shared ownership rather than individual ownership (Belk, 1984, 2010; Belk & Llamas, 2013; Swaminathan, Page, & Gürhan-Canli, 2007).

While the notion of self-construal might make it seem so, the idea of the self is not purely a private psychological construct. More than 100 years ago Charles Cooley (1902) theorized that others act as a looking glass (mirror) through which we perceive our selves. That is, we have difficulty forming an image of ourselves without the reactions and feedback of others. Moreover, we shape our behaviour to fit our understanding of others' perceptions of us. And we have multiple social groups (e.g., parents, friends, work colleagues, social groups) whose expectations we try to fulfil (Hogg & Michell, 1996; Schenk & Holman, 1980) by playing different roles and enacting different selves according to the situation and audience (Ahuvia, 2005; Bahl & Milne, 2010). These selves are often referred to as social identities (Kleine, Kleine, & Kernan, 1993). We also diverge from the idea of having a purely singular private self through social comparisons in which we compare ourselves with others (Festinger, 1954), including advertising models (Häfner, 2004; Richins, 1991). In this sense we exist as individual selves only vis-à-vis others to or from whom we may be similar or different.

There are also questions of whether the self can be said to exist at all. This is not a reference to the Buddhist concept of *anatta* or no self, which is held to be an ideal state. Rather, it is an argument that we unconsciously adapt to the expectations of those around us to such a degree that our apparently individualistic choices are merely an illusion (Hood, 2012; Pettigrew, 2002). A related but reversed argument is that in a decentred postmodern world of fragmented identity we have such a surfeit of choices that we lack a coherent sense of who we are (Elliott & Wattanasuwan, 1998). And Cushman (1990) suggests that the post-World War II Western self has been emptied out by the decline of family and community and that as a result, the self "seeks the experience of being continually filled up by consuming goods, calories, experiences, politicians, romantic partners and empathic therapists in an attempt to combat the growing alienation and fragmentation of its era" (p. 600). This leads to a consideration of the role of possessions and brands in constituting our selves.

In what follows I begin by reviewing various ways in which the link between people and their possessions has been considered. I then consider how the concept of the extended self needs to be revised and extended because of the affordances of digital media. I go on to examine evidence of how our consumption impacts others' impressions of us. And I finally offer some conclusions and suggested topics for further research.

Consumption and the self

As Bagozzi (2013) observes, "It might be said that consumption begins and ends with the self" (p. 255). He means by this that regardless of whether the attempt is to develop and enhance an independent self or to develop an aggregate interdependent self through enhancing the group, consumption and possessions play a key role in our consumer society. Stated differently, a concern with developing and enhancing independent self should lead to consumption patterns that involve "standing out", while concern with developing and enhancing interdependent self should be more consistent with consumption patterns that involve "fitting in" (Weisz, Rothbaum, & Blackburn, 1984). In different vocabularies, standing out via consumption can be seen as conspicuous consumption (Mason, 1981; Veblen, 1899), while fitting in can be seen as social conformity. Consumer choices generally seek to balance the desires for uniqueness and assimilation to the group (Berger & Heath, 2007; Chan, Berger, & Boven, 2012). But this does not necessarily mean that fitting in involves more modest consumption. Chadha and Husband (2006) report survey results from Tokyo women in their twenties showing that 94 per cent say they own a Louis Vuitton item, 92 per cent say they own Gucci, and 57 and 51 per cent, respectively, say they own Gucci and Prada. When this many people own these luxury brands, what would stand out would be NOT owning such brands. Wong and Ahuvia (1998) explain this phenomenon in terms of striving to enhance family face, also suggesting an extra-individual emphasis on the aggregate self. Because conspicuous goods are more clearly value expressive than inconspicuous goods, they have a disproportionate influence on self-concept (Sirgy, Johar, & Wood, 1986; Wright, Claiborne, & Sirgy, 1992). The same is true of highly aesthetic products (Townsend & Sood, 2012). There is also some evidence that among those with high cultural capital (Bourdieu, 1984), more subtle aesthetic consumption is preferred over ostentatious conspicuous consumption in signalling status (Berger & Ward, 2010; Chung & Fischer, 2001; Postrel, 2008).

Cultural capital is a form of symbolic capital developed through upbringing, education and environment (*habitus*) according to Bourdieu (1984). Other forms of capital include economic capital (how much money and resources we have) and social capital (the friends and family we may draw upon). Because cultural capital is required to knowledgeably discuss possessions like art, automobiles, music and furnishings, mere possession of status objects is not enough to gain a particular desired status (Bourdieu, 1984; Holt, 1998). And because lower classes attempt to acquire cultural capital or at least the outward signs of showing the same taste as high cultural capital (HCC) groups (Simmel's 1904 "trickle-down effect"), there is an incentive for HCC groups to turn to less conspicuous consumption that is harder for members of low cultural capital (LCC) groups to decode and imitate (Eckhardt, Belk, & Wilson, 2014).

However, conspicuous, aesthetic and luxury consumption constitute a broad brush approach to understanding the relationship between consumption and self, and standing out versus fitting in is only one of a number of different theoretical perspectives for understanding this relationship. Some of the earliest theorizations of the self–consumption relationship in consumer research posited congruence between a consumer's self-concept and the perceived characteristics of the brands the consumer purchases and owns (Landon, 1974; Sirgy, 1982). Belk (1988) critiqued this theory on three grounds. First, he argued, a person can hold an object like the Statue of Liberty to be a part of self-concept without believing that the traits of the statue and the self need to be similar. Secondly, besides pre-purchase brand characteristics, an object's relevance to self can also involve products rather than brands (e.g., wine for wine connoisseurs) as well as post-acquisition objects with which we have bonded (e.g., our pet). And third, rather than single products or brands representing the self, it is more likely an ensemble or brand constellation that is seen to depict our self (Arsel & Bean, 2013; McCracken, 1986; Solomon & Assael, 1987).

Instead, Belk (1988) suggested the concept of the extended self, focusing on the implications of other people as well as possessions in enlarging our individual self and our various levels of aggregate self (e.g., family, community, nation). Part of the notion of extended self involves "singularizing" branded commodities purchased in the marketplace and turning them into non-fungible possessions (Appadurai, 1986; Kopytoff, 1986). It is an empirical question which possessions consumers hold most central to their extended selves, and our most cathected possessions tend to differ by age and gender (Csikszentmihalyi & Rochberg-Halton, 1981). Even body parts and internal organs (arguably our dearest, if non-visible, possessions) have been found to be perceived as part of our extended self (Belk, 1992b). In fact, the body is a rather central part of our conception of self (Belk, 1987; Joy & Venkatesh, 1994; Thompson &

Hirschman, 1995). Other possessions are, in a sense, added onto the body, which is the starting point for self-knowledge. Because of this, parents are apt to attempt to shape the self-concepts of their children by giving them what they see as age- and gender-appropriate toys, clothing and furnishings.

While the initial formulation of the extended self (Belk, 1988) posited a singular core self, subsequent investigations have detected multiple conflicting extended selves, such as family versus work self (Tian & Belk, 2005). In addition, there are objects that contribute to the family sense of self rather than to the individual sense of self (e.g., Epp & Price, 2010). And there are multiple selves over the life course (Ahuvia, 2005; Bahl & Milne, 2010; Belk, 1988; Schouten, 1991).

Competing formulations have also been suggested, based primarily on Aron, Aron, Tudor and Nelson (1991). While the Belk (1988) formulation focuses on extending self via both possessions and other people, it treats possessions in the greatest depth. In contrast, the Aron et al. (1991) formulation was initially applied only to incorporating close others into our sense of self, but has subsequently been extended to incorporate loved brands or possessions as well (Ahuvia, 2005; Fournier & Mick, 1999; Kirmani, 2009). The two models also differ in whether they see the self as being extended into other people and things (Belk, 2013) or whether they envision other people and things as being incorporated into the self (Aron et al., 1991). The first formulation invokes a masculine metaphor and the second view invokes a feminine metaphor. Connell and Schau (2013) contend that both metaphoric models are needed to fully embrace self-augmentation via possessions, brands and other people.

The nature of our relationship with objects can also vary. In Fournier's (1998) view and findings, consumers form different types of relationships with brands just as they form different types of relationships with people. Thus, a relationship with a brand that we see as a casual fling is likely to involve less brand attachment than a brand with which we perceive ourselves as having a serious relationship. Attachment to and detachment from favourite possessions as a component of self have also been treated in terms of the perceived usefulness of these objects for objectifying our self-narratives (Ahuvia, 2005; Kleine, Kleine, & Allen, 1995; Schembri, Merrilees, & Kristiansen, 2010). This is a perspective that draws on Giddens' (1991) view that self is structured in terms of life narrative tales that we tell ourselves and others about who we are. Attachment and detachment are both essential inasmuch as the self-narrative continues to change as our sense of self changes (Belk, 1988). It also appears that when we do detach from possessions that have been a part of self, we prefer to transfer these possessions to others whom we see as similar to us (Lastovicka & Fernandez, 2005).

Not every possession is equally likely to become an intimate part of the extended self. While some mundane possessions can play a key role in the extended self (Kleine et al., 1993), there are those, like nomadic consumers, who form only utilitarian relationships with most possessions and for whom having many possessions can be a burden (Bardhi & Askegaard, 2009; Bardhi, Eckhardt, & Arnould, 2012; Belk, Groves, & Østergaard, 2000). Nevertheless, one of the ways through which we become attached to possessions and come to regard them as a part of our extended self is by mere possession and habituation. The endowment effect (Thaler, 1980) suggests that we become attached to what we possess or even touch, such that we are subsequently reluctant to give up such objects. From the perspective of prospect theory (Kahneman & Tversky, 1979) this is seen as arising from loss aversion, such that we place a higher value on retaining what we have than we do on gaining what we do not have (Nayakankuppam & Mishra, 2005). Seen from the perspective of the extended self, the explanation is that once we become attached to a good (Belk, 1992a; Kleine & Baker, 2004) and it becomes a part of our extended self, we are reluctant to give it up and see doing so as a threat to our sense of self and self-integrity (Chatterjee, Irmak, & Rose, 2013; Dommer & Swaminathan, 2013; Gao, Wheeler, & Shiv, 2009; Morewedge, Shu, Gilbert, & Wilson, 2009; Pierce, Kostova, & Dirks, 2003; Wicklund & Gollwitzer, 1982). Even children as young as four are found to be very reluctant to accept an exact copy of their toy in place of the original (Hood & Bloom, 2008). Adults show a similar insistence on the original for such items as their wedding rings, mobile phones and other treasured objects (Belk, 1988). There is some evidence that even touching the visual representation of a consumer good on a touch screen creates a sense of psychological ownership (Brasel & Gips, 2014).

While the initial formulation of extended self focused on singular possessions rather than commodity brands (Belk, 1988), a number of authors have also incorporated brand preferences and purchases within the concept of extended self (e.g., Belk, 2013; Escalas & Bettman, 2003; Fournier, 1998). Not only can young children detect the identity implications of various adult and child products by the time they enter grade school (Belk, Bahn, & Mayer, 1982; Belk, Mayer, & Driscoll, 1984), but they also understand the identity implications of various brands by this age (Chaplin & John, 2005; Chaplin & Lowrey, 2010; John, 1999).

Digital consumption and the self

Self-expression through consumption has changed considerably with the rise of the Internet, digital devices and digital platforms. Tian and Belk (2005) found that office workers use many "prosthetic possessions" to find information, store contact details, block out office noise and create a sense of privacy. We rely on our devices to remember phone numbers, do calculations, correct our spelling and grammar and find many pieces of information that we would have once had to remember or go to a library and look up in a book. Our reliance on Google to locate information prompted Carr (2008) to ask "Is Google making us stupid?" (i.e., is the part of memory that we outsource to Google making us less intelligent?). However, this is an old argument that goes back to the advent of books (another "cheat") and an argument between Plato and Socrates about whether books make us stupid (Manguel, 1996). Access to such information with a few strokes on our computer keyboards now greatly enlarges our access to knowledge and extends our intellectual "reach" and our sense of self.

We also now have many more platforms for expressing our identity, including blogs, forums, web pages, social media, photo and video sharing sites, online dating sites, virtual worlds, mobile and computer-based communications and interactive online game worlds. In addition, we can assert our product and brand preferences in many of these media and platforms without necessarily owning the object. For instance, we can "like", endorse, portray or discuss our dream car without owning it. Many of our former material possessions have become digital, including photos, videos, music, greeting cards, letters, magazines, newspapers, books and maps. Furthermore, we can now acquire virtual selves (avatars) and various virtual clothing, grooming, furnishings, vehicles and housing in which our avatar may interact with those of others in virtual realms. And in online games we can acquire objects such as virtual magical swords, shields and charms that have no material counterparts.

As Schau and Gilly (2003) detected early on with web pages, many digital spaces allow us to communicate personally relevant consumption information to a potentially much broader audience than we could reach with face-to-face contact. Furthermore, we can offer this representation of our selves 24/7. We are apt to disclose more personal information than we would likely find acceptable in face-to-face encounters. And we can rely on a number of new visual, graphic and verbal forms to present something closer to our ideal selves. Turkle (1984) once referred to our online activity as representing our "second self". But this was before the "break out of the visual" (Bolter, 1996) online and the development of more interactive Web 2.0. The possibilities for self-expression via our digital devices have grown enormously with the advent of popular social media like Facebook. One consequence of the interactive nature of social media is that others can post photos and comments about us and thereby help to co-construct our selves (Belk, 2013; Tufekci, 2012). Comments on our postings have been described as adding "digital patina" to our online self-constructions, making them more valuable (Davies, 2007; Odom, Sellen, Harper, & Thereska, 2012). But these comments can also help shape our behaviour, as Drenton (2012) found when she followed 13 teenage girls' Facebook activity for a month. On one occasion three of the girls were trying on glitzy dresses in a clothing store dressing room, where one took their photo in the dressing room mirror and instantaneously posted it online. Before they even left the dressing room their friends were adding comments about how cute they looked and advising that they buy the dresses.

Like the Evil Queen's magic mirror in *Snow White* (Ouellette, 2014, p. 148), we can also use such media to bolster our self-image. When we or others post a less than flattering photo that includes us, we may add our apologies for how bad we look in the picture. But this is often an invitation for reassurance, prompting our friends to tell us how good we look. Since such compliments remain on our social media page, they look like unsolicited testimonials. And we are likely to later return the favour by reassuring others of their attractiveness. Similarly, on professional social media sites like LinkedIn, when someone endorses our skills, we are likely to reciprocate and endorse theirs. In so doing we use social media to enhance our self-presentation with a little help from our friends (Belk, 2014a; Boyd, 2010).

What we see in the mirror of such social media and Web 2.0 Internet interactions can be considered a digital extension of Cooley's (1902) looking glass self. Despite the vastly increased possibilities for representing the self online, there is also a welcome or unwelcome loss of control to known and unknown others whose online activity helps to shape the way we and others view our self. Cooley (1902) posited that our self-presentation is interpreted and reflected back to us by others we encounter in daily life, thereby helping to construct the way we see ourselves. Zhao (2005) takes up Cooley's looking glass metaphor and suggests that online we have more resources available for self-presentations (Goffman, 1959). Using the Internet, we direct our self-presentation to telecopresent others – others who are not physically present, but can interact as if they were, as for instance in videoconferencing. We are also able to provide more information about our self online, engage in more self-disclosure, provide more elaborate self-narratives and possibly present multiple and "retractable" selves untethered from our bodies. But the sort of audience mirror that Zhao (2005) envisions online is a passive one, like a fixed mirror that reflects more or less what is presented. The co-construction of self that Belk (2013) envisions and that I discuss here involves a more active audience. Take the case of Justine Sacco, former senior director of corporate communications at IAC (InterActiveCorp). While on a long journey from New York to visit family in South Africa, she made a few quick Tweets from JFK and Heathrow airports, including these:

> "'Weird German Dude: You're in First Class. It's 2014. Get some deodorant' – Inner monologue as I inhale BO. 'Thank God for pharmaceuticals'."
> "Chilly – cucumber sandwiches – bad teeth. Back in London!"
> "Going to Africa. Hope I don't get AIDS. Just kidding. I'm white!"
>
> (*Ronson, 2015*)

She then wandered around Heathrow for half an hour and boarded the plane for the 11-hour flight to Cape Town. It was only while the plane was taxiing that she received a call from her best friend saying that she was the number one worldwide trend on Twitter. That's when the baffled woman had to shut off her smartphone for the flight. Although she had only 170 Twitter followers, the racist tone of her last comment caused great offence and led to viral retweets and follow-up messages like these:

> "All I want for Christmas is to see @JustineSacco's face when her plane lands and she checks her inbox/voicemail".
>
> "Oh man, @JustineSacco is going to have the most painful phone-turning-on moment ever when her plane lands".
>
> "We are about to watch this @JustineSacco bitch get fired. In REAL time. Before she even KNOWS she's getting fired".

Someone even came to the Cape Town airport and snapped and posted a photo of her leaving the plane behind the scant disguise of sunglasses. Belk (2013) and Solove (2007) detail other such incidents of public Internet shaming. While social groups have long used shaming to gain conformity to social norms, such incidents are usually small scale and soon forgotten. Not so with the Internet.

If the power of the Internet to co-construct and alter identity in the blink of the eye is not already evident, consider the following account of a small dinner party by a *New York Times* columnist:

> Over the course of the three-hour dinner, the poor sap eventually discovered, "my friends posted seven photos on Path, sent six Twitter messages (five with photos), six photos on Instagram and two people checked in on Foursquare. When I added up the collective follower counts of the people in the room, my little dinner party was potentially viewed by more people than watch The Late Show on CBS: over three million." (Two of his guests have large numbers of followers on Twitter.) And, to add insult to (self-inflicted) injury, a few days later he telephoned someone in a work-related call, only to be told by the other person – who has never crossed his threshold – how much he "just loved" the lamps hanging above the Bilton kitchen table.
>
> (*Naughton, 2012*)

Not all such co-construction is negative, of course. But the point is that it is increasingly out of our control. To this extent, we are becoming a character in our biography rather than its director.

The online "reputation economy" (Madden & Smith, 2010; Zimmer & Hoffman, 2011) works not only on individual identity on blogs, forums, sharing apps and dating and rating cites (e.g., Schoeneman 2013), but also on corporate identity co-construction on sites like Yelp, Urban Spoon, Angie's List and Amazon. The shift in power to the consumer is well recognized in the commercial realm, but less so in the personal realm. We can see the potentially devastating effects of online others in the cases of revenge porn, sabotaging our social media pages by former partners who have our passwords (Gershon, 2011) and cyberbullying. Surveillance by current or potential employers or schools can also dramatically affect lives and careers, as one rescinded early admission invitee to Bowdoin College learned when she Tweeted about their "lame presentation" (Singer, 2013).

Others can also initiate rather than respond to our digital self-presentations. They can post and tag us in photos, mention us in their social media pages, endorse our skills on LinkedIn (and expect us to reciprocate with our own "unsolicited endorsement"). As we have seen, posting selfies when trying on clothes at a retailer can garner instant feedback, shaping our self-image and purchase likelihood before we leave the dressing room (Drenton 2012). Even our pre-natal and post-mortem images can be shaped by others online (e.g., Carroll & Romano, 2010). In these and other ways our digital self is very much a co-construction rather than simply a self-presentation. Cooley's (1902) looking glass is no longer the reflector of a scripted dramaturgical presentation of self as Goffman (1959) envisioned. In the digital era it has become an improvisational stage-play with other actors who are often anonymous and unseen. Whether they are benign or malicious, they introduce an entirely new facet to the mirror of old. Besides other people helping to co-construct our individual sense of self online, the Internet also facilitates our aggregate sense of self. Adolescent girls sharing a piece of clothing (Lurie, Palca, & House, 1981) or giving each other mutual gifts (Segev, Shoham, & Ruvio, 2012) can forge bonds of mutual identity. Similarly, online sharing of information, gossip, music and video files, links to interesting URLs, photos or simply phatic text messages or emails saying little more than "I am here and you are my friend", all help to shape and reinforce a sense of shared aggregate identity. Although not all of our Facebook "friends" cohere as a group, there are other online communities – brand communities, fellow participants in online worlds, blogs and their followers, online fan communities, as well as subsets of our close Facebook friends – which do give us a sense of sharing a joint sense of self as members of the collective (e.g., Cova, Kozinets, & Shankar, 2007; Pearce, 2009; Rettberg, 2008; Schau, Muñiz, & Arnould, 2009). Besides these explicitly formed groups of others, we can also reach out electronically to more anonymous groups of others with queries such as "How do I transfer photos from my iPhone to my computer?" By posing our question to a search engine we are likely to be taken to helpful online forums, instructive YouTube videos and specialized apps that can solve our problems or inquiries. In so doing, we gain a feeling that we are not alone and can draw from the vast Internet resources of unseen others. This feeling of being a part of something that others have helped construct can also be seen as a self-extending and self-enlarging act. But McKenna and Seigman (2006) suggest that this same vast set of resources can also make us feel small and anonymous online. They propose that the marginalizing of the individual self under such circumstances makes us cling more tenaciously to aggregate group identities online. It is also ironic that spending time participating with others online may take time away from interacting with friends and family face to face.

Occupying an avatar that we have selected and modified is another way in which we present ourselves in online virtual worlds and interactive games. As Ouellette (2014) observes, "Avatars are a virtual extension of the self" (p. 140; see also Stotler and Dill's chapter on gaming). We dress, equip, customize and operate our avatar. In so doing we gradually come to feel that these alter egos are us, including taking their successes, failures and the compliments we (i.e., our avatars) receive from other avatars personally (Biocca, 1997). With avatars we are re-embodied in what is often an image of our ideal self (Kozinets & Kedzior, 2009). When avatars are assigned by an experimenter, Yee (2014) finds a "Proteus Effect", named after a shape-shifting Greek god. If the avatar is taller rather than shorter, we feel more confident; if it is more attractive rather than less so, we feel more sociable; if it is more physically fit rather than less fit, we are inclined to exercise more; and if it is older rather than younger, we are more inclined to save money. Moreover, these effects carry over to our offline lives as well. Some caution is in order, however, as it is not clear that the same Proteus Effects occur when we select or craft our own avatars. Others have suggested that besides acting as expressions and embodiments of our ideal selves, avatars allow us to explore our possible selves (Biocca, 1997; Denegri-Knott & Molesworth, 2010; Young & Whitty, 2012). There is some evidence that children are more likely to engage in such exploration with their avatars, that they can become quite attached to these avatars (Wang, Zhao, & Bamossy, 2009), and that their choices of avatars and online worlds change as they get older (Bryant & Akerman, 2009). For example, they shift from cute animal avatars during pre-adolescence to more style-conscious adolescent avatars who pay attention to "cool" clothing, grooming and brands.

Besides avatars, there is evidence that we get attached to other virtual possessions in online games and virtual worlds (Watkins & Molesworth, 2012). Denegri-Knott, Watkins and Wood (2012) find that just as consumers perform possession rituals to make new possessions feel more like they are truly ours (McCracken, 1986), consumers of virtual goods also customize homes and possessions in order to ritually possess them more fully. Furthermore, just as consumers may feel that a loss of real-world possessions is a loss of self and a threat to feelings of psychological security (Belk, 1988; Ferraro, Escalas, & Bettman, 2007), they can also feel a loss of virtual possessions as a similar blow to self (Belk, 2013). Because our computer or hard drive could crash, a virtual world or online game could shut down, or our files could become corrupt or lost, our grasp of virtual possessions is more tenuous than with material possessions. This leads some users to obsessively back up their files of digital possessions like photos or music (Odom et al., 2012). But it also results in feelings of vulnerability that are greater than is the case with real-world possessions (Watkins & Molesworth, 2012). Siddiqui and Turley (2006) also find greater uncertainty and lesser feelings of "authenticity" with virtual possessions compared with their real-world counterparts. As a result, Belk (2013) concludes that virtual possessions are "almost the same, but not quite". This suggests that virtual possessions play a less vital role in constituting the extended self than is the case with more tangible possessions. Given the sensual, multisensory and mnemonic pleasures of tangible collections as well as the lower effort required to download virtual music or other objects for a digital collection, we might expect intangible digital objects to provide an impoverished experience and a lower sense of self-investment in the collection. Indeed this is what several others have observed (e.g., Giles, Pietrzykowski, & Clark, 2007; McCourt, 2005), especially for highly involved music collectors who still prefer vinyl or CDs (Styvén, 2010). It seems likely that because digital objects are more vulnerable to loss and because they are more identical to the same object owned by others (e.g., digital music lacks the unique hisses and pops of vinyl recording), we feel they are both less ours and less "us". But perhaps a generation brought up in the current era when more and more "things" are digital will feel less tenuousness and uncertainty about their virtual possessions and make less of a distinction between digital and material possessions.

How our consumption impacts others

Apart from the status signalling that possessions may allow, if our possessions are expressive and constitutive of our selves, others should be able to make reasonable inferences about us based on our stuff. Through a series of studies, Gosling (2008) found that we can make inferences about others from seeing what and how they consume and that these inferences correspond to the way these others think about themselves and how they respond to personality inventories. For instance, showing subjects photos of others' dormitory rooms, examining their music collections, their books and their arrangement and ordering of furnishings, produced personality assessments that accurately paralleled the owners' measured personalities. Furthermore, viewing their Facebook and web pages similarly produced accurate profiles. Apparently, for other people, we are what we drive, what we wear, what we eat, what we read, what we post, what we listen to, and where and how we live and consume. There is always the possibility of false cues and misleading impression management, and not all signalling about our selves through our possessions is intentional. But by and large we do communicate a great deal about our selves through consumption. And whereas in an earlier era, with smaller towns and villages and more cohesive neighbourhoods, we might be called to account for consuming in a way that was not really "us", in more anonymous contemporary and online societies we are likely to take apparent consumption indications at face value as being indicative of who we are, regardless of whether some of our consumption, like cars, dresses and designer accessories, may be rented on a short-term basis rather than owned (Belk, 2014b).

This brings us back to social comparison considerations, but with a more critical lens. As Belk (1988) observes, consumer–object relations are almost never simply about a person and a thing. Rather, they are person–thing–other person relationships. Others' consumption patterns and regard for certain consumer goods influence our own consumption desires. When we observe others' consumption we might disdain, admire or envy them and covet their possessions in comparison with our own. Envy has traditionally been considered a negative emotion in which the envier "hopes that the envied person will lose the desired thing and may even conspire to make it happen" (Schimmel, 2008, p. 18). This is malicious envy and is seen vividly in "money burning" experiments in which the envier gives up his or her own earnings in order to reduce the income of the envied person (e.g., Zizzo, 2003; Zizzo & Oswald, 2001). But it has been suggested that affluent consumers are more often afflicted with "benign envy" in which the desire is to "level up" to the consumption of the envied person rather than "level down" by bringing this person's consumption or resources to the level of our own (Belk, 2008, 2011; D'Arms & Kerr, 2008; Smith & Kim, 2007). This is what is meant by "keeping up with the Joneses" (Matt, 2003; Stearns, 1999). There is some evidence that both benign and malicious envy may occur among consumers (Ven, 2009; Ven, Zeelenberg, & Pieters, 2009, 2011), depending on feelings of deservingness (Belk, 2011).

Conclusions and areas for future research

The contention that we are defined for ourselves and others by what we consume is not new and can be traced back at least to William James (1981 [1890], 1963 [1892]). I have argued that self is a dynamic hypothetical construct sustained by the illusion of continuity, and is nourished by the constancy of our durable possessions (Belk, 1991, 2013). Although some of the early empirical work on possessions and the extended self was quantitative (Belk, 1987), much of the subsequent empirical work has been qualitative. However, it is encouraging to see that there is now evidence for the theoretical formulation in fields as diverse as neuroscience (e.g., Kim & Johnson, 2012) and linguistics (Fost, 2013). Fost (2013), for example, argues that we so identify with some possessions that we refer to them as a part of us – e.g., "I am parked out back". Kim and Johnson (2012) found that there was increased activity in the medial prefrontal cortex when people were asked to think about self-relevant objects that belonged to them, but not when they thought about these objects belonging to others. There is also growing evidence of the self extended through possessions from experimental social psychology (e.g., Morrison & Johnson, 2011; Park & John, 2010; Rucker & Galinsky, 2009; Sundie et al., 2011; Swaminathan, Stilley, & Ahluwalia, 2009; Weiss & Johar, 2013) as well as clinical psychology (Frost & Steketee, 2010), evolutionary psychology (Nelissen & Meijers, 2011), psychoanalysis (Desmond, 2013) and cultural studies (Woodward, 2007), among other fields.

What is new and in need of further research is the growing role of digital media and communications in the presentation of self via consumption. There are a number of treatments that suggest that with the proliferation of digital representation possibilities, we now need to more self-consciously craft and monitor the self as if we were brands (Aggarwal & McGill, 2012; Labrecque, Markos, & Milne, 2011; Shepherd, 2005; Suler, 2002). If this advice results in increasingly carefully crafted online presentations of self, it may be that we have moved from ascribed identity to achieved identity to constructed identity. And as with hyperbole and exaggeration in advertising, we may also find a declining sense of sincerity and authenticity in these self-representations (Potter, 2010).

We are learning more about how and when consumers define themselves through their consumption, but we need to consider more deeply the questions of why consumers do this and with what effect on their well-being. If Cushman (1990) is right that we are trying to fill an emptiness that cannot be filled by the therapeutic culture of brand meanings that advertising advocates, we might now question whether the dematerialization of many possessions in a digital world makes us even less fulfilled. Alternatively, the interconnectedness, sharing and self-extension spurred by the Internet may provide the sorts of human relationships that increasingly seem to elude us in our face-to-face encounters. But much work remains to be done before we can begin to make such assessments.

Although some reference has been made here to differences in independent versus dependent selves and standing out versus fitting in, the impact of such cultural differences remains largely unexplored. There are not only individual levels of self, but aggregate levels of self as well (Belk, 1988), including national self-image. And national self-image involves a different sort of social comparison, not only with self and the Other or other cultures, but also imaginations of one's nation vis-à-vis other nations. And some of these comparisons are articulated and expressed through consumer goods from other material cultures. We can see, for example, that the sudden impact of goods from the New World greatly affected the national self-image of the Netherlands and its inhabitants during the Dutch Golden Age of the seventeenth century (Brook, 2009; Schama, 1988). At approximately the same time the English were experiencing a dramatic influx of Chinese goods, including tea, silk and chinaware, and using these items to envision England's position on the world stage (Jenkins, 2013; Markley, 2006; Porter, 2010). For China itself, the late nineteenth and early twentieth century before the formation of the PRC in 1949 was a similar period of a massive influx of foreigners and foreigner goods, especially in Shanghai and Canton (now Guangzhou). This too prompted a great rise in concern with Chinese identity and boycotts of foreign goods as well as campaigns to "buy national" (e.g., Dikötter, 2006; Wang, 2008). And since China reopened to the West in 1979, there has been another wave of questioning of Chinese identity in a global world full of attractive Western brands (e.g., Garon & Maclachlan, 2006; Griffiths, 2013; Lu, 2008; Tian & Dong, 2010; Wang, 2000; Zhiyan, Borgerson, & Schroeder, 2013; Zhou & Belk, 2004). The issue of global versus local brands is an important one in this context and much work remains to be done in this area as well.

References

Aggarwal, P., & McGill, A. L. (2012). When brands seem human, do humans act like brands? Automatic behavioural priming effects of brand anthropomorphism. *Journal of Consumer Research*, *39*(2), 307–323. doi: 10.1086/662614

Ahuvia, A. C. (2005). Beyond the extended self: Loved objects and consumers' identity narratives. *Journal of Consumer Research*, *32*(1), 171–184. doi: 10.1086/429607

Appadurai, A. (1986). Introduction: Commodities and the politics of value. In A. Appadurai (Ed.), *The social life of things: Commodities in cultural perspective* (pp. 3–36). Cambridge: Cambridge University Press.

Aron, A., Aron, E. N., Tudor, M., & Nelson, G. (1991). Close relationships as including other in the self. *Journal of Personality and Social Psychology*, *60*(2), 241–253. doi: 10.1037/0022-3514.60.2.241

Arsel, Z., & Bean, J. (2013). Taste regimes and market-mediated practice. *Journal of Consumer Research*, *39*(5), 899–917. doi: 10.1086/666595

Bagozzi, R. (2013). Social influence and the self. In A. A. Ruvio & R. Belk (Eds.), *The Routledge companion to identity and consumption* (pp. 255–264). London: Routledge.

Bahl, S., & Milne, G. R. (2010). Talking to ourselves: A dialogical exploration of consumption experiences. *Journal of Consumer Research, 37*(1), 176–195. doi: 10.1086/650000

Bardhi, F., & Askegaard, S. (2009). Home away from home: Home as order and dwelling in mobility. In J. F. Sherry Jr & E. Fischer (Eds.), *Explorations in consumer culture theory* (Vol. 8, pp. 83–97). London: Routledge.

Bardhi, F., Eckhardt, G. M., & Arnould, E. J. (2012). Liquid relationship to possessions. *Journal of Consumer Research, 39*(3), 510–529. doi: 10.1086/664037

Belk, R. (1984). Cultural and historical differences in concepts of self and their effects on attitudes towards having and giving. *Advances in Consumer Research, 11*(1), 753–760.

Belk, R. (1987). Identity and the relevance of market, personal, and community objects. In J. Umiker-Sebeok (Ed.), *Marketing and semiotics: New directions in the study of signs for sale* (Vol. 77, pp. 151–164). Berlin: Walter de Gruyter & Co.

Belk, R. (1988). Possessions and the extended self. *Journal of Consumer Research, 15*(2), 139–168. doi: 10.2307/2489522

Belk, R. (1991). Possessions and the sense of past. In R. Belk (Ed.), *Highways and buyways: Naturalistic research from the consumer behaviour odyssey* (pp. 114–130). Provo, UT: Association for Consumer Research.

Belk, R. (1992a). Attachment to possessions. In I. Altman & S. Low (Eds.), *Place attachment* (Vol. 12, pp. 37–62). New York, NY: Springer US.

Belk, R. (1992b). Me and thee versus mine and thine: How perceptions of the body influence organ donation and transplantation. In J. Shanteau & R. J. Harris (Eds.), *Organ donation and transplantation: Psychological and behavioural factors* (pp. 139–149). Washington, DC: American Psychological Association.

Belk, R. (2008). Envy and marketing. In R. H. Smith (Ed.), *Envy: Theory and research* (pp. 211–226). Oxford: Oxford University Press.

Belk, R. (2010). Sharing. *Journal of Consumer Research, 36*(5), 715–734. doi: 10.1086/612649

Belk, R. (2011). Benign envy. *Academy of Marketing Science Review, 1*(3–4), 117–134. doi: 10.1007/s13162-011-0018-x

Belk, R. (2013). Extended self in a digital world. *Journal of Consumer Research, 40*(3), 477–500. doi: 10.1086/671052

Belk, R. (2014a). Digital consumption and the extended self. *Journal of Marketing Management, 30*(11–12), 1101–1118. doi: 10.1080/0267257X.2014.939217

Belk, R. (2014b). You are what you can access: Sharing and collaborative consumption online. *Journal of Business Research, 67*(8), 1595–1600. doi: 10.1016/j.jbusres.2013.10.001

Belk, R., & Llamas, R. (2013). Shared possessions/shared self. In A. A. Ruvio & R. Belk (Eds.), *The Routledge companion to identity and consumption* (pp. 265–272). London: Routledge.

Belk, R., Bahn, K. D., & Mayer, R. N. (1982). Developmental recognition of consumption symbolism. *Journal of Consumer Research, 9*(1), 4–17. doi: 10.2307/2488933

Belk, R. W., Groves, R., & Østergaard, P. (2000). Aboriginal consumer culture. In R. Belk (Ed.), *Research in consumer behaviour* (Vol. 9, pp. 1–45). Greenwich, CT: JAI Press.

Belk, R., Mayer, R., & Driscoll, A. (1984). Children's recognition of consumption symbolism in children's products. *Journal of Consumer Research, 10*(4), 386–397. doi: 10.2307/2488908

Berger, J., & Heath, C. (2007). Where consumers diverge from others: Identity signaling and product domains. *Journal of Consumer Research, 34*(2), 121–134.

Berger, J., & Ward, M. (2010). Subtle signals of inconspicuous consumption. *Journal of Consumer Research, 37*(4), 555–569. doi: 10.1086/655445

Biocca, F. (1997). The cyborg's dilemma: Progressive embodiment in virtual environments [1]. *Journal of Computer-Mediated Communication, 3*(2), 12–26. doi: 10.1111/j.1083-6101.1997.tb00070.x

Bolter, J. D. (1996). Virtual reality and the redefinition of self. In L. Strate & R. Jacobson (Eds.), *Communication and cyberspace: Social interaction in an electronic environment* (pp. 105–120). Croskill, NJ: Hampton Press.

Bourdieu, P. (1984). *Distinction: A social critique of the judgement of taste*. Cambridge, MA: Harvard University Press.

Boyd, D. (2010). Friendship. In M. Ito, S. Baumer, M. Bittanti, R. Cody, B. Herr-Stephenson, H. A. Horst, P. G. Lange, D. Mahendran, K. Z. Martínez & C. Pascoe (Eds.), *Hanging out, messing around, and geeking out* (pp. 79–115). Cambridge, MA: MIT Press.

Brasel, S. A., & Gips, J. (2014). Tablets, touchscreens, and touchpads: How varying touch interfaces trigger psychological ownership and endowment. *Journal of Consumer Psychology, 24*(2), 226–233. doi: 10.1016/j.jcps.2013.10.003

Brewer, M. B., & Gardner, W. (1996). Who is this "we"? Levels of collective identity and self representations. *Journal of Personality and Social Psychology, 71*(1), 83–93. doi: 10.1037/0022-3514.71.1.83

Brook, T. (2009). *Vermeer's hat: The seventeenth century and the dawn of the global world.* London: Profile Books.

Bryant, A. J., & Akerman, A. (2009). Finding mii: Virtual social identity and the young consumer. In N. T. Wood & M. R. Solomon (Eds.), *Virtual social identity and consumer behaviour.* Armonk, NY: E. M. Sharpe.

Carr, N. (2008). Is Google making us stupid? *Yearbook of the National Society for the Study of Education, 107*(2), 89–94. doi: 10.1111/j.1744-7984.2008.00172.x

Carroll, E., & Romano, J. (2010). *Your digital afterlife: When Facebook, Flickr and Twitter are your estate, what's your legacy?* Berkeley, CA: New Riders.

Chadha, R., & Husband, P. (2006). *The cult of the luxury brand: Inside Asia's love affair with luxury.* London: Nicholas Brealey.

Chan, C., Berger, J., & Boven, L. V. (2012). Identifiable but not identical: Combining social identity and uniqueness motives in choice. *Journal of Consumer Research, 39*(3), 561–573. doi: 10.1086/664804

Chaplin, L. N., & John, D. R. (2005). The development of self-brand connections in children and adolescents. *Journal of Consumer Research, 32*(1), 119–129. doi: 10.1086/426622

Chaplin, L. N., & Lowrey, T. M. (2010). The development of consumer-based consumption constellations in children. *Journal of Consumer Research, 36*(5), 757–777. doi: 10.1086/605365

Chatterjee, P., Irmak, C., & Rose, R. L. (2013). The endowment effect as self-enhancement in response to threat. *Journal of Consumer Research, 40*(3), 460–476. doi: 10.1086/671344

Chung, E., & Fischer, E. (2001). When conspicuous consumption becomes inconspicuous: The case of the migrant Hong Kong consumers. *Journal of Consumer Marketing, 18*(6), 474–487. doi:10.1108/07363760110404378

Connell, P. M., & Schau, H. J. (2013). The symbiosis model of identity augmentation: Self-expansion and self-extension as distinct strategies. In A. A. Ruvio & R. Belk (Eds.), *The Routledge companion to identity and consumption* (pp. 21–30). London: Routledge.

Cooley, C. H. (1902). *Human nature and the social order.* New York, NY: Scribner's.

Cova, B., Kozinets, R., & Shankar, A. (2007). *Consumer tribes.* Oxford: Butterworth-Heinemann.

Csikszentmihalyi, M., & Rochberg-Halton, E. (1981). *The meaning of things: Domestic symbols and the self.* Cambridge: Cambridge University Press.

Cushman, P. (1990). Why the self is empty: Toward a historically situated psychology. *American Psychologist, 45*(5), 599–611. doi: 10.1037/0003-066X.45.5.599

D'Arms, J., & Kerr, A. (2008). Envy in the philosophical tradition. In R. H. Smith (Ed.), *Envy: Theory and research* (pp. 39–59). Oxford: Oxford University Press.

Davies, J. (2007). Display, identity and the everyday: Self-presentation through online image sharing. *Discourse: Studies in the Cultural Politics of Education, 28*(4), 549–564. doi: 10.1080/01596300701625305

Denegri-Knott, J., & Molesworth, M. (2010). Concepts and practices of digital virtual consumption. *Consumption Markets & Culture, 13*(2), 109–132. doi: 10.1080/10253860903562130

Denegri-Knott, J., Watkins, R., & Wood, J. (2012). Transforming digital virtual goods into meaningful possessions. In M. Molesworth & J. Denegri-Knott (Eds.), *Digital virtual consumption* (Vol. 23, pp. 76–91). New York, NY: Routledge.

Desmond, J. (2013). *Psychoanalytic accounts of consuming desire: Hearts of darkness.* Houndmills: Palgrave Macmillan.

Dikötter, F. (2006). *Exotic commodities: Modern objects and everyday life in China.* New York, NY: Columbia University Press.

Dommer, S. L., & Swaminathan, V. (2013). Explaining the endowment effect through ownership: The role of identity, gender, and self-threat. *Journal of Consumer Research, 39*(5), 1034–1050. doi: 10.1086/666737

Doob, L. W. (1960). *Becoming more civilized: A psychological exploration.* New Haven, CT: Yale University Press.

Drenton, J. (2012). Snapshots of the self: Exploring the role of online mobile photo sharing in identity development among adolescent girls. In A. Close (Ed.), *Online consumer behaviour: Theory and research in social media, advertising, and e-tail* (pp. 3–34). New York, NY: Routledge.

Eckhardt, G. M., Belk, R. W., & Wilson, J. A. J. (2014). The rise of inconspicuous consumption. *Journal of Marketing Management, 31*(7–8), 1–20. doi: 10.1080/0267257X.2014.989890

Elliott, R., & Wattanasuwan, K. (1998). Consumption and the symbolic project of the self. In *European advances in consumer research* (Vol. 3, pp. 17–20). Provo, UT: Association for Consumer Research.

Epp, A. M., & Price, L. L. (2010). The storied life of singularized objects: Forces of agency and network transformation. *Journal of Consumer Research*, *36*(5), 820–837. doi: 10.1086/603547

Escalas, J. E., & Bettman, J. R. (2003). You are what they eat: The influence of reference groups on consumers' connections to brands. *Journal of Consumer Psychology*, *13*(3), 339–348. doi: 10.1207/S15327663JCP1303_14

Ferraro, R., Escalas, J. E., & Bettman, J. R. (2007). Attachment style, psychological security, and reaction to special possession loss. Paper presented at Association for Consumer Research Annual Conference, Memphis, Tennessee, October, 2007.

Festinger, L. (1954). A theory of social comparison processes. *Human Relations*, 7(2), 117–140. doi: 10.1177/001872675400700202

Fost, J. (2013). The extended self, functional constancy, and personal identity. *Linguistic and Philosophical Investigations*, *12*, 47–66.

Fournier, S. (1998). Consumers and their brands: Developing relationship theory in consumer research. *Journal of Consumer Research*, *24*(4), 343–353. doi: 10.1086/209515

Fournier, S., & Mick, D. G. (1999). Rediscovering satisfaction. *Journal of Marketing*, *63*(4), 5–23. doi: 10.2307/1251971

Frost, R., & Steketee, G. (2010). *Stuff: Compulsive hoarding and the meaning of things*. New York, NY: Houghton Mifflin Harcourt.

Gao, L., Wheeler, S. C., & Shiv, B. (2009). The "shaken self": Product choices as a means of restoring self-view confidence. *Journal of Consumer Research*, *36*(1), 29–38. doi: 10.1086/596028

Garon, S. M., & Maclachlan, P. L. (2006). *The ambivalent consumer: Questioning consumption in East Asia and the West*. Ithaca, NY: Cornell University Press.

Gershon, I. (2011). *The breakup 2.0: Disconnecting over new media*. Ithaca, NY: Cornell University Press.

Giddens, A. (1991). *Modernity and self-identity: Self and society in the late modern age*. Stanford, CA: Stanford University Press.

Giles, D. C., Pietrzykowski, S., & Clark, K. E. (2007). The psychological meaning of personal record collections and the impact of changing technological forms. *Journal of Economic Psychology*, *28*(4), 429–443. doi: 10.1016/j.joep.2006.08.002

Goffman, E. (1959). *The presentation of self in everyday life*. Garden City, NY: Doubleday.

Gosling, S. (2008). *Snoop: What your stuff says about you*. New York, NY: Basic Books.

Griffiths, M. B. (2013). *Consumers and individuals in China: Standing out, fitting in*. London: Routledge.

Häfner, M. (2004). How dissimilar others may still resemble the self: Assimilation and contrast after social comparison. *Journal of Consumer Psychology*, *14*(1–2), 187–196. doi: 10.1207/s15327663jcp1401&2_21

Hogg, M. K., & Michell, P. C. N. (1996). Identity, self and consumption: A conceptual framework. *Journal of Marketing Management*, *12*(7), 629–644. doi: 10.1080/0267257X.1996.9964441

Holt, D. B. (1998). Does cultural capital structure American consumption? *Journal of Consumer Research*, *25*(1), 1–25. doi: 10.1086/209523

Hood, B. (2012). *The self illusion: How the social brain creates identity*. New York, NY: Oxford University Press.

Hood, B. M., & Bloom, P. (2008). Children prefer certain individuals over perfect duplicates. *Cognition*, *106*(1), 455–462. doi: 10.1016/j.cognition.2007.01.012

James, W. (1981 [1890]). *The principles of psychology* (Vol. 1). London: Harvard University Press.

James, W. (1963 [1892]). *Psychology*. Greenwich, CT: Fawcett.

Jenkins, E. Z. (2013). *A taste for China: English subjectivity and the prehistory of orientalism* (Vol. 3). Oxford: Oxford University Press.

John, D. R. (1999). Consumer socialization of children: A retrospective look at twenty-five years of research. *Journal of Consumer Research*, *26*(3), 183–213. doi: 10.1086/209559

Joy, A., & Venkatesh, A. (1994). Postmodernism, feminism, and the body: The visible and the invisible in consumer research. *International Journal of Research in Marketing*, *11*(4), 333–357. doi: 10.1016/0167-8116(94)90011-6

Kahneman, D., & Tversky, A. (1979). Prospect theory: An analysis of decision under risk. *Econometrica*, *47*(2), 263–291. doi: 10.2307/1914185

Kim, K., & Johnson, M. K. (2012). Extended self: Medial prefrontal activity during transient association of self and objects. *Social Cognitive and Affective Neuroscience*, 7(2), 199–207. doi: 10.1093/scan/nsq096

Kirmani, A. (2009). The self and the brand. *Journal of Consumer Psychology*, *19*(3), 271–275. doi: 10.1016/j.jcps.2009.05.011

Kitayama, S., & Park, J. (2013). Culture and the self: Implications for consumer behaviour. In A. A. Ruvio & R. W. Belk (Eds.), *The Routledge companion to identity and consumption* (pp. 5–20). London: Routledge.
Kleine, R. E., Kleine, S. S., & Kernan, J. B. (1993). Mundane consumption and the self: A social-identity perspective. *Journal of Consumer Psychology, 2*(3), 209.
Kleine, S. S., & Baker, S. M. (2004). An integrative review of material possession attachment. *Academy of Marketing Science Review, 1*, 1–29.
Kleine, S. S., Kleine, R. E., & Allen, C. T. (1995). How is a possession "me" or "not me"? Characterizing types and an antecedent of material possession attachment. *Journal of Consumer Research, 22*(3), 327–343. doi: 10.2307/2489618
Kopytoff, I. (1986). The cultural biography of things: Commoditization as process. In A. Appadurai (Ed.), *The social life of things: Commodities in cultural perspective* (pp. 64–91). Cambridge: Cambridge University Press.
Kozinets, R. V., & Kedzior, R. (2009). I, avatar: Auto-netnographic research in virtual worlds. In N. T. Wood & M. R. Solomon (Eds.), *Virtual social identity and consumer behaviour* (pp. 3–19). Armonk, NY: M.E. Sharpe.
Labrecque, L. I., Markos, E., & Milne, G. R. (2011). Online personal branding: Processes, challenges, and implications. *Journal of Interactive Marketing, 25*(1), 37–50. doi: 10.1016/j.intmar.2010.09.002
Landon, E. L., Jr. (1974). Self concept, ideal self concept, and consumer purchase intentions. *Journal of Consumer Research, 1*(2), 44–51. doi: 10.2307/2489106
Lastovicka, J. L., & Fernandez, K. V. (2005). Three paths to disposition: The movement of meaningful possessions to strangers. *Journal of Consumer Research, 31*(4), 813–823. doi: 10.1086/426616
Lu, P. X. (2008). *Elite China: Luxury consumer behaviour in China*. Singapore: Wiley.
Lurie, A., Palca, D., & House, R. (1981). *The language of clothes*. New York, NY: Random House.
Madden, M. K., & Smith, A. W. (2010). Reputation management and social media: How people monitor their identity and search for others online. *Pew Internet & American Life Project*. Retrieved from www.pewinternet.org/2010/05/26/reputation-management-and-social-media/
Manguel, A. (1996). *A history of reading*. Toronto: Alfred Knopf.
Markley, R. (2006). *The Far East and the English imagination, 1600-1730*. Cambridge: Cambridge University Press.
Markus, H. R., & Kitayama, S. (1991). Culture and the self: Implications for cognition, emotion, and motivation. *Psychological Review, 98*(2), 224–253
Mason, R. (1981). *Conspicuous consumption*. New York, NY: St. Martin's Press.
Matt, S. J. (2003). *Keeping up with the Joneses: Envy in American consumer society, 1890-1930*. Philadelphia, PA: University of Pennsylvania Press.
McCourt, T. (2005). Collecting music in the digital realm. *Popular Music and Society, 28*(2), 249–252. doi: 10.1080/03007760500045394
McCracken, G. (1986). *Culture and consumption: New approaches to the symbolic character of consumer goods and activities* (Vol. 1). Bloomington, IN: Indiana University Press.
McKenna, K., & Seigman, G. (2006). Considering the interactions: The effects of the internet on self and society. In R. Kraut, M. Brynin & S. Kiesler (Eds.), *Computers, phones, and the internet: Domesticating information technology* (Vol. 2). Oxford: Oxford University Press.
Morewedge, C. K., Shu, L. L., Gilbert, D. T., & Wilson, T. D. (2009). Bad riddance or good rubbish? Ownership and not loss aversion causes the endowment effect. *Journal of Experimental Social Psychology, 45*(4), 947–951. doi: 10.1016/j.jesp.2009.05.014
Morrison, K. R., & Johnson, C. S. (2011). When what you have is who you are: Self-uncertainty leads individualists to see themselves in their possessions. *Personality and Social Psychology Bulletin, 37*(5), 639–651. doi: 10.1177/0146167211403158
Naughton, J. (2012, October 21). How social networks can destroy your social life. *The Guardian*. Retrieved from www.theguardian.com/technology/2012/oct/21/john-naughton-foursquare-social-networking
Nayakankuppam, D., & Mishra, H. (2005). The endowment effect: Rose-tinted and dark-tinted glasses. *Journal of Consumer Research, 32*(3), 390–395. doi: 10.1086/497550
Nelissen, R. M. A., & Meijers, M. H. C. (2011). Social benefits of luxury brands as costly signals of wealth and status. *Evolution and Human Behaviour, 32*(5), 343–355. doi: 10.1016/j.evolhumbehav.2010.12.002
Odom, W., Sellen, A., Harper, R., & Thereska, E. (2012). Lost in translation: Understanding the possession of digital things in the cloud. Paper presented at the *SIGCHI Conference on Human Factors in Computing Systems*, Austin, TX.
Ouellette, J. (2014). *Me, myself and why: Searching for the science of self*. New York, NY: Penguin.

Park, J. K., & John, D. R. (2010). Got to get you into my life: Do brand personalities rub off on consumers? *Journal of Consumer Research, 37*(4), 655–669. doi: 10.1086/655807

Pearce, C. (2009). *Artemesia, communities of play: Emergent cultures in multiplayer games and virtual worlds*. Cambridge, MA: The MIT Press.

Pettigrew, S. (2002). Consumption and the self concept. *Media and Culture, 5*(3), 1–3.

Pierce, J. L., Kostova, T., & Dirks, K. T. (2003). The state of psychological ownership: Integrating and extending a century of research. *Review of General Psychology*, 7(1), 84–107. doi: 10.1037/1089-2680.7.1.84

Porter, D. (2010). *The Chinese taste in eighteenth-century England*. New York, NY: Cambridge University Press.

Postrel, V. (2008, July 1). Inconspicuous consumption: A new theory of the leisure class. *The Atlantic*. Retrieved from www.theatlantic.com/magazine/archive/2008/07/inconspicuous-consumption/306845/

Potter, A. (2010). *The authenticity hoax: How we get lost finding ourselves*. Toronto: McClelland & Stewart.

Rettberg, J. W. (2008). *Blogging*. Cambridge: Polity.

Richins, M. L. (1991). Social comparison and the idealized images of advertising. *Journal of Consumer Research, 18*(1), 71–83. doi: 10.2307/2489486

Ronson, J. (2015, February 12). How one stupid tweet blew up Justine Sacco's life. Opinion. *The New York Times*. Retrieved from www.nytimes.com/2015/02/15/magazine/how-one-stupid-tweet-ruined-justine-saccos-life.html?_r=0

Rucker, D. D., & Galinsky, A. D. (2009). Conspicuous consumption versus utilitarian ideals: How different levels of power shape consumer behaviour. *Journal of Experimental Social Psychology, 45*(3), 549–555. doi: 10.1016/j.jesp.2009.01.005

Schama, S. (1988). *The embarrassment of riches: An interpretation of Dutch culture in the Golden Age*. Berkeley, CA: University of California Press.

Schau, H. J., & Gilly, M. C. (2003). We are what we post? Self-presentation in personal web space. *Journal of Consumer Research, 30*(3), 385–404. doi: 10.1086/378616

Schau, H. J., Muñiz, A. M., & Arnould, E. J. (2009). How brand community practices create value. *Journal of Marketing, 73*(5), 30–51. doi: 10.1509/jmkg.73.5.30

Schembri, S., Merrilees, B., & Kristiansen, S. (2010). Brand consumption and narrative of the self. *Psychology and Marketing, 27*(6), 623–637. doi: 10.1002/mar.20348

Schenk, C. T., & Holman, R. H. (1980). A sociological approach to brand choice: The concept of situational self-image. *Advances in consumer research* (Vol. 7, pp. 610–614). Ann Arbor, MI: Association for Consumer Research.

Schimmel, S. (2008). Envy in Jewish thought and literature. In R. H. Smith (Ed.), *Envy: Theory and research* (pp. 17–38). Oxford: Oxford University Press.

Schouten, J. W. (1991). Selves in transition: Symbolic consumption in personal rites of passage and identity reconstruction. *Journal of Consumer Research*, 17(4), 412–425. doi: 10.2307/2626836

Segev, R., Shoham, A., & Ruvio, A. (2012). What does this gift say about me, you, and us? The role of adolescents' gift giving in managing their impressions among their peers. *Psychology & Marketing, 29*(10), 752–764. doi: 10.1002/mar.20561

Shepherd, I. D. H. (2005). From cattle and coke to Charlie: Meeting the challenge of self marketing and personal branding. *Journal of Marketing Management, 21*(5/6), 589–606.

Siddiqui, S., & Turley, D. (2006). Extending the self in a virtual world. *Advances in Consumer Research, 33*(1), 647–648.

Simmel, G. (1904). Fashion. *International Journal of Sociology, 8*, 124–147.

Singer, N. (2013, November 9). They loved your G.P.A. Then they saw your tweets. *The New York Times*. Retrieved from www.nytimes.com/2013/11/10/business/they-loved-your-gpa-then-they-saw-your-tweets.html?_r=0

Sirgy, M. J. (1982). Self-concept in consumer behaviour: A critical review. *Journal of Consumer Research, 9*(3), 287–300. doi: 10.2307/2488624

Sirgy, M. J., Johar, J. S., & Wood, M. (1986). Determinants of product value-expressiveness: Another look at conspicuousness, differentiation, and common usage. Paper presented at the *Academy of Marketing Science (AMS) Annual Conference*, Atlanta, Georgia.

Smith, R. H., & Kim, S. H. (2007). Comprehending envy. *Psychological Bulletin, 133*(1), 46–64. doi: 10.1037/0033-2909.133.1.46

Solomon, M. R., & Assael, H. (1987). The forest or the trees?: A gestalt approach to symbolic consumption. In J. Umiker-Sebeok (Ed.), *Marketing and semiotics: New directions in the study of signs for sale* (pp. 189–218). Bloomington, IN: Indiana University Press.

Solove, D. J. (2007). *The future of reputation: Gossip, rumor, and privacy on the internet.* New Haven, CT: Yale University Press.

Stearns, P. N. (1999). *Battleground of desire: The struggle for self-control in modern America.* New York, NY: New York University Press.

Styvén, M. E. (2010). The need to touch: Exploring the link between music involvement and tangibility preference. *Journal of Business Research, 63*(9–10), 1088–1094. doi: 10.1016/j.jbusres.2008.11.010

Suler, J. (2002). Identity management in cyberspace. *Journal of Applied Psychoanalytic Studies, 4*(4), 455–459. doi: 10.1023/A:1020392231924

Sundie, J. M., Kenrick, D. T., Griskevicius, V., Tybur, J. M., Vohs, K. D., & Beal, D. J. (2011). Peacocks, Porsches, and Torstein Veblen: Conspicuous consumption as a sexual signaling system. *Journal of Personality and Social Psychology, 100*(4), 664–680. doi: 10.1037/a0021669

Swaminathan, V., Page, K. L., & Gürhan-Canli, Z. (2007). "My" brand or "our" brand: The effects of brand relationship dimensions and self-construal on brand evaluations. *Journal of Consumer Research, 34*(2), 248–259. doi: 10.1086/518539

Swaminathan, V., Stilley, K. M., & Ahluwalia, R. (2009). When brand personality matters: The moderating role of attachment styles. *Journal of Consumer Research, 35*(6), 985–1002. doi: 10.1086/593948

Thaler, R. (1980). Toward a positive theory of consumer choice. *Journal of Economic Behaviour & Organization, 1*(1), 39–60. doi: 10.1016/0167-2681(80)90051-7

Thompson, C. J., & Hirschman, E. C. (1995). Understanding the socialized body: A poststructuralist analysis of consumers' self-conceptions, body images, and self-care practices. *Journal of Consumer Research, 22*(2), 139–153. doi: 10.2307/2489808

Tian, K., & Belk, R. (2005). Extended self and possessions in the workplace. *Journal of Consumer Research, 32*(2), 297–310. doi: 10.1086/432239

Tian, K., & Dong, L. (2010). *Consumer-citizens of China: The role of foreign brands in the imagined future China.* London: Routledge.

Townsend, C., & Sood, S. (2012). Self-affirmation through the choice of highly aesthetic products. *Journal of Consumer Research, 39*(2), 415–428. doi: 10.1086/663775

Tuan, Y. (1982). *Segmented worlds and self: Group life and individual consciousness.* Minneapolis, MN: University of Minnesota Press.

Tufekci, Z. (2012). We were always human. In N. Whitehead & M. Wesch (Eds.), *Human no more: Digital subjectivities, un-human subjects, and the end of anthropology* (pp. 33–47). Boulder, CO: University Press of Colorado.

Turkle, S. (1984). *The second self: Computers and the human spirit.* New York, NY: Simon & Schuster.

Veblen, T. (1899). *The theory of the leisure class.* New York, NY: Macmillan.

Ven, N. v. d. (2009). *The bright side of a deadly sin: The psychology of envy* (Doctoral dissertation). Tilburg University, Amsterdam.

Ven, N. v. d., Zeelenberg, M., & Pieters, R. (2009). Leveling up and down: The experiences of benign and malicious envy. *Emotion, 9*(3), 419–429. doi: 10.1037/a0015669

Ven, N. V. d., Zeelenberg, M., & Pieters, R. (2011). The envy premium in product evaluation. *Journal of Consumer Research, 37*(6), 984–998. doi: 10.1086/657239

Wang, C., Bristol, T., Mowen, J. C., & Chakraborty, G. (2000). Alternative modes of self-construal: Dimensions of connectedness-separateness and advertising appeals to the cultural and gender-specific self. *Journal of Consumer Psychology, 9*(2), 107–115.

Wang, J. (2000). *Foreign advertising in China: Becoming global, becoming local.* Ames, IA: State University Press.

Wang, J. (2008). *Brand new China: Advertising, media and commercial culture.* Cambridge, MA: Harvard University Press.

Wang, J. J., Zhao, X., & Bamossy, G. J. (2009). The sacred and the profane in online gaming: A netnographic inquiry of Chinese gamers. In N. T. Wood & M. R. Solomon (Eds.), *Virtual social identity and consumer behaviour* (pp. 109–124). Armonk, NY: E. M. Sharpe.

Watkins, R., & Molesworth, M. (2012). Attachment to digital virtual possessions in videogames. In R. Belk, S. Askegaard & L. Scott (Eds.), *Research in consumer behaviour* (Vol. 14, pp. 153–170). Bingley: Emerald Group.

Weiss, L., & Johar, G. V. (2013). Egocentric categorization and product judgment: Seeing your traits in what you own (and their opposite in what you don't). *Journal of Consumer Research, 40*(1), 185–201. doi: 10.1086/669330

Weisz, J. R., Rothbaum, F. M., & Blackburn, T. C. (1984). Standing out and standing in: The psychology of control in America and Japan. *American Psychologist, 39*(9), 955–969. doi: 10.1037/0003-066X.39.9.955

Wicklund, R. A., & Gollwitzer, P. M. (1982). *Symbolic self-completion*. Hillsdale, NJ: Erlbaum.

Wong, N., & Ahuvia, A. C. (1998). Personal taste and family face: Luxury consumption in Confucian and Western societies. *Psychology and Marketing, 15*(5), 423–441. doi: 10.1002/(SICI)1520-6793(199808)15:5<423::AID-MAR2>3.0.CO;2-9

Wong, P., & Hogg, M. (2013). Exploring cultural differences in the extended self. In A. A. Ruvio & R. Belk (Eds.), *The Routledge companion to identity and consumption* (pp. 99–108). London: Routledge.

Woodward, I. (2007). *Understanding material culture*. London: Sage.

Wright, N. D., Claiborne, C. B., & Sirgy, M. J. (1992). The effects of product symbolism on consumer self-concept. *Advances in Consumer Research, 19*(1), 311–318.

Yee, N. (2014). *The protest paradox: How online games and virtual worlds change us – and how they don't*. New Haven, CT: Yale University Press.

Young, G., & Whitty, M. T. (2012). *Transcending taboos: A moral and psychological examination of cyberspace*. New York, NY: Routledge.

Zhao, S. (2005). The digital self: Through the looking glass of telecopresent others. *Symbolic Interaction, 28*(3), 387–405. doi: 10.1525/si.2005.28.3.387

Zhiyan, W., Borgerson, J., & Schroeder, J. (2013). *From Chinese brand culture to global brands: Insights from aesthetics, fashion and history*. London: Palgrave Macmillan.

Zhou, N., & Belk, R. W. (2004). Chinese consumer readings of global and local advertising appeals. *Journal of Advertising, 33*(3), 63–76. doi: 10.1080/00913367.2004.10639169

Zimmer, M., & Hoffman, A. (2011). Privacy, context, and oversharing: Reputational challenges in a Web 2.0 world. In H. Masum & M. Tovey (Eds.), *The reputation society: How online opinions are reshaping the offline world* (pp. 175–184). Cambridge, MA: MIT Press.

Zizzo, D. J. (2003). Money burning and rank egalitarianism with random dictators. *Economics Letters, 81*(2), 263–266. doi: 10.1016/S0165-1765(03)00190-3

Zizzo, D. J., & Oswald, A. J. (2001). Are people willing to pay to reduce others' incomes? *Annales d'Économie et de Statistique, 63/64*, 39–65. doi: 10.2307/20076295

10

Revisiting self-congruity theory in consumer behaviour

Making sense of the research so far

M. Joseph Sirgy, Dong-Jin Lee and Grace B. Yu

Before discussing the research related to self-congruity, we need to help the novice reader understand what self-congruity is. Self-congruity is the psychological process and outcome that a consumer engages in given that the consumer compares his or her perception of a brand image (more specifically, brand personality or brand-user image) with his or her own self-concept (e.g., actual self-image). Differently put, it is the process and outcome directly related to the consumer's identification with a brand. For example, a consumer may perceive users of an Apple computer to be creative and he or she may think that he or she is creative (match between brand personality and actual self-image). In this instance, we refer to this process as self-congruity, and the outcome is essentially a high level of identification with the brand (or high level of self-congruity). Over the last 30+ years, much research has been done on self-congruity theory in consumer behaviour and marketing. For literature reviews, see Claiborne and Sirgy (1990); Johar and Sirgy (1991); Sirgy (1982, 1985a, 1985b, 1986); Sirgy, Johar, Samli and Claiborne (1991); Sirgy, Grewal and Mangelburg (2000); Sirgy and Su (2000); and more recently a meta-analysis by Aguirre-Rodriguez, Bosnjak and Sirgy (2012).

What is the role of self-congruity in consumer behaviour? Studies found that self-congruity plays an important role in creating consumer value (e.g., Holloway & Plant, 1988; Moliner, Sánchez, Rodríguez, & Callarisa, 2007), generating sustainable competitive advantage and brand equity (e.g., Aguirre-Rodriguez et al., 2012). Studies also found that self-congruity influences consumption behaviour–pre-purchase behaviour (e.g., consumer attitude towards the product, preference for a brand, willingness to purchase the brand, and brand choice) and post-purchase behaviour (e.g., satisfaction with the brand, brand trust and commitment to the brand and word-of-mouth related to the brand). Despite the plethora of research on self-congruity in various contexts (Aguirre-Rodriguez et al., 2012), there is a need to integrate the study findings in an overall theoretical framework.

This chapter reviews the current state of self-congruity research in consumer psychology with the goal of generating a set of theoretical propositions to spur future research. The chapter is organized as follows. First, we will review four different types of self-congruity (actual, ideal, social and ideal social self-congruity) along with their motivations. Second, we will discuss the bias effect of self-congruity on functional congruity. Third, we will then present a set of moderators under which self-congruity is likely to have a significant influence on pre- and post-purchase consumer behaviours. Finally, future research directions are discussed.

Towards an integrated model of self-congruity

An integrated model of self-congruity is developed in this section and is shown in Figure 10.1. Self-congruity is a process involving a comparison between the consumer's self-concept and brand personality with an outcome of high or low self-congruity. Functional congruity, in contrast, involves a comparison between the consumer's expectations and actual perceptions of the brand's utilitarian attributes with an outcome of high or low functional congruity. The conceptual model shown in the figure argues that both self-congruity and functional congruity influence consumers' perception of value, pre-purchase behaviour (i.e., brand evaluation, brand choice) and post-purchase behaviour (i.e., brand satisfaction, brand trust and commitment, word-of-mouth communications). We propose that that the strength of self-congruity effect is moderated by a set of consumer characteristics, brand characteristics and the cultural context. Specifically, we surmise that the strength of self-congruity effect is moderated by consumer characteristics (consumer age, consumer involvement, consumer product knowledge, childhood brand attachment), brand characteristics (brand conspicuousness, brand identity salience) and the cultural context (individualism vs. collectivism). One of the central concepts in the integrated self-congruity model is consumer self-concept, which we discuss first.

Consumer self-concept

Much research in self-congruity in consumer psychology has identified four dimensions of consumer self-concept to explain and predict consumer behaviour. These are the actual self-image, the ideal self-image, the social self-image and the ideal social self-image (Sirgy, 1982; Sirgy & Su, 2000). The *actual self-image* is defined as how consumers see themselves actually.

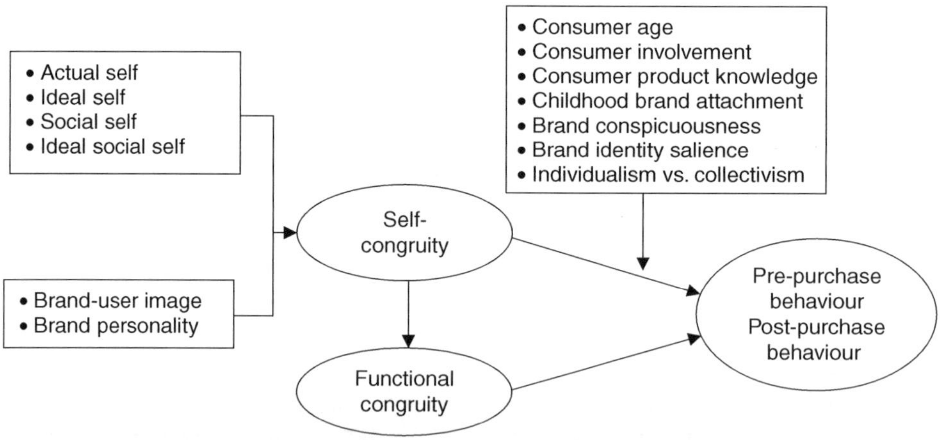

Figure 10.1 An integrated model of self-congruity.

Notes: Self-congruity is a formative concept made up of four dimensions, namely actual self-congruity, ideal self-congruity, social self-congruity, and ideal social self-congruity. Actual self-congruity is motivated by the need for self-consistency, ideal self-congruity is motivated by the need for self-esteem, social self-congruity is motivated by the need for social consistency, and the ideal social self-congruity is motivated by the need for social approval.

The actual self refers to a representation of image attributes that the individual believes he or she possesses (Higgins, 1987, 1989). The *ideal self-image* is defined as how consumers would like to see themselves. The ideal self refers to a representation of image attributes that the individual wishes or hopes to possess (Higgins, 1987, 1989). The *social self-image* is defined as how consumers believe they are seen by significant others. The *ideal social self-image* is defined as how consumers would like to be seen by significant others. The four dimensions of self-concept are activated by a set of product and consumer characteristics.

Brand-user image and brand personality

Brand image studies have documented much evidence suggesting that brand personality is an important factor influencing consumer choice (e.g., Ekinci, 2003; Ekinci & Hosany, 2006; Murphy, Benckendorff, & Moscardo, 2007a, 2007b). For example, Aaker and colleagues (e.g., Aaker, 1997; Aaker & Fournier, 1995) proposed that consumers perceive brands as having personalities in terms of five traits: sincerity, excitement, competence, sophistication and ruggedness. Consumers also consider whether the brand personality matches with their self-image when making a purchase decision. As such, Ekinci (2003) proposed that firms should establish a brand personality and make links to the self-image.

Brand image studies have also documented the effect of brand-user image on consumer behaviour (Sirgy, 1982; Sirgy & Su, 2000). Brand-user image focuses on the stereotypic perception of the typical brand user. For example, when consumers think about the image of the Apple computer, they may conjure up an image of the typical user as being "creative", "artistic", "hip" and "maverick". Such an image may relate directly to Aaker's notion of brand personality in relation to "excitement" and "competence". As such, both brand-user image and brand personality are involved in self-congruity influencing consumer behaviour (e.g., Boksberger, Dolnicar, Laesser, & Randle, 2011; Ekinci & Riley, 2003; Murphy et al., 2007a, 2007b). Having described brand personality and consumer self-concept, we now present the concept of the match between the brand personality and the consumer self-concept, namely self-congruity.

Self-congruity effects

Consumers' self-congruity reflects the match between consumers' self-concept and brand personality or brand-user image. Self-congruity with brand-user image refers to the perceived similarity a potential buyer sees between the typical user of a brand and himself or herself (Sirgy et al., 1997). Research has demonstrated that self-congruity with brand-user image is a stronger predictor of brand attitude and brand loyalty than self-congruity with brand personality in the context of luxury fashion brands (Liu, Li, Mizerski, & Soh, 2012).

Self-congruity has also a significant influence on consumers' value perception and pre-purchase behaviour such as brand evaluation and brand choice (Beerli, Meneses, & Gil, 2007; Boksberger et al., 2011; Chon, 1990, 1992; Hosany, 2012; Hung & Petrick, 2011; Kastenholz, 2004; Litvin & Goh, 2002). Consumers prefer brands that match well with their self-concept. Incongruity with their self-concept tends to cause dissonance and psychological discomfort that threaten the person's belief about the self (Sirgy, 1985b).

Moreover, consumers' self-congruity has a significant impact on consumers' post-purchase behaviour (i.e., customer satisfaction, trust and commitment to the brand, word-of-mouth communications; Aguirre-Rodriguez et al., 2012; Kressman, Sirgy, Herrmann, Huber, & Lee, 2006; Yim, Chan, & Hung, 2007). In other words, the greater the match between the brand personality and consumers' self-concept, the greater the chance that consumers will be satisfied with the brand, will feel trust for the company behind the brand, will feel committed to repurchase the same brand, will promote the brand to others and will communicate customer satisfaction. In addition, self-congruity directly increases product involvement (Kressman et al., 2006) and moderates the effect of attractiveness of alternatives on customer responses (Yim et al., 2007). That is, the greater the match between the brand personality and consumers' self-concept, the greater the chance that consumers will feel a sense of heightened involvement with the brand, which in turn will increase consumers' preference for the focal brand and decrease preference for competing brands.

Based on the discussion, it can be proposed that

> P1: Self-congruity (actual, ideal, social and ideal social self-congruity) influences consumers' pre-purchase behaviour (e.g., brand preference and choice) and post-purchase behaviour (e.g., consumer satisfaction, word-of-mouth communication and brand loyalty).

Having discussed the consumer behaviour outcomes that are influenced by self-congruity, we now turn to the self-concept motives – needs that drive consumer behaviour.

Dimensions of self-congruity and self-concept motives

What are the dimensions of self-congruity, and why does self-congruity have a significant influence on a broad range of consumer behaviours? Sirgy (1982) identified four self-concept motives (self-consistency, self-esteem, social consistency and social approval) corresponding to four self-concept dimensions (actual, ideal, social and ideal social self-image), resulting in four types of self-congruity: actual, ideal, social and ideal social-self-congruity. Specifically, self-congruity has a significant influence on perception of value and pre-consumption and post-consumption behaviours because self-congruity leads to the satisfaction of self-concept needs: the need for self-consistency, the need for self-esteem, the need for social consistency and the need for social approval.

Actual self-congruity is the mechanism that provides consumers with satisfaction of the self-consistency need (e.g., expression of their actual self-image through brand consumption). Consumers' need for self-consistency reflects their desire to engage in behaviours that are consistent with their own identity (Sedikides & Strube, 1995). The psychological dynamics of this need is particularly important when consumers have strong beliefs about their own identity (Burke & Stets, 2009; Gregg, Sedikides, & Gebauer, 2012). Similarly, ideal self-congruity provides consumers with the mechanism to meet the need for self-esteem (e.g., expression of desirable self-image through brand consumption). Consumers' need for self-esteem reflects their desire to enhance the positivity or decrease the negativity of the self-concept (Sedikides & Strube, 1995). This dynamic is particularly important for consumers with a high level of self-monitoring as well as consumers with an independent self-construal (Brown & Gallagher, 1992; Gregg et al., 2012; Sedikides & Strube, 1995). Social self-congruity is motivated by the need for social consistency (e.g., expression of compliance and conformity with group norms). In contrast, ideal social self-congruity is motivated by the need for social approval (e.g., gaining recognition from an aspirational group; Sirgy, 1982). In the following section, we will discuss the dimensions of self-congruity and self-concept motives in some more detail.

Actual self-congruity and the self-consistency motive

Actual self-image is defined as how consumers see themselves. Studies on the predictiveness of *actual self-congruity* and the *self-consistency* motive show that actual self-congruity is a strong predictor of brand choice (e.g., Beerli et al., 2007; Hung & Petrick, 2011; Klenosky, Charles, & Michael, 1993; Pizam & Calantone, 1987; Sheldon & Mark, 1987; Witt & Martin, 1987). Self-verification theory has long asserted that people are motivated to verify or confirm currently held self-views (Burke & Stets, 2009). Verification of self-concept increases self-confidence, facilitates social interactions and generates positive attitude towards the product (Swann, Stein-Seroussi, & Giesler, 1992). In contrast, lack of verification of self-concept results in negative feelings such as distress and anxiety (Burke & Stets 2009). Empirical studies have found that consumers tend to choose a certain brand whose images match their actual self-image or personal values (e.g., Ascher, 1985; Hsieh & O'Leary, 1994; Jackson, 1973). Research has also found that tourists are motivated to visit destination sites that reinforce their conceptions of who they are, and doing so satisfies the need for self-consistency (e.g., Prentice, Guerin, & McGugan, 1998).

Ideal self-congruity and the self-esteem motive

With respect to *ideal self-congruity*, a consumer's ideal self motivates their behaviour in the marketplace through the *need for self-esteem*. Consumers want to present their self-image as positively as possible by purchasing brands consistent with their ideal self-image. Consumers also want to enhance their image by being associated with firms with desirable images (Bhattacharya & Sen, 2003). Attainment of an ideal self-image results in self-esteem (e.g., Cast & Burke, 2002; Shang, Reed, & Croson, 2008). In other words, consumers have ideal images of themselves, and realizing these ideal images boosts their self-esteem (e.g., Amin, 1979; Ascher, 1985). Many studies have found that ideal self-congruity is a strong predictor of consumer choice (e.g., Beerli et al., 2007; Ekinci, Dawes, & Massey, 2008; Hung & Petrick, 2011).

Social self-congruity and the social consistency motive

Social self-congruity refers to how consumers *believe they are seen by others* in relation to the brand image. Consumers' social self-image influences consumer behaviour through the *social consistency motive* in that consumers are motivated to maintain the image of how a consumer believes they are viewed by others (the social self).

Consumers have social identity based on their identification with groups or social categories (Reed, Forehand, Puntoni, & Wallop, 2012). Consumers' social identity becomes salient when their social category becomes accessible and important. Reinforcement of social identity through the purchase of a product increases consumers' sense of belongingness and good feelings about the self (e.g., Burke & Stets, 2009). In contrast, lack of reinforcement of social identity produces anxiety and other negative feelings about the self (Large & Marcussen, 2000). For example, consumers feel uncomfortable taking actions that are inconsistent with how they believe others see them. Suggestive evidence of this phenomenon comes from studies linking consumers' reference group influence with brand choice (e.g., Mansfeld, 1992; Pearce, 1989; Robinson, 1979). Consumers rely on the norms of their reference groups in forming brand purchase intentions (Hung & Petrick, 2011).

Ideal social self-congruity and the social approval motive

Ideal social self-congruity refers to how consumers *would like to be seen by others* in relation to the brand image. The ideal social self-image affects consumers' brand choice through the *social approval motive*. In other words, consumers are motivated to do things that will cause others to think highly of them. They believe that acting in ways that realize the ideal social self-image is likely to earn approval from others. Actions inconsistent with the ideal social self-image may lead to social disapproval (e.g., Coleman, 1983; Crompton, 1979; Graburn, 1983; Matra, 1984; Moeran, 1983; Reimer, 1991; Riley, 1995).

In sum, we can capture the above discussion in terms of a major theoretical proposition that can be stated as follows:

> P2: Actual self-congruity is motivated by the need for self-consistency, ideal self-congruity is motivated by the need for self-esteem, social self-congruity is motivated by the need for social consistency and ideal social self-congruity is motivated by the need for social approval.

Relative predictiveness of self-congruity effects

In this section we will discuss the relative efficacy of self-congruity effects by first making a distinction between private and public forms of self-congruity and then focusing on the distinction between the enhancement and the consistency aspects of self-congruity.

Private self-congruity vs. public self-congruity

What is the relative efficacy of private self-congruity (actual and ideal self-congruity) vs. public self-congruity (social and ideal social self-congruity) on consumer behaviour? Through a meta-analysis, Aguirre-Rodriguez et al. (2012) tested the predictiveness of private self-congruity versus social self-congruity on consumer attitude, intentions and behaviour. They found that private self-congruity was a stronger predictor of consumer behaviour than public self-congruity. This is because private self-motives capture both inner and social standards of the self (Aguirre-Rodriguez et al., 2012). That is, consumers' efforts to achieve private self-congruity reflect the efforts to obtain satisfaction of private-self needs (i.e., self-verification and enhancement) as well as public-self needs (i.e., social assimilation and approval) (Ruvio, 2008). In contrast, consumers' efforts to achieve public self-congruity reflect the efforts to obtain satisfaction of public-self needs only. As private self-congruity is related to multiple self needs, the private self is likely to be more salient in a purchasing situation. Consider the distinction between children and adult consumers. Children's consumer behaviour is mostly influenced by the public self, given the fact that their self-concept is moulded by their perceptions of how people view them. In contrast, adults' self-concept is already moulded – they have concepts of themselves that reflect both their private and their public self. More specifically, their public self is likely to be already incorporated into their private self. This observation will be discussed further in the context of Proposition 6. Thus, one can argue that private self-congruity effects are greater than public self-congruity effects. Based on the above discussion, we suggest the following theoretical proposition:

> P3: Private self-congruity (actual and ideal self-congruity) effects are likely to be stronger than public-self congruity (social and ideal social self-congruity) effects.

Enhancement versus consistency

Ekinci et al. (2008) tested the predictiveness of actual versus ideal self-congruity on consumer satisfaction in the travel context. They found that ideal self-congruity was a stronger predictor of consumer satisfaction than actual self-congruity. This may be due to the possibility that consumer's self-enhancement motive is stronger than the self-consistency motive in a travel context. Consumers want to present themselves as positively as possible, especially when they use self-expressive services such as travel (Aguirre-Rodriguez et al., 2012; Dolich, 1969). This finding was further reinforced by studies by Hosany and Martin (2012). That is, consumers are more motivated to express their ideal self-image than their actual self-image. Based on the discussion, we suggest the following proposition:

> P4: Enhancement-type self-congruity (ideal and ideal social self-congruity) effects are likely to be stronger than consistency-type self-congruity (actual and social self-congruity) effects in relation to the purchase and consumption of goods and services that allow consumers to approach or realize their ideal self.

The effect of self-congruity on functional congruity

Functional congruity is an evaluation process that focuses on the perceived utilitarian aspects of the brand in reference to some ideal aspects. For example, a consumer may consider durability, functionality, price of alternative brands and quality of the associated services and accessories. These criteria used in decision making are utilitarian or *functional* in nature, compared with *symbolic* criteria such as brand personality or brand-user image.

When consumers experience high levels of self-congruity with a brand, they are likely to evaluate the brand more favourably (Kressman et al., 2006; Yim et al., 2007). This self-congruity bias occurs since consumers form the first impression based on the outcome of the self-congruity process. If the first impression is positive, then it is likely that further information processing may be biased in the positive direction. Consumers who experience high self-congruity tend to favourably process the utilitarian attributes, and vice versa (Chon & Olsen, 1991; Sirgy & Su, 2000). That is, consumers who experience a match between the brand personality (or brand-user image) and their self-concept are likely to process the utilitarian attributes of the brand in a favourable light, thus increasing the likelihood of forming an overall favourable attitude towards the brand. Conversely, those who experience a mismatch are likely to process the utilitarian attributes of a brand in an unfavourable light, thus increasing the likelihood of forming an unfavourable brand image. Research has shown that functional congruity is significantly influenced by the four types of self-congruity (actual, ideal, social and ideal social) (e.g., Hung & Petrick, 2011). It should be noted that the effect of self-congruity on functional congruity is greater when consumers are highly involved with the product than when consumers are less involved with the product (Kressman et al., 2006). Based on the discussion, the following proposition is introduced:

> P5: Self-congruity has a positive influence on functional congruity.

Moderators of self-congruity effect

As previously mentioned, self-congruity effect is the degree to which consumers' actual, ideal, social and ideal social self-congruity influences consumer pre-purchase (e.g., brand preference, brand choice) and post-purchase behaviour (e.g., consumer satisfaction, word-of-mouth communication, brand loyalty). Under what conditions is self-congruity effect likely to be stronger? In the next section, we will discuss the moderators of self-congruity effects.

Consumer characteristics

In this section we will discuss the effect of several consumer factors, namely consumer age, consumer involvement, consumer product knowledge and consumer childhood brand attachment, on self-congruity effect.

Consumer age

Young consumers are likely to be more image conscious than older consumers. Young consumers have a heighted attention to public self-image – they are likely to be influenced by how others perceive them (e.g., Davis & Franzoi, 1991; Rosenburg, 1986). As such, they are likely to be fashion oriented and strive to express their identity through brand consumption. This means that young consumers are likely to be more influenced by public forms of self-congruity (social and ideal social self-congruity) than private forms (actual and ideal self-congruity). In contrast, older consumers have stable personal identity and self-concept; thus, they are less likely to be influenced by the private self (i.e., actual and ideal self-congruity) (Harter, 1999). As such, we put forward the following theoretical proposition:

> P6: Consumer behaviour of young consumers is likely to be more influenced by public forms of self-congruity (social and ideal social self-congruity) than private forms (actual and ideal self-congruity). Conversely, consumer behaviour of older consumers is likely to be more influenced by private forms of self-congruity (actual and ideal self-congruity) than public forms (social and ideal social self-congruity).

Consumer involvement

Both functional and self-congruity have been suggested to influence consumer choice of brand (e.g., Blank, 1989; Chiang, Chen, Huang, & Hsueh, 2012; Chon & Olsen, 1991; Dann, 1981; Riley, 1995). The relative weights given to each may depend on a number of situational- and consumer-related characteristics such as consumer knowledge, prior experience, involvement with brand selection and time pressure (Sirgy & Su, 2000). For example, research by Beerli et al. (2007) has suggested that compared with functional congruity, the effect of self-congruity on brand choice is stronger when consumers are highly involved with the product class (high involvement with product class) and when consumers are less involved with the decision-making process (low involvement with the decision-making process; Beerli et al., 2007).

With regard to consumer involvement, we should distinguish between two types of involvement: involvement in the decision-making process (i.e., involvement with the process of selecting a certain brand) and involvement with product class (i.e., involvement with the consumption of the product). For example, a minivan is a product class while a Toyota minivan is a particular brand of this product class. These two types of involvement are expected to play very different roles in moderating the self-congruity effect on consumer behaviour. When a consumer is not involved in the decision-making process (e.g., less caring about collecting information to make an intelligent decision), he or she is likely to process the information using a decision heuristic (e.g., brand-user image, image of the brand spokesperson). In this case an evaluation of the brand based on a self-congruity process serves the consumer's goal well. This consumer is likely to engage in holistic information processing with limited cognitive elaboration. Thus, the self-congruity effect is likely to be strong when the consumer is less involved with the decision-making process and processes the information with a limited cognitive elaboration (Aguirre-Rodriguez et al., 2012).

When consumers are emotionally involved with the consumption of the product class, they are likely to experience a strong self-congruity effect. When consumers are involved with a product class, they will associate more self-related meanings with the product category. As such, the product is likely to play an important role in defining the person's identity. Thus, consumers with a high level of product category involvement are likely to care greatly about the self-image associated with product use. Further, research has provided evidence suggesting that the self-congruity effect is stronger when consumers are highly involved with the product category than when they are not involved with the product category (e.g., Beerli et al., 2007; Hou, Lin, & Morais, 2005; Prayag & Ryan, 2012; Kressman et al., 2006). Based on the discussion, we can articulate the following propositions:

> P7: Consumers with a low (high) involvement with the decision-making process are likely to experience a strong (weak) self-congruity effect.
>
> P8: Consumers with a high (low) involvement with the product category are likely to experience a strong (weak) self-congruity effect.

Consumer product knowledge

According to the life cycle model of consumption, consumers go through a series of consumption experiences including product acquisition, possession, consumption, maintenance and disposal. The strength of self-congruity effect depends on consumer knowledge and experience with the product.

When consumers have limited knowledge or experience about the product, they are likely to experience a strong self-congruity effect. This is because consumers with limited knowledge or experience are likely to evaluate the product in a holistic manner; and thus, they rely on self-congruity as decision heuristics in their brand evaluation (Aguirre-Rodriguez et al., 2012). For example, research has shown that the effect of self-congruity on store loyalty is greater for those consumers with limited knowledge and experience than for those with much knowledge (Sirgy et al., 2000). Thus, we surmise that self-congruity effect is strong when consumers' knowledge about the product is very low. This is because consumers with limited product knowledge are likely to rely on extrinsic cues (e.g., brand image) in evaluating the brand.

When consumers have a moderate level of product knowledge, they tend to consider the functional aspects of the product and rely on the factual and functional information in evaluating brands. Hence, consumers with a moderate degree of knowledge about the product are likely to experience weak self-congruity effects in evaluating brands.

When consumers are highly knowledgeable about the product, the effect of functional attributes on brand evaluation diminishes over time. Knowledgeable consumers tend to process the product information at a more abstract level, which is more consistent with a strong self-congruity effect. It has been found that self-congruity effects are stronger when consumers are knowledgeable about the product (Barone, Shimp, & Sprott, 1999). When consumers are highly knowledgeable, many of the functional attributes become translated into abstract and self-related cognitions (e.g., Dietz & Stern, 1995; Frank, 1988; Hogarth & Reder, 1987; Janis, 1977; Kahneman, Slovic, & Tversky, 1987). Thus, the self-congruity effect is likely to be strong when consumers are very knowledgeable about the product. In summary, we offer the following proposition:

> P9: Consumers with a high or a low level of product knowledge are likely to experience a stronger self-congruity effect than consumers with a moderate level of product knowledge.

Childhood brand attachment

People's earliest and defining brand experiences play a significant role in brand meaning (Braun-LaTour, LaTour, & Zinkhan, 2007). Brand attachment is a strong emotional bond with a brand. When a child is attached to a brand, the child is likely to care about the brand and regard the brand as an expression of self. That is, childhood experience of emotional attachment to a brand leads consumers to have a feeling of identification with a brand. When children experience a strong brand attachment experience, they are likely to incorporate the brand image as part of their social identity (Belk, 1988).

We posit that consumers are likely to experience a strong self-congruity effect with a brand when they have a strong brand attachment experience during their childhood. This is because brand experiences in childhood influence brand experiences in adulthood (Lee, 2001). Self-verification theory maintains that people are motivated to verify or confirm currently held persistent self-beliefs (Burke & Harrod, 2005; Burke & Stets, 2009). Hence, we propose the following:

> P10: Consumers are likely to experience a stronger self-congruity effect with a brand when they have strong rather than weak attachment to that brand during their childhood.

Brand characteristics

In this section we will discuss the moderating effects of two brand factors, namely brand conspicuousness and brand identity salience.

Brand conspicuousness

Research suggests that the effect of self-congruity on consumer behaviour is likely to be strong when the brand product is consumed conspicuously rather than inconspicuously. A conspicuous brand refers to a brand that is consumed in public and that symbolizes prestige and social status of the user (Eastman, Goldsmith, & Flynn, 1999; Veblen, 1934). This effect may occur because consumers are likely to be conscious of their public self-image. They are motivated to purchase symbolic brands as an expression of their public self-image (Berger & Heath, 2007, 2008). When a certain brand is consumed in private (i.e., inconspicuously), consumers do not feel the need to express and enhance their self-image. That is, the effect of public self-congruity on brand choice is greater than the effect of private self-congruity when the brand is consumed in public and has a high visibility.

> P11: Consumers experience a stronger self-congruity effect when the brand is consumed conspicuously rather than inconspicuously.

Brand identity salience

Self-concept is multidimensional and made up of several identities (Reed et al., 2012). Identity refers to a set of meaning one holds as a group member, as a role holder or as a person. That is, identity holds the meaning that defines who we are. People vary in the degree to which a particular identity occupies a central role, meaning that the particular schema is more readily available for processing or acting upon social information (Aquino, Freeman, Reed, Lim, & Felps, 2009; Burke & Stets, 2009; Reed et al., 2012). An identity is likely to be salient when an individual thinks the focal identity to be important, when the individual is committed to that identity and when the same identity plays a central role within the self-concept (Burke, 1980; Callero, 1985; McCall & Simmons, 1978; Reed et al., 2012; Simpson & Siguaw, 2008; Stryker, 1968; Turner, 1978). The reader should note that the relative salience of a given identity changes over time and is influenced by situational factors (Agrawal & Maheswaran, 2005; Hart, Atkins, & Ford, 1998).

A brand can have an impact on the salience of an identity when the brand image represents an important and committed identity and/or the brand plays an important role in meeting self-related needs. Brand identity salience means the degree to which a brand contributes to the salience of a specific consumer identity. It is a situational factor that increases the importance and accessibility of a specific identity related to brand image or brand personality.

One can argue that consumers are likely to experience a stronger self-congruity effect when identity salience of a brand is high rather than low. This is because consumers are likely to be involved and emotionally attached to a brand when the brand image contributes to the salience of a specific identity. When consumers have a salient identity related to a brand, they are likely to evaluate the identity-relevant attributes of a brand positively and strongly (Aquino et al., 2009; Reed, 2004). As a result, the influence of self-congruity on consumer behaviour is amplified. Based on this discussion, we put forth the following theoretical proposition:

> P12: Consumers are likely to experience a stronger self-congruity effect when identity salience of a brand is high rather than low.

Cultural characteristics

In this section we will discuss only one moderator of the self-congruity effect, namely individualism versus collectivism.

Individualism vs. collectivism

Individuals in different cultures have different self-construals – the individual's sense of self in relation to others, reflecting the extent to which the individual views himself or herself as an independent entity or as an entity dependent on others (Agrawal & Maheswaran, 2005; Triandis, 1996).

Consumers in an individualistic culture have independent self-construals. Independent self-construal is a bounded, unitary, stable self that is separated from the social context (Geertz, 1975; Markus & Kitayama, 1991; Singelis, 1994). Consumers in an individualistic culture tend to view themselves as separate and autonomous; they are less influenced by the opinion of others (Heine, Lehman, Markus, & Kitayama, 1999; Triandis, 2001). For them, maintaining consistency in self-concept is important regardless of social contexts (Cross, Gore, & Morris, 2003; Suh, 2002). Studies have found that the effect of *private* self-congruity on brand choice is likely to be greater for consumers in an individualistic culture than for consumers in a collectivistic culture (Litvin & Kar, 2003; Sung & Choi, 2012). This is because consumers in individualistic cultures have independent self-construal; self-consistency is very important for them (Cross et al., 2003).

In contrast, consumers in a collectivistic culture tend to have an interdependent self-construal, and they define their self-concept in terms of important relationships, group membership and social roles (Markus & Kitayama, 1991; Singelis, 1994). As consumers in a collectivistic culture view themselves as interdependent with their social network, they are influenced significantly by the opinion of others (Heine et al., 1999; Triandis, 2001). For interdependent consumers, adapting to the social context and maintaining group harmony are important in consumer decision making (Cross et al., 2003; Triandis, 2001). Research has found that *social* self-congruity effects are stronger for the consumers in a collectivistic culture than in an individualistic culture. This is because consumers in a collectivistic culture have interdependent self-construal (Kim & Hyun, 2013; Sirgy et al., 1991). Consumers with interdependent self-construal are likely to emphasize their public self-image through brand symbolism. Thus, consumers in a collectivistic culture are likely to experience a strong *social* self-congruity effect. Based on the above discussion, it can be proposed that

> P13: Consumers in individualistic cultures are likely to experience a stronger private self-congruity effect (actual self-congruity and ideal self-congruity) than consumers in collectivistic cultures.
>
> P14: Consumers in collectivistic cultures are likely to experience a stronger public self-congruity effect (social self-congruity and ideal social self-congruity) than consumers in individualistic cultures.

Conclusion

This chapter is designed to review the research literature of self-congruity in a systematic manner and to develop an integrated model of self-congruity in consumer behaviour. The chapter reviews the current state regarding self-congruity theory with specific theoretical propositions designed to spur future research.

There are several future research questions that are worth future efforts. *First*, most studies on self-congruity are conducted using cross-sectional study designs. Future research should focus more on longitudinal studies tracing the changes of self-congruity with a brand over time. This would be important because meaning of a brand and salience of a particular self-concept may change over time (Aquino et al., 2009; Hart et al., 1998).

Second, most studies on self-congruity seem to focus on overall self-congruity. Despite efforts to compare relative predictiveness among the self-congruity dimensions, we still have a limited understanding of the underlying conditions that moderate the relative predictiveness of various forms of self-congruity (actual, ideal, social and ideal social self-congruity). That is, it is important to identify specific conditions under which a specific type of self-congruity becomes more predictive of consumer behaviour. For example, one can argue that actual self-congruity becomes more important when consumers have strong perceptions about the brand personality and their actual self-image in relation to that brand personality. As such, they are likely to be motivated to maintain and possibly reinforce their actual self-image through brand consumption. In contrast, one can argue that ideal self-congruity may play a prominent role in predicting consumer behaviour when consumers are certain about positive brand-user image portrayed by the brand; and if so, they become motivated to realize that ideal self-image through brand consumption. As such, ideal self-congruity may be more predictive of consumer behaviour for those consumers with low self-esteem, high self-monitoring and narcissism (Brown & Gallagher, 1992; Sedikides & Strube, 1995). More research is needed in this area.

Third, most studies on self-congruity seem to focus on self-congruity effects in relation to rational brand choice. We still have a limited understanding of the effect of self-congruity on consumer affect and emotions. Self-discrepancy theory posits that significant discrepancies between the ideal self and the actual self may induce dejection emotions such as disappointment and dissatisfaction (Higgins, 1989). Future studies should examine the effects of these self-discrepancies on consumer emotions (Burke & Stets, 2009). In addition, future research could examine the effectiveness of consumers' various coping strategies arising from experiences representing self-incongruity related to the actual, ideal, social and ideal social self.

Fourth, most self-congruity studies are conducted by focusing on a single product category in which respondents evaluate a product in a vacuum. Such research lacks ecological validity. Future research should examine the role of self-congruity in the context of attractive alternatives, service failure and switching barriers.

Fifth, most self-congruity studies focus on a single brand. Consumers may experience self-congruity effects with the firm as well as the brand. For example, research can be conducted to examine the effects of self-congruity with sponsorship activities (cf. Sirgy, Lee, Johar, & Tidwell, 2008) and/or corporate social responsibility activities (cf. Marin & Ruiz, 2006). Future research should examine how self-congruity with a brand interacts with self-congruity with the firm (and possibly with endorser activities) in influencing consumer behaviour.

Sixth, most studies on self-congruity focus on self-congruity effects on consumer behaviour with the assumption that the effects are symmetric – high levels of self-congruity produce proportional positive effects on consumer behaviour, whereas low levels of self-congruity produce proportional negative effects. Are self-congruity effects symmetric? If so, under what conditions and why?

Seventh, most studies on self-congruity assume that only one type of self-congruity is salient in a given condition. Yet, one can argue that consumers may have multiple identities that can be simultaneously salient in that situation. For example, consumers may be motivated by both need for self-esteem and social approval with an equal importance in a purchasing situation. Future research could examine how consumers manage conflict between or among the self-concept motives.

Eighth, this overview focused on only one dimension of culture (individualism vs. collectivism) moderating self-congruity effects. Future research could examine the role of other cultural dimensions (e.g., femininity vs. masculinity) affecting the relative predictiveness of private (actual and ideal) versus public (social and ideal social) forms of self-congruity on consumer behaviours.

In summary, the goal of this chapter was to revisit the research conducted in this area and to cast this research in a theoretical net. The goal was to guide future research on self-congruity. We hope that scholars interested in the concept of self-congruity will continue to develop good theory and method in this line of research.

References

Aaker, J. (1997). Dimensions of brand personality. *Journal of Marketing Research*, *34*, 347–356.

Aaker, J., & Fournier, S. (1995). A brand as a character, a partner and a person: Three perspectives on the question of brand personality. *Advances in Consumer Research*, *22*, 391–395.

Agrawal, N., & Maheswaran, D. (2005). The effects of self-construal and commitment on persuasion. *Journal of Consumer Research*, *32*, 841–849.

Aguirre-Rodriguez, A., Bosnjak, M., & Sirgy, M.J. (2012). Moderators of the self-congruity effect on consumer decision-making: A meta-analysis. *Journal of Business Research*, *65*, 1179–1188.

Amin, S. (1979). *Classe et Nation*. Paris: Editions de Minuit.

Aquino, K., Freeman, D., Reed II, A., Lim, V. K., & Felps, W. (2009). Testing a social-cognitive model of moral behaviour: The interactive influence of situations and moral identity centrality. *Journal of Personality and Social Psychology, 97*, 123–141.

Ascher, F. (1985). *Tourism: Transnational corporations and cultural identities*. Oxfordshire: cabdirect.

Barone, M. J., Shimp, T. A., & Sprott, D. E. (1999). Product ownership as a moderator of self-congruity effects. *Marketing Letters, 10*, 75–85.

Beerli, A., Meneses, G. D., & Gil, S. M. (2007). Self-congruity and destination choice. *Annals of Tourism Research, 34*, 571–587.

Belk, R. W. (1988). Possessions and the extended self. *Journal of Consumer Research, 15*, 139–168.

Berger, J., & Heath, C. (2007). Where consumers diverge from others: Identity-signaling and product domains. *Journal of Consumer Research, 34*, 121–134.

Berger, J., & Heath, C. (2008). Who drives divergence? Identity-signaling, outgroup dissimilarity, and the abandonment of cultural tastes. *Journal of Personality and Social Psychology, 95*, 593–607.

Bhattacharya, C. B., & Sen, S. (2003). Consumer-company identification: A framework for understanding consumers' relationships with companies. *Journal of Marketing, 67*, 76–88.

Blank, U. (1989). *The community tourism industry imperative: The necessity, the opportunities, its potential*. State College, PA: Venture.

Boksberger, P., Dolnicar, S., Laesser, C., & Randle, M. (2011). Self-congruity theory: To what extent does it hold in tourism? *Journal of Travel Research, 50*, 454–464.

Braun-LaTour, K., LaTour, M., & Zinkhan, G. (2007). Using childhood memories to gain insight into brand meaning. *Journal of Marketing, 71*, 45–60.

Brown, J. D., & Gallagher, F. M. (1992). Coming to terms with failure: Private self-enhancement and public self-effacement. *Journal of Experimental Social Psychology, 28*, 3–22.

Burke, P. J. (1980). The self: Measurement requirements from an interactionist perspective. *Social Psychology Quarterly, 43*, 18–29.

Burke, P. J., & Harrod, M. M. (2005). Too much of a good thing? *Social Psychology Quarterly, 68*, 359–374.

Burke, P. J., & Stets, J. E. (2009). *Identity theory*. Oxford: Oxford University Press.

Callero, P. L. (1985). Role-identity salience. *Social Psychology Quarterly, 48*, 203–215.

Cast, A. D., & Burke, P. J. (2002). A theory of self-esteem. *Social Forces, 80*, 1041–1068.

Chiang, C.-C., Chen, Y.-C., Huang, L.-F., & Hsueh, K.-F. (2012). Destination image and marketing strategy: An investigation of MICE travelers to Taiwan. *Journal of American Academy of Business, 18*, 224–231.

Chon, K. (1990). The role of destination image in tourism: A review and discussion. *The Tourist Review, 45*, 2–9.

Chon, K. (1992). Self-image/destination-image congruity. *Annals of Tourism Research, 19*, 360–363.

Chon, K., & Olsen, M. D. (1991). Functional and symbolic congruity approaches to consumer satisfaction/dissatisfaction in tourism. *Journal of the International Academy of Hospitality Research, 3*, 2–22.

Claiborne, C. B., & Sirgy, M. J. (1990). Self-congruity as a model of attitude formation and change: Conceptual review and guide for future research. In B. J. Dunlap (Ed.), *Developments in Marketing Science* (Vol. 13, pp. 1–17). Cullowhee, NC: Academy of Marketing Science.

Coleman, R. (1983). The continuing significance of social class to marketing. *Journal of Consumer Research, 10*, 265–280.

Crompton, J. (1979). Motivations for pleasure vacation. *Annals of Tourism Research, 6*, 404–424.

Cross, S. E., Gore, J. S., & Morris, M. L. (2003). The relational-interdependent self-construal, self-concept consistency, and well-being. *Journal of Personality and Social Psychology, 85*, 933–944.

Dann, G. (1981). Tourism motivation: An appraisal. *Annals of Tourism Research, 9*, 87–219.

Davis, M. H., & Franzoi, S. L. (1991). Stability and change in adolescent self-consciousness and empathy. *Journal of Research in Personality, 25*, 70–87.

Dietz, T., & Stern, P. C. (1995). Toward a theory of choice: Socially embedded preference construction. *Journal of Socio-Economics, 24*, 261–279.

Dolich, I. J. (1969). Congruence relationships between self-images and product brands. *Journal of Marketing Research, 6*, 80–84.

Eastman, J. K., Goldsmith, R. E., & Flynn, L. R. (1999). Status consumption in consumer behaviour: Scale development and validation. *Journal of Marketing Theory and Practice*, 7, 41–52.

Ekinci, Y. (2003). From destination image to destination branding: An emerging area of research. *e-Review of Tourism Research, 1*, 21–24.

Ekinci, Y., & Hosany, S. (2006). Destination personality: An application of brand personality to tourism destinations. *Journal of Travel Research, 45*, 127–139.

Ekinci, Y., & Riley, M. (2003). An investigation of self-concept: Actual and ideal self-congruence in the context of service evaluation. *Journal of Retailing and Consumer Services, 10*, 201–214.

Ekinci, Y., Dawes, P. L., & Massey, G. R. (2008). An extended model of the antecedents and consequences of consumer satisfaction for hospitality services. *European Journal of Marketing, 42*, 35–68.

Frank, R. H. (1988). *Within reason: The strategic role of emotions*. New York, NY: Norton.

Geertz, C. (1975). On the nature of anthropological understanding. *American Scientist, 63*, 47–53.

Graburn, N. (1983). The anthropology of tourism. *Annals of Tourism Research*, 10, 9–13.

Gregg, A. P., Sedikides, C., & Gebauer, J. E. (2012). Dynamics of identity: Between self-enhancement and self-assessment. In S. Schwartz, K. Luyckx & V. L. Vignoles (Eds.), *Handbook of identity theory and research* (Vol. 1, pp. 305–327). New York, NY: Springer.

Hart, D., Atkins, R., & Ford, D. (1998). Urban America as a context for the development of moral identity in adolescence. *Journal of Social Issues, 54*, 513–530.

Harter, S. (1999). *The construction of self: A developmental perspective*. New York, NY: Guilford Press.

Heine, S. J., Lehman, D. R., Markus, H. R., & Kitayama, S. (1999). Is there a universal need for positive self-regard? *Psychological Review, 106*, 766–794.

Higgins, E. T. (1987). Self-discrepancy: A theory relating self and affect. *Psychological Review, 94*, 319–340.

Higgins, E. T. (1989). Self-discrepancy theory: What patterns of self-beliefs cause people to suffer. In L. Berkowitz (Ed.), *Advances in Experimental Social Psychology* (pp. 93–135). San Diego, CA: Academic Press.

Hogarth, R. M., & Reder, M. W. (Eds.) (1987). *Rational choice: The contrast between economics and psychology*. Chicago, IL: University of Chicago Press.

Holloway, J. C., & Plant, R. V. (1988). *Marketing for tourism*. Southport: Pitman.

Hosany, S. (2012). Appraisal determinants of tourist emotional responses. *Journal of Travel Research, 51*, 303–314.

Hosany, S., & Martin, D. (2012). Self-image congruence in consumer behaviour. *Journal of Business Research, 65*, 685–691.

Hou, J.-S., Lin, C.-H., & Morais, D. B. (2005). Antecedents of attachment to a cultural tourism destination: The case of Hakka and Non-Hakka Taiwanese Visitors to Pie-Pu, Taiwan. *Journal of Travel Research, 44*, 221–231.

Hsieh, S., & O'Leary, J. T. (1994). A travel decision model for Japanese pleasure travel. In *Tourism: The economy's silver lining* (pp. 94–104). Wheat Ridge, CO: Travel and Tourism Research Association.

Hung, K., & Petrick, J. F. (2011). The role of self- and functional-congruity in cruising intentions. *Journal of Travel Research, 50*, 100–112.

Jackson, G. (1973). A preliminary bicultural study of value orientations and leisure attitudes. *Journal of Leisure Research, 5*, 10–20.

Janis, L. M. (1977). *Decision making: A psychological analysis of conflict, choice and commitment*. New York, NY: Free Press.

Johar, J. S., & Sirgy, M. J. (1991). Value expressive versus utilitarian appeals: When and why to use which appeal. *Journal of Advertising, 20*, 23–34.

Kahneman, D., Slovic, P., & Tversky, A. (Eds.) (1982). *Judgment under uncertainty: Heuristics and biases*. Cambridge, UK: Cambridge University Press.

Kastenholz, E. (2004). Assessment and role of destination-self-congruity. *Annals of Tourism Research, 31*, 719–723.

Kim, J., & Hyun, Y. (2013). The importance of social and ideal social dimensions in self congruity research. *Asian Journal of Social Psychology, 16*, 39–49.

Klenosky, D. B., Charles, E. G., & Michael, M. (1993). Understanding the factors influencing ski destination choice: A means-end analytic approach. *Journal of Leisure Research, 24*, 362–379.

Kressmann, F., Sirgy, M. J., Herrmann, A., Huber, F., & Lee, D. J. (2006). Direct and indirect effects of self-image congruence on brand loyalty. *Journal of Business Research, 59*, 955–964.

Large, M. D., & Marcussen, K. (2000). Extending identity theory to predict differential forms and degrees of psychological distress. *Social Psychology Quarterly, 63*, 49–59.

Lee, C. C. (2001). Predicting tourist attachment to destinations. *Annals of Tourism Research, 28*, 229–232.

Litvin, S. W., & Goh, H. (2002). Self-image congruity: A valid tourism theory? *Tourism Management, 23*, 81–83.

Litvin, S. W., & Kar, G. H. (2003). Individualism/collectivism as a moderating factor to the self-image congruity concept. *Journal of Vacation Marketing, 10*, 23–32.

Liu, F., Li, J., Mizerski, D., & Soh, H. (2012). Self-congruity, brand attitude, and brand loyalty: A study on luxury brands. *European Journal of Marketing, 46*, 922–937.

Mansfeld, Y. (1992). *Tourism: Toward a behavioural approach*. Oxford: Pergamon Press.
Marin, L., & Ruiz, S. (2006). "I need you too!" Corporate identity attractiveness for consumers and the role of social responsibility. *Journal of Business Ethics*, *71*, 245–260.
Markus, H., & Kitayama, S. (1991). Culture and the self: Implications for cognition, emotions, and motivation. *Psychological Review*, *98*, 224–253.
Matra, J. (1984). *Social inequality, stratification, and mobility*. Englewood Cliffs, NJ: Prentice Hall.
McCall, G., & Simmons, J. (1978). *Identities and interactions* (revised ed.). New York, NY: The Free Press.
Moeran, B. (1983). The language of Japanese tourism. *Annals of Tourism Research*, *10*, 93–108.
Moliner, M. A., Sánchez, J., Rodríguez, R. M., & Callarisa, L. (2007). Perceived relationship quality and post-purchase perceived value: An integrative framework. *European Journal of Marketing*, *41*, 1392–1422.
Murphy, L., Benckendorff, P., & Moscardo, G. (2007a). Destination brand personality: Visitor perceptions of a regional tourism destination. *Tourism Analysis*, *12*, 419–432.
Murphy, L., Benckendorff, P., & Moscardo, G. (2007b). Linking travel motivation, tourist self-image and destination brand personality. *Journal of Travel and Tourism Marketing*, *22*, 45–59.
Pearce, G. D. (1989). *Tourist development*. Harlow, Essex: Longman, Burnt Mill.
Pizam, A., & Calantone, R. (1987). Beyond psychographics – values as determinants of tourist behaviour. *International Journal of Hospitality Management*, *6*, 177–181.
Prayag, G., & Ryan, C. (2012). Antecedents of tourists' loyalty to Mauritius: The role and influence of destination image, place attachment, personal involvement, and satisfaction. *Journal of Travel Research*, *51*, 342–356.
Prentice, R. C., Guerin, S., & McGugan, S. (1998). Visitor learning at a heritage attraction: A case study of discovery as a media product. *Tourism Management*, *19*, 5–23.
Reed II, A. (2004). Activating the self-importance of consumer selves: Exploring identity salience effects on judgments. *Journal of Consumer Research*, *31*, 286–295.
Reed II, A., Forehand, M. R., Puntoni, S., & Warlop, L. (2012). Identity-based consumer behaviour. *International Journal of Research in Marketing*, *29*, 310–321.
Reimer, G. (1991). Packaging dreams: Canadian tour operators at work. *Annals of Tourism Research*, *18*, 501–512.
Riley, R. W. (1995). Prestige worthy tourist behaviour. *Annals of Tourism Research*, *22*, 630–649.
Robinson, H. (1979). *A geography of tourism*. Plymouth: Macdonald and Evans.
Ruvio, A. (2008). Unique like everybody else? The dual role of consumers' need for uniqueness. *Psychology and Marketing*, *25*, 444–464.
Sedikides, C., & Strube, M. J. (1995). The multiply motivated self. *Personality and Social Psychology Bulletin*, *21*, 1330–1335.
Shang, J., Reed, A., & Croson, R. (2008). Identity congruency effects on donations. *Journal of Marketing Research*, *45*, 351–361.
Sheldon, P. J., & Mark, J. (1987). The demand for package tours: A mode choice model. *Journal of Travel Research*, *24*, 16–23.
Simpson, P. M., & Siguaw, J. A. (2008). The role of traveler type, residents, and identity salience. *Journal of Travel Research*, *47*, 167–182.
Singelis, T. M. (1994). The measurement of independent and interdependent self construals. *Personality and Social Psychology Bulletin*, *20*, 580–591.
Sirgy, M. J. (1982). Self-concept in consumer behaviour: A critical review. *Journal of Consumer Research*, *9*, 287–300.
Sirgy, M. J. (1985a). Self-image/product-image congruity and consumer decision making. *International Journal of Management*, *2*, 49–63.
Sirgy, M. J. (1985b). Using self-congruity and ideal congruity to predict purchase motivation. *Journal of Business Research*, *13*, 195–206.
Sirgy, M. J. (1986). *Self-congruity: Toward a theory of personality and cybernetics*. New York, NY: Praeger.
Sirgy, M. J., & Su, C. (2000). Destination image, self-congruity, and travel behaviour: Toward an integrative model. *Journal of Travel Research*, *38*, 340–352.
Sirgy, M. J., Grewal, D., & Mangelburg, T. (2000). Retail environment, self-congruity, and retail patronage: An integrative model and a research agenda. *Journal of Business Research*, *49*, 27–138.
Sirgy, M. J., Johar, J. S., Samli, A. C., & Claiborne, C. B. (1991). Self-congruity versus functional congruity: Predictors of consumer behaviour. *Journal of the Academy of Marketing Science*, *19*, 363–375.

Sirgy, M. J., Lee, D. J., Johar, J. S., & Tidwell, J. (2008). Effect of self congruity with sponsorship on brand loyalty. *Journal of Business Research, 61*, 1091–1097.

Sirgy, M. J., Grewal, D., Mangleburg, T.F., Park, J. O., Chon, K. S., Claiborne, C. B., …, & Berkman, H. (1997). Assessing the predictive validity of two methods of measuring self-image congruence. *Journal of the Academy of Marketing Science, 25*, 229–241.

Stryker, S. (1968). Identity salience and role performance: The relevance of symbolic interaction theory for family research. *Journal of Marriage and Family, 30*, 558–564.

Suh, E. M. (2002). Culture, identity consistency, and subjective well being. *Journal of Personality and Social Psychology, 83*, 1378–1391.

Sung, Y., & Choi, S. M. (2012). The influence of self-construal on self-brand congruity in the United States and Korea. *Journal of Cross-Cultural Psychology, 43*, 151–166.

Swann, W. B., Stein-Seroussi, A., & Giesler, R. B. (1992). Why people self-verify. *Journal of Personality and Social Psychology, 62*, 392–401.

Triandis, H. C. (1996). The psychological measurement of cultural syndromes. *American Psychologist, 51*, 407–415.

Triandis, H. (2001). Individualism-collectivism and personality. *Journal of Personality, 69*, 907–924.

Turner, R. H. (1978). The role and the person. *American Journal of Sociology, 84*, 1–23.

Veblen, T. (1934). *The theory of the leisure class*. New York, NY: Random House.

Witt, S. F., & Martin, C.A. (1987). Econometric models for forecasting international tourism demand. *Journal of Travel Research, 25*, 23–30.

Yim, K. C., Chan, K. W., & Hung, K. (2007). Multiple reference points in service evaluations: Roles of alternative attractiveness and self-image congruity, *Journal of Retailing, 83*, 147–157.

11

Social comparison processes in advertisement

On the relative sales-value of beauty

Michael Häfner

When the renowned behaviourist John B. Watson was among the first in the 1920s to utilize beauty as a marketing tool, he seemed to be doing something straightforward. Who does not prefer being exposed to beautiful as compared with less beautiful people? Needless to say, when we see someone beautiful we somehow get attracted to him or her. Hence, Watson might have thought, people should also prefer buying products that are presented by or alongside beautiful people, which presumably made him use seductively attractive "testimonials" in his advertisement campaigns (Buckley, 1982). Whether or not it is Watson who earns the credit for introducing beauty as a marketing tool, still nowadays most marketers would intuitively agree that "beauty sells".

(Un)fortunately, the story is not as simple as stated earlier. Over the last decade, consumers, marketers and also scientists have become increasingly aware that beauty is both a blessing and a curse. We are not necessarily and always attracted to beautiful others. Sometimes, others are so beautiful that they make us aware of our own shortcomings. Rather than being attracted to them, we then often take a step back from the threat these overly beautiful others (e.g., advertisement models) pose to our self-image. I will argue in the present chapter not only that this (sometimes even literal; see Fayant, Muller, Nurra, Alexopoulos, & Palluel-Germain, 2011) step back constitutes a different consequence from the (assimilative) response described already, but that this adverse, contrastive consequence originates in different psychological processes. Specifically, the latter *contrast effect* can best be described as the consequence of a social comparison process, whereas the former *assimilation effect* can best be described as a simple priming effect. In an effort to build up this argument, I shall describe the thesis that beauty shines: I will explain the mechanisms underlying priming and conditioning effects at some greater detail and briefly review relevant literature. I shall then turn to the explanation of the antithesis, namely that beauty may also backfire. Specifically, I will describe the social comparison logic and provide a (critical) review on how comparison processes may shape (consumer) behaviour. In an effort to reconcile these two different takes on how beauty may affect consumer behaviour, I shall then come to the synthesis by describing concrete context variables out of the consumer world rendering one (e.g., priming) or the other (i.e., social comparison) process and the respective outcomes (assimilation or contrast) more likely. Note that the literature reviewed in the present chapter may sometimes appear a bit outdated. However, after a very productive renaissance of social comparison research in the early 2000s, the interest in this topic slowly decreased. Moreover, there is not very much systematic applied research that has tried to translate basic findings to, for instance, the consumer domain. I have nevertheless tried to integrate as much classic and recent literature as possible into my own thoughts on how beauty may affect consumer behaviour.

Thesis: Beauty shines

As simple and straightforward as the hypothesis "beauty sells" may sound, psychologically speaking, a whole array of processes is usually subsumed under this label. There are many ways in which beauty can "spill over" or "shine" on whatever is close to it in space or time. For instance, people have the tendency to perceive beautiful others as more positive, because people tend to believe that "what is beautiful is good" (Dion, Berscheid, & Walster, 1972). Moreover, a product that is repeatedly presented by a beautiful model may gain extra appeal, or the beauty of a promoter may directly affect our choices (see also Bloch & Richins, 1992; Buunk & Dijkstra, 2011). Taken together, it can thus be concluded that people readily use beauty as a cue in their judgements and the decisions they make, both implicitly and explicitly, even if beauty is fairly unrelated to the given domain of behaviour (e.g., Landy & Sigall, 1974). But what exactly are the psychological mechanisms underlying these "beauty-biases"? The following paragraphs provide a brief overview over the psychological principles describing how beauty can shine on evaluations and decisions.

Before answering the question *how* beauty can shine on, for instance, products, beauty has to be defined. Obviously, this is not an easy endeavour. First of all, beauty is in the eye of the beholder and as such also dependent on cultural backgrounds and norms (Yin & Pryor, 2012). Despite this diversity in what exactly is defined as beautiful at a given time in a given culture, beauty seems to be stereotypically associated with positive features (i.e., the so-called physical attractiveness stereotype): From early childhood on, people "learn" that beautiful people are better, warmer, more successful and the like (Dion et al., 1972; Sullivan, 1993; Yin & Pryor, 2012). As a consequence, this "knowledge" is readily applied to whoever is beautiful across the world (for a meta-analytic review see Eagly, Ashmore, Makhijani, & Longo, 1991).

Research investigating the hows and whys of this stereotyping process mainly focuses on evaluations of the beautiful target person rather than on evaluations of products advertised along the beautiful standard. Though this focus on person perception is a bit off-focus to the present chapter, these findings make an important contribution: Regardless of the many different specific definitions of what is beautiful, the connotation of beauty is largely positive across many different cultures (Yin & Pryor, 2012), thereby contributing to the powerful effect beauty may have on consumer behaviour. But how exactly are the positive features associated with beauty spreading to the products promoted alongside it? Broadly speaking, there are two different psychological mechanisms through which the positive features of beauty can be transferred to other objects. First, beauty can function as an unconditioned stimulus that transfers its positive valence to a conditioned stimulus (i.e., a product) through *learning* or *classical conditioning* (Pavlov, 2003). Second, beauty can also directly affect judgements and decisions close in space and time through *priming* (Higgins, 1996).

Following a Pavlovian classical conditioning logic, Watson was among the first to show in one of his anecdotally conveyed consumer studies that beauty can serve as an unconditioned stimulus whose positive valence can spread to the valence of a conditioned stimulus, provided that both are presented *repeatedly* in sequence (Buckley, 1982). As such, he used attractive women to sell cigarettes not only to women (who might identify with the women or be attracted to the brand through the attractiveness stereotype) but also to men, with the intention to make men acquire a more positive representation of the cigarette brand through the learned association of it with the beautiful woman. After a while, the cigarette brand alone would be enough to trigger the positive feelings originally triggered by the beautiful woman. As a result of a repeated learning experience, the brand would thereby gain a more positive representation.

More recently, research on so-called priming effects (for reviews see Förster & Liberman, 2007; Higgins, 1996) established the notion that this gradual transfer can also take place "on the spot": Judgements and decision making are influenced by information that is accessible when judging or deciding. Therefore, judgements and decision making are often biased in a positive direction when, for instance, beautiful models are presented alongside products. Importantly, this "online effect" is effective as long as both stimuli (e.g., a beautiful model and a product) are presented close in time and space. Once time or space between the stimuli increases, priming becomes less likely and weaker.

Whether or not they have detailed knowledge about the fairly divergent cognitive processes underlying the two mechanisms through which beauty can shine on judgements and decision making, marketers seem to strongly believe in the power of the "beauty shines" formula and often use it in advertising. Actually, one may get the impression that in an effort to really make the formula work, marketers have done their best in boosting this sales technique by using more and more extremely beautiful models. The (extreme) use of (extreme) beauty as a marketing tool may, however, also backfire, but this will be the topic of the next section of this chapter.

Antithesis: Beauty threatens

Over time, the socio-cultural norms defining what is beautiful and what is not shifted. Beauty was more and more associated with thinness, fitness and other, often *unfeasible*, attributes (e.g., Malkin, Wornian, & Chrisler, 1999; Saad, 2004). Along with this, also marketing campaigns changed and featured more and more extreme models in accordance with the current *Zeitgeist* and fashion. Taken together with the increasingly accessible mass media (magazines, TV, Internet etc.), these socio-cultural changes contributed to the fact that beauty was no longer just a subtle cue that was presented along with certain products; beauty and the models embodying beauty became widely shared standards (Richins, 1991, 1995; Thompson, Heinberg, Altabe, & Tantleff-Dunn, 1999; Tiggemann, 2002). Though this shift per se is not a problem, the extremity of the models can be. With the "enthronization" of the models to shared, normative standards, perceivers trying to live up to their queens and kings start to compare to them (Festinger, 1954). Unfortunately, the problem with *unfeasible* standards is that comparisons with them are very likely to end in negative, threatening self-evaluations highlighting one's own shortcomings (see Groesz, Levine, & Murnen, 2002 for a meta-analytic review). This higher likelihood of adverse outcomes led many researchers to come up with the antithesis, namely that beauty does not shine but rather casts a shadow on the perceiver and should thus not necessarily be used to market products. Recent shower gel campaigns with less extreme standards and the abandonment of supermodels in some fashion magazines are examples of this latest trend (e.g., Unilever, 2005).

In what follows, I will start off by briefly describing the cognitive-motivational processes underlying comparison processes in general. I will then, on the one hand, critically discuss evidence speaking to the above notion that comparisons with beauty standards typically end in adverse consequences for the perceiver. On the other hand, I will also discuss evidence speaking against this notion and showing that social comparisons are flexible, even to extreme standards.

The general idea that people compare themselves with others stems from Leon Festinger, who formulated a theory of *social comparison* (1954). His core assumption was that in order to be able to more accurately judge the self, people compare themselves with relevant others. Whereas Festinger originally assumed that comparisons have only one direction, namely *towards* the standard (i.e., *assimilation*), a large number of studies, including those investigating comparisons with advertisement models, paint a different picture. As such, Groesz et al. (2002) found small to moderate effects in the opposite direction in their meta-analysis: Typically, women come to see their own body image in stark contrast to the ideal presented in most advertisement campaigns. But how can this effect be explained? What are the psychological mechanisms transforming perceived beauty into a threat to the self?

The observation that extreme standards of comparison can actually end in contrastive self-evaluations for the perceiver can be accounted for by a number of different social comparison models (e.g., Lockwood & Kunda, 1997; Mussweiler, 2003; Schwarz & Bless, 1992; for a recent overview see Corcoran, Crusius, & Mussweiler, 2011). For example, Lockwood and Kunda (1997) illustrated the effects of social comparisons in an interesting experiment with accountancy students. These researchers exposed first- and fourth-year students to an extremely successful fourth-year fellow accountancy student. Even though the standard was exactly the same (and also the same extreme) for both groups, the standard yielded dramatically different outcomes for the two different groups. Whereas first-year students assimilated towards the "superstar" and rated their own abilities and prospects of success as higher, fourth-year students contrasted away from the same superstar in their self-evaluations and predicted their chances of being successful as low. According to Lockwood and Kunda, this effect is due to the perceived *attainability* of the standard. Specifically, they assume that the older superstar motivates the young students because he embodies what they are willing to attain and thus also think they actually can attain. Conversely, the superstar seems too far away and unattainable for the same-age fellow students, who actually have no more time to "close the gap", and is thus threatening to them. Though the standard excelled in terms of academic success in the present research, the example easily translates to beauty and makes another interesting point: Beauty is not only relative and therefore in the eye of the beholder, but beauty or attractiveness can be fuelled by various sources, such as professional success or a perfect body image.

Be that as it may, Lockwood and Kunda (1997) were interested in showing that perceived attainability moderates comparison outcomes: What seems attainable is assimilated; what is unattainable is contrasted. This is, however, only one of several cognitive-motivational processes that have been highlighted as driving forces in comparison processes. Schwarz and Bless (1992), for instance, focus on inclusion versus exclusion processes, and Mussweiler's (2003) model describes the effects of perceived similarities vs. dissimilarities to a given standard. As different as these process accounts are, there is a common denominator connecting all models. Specifically, all process variables described in the already mentioned models have to do with the perception/experience of social proximity or distance in one way or another: An individual who is close to us is usually perceived to be more similar, and more attainable, and is thus also included in the self more readily. Conversely, someone who is perceived as rather distant is typically also perceived as dissimilar to us, less attainable and will therefore not easily be included into the self (Häfner, 2012; Häfner & Schubert, 2009).

Regardless of which of the models one favours in explaining why, for instance, extreme standards of beauty are likely to trigger contrastive social comparisons, all of them allow two further conclusions. First and foremost, the extremity of a given standard is no longer a static attribute inherent in a given standard (see e.g., Herr, 1986), but can rather be seen as the outcome of a constructive cognitive-motivational process. In other words, a standard is what a person makes of it. Just as in the experiment of Lockwood and Kunda (1997) discussed previously, people create their own standards. To some a superstar may seem fairly close, whereas others construct themselves in a large distance from the exact same standard. Second, and importantly, this implies that even comparisons with very extreme models do not necessarily have to end in contrastive outcomes. The latter assumption is nicely illustrated in an experiment by Brown, Novick, Lord and Richards (1992). When participants in their experiment learned that they shared their date of birth with a depicted supermodel, they assimilated their self-views towards the image of the model in a subsequent self-evaluation. Participants without any further information about the ostensibly shared birthdate contrasted away in their self-evaluations. The subtle and fairly unrelated information about the birthday thus helped to reduce the perceived distance from the given standard, directly pointing to the important role perceived distance plays in giving direction to social comparisons.

In sum, social comparison processes can thus be described as extremely flexible processes that are shaped by many different factors. Regardless of this general conclusion, however, many real-life observations show without a doubt that the internalization of the beauty ideal is associated with dramatic negative consequences for many young women: Continuous exposure to beauty models in fashion magazines, on television and in advertisement campaigns has been shown to be associated with disordered eating behaviour, body dissatisfaction and an unhealthy drive for thinness and dieting (e.g., Halliwall, & Dittmar, 2005; see also this volume; Harrison & Cantor, 1997; Krahé & Krause, 2010; Stice & Shaw, 1994; Swami et al., 2010; Tiggemann, 2002). Hence, the interesting question arises of how these ostensibly opposing findings can be reconciled. How is it possible that, on the one hand, theory seems to imply that social comparison processes (even with extreme standards like advertisement models) should be flexible and in the service of evaluating the self more accurately, whereas on the other hand real life seems to prove that comparisons with advertisement models usually end adversely?

Before I argue for the consideration of certain context variables moderating the impact beauty may have on the perceiver/consumer, let me briefly summarize the main conclusions of the social comparison perspective on beauty as a marketing tool: When beauty turns into a standard (of comparison), it may also backfire in its impact on the consumer, as there are two opposing directions a social comparison may take. Depending on what the perceiver subjectively makes of the standard, either assimilation (i.e., "becoming the standard") or contrast (i.e., "distancing from the standard") may be the consequence.

Synthesis: Beauty in context

When looking at the aforementioned controversy, one might simply argue that theory and practice are different sides of a coin. Though theoretically social comparisons should be flexible, even with extreme standards like supermodels (e.g., Häfner, 2004; Brown et al., 1992), practice teaches us that it is virtually impossible for people to construct the current beauty ideal such that it could lead to assimilative self-evaluations (e.g., Groesz et al., 2002).

Rather than following this, in my eyes, premature conclusion, I shall try to identify and describe three instances where it *is* possible *and likely* that beauty shines on the perceiver and when it is likely that beauty leads to less harmful comparative processes. Specifically, I shall first discuss findings showing that comparison with the current beauty ideal is less mandatory than is implied by quite a lot of research. I will argue that threatening comparisons are sometimes avoided and that the involvement of the self (i.e., self-consciousness or self-awareness), the relevance of a given standard and the availability of cognitive resources are important context variables determining when people compare and when they do not. Second, I shall turn to research showing that if people compare themselves with extreme role models, the outcomes are not necessarily adverse, even in a real-life context. Specifically, I will discuss research showing that if people have the chance to shift the dimension of comparison, they will do so in order to protect their threatened self. Finally, I will discuss concrete moderators of comparison processes that can be used in campaigns in order to avoid adverse comparisons in the perceiver.

To compare or not to compare?

As stated before, Festinger (1954) promoted the general idea that, in order to come to a more accurate picture of the self, people have a natural tendency to compare themselves with relevant others. Hence, the important question one has to answer is whether or when people do really want to have an accurate image of the self and whether or when beauty constitutes a *relevant* standard. Of course, one could argue along the lines of socio-cultural models stating that beauty has become such a dominant and omnipresent goal that people are almost obliged to compare in the eye of beauty (e.g., Richins, 1995). I will, however, argue more social psychologically; that is, I will try to identify context variables that render beauty either a standard or a prime. Stated differently, I start off by asking the simple question of what it takes to compare. Basically, two things are necessary to be able to compare. First, the self has to be activated or conscious; otherwise involvement is so low that comparisons are unlikely. Second, the potential standard of comparison has to be (judged as) relevant; otherwise the "standard" is not a standard. In what follows I will outline these two hypotheses in greater detail and discuss first evidence speaking to them. Furthermore, I shall try to develop perspectives for future research on the basis of these hypotheses, as research concerning these hypotheses is scarce.

Self-consciousness

Clearly, there is no possibility of comparing the self with a given standard, if there is no self. In other words, if the self is not "activated" in a given situation, if people are not aware of themselves, comparisons should be less likely. For priming effects, however, the self is not a crucial ingredient, as the prime (i.e., beauty) can affect judgements without activating the self (Förster & Liberman, 2007). Hence, whether an attractive model will serve as a standard or a prime should depend upon whether the self is activated or not.

The crucial question is, then, when advertisement campaigns activate the self and when they do not. Straightforwardly, it can be argued that if models explicitly address the perceiver or testify the gains of an advertised product or service with their attributes, then the self of the perceiver is likely to be involved. For instance, imagine an extremely beautiful model claiming, "You will be beautiful and feel great if you wear this lingerie". In such a situation perceivers are likely to try to answer the question of whether this is or can be true for them by comparing themselves with the model. "Can I ever be like that? Will the product do the trick for me?" Hence, in this case the ad suggests the model's attractiveness is related to or "caused" by the product, and thus the model becomes a (self-) relevant standard (of comparison) (see Tesser, 1988). Though the outcome of the subsequent comparison process is in principle flexible, the distance between the standards usually used in such a context and the perceiver is likely to trigger contrastive comparisons (e.g., Häfner, 2004; Häfner & Schubert, 2009).

If, on the other hand, the perceiver is *not* explicitly addressed or the model's attractiveness is not presented as related to or caused by the product in an advertisement campaign, the self is not likely to be activated, rendering comparison unlikely. For instance, try to imagine the above model in her lingerie again, this time, however, advertising a chair for a furniture company.

Even though visually, the advertisement campaign may be very similar to the one above, the consequences for the self should be different. As the model is probably not known for her excellent furniture taste, nor has her beauty anything to do with the chair she is sitting on, the model is not likely to be used as a standard of comparison in such a setting. Her attractiveness is not related to or caused by the product and can thus "simply" shine on the product. In other words, in this instance beauty may serve as a prime or an unconditioned stimulus.

To sum up, the extent to which perceivers' selves are involved should determine whether comparison or priming processes are likely to take over. Specifically, if advertisement models directly address perceivers or stand for the product with their own attributes, these models are likely to constitute standards of comparison. If the self is not involved (i.e., the model does not directly address the perceiver, or the model's attractiveness is not presented as related to or caused by the product) the model serves as a prime and her attractiveness will shine on subsequent judgements. Despite the fact that there is first evidence showing that the activation of the self (through gender priming) influences social comparisons in the predicted direction (Buunk & Dijkstra, 2011), there is not yet a direct test of the straightforward hypothesis that self-consciousness is a *necessary* prerequisite for social comparisons to take place. Furthermore, the practical implications this logic has for the design of communication campaigns (e.g., is the product being advertised by a beautiful model related to her beauty or not?) have, to the best of my knowledge, not yet been investigated. Both would, however, largely advance our knowledge on how exactly and when exactly beauty works as a marketing tool. Following the above logic, the interesting and counterintuitive prediction would be that the less beauty is related to the product being advertised, the better beauty should help to sell the product.

Relevance of a given standard

Closely related to what I discussed previously are considerations about whether or not people really compare themselves with *any* given standard. Though not spelled out this explicitly by Festinger (1954), the idea that people use comparisons to come to more accurate evaluations of the self implies that whenever people have a chance to – and as there is no such thing as a social vacuum, this is virtually always the case (see also Mussweiler, 2003) – they will compare themselves with their social environment. But what if people know what the outcome of a given comparison will look like? What if it is obvious that they are too far off the standard, or, as stated in terms of Tesser's (1988) ideas, what if a given standard is simply *irrelevant*?

First, there is quite some evidence showing that if a given standard is less relevant, for instance because the standard belongs to an out-group, comparison effects are also less intense (e.g., Blanton, Crocker, & Miller, 2000; Major, Sciacchitano, & Crocker, 1993). Second, there is a whole research tradition investigating individual differences in the chronic tendency to compare oneself with other people. According to this research, there are fairly stable differences in the so-called *social comparison orientation* (see Buunk & Gibbons, 2006; Gibbons & Buunk, 1999) rendering, per definition, comparison less relevant for some people. Of course, this research provides only indirect evidence for the notion that sometimes comparisons (or a given standard) are irrelevant and are therefore ignored or avoided. However, inspired by this research tradition are studies on (strategic) choices of comparison standards in cancer patients (e.g., Collins, 1996; Taylor & Lobel, 1989; Van der Zee, Oldersma, Buunk, & Bos, 1998). This research clearly shows that not always do all potentially available standards also serve as actual standards, but that strategic choices play an important role. As such, it was shown that cancer patients do sometimes prefer to compare in an upward manner (i.e., with patients who are better off than they are) and sometimes in a downward manner (i.e., with patients who are worse off than they are). Third, there is quite a lot of research demonstrating that people mainly compare themselves with so-called routine standards (e.g., Corcoran & Mussweiler, 2009; Rüter & Mussweiler, 2005). These routine standards are easy-to-access standards that are highly available, like, for instance, good friends. These routine standards are likely to be picked as comparison standards across many different situations, thereby making comparisons fast and easy. Sure, it could be argued that beauty is more and more accessible and can therefore also become a routine standard. Be that as it may, I would at least argue that this should only be the case for a relatively small group of people. Usually, good friends and other close people are used as standards, which implies that more extreme and distant standards do not typically serve as common standards. Fourth, and finally, cultural norms and standards should also determine how far beauty constitutes a relevant standard in a given society, for certain age groups or for a specific gender. Despite the fact that beauty seems to be perceived positively in most cultures (Yin & Pryor, 2012), and despite the fact that there is amazingly little research on how cultural norms and social comparison processes interact (for exceptions see, e.g., Buunk, Carmona, Peiró, Dijkstra & Dijkstra, 2011; Lockwood, Shaughnessy, Fortune & Tong, 2012; White & Lehman, 2005), it is obvious that culture is an important determinant of how routinely, with whom and in which direction people compare themselves with standards of beauty. When drawing on work on self-construals (e.g., Kühnen, Hannover, & Schubert, 2001), one could, for example, hypothesize that comparisons might be a more common and more important culture technique in individualistic cultures where it is important to find one`s distinct spot as compared with collectivist cultures where it is important to belong to the group (see also Buunk et al., 2011). As stated previously, these hypotheses have to remain speculative, however, as there is by far too little research as to warrant strong predictions.

Taken together, it therefore seems safe to doubt that extremely beautiful advertisement models are *the* reason for eating disorders or other dramatic consequences. On the contrary, on the basis of the already mentioned research, one could come up with the rather extreme conclusion that in many, many situations, extreme standards of beauty can and will be recognized as too extreme and therefore irrelevant standards of comparison that may then be either ineffective to the self or even come at positive effects to the self through priming. Moreover, the first two variables I discussed as potential moderators of whether or not people compare, self-consciousness and relevance of the standard, imply another important moderator, namely cognitive capacity. I shall therefore end this section on the possibility to avoid comparisons by briefly discussing research investigating the role of cognitive capacity in social comparison processes.

Cognitive capacity

As social comparisons ask for at least minimal involvement or consciousness of the self and an active comparison of the self with a given standard, it seems straightforward to conclude that it is cognitively more consuming to compare than not to compare. Thus, people should be less likely to compare when cognitive resources are scarce. Interestingly, there is not much research addressing this question, which would, however, be of great interest to the consumer domain, as consumption situations and the processing of advertisements are typically associated with low cognitive effort (Cialdini & Goldstein, 2004). But are people really less likely to compare themselves with beauty ideals when their cognitive capacities are low? Together with Debra Trampe, I conducted a series of studies to answer this question (Häfner & Trampe, 2009). In these relatively simple studies, in which we manipulated cognitive load and measured self-evaluations in response to depictions of advertisement campaigns with beautiful (and average) models, we found that comparative contrast was much less likely under conditions of cognitive load. Apparently, when our participants had to remember an eight-digit number, they were unable to compare themselves with the standard and simply "basked in the beauty" of the supermodels or the usualness of the average models, respectively.

Unfortunately, to my best knowledge, there is no more empirical evidence for the notion that comparisons do need more cognitive capacity than, for instance, priming. Taken together with all of the research I reviewed, I nevertheless feel confident in concluding that social comparisons are less ubiquitous than often assumed. Apart from the fact that people need cognitive capacity in order to compare (which they often lack or are not motivated to invest in comparisons), people have various ways to "escape" comparisons and make use of them, especially when facing threatening comparison information, like, for instance, extreme standards of beauty. In no way does this imply that avoiding comparisons is the default. I simply argue that there is a lot of research directly or indirectly showing that social comparisons do not necessarily and always take place. In these instances, when people do not compare, priming effects become more likely, in which beauty shines on whatever is presented alongside it. In the end, it is therefore neither Watson nor Festinger who is right, but both! Beauty can be a blessing and a curse also in advertising.

How to compare?

Previously, I presented evidence showing that comparisons with beautiful models are less mandatory than portrayed in some research. In this section, I will go one step further and discuss what happens when people do compare themselves with high standards of beauty. I aim to show that even if people engage in comparisons the outcomes are flexible. First, I shall therefore discuss findings showing that people can find ways to deal with threatening comparison information, namely by actually shifting the dimension of comparison. Second, I shall turn to evidence showing that even comparisons on the potentially threatening beauty dimension do not necessarily end in adverse consequences for the perceiver. There are certain instances or context factors that may favour assimilative comparisons.

Shifting dimensions to protect the self

As a host of research inspired by Tesser's Self-Evaluation Maintenance Model (SEM, 1988) shows, people find ways to deal with threatening comparison information by engaging in all sorts of defensive behaviour (Häfner et al., 2008; Hart, 2014). That is, people may react to threatening comparison information by strategically keeping up their self-value, for instance by stressing positive features of the self on an unrelated dimension: "The model may be beautiful and thin but I am much more athletic!" Often, such defensive strategies involve shifting away from the salient dimension of comparison.

Interestingly, such a shift of comparison dimension has at least two consequences: First, the threatened features of the self – which trigger the defensive mechanism – are highly accessible as a consequence of the exposure to the social comparison information. Second, however, defensive, reparative self-knowledge is activated in parallel. Hence, both negative (contrastive) and positive (defensive) features of the self should be highly accessible after exposure to threatening standards. I refer to this interesting feature because it may be an explanation for why defensive outcomes are not typically reported in research on comparisons with media images: Most of the time defensive self-evaluations are simply not assessed, as such research (also theoretically) focuses on adverse consequences (see also Häfner, 2004; Häfner et al., 2008). Hence, the dependent variables assessed in most of this research (naturally) centre around the one salient dimension that is associated with the standard of comparison. For one thing, this might imply that reparation cannot be found, as it is simply not measured. For another thing, this could also imply that reparation cannot take place at all, as if there is no question steering people's thoughts to reparative dimensions, there is "no space" to repair because what people think about circles around the threatened self.

It was exactly this reasoning that we put to an empirical test (Häfner et al., 2008; see also Sobol & Darke, 2014; Tiggemann & Polivy, 2010). Specifically, we manipulated the questions viewers were asked after exposure to idealized media images. In one condition, viewers were directly asked to evaluate the feature of the self that was portrayed to perfection by a media image (e.g., we asked how feminine our female participants felt). In another condition, we first asked them to provide their self-evaluations for a non-salient, reparative feature of the self (e.g., how athletically able they felt). As predicted, we found that focusing on the salient features likely ended in contrastive comparisons. However, focusing first on reparative features of the self was likely to end in much less threatening consequences. In this condition, participants successfully repaired their self-value and reported an overall more positive picture of the self (e.g., "I might not be as feminine as she is, but I am definitely doing fine with respect to athletic ability").

Taken together, one can thus conclude that if there is space to repair the self, people do actively use it to repair the self. These reparative processes do not only come at the advantage of protecting the self, but can even boost the self and behaviour (Sobol & Darke, 2014). But what does this mean for consumer issues? This evidence might imply that *marketers* need to care less about what kind of models they use to advertise their products. At the end of the day, the flexible customers seem to be ready to deal with the beauty standards set by marketers, don't they? In principle they should be. However, advertising campaigns are often designed so that there is really no way for consumers to deal with beauty, as it is often presented as an exclusive, salient good. Unfortunately, there is even reason to believe that the, in this case, likely adverse consequences for the perceiver actually help marketers. For instance, Wan, Ansons, Chattopadhyay and Leboe (2013) show that consumers who come to a negative image of the self through comparison with a beautiful advertisement model react with a more positive evaluation of the product and vice versa. From a distance logic point of view, these very interesting findings seem to make perfect sense: The perceived distance to the model that triggers negative self-evaluations can be reduced through the purchase of the product, which makes one resemble the dissimilar model just a little bit more (see also Häfner, 2004). Ultimately, this finding may thus also explain not only why the "beauty sells" heuristic is still present in the heads of marketers but also why it really seems to work.

Regardless of these last considerations, which – in light of minimal research – have to remain speculative, the findings urge the question under which circumstances (i.e., which context factors or moderating variables) comparisons to extreme beauty standards go in which direction. I shall therefore now look at factual comparison processes and whether or not they can be flexible even if they are related to extreme beauty.

Flexible comparisons

In this last section I will briefly review literature showing that even if standards of extreme beauty serve as comparison information, they can lead to comparative assimilation. Some of this research has already been reviewed (e.g., Häfner, 2004; Lockwood & Kunda, 1997; Brown et al., 1992), while other work is new, but all of the evidence has in common that it directly speaks to the basic social psychological idea that social comparisons are extremely flexible (see also Corcoran et al., 2011), and so they are in the context of beauty and advertising! Hence, there have to be certain context variables that push comparisons in one or the other direction. Unlike in the previous sections, I will directly start off with the conclusion and only then discuss specific research to back up the conclusion. I will do so because this will provide a common framework to the studies and it will allow me to end with relatively concrete suggestions as to when beauty is likely to trigger contrastive or assimilative comparisons. I hope these suggestions are also of value to marketers who plan and design their campaigns, and as such they are a useful summary of all the thoughts in this chapter.

So, what is the conclusion? The conclusion is that social comparisons are flexible and that it is not the standard or the perceiver that determines the direction of a social comparison but that it is rather their interaction that does the trick. A standard is only what the perceiver makes of it. Therefore, comparisons are not only flexible but also highly subjective and dependent on numerous cognitive-motivational processes. As diverse as these processes are, they all seem to be linked to the construction of social closeness and distance (Häfner, 2012; Häfner & Schubert, 2009). Generally speaking, one could thus conclude that whenever there is a chance that beauty standards can be constructed in relative closeness to the self they should lead to assimilation, whereas distance should be associated with contrast. But how can extreme beauty ever be constructed to be close to the average perceiver?

First and foremost, all direct hints bringing beauty closer to the self can help with experiencing closeness. That this works even for fairly subtle cues was demonstrated in a study in which I presented participants with different claims accompanied by extremely beautiful models (Häfner, 2004). Some of the claims pointed to similarities ("same body same feeling") and some to dissimilarities ("feel the difference"). As expected, these subtle differences tipped self-evaluations in completely different directions: Only those who were slightly pushed to construct the standards at a distance from them contrasted away in their self-evaluations. Those who "saw" similarities assimilated towards the standard. Whereas I presented the subtle cues in a semantic fashion, it is easily conceivable that also other cues would work: Exclusive, distant, clinical settings like in editorials or high fashion magazines often directly imply distance and should therefore be more likely to trigger self-evaluative contrast. Next-door, casual and easy-going settings should, on the other hand, promote a closer construction of the standard and should thus also promote assimilation.

The latter process – "easy-goingness" – brings me to the second concrete variable that has an influence on how standards are constructed. Specifically, in a set of studies my colleagues and I have investigated the role of fluency or ease of processing on the construction of beauty standards (Häfner, 2009, 2012; Häfner & Schubert, 2009). What we found is that whatever enhances processing the standard (e.g., knowing the standard well, easy-to-digest presentation, etc.) also helps to construct the self close to the standard. As such, well-known "supermodels" led, for instance, to more assimilation than their unknown lookalikes. For the marketing practice, this might imply that introducing *one* face for a given product leads to less adverse consequences than using multiple standards. Moreover, fluency could also be reached by having highly recognizable campaigns in which beauty is presented in always the same setting. Another interesting way in which fluency experiences could be enhanced is by mimicry: In a set of studies I conducted together with Thomas Schubert (Häfner & Schubert, 2015) we found that a smile on the face brings people closer to comparison standards and a frown brings them further away from the same standard. Whereas we induced the smile (or frown) by subtle instructions (i.e., we asked our participants to either lift up their cheeks or to bring their eyebrows together), it is conceivable that people would adopt a smile (or a frown!) of the standard they are confronted with. This takes me once more to the editorials in which models are often depicted with cool, cold facial expressions that would thereby foster distancing from them. Happy models, as often depicted in fashion catalogues, should, conversely, be infectious in their laughter, thereby rendering assimilation more likely. Again, I have to point out that these last considerations are speculations based on only very scarce research. Nevertheless, I do hope they stimulate further research on this fascinating topic.

Summary and conclusion

I have ended with a handful of concrete suggestions as to under which circumstances extreme standards of beauty lead to negative consequences in the perceiver and when they do not. Put simply, this is also the conclusion of the whole chapter: Social comparison processes – if they take place – are extremely flexible, regardless of what constitutes the standard. I have tried to build up arguments leading to this conclusion by briefly discussing and integrating two apparently opposing positions. Rather than hoping to convince every reader of the correctness of this logic, I hope to sensitize the reader to the fact that beauty can be approached in very different ways. In the most simple and direct way, beauty can shine on whatever is presented close in time and space to it. Another way – and I mean this literally as in another psychological process – to approach beauty is to use it as a standard with which the self can be compared.

Of course, this is by no means an exhaustive take on the effects of beauty on the perceiver and/or consumer. I largely neglected, for instance, a broad literature on individual differences that moderate social comparisons (e.g., Buunk & Gibbons, 2006) and I did so for the sake of saving space for clarifying the cognitive-motivational underpinnings of social comparison and priming processes. To me, and hopefully also to the reader, a profound knowledge of these processes seems more basic and more helpful for breaking new ground in the future.

References

Blanton, H., Crocker, J., & Miller, D. T. (2000). The effects of in-group versus out-group social comparison on self-esteem in the context of a negative stereotype. *Journal of Experimental Social Psychology*, 36, 519–530.

Bloch, P. H., & Richins, M. L. (1992). You look "mahvelous": The pursuit of beauty and the marketing concept. *Psychology and Marketing*, *9*, 3–15.

Brown, J. D., Novick, N. J., Lord, K. A. & Richards, J. M. (1992). When Gulliver travels: Social context, psychological closeness, and self-appraisals. *Journal of Personality and Social Psychology*, *62*, 717–727.

Buckley, K. W. (1982). The selling of a psychologist: John Broadus Watson and the application of behavioral techniques to advertising. *Journal of the History of the Behavioural Sciences*, *18*, 207–221.

Buunk, A. P., & Dijkstra, P. (2011). Does attractiveness sell? Women's attitude toward a product as a function of model attractiveness, gender priming, and social comparison orientation. *Psychology & Marketing*, *28*, 958–973.

Buunk, A. P., & Gibbons, F. X. (2006). Social comparison orientation: A new perspective on those who do and those who don't compare with others. In S. Guimond (Ed.), *Social comparison and social psychology: Understanding cognition, intergroup relations and culture* (pp. 15–33). Cambridge: Cambridge University Press.

Buunk, A. P., Carmona, C., Peiró, J. M., Dijkstra, A., & Dijkstra, P. (2011). Social comparison at work: The role of culture, type of organization and gender. *Crosscultural Communication*, 7, 14–21.

Cialdini, R. B., & Goldstein, N. J. (2004). Social influence: Compliance and conformity. *Annual Review of Psychology*, *55*, 591–621.

Collins, R. L. (1996). For better or worse: The impact of upward social comparison on self-evaluations. *Psychological Bulletin*, *119*, 51–69.

Corcoran, K., & Mussweiler, T. (2009). The efficiency of social comparisons with routine standards. *Social Cognition*, *27*, 939–948.

Corcoran, K., Cruisus, J., & Mussweiler, T. (2011). Social comparison: Motives, standards, and mechanisms. In D. Chadee (Ed.), *Theories in social psychology* (pp. 119–139). Oxford, UK: Wiley-Blackwell.
Dion, K., Berscheid, E., & Walster, E. (1972). What is beautiful is good. *Journal of Personality and Social Psychology, 24*, 285–290.
Eagly, A. H., Ashmore, R. D., Makhijani, M. G., & Longo, L. C. (1991). What is beautiful is good, but ...: A meta-analytic review of research on the physical attractiveness stereotype. *Psychological Bulletin, 110*, 109–128.
Fayant, M.-P., Muller, D., Nurra, C., Alexopoulos, T., & Palluel-Germain, R. (2011). Moving forward is not only a metaphor: Approach and avoidance lead to self-evaluative assimilation and contrast. *Journal of Experimental Social Psychology, 47*, 241–245.
Festinger, L. (1954). A theory of social comparison processes. *Human Relations*, 7, 117–140.
Förster, J., & Liberman, N. (2007). Knowledge activation. In A. W. Kruglanski and E. T. Higgins (Eds.), *Social psychology: Handbook of basic principles* (2nd ed., pp. 201–231), New York, NY: Guilford Press.
Gibbons, F. X., & Buunk, A. P. (1999). Individual differences in social comparison: Development of a scale of social comparison orientation. *Journal of Personality and Social Psychology, 76*, 129–142.
Groesz, L. M., Levine, M. P., & Murnen, S. K. (2002). The effect of experimental presentation of thin media images on body satisfaction: A meta-analytic review. *International Journal of Eating Disorders, 31*, 1–16.
Häfner, M. (2004). How dissimilar others may still resemble the self: Assimilation and contrast after social comparison. *Journal of Consumer Psychology, 14*, 187–196.
Häfner, M. (2009). Knowing you, knowing me: Familiarity moderates comparison outcomes to idealized media images. *Social Cognition, 27*, 496–508.
Häfner, M. (2012). Assimilation or contrast? How fluency channels comparison processing. In R. Greifeneder & C. Unkelbach (Eds.), *The experience of thinking: How feelings from mental processes influence cognition and behaviour* (pp. 119–132). London: Psychology Press.
Häfner, M., & Schubert, T. (2009). Feel the difference! The influence of ease experiences on the direction of social comparison. *Journal of Experimental Social Psychology, 45*, 291–294.
Häfner, M., & Schubert, T. (2015). *In the face of comparison information: On the proprioceptive underpinnings of spontaneous social comparisons* (Manuscript in preparation). University of the Arts, Berlin.
Häfner, M., & Trampe, D. (2009). When thinking is beneficial and when it is not: The effects of round and thin advertising models. *Journal of Consumer Psychology, 19*, 619–628.
Häfner, M., Jagsch, O., Kund, A., Mager, S., Türk-Pereira, P., & Zimmermann, A. (2008). The female may feel male: Defending against the adverse consequences of exposure to idealized media images. *Journal of Social and Clinical Psychology, 27*, 778–808.
Harrison, K., & Cantor, J. (1997). The relationship between media exposure and eating disorders. *Journal of Communication, 47*, 40–67.
Hart, J. (2014). Towards an integrative theory of psychological defense. *Perspectives on Psychological Science, 9*, 19–39.
Herr, P. M. (1986). Consequences of priming: Judgment and behaviour. *Journal of Personality and Social Psychology, 51*, 1106–1115.
Higgins, E. T. (1996). Knowledge activation: Accessibility, applicability, and salience. In E. T. Higgins & A. W. Kruglanski (Eds.), *Social psychology: Handbook of basic principles* (pp. 133–168). New York, NY: Guilford Press.
Krahé, B., & Krause, C. (2010). Presenting thin media models affects women's choice of diet or normal snacks. *Psychology of Women Quarterly, 34*, 349–355.
Kühnen, U., Hannover, B., & Schubert, B. (2001). The semantic-procedural interface model of the self: The role of self-knowledge for context-dependent versus context-independent modes of thinking. *Journal of Personality and Social Psychology, 80*, 397–409.
Landy, D., & Sigall, H. (1974). Beauty is talent: Task evaluation as a function of the performer's physical attractiveness. *Journal of Personality and Social Psychology, 29*, 299–304.
Lockwood, P., & Kunda, Z. (1997). Superstars and me: Predicting the impact of role models on the self. *Journal of Personality and Social Psychology, 73*, 91–103.
Lockwood, P., Shaughnessy, S. C., Fortune, J. L., & Tong, M. O. (2012). Social comparisons in novel situations: Finding inspiration during life transitions. *Personality and Social Psychology Bulletin, 38*, 985–996.
Major, B., Sciacchitano, A., & Crocker, J. (1993). In-group versus out-group comparisons and self-esteem. *Personality and Social Psychology Bulletin, 19*, 711–721.
Malkin, A. R., Wornian, K., & Chrisler, J. C. (1999). Women and weight: Gendered messages on magazines covers. *Sex Roles, 40*, 647–655.

Mussweiler, T. (2003). Comparison processes in social judgment: Mechanisms and consequences. *Psychological Review, 110*, 472–489.
Pavlov, I. P. (2003). *Conditioned reflexes: An investigation of the physiological activity of the cerebral cortex*. Mineola, NY: Dover.
Richins, M. L. (1991). Social comparison and the idealized images of advertising. *Journal of Consumer Research, 19*, 71–83.
Richins, M. L. (1995). Materialism, desire, and discontent. Contributions of idealized advertising images and social comparison. In R. P. Hill (Ed.), *Marketing and consumer research in the public interest* (pp. 109–132). London: Sage.
Rüter, K., & Mussweiler, T. (2005). Bonds of friendship – comparative self-evaluations evoke the use of routine standards. *Social Cognition, 23*, 137–160.
Saad, G. (2004). Applying evolutionary psychology in understanding the representation of women in advertisements. *Psychology & Marketing, 21*, 593–612.
Schwarz, N., & Bless, H. (1992). Constructing reality and its alternatives: An inclusion/exclusion model of assimilation and contrast effects in social judgment. In L. Martin & A. Tesser (Eds.), *The construction of social judgment* (pp. 217–245). Hillsdale, NJ: Erlbaum.
Sobol, K., & Darke, P. R. (2014). I'd like to be that attractive, but at least I'm smart: How exposure to ideal advertising models motivates improved decision-making. *Journal of Consumer Psychology, 24*, 533–540.
Stice, E., & Shaw, H. (1994). Adverse effects of the media portrayed thin-ideal on women and linkages to bulimic symptomatology. *Journal of Social and Clinical Psychology, 13*, 288–308.
Sullivan, D. (1993). Cosmetic surgery: Market dynamics and medicalization. *Research in the Sociology of Health Care, 10*, 97–115.
Swami, V., et al. (2010). The attractive female body weight and female body dissatisfaction in 26 countries across 10 world regions: Results of the international body project I. *Personality and Social Psychology Bulletin, 36*, 309–325.
Taylor, S. E., & Lobel, M. (1989). Social comparison activity under threat: Downward evaluation and upward contacts. *Psychological Review, 96*, 569–575.
Tesser, A. (1988). Toward a self-evaluation maintenance model of social behaviour. In L. Berkowitz (Ed.), *Advances in experimental social psychology* (Vol. 21, pp. 181–227). San Diego, CA: Academic Press.
Thompson, J. K., Heinberg, L. J., Altabe, M., & Tantleff-Dunn, S. (1999). *Exacting beauty: Theory, assessment, and treatment of body image disturbance*. Washington, DC: American Psychological Association.
Tiggemann, M. (2002). Body image development: Media influences. In T. F. Cash & T. Pruzinsky (Eds.), *Body images: A handbook of theory, research, and clinical practice*. New York, NY: Guilford Press.
Tiggemann, M., & Polivy, J. (2010). Upwards and downwards: Social comparison processing of thin idealized media images. *Psychology of Women Quarterly, 34*, 356–364.
Unilever (2005). Unilever annual review and summary financial statement 2005. Retrieved from www.unilever.com/Images/2005-annual-review-english_tcm244-424082_en.pdf
Van der Zee, K., Oldersma, F., Buunk, B. P., & Bos, D. M. (1998). Social comparison preferences among cancer patients as related to neuroticism and social comparison orientation. *Journal of Personality and Social Psychology, 75*, 801–810.
Wan, F., Ansons, T. L., Chattopadhyay, A., & Leboe, J. P. (2013). Defensive reactions to slim female images in advertising: The moderating role of mode of exposure. *Organizational Behaviour and Human Decision Processes, 120*, 37–46.
White, K., & Lehman, D. R. (2005). Culture and social comparison seeking: The role of self-motives. *Personality and Social Psychology Bulletin, 31*, 232–242.
Yin, B. & Pryor, S. (2012). Beauty in the age of marketing. *Review of Business and Finance Case Studies, 3*, 119–132.

12

Applying universal dimensions of social perception to consumer context

An extension of the SCM/BIAF models with the relevance principle

Magdalena J. Zawisza

In 2010, the year of its 100th anniversary, BP experienced serious troubles: The explosion at its Deepwater Horizon platform resulted in some estimated 200 million gallons of oil spilling over the Gulf of Mexico. The initial attitude of finger pointing and downplaying the problem seriously dented the brand image of this leading oil company. The brand was seen as neither caring (to its consumers and the environment) nor competent (in managing its technology and the disaster itself; Kervyn, Chan, Malone, Korpusik, & Ybarra, 2014). Following the disaster, sales and brand loyalty dropped to 40 per cent below those of Shell (Malone & Fiske, 2013). The BP example illustrates the importance of two dimensions of social perception within a consumer context: warmth and competence. This chapter will first introduce these dimensions alongside related social psychological theories, e.g., Stereotype Content Model (SCM; Fiske, Cuddy, Glick, & Xu, 2002) and its extension (Behaviours form Intergroup Affect and Stereotypes – the BIAS Map; Cuddy, Fiske, & Glick, 2007). In doing so, it will also discuss the issue of primacy of warmth over competence in human perception alongside a competing model, the Double Interest Account (DIA; Wojciszke & Abele, 2008). Having set the scene, the chapter will then move on to overview and evaluate the attempts made to apply the SCM model to brand perception: the BIAF model (Brands as Intentional Agents Framework; Kervyn, Fiske, & Malone, 2012). Furthermore, the chapter will identify the contradictions that have already emerged from the very recent empirical literature. This will provide background to the main argument of the chapter: that such contradictions do not necessary undermine the SCM/BIAF model – instead they point to the need for extending the model by incorporating a *relevance principle* (Zawisza & Pittard, 2015). Within this chapter the following two key questions will be discussed: To what extent do the universal dimensions of social perception apply to perception of brands? and Does the importance of warmth and competence differ depending on variables present in consumer context but absent in social perception of humans? The chapter will end by discussing directions for future research and practical implications.

The universal dimensions of social perception

A vast body of research in social psychology has identified warmth (W) and competence (C) as universal dimensions of social judgement which determine perception of groups, individuals and the self (Fiske, Cuddy, & Glick, 2007; Judd, James-Hawkins, Yzerbyt, & Kashima, 2005; Wojciszke & Abele, 2008). While they are referred to by different names (e.g., agency vs communion, other- vs. self-profitability, socially vs. intellectually good or bad, morality vs. competence), they share similarities: The W dimension pertains to social relations and the C dimension to task orientation and goal achievement (Wojciszke & Abele, 2008). Together they are said to explain 82 per cent of social perception (Cuddy et al., 2007; Wojciszke, Bazinska, & Jaworski, 1998) and are therefore often referred to as the Big Two (Abele & Bruckmüller, 2011). Adjectives that describe W are warm, kind, helpful and honest, while C is described by characteristics such as efficient, competent and active. Negative manifestations of warmth (i.e., lack of warmth) are captured by adjectives such as deceitful, unkind and abusive, while lack of competence is described by traits such as uneducated, sloppy and lazy (Kenworthy & Taush, 2008). The roots of these two dimensions are argued to be socio-structural and evolutionary (Fiske et al., 2002): The basic "friend vs. foe" distinction helps us navigate the social world, where warmth informs us of the other's intentions and, on the other hand, competence informs us of their ability to enact these intentions.

Arguably one of the most condensed forms of social perception is encapsulated in stereotypes. Fiske et al. (2002) have developed a mixed Stereotype Content Model (SCM), which proposes that the content of most stereotypes is ambivalent – that is, it is literally an evaluative mix of warmth and competence where one may be high and the other low. According to the model, the social structure of the in- and out-groups and the nature of their interdependence jointly define not only the content of stereotypes but also the emotional and behavioural responses to the stereotyped groups. For example, status defines competence and the nature of interdependence between the groups defines warmth (e.g., an out-group that is deemed cooperative is perceived as warm and a competitive one as cold). Warmth refers to orientation towards (or against) others while competence refers to (in)ability to achieve status. It is often the case that social groups are stereotyped as high on warmth but low on competence and vice versa. These two core dimensions of stereotypes are orthogonal and allow classification of stereotypes into four types depending on their content: paternalistic (low on competence and high on warmth), envious (high on competence and low on warmth), contemptuous (low–low) and admiration (high–high). SCM gained empirical support when tested on different global stereotypes (Fiske et al., 2002), as well as on subgroups of global stereotypes such as Asians (Fiske, Xu, Cuddy, & Glick, 1999), Blacks (Fiske et al., 2002), gays (Clausell & Fiske, 2005), elderly people (Cuddy, Norton, & Fiske, 2005), nationalities (Lee & Fiske, 2006) and women and men (Eckes, 2002). For example, housewives are seen as high on W and low on C (people like them but do not respect them) while business people (be they women or men) are seen as competent but cold (people respect them but do not necessarily like them; Eckes, 2002). In fact, the two dimensions have been argued to be universal – data from surveys spanning 36 countries across five continents confirmed that perception of social groups is organized along the two key dimensions of warmth and competence (Cuddy et al., 2007).

Importantly, the stereotype content has consequences. Specifically, it influences the affective and behavioural response to the stereotyped social groups (Cuddy et al., 2007). According to SCM extension – the BIAS Map (Cuddy et al., 2007) – specific stereotype content elicits specific emotions. For example, paternalistic stereotypes elicit feelings of pity (e.g., the said housewives), groups which are high on C and low on W are envied (e.g., the rich), those perceived as neither warm nor competent are treated with contempt (e.g., the homeless), and admiration is the emotional response reserved for groups perceived as high on both W and C (e.g., celebrities, in-groups). Moreover, the BIAS Map further proposes that these emotions lead to specific behaviours towards the targets of the stereotypes (Cuddy et al., 2007). For example, pity, being an ambivalent emotion, triggers either helping behaviour (i.e., active facilitation) or avoidance and neglect (i.e., passive harm). Similar behavioural ambivalence is elicited by envious stereotypes. Since envy combines both respect and resentment, the behavioural outcome of this emotion can be twofold: cooperation for convenience (i.e., passive facilitation) or scapegoating (i.e., active harm) – the latter being particularly likely in times of social instability. Contempt or disgust, being univalenced emotions, activate harming behaviours – both active and passive (e.g., forcefully expelling individuals or social exclusion). On the other hand, admiration, which is a uniformly positive emotion, motivates both active and passive positive behaviours (e.g., positive contact and cooperation).

This transference of stereotype content into emotions and then behaviours makes the SCM and BIAS models promising for the context of consumer behaviour. From that perspective it would be useful to know which of the two, competence or warmth, presides over the cognitive, affective and behavioural reactions to the stereotyped groups. SCM proposes that a "friend or foe" decision is more important, from an evolutionary point of view (e.g., survival), than determining how capable others are as friends or foes (Fiske et al., 2007). Indeed, primacy of W over C has been shown in various socio-psychological studies involving (a) identification on lexical decision tasks; (b) forming global impressions of groups or individuals; and (c) meaning stability across cultures (see Judd et al., 2005; Wojciszke & Abele, 2008 for overviews). However, according to Wojciszke's (2005) DIA, the primary role of either of these two dimensions (i.e., the primacy effect) depends on social distance (e.g., whether we evaluate a close friend or a distant other). Specifically, in various social situations individuals take the roles of either actors or observers. Observers assume the perspective of the receiver of an action and thus are more interested in the actor's W (aka communion or other-profitability) than in their C (aka agency or self-profitability). However, those acting have a greater interest in C (self-profitability). Moreover, others are differentially related to the self. For example, in situations of interdependence people will evaluate the others similarly to themselves (greater emphasis on C than W). So the typical primacy effect of W over C proposed by SCM reverses in evaluations of close friends, where C matters more than W (Wojciszke & Abele, 2008). Indeed, the primacy of W over C has been shown to be moderated by social distance between the self and others: Wojciszke and Abele (2008) found that changes in a target's evaluation were dependent on the observer's perspective – there was a "W over C" advantage in forming perceptions of socially distant others (i.e., interest in their other-profitability), but information about C (i.e., interest in self-profitability) was more important in forming evaluations of close friends or the self.

As discussed thus far, and despite the debate surrounding the primacy of warmth, the notions of W and C have been firmly established in social psychological literature and the dimensions have gained the status of universal in the realm of social perception (Cuddy et al., 2007). The question here is, however: To what extent could they inform perception in consumer context? Initial attempts to apply the SCM framework to brand perception have already been made and, as will be noted next, they do show promise. However, not all the theoretical nuances already outlined here found their recognition in the proposed adaptation of the SCM model to consumer context – the focus of the following sections.

Warmth and competence in the consumer setting – the BIAF model

The idea that humans and brands may be perceived similarly is not new (Aaker, 1997; Fournier, 1998; Fournier & Alvarez, 2012). However, consumer psychologists have only recently started to test whether, and how, the dimensions of warmth and competence apply to the consumer context (Infanger & Sczesny, 2015; Kervyn et al., 2012; Zawadzka, 2015; Zawisza & Cinnirella, 2010; Zawisza, Cinnirella, & Zawadzka, 2006; Zawisza & Pittard, 2015). Kervyn et al. (2012) have extended SCM formally to the perception of brands and have proposed the BIAF model. They take the view that "people were the first brands and that branded trade and commerce have simply adapted human interaction processes to simplify and aid human choices" (Kervyn et al., 2012, p. 207). In other words, social perception principles should apply to the perception of brands. Specifically, Kervyn and colleagues argue that actions of corporations behind the brands are not perceived as outcomes of the underlying human activity (e.g., coordinated behaviours and decisions of teams of individuals such as the management). Instead, the brands themselves are perceived as so-called "intentional agents" (Kervyn et al., 2014). Thus, perceivers (in this case consumers) apply similar questions to such intentional agents (i.e., brands or corporations) as to individuals or groups they encounter in their social world. Importantly, this includes the questions of warmth and competence. Brands become social objects, and thus are considered by consumers in terms of their intentions and abilities in enacting these intentions. The intentions determine perceived brand W and the abilities determine perceived brand C. These dimensions of intentions and ability are arguably synonymous with the original W and C dimensions in SCM (Bennett & Hill, 2012) or may be inferred from brands' W and C (MacInnis, 2012).

Both experimental and correlational data have supported the model (Kervyn et al., 2012). For example, perception of fictitious brands' C and W differed as a function of their manipulated intentions and ability in line with SCM. Moreover, different types of real brands clustered in accordance with the intentions and ability dimensions as predicted: Popular brands such as Campbell and Hershey were seen as able and well intentioned (high on W and C); subsidized brands (e.g., Amtrak or NGOs) were seen as well-intentioned but less able (high on W but low C); luxury brands (e.g., Porsche and Rolex) were perceived as able but less well intentioned (high C but low W); and, lastly, troubled brands such as BP were seen as low on both intentions and ability (low on both C and W). Thus, these four types of brand stereotypes resemble the envious, paternalistic, contemptuous and admiration stereotypes of social groups from SCM. Further, W and C predicted purchase intent (PI) and brand loyalty independently of each other (Kervyn et al., 2012). More recently, Ivens, Leischnig, Miuller and Valta (2015) have provided further support for the proposition that brands are stereotyped in a similar fashion to people. They found that the brand stereotypes (troubled, subsidized, popular and luxury types) have consequences for emotional and behavioural reactions to these brands, which are in line with the BIAS framework applied to social perception (Cuddy et al., 2007). For example, both W and C predict specific feelings about brands (e.g., admiration) and both W and C mediate the relationship between brand personality (the basis for the brand stereotypes) and consumer emotions to the brands (e.g., admiration, envy, pity or contempt). Moreover, univalent emotions (contempt and admiration) had a stronger effect on brand responses such as attitude to brand and behavioural intentions than ambivalent emotions (e.g., envy or pity).

However, emerging research generally provides more consistent support for the applicability of SCM in consumer context at the level of brand perception but less so at the level of determining PI. For example, Zawisza (2006) showed that non-traditional male portrayals and traditional female portrayals, both of which represent the warm paternalistic stereotypes, resulted in a greater effectiveness of mock print ads for vitamin products. Zawisza and Cinnirella (2010) replicated this finding for advertisements for mineral water and showed, in two experiments, that paternalistic female (housewife) and male (househusband) portrayals were more effective than envious ones (businesswoman and businessman, respectively) irrespective of whether they broke or followed the traditional gender roles. The authors attributed their findings mainly to the warmth (liking) component of the paternalistic stereotypes and the primacy of warmth over competence (Fiske et al., 2007). They also noted that ad liking has been identified as one of the strongest predictors of ad effectiveness (Du Plessis, 2005), and thus it may have been the liking of the models used in the ads that translated into the observed advertising effectiveness. This has in fact recently been confirmed directly by Infanger and Sczesny (2015) on similar adverts. That is, irrespective of whether the product advertised (baby food and financial services) matched the W or C dimensions of the endorser, the endorser's warmth predicted the ad effectiveness (attitude to ad and brand) better than their competence. Moreover, this effect was indeed mediated by the endorser's likeability.

Interestingly, this primacy of W over C in explaining advertising effectiveness seems to also apply cross-culturally. Using a different product and brand (orange juice), Zawisza, Luyt and Zawadzka (in preparation a, b) found that, in countries as diverse as the United Kingdom, Poland and South Africa, the paternalistic housewife portrayals triggered significantly more positive thoughts and feelings about the adverts than the envious businesswomen. These responses also correlated positively and significantly with PI for the advertised orange juice (Zawisza et al., in preparation a). In the same countries, adverts that used the paternalistic portrayal of househusbands were also more effective than those that used the envious stereotypes of businessmen (Zawisza et al., in preparation b). Individual gender attitudes had little influence over these preferences and mattered only in the most gender-conservative country of the three: South Africa. That is, the greater the gender-conservativeness of the South African participants, the more they preferred the traditional stereotype of businessmen (Zawisza et al., in preparation b) and housewives (Zawisza et al., in preparation a) compared with the non-traditional alternatives of a househusband and a businesswoman, respectively. Furthermore, Xu, Leung, & Yan (2013) showed that brands from countries of origin that were named as warm versus cold and competent versus incompetent largely scored as expected on the W and C dimension. Of relevance, PI, in this case for fruit juice and disposable batteries, was, again, determined more by W than by C – a finding similar to that reported by Zawisza and colleagues (2010; in preparation a and b) on different low-involving products (mineral water and orange juice) and in different countries.

SCM has also been successfully applied to perception of firms. For example, Yang and Aggarwal (2014) provide indirect evidence that small firms are perceived as warmer but less competent than bigger firms. Aaker, Vohs and Mogilner (2010), on the other hand, showed that non-profit companies were perceived as warmer but less competent than for-profit ones. However, contrary to the studies cited above, they also reported that it was the non-profit firms' perceived lack of *competence* that contributed to diminished PI (for products such as laptop bags and physical activity trackers). Boosting non-profit firms' perceived competence (by manipulating the source's credibility or priming competence with visuals of money) neutralized differences in PI between the for- and non-profit brands. The authors thus concluded that utilizing the admiration stereotype (high W and C) may be the most successful marketing strategy – the so-called "golden quadrant". However, the "admiration" (or competence boost) strategy applied to non-profit firms in this study still did not result in PI higher than that of for-profit firms. Indeed, the authors stated that C is more important than W in determining PI and briefly speculated that W may be more important for services that require trust (e.g., hospitals). In their further work, Aaker, Garbinsky and Vohs (2012) have attempted to provide additional support for the "golden quadrant" hypothesis: They reported that PI was boosted by brands' C and the C × W interaction across various brands and product categories (fast food, fuel, orange juice and painkillers). Thus, as in their previous study, the "golden quadrant" actually appeared to be skewed towards the C dimension even though competence's influence on PI was partially mediated by admiration.

However, their findings were averaged across different products and thus no insight is provided into whether the "golden quadrant" applies equally to all products. One study that kept the (hedonic) product constant (beer) was that of Zawadzka (2015). She also found that the competent positioning of that product was somewhat preferred over the warm one. It is not clear, however, whether this difference was down to the mere W and C content of these ads or other elements of the graphical content manipulated there. Bratanova, Kervyn and Klein (2015), on the other hand, found an independent influence of W and C on perceived taste of water and a new chocolate brand as well as on PI, brand loyalty and brand engagement of the latter product.

Developing the BIAF/SCM model for use in the consumer context

The emerging research shows promise for advertisers, but it is not free of contradictions. As seen above, SCM/BIAF seems to hold for the perception of gendered ads, non-profit versus for-profit firms, various types of brands (luxury, troubled, subsidized, popular) and products from different countries of origin. However, there is less agreement when it comes to the importance of W and C in determining PI for these brands. For example, some studies suggest greater importance of warmth over competence (Infanger & Sczesny, 2015; Xu et al., 2013; Zawisza & Cinnirella, 2010; Zawisza, 2006; Zawisza et al., in preparation a, b) or the reverse (Aaker et al., 2010; Zawadzka, 2015). Others advocate independent (Bennett & Hill, 2012; Kervyn et al., 2012; Bratanova et al., 2015) or combined (Aaker et al., 2012) importance of both high warmth and competence – the already mentioned "golden quadrant" (though in Aaker et al., 2012 the "golden quadrant" is somewhat skewed towards greater importance of competence).

Arguably, such contradictions do not undermine the applicability of these two dimensions to the consumer context. Rather, they indicate that the importance of W and C for PI may differently depend on other variables present, for example, in advertising but absent in social perception. In other words, they point to the need to extend the SCM/BIAF model for use in the consumer context (Zawisza & Pittard, 2015). In order to take a closer look at these consumer-specific variables, the chapter now turns to an overview of the major factors that have been identified as needed additions to the model and then proposes a more integrated model, which includes the *relevance principle*. Specifically, it is proposed here that variables such as product type (Aaker et al., 2012; Fiske, Malone, & Kervyn, 2012), targets' individual differences (Bennett & Hill, 2012; Fournier & Alvarez, 2012) and advertising appeal type (Zawisza & Pittard, 2015) may influence the relative importance of warmth and competence in determining advertising effectiveness. These three types of variables are key factors relevant to advertising context and thus are the focus of the following discussion.

Product type and SCM/BIAF

Most of the studies overviewed neglect the importance of product type. Even those that do look at various types of products (Aaker et al., 2012; Bennett & Hill, 2012; Kervyn et al., 2012) provide only cumulative data without analyzing the effects of product or brand category on PI. While Aaker et al. (2010) did speculate that W may be more important than C for products requiring trust relationships, they did not test this possibility. To date, the only investigations that have looked into product type explicitly within the SCM/BIAF framework are those by

Xu et al. (2013) and Infanger and Sczesny (2015). Infanger and Sczesny (2015) looked at the match between the endorser's warmth vs. competence and warm vs. comment products (baby food vs. financial services, respectively). While these authors did not measure PI, they found the advantage of the endorser's W (over C) in determining ad effectiveness, although the C dimension did matter for the effectiveness of the competent product. Moreover, they also speculated that the C dimension may be particularly important in determining the effectiveness of high-status products, as C is determined by perceived status in social perception (Cuddy et al., 2007). Xu et al. (2013), on the other hand, looked at hedonistic (fruit juice) and utilitarian (disposable batteries) products and reported that PI for both products was predicted by both W and C, though the predictive power of W was the stronger of the two. Moreover, C (but not W) ceased to be a significant predictor of PI after product failure in both cases. The authors called for more research to establish whether the same would apply to high-involving products.

Keller (2012) speculates that brand credibility (W and C) may be especially important in low-involving situations, when people rely on heuristics in their decisions, as well as in high-involving situations. This may be particularly relevant to product type. While various product classifications exist (credence vs. search, hedonistic vs. utilitarian, gendered vs. gender neutral), product involvement is recognized as one of the most important factors determining advertising effectiveness (McGrath & Mahood, 2004; Te'eni-Harari, Lehman-Wilzig, & Lampert, 2009). Following Petty and Cacioppo's (1983) rationale, high-involving products (e.g., cars), as opposed to low-involving ones (e.g., juice or toothpaste), are those which require careful pre-purchase consideration, as they carry significant financial or other consequences. Arguably, as high-involving products require competence in evaluating the product's properties to diminish possible risk, it is possible that an appeal which stresses C (over W) would be more effective for such products than one which stresses W (over C). For low-involving products, on the other hand, a simple affective positivity heuristic may be in operation whereby the likeable warm strategy may be more effective than the competent one. Indeed, studies that used low-involving products (e.g., vitamin products (Zawisza, 2006), mineral water (Zawisza & Cinnirella, 2010), fruit juice or disposable batteries (Xu et al., 2013), orange juice (Zawisza et al., 2015a,b), unisex perfume or baby food (Infanger & Sczesny, 2015) tend to report greater importance of W over C in determining PI. On the other hand, studies that use somewhat higher-involving products such as eco-friendly laptop bags, activity trackers or financial services report greater predictive power of C (over W) for PI (Aaker et al., 2010; Infanger & Sczesny, 2015). Interestingly, studies that combine data across various categories of products tend to return findings suggesting the combined (Aaker et al., 2012) or independent (Bennett & Hill, 2012; Kervyn et al., 2012) importance of both W and C in predicting PI.

Zawisza and Pittard (2015, Experiment 1) provide thus far the only empirical investigation of the possibility that the level of product involvement may determine the importance of warmth vs. competence for PI. Specifically, they predicted that high-involving products (smartphones) would trigger higher PI when advertised using a competent (vs. warm) ad strategy and low-involving products (toothpaste) would trigger higher PI when advertised using a warm (vs. competent) ad strategy. Their findings confirmed these hypotheses, providing direct evidence for the argument that the "golden quadrant" shifts according to product type. That is, in some situations (e.g., for low-involving products) it is the W dimension that is more important for PI, and in others (e.g., for high-involving products) it is the C dimension that plays a greater role.

However, it is also possible that the effectiveness of the W versus C approaches differs further as a function of personal characteristics – another factor present in the consumer context but not included in the SCM/BIAF models. As explained later, for some people a W ad strategy may be more effective than C even when the product is high involving (Zawisza & Pittard, 2015).

Consumer individual differences and SCM

Both demographic and psychological individual differences are arguably a crucial aspect of marketing research (Bennett & Hill, 2012; Fournier & Alvarez, 2012) and thus in need of analysis alongside the dimensions of W and C. Indeed, Bennett and Hill (2012) showed that consumers' demographic profile influences the perception of W but not C: Brands were generally perceived as less warm by older and better-educated consumers. The authors attribute the lack of effects on the competence dimension to its cognitive and, thus, objective (as opposed to affective and, thus, subjective) nature. Fournier and Alvarez (2012), on the other hand, discuss the role of psychological characteristics in determining brands' perceived W and C. They note that people vary in the degree to which they anthropomorphize brands, and thus, in the extent to which they may attribute intentional agency to them. Zawadzka (2015), on the other hand, has recently shown that the match between consumers' self-perceptions as warm and competent and the brands' W and C scores affect brand preferences: The more participants perceived themselves as competent, the more they favoured a competent beer brand as opposed to a warm one and vice versa (those who thought of themselves as warm preferred a warm rather than a competent brand of beer). An individual's commercial attachment style, akin to attachment style in human relations, may also influence a brand's perceived W and C. For example, MacInnis (2012) proposes that W may be particularly important (and more so than C) for individuals who are high (vs. low) on anxiety in their brand relationship style. Such consumers, it is argued, are insecure in their relationship with the brand and thus need reassurance. While this refers to brand attachment styles, indirect evidence for a more generalized need for W in situations of consumer threat and uncertainty comes from Xu et al. (2013). They report greater importance of W (over C) in determining PI in cases of product failure (salmonella contamination in the case of fruit juice, or fire hazard due to faulty disposable batteries). Both of their products were also low involving. As seen from the above, the low-involving and anxiety-provoking nature of the product should make the W dimension more relevant to advertising effectiveness. What would happen, however, if the product was anxiety provoking and high involving?

Thus far, the only piece of research which has investigated high-involving but anxiety-provoking products within the SCM/BIAF framework explicitly is that of Zawisza and Pittard (2015, Experiment 2). The authors manipulated the ad type in terms of its warmth and competence (e.g., via using paternalistic househusband vs envious businessman portrayals in ads for smartphones) and measured participants' smartphone anxiety. They expected that the greater effectiveness of a C (over W) ad strategy for high-involving smartphone products, as predicted in Experiment 1, would not hold for consumers high on smartphone anxiety. Instead, they expected, and found, that consumers' anxiety would overwrite this effect. Specifically, the competent advert strategy was less effective for individuals who had high smartphone anxiety than for those who were less anxious. Instead, high smartphone-anxious individuals preferred the warm ad type strategy over the competent one. These findings provided evidence that individual differences in anxiety levels shift the "golden quadrant" yet again: They determine which of the two advertising strategies, W or C, is more effective, even in the case of a high-involving product type, which typically (e.g., for non-anxious individuals) would be more desired when coupled with a competent ad content (Zawisza & Pittard, 2015).

However, there may be other factors that may shift the "golden quadrant" in the case of high-involving products or services (Zawisza & Pittard, 2015). As explained later, framing the advertising message in terms of self- versus other-profitability may be particularly relevant in determining the importance of W and C for PI and thus could shift the "golden quadrant" again.

Self- versus other-profitable appeal type and SCM

If the primacy of W over C proposed by SCM (Fiske et al., 2007) applied uniformly to consumer context, we should see a consistent advantage of W over C in brand context as well. However, this is not the case. As mentioned earlier, when it comes to PI, both Kervyn et al. (2012) and Bennett and Hill (2012) report equal predictive power of W and C, Aaker et al. (2010) report greater importance of C over W and their interaction, while Xu et al. (2013) as well as Zawisza and colleagues (2006, 2010) report greater importance of W over C, which applied even across cultures (Zawisza et al., in preparation[a,b]). While, as already argued here, product type and individual differences may be at least in part responsible for these inconsistencies, a third possibility exists.

Fiske et al. (2012, p. 206) suggest that "brands may have a more personal contact than many out-groups do, [and] so people might differ more systematically" in their perception of brands than in the perception of social groups. This statement implies that the distance (closeness or lack of it) between the brand and the consumer's self may determine the importance of W and C in brand evaluation. Although Fiske et al. (2012) speculate that this may be unique to human–brand relationships, social psychological research indicates otherwise (Wojciszke & Abele, 2008). Indeed, as discussed, in the realm of social perception, the primacy of W over C has been shown to be moderated by the (social) distance between self and others (the DIA model; Wojciszke & Abele, 2008). Specifically, there was a "W over C" advantage in perception of others (i.e., interest in their other-profitability) but a "C over W" advantage in the case of evaluating close friends or the self (i.e., interest in self-profitability). Thus, the typical primacy of W over C reverses in evaluations of close friends.

When extrapolated back to consumer context, the DIA model offers interesting possibilities which are not acknowledged in SCM/BIAF. For example, the optimal level of W vs. C from the PI perspective may vary depending on whether the advertising appeal emphasizes self- versus other-profitability of the product or service to the consumer. This is because such framing may influence the perceived relevance of W and C to the product advertised. Surprisingly, the issue of self- versus other-profitable advertising appeal type has not been investigated widely despite its relevance to many social or charitable advertising campaigns. While a similar agentic versus communal ad strategy has been studied in the context of blood donation services (Hupfer, 2006), it was not linked there to W and C. The only study thus far that has tested this possibility directly is that by Zawisza and Pittard (2015, Experiment 3). They investigated the question of whether an advertising appeal that stressed other-profitability would be more effective when using a warm ad strategy than when using a competent one, even if the service advertised was high involving (blood donation services). Based on the DIA model (Wojciszke & Abele, 2008), they predicted that the competent ad strategy would perform better (than the warm one) in the self-profitable appeal condition. At the same time, the warm ad strategy would perform better in the other-profitable appeal condition (as compared to the self-profitable condition). They manipulated the self- vs. other-profitability of the ad by stressing the benefits of blood donation for oneself or for others, respectively, while the warmth and competence of the ads were manipulated by employing paternalistic vs. envious male gender roles of the endorser in the ads. While generally the other-profitable ad appeal for blood donation services was more effective than the self-profitable one, this main effect was indeed qualified by the expected interaction: In the self-profitable condition the service use intent was higher when the competent (vs. warm) ad content was used. The warm content (vs. competent), on the other hand, was more effective in the case of the other-profitable appeal. These findings provided support for the DIA (Wojciszke & Abele, 2008) and illustrated again that the "golden quadrant" shifted as a function of the appeal type. That is, even when the service was high involving, the relevance of W and C for PI was determined by the framing used in the ad (self- vs. other-profitable).

The overview of the literature thus far shows that while the perception of the brands seems to follow the BIAF/SCM framework robustly according to the two key dimensions of warmth and competence, the answer to the question of how these affect PI is somewhat mixed. The initially proposed "golden quadrant", understood as an admiration strategy (i.e., high W and C; Aaker et al., 2012), may not always apply in the consumer context. In fact, given the above literature, it seems that the content of the "golden quadrant" shifts as a function of variables present in the consumer context but absent in the SCM/BIAF model: product type, individual differences and appeal type (Zawisza & Pittard, 2015). Thus, arguably, the meaning of the "golden quadrant" should therefore be revised to indicate the "optimal level of W and C" rather than high levels of both (Zawisza & Pittard, 2015). The findings also indicate that the BIAF/SCM model needs to be extended. However, the observation that the "golden quadrant" shifts is only useful if we can predict the nature of such a shift. How could we integrate the findings thus far? What is the overall principle that determines the shifts? The chapter now turns to presenting an argument for addressing these questions, proposing an extension of the BIAF/SCM model by the addition of the relevance principle. Bratanova et al. (2015) recently have called for research on questions relevant to this point, although they do not relate them to the "golden quadrant" or the relevance propositions explicitly: "Does one of the two dimensions have more importance? Does the relative importance change for different outcome variables (e.g., attitudinal vs. behavioural) and/or product categories?" (p. 67).

The relevance principle

The principle of relevance (aka. congruence, match-up, fit, similarity or compatibility) has been observed across contexts as diverse as that of persuasion (Wells & Petty, 1980), occupational setting (Koenig & Eagly, 2014) and judicial verdicts (Jones & Kaplan, 2003), and has been identified as a factor that aids brands' and advertising success (Fleck & Quester, 2007). In consumer context it has been found to apply to brand extension (Fleck & Quester, 2007), sponsoring (Deitz, Myers, & Stafford, 2012), celebrity endorsement (Choi & Rifon, 2012; Fleck, Korchia, & Le Roy, 2012) or cross-modal sensory marketing with its synesthetic correspondence principle (Spence, 2012; Spence & Gallace, 2011). The definition of the phenomenon proves elusive (Fleck & Quester, 2007) and may not acknowledge the underlying element of relevance explicitly. Yet one may argue that it is the relevance of any given components to each other that determines what fits or is perceived as congruent or synesthetic. Thus, here congruence is understood explicitly in terms of relevance of the universal but orthogonal concepts of W and C to variables present in advertising context discussed above: product type, audience characteristics and advertising appeal type (Zawisza & Pittard, 2015). These variables represent the three key aspects of advertising context, which have not been linked to W and C systematically or directly (with the exception of Zawisza & Pittard, 2015 and the current chapter). As has been argued earlier, the "golden quadrant" (Aaker et al., 2012) or, more precisely, the importance of W and C for PI may "shift" as a function of the relevance of these variables to the concepts of W and C encapsulated by the endorser's image in the ad.

While the relevance principle is not a factor formally included in the original SCM/BIAF models, research on job applications, which involve self-advertising, points at the potential importance of the relevance of W and C to contextual factors. For example, compatibility between the warmth of the candidate's name and the nature of the job (e.g., requiring W vs. C) resulted in higher job suitability judgements (Copley & Brownlow, 1995). Moreover, appearing both warm and competent was especially important for out-group job applicants (e.g., of Arab origin; Agerström, Björklund, Carlsson & Rooth, 2012).

Interestingly, the principle of relevance does, though implicitly, underlie the DIA model, which competes with the SCM. That is, the DIA's principles may be reinterpreted in terms of the relevance rule as follows: The typical primacy of W over C postulated by SCM reverses when C becomes more *relevant* (than W) to the subject's position. This happens in situations of social interdependence when our typical interest in self-profitability (that is, competence) is extrapolated to the others we depend on. This is, we value C over W in the case of close others and friends. Thus, social distance determines the *relevance* of W and C in our social perceptions. While, as discussed earlier, Fiske et al. (2012, p. 206) implicitly allude to the possibility that that the distance (closeness or lack of it) between the brand and the consumer's self may determine the importance of the perceived brand W and C for PI, they do not incorporate it in the BIAF model formally and do not propose an overarching principle which would help predict *when* W and when C is more important for PI.

As already discussed, Zawisza and Pittard (2015) are the first to offer, and test, an extension of the SCM/BIAF framework by adding the relevance principle in order to predict the optimal level of W and C in an advertising campaign to stimulate PI. In their three experiments they have shown that the importance of W and C for PI – the newly defined "golden quadrant" – does indeed shift as a function of product type, individual differences and appeal type. Specifically, competence was more important (resulted in higher PI) in the case of a high-involving product (a smartphone) than in the case of a low-involving one (toothpaste), and the smartphone triggered greater PI when advertised using the competent (vs. warm) ad strategy. This is in line with previous studies, which, taken together, indicate that competence is indeed more important for high- than for low-involving products (Aaker et al., 2010), while warmth is more effective than competence for low-involving products (Infanger & Sczesny, 2015; Xu et al., 2013; Zawisza, 2006; Zawisza & Cinnirella, 2010; Zawisza et al., 2015a,b).

However, while non-anxious consumers still preferred competent (vs. warm) advertising strategy for the high-involving smartphones, smartphone-anxious individuals preferred the competent ad for this product less than non-anxious consumers. In fact, they found the warm ad strategy more effective than the competent one. Thus, the preference for C over W typical of high-involving products reverses for highly smartphone-anxious customers. By extension, it is possible that the W dimension may be particularly important for individuals who are high (vs. low) on anxiety in their brand relationship style (MacInnis, 2012) or in situations of product failure (Xu et al., 2013) which may be argued to be anxiety-provoking (e.g., fire hazard and salmonella contamination). It is thus possible that any type of anxiety or insecurity related to the product (whether residing in the consumer individual differences or the product context) may require greater emphasis on W (than C), even more so if the product is high involving.

Zawisza and Pittard (2015) showed further that the need for W triggered by anxiety may be reversed again. While the "W over C" pattern held for other-profitable advertising appeals (where the warm ad strategy triggered greater blood donation service use intent), it reversed for self-profitable ones (which were more effective when using a competent rather than a warm advertising strategy). In the latter case, the superiority of W over C proposed by SCM (Fiske et al., 2007) was reversed in line with the competing DIA approach (Wojciszke & Abele, 2008). That is, self-profitability, in the shape of blood storage for one's own use (as opposed to use by others in the other-profitability scenario), required greater emphasis on C over W even though the blood donation service may be considered anxiety provoking.

Thus, the "golden quadrant", i.e., the optimal combination of C and W, may not always require equal emphasis on both elements, or greater emphasis on C, as previously suggested

(Aaker et al., 2012). As discussed, the "golden quadrant" shifts, or changes its content, from greater emphasis on C to greater emphasis on W, depending on variables present in the consumer context but absent in social perception. On a theoretical level, this evidences the need to extend SCM/BIAF not so much by adding additional variables to the model – e.g., product type or individual difference variables as suggested by some (Aaker et al., 2012; Bennett & Hill, 2012; Fournier & Alvarez, 2012) – but by recognizing that the principle of relevance operates and determines the optimal level of W and C in a particular consumer context (Zawisza & Pittard, 2015).

Directions for future research

The proposed extension of the SCM/BIAF framework by inclusion of the relevance principle for use in the consumer context is an exciting possibility, which would enable the model to be more predictive rather than descriptive. However, thus far this proposal rests on one direct empirical study (Zawisza & Pittard, 2015) and on an overview of relevant literature, as discussed. Thus, more research is needed to address the surrounding gaps in the literature. For example, although similar patterns of greater importance of W over C for PI were found for various low-involving products (e.g., vitamin pills [Zawisza, 2006], mineral water [Zawisza & Cinnirella, 2010], fruit juice and disposable batteries [Xu et al., 2013], orange juice [Zawisza et al., 2015a,b], toothpaste [Zawisza & Pittard, 2015], unisex perfume and baby food [Infanger & Sczesny, 2015], there is lack of research on high-involving products [e.g., cars, housing, etc.] other than that on smartphones [Zawisza & Pittard, 2015]).

Other research may fruitfully explore product-category comparisons such as hedonic versus utilitarian, credence versus search and gendered versus gender-neutral products. Technological products, for example, lend themselves especially well to anthropomorphism, as do tools, transportation devices, food and drink, clothing and weapons (Mick & Fournier, 1998) and thus could be perceived especially readily in terms of W and C (Fournier & Alvarez, 2012). Anxiety-provoking goods or services, particularly if the anxiety results from the brand's involvement in a disaster of ambiguous cause (neither natural nor human related), require further and careful investigation. Kervyn et al. (2014) found that the "negativity effect on warmth" observed in social perception (negative warmth information being more damaging than negative competence information) applies also to brands' reputation management in the face of a disaster. Specifically, when the disaster is attributed to lack of warmth (as opposed to lack of competence), attempts to restore the brand's reputation by focusing on emphasizing warmth are likely to backfire even though it is warmth that is deficient in such a troubled brand. In such situations it is the competence-focused restoration campaign that is likely to be more effective. This would suggest that the relevance principle is moderated by the "negativity effect on warmth" in scenarios of managing post-disaster brand reputation. The negativity effect on warmth was also shown in cases of transgressing the stereotype-based expectations related to firm size (Yang & Aggarwal, 2014): Generally, violations of warmth expectations had more negative consequences for PI than violations of competence expectations, but this was particularly evident in the case of small (vs. bigger) firms as their stereotype implies higher warmth and thus makes such a transgression especially unexpected. Further research is needed to identify when warmth and competence are more important in determining the perception and behaviours towards products, services and brands which may be subject to the negativity effect on warmth.

Consumer psychological characteristics other than smartphone (or technology) anxiety should also be investigated. For example, consumers with high need for cognition may prefer C over W for various products. Moreover, the W versus C manipulation may have less of an effect on consumers who are low on brand anthropomorphism as they would not attribute intention/W or ability/C to brands (Fournier & Alvarez, 2012). Demographic variables may also be of importance. While gender and race were not identified by Bennett and Hill (2012) as factors differentiating the perception of brands' W and C, this was not the same for age and education: Older and more educated people perceive brands in general as colder, and thus there may be a need to offset this perception by boosting the brands' warmth when they are targeted to such demographics. Moreover, Fiske et al. (2008) does list gender among moderators of the primacy of W over C phenomenon. For example, Wojciszke et al. (1998) found that women, perhaps due to their socialization, which emphasizes warm (communal) traits (as opposed to competent ones), show stronger primacy of warmth over competence in detecting these traits. However, whether this would make them more receptive to warm (vs. competent) brands and advertising content (generally or in comparison with men) remains untested.

In the increasingly globalized markets, cross-cultural differences become an especially important consideration. While the dimensions of W and C have been shown to apply cross-culturally in social perception of groups (Cuddy et al., 2007) and brands of different origin (Xu et al., 2013), less is known about how culture may affect the relative importance of the W and C dimensions in determining consumer behaviours. Although preferences for the W and C advertising content in countries such as South Africa, the UK and Poland were similar (Zawisza et al., 2015a,b) these were rather individualistic cultures and thus research on collectivist cultures is needed. For example, Wojciszke (1997) pointed out that collectivist cultures place more emphasis on the social-moral dimension (akin to warmth) while individualist cultures emphasize competence. It is possible that people from collectivist cultures will prefer advertising campaigns or brand placements that emphasize warmth. This possibility awaits further research.

Importantly, an admiration (high W and C) ad strategy has not been tested within the relevance paradigm proposed here. Such strategy would have both high W and C elements and might therefore be optimal across all types of products, individuals and appeals. However, attempts to boost the "deficit" dimension of C in non-profit firms (Aaker et al., 2010) still did not result in significantly higher PI compared with that of for-profit companies. Nevertheless, future research could fruitfully add a third condition, admiration, when testing the relevance principle extension of the SCM/BIAF models. Other methodological considerations include the need for more experimental studies to balance the current domination of correlational studies in the emerging field of research on the application of SCM to the consumer context.

On a theoretical level, more work is needed to investigate the mechanisms via which brand personality transfers to brand stereotypes (their perceived W and C) and how the latter affect emotional and behavioural reactions to the brands (Ivens et al., 2015). For example, it is not yet known whether the transference patterns supporting SCM/BIAS models found by Ivens et al. (2015) apply also to non-profit brands, which are not perceived as higher on C than on W. The relevance principle allows predictions to be made for many contextual or individual variables. Further studies could focus on investigating the interactions between such variables and their effect on determining the importance of W and C for PI.

Conclusions

In summary, even if the same (warm vs. competent) advertising strategy is used, its effectiveness depends on variables that determine the relevance of W and C to PI. These are present in the consumer context but absent in social perception. Specifically, product involvement level, participants' levels of technology anxiety, and self- versus other-profitable advertising appeal type were identified as such. Thus, the relevance principle could fruitfully extend theoretical frameworks such as SCM or BIAF. On a practical level, in deciding whether to use a warm or a competent advertising strategy, marketers need to take into account the issue of the relevance of these dimensions to the product, the advertising campaign type and their audience or in fact any other relevant variables and their potential interactions. In the world of brand perception, unlike in the social world, the "golden quadrant" shifts according to a broader marketing context.

References

Aaker, J. L. (1997). Dimensions of brand personality. *Journal of Marketing Research, 34*(3), 347–356.

Aaker, J. L., Garbinsky, E. N., & Vohs, K. D. (2012). Cultivating admiration in brands: Warmth, competence, and landing in the "golden quadrant". *Journal of Consumer Psychology, 22*(2), 191–194. doi: 10.1016/j.jcps.2011.11.012

Aaker, J. L., Vohs, K. D., & Mogilner, C. (2010). Non-profits are seen as warm and for-profits as competent: Firm stereotypes matter. *Journal of Consumer Research, 37*(2), 224–237. doi: 10/1086/651566

Abele, A. E., & Bruckmüller, S. (2011). The bigger one of the "Big Two"? Preferential processing of communal information. *Journal of Experimental Social Psychology, 47*(5), 935–948. doi:10.1016/j.jesp.2011.03.028

Agerström, J., Björklund, F., Carlsson, R., & Rooth, D. O. (2012). Warm and competent Hassan = cold and incompetent Eric: A harsh equation of real-life hiring discrimination. *Basic and Applied Social Psychology, 34*, 359–366. doi: 10.1080/01973533.2012.693438

Bennett, A. M., & Hill, R. P. (2012). The universality of warmth and competence: A response to brands as intentional agents. *Journal of Consumer Psychology, 22*(2), 199–204. doi: 10.1016/j.jcps.2011.10.005

Bratanova, B., Kervyn, N., & Klein, O. (2015). Tasteful brands: Products of brands perceived to be warm and competent taste subjectively better. *Psychologica Belgica, 55*(2), 57–70. doi: 10.5334/pb.bf

Chebat, J. C., & Michon, R. (2003). Impact of ambient odors on mall shoppers' emotions, cognition, and spending: A test of competitive causal theories. *Journal of Business Research, 56*(7), 529–539.

Choi, S. M., & Rifon, N. J. (2012). It is a match: The impact of congruence between celebrity image and consumer ideal self on endorsement effectiveness. *Psychology & Marketing, 29*, 639–650. doi: 10.1002/mar.20550

Clausell, E., & Fiske, S. T. (2005). When do subgroup parts add up to the stereotyping whole? Mixed stereotype content for gay male subgroups explains overall ratings. *Social Cognition, 23*(2), 161–181. doi: 10.1521/soco.23.2.161.65626

Copley, J. E., & Brownlow, S. (1995). The interactive effects of facial maturity and name warmth on perceptions of job candidates. *Basic and Applied Social Psychology, 16*, 251–265. doi:10.1080/01973533.1995.9646112

Cuddy, A. J., Fiske, S. T., & Glick, P. (2007). The BIAS map: Behaviours from intergroup affect and stereotypes. *Journal of Personality and Social Psychology, 92*(4), 631. doi: 10.1037/0022-3514.92.4.631

Cuddy, A., Norton, M. I., & Fiske, S. T. (2005). This old stereotype: The pervasiveness and persistence of the elderly stereotype. *Journal of Social Issues, 61*, 265–283. doi: 10.1111/j.1540-4560.2005.00405.x

Deitz, G. D., Myers, S. W., & Stafford, M. R. (2012). Understanding consumer response to sponsorship information: A resource-matching approach. *Psychology & Marketing, 29*, 226–239. doi: 10.1002/mar.20517

Du Plessis, E. (2005). *The advertised mind: Ground-breaking insights into how our brains respond to advertising*. London: Kogan Page.

Eckes, T. (2002). Paternalistic and envious gender stereotypes: Testing predictions from the stereotype content model. *Sex Roles: A Journal of Research, 47*(3–4), 99–114. doi: 10.1023/A:1021020920715

Eisingerich, A. B., & Rubera, G. (2010). Drivers of brand commitment: A cross-national investigation. *Journal of International Marketing, 18*(2), 64–79.

Fiske, S. T., Cuddy, A., & Glick, P. (2007). Universal dimensions of social cognition: Warmth and competence. *Trends in Cognitive Sciences, 11*(2), 77–83. doi: 10.1016/j.tics.2006.11.005

Fiske, S. T., Xu, J., Cuddy, A. J., & Glick, P. (1999). (Dis)respecting versus (dis)liking: Status and interdependence predict ambivalent stereotypes of competence and warmth. *Journal of Social Issues, 55*, 473–489.

Fiske, S. T., Cuddy, A. J., Glick, P., & Xu, J. (2002). A model of (often mixed) stereotype content: Competence and warmth respectively follow from perceived status and competition. *Journal of Personality and Social Psychology, 82*(6), 878–902. doi: 10.1037/0022-3514.82.6.878

Fiske, S. T., Malone, C., & Kervyn, N. (2012). Brands as intentional agents: Our response to commentaries. *Journal of Consumer Psychology, 22*(2), 205–207. doi: 10.1016/j.jcps.2011.12.002

Fleck, N. D., & Quester, P. (2007). Birds of a feather flock together ... definition, role and measure of congruence: An application to sponsorship. *Psychology & Marketing, 24*, 975–1000. doi: 10.1002/mar.20192

Fleck, N., Korchia, M., & Le Roy, I. (2012). Celebrities in advertising: Looking for congruence or likability? *Psychology & Marketing, 29*, 651–662. doi: 10.1002/mar.20551

Fournier, S. (1998). Consumers and their brands: Developing relationship theory in consumer research. *Journal of Consumer Research, 24*(4), 343–353. doi: 10.1086/209515

Fournier, S., & Alvarez, C. (2012). Brands as relationship partners: Warmth, competence, and in-between. *Journal of Consumer Psychology, 22*(2), 177–185. doi: 10.1016/j.jcps.2011.10.003

Hupfer, M. E. (2006). Helping me, helping you: Self-referencing and gender roles in donor advertising. *Transfusion, 46*(6), 996–1005. doi: 10.1111/j.1537-2995.2006.00834.x

Infanger, M., & Sczesny, S. (2015). Communion-over-agency effects on advertising effectiveness. *International Journal of Advertising, 34*(2), 285–306. doi:10.1080/02650487.2014.993794

Ivens, B. S., Leischnig, A., Muller, B., & Valta, K. (2015). On the role of brand stereotypes in shaping consumer response toward brands: An empirical examination of direct and mediating effects of warmth and competence. *Psychology & Marketing, 32*(8), 808–820. doi: 10.1002/mar.20820

Jones, C. S., & Kaplan, M. F. (2003). The effects of racially stereotypical crimes on juror decision-making and information-processing strategies. *Basic and Applied Social Psychology, 25*, 1–13. doi:10.1207/S15324834BASP2501_1

Judd, C. M., James-Hawkins, L., Yzerbyt, V., & Kashima, Y. (2005). Fundamental dimensions of social judgement: Understanding the relations between judgements of competence and warmth. *Journal of Personality and Social Psychology, 89*(6), 899–913. doi: 10.1037/0022-3514.89.6.899

Keller, K. L. (2012). Understanding the richness of brand relationships: Research dialogue on brands as intentional agents. *Journal of Consumer Psychology, 22*(2), 186–190. doi: 10.1016/j.jcps.2011.11.011

Kenworthy, J. B., & Tausch, N. (2008). Expectations about the accuracy and stability of warmth versus competence traits: An intergroup analysis. *European Journal of Social Psychology, 38*, 1121–1129. doi: 10.1002/ejsp.543

Kervyn, N., Chan, E., Malone, C., Korpusik, A., & Ybarra, O. (2014). Not all disasters are equal in the public's eye: The negativity effect on warmth in brand perception. *Social Cognition, 32*(3), 256–275. doi: 10.1521/soco.2014.32.3.256

Kervyn, N., Fiske, S. T., & Malone, C. (2012). Brands as intentional agents framework: How perceived intentions and ability can map brand perception. *Journal of Consumer Psychology, 22*(2), 166–176. doi: 10.1016/j.jcps.2011.09.006

Koenig, A. M., & Eagly, A. H. (2014). Extending Role Congruity Theory of Prejudice to men and women with sex-typed mental illnesses. *Basic and Applied Social Psychology, 36*, 70–82. doi:10.1080/01973533.2013.856789

Lane, V. R. (2000). The impact of ad repetition and ad content on consumer perceptions of incongruent extensions. *Journal of Marketing, 64*(2), 80–91.

Lee, T. L., & Fiske, S. T. (2006). Not an outgroup, not yet an ingroup: Immigrants in the stereotype content model. *International Journal of Intercultural Relations, 30*(6), 751–768. doi: 10.1016/j.ijintrel.2006.06.005

MacInnis, D. J. (2012). "Brands as intentional agents": Questions and extensions. *Journal of Consumer Psychology, 22*(2), 195–198. doi: 10.1016/j.jcps.2011.10.004

Malone, C., & Fiske, S. T. (2013). *The human brand: How we relate to people, products, and companies.* Hoboken, NJ: Wiley.

McGrath, J. M., & Mahood, C. (2004). The impact of arousing programming and product involvement on advertising effectiveness. *Journal of Current Issues & Research in Advertising, 26*(2), 41–52. doi: 10.1080/10641734.2004.10505163

Mick, D. G., & Fournier, S. (1998). Paradoxes of technology: Consumer cognizance, emotions, and coping strategies. *Journal of Consumer Research, 25*(2), 123–143.

Petty, R. E., & Cacioppo, J. T. (1983). Central and peripheral routes to persuasion: Application to advertising. In L. Percy & A. G. Woodside (Eds.), *Advertising and consumer psychology* (pp. 3–23). Lexington, VA: Lexington Books.

Schwarz, N. (1990). Feelings as information: Informational and motivational functions of affective states. In E. T. Higgins & R. M. Sorrentino (Eds.), *Handbook of motivation and cognition: Foundations of social behaviour, Vol. 2.* (pp. 527–561). New York: Guilford Press.

Spence, C. (2012). Managing sensory expectations concerning products and brands: Capitalizing on the potential of sound and shape symbolism. *Journal of Consumer Psychology, 22*, 37–54. doi: org/10.1016/j.jcps.2011.09.004

Spence, C., & Gallace, A. (2011). Multisensory design: Reaching out to touch the consumer. *Psychology & Marketing, 28*, 267–308. doi: 10.1002/mar.20392

Te'eni-Harari, T., Lehman-Wilzig, S. N., & Lampert, S. I. (2009). The importance of product involvement for predicting advertising effectiveness among young people. *International Journal of Advertising, 28*(2), 203–229. doi: 10.2501/S0265048709200540

Wells, G. L., & Petty, R. E. (1980). The effects of overt head movements on persuasion: Compatibility and incompatibility of responses. *Basic and Applied Social Psychology, 1*, 219–230. doi:10.1207/s15324834basp0103_2

Wojciszke, B. (1997). Parallels between competence- versus morality-related traits and individualistic versus collectivistic values. *European Journal of Social Psychology, 27*(3), 245–256. doi: 10.1002/(SICI)1099-0992(199705)27:3%3C245::AID-EJSP819%3E3.3.CO%

Wojciszke, B. (2005). Morality and competence in person-and self-perception. *European Review of Social Psychology, 16*, 155–188. doi: 10.1080/10463280500229619

Wojciszke, B., & Abele, A. (2008). The primacy of communion over agency and its reversals in evaluations. *European Journal of Social Psychology, 38*, 1139–1147. doi: 10.1002/ejsp.549

Wojciszke, B., Bazinska, R., & Jaworski, M. (1998). On the dominance of moral categories in impression formation. *Personality and Social Psychology Bulletin, 24*(12), 1251–1263. doi: 10.1177/01461672982412001

Xu, H., Leung, A., & Yan, R. T. (2013). It is nice to be important, but is it more important to be nice: Country-of-origin's perceived warmth in product failures. *Journal of Consumer Behaviour, 12*, 285–292. doi: 10:1002/cb.1419

Yang, L., & Aggarwal, P. (2014). Asymmetric expectations of firms stereotyped as warm versus competent. *NA-Advances in Consumer Research, 42*, 746–747.

Zawadzka, A. M. (2015). Preference for brand images associated with competence and communion. [Preferencje wizerunków produktu kojarzonych ze sprawczością i wspólnotowością.] *Marketing and Rynek, 7*, 27–34.

Zawisza, M. (2006). *The effectiveness of advertisements which follow or break traditional gender stereotypes* (Unpublished doctoral dissertation). University of London, London.

Zawisza, M., & Cinnirella, M. (2010). What matters more: Breaking tradition or stereotype content? Envious and paternalistic gender stereotypes and advertising effectiveness. *Journal of Applied Social Psychology, 40*, 1767–1797. doi: 10.1111/j.1559-1816.2010.00639.x

Zawisza, M., Luyt, R., & Zawadzka, A. M. (in preparation a). The effectiveness of envious and paternalistic female portrayals in print advertisements: A cross-national comparison between Great Britain, Poland and South Africa.

Zawisza, M., Luyt, R., & Zawadzka, A. M. (in preparation b). The effectiveness of envious and paternalistic male portrayals in print advertisements: A cross-national comparison between Great Britain, Poland and South Africa.

Zawisza, M., Cinnirella, M., & Zawadzka, A. M. (2006). Non-traditional male gender portrayal as a persuasion tool in advertising. *Social Influence, 1*(4), 288–300. doi:10.1080/15534510601016976

Zawisza, M., & Pittard, C. (2015). When do warmth and competence sell best? The "golden quadrant" shifts as a function of congruity with the product type, targets' individual differences and advertising appeal type. *Basic and Applied Social Psychology, 37*(2), 131–141. doi: 10.1080/01973533.2015.1015130

13

Does size matter?

Media influences and body image

Megan Hurst, Helga Dittmar, Emma Halliwell and Phillippa C. Diedrichs

Body image dissatisfaction appears to have grown steadily in recent years, particularly within Western cultures: worldwide, 34–62 per cent of adolescent girls and 14–39 per cent of adolescent boys are thought to be dissatisfied with their bodies (Al Sabbah et al., 2009), and more than two-thirds of adults in the United Kingdom experience negative body image (All Party Parliamentary Group on Body Image, 2012). These figures have reached levels such that Rodin, Silberstein and Striegel-Moore's (1984) proposition of "normative discontent" has become a reality for both men and women: in the twenty-first century, it appears more unusual to find someone who is satisfied with their body than someone who is dissatisfied with it.

Although a key focus in the academic investigation of body image for some time, there is growing concern over the media's influence on body image in the popular media and in society more generally. The increase in media examinations of such issues is one indication of this increased attention, with these issues covered repeatedly in mainstream newspapers such as the *Guardian* or the *Times* in the United Kingdom. In the UK parliament, there is now an All Party Parliamentary Group on Body Image, and in 2009 a submission from over 40 academics and clinicians to the UK's Advertising Standards Authority (ASA) regarding the damaging effects of unrealistic portrayals of women's bodies in the media gained widespread media coverage. These developments are echoed internationally, with numerous countries (e.g., Israel, Australia, Canada, France and Spain) implementing social policy initiatives to address the influence of the media on body image (Paxton, in press).

Women's bodies have long been the subjects, or indeed objects, of the advertising world: since advertising's heyday in the 1920s, depictions of women and their bodies have been used to sell products in virtually all industries, from clothing and beauty products to soft drinks and waste bins (Hawkins & Nakayama, 1992). For example, one advertisement from Brabantia's 2006 campaign featured an image of toned, athletic woman wearing a sports bra and trousers lunging away from a bin, and in 2012, Diet Coke ran an advertising campaign with Jean Paul Gaultier which featured a naked Daisy Lowe painted to look like a Diet Coke bottle. Gill (2009) argues that in recent years, men's bodies have joined women's in advertising to a greater extent than ever before. With ever-increasing levels of advertising, across a wider range of media, the effects of depictions of women's and men's bodies within these are an important consideration for consumer psychology.

In this chapter, we summarize the current research literature on body image and the media. We outline the effects of the media on body image, the processes by which media images influence body image, and factors that put women and men at greater risk of experiencing negative outcomes as a result of these images. Furthermore, we highlight two key research gaps particularly relevant to consumer psychology's examination of these relationships: the focus on internalization of body-related ideals, at the expense of other cultural ideals, and the focus on visual representations of bodies in the media. Moving forward, we discuss interventions to reduce and protect against the effects of the media on body image, considering both individual interventions and broader social interventions, campaigns and policy change. In particular, we focus on policies and recommendations relating to advertising: the use of warning labels for airbrushed images and the representation of a wider range of body shapes in the media. Finally, we consider emerging areas of research that are crucial for understanding the impact of the media on women's and men's body image in twenty-first-century contexts, such as the impact of social media, or "Web 2.0".

The body perfect: Who is beautiful?

In Western cultures, where the majority of body image and media research has centred, a key focus of study has been the *size* of the ideal body portrayed in the media, particularly for women. Early work in this area highlighted the existence of a "thin ideal" for women, where less weight is more desirable (Thompson & Stice, 2001). Research suggests that depictions of women's bodies are considerably thinner than the average woman in the United States and the United Kingdom, and are becoming increasingly so. This trend can be seen in the rise in "size zero" models at fashion shows and in magazines in the 2000s (e.g. Derbyshire, 2007, January 26), but also in the growing gulf between average women's bodies and those of models and celebrities, who are of course the basis for depictions of the ideal we are presented with in the media: as celebrities and models have reduced in size (from Marilyn Monroe at a BMI of 23.3 in the 1950s to Kate Moss with a BMI of 16 in 1990s (Rehabs, n.d.), the average woman's BMI has increased over this period (from 25.2 in 1960 to 27.5 in 2000) (Flegal & Troiano, 2000; Friedman, 2003).

It is important to note that these statistics relate only to the unachievable *size* that women are increasingly expected to achieve. In addition to this trend for ever-thinner models, the rise of airbrushing and digital alteration of images in the media further contributes to unrealistic expectations for women's appearance. Images are now regularly manipulated to decrease women's waists and hips, as well as alter other aspects of appearance. Although more obvious and outrageous examples of this have been mocked and highlighted in high-profile media discussions, such as Jessica Simpson's "magically disappearing hips" (*Elle* cover image, 2008; Rehabs, 2012), this practice continues among advertisers and strongly contributes to ever-more unrealistic ideals for women's bodies.

Indeed, scholars have argued in recent years that, although the "ideal" body of any culture is generally achievable by only a select few (Calogero, Boroughs, & Thompson, 2007), the current ideals portrayed by the media in Western culture are *particularly* unachievable (Bell, 2012; Groesz, Levine, & Murnen, 2002; Harrison, 2003; Tiggemann, 2011). Harrison (2003, p. 256) refers to the emerging ideal for women as the "curvaceously thin ideal", highlighting the unachievable combination of large breasts and extreme slenderness on the rest of the body. Equally, Bell (2012) argues that the ideal has shifted from merely a "thin" ideal to a "body perfect" ideal, with women now expected not simply to be thin, but also to have "perfect" hair, teeth and skin, alongside toned (but not too sizeable) muscles, as well as large breasts. A classic example of the impossibility of this "curvaceously thin" ideal can be seen in a biometric assessment of Barbie, for many years a leading children's toy and epitome of feminine attractiveness: Barbie's proportions are likely to occur in only 1 in 100,000 women (Norton, Olds, Olive, & Dank, 1996), and Brownell and Napolitano (1995) conclude that if Barbie were a real woman, she would have too small a waist and ribcage to house her vital organs. Bell (2012) also identifies airbrushing as a potential contributor to this trend towards "body perfect" rather than simply "thin" ideals: Whereas once makeup and photography were responsible for presenting the best light for models, editors and producers now have digital manipulation at their fingertips which can remove blemishes, artificially lighten teeth and create impossible cleavage on very thin women's bodies.

Body ideals for men have similarly undergone a progression towards ever more unachievable heights of muscularity and low levels of body fat. This progression is depicted most strikingly in Pope, Olivardia, Gruber, & Borowiecki's (1999) consideration of children's action toys: Luke Skywalker and Han Solo, leading characters of the *Star Wars* films, have increased in size considerably since their introduction as action figures in the 1970s, alongside GI Joe, whose 1998 version, if life-sized, would have bigger biceps than any body-builder in history. Again, similarly to the progression of women's beauty ideals beyond size, the gradual removal of cultural stigma related to men being seen to care for their appearance and the advent of airbrushing have combined to create a more polished and unachievable "body perfect" for men as well (Reaves, Hitchen, Park, & Yun, 2004).

Although extensive, research in this area is limited by its focus on Western beauty ideals. Although growing globalization is generally assumed to result in the adoption of the Western ideal across cultures, this assumption has led to a lack of research into meaningful variations in ideals and the context in which these develop; much of the research across cultures focuses on comparing women on their internalization of the Western ideal, instead of developing an understanding of the unique ideals of these countries (e.g., Swami et al., 2010). Weight, specifically a low body weight, may be a particularly Western obsession, intensified in the context of an "obesity epidemic" and widespread availability of high-calorie food; in contrast to Western values of thinness, some work suggests that Asian and African beauty ideals in fact value greater body weight, with fat associated with wealth and status (Hall, 1995). Furthermore, the focus on weight ideals and their association with the globalization of Western media overrides a consideration of other cultural forces and their effects on beauty ideals. The popularity of "Fair and Lovely" skin lightening cream and the preference for lighter skin tone in India, for example, are perhaps better understood in the context of the country's history as a former British colony and the internalization of those colonialist views privileging white skin (e.g., Bakshi & Baker, 2011; Li, Min, Belk, Kimura, & Bahl, 2008). Future research should seek to understand the meaning of these variations in beauty ideals across cultures, to supplement the existing work quantifying these differences (Swami et al., 2010).

Media and body image: Empirical evidence

In investigating the effect of the media on women's and men's body image, research has employed two main paradigms: correlational studies and experimental exposure studies. In correlational studies, participants self-report their current use of various types of media, from magazines to television to films, and rate their body image on a range of scales from general body dissatisfaction to their anxiety relating to specific body parts. Meta-analyses of these correlational findings suggest that, in general, greater media consumption is associated with greater levels of body image disturbance among both women and men (Barlett, Vowels, & Saucier, 2008; Grabe, Ward, & Hyde, 2008). Furthermore, research suggests that it is exposure to appearance-focused media, such as music videos or soap operas in the case of television or health and fitness magazines, that is particularly detrimental for body image (e.g., Borzekowski, Robinson, & Killen, 2000; Harrison, 2003). However, it is possible that women with existing body image issues may be more likely to *choose* to consume more media, and more media that portrays images of cultural beauty ideals, rather than their consumption of this media being the *cause* of their body image concerns. Correlational studies and meta-analyses of their results cannot differentiate between these possibilities, as their measures of media consumption and body image are collected concurrently. To confirm causality, longitudinal and experimental research is necessary.

The classic media exposure experiment paradigm addresses this concern and involves participants being exposed either to media that involves bodies that are representative of the current beauty ideals or to control images or videos that do not show such bodies. Research has used a variety of stimuli, including but not limited to magazine covers, advertisements and music videos (e.g., Bell & Dittmar, 2011). After this exposure, participants record their *state* body image, that is, how they feel about their bodies *right now*. This research consistently finds that exposure to media involving depictions of idealized bodies, compared with viewing control images, results in an increase in body image concerns, disordered eating and self-objectification among women (Grabe et al., 2008; Groesz et al., 2002; Want, 2009). Experimental work with men suggests that this causal effect of idealized media representations is replicated in both genders: Men show similar negative effects to women when exposed to these images in experimental conditions, although a comparison of effect sizes suggests that men may experience smaller effects than women (Barlett et al., 2008; Blond, 2008). Among men, body part dissatisfaction appears to be most strongly associated with media exposure, ahead of *overall* body satisfaction ($d = 0.66$; Blond, 2008).

Although these findings are robust and replicated across many studies, it is important to note the limitations of this exposure paradigm. This research tends to assess only short-term exposure to these images, with participants viewing several adverts before immediately reporting their state body image, in isolation from other participants. Although this highly controlled setting allows researchers to be confident in establishing a causal effect of these images, in reality, these images are deeply embedded within the fabric of Western societies. The images used within these studies are therefore taken out of context, in terms of both the volume participants are exposed to on a daily basis and the broader social context in which this occurs.

A further important point to note is, again, the focus of these studies on Western, English-speaking countries and the effects within their populations. Given wide variations between countries in advertising spend, advertising policies and the intensity of advertising within them, it is surprising that so little research has considered the impact of exposure to media on women's or men's body image outside the "core" body image research centres (i.e., the United States, the United Kingdom, Australia and Canada; Grabe et al., 2008). The two seminal meta-analyses cited above to highlight the consistency of media effects (Barlett et al., 2008; Grabe et al., 2008) focus on research from *only* Western populations; there is therefore a critical need for a broader base of body image and media research considering a wider array of countries. What work there is cross-culturally, however, supports the findings discussed above: Exposure to the media, and Westernized media in particular, is associated with greater body dissatisfaction in women across a sample of 26 countries, from ten world regions (Swami et al., 2010). Additionally, the introduction of Western media to countries previously unexposed has provided a series of naturally occurring experiments with which to examine the effects of this media. Becker et al.'s work on the introduction of Western television to Fiji (2002) suggests that this media has a negative effect on young women's body image and disordered eating. The qualitative element of this research suggests that the introduction of television not only influenced girls' body image and eating behaviours, but also influenced their beliefs about thinness: three years after the introduction of television, the girls valued thinness more highly and highlighted the benefits of thinness for their careers and family life. The introduction of Western television appeared to have introduced not simply the images of thinness, but the messages regarding its benefits beyond attractiveness.

Overall, there is consistent and compelling evidence that the media has a negative influence on women's and men's body image. Our consideration now turns to the explanations of this effect and the factors that make women and men more vulnerable to exposure to idealized depictions of bodies within the media.

Theories of media influences on body image

Theoretical understanding of body image disturbance as a result of the media has borrowed considerably from communications and media theories. Cultivation theory (Gerbner, Gross, Morgan, & Signorielli, 1994) proposes that the more media individuals watch or consume, the more they believe that real life mirrors the world depicted in television shows and advertisements. Thus, the more women watch television and engage with other forms of media, the more they believe that the exceptionally thin bodies of the women portrayed on-screen and in print are realistic, expected and important for them to achieve, and this impacts negatively on their body image.

Socio-cultural theory positions the media as one of three key external influences on perceived pressures concerning appearance, and thus on body image, alongside parents and peers (Thompson, Coovert, & Stormer, 1999). Thus, the socio-cultural model suggests that exposure to media images of idealized bodies influences women's body image by increasing their awareness of beauty ideals, by increasing their internalization of these ideals as personal goals for their own appearance (referred to as thin ideal internalization; Thompson & Stice, 2001), and by increasing their perception of pressure to match these body ideals. Grabe et al.'s meta-analysis (2008) confirms this effect of media exposure on women's internalization of the thin ideal, although the effect size is considerably greater for correlational than for experimental studies ($r = -0.42$ vs. -0.21). Interestingly, given previous discussions surrounding the increasing pressures on women due to the increasing impossibility of beauty ideals, this meta-analysis also found that this effect was greater in more recent studies (those conducted after 2000 vs. those conducted before): It would appear that media is becoming more effective at encouraging internalization of these ideals.

A meta-analysis by Cafri, Yamamiya, Brannick, & Thompson (2005) supports the proposed effects of thin ideal internalization, awareness of the thin ideal and perceived pressures to be thin on body image concerns: All three of these variables were consistently and negatively associated with body image among women. However, awareness of the thin ideal was the weakest of these three predictors, suggesting that it is more important how women interact with this ideal, rather than whether they are aware of its existence. Indeed, research suggests that women's internalization of the thin ideal moderates the influence of media exposure (e.g., Dittmar & Howard, 2004b; Want, 2009), with women who have more strongly internalized media messages around the importance of attractiveness and thinness experiencing greater state body dissatisfaction as a result of exposure to media images of these ideal bodies. These findings are consistently replicated across countries; although the majority of these "cross-cultural" studies focus on alternative Western countries (e.g., Estonia (Tiggemann & Rüütel, 2004); France (Rodgers, Chabrol, & Paxton, 2011)), they have also found support in countries more diverse, such as India (Shroff & Thompson, 2004).

Recent theoretical work by Karazsia and colleagues (2013) integrates thin ideal internalization as both a moderator and a mediator of the relationship between media exposure and body image concerns, by focusing on the distinction of state versus trait internalization. Karazsia, van Dulmen, Wong, & Crowther (2013) propose that trait thin ideal internalization, or the extent to which women have already internalized these pressures, will moderate women's reactions to an individual exposure to the thin ideal. Specifically, women who have more strongly internalized these cultural ideals will experience greater state body image concerns, as detailed above. However, Karazsia et al. also propose that these individual exposures also result in state activation of the thin ideal, and over time, repeated activations of the thin ideal result in increases in trait thin ideal internalization, which are in turn associated with worsening trait body satisfaction. Thus, over a period of time, exposure to media increases both women's internalization of the ideals contained within it and their concerns about their own bodies. This work helps to place the exposure experiments discussed above in perspective, as single "meals" in women's "media diets" (Aubrey, 2010). However, further longitudinal research is necessary to confirm this transition from state effects to trait effects of media exposure and cultural ideal internalization on both men's and women's body image.

Another proposed cognitive process explaining the negative effects of appearance media is the idea that viewing these images can highlight the distance between how our bodies actually are and how we would ideally like them to be. Self-discrepancy theory (Higgins, 1987) suggests that a discrepancy between the actual and the ideal self will generate negative emotions, such as depression, and research has suggested that these negative feelings can extend specifically to women's perceptions of their bodies. Images of idealized women's bodies in the media have been shown to be associated with appearance-related self-discrepancies: Women describe more appearance-related gaps between their actual and ideal selves, and rate these gaps as larger and more important after viewing these models (Dittmar, Halliwell, & Stirling, 2009), and this in turn is associated with lower body satisfaction. However, in spite of their intuitive value in explaining the effects of exposure to media models, relatively little research has looked at the effects of these self-discrepancies in the long term. Some preliminary findings from a sample of over 1,000 8–15-year-old children suggest that discrepancies between the ideal and the actual self across a range of domains are both predicted by and predictive of greater internalization of cultural ideals, such as the thin ideal, over time (Dittmar et al., 2014a). Furthermore, greater ideal–actual self-discrepancies are associated with declines in well-being and body image over time.

Perhaps the most widely researched theory of media effects is social comparison theory (Festinger, 1954). Social comparison theory proposes that individuals continually evaluate themselves in order to assess their own standing on a wide range of characteristics and that individuals are motivated to engage in social comparisons not only for self-evaluation, but also for self-improvement and self-enhancement (Wood, 1989). The negative effects of media exposure are usually understood as the result of upward self-evaluative appearance comparisons with the media models. Body dissatisfaction and negative mood are a result of evaluating one's appearance against the ideals displayed in the media and not measuring up to these standards. However, some research has found immediate positive effects of media exposure among women (e.g., Henderson-King & Henderson-King, 1997; Joshi, Herman, & Polivy, 2004; Mills, Polivy, Herman, & Tiggemann, 2002; Myers & Biocca, 1992) and men (Halliwell, Dittmar, & Orsborn, 2007). These findings are consistent with a self-improvement motive for appearance comparisons whereby an individual attempts to learn how to improve or to be inspired to improve a particular attribute. Therefore, individuals who are invested in their appearance, or are actively attempting to improve their appearance, may see models as inspirational figures and use them as comparison targets for self-improvement. Given the unrealistic and unachievable nature of these appearance ideals, any positive impact will likely be short lived (Mills et al., 2002).

These theories are not mutually exclusive. Indeed, it is likely that they interconnect, with thin ideal internalization leading to men and women viewing media models as more appropriate social comparison targets, and thus engaging in more of these comparisons. Comparing oneself with media models may highlight the distance between the ideal represented by these models and the actual self, increasing the perceived size and importance of discrepancy. Finally, women who have more strongly internalized the thin ideal may find that this ideal is chronically salient, is activated more easily and therefore is more obviously distant from the actual self, resulting in more negative body image more frequently (Halliwell & Dittmar, 2006). Although these theories provide an important explanation of the processes through which the media influences women's and men's body image, a key critique is the passive position in which they place the consumer, particularly in the case of self-discrepancy theory and thin ideal internalization. Men and women are "exposed" to these images and, with very little control, they then respond to them. However, this passive conceptualization of the consumer of media may overlook the involvement of men and women in producing and promoting these images themselves, and our complicit involvement in the reproduction of these ideals (Gill, 2007). As a brief example, the influence of peers and media in the socio-cultural model (Thompson et al., 1999) is represented in separate pathways; however, this may not sufficiently represent the way these forces interact with one another. Recent work modelling social networks suggests that it is not only young women's own experiences of media that influence their body image and disordered eating, but the exposure of those around them: The media exposure of friends (and friends of friends) had a significant association with girls' body image, in addition to the effects of their own media exposure (Becker et al., 2011). These critiques of the passive consumer and representations of the media as isolated from other social influences have become more relevant with the advent of social media; here, content representing these beauty ideals is not merely advertised to a waiting audience, but posted, commented on, "liked" and re-posted by this audience and their peers. A key direction for future research may be to explore these issues of complicity and reproduction in more depth and detail.

Risk factors and protective influences for media exposure

As discussed in the previous section, women's internalization of the thin ideal has been identified as a key moderating factor in determining the effects of a single exposure to thin ideal images (Karazsia et al., 2013; Want, 2009). In addition, previous meta-analyses of experimental exposures have identified existing appearance concerns as a potential moderator: Women who already experience trait dissatisfaction with their bodies are more likely to experience the negative influences of a single exposure to media containing images of the thin ideal (Groesz et al., 2002). This has been further supported in longitudinal experimental research by Stice, Spangler and Agras (2001). In this work, adolescent girls were randomly assigned to either an appearance-focused magazine subscription or a subscription to a magazine that did not contain images of the thin ideal. Girls with high initial body image dissatisfaction and low levels of social support became increasingly dissatisfied over the course of the year if they were in the thin ideal subscription condition. Girls who were initially satisfied with their bodies and had high levels of social support were relatively protected from the detrimental effects of exposure to the appearance-focused magazine. A third well-researched moderating influence is women's body mass index (BMI): Women who are heavier for their height tend to be more negatively affected by exposure to images of thin media models (Stice, 1994; Tiggemann, 2003). This can potentially be understood in terms of social comparisons, as their bodies differ more strongly from appearance ideals.

These three factors appear closely related. Women who have more strongly internalized the thin ideal tend to be more dissatisfied with their appearance in cross-sectional studies (e.g., Cafri et al., 2005), and women with higher BMI also tend to be less satisfied with their bodies (Bucchianeri, Arikian, Hannan, Eisenberg, & Neumark-Sztainer, 2013; Van den Berg et al., 2007). Identifying these risk factors is important for future work as it suggests both whom and what to target with media and body image interventions. It suggests that those with high BMI and pre-existing body image concerns are most vulnerable, but also that by designing interventions which disrupt women's and girls' internalization of the thin ideal, we can reduce the negative effects they may experience from being exposed to it.

Among men, relatively less work has examined moderating influences on the effects of exposure, and the findings of this work are less consistent. In general, personal levels of appearance concern and appearance investment appear to have some influence on this link: studies have suggested that prior levels of dissatisfaction with muscularity and high appearance investment are associated with more negative body image among men as a result of exposure to images of the male ideal (Arbour & Ginnis, 2006; Hargreaves & Tiggemann, 2004). Other findings among male samples are not as consistent with the research around women's reactions to exposure to cultural ideals: Research has not supported the role of internalization of cultural ideals in moderating men's reactions to this media (Agliata & Tantleff-Dunn, 2004; Diedrichs & Lee, 2010), in contrast to the considerable support found for women's internalization of these as a moderator, documented earlier in this section. As the field investigating men's body image continues to develop, researchers will be able to consider these moderating factors across a range of studies, enabling a more robust estimation of their effects, as in the women's literature (e.g., Groesz et al., 2002; Want, 2009).

Recent research in body image has focused on more positive *protective* factors, as opposed to the risk factors of BMI, thin ideal internalization and existing appearance concerns. Recent research by Halliwell (2013) suggests that body appreciation protects women's body image when they are exposed to thin ideal images. Avalos, Tylka and Wood-Barcalow (2005) conceptualize positive body image as 1) an appreciation of the appearance of the body *in spite of* any deviations from cultural ideals of beauty, 2) engaging in positive behaviours to care for the body and 3) employing a self-protective cognitive style when processing appearance-related messages. It may in fact be this positive cognitive style that is particularly beneficial for women's body image.

Indeed, this critical perspective towards media representations of cultural ideals may play a particularly crucial role in protecting both men and women from the effects of exposure to them. Interventions relating to media literacy, which involve educating participants about the effects of exposure to the thin ideal, the digital manipulation of models' appearances in advertisements and underlying, profit-related motives for companies to use these images, have been increasingly recognized in the literature for having a positive effect on body image (Levine & Murnen, 2009). This critical view of the media has been suggested as a key process by which other protective factors, such as feminist beliefs and identification (Kinsaul, Curtin, Bazzini, & Martz, 2014; Myers & Crowther, 2007), buffer against the negative effects of exposure to images representing cultural ideals or awareness of these ideals in the media: Women who more strongly identify as feminist have a more critical lens through which they view and consume media, and thus may be somewhat protected from its negative effects.

Beyond the thin ideal: Materialism and body dissatisfaction

In spite of the considerable array of research conducted over the last 25 years into the relationship between the media and body image, there are still considerable gaps in our knowledge of its effects and the processes by which they occur. In reviewing the evidence outlined above, it is apparent that research into men's body image and the media, particularly with regard to moderators of this association, is considerably behind comparable research studying effects among women: There is less work considering these effects, and research has yet to consistently identify moderators of this link. Additionally, although work has begun to consider the impact of the media on adolescents, these findings are still relatively sparse and it is unclear what factors moderate these relationships among this younger age group (see Wiseman, Sunday, & Becker, 2005, for a review of media influences on adolescent body image). Given the methodological and ethical issues, it is unsurprising that there is even sparser work on body image and the media among younger children. What research there is among younger children, particularly girls, suggests that exposure to media related to appearance and the thin ideal results in greater desire to be thin and lower body satisfaction, even among 5–8-year-olds (e.g., Dittmar, Halliwell, & Ive, 2006; Dohnt & Tiggemann, 2006; Tiggemann & Slater, 2014). At the other end of the age spectrum, there is also a notable lack of consideration of these relationships among older adults: The Barlett et al. (2008) meta-analysis suggests a trend of increasing effects of the media on body image with age among men, but this becomes less informative when we consider that the *oldest* samples in this analysis were college-age men. Do older men and women become more immune to the effects of the media over time, as their identities become more secure, or does the ever-increasing divide between their bodies and the youthful ideals take an increasingly higher toll on their body image? These are questions to which the research literature at present does not provide an answer.

However, beyond these demographic issues, we would argue that the literature has focused on a very narrow element of the media in relation to body image, leaving a far larger, but more subtle, gap in our knowledge. Research into the media's effect on body image has focused predominantly on the specific images portrayed in advertisements, on the sizes of women and men represented in television and film, and on the creation of an unattainable *image* of beauty through the use of ever-thinner models and in recent years the advent of airbrushing. Although the negative effects of these images are clearly important, and for the most part are well documented in the literature outlined above, from a consumer psychology perspective, this focus on the visual representation of ideal bodies overlooks the more wide-reaching effects of the media and the greater range of content that women and men are exposed to.

We have discussed at length the impact of internalization of the thin ideal. However, as Ashikali and Dittmar (2014) highlight, this body perfect ideal is but one of several ideals portrayed in contemporary media and in advertisements (the most common stimuli used in experimental studies). These ideal representations of appearance are often used to sell products and the lifestyles attached to them; these ideals are often combined, representing an ideal life, filled with beautiful people and desirable material goods (Dittmar, 2008). Thus, the associations of these goods with success and happiness (Richins & Dawson, 1992) are also critical elements of advertising and the media which many women and men consume, and these ideals may influence body image and well-being.

Given the common co-occurrence of highly attractive models and consumer goods in advertising, a key proposition is that the internalization of the thin or muscular ideal should go hand-in-hand with internalization of the importance of possessions and money, or a materialistic value orientation. Recent work among children and adolescents suggests that this is indeed the case: In a study of 8–to 15-year-olds, children who had more strongly internalized cultural ideals of attractiveness also had more strongly internalized ideals relating to the desirability of material goods (Easterbrook, Wright, Dittmar, & Banerjee, 2014). This proposition is further supported by findings that young adults also display this association (Ashikali & Dittmar, 2012; Guðnadóttir & Garðasdóttir, 2014). This research also suggests, crucially for our interests, that the internalization of *both* of these ideals (materialism and the body perfect) is associated with more negative body image: both materialistic values and internalization of cultural ideals of attractiveness have a detrimental effect on the body image of young adults and children.

Research into goals and values more broadly supports this association: Work from self-determination theory suggests that the extrinsic goals of financial success, an attractive appearance and fame are closely related (Kasser & Ryan, 1996), and that all three are associated with lower well-being. A recent meta-analysis found that both materialistic values individually and this cluster of extrinsic goals combined were associated with lower well-being across a variety of domains (Dittmar et al., 2014b), including self-esteem. Furthermore, these goals have been associated cross-culturally, with appearance, fame and materialism loading closely together in factor analyses (e.g., Grouzet et al., 2005).

In addition to materialistic and body perfect ideals being associated at the trait level, there appears to be some support for the role of materialism in increasing women's vulnerability to negative influences of the thin ideal. Ashikali and Dittmar (2012) exposed women to materialistic adverts, such as ones advertising high-cost overseas holidays or champagne, or to non-materialistic adverts, such as ones depicting stationery or art and crafts items. Women were then exposed to personal-care product advertisements that either contained models who represented the thin ideal or did not contain images of women. Women exposed to the materialistic adverts before being exposed to the thin ideal showed the most negative effects of exposure, rating appearance as more central to their self-concept and generating more body-related self-discrepancies. Furthermore, women who were more materialistic in general (high in trait materialism) experienced these negative effects to a greater extent. In a further study, Ashikali, Dittmar, & Ayers (2014) found that adolescent girls who were higher in trait materialism experienced more body dissatisfaction after viewing a cosmetic surgery reality television show, providing further support for materialism as an important factor in explaining the media's impact on women's and potentially men's body image. Given the frequency of their pairing within advertising and beyond, future research should continue to investigate the links between and dual influences of body perfect ideals and materialistic ideals. In particular, samples for this research should be extended to men, as the majority of the work thus far has focused on women's responses to these combinations of ideals.

Recent media interventions: Media literacy, airbrushing warnings and model diversity

In 2009, Helga Dittmar, Emma Halliwell, Marika Tiggemann and Michael Levine submitted a detailed summary of the effects of ideal images and airbrushing in advertising to the Advertising Standards Authority, the UK regulatory body responsible for restricting harm caused by advertising and ensuring truthful adverts. This document was signed and supported by over 40 academic and clinical experts in the field of body image research, and argued for five policy outlines, supported by evidence from the body image literature:

1. Media literacy programmes about "perfected" models as part of school curricula to encourage critical awareness and resilience in children and adolescents.
2. Clear labelling of altered, idealized models in all other advertising.

3. Encouragement for use of diverse and healthy body sizes in all media models.
4. No altered, idealized models in advertising to children.
5. Models used in Fashion Weeks, and other media advertising, to have a health certificate from an eating disorder specialist, in order to protect their health and well-being.

In this section of the chapter, we will examine the empirical evidence for the first three of these recommendations: media literacy training programmes, the labelling of airbrushed images and the use of diverse models in media.

Recognizing that the mass media is an inescapable element of the modern world, media literacy programmes aim to help participants to understand and critically evaluate the images portrayed in the media and their relationships with them (Levine & Murnen, 2009; Levine & Smolak, 2008). Such programmes tend to involve examining and deconstructing the unrealistic images of the ideal bodies presented in the media, but also our responses to them, becoming aware of how these images can make us feel and the potential costs of pursuing them. Research suggests that media literacy interventions can be effective over a single session, but that the strongest effects are achieved in a consistent programme over a period of weeks rather than hours (Levine & Murnen, 2009). Wilksch and Wade (2009), for example, demonstrate the effectiveness of MediaSmart, a media literacy programme delivered over 8 weeks; compared with the control group, adolescent girls and boys who engaged with the programme had lower levels of shape and weight concerns, body dissatisfaction and dieting. Furthermore, Levine and Murnen (2009) highlight the consistency of media literacy training's effects on internalization of socio-cultural ideals of attractiveness, such as the thin ideal or the muscular ideal for men. Given the multifaceted role awarded to thin ideal internalization in recent theoretical work (Karazsia et al., 2013), as both a moderator and a mediator of the effects of media exposure, media literacy interventions could be a crucial tool in both treating and preventing these effects.

More recent interventions have sought to marry concepts of media literacy with another powerful cognitive process: cognitive dissonance. Cognitive dissonance occurs when individuals are required to state or argue a case for something contrary to their current beliefs (Festinger, 1957). This dissonance causes unpleasant psychological tension, which theoretically individuals resolve by altering their initial beliefs to match those they have argued for. Body image interventions have begun to harness this effect, by asking participants to argue against the appearance ideals so prominent in the media (Stice & Presnell, 2007): One example of an activity from a recent intervention involved teenage girls writing a letter to another, hypothetical girl, persuading her not to pursue the thin ideal (Halliwell & Diedrichs, 2014). The Body Project cognitive dissonance intervention has been found to be effective at reducing thin ideal internalization and body dissatisfaction for young adolescent girls (12–13 years; Halliwell & Diedrichs, 2014), and for older adolescents and adult women (Stice, Shaw, & Marti, 2007). This intervention also protected young girls from negative media exposure effects (Halliwell & Diedrichs, 2014). Some of the most successful programmes for tackling negative body image, particularly with adolescents in secondary schools, involve a combination of media literacy and cognitive dissonance elements (see Yager, Diedrichs, Ricciardelli, & Halliwell, 2013, for a review of school interventions).

As can be seen in the research literature outlined above, these individual methods of reducing media effects on body image have been effective in reducing body dissatisfaction resulting from the media in the groups that are treated with them. However, even rolling out national programmes such as these to educate or "vaccinate" (from a public health, prevention perspective) young people in schools can only ever be an *ameliorative* strategy, treating the symptoms of a media which continues to portray ever more unachievable ideals rather than changing the media content that is the proposed cause. Albee (1982) notes that no public health problem has ever been solved by treating affected individuals, or even groups of individuals: disease and disorder are eliminated through *prevention*. Thus, many campaigners have argued for interventions at the source of these images, the adverts themselves, such as warning labels regarding airbrushing and the use of average-sized models in the media.

Since Dittmar and colleagues' submission to the ASA, research into the effects of labelling images as retouched or digitally altered has blossomed. The findings from this area are mixed, however. Initial studies have suggested a protective effect of these labels: Slater, Tiggemann, Firth and Hawkins (2012) found that women who were presented with retouched images that also included a warning about this manipulation did not demonstrate the same post-test decreases in body satisfaction as women who viewed the same images without the warning label. However, studies since have not found the same beneficial effect, with either null results (Ata, Thompson, & Small, 2013; Tiggemann, Slater, Bury, Hawkins, & Firth, 2013) or negative effects for participants who were aware the images were digitally altered (Harrison & Hefner, 2014). As an emerging area of literature, it may take some time for consistency to emerge in the findings and in their interpretations. As ever, it is notable that research concerning men's responses to such warning labels is still lagging behind; to our knowledge, no research has yet considered these labels' effects on men's responses to the media. Furthermore, the labelling of images is arguably still a reactive or "treatment"-based approach: The problematic images still exist and people are still exposed to them, albeit with more awareness of the manipulation involved. Additionally, and perhaps more importantly, even if these images were not airbrushed, the models within them still represent a narrowly defined beauty ideal, given their restricted diversity in size, ethnicity and age.

In this area, and relating to the third suggestion outlined in the report to the ASA, there is considerably more evidence: Using average-size women's bodies in advertising products is associated with more positive outcomes for the women viewing these adverts and, by some accounts, for the companies involved. Whereas some research supports claims from advertisers that extreme *attractiveness* sells products and improves consumer opinions better than "standard" attractiveness (e.g., Bower & Landreth, 2001), other work suggests that this field is more mixed in its findings (Brumbaugh, 1993). However, in the case of model body *size*, research consistently finds that women rate models with average body sizes as being as effective in advertisements as models with bodies closer to the traditional thin ideal (Dittmar & Howard, 2004a; Halliwell & Dittmar, 2004; Halliwell, Dittmar, & Howe, 2005) and consumers in some cases actively discuss the desire for more realistic representations of women's bodies in particular in advertising (Diedrichs & Lee, 2011). Crucially for our consideration of the media's impact on body image, these average-size (but still attractive) models have been shown to have less negative effects on women's and men's body image, or in fact no effect: Women and men exposed to these average-sized images felt no worse about their bodies than they did before they saw these adverts (Diedrichs & Lee, 2011; Dittmar & Howard, 2004a).

Although the participants in these "average-size model" studies are hypothetical consumers, rating artificial products, the real-life case study of Dove's Real Beauty campaign appears to support these findings. From 2004, Dove's advertising team has made a conscious decision to feature a greater range of women and women's body shapes than the traditional, extremely slender ideals, terming this policy shift the "Dove Campaign for Real Beauty". Research sponsored by Dove's parent company, Unilever, suggests that consumer awareness of this decision was associated with increased interest in Dove as a brand, and with likelihood of recommending Dove to friends (Unilever, 2015): 62 per cent would recommend the brand to a friend, compared with 46 per cent who were not aware of the Dove campaign for self-esteem. Obviously, this could be viewed as problematic: Dove is a brand with a vested interest in making women feel that to some extent they *need* or *want* its products, and could be viewed as engaging in more ethical marketing practices to increase sales. However, this work does provide a concrete rebuttal of some advertisers' claims that only thin models will encourage women to buy their products, and provides campaigners with a further piece of evidence to work for change in advertising more broadly, not just within a single brand.

Moving forward: Emerging areas of research

From our consideration of research above, we believe that three key areas for research development emerge, and discuss these alongside a broader obligation among researchers to promote social change. First, it is crucial for research to continue to expand its consideration of neglected demographics. Although we discuss in particular issues relating to men's body image and to media influences over the lifespan, it is also worth noting that socio-economic, ethnic and racial diversity are also relatively rare considerations in the field of media and body image. Future work should ensure that it not only encompasses these demographics but also investigates the intersectionality of individuals' experiences, following the lead of recent work examining Black and Latina women's resistance to the thin ideal within the context of their underrepresentation in mainstream media (e.g., Capodilupo & Kim, 2014; Schooler & Daniels, 2014).

Second, in the chapter we highlight recent research that considers links between the beauty ideals that have been the focus of much body image and media research and other equally pernicious cultural ideals, such as materialism (e.g., Ashikali & Dittmar, 2012; Guðnadóttir & Garðasdóttir, 2014). Future research should seek to extend our understanding of how exposure to and internalization of *both* of these ideals is associated with men's and women's feelings about their bodies. Additionally, it may be beneficial to consider how these ideal lifestyles, of beauty and riches, are related to not just body image, but also body modification behaviours such as dieting, particularly for women, or exercise focused on appearance and muscle building, particularly for men. Finally, in a media climate increasingly concerned with celebrity, research should also consider the extrinsic goal of fame, viewed as complementary to the goals of appearance and financial success in self-determination theory (e.g., Kasser & Ryan, 1996) and increasingly implicated in women's and girls' body-related decisions and behaviours (e.g., Walter, 2010).

Third, our focus within this chapter has been on traditional, mainstream media, such as television, magazines and advertising, where images are assembled and selected by powerful corporations before being "consumed" by the public. Indeed, the vast majority of the literature on body image and the media focuses on these forms, and even that considering "new media" on the Internet has focused on this traditional media producer/media consumer divide. However, the meteoric rise of social networking and image-sharing sites, such as Facebook, Instagram and Pinterest, in recent years may put pressure on this divide: The shift to Web 2.0, or a web containing primarily user-generated, social content, challenges this structure and our ways of examining the links between body image and media. Work thus far has investigated the processes by which women and men are *influenced* by this new content in a relatively similar manner to studies involving traditional media (e.g., Fardouly, Diedrichs, Vartanian, & Halliwell, 2015; Perloff, 2014). However, as the producer/consumer divide in online media becomes ever more blurred, it will become increasingly important to understand not only individuals' responses to beauty ideals, but their complicity in reproducing them through these sites' social sharing and re-posting functions. Future work should consider women's and men's experiences not only of consuming, but of engaging with and potentially reproducing, these ideal images on the web.

As a closing point, we would propose that as body image researchers, we have an obligation to move beyond merely investigating the effects of the media on body image. Given the strong body of evidence documenting the negative impact of the media, it is crucial that we continue to strongly and publicly advocate for social policies and media campaigns challenging both the narrow representation of attractiveness provided by the media and the importance placed on attractiveness in our culture more broadly. A further crucial step in challenging these ideals and their replication may involve moving beyond merely acting as scientific experts and activists ourselves, and instead working to empower the men, women and children we work with in our research to challenge the media influences in their lives. Media literacy programmes already support our participants in developing a critical awareness of the ideals represented within the media, and how these influence body image; a key next step is supporting them to challenge these influences and ideals not just in their personal lives, but in the wider world.

References

Advertising Standards Association (2012). *Public perceptions of harm and offence in UK advertising*. Retrieved from www.asa.org.uk

Advertising Standards Association (2015). *Hot topic: Health and beauty*. Retrieved from www.asa.org.uk

Agliata, D., & Tantleff-Dunn, S. (2004). The impact of media exposure on males' body image. *Journal of Social and Clinical Psychology*, *23*, 7–22.

Al Sabbah, H., Vereecken, C. A., Elgar, F. J., Nansel, T., Aasvee, K., Abdeen, Z., ... & Maes, L. (2009). Body weight dissatisfaction and communication with parents among adolescents in 24 countries: International cross-sectional survey. *BMC Public Health*, *9*, 52. doi: 10.1186/1471-2458-9-52

Albee, G. (1982). Preventing psychopathology and promoting human potential. *American Psychologist*, *37*, 1043–1050.

All Party Parliamentary Group on Body Image (2012). *Reflections on body image*. All Party Parliamentary Group report. Retrieved from www.ncb.org.uk/media/861233/appg_body_image_final.pdf

Arbour, K. P., & Ginnis, K. A. (2006). Effects of exposure to muscular and hypermuscular media images on young men's muscularity dissatisfaction and body dissatisfaction. *Body Image*, *3*, 153–161.

Ashikali, E.-M., & Dittmar, H. (2012). The effect of priming materialism on women's responses to thin-ideal media. *British Journal of Social Psychology*, *51*, 514–533. doi: 10.1111/j.2044-8309.2011.02020.x

Ashikali, E.-M., Dittmar, H., & Ayers, S. (2014). The effect of cosmetic surgery reality TV shows on adolescent girls' body image. *Psychology of Popular Media Culture*, 7, 141–153. doi: 10.1037/ppm0000022

Ata, R. N., Thompson, J. K., & Small, B. J. (2013). Effects of exposure to thin-ideal media images on body dissatisfaction: Testing the inclusion of a disclaimer versus warning label. *Body Image*, *10*, 472–480.

Aubrey, J. S. (2010). Looking good versus feeling good: An investigation of media frames of health advice and their effects on women's body-related self-perceptions. *Sex Roles*, *63*, 50–63. doi: 10.1007/s11199-010-9768-4

Avalos, L., Tylka, T. L., & Wood-Barcalow, N. (2005). The Body Appreciation Scale: Development and psychometric evaluation. *Body Image*, *2*, 285–297. doi: 10.1016/j.bodyim.2005.06.002

Bakshi, S., & Baker, A. (2011). "I think a fair girl would have better marriage prospects than a dark one": British Indian adults' perceptions of physical appearance ideals. *Europe's Journal of Psychology*, 7, 458–486.

Barlett, C. P., Vowels, C. L., & Saucier, D. A. (2008). Meta-analyses of the effects of media images on men's body-image concerns. *Journal of Social and Clinical Psychology*, *27*, 279–310.

Becker, A. E., Burwell, R. A., Herzog, D. B., Hamburg, P., & Gilman, S. E. (2002). Eating behaviours and attitudes following prolonged exposure to television among ethnic Fijian adolescent girls. *The British Journal of Psychiatry*, *180*, 509–514.

Becker, A. E., Fay, K. E., Agnew-Blais, J., Khan, A. N., Striegel-Moore, R. H., & Gilman, S. E. (2011). Social network media exposure and adolescent eating pathology in Fiji. *The British Journal of Psychiatry*, *198*, 43–50.

Bell, B. T. (2012). *Understanding adolescent girls' vulnerability to the impact of the mass media on body image and restrained eating behaviour: The role of media type, body perfect internalisation and materialism* (Unpublished doctoral dissertation). University of Sussex, Brighton, UK.

Bell, B. T., & Dittmar, H. (2011). Does media type matter? The role of identification in adolescent girls' media consumption and the impact of different thin-ideal media on body image. *Sex Roles, 65*, 478–480.

Blond, A. (2008). Impacts of exposure to images of ideal bodies on male body dissatisfaction: A review. *Body Image, 5*, 244–250.

Borzekowski, D. L. G., Robinson, T. N., & Killen, J. D. (2000). Does the camera add 10 pounds? Media use, perceived importance of appearance and weight concerns among teenage girls. *Journal of Adolescent Health, 26*, 36–41.

Bower, A. B., & Landreth, S. (2001). Is beauty best? Highly versus normally attractive models in advertising. *Journal of Advertising, 30*, 1–12.

Brownell, K. D., & Napolitano, M. A. (1995). Distorting reality for children: Body size proportions of Barbie and Ken dolls. *International Journal of Eating Disorders, 18*, 295–298.

Brumbaugh, A. M. (1993). Physical attractiveness and personality in advertising: More than just a pretty face? In L. McAlister & M. L. Rothschild (Eds.), *Advances in consumer research* (Vol. 20, pp. 159–164). Provo, UT: Association for Consumer Research.

Bucchianeri, M. M., Arikian, A. J., Hannan, P. J., Eisenberg, M. E., & Neumark-Sztainer, D. (2013). Body dissatisfaction from adolescence to young adulthood: Findings from a 10-year longitudinal study. *Body Image, 10*, 1–7. doi: 10.1016/j.bodyim.2012.09.001

Cafri, G., Yamamiya, Y., Brannick, M., & Thompson, J. K. (2005). The influence of socio-cultural factors on body image: A meta-analysis. *Clinical Psychology: Science and Practice, 12*, 421–433.

Calogero, R. M., Boroughs, M., & Thompson, J. K. (2007). The impact of Western beauty ideals on the lives of women and men: A socio-cultural perspective. In V. Swami & A. Furnham (Eds.), *Body beautiful: Evolutionary and socio-cultural perspectives* (pp. 259–298). New York, NY: Palgrave Macmillan.

Capodilupo, C. M., & Kim, S. (2014). Gender and race matter: The importance of considering intersections in Black women's body image. *Journal of Counselling Psychology, 61*, 37–49. doi: 10.1037/a0034597.

Derbyshire, D. (2007, January 26). Fashion leaders refuse to ban size zero models. *The Telegraph*. Retrieved from www.telegraph.co.uk/news/uknews/1540595/Fashion-leaders-refuse-to-ban-size-zero-models.html

Diedrichs, P. C., & Lee, C. (2010). GI Joe or average Joe? The impact of average-size and muscular male fashion models on men's and women's body image and advertisement effectiveness. *Body Image, 7*, 218–226.

Diedrichs, P. C., & Lee, C. (2011). Waif goodbye! Average-size female models promote positive body image and appeal to consumers. *Psychology & Health, 26*, 1273–1291.

Dittmar, H. (2008). *Consumer culture, identity and well-being: The search for the "good life" and the "body perfect"*. Hove, UK: Psychology Press.

Dittmar, H., Bond, R., Hurst, M., & Kasser, T. (2014). The relationship between materialism and personal well-being: A meta-analysis. *Journal of Personality and Social Psychology, 107*, 879–924.

Dittmar, H., Bond, R., Hurst, M. & Kasser, T. (2014a). The relationship between materialism and personal well-being: A meta-analysis. *Journal of Personality and Social Psychology, 107*, 879–924.

Dittmar, H., Easterbrook, M. J., Banerjee, R., Wright, M., & Hurst, M. (2014b, June). When the pursuit of "looking good" is bad for you: Longitudinal evidence on the links between body ideal values, identity, and well-being in primary and secondary school children. Paper presented at *Appearance Matters 6*. Bristol, UK.

Dittmar, H., Halliwell, E., & Ive, S. (2006). Does Barbie make girls want to be thin? *Developmental Psychology, 42*, 283–292.

Dittmar, H., Halliwell, E., & Stirling, E. (2009). Understanding the impact of thin media models on women's body-focused affect: The roles of thin-ideal internalisation and weight-related self-discrepancy activation in experimental exposure effects. *Journal of Social and Clinical Psychology, 28*, 43–72.

Dittmar, H., & Howard, S. (2004a). Professional hazards? The impact of models' body size on advertising effectiveness and women's body-focused anxiety in professions that do and do not emphasise the cultural ideal of thinness. *British Journal of Social Psychology, 43*, 477–497.

Dittmar, H., & Howard, S. (2004b). Thin-ideal internalization and social comparison tendency as moderators of media models' impact on women's body-focused anxiety. *Journal of Social and Clinical Psychology, 23*, 768–791.

Dohnt, H., & Tiggemann, M. (2006). The contribution of peer and media influences to the development of body satisfaction and self-esteem in young girls: A prospective study. *Developmental Psychology, 42*, 929–936.

Easterbrook, M. J., Wright, M. L., Dittmar, H., & Banerjee, R. (2014). Consumer culture ideals, extrinsic motivations, and well-being in children. *European Journal of Social Psychology, 44*, 349–359.

Fardouly, J., Diedrichs, P. C., Vartanian, L., & Halliwell, E. (2015). Social comparisons on social media: The impact of Facebook on young women's body image concerns and mood. *Body Image, 13*, 38–45.

Festinger, L. (1954). A theory of social comparison processes. *Human Relations*, 7, 117–140.

Festinger, L. (1957). *A theory of cognitive dissonance*. Stanford, CA: Stanford University Press.

Flegal, K. M., & Troiano, R. P. (2000). Changes in the distribution of body mass index of adults and children in the US population. *International Journal of Obesity, 24*, 807–818.

Friedman, J. M. (2003). A war on obesity, not the obese. *Science, 299*, 856–858.

Gerbner, G., Gross, L., Morgan, M., & Signorielli, N. (1994). Growing up with television: The cultivation perspective. In J. Bryant & D. Zillman (Eds.), *Media effects: Advances in theory and research* (pp. 61–90). Hillsdale, NJ: Erlbaum.

Gill, R. (2009). Beyond the "sexualisation of culture" thesis: An intersectional analysis of "sixpacks", "midriffs" and "hot lesbians" in advertising. *Sexualities, 12*, 137–160.

Gill, R. C. (2007). Critical respect: The difficulties and dilemmas of agency and "choice" for feminism. *European Journal of Women's Studies, 14*, 69–80.

Grabe, S., Ward, L. M., & Hyde, J. S. (2008). The role of the media in body image concerns among women: A meta-analysis of experimental and correlational studies. *Psychological Bulletin, 134*, 460–475. doi: 10.1037/0033-2909.134.3.460

Groesz, L. M., Levine, M. P., & Murnen, S. K. (2002). The effect of experimental presentation of thin media images on body satisfaction: A meta-analytic review. *International Journal of Eating Disorders, 31*, 1–16. doi: 10.1002/eat.10005

Grouzet, F. M. E., Kasser, T., Ahuvia, A., Fernandez-Dols, J. M., Kim, Y., Lau, S., Ryan, R. M., Saunders, S., Schmuck, P., & Sheldon, K. M. (2005). The structure of goal contents across 15 cultures. *Journal of Personality and Social Psychology, 89*, 800–816. doi: 10.1037/0022-3514.89.5.800

Guðnadóttir, U., & Garðasdóttir, R. B. (2014). The influence of materialism and ideal body internalization on body-dissatisfaction and body-shaping behaviours of young men and women: Support for the Consumer Culture Impact Model. *Scandinavian Journal of Psychology, 55*, 151–159.

Hall, C. C. (1995). Asian eyes: Body image and eating disorders of Asian and Asian American women. *Eating Disorders: The Journal of Treatment and Prevention, 3*, 8–18.

Halliwell, E. (2013). The impact of thin idealized media images on body satisfaction: Does body appreciation protect women from negative effects? *Body Image, 10*, 509–514.

Halliwell, E., & Diedrichs, P. C. (2014). Testing a dissonance body image intervention among young girls. *Health Psychology, 33*, 201–204.

Halliwell, E., & Dittmar, H. (2004). Does size matter? The impact of model's body size on women's body-focused anxiety and advertising effectiveness. *Journal of Social and Clinical Psychology, 23*, 104–122.

Halliwell, E., & Dittmar, H. (2006). Associations between appearance-related self-discrepancies and young women's and men's affect, body satisfaction, and emotional eating: A comparison of fixed-item and participant-generated self-discrepancies. *Personality and Social Psychology Bulletin, 32*, 447–458.

Halliwell, E., Dittmar, H., & Howe, J. (2005). Short research note: The impact of advertisements featuring ultra-thin or average-size models on women with a history of eating disorders. *Journal of Community & Applied Social Psychology, 15*, 405–413.

Halliwell, E., Dittmar, H., & Orsborn, A. (2007). The effects of exposure to muscular male models among men: Exploring the moderating role of gym use and exercise motivation. *Body Image, 4*, 278–287.

Hargreaves, D. A., & Tiggemann, M. (2004). The effect of "thin ideal" television commercials on body dissatisfaction and schema activation during early adolescence. *Journal of Youth and Adolescence, 32*, 367–373.

Harrison, K. (2003). Television viewers' ideal body proportions: The case of the curvaceously thin woman. *Sex Roles, 48*, 225–264. doi: 10.1023/A:1022825421647

Harrison, K., & Hefner, V. (2014). Virtually perfect: Image retouching and adolescent body image. *Media Psychology, 17*, 134–153.

Hawkins, M. A., & Nakayama, T. K. (1992). Discourse on women's bodies: Advertising in the 1920s. In L. A. M. Perry, L. H. Turner & H. M. Sterk (Eds.), *Constructing and reconstructing gender: The links among communication, language and gender*. Albany, NY: State University of New York Press.

Henderson-King, E., & Henderson-King, D. (1997). Media effects on women's body esteem: Social and individual difference factors. *Journal of Applied Social Psychology, 27*, 399–417.

Higgins, E. T. (1987). Self-discrepancy: A theory relating self and affect. *Psychological Review, 94*, 319–340.

Joshi, R., Herman, C. P., & Polivy, J. (2004). Self-enhancing effects of exposure to thin-body images. *International Journal of Eating Disorders, 35*, 333–341.

Karazsia, B. T., van Dulmen, M. H. M., Wong, K., & Crowther, J. H. (2013). Thinking meta-theoretically about the role of internalization in the development of body dissatisfaction and body change behaviours. *Body Image, 10*, 433–441. doi: 10.1016/j.bodyim.2013.06.005

Kasser, T., & Ryan, R. M. (1996). Further examining the American dream: Differential correlates of intrinsic and extrinsic goals. *Personality and Social Psychology Bulletin, 22*, 280–287. doi: 10.1177/0146167296223006

Kinsaul, J. A., Curtin, L., Bazzini, D., & Martz, D. (2014). Empowerment, feminism, and self-efficacy: Relationships to body image and disordered eating. *Body Image, 11*, 63–67.

Levine, M. P., & Murnen, S. K. (2009). "Everybody knows that mass media are/are not [pick one] a cause of eating disorders": A critical review of evidence for a causal link between media, negative body image, and disordered eating in females. *Journal of Social and Clinical Psychology, 28*, 9–42. doi: 10.1521/jscp.2009.28.1.9

Levine, M. P., & Smolak, L. (2008). "What exactly are we waiting for?" The case for universal-selective eating disorders prevention programs. *International Journal of Child and Adolescent Health, 1*, 295–304.

Li, E. P. H., Min, H. J., Belk, R. W., Kimura, J., & Bahl, S. (2008). Skin lightening and beauty in four Asian cultures. *Advances in Consumer Research, 35*, 444–449.

Mills, J. S., Polivy, J., Herman, C. P., & Tiggemann, M. (2002). Effects of exposure to thin media images: Evidence of self-enhancement among restrained eaters. *Personality and Social Psychology Bulletin, 28*, 1687–1699.

Myers, P. N., & Biocca, F. A. (1992). The elastic body image: The effect of television advertising and programming on body image distortions in young women. *Journal of Communication, 42*, 108–133.

Myers, T. A., & Crowther, J. H. (2007). Socio-cultural pressures, thin-ideal internalization, self-objectification, and body dissatisfaction: Could feminist beliefs be a moderating factor? *Body Image, 4*, 296–308.

Norton, K. I., Olds, T. S., Olive, S., & Dank, S. (1996). Ken and Barbie at life size. *Sex Roles, 34*, 287–294.

Our rising ad dosage: It's not as oppressive as some think (2007, February 15). *Media Matters, 1–2*. Retrieved from www.mediadynamicsinc.com

Paxton, S. J. (2015). Social policy and prevention. In M. Levine & L. Smolak (Eds.), *The Wiley-Blackwell handbook of eating disorders* (pp. 655–668). Chichester, UK: Wiley.

Perloff, R. M. (2014). Social media effects on young women's body image concerns: Theoretical perspectives and an agenda for research. *Sex Roles, 71*, 363–377.

Pope, H. F., Olivardia, R., Gruber, A., & Borowiecki, J. (1999). Evolving ideals of male body image as seen through action toys. *International Journal of Eating Disorders, 26*, 65–72.

Rader Programs (2012). *Media Influence*. Retrieved January 31, 2015, from www.raderprograms.com/causes-statistics/media-eating-disorders.html

Reaves, S., Hitchon, J. B., Park, S.-Y., & Yun, G. W. (2004). If looks could kill: Digital manipulation of fashion models. *Journal of Mass Media Ethics, 19*, 56–71.

Rehabs (n.d.). Body Image and BMI: 100 Years in the US. Retrieved on 13th July 2016 from www.rehabs.com/explore/womens-body-image-and-bmi.

Rehabs (2012). Dying to be Barbie: How the media makes women anorexia. Retrieved from www.rehabs.com/explore/dyingtobebarbie

Richins, M., & Dawson, S. (1992). A consumer values orientation for materialism and its measurement: Scale development and validation. *Journal of Consumer Research, 19*, 303–316.

Rodgers, R., Chabrol, H., & Paxton, S. J. (2011). An exploration of the tripartite influence model of body dissatisfaction and disordered eating among Australian and French college women. *Body Image, 8*, 208–215.

Rodin, J., Silberstein, L., & Striegel-Moore, R. (1984). Women and weight: A normative discontent. *Nebraska Symposium on Motivation, 32*, 267–307.

Schooler, D., & Daniels, E. A. (2014). "I am not a skinny toothpick and proud of it": Latina adolescents' ethnic identity and responses to mainstream media images. *Body Image, 11*, 11–18.

Shroff, H., & Thompson, J. K. (2004). Body image and eating disturbance in India: Media and interpersonal influences. *International Journal of Eating Disorders, 35*, 198–203.

Slater, A., Tiggemann, M., Firth, B., & Hawkins, K. (2012). Reality check: An experimental investigation of the addition of warning labels to fashion magazine images on women's mood and body dissatisfaction. *Journal of Social and Clinical Psychology, 31*, 105–122.

Stice, E. (1994). Review of the evidence for a socio-cultural model of bulimia nervosa: An explanation of the mechanisms of action. *Clinical Psychology Review, 14*, 633–661.

Stice, E., & Presnell, K. (2007). *The body project: Promoting body acceptance and preventing eating disorders* (Facilitator manual). New York, NY: Oxford University Press.

Stice, E., Shaw, H., & Marti, C. N. (2007). A meta-analytic review of eating disorder prevention programs: Encouraging findings. *Annual Review of Clinical Psychology, 3*, 207–231.

Stice, E., Spangler, D., & Agras, W. S. (2001). Exposure to media-portrayed thin-ideal images adversely affects vulnerable girls: A longitudinal experiment. *Journal of Social and Clinical Psychology, 20*, 271–289. doi: 10.1521/jscp.20.3.270.22309

Swami, V., Frederick, D. A., Aavik, T., Alcalay, L., Allik, J., Anderson, D., ... & Zivcic-Becirevic, I. (2010). The attractive female body weight and female body dissatisfaction in 26 countries across 10 world regions: Results of the International Body Project 1. *Personality and Social Psychology Bulletin, 36*, 309–325.

Thompson, J. K., Coovert, M., & Stormer, S. (1999). Body image, social comparison, and eating disturbance: A covariance structure modeling investigation. *International Journal of Eating Disorders, 26*, 43–51.

Thompson, K. J., & Stice, E. (2001). Thin-ideal internalization: Mounting evidence for a new risk factor for body-image disturbance and eating pathology. *Current Directions in Psychological Science, 10*, 181–183. doi: 10.1111/1467-8721.00144

Tiggemann, M. (2003). Media exposure, body dissatisfaction and disordered eating: Television and magazines are not the same! *European Eating Disorders Review, 11*, 418–430.

Tiggemann, M. (2011). Socio-cultural perspectives on human appearance and body image. In T. F. Cash & L. Smolak (Eds.), *Body image: A handbook of science, practice, and prevention* (2nd ed., pp. 12–19). New York, NY: Guilford Press.

Tiggemann, M., & Rüütel, E. (2004). A cross-cultural comparison of body dissatisfaction in Estonian and Australian young adults and its relationship with media exposure. *Journal of Cross-Cultural Psychology, 32*, 736–742.

Tiggemann, M., & Slater, A. (2014). NetTweens: The internet and body image concerns in preteenage girls. *The Journal of Early Adolescence, 34*, 606–620. doi: 10.1177/0272431613501083

Tiggemann, M., Slater, A., Bury, B., Hawkins, K., & Firth, B. (2013). Disclaimer labels on fashion magazine advertisements: Effects on social comparison and body dissatisfaction. *Body Image, 10*, 42–53.

Unilever (2015). Improving self-esteem. Retrieved from www.unilever.com/sustainable-living-2014/improving-health-and-wellbeing/health-and-hygiene/improving-self-esteem/

Van den Berg, P., Paxton, S. J., Keery, H., Wall, M., Guo, J., & Neumark-Sztainer, D. (2007). Body dissatisfaction and body comparison with media images in males and females. *Body Image, 4*, 257–268.

Walter, N. (2010). *Living dolls: The return of sexism*. London, UK: Hachette UK.

Want, S. (2009). Meta-analytic moderators of experimental exposure to media portrayals of women on female appearance satisfaction: Social comparisons as automatic processes. *Body Image, 6*(4), 257–269.

Wilksch, S. M., & Wade, T. D. (2009). Reduction of shape and weight concern in young adolescents: A 30-month controlled evaluation of a media literacy program. *Journal of the American Academy of Child and Adolescent Psychiatry, 48*, 652–661.

Wiseman, C. V., Sunday, S. R., & Becker, A. E. (2005). Impact of the media on adolescent body image. *Child and Adolescent Psychiatric Clinics of North America, 14*, 453–471. doi: 10.1016/j.chc.2005.02.008

Wood, J. V. (1989). Theory and research concerning social comparisons of personal attributes. *Psychological Bulletin, 106*, 231–248.

Yager, Z., Diedrichs, P. C., Ricciardelli, L. A., & Halliwell, E. (2013). What works in secondary schools? A systematic review of classroom-based body image programs. *Body Image, 10*, 271–281.

14
The psychology of healthy eating

Lara Spiteri-Cornish

Eating should be a normal, pleasurable thing to do and human beings were designed to find pleasure in food (de Ridder, 2012). Yet nowadays, eating has become a complicated activity, with many people afraid of eating too much, too little or not healthily enough. Indeed, in developed societies healthy eating has increasing focus as a major determinant of population health and longevity. Dietary behaviours are associated with the serious health costs of heart disease, osteoporosis and other serious illnesses and obesity is a main area of concern in healthy eating discourse (Brug, 2008; Eldridge & Murcott, 2000; Wiggins, 2004). Over the past decade there has been a dramatic rise in obesity in the developed and, increasingly, in the developing world (Finkelstein et al., 2012; Stevens et al., 2012). Indeed, the World Health Organization attests that in the past 30 years not a single country has made serious progress in the fight against obesity, and while in 1980, 857 million people worldwide were overweight or obese, by 2013 that number had more than doubled. Today, it is estimated that nearly one-third of all living people, i.e., 2.1 billion, are either overweight or obese (World Health Organization, 2014). The increase in obesity numbers spearheaded a number of interventionist public policies and healthy eating campaigns in many industrialized countries, aiming to increase consumer awareness of the importance of eating healthily (Andreasen, 2011; Centers for Disease Control and Prevention, 2014; Department of Health, 2009). Yet dietary patterns have not improved. In the United States, for example, the Produce for Better Health Foundation (2009) found that fruit and vegetable consumption dropped by 12 per cent and 6 per cent, respectively, when compared with the previous year. The World Health Organization estimates that in more than half of European countries the individual consumption of fruits and vegetables is lower than 400g per day, and in one-third of such countries the average individual intake is less than 300g per day (European Food Information Council, 2012). The European Food Safety Authority's analysis based on national dietary surveys suggests that the recommended amount is reached in only four of the participating 11 EU Member States (European Food Information Council, 2012). In the United Kingdom, there is a significant upward trend in household expenditure on eggs, butter, beverages, sugar and preserves (National Health Service Information Centre, 2012), yet purchases of fruits and vegetables are now respectively 11.6 per cent and 9.6 per cent lower than in 2007 (National Health Service Information Centre, 2012).

For many years, obesity has been formally considered to be the most serious health issue facing the developed world (World Health Organization, 2000) and this in turn has focused attention on the role of food in society, with an emphasis on how to encourage healthier eating habits. Healthy eating can be defined as those eating behaviours that enable a person to achieve a state of complete physical, mental and social well-being, and not merely the absence of disease or infirmity (World Health Organization, 2007). The best health outcomes are associated with balanced dietary patterns that boast high intakes of fruits, vegetables and grains, not just eating or avoiding a single food (Nestle, 2007; Wansink, 2007). While this definition seems clear-cut, in the last few years the notion of healthy eating has become more ambiguous for a number of reasons. First, nutritional science is constantly evolving and increasing in complexity, and the definition of healthy foods now incorporates more elements than ever before, e.g., not just the amount of fat but the *type* of fat (Paquette, 2005). Second, the rise of nutritionism, whereby "food = nutrients = health" (Block et al., 2011, p. 5), has shifted the focus from base food products to their nutritive components (Pollan, 2009). This encourages consumers to focus more on consuming nutrients than where these nutrients come from, which in turn might result in flawed perceptions of the healthiness of foods (Spiteri-Cornish, 2012). Finally, many stakeholders in food consumption and/or population health regularly present their own views of what healthy eating behaviour should look like (Andreasen, 2011; Block et al., 2011; Lahteenmaki, 2003; Nestle, 2007; Pollan, 2009). Governments, non-governmental organizations, doctors, food manufacturers and retailers, chefs, nutritionists and a variety of other individuals and groups bombard consumers with information about the "correct" eating habits, the healthiest foods to eat and those to avoid, and the latest scientific fad or celebrity diet. This mostly results in a large majority of people feeling overwhelmed, confused and potentially discouraged by the ever-increasing amount of conflicting dietary advice (Fitzgibbon et al., 2007; Grunert et al., 2012; Mitchell, Walsh, & Yami, 2005).

Within this context of complexity, people must gather food and nutrition information from a multitude of sources, give it meaning and decide on its usefulness and applicability in their daily life (Paquette, 2005). This is extremely challenging because food choice and other dietary decisions are the result of an intricate interplay between people's psychological make-up and their physical, social and cultural environment. Theories of health behaviour attest that the likelihood that people will engage in healthy eating is greatest when they are motivated to act healthily, when they have the ability to do so and when their social and physical environment offers the right opportunities for engaging in the healthy behaviour (Brug et al., 2008). However this does not reflect most people's lives, especially those living in an industrialized and increasingly obesogenic environment.

Psychological underpinnings of healthy eating

Challenges and barriers to healthy eating

Motives to eat healthily can be categorized as either intrinsic, i.e., related to rewards that are internal to the individual, such as health optimization, or extrinsic, i.e., related to external rewards or punishment, such as approval or disapproval of others (Deci & Ryan, 2000). Extant research shows that both intrinsic and extrinsic motives impact on healthy eating intention and behaviour, yet it is evident that many people struggle with embarking on or maintaining a healthy eating regime. There are a number of reasons why engaging in healthy eating is exceedingly difficult for so many people. First, individuals' daily eating behaviour is often habitual and guided by default choices (Roberto & Kawachi, 2014). Habits are routine repetitions of behaviours prompted by environmental stimuli rather than personal goals or intentions, and breaking such automatic routines requires intense monitoring and self-regulation, both of which are effortful and demanding (Baumeister, Muraven, & Tice, 2000; Wood, Quinn, & Kashy, 2002). Second, in daily life people have a strong tendency to stay with default options, a phenomenon known as the "status quo bias" (Samuelson & Zeckhauser, 1988). Unfortunately, the vast majority of food defaults in most industrialized environments encourage unhealthy eating. A notable exception to this is the Netherlands, which in 2014 was judged to be the best country for its eating habits, with a low prevalence of diabetes and better nutritional diversity than its European rivals (Oxfam, 2014). France, Switzerland, Austria, Belgium, Denmark and Sweden are also considered to have healthier eating habits and consequently less diet-related illnesses than other wealthy developed countries, such as the United States and the United Kingdom (Oxfam, 2014; World Health Organization, 2014). These countries have high levels of obesity, generally unhealthy eating habits and food defaults that encourage overconsumption. Restaurant defaults, for example, often comprise large portion sizes and unhealthy side dishes, and frequently require those who want healthier options to request a substitute. This, however, is something that status quo bias discourages, which results in most people engaging in unhealthy eating behaviour. Default options are also influential because they shape food norms. Consistently large portion sizes, for example, convey that this is the norm, and when faced with *normal* portion sizes many people seek out more food in order to feel satisfied. Next, eating constitutes an immediate and intense gratification, while weight loss and good health are more distant rewards. This makes the self-regulation needed to resist the temptation of immediate gratification in favour of future outcomes much harder for many people (Baumeister, Bushman, & Campbell, 2000; Mischel, Cantor, & Feldman, 1996). This sense of gratification has been deemed responsible for emotional eating, whereby people indulge in energy-dense foods as a means to regulate their mood. Indeed, negative emotions have often been linked with obesogenic behaviours, which led to the development of the Emotional Eating Scale (EES) with subscales of Anger/Frustration, Anxiety and Depression (Arnow, Kenardy, & Agras, 1995). All three subscales correlated highly with measures of overconsumption of unhealthy foods, and researchers believe that for some people emotions might precipitate unhealthy eating. Stress also appears to alter overall food intake and chronic life stresses have been associated with a greater preference for energy and nutrient-dense foods, namely those that are high in sugar and fat (Torres & Nowson, 2007). Indeed, research suggests that chronic life stress may be causally linked to weight gain, and stress-induced eating may be one factor contributing to the development of obesity (Oliver, Wardle, & Gibson, 2000; Schiffman, Graham, Sattely-Miller, & Peterson-Dancy, 2000).

Finally, central to much work about obesity is the concept of self-control or self-regulation. The self is viewed as the instrument responsible for regulating an individual's activities and is often called on to suppress impulses or desires that contravene long-term goals (Baumeister, Bratslavsky, Muraven, & Tice, 1998). Extant research on self-regulation focuses on people's ability to monitor and modify behaviour, thoughts and affect in order to achieve these goals and is relevant in issues of achievement, intrinsic motivation, autonomy, self-determination and cognitive strategies in goal implementation (Efklides, Niemivirta, & Yamauchi, 2002). In such research there is a contentious area, which is the relationship between self- regulation and self-control. One distinction made by Baumeister et al. (1998) is that "some internal resource is used by the self to make decisions, respond actively, and exert self-control" (p. 1263). In this way, self-regulation can be viewed as the broader term (the internal resource), including self-control as well as active responding and decision making. In this same article, however, and in many others, self-control and self-regulation are often used interchangeably, with no clear distinction between them, and both are often viewed as "the self's capacity to alter its own states and responses" (Baumeister & Mick, 2002, pp. 670–671). Self-control is regarded as having many positive effects on health-related outcomes, such as increased levels of healthy eating, less binge eating, reduced alcohol consumption and more physical exercise (de Ridder, Lensvelt-Mulders, Finkenauer, Stok, & Baumeister, 2012; Wills, Isasi, Mendoza, & Ainette, 2007). In contrast, low self-control is linked with adverse consequences such as overindulgence in alcohol and consumption of sugary and fatty foods (de Ridder et al., 2012; Friese & Hofmann, 2009).

Attempting to understand why individuals fail to engage their self-control when this would help them achieve their goals has been the subject of much research. According to the *strength model*, also known as the *ego-strength model* or *resource model*, self-control functions like a muscle that fatigues after use and then requires rest. The strength model postulates that repeated acts of self-control, whether cognitive, emotional or behavioural, use up the limited supply, leaving people vulnerable to impulses which might contravene their goals (Baumeister et al., 2000). It is now accepted in scholarly discourse that self-control is a finite resource that is easily exhausted, creating a state of ego-depletion that makes effortful and reflective planning extremely difficult (Muraven, Tice, & Baumeister, 1998). From a healthy eating perspective, being in this state is problematic on two levels. First, when ego-depleted, people are likely to resort to non-reflective, impulsive decision-making strategies such as opting for unhealthier food choices or overeating. In addition, resource depletion has also been demonstrated to heighten sensitivity to immediate and concrete environmental influences, such as tempting energy-dense foods and other situational cues (Bruyneel, Dewitte, Vohs, & Warlop, 2006; Hofmann, Strack, & Deutsch, 2008). The strength model of self-control has been the foundation for many healthy-eating communications aiming to foster increased levels of self-control and consequently help people make healthier food choices. Yet, such efforts have met with very little success because most consumption choices are made under mindless conditions, when self-control is low habitually (Herman & Polivy, 2011; Wansink & Sobal, 2007). This concerns researchers, yet Salmon, Fennis, de Ridder, Adriaanse, & de Vet (2014) believe that low levels of self-control do not necessarily imply unhealthy food choices. The authors attest that under conditions of low self-control, people are inclined to apply impulsive decision-making strategies, such as relying on heuristics, i.e., simple decision rules that are assumed to save self-control resources by excluding part of the information (Fennis, Janssen, & Vohs, 2009; Gigerenzer & Gaissmaier, 2011; Shah & Oppenheimer, 2008). Salmon et al. (2014) believe that if people in low self-control states are primed with an influence heuristic, such as a social proof heuristic, the impact of self-control on food choice can be reversed. Regrettably, this is not a straightforward solution to unhealthy eating, as it assumes that if people were in a high self-control condition they would decide upon healthy options, which is not always the case. Indeed, people make unhealthy food choices even in high self-control conditions, which suggests that self-control is not enough to encourage healthy eating habits in the population.

Healthy eating as a goal

To counteract the problems that people have with eating healthily and encourage behaviour change, stakeholders in health and well-being regularly engage in education campaigns, offering dietary knowledge and information. Yet knowledge alone is normally insufficient for inspiring behaviour change, and converting healthy eating intentions into action is particularly difficult in light of the underlying complexities of eating behaviour (Brug, Oenema, & Ferreira 2005; Doval, 2013). Fewer than a quarter of people who embark on a healthy eating plan still follow it a year later, and around half of those with healthy eating intentions fail to act on them at all (Flay & Petraitis, 1994). People's motivation to eat healthily ebbs and flows, and many experience great difficulty in attempting to achieve their healthy eating goals. This raises questions regarding how motivation translates into action. Motivation is an important prerequisite for changing behaviour and has been central to much research about healthy eating. Deci and Ryan (2000), for example, discovered that the *reasons* behind embarking on health-related goals are central to their success, and that those who adopt goals for the wrong reasons (e.g., "to please others" versus "to be healthier and live longer") are vulnerable to giving up on them. Keatley, Clarke and Hagger (2013) elaborate on this by examining in what way implicit and explicit measures of motivation predict eating behaviour and demonstrate that healthy eating is not an activity that people are naturally inclined to do but needs to be deliberated. They discovered that while people may adopt a health goal on an explicit level (and even genuinely believe that this is what they really want), implicit measures of motivation may reveal different preferences (e.g., a preference for chocolate), and it is these preferences that usually have the most impact on behaviour.

People often experience a desire to improve their dietary habits, but if they are not really committed to their goal they are unlikely to succeed. In committing to any goal, mentally contrasting a desired future with negative reality enhances action and potential future success. In their seminal study, Johannessen, Oettingen and Mayer (2012) showed how mental contrasting can be sufficient to decrease individuals' overall caloric intake and especially their intake from unhealthy foods. They also demonstrated that the effects of contemplating healthy eating also translated to physical activity, which could be a motivation spill-over effect. The concept of health goals was also studied by Freund and Hennecke (2012), who examined the role of goal focus in weight-watching women. The results revealed that a focus on the outcome of dieting ("how much weight loss will I achieve?") had a negative impact on dieting behaviour (less weight loss and more disinhibition after lapses), whereas a focus on the process of dieting ("how will I manage my eating behaviours?") proved beneficial in terms of both actual weight loss and continued adherence to the diet. Thus, a sole focus on the desired outcome of behaviour change may interfere with the motivation needed for the difficult process of engaging in outcome-related actions.

The volitional part of behaviour change should not be underestimated, because it is evident that lack of reflection on the actual strategies to be employed for goal attainment increases the risk of failure. Conversely, having a detailed plan of action regarding how dietary changes are to be accomplished requires effort, and an emerging theme in the healthy eating research relates precisely to impact of actual or perceived exerted effort on behaviour (de Witt Huberts, Evers, & De Ridder, 2012). For example, it has been demonstrated that people who engage in health-goals-related activities often reward themselves by cheating a little on these goals. Indeed, Radtke, Scholz, Keller, Knäuper, & Hornung (2011a) and Radtke, Scholz, Keller, & Hornung (2011b) showed that compensatory health beliefs, or beliefs that the negative consequences of unhealthy behaviours can be compensated for by engaging in healthy behaviours ("Smoking is okay as long as I eat healthily"), often emerge as a result of the pressure of behaving healthily. The role of compensatory health beliefs in health-related behaviours has been studied by a number of researchers. These are defined as beliefs that the negative consequences of unhealthy behaviours can be compensated for by engaging in healthy behaviours (Radtke et al., 2011a, b). In a Danish study, compensatory behaviour, in the form of physical inactivity, was observed following vigorous exercise (Rosenkilde et al., 2012). In food-related scenarios, compensatory behaviour might be displayed in the form of indulging in low-fat foods, or overeating as a response to exercising (Church et al., 2009). Yet this type of behaviour does not work in reverse, and Church et al. found that people who overeat do not compensate by eating less at dinner, making this psychological bias harmful to health goals. Another challenge to reaching healthy eating goals is the so-called "peanuts effect" (Roberto & Kawachi, 2014). This is the tendency to discount very small individual losses and fail to consider the cumulative effect of multiple losses (Downs & Loewenstein, 2011). For example, when smaller-sized portions (e.g., 100-calorie packets) of popular foods were introduced in the market, Scott, Nowlis, Mandel, & Morales (2008) found that while these packets work well for non-dieters, for restrained eaters (most likely to purchase these products) these small packages, or *mere peanuts*, led to greater overall consumption. A related phenomenon is the *what the hell* effect, whereby restrained eaters who consume an unhealthy food while dieting decide that they may as well keep eating as they have already failed in their goal-related behaviour (Cochran & Tesser, 1996).

Notable health behaviour theories, such as Protection Motivation Theory, Theory of Planned Behaviour and Social Cognitive Theory, identify intention, regarded as the consequence of motivation, as the most proximal determinant of behaviour (Ajzen, 1991; Bandura, 1993; Bargh & Chartrand, 1999; Brug et al., 2005; Rothschild, 1999). Considering the insights of these major theories synergistically, three groups of determinants that predict intention emerge, namely attitudes, self-representation and self-efficacy (Armitage & Conner, 2000; Bestwick et al., 2013; Downs, Loewenstein, & Wisdom, 2009; Magnusson, 2010). Attitudes are based on subjective evaluations of expected positive and negative outcomes of behaviour. For many people, short-term outcomes often become more important than longer-term outcomes, and in eating behaviour two outcomes have a major impact on consumer attitudes and consequent dietary behaviour (Birch, 1999). Taste, satiety and pleasure are short-term outcomes of eating and are considered of foremost importance by most people. People tend to eat what they like and avoid foods they dislike, biologically preferring sweet and salty over other taste sensations (Capaldi, 1996). Learning theories suggest that taste preferences can be learned and unlearned and that people learn to like foods high in fat and sugar, i.e., taste-nutrient learning, when these foods are offered as rewards or consumed during pleasant circumstances. Research in food choice shows that food aesthetics, i.e., taste, texture, appearance and smell, are powerful physical reinforcers of food choice and that most consumers prefer the aesthetics of unhealthy foods (e.g., chocolate and biscuits) to those of healthy foods (e.g., fruits and vegetables) (Birch, 1999; Lahteenmaki, 2003; Nestle, 2007; Stevenson, Doherty, Barnett, Muldoon, & Trew, 2007). A second category of outcome expectations is health, which is also considered to be fundamental by most people (Lennernäs et al., 1997). Yet, in a large-scale study conducted by HealthFocus, 40 per cent of Americans and 57 per cent of Europeans attested that they rarely or never compromised on taste to improve the healthfulness of their diets (HealthFocus, 2005). Furthermore, health expectations appear to influence food choice only when health consequences are expected to be soon, severe and easily recognizable or evident (Capaldi, 1996). Energy-dense foods provide a comfortable feeling of satiety, and beliefs about the potentially negative health consequences of eating such foods often do not have a strong impact on food choice (Birch, 1999). In recent decades consumers have developed a sense of entitlement that encourages them to demand foods that are both nutritious *and* appetising, and few are willing to sacrifice one for the other (Bhaskaran & Hardley, 2002).

Self-representations or self-schemas reflect stable characteristics of the self, i.e., the values and norms people adhere to and what they perceive to be important (Conner & Armitage, 2002). Self-schemas describe the extent to which people find certain behaviours relevant to their self-image, and people with a healthy eating self-schema (people who consider themselves as a typical fruit and vegetable eater) consider healthy eating important and typical of them (Conner & Norman, 1998). Conversely, individuals who do not possess a healthy eating schematic will perceive healthy eating as outside their norm and are unlikely to engage in it.

Interestingly, however, Allom and Mullan (2012) found that while people with healthy eating self-schemas experienced more benefit from their self-regulation ability as they ate more fruits and vegetables when they intended to do so, people without a healthy eating schema ate more fruits and vegetables when they had superior self-regulation ability or when they had the habit of doing so. This suggests it is possible to compensate for not having a healthy eating self-schema by developing healthy eating habits or investing effort in self-regulation. However, the ability to self-regulate is linked with self-efficacy and some people might find this exceptionally challenging.

Self-efficacy, or perceived behavioural control, refers to the perception of, or confidence in, one's abilities and skills to engage in certain behaviours (Bandura, 2012; Conner & Armitage, 2002). People who are confident that they can decrease their intake of processed foods and eat more fruits and vegetables, for example, will be more motivated to do so even when faced with barriers (e.g., in an obesogenic environment) (Lubans et al., 2012). Self-efficacy is behaviour and context specific, however, and while some people feel confident in their ability to eat healthily in certain contexts, e.g., at home, they might feel less able to control themselves in others, e.g., at social functions (Brug, 2008). Furthermore, personal abilities and skills are likely to influence individual self-efficacy. People who have the ability to assemble a comprehensive understanding of the behaviours they want to engage in are more likely to successfully translate their motivation into action (Conner & Armitage, 2002). Indeed, many believe that an in-depth knowledge of the nature of food and nutrition, recommended dietary intake and healthy alternatives to calorific choices is a precursor to positive dietary changes and adherence to such changes. However, others contest this and attest that knowledge, while necessary, is not by itself a sufficient prerequisite for healthy eating behaviour (Brug, 2008). Another skill that heightens people's self-efficacy is their ability for self-assessment, or in the case of healthy eating, their ability to accurately assess their level of food intake, determined by their choice of food, portion size, cooking method etc. Some people are unable to undertake accurate self-assessment and instead engage in social comparative behaviour, comparing their food intake with their perceptions of what other people consume. However, during such social comparisons, many people often fall prey to the optimistic bias, often believing that they already comply with dietary recommendations even when they do not, thus eliminating any motivation to change (Bogers, Brug, van Assema, & Dagnelie, 2004; Giskes et al., 2007a). Furthermore, people are vulnerable to the planning fallacy, or the tendency to be overly optimistic about their ability to act in accordance with their goals at a later stage, e.g., to begin an exercise regimen the day after they overeat. In fact, many of these plans fail to result in any long-lasting behavioural changes.

While an emphasis upon individual aspects such as self-schemas, self-efficacy and self-regulation abounds in obesity literature, many scholars argue that the focus of such studies should shift to the environment itself, as this is only one of the main driving forces behind many unhealthy eating habits (Booth et al., 2001; Duncan, Spence, & Mummery, 2005; Kremers et al., 2006).

The obesogenic environment and eating behaviour

Ecological models of health behaviour emphasize a number of environmental factors in shaping unhealthy eating patterns (Sallis & Owen, 2003). These include social environmental influences (inter-individual influences), physical environmental influences (influences within community settings) and macro-system influences (influences at the societal level) (Story, Neumark-Sztainer, & French, 2002). Swinburn, Egger and Raza (1999) developed a matrix to help investigate obesogenic environments, i.e., environments that promote excess food consumption and sedentary lifestyles. The ANGELO (Analysis Grid for Environments Linked to

Obesity) matrix was a way of linking different classes of environmental influences with obesity and distinguished between micro- and macro-environments. Microenvironments, or those settings in which individuals meet and gather, offer opportunities for direct interaction with the environment, e.g., homes, schools, offices, supermarkets, eateries, other recreational facilities and neighbourhoods. Macro-environments encompass the more anonymous infrastructure that may encourage or discourage overeating, such as food and nutrition policies, food distribution, marketing and labelling (Swinburn et al., 1999). The matrix also distinguishes four "types" of environments. The physical environment deals with the availability of opportunities for healthy and unhealthy choices, such as points-of-purchase for different foods, and availability of healthy food options in school or work cafeterias. The economic environment denotes the costs related to healthy and unhealthy eating. The political environment signifies the rules and regulations that may influence food choice and eating behaviour (e.g., bans on vending machines in schools; calorie counts on restaurant menus). The socio-cultural environment refers to the social and cultural subjective and descriptive norms and other social influences such as social support for the adoption of health behaviour or social pressure to engage in unhealthy habits. This framework has been found useful for categorizing different environmental influences on nutrition or other health behaviours and working with communities to prioritize activities for interventions that address obesity (Swinburn et al., 1999). This framework was also adapted for use by policy makers at national level in Europe to prioritize strategies for effective food and nutrition initiatives (World Health Organization, 2012), highlighting the central role of an increasingly obesogenic environment in unhealthy eating behaviour.

Obesity and the physical environment

Social cognitive theories explicitly highlight the interaction between the individual and the environment in predicting health behaviour (Armitage & Conner, 2000). Health theories hypothesize that individuals' health behaviours are determined by their motivation and abilities, which need to be stronger in an environment that does not facilitate healthy eating (Rothschild, 1999). When obesity researchers shifted their attention from the psychological underpinnings of overeating or unhealthy eating to the role of the environment in obesity rates, the physical environment took central stage. One of the chief issues to be examined was whether consumer access to healthy versus unhealthy food was the underlying factor behind obesity. Different studies turned up conflicting results. In the United States, for example, an increase in the number of supermarkets (with their larger variety of healthy foods) was shown to be linked with an increase in fruit and vegetable consumption and a lower prevalence of obesity (Morland, Diez Roux, & Wing, 2006; Morland, Wing, & Diez Roux, 2002). Other investigations, however, such as the Brisbane Food Study or the Socioeconomic Status and Activity in Women Study, both conducted in Australia, found that the availability of healthy foods is not related to actual food-purchasing behaviour (Giskes et al., 2007b; Ball, Timperio, Giles-Corti, Roberts, & Crawford, 2007). This lack of association makes sense because the majority of individuals living in countries where obesity levels are high often have sufficient access to healthy foods. This led to another shift in focus regarding underlying causes of obesity, implicitly or explicitly highlighting the overabundant availability and accessibility of processed, unhealthy foods as the cause of overeating (Giskes et al., 2007a).

> Food processing is a fundamental aspect of human culture and industrial methods are needed to supply the nourishment of a world population now exceeding 7 billion people. The current problem is that an unhealthy dietary pattern has been created based on a manufactured,

> durable, highly palatable diet, aggressively presented on the market, ready to eat or by simple heating, composed of highly processed, cheap ingredients and additives.
>
> (Doval, 2013, p. 519)

Chandon and Wansink (2012) claim that in many developed countries, convenient, ready-to-eat food is ubiquitous, in grocery stores and coffee shops, in petrol stations, pharmacies, places of work, schools and even hospitals. Swinburn et al. (2011) believe that this type of food distribution explains, at least partially, why the total intake of calories has increased to around 3,900 kcal per person per day in the United States and between 3,400 and 3,600 kcal in other wealthy countries; the exception to this being Japan, where food intake is only 2,700 kcal per person and levels of obesity are still comparatively low. With rising income levels and global expansion of food retailing, consumption patterns, as measured by spending on different types of food products, appear to be converging across many countries worldwide (Regmi, Takeshima, & Unnerverhrm, 2008). Food products and multinational food retail franchises from the United States and other high-income countries have become increasingly common in middle-income nations such as China and Thailand, leading to a change in consumption patterns. In China, for example, fast-food sales have more than doubled between 1999 and 2005, while sales from Western-style supermarkets increased from $16 to $91 billion during the same period (Regmi & Seale, 2000). Changes in food preferences and food delivery mechanisms appear to be mutually enforcing, with worldwide tastes and diets evolving along with increasingly modern food retailing and food outlets. Researchers believe that the convergence of global eating patterns is characterized by two phases: The first refers to an increase of caloric intake resulting from an increase in overall food consumption, while the second phase, or "diet transition", sees a change in diet structure whereby consumption of cereals and vegetables decreases while that of sugar, fats, and animal and processed food products increases. While developed countries achieved this second step over a century ago, many emerging and developing countries in Asia, Central and Latin America, and to a lesser extent in Africa are following a similar pattern but at an accelerated pace, as the diet transition is reduced to 20 years in emerging countries and 40 years in developing countries (Guyomard et al., 2011; Regmi & Seale, 2010).

The converging, modern eating environment concerns many researchers in psychology, sociology, philosophy and medicine. The unrestricted access to tasty, convenient and cheap foods is seen to be the major contributor to the global growth of the obesity problem (Armitage & Conner, 2000; Brug, 2008; Brug et al., 2005; Loewenstein & O'Donoghue, 2002; de Ridder, 2014). Indulging in calorie-dense foods has become so easy that it challenges many people's ability to control their food consumption to breaking point (de Ridder, 2014). This is exacerbated by the fact that energy-dense and energy-rich foods "strongly appeal to our innate and early acquired preferences for sweet, fat and salty" (Brug et al., 2005, p. 51) and that people are biologically programmed to eat when food is plentiful (Brug, 2008). People are also susceptible to present-bias, whereby they place disproportionate emphasis on momentary gratification relative to future consequences (Frederick, Loewenstein, & O'Donoghue, 2002; O'Donoghue & Rabin, 2000). An environment where unhealthy, tasty food is readily and consistently available heightens the strength of this bias and encourages people to focus on the immediate enjoyment of the food, rather than the delayed health costs associated with eating it. The modern obesogenic environment thus places a very high burden on individual decision making in the midst of plenty. This creates scenarios where consumers need to constantly consider their motivations for health goals and their ability to regulate their impulses and resist social influences (de Ridder, 2014). This is relevant not only to those people considered to be overweight or obese but to everyone who is attempting to control food intake to enhance health and well-being.

The push and pull of healthy eating

People have "become increasingly obese while obsessing over fat, calories, and body mass index" (Block et al., 2011, p. 2). People are more conscious than ever of the link between food and health, and fixating on the calorific content of food is not only commonplace but also part of everyday social discourse. Consumer interest in calorie counting and analysis of food content is the end result of many pushes and pulls, and a response to multiple forces that create an overall nutrition environment. In the past, academic discourse has assisted the development of interventional public policies (Andreasen, 2011), along with a number of healthy eating campaigns (e.g., "Eat4Life" and "5-a-Day Campaign" in the United Kingdom). However, concerns have been raised that such communications do not fit in with lay models of healthy eating (Ikeda, 1999; Lupton & Chapman, 1995). Consequently, within psychological research there has been increased interest in the *meanings* that people ascribe to healthy eating, aiming to determine how they perceive it and how important it is for them (Dixey, 1998). Underlying such areas of research is disquiet with how healthy eating is defined and communicated, and how this is understood and put into practice by consumers. Healthy eating campaigns often focus on nutrients linked with health problems (e.g., cholesterol; saturated fats) rather than whole foods, yet consumers buy and eat *foods* and must be able to translate recommendations about nutrients into how best to purchase foods (Marks, Murray Evans, & Willig, 2000; Nestle, 2007; Pollan, 2009; Spiteri Cornish, 2012). Another concern about healthy eating communications deals with the fact that little is known about psychological and behavioural responses to healthy eating campaigns (Spiteri Cornish & Moraes, 2015). Research demonstrates that consumers are likely to experience anxiety and a desire to adopt healthy eating patterns as a result of frequent exposure to healthy eating communications (Brennan & Binney, 2010; Bublitz, Peracchio, & Block, 2010; Cho & Salmon, 2006; Festinger, 1957; Henley, Donovan, & Moorhead, 1998). Yet, while health campaigns manage to successfully raise awareness of the importance of healthy eating, the nutrition information that they offer is perceived by many as inconsistent, incomplete, confusing and contradictory across socio-demographic variables (Dallongeville, Marécaux, Cottel, Bingham, & Amouyel, 2001; Grunert et al., 2012; Handu, Monty, & Chmel, 2008; Lee, Lee, Chang, & Kim, 2009). Spiteri-Cornish and Moraes (2015) demonstrate that many consumers do respond to health communications by striving to eat healthily, but inadequate nutrition information derived from unreliable sources, flawed baseline nutrition knowledge and poor nutrition literacy hinder their efforts. Inconsistent, incomplete and contradictory information leaves many participants feeling confused about how to implement healthy eating habits (Mitchell et al., 2005; Scammon et al., 2011). Further, a lack of ability to differentiate between credible and unreliable sources of nutrition information means that many individuals blame their confusion on policy makers, and express frustration and cynicism towards vague and often contradictory communications. This in turn increases participants' reliance on food adverts, product labels and other commercial sources of ambiguous yet appealing information (Briggs, 2006; Hastak & Mazis, 2011).

Other initiatives to encourage consumers to eat more healthily involved compelling the food industry to design a food labelling system, providing calorie and nutrient information to consumers. However, evidence suggests that calorie labelling does not have the desired effect of significantly reducing the purchase or consumption of calories (Swartz, Braxton, & Viera, 2011). Indeed, labels providing nutrient information designed by various food industries lead to consumer confusion because they highlight those nutrients that the industry wants consumers to focus on, use a variety of often conflicting signals, and modify the list of nutrients according to current company strategies (Doval, 2013). Furthermore, the concept of the recommended daily allowance for calories, fat, salt and sugar is not easy to communicate or understand, considering that consumers examine food packaging for mere seconds before making a decision (Brownell & Joplan, 2011). Brownell and Joplan believe that a few "front-of-package" labels, such as the "traffic lights" system, do successfully simplify food choice for consumers, enabling them to know the nutritional value and risk associated with the product with a quick and easy look. Yet the food industry lobbied hard against it, especially with regard to the use of the red light, claiming nothing is too high in food. The traffic lights approach has been hailed by many as a tool with the ability to motivate manufacturers to reformulate their products to reduce red light qualifications, thus improving the overall quality of health food offerings. However, manufacturers have found ways to side-step this by including certain claims on food packing, such as "low-fat", "healthy living" etc., which contravene the impact of even the most effective of labelling systems. Ebneter, Latner and Nigg (2013), for example, found that people underestimate the calorie content of foods that are labelled "low-fat", hence buying and consuming more of them. In addition, these foods are also perceived as healthier than regular-labelled versions of the same food, making "low-fat" labelling a more powerful determinant of health attributions than caloric information.

This type of "health halo" effect is regularly seen among products that contain health claims (Chandon & Wansink, 2007). Indeed, the pull from policy makers to educate people about healthy food and encourage them to read labels resulted in a push response by the food industry in the form of many foods marketed as healthier or healthy in order to convey a better fit with the new healthy eating paradigm, without necessarily being healthier than the alternatives (Kleinschmidt, 2003; Lahteenmaki, 2003; Menrad, 2003; Wansink, 2007). Brownell and Joplan (2011) attest that many manufacturers are free to fortify foods with questionable nutritional value in order to create more positive labels. A category of foods that exemplifies this is functional (i.e., fortified, enhanced) foods (Heasman & Mellentin, 2001; Kleinschmidt, 2003; Lahteenmaki, 2003). The commercially oriented health credentials of these foods (e.g., chocolate cereal with added fibre, white bread with added omega-3, sweets with added vitamins) lead many consumers to believe that they are healthy alternatives to high-calorie, unhealthy foods, even though this is rarely the case (Menrad, 2003; Wansink, 2007). This, in turn, may also result in a health halo effect (Chandon & Wansink, 2007), whereby consumers overestimate the health benefits of these foods and underestimate their calories, fat and sugar content. This highlights the fact that consumers often look to the wrong "experts", such as food manufacturers, for nutrition information. Such information may then be internalized, shaping how future nutrition information is interpreted, eventually resulting in a low correlation between subjective and objective nutrition knowledge and leading to flawed dietary decisions (Mattila & Wirtz, 2002).

Obesity and the social environment

Food socialization, or the processes consumers use to learn about food, starts during childhood, and the family is generally the most important means of socialization, providing information, pressure to conform and support (Moore, Wilkie, & Lutz, 2002). Food socialization may occur via explicit, e.g., parents restricting consumption of particular foods, or implicit means, e.g., mimicking the behaviours of others (Moschis, 1985). Research highlights the pivotal role of parents in the development of optimal and suboptimal eating habits. For example, evidence shows that parents' mere presence leads children to make healthier choices for lunch, highlighting the importance of the family meal to the food socialization process (Klesges, Stein, Eck, Isbell, & Klesges, 1991). Indeed, researchers have found positive relationships between frequency of family meals and children eating healthier foods (Videon & Manning, 2003). Other studies focused more exclusively on the link between parenting style and children's eating habits. A study conducted in the Netherlands found that parental encouragement and modelling are stronger correlates of food consumption than food availability (de Bourdeaudhuij et al., 2007; Rasmussen et al., 2006; Wind et al., 2006). In relation to parenting as a socio-cultural environmental factor, there are distinct differences between general parenting styles and content-specific acts of parenting (Brug, Kremers, Lenthe, Ball, & Crawford, 2008). For example, previous research has shown that there are several child feeding practices (e.g., encouraging children to eat beyond satiety, using food as a reward) that lead to an increased risk of childhood obesity. Two recent Dutch studies among adolescents have shown that more restrictive or authoritative parenting practices are associated with lower consumption of sugary drinks and higher fruit consumption when compared with other parenting styles (de Bruijn, Kremers, de Vries, van Mechelen, & Brug, 2007; van der Horst, Kremers, Ferreira, Singh, & Brug, 2007). However, other studies show more troubling results. Brown and Ogden (2004), for example, demonstrate that children whose parents exert higher levels of control reported higher levels of unhealthy eating relative to children whose parents exerted less control. Similarly, Rhee et al. (2006) determined that children residing in a food-restrictive environment have an increased risk of being overweight, especially when the restrictiveness is not coupled with warmth and affection. Evidence also suggests that an indulgent parenting style might contribute to undesirable long-term effects on obesity in children (Olvera & Power, 2010). Thus, it is important to consider the emotional tone, in addition to the restrictiveness versus permissiveness dimensions of parental style, when examining children's responses to parental socialization efforts regarding food.

Social networks outside of the family unit also have a strong impact on people's consumption behaviour. Obesity appears to spread across social networks, stressing the impact of social factors on food consumption behaviour (Freund & Hennecke, 2012). One explanation for this is the social transmission of eating habits, whereby a strong relationship forms between social contexts and food consumed. People eat more in social situations and alter their food intake to match that of their dining companions (Robinson & Higgs, 2013). Furthermore, recent findings indicate that socially connected individuals display strong concordance in eating habits over time, suggesting that eating is strongly dominated by social factors (Pachucki, Jacques, & Christakis, 2011). Analysis of the specific processes behind the spread of eating patterns through social networks offers a number of explanations. Schultz, Nolan, Cialdini, Goldstein, & Griskevicius (2007) believe that this could be the operation of eating norms. Human beings are social beings who tend to conform to group standards, and social norms have long been thought to exert a powerful influence on behaviour (Reno, Cialdini, & Kallgren, 1993). In line with social identity theory, individuals' identification with the norm reference-group impacts their eating behaviours (Berger & Heath, 2008; Berger & Rand, 2008). People's sense of self is often guided by their identity as members of their social network, and if members within that network are perceived to engage in healthy eating patterns, they will eat more healthily to maintain their sense of identity. For many, therefore, conforming to informational eating norms may be a way of reinforcing identity to a social group, and consequently they will only engage in eating habits that are perceived as the acceptable norm (Tarrant & Butler, 2010; Turner & Oakes, 1986).

Social desirability, or the need to maintain social identity, is not enough to explain the impact of social influences on food consumption, however. Some studies show that people often conform to eating norms even when they are alone and believe they are not being observed (Pliner & Mann, 2004; Roth, Herman, Polivy, & Pliner, 2001). This led social psychologists to differentiate between the impact of injunctive and descriptive norms (Reno et al.,

1993; Schultz et al., 2007). Descriptive norms parallel informational eating norms in that they refer to information about what other people are doing. Injunctive norms, on the other hand, refer to social approval. When social approval is not guiding norm-related behaviour, for example when people eat alone, it is conceivable that descriptive norms might underlie the behaviour (Robinson, Fleming, & Higgs, 2014). Eating norms may thus act as a form of informational social influence, and the fact that a particular behaviour is undertaken by members of a social network is taken as proof of utility, or social proof (Rimal et al., 2005). Indeed, Rimal et al. (2005) propose that descriptive norms influence behaviour by altering the extent to which an individual perceives particular behaviours as valuable to them, and this might lead people to believe that it would benefit them to alter their eating patterns to be more in line with group norms. Many social psychological researchers support this theory and suggest that people use the behaviour of others as a template for how they should behave, i.e., informational social influence (Bond & Smith, 1996; Schultz et al., 2007). Thus, it is plausible that people observe eating norms in their social networks and use these norms to inform their own dietary behaviour. Perceptions about the healthiness of other people's eating habits might also influence individuals' eating patterns, which would explain why weight gain or weight loss is noticeable in social networks over time (Pachucki et al., 2011). The theory of social proximity supports this perspective and suggests that because people perceive individuals in their social circle as similar to them, they use their behaviour as an important source of information. Thus, the eating habits of close or significant others are likely to have a strong impact on people's food choice and intake (Croker, Whitaker, Cooke, & Wardle, 2009).

Conclusion

What humans should eat has become one of the most complicated and confusing questions of this generation, and different experts have widely different views as to what the answer should be. Debates about low-carb versus low-fat, high-protein versus low-calorie, and animal-based versus plant-based abound in scholarly discourse and mainstream media alike. Concurrently, food manufacturers and retailers wade into the discussion by providing brand new "healthy foods", fortifying standard foods to make them heathier and applying food labels that highlight necessary nutrients. In among all these discussions, debates, arguments, new foods, different labelling techniques and new scientific advancements in nutrition that arise regularly, people are expected to make optimal food decisions, maintain a healthy weight and eat foods that enhance longevity. They are then advised that the best ways to achieve their health goals are to engage their self-control, visualize, meditate, blog about their food-related emotions, keep food diaries, go to therapy or join supportive dieting groups. In an environment that encourages overindulgence in unhealthy foods, people have to fight to override their biological imperative to eat high-fat, high-sugar foods whenever these are available and instead choose foods that nourish them and keep them healthy. Yet, the complexity of the modern eating environment means that few people completely understand how to do this, and some believe it is not even possible.

Knowledge about food and nutrition seems to improve the quality of food consumption choices (Worsley, 2002), yet there needs to be a more overarching agreement from policy makers and other stakeholders in human health regarding the food knowledge that is communicated to people. Nutrition literacy needs then to be supplemented by the motivation to develop, engage in and maintain food-related goals, which for many people is difficult because of experienced psychological challenges (Block et al., 2011). This is made increasingly more demanding by countless marketing cues that influence consumption at an individual level (Wansink, 2007) and the fact that consumption decisions are often made with little cognitive effort or even awareness. Food consumption arises from an interplay between psychological, sociological, cultural and environmental factors, and dealing with one without considering the others will have very limited results. Emphasis on individuals to take responsibility for their own eating habits is shortsighted in light of the increasingly obesogenic environment that many people inhabit. Similarly, ignoring the role of food socialization and encouraging people to distance themselves from their social environment in their attempts to eat more healthily is also restricted in its impact. It is only when policy makers and other stakeholders come together and analyse the obesity problem from a multi-paradigm, multidisciplinary, multicultural perspective that they can begin to confront one of the biggest and most enduring problems of the twenty-first century.

Suggestions for future research

The real-world choices for an obese person trying to lose weight are complex and often confusing, and more research is needed to support attempts by stakeholders in health and well-being to improve dietary behaviour worldwide, reversing the rise in obesity and consequent lifestyle diseases. First, future research should attempt to better understand the antecedents of healthy eating behaviour in light of the modern, multifaceted obesogenic environment with all its complexities. Furthermore, positioning this research in a multicultural backdrop will enable researchers to better appreciate the impact of different food environments, combined with cultural behaviours and expectations, on eating behaviour and consequently on levels of worldwide obesity.

Second, little progress has been made so far towards achieving a more coherent, multidisciplinary understanding of healthy eating behaviour, drawing from psychology, sociology, anthropology (or biology) and other paradigms. With the threat of obesity looming high on policy makers' agendas worldwide, it is essential for professionals with different academic and ontological backgrounds and expertise to pull together and examine the different facets of healthy eating behaviour in today's obesogenic environment if they hope to develop an overarching understanding of healthy eating and fight back against obesity.

References

Ajzen, I. (1991). The theory of planned behaviour. *Organizational Behaviour and Human Decision Processes*, *50*, 179–211.

Allom, V., & Mullan, B. (2014). Individual differences in executive function predict distinct eating behaviours. *Appetite*, *80*, 123–130.

Andreasen, A. R. (2011). Rethinking the relationship between social/nonprofit marketing and commercial marketing. *Journal of Public Policy and Marketing*, *31*(1), 36–41.

Armitage, C. J., & Conner, M. (2000). Social cognition models and health behaviour: A structured review. *Psychology & Health*, *15*, 173–189.

Arnow, B., Kenardy, J., & Agras, W. S. (1995). The Emotional Eating Scale: The development of a measure to assess coping with negative affect by eating. *The International Journal of Eating Disorders*, *18*(1), 79–90.

Ball, K., Timperio, A. J., Giles-Corti, B., Roberts, R., & Crawford, D. (2007). Personal, social and environmental determinants of educational inequalities in walking: A multilevel study. *Journal of Epidemiology and Community Health*, *61*, 108–114.

Bandura, A. (1993). Perceived self-efficacy in cognitive development and functioning. *Educational Psychologist*, *28*(2), 117–148.

Bandura, A. (2012). On the functional properties of perceived self-efficacy revisited. *Journal of Management*, *38*, 9–44.

Bargh, J. A., & Chartrand, T. L. (1999). The unbearable automaticity of being. *American Psychologist*, *54*, 462–479.

Baumeister, R. F., Bratslavsky, E., Muraven, M., & Tice, D. M. (1998). Ego depletion: Is the active self a limited resource? *Journal of Personality and Social Psychology, 74*, 1252–1265.

Baumeister, R. F., Bushman, B. J., & Campbell, W. K. (2000). Self-esteem, narcissism, and aggression: Does violence result from low self-esteem or from threatened egotism? *Current Directions in Psychological Science, 9*, 26–29.

Baumeister, R. F., & Mick, D. G. (2002). Yielding to temptation: Self-control failure, impulsive purchasing, and consumer behaviour. *Journal of Consumer Research, 28*(4), 670–677.

Baumeister, R. F., Muraven, M., & Tice, D. M. (2000). Ego depletion: A resource model of volition, self-regulation, and controlled processing. *Social Cognition, 18*(2), 130–150.

Beaver, J. D., Lawrence, A. D., van Ditzhuijzen, J., Davis, M. H., Woods, A. & Calder, A. J. (2006). Individual differences in reward drive predict neural responses to images of food. *Journal of Neuroscience, 26*, 5160–5166.

Berger. J., & Heath, C. (2008). Who drives divergence? Identity-signalling, outgroup dissimilarity, and the abandonment of cultural tastes. *Journal of Personality and Social Psychology, 95*(3), 593–607.

Berger, J., & Rand, L. (2008). Shifting signals to help health: Using identity signalling to reduce risky health behaviours. *Journal of Consumer Research, 35*(1), 509–518.

Bestwick, C. S, Douglas, F. C. G., Allan, J. L., Macdiarmid, J. I., Ludbrook, A., & Carlisle, S. (2013). A perspective on the strategic approach to the complexity and challenges of behaviour change in relation to dietary health. *British Nutrition Foundation Nutrition Bulletin, 38*(1), 38–50.

Bhaskaran, S., & Hardley, F. (2002). Buyer beliefs, attitudes and behaviour: Foods with therapeutic claims. *Journal of Consumer Marketing, 19*(7), 591–606. Retrieved from www.worldcat.org/title/buyer-beliefs-attitudes-and-behaviour-foods-with-therapeutic-claims/oclc/441392599&referer=brief_results.

Birch, L. L. (1999). Development of food preferences. *Annual Review of Nutrition, 19*, 41–62.

Block, L. G., Grier, S. A., Childers, T. L., Davis, B., Ebert, J. E. J., Kumanyika, S., …, & van Ginkel Bieshaar, M. N. G. (2011). From nutrients to nurturance: A conceptual introduction to food well-being. *Journal of Public Policy & Marketing, 30*(1), 5–13.

Bogers, R. P., Brug, J., van Assema, P., & Dagnelie, P. C. (2004). Explaining fruit and vegetable consumption: The theory of planned behaviour and misconception of personal intake levels. *Appetite, 42*, 157–166.

Bond, R., & Smith, P. (1996). Culture and conformity: A meta-analysis of studies using Asch's (1952b, 1956) line judgment task. *Psychological Bulletin, 19*(1), 111–137.

Booth, S. L., Sallis, J. F., Ritenbaugh, C., Hill, J. O., Birch, L. L., Frank, L. D., …, & Hays, N. P. (2001). Environmental and societal factors affect food choice and physical activity: Rationale, influences, and leverage points. *Nutrition Reviews, 59*(3 Pt 2), S21–39; discussion S57–65.

Brennan, L., & Binney, W. (2010). Fear, guilt, and shame appeals in social marketing. *Journal of Business Research, 63*(2), 140–146.

Briggs, R. (2006). Marketers who measure the wrong thing get faulty answers. *Journal of Advertising Research, 46*(4), 462–468.

Brown, R., & Ogden, J. (2004). Children's eating attitudes and behaviour: A study of the modeling and control theories of parental influence. *Health Education Research, 19*(3), 261–271.

Brownell, K. D., & Joplan, J. P. (2011). Front-of-package nutrition labelling: An abuse of trust by the food industry. *The New England Journal of Medicine, 364*, 2373–2375.

Brug, J. (2008). Determinants of healthy eating: Motivation, abilities and environmental opportunities. *Family Practice, 25*, 50–55.

Brug, J., & de Nooijer, J. (2006). Predicting fruit consumption: Cognitions, intention and habits. *Journal of Nutrition Education and Behaviour, 38*(2), 73–81.

Brug, J., Kremers, S. P., Lenthe, F., Ball, K., & Crawford, D. (2008). Environmental determinants of healthy eating: In need of theory and evidence. *Proceedings of the Nutrition Society, 67*(3), 307–316.

Brug, J., Oenema, A., & Ferreira, I. (2005). Theory, evidence and intervention mapping to improve behavioural nutrition and physical activity interventions. *The International Journal of Behavioural Nutrition and Physical Activity, 2*(1), 2.

Bruyneel, S., Dewitte, S., Vohs, K. D., & Warlop, L. (2006). Repeated choosing increases susceptibility to affective product features. *International Journal of Research in Marketing, 23*, 215–225.

Bublitz, M. G., Peracchio, L. A., & Block, L. G. (2010). Why did I eat that? Perspectives on food decision making and dietary restraint. *Journal of Consumer Psychology, 20*(3), 239–258.

Buehler, R. G., Griffin, D., & Ross, M. (1994). Exploring the "planning fallacy": Why people underestimate their task completion times. *Journal of Personality and Social Psychology, 67*(3), 366–381.

Capaldi, E. D. (1996). *Why We Eat What We Eat*. Washington, DC: American Psychological Association.

Centers for Disease Control and Prevention (2014). Adult obesity facts. Retrieved from www.cdc.gov/obesity/data/adult.html.

Chandon, P., & Wansink, B. (2007). The biasing health halos of fast-food restaurant health claims: Lower calorie estimates and higher side-dish consumption intentions. *Journal of Consumer Research, 34*, 301–313.

Chandon, P., & Wansink, B. (2012). Does food marketing need to make us fat? A review and solutions. *Nutrition Reviews, 70*(10), 571–592.

Cho, H., & Salmon, C. T. (2006). Fear appeals for individuals in different stages of change: Intended and unintended effects and implications on public health campaigns. *Health Communication, 20*(1), 91–99.

Church, T. S., Martin, C. K., Thompson, A. M., Earnest, C. P., Mikus, C. R., & Blairm, S. N. (2009). Changes in weight, waist circumference and compensatory responses with different doses of exercise among sedentary, overweight postmenopausal women. *PLoS One, 4*(2), e4515.

Cochran, W., & Tesser, A. (1996). The "what the hell" effect: Some effects of goal proximity and goal framing on performance. In L. Martin & A. Tesser (Eds.), *Striving and feeling: Interactions among goals, affect, and self-regulation* (pp. 99–120). Mahwah, NJ: Erlbaum.

Conner, M., & Armitage, C. J. (2002). *The social psychology of food*. Buckingham: Open University Press.

Conner, M., & Norman, P. (1998). Editorial: Social cognition models in health psychology. *Psychological Health, 13*, 179–185.

Croker, H, Whitaker, K. L., Cooke, L., & Wardle, J. (2011). Do social norms affect intended food choice? *Preventive Medicine, 49*(2–3), 190–193.

Dallongeville, J., Marécaux, N., Cottel, D., Bingham, A., & Amouyel, P. (2001). Association between nutrition knowledge and nutritional intake in middle-aged men from Northern France. *Public Health Nutrition, 4*, 27–33.

de Bourdeaudhuij, I., Velde, S., Brug, J., Due, P., Wind, M., Sadvik, C., …, & Klepp, K. I. (2007). Personal, social and environmental predictors of daily fruit and vegetable intake in 11-year-old children in nine European countries. *European Journal of Clinical Nutrition, 62*, 834–841.

de Bruijn, G. J., Kremers, S. P. J., de Vries, H., van Mechelen, W., & Brug, J. (2007). Associations of social-environmental and individual-level factors with adolescent soft drink consumption: Results from the SMILE study. *Health Education Research, 22*, 227–237.

de Ridder, D. (2012). Plans, norms, motivation, and cheating a little: The curious case of healthy eating. *Psychology & Health, 27*(2), 1–6. doi: 10.1080/08870446.2012.721957

de Ridder, D. T. D., Lensvelt-Mulders, G., Finkenauer, C., Stok, F. M., & Baumeister, R. F. (2012). Taking stock of self-control: A meta-analysis of how trait self-control relates to a wide range of behaviours. *Personality and Social Psychology Review, 16*, 76–99.

de Witt Huberts, J. C., Evers, C., & de Ridder, D. T. D. (2012). License to sin: Selflicensing as a mechanism underlying hedonic consumption. *European Journal of Social Psychology, 42*(4), 490–496.

Deci, E. L., & Ryan, R. M. (2000). The "what" and "why" of goal pursuits: Human needs and the self-determination of behaviour. *Psychological Inquiry, 11*, 227–268.

Department of Health (2009). *Change 4 Life: Three year Social marketing strategy*. Retrieved from www.gov.uk/government/uploads/system/uploads/attachment_data/file/213719/dh_130488.pdf

Deutsch, M., & Gerard, H. (1955). A study of normative and informational social influences upon individual judgment. *Journal of Abnormal Social Psychology, 51*(3), 629–636.

Dixey, R. (1998) Healthy eating in schools, overweight and eating disorders –are they connected? *Educational Review*, 50, 29–35.

Doval, H. C. (2013). Healthy eating: How to achieve it? *Argentine Journal of Cardiology, 81*(6), 519–528.

Downs, J. S., & Loewenstein, G. (2011). Behavioural economics and obesity. In J. Cawley (Ed.), *The Oxford handbook of the social science of obesity*. Oxford, UK: Oxford University Press.

Downs, J. S., Loewenstein, G., & Wisdom, J. (2009) The psychology of food consumption. Strategies for promoting healthier food choices. *American Economic Review: Papers & Proceedings, 92*, 1–10.

Duncan, M. J., Spence, J. C., & Mummery, W. K. (2005). Perceived environment and physical activity: A meta-analysis of selected environmental characteristics. *International Journal of Behavioural Nutrition and Physical Activity, 2*, 11.

Ebneter, D. S., Latner, J. D., & Nigg, C. R. (2013). Is less always more? The effects of low-fat labeling and caloric information on food intake, calorie estimates, taste preference, and health attributions. *Appetite, 68*, 92–97.

Efklides, A., Niemivirta, M., & Yamauchi, H. (2002). Introduction: Some issues on self-regulation to consider. *Psychologia, 45*, 207–210.

Eldridge, J., & Murcott, A. (2000). Adolescents' dietary habits and attitudes: Unpacking the "problem" of (parental) influence. *Health, 4*, 25–49.

European Food Information (EUFIC). (2012). *Fruit and vegetable consumption in Europe – do Europeans get enough?* EUFIC Review, European Food Information Council No. 01/2012. Retrieved from www.eufic.org/article/en/page/RARCHIVE/expid/Fruit-vegetable-consumption-Europe

Fennis, B. M., Janssen, L., & Vohs, K. D. (2009). Acts of benevolence: A limited-resource account of compliance with charitable requests. *Journal of Consumer Research, 35*, 906–924.

Festinger, L. (1957). *A theory of cognitive dissonance*. Stanford, CA: Stanford University Press.

Finkelstein, E. A., Khavjou, O. A., Thompson, H., Trogdon, J. G., Pan, L., Sherry, B., & Dietz, W. (2012). Obesity and severe obesity forecasts through 2030. *American Journal of Preventive Medicine, 42*(6), 563–570.

Finucane, M. M., Stevens, G. A., Cowan, M. J., Danaei, G. F., Lin, J. K., Paciorek, C. J., …, & Ezzati, M. (2011). National, regional, and global trends in body-mass index since 1980: Systematic analysis of health examination surveys and epidemiological studies with 960 country-years and 9.1 million participants. *Lancet, 377*(9765), 557–567.

Fitzgibbon, M., Gans, K. M., Evans, W. D., Viswanath, K., Johnson-Taylor, W. L., Krebsmith, S. M., …, & Yaroch, A. L. (2007). Communicating healthy eating: Lessons learned and future directions. *Journal of Nutrition Education and Behaviour, 39*, 63–71.

Flay, B. R., & Petraitis, J. (1994). The theory of triadic influence: A new theory of health behaviour with implications for preventive interventions. *Advances in Medical Sociology, 4*, 4–19.

Frederick, S. L., Loewenstein, G., & O'Donoghue, T. (2002). Time discounting and time preference: A critical review. *Journal of Economic Literature, 40*(2), 351–401.

Freund, A. M., & Hennecke, M. (2012). Changing eating behaviour vs. losing weight: The role of goal focus for weight loss in overweight women. *Psychology & Health*, 27(Suppl. 2), 25–42.

Friese, M., & Hofmann, W. (2009). Control me or I will control you: Impulses, trait self-control, and the guidance of behaviour. *Journal of Research in Personality, 43*, 795–805.

Gigerenzer, G., & Gaissmaier, W. (2011). Heuristic decision making. *Annual Review of Psychology, 62*, 451–482.

Giskes, K., Kamphuis, C. B., van Lenthe, F. J., Kremers, S. P. J., Droomers, M., & Brug, J. (2007a). A systematic review of associations between environmental factors, energy and fat intakes among adults: Is there evidence for environments that encourage obesogenic dietary intakes? *Public Health and Nutrition, 10*(10), 1005–1017.

Giskes, K., Van Lenthe, F. J., Brug, J., Mackenbach, J. P., & Turrell, G. (2007b). Socioeconomic inequalities in food purchasing: The contribution of respondent-perceived and actual (objectively measured) price and availability of foods. *Preventive Medicine, 45*, 41–48.

Glanz, K., Basil, M., Maibach, E., Goldberg, J., & Snyder, D. (1998). Why Americans eat what they do: Taste, nutrition, cost, convenience, and weight control concerns as influences on food consumption. *Journal of the American Dietetic Association, 98*, 1118–1126.

Grunert, K. G., Wills, J., Fernandez-Celemin, L., Lahteenmaki, L., Scholderer, J., & Storcksdieck genannt Bonsmann, S. (2012). Socio-demographic and attitudinal determinants of nutrition knowledge of food shoppers in six European countries. *Food Quality and Preference, 26*(2), 166–177.

Guyomard, H., Darcy-Vrillon, B., Esnouf, C., Marin, M., Momot, A., Russel, M., & Guillou, M. (2011). *Eating patterns and food systems: Critical knowledge requirements for policy design and implementation*. INRA. Document prepared for the Commission on Sustainable Agriculture and Climate Change. Retrieved from http://ccafs.cgiar.org/sites/default/files/assets/docs/guyomard_et_al_eating_patterns_and_food_systems.pdf

Handu, D. J., Monty, C. E., & Chmel, L. M. (2008). Nutrition education improved nutrition knowledge, behaviour, and intention among youth in Chicago public schools. *Journal of the American Dietetic Association, 108*(9), A91.

Hastak, M., & Mazis, M. B. (2011). Deception by implication: A typology of truthful but misleading advertising and labelling claims. *Journal of Public Policy and Marketing, 30*(2), 157–167.

HealthFocus (2005). *HealthFocus: Study of public attitudes and actions toward shopping and eating*. St Petersburg, FL: Health Focus.

Heasman, M., & Mellentin, J. (2001). *The functional food revolution*. London: Earth Scan.

Henley, N., Donovan, R. J., & Moorhead, H. (1998). Appealing to positive motivations and emotions in social marketing: Example of a positive parenting campaign. *Social Marketing Quarterly, 4*(4), 48–53.

Herman, C. P., & Polivy, J. (2011). The self-regulation of eating: Theoretical and practical problems. In K. D. Vohs & R. F. Baumeister (Eds.), *Handbook of self-regulation: Research, theory and applications* (pp. 522–536). New York, NY: Guilford Press.

Hofmann, W., Strack, F., & Deutsch, R. (2008). Free to buy? Explaining self-control and impulse in consumer behaviour. *Journal of Consumer Psychology, 18*, 22–26.

Ikeda, J. (1999). Culture, food, and nutrition in increasingly culturally diverse societies. In J. Germov & L. Williams (Eds.), *A sociology of food and nutrition*. Oxford: Oxford University Press.

Jastreboff, A. M., Sinha, R., Lacadie, C., Small, D. M., Sherwin, R. S., & Potenza, M. N. (2013). Neural correlates of stress- and food-cue-induced food craving in obesity: Association with insulin levels. *Diabetes Care, 36*, 394–402.

Keatley, D., Clarke, D. D., & Hagger, M. S. (2013). The predictive validity of implicit measures of self-determined motivation across health-related behaviours. *British Journal of Health Psychology, 18*, 2–17.

Kleinschmidt, A. (2003). *When food isn't just food*. Research Leaflet, 2.

Klesges, R. C., Stein, R. J., Eck, L. H., Isbell, T. R., & Klesges, L. M. (1991). Parental influences on food selection in young children and its relationships to childhood obesity. *American Journal of Clinical Nutrition, 53*, 859–864.

Kremers, S. P. J., de Bruijn, G. J., Visscher, T. L. S., van Mechelen, W., de Vries, N. K., & Brug, J. (2006). Environmental influences on energy balance-related behaviours: A dual-process view. *International Journal of Behavioural Nutrition and Physical Activity, 3*, 9.

Lahteenmaki, L. (2003). Consumers and functional foods. In T. Mattila-Sandholm & M. Saarela (Eds.), *Functional dairy products*. Cambridge: Woodhead.

Lee, J. W., Lee, H. S., Chang, N., & Kim, J. M. (2009). The relationship between nutrition knowledge scores and dietary behaviour, dietary intakes and anthropometric parameters among primary school children participating in a nutrition education program. *Korean Journal of Nutrition, 42*, 338–349.

Lennernäs, M., Fjellström, C., Becker, W., Giachetti, I., Schmitt, A., Remaut de Winter, A. M., & Kearney, M. (1997). Influences on food choice perceived to be important by nationally-representative sample of adults in the European Union. *European Journal of Clinical Nutrition, 51*(suppl. 2), 8–15.

Loewenstein, G., & O'Donoghue, T. (2002). Time discounting and time preference: A critical review. *Journal of Economic Literature, 40*(2), 351–401.

Lubans, D. R., Plotnikoff, R. C., Morgan, P. J., Dewar, D., Costigan, S., & Collins, C. (2012). Explaining dietary intake in adolescent girls from disadvantaged secondary schools. A test of Social Cognitive Theory. *Appetite, 58*, 517–524.

Lupton, D., & Chapman, S. (1995). "A healthy lifestyle might be the death of you": Discourses on diet, cholesterol control and heart disease in the press and among the lay public. *Sociology of Health and Illness, 17*(4), 477–494.

Magnusson, R. S. (2010). Obesity prevention and personal responsibility: The case of front-of-pack labelling in Australia. *BMC Public Health, 10*, 662–673.

Marcelino, A. S., Adam, A. S., Couronne, T., Koster, E. P., & Sieffermann, J. M. (2001). Internal and external determinants of eating initiations in humans. *Appetite, 36*, 9–14.

Marks, D., Murray, M., Evans, B., & Willig, C. (2000). *Health psychology: Theory, research and practice*. London: Sage.

Mattila, A., & Wirtz, J. (2002). The impact of knowledge types on the consumer search process: An investigation in the context of credence services. *International Journal of Service Industry Management, 13*, 214–230.

Menrad, K. (2003). Market and marketing of functional food in Europe. *Journal of Food Engineering, 56*, 181–188.

Meule, A., Lutz, A. P., Vogele, C., & Kubler, A. (2014). Impulsive reactions to food-cues predict subsequent food craving. *Eating Behaviour, 15*, 99–105.

Mischel, W., Cantor, N., & Feldman, S. (1996). Principles of self-regulation: The nature of willpower and self-control. In E. T. Higgins & A. W. Kruglanski (Eds.), *Social psychology: Handbook of basic principles* (pp. 329–360). New York, NY: Guilford Press.

Mitchell, V., Walsh, G., & Yami, M. (2005). Towards a conceptual model of consumer confusion. *Advances in Consumer Research, 32*(1), 143–150. Retrieved from www.acrwebsite.org/

Moore, E., Wilkie, L., & Lutz, R. J. (2002). Passing the torch: Intergenerational influences as a source of brand equity. *Journal of Marketing, 66*, 21–37.

Morland, K., Diez Roux, A. V., & Wing, S. (2006). Supermarkets, other food stores, and obesity: The atherosclerosis risk in communities study. *American Journal of Preventative Medicine, 30*, 333–339.

Morland, K., Wing, S., & Diez Roux, A. V. (2002). The contextual effect of the local food environment on residents' diets: The atherosclerosis risk in communities study. *American Journal of Public Health, 92*(11), 1761–1767.

Morris, M. J., Beilharz, J. E., Maniam, J., Reichelt, A. C., & Westbrook, R. (2014). Why is obesity such a problem in the 21st century? The intersection of palatable food, cues and reward pathways, stress, and cognition. *Neuroscience and Biobehavioural Reviews*, 58, 36–45.

Moschis, G. P. (1985). The role of family communication in consumer socialization of children and adolescents. *Journal of Consumer Research, 1*, 898–913.

Muraven, M., & Baumeister, R. F. (2000). Self-regulation and depletion of limited resources: Does self-control resemble a muscle? *Psychological Bulletin, 126*(2), 247–259.

Muraven, M., Tice, D. M., & Baumeister, R. F. (1998). Self-control as limited resource: Regulatory depletion patterns. *Journal of Experimental and Social Psychology, 74*(3), 774–789.

Murdaugh, D. L., Cox, J. E., Cook, E. W., & Weller, R. E. (2012). FMRI reactivity to high-calorie food pictures predicts short- and long-term outcome in a weight-loss program. *NeuroImage, 59*(3), 2709–2721.

National Health Service Information Centre (2012). *Statistics on obesity, physical activity and diet: England.* The NHS Information Centre for Health and Social Care. Retrieved from www.hscic.gov.uk/catalogue/PUB05131/obes-phys-acti-diet-eng-2012-rep.pdf

Nestle, M. (2007). *Food politics* (10th anniversary ed.). London: University of California Press.

O'Donoghue, T., & Rabin, M. (2000). The economics of immediate gratification. *Journal of Behavioural Decision Making, 3*(2), 233–250.

Oliver, G., Wardle, J., & Gibson, L. (2000). Stress and food choice: A laboratory study. *Psychosomatic Medicine, 62*, 853–865.

Olvera, N., & Power, T. G. (2010). Parenting styles and obesity in Mexican American children: A longitudinal study. *Journal of Paediatric Psychology, 35*(3), 243–249.

Olvera, N., Sharma, S. Suminski, R., Rodriguez, A., & Power, T. G. (2007). BMI trends in Mexican American children in relation to maternal BMI. *Ethnicity & Disease, 17*, 707–713.

Oxfam (2014). Good enough to eat. Where in the world are the best and worst places to eat? Retrieved from www.oxfamamerica.org/static/media/files/Good_Enough_To_Eat_Media_brief_FINAL.pdf

Pachucki, M. A., Jacques, P. F., & Christakis, N. A. (2011). Social network concordance in food choice among spouses, friends and siblings. *American Journal of Public Health, 101*(11), 217–227.

Paquette, M. C. (2005). Perceptions of healthy eating: State of knowledge and research gaps. *Canadian Journal of Public Health, 96*(Suppl. 3), S15–19, S16–21.

Pliner, P., & Mann, N. (2004). Influence of social norms and palatability on amount consumed and food choice. *Appetite, 42*(2), 227–237.

Pollan, M. (2009). *In defense of food: An eater's manifesto.* London: Penguin.

Produce for Better Health Foundation (2009). *New report summarizes fruit and vegetable consumption data by state* (Press release: September 29, 2009). Retrieved from Produce for Better Health Foundation website: http://www.pbhfoundation.org

Radtke, T., Scholz, U., Keller, R., & Hornung, R. (2011b). Smoking is ok as long as I eat healthily. Compensatory Health Beliefs and their role for intentions and smoking within the Health Action Process Approach. *Psychology and Health, 1*, 17.

Radtke, T., Scholz, U., Keller, R., Knäuper, B., & Hornung, R. (2011a). Smoking-specific compensatory health beliefs and the readiness to stop smoking in adolescents. *British Journal of Health Psychology, 16*, 610–625.

Rasmussen, M., Krolner, R., Klepp, K. I., Lytle, L., Brug, J., Bere, E., & Due, P. (2006). Determinants of fruit and vegetable consumption among children and adolescents: Systematic review of the literature. *International Journal of Behavioural Nutrition and Physical Activity, 3*, 22.

Regmi, A., & Seale, J. L. (2010). *Cross price elasticities of demand across 114 countries.* Technical Bulletin Number 1925, Economic Research Service, US Dept. of Agriculture. Retrieved from www.ers.usda.gov/Publications/ TB1925/TB1925.pdf

Regmi, A., Takeshima, H., & Unnevehrm, L. (2008). *Convergence in global food demand and delivery.* Economic Research Report Number 56, Economic Research Service, US Dept. of Agriculture. Retrieved from www.ers. usda.gov/Publications/ERR56/ERR56.pdf

Reno, R. R., Cialdini, R. B., & Kallgren, C. A. (1993). The trans-situational influence of social norms. *Journal of Personality and Social Psychology, 64*(1), 104–112.

Rhee, K. E., Lumeng, J. C., Appugliese, D. P., Kaciroti, N., & Bradley, R. H. (2006). Parenting styles and overweight status in first grade. *Pediatrics, 117*, 2047–2054.

Rimal, R. N., & Real, K. (2003). Understanding the influence of perceived norms on behaviours. *Communication Theory, 13*, 184–203.

Roberto, C. A., & Kawachi, I. (2014). Use of psychology and behavioural economics to promote healthy eating. *American Journal of Preventive Medicine, 47*(6), 832–837.

Robinson, E., Fleming, A., & Higgs, S. (2014). Prompting healthier eating: Testing the use of health and social norm based messages. *Health Psychology, 33*(9), 1057–1064.

Robinson, E., & Higgs, S. (2013). Making food choices in the presence of "healthy" and "unhealthy" companions. *British Journal of Nutrition, 109*(4), 765–771.

Robinson, E., Robinson, T., Fleming, E. L., & Higgs, S. (2014). Prompting healthier eating: Comparing the use of health and social norm based messages. *Health Psychology, 33*, 1057–1064.

Rosenkilde, M., Auerbach, P., Reichkendler, M. H., Ploug, T., Stallknecht, B. M., & Sjödin, A. (2012). Body fat loss and compensatory mechanisms in response to different doses of aerobic exercise – a randomized controlled trial in overweight sedentary males. *American Journal of Physiology. Regulatory, Integrative and Comparative Physiology, 303*(6), R571–R579.

Roth, D. A., Herman, C. P., Polivy, J., & Pliner, P. (2001). Self-presentational conflict in social eating situations: A normative perspective. *Appetite, 36*(2), 65–171.

Rothschild, M. L. (1999). Carrots, sticks, and promises: A conceptual framework for the management of public health and the social issue behaviours. *Journal of Marketing, 63*, 24–37.

Sallis, J. F., & Owen, N. (2003). Ecological models of health behaviour. In K. Glanz, B. K. Rimer & F. M. Lewis (Eds.), *Health behaviour and health education* (3rd ed., pp. 462–485).San Francisco, CA: Jossey Bass.

Salmon, S. J., Fennis, B. M., de Ridder, D. T., Adriaanse, M. A., & de Vet, E. (2014). Health on impulse: When low self-control promotes healthy food choices. *Health Psychology, 33*(2), 103–109.

Samuelson, W., & Zeckhauser, R. (1988). Status quo bias in decision making. *Journal of Risk and Uncertainty, 1*(1), 7–59.

Scammon, D. L., Keller, P. A., Albinsson, P. A., Bahl, S., Catlin, J., Haws, K. L., …, & Schindler, R. M. (2011). Transforming consumer health. *Journal of Public Policy and Marketing, 30*(1), 14–22.

Schiffman, S. S., Graham, B. G., Sattely-Miller, E. A., & Peterson-Dancy, M. (2000). Elevated and sustained desire for sweet taste in African-Americans: A potential factor in the development of obesity. *Nutrition, 16*, 886–893.

Schultz, W. P., Nolan, J. M., Cialdini, R. B., Goldstein, N. J., & Griskevicius, V. (2007). The constructive, destructive, and reconstructive power of social norms. *Psychological Science, 18*(5), 429–434.

Scott, M. L., Nowlis, S. M., Mandel, N., & Morales, A. C. (2008). The effects of reduced food size and package size on the consumption behaviours of restrained and unrestrained eaters. *Journal of Consumer Research*, 35(3), 391–405.

Shah, A. K., & Oppenheimer, D. M. (2008). Heuristics made easy: An effort-reduction framework. *Psychological Bulletin, 134*, 207–222.

Simon, H. (2000). Bounded rationality in social science: Today and tomorrow. *Mind & Society, 1*, 25–39.

Spiteri-Cornish, L. (2012). It's good for me: It has added fibre! An exploration of the role of different categories of functional foods in consumer diets. *Journal of Consumer Behaviour, 11*(4), 292–302.

Spiteri Cornish, L., & Moraes, C. (2015). The impact of consumer confusion on nutrition literacy and subsequent dietary behaviour. *Psychology and Marketing, 32*, 558–574.

Stevens, G. A., Singh, G. M., Lu, Y., Danaei, G., Lin, J. K., Finucane, M. M., & Ezzati, M. (2012). National, regional, and global trends in adult overweight and obesity prevalences. *Population Health Metrics, 10*(1), 22.

Stevenson, C., Doherty, G., Barnett, J., Muldoon, O. T. & Trew, K. (2007). Adolescents' views of food and eating: Identifying barriers to healthy eating. *Journal of Adolescence, 30*(3), 417–434.

Story, M., Neumark-Sztainer, D., & French, S. (2002). Individual and environmental influences on adolescent eating behaviours. *Journal of the American Dietetic Association, 102*(3), S40–S51.

Suku Bhaskaran, S., & Hardley, F. (2002). Buyer beliefs, attitudes and behaviour: Foods with therapeutic claims. *Journal of Consumer Marketing, 19*(7), 591–606.

Swartz, J. J., Braxton, D., & Viera, A. J. (2011). Calorie menu labeling on quickservice restaurants menus: An updated systematic review of the literature. *International Journal of Behavioural Nutrition and Physical Activity, 8*, 135.

Swinburn, B., Egger, G., & Raza, F. (1999). Dissecting obesogenic environments: The development and application of a framework for identifying and prioritizing environmental interventions for obesity. *Journal of Preventive Medicine, 29*, 563–570.

Swinburn, B, Sacks, G., Hall, K. D., McPherson, K., Finegood, D. T., Moodie, M. L., & Gortmaker, S. L. (2011). The global obesity pandemic: Shaped by global drivers and local environments. *Lancet*, 378, 804–814.

Tarrant, M., & Butler, K. (2010). Effects of self-categorization on orientation towards health. *British Journal of Social Psychology*, *50*(1), 121–139.

Torres, S. J., & Nowson, C. A. (2007). Relationship between stress, eating behaviour and obesity. *Nutrition*, *23*(11–12), 887–894.

Turner, J., & Oakes, P. (1986). The significance of the social identity concept for social psychology with reference to individualism, interactionism and social influence. *British Journal of Social Psychology*, *25*(3), 237–252.

van der Horst, K., Kremers, S., Ferreira, I., Singh, A., & Brug, J. (2007). Perceived parenting style and practices and the consumption of sugar-sweetened beverages by adolescents. *Health Education Research*, *22*, 295–304.

Videon, T. M., & Manning, C. K. (2003). Influences on adolescent eating patterns: The importance of family meals. *Journal of Adolescent Health*, *32*(5), 365–373.

Wansink, B. (2007). *Marketing nutrition: Soy, functional foods, biotechnology, and obesity*. Chicago, IL: University of Illinois Press.

Wansink, B., & Sobal, J. (2007). Mindless eating: The 200 daily food decisions we overlook. *Environment and Behaviour*, *39*, 106–123.

Wiggins, S. (2004). Good for "you": Generic and individual healthy eating advice in family mealtimes. *Journal of Health Psychology*, *9*(4), 535–548.

Wills, T. A., Isasi, C. R., Mendoza, D., & Ainette, M. G. (2007). Self-control constructs related to measures of dietary intake and physical activity in adolescents. *Journal of Adolescent Health*, *41*, 551–558.

Wind, M., De Bourdeaudhuij, I., te Velde, S. J., Sandvik, C., Due, P., Klepp, K. I., & Brug, J. (2006). Correlates of fruit and vegetable consumption among 11-year-old Belgian-Flemish and Dutch schoolchildren. *Journal of Nutrition Education and Behaviour*, *38*, 211–221.

Wood, W., Quinn, J. M., & Kashy, D. A. (2002). Habits in everyday life: Thought, emotion, and action. *Journal of Personality and Social Psychology*, *83*(6), 1281–1297.

World Health Organization (2000). *Obesity: Preventing and managing the global epidemic*. Report of a WHO Consultation (WHO Technical Report Series 894). Retrieved from www.who.int/nutrition/publications/obesity/WHO_TRS_894/en/

World Health Organization (2007). *Basic documents* (46th ed.). (NLM Classification: WA.540 MW.6). Retrieved from http://apps.who.int/iris/handle/10665/43637

World Health Organization (2012). *Population-based approaches to childhood obesity prevention*. Retrieved from www.agitasp.org.br

World Health Organization (2014). *World health statistics 2014*. Retrieved from http://apps.who.int/iris/bitstream/10665/112738/1/9789240692671_eng.pdf?ua=1

Worsley, A. (2002). Nutrition knowledge and food consumption: Can nutrition knowledge change food behaviour? *Asia Pacific Journal of Clinical Nutrition*, *11*(3), S579–S585.

Part IV
Social and cultural influences

15

Political marketing

Theory and practice

Wojciech Cwalina, Andrzej Falkowski and Bruce I. Newman

Politicians are in the business of selling hope to people. This hope is related to convincing people that it is this particular politician or political party that guarantees successful management of national security, social stability and economic growth on behalf of the electorate. From this perspective, the major challenge to political marketing is to connect a politician's words, actions and vision into a realistic transformation of the electorate's dreams and aspirations (Newman, 1999a).

The first conceptualizing efforts related to political marketing referred to or represented the transferring of classical product marketing to the sphere of politics (e.g., Farrell & Wortmann, 1987; Kotler, 1975; Niffenegger, 1988; Shama, 1975). The starting point for this approach was the assumption that it would be a gross mistake to think that election campaigns have taken on marketing character only in recent years. Campaigning for office has always had a marketing character, and the only thing that has increased over time is the sophistication and acceleration of the use of marketing methods in politics (Kotler, 1975; Kotler & Kotler, 1999). From this perspective, political marketing was defined as "the process by which political candidates and ideas are directed at the voters in order to satisfy their political needs and thus gain their support for the candidate and ideas in question" (Shama, 1975, p. 793). Applying consumer product marketing to politics was justified by a number of similarities – similarities of concepts (e.g., consumers, market segmentation, marketing mix, image, brand loyalty, product concept and positioning) and similarities of tools (e.g., market research, communication and advertising). On the other hand, attempts were made to prove that the differences between marketing and politics were only ostensible and that they disappeared under a more thorough analysis (see Egan, 1999; Kotler, 1975).

Despite many similarities between political marketing and mainstream (product, service, not-for-profit and relationship) marketing, identifying them as the same cannot be justified. Lock and Harris (1996) point out seven major differences between the two spheres. First, those eligible to vote always choose their candidate or political party on the same day that the voting takes place. Consumers, on the other hand, can purchase their products at different times, depending on their needs and purchasing power. Second, while the consumer purchasing a product always knows its price – the value expressed in financial terms – for voters there is no price attached to their ability to make a voting decision. Making a voting decision may, but need not, be the result of analyzing and predicting the consequences of this decision in terms of possible financial losses and gains by particular voters. Third, voters realize that the choice is collective and that they must accept the final election result even if it goes against their choice. Fourth, winner takes all in political elections. The closest equivalent to commercial marketing in this case would be gaining a monopoly on the market. Fifth, the political party or candidate is a complex and intangible entity. Although in commercial marketing there are also products and, especially, services that the consumer cannot unpack and check while buying them, the proportion of such packages that cannot be unpacked is much greater in the political market. Besides, consumers may change their minds and exchange products or services almost immediately for others, if they do not like the ones that they have purchased. However, if voters decide to change their minds, they have to wait till the next election, at least for a few years. Sixth, in consumer product marketing, brand leaders tend to stay in front. In political marketing, on the other hand, many politicians and parties begin to lose support in public opinion polls after winning the election, because their decisions are not well received by various social groups (e.g., unfavourable budget decisions or tax increases).

The differences between consumer goods marketing and political marketing are big enough to make one think about developing an independent concept for studying voting behaviours. Newman (1994) believes that the key concept for political marketing is the concept of "exchange". The main purpose of the election is for voters to select their representative, who will pursue the most desired policies (Downs, 1957). Thus, when applying marketing to politics, the exchange process centres on a candidate who offers political leadership in exchange for a vote from the citizen. In other words, when voters cast their votes, a transaction takes place. They are engaged in an exchange of time and support (their vote) for the services that the party or candidate offers after election through better government. In this way, marketing offers political parties and candidates the ability to address diverse voter concerns and needs through marketing analyses, planning, implementation and control of the political and electoral campaigns.

The chapter focuses on some theoretical and empirical research on voter segmentation and positioning of candidates, which supports some assumptions of the Advanced Model of Political Marketing. The model brings together into a single framework the following two elements: the permanent political campaign and the political marketing process. These two components are realized within a particular country's political system. Particular attention will be paid to the candidate's campaign platform and image. The next paragraph describes the advanced model of political marketing in detail.

The advanced model of political marketing

The political marketing management should be analysed at two interdependent levels: the macro- and micro-levels (Cwalina, Falkowski, & Newman, 2012). In this perspective, the following macrostructures play important roles: (1) the political system and its legal regulations concerning the foundations of a particular political system (the constitution), as well as ruling, organizing elections and regulating the media market; (2) technological forces; (3) the state's demographic structure; and (4) modern concepts of marketing management and its methods (focus on voters' needs and wants; voter segmentation; candidate/party positioning; message development and dissemination; see e.g., Cwalina, Falkowski, & Newman, 2011; Lees-Marshment, 2009). Voters, politicians, political parties, opinion leaders and other organizations (e.g., lobbyists, non-governmental organizations [NGOs] or labour unions) are considered agents that function not only within these macrostructures but also within specific microstructures. Just as microeconomics and macroeconomics are the two major perspectives within the field of economics, so are the micro and macro approaches to political marketing, which represent the two major perspectives that allow one to better understand the workings of modern democracies and the processes taking place there. An approach that takes into account both levels of analysis can integrate various theories of particular political behaviour considered as part of an external macrostructure, understood as broad social, political, legal, economic and technological context, with the theories of political behaviour of individuals and institutions considered as the internal microstructure. They enjoy a lot of influence on the course of political events and the shape of the microenvironment.

Looking at political behaviours and processes from macro- and micro-perspectives simultaneously, one can better understand the working of modern democracies and the processes taking place, as well as the inherent development, threats and opportunities. Such an approach can then integrate various theories of particular political behaviour, regarded as part of an external macrostructure and understood in a broad social, political, legal, economic and technological context, forming and controlling the political behaviour of individuals and institutions. However, such an approach towards marketing can also perform a heuristic function: It is the source of new ideas and an innovative approach to explaining the existing political behaviours, as well as predicting those which might appear in the more or less remote future. In this context, marketing management functions as a lens through which a given persuasion strategy is planned and implemented.

The advanced model of political marketing proposed by Cwalina, Falkowski and Newman (2011, 2014) and presented in Figure 15.1 constitutes a proposal to explain the specificity of marketing activities in politics described above. This model is derived from the model of political marketing put forward by Newman (1994).

The advanced model of political marketing integrates the permanent political campaign and the political marketing process into a single framework. The permanent campaign is a process of continuing transformation that never stops. It transforms government into an instrument designed to sustain an elected official's public popularity (Newman, 1999a). The permanent political campaign and political marketing processes are realized within a particular country's political system. The system depends, above all, on "democracy orientation", which consists of political tradition as well as the efficiency of the developed democratic procedures (e.g., referenda, direct or indirect election of president). Democracy orientation determines how the functions of the authorities are implemented and what is the dominant object in the government structure. However, democracy orientation also defines whom the voters focus on during elections. From this perspective, one can distinguish four fundamental types of such orientation: candidate-oriented democracy (e.g., the United States), party leader-oriented democracy (e.g., the United Kingdom and Mexico), party-oriented democracy (e.g., France, Poland or Finland) and government-oriented democracy (e.g., Russia and China) (Cwalina, Falkowski, & Newman, 2011, 2012).

Depending on the democracy orientation, then, political campaigns may focus on different goals and use different means to reach them, including many of the recent innovations put forward in the two recent election campaigns of Barack Obama in 2008 and 2012, including micro-targeting, social media, voter analytics and Big Data (Newman, 2016). Nevertheless, in all democratic systems, political campaigns are permanent. The permanent campaign is a process of continuing transformation. It never stops. Therefore, distinguishing the particular stages of the campaign (pre-campaign period, campaign period and post-campaign period) is, in a sense, an artificial procedure because those particular stages often merge into one with no clear dividing lines between stages. Governing then becomes a perpetual campaign that transforms government into an instrument designed to sustain an elected official's public popularity (Newman, 1999; Williams & Newman, 2013; Gouliamos, Theocharous, & Newman, 2013).

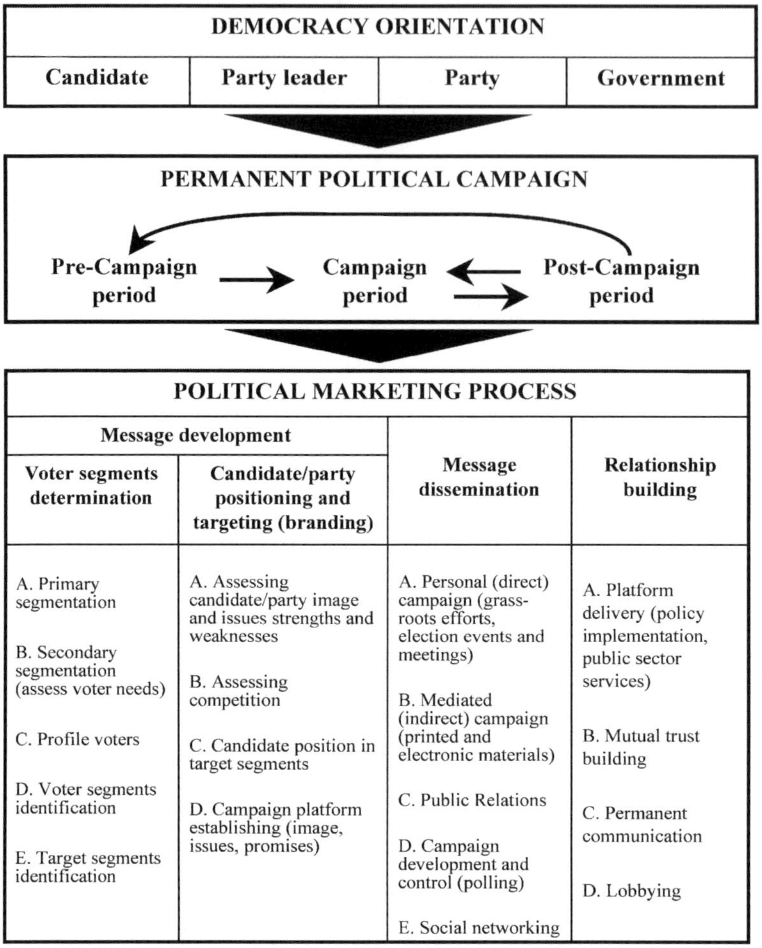

Figure 15.1 The advanced model of political marketing (Cwalina, Falkowski, & Newman, 2011, p. 74).

The political marketing process contains three key elements: politician/party message development, message dissemination and relationship building (Cwalina, Falkowski, & Newman, 2011, 2012). Message development refers to distinguishing particular groups of voters for whom an individualized and appropriate campaign platform will be designed. Determining voter segments is a process in which the electorate is broken down into segments or groupings that the candidate then targets with a particular message. In political marketing, one can distinguish two levels of voter segmentation: primary and secondary (Cwalina, Falkowski, & Newman, 2009). The primary segmentation focuses on dividing voters based on two main criteria: (1) voter party identification (particular party partisanship versus independency) and (2) voter identification strength (from heavy partisans through weak partisans to floating voters). Looking at the marketing campaign holistically, its goal should be to reinforce the decisions of the supporters and to win the support of those who are uncertain or whose preferences are not crystallized and those who still hesitate or have poor identification with a candidate or party that is close ideologically. It is these groups of voters that require more study – the secondary segmentation.

After identifying voting segments, one needs to define the candidate's position in each of the multiple stages in the process of positioning. This consists of assessing the candidate's and opponents' strengths and weaknesses. The key elements here include (1) creating an image of the candidate that emphasizes the individual's particular personality traits and (2) developing and presenting a clear position on the country's economic and social issues. These elements may be used jointly for positioning politicians via policies on issues or via image and emotions. The goal of message development is to set and establish the campaign platform. This evolves over the course of the permanent political campaign (during both the election period and the governing period). The campaign platform is defined in terms of candidate leadership, image and the issues and policies the candidate advocates. It is influenced by several factors, including the candidate, the people in the candidate's organization, the party and, most importantly, the voters.

The established political or party message is then communicated to the voter market. A personal (direct) campaign primarily refers to the grassroots effort necessary to build up a volunteer network to handle the day-to-day activities of running the campaign. The grassroots effort becomes the first information channel to transmit the candidate's message from the candidate's organization to the voters, and to transmit feedback from the voters to the candidate.

A mediated (indirect) campaign is a second information channel for the candidate. Instead of the person-to-person channel used with the direct marketing approach, this channel makes use of electronic and printed media outlets, such as television, radio, newspapers, magazines, direct mail, the Internet (e.g., email, websites, blogs), campaign literature (e.g., fliers, brochures, fact sheets), billboards and any other available forms of promotion. Political marketing also adopts new ways of communicating with the voter, mainly related to the development of new technologies, such as social networking and mobile marketing.

The third element of the political marketing process and the goal of any political party or candidate is to establish, maintain and enhance relationships with voters and other political power brokers (e.g., media, party organizations, sponsors, lobbyists, interest groups) to meet the objectives of the parties involved. This is achieved by a mutual exchange, both during the election campaign and after it, when the candidate is either ruling or in opposition to the winner. An integral element of this relationship building is the "promise concept". The key functions related to this concept are giving promises, fulfilling promises and enabling promises. Therefore, an important element of building stable relationships is trust, which is a willingness to rely on an exchange partner in whom one has confidence. To achieve trust, one also needs to establish communications channels that function on a constant basis. Therefore, in the next paragraph the accurate notion of a politician, as used in political marketing, is presented.

A politician is not a product

The key consequence of the still common myth that political marketing is similar to product marketing is that candidates are often compared to particular consumer products, such as toothpaste or a bar of soap. As Kotler and Levy (1969, p. 10) state, "political contests remind us that candidates are marketed as well as soap". From the perspective of modern political marketing, comparisons between politicians and products are outdated, are hardly appropriate and may lead to errors in planning and conducting successful election campaigns (Cwalina, Falkowski, & Newman, 2011; Harris, 2001; Lees-Marchment, 2009; Newman, 1994). The notion that candidates can be promoted in the same manner as soap has become the mechanism for decrying the side effects of political marketing. This outdated axiom still continues to be used by political actors and observers, especially media, alike. The "selling soap" analogy presumes that candidates are sold within a selling concept rather than promoted within a marketing concept.

Candidates are not "sold"; they are "marketed". First of all, the marketing concept begins with the voter, not the candidate. Following a selling concept means that the candidate looks no further than her/his own ideology to develop the campaign platform, which may not be what the electorate wants to hear. In contrast, the marketing concept dictates what candidates should do to create and retain their voters.

Newman (1994) states that if one needs to make an analogy, the candidate is like a service provider rather than a product. From this perspective, candidates offer a service to their voters, much in the same way that insurance agents offer a service to their consumers. In this case, the insurance policy becomes the product sold by the agent. However, the actual delivery of a service that candidates offer to the voter does not occur until they begin to govern. But these similarities between service and political marketing do not mean that they are identical. Among elements distinguishing political marketing, Lloyd (2005) suggests the following: (1) political outcomes are standardized at the point of "production", whereas variations arise from the way they are perceived, based upon electors' experiences and expectations; (2) political outcomes may refer to individuals or groups, and they either function independently or sum up; and (3) voters are stakeholders in the resources that create political outcomes. More importantly, the main purpose of consumer goods marketing is to increase firms' financial gain from selling their products or services. In the political marketplace, the motivations of politicians are different. Ambition lies at the heart of politics, and it thrives on the hope of preferment and the drive for office (Rohde, 1979; Schlesinger, 1966). Politicians, then, may be characterized as driven by a motivational syndrome that comprises the needs for power, status, achievement and affiliation (Winter, 1982), but they may also be driven by the need for experience seeking (Canon, 1993).

"Politics deals with a person, not a product" (O'Shaughnessy, 1987, p. 63). In every democratic country in the world, regardless of the electoral system (e.g., majority rule, first-past-the-post, proportional representation), voters cast a vote for a particular candidate – listed on the ballot with their name. They may be a representative of a political party, but they may be an "independent" candidate. In consequence, political marketing is mainly concerned with people and their relationships with each other, whereas consumer goods marketing is often concerned with people's interaction with products. Therefore, attitudes and impression-formation processes in reference to political candidates as persons also have a number of characteristics distinguishing them from consumer products. These differences are visible at neural as well as psychological and behavioural levels of information processing.

Neural differences in brand and person judgements

When thinking about objects and people, there are important differences in the processing of information, both at a neural level and in terms of self-report or behavioural measures. Using event-related functional magnetic resonance imaging (fMRI), Mitchell, Heatherton and Macrae (2002) measured neural activity of participants while they made semantic judgements about people or objects. Participants in this study responded to visually presented noun–-adjective pairs by pressing one of two response buttons if the adjective could ever be true of the noun or another button if it could not. Nouns were the name of a person (e.g., David, Emily) or an object from the categories "clothing" (e.g., glove, shirt) and "fruit" (e.g., grape, mango). Half of the adjectives could appropriately describe a person (e.g., assertive, energetic, fickle, nervous) but none of the objects, whereas the remaining half of the adjectives could describe one class of objects, but not persons or the other class of objects (e.g., clothing: patched, threadbare; fruit: sundried, seedless). The results of this experiment demonstrated a qualitative dissociation between the brain areas subserving semantic judgements about people and inanimate objects. This dissociation was evidenced both by the neuroanatomical localization of different brain areas as well as by qualitative differences in the nature of the haemodynamic time courses underlying activation in these areas. Generally, these results suggest that distinct networks of brain regions subserve the representation of semantic knowledge about people and objects.

Extending this work, participants in the next study, conducted by Mitchell, Macrae and Banaji (2005), were asked either to form an impression about or to remember the order of information presented alongside two types of target: people and inanimate objects.

During scanning, participants responded to target–statement pairs. Targets were photographs of male faces, computers and cars, and statements were sentences, which described persons (e.g., "promised not to smoke in his apartment since his roommate was trying to quit"), computers (e.g., "had coffee spilled on it last month") and cars (e.g., "recently had new fog lights installed"). Each photograph–statement pair was accompanied by one of two cues ("Form Impression" or "Remember order") that indicated, respectively, whether the impression-formation or sequencing task was to be performed on that trial. For impression-formation trials, participants were instructed to use the statement to generate an opinion about the person or object. Participants were told that, for these trials, their opinion about each target would later be measured. For sequencing trials, participants were instructed to encode the order in which statements were paired with each target. Participants were told that, for these trials, their memory for the sequences would later be tested. In actual fact, no such tests were administered. Mitchell and his collaborates (2005) found that one of the brain regions (i.e., the dorsal medial prefrontal cortex (mPFC)) was differentially activated by forming impressions of other people compared with forming impressions of inanimate objects or with intentionally encoding the order of information associated with targets of either type. These results suggest that activity of this brain region is uniquely engaged in the social-cognitive aspects of integrating information into a coherent impression of requiring reference to the psychological states of another person – and not simply forming impressions more generally.

More specifically, Yoon, Gutchess, Feinberg and Polk (2006) used fMRI to investigate whether semantic judgements about products and persons are processed similarly. The rationale for their study was the assumption that although we might describe both a friend and his car as "reliable", our meanings would surely not be identical. That is, although we may use similar vocabularies to describe judgements of persons and products, we cannot conclude that the same concepts are involved in the use of those terms. During scanning, each participant was presented with five different types of target cue items concurrently presented with an adjective (e.g., "Sprite + cheerful", "Billy Joel + sincere"). The five types of judgements corresponding to the critical treatment conditions were (a) person-self (i.e., does the adjective describe you?); (b) person-nonself (i.e., does the adjective describe the person, e.g., Billy Joel?); (c) brand-self (i.e., does the adjective describe a brand that is self-relevant, e.g., Sprite?); (d) brand-nonself (i.e., does the adjective describe a brand that is not self-relevant, e.g., Harley-Davidson?); and (e) case (i.e., is the adjective presented in uppercase or lowercase?). The results of this study supported the contention that consumers do not process descriptive judgements of products in the same manner as those applied to humans. In particular, Yoon and her collaborators found neural dissociation of cortical regions subserving descriptive judgements about products and people. Specifically, comparisons of neural responses for judgements about persons (self and nonself) and brands (self and nonself) indicated significantly greater mPFC activation for persons, and for products, activation was greater in the left inferior prefrontal cortex (LIPC), an area known to be involved in object processing. These results are consistent with and extend the studies of Mitchell and his collaborators (2002, 2005) and challenge the view that processing of products and brands is akin to that of humans. Furthermore, people are significantly more complex objects than products or brands.

Complexity of candidate's campaign platform

People need to predict what other people will do, and the other person's perceived characteristics are the basis for predicting his/her behaviour. Unlike objects, people are agents, that is, they intentionally influence the environment and attempt to control it for their own purposes (Fiske & Taylor, 2008; Kelley & Michela, 1980). Persons are "perceived as action centers and as such can do something to us. They can benefit or harm us intentionally, and we can benefit or harm them. Persons have abilities, wishes and sentiments; they can act purposefully, and can perceive or watch us" (Heider, 1958, p. 21). Thus, even when we know another person quite well, we often desire to find out *why* she is acting in a certain way. For example, when a presidential candidate during a meeting with voters takes a small child in his arms, we can think about the causes of such behaviour. If we can attribute a given action to some enduring cause (e.g., stable personality trait), we add a measure of predictability to our social world. We gain confidence that under similar conditions, this particular person will act much the same way again. For example, hugging the child by a politician is a sign that she or he is sensitive and caring. However, if we can attribute a given action to some situational factors, we can conclude that she or he behaves in this way because of circumstances: He wants to please voters and gain their support. Then, because people are so complex, because they have traits and intents hidden from view, and because they affect us in ways objects do not, social cognition automatically involves social explanation. It is more important for an ordinary person to explain why a person is fragile than to explain why a bauble that we hang on the Christmas tree is fragile (Fiske & Taylor, 2008).

One of the basic feature of person knowledge is that it frequently refers to the mental states of others (e.g., beliefs, attitudes, intentions to act, motivations, emotions, etc.), states that cannot be directly observed but may instead require generalization from one's own internal psychological properties (Fiske & Taylor, 2008). Even if we do not intend to make a person judgement or to form a person impression, but simply attend to another person's physical features and their behaviour, this is sufficient to trigger inferences about the person. These inferences are automatic and occur even if the behaviour presentation is very brief and if we do not attend carefully to the meaning of the behaviour. These spontaneous inferences are about the person and have specific implications for our representation of that person (e.g., Bargh, 1994; Uleman, Saribay, & Gonzalez, 2008). For example, Sears (1983) showed that, depending on the point at which the personhood or humanness dimension of the object in question is located, it is evaluated differently. At the personal extreme are located specific individual human beings, such as you, me, Barack Obama, Angela Merkel and the clerk at the corner drugstore. At the impersonal extreme are located wholly inanimate objects – natural, such as rocks, and human made, such as soap or soft drinks. In the middle of the personhood continuum are located collective social objects such as groups (e.g., political party or football club), aggregated people (e.g., "the aged" or "the poor") and institutions that are collections of individuals (such as the European Parliament or the United States Congress). The findings from 11 studies by Sears (1983) show that the positivity effect, i.e., the tendency towards favourable evaluation of the object, is stronger for personal objects (e.g., a particular politician or professor) than for collective social objects (e.g., politicians in general or professors in general), whereas Menon and Johar (1997) found that this effect does not manifest at all in the case of consumer experiences with products (e.g., buying a laptop).

Person perception is more complex than inanimate object perception due to the manifold observational data available and the various causes to which these data can be attributed. For this reason, one of the main purposes of political marketing is strict control over the information about the candidate (e.g., Cwalina, Falkowski, & Newman, 2015; Perloff, 2014). In general, they have to present her or him in a positive light and make her or his image and message attractive to voters and effective in gaining their support. Then, what is crucial for the specificity of political marketing is defining what the candidate offer or "political product" actually is. Butler and Collins (1994) describe it as a conglomerate consisting of three parts: the multicomponent (person/party/ideology) nature of the offer; the significant degree of loyalty involved; and the fact that it is mutable – that is, it can be changed or transformed in the post-election setting. Lees-Marshment (2003, pp. 14–15) defines a party's "product" as its behaviour that "is ongoing and offered at all times (not just elections), at all levels of party. The products include the leadership, MP's (and candidates), membership, staff, symbols, constitution, activities such as party conferences and policies".

According to Newman (1994), the real candidate election offer or "political product" is the campaign platform. It consists of a number of elements, including (1) the election manifesto of the candidate based on the political and economic guidelines of the party s/he belongs to or the organization set up for the time of the elections; (2) his/her positions on the most important problems appearing during the campaign; (3) the image of the candidate; (4) his/her reference to her/his political background and the groups of voters supporting her/him (e.g., labour unions, associations, NGOs etc.) or the authorities. These components are strongly interrelated and they are likely to influence candidate evaluation and support (Hacker, Zakahi, Giles, & McQuitty, 2000). The results of correlational analyses combining issues with candidate image conducted by Schoenwald (1987) show, for example, that an improved voter perception on the "devotes-time-to-education" attribute could translate into a better reading on caring about children, caring about state problems and being generally more human. Similarly, in an experiment conducted in Poland, Falkowski and Michalak (2014) found, using structural equation modelling, that evaluation of the candidate's electoral manifesto significantly affects the assessment of his image characteristics, but not vice versa. Participants in their experiment were initially given a description of a real politician (manifesto and personality characteristics) and then asked to evaluate various aspects of the candidate: their policy proposals, traits and physical appearance. A week later, they read a positive or negative opinion of the politician and were asked to recall their earlier evaluations. The results show that the core structure of a politician's image is based on his election policy. However, a decision on the electoral support of a politician is a result of the interaction of both election manifesto and the image of the candidate. These findings corroborate the view presented by Scammell (1996), that the role of a candidate's issue stands (presented in manifesto, interviews, press conferences, public speeches, ads, etc.) in election campaigning lies not only in their intrinsic merit but also in their ability to affect the overall image of her/his credibility and competence. This assumption is supported by Peterson (2005), who also found that in addition to the direct impact on vote choice, issue stands also matter because they determine how voters perceive candidate character. The more certain a voter is about a candidate's policy positions, the more the voter uses those positions to inform her perceptions of the candidate's personality. This relation, in turn, produces sizeable differences in whom the voter is likely to support. Therefore, it is necessary to describe the candidate's campaign platform, that is, a list of the values and actions that are supported by a political party or individual candidate, in order to appeal to the general public.

Candidate's campaign platform

The application of person knowledge demands a flexibility that is typically unnecessary for most classes of object knowledge. People must frequently track interactions among independent agents acting in complex social settings (Mitchell et al., 2002). People change over time and circumstances more than objects typically do. This can make cognitions rapidly obsolete or unreliable. The accuracy of one's cognitions about people is harder to check than the accuracy of one's cognitions about objects. It is hard to agree on whether a given person is honest, extraverted or cold, but it is quite easy to test whether a given vacuum cleaner is quiet and energy efficient (Fiske & Taylor, 2008). Moreover, people may also change upon being the target of perception. For example, they may adjust their appearance or behaviour for the demands of a given situation.

According to the advanced model of political marketing, elaborating and establishing the campaign platform is the most important element of the political marketing process (Baines, Harris, & Lewis, 2002; Cwalina, Falkowski, & Newman, 2011). It is the final effect of campaign message development that is individualized, adjusted, positioned and delivered to targeted voter segments. But the important characteristic of a campaign platform is its flexibility. It evolves together with the development of the voting campaign and changes in the electoral competition. Moreover, although the campaign platform is an overall presentation of the candidate's message, it does not mean that voters are equally focused on each of its components. The weights of particular domains of the platform may change with changes in macro- (e.g., legal regulations, demographic transitions, new media) and micro- (e.g., changes in voter beliefs, set of the candidates in particular electoral district, role of political consultants) factors influencing the political process (Cwalina, Falkowski, & Newman, 2012). Based on his model of the voter's choice behaviour, Newman (1999b; Newman & Sheth, 1985) shows that the value of information reaching the voter depends on the specific domain it concerns: issue and policies (candidate's manifesto), social imagery (perception of reference groups supportive for candidates), emotional feelings aroused by candidate, candidate image, current events (economic, social or international), personal events (situations in the personal life of the candidate) and epistemic issues (specific motives for support of a given candidate). Based on the value of the information concerning those particular domains for the voter, he distinguishes four segments of voters. *Rational voters* are primarily concerned with the policies and issues dealing with the economy, foreign policy and social issues, and these are mainly the issues they consider when making their voting decisions. *Emotional voters* are mainly concerned with the candidate's personality or image, and with particular emotions that a candidate evokes among voters, such as happiness, hope, anxiety, pride and disappointment. When making political choices, emotional voters follow their feelings. *Social voters* vote for a given candidate associated with a particular social group, including, for instance, a national minority, a particular religion or a business lobby. The fourth group, *situational voters*, are particularly sensitive in their choices to anything that has or might have happened recently: negative (e.g., higher rate of inflation or unemployment or increased corruption) or positive (e.g., increased access to education and to the Internet, lower costs of living or fewer racial tensions). The results of a cross-cultural study of presidential elections in the United States and Poland and the parliamentary election in Slovenia in 2000 conducted by Cwalina, Falkowski and Newman (2008, 2010; Cwalina, Falkowski, Newman, & Verčič, 2004) confirm that in an established democracy like the United States, voters have already learned to analyse more carefully messages from presidential campaigns. They are more focused on policies proposed by candidates and their associations with specific social groups (white-collar workers and executives in the case of George W. Bush, and the poor in the case of Al Gore). In comparison, in evolving democracies like Poland and Slovenia, the key factor in influencing voting behaviour was the affect towards the candidate elicited by his image and situational contingency (see also Falkowski & Cwalina, 2002; Newman, 2002; Verčič & Verdnik, 2002). Thus, the flexibility of candidate's campaign platforms in building his/her image is quite large.

The political message, as a part of building the campaign platform, may not only be targeted to particular segments of the marketplace; it may also influence the weights that voters ascribe to various components of a candidate's campaign platform. The psychological mechanism of this influence is priming (Cwalina, Falkowski, & Newman, 2015). Priming can influence voters by altering their perceptions of issue salience and attributes of the candidate's image as well as relative weights of these campaign platform components.

For a large part of the electorate to decide for whom to vote, party affiliation or ideological orientation is sufficient information about candidates. If it is consistent with their party identifications, it significantly modifies the judgements about candidates, as well as determining the decision to support any of them. The concept of party identification explains how the average individual manages the complexities of democratic politics. This directly relates to the concept of partisanship: long-term, affective psychological attachment to a preferred political party (Campbell, Converse, Miller, & Stokes, 1960; Green, Palmquist, & Schickler, 2002). Partisanship is, then, a heuristic for organizing political information, evaluations and behaviours (Conover & Feldman, 1981; Cwalina, Falkowski, & Newman, 2008). It is some kind of a "perceptual screen" through which individuals interpret and evaluate their political experiences. According to Dalton (2013), partisanship ties individuals to their preferred political party and its representatives. It helps orient the individual to the complexities of politics, provides a framework for assimilating political information and understanding political issues, and acts as a guide in making political judgements. Therefore, voter party identification (vs. independence), and its strength (from heavy partisans to floating voters) are two main criteria of the primary segmentation in the advanced model of political marketing, strictly connected with candidates' campaign platforms. Rahn (1993) found that in the absence of the party label, individuals can and do respond to the implications of the candidates' messages. They use policy positions in making their evaluations of the candidates and in inferences about their stands on issues. However, when voters have both particular policy information and a party label, they neglect the first and use the label in drawing inferences and evaluating candidates. Even when individuating policy information is made available in conjunction with party stereotypes, it is ignored and even distorted. The analysis conducted by Bishin, Stevens and Wilson (2005) also confirms the influence of voters' partisanship on candidate information processing. Based on data from the Voter News Service (VNS) General Election Exit Poll 2000, they found that the impact of a presidential candidate's character on voting decisions is larger for independents than for partisans. Moreover, the results suggest that for some candidates the impact of character can be decisive. More specifically, shifts in the perception of George W. Bush from truthful or fair to untruthful or unfair led the independent voters who supported him to oppose him. However, character evaluations of Al Gore did not affect voting decisions significantly.

The results of two experiments conducted by Cwalina and Falkowski (in press b) corroborate the existence of strong partisan bias in evaluation of political candidates and political parties. In the first experiment, participants, divided into three groups, were presented with the election manifesto of a fictional party – the Polish Renewal Initiative. In the first group, the party was described as a "new left-wing party", in the second as a "new right-wing party", and in the control group, the party orientation was not defined but merely referred to as "new". All respondents were shown exactly the same manifesto and next they expressed, among other things, their attitude towards it (feeling thermometer scale) and intention to vote for the party. The results showed that the leftist voters had a more negative attitude towards and lower intention to vote for the right-wing party than for the party without an ideological label and the leftist party, and the rightist voters were more negative towards the left-wing party as well as the party without an ideological label than towards the party whose label was consistent with their ideological orientation.

In the second experiment, participants were presented with a brief description of a fictional Polish politician. This description was the same for all participants except for information about his party affiliation. He was presented as a member of the Democratic Left Alliance (SLD; left-wing party) vs. the Polish People's Party (Polskie Stronnictwo Ludowe (PSL); agrarian, centre-right-wing party) vs. the Civic Platform (Platforma Obywatelska (PO); centre-right-wing party) vs. the Law and Justice (Prawo i Sprawiedliwość (PiS); right-wing party) vs. a party without a specified name ("one of the political parties"). Next, subjects, among other things, evaluated his image and the perceived belief that the politician would represent the interests of his voters well in parliament. Cwalina and Falkowski (in press b) found that the politician with party affiliation consistent with the voters' orientation was evaluated as significantly more competent than the politician with party affiliation incompatible with this orientation. Moreover, the politician with no specified party affiliation was evaluated as more competent by the right-wing than by the left-wing voters. The same pattern of results was evident in beliefs about the appropriate representation of voters by the politician.

Basic dimensions of candidate's image

The attributes used to describe persons differ substantially from those used to describe inanimate objects (e.g., products or brands). Whereas objects are primarily evaluated based on how well they function (instrumental benefits), functionality is far less important when evaluating people. Keller (1993, 2005) describes core brand performance as the heart of a brand's equity. Symbolic and psychological benefits are important, but are more useful for positioning advantages or differentiation. On the other hand, functional performance is essential to place the brand on parity with other brands in the category, and rarely can a brand overcome performance deficiencies. Similarly, Kahn and Meyer (1991) found that during product evaluation consumers emphasize the absence of utility-preserving attributes (e.g., basic quality of a stereo's sound) over absence of utility-enhancing attributes (e.g., sleek design of the stereo). This means that utility-preserving (functional) attributes create core performance of the product.

Psychological research indicates that primary, universal dimensions of social cognition include social intent for good or ill (morality or communion) and capability to enact those intentions (competence or agency) (e.g., Abele & Wojciszke, 2007; Fiske, Cuddy, & Glick, 2006; Peeters, 1992; Reeder & Brewer, 1979). Intentions are seen to follow from dispositions. Moral content dominates person perception because it typically has a direct and unconditional bearing on the well-being of other people surrounding the person who is described by the trait (including the perceiver). Competence dominates self-perception because it has a direct bearing on the well-being of the perceiver (Wojciszke, 2005). When forming global evaluations of others, the perceiver is more interested in their moral than their competence qualities and construes their behaviour in moral terms, and his or her impressions and emotional responses are more strongly based on morality than on competence considerations (Wojciszke, Bazinska, & Jaworski, 1998).

Morality and competence are also the core features of politicians' images that positively and strongly influence voters' behaviour towards them (Cwalina, Falkowski, & Newman, 2011; Druckman, Jacobs, & Ostermeier, 2004; Funk, 1999; Kinder & Sears, 1985; Kjeldahl,

Carmichael, & Mertz, 1971; Pancer, Brown, & Barr, 1999). Moreover, they are central qualities of the ideal president prototype, as shown by the results of research conducted in the United States (Kinder, Peters, Abelson, & Fiske, 1980) as well as in Poland (Cwalina & Falkowski, 2000, 2006).

For example, Wattenberg (1991; see also Miller, Wattenberg, & Malanchuk, 1986), after analyzing the evaluations of the personality features of all the candidates running for the US presidency between 1952 and 1988, found that a candidate's personal attributes can be divided into five general categories: (1) integrity – associated with the candidate's trustworthiness and incorporating comments concerning honesty, sincerity and any reference to corruption in government; (2) reliability – a candidate being dependable, strong, decisive, aggressive, stable or the converse of these; (3) competence – refers to a candidate's past experience, ability as a statesman, comprehension of political issues, realism and intelligence; (4) charisma – a candidate's leadership abilities, dignity, humbleness, patriotism and ability to get along and communicate with people; and (5) personal aspects of the candidate – appearance, age, religion, wealth, former occupation, family and so on. The results of analyses performed by Wattenberg (1991) showed that in seven cases out of ten, the candidate who got higher ratings in public opinion polls regarding the previously mentioned attributes won.

The importance of politicians' integrity and competence for the political support they receive has been the subject of sophisticated analyses by Mondak (1995a, b; McCurley & Mondak, 1995). He assumed that the goal of the voter is to identify the best candidate from those running for an office. The quality of the candidate refers to the non-political traits that can be traced in his or her behaviour, and include integrity and competence. From this perspective, an electoral system functions as a filtration mechanism in that voters strive to maximize the quality of their elected representatives. Those who do not meet these criteria remain, like sediment, at the very bottom. In order to verify these assumptions, Mondak conducted content analysis of the written descriptions of the US House members that appear in the 1972–94 volumes of the *Almanac of American Politics*. All words and phrases that spoke of a House member's competence or integrity were coded, and next they were juxtaposed with the judgements of the same candidates made by American voters in National Election Studies (NES) from 1976 to 1992. The results show that American congressmen do not treat service in the House as a stepping stone. The politicians running for higher office are – on average – evaluated as less moral than those who remain in the House of Representatives. Strategic retirement from re-election seems to be related to their morality (scandals) rather than competencies. Their competencies are on a similar level to those still holding office but their honesty is lower. Mondak's analysis also demonstrated that quality and integrity evaluations exert a strong direct effect on both the general evaluation (the NES feeling thermometer) and on the vote choice. Competence, in contrast, affects only the vote. Furthermore, challengers receive additional votes per dollar when they oppose low-quality rather than high-quality incumbents. Consequently, according to Mondak (1995a), the electoral system functions not only to weed out the worst incumbents, but also to preserve the best.

The results of an experiment conducted in Poland by Cwalina and Falkowski (2016) lead to similar conclusions. Participants read one of the four versions of a fictitious Polish parliament candidate's profile, presenting him as incompetent and immoral, competent and immoral, incompetent and moral, and competent and moral. Next, they evaluated the candidate on number variables and expressed intention to vote for him in a parliamentary election. The results show that what was crucial for voting for the politician was his morality. The support for a candidate with high morality and low competence was significantly higher than that for a candidate with low morality and high competence.

Although morality and competence are the core dimensions of the image of a politician, it does not mean that her or his positioning on election market cannot be built on the basis of other dispositions. For example, Caprara and his collaborators (Caprara & Zimbardo, 2004; Caprara, Barbaranelli, Consiglio, Picconi, & Zimbardo, 2003; Caprara et al., 2007, Caprara, Schwarz, Vecchione, & Barbaranelli, 2008) found that people vote for candidates whose personality traits are in accordance with the ideology of their preferred party and whose traits match their own traits, while Cwalina and Drzewiecka (in press; Drzewiecka & Cwalina, 2014) show positioning strategy based on politicians' leadership styles, where leaders with coercive leadership style are least preferred by voters, while voters are willing to vote for parties led by leaders with democratic, coaching and affiliative style.

Final remarks

Psychological research shows that the semantic system for person knowledge may prove to relay on mind architecture structurally similar to that underlying object knowledge. As in the case of consumer goods as well as politicians and political parties, one of the key factors of its success is building brand equity (Cwalina & Falkowski, 2015; de Chernatony & White, 2002; Keller, 2005; Smith, 2001). In consumer and political domains brand knowledge is consistent with Anderson's (1983) associative network memory model. According to this model, semantic memory or knowledge consists of a set of nodes and links. Nodes are stored pieces of information connected by links that vary in strength. A spreading activation process from node to node determines the extent of retrieval in memory. A node becomes a potential source of activation for other nodes either when external information is being encoded or when internal information is retrieved from long-term memory. Activation can spread from one node to other linked nodes in memory. When the activation of another node exceeds some threshold level, the information contained in that node is recalled. Thus, the strength of association between the activated node and all linked nodes determines the extent of spreading activation and the particular information that can be retrieved from memory. However, although the structure of consumer and political brands is similar, the content and processes in these representations are different, and have different implications for brand performance. Comparative studies in this field include Lock and Harris (1996) and Cwalina, Falkowski and Newman (2011). One of the common strategies in consumer product marketing is enhancing a physical object through abstract associations (Keller, 2005; Shostack, 1977). Its purpose is shifting attention away from pragmatic considerations about a product (such as the product's functionality) and making consumers sensitive to information that figures prominently in the interpersonal realm (such as the product's perception as "warm" or "cold"). This strategy is based on priming anthropomorphic beliefs about products and brands. The essence of anthropomorphism is attributing capacities that people tend to think of as distinctly human to non-human agents such as animals, natural entities, technological devices, things or brands (Epley, Waytz, & Cacioppo, 2007; Waytz, Cacioppo, & Epley, 2010). In this marketing approach "brand personality" has emerged as an important means of brand differentiation, and thus of increasing consumer preference. Brand personality is defined as "the set of human characteristics associated with brand" (Aaker, 1997, p. 347) or as "the set of human personality traits that correspond to the interpersonal domain of human personality and are relevant to describing brand as a relationship partner" (Sweeney & Brandon, 2006, p. 645).

The main consequence of anthropomorphism in marketing is creating empathic connection with products and brands, which is based on trust and friendship (Aaker, Fournier, & Brasel, 2004; Fournier, 1998). The results of two experiments conducted by Chandler and Schwarz (2010) show that consumers reported lower intentions to replace their car when they were induced to think about it in anthropomorphic terms. Moreover, thinking about one's car in anthropomorphic terms decoupled replacement intentions from the car's perceived quality and functionality. Instead, consumers who were primed to think about their car in anthropomorphic terms turned to information that is valued in the interpersonal domain and were less likely to replace their car when its colour was associated with (experimentally manipulated) "warm" rather than "cold" connotations. Thus, whether a target is categorized as person or inanimate object (e.g., product) has downstream consequences on what information comes to mind, what information is deemed relevant and what predictions seem plausible when thinking about the target. However, perception of products or brands in terms of human attributes is not spontaneous and automatic. Consumers must be primed in more or less subtle ways (e.g., verbal description of product in human terms in advertising; endowing product with human features such as the shape of the front grille of the car as pointing up in the shape of a smile; Aggarwal & McGill, 2007). For example, participants in Aaker's (1997, p. 350) study received instruction: "We would like you to think of each brand as if it were a person. This may *sound unusual* [emphasis added], but think of the set of human characteristics associated with each brand". Menon and Johar (1997) suggest that consumer researchers need to be cautious when applying knowledge of structure and processes dealing with person memory to the domain of products. The results of their research demonstrate that judgements related to non-social product experiences trigger processes that are different from those established for social stimuli. Product experiences are inherently less ambiguous than personal experiences, thereby entailing more concrete and less self-referent processing. Judgements of social stimuli (e.g., person, party) are likely to depend on inferred, abstract information (e.g., traits), whereas judgements of non-social stimuli (e.g., products) are likely to depend on concrete attributes. Moreover, the results of neuroimaging research on anthropomorphizing objects also show different neural patterns of dispositional inferences to objects than to people (Harris & Fiske, 2008).

Just as a person is not a product, the product will never be the person. As a consequence, identifying political brands with consumer brands may lead to errors if marketing knowledge is directly applied to politics (Newman, 2016). Future research will focus on developing a methodology for building brand value in the political marketplace. The current discussion stimulating such research can be found in the special issue of the *Journal of Political Marketing* (*14*(1–2), 2015) dedicated to political branding.

References

Aaker, J. L. (1997). Dimensions of brand personality. *Journal of Marketing Research*, *34*, 347–356.

Aaker, J., Fournier, S., & Brasel, S. A. (2004). When good brands do bad. *Journal of Consumer Research*, *31*, 1–16.

Abele, A. E., & Wojciszke, B. (2007). Agency and communion from the perspective of self versus others. *Journal of Personality and Social Psychology*, *93*, 751–763.

Aggarwal, P., & McGill, A. L. (2007). Is that car smiling at me? Schema congruity as a basis for evaluating anthropomorphized products. *Journal of Consumer Research*, *34*, 468–479.

Anderson, J. R. (1983). *The architecture of cognition*. Cambridge, MA: Harvard University Press.

Baines, P. R., Harris, P., & Lewis, B. R. (2002). The political marketing planning process: Improving image and message in strategic target areas. *Marketing Intelligence & Planning*, *20*, 6–14.

Bargh, J. A. (1994). The Four Horsemen of automaticity: Awareness, efficiency, intention, and control in social cognition. In R. S. Wyer & T. K. Srull (Eds.), *Handbook of social cognition* (pp. 1–40). Hillsdale, NJ: Erlbaum.

Bishin, B. J., Stevens, D., & Wilson, C. (2005). Truth or consequences? Character and swing voters in the 2000 election. *Public Integrity*, *7*, 129–146.

Butler, P., & Collins, N. (1994). Political marketing: Structure and process. *European Journal of Marketing*, *28*, 19–34.

Campbell, A., Converse, P. E., Miller, W. E., & Stokes, D. E. (1960). *The American voter.* New York, NY: Wiley.
Canon, D. T. (1993). Sacrificial lambs or strategic politicians? Political amateurs in U.S. House elections. *American Journal of Political Science, 37*, 1119–1141.
Caprara, G. V., & Zimbardo, P. G. (2004). Personalizing politics: A congruency model of political preference. *American Psychologist, 59*, 581–594.
Caprara, G. V., Barbaranelli, C., Fraley, R. C., & Vecchione, M. (2007). The simplicity of politicians' personalities across political context: An anomalous replication. *International Journal of Psychology, 42*, 393–405.
Caprara, G. V., Schwartz, S. H., Vecchione, M., & Barbaranelli, C. (2008). The personalization of politics: Lessons from the Italian case. *European Psychologist, 13*, 157–172.
Caprara, G. V., Barbaranelli, C., Consiglio, C., Picconi, L., & Zimbardo, P. G. (2003). Personalities of politicians and voters: Unique and synergic relationships. *Journal of Personality and Social Psychology, 84*, 849–856.
Chandler, J., & Schwarz, N. (2010). Use does not wear ragged the fabric of friendship: Thinking of objects as alive makes people less willing to replace them. *Journal of Consumer Psychology, 20*, 138–145.
Conover, P. J., & Feldman, S. (1981). The origins and meaning of liberal/conservative self-identifications. *American Journal of Political Science, 25*(4), 617–645.
Cwalina, W., & Drzewiecka, M. (in press). Who are the political leaders we are looking for? Candidate positioning in terms of leadership style: A cross-cultural empirical study in Goleman's typology. *Journal of Political Marketing.*
Cwalina, W., & Falkowski, A. (2000). Psychological mechanisms of political persuasion: The influence of political advertising on voting behaviour. *Polish Psychological Bulletin, 31*, 203–222.
Cwalina, W., & Falkowski, A. (2006). Political communication and advertising in Poland. In L. L. Kaid & C. Holtz-Bacha (Eds.), *The Sage handbook of political advertising* (pp. 325–342). Thousand Oaks, CA: Sage.
Cwalina, W., & Falkowski, A. (2015). Political branding: Political candidates positioning based on inter-object associative affinity index. *Journal of Political Marketing, 14*, 152–174.
Cwalina, W., & Falkowski, A. (2016). Morality and competence in shaping the images of political leaders. *Journal of Political Marketing, 15*(2). doi: 10.1080/15377857.2016.1151121
Cwalina, W., & Falkowski, A. (in press). Partisan schemata in biased interpretation of electoral programmes and political candidate evaluation. *Journal of Political Marketing.*
Cwalina, W., Falkowski, A., & Newman, B. I. (2008). *A cross-cultural theory of voter behaviour.* New York, NY: Haworth Press.
Cwalina, W., Falkowski, A., & Newman, B. I. (2009). Political management and marketing. In D. W. Johnson (Ed.), *Routledge handbook of political management* (pp. 67–80). New York, NY: Routledge.
Cwalina, W., Falkowski, A., & Newman, B. I. (2010). Towards the development of a cross-cultural model of voter behaviour: Comparative analysis of Poland and the US. *European Journal of Marketing, 44*, 351–368.
Cwalina, W., Falkowski, A., & Newman, B. I. (2011). *Political marketing: Theoretical and strategic foundations.* Armonk, NY: M.E. Sharpe.
Cwalina, W., Falkowski, A., & Newman, B. I. (2012). The macro and micro views of political marketing: The underpinnings of a theory of political marketing. *Journal of Public Affairs, 12*, 254–269.
Cwalina, W., Falkowski, A., & Newman, B. I. (2014). Advanced theory of political marketing. In T. Marek, W. Karwowski, M. Frankowicz, J. Kantola & P. Zgaga (Eds.), *Human factors of a global society: A system of systems perspective* (pp. 245–254). Boca Raton, FL: CRC Press.
Cwalina, W., Falkowski, A., & Newman, B. I. (2015). Persuasion in the political context: Opportunities and threats. In D. W. Stewart (Ed.), *Handbook of persuasion and social marketing* (Vol. 1, pp. 61–128). Santa Barbara, CA: Praeger/ABC-CLIO, LLC.
Cwalina, W., Falkowski, A., Newman, B. I., & Verčič, D. (2004). Models of voter behaviour in traditional and evolving democracies: Comparative analysis of Poland, Slovenia, and U.S. *Journal of Political Marketing, 3*, 7–30.
Dalton, R. J. (2013). *The apartisan American: Dealignment and changing electoral politics.* Washington, DC: CQ Press.
de Chernatony, L., & White, J. (2002). New Labour: A study of the creation, development and demise of a political brand. *Journal of Political Marketing, 1*, 45–52.
Downs, A. (1957). *An economic theory of democracy.* New York, NY: HarperCollins.
Druckman, J. M., Jacobs, L. R., & Ostermeier, E. (2004). Candidate strategies to prime issues and image. *Journal of Politics, 66*, 1180–1202.

Drzewiecka, M., & Cwalina, W. (2014). What political leadership styles do we prefer? Cross-cultural study in Goleman's typology of leadership. *SCIECONF – Proceedings in Scientific Conference, 2*, 161–166.

Egan, J. (1999). Political marketing: Lessons from the mainstream. *Journal of Marketing Management, 15*, 495–503.

Epley, N., Waytz, A., & Cacioppo, J. T. (2007). On seeing human: A three-factor theory of anthropomorphism. *Psychological Review, 114*, 864–886.

Falkowski, A., & Cwalina, W. (2002). Structural models of voter behaviour in the 2000 Polish presidential election. *Journal of Political Marketing, 1*, 137–158.

Falkowski, A., & Michalak, M. (2014). Backward framing and memory evaluation in political elections. *Journal of Political Marketing, 13*, 85–107.

Farrell, D. M., & Wortmann, M. (1987). Parties' strategies in the electoral market: Political marketing in West Germany, Britain and Ireland. *European Journal of Political Research, 15*, 297–318.

Fiske, S. T., Cuddy, A. J. C., & Glick, P. (2006). Universal dimensions of social cognition: Warmth and competence. *Trends in Cognitive Sciences, 11*, 77–83.

Fiske, S. T., & Taylor, S. E. (2008). *Social cognition: From brains to culture*. New York, NY: McGraw-Hill.

Fournier, S. (1998). Consumers and their brands: Developing relationship theory in consumer research. *Journal of Consumer Research, 24*, 343–373.

Funk, C. L. (1999). Bringing the candidate into models of candidate evaluation. *Journal of Politics, 61*, 700–720.

Gouliamos, K., Theocharous, A., & Newman, B. I. (Eds.) (2013). *Political marketing: Strategic campaign culture*. New York, NY: Routledge.

Green, D., Palmquist, B., & Schickler, E. (2002). *Partisan hearts and minds: Political parties and the social identities of voters*. New Haven, CT: Yale University Press.

Hacker, K. L., Zakahi, W. R., Giles, M. J., & McQuitty, S. (2000). Components of candidate images: Statistical analysis of the issue-persona dichotomy in the presidential campaign of 1996. *Communication Monographs, 67*, 227–238.

Harris, L. T., & Fiske, S. T. (2008). The brooms in Fantasia: Neural correlates of anthropomorphizing objects. *Social Cognition, 26*, 210–223.

Harris, P. (2001). To spin or not to spin that is the question: The emergence of modern political marketing. *Marketing Review, 2*, 35–53.

Heider, F. (1958). *The psychology of interpersonal relations*. Hoboken, NJ: Wiley.

Kahn, B. E., & Meyer, R. J. (1991). Consumer multi-attribute judgments under attribute-weight uncertainty. *Journal of Consumer Research, 17*, 508–522.

Keller, K. L. (1993). Conceptualizing, measuring, managing customer-based brand equity. *Journal of Marketing, 57*, 1–22.

Keller, K. L. (2005). *Strategic brand management: Building, measuring, and managing brand equity*. Englewood Cliffs, NJ: Prentice-Hall.

Kelley, H. H., & Michela, J. L. (1980). Attribution theory and research. *Annual Review of Psychology, 31*, 457–501.

Kinder, D. R., Peters, M. D., Abelson, R. P., & Fiske, S. T. (1980). Presidential prototypes. *Political Behaviour, 2*, 315–337.

Kinder, D. R., & Sears, D. O. (1985). Public opinion and political action. In G. Lindzey & E. Aronson (Eds.), *Handbook of social psychology* (Vol. 2, pp. 659–741). New York, NY: Random House.

Kjeldahl, B. O., Carmichael, C. W., & Mertz, R. J. (1971). Factors in a presidential candidate's image. *Speech Monographs, 38*, 129–131.

Kotler, P. (1975). Overview of political candidate marketing. In M. J. Schlinger (Ed.), *Advances in consumer research* (Vol. 2, pp. 761–769). Provo, UT: Association for Consumer Research.

Kotler, P., & Kotler, N. (1999). Political marketing. Generating effective candidates, campaigns, and causes. In B. I. Newman (Ed.), *Handbook of political marketing* (pp. 3–18). Thousand Oaks, CA: Sage.

Kotler, P., & Levy, S. J. (1969). Broadening the concept of marketing. *Journal of Marketing, 33*, 10–15.

Lees-Marshment, J. (2003). Political marketing: How to reach that pot of gold. *Journal of Political Marketing, 2*, 1–32.

Lees-Marshment, J. (2009). *Political marketing: Principles and applications*. London: Routledge.

Lloyd, J. (2005). Square peg, round hole? Can marketing-based concepts such as "product" and the "marketing mix" have a useful role in the political arena? In W. W. Wymer Jr & J. Lees-Marshment (Eds.), *Current issues in political marketing* (pp. 27–46). Binghamton, NY: Haworth Press.

Lock, A., & Harris, P. (1996). Political marketing – vive la différence! *European Journal of Marketing, 30*, 14–24.

McCurley, C., & Mondak, J. J. (1995). Inspected by #1184063113: The influence of incumbents' competence and integrity in U.S. House elections. *American Journal of Political Science, 39*, 864–885.

Menon, G., & Johar, G. V. (1997). Antecedents of positivity effects in social versus nonsocial judgments. *Journal of Consumer Psychology, 6*, 313–337.

Miller, A. H., Wattenberg, M. P., & Malanchuk, O. (1986). Schematic assessments of presidential candidates. *American Political Science Review, 80*, 521–540.

Mitchell, J. P., Heatherton, T. F., & Macrae, C. N. (2002). Distinct neural systems subserve person and object knowledge. *Proceedings of the National Academy of Sciences of the United States of America, 99*, 15238–15243.

Mitchell, J. P., Macrae, C. N., & Banaji, M. R. (2005). Forming impressions of people versus inanimate objects: Social-cognitive processing in the medial prefrontal cortex. *NeuroImage, 26*, 251–257.

Mondak, J. J. (1995a). Elections as filters: Term limits and the composition of the U.S. House. *Political Research Quarterly, 48*, 701–727.

Mondak, J. J. (1995b). Competence, integrity, and the electoral success of congressional incumbents. *Journal of Politics, 57*, 1043–1069.

Newman, B. I. (1994). *The marketing of the president: Political marketing as campaign strategy*. Thousand Oaks, CA: Sage.

Newman, B. I. (1999a). *The mass marketing of politics: Democracy in an age of manufactured images*. Thousand Oaks, CA: Sage.

Newman, B. I. (1999b). A predictive model of voter behaviour: The repositioning of Bill Clinton. In B. I. Newman (Ed.), *Handbook of political marketing* (pp. 259–282). Thousand Oaks, CA: Sage.

Newman, B. I. (1999c). Handbook of political marketing. Thousand Oaks, CA: Sage.

Newman, B. I. (2002). Testing a predictive model of voter behaviour on the 2000 U.S. presidential election. *Journal of Political Marketing, 1*, 159–173.

Newman, B. I. (2016). *The marketing revolution in politics: What recent U.S. presidential campaigns can teach us about effective marketing*. Toronto, Canada: Rotman-University of Toronto Press.

Newman, B. I., & Sheth, J. N. (1985). A model of primary voter behaviour. *Journal of Consumer Research, 12*, 178–187.

Niffenegger, P. B. (1988). Strategies for success from the political marketers. *Journal of Services Marketing, 2*, 15–21.

O'Shaughnessy, N. (1987). America's political market. *European Journal of Marketing, 21*, 60–66.

Pancer, S. M., Brown, S. D., & Barr, C. W. (1999). Forming impression of political leaders: A cross-national comparison. *Political Psychology, 20*, 345–368.

Peeters, G. (1992). Evaluative meanings of adjectives in vitro and in context: Some theoretical implications and practical consequences of positive-negative asymmetry and behavioural-adaptive concepts of evaluations. *Psychologia Belgica, 32*, 211–231.

Perloff, R. M. (2014). *The dynamics of political communication: Media and politics in a digital age*. New York, NY: Routledge.

Peterson, D. A. M. (2005). Heterogeneity and certainty in candidate evaluations. *Political Behaviour, 27*, 1–24.

Rahn, W. M. (1993). The role of partisan stereotypes in information processing about political candidates. *American Journal of Political Science, 37*, 472–496.

Reeder, G. D., & Brewer, M. D. (1979). A schematic model of dispositional attributions in interpersonal perception. *Psychological Review, 86*, 61–79.

Rohde, D. W. (1979). Risk-bearing and progressive ambition: The case of members of the United States House of Representatives. *American Journal of Political Science, 23*, 1–26.

Scammell, M. (1996). The odd couple: Marketing and Maggie. *European Journal of Marketing, 30*, 114–126.

Schlesinger, J. (1966). *Ambition and politics: Political careers in the United States*. Chicago, IL: Rand McNally.

Schoenwald, M. (1987). Marketing a political candidate. *Journal of Consumer Marketing, 4*, 57–63.

Sears, D. O. (1983). The person-positivity bias. *Journal of Personality and Social Psychology, 44*, 233–250.

Shama, A. (1975). Applications of marketing concepts to candidate marketing. In M. J. Schlinger (Ed.), *Advances in consumer research* (Vol. 2, pp. 793–801). Provo, UT: Association for Consumer Research.

Shostack, G. L. (1977). Breaking free from product marketing. *Journal of Marketing, 41*, 73–80.

Smith, G. (2001). The 2001 general election: Factors influencing the brand image of political parties and their leaders. *Journal of Marketing Management, 17*, 989–1006.

Sweeney, J. C., & Brandon, C. (2006). Brand personality: Exploring the potential to move from factor analytical to circumplex models. *Psychology & Marketing*, *23*, 639–663.
Uleman, J. S., Saribay, S. A., & Gonzalez, C. M. (2008). Spontaneous inferences, implicit impressions, and implicit theories. *Annual Review of Psychology*, *59*, 329–360.
Verčič, D., & Verdnik, I. (2002). Models of voter behaviour: The Slovenia parliamentary elections. *Journal of Political Marketing*, *1*, 123–135.
Wattenberg, M. P. (1991). *The rise of candidate-centered politics: Presidential elections of the 1980s*. Cambridge, MA: Harvard University Press.
Waytz, A., Cacioppo, J., & Epley, N. (2010). Who sees human? The stability and importance of individual differences in anthropomorphism. *Perspectives on Psychological Science*, *5*, 219–232.
Williams, C. B. & Newman, B. I. (Eds.) (2013). *Political marketing in retrospective and prospective*. New York, NY: Routledge.
Winter, D. G. (1982). Motivation and performance in presidential candidates. In A. J. Stewart (Ed.), *Motivation and society* (pp. 244–273). San Francisco, CA: Jossey-Bass.
Wojciszke, B. (2005). Affective concomitants of information on morality and competence. *European Psychologist*, *10*, 60–70.
Wojciszke, B., Bazinska, R., & Jaworski, M. (1998). On the dominance of moral categories in impression formation. *Personality and Social Psychology Bulletin*, *24*, 1251–1263.
Yoon, C., Gutchess, A. H., Feinberg, F., & Polk, T. A. (2006). A functional magnetic resonance imaging study of neural dissociations between brand and person judgments. *Journal of Consumer Research*, *33*, 31–40.

16

Religion and consumer behaviour

Elizabeth A. Minton and Lynn R. Kahle

It's not hard to make decisions when you know what your values are.

Roy Disney

The former senior executive of Walt Disney Company said it well – decisions are guided by values. But where do values come from? One of the foundational sources of a consumer's values is religion. Throughout this chapter, the importance of both religious and non-religious belief systems in the study of consumer behaviour will be emphasized, an overview of past research in the area will be provided, relevant theories will be discussed and beneficial areas for future research will be identified.

Overview

Importance of religion to consumer behaviour

Religion pervades society. Over 70 per cent of people in the world are religious Hunt & Penwell, 2008). From a macromarketing perspective, religion influences the processes by which economic activity occurs in the marketplace. As Mittelstaedt (2002) describes, religion influences what, how, when and where marketplace exchanges occur. For example, religion can prohibit or encourage sales of certain products (e.g., alcohol prohibitions) or limit when a product can be sold (e.g., not on a holy day). From a micro perspective, religion influences core value development (Minton & Kahle, 2013; Pargament, 2001; Roccas, 2005), which then influences individual consumers' decisions and behaviours in the marketplace (Kahle, 1996; Kahle & Valette-Florence, 2012; Sheth, 1983).

More specifically, MacInnis and Folkes (2010) define consumer behaviour as involving the acquisition, consumption and disposal of goods. Religion melds well with this definition given that religion influences acquisition (e.g., where one shops, information sources sought), consumption (e.g., what products one will eat, any blessing or spiritual ritual performed before consumption) and also disposal of goods (e.g., views on sustainability, repurposing for the poor). Rinallo, Scott and Maclaran (2012) also support religion's pertinence to consumer behaviour in describing four ways that religion and the marketplace merge: (1) sacralization of the mundane (e.g., mundane grape juice being sacred in Christian communion), (2) spiritual meanings in consumption (e.g., how consumption fuels sacrality, such as in collecting), (3) commodification of the spiritual (e.g., marketing religious services), and (4) consumption of spiritual goods (e.g., sale of Buddha figures). Minton and Kahle (2013) suggest that a fifth element be added: adaptation to the sacred, which describes how businesses and policy members alter business practices to better serve religious consumers. Although sacrality research and understanding how to market religious goods and services are important, this chapter is focused most prominently on differences among religious and non-religious consumers and how these differences play out in the marketplace.

Defining religion

The term *religion* has been used to describe many things – from one's beliefs to how fervently one participates in a behaviour. For example, you might hear, "She is a religious person", "He religiously brushes his teeth" or "TV is their religion". These different interpretations of religion likely come from the Latin word *religio*, which means to do something with scrupulous attention to detail (Bowker, 2006) – whether that be scrupulous attention to the core tenets of scripture or to how one cares for one's health. Although *religion* and related words have multiple meanings, this chapter focuses on the more traditional meaning of religion as referring to one's beliefs. Providing a specific definition for religion is challenging given the need to encompass monotheistic religions (belief in just one God), polytheistic religions (belief in multiple gods), as well as religions that believe in other spirits, beings or purposes (e.g., the Buddhist's search for spiritual enlightenment or the Confucian's alignment with Confucius' teachings) (Hood, Hill, & Spilka, 2009).

Despite these challenges, most researchers agree that there are two main components of religion: (1) religious affiliation and (2) religiosity (Bailey & Sood, 1993; Essoo & Dibb, 2004; Hood et al., 2009; Minton & Kahle, 2013). Religious affiliation answers the question of *what* a consumer believes, whereas religiosity answers the question of *how* strongly a consumer believes There are many different definitions for religious affiliation and religiosity, which vary based on the purpose and context of research studies (Wilkes, Burnett, & Howell, 1986). Minton and Kahle (2013) developed definitions for these terms based on a comprehensive review of research in religion and marketing. These authors define religious affiliation as "a commonly held set of beliefs and values that guide external behaviour and an internal search for meaning". Accompanying religious affiliation, Minton and Kahle (2013) define religiosity as "the degree to which one holds religious beliefs and values through an internal spiritual connection and external religious practices and behaviours".

Measuring religion

Research in the domain of consumer behaviour often measures religion either by assessing religiosity (Burroughs & Rindfleisch, 2002; Chamberlain & Zika, 1988; Chandrasekaran & Tellis, 2008; Clark & Dawson, 1996; Saroglou, Pichon, Trompette, Verschueren, & Dernelle, 2005; Shachar, Erdem, Cutright, & Fitzsimons, 2011; Vitell & Paolillo, 2003) or by assessing religious affiliation (Al-Olayan & Karande, 2000; Alserhan, 2010; Muhamad & Mizerski, 2010; Zinnbauer et al., 1997), but infrequently measures both (Minton & Kahle, 2013). Given the previous discussion about the correlation between religious affiliation and religiosity, future research would highly benefit from assessing both religious affiliation and religiosity together (Essoo & Dibb, 2004; Minton & Kahle, 2013). Without both, researchers are left either knowing how strongly a consumer believes but not knowing what they are believing in beyond general religious values (e.g., caring for others) or knowing what a consumer believes but not knowing how strongly the consumer adheres to those beliefs (e.g., the idea of the C of E Christian who attends religious services only on Christmas and Easter).

In measuring either religiosity or religious affiliation, many challenges arise that researchers need to be aware of (Bader & Finke, 2014). When measuring religiosity in particular, a wide variety of scales are available, thereby making choice of scale as well as comparability among studies using different scales difficult (Minton & Kahle, 2013). In Hill and Hood's (1999) book of religiosity scales, 126 different academically supported scales are identified. Religiosity scales range in their emphasis on consumer spirituality (Seidlitz et al., 2002), cross-cultural applicability (Dejong, Faulkner, & Warland, 1976; Muhamad & Mizerski, 2010), in-depth understanding of one specific religious affiliation (King & Hunt, 1972) or general religiosity (Himmelfarb, 1975; Wilkes et al., 1986). It is beneficial to note that religion encompasses more institutional formalities, while spirituality encompasses more intangible elements (Emmons & Paloutzian, 2003; Hill et al., 2000; Hood et al., 2009; Zinnbauer et al., 1997). The religiosity scale developed by Wilkes et al. (1986) was one of the first scales used specifically for consumer behaviour research. However, this scale consists of only four items (church attendance, importance of religious values, confidence in religious values and self-perceived religiosity), thereby limiting the validity of the measure. Researchers must balance the potentially increased validity from having more items, such as using Himmelfarb's (1975) 41-item religiosity scale, with time and funding constraints.

Stark and Glock (1968) emphasize the need to explore three dimensions of religiosity: affective, behavioural and cognitive religiosity. Affective religiosity corresponds most closely with spirituality, behavioural religiosity with external activities such as religious service attendance, and cognitive religiosity with knowledge of religious doctrine. Each of these attributes contributes to a comprehensive understanding of religiosity. Around the same time that Stark and Glock (1968) proposed the three-dimension model of religiosity, Allport and Ross (1967) brought forth discussion of intrinsic and extrinsic religiosity. As Allport and Ross (1967) state, "the extrinsically motivated person uses his religion, whereas the intrinsically motivated person lives his religion" (p. 434). Intrinsic religiosity is most closely connected with Stark and Glock's (1968) affective religiosity component, while extrinsic religiosity is most closely connected with their behavioural religiosity component. Both Stark and Glock (1968) and Allport and Ross (1967) emphasize that religiosity can be seen as a continuum where consumers can be low on all dimensions of religiosity (e.g., an Atheist), vary on the dimensions (e.g., be more behaviourally/extrinsically religious) or be high on all dimensions (e.g., a very active and spiritual religious consumer).

In a review of religiosity studies, Donahue (1985) found that intrinsic religiosity has an average correlation of 0.76 with various religious commitment measures, while extrinsic religiosity is only correlated 0.03 with the same measures. Similarly, intrinsic religiosity is correlated with religious belief measures at 0.39, while extrinsic religiosity is only correlated with religious belief measures at 0.16. Recent research has suggested a need to go beyond Allport and Ross's (1967) two-factor model of religiosity (Kirkpatrick & Hood, 1990) and instead address a broader three-component model of religiosity featuring affective, behavioural and cognitive elements. There is still no perfect three-component measure of religiosity that is applicable to all religious affiliations in all cultures. Future research would benefit from developing and validating such a measure.

Challenges also arise in measuring religious affiliation. While one can ask a consumer's broad religious affiliation (e.g., Hindu, Christian, Buddhist, Muslim), beliefs within each of these religious groups can vary greatly (Muhamad & Mizerski, 2010; Rhodes, 2005). Many research studies accompany a question on broad religious affiliation with a measure of religious fundamentalism (e.g., assessing whether religious doctrine is literal or can be adapted to current times, views on the role of women). Smith's (1990) classification system is one measure of fundamentalism for Christian denominations that classifies religions as either liberal, moderate or conservative. This same classification system can be used with other religious affiliations.

Even with these two measures of religious affiliation (broad religious group and fundamentalism), Bader and Finke (2014) recommend further analysis to gain an accurate understanding of one's beliefs. These authors suggest that religious affiliation may be best measured using questions assessing core truths of one's beliefs, such as beliefs about the origin of human life, the existence of heaven and hell or the accuracy of evolutionary theories. Whether measuring religious affiliation or religiosity, Bader and Finke (2014) conclude by saying that "developing survey measures of religion is deceptively difficult, and researchers would benefit from carefully examining past attempts in detail" (p. 661). In other words, researchers seeking to understand the relationship between religion and consumer behaviour should begin with previous measures of religiosity and religious affiliation. Those measures can be adapted, if needed, to address validity-related weaknesses or contextual applicability rather than trying to reinvent the wheel by developing new measures of religiosity and religious affiliation.

Major religious groups

Before delving into past research examining religion's influence on consumer behaviour, it may be beneficial to many readers to provide a brief overview of the largest religious (Hinduism, Buddhism, Confucianism, Taoism, Christianity, Islam, Judaism) and non-religious belief systems (Agnosticism, Atheism). With the exception of Islam, where Muslims are the followers of Islam, followers of a religious affiliation are generally known by a variation of the religious affiliation name (e.g., Hindus follow Hinduism, Buddhists follow Buddhism, Christians follow Christianity).

Within religious belief systems, James (1902) distinguished between Western and Eastern religions. Followers of Western religions (Christians, Jews, Muslims) believe in one God (monotheistic), are rooted in Abrahamic traditions (where God revealed Himself to Abraham, a spiritual role model), provide revelation through prophets, strive to obey religious doctrine and acknowledge heavenly existence as life's goal. In contrast, followers of Eastern religions (Hinduism, Buddhism, Taoism, Confucianism) believe in multiple gods (polytheistic) or spiritual variations, are rooted in meditative traditions, provide revelation through the awakened one, strive to seek understanding and acknowledge enlightenment as life's goal. More simply, followers of Western religions believe in common truth that all accept, while followers of Eastern religions believe that each individual seeks their own truth through connection with a divine being or spirit (Hofstede, 1994; Hunt & Penwell, 2008).

In contrast to followers of religious belief systems, Atheists and Agnostics believe that there is no God (Atheists) or that it is impossible to know whether or not there is a God (Agnostics) (Johnson, Grim, Bellofatto, & Berger, 2013). Although many might argue that Atheists and Agnostics do not have a belief system, their position on the origin of the world and evolution of the human species represents foundations for a belief system. Thus, research examining religion would benefit from taking a broader approach to seeing how one's belief system (whether rooted in religious tradition or not) influences consumer behaviour. For example, a non-religious consumer may feel a much greater need to participate in sustainable behaviours to preserve the planet for generations to come, while a religious consumer may feel less of a need given the expectation of reaching enlightenment or a religious saviour soon to come. This is just one example of many where religious and non-religious consumers have differing perspectives that may lead to alternative consumer actions and behaviours. See Table 16.1 for

Table 16.1 Summary of beliefs and prominence of major religious and non-religious affiliations

Religion	*Followers*	*Number worldwide*[1]	*Major divisions*	*Main beliefs*[2]	*Holy book*
Western					
Christianity	Christians	2.2 billion	Protestant, Catholic, Orthodox	There is one God. He created the world. Jesus is the son of God and died on a cross as a sacrifice for the sins of mankind. People can be saved from eternal life in hell by asking for forgiveness of sins and believing in God.	Bible
Judaism	Jews	16 million	Conservative, Reformed, Orthodox, Unaffiliated	There is one God. He created the world. In contrast to Christianity and Islam, Jews believe a saviour of the world has yet to come and therefore only believe in the first half of the Christian Bible. Jews believe in three fundamental truths: *torah* (religious study), *avodah* (worship) and *gemilut chasadim* (giving back/repairing the world).	Torah
Islam	Muslims	1.2 billion	Sunni, Shi'ite	There is one God, Allah. He created the world. Muhammad received divine inspiration from Allah to write the holy book. Islam is built on five pillars: *shahada* (professing one's faith), *salat* (prayer five times per day), *saum* (fasting during the month of Ramadan), *zakat* (charity tax to poor) and *hajj* (pilgrimage to Mecca).	Qur'an
Eastern					
Hinduism	Hindus	1 billion	Shaivism, Shaktism, Vaishnavism, Smartism	Beliefs differ based on which scriptures are followed. A cycle of rebirth occurs for one's soul through reincarnation until all harmful actions of one's life are resolved. Hinduism is built on three pillars of practice: temple worship, scripture and religious traditions. Hindus practice *ahimsa* (non-violence) and view cows as sacred.	Vedas (consisting of Samhitas, Brahmamas, Upanishads and Sutras)

Buddhism	Buddhists	350 million	Zen, Theravada, Tibetan	Follows teachings of Buddha and seek mental departure from the physical world. Buddhists follow four noble truths: *dukkha* (suffering/stress, defining aspect of life); *dukkha* is caused by *tanha* (material attachment); *dukkha* ends with *nirvana* (reaching heavenly state devoid of suffering) and ending dukkha is reached by the Eightfold Path to enlightenment (right thought/attitude, intention, speech, conduct/action, livelihood/occupation, effort, awareness and concentration).	Tripitaka and Sutras
Confucianism/ Taoism	Confucians, Taoists or Daoists	6 million Confucians, 20 million Taoists	Religious, Philosophical	More of a philosophy than a religion. Confucians follow the teachings of Confucius focusing on humanism and transcendence with an emphasis on moral rule. Taoists focus on internal transformation resulting in morally good societies and actions. At the centre of both Confucianism and Taoism are morally good thoughts and actions.	Analects (Confucians), Tao Te Ching and Chuang Tzu (Taoists)
Non-religious					
Agnosticism	Agnostics	700 million[3]	NA	Believe that the origins of the world are unknowable. Agnostics do not support or deny evidence for God or other divine beings.	NA
Atheism	Atheists	150 million[3]	NA	Believe that there is no God, divine being or other spirit. Many Atheists adhere to the scientific rationale of the "big bang" beginning to the universe as well as evolution to describe how human life formed.	NA

Notes

1 Numbers of followers worldwide are estimates provided by Hunt and Penwell (2008).

2 Beliefs are adapted from Hunt and Penwell (2008) and Bowker's (2005) review of world religions.

3 These numbers are very rough estimates provided by *The world's religions in figures* (Johnson et al., 2013).

a comparison of the major religious and non-religious belief systems, their prominence around the world and key features of each belief system.

Past research

Research examining religion's influence on consumer behaviour began in the mid-1970s. This early research focused on exploring whether religion could be a viable market segmentation variable. Thompson and Raine (1976) explored correlations between religious groups and furniture sales, finding minimal correlations. Engel (1976) explored psychographic profiles of religious consumers, finding differences among religious denominations in attitudes towards controversial behaviours (e.g., drinking, smoking). These initial studies promote religion as a possible segmentation variable, though they do not support findings with sufficient theory to explain why religious consumers should differ on consumption-related attitudes and behaviours. Although more recent research has improved by being grounded in theory (Bailey & Sood, 1993; Hirschman, 1983; LaBarbera, 1987; McDaniel & Burnett, 1990; Mittelstaedt, 2002; Rindfleisch, Burroughs, & Wong, 2009; Sood & Nasu, 1995; Taylor, Halstead, & Haynes, 2010; Wilkes et al., 1986), future research needs to further integrate theory in research on religion and consumer behaviour. Past research on religion will now be reviewed in several subtopics within consumer behaviour.

Ethics

Ethics and religion are highly intertwined, given prescriptions in religious scripture regarding ethical behaviour (e.g., be truthful, do not retaliate, do not steal) (Minton & Kahle, 2013). Hunt and Vitell (2006), two well-known business ethics researchers, assert that any theory of marketing ethics should incorporate religion. While the influence of religion on most consumer behaviours is underexplored, the field of ethics and moral decision making has been well explored. It is beyond the scope of this chapter to review all of the research on religion and consumer ethics, so this chapter highlights several prominent research topics. Those interested in religion and consumer ethics are encouraged to search through articles in the *Journal of Business Ethics* and also conduct forward and backward citation searches on the articles cited herein.

Intrinsic religiosity, but not extrinsic religiosity, is positively correlated with ethical consumer behaviours (Patwardhan, Keith, & Vitell, 2012; Vitell, Paolillo, & Singh, 2005). In other words, consumers who have internalized their religion are more likely to be ethical than consumers who are only participating in religious behaviours, such as attending religious services. This follows our previous discussion regarding Allport and Ross's (1967) intrinsic and extrinsic dimensions of religiosity. In a related study, Vitell and Paolillo (2003) found that religious consumers are more likely to be ethical idealists (always following moral rules) rather than ethical relativists (using judgement in following moral rules). Among religious consumers, Buddhists are generally more ethically relative in comparison with Muslims and southern Christians, who are more ethically idealist (Cornwell et al., 2005). Views towards ethical idealism/relativism influence consumers' perceptions of corporate activities as well as personal behaviour in the marketplace, such as lying about product performance when trying to return a product or alerting a cashier about being given too much change in a transaction.

Ethical values also influence attitudes towards marketing controversial products. Muslims are more likely than Buddhists, Christians and non-religious consumers to be offended by advertisements featuring gender/sex-related products, health-care products and addictive products (e.g., alcohol) (Fam, Waller, & Erdogan, 2004). Religious prescriptions relating to the role of women in society or abstaining from addictive products likely influence the level of offence perceived by product advertisements. In a different study, perceptions of fair trade products were assessed, finding that Buddhists were the most likely to support fair trade producers in comparison with consumers of other religious affiliations (Doran & Natale, 2011). Doran and Natale (2011) describe that weak effect sizes for the relationship between religion and purchase of fair trade products may be due to a disconnect between caring attitudes and behaviours. Future research would benefit from exploring why this attitude-behaviour gap exists and methods for narrowing this gap specifically for religious or non-religious consumers.

General shopping behaviours

Although a plethora of research has explored how religion influences ethics in the marketplace, much less research has examined the influence of religious and non-religious belief systems on general shopping behaviours. Unfortunately, the few studies that have examined general shopping behaviours are often correlational in nature and lacking substantial theory to explain why correlational effects exist. For example, early research found that Jewish consumers were more innovative and more likely to be opinion leaders than Catholic, Protestant, Hindu, Muslim or Buddhist consumers (Hirschman, 1981). In a similar study, Catholics were found to be more innovative in consumption decisions relating to dancing, transportation options and sports. Although some conjectures are made as to why these effects occur (e.g., Jews are encouraged to be opinion leaders in seeking knowledge in the church) (Hirschman & Holbrook, 1982), further theory is needed to support these findings.

In other correlational research, Catholics are shown to be more thoughtful, traditional and demanding in searching for a TV in comparison with Hindus (Essoo & Dibb, 2004). In evaluating stores, price, reputation and product selection are most important to Muslims, while general atmospherics are more important to Hindus (Mokhlis, 2009). With regard to brands, Buddhist and Christian fundamentalists are more likely to be brand loyal than their more moderate or liberal counterparts (Rindfleisch, Burroughs, & Wong, 2005). In general, the more religious a consumer, the less likely they are to seek branded products to contribute to their self-worth (Shachar et al., 2011). To gain a more accurate understanding of religiosity's influence on general shopping behaviours, researchers need to explore various dimensions of religiosity, such as Stark and Glock's (1968) affective, behavioural and cognitive components of religiosity or Allport and Ross's (1967) intrinsic and extrinsic dimensions of religiosity. For example, one study finds that intrinsically religious consumers are more impulsive and less price conscious in contrast to extrinsically religious consumers (Mokhlis, 2006). Granted, a consumer can be both intrinsically and extrinsically religious, but these comparisons are made between consumers who are high in one dimension and low in another (e.g., a consumer who attends religious services frequently but has no internal spiritual connection).

Religiosity also influences reactions to product cost, with highly religious Protestants more likely to seek out products on sale and to be open to purchasing foreign products in comparison with less religious Protestants (Sood & Nasu, 1995). This general tendency to seek out products on sale may be confounded by prior research examining religiosity as a one-dimension factor. For example, Minton (2015) shows that religiosity leads to greater trust in advertising, although this trust varies by religiosity dimension (affective, behavioural or cognitive religiosity).

Given Mokhlis' (2006) research, it could be expected that extrinsically religious consumers would seek out products on sale more than intrinsically religious consumers. Again, conjectures regarding the reason for these effects could be generated (e.g., emphasis on frugality in religious scripture), but stronger theory is needed in all research assessing religion's influence on consumer behaviour. Such a stronger connection to theory may enhance the adoption of religion into mainstream marketing literature. Additionally, integrating discussion on both religious affiliation and religiosity as well as multiple dimensions of religiosity could increase the predictive ability of religiosity in describing consumer behaviours.

Sustainability

Sustainability can be seen as a subset of general shopping behaviours because views towards sustainability influence what products a consumer purchases (e.g., organic foods, low-chemical cleaning products) and also where a consumer shops (e.g., stores that participate in sustainable practices). Sarre (1995) explains that followers of Western religions (Christianity, Judaism, Islam) believe that God is dominant over nature, while followers of Eastern religions (Buddhism, Hinduism, Confucianism, Taoism) believe in the pantheistic view that God is in and through all elements of nature (e.g., a tree is God, water is God). Non-religious consumers, on the other hand, generally believe that Earth was created by the "Big Bang", thereby prescribing no spiritual or divine connection to the world. According to White's (1967) thesis, Western religious followers should be the least sustainable in comparison with Eastern and non-religious followers because these Western followers believe that the world is likely to end soon when a saviour returns. Additionally, prescriptions in religious scripture emphasize man's dominance over nature (e.g., man naming animals). More recent research supports this view that Western religious consumers are generally less sustainable in their behaviour in comparison with their Eastern and non-religious counterparts (Djupe & Gwiasda, 2010; Wolkomir, Futreal, Woodrum, & Hoban, 1997; Woodrum & Wolkomir, 1997). In addition to exploring differences between religious affiliations, prior research has also examined confounding factors such as political affiliation, education, gender and income (Wolkomir et al., 1997; Woodrum & Wolkomir, 1997).

Specifically within Christianity, fundamentalist consumers (i.e., those who believe religious scripture is infallible) are less likely to have sustainable attitudes (e.g., believe that caring for the environment is critical) or to participate in sustainable behaviours (e.g., recycle, purchase organic produce) in comparison with more liberal consumers (i.e., those who believe that religious scripture should be adapted to modern times) (Minton, 2013, 2014). On a broader scale, Kalamas, Cleveland and Laroche (2014) found that consumers who attribute environmental change (e.g., global warming) to powerful others (e.g., a God or divine being) are more likely to participate in sustainable behaviours than consumers who attribute environmental change to chance or fate. Other research has shown little effect of religion on sustainable consumption (Martin & Bateman, 2014), although these results may be due to inadequate variance in the sample source. Research on religion benefits greatly from a diverse sample, allowing for differing religious views and levels of religiosity. However, one should strive for diversity while also controlling for the effects of culture. For example, comparing Christians in the United States with Buddhists in South Korea would confound the effect of religious affiliation with culture. Instead, a better-designed study would examine religious affiliations within one culture, such as was done by Minton, Kahle and Kim (2015) in examining Buddhists and Christians within one country. Such comparison is difficult, however, given that most countries feature majority (minority) religions and it is easier (harder) to locate adherents to these religions and survey them.

Health

Although most research on health is conducted outside the field of marketing, a large body of literature shows that religiosity is positively correlated with general healthiness

(Emmons & Paloutzian, 2003). Religious consumers have greater overall well-being than non-religious consumers (Chamberlain & Zika, 1988; LaBarbera & Gurhan, 1997; Witter, Stock, Okun, & Haring, 1985). These effects occur even after controlling for a host of demographic variables. This is a good time to note that all studies on religion and consumer behaviour should factor in demographic covariates. Prior research has found that age (Babakus, Cornwell, Mitchell, & Schlegelmilch, 2004; Bailey & Sood, 1993; Muhamad & Mizerski, 2007; Ong & Moschis, 2006; Wilkes et al., 1986), education (Bailey & Sood, 1993) and marital status (Muhamad & Mizerski, 2007) can interact with religion's effect on consumer behaviour. Consumers who are older, less educated and married are more likely to be religious. However, the effect of demographic variables also varies greatly by broad religious affiliation and denomination/subgroup within that broad affiliation. Demographic variables of gender (Babakus et al., 2004; Bailey & Sood, 1993) and income (Bailey & Sood, 1993) have generally shown no significant interactions with religion in influencing consumer behaviour.

Focusing back on health, religious consumers have been shown to be less depressed, be less likely to abuse drugs and alcohol, and live longer than non-religious consumers (Azar, 2010). Additionally, highly religious consumers generally are more tender minded and have higher superego strength (Barton & Vaughan, 1976). In a review of religion and health studies, Seeman, Dubin and Seeman (2003) found that religion positively contributes to cardiovascular, neuroendocrine and immune functioning. These positive health trends are at least partially a result of the religious consumer's greater supply of coping mechanisms (e.g., the ability to seek support from a God or divine being) in comparison with the coping mechanisms available to non-religious consumers. Also, Lawler-Row (2010) finds that the forgiveness a religious consumer feels after praying to a God or divine being leads to less depression and greater general health as a result of decreased guilt and stress.

These differences in healthiness between religious and non-religious consumers have many implications for marketers. First, organizations supplying health care (e.g., hospitals, health clinics) may approach marketing strategy differently when aiming towards religious and non-religious consumers based on their health needs and ways of coping. Second, speciality psychiatry services can be designed to assist coping for religious and non-religious consumers. Third, manufacturers of health products may consider different marketing strategies based on whether the health product will be supplemented with supernatural intervention. Of course, any religious-based market segmentation strategy should be approached cautiously so as not to alienate religious and non-religious consumers alike.

Similar to healthiness, religious consumers have been shown to be happier and have greater life satisfaction than non-religious consumers across studies in both the United States and Singapore (Swinyard, Kau, & Phua, 2001). However, consumers who are only behaviourally/extrinsically religious (i.e., no internal personal connection with a God or divine being) are much less likely to experience increased life satisfaction or happiness. Religious consumers are also less likely to exhibit aggression and more likely to be altruistic and extend empathy towards others, thereby contributing to increased happiness (Saroglou et al., 2005). Burroughs and Rindfleisch (2002) find that consumer well-being and materialism are negatively correlated for highly religious consumers, suggesting that highly religious consumers feel pressure to turn to a God or divine being rather than material possessions to gain happiness in life. Given this increased anti-materialistic pressure for highly religious consumers, future research would benefit from exploring how highly religious consumers respond to brands conveying a materialistic message differently from less or non-religious consumers.

Theory, religion and consumer behaviour

Numerous theories describing how religion influences behaviour have been proposed in the psychology literature. These theories address cognitive, psychoanalytic, positive psychology and humanistic perspectives on the psychology of religion. These theories are reviewed before theories relevant to non-religious belief systems (evolutionary theory) are reviewed. Finally, theory relevant more specifically to the study of religion and consumer behaviour will be discussed.

James (1902) came from a cognitive perspective and was well known for distinguishing between psychological processes involved in institutional religion versus personal religion. James theorized that institutional religion served the purpose of social structure. Personal religion, on the other hand, was adapted based on a pragmatic approach whereby religious practices that contributed to one's walk in life were held on to and other practices that did not help in one's walk in life were discarded. Adler and Jahn (1933) came from a similar cognitive perspective in suggesting that religion's purpose is to deal with the inferiority one feels in life by striving to be in connection with a perfect and supreme God or divine being. Freud (1985) came from a psychoanalytic perspective and proposed that religion served to fill a need in one's life that was not previously filled. Western religions often refer to God as a heavenly father, and Freud theorized that children develop an attachment to a heavenly father as a result of inadequate connection to their physical father. Freud's initial theories have since developed into attachment theory, a type of coping theory, which describes how the connection between a child and a parent early in life influences the child's religiosity later in life (Bowlby, 1977). Jung (1966) approached religion from a positive psychology perspective in emphasizing conscious and unconscious thought and describing religion as a collection of unconscious thought that allowed social wisdom to be transmitted through generations. Maslow (1970) followed a humanistic approach to religion in describing that religious consumers are more likely to reach self-actualization and that religion contributes to one's ability to have peak experiences. Similarly, Frankl (1959) emphasized humanistic tendencies in religion, although from a negative perspective. Frankl suggested that outside work and other activities, there is emptiness as to one's purpose and meaning in life, and religion helps to fill this void. Each of these theories has received at least some support, but none is regarded as the only theory explaining how religion influences behaviour. The authors of one of the best-known psychology of religion books today state the theory situation in the field of psychology well: "Within the psychology of religion, the cry for good theory remains at the level of cacophony" (Hood et al., 2009, p. 503).

In contrast to these theories of religion, the most prominent theory that non-religious consumers support is evolutionary theory. However, some consumers support both religious and evolutionary theories. Darwin (1859) proposed the theory of evolution, which states that humans today are descendants of primordial life from billions of years ago. Darwin's theory of evolution is based on natural selection, whereby creatures that are the strongest and fittest will survive, while those that are the weakest will die. Similarly, features of animals that are unneeded for survival will fade away, while features needed for survival are kept and enhanced through generations of evolution. Evolutionary theory has been used to explain many behaviours today, such as signalling activities in consumption behaviours, attractive dress as a precursor to mating rituals, financial and physical risk taking, and more (Saad, 2007; Saad & Gill, 2000).

The theories just described provide insight into the influence of belief systems on behaviour. Discussion now will turn to more specific theories that can be used in examining how religious or non-religious beliefs influence consumer behaviour. Attribution theory explains how consumers describe the source of actions as either internal to one's self or external, from things in the environment (Kelley & Michela, 1980). When applied to religion, two external attributions become possible – one to the physical environment and a second to the divine environment (Spilka & Schmidt, 1983; Spilka, Shaver, & Kirkpatrick, 1985; c.f., Minton, 2016). For example, imagine a consumer who visits a retail store only to encounter a rude employee. A consumer could attribute this experience to themselves and state that they provoked the employee to be rude. The consumer could also attribute the poor experience to the store for not adequately training or managing the employee. Finally, the consumer could attribute the experience to the divine environment and see this as a time God either wants the consumer to learn patience or has led the consumer to help the employee during a time of need. Research would benefit from exploring when consumers make attributions to the divine environment and how such attributions change successive consumer attitudes and behaviours.

While attribution theory is relevant when describing how consumers explain behaviour, self-determination theory is relevant when describing how consumers are motivated to perform a behaviour. More specifically, self-determination theory posits that there are controlled and autonomous motives. Controlled motives are based on regulations and policies, while autonomous motives are developed from within (Deci & Ryan, 2012; Moller, Ryan, & Deci, 2006; Ryan & Deci, 2000). Values rooted in a religious or non-religious belief system will primarily influence autonomous motives. For example, belief system values relating to the environment (e.g., the Atheist's desire to sustain the planet for generations to come) may autonomously motivate purchase of biodegradable plastic bags to help the environment. When autonomous motives do not influence behaviour, controlled motives (e.g., government taxes on non-biodegradable plastic bags) may lead to behaviour change. Autonomous and controlled motives can also work together to influence behaviour. Future research would benefit from exploring in what situations religious or non-religious beliefs influence autonomous motives. Additionally, further research should investigate ways to activate or prime such beliefs so as to increase reliance on autonomous motives.

Also relevant to the study of religion in consumer behaviour are social learning theories that describe where marketplace attitudes and behaviours originate from. The persuasion knowledge model states that knowledge of persuasion tactics is developed at a young age (Friestad & Wright, 1994, 1995). Friestad and Wright (1995) add that one of the primary sources of persuasion knowledge is the culture surrounding a consumer, which is influenced by religion. According to social learning theory, consumers learn attitudes and behaviours by observing those around them (Bandura, 1971). Thus, consumers who regularly participate in religious activities are more likely to learn attitudes and behaviours similar to other religious consumers. Religious belief systems (as opposed to non-religious belief systems) are more closely tied to social learning theory, given more frequent opportunities to participate in organized religious activities (as opposed to organized activities for Atheists or Agnostics). Additionally, highly religious consumers in general are more active participants in civic groups than less or non-religious consumers (Berggren & Bjørnskov, 2011; Welch, Sikkink, & Loveland, 2007). Building on social learning theory, information integration theory explains how consumers adapt prior attitudes and behaviours based on new information (Anderson, 1981). Future research would benefit from exploring how religion influences adaptation of new marketplace information into prior schemas as well as differences between religious and non-religious consumers in persuasion knowledge.

In addition to the persuasion knowledge model, social relations theory helps to describe interactions among consumers or between consumers and employees. Social relations theory posits that interactions and resulting judgements are a social construction of the perceiver (e.g., the consumer), the target (e.g., the employee) and any prior interactions between the perceiver and the target (Kenny, 1994; Kenny & La Voie, 1984). Research on out-group bias consistently shows that consumers have more favourable impressions of members of their in-group and less favourable impressions of members of their out-group (Hewstone, Rubin, & Willis, 2002; Islam & Hewstone, 1993; White & Dahl, 2007). For example, a religious consumer would be positively biased towards other religious consumers, just as a non-religious consumer would be positively biased towards other non-religious consumers. However, prior research has shown that poorly performing companies that use religious symbols can actually lead religious consumers to like a company less than if no religious symbol were used (Taylor et al., 2010). Thus, future research would benefit from exploring when conveying religious information is beneficial for a business in attracting consumers and improving business in contrast to when such information leads to decreased firm performance.

Such in-group favouritism effects are even more profound for dissociative reference groups in which consumers seek to avoid an out-group (Berger & Heath, 2008; White & Dahl, 2007). Research on dissociative reference groups builds on social identity theory whereby consumers develop their own sense of identity in relation to other consumers (Tajfel & Turner, 1979). Dissociative reference groups are highly applicable to religion, as religious consumers generally want to avoid being considered non-religious, just as non-religious consumers generally want to avoid being considered religious. Consumers are likely to take actions to divest themselves of any association with a dissociative reference group (Berger & Heath, 2008). Future research would benefit from exploring the actions that consumers take to avoid being considered part of their dissociative reference group. Also, further investigation would be beneficial to understand what actions companies take that may communicate information perceived as coming from a dissociative reference group. As discussion moves more specifically to future research considerations, it is important to emphasize that the theories just described are several relevant theories to the study of religious and non-religious belief systems and consumer behaviour, but in no way is this an exhaustive list.

Future research

Future research examining religion's influence on consumer behaviour should focus on five areas: (1) expansion to a wider variety of religious affiliations and cultures, (2) exploration as to how religiosity dimensions differentially influence consumer behaviours, (3) connection of various contexts to a stronger foundation in theory, (4) examination of how the relationship between belief systems and consumer behaviour can be used to increase pro-social behaviours among religious and non-religious consumers alike and (5) investigation as to how one's belief system can be activated to influence consumer behaviour.

First, much of the past research examining religion's influence on consumer behaviour has been conducted in single countries (e.g., the United States, Malaysia). Comparisons among countries could provide understanding as to how culture influences religion's effect on consumers as well as differences between consumers who follow a minority versus a majority religion (Hirschman, Ruvio, & Touzani, 2011; Yang & Ebaugh, 2001). Research also needs to explore a wider variety of religious affiliations. Comprehensive studies should examine the major Western religious groups (Christians, Jews, Muslims), Eastern religious groups (Hindus, Buddhists, Confucians, Taoists) and non-religious groups (Agnostics, Atheists). Very little research has examined differences between Agnostics and Atheists. Future research may also explore the effect of spirituality or non-traditional religions on attitudes and behaviours in the marketplace.

Second, most research on religion that incorporates religiosity examines religiosity as a one-dimension construct. Oftentimes, this construct is measured with just a handful of items

(Wilkes et al., 1986), potentially compromising the validity of that construct. Future research needs to consider more comprehensive assessment items that explore different dimensions of religiosity. Allport and Ross (1967) introduced intrinsic and extrinsic dimensions of religiosity, which have been shown to influence consumer behaviour differently (Mokhlis, 2006; Patwardhan et al., 2012; Swinyard et al., 2001; Vitell et al., 2005). Stark and Glock (1968) introduced a more comprehensive model of religiosity featuring three dimensions: affective, behavioural and cognitive religiosity. Such a three-dimension view of religiosity has only recently been used, such as by Minton (2015). In Minton's (2015) research, affective and cognitive religiosity influence attitudes and behaviours in the marketplace much more than behavioural religiosity. Future research should confirm and extend such effects.

Third, much of the past research examining religion's effect on consumer behaviour has been correlational in nature (Minton & Kahle, 2013). Future research would greatly benefit from a stronger connection to theory to explore and explain why a consumer's religious or non-religious belief system should influence their behaviour. In the previous section, numerous theories relevant to the study of religion's influence on consumer behaviour today were reviewed, including attribution theory, self-determination theory, the persuasion knowledge model, social learning theory, information integration theory, social relations theory and social identity theory. These theories represent a starting point for research in the area, although this is not an exhaustive list by any means. Researchers should search the psychology, religion and sociology literature, in particular, to identify theories relevant to religion and marketing research. Theory should be selected and adapted based on the context and purposes of the study.

Fourth, more exploration is needed as to how knowledge of a consumer's beliefs and devotion to those beliefs can be used to influence pro-social behaviours. Critics of religion and consumer behaviour research have often lamented that they feel information on a consumer's beliefs will be used to manipulate them. However, more research on how religion can be used to promote positive behaviours rather than pure manipulation for the purposes of selling a product or service is needed. Prior research has shown that religious consumers are more pro-social in general (Saroglou et al., 2005), but other research suggests that religious consumers are less sustainable (i.e., suggesting religious consumers are less pro-social) (Minton, 2013, 2014; L. White, 1967; Wolkomir et al., 1997; Woodrum & Wolkomir, 1997). Future research would benefit from exploring how religious and non-religious consumers alike can be encouraged to participate in pro-social behaviours that these groups of consumers do not currently engage in. For example, future research could examine stealing, gift giving, sharing or collaborative consumption and the associated relationship with religious affiliation and religiosity.

Lastly (although certainly not the last possible area for future research), research would benefit from exploring how to activate a consumer's belief system. Prior research in psychology has shown that priming religion can increase pro-social behaviours (Shariff & Norenzayan, 2007), increase submissive thoughts (Saroglou, Corneille, & Van Cappellen, 2009) and decrease distress and defensiveness (Inzlicht & Tullett, 2010). However, when non-religious consumers are primed with religion, distress and defensiveness are increased (Inzlicht & Tullett, 2010). Thus, priming religion is not universally positive. Future research should explore how religious priming techniques already being used in the psychology, sociology and religion literature can be applied in the consumer behaviour domain to positively influence religious and non-religious consumers alike. Most interestingly, future research needs to explore what type of religious prime (e.g., word primes, sentence unscramble, writing tasks, visual primes or masked primes) works best to prime behaviour and can be integrated into marketing communications, with the expectation that some types of religious primes may work best in some situations, whereas other types of religious primes may work better in other situations.

Implications

Research on religion's influence on consumer behaviour has many potential implications for practice. Anyone involved in international marketing needs to be intimately aware of the religious beliefs of their consumers in every country their company operates in (Minton & Kahle, 2013). Market offerings may need to be adapted based on what consumers find offensive, acceptable or desirable. Additionally, those involved in international marketing need to be aware of the religious traditions of other cultures when meeting with potential clients, talking with the press or communicating with employees in another country.

Regardless of the multinational status of a firm, religion is a viable market segmentation tool for all businesses –by religious affiliation as well as level of religiosity. Segmenting by religious affiliation is easier than ever before with the proliferation of social media and access to personal data on consumers (Kahle & Valette-Florence, 2012). Businesses may desire to create specialized products for religious consumers or adapt advertising to better target certain religious or non-religious groups. Even if no adaptations are made, understanding the religious background of a target market will lead to insight into consumers that can assist in interactions with consumers, new product development in the future or even the timing of product availability and selection of distribution channels.

On a broader scale, research on religion's influence on consumer behaviour can also inform public policy development and refinement. Prior research has already shown that religion can influence where and when trade occurs as well as what is traded in the marketplace (Mittelstaedt, 2002). Thus, religion is already intertwined in governmental activities. Policy makers interested in social change may benefit from targeting religious groups and communicating social change messages that are relevant to the religious group's belief system. Additionally, there is frequent discussion about equal opportunity, so research findings could educate policy makers as to areas where religious or non-religious consumers are not being provided with equal opportunity in the marketplace.

In addition to benefits for business and policy makers, research on religious and non-religious belief systems can empower consumers to understand how their belief system influences their attitudes and behaviours. Such knowledge can allow consumers to make more accurate judgements in the marketplace, reduce the threat of being taken advantage of and enable a more transparent marketplace.

Conclusion

Everyone has a belief system. Such belief systems can be rooted in religious (e.g., Buddhist, Christian, Hindu, Muslim) or non-religious (e.g., Atheist, naturalist, humanist, Agnostic) sources, but all belief systems influence consumer attitudes and behaviours. For many, belief systems represent the core values a consumer holds, which guide daily life, often more than consumers realize. Although some research has examined the influence of these belief systems on consumer behaviour, much more research in this area is needed. Such research can be built from the perspective of religion being an individual difference variable that influences a wide variety of consumer outcomes, ranging from decision making to familial relations to brand evaluations and many more.

Referring back to our quote at the beginning of this chapter by Roy Disney, "It's not hard to make decisions when you know what your values are". Consumers look to their core values in making decisions, particularly for more involved decision making. With that being said, values rooted in belief systems also subconsciously influence less involved decisions and a wide variety of attitudes and behaviours in the marketplace. Businesses, consumers and policy makers alike can benefit greatly from understanding a consumer's core values rooted in religious and non-religious belief systems. Such beliefs already pervade society. Now is the time to understand how these beliefs influence consumers and the marketplace.

References

Adler, A., & Jahn, E. (1933). *Religion and psychology*. Frankfurt am Main: Fischer Verlag.

Al-Olayan, F. S., & Karande, K. (2000). A content analysis of magazine advertisements from the United States and the Arab world. *Journal of Advertising, 29*(3), 69–82.

Allport, G. W., & Ross, J. M. (1967). Personal religious orientation and prejudice. *Journal of Personality and Social Psychology, 5*(4), 432–443.

Alserhan, B. A. (2010). Islamic branding: A conceptualization of related terms. *Journal of Brand Management, 18*(1), 34–49.

Anderson, N. H. (1981). *Foundations of information integration theory*. New York, NY: Academic Press.

Azar, B. (2010). A reason to believe. *Monitor on Psychology*, 52–56.

Babakus, E., Cornwell, T., Mitchell, V., & Schlegelmilch, B. (2004). Reactions to unethical consumer behaviour across six countries. *Journal of Consumer Marketing, 21*(4), 254–263.

Bader, C. D., & Finke, R. (2014). Toward assessing and improving survey questions on religion: The ARDA's measurement wizard. *Journal for the Scientific Study of Religion, 53*(3), 652–661.

Bailey, J. M., & Sood, J. (1993). The effects of religious affiliation on consumer behaviour: A preliminary investigation. *Journal of Managerial Issues, 5*(3), 328–352.

Bandura, A. (1971). *Social learning theory*. New York, NY: General Learning Press.

Barton, K., & Vaughan, G. M. (1976). Church membership and personality: A longitudinal study. *Social Behaviour and Personality, 4*(1), 11–16.

Berger, J., & Heath, C. (2008). Who drives divergence? Identity signaling, outgroup dissimilarity, and the abandonment of cultural tastes. *Journal of Personality and Social Psychology, 95*(3), 593–607.

Berggren, N., & Bjørnskov, C. (2011). Is the importance of religion in daily life related to social trust? Cross-country and cross-state comparisons. *Journal of Economic Behaviour & Organization, 80*(3), 459–480.

Bowker, J. (2005). *The concise Oxford dictionary of world religions*. New York, NY: Oxford University Press.

Bowker, J. (2006). *World religions: The great faiths explored and explained*. New York, NY: Dorling Kindersley.

Bowlby, J. (1977). The making and breaking of affectional bonds. *The British Journal of Psychiatry, 130*(3), 201–210.

Burroughs, J. E., & Rindfleisch, A. (2002). Materialism and well-being: A conflicting values perspective. *Journal of Consumer Research, 29*(3), 348–370.

Chamberlain, K., & Zika, S. (1988). Religiosity, life meaning and wellbeing : Some relationships in a sample of women. *Journal for the Scientific Study of Religion, 27*(3), 411–420.

Chandrasekaran, D., & Tellis, G. J. (2008). Global takeoff of new products: Culture, wealth, or vanishing differences? *Marketing Science, 27*(5), 844–860.

Clark, J. W., & Dawson, L. E. (1996). Personal religiousness and ethical judgements: An empirical analysis. *Journal of Business Ethics, 15*(3), 359–372.

Cornwell, B., Cui, C. C., Mitchell, V., Schlegelmilch, B., Dzulkiflee, A., & Chan, J. (2005). A cross-cultural study of the role of religion in consumers' ethical positions. *International Marketing Review, 22*(5), 531–546.

Darwin, C. (1859). *On the origin of species by means of natural selection*. London: John Murray.

Deci, E., & Ryan, R. M. (2012). Self-determination theory. In P. A. M. Van Lange, A. W. Kruglanski & E. T. Higgins (Eds.), *Handbook of theories of social psychology* (pp. 416–437). Thousand Oaks, CA: Sage.

Dejong, G. F., Faulkner, J. E., & Warland, R. H. (1976). Dimensions of religiosity reconsidered: Evidence from a cross-cultural study. *Social Forces, 54*(4), 866–889.

Djupe, P. A., & Gwiasda, G. W. (2010). Evangelizing the environment: Decision process effects in political persuasion. *Journal for the Scientific Study of Religion, 49*(1), 73–86.

Donahue, M. J. (1985). Intrinsic and extrinsic religiousness: The empirical research. *Journal for the Scientific Study of Religion, 24*(4), 418–423.

Doran, C., & Natale, S. (2011). Empatheia and caritas: The role of religion in fair trade consumption. *Journal of Business Ethics, 98*(1), 1–15.

Emmons, R. A., & Paloutzian, R. F. (2003). The psychology of religion. *Annual Review of Psychology, 54*(1), 377–402.
Engel, J. (1976). Psychographic research in a cross-cultural non product setting. *Advances in Consumer Research, 3*, 98–101.
Essoo, N., & Dibb, S. (2004). Religious influences on shopping behaviour: An exploratory study. *Journal of Marketing Management, 20*(7), 683–712.
Fam, K. S., Waller, D. S., & Erdogan, B. Z. (2004). The influence of religion on attitudes towards the advertising of controversial products. *European Journal of Marketing, 38*(5/6), 537–555.
Frankl, V. E. (1959). *Man's search for meaning*. New York, NY: Simon and Schuster.
Freud, S. (1985). *The origins of religion: Totem and taboo, Moses and monotheism and other works*. London: Penguin.
Friestad, M., & Wright, P. (1994). The persuasion knowledge model: How people cope with persuasion attempts. *The Journal of Consumer Research, 21*(1), 1–31.
Friestad, M., & Wright, P. (1995). Persuasion knowledge: Lay people's and researchers' beliefs about the psychology of advertising. *Journal of Consumer Research, 22*(1), 62–74.
Hewstone, M., Rubin, M., & Willis, H. (2002). Intergroup bias. *Annual Review of Psychology, 53*(1), 575–604.
Hill, P., & Hood, R. (1999). *Measures of religiosity*. Birmingham, AL: Religious Education Press.
Hill, P. C., Pargament, K. I., Hood, R. W., McCullough, M. E., Swyers, J. P., Larson, D. B., & Zinnbauer, B. J. (2000). Conceptualizing religion and spirituality: Points of commonality, points of departure. *Journal for the Theory of Social Behaviour, 30*(1), 51–77.
Himmelfarb, H. S. (1975). Measuring religious involvement. *Social Forces, 53*(4), 606–618.
Hirschman, E. C. (1981). American Jewish ethnicity: Its relationship to some selected aspects of consumer behaviour. *Journal of Marketing, 45*(3), 102–110.
Hirschman, E. C. (1983). Religious affiliation and consumption processes: An initial paradigm. *Research in Marketing, 6*, 131–170.
Hirschman, E. C., & Holbrook, M. B. (1982). Hedonic consumption: Emerging concepts, methods and propositions. *The Journal of Marketing, 46*(3), 92–101.
Hirschman, E. C., Ruvio, A. A., & Touzani, M. (2011). Breaking bread with Abraham's children: Christians, Jews and Muslims' holiday consumption in dominant, minority and diasporic communities. *Journal of the Academy of Marketing Science, 39*(3), 429–448.
Hofstede, G. (1994). Management scientists are human. *Management Science, 40*(1), 4–13.
Hood, R. W. Jr, Hill, P. C., & Spilka, B. (2009). *The psychology of religion: An empirical approach* (4th ed.). New York, NY: Guilford Press.
Hunt, J., & Penwell, D. (2008). *AMG's handi-reference world religions and cults*. Chattanooga, TN: AMG.
Hunt, S. D., & Vitell, S. J. (2006). A general theory of marketing ethics: A revision and three questions. *Journal of Macromarketing, 26*(2), 1–11.
Inzlicht, M., & Tullett, A. M. (2010). Reflecting on god: Religious primes can reduce neurophysiological response to errors. *Psychological Science, 21*(8), 1184–1190.
Islam, M. R., & Hewstone, M. (1993). Intergroup attributions and affective consequences in majority and minority groups. *Journal of Personality and Social Psychology, 64*(6), 936–950.
James, W. (1902). *The varieties of religious experience*. New York, NY: Touchstone.
Johnson, T. M., Grim, B. J., Bellofatto, G. A., & Berger, P. L. (2013). *The world's religions in figures: An introduction to international religious demography*. Malden, MA: Wiley-Blackwell.
Jung, C. G. (1966). *Psychology and religion*. New York, NY: Yale University Press.
Kahle, L. R. (1996). Social values and consumer behaviour: Research from the list of values. In C. Seligman, J. M. Olson & M. P. Zanna (Eds.), *The psychology of values: The Ontario symposium* (Vol. 8). Mahwah, NJ: Erlbaum.
Kahle, L. R., & Valette-Florence, P. (2012). *Marketplace lifestyles in an age of social media*. Armonk, NY: M.E. Sharpe.
Kalamas, M., Cleveland, M., & Laroche, M. (2014). Pro-environmental behaviours for thee but not for me: Green giants, green gods, and external environmental locus of control. *Journal of Business Research, 67*(2), 12–22.
Kelley, H. H., & Michela, J. L. (1980). Attribution theory and research. *Annual Review of Psychology, 31*(1), 457–501.
Kenny, D. A. (1994). *Interpersonal perception: A social relations analysis*. New York, NY: Guilford Press.
Kenny, D. A., & La Voie, L. (1984). The social relations model. *Advances in Experimental Social Psychology, 18*, 142–182.

King, M. B., & Hunt, R. A. (1972). Measuring the religious variable: Replication. *Journal for the Scientific Study of Religion, 11*(3), 240–251.

Kirkpatrick, L. A., & Hood, Jr, R. W. (1990). Intrinsic-extrinsic religious orientation: The boon or bane of contemporary psychology of religion? *Journal for the Scientific Study of Religion, 29*(4), 442–462.

LaBarbera, P. A. (1987). Consumer behaviour and born again Christianity. *Research in Consumer Behaviour, 2*, 193–222.

LaBarbera, P. A., & Gurhan, Z. (1997). The role of materialism, religiosity, and demographics in subjective well-being. *Psychology & Marketing, 14*(1), 71–97.

Lawler-Row, K. A. (2010). Forgiveness as a mediator of the religiosity–health relationship. *Psychology of Religion and Spirituality, 2*(1), 1–16.

MacInnis, D. J., & Folkes, V. S. (2010). The disciplinary status of consumer behaviour: A sociology of science perspective on key controversies. *Journal of Consumer Research, 36*(6), 899–914.

Martin, W. C., & Bateman, C. R. (2014). Consumer religious commitment's influence on ecocentric attitudes and behaviour. *Journal of Business Research, 67*(2), 5–11.

Maslow, A. H. (1970). *Religions, values, and peak-experiences.* New York, NY: Penguin.

McDaniel, S., & Burnett, J. (1990). Consumer religiosity and retail store evaluative criteria. *Journal of the Academy of Marketing Science, 18*(2), 101–112.

Minton, E. A. (2013). Religion and religiosity's influence on sustainable consumption behaviours. In L. R. Kahle & E. Gurel-Atay (Eds.), *Communicating sustainability for the green economy* (pp. 73–87). Armonk, NY: M.E. Sharpe.

Minton, E. A. (2014). How religious affiliation grouping influences consumer behaviour findings. In J. Stolz & J.-C. Usunier (Eds.), *Religions as brands. New perspectives on the marketization of religion and spirituality* (pp. 157–173). Oxford, UK: Ashgate.

Minton, E. A. (2015). In advertising we trust: Religiosity's influence on marketplace and relational trust. *Journal of Advertising, 44*(4), 1–12.

Minton, E. A. (2016). Sacred attributions: Implications for behaviour in the marketplace. *Psychology & Marketing, 33*(6), 437–448.

Minton, E. A., & Kahle, L. R. (2013). *Belief systems, religion, and behavioural economics: Marketing in multicultural environments.* New York, NY: Business Expert Press.

Minton, E. A., Kahle, L. R., & Kim, C.-H. (2015). Religion and motives for sustainable behaviours: A cross-cultural comparison and contrast. *Journal of Business Research*, in press.

Mittelstaedt, J. (2002). A framework for understanding the relationships between religions and markets. *Journal of Macromarketing, 22*(1), 6–18.

Mokhlis, S. (2006). The effect of religiosity on shopping orientation: An exploratory study in Malaysia. *Journal of American Academy of Business, 9*, 64–74.

Mokhlis, S. (2009). Religious differences in some selected aspects of consumer behaviour: A Malaysian study. *Journal of International Management, 4*(1), 67–76.

Moller, A. C., Ryan, R. M., & Deci, E. L. (2006). Self-determination theory and public policy: Improving the quality of consumer decisions without using coercion. *Journal of Public Policy & Marketing, 25*(1), 104–116.

Muhamad, N., & Mizerski, D. (2007). Muslim religious commitment related to intention to purchase taboo products. *Journal of Business and Policy Research, 3*, 74–85.

Muhamad, N., & Mizerski, D. (2010). The constructs mediating religions' influence on buyers and consumers. *Journal of Islamic Marketing, 1*(2), 124–135.

Ong, F. S., & Moschis, G. P. (2006). Religiosity and consumer behaviour: A cross-cultural study. Paper presented at the *International Conference on Business and Information*, Singapore.

Pargament, K. I. (2001). *The psychology of religion and coping: Theory, research, practice.* New York, NY: Guilford Press.

Patwardhan, A. M., Keith, M. E., & Vitell, S. J. (2012). Religiosity, attitude toward business, and ethical beliefs: Hispanic consumers in the United States. *Journal of Business Ethics, 110*(1), 61–70.

Rhodes, R. (2005). *The complete guide to Christian denominations.* Eugene, OR: Harvest House.

Rinallo, D., Scott, L., & Maclaran, P. (2012). *Consumption and spirituality.* New York, NY: Routledge.

Rindfleisch, A., Burroughs, J. E., & Wong, N. (2005). Religiosity and brand commitment: A multicultural perspective. *Asia Pacific Advances in Consumer Research, 6*, 153–154.

Rindfleisch, A., Burroughs, J. E., & Wong, N. (2009). The safety of objects: Materialism, existential insecurity, and brand connection. *Journal of Consumer Research, 36*(1), 1–16.

Roccas, S. (2005). Religion and value systems. *Journal of Social Issues, 61*(4), 747–759.

Ryan, R. M., & Deci, E. L. (2000). Self-determination theory and the facilitation of intrinsic motivation, social development, and well-being. *American Psychologist, 55*(1), 68–78.
Saad, G. (2007). *The evolutionary bases of consumption*. Mahwah, NJ: Erlbaum.
Saad, G., & Gill, T. (2000). Applications of evolutionary psychology in marketing. *Psychology and Marketing, 17*(12), 1005–1034.
Saroglou, V., Corneille, O., & Van Cappellen, P. (2009). "Speak, Lord, your servant is listening": Religious priming activates submissive thoughts and behaviours. *The International Journal for the Psychology of Religion, 19*(3), 143–154.
Saroglou, V., Pichon, I., Trompette, L., Verschueren, M., & Dernelle, R. (2005). Prosocial behaviour and religion: New evidence based on projective measures and peer ratings. *Journal for the Scientific Study of Religion, 44*(3), 323–348.
Sarre, P. (1995). Towards global environmental values: Lessons from Western and Eastern experience. *Environmental Values, 4*(2), 115–127.
Seeman, T. E., Dubin, L. F., & Seeman, M. (2003). Religiosity/spirituality and health: A critical review of the evidence for biological pathways. *American Psychologist, 58*(1), 53–63.
Seidlitz, L., Abernethy, A. D., Duberstein, P. R., Evinger, J. S., Chang, T. H., & Lewis, B. L. (2002). Development of the spiritual transcendence index. *Journal for the Scientific Study of Religion, 41*(3), 439–453.
Shachar, R., Erdem, T., Cutright, K. M., & Fitzsimons, G. J. (2011). Brands: The opiate of the nonreligious masses? *Marketing Science, 30*(1), 92–110.
Shariff, A. F., & Norenzayan, A. (2007). God is watching you: Priming God concepts increases prosocial behaviour in an anonymous economic game. *Psychological Science, 18*(9), 803–809.
Sheth, J. N. (1983). An integrative theory of patronage preference and behaviour. In W. R. Darden & R. F. Lusch (Eds.), *Patronage behaviour and retail management* (pp. 9–28). New York, NY: North-Holland.
Smith, T. W. (1990). Classifying Protestant denominations. *Review of Religious Research, 31*(3), 225–245.
Sood, J., & Nasu, Y. (1995). Religiosity and nationality: An exploratory study of their effect on consumer behaviour in Japan and the United States. *Journal of Business Research, 34*(1), 1–9.
Spilka, B., & Schmidt, G. (1983). General attribution theory for the psychology of religion: The influence of event-character on attributions to god. *Journal for the Scientific Study of Religion, 22*(4), 326–339.
Spilka, B., Shaver, P., & Kirkpatrick, L. A. (1985). A general attribution theory for the psychology of religion. *Journal for the Scientific Study of Religion, 24*(1), 1–20.
Stark, R., & Glock, C. Y. (1968). *American piety: The nature of religious commitment*. Los Angeles, CA: University of California Press.
Swinyard, W. R., Kau, A.-K., & Phua, H.-Y. (2001). Happiness, materialism, and religious experience in the US and Singapore. *Journal of Happiness Studies, 2*(1), 13–32.
Tajfel, H., & Turner, J. (1979). An integrative theory of intergroup conflict. *The social psychology of intergroup relations* (Vol. 33, pp. 33–47).
Taylor, V., Halstead, D., & Haynes, P. (2010). Consumer responses to Christian religious symbols in advertising. *Journal of Advertising, 39*(2), 79–92.
Thompson, H., & Raine, J. (1976). Religious denomination preference as a basis for store location. *Journal of Retailing, 52*(2), 71–78.
Vitell, S. J., & Paolillo, J. G. P. (2003). Consumer ethics: The role of religiosity. *Journal of Business Ethics, 46*(2), 151–162.
Vitell, S. J., Paolillo, J. G. P., & Singh, J. J. (2005). Religiosity and consumer ethics. *Journal of Business Ethics, 57*(2), 175–181.
Welch, M. R., Sikkink, D., & Loveland, M. T. (2007). The radius of trust: Religion, social embeddedness and trust in strangers. *Social Forces, 86*(1), 23–46.
White, K., & Dahl, D. W. (2007). Are all out-groups created equal? Consumer identity and dissociative influence. *Journal of Consumer Research, 34*(4), 525–536.
White, L. (1967). The historical roots of our environmental crisis. *Science, 155*(3767), 1203–1207.
Wilkes, R. E., Burnett, J. J., & Howell, R. D. (1986). On the meaning and measurement of religiosity in consumer research. *Journal of the Academy of Marketing Science, 14*(1), 47–56.
Witter, R. A., Stock, W. A., Okun, M. A., & Haring, M. J. (1985). Religion and subjective well-being in adulthood: A quantitative synthesis. *Review of Religious Research, 26*(4), 332–342.
Wolkomir, M. J., Futreal, M., Woodrum, E., & Hoban, T. (1997). Denominational subcultures of environmentalism. *Review of Religious Research, 38*(4), 325–343.

Woodrum, E., & Wolkomir, M. J. (1997). Religious effects on environmentalism. *Sociological Spectrum, 17*(2), 223–234.

Yang, F., & Ebaugh, H. R. (2001). Religion and ethnicity among new immigrants: The impact of majority/minority status in home and host countries. *Journal for the Scientific Study of Religion, 40*(3), 367–378.

Zinnbauer, B. J., Pargament, K. I., Cole, B., Rye, M. S., Butter, E. M., Belavich, T. G., . . . Kadar, J. L. (1997). Religion and spirituality: Unfuzzying the fuzzy. *Journal for the Scientific Study of Religion, 36*(4), 549–564.

17

The psychological consequences of money for economic and social relationships

Tomasz Zaleskiewicz and Agata Gasiorowska

Money is one of the most ubiquitous and exceptional elements in society. From an economic point of view, it is a universal, instrumental and market-driven force that may be defined by the functions it provides. Mansfield (1992) argues that money is everything that fulfils the typical functions of money. Money serves as a medium of exchange, a means of storing wealth and value, a means of evaluation and a unit of measurement used to value goods or services (Begg, Fischer, & Dornbusch, 2002). Theories of money in economics are based on a model of rational behaviour and are typically concerned with the macroeconomic level of analysis. Psychological approaches to money focus on the peculiarities of human attitudes and behaviours (Lea, Tarpy, & Webley, 1987). From the psychological or anthropological point of view, money is not universal, because some of its forms are strictly reserved for special situations or unique social groups (Belk & Wallendorf, 1990). For example, Zelizer (1989) shows that some traditional communities identify gender of money: women use different forms of money than men. Numerous studies have documented that money serves important symbolic and affective functions and is a resource in interpersonal and intrapersonal regulation (Lea & Webley, 2006).

Money plays an important role in consumption not only in an economic (transactional) but also in a psychological or cultural sense. Conspicuous consumption and materialism are two defining features of contemporary Western culture (Kasser & Kanner, 2004). People strive, sometimes obsessively, to accumulate money and material possessions in vast excess above what is necessary to survive and prosper, and some people centre their lives around the accumulation of wealth at the expense of other values that might be more conducive to happiness (Dittmar, Bond, Hurst, & Kasser, 2013; Kasser, 2003). The fact that people are preoccupied with accumulating money and material possessions far beyond what would be necessary to survive and thrive requires an explanation, and scholars have long posited that people use money as a way to fulfil more complicated psychological needs. For example, money might enhance autonomy (Dewitte, 2006), be associated with feelings of strength, self-efficacy and confidence (Gasiorowska, 2014; Pessiglione et al., 2007; Zhou, Vohs, & Baumeister, 2009), buffer pain and social exclusion (Zhou et al., 2009), compensate for a lack of power (Dubois, Rucker, & Galinsky, 2010; Gal, 2012) and help to secure meaning and transcend death (Zaleskiewicz, Gasiorowska, & Kesebir, 2013; Zaleskiewicz, Gasiorowska, Kesebir, Luszczynska, & Pyszczynski, 2013).

The present chapter provides an insight into the understanding of money as a symbol of the market pricing approach to social relationships. We review and summarize the current state of literature on money, arguing that money affects consumers' behaviours, changing their mindset from communal-oriented (based on non-contingent support of other's welfare) to exchange-oriented (based on expectations to receive a comparable benefit in exchange for benefit given). Money is perhaps the most prominent instantiation of a market mode, and exchange relationships seem to be automatically linked with money. Introducing monetary payments to relationships formed as communal changes them into market-like practices (Ariely, Bracha, & Meier, 2009; Gneezy & Rustichini, 2000a, b; Heyman & Ariely, 2004; Sandel, 2012). What is more, people do not have to use real money in a relationship to experience this shift. It has been empirically shown in both adults and children that even reminders of the concept of money cause mindsets, preferences and behaviours to be congruent with exchange relationships (Gasiorowska, Zaleskiewicz, & Wygrab, 2012; Gasiorowska, Chaplin, Zaleskiewicz, Wygrab, & Vohs 2016; Vohs, Mead, & Goode, 2006). Before we turn to a more detailed description of these psychological effects of money, we present a general description of different types of relationships that people can engage in, and show how monetary payments and money per se cause a shift from one type of relationship to another.

Types of social and economic relationships

People engage in different types of relationships to get their needs satisfied. Many of these relationships are social in nature, because they involve other individuals or groups, but we could also consider people's relations with organizations, products or brands (Aggarwal, 2004). All these relationships differ among each other in terms of both formal and psychological characteristics, and only some of them involve money. The nature of the relationship typically determines how social interaction is generated, interpreted and evaluated. Even if the interaction is economic in nature, the way it is perceived by the actors might have long-term psychological consequences.

Social scientists have undertaken several attempts to offer a coherent typology of social relationships. One of the most widely cited and discussed models was proposed by Margaret Clark and Judson Mills (Clark & Mills, 1993, 2012), who showed that people might engage in communal or exchange relations. The two types of relationships are governed by different rules of behaviour and require different mindsets. The nature of communal relationships that typically do not involve money implies that "benefits are given without the donor or the recipient feeling the recipient has an obligation to repay" (Clark & Mills, 2012, p. 234). Benefits may take many forms, such as goods and services, but also compliments, support in reaching a goal or symbols of caring such as flowers. As the two authors suggest, communal relationships are often asymmetrical. It means that people give benefits not because they expect anything in return, but because they want to increase the recipient's welfare or happiness. In other words, non-contingent helping is arguably the *sine qua non* of communal relationships, and offering and giving help are prominent signals that the helper expects from a communal relationship (Clark, Ouellette, Powell, & Milberg, 1987). People being in a communal mode find it natural to be helpful, altruistic and generous, and friendship or social interactions within a family can exemplify such relationships (Clark & Mills, 1993).

In contrast, exchange relationships imply that "the receipt of a benefit incurs an obligation (debt) to return a comparable benefit" (Clark & Mills, 2012, p. 233). When people engage in such relationships, they care about how much they get out after having invested something and whether the repayment is of a comparable value. For that reason, exchange relationships typically involve money as the easiest means of calculating and expressing value. Market mode or exchange relationships emphasize rationality, logical thinking, efficiency, self-control and equal exchange, not allowing intimacy and emotional connectedness (Mead & Stuppy, 2014). Examples of exchange relationships are those between acquaintances or between strangers meeting for the first time, where there is no assumption that partners want to form a communal relationship (Clark & Mills, 2012). However, the canonical exemplification of market relationships is any kind of business relationship, in which people pay with money (in the case of trade) or are paid (in the case of providing services). What is important from our point of view is that within the market mode agentic performance is crucial, and the engagement and effort are related to monetary compensation that should increase with effort and the performance level (Gneezy & Rustichini, 2000b).

The relationships in which people engage might be communal or exchange in nature. For example, the relationship between a parent and a child is a typical example of communal relations, and working for payment is a natural exemplification of exchange relations. However, there are also numerous relationships that are more ambiguous. As Clark and Mills (2012) indicate, teachers who take care of young students at school do not expect a direct payment from children, but receive a salary for these services from the school administration. In such unclear relationships, people search for cues to interpret in either communal or exchange terms, and money is one such cue. For example, when money is involved in ambiguous relationships, people tend to define this relation as an exchange type rather than a communal type (Clark & Mills, 2012; Heyman & Ariely, 2004). What happens, however, if money is involved in relationships that are definitely communal in nature? Several studies have shown that introducing monetary payments to relationships formed as communal changes them into market-like practices, or at least impairs attitudes and behaviours that are characteristic of relations based on social norms (Ariely et al., 2009; Gneezy & Rustichini, 2000a, b; Heyman & Ariely, 2004; Sandel, 2012). Moreover, people do not have to use money in a relationship to experience this shift: Research has shown that people (both adults and children) when reminded of money (compared with other concepts) behave less pro-socially and more agentially (Vohs et al., 2006), which suggests that money does not aid the types of behaviours found in warm, communal relationships. In contrast, money primes (compared with neutral primes) led people to be better performers, to be more motivated and to show a drive to excel at work. Those behaviours indicate efforts to be efficacious producers, which are valued in the marketplace and typical of relationships based on market pricing (Heyman & Ariely, 2004).

In the following part of this chapter we review two groups of studies. The first group shows the effects of introducing real monetary payments to either ambiguous or communal relations. The second group demonstrates the psychological consequences of priming the concept of money for such social relations.

The effects of monetary payments on modes of relating

As we have already pointed out in this chapter, money is perhaps the most prominent instantiation of market mode, and exchange relationships seem to be automatically linked with money. For that reason, introducing monetary payments to communal relationships changes them into exchange relationships. This means that involving money in an interaction between people might modify the rules regulating such interaction.

One of the most striking illustrations of the effects described above was presented by Gneezy and Rustichini (2000a). The two authors conducted a field study to test the consequences of introducing monetary fines for parents who arrive late to collect their children from day-care centres. The centres that participated in the experiment operated from 7.30 a.m. to 4 p.m., and there was no fine for coming late. In addition, no information was given on what happens if parents collect children later than 4 p.m. When parents did not arrive on time, the teacher had to wait with the children. If monetary fines were not present, parents might have perceived the situation in terms of the communal relationship. Arriving late to collect children would then be incongruent with a social norm, because teachers were forced to stay after closing time without any additional payment. On the contrary, arriving on time means in this context that parents do not want to take advantage of the teachers' kindness. What happened if monetary fines for coming late were introduced? The authors observed ten day-care centres over a period of 20 weeks. The first 4 weeks was a period without financial fine. The monetary payment was implemented at the beginning of the fifth week in six out of the ten day-care centres. The results were striking: The number of parents' late arrivals at the day-care centre increased after the monetary fine was introduced. Moreover, the higher number of parents coming late remained stable even if the fine was removed at the beginning of the 17th week. It seems that the implementation of a monetary fine transformed the communal-type relationship to an exchange-type relationship. As the two authors argue, parents tended to perceive the fine as a price that had to be paid in exchange for collecting children too late. Teachers' additional work after closing time did not have to be seen as a charity, but as a service that could be purchased for money (Gneezy & Rustichini, 2000a).

When people participate in communal relationships and give benefits to other individuals or the group, they do not expect repayment (Clark & Mills, 1993, 2012). For example, parents pay for their children's education, but this type of favour is non-contingent. In the case of market pricing relations, people not only desire repayment, but also presume that the compensation will be of a comparable value. What are the psychological consequences of violating this expectation? To answer this question, Gneezy and Rustichini (2000b) examined the relation between monetary compensation for an activity and the performance level of that activity. They manipulated the amount of payment for completing a cognitive task (answering 50 questions taken from an IQ test). In one of the experimental conditions no payment was implemented. Participants were simply asked to answer as many questions as they could. The participants might have perceived this situation as a communal relationship, because completing the task properly would be similar to doing the experimenter a favour. In other groups (i.e., experimental conditions) three different values of a monetary payment for each question with a correct answer were used. On the basis of economic theory assumptions, one might expect a positive correlation between the level of performance and the amount of payment, because incentives increase effectiveness by definition. Indeed, the average number of questions answered correctly was 23 in the group with the lowest salary and increased significantly (to approximately 34 questions) in the two groups with the higher salary. However, Gneezy and Rustichini (2000b) found that the average effectiveness in the no-payment condition was better in comparison with the low-payment condition (approximately 28 correct answers were observed in the no-salary group). These results suggest that introducing money changed the perception of the situation: The communal relationship was replaced by the market pricing relationship, in which people care about the value of the payment and determine the amount they work according to the payment.

The effects described above were replicated by Heyman and Ariely (2004), who compared people's willingness to help in situations in which monetary repayments were or were not used. Helping colleagues or neighbours is a typical example of the communal relationship: People altruistically support each other regardless of the value of compensation and sometimes even do not accept money as a repayment for help (Webley & Lea, 1993). Involving money invokes market pricing-oriented norms and mindsets, and motivates individuals to search for a symmetrical relation between effort and payment. Heyman and Ariely (2004) conducted three experiments to confirm these assumptions. In one of the studies participants were asked to do a simple task. In the control condition students did not receive any payment. In two other groups monetary payment was introduced and had a different value depending on the experimental condition. The authors reported that effort in the no-payment group was similar to that in the medium-payment group, but significantly below that in the low-payment group. These results showed again that when a situation is framed as communal, people interpret their effort in terms of gifts or favours and work as hard as if they were paid at least a medium salary. On the contrary, in the market pricing mode people track the relation between effort and repayment and become reluctant to offer their engagement (e.g., work) when they perceive the compensation as unsatisfactory (Heyman & Ariely, 2004).

Implementing money to the social relationship changes its nature from communal to exchange type, and might also impact the psychological processes involved. For example, expressing and identifying emotions is natural for communal relationships, because they are typically associated with empathy (for example, "I help you, because I want you to be happier"). Therefore, we might predict that implementing money in a social relationship would have a harmful effect on emotional processes. This prediction was empirically supported in a series of experiments carried out by Ma-Kellams and Blascovich (2013). These authors studied the effects of monetary incentives on empathic accuracy and expected that introducing financial payments would impair the accuracy with which people uncover others' feelings. In one of the studies, participants watched individuals discussing recent emotional experiences and were asked to infer feelings expressed by these individuals. Performance in this task was either related to monetary payment or not. Results perfectly confirmed the authors' expectations: Participants in the experimental condition (with monetary payment) demonstrated a worse performance in detecting emotions than participants in the control condition (without monetary payment). This means that using money in a situation that is typically defined as communal has a negative effect on performance. This effect was also replicated in the second experiment conducted by the same authors (Ma-Kellams & Blascovich, 2013).

Another demonstration of an impairing influence of the implementation of money into the communal-type situation was presented by Ariely et al. (2009). These authors studied how introducing material rewards changes people's motivation to behave pro-socially. On the theoretical level they differentiated three types of motivations: intrinsic motivation (pro-social behaviour has a value per se), extrinsic motivation (people behave pro-socially because they expect a monetary compensation) and image motivation (people behave pro-socially because they want others to perceive them as benevolent). The authors of this study hypothesized that monetary incentives would impair participants' effort in a pro-social act when their decisions were public (in comparison to a situation in which a decision was private). They argued that in public situations monetary incentives could crowd out image motivation and, therefore, become counterproductive. However, the above assumption seems to be also congruent with the distinction between communal and exchange relationships. While exchange relationships may be both anonymous and public, communal relationships are typically public, because they are associated with keeping close ties (Ariely et al., 2009).

To test their hypotheses, Ariely et al. (2009) conducted an experimental study, in which two factors were manipulated: context (public vs. private) and motivation (intrinsic vs. extrinsic). The participants were asked to do a task in which higher effort indicated more pro-social behaviour. The authors found that people put more effort into the public than the private condition. This is not surprising, taking into account that communal relationships are public, as we have already noted. Moreover, monetary incentives increased effort, but only in the private condition (compared with the public condition). The latter outcome suggests that monetary payments are not useful when people act in the communal mode.

Empirical outcomes presented so far have demonstrated that inducing money in the form of a financial payment (incentive) changes social relationships. However, people maintain not only social relations, but also relations with non-social objects such as brands and companies. Therefore, implementing communication referring to arguments associated with money may impair the consumer–company relationship when this relationship is based on communal values. This problem was empirically examined by Aggarwal (2004), who expected that violation of norms characteristic of communal relationships between a bank and its customer would negatively affect the appraisal of marketing actions and the general evaluation of the bank. The author used two different scenarios to prime either communal or exchange relationship norms. The participants were asked to imagine that they requested help from a bank and, depending on the experimental condition, had to pay a service fee or not. It has been assumed that charging customers for a specific service is congruent with norms typical of the exchange relationship, but incongruent with communal relationship norms. Therefore, in the latter case, it should have an impairing effect on how the customer perceives the bank and how she or he evaluates the brand. Empirical evidence supported this theoretical argumentation. When information about the necessity to pay for a service was provided, participants in the communal relationship condition evaluated both marketing action and the brand lower than participants in the exchange relationship condition. These results suggest that money may impair not only social relations but also relations between customers and brands or companies, assuming that the initial relationship is communal in nature.

Summing up, people clearly differentiate between the two types of relationships: communal (sharing) and exchange (market pricing). Both types of relations have their own characteristics, have separate features and do not mix with each other. One factor that seems to be crucial for the communal–exchange distinction is money. Money is inseparably associated with exchange relationships and is never present in communal relationships. The experiments presented in this section documented that introducing monetary payments to the communal relationship changes people's attitudes and behaviours. However, a growing collection of studies has recently shown that even subtle reminders of money have an effect on the quality of social interactions. In other words, it is not necessary to implement real money to make people think about social relations in terms of economic transactions. In the next part of this chapter, we review studies showing the psychological consequences of priming the concept of money.

Money primes and the shift from communal to market mode

As mentioned in the introduction, the connection between money and market mode seems to reach far beyond the economic functions of money (means of exchange, units of account and means of storing value). Money is such a strong symbol of market mode that even subtle money primes can cause people's behaviours and preferences to be more congruent with exchange and less congruent with communal relationships. The best-known and most widely cited research on this topic has been conducted by Vohs, Mead and Goode (2006, 2008). It has shown that after being reminded of money, compared with other concepts, people become less helpful and more agentive. The effects of money priming have been replicated in independent laboratories in many countries around the world, such as Belgium (Quoidbach, Dunn, Petrides, & Mikolajczak, 2010; Van Laer, De Ruyter, & Cox, 2013), Canada (Kushlev, Dunn, & Ashton-James, 2012;), France (Guéguen & Jacob, 2013), India (Mukherjee, Manjaly, &

Nargundkar, 2013), Poland (Gasiorowska & Helka, 2012), Switzerland (Reutner & Wänke, 2013), and the United States (Chatterjee, Rose, & Sinha, 2013; Mogilner, 2010; Molinsky, Grant, & Margolis, 2012), suggesting that these effects are cross-culturally universal. Moreover, the shift from communal mode to market mode triggered by money primes can be observed not only in adults, but also in adolescents (Roberts & Roberts, 2012) and even in very young children (Gasiorowska et al., 2012; Gasiorowska et al., 2016). In the next part of this chapter we will explain the methodological issues related to money-priming experiments and take a closer look at the whole host of studies in which mere reminders of money shifted people into market mode, which conflicts with the communal mode.

What is money priming?

Money priming is a novel experimental method employed to understand the psychology of money that has recently been tested on adults and children. In these experiments participants arrive at the laboratory individually and are randomly exposed to concepts related to either money or other objects. The procedure of money priming begins usually with the performance of a task that is associated with money per se, but not with giving, getting, earning or losing it. In experiments based on money priming, participants did not have to deal with real gains or losses, and often did not even have contact with real money. Instead, they were asked to solve word-descrambling tasks with words related to money, to perform tasks while being in close proximity to banknotes lying on the table, or to imagine that they possessed a big amount of money (Briers, Pandelaere, Dewitte, & Warlop, 2006; Gino & Pierce, 2009; Mogilner, 2010; Vohs et al., 2006). In other studies, researchers exposed participants to pictures and animations with coins and notes, such as posters on the wall, screensavers or images in the background of the questionnaire (Caruso, Mead, & Vohs, 2009; Mead & Baumeister, 2009; Quoidbach et al., 2010; Vohs et al., 2006). Sometimes people also had physical contact with money and were asked to touch, sort or count it (Gasiorowska et al., 2012, in review; Guéguen & Jacob, 2013; Reutner & Wänke, 2013; Zaleskiewicz et al., 2013; Zhou et al., 2009). Two things are common to all these manipulations. First, the instruction presented to participants did not refer directly to money. Second, participants were not paid or rewarded on the basis of their performance. In other words, people in such experiments did not change their behaviour or preferences because they wanted to receive the desired reward in cash. As in other experiments based on the priming procedure, participants were not aware that the first task (or the background of the questionnaire, posters on the wall etc.) was in any way related to the next one. What is more, they did not realize that the first task had any effect on their subsequent decisions, behaviours and preferences. In the next part of this chapter we review studies showing how the exposure to money shifts people to market mode and makes them behave in accordance with norms typical of exchange but not communal relationships.

Money primes trigger behaviour and preferences consistent with market mode

On the one hand, being in a communal relationship inevitably requires taking other people into consideration, and being sensitive not only to their needs or requests for help, but also to their emotions and the fact that they could have a different point of view. On the other hand, the market mindset promotes self-interest, rationality and efficiency, with a diminished regard for others (Clark & Mills, 1993, 2012). Recent studies have indeed shown that money is related to self-focus, autonomy and independence. For example, Reutner and Wänke (2013) argued that people reminded of money became more self-oriented, because money shifted their focus more towards self-related needs and less towards the needs of other people. In line with this reasoning, they found that money-primed participants, compared with participants not primed with money, were more vulnerable to following recommendations based on self-related arguments of social campaigns, such as arguing to reduce meat intake and arguing against smoking cigarettes, and that they were less prone to follow recommendations based on other-related arguments. For people primed with money, self-related arguments were perceived as more convincing, because activating the concept of money caused them to be focused on personal advancement, their own needs and benefits.

This result was also replicated in our research (Gasiorowska, 2014). We asked our participants to perform a task that required building words either related or unrelated to money from provided syllables, and then to watch one of two commercials presenting a very sophisticated hi-fi product. One version of the commercial used arguments related to the independent self, while the other used arguments related to the interdependent self. We found that when the product was presented with self-related arguments, participants primed with money assessed it as a better one and were eager to pay a higher price than participants from a control condition. When the commercial used group-related arguments, the pattern of results reversed (Gasiorowska, 2014).

We also showed directly that money changes self-construal to be more coherent with a market mode and less coherent with a communal mode, leading people to focus on the self (Gasiorowska, 2014). First, we asked individuals to participate in a working memory test and try to remember details from either a high-nominal banknote or an abstract picture. Then, they completed a Twenty Statements Test (Kuhn & McPartland, 1954), in which they responded to the question of "Who I am?" by filling in answers to the prompt "I am" twenty times. We found that reminders of money influenced both independent and interdependent self-construal. Participants in the money-primed condition saw themselves in a more independent manner and a slightly less interdependent manner than those in the control condition (Gasiorowska, 2014).

Up to this point, we demonstrated that money primes trigger self-interest and self-focus. Indeed, the money and market mindset prioritizes self-interest and egocentrism, but also rationality, logical thinking, efficiency and hard work. This is also what we see in experiments where money is cued. In a study conducted by Mogilner (2010), participants solved a scrambled word task, and then were left for some time in the cafeteria, surreptitiously observed by the experimenter's confederate. It revealed that those participants who were primed with money spent more time reading or working on their laptops (excluding time spent on social networking sites) and less time talking with other people at the cafe, talking on a mobile phone or texting (Mogilner, 2010). Just a mere reminder of money motivated people to work more (activity typical of exchange relationships) at the cost of socializing less (activity typical of communal mode).

When people are in a market mode, the notions of rationality and efficiency heavily influence their behaviours and preferences. For example, some research suggests that the psychological effects of money include enhancing the belief that people can achieve their goals as well as their persistence in reaching those goals. In a simple experiment conducted by Mukherjee et al. (2013), participants who had a picture of money in the background of their questionnaire reported higher feelings of self-efficacy compared with those from the control group. In another study, people who counted money declared that they felt stronger than those who counted slips of paper (Zhou et al., 2009). In one of our studies we asked participants to memorize details from either a valuable banknote or an abstract picture, and then asked them to fill in the agency–communion scale (Abele & Wojciszke, 2007) with two additional items: "self-sufficient" and "strong". Agency and communion are the two basic dimensions for judging self and others, similar to the distinction between independence and interdependence, or between competence and warmth (Abele & Wojciszke, 2007). According to Abele and

Wojciszke (2007), agency emerges from striving to individuate the self and involves such qualities as ambition, dominance, competence and efficiency in goal attainment. On the other hand, communion emerges from striving to integrate the self in a larger social unit through caring for others, and involves such qualities as focus on others, cooperation and emotional expression. For that reason, we might assume that agency is a feature required and valued in exchange relationships and in market mode, while a high level of communion is typical of communal relationships. Indeed, we found that money-primed participants, compared with those not primed with money, declared that they were more agentive, stronger and slightly more self-sufficient, but the level of declared communion did not differ between the two groups. To sum up, the concept of money is closely related to the idea of expertise, and priming money can boost agency and competence ascribed to self and to others (Aaker, Vohs, & Mogilner, 2010; Gasiorowska, 2014).

Activating the concept of money not only makes people feel that they are competent and agentive, but also makes them behave in that way. In experiments conducted by Vohs et al. (2006), participants reminded of money wanted to take more work on themselves, and worked longer on a challenging task, even when they had an opportunity to work with others or to ask for help. We also demonstrated that these effects are present when young children at the age of 3-6 years are reminded of money (Gasiorowska et al., 2016). First, children who had been handling coins as opposed to paper discs persisted longer on an extremely difficult jigsaw puzzle before they gave up or asked for help. In another study, we instructed children to handle money or other objects (depending on experimental condition), and then asked them to work on a difficult labyrinth task with the option of quitting. As predicted, children who had been exposed to money were more agentic than other children. They worked harder and achieved better outcomes (Gasiorowska et al., 2016).

Because persistence in non-solvable tasks is frequently used as a measure of self-regulation, it seems plausible to assume that money primes increased self-control, an important feature of agentive self. Recently, Boucher and Kofos (2012) have reported findings on the relation between self-control and the psychological meaning of money. In two experiments, they showed that participants who experienced ego depletion through exerting self-control and were then primed with money performed better on the control-demanding Stroop task and were more persistent in an anagram task relative to those who were not primed with money after depletion. Boucher and Kofos (2012) also demonstrated that the effect of money reminders on performance among depleted participants was mediated by the subjective difficulty of the second task. Therefore, it was not that money-primed participants were more motivated during the second self-control task, but they thought that the task was less difficult and required less effort (Boucher & Kofos, 2012).

To sum up, we demonstrated that money is a cue to market mode, as even subtle reminders of money trigger various behaviours and preferences that are typical of exchange relationships: self-focus and self-interest, but also enhanced agency and self-control. In the next part of this chapter we will take a closer look at the other side of the psychological consequences of money – its power to hamper communal relationships.

Money primes hamper behaviour and preferences consistent with communal mode

As already discussed in this chapter, money activates self-focus and self-enhancement goals that are directly related to exchange relationships (Gasiorowska, 2014; Mead & Stuppy, 2014). This means, however, that it might restrain behaviours typical of communal relationships, such as a focus on other people and other-oriented goals. Money allows individuals to acquire what they need for survival, minimizing their need to get along with others and their dependence on others (Zhou et al., 2009). Money seems to increase egocentrism – the fundamental tendency to interpret the world in terms of the self and to ignore the other aspects of social life. In research conducted by Caruso, Mead and Vohs (2009), money led to ignoring the perspective of others, because people reminded of money were less willing to correct their egocentric viewpoint. Caruso et al. (2009) asked participants to draw the symbol $ (money-related) or symbol S (not related to money) on their forehead. A greater proportion of participants drew the symbol on their forehead egocentrically, as though the writers would read it themselves. This suggests that they were less able to adopt the visual perspective of others. Moreover, in another experiment conducted by Caruso et al. (2009), money primes led to the committing of more errors when recalling information about another person, but not when recalling non-social data. In another study, people reminded of money showed a higher level of egocentric projections. Their predictions of another's beliefs about abortion were much more similar to their own opinions compared with the predictions produced by participants from a control condition (Caruso et al., 2009).

Studies on the psychological consequences of money also reveal that people reminded of money not only have problems with overcoming the egocentric perspective and taking the perspective of others, but also experience a reduced desire for social connectedness on different levels. For example, they preferred to keep a physical distance from other people, and to work or spend their leisure time alone rather than with others (Park, Gasiorowska, & Vohs, in review; Vohs et al., 2006). In addition, money reminders reduced the use of self-presentation strategies and interpersonal likeability. In an experiment conducted by Mead and Baumeister (2009), money-primed participants (compared with controls) were rated by independent judges as less likeable and less friendly during the interaction, which indicates that they were less involved in making a good impression on their future conversation partners. In other words, the implementation of money-related concepts reduced the likelihood that people would self-present to a new acquaintance – behaviour that is essential for a potential communal relationship.

Reminders of money might also alter the emotional state when it comes to social relations. For example, counting money instead of papers significantly reduced suffering induced by social rejection, but did not alter social distress in the non-rejected participants (Zhou et al., 2009). Other studies showed that money causes individuals to view themselves in a less relational manner, impairing their compassion and empathy. Activating the concept of money reduced the compassion that individuals expressed to others and lowered the feeling of empathy for persons who were suffering, such as a homeless person and an alleged terrorist who was being starved (Caruso et al., 2013). This effect was also observed in managers from Fortune 100 financial companies, who were less prone to take responsibility for the customer's case and did not want to take the perspective of the customer when they first solved a money-related crossword puzzle (Van Laer et al., 2013). In a different study, the effect of money primes on reduced compassion was mediated by lowered feelings of empathy and heightened perceptions of unprofessionalism in expressing emotions (Molinsky et al., 2012). All these results confirm our argumentation that money leads to indifference to other people, mostly because being in market mode and highly concentrated on self contradicts caring about others. Caring about others is not the only sign of being in a communal mode. What is even more important, people being in such a mode find it natural to be helpful, altruistic and generous (Fiske, 1992, 2004; Fiske & Haslam, 2005). Offering, giving and accepting help signal that the helper wants to form a communal and not an exchange relationship (Clark et al., 1987). Since money is the essence of market mode, it should hinder the behaviours and preferences that are typical of communal mode. Some studies indeed showed these effects. For example, Vohs et al. (2006, 2008) demonstrated that participants exposed to money were less likely to help either the experimenter or the other participant in the study than those exposed to neutral primes. In a field experiment conducted by Guéguen and Jacob (2013), people who took cash from an ATM (compared with those who just passed an ATM) were less likely to help the experimenter by participating in the study and also were less prone to warn a passer-by that she had dropped her ticket. In other experiments, money primes reduced the willingness to volunteer time to others in need (Chatterjee et al., 2013; Pfeffer & DeVoe, 2009). The effect of reduced willingness to help was observed not only when participants were supposed to help a stranger, but also when the individual who needed help was their partner in a romantic relationship (Mead, Vohs, Savini, Stillman, & Baumeister, 2010). Assuming that a romantic relationship is a strong communal domain that endorses a code of caring for others, this is a robust argument that money causes a shift from communal mode to market mode. Moreover, our recent research showed that even very young children aged from 3 to 6 years who had previously counted or sorted money were less helpful to the experimenter than those who had interacted with non-monetary objects (Gasiorowska et al., 2012, 2016).

Reminding people of money affects not only willingness to share time and make an effort in the interest of other people, but also readiness to share precious resources. Money primes decreased the willingness to donate as well as real donations for different charities (Chatterjee et al., 2013; Roberts & Roberts, 2012; Vohs et al., 2006). When compared with those reminded of neutral concepts, participants reminded of money sent a smaller part of their endowment to the receiver in a dictator game (Gasiorowska & Helka, 2012), and declared that they would like to spend less money on Christmas gifts for their relatives or a birthday present for their best friend (Gasiorowska, 2013).

Activating the concept of money also had a negative effect on generosity when we investigated behaviours and preferences of young children (Gasiorowska et al., 2012). The tendency to make egalitarian (i.e., non-selfish) choices was weaker in children who saw a poster presenting money and talked about it, or who sorted coins, than in those who performed other tasks. More precisely, children reminded of money showed a lower level of generosity, as they preferred not to share their stickers with the anonymous partner to a greater extent than children not reminded of money. We also asked our participants to choose between 1) allocating one sticker to themselves and one to their partners (1,1), and 2) allocating one sticker to themselves and nothing to the partners (1,0). According to Fehr, Bernhard and Rockenbach (2008), this kind of dilemma measures an elementary form of pro-sociality, as choosing the (1,1) option over the (1,0) option means delivering a benefit to the partner at no cost, and the decision maker receives one sticker regardless of the decision made. Even in such a case, activating the concept of money decreased children's pro-sociality and reduced the inclination to give a sticker to an anonymous partner (Gasiorowska et al., 2012).

Why are people reminded of money less pro-social? Does it mean that money directly impairs interpersonal harmony and hinders communal relationships? We do not think so. We would rather assume that the main psychological effect of money is the salience of market mode, and that diminished empathy, helpfulness and pro-sociality are just a by-product. For example, as money primes boost perceived agency and competence assigned to self and to other objects (Aaker et al., 2010; Gasiorowska, 2014), they might also cause a perception of other people as more agentic and competent. We suppose that people reminded of money do not want to help others, not because they are anti-social, but because they think that others are able to cope by themselves and do not expect help. In other words, they perceive both themselves and others as being in a market mode.

Summary

Money changes people's behaviour as well as their cognitive, motivational and emotional state (Briers et al., 2006; Vohs et al., 2006; Zhou et al., 2009). The effects of money may be observed in situations when people deliberately think about monetary consequences of their actions, but also when people are not conscious that they are affected by money cues. Introducing money to a relationship, or even reminders of money, activates the set of self-enhancement goals driving self-oriented behaviours, which is coherent with the market/exchange mindset. At the same time, the appearance of money suppresses other-oriented goals and impairs pro-social behaviours. Dealing with money activates the structures of knowledge that are incompatible with the pursuit of social harmony (Bijleveld & Aarts, 2014). For that reason, we believe that a contemporary society that bombards people with material and monetary cues can shift people's mindsets into a market mode, a self-centred mindset that hampers harmonious and deep social relationships.

The whole area of research on money reminders as a cue to market mode is quite new but very promising. Still, some issues remain uncovered. For example, what is the mechanism behind associating money with market mode, which causes even young children to possess such associations? To what degree are these associations transmitted from parents, who demonstrate a market mode mentality when interacting with their children? What is the role of the media and contemporary consumer culture in forming associations between money and market mode in the process of mental development?

The second intriguing issue worthy of being studied is related to the role money plays in mixed situations that include cues for both exchange and communal relationships. One example of such a situation could be a joint effort task, in which participants are paid for effort (exchange cue), but they must also cooperate to be more successful (communal cue). Another case of such a mixed situation would be an interpersonal interaction demanding trust. Although typically perceived as a characteristic of a close relationship, trust seems to be as crucial to economic transactions as self-interest is (Berg, Dickhaut, & McCabe, 1995; Fukuyama, 1996). If so, then we might assume that money priming will hamper trust when there is no exchange or economic transaction involved, but the situation is directly framed as a transaction.

Finally, a problem that deserves to be examined in future research is the degree to which the effects of money reminders are universal across cultures. It is worth noticing here that the effects of money priming are not universal among individuals, and can be observed to a higher degree in those who assign symbolic, affective meaning to money than in those who perceive money only in instrumental, economic terms (Gasiorowska, 2014). For that reason, it would be interesting to extend these individual differences to cross-cultural differences. It is possible that economic inequality, measured for example with the Gini index, would serve as a moderator of money-priming effect in cross-national research. As inequality erodes trust and increases anxiety (Wilkinson & Pickett, 2009), we believe that future research might show stronger effects of money priming in people from economically unequal societies than in those from more equal ones.

To conclude, this chapter provides an insight into the understanding of the psychology of money, an area that has recently witnessed an extensive increase in research attention. We noted that consumer research typically defines money in terms of a universal economic force that allows people to fulfil needs and purchase goods. In other words, economic and consumer sciences perceive money as nothing more than a means of exchange. Psychological science, on the other hand, proposes and empirically demonstrates that money might become an end in itself and influence the world of social relations as well as intrapersonal regulations. We summarized the current state of the empirical literature on money, arguing that money affects consumers' attitudes and behaviours on both the conscious (when consumers deliberate about monetary consequences of their actions) and the unconscious level (when consumers are affected by incidental cues related to money). We also demonstrated that money is strongly connected to self-focus and, therefore, has an effect on intrapersonal and interpersonal processes not only in adults but also in children. Finally, we provided some reference to new directions for research in the field of the psychology of money.

Acknowledgements

This work was supported by the SWPS University of Social Sciences and Humanities (Project BST/WROC/2015/04) and the Polish National Science Centre (Grant DEC-2013/11/B/HS6/01316).

References

Aaker, J. L., Vohs, K. D., & Mogilner, C. (2010). Non-profits are seen as warm and for-profits as competent: Firm stereotypes matter. *Journal of Consumer Research, 37*(2), 224–237.

Abele, A. E., & Wojciszke, B. (2007). Agency and communion from the perspective of self versus others. *Journal of Personality and Social Psychology, 93*(5), 751–763.

Aggarwal, P. (2004). The effects of brand relationship norms on consumer attitudes and behaviour. *Journal of Consumer Research, 31*, 87–101.

Ariely, D., Bracha, A., & Meier, S. (2009). Doing good or doing well? Image motivation and monetary incentives in behaving prosocially. *American Economic Review, 99*, 544–555.

Begg, D., Fischer, S., & Dornbusch, R. (2002). *Economics*. Maidenhead, Berkshire: McGraw-Hill Higher Education.

Belk, R. W., & Wallendorf, M. (1990). The sacred meaning of money. *Journal of Economic Psychology, 11*, 35–67.

Berg, J., Dickhaut, J., & McCabe, K. (1995). Trust, reciprocity, and social history. *Games and Economic Behaviour, 10*, 122–142.

Bijleveld, E., & Aarts, H. (2014). A psychological perspective on money. In E. H. Bijleveld & H. Aarts (Eds.), *The psychological science of money* (pp. 3–19). New York, NY: Springer.

Boucher, H. C., & Kofos, M. N. (2012). The idea of money counteracts ego depletion effects. *Journal of Experimental Social Psychology, 48*(4), 804–810.

Briers, B., Pandelaere, M., Dewitte, S., & Warlop, L. (2006). Hungry for money: On the exchangeability of financial and caloric resources. *Psychological Science, 17*, 939–943.

Caruso, E. M., Mead, N., & Vohs, K. D. (2009). There's no "you" in money: Thinking of money increases egocentrism. *Advances in Consumer Research, 36*, 208–209.

Caruso, E. M., Vohs, K. D., Baxter, B., & Waytz, A. (2013). Mere exposure to money increases endorsement of free market systems and social inequality. *Journal of Experimental Psychology: General, 142*(2), 301–306.

Chatterjee, P., Rose, R. L., & Sinha, J. (2013). Why money meanings matter in decisions to donate time and money. *Marketing Letters, 24*, 109–118.

Clark, M. S., & Mills, J. R. (1993). The difference between communal and exchange relationships: What it is and is not. *Personality and Social Psychology Bulletin, 19*, 684–691.

Clark, M. S., & Mills, J. R. (2012). A theory of communal (and exchange) relationships. In P. A. M. Van Lange, A. W. Kruglanski & E. T. Higgins (Eds.), *Handbook of theories of social psychology* (Vol. 2, pp. 232–250). Los Angeles, CA: Sage.

Clark, M., Ouellette, R., Powell, M., & Milberg, S. (1987). Recipient's mood, relationship type, and helping. *Journal of Personality and Social Psychology, 53*, 94–103.

Dewitte, S. (2006). Money and the autonomy instinct. *Brain and Behavioural Sciences, 29*(2), 184–185.

Dittmar, H., Bond, R., Hurst, M., & Kasser, T. (2013). The relationship between materialism and personal well-being: A meta-analysis. *Journal of Personality and Social Psychology, 107*, 879–924.

Dubois, D., Rucker, D. D., & Galinsky, A. D. (2010). The accentuation bias: Money literally looms larger (and sometimes smaller) to the powerless. *Social Psychological and Personality Science, 1*(3), 199–205.

Fehr, E., Bernhard, H., & Rockenbach, B. (2008). Egalitarianism in young children. *Nature, 454*(7208), 1079–1084.

Fiske, A. P. (1992). The four elementary forms of sociality: Framework for a unified theory of social relations. *Psychological Review, 99*, 689–723.

Fiske, A. P. (2004). Relational Models Theory 2.0. In N. Haslam (Ed.), *Relational Models Theory: A contemporary overview* (pp. 3–26). Mahwah, NJ: Erlbaum.

Fiske, A. P., & Haslam, N. (2005). The four basic social bonds: Structures for coordinating interaction. In M. Baldwin (Ed.), *Interpersonal cognition* (pp. 267–298). New York, NY: Guilford Press.

Fukuyama, F. (1996). *Trust: The social virtues and the creation of prosperity*. New York, NY: The Free Press.

Gal, D. (2012). A mouth-watering prospect: Salivation to material reward. *Journal of Consumer Research, 38*(6), 1022–1029.

Gasiorowska, A. (2013). Psychologiczne skutki aktywacji idei pieniędzy a dawanie prezentów [The psychological consequences of mere exposure to money and gift-giving]. *Psychologia Społeczna, 8*, 156–168.

Gasiorowska, A. (2014). *Psychologiczne znaczenie pieniędzy. Dlaczego pieniądze wywołują koncentrację na sobie*. [The psychological meaning of money. Why money induces self-focus]. Warsaw: Wydawnictwo Naukowe PWN.

Gasiorowska, A., & Helka, A. (2012). Psychological consequences of money and money attitudes in dictator game. *Polish Psychological Bulletin, 3*(1), 20–26.

Gasiorowska, A., Zaleskiewicz, T., & Wygrab, S. (2012). Would you do something for me? The effects of money activation on social preferences and social behaviour in young children. *Journal of Economic Psychology, 33*, 603–608.

Gasiorowska, A., Chaplin, L., Zaleskiewicz, T., Wygrab, S., & Vohs, K. (2016). Money cues increase agency and decrease prosociality among children: early signs of market mode behaviours. *Psychological Science, 27*, 331–344.

Gino, F., & Pierce, L. (2009). The abundance effect: Unethical behaviour in the presence of wealth. *Organizational Behaviour and Human Decision Processes, 109*(2), 142–155.

Gneezy, U., & Rustichini, A. (2000a). A fine is a price. *Journal of Legal Studies, XXIX*, 1–18.

Gneezy, U., & Rustichini, A. (2000b). Pay enough or don't pay at all. *Quarterly Journal of Economics, August*, 791–810.

Guéguen, N., & Jacob, C. (2013). Behavioural consequences of money: When the automated teller machine reduces helping behaviour. *The Journal of Socio-Economics, 47*, 103–104.

Heyman, J., & Ariely, D. (2004). Effort for payment. *Psychological Science, 15*, 787–793.

Kasser, T. (2003). *The high price of materialism*. Cambridge, MA: The MIT Press.

Kasser, T., & Kanner, A. D. (2004). *Psychology and consumer culture. The struggle for a good life in a materialistic world*. Washington, DC: American Psychological Association.

Kuhn, M. H., & McPartland, T. S. (1954). An empirical investigation of self-attitudes. *American Sociological Review, 19*(1), 68–76.

Kushlev, K., Dunn, E. W., & Ashton-James, C. E. (2012). Does affluence impoverish the experience of parenting? *Journal of Experimental Social Psychology, 48*, 1381–1384.

Lea, S. E. G., Tarpy, R. M., & Webley, P. (1987). *The individual in the economy*. Cambridge: Cambridge University Press.

Lea, S. E. G., & Webley, P. (2006). Money as tool, money as drug: The biological psychology of a strong incentive. *Behavioural and Brain Sciences, 29*, 161–209.

Ma-Kellams, C., & Blascovich, J. (2013). The ironic effect of financial incentives on empathic accuracy. *Journal of Experimental Social Psychology, 49*, 65–71.

Mansfield, E. (1992). *Principles of macroeconomics*. New York, NY: W. W. Norton.

Mead, N., & Baumeister, R. (2009). Money reduces self-presentation and interpersonal likability in novel social situations. *Advances in Consumer Research, 36*, 208.

Mead, N. L., & Stuppy, A. (2014). Money can promote or hinder interpersonal harmony. In E. H. Bijleveld & H. Aarts (Eds.), *The psychological science of money* (pp. 243–262). New York, NY: Springer.

Mead, N., Vohs, K. D., Savini, K., Stillman, T., & Baumeister, R. (2010). Reminders of money weaken sociomoral responses. *Advances in Consumer Research, 37*, 36.

Mogilner, C. (2010). The pursuit of happiness: Time, money, and social connection. *Psychological Science, 21*(9), 1348–1354.

Molinsky, A. L., Grant, A. M., & Margolis, J. D. (2012). The bedside manner of homo economicus: How and why priming an economic schema reduces compassion. *Organizational Behaviour and Human Decision Processes, 119*, 27–37.

Mukherjee, S., Manjaly, J. A., & Nargundkar, M. (2013). Money makes you reveal more: Consequences of monetary cues on preferential disclosure of personal information. *Frontiers in Psychology*, *4*, 839. Retrieved from http://dx.doi.org/10.3389/fpsyg.2013.00839

Park, J., Gasiorowska, A., & Vohs, K. D. (in review). Self-affirmation has the power to offset the harmful effects of money reminders. *Journal of Personality and Social Psychology*.

Pessiglione, M., Schmidt, L., Draganski, B., Kalisch, R., Lau, H., Dolan, R. J., & Frith, C. D. (2007). How the brain translates money into force: A neuroimaging study of subliminal motivation. *Science*, *316*, 904–906.

Pfeffer, J., & DeVoe, S. E. (2009). Economic evaluation: The effect of money and economics on attitudes about volunteering. *Journal of Economic Psychology*, *30*, 500–508.

Quoidbach, J., Dunn, E. W., Petrides, K. V., & Mikolajczak, M. (2010). Money giveth, money taketh away: The dual effect of wealth on happiness. *Psychological Science*, *21*, 759–763.

Reutner, L., & Wänke, M. (2013). For my own benefit or for the benefit of others: Reminders of money moderate the effects of self-related versus other-related persuasive arguments. *Social Psychological and Personality Science*, *4*(2), 220–223.

Roberts, J. A., & Roberts, C. R. (2012). Money matters: Does the symbolic presence of money affect charitable giving and attitudes among adolescents? *Young Consumers: Insight and Ideas for Responsible Marketers*, *13(4)*, 329–336.

Sandel, M. J. (2012). *What money can't buy: The moral limits of markets*. New York, NY: Farrar, Straus and Giroux.

Van Laer, T., De Ruyter, K., & Cox, D. (2013). A walk in customers' shoes: How attentional bias modification affects ownership of integrity-violating social media posts. *Journal of Interactive Marketing*, *27*, 14–27.

Vohs, K. D., Mead, N. L., & Goode, M. R. (2006). The psychological consequences of money. *Science*, *314*, 1154–1156.

Vohs, K. D., Mead, N. L., & Goode, M. R. (2008). Merely activating the concept of money changes personal and interpersonal behaviour. *Current Directions in Psychological Science*, *17*, 208–212.

Webley, P., & Lea, S. E. G. (1993). The partial unacceptability of money in repayment for neighborly help. *Human Relations*, *46*, 65–76.

Wilkinson, R. G., & Pickett, K. (2009). *The spirit level: Why more equal societies almost always do better*. London: Allen Lane.

Zaleskiewicz, T., Gasiorowska, A., & Kesebir, P. (2013). Saving can save from death anxiety: The effects of mortality salience on financial choices. *PLoS ONE*, *8*(11), e79707. doi: 10.1371/journal.pone.0079407

Zaleskiewicz, T., Gasiorowska, A., Kesebir, P., Luszczynska, A., & Pyszczynski, T. (2013). Money and the fear of death: The symbolic power of money as an existential anxiety buffer. *Journal of Economic Psychology*, *36*, 55–67.

Zelizer, V. A. (1989). The social meaning of money: "Special Monies". *The American Journal of Sociology*, *95*, 342–377.

Zhou, X., Vohs, K. D., & Baumeister, R. F. (2009). The symbolic power of money: Reminders of money alter social distress and physical pain. *Psychological Science*, *20*, 700–706.

18

Young children as consumers

Their vulnerability to persuasion and its effect on their choices

Dick Mizerski, Shasha Wang, Alvin Lee and Claire Lambert

The psychological study of children as consumers has been investigated over the past 70 years. Lester Guest authored what was arguably the first study of children as a future consuming market in the *Journal of Applied Psychology* article "The genesis of brand awareness" (Guest, 1942). Guest discusses an experiment on a sample of 8–18-year-olds who reported their recognition of brand names in several product categories, and argues that brand name recognition is an indicator of their future brand preferences and choices. Guest (1942, p. 803) proposes that the children will have "brand knowledge" for the brands they recognize by name alone. He further argues that the children's recognition of a brand may strongly influence their later preferences. Guest's (1948, 1955) later articles were based on follow-up longitudinal surveys of his original sample and failed to find a link between children's early brand name recognition and their later purchase and use of the brand. Nonetheless, these theoretical assumptions and the measure of memory continue to be used in research on children (Fischer, Schwartz, Richards, Goldstein, & Rojas, 1991; Pierce, Choi, Gilpin, Farkas, & Berry, 1998). The early interest of marketers in children as a future market later evolved into their interest in children as a market to target.

In his best-selling sociology book *The Lonely Crowd*, David Riesman (1953, p. 98) proposes that the future occupation of children is to be "skilled consumers" who can distinguish between different brands. In other words, children trained to be able to choose brands with few if any differentiating factors are a market in themselves, as well as in the future when they become adults. In *The Hidden Persuaders*, Vance Packard (1957) argues that consumers of all ages are manipulated to believe marketers' claims and buy their brands. This ability to manipulate is based on psychology and motivational research techniques. Packard devotes a chapter, titled "The psycho-seduction of children", to research on children to better understand how they will behave in the marketplace. He claims that brand exposure to young children can condition them to become adults trained to buy products on cue. While Packard's claims about the effects of subliminal advertising and the use of motivation research have been discredited, his reporting shows that marketers had a strong interest in targeting and obtaining revenue from young children in the 1950s. Marketers increased their targeting of young children with extensive TV advertising and TV programmes developed specifically to expose the young audience to the advertising.

This chapter continues the narrative of how academic researchers, groups of concerned parents and government responses increased the general belief that children are vulnerable to marketers' sophisticated and sometimes deceptive messages (Beales, 2003). The present review provides a chronological and critical overview of the current state of research about the vulnerability of children to persuasive messages such as in TV commercials and advergames. Advergames are online games built around a brand to advertise the brand as children play the game. The child's knowing about commercial persuasion is widely thought to provide a defence against persuasive messages. This knowledge is theorized to lead the children to be sceptical of claims made about brands advertised, and to want the brand less (An, Jin, & Park, 2014; Buijzen, 2007; Robertson & Rossiter, 1974; Ward, 1972). Evidence of inadequate knowledge of commercial persuasion even into late adolescence (Carter, Patterson, Donovan, Ewing, & Roberts, 2011; Hastings et al., 2003) has been used to prompt strict regulations and bans on targeting children in many countries. However, findings from 40 years of studies conducted in a range of countries and cultures challenge the view that young children use that knowledge in their responses to commercials. Similarly, evidence of a causal link between children's susceptibility to use "consumer vice" products such as cigarettes or alcohol and their receptivity or vulnerability to commercial messages for those products has had a strong effect on litigation and legislation in many countries. Nonetheless, questions about the methods used to determine "susceptibility" have challenged the veracity of the findings for these products. This chapter will compare the two paradigms about vulnerability to commercial messages and provide conclusions from the research.

Children as a market

Packard was early in anecdotally reporting marketers' efforts to understand children as a consuming market in their own right, not just a cohort for future consumption. He discusses the early 1950s work of Austrian psychologist Ernest Dichtor, who covertly observed young children viewing TV and commercials to better understand how to influence their choices. Children were a market to obtain revenue, but they were not discussed as especially vulnerable to persuasion.

James McNeal's (1964) chapter in the book *Children as Consumers* was the first academic report on how children behave and make decisions so that they can be appreciated as a consumer market in their own right. William Wells' (1965) early work "Communicating with children" also supports this view, probing the potential effects of TV advertising as it became the most popular and effective medium to target children. He also developed the first scale (smiling versus frowning faces) to empirically capture his young subjects' affective responses to TV commercials and the brands they advertised. Both McNeal's (1964) book and Wells' (1965) article argue that children constitute a significant market, that they wield influence on other buyers and that they are affected by marketing tactics.

The large (60 per cent) increase in the number of children under the age of five (baby boomers) around the world after World War II increased marketers' recognition that young children are profitable consumers. The research on children followed this population growth trend with over 50 articles published about children as consumers in the 1960s, and more than 300 by the late 1970s. The research was published in a broad range of journals and disciplines (McNeal, 1992). While early research (Guest, 1942) viewed children as a future market, the more contemporary view in the literature is that children are themselves consumers (Ross et al., 1984), who often lack a cognitive defence against marketer persuasion efforts such as advertising (Hastings et al., 2003), offerings of toy premiums (McAlister & Cornwell, 2012) and online content such as advergames (Mallinckrodt & Mizerski, 2007). This vulnerability is argued by the Institute of Medicine (2005) to lead to lifelong poor choices, which affect quality of life and mortality.

While this view of children as vulnerable consumers first developed in the popular press, it has since captured widespread acceptance (Beales, 2003; Brucks, Armstrong, & Goldberg, 1988; McAlister & Cornwell, 2012). Researchers from a variety of disciplines have produced studies featuring a range of measures of vulnerability to marketing activity. Although these investigations have increased our understanding of the reasons for children's vulnerability to commercial persuasion, there is inconsistent evidence that links this vulnerability to their consumption of brands advertised and promoted. Does children's vulnerability to persuasive messages such as in TV commercials and advergames affect their choice of brands or products?

Children as vulnerable consumers

In the early 1970s, the benign view of children as simply a new market was replaced with a view of children as vulnerable to persuasive messages and promotion offers from marketers. For example, Blatt, Spencer and Ward (1972) used personal interviews of kindergarten children (below age 5) and found them to be confused about the general purpose of ads. Second-graders (ages 7–8), on the other hand, had a basic understanding of the general purpose of ads. Older children understood beyond the intent of the ad; for instance, fourth-graders (ages 9–10) could comment on the construction of the commercials and the special techniques used to create the reality of the ad. By sixth grade (age 12), children could rationally evaluate advertisements.

The idea of children as vulnerable consumers focused research towards understanding how children relate and respond to advertisements. Ward (1972) used the age-sensitive development categories initially proposed by Blatt et al. (1972) for developing his personal 1-hour interviews with 5–12-year-old US children. He found the children's responses to questions about TV commercials to be related to their stages of cognitive development as they age. Indeed, both psychologists (Piaget, 1962) and marketing researchers (John, 1999) believe that young children's ability to understand persuasive messages develops with age, and this enables a child to better cognitively defend against persuasion. In line with this viewpoint, Ward (1972) reported that younger children had little knowledge about persuasive commercial messages (e.g., they may not know the difference between a TV programme and a TV commercial), and few questioned the credibility of commercials. Older children showed more insight and could identify the selling intent of commercials, or that they aimed to help people buy things by reducing confusion.

Ward's report (1972) began the theory of what is often referred to as "persuasion knowledge". The theory posits that having knowledge about the persuasive nature of commercial messages is causally associated with the children's perceptions of the truthfulness of advertising messages. Ward (1972) highlighted the positive effects of age on children's scepticism and mistrust of what ads claimed. The older the children, the more knowledgeable they are of the intentions of persuasive messages, and the more sceptical they will be of the message. In their later book, Ward, Wackman and Wartella (1977) assert that commercials motivate children to buy products or make purchase requests. However, neither Ward (1972) nor Ward et al. (1977) tested the relationship between having knowledge of the persuasive nature of TV commercials and the children's responses to the brands advertised.

The argument about children's lack of persuasion knowledge (i.e., the knowledge that commercial messages have persuasive intent) has become a simple and compelling concept, and provided the basis for measuring children's vulnerability to commercial persuasion (Carter et al., 2011; Hastings et al., 2003; Institute of Medicine, 2005). There is extensive literature on what may lead children to become knowledgeable and sceptical consumers (e.g., Brucks et al., 1988; Feshbach, Feshbach, & Cohen, 1982; Wright, Friestad, & Boush, 2005), but relatively few studies explicitly test the effects of children having this knowledge.

A competing paradigm of children's vulnerability to marketing promotion has been proposed by the health communications and medical literature. This literature reports studies that attempt to predict a child's use of adults-only products (e.g., alcohol, tobacco, gambling) and identifies the causes for their use. This research claims a causal link between children's susceptibility to use a product (a trait) and their receptivity to marketer advertising and promotion (Pierce et al., 1998). The methods and findings of this research will be examined following a discussion of persuasion knowledge and vulnerability.

It should be noted that a related construct, "consumer susceptibility to interpersonal influence" – a person's need to identify with or enhance their image in the eyes of significant others (Bearden, Netemeyer, & Teel, 1989) – is not covered here because it does not directly concern children's responses to commercial communications.

Children's vulnerability and their responses to the ad and brand

Robertson and Rossiter (1974) published what is arguably the first report of a significant association between children's knowledge of commercial persuasion and their responses to brands advertised. In two longitudinal studies they reported on four waves of personal interviews with 289 male US primary school students; these are referred to as waves 1, 2, 3 and 4. The sample consisted of first (ages 6–7), third (ages 8–9) and fifth (ages 10–11) graders. Using "attribution theory" (Mizerski, Golden, & Kernan, 1979) to explain children's processing of advertising messages, Robertson and Rossiter (1974) proposed that children are motivated to understand their environment by attributing causal links to the intent of TV advertisements. In interview waves 1 and 2, they found that children believed marketers had both "assistive" and "persuasive" intentions for showing TV commercials. Assistive intent refers to attributing the commercial's intent to assist the buyer or consumer – an intent first noticed by Ward (1972). However, Robertson and Rossiter (1974) found that only the children's knowledge of commercials' persuasive intent and children's motivation to consume the advertised brands were related to the evaluation of TV advertising. The authors argued that a child's knowledge about commercial persuasive messages lowered the child's trust and liking of the ads, and decreased their motivation to consume the brands advertised. However, the questions and the children's responses regarded TV ads in general, not specific ads for brands.

In interview waves 3 and 4, Rossiter and Robertson (1974) introduce the concept of "cognitive defence", that is, the protection a child has in their responses to the advertising and the brands advertised when they have knowledge of commercial persuasion. The initial relationship Robertson and Rossiter found between attribution of persuasive intent to advertising and children's responses to the ads and brands was no longer significant when viewed over interview waves 3 and 4. Rossiter and Robertson attributed this non-significant response to a "Christmas barrage" of TV commercials that overwhelmed children's defences against advertising. However, no measures of advertising intensity or other indicators of the Christmas barrage were reported.

Rossiter and Robertson (1974) may have failed to establish a relationship between children's ability to distinguish the persuasive intent of commercials and children's preference for the brands advertised because of a methodological bias in their cross-sectional study. The lengthy and wide-ranging in-depth interviews may have introduced "self-generated validity" (Feldman & Lynch, 1988) or social desirability (Brucks et al., 1988) biases in the children's responses. For example, in interview waves 1 and 2 (Robertson & Rossiter, 1974), children reported their viewing, beliefs and affect (liking) towards ads and products advertised and their consumption of advertised products. This method could have contributed to the correlations obtained (Brucks et al., 1988). In interview waves 3 and 4, Rossiter and Robertson (1974) separated the questions about the children's persuasion knowledge from their responses to the advertised brands by a period of four to five weeks. This delay may have reduced the conditions for self-generated validity. Therefore, the finding of a non-significant association between children's persuasion knowledge and their responses to the brands advertised may be less biased and more accurate than the Rossiter & Rossiter (1974) finding of an association.

Studies by Ward (1972), Ward et al. (1977), Robertson and Rossiter (1974), Calder, Robertson and Rossiter (1975) and Adler and Friedlander (1980) formed the theoretical basis for the argument that young children largely do not understand, or do not have the ability to understand, the persuasive intention of TV commercials (Ratner, Hellegers, & Ogg, 1978). Importantly, the theory of persuasion knowledge investigated by these authors had practical implications for public policy.

At a time when producers of cereals and confections (particularly of those with "excessive" sugar) were criticized for placing TV commercials in programmes targeted to children, the US Federal Trade Commission (FTC) began an investigation into the marketing of such goods and toys to children. The investigation was inspired by requests from non-government action groups (e.g., Action for Children's Television, Center for Science in the Public Interest and Consumers Union of America) to regulate TV advertising to guard vulnerable young children against commercial persuasion (Beales, 2003; Feshbach et al., 1982). The FTC's Notice of Proposed Rulemaking (1978) suggested remedies including bans on all advertising for products directed at or viewed by audiences with significant numbers of children too young to comprehend the selling intent of advertising (Beales, 2003). The FTC initially proposed that children up to 8 years old were vulnerable, but later reduced the age to six and under. The FTC also explored alternative remedies, including informative advertising funded by the advertisers of highly cariogenic foods (i.e., foods leading to tooth decay), teaching children about the persuasive intent of advertising (Beales, 2003; Ratner et al., 1978).

Although consumer groups strongly supported the investigation, the majority of the FTC commissioners voted to close the investigation and rule-making process. They stated that although child-oriented TV advertising was established as a genuine cause for public concern, no workable solutions were apparent for the commission to implement (Beales, 2003). While politics stopped legislation in the United States, research and legislation on children's lack of a cognitive defence to marketing efforts increased worldwide (Hastings et al., 2003).

Replicating the effects of persuasion knowledge

Research testing the veracity of the assumptions about children's knowledge of, and vulnerability to, commercial persuasion continues to explore the boundary of its effects. These studies report on a range of products promoted using persuasive messages from different media and are mostly based on the theories of information processing. After information processing was formally adapted to consumer research (e.g., Bettman, 1979; Bettman & Park, 1980), studies tended to test whether techniques encouraging children to use their knowledge would create a cognitive defence against persuasive commercial messages (Christenson, 1982). Other research investigated whether new digital media (Mallinckrodt & Mizerski, 2007; Panic, Cauberghe, & De Pelsmacker, 2013) or creative techniques such as product placement (Acharya, 2009) could bypass the children's cognitive defences. The following section reviews this research.

Twenty studies have tested the relationship between children knowing about commercial persuasion and their responses to ads and/or the brands advertised (see Table 18.1). Because all of the studies explore how children process advertising, they share a common

Table 18.1 Studies testing the effect of persuasion knowledge in children's reactions toward advertisements and the advertised brands/products

				Advertisements			*Brands/products*			
Author	*Method (age in years, sample size)*	*Reason use PK*	*Measures*	*Truth of ads*	*Affect/ like ads*	*Brand recall*	*Brand preference*	*Intend request/ buy*	*Influence friends*	*Choice*
Ward (1972)	Interview (5–12, n = 67)	Auto	DA, II and SBI	N						
Ward et al. (1974)	Interview	Auto	SBI	N						
Robertson and Rossiter (1974)	Interview (5, 7, 9, n = 289)	Auto	SBI, II, SO and DA	M	M			M		
Rossiter and Robertson (1974)	Interview (5, 7, 9, n = 289)	Auto	Cognitive defence	N	N			NE		
Christenson (1982)	Experiment (5, 6, 9, 10, n = 90)	Cued by warning	PBI	M			NE			
Feshbach et al. (1982)	Experiment (6, 8, n = 267)	Cued by training	Train PK	N			N	N		
Ross et al. (1984)	Experiment (8–14, n = 415)	Auto	SO				NE			
Sanft (1986)	Experiment (5, 6, n = 19)	Cued by training	Train SBI			P	NE			
Brucks et al. (1988)	Experiment (9–10, n = 102)	Cued by training	Train PK	N						
Boush et al. (1994)	Survey (11–13, n = 426)	Auto	SO	N						
Buijzen (2007)	Experiment (5–10, n = 206)	Cued by training	PBI and change perception	NE	N			NE		
Mallinckrodt and Mizerski (2007)	Experiment (5–8, n = 295)	Auto	SO, PBI and UI				NE	NE		
An and Stern (2011)	Experiment (8, n = 112)	Cued by break	UI, SO and II			NE	NE			

Acharya (2009)	Experiment (6–14, n = 296)	Auto	DA and UI					NE	P	NE
Rozendaal et al. (2009)	Survey (8–12, n = 296)	Auto	DA, SBI and change attitude				NE			
Van Reijmersdal et al. (2012)	Experiment (7–12, n = 105)	Cued by brand or involvement	SO and UI		NE	NE	NE			
Panic et al. (2013) – TV commercial	Experiment (7–10, n = 254)	Cued by break\auto	SO and SBI					N		
Panic et al. (2013) – advergame	Experiment (7–10, n = 28)		SO and SBI					NE		
Rozendaal et al. (2013)	Experiment (9–12, n = 155)	Cued by medium	DA, UI, SO and change attitude					M		
An et al. (2014)	Experiment (8, 9, n = 129)	Cued training	DA	N				NE		
Verhellen et al. (2014)	Experiment (11–14, n = 125)	Cued by medium	SO and change attitude				N	NE		

Notes
DA: distinguish advertisement from non-advertisement programmes; II: informative intent (to provice information); SBI: self-buying intent (to buy the brand); SO: know the source (people who made it); PBI: parent-buying intent (to ask parents to buy); UI: using intent (to use the brand).

M: mixed results; N: negative; P: positive; NE: no effect; blank – the relationship was not tested in the study.

information-processing paradigm. However, they differ in the proposed reasons for why children would use their persuasion knowledge. Each study assumes one of two such reasons. The research before 1980 and a minority after 1980 assume that a child with appropriate knowledge of commercial persuasion would use it as an "automatic" response (Mallinckrodt & Mizerski, 2007). On the other hand, more than twice as many studies published since 1980 assumed that a cue of some sort (e.g., ad break, warning, involvement, medium, training) was necessary to "activate" (An & Stern, 2011; Brucks et al., 1988; Van Reijmersdal, Rozendaal & Buijzen, 2012; Verhellen, Oates, De Pelsmacker, & Dens, 2014), "provoke" (Panic et al., 2013) or "prompt" (Buijzen, 2007) children's use of their persuasion knowledge. This is sometimes referred to as "cue theory" for information processing (Panic et al., 2013).

The use of persuasion knowledge when cued by training

Of the ten studies that tested some type of cue, the most frequent approach (six studies) proposes training young children about persuasion so that they will be more sceptical of advertising content and intention. This process of learning scepticism towards the message is expected to decrease desire for the brand advertised. Feshbach et al. (1982) conducted an experiment with 267 second-grade (ages 6–7) and fourth-grade (ages 8–9) children. They trained the two groups of children with different approaches (motivational versus economic) for 30 minutes, three times over five days. The content of the training material was not reported except that it featured material that taught children to distinguish TV programmes from commercials and provided an understanding of the roles of actors. The authors reported a large number of significant effects of the training, including that the children "rated advertised products as less desired, were more aware of the information value, found commercials less credible, were less apt to choose an advertised product over an unadvertised product in a simulated behavioural choice, had a better understanding of the commercials, [and] were less accepting of commercials than were the control children" (Feshbach et al. Cohen, 1982, p. 396). Unfortunately, specifics of the measures used were left out of the report, and lack of error level adjustments for multiple comparisons makes it difficult to gauge the veracity of the findings.

Christenson (1982) conducted experiments exposing children to a TV public service announcement (PSA) that taught them about the persuasive intent of TV commercials, and that they should distrust claims ads make. He argued that the PSA messages were a cue to help young children "link" the hidden persuasive intention of TV advertisements to low trustfulness of TV advertisements. He found that younger children (ages 7–9) who were exposed to the PSA tended to be sceptical towards the advertisement, but unexpectedly this tendency was not found among older children (ages 10–11). However, when Christenson compared the PSA and ad exposure children with a control group, the two groups of children did not have significantly different perceptions of or attitudes to the advertised brands.

Sanft (1986) argues that a child's knowledge base is the critical difference between younger and older children, proposing that younger children would respond like their older peers if they had the same relevant knowledge base. Sanft tested 19 5- and 6-year-old US children over two different periods. All the children watched four TV commercials for breakfast cereal in the first meeting. A control group was dismissed to be reinterviewed several days later, while the treatment group were briefed about the persuasive nature of the ads they had just seen – this sought to alert them to the two areas often argued to be the basis for persuasion knowledge: distinguishing between ads and entertainment, and the intent of the ad. Following this briefing the treatment group was shown two more TV commercials from Saturday morning cartoon shows. The instructor again discussed the persuasive nature of the ads. The following week, both the treatment and control groups were shown four TV commercials, after which they were interviewed about the persuasive nature of TV commercials. The treatment group tended to have higher recall of brand information. However, knowing the persuasive purpose of the ads did not affect their memory for brand information or preference for the brands advertised.

Brucks et al. (1988) use a measure of children's counterarguments (Petty & Cacioppo, 1981) as evidence of children's "cognitive defences" for resisting TV ad persuasion. They argue that there is a lack of support for children's knowledge of "selling intent" being sufficient to resist persuasion and the expectation that children should be able to discount the advertiser's message. Brucks et al. (1988) suggest that cognitive defences against advertising will only have an effect when cued by a stimulus that activates this knowledge. They found that 9- and 10-year-olds in their experimental group (instructed, so assumed high knowledge) with a cue (an exam) were more sceptical towards ads because they reported a higher number of counterarguments compared with children who did not receive a cue or had low knowledge. The experimental group was also more likely to be sceptical and critical of the ad's "deceptiveness". Nonetheless, Brucks et al. (1988) admit that children's counterarguments towards advertising may not be effective in decreasing the effects of persuasion on a child's responses. High counterarguers may want the advertised brand as much as low-counterarguing children.

Buijzen (2007) contends that information-processing research infers that children 12 and younger need to have prompts and cues to apply persuasion knowledge. She used an experimental design with two treatment groups and one control group of 206 5–10-year-old Dutch children. The treatment groups viewed a series of TV commercials where the researcher provided comments (cues) about the commercials between ads. Buijzen used a "factual intervention" treatment as a cue to provide facts about the advertised product and the commercial. Buijzen also used another "evaluative intervention" cue treatment, where she casually stated negative evaluations of the advertised product and the commercial to a treatment group. The control group received no comments and thus no cues. The children's persuasion knowledge was measured by whether they recognized the selling intent of the advertisements, and whether they believed the advertised toys were more attractive than the control group. Buijzen found that the children who were taught about the persuasive nature of advertising tended to like the advertisements less than children without persuasion knowledge. However, no effect of the training intervention was found for their intention to request the products advertised. In addition to the "training-type" interventions used by Buijzen to impart awareness of persuasion knowledge in children, other researchers have used "informing-type" interventions.

Training to activate persuasion knowledge when children use digital media

Informative intervention may take the form of an advertisement break that informs viewers about an upcoming advertisement. Contrary to expectation, training-type interventions do not affect young children's reactions to advertising (e.g., whether they like the ad) or to the advertised brand (e.g., whether they like or prefer the brand compared with an unadvertised brand). However, most informative interventions are tested using interactive Internet-based media such as advergames. The interactive nature of advergames is quite different from the primarily passive nature of audience exposure to TV commercials (Krugman, 1965; Mallinckrodt & Mizerski, 2007). Perhaps the demanding requirement of interactivity for advergames prevents the effects of interventions such as training.

An et al. (2014) tested informative interventions and cited evidence that the majority of children under age ten do not recognize the role of advertising or its persuasive intent in the context of advergames. This research used the adult-based persuasion knowledge model

(Friestad & Wright, 1994) and reasoned that young children must recognize the message as an ad in order to be sceptical of it, and scepticism would diminish their desire for the advertised product. However, the Internet medium that hosts advergames makes it difficult for young children to recognize the source of an advergame, and the interactive nature of the medium may mask the intent of the advergames. A South Korean study of 129 8- and 9-year-olds by An and Stern (2011) tested whether children could be taught "advertising literacy" and whether this training could help children learn that advergames were a type of advertising. An and Stern also proposed that scepticism of the advergame would increase children's recognition that it was advertising. Most of the trained advergame-knowledgeable children (78.8 per cent) in their experiment could identify advergames as advertisements. Surprisingly, some children in the control group, who did not receive advertising literacy training, could also identify advergames as ads. Nonetheless, knowing the intent and identifying the advergame as advertising were not associated with children's brand preferences. Following these studies, researchers proceeded to examine whether a "signal" such as an ad break would be a sufficient stimulus for children to begin using their persuasion knowledge when exposed to advergames.

"Ad breaks" as cues for persuasion knowledge

Two studies tested whether children could be trained to recognize a signal as a cue for an upcoming commercial message and whether this cue would prompt them to use their persuasion knowledge. An and Stern (2011) tested whether a separating device (known as a "break" or a "bumper") in an advergame could activate children's persuasion knowledge and counter-argument abilities against the claims in an ad. Using 112 fourth-grade children (ages 8–11, older than the age that some view as most vulnerable) (Beales, 2003), the experiment tested audio and visual variations of an ad break containing a warning that the advergame had commercial content. This was implemented before children played the advergame. While the message may be viewed as training, the source of the message was not clearly identified. The message also did not differentiate the commercial and entertainment aspects of the advergame or state the persuasive intent of the message source. Children who saw the breaks reported decreased memory of the advergame and affect for the brand. However, the use of a break was not associated with children's knowledge of the persuasive intent of the advergame.

To investigate differences in the effectiveness of ad breaks between advergames and TV commercials, Panic et al. (2013) tested 254 Belgian children (mean age of eight). They found that children who played advergames with or without a break reported lower persuasion knowledge than children who watched TV commercials. Of those who had persuasion knowledge, those exposed to TV ads reported a lower intention to request the advertised product. This finding appears to support the effects of "masked" marketing (Petty & Andrews, 2008), which make it more difficult to identify the commercial source of the message in advergames. However, the differences reported ceased to be statistically significant when the necessary adjustments to the error level (e.g., Bonferroni) were applied. The authors used a second study to determine whether the apparent "media effect" on purchase knowledge was simply due to the appealing nature of the advergame format. The study compared the effects of an advergame for potato chips with a health advergame on 8-year-old Belgian children. They reported no significant differences in either children's attitudes towards the advergame or their behavioural intention towards the outcome promoted in the advergames. In other words, the children's persuasion knowledge exerted no effect on their intention to request the brand advertised in the advergame. Panic et al. (2013) argued that, compared with TV advertisements, advergames may evoke less critical message processing by children as they may be less suspicious of ulterior motives.

New media such as advergames make it more difficult for children to recognize the source of the message and understand the persuasive intent of the source. Reflecting this, Verhellen et al. (2014) argue that integrated marketing communications reduce children's use of their persuasion knowledge. They proposed that persuasion knowledge must be "activated" or cued for children to recognize the nature of a persuasive message. To test this, they compared four groups of children: some viewed a TV commercial for a brand of popsicle, some viewed a trailer (recorded highlights) for an advergame featuring the brand of popsicle viewed on TV, others viewed the trailer and played the advergame (integrated media) while others just played the advergame without viewing the trailer. The combination of the trailer and the advergame was proposed to generate the lowest persuasion knowledge, the lowest brand recall and the highest brand attitude and brand choice compared with the TV ad. Their experiment tested 125 11–14-year-olds (a much older cohort than most view as "vulnerable") (Beales, 2003) and found that the group exposed to the advergame had more difficulty recognizing the persuasive message. While children's persuasion knowledge did not differ by group, those with persuasion knowledge exposed to a "trailer" for the game and who also played the advergame had lower attitude towards the brand. However, this finding was not statistically significant after being adjusted for the four group comparisons with a Bonferroni correction for error level. Attitude towards the brand was not moderated or affected by the child's persuasion knowledge.

In an experiment similar to that by Verhellen et al. (2014), Van Reijmersdal et al. (2012) examined the effect of message recall, recognition and brand attitude on children's persuasion knowledge. Specifically, Van Reijmersdal et al. (2012) tested whether brand prominence in an advergame and the children's involvement in the game influenced their cognitive (brand recall and recognition) and affective (attitude towards the brand and advergame) responses to brand placement. They were also interested in whether the child's persuasion knowledge moderated these responses. One hundred and five 7–12-year-old Dutch children played one of two advergames representing two levels of brand prominence: subtle and prominent. The children's persuasion knowledge was operationalized as understanding the source of the placement of the brand in the game and the persuasive intent of the placement. They found that prominence of the brand within the game significantly affected the children's ability to recall and recognize the advertised brand. Neither involvement with the game nor the children's knowledge of the persuasive nature of advertising in games influenced their memory of the brand or affect towards the game or brand. Similarly to Mallinckrodt and Mizerski (2007) and Livingstone and Helsper (2006), Van Reijmersdal et al. (2012) found that older children with persuasion knowledge were more influenced by the commercial message than younger children.

The body of experiments reviewed in this section can be described as a systematic attempt to test remedies that activate children's persuasion knowledge when they face TV and advergame commercial persuasive messages. Although children can generally tell the difference between a TV ad and entertainment content, the separation of content from advertising is less clear for advergames. Taken together, the results reported can best be described as inconclusive. There are many non-significant results that suggest the proposed remedies do not affect children's recognition, liking or recall of the different advertisements and their intentions. This lack of positive findings arises despite the systematic examination of ad elements such as copy that manipulate an ad's deceptiveness, scepticism, different interventions and counterarguments, alerts, ad variations, different media (TV versus advergames) and signals to trigger and activate children's persuasion knowledge. Moreover, although the studies have been carried out in multiple countries, presumably with children from various cultural backgrounds (from South Korea to Belgium), few differences in reactions and perceptions are reported in the results. This suggests that children from different countries may interact with commercially persuasive messages in similar ways. Although this set of studies that tested cue, signal, training and interventions reported little success, older studies have reported more promising findings.

Automatic use of persuasion knowledge

The early work of Ward (1972; Ward et al., 1977), Robertson and Rossiter (1974; Rossiter & Robertson, 1974) and six studies since (see Table 18.1) assume that children with persuasion knowledge use it automatically to adjust their responses to commercial messages and the brands or products advertised in those messages. Such studies find more evidence than cue-focused studies that persuasion knowledge is associated with children's responses to the ad. However, they also find less evidence that children's persuasion knowledge is associated with affective or intended responses to the advertised brand.

Ross et al. (1984), for example, experimentally tested whether ads with celebrity endorsements affected the responses of 8–14-year-old US boys to a TV commercial. They also tested the effect of children's knowledge on their responses, for instance, knowledge of the source, awareness that the advertisements were staged and made in a studio, or that the announcer had rehearsed and was paid. These areas of knowledge are similar to distinguishing between advertising and entertainment on TV. The age of the boys was older than some view as vulnerable (Beales, 2003). Nonetheless, the children's age had a positive effect on their knowledge about TV advertising. As hypothesized, the authors found that celebrity endorsements prompted the children to have more trust in the ad. Children's knowledge of persuasion had no effect on their preference for the brand advertised.

Boush, Friestad and Rose (1994) examined adolescents' development of their knowledge of the persuasive nature and scepticism towards different TV advertising tactics over time. They conducted a longitudinal survey on 426 US adolescents in sixth to eighth grade (about ages 11 to 13). This age group was substantially older than the children typically studied for persuasion knowledge, and thus misses many years of children's development in this area. Similarly to the Rossiter and Robertson (1974) study, no ads were shown and the children were asked about advertising in general. Scepticism was tested by measuring the adolescents' disbelief in ad claims and their mistrust in advertiser motives. While Boush et al. (1994) found the children mistrustful of the ad claims and motives, the method of interviewing might have biased the responses (Feldman & Lynch, 1988) in a similar way as in the case of Robertson and Rossiter (1974), that is, advertising in general was queried rather than whether a child's knowledge of persuasion was used to process a specific ad targeted to them. To avoid these issues, researchers thereafter used experimental-based studies that tested specific branded products.

Mallinckrodt and Mizerski (2007) experimentally tested 295 5–8-year-old West Australian children playing an advergame. They argued that discounting the message as an advertisement should lower children's desire for the brand. Specifically, children would find it difficult to identify the source of an advergame because it was a form of "masked" (Petty & Andrews, 2008) or "stealth" marketing (Martin & Smith, 2008). Children who were aware of the persuasive nature of advertising (i.e., who could identify the source and intentions of the advergame) were expected to have lower affect towards the advergame, the brand (Froot Loops cereal) and the cereal category compared with other healthy and unhealthy food categories. These knowledgeable children were also expected to prefer and request the brand less than children without persuasion knowledge. As with most previous research, the children's knowledge of persuasion was positively related to their age. However, the knowledgeable children, those who knew the intent and the source of game, did not report lower affect towards the advergame, Froot Loops cereal or the cereal category than the less knowledgeable children. More surprisingly, the children with persuasion knowledge had a greater intent to request the Froot Loops brand over other brands of cereal. This finding is opposite to that hypothesized, but has also been reported in several studies testing the effects of advertising knowledge (for a review see Livingstone & Helsper, 2006). Other studies have found similar effects and offer possible explanations for this unanticipated reaction.

Acharya (2009) tested the effect of children's knowledge of persuasion on their intent to request a brand after covert exposure to product placement for an upcoming movie in a magazine targeted at them. Similarly to advergames, product placement is viewed as an example of stealth or masked marketing because it obscures the difference between commercial and entertainment content (Martin & Smith, 2008). Acharya (2009) reported that having persuasion knowledge of the placement did not increase children's request to watch the movie advertised. Similarly, Rozendaal, Buijzen and Valkenburg (2009) reported that having persuasion knowledge did not increase or decrease desire for an advertised product. Specifically, they tested the effect of Dutch children's knowledge of advertising persuasion (n = 296, ages 8–12) on their desire for the products advertised and reported no link between these elements. Contrary to expectation, children younger than ten with knowledge of persuasion tended to report a greater desire for products advertised than less knowledgeable children under 10 years old.

While this finding contradicts the authors' expectations, it is similar to findings of Mallinckrodt and Mizerski (2007) and Acharya (2009) and is discussed in the review of advertising knowledge by Livingstone and Helsper (2006). There seems to be an age effect whereby as children grow older and get better at identifying an advertisement, they also begin to want the advertised product more. This is logical, as many studies talk about the development of persuasion knowledge in children, implying that there is a temporal effect. As children become more aware of products, they become more knowledgeable as consumers. It is also known that they use advertising and peers as sources of information about the products that they would like to use.

The veracity of children's knowledge of persuasion

The research reviewed to this point shows that the majority of children beyond 8 years old have some knowledge of the persuasive nature of commercials, and the age of the child tends to be positively related to their development of this knowledge. Some research finds that children up to 16 years old do not have adequate knowledge of persuasion (Carter et al., 2011; Hastings et al., 2003), while other research finds that much younger children have knowledge of the persuasive nature of a TV commercial, advergame or product placement (McAlister & Cornwell, 2012).

The construct of "advertising knowledge" is favoured by communications researchers and most typically is operationalized by questioning children about how ads are constructed and about the techniques used in TV commercials (e.g., endorsements; see Livingstone & Helsper, 2006). Understanding how ads "work" is assumed to make the child more sceptical of the claims made and the reality of the brand advertised (Panic et al., 2013; Ward, 1972). However, the truth behind this assumption remains unclear, particularly when children are exposed to newer media formats such as digital media, which increasingly blurs the line between advertising and entertaining content (Mallinckrodt & Mizerski, 2007; Martin & Smith, 2008; Petty & Andrews, 2008). In fact, advertising has now become entertainment; for example, advergames and online video advertisements are designed to be entertainment.

In contrast, the construct favoured by consumer researchers consists of the child knowing that advertising is different from entertainment, and knowing that the intent of the marketer is to persuade. This knowledge is assumed to give children a cognitive defence against persuasive messages such as that assumed by advertising knowledge research. In many studies, a mix of questions about advertising techniques and intention of the advertiser is employed to operationalize the construct now referred to as persuasion knowledge (Friestad & Wright, 1994). However, children knowledgeable about both persuasion and advertising tend to be more sceptical of the persuasive message than less knowledgeable children – the point of convergence between the two approaches.

Of the 20 studies that tested the effects of children's persuasion knowledge (Table 18.1), 11 studies tested these effects on children's responses to the message. Eight of the 11 studies (73 per cent) found that as children's knowledge of persuasion increases, they tend to respond more negatively to the message. This proportion of support is relatively consistent across a wide range of methods used, ages, cultures and countries sampled. When children's scepticism is measured, it is positively related to their knowledge of persuasion and negatively related to their responses to the ad.

Most of the studies that failed to find a relationship between the knowledge and responses to the ads were studying online advergames. This medium appears be more difficult for children to understand because of its stealth or masked nature (Martin & Smith, 2008; Petty & Andrews, 2008). Children tend to find it difficult to differentiate commercial and entertainment content and to use their knowledge of persuasive intent (Mallinckrodt & Mizerski, 2007). On the other hand, Acharya (2009) found that most children in her study were able to identify stealth or masked product placement in a child's magazine. This may be due to magazines being less cognitively demanding and absorbing than online advergames. Thus, the problem of identification may be restricted to electronic media.

Thirteen of the 20 studies (81 per cent) reviewed (Table 18.1) tested whether children's knowledge of commercial persuasion affected their response to the brand or product advertised. Only four of the 13 studies (31 per cent) found any relationship between the child's knowledge and their responses. Two additional studies (Mallinckrodt & Mizerski, 2007; Van Reijmersdal et al., 2012) that tested advergames as the media found that older children with knowledge tended to want the advertised brand more than younger children without knowledge – an association opposite to that proposed by the persuasion knowledge model (Friestad & Wright, 1994). This may be due to the higher cognitive processing load associated with playing advergames, and their immersive and interactive nature, with components of the game helping to build a child's knowledge of the advertised product.

Of the four studies in Table 18.1 reporting that higher persuasion knowledge decreased children's responses to the advertised brand or product, three appear to suffer from method artefacts. Robertson and Rossiter (1974) were unable to replicate their findings with a longitudinal sample, while Verhellen et al. (2014) failed to account for frequency of exposure in their findings. Feshbach et al. (1982) found effects of persuasion knowledge training, but they report insufficient details of the treatments and measures used. Panic et al.'s (2013) result ceased to be significant after Bonferroni correction for family-wise error was applied. Clearly, more research is required to understand this issue. The limited effect of persuasion knowledge on children's responses to the product suggests that young children can be sceptical of persuasive messages from advertisers, yet they still want the product.

This conundrum may be due to the smaller base of knowledge about young children compared with adults. The young children with persuasion knowledge may not have sufficient knowledge beyond understanding persuasion. This may include not understanding the work or effort required to pay for the goods advertised (Mallinckrodt & Mizerski, 2007). If the product was free, which is mostly the case for young children as someone else usually pays for it, then one would expect that the ad claims about the product would be less salient in their choices. That is why the persuasion knowledge model (Friestad & Wright, 1994) may not fit the information processing and decision making of young children. However, this explanation is less compelling for the older children with persuasion knowledge who still want the product (e.g., Mallinckrodt & Mizerski, 2007; Van Reijmersdal et al., 2012).

Children's vulnerability: "Susceptibility" and "receptivity"

Current research on the vulnerability of adolescents and teenagers to consumer vice products often uses models of receptivity and susceptibility (Altman, Levine, Coeytaux, Slade, & Jaffe, 1996). These are health communication models that adopt a hierarchy of effects (Palda, 1966; Pierce et al., 1998) perspective on advertising effects. This area of research argues that the audience of brand or product advertising moves through stages of responses, from cognitive to affective to behaviour. This receptivity/susceptibility model finds positive causal links between children's receptiveness to advertising messages and their susceptibility to use unhealthy substances such as tobacco (Unger, Johnson, & Rohrbach, 1995), alcohol or marijuana (Longshore, Ellickson, McCaffrey, & Clair, 2007). This receptivity/susceptibility paradigm became the leading model for studying epidemiology in the health communications field (Pierce et al., 1998). Figure 18.1 shows the identification of a child "susceptible" to an event such as trying or taking up smoking. The receptivity questions ask about ownership of product samples, exposure to advertising, and peers and family product use. The model uses a process of asking a sample of children (9 years and older) to respond to a series of survey questions over the phone. The child's susceptibility to smoking increases with each answer that does not strongly rule out smoking (i.e., only "definitely not" answers).

The concept of persuasion knowledge is cognitively based and requires the child to analyse the persuasive nature of the advertising message. The Pierce et al. (1998) receptivity component of the model differs from persuasion knowledge models as it is memory-based and argues that adolescents are receptive to commercial persuasion depending largely on their memory of advertising and promotion. The child's ability to remember brands, advertising and receiving promotion items such as T-shirts is positively related to their receptivity. Children who are receptive to the advertising of adults-only vice products and susceptible to try the product or brand have a significantly higher probability of experimenting and using the product than less susceptible children. Persuasion knowledge and receptivity/susceptibility have not been used in the same study, although both have been applied in the area of fast food (e.g., Adachi-Mejia et al., 2011). This lack of integration may change as more products are judged unhealthy and a risk to children (Institute of Medicine, 2005).

The receptivity/susceptibility model is a good predictor of smoking initiation, and has been extensively replicated for a range of products such as alcohol and illegal drugs (Henriksen, Feighery, Schleicher, & Fortmann, 2008). A Google Scholar search (August 2015) revealed that the model has been replicated in at least 106 peer-reviewed articles using longitudinal and cross-sectional adolescent health surveys around the world. As long as the replications of the model are exact, the results are very stable across national boundaries, using adolescent samples that are normally drawn from school-aged children. Nonetheless, the research has been criticized. For example, Lee, Lam, Mizerski, & Mizerski (2005) and Lee and Lam (2005) tested the model on the original data and found that methodological problems led to a bias in the findings. Several critics noted that the sample-selection method introduced systematic attrition bias into the research (Heckman, 2007; Lee, 2008; Lee & Mizerski, 2007), which affects the findings. Geweke and Donald (2002) re-examined the Pierce et al. (1998) data and found

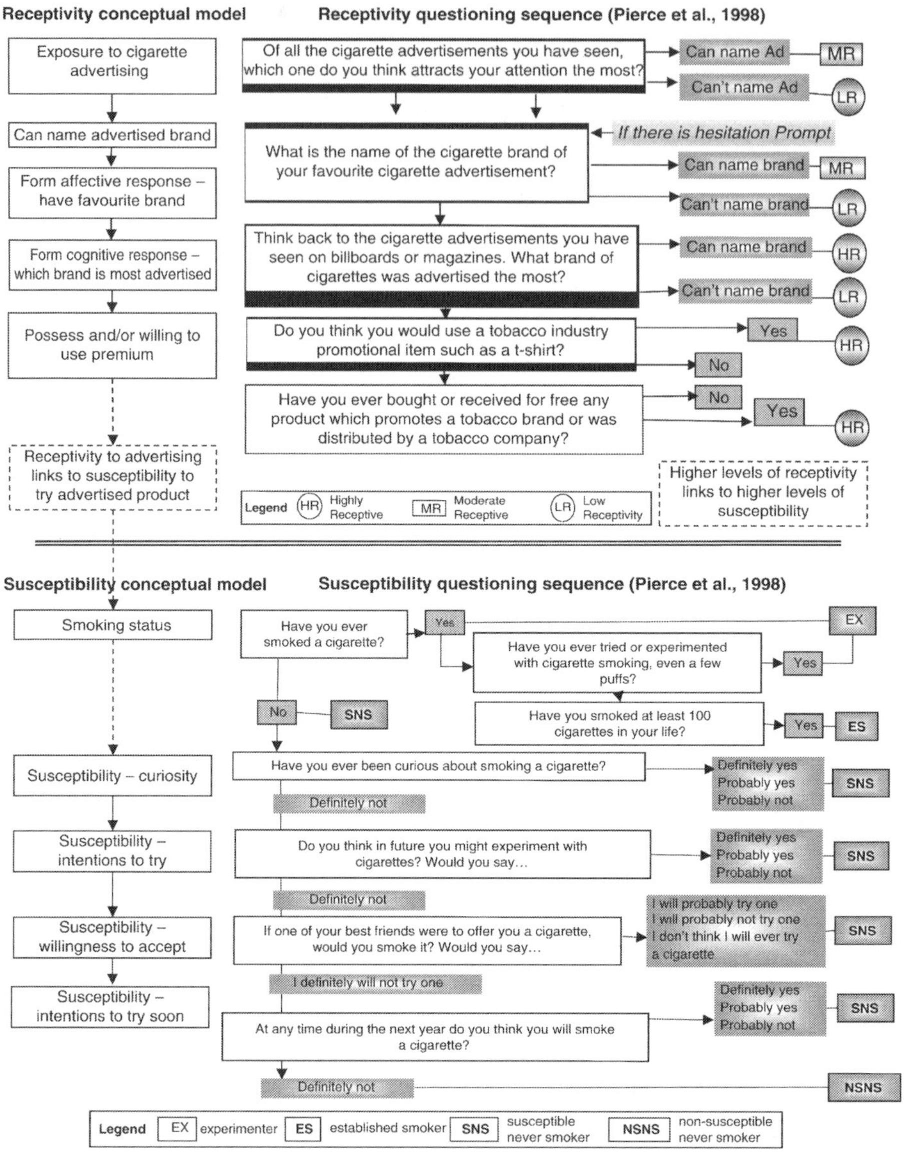

Figure 18.1 Receptivity and susceptibility conceptual model and questioning sequence.

systematic flaws in the data-collection methods, sampling procedures, analytical methods and interpretation of analyses. For example, Heckman (2007) and Geweke and Donald (2002) find that the same questions are used to measure receptivity and susceptibility, so there is a clear measurement artefact when testing the relationship between the two. Nonetheless, results from the Pierce et al. (1998) receptivity/susceptibility model are very stable when replication of sampling, measures and analysis is consistent (NCI, 2013).

While there is a lack of empirical support for the theories of children's vulnerability to persuasive messages linked to their responses to advertised brands, advocates have compelling narratives that informed public policies restricting children's exposure to those messages (Hastings et al., 2003; Pierce et al., 1998; Wilcox et al., 2004). It is natural to believe that young children are vulnerable to marketers and need protection, but findings show that the link between vulnerability and choices is still unclear. Is it justified to lament a lack of persuasion knowledge in children and call for restrictions on targeting children under 16 (Carter et al., 2011) without finding consistent evidence for negative effects of this deficit? If having persuasion/advertising knowledge or memory of advertising is not necessarily associated with the child's responses to the advertised brand, how important is it that the child has this knowledge? We argue that developing scepticism of persuasive messages is likely to be beneficial for young children, even if only so that they can use this knowledge when they later make their own consumer decisions. However, the findings regarding online media reveal children's difficulty identifying messages as persuasive. Online media are heavily used by children, and often contain persuasive messages masked as entertainment. If young children cannot identify the message as persuasive, can they be sceptical about the message?

Although a range of Eastern and Western countries have been sampled in the research reviewed, the samples tend to comprise primarily urban middle- to upper-class subjects. Perhaps this commonality lowers the possibility of finding cultural effects in the research. A broader range of research subjects is needed. To date, no researcher has undertaken a cross-cultural study, although the need for this type of research is noted in meta-analytical reviews in the literature (John, 1999; Livingstone & Helsper, 2006).

Finally, many measures of persuasion knowledge have been used. These measures take the form of either a single-item or a multi-item reflective measure. Perhaps many findings would be different if the construct of persuasion knowledge were captured with a formative rather than a reflective measure (Coltman, Devinney, Midgley, & Venaik, 2008). The association between a child's age and their vulnerability is found consistently in studies of persuasion knowledge, receptivity and susceptibility. This relationship suggests that children's persuasion knowledge and their susceptibility develop over time.

References

Acharya, D. (2009). *Product placement in print media and its effect on children and their responses* (Doctoral thesis). The University of Western Australia, Perth. Retrieved from https://repository.uwa.edu.au/R/-?func=dbin-jump-full&object_id=3829&local_base=GEN01-INS01

Adachi-Mejia, A. M., Sutherland, L. A., Longacre, M. R., Beach, M. L., Titus-Ernstoff, L., Gibson, J. J., & Dalton, M. A. (2011). Adolescent weight status and receptivity to food TV advertisements. *Journal of Nutrition Education and Behaviour, 43*(6), 441–448.

Adler, R. P., & Friedlander, B. Z. (1980). *The effects of television advertising on children: Review and recommendations*. Lexington, MA: D. C. Heath.

Altman, D. G., Levine, D. W., Coeytaux, R., Slade, J., & Jaffe, R. (1996). Tobacco promotion and susceptibility to tobacco use among adolescents aged 12 through 17 years in a nationally representative sample. *American Journal of Public Health, 86*(11), 1590–1593.

An, S., Jin, H. S., & Park, E. H. (2014). Children's advertising literacy for advergames: Perception of the game as advertising. *Journal of Advertising, 43*(1), 63–72.

An, S., & Stern, S. (2011). Mitigating the effects of advergames on children. *Journal of Advertising, 40*(1), 43–56.

Beales, J. H. (2003). Advertising to kids and the FTC: A regulatory retrospective that advises the present. *George Mason Law Review, 12*, 873–894.

Bearden, W. O., Netemeyer, R. G., & Teel, J. E. (1989). Measurement of consumer susceptibility to interpersonal influence. *Journal of Consumer Research, 15*(4), 473–481.

Bettman, J. R. (1979). *An information processing theory of consumer choice*. Reading, MA: Addison Wesley.

Bettman, J. R., & Park, C. W. (1980). Effects of prior knowledge and experience and phase of the choice process on consumer decision processes: A protocol analysis. *Journal of Consumer Research*, 7(3), 234–248.

Blatt, J., Spencer, L., & Ward, S. (1972). A cognitive development study of children's reactions to television advertising. *Television and Social Behaviour, 4*, 452–466.

Boush, D. M., Friestad, M., & Rose, G. M. (1994). Adolescent skepticism toward TV advertising and knowledge of advertiser tactics. *Journal of Consumer Research, 21*(1), 165–175.

Brucks, M., Armstrong, G. M., & Goldberg, M. E. (1988). Children's use of cognitive defenses against television advertising: A cognitive response approach. *Journal of Consumer Research, 14*(4), 471–482.

Buijzen, M. (2007). Reducing children's susceptibility to commercials: Mechanisms of factual and evaluative advertising interventions. *Media Psychology, 9*(2), 411–430.

Calder, B. J., Robertson, T. S., & Rossiter, J. R. (1975). Children's consumer information processing. *Communication Research, 2*(3), 307–316.

Carter, O. B. J., Patterson, L. J., Donovan, R. J., Ewing, M. T., & Roberts, C. M. (2011). Children's understanding of the selling versus persuasive intent of junk food advertising: Implications for regulation. *Social Science & Medicine, 72*(6), 962–968.

Christenson, P. G. (1982). Children's perceptions of TV commercials and products: The effects of PSAs. *Communication Research, 99*(4), 491–524.

Coltman, T, Devinney, T. M., Midgley, D. F., & Venaik, S. (2008). Formative versus reflective measurement models: Two applications of formative measurement. *Journal of Business Research, 61*(12), 1250–1262.

Feldman, J. M., & Lynch, J. G. (1988). Self-generated validity and other effects of measurement on belief, attitude, intention, and behaviour. *Journal of Applied Psychology, 73*(3), 421–435.

Feshbach, S., Feshbach, N. D., & Cohen, S. E. (1982). Enhancing children's discrimination in response to television advertising: The effects of psychoeducational training in two elementary school-age groups. *Developmental Review, 2*(4), 385–403.

Fischer, P. M., Schwartz, M. P., Richards, J. W., Goldstein, A. O., & Rojas, T. H. (1991). Brand logo recognition by children aged 3 to 6 years: Mickey Mouse and Old Joe the Camel. *Journal of the American Medical Association, 266*(22), 3145–3148.

Friestad, M., & Wright, P. (1994). The persuasion knowledge model: How people cope with persuasion attempts. *Journal of Consumer Research, 21*(1), 1–31.

Geweke, J., & Donald, M. L. (2002). Pitfalls in drawing policy conclusions from retrospective survey data: The case of advertising and underage smoking. *Journal of Risk and Uncertainty, 25*(2), 111–131.

Guest, L. (1942). The genesis of brand awareness. *Journal of Applied Psychology, 26*(6), 800–808.

Guest, L. (1948). The public's attitudes toward psychologists. *American Psychologist, 3*(4), 135–139.

Guest, L. (1955). Brand loyalty – twelve years later. *Journal of Applied Psychology, 39*(6), 405–408.

Hastings, G., Stead, M., McDermott, L., Forsyth, A., MacKintosh, A. M., Rayner, M., Godfrey, C., Caraher, M., & Angus, K. (2003). *Review of research on the effects of food promotion to children*. Glasgow, University of Strathclyde: Centre for Social Marketing.

Heckman, J. J. (2007). *Written direct examination of James J. Heckman (USA v Philip Morris USA Inc ed.).* Washington, DC: United States District Court.

Henriksen, L., Feighery, E. C., Schleicher, N. C., & Fortmann, S. P. (2008). Receptivity to alcohol marketing predicts initiation of alcohol use. *Journal of Adolescent Health, 42*(1), 28–35.

Institute of Medicine (2005). *Dietary reference intakes for energy, carbohydrate, fiber, fat, fatty acids, cholesterol, protein and amino acids.* Panel on Macronutrients, Panel on the Definition of Dietary Fiber, Subcommittee on Upper Reference Levels of Nutrients, Subcommittee on Interpretation and Uses of Dietary Reference Intakes, and the Standing Committee on the Scientific Evaluation of Dietary Reference Intakes, Food and Nutrition Board. Washington, DC: National Academies Press.

John, D. R. (1999). Consumer socialization of children: A retrospective look at twenty-five years of research. *Journal of Consumer Research, 26*(3), 183–213.

Krugman, H. E. (1965). The impact of television advertising: Learning without involvement. *Public Opinion Quarterly, 29*(3), 249-356.

Lee, A. (2008). *Retesting the link between youth receptivity to tobacco promotion and their susceptibility to smoke* (Doctoral thesis). The University of Western Australia, Perth. Retrieved from http://research-repository.uwa.edu.au/en/publications/retesting-the-link-between-youth-receptivity-to-tobacco-promotion-and-their-susceptibility-to-smoke(264da4ee-d999-4a53-aa3c-da6bf3a4f86c).html?uwaCustom=thesis

Lee, A., & Lam, D. C. S. (2005). How well does the index of receptivity to tobacco industry promotion discriminate between smoking and never smoking adolescents? Paper presented at the *Australian and New Zealand Marketing Academy Conference*. Perth, Australia.

Lee, A., Lam, D. C. S., Mizerski, D., & Mizerski, K. (2005). Investigating the construct of adolescent receptivity to tobacco advertising and promotion. Paper presented at the *American Advertising Association Asia Pacific Conference*. Hong Kong.

Lee, A., & Mizerski, D. (2007). Extreme response bias in measuring susceptibility to smoking. Paper presented at the *Australia and New Zealand Marketing Association Conference*. Dunedin, New Zealand.

Livingstone, S., & Helsper, E. J. (2006). Does advertising literacy mediate the effects of advertising on children? A critical examination of two linked research literatures in relation to obesity and food choice. *Journal of Communication, 56*(3), 560–584.

Longshore, D., Ellickson, P. L., McCaffrey, D. F., & Clair, P. A. S. (2007). School-based drug prevention among at-risk adolescents: Effects of ALERT plus. *Health Education & Behaviour, 34*(4), 651–668.

Mallinckrodt, V., & Mizerski, D. (2007). The effects of playing an advergame on young children's perceptions, preferences, and requests. *Journal of Advertising, 36*(2), 87–100.

Martin, K. D., & Smith, N. C. (2008). Commercializing social interaction: The ethics of stealth marketing. *Journal of Public Policy & Marketing, 27*(1), 45–56.

McAlister, A. R., & Cornwell, T. B. (2012). Collectible toys as marketing tools: Understanding preschool children's responses to foods paired with premiums. *Journal of Public Policy & Marketing, 31*(2), 195–205.

McNeal, J. U. (1964). *Children as consumers: Issue 9 of Studies in Marketing Series*. Austin, TX: Bureau of Business Research, University of Texas.

McNeal, J. U. (1992). *Kids as customers: A handbook of marketing to children*. Lanham, MD: Lexington Books.

Mizerski, R. W., Golden, L. L., & Kernan, J. B. (1979). The attribution process in consumer decision making. *Journal of Consumer Research, 6*(2), 123–140.

NCI (2013). *NCI measures guide for youth tobacco research: Susceptibility to smoking*. Retrieved from http://cancercontrol.cancer.gov/brp/tcrb/guide-measures/index.html

Packard, V. (1957). *The hidden persuaders*. New York, NY: David McKay.

Palda, K. S. (1966). The hypothesis of a hierarchy of effects: A partial evaluation. *Journal of Marketing Research, 3*(1), 13–24.

Panic, K., Cauberghe, V., & De Pelsmacker, P. (2013). Comparing TV ads and advergames targeting children: The impact of persuasion knowledge on behavioural responses. *Journal of Advertising, 42*(2–3), 264–273.

Petty, R. D., & Andrews, J. C. (2008). Covert marketing unmasked: A legal and regulatory guide for practices that mask marketing messages. *Journal of Public Policy & Marketing, 27*(1), 7–18.

Petty, R. E., & Cacioppo, J. T. (1981). Issue involvement as a moderator of the effects on attitude of advertising content and context. *Advances in Consumer Research, 8*(1), 20–24.

Piaget, J. (1962). The stages of the intellectual development of the child. *Bulletin of the Menninger Clinic, 26*, 120–128.

Pierce, J. P., Choi, W. S., Gilpin, E. A., Farkas, A. J., & Berry, C. C. (1998). Tobacco industry promotion of cigarettes and adolescent smoking. *Journal of the American Medical Association, 279*(7), 511.

Ratner, E. M., Hellegers, J. F., & Ogg, R. C. (1978). *FTC staff report on television advertising to children*. Washington, DC: US Government Printing Office.

Riesman, D. (1953). *The lonely crowd: A study of the changing American character* (Vol. 16). New York, NY: Doubleday Anchor Books.

Robertson, T. S., & Rossiter, J. R. (1974). Children and commercial persuasion: An attribution theory analysis. *Journal of Consumer Research, 1*(1), 13–20.

Ross, R. P., Campbell, T., Wright, J. C., Huston, A. C., Rice, M. L., & Turk, P. (1984). When celebrities talk, children listen: An experimental analysis of children's responses to TV ads with celebrity endorsement. *Journal of Applied Developmental Psychology, 5*(3), 185–202.

Rossiter, J. R., & Robertson, T. S. (1974). Children's TV commercials: Testing the defenses. *Journal of Communication, 24*(4), 137–144.

Rozendaal, E., Buijzen, M., & Valkenburg, P. (2009). Comparing children's and adults' cognitive advertising competences in the Netherlands. *Journal of Children and Media, 4*(1), 77–89.

Rozendaal, E., Slot, N., van Reijmersdal, E. A., & Buijzen, M. (2013). Children's responses to advertising in social games. *Journal of Advertising, 42*(2–3), 142–54.

Sanft, H. (1986). The role of knowledge in the effects of television advertising on children. *Advances in Consumer Research, 13*(1), 147–152.

Unger, J. B., Johnson, C. A., & Rohrbach, L. A. (1995). Recognition and liking of tobacco and alcohol advertisements among adolescents: Relationships with susceptibility to substance use. *Preventive Medicine, 24*(5), 461–466.

Van Reijmersdal, E. A., Rozendaal, E., & Buijzen, M. (2012). Effects of prominence, involvement, and persuasion knowledge on children's cognitive and affective responses to advergames. *Journal of Interactive Marketing, 26*(1), 33–42.

Verhellen, Y., Oates, C., De Pelsmacker, P., & Dens, N. (2014). Children's responses to traditional versus hybrid advertising formats: The moderating role of persuasion knowledge. *Journal of Consumer Policy, 37*(2), 235–255.

Ward, S. (1972). Children's reactions to commercials. *Journal of Advertising Research, 12*(2), 37–45.

Ward, S., Wackman, D. B., & Wartella, E. (1977). *How children learn to buy: The development of consumer information-processing skills*. Oxford, UK: Sage.

Wells, W. D. (1965). Communicating with children. *Journal of Advertising Research, 5*(2), 2–14.

Wilcox, B. L., Kunkel, D., Cantor, J., Palmer, E., Linn, S., & Dowrick, P. (2004). *Report of the American Psychological Association Task Force on advertising and children*. Washington, DC: American Psychological Association.

Wright, P., Friestad, M., & Boush, D. M. (2005). The development of marketplace persuasion knowledge in children, adolescents, and young adults. *Journal of Public Policy & Marketing, 24*(2), 222–233.

Part V

Decision making, attitudes and behavioural research

19

Framing effects in consumer judgement and decision making

Tobias Krüger, Tobias Vogel and Michaela Wänke

Do consumers care whether ground beef is advertised as 75 per cent lean or 25 per cent fat? Does it matter whether a gamble offers $50 for sure or a 50 per cent chance to win $100 and a 50 per cent chance to win nothing? Does it make a difference whether a doctor communicates the outcome of a medical treatment as successful in 80 per cent of all cases or as not successful in 20 per cent of all cases?

From a normative point of view, the answer to these questions is pretty straightforward: it shouldn't. Expected utility theory assumes human behaviour to be governed by various axioms of rationality (von Neumann & Morgenstern, 1947); rational decision makers choose according to a prospect's expected utility and not according to the way in which it is portrayed. Granting that 25 per cent fat is the same in other words as 75 per cent lean, and 80 per cent survival is the same as 20 per cent mortality, the different descriptions should not affect consumers' choice of ground beef or patients' choice of a medical treatment. Put more generally, the way in which a decision is presented, its *framing*, should not affect a decision maker's preference as long as expected utilities stay invariant.

Yet, decades of research have found that framing can have dramatic consequences for people's preferences and choices (Keren, 2011a, b; Kühberger, 1998; Levin, Schneider, & Gaeth, 1998). Despite their logical equivalence, people prefer ground beef that is 75 per cent lean over ground beef that is 25 per cent fat (Levin & Gaeth, 1988), a gamble that offers $50 for sure over a gamble that offers a 50 per cent chance to win $100 (cf. Tversky & Kahneman, 1981) and a medical treatment that is successful in 80 per cent of all cases over a treatment that is not successful in 20 per cent of all cases (Wilson, Kaplan, & Schneiderman, 1987).

Questioning fundamental axioms of rational choice, framing effects are at the heart of the rationality debate of human decision making (Shafir & LeBoeuf, 2002). The present chapter will sketch this interesting debate as well as its implications for consumer behaviour. We will first derive a general definition of what can be considered a framing effect. Next, to organize the comprehensive literature, we will discuss the most prevalent typologies with representative findings in the realm of consumer judgement and decision making and the most common accounts of framing effects. Finally, we will broaden the perspective by discussing moderators to see whether framing effects can be switched off, and by reviewing specific applications of the framing idea in the field of consumer research.

What are framing effects?

Framing effects are said to occur when *equivalent* presentations of the same decision problem lead to systematically different decisions (Sher & McKenzie, 2006). Thus, at their core, framing effects are about the communication of a decision problem (Keren, 2011a) and are typically concerned with how choice alternatives are described and through which response mode answers are elicited. To define what can be considered a framing effect (and not just a preference between two actually different options), the equivalence of the frames is a critical criterion. Indeed, preference asymmetries across choice options that factually differ in their expected utilities would not violate normative principles of rational choice, nor would they be considered as framing effects. Preferences for a medical treatment with a 50 per cent success rate over a treatment with a 60 per cent failure rate are easily explained via differences in expected utilities without drawing on any psychological account about the representation of the decision problem. It is the preference of a treatment with a 50 per cent success rate over one with a 50 per cent failure rate that cannot be accounted for by a rational actor's expected utilities, as both outcomes are mathematically or logically equivalent.

Obviously, according to this definition, the standard of equivalence – like logical, formal or mathematical equivalence – is essential for the demarcation of the effect. We will come back to a discussion of useful definitions of equivalence in a later section of this chapter. First, we will provide a general overview of the most important framing effects within common framing typologies.

Typologies and examples of framing effects

To consolidate the vast and diverse literature on framing effects, several attempts have been made to establish typologies that organize the plethora of findings. Subdividing framing effects may be useful to the extent that different psychological mechanisms come into play in different areas of framing research. Thus, theoretical explanations for why framing effects occur are manifold and have to be tailored to the specific nature of the decision problem.

Probably the most widely cited typology of framing effects has been suggested by Levin et al. (1998). Based on (a) what is framed, (b) what the frame affects and (c) how the effect is measured, the authors propose three distinct types of framing effects – *risky choice framing*, *attribute framing* and *goal framing* – with the goal to resolve seemingly non-integrable, contradictory patterns of results from previous research and to tailor specific accounts and underlying mechanisms to a particular subset of findings.

Risky choice framing

In risky choice framing, people are confronted with two choice options that differ in their degree of risk. These options are either framed positively (i.e., in terms of gains) or negatively (i.e., in terms of losses). The most prominent example of risky choice framing – the *Asian disease problem* – was published in a seminal article by Tversky and Kahneman (1981). In the Asian disease problem, participants are informed that an unusual Asian disease is expected to kill 600 people, but that there are two alternative programmes to combat the disease. The participants' task is to choose between the two programmes. In the positive and the negative framing condition, the outcome of the two programmes is described in terms of people saved and people dying, respectively. Essentially for a risky choice framing, the two options in each programme differ in their degree of risk – that is, in both conditions there is one programme with a riskless outcome (i.e., 200 people surviving; 400 people dying) and one programme with an outcome that involves a specified degree of risk (i.e., one-third probability that 600 people are saved and two-thirds probability that no people are saved; a one-third probability that nobody will die and a two-thirds probability that 600 people will die).

Participants' choices in the Asian disease problem reflect a *preference reversal* across the two framing conditions: Whereas the majority of participants in the positive framing condition (72 per cent) prefer the riskless option, the majority of participants in the negative framing condition (78 per cent) prefer the risky option. Thus, despite the logical equivalence of the frames, choices differ substantially as a function of the frames' valence. As predicted by prospect theory, people are risk averse in the domain of gains and risk seeking in the domain of losses (Kahneman & Tversky, 1979; Tversky & Kahneman, 1981). We will elaborate on the theory and specific explanations for risky choice framing at a later point in this chapter.

Although much of the research concerning risky choice framing has been concerned with the Asian disease problem and its variants, risky choice framing has also received much attention in the field of consumer and marketing research. For instance, in a hypothetical scenario, Qualls and Puto (1989) asked a random sample of professional fleet managers to make a choice between awarding a maintenance contract for a fleet to one of two providers. Critically, one provider offered a fixed rate (riskless option), whereas the other provider offered a rate dependent on the number of vehicles in the fleet, which was not entirely predictable (risky option). Consistent with Tversky and Kahneman's (1981) earlier research, the fleet managers were more likely to choose the fixed rate and the flexible rate when the options were framed as positive and negative, respectively. Even financial planners, who deal with the evaluation of risky prospects as part of their professional life, were shown to be susceptible to risky choice framing in a problem conceptually analogous to the Asian disease dilemma in the domain of investment strategies (Roszkowski & Snelbecker, 1990).

Since Tversky and Kahneman's (1981) original publication of the Asian disease problem, a large number of studies across a wide range of domains have replicated the original results. A meta-analysis by Kühberger (1998) reported an average effect size of $d = 0.31$ across 136 studies that were concerned with risky decisions. Effects tended to be stronger when an experimental paradigm was similar to Tversky and Kahneman's – for instance, with regard to response mode (choice vs. ratings), and differences in the level of risk between the two options (qualitatively vs. quantitatively).

Attribute framing

The second class of Levin, Schneider and Gaeth's (1998) typology, attribute framing, is concerned with the most simple case of valence framing: A single attribute of a decision object is either framed in positive or in negative terms. Just as the glass can be half full or half empty, performance can be described in terms of success or failure rates, medical treatments in terms of survival or mortality rates, a conference in terms of what percentage of papers is accepted or rejected, or consumer satisfaction in terms of percentage of satisfied or of dissatisfied consumers (Beach, Puto, Heckler, Naylor, & Marble, 1996). As long as the dichotomous probabilities add up to 1, one frame is mathematically equivalent to the other – communicating the success rate logically implies the failure rate and vice versa.

Our introductory example of ground beef represents one of the most prominent examples of attribute framing (Levin, 1987; Levin & Gaeth, 1988). Consumers evaluated the quality of ground beef that was labelled as "75 per cent lean ground beef" (positive frame) more favourably than when it was labelled as "25 per cent fat ground beef" (negative frame) despite the logical equivalence of the two frames. Similarly, consumers evaluated soup advertised as 95 per cent fat free as healthier than a soup advertised as 5 per cent fat (Sanford, Fay, Stewart, & Moxey, 2002). Not surprisingly nutrients deemed unhealthy are often advertised in a positive frame, as an abundance of product claims as X per cent fat free (salt free, etc.) shows. This kind of framing can be extended to many attributes that involve numerical quantities; for example, X per cent of the parts were made by American (domestic) versus non-American (foreign) workers (Levin, Jasper, & Gaeth, 1996). Likewise in the medical domain, a treatment is evaluated as more effective and is more likely to be recommended to another person or a family member when it is described with a "50 per cent success rate" rather than a "50 per cent failure rate" (Levin, Schnittjer, & Thee, 1988).

In contrast to risky choice framing, which involves the joint evaluation of two alternative options (e.g., the two different programmes in the Asian disease dilemma), attribute framing involves only a single alternative that is evaluated in isolation (e.g., ground beef). Note that this also changes the nature of preference reversals (also called *bidirectional framing effect*; see Wang, 1996): In attribute framing, a preference reversal can only be obtained in terms of a majority of participants favouring an option (e.g., purchasing ground meat) in one framing condition and a majority of participants *not* favouring the option in the other condition.

In general, research on attribute framing quite consistently provides evidence for a *valence-consistent shift*: Choice options are evaluated more positively when presented in positive rather than in negative terms. Although there is evidence for moderators in attribute framing (e.g., Freling, Vincent, & Henard, 2014), in their review, Levin et al. (1998) do not report a single study in which a negative frame produces more favourable evaluations than the respective positive frame and conclude that the research on attribute framing "presents the clearest evidence of a homogeneous phenomenon" (p. 160) from all the three types of framing effects within their taxonomy.

Differences in category accessibility and priming have been discussed (Levin et al., 1998) as a potential explanation to account for the occurrence of attribute framing effects – positive and negative frames produce predominantly positive and negative associations, respectively. We will elaborate on the mechanisms behind attribute framing after discussing goal framing, the third and final class in Levin et al.'s (1998) taxonomy.

Goal framing

Goal framing is concerned with the potentially beneficial consequences of engaging in a certain behaviour versus the potentially detrimental consequence of not engaging in it. Thus, it refers to the goal – attaining a gain versus avoiding a loss – which an individual adopts when performing a certain behaviour. For example, the decision to change the energy provider can be framed as saving money (gain) when changing the provider or as suffering from unnecessary costs (loss) if one does not switch from the old provider.

Goal framing is similar to attribute framing, as it involves the judgement of a single rather than multiple options (see, e.g., Meyerowitz & Chaiken, 1987). It is, however, different from attribute framing, as both frames describe a behaviour as concordantly good (or concordantly bad). Goal frames do not characterize a specific aspect as positive in one framing condition and as negative in the other condition (such as presenting ground beef either as lean or as fat). Instead, goal framing focuses on a behaviour's positive consequences; yet, these consequences are either presented as positive because of gaining something (e.g., save money) or they are presented as positive because of not losing something (e.g., avoid unnecessary costs). Thus, in goal framing, both frames promote the same action or result (e.g., change energy provider) but for different reasons, whereas in attribute framing, an object's attribute is either presented in positive or in negative terms.

Levin and colleagues propose loss aversion as an underlying mechanism to explain goal framing. Because losses loom larger than gains (Tversky & Kahneman, 1991), people should be more likely to take an action that avoids a loss rather than one that attains a gain (see also the specific section on accounts of framing).

Much research on goal framing is motivated by how appeals should be framed to be most persuasive. The simple prediction is that pointing out how a behaviour can prevent losses should be more effective in motivating the behaviour than pointing out how the same behaviour attains gains. In a field experiment conducted by Ganzach and Karsahi (1995; see also Thaler, 1980), credit card owners received a marketing pamphlet that framed the benefits of credit card usage either in terms of gains obtained from using the card (e.g., paying by card is convenient; no danger that money will be lost or stolen) or in terms of losses suffered from not using it (e.g., paying by cash is less convenient; there is a danger that money will be lost or stolen). Results of 246 credit card owners indicated that 54.8 per cent of the customers in the loss-frame condition and 23.6 per cent of the customers in the gain-frame condition used their credit card within the first month after receiving the pamphlet. Also, customers in the loss-frame condition charged their credit card with more than twice the amount as those in the gain-frame condition. Thus, the loss-frame pamphlet was much more effective in promoting credit card usage than the gain-frame pamphlet in several respects.

Whether gain-framed or loss-framed messages or appeals are more persuasive has been extensively researched with respect to health behaviour and consumption of health-related products. In line with the credit card example above, a widely cited article by Meyerowitz and Chaiken (1987) presents evidence for women's higher engagement rates in breast self-examination (BSE) under a loss versus a gain frame. In the loss-frame condition, participants were told that "women who *do not do* BSE have a *decreased* chance of finding a tumour", whereas, in the gain-frame condition, participants were told that "women who *do* BSE have an *increased* chance of finding a tumour" (p. 504). Results indicate that women who were made aware of the negative consequences from not doing BSE had a more positive attitude towards it than women who were made aware of the positive consequences from doing BSE. Moreover, in a follow-up study four months after the initial experimental session, women in the loss-frame condition reported a higher frequency of actually having performed BSE than women in the gain-frame condition. Similarly to Meyerowitz and Chaiken's results, a loss-framed advertising slogan for a grape juice ("don't miss out on preventing clogged arteries") elicited more liking for the brand than an analogous gain-framed slogan ("prevent clogged arteries") (Lee & Aaker, 2004).

Yet, the literature is not as consistent as one would want it to be, as there are also findings for gain-framed advertising appeals to be more persuasive (e.g., Rothman, Martino, Bedell, Detweiler, & Salovey, 1999). Indeed, Rothman and Salovey (1997) claimed loss frames to be more effective only for promoting behaviour that detects health problems, such as BSE, but gain frames to be more effective for promoting behaviour that prevents the onset of a disease. Although results regarding the effectiveness of an ad for a mouth rinse are in line with this claim (Rothman et al., 1999), they are inconsistent with Lee and Aaker's (2004) findings reported above.

To make matters even more complicated for applied purposes, it is not always clear whether the gain or loss relates to the action and non-action (attaining health or preventing misery vs. missing out on attaining health or failing to prevent misery), as in the research cited above, or to the focused end-state (health or happiness vs. disease or misery). Obviously, there are several critical variables that moderate the effects of goal framing (see the section below on moderators of framing).

Alternative typologies of framing effects

Levin and colleagues' (1998) classification and, in particular, their claim that different types of framing map onto distinct underlying mechanisms has not remained without criticism. Keren (2011a) questioned, among other things, whether the underlying processes of the three types are indeed distinctively different, and pointed out that the categories are not necessarily conceptually different but may be overlapping. The latter, however, might also apply to alternative typologies that aim to organize the framing literature. In any case, several authors have suggested alternative typologies to organize the literature.

For instance, Soman (2004) suggested differentiating between *outcome framing*, *structure framing* and *task framing*, which refer to different components of a decision problem. In his framework, outcome framing characterizes the way in which an outcome is described, such as when communicating a numerical quantity in terms of gains versus losses (Tversky & Kahneman, 1981), or when scaling an amount of money in different currencies (Raghubir & Srivastava, 2002). Likewise, monetary outcomes can be framed in terms of amount of interest or rate of interest. In this regard, Soman also subsumes one particularly interesting variant of framing as outcome framing, namely the aggregation and disaggregation of gains and losses. The same costs can result from a base price and a surcharge or a higher base price and a rebate. In one study, participants preferred an insurance with a \$1,600 premium per year that offered a \$600 rebate in the case of not filing any claims over an insurance with a \$1,000 premium that included a deductible of \$600 (Johnson, Hershey, Meszaros, & Kunreuther, 1993). In both cases consumers had to pay \$1,600 in the case of a claim and \$1,000 in the case of no claim. However, first, the difference in subjective utility between the loss of \$1,600 and \$1,000 is more than compensated by the gain of \$600, and second, adding the subjective utilities of the losses of \$1,000 and \$600 is more negative than the result from the loss of \$1,600 (see prospect theory account below). Note that in this case, although both options look mathematically equivalent, in real life the option with the rebate actually implies losing the opportunity to invest the \$600 and is therefore the worse option.

A popular strategy in pricing is to break down or segregate costs into smaller units to make them seem less severe. According to such a *pennies-a-day strategy*, a few cents per day seem negligible and are accepted more willingly than a larger yearly fee (Gourville, 1998). Contrariwise, aggregation of small savings into larger sums makes them look more significant: Consumers required a mean saving of \$56 per year to switch their telephone company, but it took monthly savings of \$11.75 (equivalent to \$141 a year) on average to make them switch (Gourville, 1998). Interestingly, the preference for segregation of costs over aggregation is inconsistent with prospect theory. Apparently small losses are truly neglected.

The second class in Soman's (2004) taxonomy, structure framing, refers to the arrangement of the decision problem and concerns, for instance, whether information is presented sequentially rather than at once (Tversky & Kahneman, 1981), or whether several aspects of a decision are presented in isolation versus as a compound (Soman & Gourville, 2001).

Finally, task framing refers to the nature of the response task that is used to elicit the answer, such as choosing versus rejecting one of two options (Shafir, 1993). An interesting application of task framing is found in customization: Often consumers can configure their purchase by adding options to a base model or starting from scratch. In other cases, the default comes fully equipped but consumers can choose to drop features. In line with loss aversion, a laboratory study found that consumers ended up with more options and a more expensive purchase when they stripped down a default model compared with beefing up the base model (Park, Jun, & MacInnis, 2000). In this vein, many studies showed that when a default option is provided consumers are likely not to change it (e.g., Johnson & Goldstein, 2003). For instance, due to different insurance laws in two US states a comparison between the two states provides a natural experiment (Johnson et al., 1993). In one US state where a motor insurance premium included the right to sue for pain and suffering, about 75 per cent of drivers retained that right and only about 25 per cent waved that right for a lower insurance premium. In the neighbouring state, where the default insurance did not contain the right to sue for pain and suffering, only about 20 per cent chose to pay extra to acquire that right.

Another recurring theme throughout several framing typologies is the distinction between *framing in a strict sense* and *framing in a loose sense*, which is concerned with different definitions of equivalence across the frames (Keren, 2011a; Kühberger, 1998). Framing in a strict sense refers to logical or mathematical equivalence such as in the Asian disease dilemma. Framing in a loose sense refers to linguistic re-descriptions of the same decision problem or to changes in the response mode such as, for instance, when framing a task as contributing to versus withdrawing from a public resource pool (Aquino, Steisel, & Kay, 1992) or when choosing versus rejecting one out of two options (Shafir, 1993).

Finally, Druckman (2001, 2011) differentiates between *frames in communication* and *frames in thought* (for a similar distinction, see Kahneman, 2000). Frames in communication characterize specific emphases on a message's content such as, for example, the importance of economic issues in a political debate. Frames in thought, in contrast, refer to an individual's construal of a particular message: A person with an economic frame of mind may look specifically for economy-related information in a political message. Thus, in many situations, frames in communication versus frames in thought are concerned with a speaker's utterance and a listener's interpretation, respectively.

Summary discussion

Framing is a multidimensional construct. Indeed, highlighting the need for well-conceived typologies, several authors have called for an organization of the literature in order to clarify the plethora of theoretical constructs and experimental paradigms that have been used in the past (Druckman, 2001; Keren, 2011a; Levin et al., 1998). From a theoretical perspective, these taxonomies are essential to understand the distinct psychological mechanisms that are involved in the different types of framing effects. In the next section, we will discuss the specific accounts that have been put forward to explain the occurrence of framing effects and how they map onto the different types discussed.

Beyond the various accounts of framing, differences between the types of framing effects can also be found at the empirical level. In their narrative review, Levin et al. (1998) found the valence-consistent shift in attribute framing to be the most consistent framing effect within their classification system. Yet, in terms of effect sizes, Piñon and Gambara (2005) found attribute framing ($d = 0.260$) to produce smaller effect sizes than the risky choice ($d = 0.437$) and the goal-framing paradigm ($d = 0.444$). Thus, framing effects do not only differ in terms of their theoretical foundations, but also in terms of their empirical strength.

Accounts of framing effects

Prospect theory

To explain the preference reversal obtained in the original demonstration of the Asian disease problem and other risky choice frames, Tversky and Kahneman (1981) drew on *prospect theory* as a descriptive model of decision making under uncertainty (Kahneman & Tversky, 1979). At its core, prospect theory suggests a value function whereby a subjective value is assigned to each possible (objective) outcome. Three basic principles characterize this value function: First, outcomes are construed either as positive deviations (gains) or as negative deviations (losses) from a reference point. Second, the function is concave in the domain of gains and convex in the domain of losses. Thus, for instance, the difference between $10 and $20 is perceived as greater than the mathematically identical difference between $110 and $120. Third, the value function is steeper for losses than for gains, implying a larger negative impact of losing $10 than the corresponding positive impact of winning $10.

Now, consider the subjective utilities that are implied by the different outcomes of the Asian disease problem within this framework (see Figure 19.1). Due to the value function's shape, 200 people being saved has a higher utility than a one-third probability that 600 people will be saved. As a consequence, the sure option is preferred when the choice is framed in terms of "lives saved". In contrast, when talking about "lives lost", the sure option of 400 people dying is less attractive than a two-thirds probability of all 600 people dying. Thus, due to the concavity and convexity of the value function, the certain and the risky option are asymmetrically attractive for gains and losses.

A similar account based on prospect theory (Kahneman & Tversky, 1979) has been suggested to explain goal framing. However, instead of focusing on the value function's negatively accelerating shape, the explanation for goal framing is based on the function's different slopes for gains versus losses. According to the notion of *loss aversion* (Tversky & Kahneman, 1991), a negative outcome has a larger absolute value than the identical positive outcome – the value function's slope is steeper in the negative than in the positive domain. Thus, with regard to goal framing, the consequences of an action weigh heavier when it is framed as avoiding losses rather than as obtaining benefits. For example, Meyerowitz and Chaiken's (1987) classical finding of higher rates of BSE performance in the loss-frame condition can be explained by the value function's steeper slope in the negative domain – the decreased chance of finding a tumour when not engaging in BSE weighs heavier than the increased chance of finding one when engaging in it.

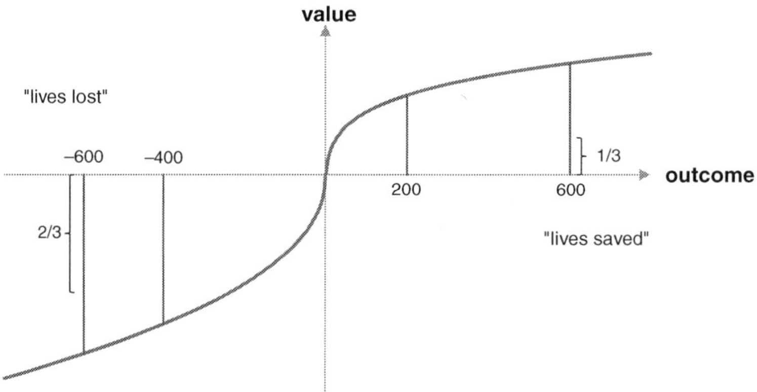

Figure 19.1 The Asian disease dilemma explained by prospect theory's value function.

Note: In the domain of gains ("lives saved"), the value of saving 200 lives is more positive than one-third of the value of saving 600 lives. In the domain of losses ("lives lost"), however, the value of 400 people dying is more negative than two-third of the value of 600 people dying. As a consequence, the certain option is preferred in the domain of gains, whereas the uncertain option is preferred in the domain of losses.

Prospect theory serves as an empirically well-founded framework that helps in understanding and integrating framing effects of various typologies (e.g., risky choice framing, goal framing, outcome framing, task framing). Yet, Kahneman and Tversky (1979) introduced the theory as a *descriptive model* of decision making under risk rather than as an *explanation* of such behaviour. For prospect theory to be regarded as an actual explanation for framing effects, it needs to be backed up by psychological principles that provide reasons for the specific slope and shape of the value function. For instance, the value function's differences in slope for gains versus losses may be rooted in a general *negativity bias* of giving greater weight to negative as compared with positive information (Rozin & Royzman, 2001). Likewise, the function's concavity and convexity may be attributable to such fundamental psychophysical laws as the Weber–Fechner law and the economical principle of diminishing marginal utility.

Category accessibility and priming

Perception and cognition are essentially guided by mental categorization processes (Bruner, 1957). Human information processing is characterized by pre-organizing informational input and by differentiating it along the mental structures that are activated at the moment of encoding. Activated concepts *prime* the activation of related concepts. Different semantics evoke different associations.

Drawing on category accessibility and priming as fundamental principles of human cognition, Levin and colleagues (1998) suggested an account for attribute framing. In attribute framing, logically identical information is presented either in positive or in negative terms, such as success versus failure rates or winning versus losing proportions. As a consequence, the frames should evoke different associations in the recipient's mind: Success rates and winning proportions activate predominantly positive associations; failure rates and losing proportions active mostly negative associations.

For instance, in Levin and Gaeth's (1988) study on the framing of ground beef that was already introduced at the beginning of this chapter, one may easily imagine that upon hearing the word *fat* the consumer thinks of fat, how it looks, how it tastes and how unhealthy it is. In contrast, the word *lean* elicits completely different associations about the beef, such as healthiness or high nutritional value. Indeed, support for this idea of spreading activation can be found in the additional measures that were assessed in the study. The framing manipulation did not only affect judgements directly related to the greasiness of the beef, but also judgements related to its taste experience.

Related arguments to explain attribute framing have been put forward based on the notion of *confirmation bias* (Klayman & Ha, 1987): Once a certain evaluative tone – be it positive or negative – is communicated by the framing manipulation, people are more likely to continue their information search in a confirmative rather than a disconfirmative fashion. Thus, when hearing about the success rate of a medical treatment, people are more likely to generate information that supports the treatment's success rather than its failure and vice versa. As a result, their information sample will be skewed towards the evaluative tone of the frame and preferences are formed correspondingly.

Compatibility

Compatibility has been suggested as another account of attribute framing, drawing on principles that are similar to category accessibility and priming (Keren, 2011a). According to the *compatibility principle*, "the weight of a stimulus attribute is enhanced to the extent that it is compatible with the required response" (Shafir, 1995, p. 248). For instance, when the stimulus material is presented in an auditory mode, a vocal response is faster than a pointing response due to the higher correspondence between presentation and response mode. Any transformation of incompatible input and output modes requires additional mental processing that is potentially effortful and error prone (Slovic, Griffin, & Tversky, 1990).

In framing research, the compatibility principle is particularly applicable to situations in which the manipulation concerns the response mode used to elicit the answer, such as choosing versus rejecting, or expressing like versus expressing dislike (i.e., task framing; Soman, 2004). In a series of decision problems, Shafir (1993) provided participants with impoverished options that had mostly average attributes as well as with enriched options that had both many positive and many negative attributes. For instance, in one of their studies, participants chose between two vacation packages for spring break. Package A came with "average weather, average beaches, medium-temperature water, and average nightlife", whereas package B came with "lots of sunshine, gorgeous beaches, very cold water and no nightlife". Because of the higher compatibility of positivity and choosing, and negativity and rejecting, the enriched option was both more often chosen and more often rejected than the impoverished option. Similar findings that support the significance of the compatibility principle have been documented for choosing versus matching tasks when evaluating the quality of bets (Slovic, 1995).

Conversational logic and implicatures

At its heart, framing is concerned with communication. Any information that is communicated by a frame – particularly when it is conveyed in an impoverished informational environment such as in a scientific experiment – is enriched with the receiver's pragmatic inferences about the sender's intentions. The conversational account focuses on the principles of cooperative communication to explain framing effects.

According to Grice (1975), effective communication is based on *conversational implicatures*. Implicatures characterize the meaning of an utterance that goes beyond its literal or strictly implied message. For instance, logically the utterance "Tom had two beers yesterday" implies that Tom had two or more beers: Even if he had five beers, the utterance would still be true. Based on the logic of conversation, however, most listeners would infer that Tom had *exactly* two beers, because otherwise an utterance such as "Tom had at least two beers yesterday" would have been more appropriate (for a review, see Wänke, 2007).

The idea that utterances carry information beyond their literal content and, therefore, convey different implicatures can be applied to framing (McKenzie & Nelson, 2003; Sher & McKenzie, 2006; Wänke, 2007). Sher & McKenzie (2006) argued that a chosen frame *leaks information* that is not part of the explicit description but part of the background knowledge the person choosing the frame has. Whereas the amount of water in a glass is exactly the same when the glass is described as half empty or half full, the chosen frame may convey other information. When the glass is described as half full it evokes comparison with an empty glass or one that was empty before, whereas describing the glass as half empty tacitly implies a deviation from a full glass. In other words, although formally equivalent, both statements differ in their pragmatic meaning. Likewise, McKenzie and Nelson (2003) showed that when the outcome of a new therapy lay above the previous survival rate for a disease, a large majority of speakers chose to express this rate in a survival frame (e.g., 25 per cent survival). In contrast, a mortality frame was chosen when the survival rate lay below a previous reference point. From this perspective, sensitivity to communicated frames is highly rational and it makes sense to prefer a therapy that is described in terms of its survival rate compared with one for which its mortality rate is given.

In this realm, it is interesting to note that framing effects in the Asian disease problem disappeared when the problem was presented as a statistical rather than a medical problem (Bless, Betsch, & Franzen, 1998). In fact, when participants considered the task as a statistical problem, either of the two options was chosen by about 50 per cent, which suggests that they realized that both options were statistically equivalent and chose at random. Presumably, choice of words was seen as less diagnostic when the task was to calculate expected values.

Speakers do not only choose slightly different words to express different things. The way something is framed apparently also carries meaning for the receiver. A similar example comes from comparative questions. For example, when asked whether traffic contributes more than industry or less than industry to air pollution, 45 per cent of the respondents thought that traffic contributes more. When the question was framed differently and respondents were asked whether industry contributes more than traffic or less than traffic to air pollution, only 24 per cent thought that traffic was the main polluter (Wänke, 1996; Wänke, Schwarz, & Noelle-Neumann, 1995). The reason for such asymmetric comparison judgements lies in respondents focusing on the (grammatical) subject of the comparison and neglecting the referent (Tversky, 1977). Presumably they assume that the speaker chose this particular comparison object as the subject because this is the target of interest (Wänke & Reutner, 2011). In a similar vein, pragmatic assumptions can account for task-framing effects: Apparently people understand defaults as recommended options and are therefore hesitant to depart from them, and accept the default (Johnson & Goldstein, 2003; McKenzie, Liersch, & Finkelstein, 2006).

Moderators of framing effects

While theoretical explanations are still being debated, there is little doubt regarding the phenomenon's significance for applied fields. Framing allows shifting preferences without changing an object's actual properties by merely altering the object description or the response format. In this vein, products and services can gain an advantage over their competitors, rendering framing a powerful strategy for practitioners, from policy makers through advertisers to salespeople. In order to better understand under which conditions framing effects occur in applied settings, researchers in the areas of marketing, consumer and health psychology have dedicated much of their work to what moderates framing effects on persuasion and decision making (Covey, 2014; Updegraff & Rothman, 2013). In the remainder of this section, we want to introduce various receiver characteristics that qualify whether framing can be assumed to have an effect on consumer choice. We will then turn to the framing of persuasive messages, and consider which frame is expected to work best with whom. Finally, we will broaden our perspective on framing research and discuss findings from related areas that are still very much related to the idea of framing, although they may not fulfil the equivalence criterion in its strictest sense.

When framing choice options fizzle out

From a marketing perspective, you may wonder whether framing is a viable technique for promoting your product to the clientele in mind. From a consumer perspective, however, you may consider framing a manipulation of your self-guided choice (Brehm, 1966). Furthermore, assuming invariant product utility across frames, falling prey to frames comes at the risk of making a bad choice. From either perspective, the question arises whether there are conditions under which framing effects are likely to fizzle out.

To a great extent, this question has been addressed from the perspective of dual-process models of decision making (Epstein, 1998; James, 1890) and attitude change (Chaiken & Eagly, 1989; Petty & Cacioppo, 1986) (cf. Chapter 21, this volume). These models propose two modes of thinking as a common denominator, one of which is analytical and the other relies on affect and simple heuristics. Whether people process information analytically or in a heuristic way depends on people's processing motivation and capacity (Chaiken & Eagly, 1989; Petty & Cacioppo, 1986). Only if processing motivation and capacity are high enough are people likely to think analytically, and therefore, to discount the irrelevant information provided by the frame (see Kahneman & Frederick, 2007).

In line with this notion, the need for cognition (Cacioppo & Petty, 1982), a construct used to describe inter-individual differences in intrinsic processing motivation, has been identified as a moderator of framing effects. That is, studies show that choices are less affected by frames for individuals high rather than low in need for cognition (Simon, Fagley, & Halleran, 2004; Smith & Levin, 1996). McElroy and Seta (2003) further found that individuals with a disposition to think analytically are less influenced by choice framing than are less analytical individuals.

More compelling evidence for the causal role of processing motivation in resisting framing effects is obtained from studies in which processing motivation is manipulated experimentally. McElroy and Seta (2003) varied the personal relevance of the decision. Only in the low-involvement condition were framing effects obtained. In other studies, processing style was manipulated in a more direct manner. In order to induce an affective processing style, Fagley, Coleman and Simon (2010) made participants focus on their feelings by asking them "to take a moment and imagine the feelings [they] would have" (p. 267) in the specific situation. Indeed, framing effects on risky choice increased for participants who had received this instruction.

As mentioned before, analytical processing does not only depend on processing motivation; consumers also have to be capable of analyzing the information. Provided with a risky choice, for instance, only consumers capable of calculating the expected utility of both options will be able to realize their objective equivalence. Indeed, empirical findings suggest that high maths skills enable consumers to compare alternatives and buffer against framing effects on risky choice (Peters, 2012; Peters et al., 2006), at least for individuals motivated to elaborate on the information (Simon et al., 2004). This finding is complemented by studies demonstrating that susceptibility to framing effects may be reduced when information is not provided in an abstract numerical format but in a format familiar to the decision maker (Garcia-Retamero & Dhami, 2013).

Capacity constraints, however, are not a necessary condition for framing effects to occur. In fact, a cognitive load manipulation did not alter the influence of a win vs. loss frame on risky decisions. Yet, cognitive load had a main effect on decisions for the sure option. People for whom capacity was reduced by high load tended to choose the easy-to-calculate sure option more often than those in the low-load condition (Whitney, Rinehart, & Hinson, 2008). Future research is needed to corroborate the notion that easy-to-calculate options are preferred over hard-to-calculate ones – a finding that was in line with the heuristic use of processing fluency as a basis for evaluations (Winkielman, Halberstadt, Fazendeiro, & Catty, 2006). Pertinent to the starting question, however, there was also a main effect of the frame: Win frames as opposed to loss frames caused more risk-averse choices in both the load and the no-load condition. One may speculate that despite unconstrained capacity, participants' motivation to carefully process the information was not high enough.

From the perspective of practitioners, framing appears a viable strategy for shifting preferences, at least if consumers are either unmotivated or unable to engage in analytical thinking. Arguably, in real life these conditions are often met. Consumers tend to be cognitive misers; thus heuristic processing may be the default rather than the exception (see Chaiken & Ledgerwood, 2012). Yet, conditions of minimal capacity and motivation do not necessarily constitute a good soil for framing effects. The processing of the frame and its integration into the decision already require some motivation and capacity. When under severe time constraints, individuals actually disregard the framing information and choices thus remain unaffected (Igou & Bless, 2007).

Framing persuasive messages to match the receiver

One research domain that markedly advanced the identification of moderating conditions is persuasion research. In principle, the effects obtained in the studies on choice also pertain to the framing in the domain of persuasion. For instance, the persuasive impact of irrelevant information is increased for individuals low as opposed to high in need for cognition (e.g., Haugtvedt, Petty, & Cacioppo, 1992) or personal involvement (e.g., Petty, Cacioppo, & Schumann, 1983). However, the question addressed in persuasion research goes beyond identifying whether frames do have an effect or not. It addresses the question of whether it was worth fitting the message frames with the receiver characteristics (e.g., Cesario, Higgins, & Scholer, 2008; Higgins, 2000, 2005; Rothman et al., 1999).

Given the prominence of dual-process theories of persuasion, it may not come as a surprise that the differential framing effects on persuasion have been studied for indicators of processing motivation and capacity. In this vein, researchers analyzed whether the effectiveness of different goal frames (e.g., consuming fruit boosts your health vs. *not* consuming fruit makes you sick) is moderated by inter-individual differences concerning processing motivation. However, a meta-analysis (Covey, 2014) did not find unambiguous results: Some studies suggest that positive frames are more effective for motivated than unmotivated receivers, while other studies lead to the opposite conclusion.

A theoretical framework more closely related to the question of how to match a frame with a receiver is regulatory focus theory (Higgins, 1997). According to this theory, goal attainment is achieved via two foci, a promotion and a prevention focus. In a promotion focus, individuals strive for self-fulfilment and aspiration; in a prevention focus, they try to fulfil their duties and obligations. In the former, goal attainment is characterized by eagerness, in the latter by vigilance. Finally, in a promotion focus people tend to be sensitive toward possible gains, but a prevention focus sensitises people towards positive losses. Hence, a gain frame has been proposed and demonstrated to create a fit with a promotion focus, but loss frames should be more appealing when recipients are in a prevention focus (Cesario, Grant, & Higgins, 2004; Lee & Aaker, 2004; Yi & Baumgartner, 2008). Note that a fit does not require matching the frame with a dispositional focus. The situational regulatory focus can be induced by the message itself. That is, a message that highlights a promotion goal (e.g. get energize) is more persuasive when it suggests a desirable outcome (e.g., "Boost your energy!) than when it implies an undesirable outcome of an inaction (e.g., "Do not miss boosting your energy!"). Vice versa, a message concentrating on a prevention goal (e.g. prevent disease) is less effective when it highlights what can be gained (e.g., "Avoid a cold!") than when aversive consequences resulting from inaction are implied (e.g., "Do not miss avoiding a cold!") (see Lee & Aaker, 2004).

Framing in different cultures

As discussed before, framing can be conceived as a linguistic phenomenon (Keren, 2011b). Given that languages differ across cultures, culture can be expected to be a pertinent moderator of framing. For instance, a product label may sound attractive to speakers of one language, but sound unpleasant to speakers of another. In still other languages, the label may even have negative semantic connotations, demonstrating that global marketers should be careful when choosing product and service names. Arguably, marketers at the Japanese manufacturer Mitsubishi were unaware that the name of their off-road car "Pajero" is offensive among Spanish-speaking persons.

However, marketing communication may not only get lost in translation. Different cultures have their unique values, and international campaigns, therefore, should also consider which attributes, goals and existential values are rewarding in a given culture above and beyond linguistic differences (Airhihenbuwa, 1995).

The majority of research on cultural influences on framing effects contrasted Eastern and Western cultures. A notable finding is that framing in its broadest sense is not bound to Western cultures, but framing effects on evaluations and judgements occur across cultures (Sharp & Salter, 1997). Hence, classic framing effects captured by prospect theory (Kahneman & Tversky, 1979) are descriptive of Asian people's decisions, too. However, effects may differ in size. For instance, Koreans and Chinese are more optimistic than Americans, and as a consequence they are typically less loss averse (Arkes, Hirshleifer, Jiang, & Lim, 2010).

Other researchers focused on risk attitudes. Whereas some studies suggest that decision makers from Eastern cultures are more risk seeking than decision makers from Western cultures (Marshall, Huan, Xu, & Nam, 2011), others indicate the opposite conclusion (Colgate, Tong, Lee, & Farley, 2007). Such discrepancies may partly reflect different operationalizations. However, they may also reflect differences in risk-seeking behaviour across domains: While Chinese are typically more risk seeking in the financial domain, Americans are typically more risk seeking in medical and academic decisions – an effect that can be explained by the fact that members of collectivist societies such as China are more likely to receive financial support if they are in need (Hsee & Weber, 1999). Importantly, and in line with prospect theory, people seem to be risk averse with regard to gains, but risk seeking with regard to losses, across a wide range of cultures (Rieger, Wang, & Hens, 2014).

Besides the mere geographical distinction, researchers usually refer to psychological mindsets when studying differences between Eastern and Western cultures. Most prominently, cultures are described with regard to predominant value orientations (i.e., collectivist vs. individualist; see Hofstede, 1984; Triandis, 2001) and how people construe their selves (i.e., interdependent vs. independent; see Markus & Kitayama, 1991). From this perspective, people from Eastern cultures differ from their Western counterparts in that they put more weight on the wealth of their group (i.e., collectivist value orientation) than on their own, and that they define themselves regarding their social relations (i.e., an interdependent self-construal) rather than their personal values and opinions. Such constructs may actually serve to explain observed cultural variation in the aforementioned effects (Arkes et al., 2010; Rieger et al., 2014). As such, risk aversion in the domain of gains is more pronounced in collectivistic countries, while risk seeking in losses is reduced in those countries, which can be explained via the better societal safety net in interdependent cultures (for the "cushion hypothesis", see Hsee & Weber, 1999). Crucially, since these variables strongly affect information processing (Oyserman & Lee, 2008), it is one step further to predict that culture moderates the effectiveness of message frames. In this line of thinking, Mandel (2003) replicated this pattern of risk-seeking preferences across independent versus interdependent cultures when priming US-American participants with the different cultural mindsets (however, see also Hamilton & Biehal, 2005).

Lee, Aaker and Gardner (2000) proposed and found that interdependent selves would be more responsive to prevention-focused information. In line with their reasoning, they showed that Eastern participants are more prevention focused than their Western counterparts. Remember that a prevention focus is typically associated with a higher sensitivity for losses (vs. gains). Accordingly, loss-framed messages were relatively more persuasive than win-framed messages in a sample with an East Asian background as compared with a sample of white Britons (Uskul, Sherman, & Fitzgibbon, 2009; see also Lechuga, Swain, & Weinhardt, 2011), a finding inviting future research on moderators of culture-dependent optimism.

Fit effects beyond framing

In the previous paragraphs we have reported a series of fit effects. Hence, the application of well-studied frames (e.g., positive vs. negative frame; gain vs. loss frame) in persuasion can be optimized by matching the frames with characteristics of the target clientele (i.e., their cognitive mindsets, their culture etc.). Given the practical significance of matching messages with the receiver, fit effects have been studied for numerous message aspects other than the frames reported in this chapter. Many of those fit effects suppose a rather broad definition of framing based on a very lenient conceptualization of equivalence across the frames. However, the respective message variation is often referred to as framing, and due to their practical relevance we reiterate some of them here.

One example is that messages can consist of language describing either an endorser's thoughts or an endorser's feelings. It has been shown that the former works better with persons who tend to evaluate things based on their thoughts (i.e., cognitively oriented persons) and men, whereas the latter works better with people who tend to evaluate issues based on their affective reactions (i.e., affectively oriented persons) and women (Mayer & Tormala, 2010). Thus, companies should carefully consider their clientele when phrasing advertising copy that "they feel" or "think" that consumers will "enjoy" or "profit from" their new product.

Further, many studies have elaborated on the interplay of linguistic frames and processing styles on persuasion outcomes. For instance, against the backdrop of construal level theory (Trope & Liberman, 2010), the persuasive impact of describing a product's benefits in concrete versus abstract terms depends on temporal distance. Some weeks prior to the release, an upcoming computer should be advertised by an abstract description (e.g., "The computer includes modern processor technology"). At the point of sale, however, it was advisable to describe the product in a concrete fashion (e.g., "The computer has a 3.9 GHz i7-Haswell processor"). A series of other message characteristics (e.g., highlighting why to use the product vs. how to use it) has been shown to create a fit effect with temporal distance on persuasive outcomes (e.g., Fujita, Eyal, Chaiken, Trope, & Liberman, 2008). Whereas consumers could aggregate concrete features into an abstract category, disaggregation from abstract to concrete is much more difficult or even impossible. Note that, in this context, the equivalence of the frames is much more debatable than in classical risky choice or attribute framing, where equivalence at least in logical terms is incontestable. Thus, one may argue whether these findings should still be considered as framing effects. We will elaborate on this discussion of equivalence and the resultant definition of framing in the subsequent section.

Equivalence and the rationality debate

Framing effects gain much of their appeal from the fact that preference shifts or even reversals are obtained for *equivalent* choice alternatives that differ only in the way in which they are presented. Indeed, the rationality debate that accompanied framing research from its very beginning – namely, the discussion of whether framing effects violate the invariance axiom of rational choice (Tversky & Kahneman, 1986) – is only pertinent in the light of some reasonable standard of equivalence. Preference reversals across *inequivalent* choice options neither represent a challenge to human rationality nor violate normative theories of choice (cf. Thaler, 1980).

The definition of equivalence thus is of central relevance when talking about framing effects – but what exactly does it mean for frames to be *equivalent*? Arguably, there is more than a single standard according to which one might define whether two frames may be considered equivalent. Indeed, a glance at the literature reveals that equivalence has been characterized in many different ways, such as, for instance, as "objective" (Levin et al., 1998), "unquestionable" (Quattrone & Tversky, 1988), "effective" (Tversky & Kahneman, 1981) or "formal" equivalence (Kühberger, 1998). However, the value of adding such adjectives with regard to clarifying the notion of equivalence has been questioned (Sher & McKenzie, 2006). Adding a qualifying adjective may simply raise the question of how to define the respective qualifier – what exactly does it mean for two frames to be "objectively" or "formally" equivalent?

Qualifying equivalence as "logical" or "mathematical" equivalence, however, is a different case. Logical equivalence can be unambiguously defined by computing the expected utilities implied by each frame. However, as Sher and McKenzie (2006, 2011) argue, there is no normative problem with logically equivalent frames generating preference asymmetries. Let us assume that there are two logically equivalent frames, A and B. Whenever there is some background condition C (not explicitly stated in either frame A or frame B), whose likelihood differs as a function of whether frame A or frame B was chosen, the mere fact that the speaker chose A rather than B leaks information about the likelihood of C. Given that C bears some relevance to the decision problem, preference asymmetries across the two frames A and B can be attributed to differences in the likelihood of C and, therefore, may be entirely reasonable from a rational point of view.

For instance, in one of their studies (Sher & McKenzie, 2006), participants received one empty cup and one cup filled with water at the beginning of the experiment. Then, they were asked to pour half of the water from one cup into the other. After this procedure, both cups were roughly identically filled with water. Nevertheless, when instructed to move "the half empty" (vs. "the half full") cup to one of the corners of the table, 69 per cent (vs. 46 per cent) of the participants chose the cup that was full at the beginning of the experiment. Thus, despite their logical equivalence, the two frames "half empty" and "half full" conversationally leaked different information about which cup the experimenter wanted to be moved and thereby affected participants' choices.

Based on their research, Sher and McKenzie (2006) suggest *information equivalence* as a benchmark when considering framing effects to be at odds with rational decision making. Information equivalence refers to the idea that frames need to be not only be logically equivalent, but also equivalent in terms of their information leakage, that is, in terms of the pragmatic intents that can be inferred from the mere usage of the particular frame. In the water cup experiment, the two frames evoked different inferences about the experimenter's intentions and thus were not informationally equivalent. Note that in the light of this argument, judgements about human rationality derived from framing research have to be considered much more carefully, because participants' responses are interpreted as picking up on subtle linguistic cues (such as the experimenter's choice of words) rather than as not following basic rules of logical reasoning.

Arguably, the concept of information equivalence may be considered a very strict conceptualization of the equivalence idea. Yet, it illustrates the importance of thoroughly analyzing the particular equivalence standard before prematurely calling human rationality into question.

To reconcile different concepts of equivalence, Keren (2011a) recently suggested not defining equivalence as a universal property, but restricting it to particular dimensions. For instance, in the 75 per cent lean versus 25 per cent fat ground beef example, the two frames indeed are logically equivalent. Yet, at the same time, they were shown to differ on the trustworthiness dimension – a butcher presenting his beef in terms of 25 per cent fat is considered more trustworthy than a butcher relying on the 75 per cent lean frame (for trust–choice incompatibility, see Keren, 2007). Thus, any identification of equivalence between two frames should address the specific dimensions that are involved (and probably also relevant dimensions that are not involved). Likewise, any conclusion about human rationality has to be considered in the light of the particular equivalence standard. Not detecting logical differences between simple percentages would surely qualify as irrational behaviour. However, being able to notice small linguistic nuances and interpreting them as hints towards a certain option appears to be quite rational from a pragmalinguistic perspective.

Above and beyond the rationality debate, framing effects are intriguing for being necessarily involved in real-world decision making. At the end of the day, any decision has to be framed in a certain way, which may substantially influence the decision outcome. A superficially small policy change regarding organ donation from an opt-in to an opt-out default can increase the donor rates by almost 60 per cent (Johnson & Goldstein, 2003). Governments cannot avoid making a decision about which choice model to adopt. In this regard, insights from the behavioural sciences into the pervasive influence of framing effects can be used in order to make informed decisions about how to optimally construct a choice context.

References

Airhihenbuwa, C. O. (1995). *Health and culture: Beyond the Western paradigm*. Thousand Oaks, CA: Sage.

Aquino, K., Steisel, V., & Kay, A. (1992). The effects of resource distribution, voice, and decision framing on the provision of public goods. *Journal of Conflict Resolution, 36*, 665–687.

Arkes, H. R., Hirshleifer, D., Jiang, D., & Lim, S. S. (2010). A cross-cultural study of reference point adaptation: Evidence from China, Korea, and the US. *Organizational Behaviour and Human Decision Processes, 112*, 99–111.

Beach, L. R., Puto, C. P., Heckler, S. E., Naylor, G., & Marble, T. A. (1996). Differential versus unit weighting of violations, framing, and the role of probability in image theory's compatibility test. *Organizational Behaviour and Human Decision Processes, 65*, 77–82. doi: 10.1006/obhd.1996.0007

Bless, H., Betsch, T., & Franzen, A. (1998). Framing the framing effect: The impact of context cues on solutions to the "Asian disease" problem. *European Journal of Social Psychology, 28*, 287–291.

Brehm, J. W. (1966). *A theory of psychological reactance*. New York, NY: Academic Press.

Bruner, J. S. (1957). On perceptual readiness. *Psychological Review, 64*, 123–154.

Cacioppo, J. T., & Petty, R. E. (1982). The need for cognition. *Journal of Personality and Social Psychology, 42*, 116.

Cesario, J., Grant, H., & Higgins, E. T. (2004). Regulatory fit and persuasion: Transfer from "feeling right". *Journal of Personality and Social Psychology, 86*, 388.

Cesario, J., Higgins, E. T., & Scholer, A. A. (2008). Regulatory fit and persuasion: Basic principles and remaining questions. *Social and Personality Psychology Compass, 2*, 444–463.

Chaiken, S., Liberman, A., & Eagly, A. H. (1989). Heuristic and systematic information processing within and beyond the persuasion context. In J. S. Uleman & J. A. Bargh (Eds.), *Unintended thought* (pp. 212–252). New York, NY: Guilford Press.

Chaiken, S., & Ledgerwood, A. (2012). A theory of heuristic and systematic information processing. In P. A. M. Van Lange, A. W. Kruglanski & E. T. Higgins (Eds.), *Handbook of theories of social psychology* (Vol. 1, pp. 246–266). Thousand Oaks, CA: Sage.

Colgate, M., Tong, V. T.-U., Lee, C. K.-C., & Farley, J. U. (2007). Back from the brink: Why customers stay. *Journal of Service Research, 9*, 211–228.

Covey, J. (2014). The role of dispositional factors in moderating message framing effects. *Health Psychology, 33*, 52.

Druckman, J. N. (2001). The implications of framing effects for citizen competence. *Political Behaviour, 23*, 225–256.

Druckman, J. N. (2011). What's it all about? Framing in political science. In G. Keren (Ed.), *Perspectives on framing*, (pp. 279–304.) New York, NY: Psychology Press.

Epstein, S. (1998). Cognitive-experiential self-theory. In D. F. Barone, M. Hersen & V. B. Van Hasselt (Eds.), *Advanced personality* (pp. 211–238). New York, NY: Plenum Press.

Fagley, N., Coleman, J. G., & Simon, A. F. (2010). Effects of framing, perspective taking, and perspective (affective focus) on choice. *Personality and Individual Differences, 48*, 264–269.
Freling, T. H., Vincent, L. H., & Henard, D. H. (2014). When not to accentuate the positive: Re-examining valence effects in attribute framing. *Organizational Behaviour and Human Decision Processes, 124*, 95–109.
Fujita, K., Eyal, T., Chaiken, S., Trope, Y., & Liberman, N. (2008). Influencing attitudes toward near and distant objects. *Journal of Experimental Social Psychology, 44*, 562–572. doi: 10.1016/j.jesp.2007.10.005
Ganzach, Y., & Karsahi, N. (1995). Message framing and buying behaviour: A field experiment. *Journal of Business Research, 32*, 11–17.
Garcia-Retamero, R., & Dhami, M. K. (2013). On avoiding framing effects in experienced decision makers. *The Quarterly Journal of Experimental Psychology, 66*, 829–842.
Gourville, J. T. (1998). Pennies-a-day: The effect of temporal reframing on transaction evaluation. *Journal of Consumer Research, 24*, 395–403.
Grice, H. P. (1975). Logic and conversation. In P. Cole & J. L. Morgan (Eds.), *Syntax and semantics 3: Speech acts* (pp. 41–58). New York, NY: Academic Press.
Hamilton, R. W., & Biehal, G. J. (2005). Achieving your goals or protecting their future? The effects of self-view on goals and choices. *Journal of Consumer Research, 32*, 277–283. doi: 10.1086/432237
Haugtvedt, C. P., Petty, R. E., & Cacioppo, J. T. (1992). Need for cognition and advertising: Understanding the role of personality variables in consumer behaviour. *Journal of Consumer Psychology, 1*, 239–260.
Higgins, E. T. (1997). Beyond pleasure and pain. *American Psychologist, 52*, 1280.
Higgins, E. T. (2000). Making a good decision: Value from fit. *American Psychologist, 55*, 1217.
Higgins, E. T. (2005). Value from regulatory fit. *Current Directions in Psychological Science, 14*, 209–213.
Hofstede, G. (1984). The cultural relativity of the quality of life concept. *Academy of Management Review, 9*, 389–398.
Hsee, C. K., & Weber, E. U. (1999). Cross-national differences in risk preference and lay predictions. *Journal of Behavioural Decision Making, 12*, 165–179.
Igou, E. R., & Bless, H. (2007). On undesirable consequences of thinking: Framing effects as a function of substantive processing. *Journal of Behavioural Decision Making, 20*, 125–142.
James, W. (1890). *The principles of psychology*. New York, NY: Henry Holt.
Johnson, E. J., & Goldstein, D. (2003). Do defaults save lives? *Science, 302*, 1338–1339.
Johnson, E. J., Hershey, J., Meszaros, J., & Kunreuther, H. (1993). Framing, probability distortions, and insurance decisions. *Journal of Risk and Uncertainty, 7*, 35–51.
Kahneman, D. (2000). Preface. In D. Kahneman & A. Tversky (Eds.), *Choices, values, and frames* (pp. ix–xvii). Cambridge: Cambridge University Press.
Kahneman, D., & Frederick, S. (2007). Frames and brains: Elicitation and control of response tendencies. *Trends in Cognitive Sciences, 11*, 45–46.
Kahneman, D., & Tversky, A. (1979). Prospect theory: An analysis of decision under risk. *Econometrica: Journal of the Econometric Society, 47*(2), 263–291.
Kahneman, D., & Tversky, A. (1984). Choices, values, and frames. *American Psychologist, 39*, 341.
Keren, G. (2007). Framing, intentions, and trust–choice incompatibility. *Organizational Behaviour and Human Decision Processes, 103*, 238–255.
Keren, G. (2011a). On the definition and possible underpinnings of framing effects: A brief review and a critical evaluation. In G. Keren (Ed.), *Perspectives on framing* (pp. 3–33). New York, NY: Psychology Press.
Keren, G. (2011b). *Perspectives on framing*. New York, NY: Taylor & Francis US.
Klayman, J., & Ha, Y.-W. (1987). Confirmation, disconfirmation, and information in hypothesis testing. *Psychological Review, 94*, 211–228.
Kühberger, A. (1998). The influence of framing on risky decisions: A meta-analysis. *Organizational Behaviour and Human Decision Processes, 75*, 23–55.
Lechuga, J., Swain, G. R., & Weinhardt, L. S. (2011). Impact of framing on intentions to vaccinate daughters against HPV: A cross-cultural perspective. *Annals of Behavioural Medicine, 42*, 221–226.
Lee, A. Y., & Aaker, J. L. (2004). Bringing the frame into focus: The influence of regulatory fit on processing fluency and persuasion. *Journal of Personality and Social Psychology, 86*, 205.
Lee, A. Y., Aaker, J. L., & Gardner, W. L. (2000). The pleasures and pains of distinct self-construals: The role of interdependence in regulatory focus. *Journal of Personality and Social Psychology, 78*, 1122.
Levin, I. P. (1987). Associative effects of information framing. *Bulletin of the Psychonomic Society, 25*, 85–86.
Levin, I. P., & Gaeth, G. J. (1988). How consumers are affected by the framing of attribute information before and after consuming the product. *Journal of Consumer Research, 15*(3), 374–378.

Levin, I. P., Jasper, J. D., & Gaeth, G. J. (1996). Measuring the effects of framing country-of-origin information: A process tracing approach. *Advances in Consumer Research*, *23*, 385–389.

Levin, I. P., Schneider, S. L., & Gaeth, G. J. (1998). All frames are not created equal: A typology and critical analysis of framing effects. *Organizational Behaviour and Human Decision Processes*, *76*, 149–188.

Levin, I. P., Schnittjer, S. K., & Thee, S. L. (1988). Information framing effects in social and personal decisions. *Journal of Experimental Social Psychology*, *24*, 520–529.

Mandel, N. (2003). Shifting selves and decision making: The effects of self-construal priming on consumer risk-taking. *Journal of Consumer Research*, *30*, 30–40. doi: 10.1086/374700

Markus, H. R., & Kitayama, S. (1991). Culture and the self: Implications for cognition, emotion, and motivation. *Psychological Review*, *98*, 224–253.

Marshall, R., Huan, T.-C. T., Xu, Y., & Nam, I. (2011). Extending prospect theory cross-culturally by examining switching behaviour in consumer and business-to-business contexts. *Journal of Business Research*, *64*, 871–878.

Mayer, N. D., & Tormala, Z. L. (2010). "Think" versus "feel" framing effects in persuasion. *Personality and Social Psychology Bulletin*, *36*, 443–454.

McElroy, T., & Seta, J. J. (2003). Framing effects: An analytic–holistic perspective. *Journal of Experimental Social Psychology*, *39*, 610–617.

McKenzie, C. R., & Nelson, J. D. (2003). What a speaker's choice of frame reveals: Reference points, frame selection, and framing effects. *Psychonomic Bulletin & Review*, *10*, 596–602.

McKenzie, C. R., Liersch, M. J., & Finkelstein, S. R. (2006). Recommendations implicit in policy defaults. *Psychological Science*, *17*, 414–420.

Meyerowitz, B. E., & Chaiken, S. (1987). The effect of message framing on breast self-examination attitudes, intentions, and behaviour. *Journal of Personality and Social Psychology*, *52*, 500.

Oyserman, D., & Lee, S. W. (2008). Does culture influence what and how we think? Effects of priming individualism and collectivism. *Psychological Bulletin*, *134*, 311.

Park, C. W., Jun, S. Y., & MacInnis, D. J. (2000). Choosing what I want versus rejecting what I do not want: An application of decision framing to product option choice decisions. *Journal of Marketing Research*, *37*, 187–202.

Peters, E. (2012). Beyond comprehension: The role of numeracy in judgments and decisions. *Current Directions in Psychological Science*, *21*, 31–35.

Peters, E., Västfjäll, D., Slovic, P., Mertz, C., Mazzocco, K., & Dickert, S. (2006). Numeracy and decision making. *Psychological Science*, *17*, 407–413.

Petty, R. E., & Cacioppo, J. T. (1986). The elaboration likelihood model of persuasion. *Advances in Experimental Social Psychology*, *19*, 123–205.

Petty, R. E., Cacioppo, J. T., & Schumann, D. (1983). Central and peripheral routes to advertising effectiveness: The moderating role of involvement. *Journal of Consumer Research*, *10*(2), 135–146.

Piñon, A., & Gambara, H. (2005). A meta-analytic review of framing effect: Risky, attribute and goal framing. *Psicothema*, *17*, 325–331.

Qualls, W. J., & Puto, C. P. (1989). Organizational climate and decision framing: An integrated approach to analyzing industrial buying decisions. *Journal of Marketing Research*, *26*, 179–192. doi: 10.2307/3172604

Quattrone, G. A., & Tversky, A. (1988). Contrasting rational and psychological analyses of political choice. *American Political Science Review*, *82*, 719–736.

Raghubir, P., & Srivastava, J. (2002). Effect of face value on product valuation in foreign currencies. *Journal of Consumer Research*, *29*, 335–347.

Rieger, M. O., Wang, M., & Hens, T. (2014). Risk preferences around the world. *Management Science*, *61*, 637–648. doi: 10.1287/mnsc.2013.1869

Roszkowski, M. J., & Snelbecker, G. E. (1990). Effects of "framing" on measures of risk tolerance: Financial planners are not immune. *Journal of Behavioural Economics*, *19*, 237–246.

Rothman, A. J., Martino, S. C., Bedell, B. T., Detweiler, J. B., & Salovey, P. (1999). The systematic influence of gain-and loss-framed messages on interest in and use of different types of health behaviour. *Personality and Social Psychology Bulletin*, *25*, 1355–1369.

Rothman, A. J., & Salovey, P. (1997). Shaping perceptions to motivate healthy behaviour: The role of message framing. *Psychological Bulletin*, *121*, 3.

Rozin, P., & Royzman, E. B. (2001). Negativity bias, negativity dominance, and contagion. *Personality and Social Psychology Review*, *5*, 296–320.

Sanford, A. J., Fay, N., Stewart, A., & Moxey, L. (2002). Perspective in statements of quantity, with implications for consumer psychology. *Psychological Science*, *13*(2), 130–134.

Shafir, E. (1993). Choosing versus rejecting: Why some options are both better and worse than others. *Memory & Cognition*, *21*, 546–556.

Shafir, E. (1995). Compatibility in cognition and decision. *Decision making from a cognitive perspective: Advances in research and theory*, *32*, 247.

Shafir, E., & LeBoeuf, R. A. (2002). Rationality. *Annual Review of Psychology*, *53*, 491–517.

Sharp, D. J., & Salter, S. B. (1997). Project escalation and sunk costs: A test of the international generalizability of agency and prospect theories. *Journal of International Business Studies*, *28*, 101–121. doi: 10.2307/155450

Sher, S., & McKenzie, C. R. (2006). Information leakage from logically equivalent frames. *Cognition*, *101*, 467–494.

Sher, S., & McKenzie, C. R. (2011). Levels of information: A framing hierarchy. In G. Keren (Ed.), *Perspectives on framing*, (pp. 35–63) New York, NY: Psychology Press.

Simon, A. F., Fagley, N. S., & Halleran, J. G. (2004). Decision framing: Moderating effects of individual differences and cognitive processing. *Journal of Behavioural Decision Making*, *17*, 77–93.

Slovic, P. (1995). The construction of preference. *American Psychologist*, *50*, 364–371.

Slovic, P., Griffin, D., & Tversky, A. (1990). Compatibility effects in judgment and choice. In R. M. Hogarth (Ed.), *Insights in decision making: A tribute to Hillel J. Einhorn* (pp. 5–27). Chicago, IL, US: University of Chicago Press.

Smith, S. M., & Levin, I. P. (1996). Need for cognition and choice framing effects. *Journal of Behavioural Decision Making*, *9*, 283–290.

Soman, D. (2004). Framing, loss aversion, and mental accounting. In D. J. Koehler, N. Harvey, D. J. Koehler & N. Harvey (Eds.), *Blackwell handbook of judgment and decision making* (pp. 379–398). Malden, MA: Blackwell Publishing.

Soman, D., & Gourville, J. T. (2001). Transaction decoupling: How price bundling affects the decision to consume. *Journal of Marketing Research*, *38*, 30–44.

Thaler, R. H. (1980). Toward a positive theory of consumer choice. *Journal of Economic Behaviour & Organization*, *1*, 39–60.

Triandis, H. C. (2001). Individualism and collectivism: Past, present, and future. *The handbook of culture and psychology* (pp. 35–50). New York, NY: Oxford University Press.

Trope, Y., & Liberman, N. (2010). Construal-level theory of psychological distance. *Psychological Review*, *117*, 440–463.

Tversky, A. (1977). Features of similarity. *Psychological Review*, *84*, 327–352.

Tversky, A., & Kahneman, D. (1981). The framing of decisions and the psychology of choice. *Science*, *211*, 453–458.

Tversky, A., & Kahneman, D. (1986). Rational choice and the framing of decisions. *Journal of Business*, *59*, 251–278.

Tversky, A., & Kahneman, D. (1991). Loss aversion in riskless choice: A reference-dependent model. *The Quarterly Journal of Economics*, 1039–1061.

Updegraff, J. A., & Rothman, A. J. (2013). Health message framing: Moderators, mediators, and mysteries. *Social and Personality Psychology Compass*, 7, 668–679.

Uskul, A. K., Sherman, D. K., & Fitzgibbon, J. (2009). The cultural congruency effect: Culture, regulatory focus, and the effectiveness of gain- vs. loss-framed health messages. *Journal of Experimental Social Psychology*, *45*, 535–541.

von Neumann, J., & Morgenstern, O. (1947). *Theory of games and economic behaviour* (2nd ed.). Princeton, NJ: Princeton University Press.

Wang, X. T. (1996). Framing effects: Dynamics and task domains. *Organizational Behaviour and Human Decision Processes*, *68*, 145–157.

Wänke, M. (1996). Comparative judgments as a function of the direction of comparison versus word order. *Public Opinion Quarterly*, *60*, 400–409.

Wänke, M. (2007). What is said and what is meant: Conversational implicatures in natural conversations, research settings, media and advertising. In K. Fiedler (Ed.), *Social communication* (pp. 223–255). New York, NY: Psychology Press.

Wänke, M., & Reutner, L. (2011). Direction-of-comparison effects: How and why comparing apples with oranges is different from comparing oranges with apples. In G. Keren (Ed.), *Perspectives on framing* (pp. 177–193). New York, NY: Psychology Press.

Wänke, M., Schwarz, N., & Noelle-Neumann, E. (1995). Asking comparative questions: The impact of the direction of comparison. *Public Opinion Quarterly*, *59*, 347–372.

Whitney, P., Rinehart, C. A., & Hinson, J. M. (2008). Framing effects under cognitive load: The role of working memory in risky decisions. *Psychonomic Bulletin & Review, 15*, 1179–1184.
Wilson, D. K., Kaplan, R. M., & Schneiderman, L. J. (1987). Framing of decisions and selections of alternatives in health care. *Social Behaviour, 2*, 51–59.
Winkielman, P., Halberstadt, J., Fazendeiro, T., & Catty, S. (2006). Prototypes are attractive because they are easy on the mind. *Psychological Science, 17*, 799–806.
Yi, S., & Baumgartner, H. (2008). Motivational compatibility and the role of anticipated feelings in positively valanced persuasive message framing. *Psychology & Marketing, 25*, 1007–1026.

20

Enhancing consumer behaviour with implementation intentions

Peter M. Gollwitzer, Maik Bieleke and Paschal Sheeran

Implementation intentions (Gollwitzer, 1993, 1999, 2014) are if-then plans that help individuals attain their goals. Implementation intentions have proven beneficial in various domains in which individuals fall short of attaining their goals, from health behaviour through academic achievement to interpersonal issues (for reviews, see Adriaanse, Vinkers, De Ridder, Hox, & De Wit, 2011; Bélanger-Gravel, Godin, & Amireault, 2013; Gollwitzer & Sheeran, 2006; Gollwitzer, 2014; Hagger & Luszczynska, 2014). The aim of this chapter is to present research on how implementation intentions influence the affective, cognitive and conative components of consumer behaviour. We outline the nature of implementation intentions and describe moderators and mediators identified in previous research. Next, we adopt the perspective of comprehensive models of consumer behaviour (e.g., Bettman, 1979; Blackwell, Miniard, & Engel, 2006; Howard & Sheth, 1969) and systematically review implementation intention effects along the lines of these models. Specifically, we describe how implementation intentions affect information acquisition (i.e., perception, processing and comprehension), components of the decision process (i.e., pre- and post-decisional evaluation) and internal and external influences on behaviour (i.e., affect, norms, priming and mimicry) in consumer context. We conclude by outlining topics for future research on implementation intentions in the domain of consumer behaviour.

What are implementation intentions and how do they work?

Forming implementation intentions (Gollwitzer, 1993, 1999, 2014) is a self-regulatory tool that helps to successfully attain one's goal intentions. Whereas goal intentions focus on desired future behaviours or outcomes ("I intend to reach outcome O!" or "I will perform behaviour B!"), implementation intentions specify a critical situation and link it to a goal-directed response in an if-then format: "*If* situation S is encountered, *then* I will initiate response R!" The if-component contains a good opportunity to act or an obstacle to goal attainment, while the then-component specifies the response to be initiated. The mental representation of the critical situation specified in the if-part of an implementation intention becomes a highly activated and easily accessible cue. As a consequence, the specified cue is more readily detected (e.g., Aarts, Dijksterhuis, & Midden, 1999; Webb & Sheeran, 2007) as it benefits from an attentional advantage (i.e., it draws attention) (Achtziger, Bayer, & Gollwitzer, 2012; Wieber & Sassenberg, 2006). Linking the situation to a response moreover creates a strong mental association between situation and response, enabling immediate (e.g., Gollwitzer & Brandstätter, 1997; Orbell & Sheeran, 2000) and efficient (e.g., Brandstätter, Lengfelder, & Gollwitzer, 2001; Lengfelder & Gollwitzer, 2001) initiation of the response without needing further conscious intent (Bayer, Achtziger, Gollwitzer, & Moskowitz, 2009; Sheeran, Webb, & Gollwitzer, 2005). The heightened cue accessibility and the automatic initiation of the respective response together mediate the beneficial effects of implementation intentions on rates of goal attainment (e.g., Parks-Stamm, Gollwitzer, & Oettingen, 2007; Webb & Sheeran, 2007, 2008).

In sum, forming implementation intentions enables consumers to strategically automate a desired behaviour, and this is of tremendous importance in particular for regulating antagonistic, unwanted automatic behaviours. Consider the case of habits, developed by repeatedly performing a behaviour in a certain context (e.g., Wood & Neal, 2009). Once habitual behaviours are established, they are triggered automatically by the context and thus are hard to replace by voluntary alternative behaviours. For instance, people find it difficult to start recycling their waste using special recycling containers, given that they are used to disposing of all kinds of different waste into one single dustbin. However, forming implementation intentions helps people to strategically automate new alternative behaviours, levelling out the automaticity advantage of habitual behaviours. All they have to do is to link the critical context (e.g., disposing waste) with the wanted alternative behaviour (e.g., recycling into the designated containers) in an if-then format (see Holland, Aarts, & Langendam, 2006).

A meta-analysis (Gollwitzer & Sheeran, 2006) involving over 8,000 participants in 94 independent studies revealed a medium-to-large effect size of implementation intentions on the rate of goal attainment ($d = 0.65$) beyond the effect of holding a mere goal intention ($d = 0.36$) (Webb & Sheeran, 2006). For instance, imagine consumers intending to buy a tablet computer having carefully compared the pros and cons of different brands via Internet comparison pages and test reports. These consumers might find it difficult to use the detailed information about the different products and instead rely on salient but superficial features (e.g., appearance) once they are in the shop. To effectively overcome this difficulty, consumers could form an implementation intention like "If I make my purchase decision, then I will first consider the comparative information I have about the different brands!"

When do implementation intentions work most effectively?

Different moderating and mediating processes of implementation intention effects have been identified (Gollwitzer & Sheeran, 2006; Prestwich & Kellar, 2014). For example, people must be committed to the underlying goal intention for implementation intentions to have effects on goal attainment (Achtziger et al., 2012; Orbell, Hodgkins, & Sheeran, 1997; Sheeran et al., 2005). Beyond this moderator, research has also identified circumstances under which implementation intentions work more effectively. For instance, heightened self-efficacy boosts implementation intention effects (Koestner et al., 2006; Wieber, Odenthal, & Gollwitzer, 2010), especially when goal attainment is difficult (e.g., purchasing a computer that matches one's skills and needs). Recent research has examined how mindsets, personal feelings of control and the number of goals and plans influence the effectiveness of implementation intentions.

Concrete versus abstract mindsets

Consumers often face a tradeoff between having a powerful strategy that helps them attain a certain goal and a more flexible strategy that can be adapted to changing requirements.

For instance, in familiar situations like shopping in a local grocery, consumers usually know what action is most instrumental to achieve their goals (e.g., buying vegetables to eat healthily or cheaper brands to save money) and may primarily struggle with implementing this action because of antagonistic habitual behaviours (e.g., buying fast food or always buying products of the same brand). These situations call for one powerful strategy rather than a set of strategies to be used flexibly. Unfamiliar situations such as investing in an emerging new stock market, on the other hand, do not usually allow consumers to identify a single most instrumental action in advance. Instead, consumers should flexibly take advantage of alternative, non-planned means as they emerge rather than implementing a pre-specified action. How can this tradeoff between effectiveness and flexibility be solved when using implementation intentions? It turns out that an appropriate mindset might be the key.

Wieber, Sezer and Gollwitzer (2014, Study 1) tested the effects of mindsets on implementation intentions in a situation with a single instrumental action. Specifically, participants were asked to perform two rounds of a handgrip task. After the first round, participants formed an implementation intention ("And if my muscles start hurting, then I will ignore the pain!") in addition to the goal to perform well. Then, an ostensibly unrelated questionnaire on personal relationships followed that induced a concrete versus an abstract mindset by asking participants *how* versus *why* they form and maintain personal relationships, respectively. This mindset manipulation influenced the effectiveness of implementation intentions in the second round of the handgrip task: How-mindset participants performed better than why-mindset participants. Apparently, the how-mindset facilitated the stimulus-controlled automaticity of implementation intentions (Gilbert, Gollwitzer, Cohen, Oettingen, & Burgess, 2009). These findings suggest that consumers who want to use an implementation intention to buy vegetables instead of fast food should envision *how* they act upon this plan, thus inducing a concrete mindset, rather than deliberating about *why* they want to eat more healthily.

Can mindsets enhance the flexibility of goal striving by implementation intentions as well? Bayuk, Janiszewski and Laboef (2010) investigated implementation intentions related to saving goals to address this question. Participants were instructed to write down how or why they save money to put them into a concrete versus abstract mindset, respectively. Afterwards, they were presented with several non-planned means of attaining their saving goals and rated the likelihood of using them. Participants were more likely to resort to non-planned behaviours when they adopted an abstract why-mindset as compared to a concrete how-mindset. Together with the results from Wieber et al. (2014), this study suggests how mindsets can solve the tradeoff between effectiveness and flexibility when using implementation intentions. Consumers who want to maximize the effectiveness of implementation intentions should adopt a concrete mindset (e.g., asking themselves *how* they aim to achieve their goals), whereas consumers who wish to maintain as much flexibility as possible should rather adopt an abstract mindset (e.g., asking themselves *why* they aim to achieve their goals).

Personal feelings of control

Moods can have strong effects on consumers' information processing and preferences. For instance, people process information about persuasive messages more carefully in a sad compared to an angry mood (e.g., Bodenhausen, Sheppard, & Kramer, 1994; Tiedens & Linton, 2001). Moreover, people in a sad mood prefer vacation destinations that promote relaxation rather than activity, while those in an angry mood prefer activity over relaxation (Rucker & Petty, 2004).

Of importance for implementation intention research, being in a sad versus angry mood is also associated with low versus high feelings of control (Keltner, Ellsworth, & Edwards, 1993).

Since forming implementation intentions and acting upon them is a form of action control, one might ask whether being in a sad versus angry mood affects the formation and effectiveness of implementation intentions. Maglio, Gollwitzer and Oettingen (2014) recently addressed this question from the perspective of emotion appraisal theories (Smith & Ellsworth, 1985) by experimentally inducing anger and sadness. For example, in one of their studies, participants named an important academic goal. In an ostensibly unrelated second task, they were instructed to take the perspective of a person who was treated unfairly (anger induction), experienced a personal loss (sadness induction) or prepared a shopping list (neutral affect). Next, participants returned to their initial task and were asked to complete sentence stems to describe how they think about their academic goal. Results showed that participants in the anger condition were significantly more likely to think about their goal in terms of if-then (implementation intention) statements than participants in the sadness condition. Subsequent experiments (Maglio et al., 2014, Studies 2 and 3) confirmed that this effect was mediated by feelings of personal control. Importantly, findings showed that angry individuals were not only more likely to form implementation intentions, but they also executed the planned behaviour more effectively. In sum, this line of research suggests that consumers in sad moods benefit less from implementation intentions, as being in a sad mood is associated with reduced personal control.

Number of goals and plans

Another important aspect regarding the strength of implementation intentions is setting an appropriate number of goals and plans. Forming single implementation intentions for goals leads to better goal attainment than forming several plans (Verhoeven, Adriaanse, Ridder, Vet, & Fennis, 2013). Verhoeven and her colleagues invited women with an intention to reduce their consumption of unhealthy snacks and asked them to initially monitor their snacking behaviour for three days by keeping a consumption diary (baseline measure). After participants had returned their diaries, they were instructed to specify either one or three implementation intentions. In the following three days, participants were again provided with a diary to monitor their snacking behaviour (follow-up measure). Participants with a single implementation intention snacked on fewer occasions and had a lower caloric intake in the follow-up measure compared to the baseline, whereas no change was observed in the condition with three implementation intentions. In a follow-up study (Verhoeven et al., 2013, Study 2), the authors argued that single plans might be superior because they avoid information interference (Kruglanski et al., 2002). In line with this reasoning, goal attainment was still optimal when participants formed multiple plans each targeting different (versus single) goals. The conclusion that can be drawn from this line of research is that consumers may formulate several implementation intentions but these should target different goals.

Moreover, consumers should feel able to manage the multiple goals they are pursuing when furnishing them with several implementation intentions. Dalton and Spiller (2012) assigned participants to single or multiple goals (e.g., "read a book for pleasure") to be achieved in the next couple of days and induced implementation intentions by asking them how, when and where they would try to achieve their goal(s). Afterwards, participants rated their commitment to each assigned goal and also to five non-assigned goals. On each of the following five days, they reported activities related to assigned and non-assigned goals and whether they had already achieved these goals. Beneficial effects of implementation intentions were observed for a single assigned (versus non-assigned) goal but not multiple assigned (versus non-assigned) goals. Moreover, commitment of single assigned goals was increased relative to non-assigned goals, whereas commitment to multiple assigned goals was rather low and similar to non-assigned goals. The authors attribute these differences in goal commitment and the resulting effectiveness of implementation intentions to changes in perceived goal difficulty: Planning for multiple goals highlights the difficulty of goal achievement and thus lowers goal commitment. In line with this reasoning, no differences in the effectiveness of implementation intentions for single versus multiple goals emerged when participants perceived the attainment of multiple goals as manageable (Dalton & Spiller, 2012, Study 3). Thus, forming implementation intentions for several goals is effective when attainment seems feasible and goal commitment remains high.

Taken together, the studies by Verhoeven et al. (2013) and Dalton and Spiller (2012) provide guidance for consumers who want to attain multiple goals and use implementation intentions to facilitate goal attainment. When the goals pertain to the same domain (e.g., snacking habits) it is advisable to furnish only one of these goals with an implementation intention; goals pertaining to different domains (e.g., snacking habits and thriftiness), might however each be furnished with an implementation intention. However, in the latter case consumers should be careful not to choose conflicting goals and make sure that their attainment is manageable.

Information acquisition, decision processes and behavioural influences

Comprehensive models of consumer behaviour (e.g., Bettman, 1979; Blackwell et al., 2006; Howard & Sheth, 1969) share a focus on three central aspects: information acquisition (e.g., perception, processing and comprehension), the decision process (e.g., pre- and post-decisional evaluation) and internal and external influences on behaviour (e.g., affect, norms, priming and mimicry). Again, it may be helpful to imagine a consumer who intends to buy a tablet computer. First, information about the different brands must be acquired by reading relevant pieces of information (e.g., product tests in the Internet), processing their content (e.g., attending to relevant technical features) and comprehending them in an unbiased manner (e.g., ignoring stereotypes about the country of origin). Second, available information must be evaluated (e.g., weighing the pros and cons of different brands) and updated (e.g., according to new information received in the store) during the actual decision process. Third, the decision must be protected against undesired internal (e.g., hinging the decision on an incidental mood) and external (e.g., being mimicked by the salesperson) factors that might influence the decision. Even in this simple purchase example, consumer behaviour depends on a complex interaction of several features that are often difficult to control. For instance, consumers may experience problems in acquiring relevant information (e.g., Jacoby, Chestnut, & Silberman, 1977) or find it hard to ignore irrelevant information (e.g., Meyvis & Janiszewski, 2002). Even if people have acquired relevant information, though, they may still fail to evaluate and integrate this knowledge properly (e.g., Hutchinson & Alba, 1991; Staw, 1981). As a consequence, a need for strategies that enhance consumer decision making has been recognized (e.g., Bazerman, 2001). Implementation intentions are such a strategy.

Can implementation intentions enhance information acquisition?

Perception

Consumers are often confronted with a lot of information, as companies are competing for customers' attention in a clutter of package designs, ads and product information (S.P. Anderson & de Palma, 2013; Pieters, Warlop, & Wedel, 2002). However, consumers need only a little of this information to attain their goals (e.g., identifying special offer displays in the supermarket when pursuing a thriftiness goal). Can implementation intentions facilitate the perception of such goal-relevant information? We addressed this question based on the observation that people can *consciously* process only one stimulus at a given time and must postpone conscious processing of other stimuli until processing of the current stimulus is complete (e.g., Pashler, 1994). Differences in perceptual performance can thus be investigated by presenting two successive stimuli: When the second stimulus appears after a long delay, a higher quality of perception will allow a more immediate initiation for processing the second stimulus. However, when the second stimulus appears after a short delay, perception quality does not matter because there is plenty of time for perceiving the second stimulus. In line with this reasoning, implementation intentions should lead to faster responses towards the second stimulus for long but not for short delays, assuming that they indeed affect perception quality.

Janczyk, Dambacher, Bieleke and Gollwitzer (2015, Study 2) tested this interaction hypothesis in an experiment involving a first auditory stimulus (i.e., a tone presented via headphones) and a second visual stimulus (i.e., horizontally arranged squares). At the start of a trial, a tone was presented and three unfilled squares appeared on the screen. After one of three possible delays, either one or two squares were coloured in white. Participants had to classify the pitch of the tone and the position of the filled squares. Importantly, trials with one filled square were associated with implementation intentions (e.g., "If the left square becomes white, press the left key!"), in contrast to control trials with two filled squares in which participants were free to choose a response. In line with the interaction hypothesis derived above, responses to the second stimulus were faster in implementation intention compared to control trials for the longest delay but not for the two shorter delays. This finding indicates that implementation intentions enhance the perception of stimuli, potentially helping consumers to efficiently perceive goal-relevant information as it emerges (e.g., special offer displays in the supermarket).

Processing

Perceiving goal-relevant information is the initial step in information acquisition – but can implementation intentions also enhance its processing, in particular in the presence of distracting irrelevant information? For instance, consumers with the goal of buying organic food might search a grocery store primarily for products carrying a special organic label. This can be an arduous task, given the sheer amount of available products and the quantity of information displayed on the packages that is irrelevant to the organic shopping goal. Those consumers would benefit from a strategy that facilitates their attentional selectivity for processing goal-relevant information. Can implementation intentions enhance the attention for a goal-relevant piece of information in such a selective way? Bieleke, Dambacher, Hübner and Gollwitzer (2016, Study 3) made use of a computational model of selective attention (Hübner, Steinhauser, & Lehle, 2010) to address this question. In each trial of the study, stimuli consisted of one relevant item flanked by distracting items. Participants classified the relevant item while trying to ignore the flanking items and formed an implementation intention for one of the relevant items (e.g., "And if I see the number 2, then I will immediately press the left mouse button!"). Accordingly, processing efficiency in implementation intention trials could be compared with the baseline efficiency achieved in control trials. Fitting response time and error distributions to the computational model revealed a higher efficiency of information processing in implementation intention trials compared to standard trials: participants were more efficient in weighting and filtering sensory information, identifying the stimulus and selecting the respective response. As a consequence, they were able to classify relevant items faster and this was achieved without a drop in accuracy. Accordingly, these results suggest that implementation intentions enhance efficiency of information processing, a feature that consumers can use to selectively attend to goal-relevant information and to shield it from irrelevant, distracting information (e.g., when searching for products with an organic label).

Comprehension

Even if consumers manage to perceive and process relevant information, they still need to arrive at an unbiased understanding of that information. This is particularly difficult when stereotypes or attitudes that can bias comprehension are activated outside of awareness (e.g., Greenwald & Banaji, 1995; Maison, Greenwald, & Bruin, 2004). Instead of judging a product solely by decision-relevant attributes like functionality or price, for instance, consumers often rely on judgements that are elicited by attitudes towards the product's country of origin (Liu & Johnson, 2005) or stereotypes evoked by the salesperson (Babin, Boles, & Darden, 1995). Similarly, the mere activation of stereotypes about one's group may decrease the likelihood of purchasing goods from out-group members independent of product quality (Lee, Kim, & Vohs, 2011). How can consumers use implementation intentions to protect comprehension from these biasing effects?

Mendoza, Gollwitzer and Amodio (2010, Study 1) tested whether implementation intentions can overcome bias engendered by automatically activated racial stereotypes. They used a computerized task that assesses how object categorization is biased by racial stereotypes. Specifically, participants were presented with images of black or white males holding either a gun or a neutral object (e.g., wallet or phone) and had to press a "shoot" button if the presented person carried a gun. As expected, participants displayed a strong racial bias reflected in higher error rates for stereotype-incongruent (e.g., black males holding a wallet) as compared to stereotype-congruent (black males holding a weapon) stimuli. However, participants who had formed the implementation intention "If I see a person, then I will ignore his race!" committed significantly fewer classification errors, indicating improved information comprehension. Further analyses revealed that this effect was caused by a reduction of the automatic activation of stereotypes.

Although highly effective, ignoring stereotypical information is not a viable strategy when people are not even aware of stereotype biases. For these situations, Webb, Sheeran and Pepper (2012) have tested implementation intentions that replace the automatically activated stereotypical response by a desired response. In one of their studies, the authors turned toward automatic responses to Muslim versus Scottish names and the attributes of terrorism versus peace. Participants were shown a pair of categories (e.g., Scottish and terrorism) at the top of the computer screen and had to press a button when a word belonging to one of those categories appeared below (e.g., Douglas or Bomb). The authors expected worse performance for incongruent (i.e., Muslim-peace) compared to congruent category (i.e., Muslim-terrorism) pairings and this hypothesis found support in a condition with standard task instructions. However, when participants had received an implementation intention specifying an alternative response in the critical situation, no differences between Muslim-terrorism and Muslim-peace pairings were observed. Further analyses revealed that this effect was due to a stronger association between Muslim and peace forged in the implementation intention condition.

Taken together, the research by Mendoza et al. (2010) and Webb et al. (2012) suggests that implementation intentions help consumers to base their decisions on properly comprehended rather than stereotypical information. This has immediate effects on decision quality; for instance, comparing products across important dimensions (e.g., price, functionality and sustainability) will probably lead to better decisions than judging the products by stereotypes about their country of origin.

Can implementation intentions facilitate the decision process?

In the decision process, consumers need to evaluate pre-decisional information (e.g., pros and cons of different alternatives) and post-decisional information (e.g., feedback) in order to make good decisions. In the following part, we review studies on how implementation intentions can facilitate information evaluation to enhance the decision process.

Pre-decisional evaluation

Consumer decisions often occur in interaction with other group members (e.g., relatives, colleagues or peers). In these cases, goal striving becomes a collective endeavour and it is important that group members share information that is relevant for making good decisions, and that they overcome obstacles to goal attainment conjointly. Thürmer, Wieber and Gollwitzer (2015) turned to problems which can be optimally solved only when group members share individually available information (Stasser & Titus, 1985) to test whether implementation intentions can facilitate the exchange and integration of decision-relevant information in groups. Participants faced different problems (e.g., renting an apartment) and initially had to make a decision based on their private information about various options. Afterwards they were given the opportunity to exchange information regarding these options with two other group members. By design, considering information held by others was the best way to solve the problems as privately held information favoured an inferior option. Optimal decisions therefore required participants to review new information about previously non-preferred options and to revise their initial choice. Prior to the task, participants set the goal to find the optimal decision alternative and control group participants received the additional strategy to "go over the advantages of the non-preferred alternatives again". Implementation intention participants received a similar strategy in an if-then format: "And when we finally take the decision sheet to note our preferred alternative, then we will go over the advantages of the non-preferred alternatives again!" It was observed that control group participants made optimal decisions significantly less often than implementation intention participants. Content analyses of the group discussions revealed that implementation intention groups discussed a larger percentage of unshared information, and this enhanced information exchange in turn may have enabled them to better revise their initial decisions. These results suggest that implementation intentions can benefit consumer decision making in groups by facilitating the exchange and integration of decision-relevant information.

Post-decisional evaluation

People have difficulties in revising decisions in line with emerging negative feedback (Henderson, Gollwitzer, & Oettingen, 2007), and even persist in investing resources in an evidently vain course of action – a phenomenon referred to as the *sunk cost fallacy* (e.g., Arkes & Blumer, 1985; Staw, 1981). This problem pertains, for instance, to consumers taking an already paid for vacation even when they already regret the choice of the vacation resort (Arkes & Blumer, 1985), managers evaluating employees that they were responsible for hiring more favourably, irrespective of the employees' performance (Bazerman, Beekun, & Schoorman, 1982) and inventors continuously spending money, time and effort on a project despite professional advice to quit (Åsterbro, Jeffrey, & Adomdza, 2007).

Given the ubiquity and severe consequences of the sunk cost fallacy (reviews by Roth, Robbert, & Straus, 2015; Sleesman, Conlon, McNamara, & Miles, 2012), Wieber, Thürmer and Gollwitzer (2015, Study 1) investigated whether implementation intentions can be used to enhance the integration of decision-relevant feedback. They asked triads of participants to assume the role of a city council responsible for a kindergarten construction project. The task consisted of three consecutive phases in which participants decided on their investments in the project. Prior to the task, participants formed the goal "We want to make the optimal investment decision in each phase!" Goal intention participants added the control strategy "We want to judge the project as neutral observers who are not responsible for earlier investment decisions!", whereas implementation intention participants added the if-then plan: "If we are about to make an investment decision, then we will judge the project as neutral observers who are not responsible for earlier decisions!" In the task, a sunk cost problem was created by providing feedback about the current status of the project before the investment decision in each phase. This feedback was extremely positive at the beginning (e.g., donation of a developable plot) and encouraged a high level of initial investment. However, the feedback became more and more discouraging as participants progressed through the task (e.g., detection of oil contaminations in the sandpit) and thus called for a reduction in investments.

Replicating prior research on the sunk cost fallacy, goal intention participants did not adjust their investment levels to the increasingly poor prospects of the kindergarten project. In contrast, implementation intention participants integrated the feedback in their decisions and reduced their investment level accordingly. Following up on the mechanisms of this effect, Wieber et al. (2015, Study 2) observed no differences between conditions in the amount of time spent on arriving at their decisions, but found that the concepts used in the provided strategies (i.e., "decide", "invest") were more accessible for implementation intention participants as compared to goal intention participants. This suggests that implementation intentions curbed the sunk cost fallacy by automating a complex information evaluation process rather than by amplifying information search.

Can implementation intentions control internal and external influences on consumer behaviour?

Several factors can exert unwanted influence on consumers' decision making. Below, we discuss how implementation intentions can help people better manage both internal (i.e., affect and norms) and external (i.e., priming and mimicry) influences.

Negative mood and feelings

Emotions have an important impact on consumer behaviour (e.g., Bagozzi, Gopinath, & Nyer, 1999). For instance, it has been argued that more hours of daylight and sunshine increase stock market returns by inducing positive mood and increasing the willingness to take risks (Hirshleifer & Shumway, 2003; Kamstra, Kramer, & Levi, 2003). However, moods and emotions often have unwanted effects on information processing and decision making (review by Pham, 2007), thus hindering goal attainment. Can consumers use implementation intentions to regulate unwanted affective influences? Plenty of research suggests an affirmative answer to this question (meta-analysis by Webb, Schweiger Gallo, Miles, Gollwitzer, & Sheeran, 2012) and we provide two examples relevant for consumer behaviour.

Webb, Sheeran, et al. (2012, Study 2) found that implementation intentions help regulate detrimental effects of negative mood and arousal on risk-taking. In one of their studies, participants were placed in an aroused (versus neutral) mood and subsequently made a series of risky betting decisions. For each decision, they were presented with red and blue boxes at varying ratios (from 9:1 to 1:9) and told that a token was hidden behind one of these boxes. Participants could then bet money on the colour of the box with the token. In this task, dealing with risks in a sophisticated manner required sensitivity to the relative risk associated with a betting decision (e.g., taking more risks when the ratio was 9:1 rather than 6:4). Participants with an implementation intention ("If I am asked to make a bet, then I will pay close attention to the number of red versus blue boxes!") conformed to this reasoning and remained sensitive to relative risks even when put in an aroused mood. In contrast, participants with the mere goal intention to perform well made similar betting decisions independent of the box ratio, indicating that they paid little attention to relative risks.

Another example for unwanted affective influences on consumer behaviour is the feeling of doubt and worry which accompanies self-handicapping (Jones & Berglas, 1978). For instance, consumers may adopt low goals to avoid disappointment after failure (Cho & Johar, 2011) or refrain from buying goods they want because they might later regret the purchase (Bolton & Alba, 2012). To investigate whether implementation intentions can help regulate the doubts and worries that lead to self-handicapping, Thürmer, McCrea and Gollwitzer (2013) asked participants to take a test supposedly called CFIT and described it as a measure of either intelligence (highly threatening) or perception style (less threatening). When facing the highly threatening intelligence test rather than the perception style test, participants with the mere goal intention to perform well ("I want to achieve my maximum result in the CFIT!") reported to be more stressed in their everyday life (claimed self-handicap: Study 1) and chronic self-handicappers even prepared less adequately for the test (behavioural self-handicap: Study 2). However, both effects were eliminated when participants formed an additional implementation intention ("And when I start with Part 2 of the study, then I will ignore my worries and tell myself: I can do it!"). Together with the study by Webb, Sheeran, et al. (2012), these findings suggest that implementation intentions can aid consumers in regulating undesired effects of moods and emotions on behaviour.

The mood and emotion effects outlined above are instances of incidental affect, that is, affect that is generated by the situation that then informs peoples' stimulus-relevant responses. It is also important to consider *integral affect,* or the affect engendered by the stimulus (consumer product) itself, as optimal consumer decisions can be derailed not only by current moods and emotions, but also by overweighing feelings about a product at the expense of thoughts about the product's utility (pros vs. cons). Sheeran, Webb and Gollwitzer (2016) investigated whether implementation intentions could help people to override their positive feelings towards a target behaviour and make a decision that was more in line with their thinking. UK students indicated their thoughts and feelings about getting drunk. In general, participants thought that drunkenness was a bad idea (negative thoughts) but rather enjoyable (positive feelings). One-half of the sample formed an implementation intention to help them manage their positive affect towards drunkenness (i.e., "If I have the urge to get drunk, then I instantly ignore that feeling and tell myself 'I can get drunk another night!'"). Findings showed that control participants had decided to get drunk 25 per cent more often over the subsequent week compared to implementation intention participants. Moreover, whereas feelings about drunkenness predicted decisions for control participants, feelings were no longer influential when an if-then plan had been formed. For implementation intention participants, only their thoughts about drunkenness predicted the decisions they had made.

Social norms

Many consumers who enter a shop with a specific purchase in mind make additional, unplanned purchases (impulse shopping) (Kollat & Willett, 1967; Rook, 1987). Impulse shopping is a widespread behaviour that elicits shame and guilt as a psychological consequence beyond the financial problems created by excess spending (Yi & Baumgartner, 2011). Many consumers have difficulties gaining control over their shopping impulses (Verplanken & Sato, 2011; Vohs & Faber, 2007); a problem that is amplified when shopping in groups due to the activation of indulgence norms (Luo, 2005; Mangleburg, Doney, & Bristol, 2004). Can consumers shield their shopping preferences from these undesired social norms by using implementation intentions? To answer this question, Thürmer, Wieber and Gollwitzer (2016, Study 2) established social norms by asking participants to read vignettes describing activities that are common in interactions with friends from home (indulgence norm) or student peers (frugality norm). Afterwards, they were asked to participate in a consumption study requiring them to shop for food items to cook a meal for either friends or peers. In preparation for this task, some participants received implementation intention instructions ("If we want to put something in our shopping cart, then we will take only what we really need!"), whereas others received control plan instructions without the if-then link ("We will only put things in our shopping cart that we really need!") or plans lacking a helpful strategy ("If we want something that we really need, then we will put it in our shopping cart!"). In line with prior research (Luo, 2005), participants selected more products that were not necessary for preparing the meal when shopping for their friends from home rather than student peers, indicating greater impulse shopping due to a stronger indulgence norm. However, implementation intentions significantly reduced this norm effect, especially when using the if-then format. Thus, implementation intentions protected consumers from acting in line with an activated social indulgence norm.

Priming

It has been suggested that consumer behaviour is influenced by priming, the conscious or non-conscious activation of an action-related construct or goal (e.g., Bargh, 2002; Dijksterhuis, Smith, Baaren, & Wigboldus, 2005). As an instance of goal priming, consumers who were primed with prestige versus thrift goals became more likely to subsequently purchase expensive goods (Chartrand, Huber, Shiv, & Tanner, 2008). Beyond creating preference change, however, priming may also negatively affect consumer well-being. For example, cute product primes foster indulgent consumer behaviour (Nenkov & Scott, 2014) and social primes manage to activate alcohol consumption (Sheeran, Aarts, et al., 2005). It is difficult to control these priming effects on behaviour because people are commonly not aware of them (Oettingen, Grant, Smith, Skinner, & Gollwitzer, 2006; Wilson & Brekke, 1994).

Implementation intentions have recently been shown to provide strategic control of priming effects (Gollwitzer, Sheeran, Trötschel, & Webb, 2011; Webb, Sheeran, & Gollwitzer, 2012). For instance, one study tested whether implementation intentions can be used to control the effects of social goal primes on the readiness to drink alcohol. Participants were told that they would work on a verb identification task as part of a language study. Prior to this task, they were asked to answer two ostensibly unrelated questionnaires. The first questionnaire manipulated the kind of implementation intention; half of the participants formed an implementation intention to prevent excessive drinking (related condition), whereas the remaining half formed an implementation intention geared at preventing excessive snacking (unrelated condition). The implementation intentions were formed by completing the sentence "As soon as I think about drinking [eating snack food], then I will ignore these thoughts and tell myself to…!" The second questionnaire was introduced as a survey of students' university life. The goal prime was manipulated by asking questions that were either related to socializing (social goal prime) or studying behaviour (academic goal prime). In the subsequent verb identification task, participants were instructed to judge as fast and as accurately as possible whether a string of letters was a verb or not. In some trials the verb *drinking* was presented, and response times in these trials were averaged into a measure of the readiness to drink. Results showed a greater readiness to drink (as indexed by shorter response times to the word drinking) for the social compared to the academic goal prime. However, this priming effect emerged only when participants formed an unrelated implementation intention, and was absent when participants had formed an implementation intention to ignore drinking-related thoughts. These findings suggest that people can ward off unwanted priming effects by using implementation intentions.

Mimicry

Another powerful external influence on consumer behaviour is mimicry, the automatic imitation of behaviours (Chartrand & Bargh, 1999). Being mimicked can bias consumer decisions by increasing persuasiveness and rapport. For instance, restaurant guests give larger tips when being mimicked by the service person (van Baaren, Holland, Steenaert, & van Knippenberg, 2003), and customers are more likely to comply with the suggestions of a mimicking salesperson (Jacob, Guéguen, Martin, & Boulbry, 2011). Similarly, the success of launching new (and potentially superior) products may not only depend on objective criteria like functionality and price but also on mimicry effects on liking (Tanner, Ferraro, Chartrand, Bettman, & Van Baaren, 2014). As these examples suggests, the effects of mimicry on choice may not represent consumers' actual preferences. Hence, a strategy to control mimicry effects on consumer behaviour could help to better align consumer preferences and behaviour.

In a recent study, Wieber, Gollwitzer and Sheeran (2014, Study 2) tested whether implementation intentions can be used to regulate the automatic effects of being mimicked on the decision to spend money. In their study, participants were first instructed to adopt the goal of being thrifty ("I want to be thrifty with my money!"). One-half of the participants then added a control strategy ("I will save my money for important investments!"), whereas the remaining half added an implementation intention ("And if I am tempted to buy something, then I will tell myself: I will save my money for important investments!"). In a subsequent, allegedly unrelated interview about students' satisfaction, participants were either mimicked by the experimenter (i.e., imitation of body postures) or not. At the end of the interview, the experimenter asked for a favour: to exchange their monetary compensation for left over coffee vouchers and chocolate bars (thereby challenging participants' thriftiness goal by providing the chance to spent money on food items). It was found that participants with the control strategy spent more money when being mimicked by the interviewer than when not being mimicked. In contrast, implementation intention participants always spent only a small fraction of their money irrespective of the mimicry manipulation. Apparently, implementation intentions could regulate the biasing effects of mimicry on consumer behaviour.

The cross-cultural generalizability of implementation intentions

An implementation intention is a simple conditional statement using an if-then format, specifying that *if* a certain condition is met, *then* it will be followed by a consequence. If-then conditionals are considered to be an integral constituent of human cognition and thinking (J.R. Anderson, 1983; Johnson-Laird & Byrne, 2002; Stalnaker, 1981), and rank among those linguistic universals that appear consistently across all languages (Greenberg, 1963). Indeed, children as young as two-years old (Scholnick & Wing, 1991, 1992) and even apes (Premack & Premack, 1972) are able to grasp the concept of if-then conditionals. What renders forming implementation intentions a distinct self-regulation strategy simply pertains to the content used in the if-then conditional statement: The if-part specifies an opportune situation for attaining a goal, while the then-part specifies an instrumental, goal-directed behaviour. Thus, forming an implementation intention exploits a fundamental and natural way of how humans across cultures represent conditional information in their cognition and language in order to facilitate goal attainment. This simplicity is an appealing feature of implementation intentions for consumers because it renders them independent of cultural differences. However, the fact that the formation of implementation intentions is generalizable across cultures does not imply that the effects of forming them are generalizable as well; instead, there are multiple ways of how cultural differences might influence implementation intention effects and we shall present one example for illustration.

At the outset of our chapter, we have described a couple of variables that moderate the effectiveness of implementation intentions. Any systematic cultural difference in these moderating variables should in turn also influence the effects of implementation intentions. For instance, recall the observation that concrete mindsets facilitate the effectiveness of implementation intentions, whereas abstract mindsets enhance the flexibility to switch to non-planned means to attain a goal (Bayuk et al., 2010; Wieber et al., 2014). Are there systematic cultural differences with regard to whether people chronically adopt concrete versus abstract mindsets? A large body of research indicates that this is indeed the case: People from Eastern cultures adopt more direct and concrete modes of thought than Westerners (e.g., Choi, Dalal, Kim-Prieto, & Park, 2003; Nisbett, Peng, Choi, & Norenzayan, 2001). This fact is also reflected in the stronger use of verbs over adjectives in Eastern compared to Western languages, which allows comparatively more concrete and action-focused expressions in Eastern cultures (Maass, Karasawa, Politi, & Suga, 2006).

Chronic cultural differences in the reliance on concrete versus abstract mindsets will likely have consequences for implementation intention effects. For instance, it seems conceivable that the more concrete mindsets adopted by Easterners enhance the effectiveness of implementation intentions, whereas the more abstract mindsets held by Westerners should facilitate the flexibility in switching to alternative non-planned means. To date, research on such cultural effects regarding implementation intentions has not yet been conducted. However, it should be noted that cultural differences – such as those pertaining to mindsets – can be subject to situational influences and thus highly malleable (e.g., Oettingen, Sevincer, & Gollwitzer, 2008; Oyserman, 2011). For instance, participants in the Wieber et al. (2014) study could adopt a concrete versus an abstract mindset by merely asking how and why questions, respectively. In sum, we consider implementation intentions to be a self-regulation strategy that is fairly generalizable across cultures, and where cultural differences pertain to moderators of implementation intentions, we expect them to influence the effectiveness of implementation intentions.

Future directions

What is the optimal format of implementation intentions?

In the studies described so far implementation intentions were presented in a verbal if-then format. Is that format optimal or can the effects be augmented by additionally visualizing the situational cue and the response specified in the if-then plan? From laboratory tasks with rather abstract stimuli and tasks it is known that verbal, visual and combined verbal-visual implementation intention formats are equally effective (e.g., Burkard, Rochat, & Van der Linden, 2013; McFarland & Glisky, 2012; Meeks & Marsh, 2010). However, in everyday life settings using richer stimuli (e.g., food products) implementation intentions effects can indeed be augmented by visualizing the plan contents (e.g., Knäuper et al., 2011; Knäuper, Roseman, Johnson, & Krantz, 2009). For instance, Knäuper et al. (2011) investigated the effectiveness of implementation intentions in increasing fruit consumption. After asking participants to form standard verbal implementation intentions, the authors encouraged them to visualize the critical cues (e.g., seeing fruits at the cafeteria) and the cue-response links (e.g., taking and eating fruits when they are encountered). This verbal-visual implementation intention induction was observed to be more effective in increasing fruit consumption than the standard verbal implementation intention, indicating that consumers benefit from visualizing cues and responses in addition to formulating an if-then plan.

Granted that visualizing plan contents enhances the effectiveness of implementation intentions, one might wonder whether the visualization of cues and responses may already lead to the formation of if-then plans. Fennis, Adriaanse, Stroebe and Pol (2011) examined this question by presenting participants with a webpage advocating the usage of a pocket-guide listing fair-trade products to facilitate sustainable consumption. Importantly, the webpage described different situational cues (e.g., writing a shopping list, putting products in the shopping basket) and also provided an instrumental means (i.e., using the pocket-guide to check whether a product is fair-trade) without ever providing a verbal if-then plan. Nevertheless, the authors observed that a vivid description of the plan contents strengthened the accessibility of situational and response cues (e.g., "shopping list", "checking") and resulted in more actual purchases of sustainable products. These results are promising because they indicate that implementation intentions can be conveyed to consumers even when an explicit instruction to form if-then plans is impracticable.

Mentally contrasting wishes and obstacles

Forming implementation intentions has mainly been studied as a self-regulation strategy that is given to people in a paternalistic manner. Recently, a self-regulation strategy called *mental contrasting with implementation intentions* (MCII) (e.g., Oettingen, 2012, 2014) has been designed to allow people to personalize the content of the if- and then-parts of their implementation intentions. In mental contrasting, people are first encouraged to elaborate on their wishes and imagine the most desired outcomes of their fulfilment. Then they are asked to contrast these outcomes with the personal obstacles that stand in the way of achieving these outcomes. Mentally contrasting desired outcomes versus real-world obstacles creates a propensity to plan and enables a person to identify powerful, idiosyncratic barriers to wish fulfilment. Once these obstacles are identified, the person is ready to form if-then plans that link the presence of the obstacles to instrumental responses that are helpful in overcoming those obstacles (e.g., "If I encounter [my obstacle], then I will [my response to effectively manage the obstacle]!").

Mental contrasting has been found to benefit the effects of implementation intentions (e.g., Adriaanse et al., 2010; Kirk, Oettingen, & Gollwitzer, 2013). For example, MCII proved more effective in helping college students to break snacking habits than forming implementation intentions on their own. Importantly, mental contrasting increased perceived clarity about the personal obstacles involved in reducing unhealthy snacking. When Adriaanse, de Ridder and de Wit (2009) compared the effectiveness of if-then plans that were personalized vs. kept general (i.e., specifically referred to each participant's unique action control problem vs. a general action control problem), the personalized if-then plans turned out to be more effective. Information about MCII and how it can be applied is freely available at *woopmylife.org* (WOOP stands for the MCII components: Wish, Outcome, Obstacle and Plan).

Conclusion

In the present chapter, we have discussed implementation intentions as a self-regulatory tool that can be used to enhance consumer behaviour. Moderating and mediating processes that facilitate the effectiveness of implementation intentions were outlined, and implementation intentions were demonstrated to enhance the three central aspects of consumer behaviour: information acquisition, information elaboration during the decision process and the control of internal and external influences on behaviour. These beneficial effects of implementation intentions can enable consumers to improve their rates of goal attainment, and are known to be especially effective when people experience difficulties in achieving their goals (Gollwitzer & Sheeran, 2006). Moreover, evolving research on the personalization and optimization of implementation intentions using MCII and visualization suggests that implementation intentions can be conveyed to consumers in an easy and individually tailored manner.

Acknowledgements

The contributions of Peter M. Gollwitzer and Maik Bieleke were supported by the German Research Foundation (DFG) through research unit FOR 1882 Psychoeconomics.

References

Aarts, H., Dijksterhuis, A., & Midden, C. (1999). To plan or not to plan? Goal achievement or interrupting the performance of mundane behaviours. *European Journal of Social Psychology, 29*, 971–980.

Achtziger, A., Bayer, U. C., & Gollwitzer, P. M. (2012). Committing to implementation intentions: Attention and memory effects for selected situational cues. *Motivation and Emotion, 36*, 287–300. doi: 10.1007/s11031-011-9261-6

Adriaanse, M. A., de Ridder, D. T. D., & de Wit, J. B. F. (2009). Finding the critical cue: Implementation intentions to change one's diet work best when tailored to personally relevant reasons for unhealthy eating. *Personality & Social Psychology Bulletin, 35*, 60–71. doi: 10.1177/0146167208325612

Adriaanse, M. A., Oettingen, G., Gollwitzer, P. M., Hennes, E. P., De Ridder, D. T. D., & De Wit, J. B. F. (2010). When planning is not enough: Fighting unhealthy snacking habits by mental contrasting with implementation intentions (MCII). *European Journal of Social Psychology, 40*, 1277–1293. doi: 10.1002/ejsp

Adriaanse, M. A., Vinkers, C. D. W., De Ridder, D. T. D., Hox, J. J., & De Wit, J. B. F. (2011). Do implementation intentions help to eat a healthy diet? A systematic review and meta-analysis of the empirical evidence. *Appetite, 56*, 183–193. doi: 10.1016/j.appet.2010.10.012

Anderson, J. R. (1983). A spreading activation theory of memory. *Journal of Verbal Learning and Verbal Behaviour, 22*, 261–295. doi: 10.1016/S0022-5371(83)90201-3

Anderson, S. P., & de Palma, A. (2013). Shouting to be heard in advertising. *Management Science, 59*, 1545–1556. doi: 10.1287/mnsc.1120.1682

Arkes, H. R., & Blumer, C. (1985). The psychology of sunk cost. *Organizational Behaviour and Human Decision Processes, 35*, 124–140.

Åsterbro, T., Jeffrey, S. A., & Adomdza, G. K. (2007). Inventor perseverance after being told to quit: The role of cognitive biases. *Journal of Behavioural Decision Making, 272*, 253–272. doi: 10.1002/bdm.554

Babin, B. J., Boles, J. S., & Darden, W. R. (1995). Salesperson stereotypes, consumer emotions, and their impact on information processing. *Journal of the Academy of Marketing Science, 23*, 94–105.

Bagozzi, R. P., Gopinath, M., & Nyer, P. U. (1999). The role of emotions in marketing. *Journal of the Academy of Marketing Science, 27*, 184–206. doi: 10.1177/0092070399272005

Bargh, J. A. (2002). Losing consciousness: Automatic influences on consumer judgment, behaviour, and motivation. *Journal of Consumer Research, 29*, 280–285. doi: 10.1086/341577

Bayer, U. C., Achtziger, A., Gollwitzer, P. M., & Moskowitz, G. B. (2009). Responding to subliminal cues: Do if-then plans facilitate action preparation and initiation without conscious intent? *Social Cognition, 27*, 183–201.

Bayuk, J. B., Janiszewski, C., & LeBoeuf, R. A. (2010). Letting good opportunities pass us by: Examining the role of mindset during goal pursuit. *Journal of Consumer Research, 37*, 570–583. doi: 10.1086/654892

Bazerman, M. H. (2001). Consumer research for consumers. *Journal of Consumer Research, 27*, 499–504. doi: 10.1086/319624

Bazerman, M. H., Beekun, R. I., & Schoorman, F. D. (1982). Performance evaluation in a dynamic context: A laboratory study of the impact of a prior commitment to the ratee. *Journal of Applied Psychology, 67*, 873–876. doi: 10.1037//0021-9010.67.6.873

Bélanger-Gravel, A., Godin, G., & Amireault, S. (2013). A meta-analytic review of the effect of implementation intentions on physical activity. *Health Psychology Review*, 7, 23–54. doi: 10.1080/17437199.2011.560095

Bettman, J. R. (1979). *An information processing theory of consumer choice*. Reading, MA: Addison-Wesley.

Bieleke, M., Dambacher, M., Hübner, R., & Gollwitzer, P. M. (2016, Study 3). *If-then planning enhances selective attention: A diffusion model approach*. Manuscript in preparation.

Blackwell, R. D., Miniard, P. W., & Engel, J. F. (2006). *Consumer behaviour*. Mason, OH: Thomson/South-Western.

Bodenhausen, G. V, Sheppard, L. A., & Kramer, G. P. (1994). Negative affect and social judgment: The differential impact of anger and sadness. *European Journal of Social Psychology, 24*, 45–62. doi: 10.1002/ejsp.2420240104

Bolton, L. E., & Alba, J. W. (2012). When less is more: Consumer aversion to unused utility. *Journal of Consumer Psychology, 22*, 369–383. doi: 10.1016/j.jcps.2011.09.002

Brandstätter, V., Lengfelder, A., & Gollwitzer, P. M. (2001). Implementation intentions and efficient action initiation. *Journal of Personality and Social Psychology, 81*, 946–960. doi: 10.1037//0022-3514.81.5.946

Burkard, C., Rochat, L., & Van der Linden, M. (2013). Enhancing inhibition: How impulsivity and emotional activation interact with different implementation intentions. *Acta Psychologica, 144*, 291–297. doi: 10.1016/j.actpsy.2013.07.008

Chartrand, T. L., & Bargh, J. A. (1999). The chameleon effect: The perception-behaviour link and social interaction. *Journal of Personality and Social Psychology, 76*, 893–910. doi: 10.1037//0022-3514.76.6.893

Chartrand, T. L., Huber, J., Shiv, B., & Tanner, R. J. (2008). Nonconscious goals and consumer choice. *Journal of Consumer Research, 35*, 189–201. doi: 10.1086/588685

Cho, C. K., & Johar, G. V. (2011). Attaining satisfaction. *Journal of Consumer Research, 38*, 622–631. doi: 10.1086/660115

Choi, I., Dalal, R., Kim-Prieto, C., & Park, H. (2003). Culture and judgment of causal relevance. *Journal of Personality and Social Psychology, 84*, 46–59. doi: 10.1037/0022-3514.84.1.46

Dalton, A. N., & Spiller, S. A. (2012). Too much of a good thing: The benefits of implementation intentions depend on the number of goals. *Journal of Consumer Research, 39*, 600–614. doi: 10.1086/664500

Dijksterhuis, A., Smith, P. K., Baaren, R. B. Van, & Wigboldus, D. H. J. (2005). The unconscious consumer: Effects of environment on consumer behaviour. *Journal of Consumer Psychology, 15*, 193–202. doi: 10.1207/s15327663jcp1503_3

Fennis, B. M., Adriaanse, M. A., Stroebe, W., & Pol, B. (2011). Bridging the intention–behaviour gap: Inducing implementation intentions through persuasive appeals. *Journal of Consumer Psychology, 21*, 302–311. doi: 10.1016/j.jcps.2010.12.003

Gilbert, S. J., Gollwitzer, P. M., Cohen, A.-L., Oettingen, G., & Burgess, P. W. (2009). Separable brain systems supporting cued versus self-initiated realization of delayed intentions. *Journal of Experimental Psychology. Learning, Memory, and Cognition, 35*, 905–915. doi: 10.1037/a0015535

Gollwitzer, P. M. (1993). Goal achievement: The role of intentions. *European Review of Social Psychology, 4*, 141–185.

Gollwitzer, P. M. (1999). Implementation intentions: Strong effects of simple plans. *American Psychologist, 54*, 493–503.

Gollwitzer, P. M. (2014). Weakness of the will: Is a quick fix possible? *Motivation and Emotion, 38*, 305–322. doi: 10.1007/s11031-014-9416-3

Gollwitzer, P. M., & Brandstätter, V. (1997). Implementation intentions and effective goal pursuit. *Journal of Personality and Social Psychology, 73*, 186–199.

Gollwitzer, P. M., & Sheeran, P. (2006). Implementation intentions and goal achievement: A meta-analysis of effects and processes. *Advances in Experimental Social Psychology, 38*, 69–119.

Gollwitzer, P. M., Sheeran, P., Trötschel, R., & Webb, T. L. (2011). Self-regulation of priming effects on behaviour. *Psychological Science, 22*, 901–907. doi: 10.1177/0956797611411586

Greenberg, J. H. (1963). Some universals of grammar with particular reference to the order of meaningful elements. In J. H. Greenberg (Ed.), *Universals of language* (pp. 73–113). Cambridge, MA: MIT Press.

Greenwald, A. G., & Banaji, M. R. (1995). Implicit social cognition: Attitudes, self-esteem, and stereotypes. *Psychological Review, 102*, 4–27. doi: 10.1037//0033-295X.102.1.4

Hagger, M. S., & Luszczynska, A. (2014). Implementation intention and action planning interventions in health contexts: State of the research and proposals for the way forward. *Applied Psychology. Health and Well-Being, 6*, 1–47. doi: 10.1111/aphw.12017

Henderson, M. D., Gollwitzer, P. M., & Oettingen, G. (2007). Implementation intentions and disengagement from a failing course of action. *Journal of Behavioural Decision Making, 102*, 81–102. doi: 10.1002/bdm.553

Hirshleifer, D., & Shumway, T. (2003). Good day sunshine: Stock returns and the weather. *Journal of Finance, 58*, 1009–1032.

Holland, R. W., Aarts, H., & Langendam, D. (2006). Breaking and creating habits on the working floor: A field-experiment on the power of implementation intentions. *Journal of Experimental Social Psychology, 42*, 776–783. doi: 10.1016/j.jesp.2005.11.006

Howard, J. A., & Sheth, J. N. (1969). *The theory of buyer behaviour*. New York, NY: Wiley & Sons.

Hübner, R., Steinhauser, M., & Lehle, C. (2010). A dual-stage two-phase model of selective attention. *Psychological Review, 117*, 759–84. doi: 10.1037/a0019471

Hutchinson, J. W., & Alba, J. W. (1991). Ignoring irrelevant information: Situational determinants of consumer learning. *Journal of Consumer Research, 18*, 325–345.

Jacob, C., Guéguen, N., Martin, A., & Boulbry, G. (2011). Retail salespeople's mimicry of customers: Effects on consumer behaviour. *Journal of Retailing and Consumer Services, 18*, 381–388. doi: 10.1016/j.jretconser.2010.11.006

Jacoby, J., Chestnut, R. W., & Silberman, W. (1977). Consumer use and comprehension of nutrition information. *Journal of Consumer Research, 4*, 119–128.

Janczyk, M., Dambacher, M., Bieleke, M., & Gollwitzer, P. M. (2015). The benefit of no choice: Goal-directed plans enhance perceptual processing. *Psychological Research, 79*, 206–220. doi: 10.1007/s00426-014-0549-5

Johnson-Laird, P. N., & Byrne, R. M. J. (2002). Conditionals?: A theory of meaning, pragmatics, and inference. *Psychological Review, 109*, 646–678. doi: 10.1037//0033-295X.109.4.646

Jones, E. E., & Berglas, S. (1978). Control of attributions about the self through self-handicapping strategies: The appeal of alcohol and the role of underachievement. *Personality and Social Psychology Bulletin, 4*, 200–206.

Kamstra, M. J., Kramer, L. A., & Levi, M. D. (2003). Winter blues: A SAD stock market cycle. *American Economic Review, 93*, 324–343.

Keltner, D., Ellsworth, P. C., & Edwards, K. (1993). Beyond simple pessimism: Effects of sadness and anger on social perception. *Journal of Personality and Social Psychology, 64*, 740–752. doi: 10.1037/0022-3514.64.5.740

Kirk, D., Oettingen, G., & Gollwitzer, P. M. (2013). Promoting integrative bargaining: Mental contrasting with implementation intentions. *International Journal of Conflict Management, 24*, 148–165. doi: 10.1108/10444061311316771

Knäuper, B., Roseman, M., Johnson, P. J., & Krantz, L. H. (2009). Using mental imagery to enhance the effectiveness of implementation intentions. *Current Psychology, 28*, 181–186. doi: 10.1007/s12144-009-9055-0

Knäuper, B., McCollam, A., Rosen-Brown, A., Lacaille, J., Kelso, E., & Roseman, M. (2011). Fruitful plans: Adding targeted mental imagery to implementation intentions increases fruit consumption. *Psychology & Health, 26*, 601–617. doi: 10.1080/08870441003703218

Koestner, R., Horberg, E. J., Gaudreau, P., Powers, T., Di Dio, P., Bryan, C., Jochum, R., & Salter, N. (2006). Bolstering implementation plans for the long haul: The benefits of simultaneously boosting self-concordance or self-efficacy. *Personality & Social Psychology Bulletin, 32*, 1547–1558. doi: 10.1177/0146167206291782

Kollat, D. T., & Willett, R. P. (1967). Customer impulse purchasing behaviour. *Journal of Marketing Research, 4*, 21–31.

Kruglanski, A. W., Shah, J. Y., Fishbach, A., Friedman, R., Chun, W. Y., & Sleeth-Keppler, D. (2002). A theory of goal sytems. *Advances in Experimental Social Psychology, 34*, 331–378.

Lee, K., Kim, H., & Vohs, K. D. (2011). Stereotype threat in the marketplace: Consumer anxiety and purchase intentions. *Journal of Consumer Research, 38*, 343–357. doi: 10.1086/659315

Lengfelder, A., & Gollwitzer, P. M. (2001). Reflective and reflexive action control in patients with frontal brain lesions. *Neuropsychology, 15*, 80–100. doi: 10.1037/0894-4105.15.1.80

Liu, S. S., & Johnson, K. F. (2005). The automatic country-of-origin effects on brand judgments. *Journal of Advertising, 34*, 87–97. doi: 10.1080/00913367.2005.10639183

Luo, X. (2005). How does shopping with others influence impulsive purchasing? *Journal of Consumer Psychology, 15*, 288–294. doi: 10.1207/s15327663jcp1504_3

Maass, A., Karasawa, M., Politi, F., & Suga, S. (2006). Do verbs and adjectives play different roles in different cultures? A cross-linguistic analysis of person representation. *Journal of Personality and Social Psychology, 90*, 734–750. doi: 10.1037/0022-3514.90.5.734

Maglio, S. J., Gollwitzer, P. M., & Oettingen, G. (2014). Emotion and control in the planning of goals. *Motivation and Emotion, 38*, 620–634. doi: 10.1007/s11031-014-9407-4

Maison, D., Greenwald, A. G., & Bruin, R. H. (2004). Predictive validity of the implicit association test in studies of brands, consumer attitudes, and behaviour. *Journal of Consumer Psychology, 14*, 405–415. doi: 10.1207/s15327663jcp1404_9

Mangleburg, T. F., Doney, P. M., & Bristol, T. (2004). Shopping with friends and teens' susceptibility to peer influence. *Journal of Retailing, 80*, 101–116. doi: 10.1016/j.jretai.2004.04.005

McFarland, C., & Glisky, E. (2012). Implementation intentions and imagery: Individual and combined effects on prospective memory among young adults. *Memory & Cognition, 40*, 62–69. doi: 10.3758/s13421-011-0126-8

Meeks, J. T., & Marsh, R. L. (2010). Implementation intentions about nonfocal event-based prospective memory tasks. *Psychological Research, 74*, 82–89. doi: 10.1007/s00426-008-0223-x

Mendoza, S. A., Gollwitzer, P. M., & Amodio, D. M. (2010). Reducing the expression of implicit stereotypes: Reflexive control through implementation intentions. *Personality & Social Psychology Bulletin, 36*, 512–23. doi: 10.1177/0146167210362789

Meyvis, T., & Janiszewski, C. (2002). Consumers' beliefs about product benefits: The effect of obviously irrelevant product information. *Journal of Consumer Research, 28*, 618–635. doi: 10.1086/338205

Nenkov, G. Y., & Scott, M. L. (2014). "So cute I could eat it up": Priming effects of cute products on indulgent consumption. *Journal of Consumer Research, 41*, 326–341. doi: 10.1086/676581

Nisbett, R. E., Peng, K., Choi, I., & Norenzayan, A. (2001). Culture and systems of thought: Holistic versus analytic cognition. *Psychological Review, 108*, 291–310. doi: 10.1037/0033-295X.108.2.291

Oettingen, G. (2012). Future thought and behaviour change. *European Review of Social Psychology, 23*, 1–63. doi: 10.1080/10463283.2011.643698

Oettingen, G. (2014). *Rethinking positive thinking: Inside the new science of motivation*. New York, NY: Penguin.

Oettingen, G., Sevincer, A. T., & Gollwitzer, P. M. (2008). Goal pursuit in the context of culture. In R. Sorrentino & S. Yamaguchi (Eds.), *The handbook of motivation and cognition across cultures* (pp. 191–211). San Diego, CA: Elsevier/Academic Press.

Oettingen, G., Grant, H., Smith, P. K., Skinner, M., & Gollwitzer, P. M. (2006). Nonconscious goal pursuit: Acting in an explanatory vacuum. *Journal of Experimental Social Psychology, 42*, 668–675. doi: 10.1016/j.jesp.2005.10.003

Orbell, S., Hodgkins, S., & Sheeran, P. (1997). Implementation intentions and the theory of planned behaviour. *Personality & Social Psychology Bulletin, 23*, 945–954. doi: 10.1177/0146167297239004

Orbell, S., & Sheeran, P. (2000). Motivational and volitional processes in action initiation: A field study of the role of implementation intentions. *Journal of Applied Social Psychology, 30*, 780–797. doi: 10.1111/j.1559-1816.2000.tb02823.x

Oyserman, D. (2011). Culture as situated cognition: Cultural mindsets, cultural fluency, and meaning making. *European Review of Social Psychology, 22*, 164–214. doi: 10.1080/10463283.2011.627187

Parks-Stamm, E. J., Gollwitzer, P. M., & Oettingen, G. (2007). Action control by implementation intentions: Effective cue detection and efficient response initiation. *Social Cognition, 25*, 248–266.

Pashler, H. (1994). Dual-task interference in simple tasks: Data and theory. *Psychological Bulletin, 116*, 220–244. doi: 10.1037//0033-2909.116.2.220

Pham, M. T. (2007). Emotion and rationality: A critical review and interpretation of empirical evidence. *Review of General Psychology, 11*, 155–178. doi: 10.1037/1089-2680.11.2.155

Pieters, R., Warlop, L., & Wedel, M. (2002). Breaking through the clutter: Benefits of advertisement originality and familiarity for brand attention and memory. *Management Science, 48*, 765–781. doi: 10.1287/mnsc.48.6.765.192

Premack, A. J., & Premack, D. (1972). Teaching language to an ape. *Scientific American, 227*, 92–99. doi: 10.1038/scientificamerican1072-92

Prestwich, A., & Kellar, I. (2014). How can the impact of implementation intentions as a behaviour change intervention be improved? *European Review of Applied Psychology, 64*, 35–41. doi: 10.1016/j.erap.2010.03.003

Rook, D. W. (1987). The buying impulse. *Journal of Consumer Research, 14*, 189–199.

Roth, S., Robbert, T., & Straus, L. (2015). On the sunk-cost effect in economic decision-making: A meta-analytic review. *Business Research, 8*, 99–138. doi: 10.1007/s40685-014-0014-8

Rucker, D. D., & Petty, R. E. (2004). Emotion specificity and consumer behaviour: Anger, sadness, and preference for activity. *Motivation and Emotion, 28*, 3–21. doi: 10.1023/B:MOEM.0000027275.95071.82

Scholnick, E. K., & Wing, C. S. (1991). Speaking deductively: Preschoolers' use of If in conversation and in conditional inference. *Developmental Psychology, 27*, 249–258. doi: 10.1037/0012-1649.27.2.249

Scholnick, E. K., & Wing, C. S. (1992). Speaking deductively: Using conversation to trace the origins of conditional thought in children. *Merrill-Palmer Quarterly, 38*, 1–20.

Sheeran, P., Webb, T. L., & Gollwitzer, P. M. (2005). The interplay between goal intentions and implementation intentions. *Personality & Social Psychology Bulletin, 31*, 87–98. doi: 10.1177/0146167204271308

Sheeran, P., Webb, T. L., & Gollwitzer, P. M. (2016). *Guidance of behaviour by thoughts versus feelings: Situational and strategic determinants*. Manuscript under review.

Sheeran, P., Aarts, H., Custers, R., Rivis, A., Webb, T. L., & Cooke, R. (2005). The goal-dependent automaticity of drinking habits. *British Journal of Social Psychology, 44*, 47–63. doi: 10.1348/014466604X23446

Sleesman, D. J., Conlon, D. E., McNamara, G., & Miles, J. E. (2012). Cleaning up the big muddy: A meta-analytic review of the determinants of escalation of commitment. *Academy of Management Journal, 55*, 541–562. doi: 10.5465/amj.2010.0696

Smith, C. A., & Ellsworth, P. C. (1985). Patterns of cognitive appraisal in emotion. *Journal of Personality and Social Psychology, 48*, 813–838. doi: 10.1037//0022-3514.48.4.813

Stalnaker, R. C. (1981). A theory of conditionals. In W. L. Harper, R. Stalnaker & G. A. Pearce (Eds.), *Ifs: Conditionals, belief, decision, chance, and time* (pp. 41–55). Dordrecht, Netherlands: Reidel.

Stasser, G., & Titus, W. (1985). Pooling of unshared information in group decision making: Biased information sampling during discussion. *Journal of Personality and Social Psychology, 48*, 1467–1478. doi: 10.1037//0022-3514.48.6.1467

Staw, B. M. (1981). The escalation of commitment to a course of action. *Academy of Management Review, 6*, 577–587. doi: 10.1016/0749-5978(85)90049-4

Tanner, R. J., Ferraro, R., Chartrand, T. L., Bettman, J. R., & Van Baaren, R. (2014). Of chameleons and consumption: The impact of mimicry on choice and preferences. *Journal of Consumer Research, 34*, 754–766.

Tiedens, L. Z., & Linton, S. (2001). Judgment under emotional certainty and uncertainty: The effects of specific emotions on information processing. *Journal of Personality and Social Psychology, 81*, 973–988. doi: 10.1037/0022-3514.81.6.973

Thürmer, J. L., McCrea, S. M., & Gollwitzer, P. M. (2013). Regulating self-defensiveness: If-then plans prevent claiming and creating performance handicaps. *Motivation and Emotion, 37*, 712–725. doi: 10.1007/s11031-013-9352-7

Thürmer, J. L., Wieber, F., & Gollwitzer, P. M. (2015). A self-regulation perspective on hidden-profile problems: If–then planning to review information improves group decisions. *Journal of Behavioural Decision Making, 28*, 101–113. doi: 10.1002/bdm.1832

Thürmer, J. L., Wieber, F., & Gollwitzer, P. M. (2016). *Why does observing peer habits increase impulse buying? Processes and Remedies*. Unpublished manuscript. University of Konstanz.

Van Baaren, R. B., Holland, R. W., Steenaert, B., & van Knippenberg, A. (2003). Mimicry for money: Behavioural consequences of imitation. *Journal of Experimental Social Psychology, 39*, 393–398. doi: 10.1016/S0022-1031(03)00014-3

Verhoeven, A. A. C., Adriaanse, M. A., Ridder, D. T. D. D. E., Vet, E. D. E., & Fennis, B. O. B. M. (2013). Less is more: The effect of multiple implementation intentions targeting unhealthy snacking habits. *European Journal of Social Psychology, 43*, 344–354. doi: 10.1002/ejsp.1963

Verplanken, B., & Sato, A. (2011). The psychology of impulse buying: An integrative self-regulation approach. *Journal of Consumer Policy, 34*, 197–210. doi: 10.1007/s10603-011-9158-5

Vohs, K. D., & Faber, R. J. (2007). Spent resources: Self-regulatory resource availability affects impulse buying. *Journal of Consumer Research, 33*, 537–547. doi: 10.1086/510228

Webb, T. L., & Sheeran, P. (2006). Does changing behavioural intentions engender behaviour change? A meta-analysis of the experimental evidence. *Psychological Bulletin, 132*, 249–268. doi: 10.1037/0033-2909.132.2.249

Webb, T. L., & Sheeran, P. (2007). How do implementation intentions promote goal attainment? A test of component processes. *Journal of Experimental Social Psychology*, *43*, 295–302. doi: 10.1016/j.jesp.2006.02.001

Webb, T. L., & Sheeran, P. (2008). Mechanisms of implementation intention effects: The role of goal intentions, self-efficacy, and accessibility of plan components. *The British Journal of Social Psychology*, *47*, 373–395. doi: 10.1348/014466607X267010

Webb, T. L., Sheeran, P., & Pepper, J. (2012). Gaining control over responses to implicit attitude tests: Implementation intentions engender fast responses on attitude-incongruent trials. *British Journal of Social Psychology*, *51*, 13–32. doi: 10.1348/014466610X532192

Webb, T. L., Sheeran, P., Gollwitzer, P. M., & Trötschel, R. (2012). Strategic control over the unhelpful effects of primed social categories and goals. *Zeitschrift für Psychologie*, *220*, 187–193. doi: 10.1027/2151-2604/a000112

Webb, T. L., Schweiger Gallo, I., Miles, E., Gollwitzer, P. M., & Sheeran, P. (2012). Effective regulation of affect: An action control perspective on emotion regulation. *European Review of Social Psychology*, *23*, 143–186. doi: 10.1080/10463283.2012.718134

Webb, T. L., Sheeran, P., Totterdell, P., Miles, E., Mansell, W., & Baker, S. (2012). Using implementation intentions to overcome the effect of mood on risky behaviour. *British Journal of Social Psychology*, *51*, 330–45. doi: 10.1348/014466610X533623

Wieber, F., & Sassenberg, K. (2006). I can't take my eyes off of it – Attention attraction effects of implementation intentions. *Social Cognition*, *24*, 723–752.

Wieber, F., Odenthal, G., & Gollwitzer, P. M. (2010). Self-efficacy feelings moderate implementation intention effects. *Self and Identity*, *9*, 177–194. doi: 10.1080/15298860902860333

Wieber, F., Sezer, L. A., & Gollwitzer, P. M. (2014). Asking "why" helps action control by goals but not plans. *Motivation and Emotion*, *38*, 65–78. doi: 10.1007/s11031-013-9364-3

Wieber, F., Gollwitzer, P. M., & Sheeran, P. (2014). Strategic regulation of mimicry effects by implementation intentions. *Journal of Experimental Social Psychology*, *53*, 31–39. doi: 10.1016/j.jesp.2014.02.002

Wieber, F., Thürmer, J. L., & Gollwitzer, P. M. (2015). Attenuating the escalation of commitment to a faltering project in decision-making groups: An implementation intention approach. *Social Psychological and Personality Science*, *6*, 587-595. doi: 10.1177/1948550614568158

Wilson, T. D., & Brekke, N. (1994). Mental contamination and mental correction: Unwanted influences on judgments and evaluations. *Psychological Bulletin*, *116*, 117–142. doi: 10.1037/0033-2909.116.1.117

Wood, W., & Neal, D. T. (2009). The habitual consumer. *Journal of Consumer Psychology*, *19*, 579–592. doi: 10.1016/j.jcps.2009.08.003

Yi, S., & Baumgartner, H. (2011). Coping with guilt and shame in the impulse buying context. *Journal of Economic Psychology*, *32*, 458–467. doi: 10.1016/j.joep.2011.03.011

21

The elaboration likelihood model

Understanding consumer attitude change

Jacob Teeny, Pablo Briñol and Richard E. Petty

From billboards to magazine ads to television commercials, most instances of marketing are an attempt to persuade consumers to have a more favourable attitude towards a product, brand, company or service and ultimately influence purchase decision. Attitudes, as used in this chapter and throughout the literature, are summary evaluations indicating what people like and dislike. Although the end goal of a marketing campaign is undoubtedly to motivate behaviour or consumption of a product, a good first step is to persuade the consumer to have a favourable attitude towards the product. Importantly, not all attitudes are equally effective in guiding behaviour, and we will describe how attitudes can differ not only in their valence, but also in how consequential they are. Understanding both how to change attitudes and make them consequential requires consideration of the basic processes by which persuasion occurs.

In this chapter, we review how persuasion arises, particularly in the domain of marketing and consumer behaviour. To organize the processes and findings presented throughout, we use the Elaboration Likelihood Model (ELM) (Petty & Cacioppo, 1986; Petty & Briñol, 2012) as a conceptual framework. The chapter is divided into six sections: (a) the structure of communication and the three key factors of persuasion, (b) the Elaboration Likelihood Model, (c) the multiple roles that communication factors can have in persuasion, (d) the role of tailoring or matching in persuasion, and (e) future directions for consumer persuasion.

Communication factors in persuasion

Persuasion refers to any attempt to alter the contents of someone's mind. Although persuasion can be used to change many things such as a person's specific *beliefs* (e.g., a particular brand of soda has the healthiest ingredients), the literature tends to focus on people's *attitudes*, that is, people's general, summary evaluations (i.e., their positivity or negativity) towards a person, issue or object (Petty, Briñol, & DeMarree, 2007) including products and brands. People tend to behave in accordance with their attitudes – purchasing the products they like, avoiding the ones they don't – so by influencing relevant attitudes through persuasion, one is affecting the likelihood that people will engage in attitude-relevant behaviour, especially if the attitude induced is a strong one (for a review, see Petty & Krosnick, 1995).

When the situation allows for persuasion to occur, a person or a group of people (i.e., the *recipient* or the consumer) receives an appeal (i.e., a *communication*, such as an advertising message or a simple purchase request) from another person or group or company (i.e., the *source* or marketer) in a particular setting (i.e., the *context*). Successful persuasion is said to occur when the recipient's attitude is modified in the desired direction. Although this chapter focuses on attitude change as the key dependent variable, the same persuasion procedures can also be useful for understanding how to influence beliefs, behavioural intentions and other non-evaluative judgements and decisions.

It is also worth noting that the work reviewed in this chapter focuses on the longstanding tradition of assessing the impact of persuasion on the deliberative self-reports of people's attitudes (Haugtvedt & Kasmer, 2008; Petty & Wegener, 1998a). However, the impact of consumer persuasion can be also assessed with measures that tap the more automatic evaluations associated with objects, issues and people (Petty, Fazio, & Briñol, 2009; Gawronski & Payne, 2010). Techniques that assess automatic evaluative associations without directly asking people to report their attitudes are often referred to as *implicit measures* (for a review in the consumer domain, see Perkins & Forehand, 2010). From the perspective of the ELM, sufficient research now makes it clear that the same fundamental processes described in this chapter for understanding changes in explicit measures of attitudes are also useful for understanding changes in automatic evaluations (Briñol, Petty, & McCaslin, 2009).

Source factors

Source factors are the aspects of a person or collection of persons (including companies and other institutions) that are delivering the message. Perhaps the most common source factor studied in the literature is credibility (Kelman & Hovland, 1953). Credibility refers to two aspects of the source: expertise (i.e., how much knowledge the source possesses) and trustworthiness (i.e., the intention of the source to be honest). Early research found that audiences were generally more persuaded when the source of a message was an expert (Rhine & Severance, 1970) or viewed as trustworthy (Mills & Jellison, 1967; Patzer, 1983), though there were notable exceptions (see Briñol & Petty, 2009, for a review on persuasive sources).

In addition to credibility, people's attitudes can also be influenced by the physical attractiveness (Deshields Jr., Kara, & Kaynak, 1996; Kahle & Homer, 1985), the perceived similarity (Brock, 1965) and the general likability (Benoy, 1982) of the person delivering the message. Also, sources that are perceived to be warm or competent (Aaker, Vohs, & Mogilner, 2010) and sources that come from the majority compared to the minority (Martin & Hewstone, 2008) have been capable of enhancing persuasion. Finally, a source's power – his or her control over resources – can also render a source more influential (e.g., Festinger & Thibaut, 1951; Yukl & Falbe, 1991; see Briñol, Petty, Durso, & Rucker, 2015 for a review on powerful sources). Although these simple main effects (more positive sources inducing more persuasion) are common in the literature, we will see shortly that positive sources can sometimes lead to less persuasion depending on the process by which the source factor operates.

Message factors

Message factors comprise what the source says in the message or how the message is organized and structured. A critical aspect of the message is the persuasiveness of its arguments (Petty, Wells, & Brock, 1976). Strong arguments are those that describe consequences or attributes of the object, product, service or brand that are perceived to be desirable, likely, important and novel (Petty & Wegener, 1991). Likewise, messages offering more arguments in favour of the object can be more persuasive than messages with fewer ones (Silvera, Josephs, & Giesler, 2002; see Petty & Cacioppo, 1984a, for a review on number of arguments).

The type of information a message or an advertisement presents, can also impact its persuasiveness. Such factors include whether the message is simple or complex (Ahearne, Gruen, & Saxton, 2000; Yalch & Elmore-Yalch, 1984), concrete or abstract (Fujita et al., 2008; Spassova & Lee, 2013), contains humour (which varies by culture) (Alden, Hoyer, & Lee, 1993), is low or high in imagery (Petrova & Cialdini, 2008), contains stories or narratives (Green, Brock, & Kaufman, 2004), whether its information argues only in favour of the advocated position (i.e., one-sided) or for both sides (i.e., two-sided; Hovland, Lumsdaine, & Sheffield, 1949; Eisend, 2006) or is pro or counter-attitudinal (see Clark & Wegener, 2013, for a review on message direction). Although early research tended to show that message factors only worked in one direction (e.g., more arguments leading to more persuasion), it is possible for all message features to produce a diversity of results as we'll see later. For example, adding more arguments can lead to less persuasion if those arguments are weak and people are thinking carefully (Petty & Cacioppo, 1984a).

Recipient factors

Recipient factors refer to aspects of the individuals receiving the message (i.e., the audience). These factors can range from demographic features such as one's gender to persistent characteristics such as one's intelligence and personality type (Brinol & Petty, 2005). Even the society in which one was raised, be it individualistic or collectivistic, can influence the effectiveness of a persuasive appeal (Shavitt, Nelson & Yean, 1997). Additionally, recipient factors can be more transitory such as whether the audience is momentarily feeling powerful or happy (see Petty & Briñol, 2015a, for a review on emotion and persuasion). Similar to source and message factors, some early research showed that recipient factors produced main effects on persuasion. For example, as intelligence decreased, the likelihood of persuasion tended to increase (Rhodes & Wood, 1992). Conversely, as consumers became more knowledgeable about marketing tactics, persuasion tended to be reduced (Friestad & Wright, 1994; Obermiller & Spangenberg, 1998), whereas making recipients happy (e.g., with pleasant music in an ad) tended to increase persuasion (DeCarlo & Barone, 2009; Gorn, 1982). However, as we describe later in this chapter, these main effect results represent only part of the picture, and they can reverse depending on the circumstances.

Thus, whether it is aspects of the source, the advertisement itself, or the individual who receives the message, there are a multitude of variables that can affect consumer persuasion. However, research over the years has shown that some of the same source, message and recipient factors that increase persuasion are also capable of decreasing it. Although researchers quarrelled about inconsistencies like these for decades, an examination of the psychological processes responsible for attitude change can organize and explain these seemingly contradictory results. We turn to these processes next.

Processes of persuasion

Over the past 50 years, numerous theories have tried to account for the psychological processes involved in attitude change (for a historical review, see Briñol & Petty, 2012). At the outset, persuasion researchers tended to focus on a single outcome for any variable (e.g., positive emotions should always increase persuasion) and a single process by which a variable had its effect (see Petty, 1997; Petty & Briñol, 2008); though as noted, the accumulating research showed that a given feature sometimes increased persuasion whereas at other times it decreased it. Furthermore, some attitude changes lasted longer and were more likely to guide behaviour than other changes.

Contemporary theories of persuasion have been generated to articulate the multiple ways in which variables can affect attitudes in different situations. In the present review, we focus on the Elaboration Likelihood Model (ELM) (Petty & Cacioppo, 1986; Petty & Wegener, 1998a; Petty & Briñol, 2012). Other dual process and dual system approaches following the ELM share some similar features (e.g., the heuristic-systematic model) (Chaiken, Liberman, & Eagly, 1989) (and the unimodal) (Kruglanski & Thompson, 1999), but the ELM continues to be the one guiding more research on persuasion and attitude strength (see Sherman, Gawronski, & Trope, 2012, for other dual process/system approaches to judgement).

The elaboration likelihood model

According to the ELM We have the very same citations in the previous paragraph, so maybe we can just drop them here the psychological processes responsible for the effects of variables on attitude change can be organized into a finite set that operate at different points along an elaboration continuum, going from very low (even automatic) thinking to very high. The theory predicts that under low thinking conditions, variables influence attitudes by operating as simple judgement cues or heuristics (e.g., I like your product because I like you). When the likelihood of thinking is relatively high, variables can impact the extent of influence by more thoughtful means such as by influencing the direction of the thoughts that come to mind (i.e., whether they are favourable or unfavourable), serving as a piece of evidence (i.e., an argument) to be scrutinized, or impacting the confidence people have in the thoughts they generated and thus how much the recipient relies upon those thoughts. The theory furthermore asserts that when elaboration is not constrained to be very low or high, variables can influence attitudes by affecting the amount of thinking that occurs. Thus, as we explain and provide evidence for next, the ELM describes several processes by which variables can affect persuasion in different situations.

Affecting the amount of thinking

One way in which a variable can affect persuasion is through increasing or decreasing the motivation or ability to think about the influence attempt. For example, people might not have the ability to think about a complex or long message unless it is presented more than one time. That is, message repetition is one variable that enables people to engage in greater thinking (Cacioppo & Petty, 1979, 1989; Gorn & Goldberg, 1980; Ratneshwar & Chaiken, 1991). In contrast, if the speaker talks too fast, thinking about the message is disrupted (Smith & Shaffer, 1995). Increasing thinking tends to enhance persuasion if the arguments are strong but reduces it if they are weak. The reverse is true for reducing thinking. To demonstrate this effect with disrupted thinking, Petty, Wells and Brock (1976) gave students strong or weak arguments in favour of a tuition increase, while at the same time the students either did or did not have to engage in a distracting secondary task. When strong arguments were presented, distraction disrupted thinking and diminished persuasion by reducing the favourable thoughts that would have been generated. When weak arguments were presented, however, disrupting thinking actually enhanced persuasion by reducing the counterarguing that would have occurred. Following this study, a manipulation of argument quality has been used in many additional studies to gauge the impact a variable has on message processing. That is, the argument quality effect on attitudes should become larger as message processing is increased and reduced as processing is disrupted. Furthermore, just as there are different situational factors that influence a person's ability to process a message (e.g., repetition, distraction), there are also individual differences influencing ability to think such as the amount of accessible knowledge on the topic (Wood, Rhodes, & Biek, 1995) and previous experience (Wu & Shaffer, 1987).

Now, even if a consumer has all day to elaborate upon an advertisement, should the consumer have no interest in the product advertised, any persuasive appeal on its behalf will not be processed very carefully. Therefore, in addition to ability, the person must also be motivated to think about the message. Although there are many determinants, perhaps the most important is the message's perceived *personal relevance* (Petty & Cacioppo, 1979b, 1990). Whenever the message can be linked to some aspect of the message recipient's "self", such as through the recipient's values, goals, outcomes and identities, it can enhance self-relevance and increase the likelihood of processing the message (e.g., Blankenship & Wegener, 2008; Fleming & Petty, 2000). In an early consumer demonstration of this, Petty, Cacioppo and Schumann (1983) varied participant's interest in an advertisement for the "Edge Razor" by informing them that they would receive a razor for participating in the experiment (high relevance) or a tube of toothpaste (low relevance). Subsequently, participants were exposed to a razor advertisement containing either strong (e.g., "In direct comparison tests, the Edge blade gave twice as many close shaves as its nearest competitor") or weak (e.g., "In direct comparison tests, the Edge blade gave no more nicks or cuts than its competition") arguments. Petty et al. found larger argument quality effects (i.e., more persuasion for the strong than weak arguments) when the razor advertisement was high as opposed to low in personal relevance.

Other variables that have been shown to impact the amount of thinking include messages with personalized addresses (Howard & Kerin, 2004), the use of rhetorical questions (Ahluwalia, Burnkrant, Mick, & Brucks, 2004; Petty, Cacioppo, & Heesacker, 1981), one's level of anxiety (Sengupta & Venkataramani, 2001) and one's doubt or uncertainty regarding the message (Ziegler, Diehl, & Ruther, 2002). Individual traits also affect one's motivation to think such as one's *need for cognition*, that is, one's desire to engage in thoughtful, cognitive activities (e.g., Cacioppo, Petty, & Morris, 1983). Individuals high in need of cognition are more influenced by the quality of a message and less by simple cues than those low in need of cognition (for reviews, see Cacioppo, Petty, Feinstein, & Jarvis, 1996; Petty, Briñol, Loersch, & McCaslin, 2009). A recent meta-analysis (Carpenter, 2014) found 134 studies with over 15,000 participants testing the ELM hypothesis that variables affecting thinking would interact with argument quality to produce persuasion and concluded that the available data were consistent with the ELM predictions.

Low thinking processes

When motivation and/or ability to think about the persuasive proposal are relatively low, according to the ELM (Petty & Wegener, 1998a), source, message and recipient variables are likely to exert their influence by serving as simple cues or input to simple heuristics. Heuristics are rules of thumb such as "foods recommended by the doctor in this ad are probably good for me" (Chaiken, 1980). The ELM predicts that when thinking is low, people do not rely much on a personal assessment of the merits of the consumer proposal in forming their attitudes but rely instead on a variety of simple cues from the source, the message or the situation that become associated with the product or serve as input to a simple decision rule.

Under conditions of low elaboration, source variables such as credibility have been shown to serve as a simple positive cue to persuasion. For example, when messages deal with unimportant or irrelevant issues (low motivation to think), irrespective of the actual merits of the arguments presented, individuals are likely to be more persuaded by credible sources compared to non-credible sources (Petty, Cacioppo, & Goldman, 1981). This can be understood as resulting from the use of a simple heuristic or association such as, "If an expert and trustworthy source supports this position, it must be good". Other variables have shown similar cue effects under low thinking conditions, such as source attractiveness (Chaiken, 1987), source majority status (Horcajo, Briñol, & Petty, 2014), length of the message (Petty & Cacioppo, 1984a) or recipient mood (Petty, Schumann, Richman, & Strathman, 1993).

In addition to heuristics, low elaboration consumers can be influenced by simple associative connections, as in the case of evaluative conditioning where repeatedly pairing an attitude object with something good enhances positive evaluations (Razran, 1940; Staats & Staats, 1958). When thinking is low, one noteworthy feature of variables serving as simple cues is that they impact attitudes in the direction of their valence. For example, if attractiveness of the source and being happy are positively valenced, they will result in more positive attitudes. When these same variables serve in other roles, though, their impact on attitudes need not be positive.

High thinking processes

When motivation and ability to think are high, people will engage in careful thought, assessing the relevance and the merits of *all* of the information available. As already explained, in such situations, the quality or cogency of the information presented will be an important determinant of how effective the persuasion attempt is. Below we articulate additional processes that variables can influence when thinking is high.

Biasing thoughts

When thinking is high, variables can bias the nature of the thoughts that are generated. That is, some features of the persuasion context increase the likelihood of favourable thoughts being elicited, whereas others increase the likelihood of unfavourable thoughts. For example, if people are put in a good mood prior to hearing an involving message, their thoughts will be biased in favour of the message (Petty et al., 1993). On the other hand, instilling "reactance" (Brehm, 1966) in message recipients by telling them that they have no choice but to be persuaded on an important issue motivates counterarguing (or negative thoughts), even when the arguments used are strong (Petty & Cacioppo, 1979a). Biased thinking, then, whether favourable or unfavourable, often reduces the impact of message quality on persuasion compared to objective thinking.

In general, any time a message takes a position opposed to one's attitudes, values, personal identity or preferred outcome, people will tend to be biased against it. When a message takes a position in favour of those variables, though, people will be biased in favour of it (Petty & Cacioppo, 1990; see Clark & Wegener, 2013, for a review). To be clear, and as noted earlier, when a message is framed as relevant to one's values, identity or preferred outcomes, the *extent* of information processing is affected, but when a message takes a particular position on them, the *valence* of the processing can be affected. However, the potential for biased thinking to occur is enhanced when the message itself is somewhat ambiguous so that the recipient can interpret it in either a favourable or unfavourable way (Chaiken & Maheswaran, 1994).

Serving as an argument

Under high elaboration conditions, variables can also serve as arguments. When processing carefully, all aspects of the communication are scrutinized as to whether or not they provide evidence for changing an attitude or adopting the advocated position. For example, the attractiveness of a source could be considered an argument for relevant advocacies such as for beauty products, but will likely operate through other processes for proposals and products unrelated to looks (Petty & Cacioppo, 1984b; cf., Pierro, Mannetti, Kruglanski, & Sleeth-Keppler, 2004). Similarly, one's culture can also moderate whether a variable is treated as a cue or an argument. For example, in independent cultures, where people emphasize viewing the self as unique or distinct to others (e.g., Hui & Triandis, 1986), consensus support for an attitudinal position is perceived as a simple cue and works best when thinking is relatively low. However, in collectivist cultures, where people emphasize viewing the self as interconnected to others, consensus information can be perceived as an argument and works when thinking is high (Aaker & Maheswaran, 1997).

For a variable to serve as an argument it has to be evaluated as direct evidence for the merits of the attitude object. For example, Martin, Abend, Sedikides and Green (1997) examined how participants evaluated a story that was designed to make them happy or sad. Because a core goal of the story was the mood it was supposed to evoke, participants' moods could be viewed as a relevant argument. Thus, if a story were designed to make people sad, actually feeling sad would be a strong argument in favour of the merits of the story; however, feeling happy would make the story seem less effective. Although negative emotions such as sadness or fear could serve as negative cues for disliking if thinking is low, it can lead to positive evaluations if these are the intended states and thinking is high.

Validation

When thinking is high, there is yet another process through which a variable can influence the degree of persuasion: thought validation. Recent research suggests that people not only have thoughts, but they can have thoughts about their thoughts, or *metacognitions* (Petty, Briñol, Tormala, & Wegener, 2007; Briñol & DeMarree, 2012). One feature of thoughts that has proven to be useful is the confidence with which people hold their thoughts. That is, two consumers can have the same favourable thought about the message (e.g., iPhones have long battery life), but one consumer can have considerably more confidence in the validity of that thought than another person. Similarly, two consumers might have the very same thought about a product, but one of them may feel better about that thought (e.g., this thought makes me feel good), using it more when forming a final evaluation about the product (Briñol, Petty, & Barden, 2007). According to the *self-validation hypothesis* (Petty, Briñol, & Tormala, 2002), influencing thought-confidence and thought-liking when thinking is high can increase or decrease the persuasiveness of the appeal depending on the dominant direction of thoughts. In support of this idea, Briñol, Petty and Tormala (2004) found that when the thoughts in response to an advertisement were primarily favourable, increasing confidence in their validity increased consumer persuasion, but increasing doubt in their validity decreased consumer persuasion. When the thoughts to a message were mostly unfavourable, however, increasing confidence in their validity reduced persuasion, but undermining confidence increased it.

Research on self-validation has shown that this mechanism can account for some already established persuasion outcomes (e.g., more persuasion with happy rather than sad mood, with high over low credibility sources, when argument generation is easy rather than difficult), but by a different process than postulated previously (see Briñol & Petty, 2009, for a review). It is worth noting that self-validation processes have two boundary conditions: (1) there must be relatively *high* levels of thinking, and (2) the confidence should be salient *during* or *following* thought generation rather than *prior* to it. If confidence is salient prior to thinking, it tends to reduce the amount of thinking by validating one's initial viewpoint thereby reducing the need for processing new information (Tiedens & Linton, 2001).

Correction for perceived bias

Finally, under high elaboration conditions, variables can lead individuals to notice and respond to a potential bias in their thinking and attempt to correct for such bias. Specifically, because people are motivated to hold correct attitudes, under careful scrutiny they might detect factors that they believe are biasing their judgements and make an effort to correct for them (e.g., if an emotion induction in an advertisement was seen as particularly blatant [DeSteno et al., 2004]). If people have doubt in their thoughts because they fear that their thoughts might have stemmed from some biasing factor in the situation or some prejudice they have, they could attempt to explicitly correct for their biased thoughts in accordance with the mechanism specified by the Flexible Correction Model (FCM) (see Wegener & Petty, 1997, for a review). That is, people might estimate the magnitude and direction of the perceived biasing effect on their judgements and attempt to adjust for it. To the extent that they correct too much, reverse effects of variables can be obtained (Petty & Wegener, 1993; Wegener & Petty, 1995; Wilson & Brekke, 1994).

For example, in one study (Petty, Wegener, & White, 1998), when people became aware that a likable source might be biasing their attitudes, they became more favourable towards the proposal when it was endorsed by a dislikeable than a likable source. Such explicit corrections typically require relatively high degrees of thinking. However, if certain corrections are practiced repeatedly, they can require less effort and even become automatic (e.g., Glaser & Banaji, 1999; Maddux et al., 2005). Of course, people must be motivated and aware of a bias in order to correct for it (for further discussion, see Wegener & Petty, 1994).

Consequences of different processes

According to the ELM, attitudes formed or changed through high thinking processes are more consequential (stronger) than those changed through low thinking processes (Petty, Haugtevdt & Smith, 1995, for a review). That is, although some attitudes are weak and relatively inconsequential, others have greater impact. The term *attitude strength* is used to describe the quality of attitudes that allows them to persist over time, resist persuasion, affect information processing and guide behaviour (Petty & Krosnick, 1995). Some of the features associated with strong attitudes include the following: low ambivalence (Armitage & Conner, 2000), high accessibility (Bassili & Fletcher, 1991; Fazio et al., 1982; Hodges & Wilson, 1994) high commitment (Kiesler, 1971) and high attitude certainty (Bassili, 1996; Rucker, Tormala, Petty, & Briñol, 2014). Possessing these features increases the strength of an attitude and thus the likelihood that an individual will use and maintain that attitude over time.

Importantly, elaboration increases the likelihood that a newly changed attitude will possess the several features of a strong attitude (see Petty et al., 1995, for a review). There are both structural and metacognitive reasons for this. First, as thinking increases during attitude change, people should acquire more support for their attitudes and their attitudes should become more accessible and well-integrated in the knowledge structure. Second, people often become more committed to and confident in their views with greater thinking. Each of these factors would increase the likelihood that an attitude would be consequential.

One example of the link between elaboration and strength comes from a study by Haugtvedt and Petty (1992). In this research, individuals who varied in their need for cognition were exposed to a television ad for an answering machine in the context of a television programme.

The ad was designed to contain compelling arguments as well as positive cues so that comparably favourable attitudes would be induced regardless of the level of thinking. Attitudes towards the answering machine were measured immediately following the ad and then again two days later. At the delayed period, need for cognition predicted the extent of persistence (i.e., the amount of attitude change) of the initial attitude. That is, those higher in need for cognition (who would have processed the message carefully initially) tended to persist in their new favourable attitudes, but those lower in need for cognition (who would have relied on simple cues at the time of initial exposure) did not (see Boninger et al., 1990; Chaiken, 1980, for similar results).

In summary, through the mechanism of both low and high thinking, we can now understand when and why certain variables affect persuasion. Knowing the mechanism is important because as just noted, according to the ELM, when variables produce attitude change through high thinking processes, the new attitudes are more persistent, resistant to further change, and predictive of behaviour than when the same changes occur via low thinking processes.

Multiple roles for persuasion variables

So far, we have examined the factors of persuasion in the separate contexts of high, low and unconstrained thinking. However, the same variable that served as a cue under low thinking conditions could serve as an argument under high thinking and affect the amount of thinking when it is unconstrained. Next, we provide an example from research on one variable to illustrate how any given variable can affect attitudes in each of the roles postulated. For our example, consider whether the message recipient is in a relatively happy or sad state. How should this affect persuasion?

First off, one's emotional state can affect the amount of thinking one does about a message when thinking is unconstrained. Typically, sadness tends to increase elaborative processing over happiness because it indicates that something is wrong and needs to be addressed (Schwarz, Bless, & Bohner, 1991). In contrast, happiness indicates that things are fine the way they are (Worth & Mackie, 1987). However, if thinking is already low (e.g., because of distraction), being happy can increase persuasion compared to sadness through the peripheral route by serving as a simple associative cue or input to a decision rule ("If I feel good, I must like it") (e.g., Bosmans & Baumgartner, 2005). On the other hand, if thinking is high, feeling happy can enhance persuasion by biasing the direction of one's thoughts, increasing the number of positive thoughts one generates towards the appeal (Petty et al., 1993) or making good consequences seem more likely and bad consequences seem less likely (Wegener, Petty, & Klein, 1994). If relevant to the persuasive appeal, happiness can also be evaluated as an argument for the attitude object (Martin et al., 1997).

In addition to these primary cognitions, emotions can also affect the perceived validity of one's thoughts when the feelings follow (rather than precede) processing, by increasing or decreasing the certainty one has in one's thoughts. For example, if people feel happy following the generation of positive thoughts, they will rely on them more and be more persuaded, but if happiness follows generation of negative thoughts, people will rely on them more and be less persuaded than if sadness follows thought generation (Briñol et al., 2007).

However, if emotions are made too salient such that individuals perceive them to be biasing their thoughts (e.g., consumers perceive a happy TV programme is affecting their ensuing evaluation of a commercial), the individual will be motivated to correct his or her attitude and effects opposite to the perceived bias (Berkowitz, Jaffe, Jo, & Troccoli, 2000). Importantly, induced emotions can result in the same degree of attitude change regardless of the process (Petty et al., 2003), but when emotion acts under high elaboration to increase persuasion, the attitude change will last longer, be more resistant to persuasion, and be more likely guide attitude consistent behaviour (see Petty & Briñol, 2015a, for a review).

Other prominent variables in communication, that is, features of the source such as credibility and attractiveness, have also been shown to demonstrate these varied outcomes, such as affecting the amount of thinking one does when it is unconstrained (Puckett, Petty, Cacioppo, & Fisher, 1983) and serving as a simple peripheral cue when thinking is low (Priester & Petty, 1995). However, when thinking is high, these same variables can and serve as a substantive argument (Petty & Cacioppo, 1984b), bias thoughts (Chaiken & Maheswaran, 1994), affect the perceived validity of one's thoughts (Briñol et al., 2004) as well as influence someone to correct for a perceived bias in their attitude (Petty, Wegener & White, 1998). To date, a number of other variables have been shown to operate in these multiple roles in the predicted circumstances. These include recipient power (Briñol et al., 2015), ease of retrieval (Briñol, Tormala, & Petty, 2013) and bodily responses (Briñol, Petty, & Wagner, 2012), to name just a few (for a review, see Petty & Briñol, 2015b).

Matching

Up to this point, we have focused on the multiple processes by which communication factors in isolation can impact attitudes and persuasion in different situations. However, these individual variables can also interact with each other in affecting persuasion processes and outcomes. To highlight this interplay, we next focus on the outcomes of when a variable within the recipient, message, and/or source *matches* another factor of the persuasion situation (for more extensive reviews on matching, see Briñol & Petty, 2006; Petty, Wheeler, & Bizer, 2000; Salovey & Wegener, 2003).

We begin with the well-validated notion that people tend to like things that are associated with themselves more than things that are associated with others (e..g, Kahneman, Knetsch, & Thaler, 1990). For example, people overvalue their in-group compared to out-groups (Tajfel, 1981) and find their own arguments more convincing than those generated by others (Greenwald & Albert, 1968). People also value and are more interested in things associated with themselves, as shown with self-relevance increasing information processing (Petty & Cacioppo, 1979b). Furthermore, most people tend to find things associated with themselves easier to process (Briñol et al., 2013). Thus, based on these features (familiarity, liking and interest), matching a message to the self has the potential to impact attitudes and persuasion through the same multiple processes documented previously.

Currently, many different types of matching have been demonstrated throughout the literature. For example, research has shown that by matching a quality of the message's source, such as the gender, to that of the recipient (e.g., a woman delivering an appeal to a woman) can increase the persuasiveness of the message (see Fleming & Petty, 2000). Other examples of variables that have shown this main effect for matching include need for cognition (Bakker, 1999), sensation seeking (Palmgreen, Stephenson, Evertt, Baseheart, & Francies, 2002), the functional basis of attitudes (Pratkanis & Gilner, 2005) and affect versus cognition (Fabrigar & Petty, 1999). Even one's culture can account for this effect. For example, advertisements appealing to one's independence and personal success are more persuasive to people from Western countries (i.e., individualistic cultures which promote traits like these) than people from Eastern countries (i.e., collectivist cultures). However, the opposite is true for advertisements appealing to collectivist values, like in-group benefits and family integrity (Han & Shavitt, 1994; Zhang & Gelb, 1996). However, without understanding the process through which matching can increase (or decrease) persuasion, we cannot account for when it will or will not occur. By applying the ELM, though, we can begin to better understand these effects.

Understanding matching with the ELM

According to the ELM, matching can influence attitudes by the same fundamental processes described so far for variables like emotion and source credibility (e.g., see Petty, Barden, & Wheller, 2009). For example, one of the variables that has been studied the most with respect to matching is *self-monitoring*, or the degree to which one orients him or herself towards social approval (Snyder, 1974). High self-monitors are very attentive to modifying their behaviour to their current social circumstances, whereas low self-monitors are more motivated to be consistent with their internal beliefs and values. In a study by Petty and Wegener (1998b), researchers matched or mismatched advertisements with cogent or flimsy arguments to individuals who differed in levels of self-monitoring. That is, high and low self-monitors either read social image (e.g., how good a product makes you look) or quality (e.g., how efficient a product is) appeals that contained either strong or weak arguments. For the participants who read advertisements that matched their self-monitoring status (i.e., social image messages for high self-monitors and quality messages for low self-monitors), the strength of the arguments had a larger effect on attitudes compared to those who received mismatched advertisements, an indication that matching enhanced information processing thereby increasing the impact of message quality on attitudes (see also DeBono & Harnish, 1988; Fujita et al., 2008; Peracchio & Meyers-Levy, 1997; Wan & Rucker, 2013; Wheeler, Petty, & Bizer, 2005).

When the likelihood of elaboration is constrained to be low, however, a match between the message and the consumer is more likely to influence attitudes by serving as a simple cue (e.g., DeBono, 1987). For example, if a source simply asserts that the arguments are consistent with a low self-monitor's values, if thinking is not high, this simple match to the self can produce persuasion with the reasoning, "If it links to my values, it must be good!" In contrast, when thinking is set to a high level (e.g., a topic of high personal interest; high accountability for a decision), then matching could enhance persuasion by biasing the direction of thinking. Indeed, some research suggests that high self-monitors are more motivated to generate favourable thoughts to messages that make an appeal to image rather than an appeal to values (e.g., Lavine & Snyder, 1996).

Yet another role for matching is provided by the self-validation hypothesis. For example, Evans and Clark (2012) showed that thought-confidence increased when the characteristics of the source matched (vs. mismatched) the characteristic of the recipient. These researchers showed that high (vs. low) self-monitors relied more on their thoughts when the source was attractive (vs. credible), which increased persuasion for positive thoughts but decreased persuasion for negative thoughts (for an additional example of matching increasing thought validation, see Huntsinger, 2013). This metacognitive role would be more likely to occur under relatively high elaboration conditions and when the match follows message processing.

Future avenues in matching research

In this chapter, we have shown matching is relatively prolific throughout the literature; however, there are still areas and applications of matching that have yet to be fully examined. In the final section of this chapter, we discuss areas that matching research has begun to explore but deserve further consideration.

Correcting for matching

Similar to the communication variables discussed previously, if people are made aware of the potential bias induced by matching, they may be prone to correct for it. For example, if a consumer recognizes that an ad is being specifically matched to him or her to increase persuasion, he or she may intentionally correct in the opposite direction of the appeal's intention. In one study, Cessario, Grant and Higgins (2004) manipulated whether or not a persuasive appeal for an after-school programme matched the individual's strategy for goal pursuit (i.e., either promotion-focused or prevention-focused) and whether or not the individuals were made aware of the biasing effects of matched messages. Although naive participants found the matched message to be more persuasive, those who were made aware of the effect by highlighting the source for their feelings of "rightness" corrected for their bias and actually found the *mismatched* message more persuasive.

Other research has also revealed that personalized (i.e., matched) messages may not always be more effective – or at least these favourable personalization effects are subject to moderation by external factors (as meta-analyzed in Noar et al., 2007). For example, when people don't see a legitimate reason for why their personal information was used in a highly personalized message, effectiveness is decreased (White, Zahay, Thorbjørnsen, & Shavitt, 2008). Similarly, highly personalized messages may not generate desirable responses from individuals who possess interdependent or collectivist tendencies (versus those with independent tendencies; Li, Kalyanaraman, & Du, 2011; Kramer, Spolter-Weisfeld, & Thakkar, 2007). Moreover, when people anticipate feelings of regret associated with personalized products, they may select standard ones instead (Syam, Krishnamurthy, & Hess, 2008).

When matching decreases (vs. increases) thinking

The thrust of evidence so far has demonstrated how matching often increases influence, and one mechanism for this is that matching increases thinking about the arguments when it is not otherwise constrained. The question remains though: Are there boundary conditions wherein matching can sometimes decrease thinking? Petty and Wegener (1998a, p. 230) suggested that "if people form stronger expectations about what a message will say … they would be more surprised when the message violates these expectations". That is, if one expects a persuasive message to match the participant's already held views, he or she may be less likely to scrutinize the message due to the belief that he or she already knows what to expect (Hastie, 1984; Maheswaren & Chaiken, 1991). In contrast, if people are surprised by the position taken, information processing will be increased (Baker & Petty, 1994). Previously, we reviewed evidence demonstrating how matching could increase elaboration by making the message content seem more self-relevant to the recipient. What happens, however, when matching instead leads the recipient to simply perceive the message content as expected or already known?

Some initial work on this comes from Smith and Petty (1996) who found that if a message mismatched what people expected (e.g., if the participants expected a positively-framed message and received a negatively-framed one), argument quality had a larger impact on attitudes than if the position matched what was expected, implying greater message scrutiny. A cross-cultural study (Aaker & Williams, 1998) also examined this expectancy violation with advertisements for camera film in both the United States and China. In the U.S., consumers are accustomed to ads that use Western-valued emotions (e.g., delight), whereas in China, consumers are accustomed to ads that use Eastern-valued emotions (e.g., calmness). Thus, when researchers mismatched ad expectations (e.g., a delight-focused appeal for the Chinese), they found greater argument quality effects than when the ad was matched.

Additional evidence for this mismatching increasing processing effect comes from Ziegler (2010) who put participants in either a good or bad mood and then manipulated the source of a message to have high or low likability. Past research has shown that people come to have mood-congruent expectations for the valence of a source (e.g., a positive mood leads to expectations of a positive source) (Mayer, Gaschke, Braverman & Evans, 1992). Therefore, a match to expectations in this instance would be constituted under the good mood/likable source condition and the bad mood/unlikable source condition. Once more, if expectancy violation leads to more processing than confirmation, the mismatching condition should lead to greater argument quality effects than matching would – which was exactly what was found (see also Baker & Petty, 1994; Ziegler, 2010; Ziegler et al., 2002). In brief, these studies show that if matching is to expectations, it is the mismatching condition that leads to greater scrutiny (due to surprise). On the other hand, if matching is to the self, then the matching condition produces the greater scrutiny (due to the enhanced interest from personal relevance).

In addition to surprise and expectancy violation paradigms, there might be other processes and conditions under which matching could decrease thinking. For example, if the confidence that emerges from matching validates the belief that one already knows enough about the topic, or if it increases the sense of validity in one's existing attitude, then matching would be expected to undermine thinking. This would be most likely when the sense of matching precedes the processing of the message.

Matching and self-persuasion

All of the matching research reviewed so far has shown how matching influences responses to messages generated by external sources. However, one new avenue for exploring matching is within the realm of self-persuasion, and specifically, its relation to argument generation (rather than reception). Prior research has shown that matching can influence the number and the content of thoughts people generate in response to persuasive messages generated by others. A relevant question, then, is to what extent matching can also influence the thoughts consumers themselves generate in the absence of persuasive messages.

Imagine for a moment that a consumer is trying to convince him or herself to purchase a new treadmill instead of a television. In the absence of any kind of persuasive appeal from a company, what kind of arguments will the consumer generate to influence his or her decision? In one study by Shavitt, Lowery and Han (1992), individuals who were high versus low in self-monitoring were presented with consumer products that could be ambiguously categorized as either utilitarian or social identity based (e.g., watches and sunglasses). Participants were then asked to generate and design ads that would "explicitly appeal to themselves". Paralleling prior matching effects, low self-monitors constructed ads composed mostly of utilitarian arguments, whereas high-self monitors made ads mostly composed of social identity-based arguments.

Another example of this effect comes from Rucker and Galiniski (2009) who examined power. The researchers proposed that powerful people value products for their quality or functionality (because such features support their own argentic goals), whereas less powerful people value products for their ability to confer status (because these features promote their goals of attaining the esteem of others). Thus, when participants were asked to generate slogans for a BMW, the results showed that participants assigned to the high-power condition tended to focus their slogans on performance, whereas those in the low-power condition tended to focus their slogans on prestige. Together, these two studies suggest that people tend to generate arguments that match their own personality or cognitive style, exactly those arguments that tend to be the most effective when generated by others.

In their analysis of self-persuasion, Maio and Thomas (2007) described two types of strategies: epistemic and teleological. Epistemic strategies try to restructure one's cognitions to align with the desired outcome attitude (e.g., reinterpreting undesired attributes of an object to be more positive).

In contrast, teleological strategies attempt to reduce the accessibility of the undesired attitude (e.g., suppressing or distracting oneself from an undesired attribute). Resch and Lord (2011) speculated that epistemic strategies would require greater cognitive processing because they involve generating new thoughts, whereas teleological techniques require greater self-control because they require managing current thoughts. Following a matching logic, Resch and Lord (2011) found that when participants high in Need for Cognition used epistemic strategies (the more cognitively demanding type), it resulted in greater self-persuasion. However, when participants high in self-control used teleological strategies (a task requiring self-control to maintain active thought suppression) (Tangney, Baumeister, & Boone, 2004), it resulted in greater self-persuasion.

A final illustration of this phenomenon comes from research in which people match the effort they invest in generating arguments with the perceived demands of the task. Specifically, research conducted by Briñol, McCaslin and Petty (2012) began with the assumption that people hold the reasonable belief that generating arguments to persuade themselves is more difficult when the topic is counter-attitudinal rather than pro-attitudinal, and they further believe that they know their own opinions better than they know the opinions of others (cf., Dunning, 2012). Because of this, when the topic of the persuasion task is counter-attitudinal, people invest more effort in generating a message designed to persuade themselves than in generating arguments to convince another person of the same position. That is, people can be sure that they are opposed but are less sure of the opposition of the other; thus, they work harder to persuade themselves. The reverse is the case when the message is pro-attitudinal. Here, people invest less effort in generating arguments designed to persuade themselves than another person because they are less sure that the other person already agrees. When the impact on actual self-persuasion was assessed, it followed directly from the effort expended in the persuasion task.

In sum, the concept of matching has been demonstrated in the domain of externally originated persuasion and for self-persuasion. Little work, however, has addressed the relevance of matching for when people spontaneously advocate to others such as in the domain of Word of Mouth effects (Berger, 2014). For example, are advertisements that match a dimension of someone's personality (e.g., extraversion) more likely to be shared subsequently with other people believed to also have that personality dimension (e.g., other extraverted people)? Or more generally, to what extent do people tell others about products and services when they think the others are similar versus dissimilar to them? Future research can benefit from examining whether these and other forms of matching affect the source's willingness to engage in word of mouth influence.

Concluding remarks

We have focused on how source, recipient and context variables can produce (or not produce) persuasion by a variety of high and low effort processes that operate along an elaboration continuum. Although attitude change is possible as a result of relatively low thought processes (e.g., relying on simple cues and inferences), these changes are not as consequential as those induced via high thought processes. In parallel, many of the same psychological processes and outcomes that have been observed in research on receiving and processing external messages have also been observed when consumers generate their own messages in the absence of external information – an area of research worth further exploration. Other important research questions to pursue include: When do people spontaneously attempt to self-persuade themselves? Do they tend to do so through peripheral cues or central arguments? Do matching and mismatching effects work similarly in this context? In sum, the present review not only examined the psychological processes relevant for understanding the influence of single variables; it also addressed instances where multiple variables, such as in matching effects, interact to provide a host of outcomes.

References

Aaker, J. L., & Maheswaran, D. (1997). The effect of cultural orientation on persuasion. *Journal of Consumer Research*, *24*(3), 315–328.

Aaker, J., Vohs, K. D., & Mogilner, C. (2010). Nonprofits are seen as warm and for-profits as competent: Firm stereotypes matter. *Journal of Consumer Research*, *37*(2), 224–237.

Aaker, J. L., & Williams, P. (1998). Empathy versus pride: The influence of emotional appeals across cultures. *Journal of Consumer Research*, *25*(3), 241–261.

Ahearne, M., Gruen, T., & Saxton, M. K. (2000). When the product is complex, does the advertisement's conclusion matter? *Journal of Business Research*, *48*(1), 55–62.

Ahluwalia, R., Burnkrant, R. E., Mick, D. G., & Brucks, M. (2004). Answering questions about questions: A persuasion knowledge perspective for understanding the effects of rhetorical questions. *Journal of Consumer Research*, *31*(1), 26–42.

Alden, D., Hoywer, W., & Lee, C. (1993). Identifying global and culture-specific dimensions of humor in advertising: A multinational analysis. *Journal of Marketing*, *57*(2), 64–75.

Armitage, C. J., & Conner, M. (2000). Attitudinal ambivalence: A test of three key hypotheses. *Personality and Social Psychology Bulletin*, *26*(11), 1421–1432.

Baker, S. M., & Petty, R. E. (1994). Majority and minority influence: Source-position imbalance as a determinant of message scrutiny. *Journal of Personality and Social Psychology*, *67*, 5–19.

Bakker, A. B. (1999). Persuasive communication about AIDS prevention: Need for cognition determines the impact of message format. *AIDS Education and Prevention*, *11*, 150–162.

Bassili, J. N. (1996). Meta-judgmental versus operative indices of psychological properties: The case of measures of attitude strength. *Journal of Personality and Social Psychology*, *71*, 637–653.

Bassili, J. N., & Fletcher, J. F. (1991). Response-time measurement in survey research a method for CATI and a new look at non-attitudes. *Public Opinion Quarterly*, *55*(3), 331–346.

Benoy, J. W. (1982). The credibility of physically attractiveness communicators: A review. *Journal of Advertising*, *11*, 15–24.

Berger, J. (2014). Word of mouth and interpersonal communication: A review and directions for future research. *Journal of Consumer Psychology*, *24*(4), 586–607.

Berkowitz, L., Jaffee, S., Jo, E., & Troccoli, B. T. (2000). On the correction of feeling-induced judgmental biases. In J. P. Forgas (Ed.), *Feeling and thinking: The role of affect in Social Cognition* (pp. 131–152). Cambridge, England: Cambridge University Press.

Blankenship, K. L., & Wegener, D. T. (2008). Opening the mind to close it: Considering a message in light of important values increases message processing and later resistance to change. *Journal of Personality and Social Psychology*, *94*(2), 196–213.

Boninger, D. S., Brock, T. C., Cook, T. D., Gruder, C. L., & Romer, D. (1990). Discovery of a reliable attitude change persistence resulting from a transmitter set. *Psychological Science*, *1*, 268–271.

Bosmans, A., & Baumgartner, H. (2005). Goal-relevant emotional information: When extraneous affect leads to persuasion and when it does not. *Journal of Consumer Research*, *32*(3), 424–434.

Brehm, J. W. (1966). *A theory of psychological reactance*. New York, NY: Academic Press.

Briñol, P., & DeMarree, K. G. (2012). *Social metacognition: Thinking about thinking in social psychology*. New York, NY: Psychology Press.

Briñol, P., McCaslin, M. J., & Petty, R. E. (2012). Self-generated persuasion: Effects of the target and direction of arguments. *Journal of Personality and Social Psychology*, *102*, 925–940.

Briñol, P., & Petty, R. E. (2005). Individual differences in attitude change. In D. Albarracin, B. T. Johnson & M. P. Zanna (Eds.), *The handbook of attitudes and attitude change* (pp. 575–615). Mahwah, NJ: Lawrence Erlbaum Associates.

Briñol, P., & Petty, R. E. (2006). Fundamental processes leading to attitude change: Implications for cancer prevention communications. *Journal of Communication*, *56*, S81–S104.

Briñol, P., & Petty, R. E. (2009). Persuasion: Insights from the self-validation hypothesis. *Advances in Experimental Social Psychology*, *41*, 69–118.

Briñol, P., & Petty, R. E. (2012). The history of attitudes and persuasion research. In A. Kruglanski & W. Stroebe (Eds.), *Handbook of the history of social psychology* (pp. 285–320). New York, NY: Psychology Press.

Briñol, P., & Petty, R. E. (2015). Elaboration and validation processes: Implications for media attitude change. *Media Psychology*, *18*, 267–291.

Briñol, P., Petty, R. E., Durso, R. O., & Rucker, D. D. (2016). Power and persuasion: Processes by which power influences evaluative judgments. *Unpublished Manuscript*. Columbus, OH.

Briñol, P., Petty, R. E., & McCaslin, M. J. (2009). Changing attitudes on implicit versus explicit measures: What is the difference? In R. E. Petty, R. H. Fazio & P. Briñol (Eds.), *Attitudes: Insights from the new implicit measures* (pp. 285–326). New York, NY: Psychology Press.

Briñol, P., Petty, R. E., & Tormala, Z. L. (2004). Self-validation of cognitive responses to advertisements. *Journal of Consumer Research*, *30*, 559–573.

Briñol, P., Petty, R. E., & Wagner, B. C. (2012). Embodied validation: Our body can change and also validate our thoughts. In P. Briñol & K. G. DeMarree (Eds.), *Social metacognition* (pp. 219–240). New York, NY: Psychology Press.

Briñol, P., Petty, R. E., & Barden, J. (2007). Happiness versus sadness as a determinant of thought confidence in persuasion: A self-validation analysis. *Journal of Personality and Social Psychology*, 93, 711–727.

Briñol, P., Rucker, D. D., & Petty, R. E. (2015). Naïve theories about persuasion: Implication for information processing and consumer attitude change. *International Journal of Advertising*, 34, 85–106.

Briñol, P., Tormala, Z. L., & Petty, R. E. (2013). Ease and persuasion: Multiple processes, meanings, and effects. In C. Unkelbach & R. Greifeneder (Eds.), *The experience of thinking: How the fluency of mental processes influences cognition and behaviour* (pp. 101–118). London: Psychology Press.

Brock, T. C. (1965). Communicator-recipient similarity and decision change. *Journal of Personality and Social Psychology*, *1*(6), 650–654.

Cacioppo, J. T., & Petty, R. E. (1979). The effects of message repetition and position on cognitive responses, recall, and persuasion. *Journal of Personality and Social Psychology*, *37*, 97–109.

Cacioppo, J. T., & Petty, R. E. (1989). Effects of message repetition on argument processing, recall, and persuasion. *Basic and Applied Social Psychology*, *10*, 3–12.

Cacioppo, J. T., Petty, R. E., Feinstein, J., & Jarvis, W. B. G. (1996). Dispositional differences in cognitive motivation: The life and times of individuals varying in need for cognition. *Psychological Bulletin*, *119*, 197–253.

Cacioppo, J. T., Petty, R. E., & Morris, K. (1983). Effects of need for cognition on message evaluation, argument recall, and persuasion. *Journal of Personality and Social Psychology*, *45*, 805–818.

Carpenter, C. J. (2014). A meta-analysis of the ELM's argument quality X processing type predictions. *Human Communication Research*, *41*, 501–534.

Cesario, J., Grant, H., & Higgins, E. T. (2004). Regulatory fit and persuasion: Transfer from "feeling right". *Journal of Personality and Social Psychology*, *86*(3), 388–404.

Chaiken, S. (1980). Heuristic versus systematic information processing in the use of source versus message cues in persuasion. *Journal of Personality and Social Psychology*, *39*, 752–766.

Chaiken, S. (1987). The heuristic model of persuasion. In M. P. Zanna, J. Olson & C. P. Herman (Eds.), *Social influence: The Ontario symposium* (Vol. 5, pp. 3–39). Hillsdale, NJ: Lawrence Erlbaum Associates.

Chaiken, S. L., Liberman, A., & Eagly, A. H. (1989). Heuristic and systematic processing within and beyond the persuasion context. In J. S. Uleman & J. A. Bargh (Eds.), *Unintended thought* (pp. 212–252). New York, NY: Guilford Press.

Chaiken, S., & Maheswaran, D. (1994). Heuristic processing can bias systematic processing: Effects of source credibility, argument ambiguity, and task importance on attitude judgment. *Journal of Personality and Social Psychology*, *66*, 460–473.

Clark, J. K., & Wegener, D. T. (2013). Message position, information processing, and persuasion: The Discrepancy Motives Model. In P. Devine & A. Plant (Eds.), *Advances in experimental social psychology* (Vol. 47, pp. 189–232). San Diego, CA: Academic Press.

DeBono, K. G. (1987). Investigating the social adjustive and value expressive functions of attitudes: Implications for persuasion processes. *Journal of Personality and Social Psychology*, *52*, 279–287.

DeBono, K. G., & Harnish, R. J. (1988). Source expertise, source attractiveness, and processing or persuasive information: A functional approach. *Journal of Personality and Social Psychology*, *55*, 541–546.

DeCarlo, T. E., & Barone, M. J. (2009). With suspicious (but happy) minds: Mood's ability to neutralize the effects of suspicion on persuasion. *Journal of Consumer Psychology*, *19*(3), 326–333.

DeShields Jr., O. W., Kara, A., & Kaynak, E. (1996). Source effects in purchase decisions: The impact of physical attractiveness and accent of salesperson. *International Journal of Research in Marketing*, *13*(1), 89–101.

DeSteno, D., Petty, R. E., Rucker, D. D., Wegener, D. T., & Braverman, J. (2004). Discrete emotions and persuasion: The role of emotion-induced expectancies. *Journal of Personality and Social Psychology, 86*, 43–56.

Dunning, D. (2012). *Self-insight: Roadblocks and detours on the path to knowing thyself.* New York, NY: Psychology Press.

Eisend, M. (2006). Two-sided advertising: A meta-analysis. *International Journal of Research in Marketing, 23*(2), 187–198.

Evans, A. T., & Clark, J. K. (2012). Source characteristics and persuasion: The role of self-monitoring in self-validation. *Journal of Experimental Social Psychology, 48*, 383–386.

Fabrigar, L. R., & Petty, R. E. (1999). The role of the affective and cognitive bases of attitudes in susceptibility to affectively and cognitively based persuasion. *Personality and Social Psychology Bulletin, 25*, 363–381.

Fazio, R. H., Chen, J. M., McDonel, E. C., & Sherman, S. J. (1982). Attitude accessibility, attitude-behaviour consistency, and the strength of the object-evaluation association. *Journal of Experimental Social Psychology, 18*(4), 339–357.

Festinger, L., & Thibaut, J. (1951). Interpersonal communication in small groups. *The Journal of Abnormal and Social Psychology, 46*(1), 92–99.

Fleming, M. A., & Petty, R. E. (2000). Identity and persuasion: An elaboration likelihood approach. In D. J. Terry & M. A. Hogg (Eds.), *Attitudes, behaviour, and social context: The role of norms and group membership* (pp. 171–199). Mahwah, NJ: Lawrence Erlbaum Associates.

Friestad, M., & Wright, P. (1994). The Persuasion Knowledge Model: How people cope with persuasion attempts. *Journal of Consumer Research, 21*, 1–31.

Fujita, K., Eyal, T., Chaiken, S., Trope, Y., & Liberman, N. (2008). Influencing attitudes toward near and distant objects. *Journal of Experimental Social Psychology, 44*(3), 562–572.

Gawronski, B., & Payne, B. K. (Eds.) (2010). *Handbook of implicit social cognition: Measurement, theory, and applications.* New York, NY: Guilford Press.

Glaser, J., & Banaji, M. R. (1999). When fair is foul and foul is fair: Reverse priming in automatic evaluation. *Journal of Personality and Social Psychology, 77*, 669–687.

Gorn, G. J. (1982). The effects of music in advertising on choice behaviour: A classical conditioning approach. *Journal of Marketing Research, 46*, 94–101.

Gorn, G. J., & Goldberg, M. E. (1980). Children's responses to repetitive television commercials. *Journal of Consumer Research, 6*(4), 421–424.

Green, M. C., Brock, T. C., & Kaufman, G. F. (2004). Understanding media enjoyment: The role of transportation into narrative worlds. *Communication Theory, 14*(4), 311–327.

Greenwald, A. G., & Albert, R. D. (1968). Acceptance and recall of improvised arguments. *Journal of Personality and Social Psychology, 8*, 31–34.

Han, S. P., & Shavitt, S. (1994). Persuasion and culture: Advertising appeals in individualistic and collectivistic societies. *Journal of Experimental Social Psychology, 30*(4), 326–350.

Hastie, R. (1984). Causes and effects of causal attribution. *Journal of Personality and Social Psychology, 46*(1), 44–56.

Haugtvedt, C. P., & Kasmer, J. A. (2008). Attitude change and persuasion. In C. P. Haugtvedt, P. M. Herr & F. R. Kardes (Eds.), *Handbook of consumer psychology* (pp. 419–436). New York, NY: Lawrence Erlbaum Associates.

Haugtvedt, C. P., & Petty, R. E. (1992). Personality and persuasion: Need for cognition moderates the persistence and resistance of attitude changes. *Journal of Personality and Social Psychology, 63*, 308–319.

Hodges, S. D., & Wilson, T. D. (1994). Effects of analyzing reasons on attitude change: The moderating role of attitude accessibility. *Social Cognition, 11*, 353–366.

Horcajo, J., Briñol, P., & Petty, R. E. (2014). Multiple roles for majority versus minority source status on persuasion: When source status follows the message. *Social Influence, 9*, 37–51.

Hovland, C. I., Lumsdaine, A. A., & Sheffield, F. D. (1949). *Experiments on mass communication.* Princeton, NJ: Princeton University Press.

Howard, D. J., & Kerin, R. A. (2004). The effects of personalized product recommendations on advertisement response rates: The "Try This. It Works!" Technique. *Journal of Consumer Psychology, 14*(3), 271–279.

Hui, C. H., & Triandis, H. C. (1986). Individualism–collectivism: A study of cross-cultural researchers. *Journal of Cross-Cultural Psychology, 17*(2), 225–248.

Huntsinger, J. R. (2013). Incidental experiences of affective coherence and incoherence influence persuasion. *Personality and Social Psychology Bulletin, 39*, 792–802.

Kahle, L. R., & Homer, P. M. (1985). Physical attractiveness of the celebrity endorser: A social adaptation perspective. *Journal of Consumer Research, 11*(4), 954–961.

Kahneman, D., Knetsch, J. L., & Thaler, R. H. (1990). Experimental tests of the endowment effect and the coase theorem. *Journal of Political Economy, 98*, 1325–1348.

Kelman, H. C., & Hovland, C. I. (1953). "Reinstatement" of the communicator in delayed measurement of opinion change. *Journal of Abnormal and Social Psychology, 48*, 327–335.

Kiesler, C. A. (1971). *The psychology of commitment: Experiments linking behaviour to beliefs*. New York, NY: Academic Press.

Kramer, T., Spolter-Weisfeld, S., & Thakkar, M. (2007). The effect of cultural orientation on consumer response to personalization. *Marketing Science, 26*(2), 246–258.

Krosnick, J. A., & Petty, R. E. (1995). Attitude strength: An overview. In R. E. Petty & J. A. Krosnick (Eds.), *Attitude strength: Antecedents and consequences* (pp. 1–24). Mahwah, NJ: Lawrence Erlbaum Associates.

Kruglanski, A. W., & Thompson, E. P. (1999). Persuasion by a single route: A view from the unimodel. *Psychological Inquiry, 10*(2), 83–109.

Lavine, H., & Snyder, M. (1996). Cognitive processing and the functional matching effect in persuasion: The mediating role of subjective perceptions of message quality. *Journal of Experimental Social Psychology, 32*(6), 580–604.

Li, C., Kalyanaraman, S., & Du, Y. R. (2011). Moderating effects of collectivism on customized communication: A test with tailored and targeted messages. *Asian Journal of Communication, 21*(6), 575–594.

Maddux, W. W., Barden, J., Brewer, M. B., & Petty, R. E. (2005). Saying no to negativity: The effects of context and motivation to control prejudice on automatic evaluative responses. *Journal of Experimental Social Psychology, 41*, 19–35.

Maheswaran, D., & Chaiken, S. (1991). Promoting systematic processing in low-motivation settings: Effect of incongruent information on processing and judgment. *Journal of Personality and Social Psychology, 61*(1), 13–25.

Maio, G. R., & Thomas, G. (2007). The epistemic-teleologic model of deliberate self-persuasion. *Personality and Social Psychology Review, 11*(1), 46–67.

Martin, L., Abend, T., Sedikides, C., & Green, J. D. (1997). How would I feel if...?: Mood as input to a role fulfilment evaluation process. *Journal of Personality and Social Psychology, 73*, 242–253.

Martin, R., & Hewstone, M. (2008). Majority versus minority influence, message processing and attitude change: The source-context-elaboration model. In M. P. Zanna (Ed.), *Advances in experimental social psychology* (Vol. 40, pp. 237–326). San Diego, CA: Academic Press.

Mayer, J. D., Gaschke, Y. N., Braverman, D. L., & Evans, T. W. (1992). Mood-congruent judgment is a general effect. *Journal of Personality and Social Psychology, 63*(1), 119.

Mills, J., & Jellison, J. M. (1967). Effect on opinion change of how desirable the communication is to the audience the communicator addressed. *Journal of Personality and Social Psychology*, 6, 98–101.

Noar, S. M., Benac, C. H., & Harris, M. S. (2007). Does tailoring matter? Meta-analytic review of tailored print health behaviour change interventions. *Psychological Bulletin, 133*(4), 673–693.

Obermiller, C., Spangenberg, E., & MacLachlan, D. L. (2005). Ad skepticism: The consequences of disbelief. *Journal of Advertising, 34*(3), 7–17.

Palmgreen, P., Stephenson, M. T., Everett, M. W., Baseheart, J. R., & Francies, R. (2002). Perceived message sensation value (PMSV) and the dimensions and validation of a PMSV scale. *Health Communication, 14*(4), 403–428.

Patzer, G. L. (1983). Source credibility as a function of communicator physical attractiveness. *Journal of Business Research, 11*(2), 229–241.

Perkins, A., & Forehand, M. (2010). Implicit social cognition and indirect measures in consumer behaviour. In B. Gawronski & B. K. Payne (Eds.), *Handbook of implicit social cognition: Measurement, theory, and applications* (pp. 535–547). New York: Guilford Press.

Petrova, P. K., & Cialdini, R. B. (2008). Evoking the imagination as a strategy of influence. In C. P. Haugtvedt, P. M. Herr & F. R. Kardes (Eds.), *Handbook of consumer psychology* (pp. 505–524). New York, NY: Lawrence Erlbaum Associates.

Petty, R. E. (1997). The evolution of theory and research in social psychology: From single to multiple effect and process models. In C. McGarty & S. A. Haslam (Eds.), *The message of social psychology: Perspectives on mind in society* (pp. 268–290). Oxford, UK: Blackwell Publishers.

Petty, R. E., Barden, J., & Wheeler, S. C. (2009). The elaboration likelihood model of persuasion: Developing health promotions to produce sustained behaviour change. In R. J. DiClemente,

R. A. Crosby & M. Kegler (Eds.), *Emerging theories in health promotion practice and research* (2nd ed., pp. 185–214). San Francisco, CA: Jossey-Bass.

Petty, R. E., & Briñol, P. (2008). Persuasion: From single to multiple to meta-cognitive processes. *Perspectives on Psychological Science*, *3*, 137–147.

Petty, R. E., & Briñol, P. (2012). The Elaboration Likelihood Model. In P. A. M. Van Lange, A. Kruglanski & E. T. Higgins (Eds.), *Handbook of theories of social psychology* (Vol. 1, pp. 224–245). Los Angeles, CA: Sage.

Petty, R. E., & Briñol, P. (2015a). Emotion and persuasion: Cognitive and meta-cognitive processes impact attitudes. *Cognition and Emotion*, *29*, 1–26.

Petty, R. E., & Briñol, P. (2015b). Processes of social influence through attitude change. In E. Borgida & J. Bargh (Eds.), *APA handbook of personality and social psychology: Attitudes and social cognition* (Vol. 1, pp. 509–545). Washington, DC: APA Books.

Petty, R. E., Briñol, P., & DeMarree, K. (2007). The meta-cognitive model (MCM) of attitudes: Implications for attitude measurement, change, and strength. *Social Cognition*, *25*, 657–686.

Petty, R. E., Briñol, P., Loersch, C., & McCaslin, M. J. (2009). The need for cognition. In M. R. Leary & R. H. Hoyle (Eds.), *Handbook of individual differences in social behaviour* (pp. 318–329). New York, NY: Guilford Press.

Petty, R. E., Briñol, P., & Tormala, Z. L. (2002). Thought confidence as a determinant of persuasion: The self-validation hypothesis. *Journal of Personality and Social Psychology*, *82*, 722–741.

Petty, R. E., Briñol, P., Tormala, Z. L., & Wegener, D. T. (2007). The role of meta-cognition in social judgment. In A. W. Kruglanski & E. T. Higgins (Eds.), *Social psychology: Handbook of basic principles* (2nd ed., pp. 254–284). New York, NY: Guilford Press.

Petty, R. E., & Cacioppo, J. T. (1979a). Effects of forewarning of persuasive intent and involvement on cognitive responses and persuasion. *Personality and Social Psychology Bulletin*, *5*, 173–176.

Petty, R. E., & Cacioppo, J. T. (1979b). Issue involvement can increase or decrease persuasion by enhancing message-relevant cognitive responses. *Journal of Personality and Social Psychology*, *37*, 1915–1926.

Petty, R. E., & Cacioppo, J. T. (1984a). The effects of involvement on response to argument quantity and quality: Central and peripheral routes to persuasion. *Journal of Personality and Social Psychology*, *46*, 69–81.

Petty, R. E., & Cacioppo, J. T. (1984b). Source factors and the elaboration likelihood model of persuasion. *Advances in Consumer Research*, *11*(1), 668–672.

Petty, R. E., & Cacioppo, J. T. (1986). The Elaboration Likelihood Model of persuasion. *Advances in Experimental Social Psychology*, *19*, 123–205. [PB]

Petty, R. E., & Cacioppo, J. T. (1990). Involvement and persuasion: Tradition versus integration. *Psychological Bulletin*, *107*, 367–374.

Petty, R. E., Cacioppo, J. T., & Goldman, R. (1981). Personal involvement as a determinant of argument-based persuasion. *Journal of Personality and Social Psychology*, *41*, 847–855.

Petty, R. E., Cacioppo, J. T., & Heesacker, M. (1981). The use of rhetorical questions in persuasion: A cognitive response analysis. *Journal of Personality and Social Psychology*, *40*, 432–440.

Petty, R. E., Cacioppo, J. T., & Schumann, D. (1983). Central and peripheral routes to advertising effectiveness: The moderating role of involvement. *Journal of Consumer Research*, *10*, 135–146.

Petty, R. E., Haugtvedt, C., & Smith, S. M. (1995). Elaboration as a determinant of attitude strength: Creating attitudes that are persistent, resistant, and predictive of behaviour. In R. E. Petty & J. A. Krosnick (Eds.), *Attitude strength: Antecedents and consequences* (pp. 93–130). Mahwah, NJ: Lawrence Erlbaum Associates.

Petty, R. E., & Krosnick, J. A. (Eds.) (1995). *Attitude strength: Antecedents and consequences*. Mahwah, NJ: Lawrence Erlbaum Associates.

Petty, R. E., Schumann, D. W., Richman, S. A., & Strathman, A. J. (1993). Positive mood and persuasion: Different roles for affect under high and low elaboration conditions. *Journal of Personality and Social Psychology*, *64*, 5–20.

Petty, R. E., & Wegener, D. T. (1991). Thought systems, argument quality, and persuasion. In R. S. Wyer & T. K. Srull (Eds.), *Advances in social cognition* (Vol. 4, pp. 147–161). Hillsdale, NJ: Lawrence Erlbaum Associates.

Petty, R. E., & Wegener, D. T. (1993). Flexible correction processes in social judgment: Correcting for context induced contrast. *Journal of Experimental Social Psychology*, *29*, 137–165.

Petty, R. E., & Wegener, D. T. (1998a). Attitude change: Multiple roles for persuasion variables. In D. Gilbert, S. Fiske & G. Lindzey (Eds.), *The handbook of social psychology* (4th ed., Vol. 1, pp. 323–390). New York, NY: McGraw-Hill.

Petty, R. E., & Wegener, D. T. (1998b). Matching versus mismatching attitude functions: Implications for scrutiny of persuasive messages. *Personality and Social Psychology Bulletin, 24*, 227–240.

Petty, R. E., & Wegener, D. T. (1999). The Elaboration Likelihood Model: Current status and controversies. In S. Chaiken & Y. Trope (Eds.), *Dual process theories in social psychology* (pp. 41–72). New York, NY: Guilford Press.

Petty, R. E., Wegener, D. T., & White, P. (1998). Flexible correction processes in social judgment: Implications for persuasion. *Social Cognition, 16*, 93–113.

Petty, R. E., Wells, G. L., & Brock, T. C. (1976). Distraction can enhance or reduce yielding to propaganda: Thought disruption versus effort justification. *Journal of Personality and Social Psychology, 34*, 874–884.

Petty, R. E., Wheeler, S. C., & Bizer, G. (2000). Matching effects in persuasion: An elaboration likelihood analysis. In G. Maio & J. Olson (Eds.), *Why we evaluate: Functions of attitudes* (pp. 133–162). Mahwah, NJ: Lawrence Erlbaum Associates.

Pierro, A., Mannetti, L., Kruglanski, A. W., & Sleeth-Keppler, D. (2004). Relevance override: On the reduced impact of "cues" under high-motivation conditions of persuasion studies. *Journal of Personality and Social Psychology, 86*(2), 251–264.

Pratkanis, A. R., & Gliner, M. D. (2005). And when shall a little child lead them? Evidence for an altercasting theory of source credibility. *Current Psychology: Developmental, Learning, Personality, Social, 23*(4), 279–304.

Priester, J. M., & Petty, R. E. (1995). Source attributions and persuasion: Perceived honesty as a determinant of message scrutiny. *Personality and Social Psychology Bulletin, 21*, 637–654.

Puckett, J. M., Petty, R. E., Cacioppo, J. T., & Fisher, D. L. (1983). The relative impact of age and attractiveness stereotypes on persuasion. *Journal of Gerontology, 38*, 340–343.

Ratneshwar, S., & Chaiken, S. (1991). Comprehension's role in persuasion: The case of its moderating effect on the persuasive impact of source cues. *Journal of Consumer Research, 18*, 52–62. doi: 10.1086/209240.

Razran, G. H. (1940). Conditioned response changes in rating and appraising socio-political slogans. *Psychological Bulletin, 37*(48), 481.

Resch, H. L., & Lord, C. G. (2011). Individual differences in using epistemic and teleologic strategies for deliberate self-persuasion. *Personality and Individual Differences, 50*(5), 615–620.

Rhine, R., & Severance, L. (1970). Ego-involvement, discrepancy, source credibility, and attitude change. *Journal of Personality and Social Psychology, 16*, 175–190.

Rhodes, N., & Wood, W. (1992). Self-esteem and intelligence affect influenceability: The mediating role of message reception. *Psychological Bulletin, 111*, 156–171

Rucker, D. D., & Galinsky, A. D. (2009). Conspicuous consumption versus utilitarian ideals: How different levels of power shape consumer behaviour. *Journal of Experimental Social Psychology, 45*(3), 549–555.

Rucker, D. D., Petty, R. E., & Briñol, P. (2015). Social psychological foundations of social marketing. In D. Stewart (Ed.), *Handbook of persuasion and social marketing* (Vol. 1, pp. 27–60). Santa Barbara, CA: Praeger Publishers.

Rucker, D. D., Petty, R. E., & Priester, J. R. (2007). Understanding advertising effectiveness from a psychological perspective: The importance of attitudes and attitude strength. In G. J. Tellis & T. Ambler (Eds.), *The handbook of advertising* (pp. 73–88). Thousand Oaks, CA: Sage.

Rucker, D. D., Tormala, Z. L., Petty, R. E., & Briñol, P. (2014). Consumer conviction and commitment: An appraisal-based framework for attitude certainty. *Journal of Consumer Psychology, 24*, 119–136.

Salovey, P., & Wegener, D. T. (2003). Communicating about health: Message framing, persuasion, and health behaviour. In J. Suls & K. A. Wallston (Eds.), *Social psychological foundations of health and illness* (pp. 54–81). Malden, MA: Blackwell Publishing.

Schwarz, N., Bless, H., & Bohner, G. (1991). Mood and persuasion: Affective status influence the processing of persuasive communications. In M. P. Zanna (Ed.), *Advances in experimental social psychology* (Vol. 24, pp. 161–197). San Diego, CA: Academia Press.

Sengupta, J., & Venkataramani Johar, G. (2001). Contingent effects of anxiety on message elaboration and persuasion. *Personality and Social Psychology Bulletin, 27*(2), 139–150.

Shavitt, S., Lowrey, T. M., & Han, S. P. (1992). Attitude functions in advertising: The interactive role of products and self-monitoring. *Journal of Consumer Psychology, 1*(4), 337–364.

Shavitt, S., Nelson, M. R., & Yuan, R. M.-L. (1997). Exploring cross-cultural differences in cognitive responding to ads. In M. Brucks & D. J. MacInnis (Eds.), *Advances in consumer research* (Vol. 24, pp. 245–250). Provo, UT: Association for Consumer Research.

Sherman, J., Gawronski, B., & Trope, Y. (Eds.) (2012). *Dual-process theories of the social mind*. New York, NY: Guildford Press.

Silvera, D. H., Josephs, R. A., & Giesler, R. B. (2002). Bigger is better: The influence of physical size on aesthetic preference judgments. *Journal of Behavioural Decision Making*, *15*(3), 189–202.

Smith, S. M., & Petty, R. E. (1995). Personality moderators of mood congruency effects on cognition: The role of self-esteem and negative mood regulation. *Journal of Personality and Social Psychology*, *68*, 1092–1107.

Smith, S. M., & Shaffer, D. R. (1995). Speed of speech and persuasion: Evidence for multiple effects. *Personality and Social Psychology Bulletin*, *21*, 1051–1060.

Snyder, M. (1974). Self-monitoring of expressive behaviour. *Journal of Personality and Social Psychology*, *30*, 526–537.

Spassova, G., & Lee, A. Y. (2013). Looking into the future: A match between self-view and temporal distance. *Journal of Consumer Research*, *40*(1), 159–171.

Staats, C. K., & Staats, A. W. (1957). Meaning established by classical conditioning. *Journal of Experimental Psychology*, *54*, 74–80.

Syam, N., Krishnamurthy, P., & Hess, J. D. (2008). That's what I thought I wanted? Miswanting and regret for a standard good in a mass-customized world. *Marketing Science*, *27*(3), 379–397.

Tajfel, H. (1982). Social psychology of intergroup relations. *Annual Review of Psychology*, *33*(1), 1–39.

Tangney, J. P., Baumeister, R. F., & Boone, A. L. (2004). High self-control predicts good adjustment, less pathology, better grades, and interpersonal success. *Journal of Personality*, *72*(2), 271–324.

Tiedens, L. Z., & Linton, S. (2001). Judgment under emotional certainty and uncertainty: The effects of specific emotions on information processing. *Journal of Personality and Social Psychology*, *81*(6), 973–988.

Wegener, D. T., & Petty, R. E. (1994). Mood management across affective states: The hedonic contingency hypothesis. *Journal of Personality and Social Psychology*, *66*, 1034–1048.

Wegener, D. T., & Petty, R. E. (1995). Flexible correction processes in social judgment: The role of naive theories in corrections for perceived bias. *Journal of Personality and Social Psychology*, *68*, 36–51.

Wegener, D. T., & Petty, R. E. (1997). The flexible correction model: The role of naive theories of bias in bias correction. In M. P. Zanna (Ed.), *Advances in experimental social psychology* (Vol. 29, pp. 141–208). San Diego, CA: Academic Press.

Wegener, D. T., Petty, R. E., & Klein, D. J. (1994). Effects of mood on high elaboration attitude change: The mediating role of likelihood judgments. *European Journal of Social Psychology*, *23*, 25–44.

Wheeler, S. C., Petty, R. E., & Bizer, G. Y. (2005). Self-schema matching and attitude change: Situational and dispositional determinants of message elaboration. *Journal of Consumer Research*, *31*, 787–797.

White, T. B., Zahay, D. L., Thorbjørnsen, H., & Shavitt, S. (2008). Getting too personal: Reactance to highly personalized email solicitations. *Marketing Letters*, *19*(1), 39–50.

Wilson, T. D., & Brekke, N. (1994). Mental contamination and mental correction: Unwanted influences on judgments and evaluations. *Psychological Bulletin*, *116*, 117–142.

Wood, W., Rhodes, N., & Biek, M. (1995). Working knowledge and attitude strength: An information processing analysis. In R. E. Petty & J. A. Krosnick (Eds.), *Attitude strength: Antecedents and consequences*. Hillsdale, NJ: Lawrence Erlbaum Associates.

Worth, L. T., & Mackie, D. M. (1987). Cognitive mediation of positive affect in persuasion. *Social Cognition*, *5*, 76–94.

Wu, C., & Shaffer, D. R. (1987). Susceptibility to persuasive appeals as a function of source credibility and prior experience with the attitude object. *Journal of Personality and Social Psychology*, *52*(4), 677.

Yalch, R. F., & Elmore-Yalch, R. (1984). The effect of numbers on the route to persuasion. *Journal of Consumer Research*, 522–527.

Yukl, G., & Falbe, C. M. (1991). Importance of different power sources in downward and lateral relations. *Journal of Applied Psychology*, *76*(3), 416.

Zhang, Y., & Gelb, B. D. (1996). Matching advertising appeals to culture: The influence of products' use conditions. *Journal of Advertising*, *25*(3), 29–46.

Ziegler, R. (2010). Mood, source characteristics, and message processing: A mood-congruent expectancies approach. *Journal of Experimental Social Psychology*, *46*(5), 743–752.

Ziegler, R., Diehl, M., & Ruther, A. (2002). Multiple source characteristics and persuasion: Source inconsistency as a determinant of message scrutiny. *Personality and Social Psychology Bulletin*, *28*(4), 496–508.

22

Transactions as tradeoffs between costs and benefits

Bernadette Kamleitner and Ruta Ruzeviciute

Consumer behaviour often involves a factual tradeoff between costs and benefits. Going to the theatre involves obtaining a potentially entertaining and fun experience in return for a certain amount of money and the hassle involved in getting the ticket. Borrowing a pint of milk from a neighbour involves the benefits of being able to have a café latte or a happy pet cat. It also involves having to leave the couch and it may mean incurring some social debt to the neighbour who may come knocking to get your last drop of milk another time.

All consumer decisions involve advantages and disadvantages, costs and benefits. How consumers perceive specific costs and benefits, how much attention they pay to them, and how strongly they weigh them has long been recognized as a key driver of the decisions consumers make (Beach & Mitchell, 1978; Bettman, Johnson, & Payne, 1991, Epstein, 2003; Kahneman, 2003; Tversky & Kahneman, 1981). For example, whether or not a person perceives and pays any attention to the social debts involved in borrowing a pint of milk depends on the specific individual and her setting including the cultural background (Patterson & Smith, 2003; Shane, 1992; Wandersman, Florin, Friedmann, & Meier, 1987).

The premise has been that consumers would compare the costs and benefits of an option to determine whether the option involves a net benefit or a net cost (Thaler, 1985; Tversky & Kahneman, 1981; Zeithaml, 1988). The powerbase of this premise lies in its often implicit nature (Kamleitner & Hölzl, 2009). Many theories such as utility theories, exchange theories and decision theories inherently assume that individuals compare costs and benefits and are guided by the net outcome (utility, value or worth) of this comparison (Cronin, Brady, Brand, Hightower, & Shemwell, 1997; Handy et al., 2000; Monroe, 1990; Thaler, 1985; Woodruff, 1997; Zeithaml, 1988). Even theories deviating from the assumption of rational behaviour frequently assume that consumers will at least mentally connect and consider both costs and benefits. For example, the sunk cost effect (e.g., Arkes & Blumer, 1985; He & Mittal, 2007) – i.e., the finding that past investments influence future spending decisions – necessitates that people mentally link costs and benefits. Another example is mental accounting which assumes that spending within one category (mental budget) decreases the probability of further spending in that category (Heath & Soll, 1996; Thaler, 1999); again a mental link between costs and benefits is vital.

In this chapter we ask whether individuals really do and can make these comparisons. We take a close look at the notion of behaviour as the outcome of cost–benefit tradeoffs. We do so by dissembling cost–benefit tradeoffs into their three constituent parts: the perception of costs, the perception of benefits and the mental link (cost–benefit associations) needed for their tradeoff. First, we question whether consumers are at all capable of and willing to engage in mental tradeoffs. Drawing on the notion of and insights on cost–benefit associations we will show that consumers are neither capable nor willing to universally engage in mental cost–benefit tradeoffs. Digging deeper we will zoom in on the very fabric of benefits and costs. We will elaborate on the notion of benefits and costs and we will question whether a distinguishing line can be drawn between them. In sum, this chapter reviews and questions what is actually known about a phenomenon that has tended to be taken for granted since the origins of consumer research.

Do consumers mentally link costs and benefits?

Sometimes, accruing or thinking about benefits makes people think of the cost involved in obtaining these benefits and sometimes, incurring or thinking of cost makes people think of the benefits obtained for those costs (Kamleitner & Hölzl, 2009). Such cost–benefit associations are needed if consumers are to decide on the favourability of the net outcome, i.e., when they make cost–benefit tradeoffs (Prelec & Loewenstein, 1998). Yet, not much is known about when and why these associative thoughts occur and what they effectuate.

A metaphor proves useful in explaining why cost–benefit associations are a potentially powerful construct. Imagine a city divided by a river. On one side of the river all the most beautiful sights, people, and enjoyments can be found. This is the benefit district. On the other side of the river all the most dodgy places, criminals and disadvantages can be found. This is the cost district. A person deciding on whether to move to this city may want to take a look at the entire city and decide whether, on the whole, it is a place worth moving to. To what extent this will in fact become a comprehensive impression depends on the bridges, i.e., the metaphorical cost–benefit associations, connecting the two districts. If there are no bridges, the person is likely to see only one part of the city. Whichever part this is, it is likely to be viewed in its purest and unmitigated form because no bridges also mean that inhabitants from the two districts cannot mingle.

Theories that deal with these metaphorical bridges and their implications, i.e., theories that address cost–benefit associations, are sparse. Aside from several theories addressing these associations indirectly (for a review of those theories see Kamleitner & Hölzl, 2009) only work on credit use (Kamleitner, Hoelzl, & Kirchler, 2010; Kamleitner, Hornung, & Kirchler, 2011; Kamleitner & Kirchler, 2006) and the theory of prospective double-entry mental accounting (Prelec & Loewenstein, 1998) do so directly.

Prospective double-entry mental accounting describes "the reciprocal interactions between the pleasure of consumption and the pain of paying" (Prelec & Loewenstein, 1998, p. 4); in other words it models (anticipated) mental cost–benefit associations. Within this theory these associations are termed "coupling". Two coupling coefficients, α and β, describe the degree and the direction of these associations. The coefficient α describes the association from benefit/consumption to cost/payment, i.e., the extent to which consumption pleasure evokes thoughts of pain of payment. Going back to the metaphor, it describes whether there is a bridge that lets inhabitants of the cost district move over to and influence the benefit district. The coefficient β describes the association from cost/payment to benefit/consumption, i.e., the extent to which pain of payment evokes thoughts of consumption pleasure (Prelec & Loewenstein, 1998). With regard to the metaphor, it describes whether inhabitants of the benefit district can move over and mingle with inhabitants of the cost district. Within this theory, asymmetric associations (i.e., one-way bridges) are possible though they are rarely assumed or investigated.

Nonetheless some empirical insights exist. The underlying research is primarily situated in the context of loans and, in particular, in post-purchase settings (Hoelzl, Pollai, & Kamleitner,

2007; Kamleitner, Hoelzl, & Kirchler, 2008; Kamleitner & Kirchler, 2006). Results converge in showing that there are considerable individual differences in the cost–benefit association patterns measured as the automaticity with which costs evoke thoughts of benefits and vice versa. Furthermore, results suggest that the association is asymmetric for most consumers with the cost-to-benefit association (coefficient β) being stronger. To which extent this also holds for consumption decisions has yet to be investigated.

Several direct and indirect insights into the causes of cost–benefit associations do, however, suggest that strong reciprocal cost–benefit associations cannot be taken for granted. We first discuss the consequences of weak or missing cost–benefit associations before delving into possible reasons for variations in cost–benefit association patterns.

What are the consequences of varying cost–benefit associations?

Cost–benefit associations presumably influence experiences, cognitions and behaviour across all stages of consumer behaviour; after all they may arise any time a consumer thinks of costs or benefits. The bridge metaphor serves to illustrate the encompassing influence. Whether there are bridges available determines who can move where and how the city as well as the two districts can be experienced. The first consequence to note is an influence on memory (Kamleitner & Hölzl, 2009). Strong associations entail that salience of one concept leads to salience of the associated concept. The associated cognition, hence, becomes mentally more present and, in turn, easier to recall (cf. Anderson, 2013). Metaphorically speaking a person in the benefit district may forget about the cost district if there are no reminding bridges connecting the districts. Since people tend to more frequently think about consumption benefits (Kamleitner et al., 2010), this matters in particular for the benefit-to-cost association. Indeed, Soman (2001) found that students leaving a bookstore were significantly less able to remember the amount spent when they had paid with credit card, a mechanism that reduces cost–benefit associations, than when they had paid in cash, a mechanism that strengthens cost–benefit associations (see also Srivastava & Raghubir, 2002). Not only were those paying by credit card less able to remember the amount, they also underestimated the amount spent. In a related vein, Kamleitner and Hölzl (2009) report that strong cost–benefit associations may increase the salience of opportunity costs.

The next consequence relates to perceived utility. The two directions of association are supposed to have differential effects (Prelec & Loewenstein, 1998): If strong associations from costs to benefits are established, this is supposed to reduce the disutility of payment because it makes people aware of what they are paying for. If strong associations from benefits to costs are established, this is supposed to reduce consumption utility because consumers no longer can consume a product as if it were free. Consequently, a strong cost-to-benefit association combined with a weak benefit-to-cost association is assumed to boost hedonic efficiency: Consumption feels free while payments are buffered by thoughts of benefits (Prelec & Loewenstein, 1998). Moving back to the metaphor: The benefit district remains untarnished while the cost district is either totally disregarded or beautified by transfers from the benefit district.

In contrast, strong reciprocal associations are assumed to boost decision efficiency because people are (painfully) aware of the costs of consumption and are hence more likely to regulate their spending (Prelec & Loewenstein, 1998). In terms of the metaphor, inhabitants of both districts are mingling lively and the city is seen for what it is. Cost–benefit tradeoffs are possible and net utilities can be inferred.

Although the hedonic consequences of cost–benefit associations are intuitively appealing there is not much research backing them. Several studies in a personal loan context showed that benefit-to-cost associations have an impact on cost perceptions rather than on benefit perceptions (Kamleitner et al., 2008). If an object that is consumed makes people think of the cost, the costs are perceived as considerably more onerous. Whereas these results indicate that cost–benefit associations are in fact consequential in experiential terms, they also indicate the phenomenon's complexity (for a discussion of possible metacognitive processes, see Kamleitner et al., 2008).

Because cost–benefit associations presumably influence consumers' actual as well as anticipated utilities, they can also influence if and when which purchase is made and how (cf. Heath & Fennema, 1996; Prelec & Loewenstein, 1998). For example, Kamleitner and Hölzl (2009) suggest that cost–benefit associations may affect which options are preferred. Cheaper but less attractive options may become more appealing to those who strongly associate costs and benefits than to those who do not. When consumption and payment occur also likely relates to the strength of cost–benefit associations. Consumers who do not associate benefits with costs are assumed to prefer to consume first and pay later, whereas the opposite may be true for consumers with strong cost–benefit associations (Prelec & Loewenstein, 1998).

The behavioural consequence of cost–benefit associations that we know most about sets in after an object has been acquired, during the consumption phase. Several studies suggest that the weaker the cost–benefit association, the more people consume how they want instead of how they think they should (e.g., Kivetz, 1999; Stremersch & Tellis, 2002). The underlying rationale is that in the absence of cost–benefit associations, consumers are tempted to consume as if an object is free. For example, services with unlimited usage will be used less frequently because there is no need to get as much for your money as possible. In turn, cost–benefit associations may influence the care people take of their goods and repurchasing behaviour (cf. Heath & Fennema, 1996; Soman & Gourville, 2001).

What determines whether cost–benefit associations are established?

The actual cost–benefit association pattern is likely to depend on a variety of interacting causes (Kamleitner, 2009; Prelec & Loewenstein, 1998). Cost–benefit associations can be a situational by-product. They can, however, also depend on personal characteristics (some people have an eye for bridges), and be driven motivationally. With regard to personal characteristics, some researchers have speculated that tightwads are more likely to engage in strong cost–benefit associations than spendthrifts (Kivetz, 1999; Prelec & Loewenstein, 1998). Lay intuitions back that speculation and suggest that people who care about costs are more likely to associate costs and benefits (Kamleitner, 2009). This opens the floor for potential cultural differences (Tatzel, 2002). To date, the influence of culture on the propensity to establish cost–benefit associations has not been addressed. There are, however, hints at their existence. In particular, evidence on cultural differences in sunk cost effects (Keil et al., 2000; Pattaratanakun & Mak, 2015; Salter & Sharp, 2001; Sharp & Salter, 1997) points in that direction. Sunk cost effects are a phenomenon that presupposes a mental association between sunk cost and benefits. Cross-cultural differences in this effect may signal respective differences in cost–benefit associations.

Beyond being driven by personal and cultural influences, consumers may exhibit different degrees of cost–benefit associations because it may make them feel better. Consumers may be motivated to influence cost–benefit associations because they affect experienced utility. For example, Soman and Gourville (2001) found that people may purposefully disassociate benefits of a bundle (theatre tickets or ski tickets) from its cost depending on the attractiveness of alternative benefits. When people were highly motivated to forgo consumption (attend a prepaid play or go skiing) because of an attractive alternative (e.g., a tempting party) or because the consumption became unattractive (e.g., skiing in poor conditions), they were likely to disassociate benefits from costs; presumably because disassociation released consumption pressure.

Consumers trying to avoid a mental bridge between costs and benefits of a transaction can draw on a range of possible mechanisms. For instance, framing a purchase as an investment (thus making the cost invisible) may be an efficient strategy to weaken cost–benefit associations (Kivetz, 1999). Moreover, consumers can engineer and seek situations that strengthen or weaken cost–benefit associations. In doing so, consumers can draw on a well-sorted tool box because any aspect that affects whether costs and benefits are perceived as somehow "belonging together" can foster their association (cf. Henderson & Peterson, 1992; Kamleitner & Hölzl, 2009). For example, temporal proximity and causal relatedness of outcomes (here: costs and benefits) enhance the likelihood of their mental association and integration (e.g., Gourville & Soman, 1998; Hirst, Joyce, & Schadewald, 1994; Linville & Fischer, 1991; Soman & Lam, 2002; Thaler, 1985). The complexity of the cost–benefit relationship also affects their mental association. The more benefits and/or costs there are and the more ambiguity to the cost of a particular consumption there is, the more difficult it becomes to associate single benefits with costs and vice versa (Prelec & Loewenstein, 1998). In particular, situations in which the relationship of costs to benefits is one-to-many or many-to-many (e.g., fixed-fees, bundles) hamper the establishment of cost–benefit associations.

Association can only occur for concepts that are salient and mentally accessible. In particular the method of payment has been assumed to influence cost–benefit associations via its influence on cost salience (Prelec & Loewenstein, 1998). For example, handing cash over a cash desk is more salient (Soman, 2001, 2003; Srivastava & Raghubir, 2002) and will, thus, lead to stronger cost–benefit associations than paying by credit card. Absolute magnitude and importance are influencing salience and, thus, associability, too. For example, very small amounts may hinder cost–benefit associations if they are categorized as zero (Ariely & Silva, 2002). In contrast, very high costs are likely to come to mind often. The same holds for benefits where large quantities have also been shown to increase salience (Chandon & Wansink, 2002) and, thus, associability.

Taken together, insights on cost–benefit associations unveil a complex interplay of situational, individual, motivational and potentially cultural factors that jointly affect cognitions, perceptions and behaviours. What we have not yet addressed is what costs and benefits actually are. We are by no means alone in this failure. The vast majority of the existing literature treated the metaphorical cost and benefit "districts" as self-explanatory notions. In the next step, we are going to zoom in on these districts.

What perspectives on costs and benefits are there?

Broadly speaking, costs and benefits relate to the perceived disadvantages and advantages of an object or course of action (Cronin et al., 1997; Zeithaml, 1988). Importantly, costs and benefits can be conceptualized at different levels of abstraction. When, for example, contemplating the purchase of an apple, one could contemplate its costs and benefits in terms of concrete attributes, such as its colour, shape and price. Alternatively, one could contemplate costs and benefits in more abstract terms, such as perceived healthiness or freedom of choice.

The idea that costs and benefits can be viewed in terms of different levels of abstraction dates back to the well-known "Means–End Chain" model (Gutman, 1982). It describes how consumers may (unconsciously) translate concrete product attributes (e.g., colour of the apple) into meaningful costs and benefits at a higher level of abstraction (e.g., healthiness). The assumption is that products are not bought for their concrete attributes but for their higher level consequences, i.e., for what they mean.

Concrete attributes hold, nonetheless, an important place in the consumer literature (cf. Woodruff, 1997; Zeithaml, 1988). The abstraction level consumers adopt effectively influences the choices they make and the biases they are prone to exhibit (Khan, Zhu, & Kalra, 2011). What is more, the abstraction level that matters most to consumers may depend on the stage of the consumption process and characteristics of the individual. Although attribute-based costs and benefits are particularly prominent in purchase situations (Woodruff, 1997), consumers having little experience with an object might base their judgement on higher level attributes, such as brand or communicated image (Zeithaml, 1988). In contrast, more abstract advantages and disadvantages are likely to become more salient during consumption and post-consumption stages (Woodruff, 1997). Moreover, the existing literature suggests that the level of abstraction at which costs and benefits are framed may also be dependent on macro-level factors such as culture (e.g., Trope & Liberman, 2010; Vohs, Mead, & Goode, 2006).

An overlap in the literature on benefits and their perception with literature on costs and their perception may seem intuitive. Yet there is barely any overlap (for very context specific exceptions see for example Reynolds & Beatty, 1999; Ruth, 2001; Strader & Shaw, 1999). Although both terms are usually treated as antipodes (advantages vs. disadvantages), they are not always considered simultaneously. Specific streams of literature on customer value and cost–benefit tradeoffs provide noteworthy exceptions (e.g., Zeithaml, 1988). However, the focus in this literature is on "what I get for what I give" (Zeithaml, 1988, p. 13), i.e., on the tradeoff rather than on what is being traded off. Consequently, benefits and costs are not always treated at the same level of abstraction: While benefits are usually treated on higher abstraction levels (e.g., quality) (Monroe, 1990; Zeithaml, 1988), costs are primarily considered at attribute level (e.g., money) (Monroe, 1990). In the next sections we review the status quo on conceptualizations of benefits and cost respectively.

What (types of) benefits are there?

To better understand the notion of benefit, we entered it as a search term. Even restricting the search to the consumer literature, the search results tend to draw the picture of a fragmented and context-specific literature base. For example, there is research on very narrow and specific benefits in advertising (Ruth, 2001), brand communities (Gummerus, Liljander, Weman, & Pihlström, 2012), brand management (Park et al., 1986) and education (Chen et al., 2008). It also became apparent that the term *benefit* tends to be used without a perceived need to define it, and that what we would have considered benefits may come under several names (e.g., advantage, value). Since a lack of definition also means that it is hard to determine whether related notions are relevant, we suggest the following working definition for the purposes of this review. We refer to a benefit as any subjective advantage or gain that manifests at any level of abstraction.

Low abstraction level benefits relate to concrete, favourable attributes such as size, colour, sweetness or any other concrete feature inherent to an object or course of action. An important characteristic of low-level benefits is that they can be objectively described and measured. The subjective dimension only becomes relevant when these attributes are evaluated. For example, a specific size of a phone could be perceived as too big and unfavourable by one person but as just right by another person. Concrete attributes only can be considered benefits, if they are perceived as an advantage or plus point. Concrete attribute advantages can then be further abstracted to more abstract benefits, such as "a big phone suggests security" (Gutman, 1982). However, as concrete attributes are highly context specific, it is no surprise that most existing classifications of benefits (see Table 22.1) instead focus on higher levels of abstraction, such as relationship or economic benefits (e.g., Gummerus et al., 2012; Gwinner, Gremler, & Bitner,

Table 22.1 An overview of categorizations of values/benefits

Source	*Context*	*Benefit/value*	*Definition sketch*
Holbrook (1994)	Consumption (*in general*)	Efficiency value	(Or convenience) is derived through active manipulation of an object to accomplish a self-directed goal
		Excellence value	(Or quality) aims at achieving self-oriented goals through distanced appreciation
		Politics value	(Or success) – value that originates from an endeavor to achieve success through favourable response of others
		Esteem value	(Or reputation) is derived from a reflection about own status, based on approval from others
		Play value	(Or fun) – value results from active engagement with an activity that is enjoyed for its mere pleasure
		Aesthetics value	(Or beauty) – value results from reactive appreciation of an object as an end in itself
		Morality value	(Or virtue) – value arises from actions or objects that are intrinsically interested in the well being of others
		Spirituality value	(Or faith/ecstasy) – the intrinsic value derived from spiritual faith
Sheth et al. (1991)	Acquisition and consumption (*in general*)	Functional value	The utility gained from the products' ability to demonstrate "functional, physical, utilitarian" performance. Functional value is inherent to alternative's attributes or characteristics
		Social value	The signalling power of the product (or alternative) derived through association with certain reference groups
		Emotional value	The product's ability to instigate feelings or affective states
		Epistemic value	The utility gained through instigated and/or satisfied curiosity, need for knowledge and novelty
		Conditional value	Utility that occurs just in specific situations
Sweeney and Soutar (2001)	Acquisition of durable good	Emotional value	The utility derived from the feelings or affective states that a product generates
		Social value	The utility derived from the product's ability to enhance social self-concept
		Functional value (price/value for money)	The utility derived from the product due to the reduction of its perceived short term and longer term costs
		Functional value (performance/ quality)	The utility derived from the perceived quality and expected performance of the product

(*Continued*)

Table 22.1 (Continued)

Source	*Context*	*Benefit/value*	*Definition sketch*
Park et al. (1986)	Strategic brand management	Functional benefit	Fulfils needs that aim at solving consumption-related issues
		Symbolic benefit	Tackles needs of identity-signalling (e.g. self-enhancement, group membership, ego-identification)
		Experiential benefit	Provides sensory and cognitive stimulation and pleasure derived from it
Babin et al. (1994)	Services (*shopping*)	Utilitarian value	Instrumental value that is derived from goal-driven shopping behaviour
		Hedonic value	Non-instrumental value that is derived from playfulness and enjoyment of shopping experience
Gummerus et al. (2012)	Online community engagement	Practical benefit	Instrumental benefits that are derived through information advantage
		Social benefit	Arises from interaction between the company and the customer, could imply value derived through friendship or recognition
		Social enhancement	Relates to the need for recognition and belonging to a certain group
		Entertainment benefit	Originates from fun and relaxation based on experiential value
		Economic benefit	Refers to utilitarian advantages that a brand community could provide, such as money or time savings
Gwinner et al. (1998)	Services	Relationship benefit	The benefit derived through service beyond the value of the core product or service received
		Confidence benefit	Risk reduction benefit resulting in increased choice confidence
		Social benefit	Psychological benefit derived from a friend-like relation
		Special treatment benefit	Satisfaction-related benefit derived from preferential treatment

1998; Park et al., 1986). When it comes to classifications of abstract benefits, two streams of literature that hardly ever use the term *benefit* also become relevant: literature on different types of utility (e.g., Lichtenstein, Netemeyer, & Burton, 1990; Thaler, 1985) and multidimensional value (e.g., Babin, Darden, & Griffin, 1994; Holbrook, 1994; Sheth, Newman, & Gross, 1991). Note that in this section we are not referring to a unidimensional meaning of value (Sánchez-Fernández & Iniesta-Bonillo, 2007) which refers to value as the net result of cost benefit trade-offs, i.e., "what I get for what I give" (Zeithaml, 1988, p. 13). Here we focus on literature on types of value. This literature treats overall value as a composite construct originating from multiple values (Holbrook, 1994; Sheth et al., 1991) which roughly correspond to high abstraction benefits.

The multidimensional value literature serves as a valuable source of insights on different types of abstract benefits. Table 22.1 provides an overview of most benefit and value typologies. One of the most comprehensive and influential value typologies was proposed by Holbrook (1994).

He distinguishes three separate dimensions of value: instrumentality (intrinsic vs. extrinsic), orientation (self-oriented vs. other-oriented) and activation (active vs. reactive value). Value instrumentality refers to whether a benefit generates value by acting as a means towards a goal or whether it is valued in its own right. Value orientation refers to whether value is derived from a self or other perspective, and value activation refers to whether value can be obtained actively or passively. Based on this three-dimensional scheme, Holbrook (1994) derived a matrix with eight types of value: Efficiency, excellence, politics, esteem, play, aesthetics, morality, spirituality (see Table 22.1 for definitions). Subsequent research (Babin et al., 1994; Overby & Lee, 2006) has picked up and built on the dimension of value instrumentality, value activation and orientation dimensions has been comparably discarded. A somewhat different approach in determining types of values has been taken by Sheth et al. (1991). Instead of developing a multidimensional framework, he defined five basic values – functional, social, emotional, epistemic, conditional – that are assumed to motivate purchase behaviour. This framework, too, has inspired other researchers (e.g., Sweeney & Soutar, 2001). Although later frameworks proposed some changes, as Table 22.1 shows, most of them agree on functional, social and emotional components. The particular weights assigned to specific values are, however, subjective and open to individual and cultural differences (Holbrook, 1994; Sheth et al., 1991). In fact, empirical evidence shows that even established theories such as Maslow's hierarchy of needs do not necessarily generalize across cultures (Hofstede, 1984); with self-actualization dominating in Western and group harmony and status in Eastern cultures. Apart from the question what specific benefits may dominate in particular contexts, the question of what the prevailing level of abstraction in the conceptualization of benefits may be remains still open.

What level of abstraction dominates for the term benefit*?*

Whether and when concrete benefits are turned into more abstract benefits is an open question. When we buy our daily pint of milk (low involvement situation), or when we choose an object we genuinely like for its concrete features, such as smell or the feel while touching it, specific attributes may be on consumers' minds the most. However, what if people are simply asked to come up with benefits? Which level of abstraction prevails when the mere notion of benefits is evoked?

To explore whether spontaneous benefit associations tend to be more concrete or abstract, we conducted a free-association test and asked 20 people to name everything that comes to mind when they think of the word *benefit*. In total, 60 associations were generated. On the basis of the abstraction level of the words and expressions named (Trope & Liberman, 2010), i.e., abstract vs. concrete features, detailed vs. holistic description, superordinate vs. subordinate category, adjective vs. verb, two coders classified associations as concrete or abstract. Differences between the coders were reconciled through discussion. The coding yielded 77 per cent abstract benefits (e.g., freedom, meaning of life, health, sustainability) and 16 per cent concrete benefits (e.g., flat, student transit pass, coffee, bicycle). 7 per cent of association could not be assigned to any category (e.g., diminishing returns, maximum sum of utilities).

Given that the keyword was rather abstract in itself, it is not surprising that the majority of associations was abstract also. In that sense, consumers own conceptualization of the term benefits seems to align with the way the term has been predominantly treated in the literature: in abstract terms. It is, however, noteworthy that there were still a sizable number of concrete *benefits* named. This suggests that future research would do well to consider benefits at different abstraction levels. It also poses an added complication for the analysis of cost–benefit associations. It may well be that the level of abstraction at which benefits are considered interacts with the propensity to establish cost–benefit associations.

What (types of) costs are there?

Moving on to costs, the literature provides a less fragmented picture. Unlike the typology of consumer benefits, the classification of costs seems to be rather straightforward. The literature tends to agree that the main costs of consumer experience involve disadvantages related to monetary (e.g., money required in exchange to certain good), physical (e.g., efforts to perform certain act), psychological (e.g., sacrifice of emotional well-being in exchange for certain good) or timer costs (Kotler, 2000; Verhallen & Pieters, 1984; Zeithaml, 1988). It is important to note that even highly contextualized studies (e.g., switching costs) (Burnham, Frels, & Mahajan, 2003) refer to the same base of costs. Some more specific costs, such as risk costs, distribution costs or taxes (Strader & Shaw, 1999) are only added so as to capture a phenomenon in its full depth (e.g., online shopping). Unlike specific types of benefits (see Table 22.1), specific types of costs tend to be treated as self-explanatory and most sources make do without a definition.

Looking across different types of costs (Kotler, 2000; Verhallen & Pieters, 1984; Zeithaml, 1988) the following working definition emerges: We refer to a cost as any subjective disadvantage or loss that manifests at any level of abstraction and constitutes a sacrifice needed to obtain a benefit. The last part of the definition is an important addition that constitutes a crucial difference between the cost and benefit literatures, while at the same time connecting them: The term *cost* appears to be only used with reference to one or multiple benefits. The term *benefit* does not seem to need such a referent. This observation goes well in hand with the aforementioned fact that cost-to-benefit associations tend to be stronger than vice versa.

Another difference to the benefit literature emerges with regard to the prevailing level of abstraction. Costs also may be viewed from different levels of abstraction and some types of costs, in particular psychological costs, tend to be generally abstract. However, the literature (e.g., Monroe, 1990) primarily focuses on one specific and concrete type of costs: price. Whereas most literature on consumer choices treats price as a low-level attribute, some authors (e.g., Lichtenstein & Burton, 1989; Zeithaml, 1988) distinguish between objective and perceived prices that can be conceptualized at different levels of abstraction. In fact, following the logic of the means–end chain, consumers could translate the concrete feature price into more abstract forms of sacrifice, such as "paying a high price curbs (financial) freedom". In line with our conceptualization of cost, we posit that price only becomes a low-level cost or sacrifice when a person attaches negative valence to it. Extensive literature on the Veblen effect (Truong, 2010; Veblen, 1994/1899) and luxury consumption suggests that a high price is not necessarily perceived as a cost but may also be perceived as a benefit with signalling value.

Whether consumers, like researchers, predominantly conceptualize cost in terms of low level, concrete attributes is an open question. Its answer is, however, likely useful in explaining how decisions come about and how consumers feel about objects and courses of action they have already taken. We assume that in choice situations in particular, monetary costs tend to be primarily viewed at lower levels of abstraction. The rationale for this assumption is that price acts as an easily comparable, concrete attribute. However, further research is necessary to determine which level of abstraction consumers predominantly use, and when.

What level of abstraction dominates for the term cost?

To explore which level of abstraction the term *cost* itself evokes, we conducted a free-association test analogous to the one described above for benefits. In total, 79 cost associations were generated by 20 individuals. This means that the same people came up with 32 per cent more associations when the stimulus word was costs than when it was benefit. Given that lower level abstractions also tend to be more detailed, the differences in the number of associations may provide a first hint that in fact, costs are viewed at a lower level of abstraction.

We again coded all associations into a simplified dichotomy of concrete versus abstract and reconciled potential coding differences. 32 per cent of associations referred to concrete, low-level abstraction costs (e.g., mobile phone, gas, car), 62 per cent to high level abstraction costs (e.g., time, leisure, investment) and 6 per cent could not be assigned to any category (e.g., liquidity leakage, cost/benefit calculation).

Although the majority of associations was again comparably abstract, results show that the number of concrete associations is twice as high as when the stimulus word was *benefit*. This provides some hint that the notion of cost is seen as generally less abstract than the notion of benefits.

Can costs and benefits be reliably distinguished?

The discussion in the previous sections showed that the distinction between costs and benefits is only clear when arguments are framed at a high abstraction level, i.e., when the broader meaning moves into the focus (e.g., Gummerus et al., 2012; Gwinner et al., 1998). At a low level of abstraction, concrete attributes, features and facts only turn into benefits and costs via a process of subjective evaluation (c.f. Zeithaml, 1988). In the example of the phone, the size of a phone could be both, that is, advantage/benefit or disadvantage/cost, depending on the preferences of the evaluating person. The same holds for price. A consumer with a high income could perceive a $599 phone as "good value for money/effort/time" whereas a less well-off consumer might not, unless the high price is used as a conspicuous social signal (Braun & Wicklund, 1989).

Existing research holds many examples to show that the evaluation of attributes is a matter of context and presentation. Even slight changes in the situational setup may suffice to instigate preference reversals (e.g., Boland, Brucks, & Nielsen, 2012; Bonini & Rumiati, 2002; Christopoulos, Kokkinaki, Harvey, & Sevdalis, 2011). For example, the notion of transaction utility suggests that the same price is evaluated differently depending on which context-specific reference price is salient (Thaler, 1985). A price of $5 may be a favourable bargain for a beer at a bar but a costly rip off for the same beer in the supermarket.

Interestingly much of this literature and in particular literature focusing on preference reversals does not assume a change of valence. Rather, it assumes that malleability in judgements and choices is the result of a change in the weights assigned to attributes and features (e.g., Chakravarti, Grenville, Morwitz, Tang, & Ülkümen, 2013; Ge, Häubl, & Elrod, 2012; Laran & Wilcox, 2011; Willemsen & Keren, 2004). The fact that individual judgements are needed to determine whether an attribute is in fact a benefit or a cost is often ignored by the literature (for example in research on attraction and compromise effects) (Malkoc, Hedgcock, & Hoeffler, 2013; Simonson, 1989). In other words, much literature assumes that features such as price or quality are always perceived as costs and benefits respectively but that they do not equally matter across situations.

In this last section we question whether this assumption may always be warranted. Can one be sure that an attribute that has been identified as a cost or benefit by one participant would be understood the same way by another?

To get a preliminary answer to this question, we asked 67 participants (49 women, mean age 30.5 years) to immerse themselves into the situation of shopping online for a new bedding set. After being provided with a reference price, participants were exposed to a realistic online product description. A picture of a bedding set was accompanied by a description of a

Table 22.2 The proportion of cost and benefit classifications with regard to concrete attributes

Aspect	*Cost association*	*Benefit association*	*Neither*
Price of the bedding	41.5%	41.5%	17%
Shipping costs	35%	32%	33%
Shopping experience	11%	48%	41%
The feel of the bedding	11%	76%	11%
Design of the bedding	14%	75%	13%

number of features and aspects. The features and aspects captured both typical cost (price of the bedding, shipping costs) and benefits (feel of the bedding, design of the bedding). Subsequently, participants were requested to indicate whether they would buy the bedding and whether they considered the features and aspects of the offer a cost/disadvantage, a benefit/advantage or neither. The prevailing assumption would be that price-related components are considered disadvantageous costs, whereas feel and design are most likely benefits.

Table 22.2 shows the respective actual classifications. Seemingly intuitive price and cost associations failed to show a uniform pattern. Both the price of the bedding and shipping costs were as often deemed a cost as they were deemed a benefit. Although for all other aspects benefit classifications dominated, there was still variation in the way different aspects were classified.

These results show that the perception of costs and benefits is highly subjective. In case of concrete features and aspects, it is down to an individual's interpretation on what to consider a cost or a benefit. Even in simple and presumably clear-cut scenarios and for stereotypical costs such as shipping cost, individual cognitive reference points appear to matter. On one side this finding sits well with a large existing body of evidence (Dholakia & Simonson, 2005; Thaler, 1985). On the other side, it suggests that perhaps many studies still do not go far enough in making sure that the valence is kept constant across participants.

Conclusion and implications

This chapter focused on two terms that lie at the heart of an often implicitly assumed tradeoff and that are generally treated as self-explanatory: costs and benefits. As is often the case with presumably self-explanatory notions, a closer look has identified the topic to be as broad and multifaceted as it is challenging. It touches on and is influenced by many concepts and theories of the entire field of consumer research. Consequently, any new insights on costs, benefits and their association are likely to be relevant to researchers investigating consumer decision making, consumption processes, perception and so forth. In this final section we condense the insights achieved and point to what we consider the most pressing questions for the future of this ill-defined field. We start with the notions of costs and benefits in isolation and then loop back to implications and insights arising for the notion of cost–benefit associations.

Understanding costs and benefits

Overall, it becomes clear that it is hardly possible to provide a straightforward answer to the question – what are costs and benefits? The answer is only relatively clear, if abstract notions of costs and benefits are considered. Once a low level of abstraction is applied and concrete features and attributes move into focus, the personally attributed valence is the only dimension that sets costs and benefits apart. When consumers evaluate an attribute, a small shift in situational and personal cues (memories, situational priming etc.) could determine whether the same attribute becomes a benefit or a cost – advantage or disadvantage.

These observations raise the question as to whether experimental manipulations sometimes have (also) influenced decisions because turned a presumable cost feature into a perceived benefit or vice versa (e.g., price as cost vs. price as benefit). It might be interesting for future research working with concrete level descriptions to include measures that enable disentanglement of attribute classification (cost–benefit) and weights (for the broader implications in terms of measurement cf. McGraw, Larsen, Kahneman, & Schkade, 2010). Moreover, although the means-end-chain framework allows for one concrete attribute to trigger multiple higher level costs and benefits, the possibility that the same attribute may be even simultaneously cost or benefit has barely ever been considered. This possibility too may constitute an interesting direction for future research.

The apparent malleability of costs and benefits at low levels of abstraction makes them a particularly interesting and challenging topic. Nonetheless, this chapter has shown that all levels of abstraction are relevant. Even the keywords, *benefits* and *costs*, were shown to bring to mind both abstract and concrete associations. Interestingly, the degree to which a specific abstraction level appears to determine considerations (by consumers and the literature) appears to vary across benefits and costs. What we observe is that benefits are usually considered as abstract, attribute-induced meaning derivatives (e.g., small package → consumption convenience), whereas costs tend to be considered as low-level attributes, such as price.

An important point to raise in this context is the potential moderating role of culture. Cultural differences are likely to occur at each step of the way. Culture is prone to affect whether an aspect is perceived as a cost or as a benefit (e.g., for variations in the understanding of price, see Sternquist, Byun, & Jin, 2004), at which level of abstraction it is perceived and whether it is mentally connected to other costs and benefits. Culture manifests in various ways including language, artefacts, values and beliefs (e.g., De Mooij & Hofstede, 2002; Soares et al., 2007). All these variables may influence the way we think and behave (Sojka & Tansuhaj, 1995). In particular, language acts as a code and scheme for everyday life representations and thereby holds the power to influence the structure of one's thoughts (Douglas, 1979; Sojka & Tansuhaj, 1995) including the level of abstractness (Stapel & Semin, 2007). For example, Western languages tend to include more abstract language elements, such as adjectives, whereas Eastern languages tend to be more context specific and focus on more concrete elements, such as verbs (Maass et al., 2006). Knowing that languages differ in terms of the prevailing level of abstractness suggests that the abstractness with which costs and benefits are framed also differs across language groups and cultures.

A similar argument holds for the role of artefacts and possessions representing cultural values. They, too, can shape people's thought structure (Sojka & Tansuhaj, 1995). In societies in which cultural meaning is defined by possessions, for example in the U.S., attribute-level information tends to be assigned more importance than symbolic meaning (Wallendorf & Arnould, 1988). The prevailing associations with costs and benefits for such cultures may be also more concrete. Similarly, beliefs and values embedded in a culture might influence perceptions and thoughts (c.f. De Mooij & Hofstede, 2002; Soares et al., 2007). In particular, cultural values that define the relation with others are of importance. For instance, more individualism and self-focus are associated with favouring individual-centred (Holbrook, 1994) and less social (Sheth et al., 1991) values, and with framing costs at low levels of abstraction (Vohs et al., 2006). The interpretation of concrete attributes constituting certain values might also differ. For example, aesthetics matters across culture (Holbrook, 1994). However, the interpretations of what is beautiful diverge: For masculine cultures "big" is beautiful whereas feminine cultures favour "small" as an attribute (De Mooij & Hofstede, 2002).

The list of potential cultural differences goes on. For example, power distance facilitates high abstraction thinking, such as wide categorization (Smith & Trope, 2006), and an attentional focus on central rather than peripheral information (Overbeck & Park, 2001). Similarly short-term orientation, generally inherent in Western cultures (De Mooij & Hofstede, 2002), might foster myopic behaviour and thus motivate more concrete thinking (Trope & Liberman, 2010). Taken together, the time appears ripe to empirically drill into the question of cultural differences if we aim to get a better grip on our understanding of costs and benefits and, by extension, their association.

Understanding cost–benefit associations

Cost–benefit associations are a widely applied implicit assumption as well as a scarcely investigated phenomenon. The preceding review on the notions of costs and benefits in isolation shed some light on why direct research on cost–benefit associations may be that scarce: Benefits and costs can be simultaneously considered at different levels of abstraction, and it is not straightforward as to what exactly the perceived benefits and costs are in a given situation.

Turning back to our initial metaphor, this means that the cost or benefit districts may be anything but clearly marked and be hidden by a constant layer of fog or smog. They might effectively elude a closer look. Moreover, their respective inhabitants may not always easily be distinguishable. Sticking to this metaphor it may mean at least two things: First, because the districts are not easily recognizable for what they are, there may be little motivation to build a bridge between them. The potentially ambiguous notion of costs and benefits may hamper their association (e.g., Prelec & Loewenstein, 1998). Second, even if costs and benefits were well defined, they may potentially remain at different levels of abstraction. Again, this may influence the degree and direction in which cost–benefit associations are established. Presumably, the more concrete notion will be more likely to bring to mind the more abstract notion rather than vice versa. Actual insights on how the level of abstraction and a potential asymmetry in abstraction levels between costs and benefits affects experiences and behaviours are missing.

Evidently, many questions on cost–benefit associations remain open. Given the multiplicity, potential vagueness and ambiguity of the involved notions of costs and benefits, their measurement is potentially one of the biggest challenges. Although existing research has managed to provide some helpful insights with rather direct questions, there certainly is room for the development of more fine-grained measures.

In light of apparent conceptual and methodological challenges it may seem tempting to forgo the empirical study of cost–benefit associations altogether. We believe that doing so would mean losing out on potentially far-reaching insights. There is no doubt that (a) cost–benefit associations influence consumer experiences and behaviour and that (b) they are malleable with regard to personal, cultural and situational characteristics (e.g., payment method or bundle offers).

The list of potential beneficiaries of a deeper understanding of cost–benefit associations is long. Research on decision making and consumption (in particular those fields that implicitly assume cost–benefit associations) would certainly benefit from a better understanding of the effects and causes of different cost–benefit association patterns; so would public policy makers and marketers who might be interested in how their respective toolboxes affect cost–benefit associations.

Doubtless much more research is needed to fully understand the underlying processes, dynamics and moderators (see Kamleitner, 2009; Kamleitner & Hölzl, 2009 for further concrete directions of future research). What we can, however, say for sure is that the often implicit assumption that consumers engage in a tradeoff between costs and benefits is not generally warranted.

The final point we would like to stress in this review is one particularly promising direction of future research. It appears promising because it connects insights on the notions of costs and benefits. The literature assumes that the way people think about benefits changes over time (Woodruff, 1997). Since the way people think about benefits and costs is likely to affect the degree to which they can establish cost–benefit associations, it would be interesting to investigate the temporal dynamics of cost–benefit associations. It may be that temporal changes in cost–benefit associations over time (Kamleitner & Kirchler, 2006) primarily reflect changes in the conceptualizations of costs and benefits. Insights like these would simultaneously enhance our understanding of costs and benefits, of the dynamics of their associations and of the consumption process in general. In other words, it would simultaneously enhance our knowledge about several parameters that are fundamental to the study of consumer behaviour.

References

Anderson, J. R. (2013). *Language, memory, and thought*. New York, NY: Psychology Press.

Ariely, D., & Silva, J. (2002). Payment method design: Psychological and economic aspects of payments. *MIT Sloan School of Management Paper 196*.

Arkes, H. R., & Blumer, C. (1985). The psychology of sunk cost. *Organizational Behaviour and Human Decision Processes*, *35*(1), 124–140.

Babin, B. J., Darden, W. R., & Griffin, M. (1994). Work and/or fun: Measuring hedonic and utilitarian shopping value. *Journal of Consumer Research*, *20*(4), 644–656.

Beach, L. R., & Mitchell, T. R. (1978). A contingency model for the selection of decision strategies. *Academy of Management Review*, *3*(3), 439–449.

Bettman, J. R., Johnson, E. J., & Payne, J. W. (1991). Consumer decision making. In T. S. Robertson & H. H. Kassarjian (Eds.), *Handbook of consumer theory and research*. Englewood Cliffs, NJ: Prentice Hall.

Boland, W. A., Brucks, M., & Nielsen, J. H. (2012). The attribute carryover effect: What the "runner up" option tells us about consumer choice processes. *Journal of Consumer Research*, *38*(5), 872–885.

Bonini, N., & Rumiati, R. (2002). Acceptance of a price discount: The role of the semantic relatedness between purchases and the comparative price format. *Journal of Behavioural Decision Making*, *15*(3), 203–220.

Braun, O. L., & Wicklund, R. A. (1989). Psychological antecedents of conspicuous consumption. *Journal of Economic Psychology*, *10*(2), 161–187.

Burnham, T. A., Frels, J. K., & Mahajan, V. (2003). Consumer switching costs: A typology, antecedents, and consequences. *Journal of the Academy of Marketing Science*, *31*(2), 109–126.

Chakravarti, A., Grenville, A., Morwitz, V. G., Tang, J., & Ülkümen, G. (2013). Malleable conjoint partworths: How the breadth of response scales alters price sensitivity. *Journal of Consumer Psychology*, *23*(4), 515–525. doi: 10.1016/j.jcps.2012.10.013

Chandon, P., & Wansink, B. (2002). When are stockpiled products consumed faster? A convenience-salience framework of postpurchase consumption incidence and quantity. *Journal of Marketing Research*, *39*(3), 321–335.

Chen, C., Jones, K. T., & Mcintyre, D. D. (2008). Analyzing the factors relevant to students' estimations of the benefits and costs of pursuing an accounting career. *Accounting Education*, *17*(3), 313–326.

Christopoulos, G., Kokkinaki, F., Harvey, N., & Sevdalis, N. (2011). Paying for no reason? (Mis-) perceptions of product attributes in separate vs. joint product evaluation. *Journal of Economic Psychology*, *32*(5), 857–864. doi: 10.1016/j.joep.2011.05.003

Cronin, J. J., Brady, M. K., Brand, R. R., Hightower, R., & Shemwell, D. J. (1997). A cross-sectional test of the effect and conceptualization of service value. *Journal of Services Marketing*, *11*(6), 375–391. doi:10.1108/08876049710187482

De Mooij, M., & Hofstede, G. (2002). Convergence and divergence in consumer behaviour: Implications for international retailing. *Journal of Retailing*, *78*(1), 61–69.

Dholakia, U. M., & Simonson, I. (2005). The effect of explicit reference points on consumer choice and online bidding behaviour. *Marketing Science, 24*(2), 206–217.

Douglas, S. P. (1979). A cross-national exploration of husband-wife involvement in selected household activities. *Advances in Consumer Research, 6*, 364–371.

Epstein, S. (2003). Cognitive-experiential self-theory of personality. In T. Millon & M. J. Lerner (Eds.), *Comprehensive handbook of psychology* (Vol. 5: *Personality and social psychology*, pp. 159–184). Hoboken, NJ: Wiley.

Ge, X., Häubl, G., & Elrod, T. (2012). What to say when: Influencing consumer choice by delaying the presentation of favorable information. *Journal of Consumer Research, 38*(6), 1004–1021.

Gourville, J. T., & Soman, D. (1998). Payment depreciation: The behavioural effects of temporally separating payments from consumption. *Journal of Consumer Research, 25*(2), 160–174.

Gummerus, J., Liljander, V., Weman, E., & Pihlström, M. (2012). Customer engagement in a Facebook brand community. *Management Research Review, 35*(9), 857–877. doi: 10.1108/01409171211256578

Gutman, J. (1982). A means-end chain model based on consumer categorization processes. *Journal of Marketing, 46*(2), 60–72.

Gwinner, K. P., Gremler, D. D., & Bitner, M. J. (1998). Relational benefits in services industries: The customer's perspective. *Journal of the Academy of Marketing Science, 26*(2), 101–114.

Handy, F., Cnaan, R. A., Brudney, J. L., Ascoli, U., Meijs, L. C. M. P., & Ranade, S. (2000). Public perception of "Who is a volunteer": An examination of the net-cost approach from a cross-cultural perspective. *Voluntas: International Journal of Voluntary and Nonprofit Organizations, 11*(1), 45–65. doi: 10.2307/27927669

He, X., & Mittal, V. (2007). The effect of decision risk and project stage on escalation of commitment. *Organizational Behaviour and Human Decision Processes, 103*(2), 225–237.

Heath, C., & Fennema, M. G. (1996). Mental depreciation and marginal decision making. *Organizational Behaviour and Human Decision Processes, 68*(2), 95–108.

Heath, C., & Soll, J. B. (1996). Mental budgeting and consumer decisions. *Journal of Consumer Research, 23*(1), 40–52.

Henderson, P. W., & Peterson, R. A. (1992). Mental accounting and categorization. *Organizational Behaviour and Human Decision Processes, 51*(1), 92–117.

Hirst, E. D., Joyce, E. J., & Schadewald, M. S. (1994). Mental accounting and outcome contiguity in consumer-borrowing decisions. *Organizational Behaviour and Human Decision Processes, 58*(1), 136–152.

Hoelzl, E., Pollai, M., & Kamleitner, B. (2007). *Experience and its fit with prediction and recollection: The case of perceived change in loan burden.* Manuscript under review.

Hofstede, G. (1984). The cultural relativity of the quality of life concept. *Academy of Management Review, 9*(3), 389–398.

Holbrook, M. (1994). The nature of customer value: An axiology of services in the consumption experience. In R. Rust & R. Oliver (Eds.), *Service quality: New directions in theory and practice* (pp. 21–71). Newbury Park, CA: Sage.

Kahneman, D. (2003). A perspective on judgment and choice: Mapping bounded rationality. *American Psychologist, 58*(9), 697–720.

Kamleitner, B. (2009). Cost–benefit-associations: A powerful but understudied construct. In F. Saito (Ed.), *Consumer behaviour* (pp. 227–237). Hauppauge, NY: Nova Science Publishers.

Kamleitner, B., Hoelzl, E., & Kirchler, E. (2008). Experiencing costs and benefits of a loan transaction: The role of cost–benefit associations. *Working Paper.*

Kamleitner, B., Hoelzl, E., & Kirchler, E. (2010). Experiencing costs and benefits of a loan transaction: The role of cost–benefit associations. *Journal of Economic Psychology, 31*(6), 1047–1056

Kamleitner, B., & Hoelzl, E. (2009). Cost–benefit-associations and financial behaviour. *Applied Psychology: An International Review, 58*(3), 435–452.

Kamleitner, B., Hornung, B., & Kirchler, E. (2011). Over-indebtedness and the interplay of factual and mental money management: An interview study. *New Zealand Economic Papers, 45*(1), 139–160.

Kamleitner, B., & Kirchler, E. (2006). Personal loan users' mental integration of payment and consumption. *Marketing Letters, 17*(4), 281–294.

Keil, M., Tan, B. C. Y., Wei, K.-K., Saarinen, T., Tuunainen, V., & Wassenaar, A. (2000). A Cross-cultural study on escalation of commitment behaviour in software projects. *Mis Quarterly, 24*(2), 299–325. doi: 10.2307/3250940

Khan, U., Zhu, M., & Kalra, A. (2011). When tradeoffs matter: The effect of choice construal on context effects. *Journal of Marketing Research (JMR), 48*(1), 62–71.

Kivetz, R. (1999). Advances in research on mental accounting and reason-based choice. *Marketing Letters, 10*(3), 249–266.
Kotler, P. (2000). *Marketing management: The millennium edition*. New York, NY: Prentice Hall.
Laran, J., & Wilcox, K. (2011). Choice, rejection, and elaboration on preference-inconsistent alternatives. *Journal of Consumer Research, 38*(2), 229–241. doi: 10.1086/659040
Lichtenstein, D. R., & Burton, S. (1989). The relationship between perceived and objective price-quality. *Journal of Marketing Research, 26*(4), 429–443. doi: 10.2307/3172763
Lichtenstein, D. R., Netemeyer, R. G., & Burton, S. (1990). Distinguishing coupon proneness from value consciousness: An acquisition-transaction utility-theory perspective. *Journal of Marketing, 54*(3), 54–67.
Linville, P. W., & Fischer, G. W. (1991). Preferences for separating or combining events. *Journal of Personality and Social Psychology, 60*(1), 5–23.
Maass, A., Karasawa, M., Politi, F., & Suga, S. (2006). Do verbs and adjectives play different roles in different cultures? A cross-linguistic analysis of person representation. *Journal of Personality and Social Psychology, 90*(5), 734.
Malkoc, S. A., Hedgcock, W., & Hoeffler, S. (2013). Between a rock and a hard place: The failure of the attraction effect among unattractive alternatives. *Journal of Consumer Psychology, 23*(3), 317–329. doi: 10.1016/j.jcps.2012.10.008
McGraw, A. P., Larsen, J. T., Kahneman, D., & Schkade, D. (2010). Comparing gains and losses. *Psychological Science, 21*(10), 1438–1445. doi: 10.1177/0956797610381504
Monroe, K. B. (1990). *Pricing: Making profitable decisions*. New York, NY: McGraw-Hill.
Overbeck, J. R., & Park, B. (2001). When power does not corrupt: Superior individuation processes among powerful perceivers. *Journal of Personality and Social Psychology, 81*(4), 549–565.
Overby, J. W., & Lee, E.-J. (2006). The effects of utilitarian and hedonic online shopping value on consumer preference and intentions. *Journal of Business Research, 59*(10–11), 1160–1166. doi: 10.1016/j jbusres.2006.03.008
Park, C. W., Jaworski, B. J., & MacInnis, D. J. (1986). Strategic brand concept-image management. *Journal of Marketing, 50*(4), 135–145. doi: 10.2307/1251291
Pattaratanakun, J. A., & Mak, V. (2015). Culture moderates biases in search decisions. *Psychological Science, 26*(8), 1229–1240. doi: 10.1177/0956797615583979
Patterson, P. G., & Smith, T. (2003). A cross-cultural study of switching barriers and propensity to stay with service providers. *Journal of Retailing, 79*(2), 107–120. doi: 10.1016/S0022-4359(03)00009-5
Prelec, D., & Loewenstein, G. (1998). The red and the black: Mental accounting of savings and debt. *Marketing Science, 17*(1), 4–28.
Reynolds, K. E., & Beatty, S. E. (1999). Customer benefits and company consequences of customer-salesperson relationships in retailing. *Journal of Retailing, 75*(1), 11–32.
Ruth, J. A. (2001). Promoting a brand's emotion benefits: The influence of emotion categorization processes on consumer evaluations. *Journal of Consumer Psychology, 11*(2), 99–113.
Salter, S. B., & Sharp, D. J. (2001). Agency effects and escalation of commitment: Do small national culture differences matter? *International Journal of Accounting, 36*(1), 33–45. doi: 10.1016/S0020-7063(01)00084-X
Sánchez-Fernández, R., & Iniesta-Bonillo, M. Á. (2007). The concept of perceived value: A systematic review of the research. *Marketing Theory*, 7(4), 427–451.
Shane, S. A. (1992). The effect of cultural differences in perceptions of transaction costs on national differences in the preference for licensing. *Academy of Management Proceedings, 1992*(1), 122–126. doi: 10.5465/ambpp.1992.17515164
Sharp, D. J., & Salter, S. B. (1997). Project escalation and sunk costs: A test of the international generalizability of agency and prospect theories. *Journal of International Business Studies, 28*(1), 101–121. doi: 10.2307/155450
Sheth, J. N., Newman, B. I., & Gross, B. L. (1991). Why we buy what we buy: A theory of consumption values. *Journal of Business Research, 22*(2), 159–170. doi: 10.1016/0148-2963(91)90050-8
Simonson, I. (1989). Choice based on reasons: The case of attraction and compromise effects. *Journal of Consumer Research, 16*(2), 158. doi: 10.1086/209205 %U http://www.journals.uchicago.edu/doi/abs/10.1086/209205
Smith, P. K., & Trope, Y. (2006). You focus on the forest when you're in charge of the trees: Power priming and abstract information processing. *Journal of Personality and Social Psychology, 90*(4), 578–596.

Soares, A. M., Farhangmehr, M., & Shoham, A. (2007). Hofstede's dimensions of culture in international marketing studies. *Journal of Business Research, 60*(3), 277–284. doi: 10.1016/j.jbusres.2006.10.018

Sojka, J. Z., & Tansuhaj, P. S. (1995). Cross-cultural consumer research: A twenty-year review. *Advances in Consumer Research, 22*, 461–474.

Soman, D. (2001). Effects of payment mechanism on spending behaviour: The role of rehearsal and immediacy of payments. *Journal of Consumer Research, 27*(4), 460–474.

Soman, D. (2003). The effect of payment transparency on consumption: Quasi-experiments from the field. *Marketing Letters, 14*(3), 173–183.

Soman, D., & Gourville, J. T. (2001). Transaction decoupling: How price bundling affects the decision to consume. *Journal of Marketing Research, 38*(1), 30–44.

Soman, D., & Lam, V. M. W. (2002). The effects of prior spending on future spending decisions: The role of acquisition liabilities and payments. *Marketing Letters, 13*(4), 359–372.

Srivastava, J., & Raghubir, P. (2002). Debiasing using decomposition: The case of memory-based credit card expense estimates. *Journal of Consumer Psychology, 12*(3), 253–264.

Stapel, D. A., & Semin, G. R. (2007). The magic spell of language: Linguistic categories and their perceptual consequences. *Journal of Personality and Social Psychology, 93*(1), 23–33.

Sternquist, B., Byun, S.-E., & Jin, B. (2004). The dimensionality of price perceptions: A cross-cultural comparison of Asian consumers. *International Review of Retail, Distribution and Consumer Research, 14*(1), 83–100. doi: 10.1080/0959396032000154310

Strader, T. J., & Shaw, M. J. (1999). Consumer cost differences for traditional and Internet markets. *Internet Research, 9*(2), 82–92. doi: 10.1108/10662249910264819

Stremersch, S., & Tellis, G. J. (2002). Strategic bundling of products and prices: A new synthesis for marketing. *Journal of Marketing, 66*(1), 55–72.

Sweeney, J. C., & Soutar, G. N. (2001). Consumer perceived value: The development of a multiple item scale. *Journal of Retailing*, 77(2), 203–220.

Tatzel, M. (2002). "Money worlds" and well-being: An integration of money dispositions, materialis, and price-related behaviour. *Journal of Economic Psychology, 23*, 103–126.

Thaler, R. H. (1985). Mental accounting and consumer choice. *Marketing Science, 4*(3), 199–214.

Thaler, R. H. (1999). Mental accounting matters. *Journal of Behavioural Decision Making, 12*(3), 183–206.

Trope, Y., & Liberman, N. (2010). Construal-level theory of psychological distance. *Psychological Review, 117*(2), 440.

Truong, Y. (2010). Personal aspirations and the consumption of luxury goods. *International Journal of Market Research, 52*(5), 653–671. doi: Doi 10.2501/S1470785310201521

Tversky, A., & Kahneman, D. (1981). The framing of decisions and the psychology of choice. *Science, 211*(4481), 453–458.

Veblen, T. (1994/1899). *The theory of the leisure class*. New York, NY: Penguin Books.

Verhallen, T. M. M., & Pieters, R. G. M. (1984). Attitude theory and behavioural costs. *Journal of Economic Psychology, 5*(3), 223–249. doi: 10.1016/0167-4870(84)90024-2

Vohs, K. D., Mead, N. L., & Goode, M. R. (2006). The psychological consequences of money. *Science, 314*(5802), 1154–1156.

Wallendorf, M., & Arnould, E. J. (1988). "My favorite things": A cross-cultural inquiry into object attachment, possessiveness, and social linkage. *Journal of Consumer Research, 14*(4), 531–547. doi: 10.2307/2489159

Wandersman, A., Florin, P., Friedmann, R., & Meier, R. (1987). Who participates, who does not, and why? An analysis of voluntary neighborhood organizations in the United States and Israel. *Sociological Forum, 2*(3), 534–555. doi: 10.1007/BF01106625

Willemsen, M. C., & Keren, G. (2004). The role of negative features in joint and separate evaluation. *Journal of Behavioural Decision Making, 17*(4), 313–329.

Woodruff, R. B. (1997). Customer value: The next source for competitive advantage. *Journal of the Academy of Marketing Science, 25*(2), 139.

Zeithaml, V. A. (1988). Consumer perceptions of price, quality, and value: A means-end model and synthesis of evidence. *Journal of Marketing, 52*(3), 2–22.

23

Naïve theories about marketing and consumption in consumer inference

Hélène Deval, Maria L. Cronley, Susan Powell Mantel and Frank R. Kardes

Consumers frequently have to evaluate products and make decisions based on limited or incomplete information. In fact, in today's world, consumers rarely have complete information regarding products about which they form judgements and make decisions. Second-hand sources like advertising or word-of-mouth communications typically provide some information about product attributes and benefits, but it is rarely exhaustive. Consumers could search out additional information through product websites, or public product evaluation sources (e.g., Consumer Reports), but they do not often invest the time or effort for all but the most important purchase decisions. Instead, consumers use a variety of inferential strategies to fill the gaps in their product knowledge prior to making judgements and choices (Gunasti & Ross, 2009; Kardes, Posavac, & Cronley, 2004). For example, consumers will often infer the level of a missing attribute (Dick, Chakravarti, & Biehal, 1990), or infer a product's overall quality (Kardes et al., 2004) or even the social signalling potential of a product (Berger & Heath, 2007) and use these inferences to make a purchase decision. In certain cases, these inference rules can be used even when more detailed information is available. Sometimes, for example, consumers do not necessarily lack information, but do not have the time, energy and/or motivation to process all that is available and, therefore, resort to making an inference from easily accessible cues to form a judgement.

This chapter focuses on how the intersection of a consumer's previously held naïve theories and situational factors influences information evaluation; more specifically, naïve theories, common sense and informal explanations that people use to simplify their life, drive inferences and subsequent judgements about the situation itself, the product and the decision. Common naïve consumer theories exist in all cultures, span across contexts related to price, quality, brand name, cultural stereotypes and product performance information, to name just a few elements, and thus influence how consumers will respond to a variety of marketing contexts. At the same time, situational factors that may bias consumer decision frames and thus influence information processing and judgement include time constraints, the desire to evaluate and think about the information, situational expertise, cognitive stress and attitude relevance.

Various heuristic processes have been proposed and tested over the years to explain how consumers choose to utilize the information that is presented or that is accessible in making a product judgement or choice. As the field has progressed, review pieces have tried to generalize across these heuristic theories forming overarching frameworks that help understand the efficiencies used by consumers when managing limited time and/or limited information. For example, the selective hypothesis testing framework (Sanbonamatsu, Posavac, Kardes, & Mantel 1998) suggests that each situation is evaluated based on the perceptual frame at the start of the evaluation (i.e., the select hypothesis). That is, an initial hypothesis is generated and then information that is consistent with that initial hypothesis is weighted heavier than information that is inconsistent. More recently, Shah and Oppenheimer (2008) suggest a framework to classify the various heuristic theories based on the stage of the formal decision process at which the heuristic process simplifies the judgement. That is, many heuristic processes induce people to (1) examine fewer pieces of information, (2) reduce the difficulty associated with retrieving and storing information, (3) simplify the weighting for the different cues, (4) integrate less information, and/or (5) examine fewer alternatives. In both frameworks, the information processor tries to efficiently process available information, and the outcome is influenced by the initial situation, motivation to process and the availability/ease of access of information.

As an example, we can consider the use of a brand name as a heuristic. In the absence of any other piece of information, the brand name will be used to infer missing information and build an evaluation of the brand (Chisnall, 1974). Alternatively, the brand name might be used as a heuristic, even if other information is present, by causing the consumer to reduce the effort necessary to evaluate a product and its various features (Maheswaran, Mackie, & Chaiken, 1992). The extent to which the brand name is processed has been described by the Elaboration Likelihood Model (ELM) (Petty, Cacioppo, & Schumann, 1983; Petty & Wegener, 1999; Wheeler, Petty, & Bizer, 2005) and the Heuristic-Systematic Model (HSM) Chen & Chaiken, 1999; Maheswaran et al., 1992; Ratneshwar & Chaiken, 1991). If consumers are following the peripheral route (ELM) or the heuristic route (HSM) the brand name may be processed superficially based on its form, colours, implied feelings etc.; however, if consumers are following the central route (ELM) or the Systematic route (HSM), the brand name may be considered for the attributes that the brand represents. While heuristics, such as brand name, allow consumers to efficiently process information and navigate the complexities of life while still making relatively good decisions, the heuristic strategy does, however, create room for bias and that bias can lead to less than optimal judgements or decisions.

Examples of consumer bias resulting in potentially poor decisions are numerous and can occur at every stage of information processing from attention to choice (Kardes & Wyer, 2013). The consumer encounters information, parses the information in an ostensibly efficient manner and attempts to simplify the complexity of the potential variables influencing a decision occasion. One method by which consumers simplify the world is by relying on personal history or common sense. That is, they start with an assumption that is based on a naïve theory of how things relate to each other. They interpret the available information in light of informal, common-sense associations that are based on exemplars observed in everyday life. Consumers use naïve theories to simplify the world because the relationships generally hold true, but in some circumstances the naïve theory can divert the decision off course and insert a bias into the situation. Ultimately, that resulting bias can lead to dissatisfaction, stress, regret or suboptimal choices. To better understand how the use of a naïve theory in a particular context or situation can both simplify decision making but also lead to bias and suboptimal decisions, understanding how naïve theories are formed and used across concepts is helpful. The next section breaks down the anatomy of naïve theories.

The formation of naïve theories

The established definition of naïve theories was constructed by Furnham (1988) to be an informal, common-sense explanation people use in their everyday lives to make sense of their environment, and these accounts often diverge from formal "scientific" descriptions of what actually happens. The research in this area has identified several components necessary to have a naïve theory: ontological commitments or categorical associations, causal laws, coherence or the interrelatedness of beliefs (Carey, 1985; Gelman & Noles, 2011).

The ontological commitments relate to the category to which the object is perceived to belong and the properties associated with items typically in that group. To borrow one of Gelman and Noles' examples (2011), a $20 bill can be viewed as a flammable piece of paper or a unit of exchange depending on the category to which the $20 bill is assumed to belong – a physical object subject to physical laws or an economic entity subject to economic theories.

The second necessary component of a naïve theory is a causal relationship between several elements of the situation. That is, the relationship between elements of the environment are related in an "if X then Y" structure (Gelman & Noles, 2011). For example, if a product is expensive then it must be well made, or if a product is rare then it must be valuable. This causal link is what differentiates a theory from a simple script.

Finally, the coherence element suggests that various categories of beliefs follow similar rules – that is, some beliefs are interrelated and do not exist as isolated propositions. For example, in studying perceptions about important human attributes, Dweck and her collaborators (e.g., Blackwell, Trzesniewski, & Dweck, 2007; Chiu, Hong, & Dweck, 1997; Dweck, Chiu, & Hong, 1995) studied the differences between two competing naïve theories: entity theory and incremental theory. Both of these naïve theories refer to the assumptions people may make about the malleability of attributes associated with a person. Those that hold the "entity" naïve theory may believe that humans are non-malleable entities and their personal attributes are fixed (i.e., non-malleable) over time. Conversely, those that hold the "incremental" naïve theory may believe that human attributes are malleable and can be changed and developed. The idea of coherence suggests that, in order to be a naïve theory, the concept of "entity" vs. "incremental" will be held consistently for a large set of important attributes. That is, if a person holds the "entity" naïve theory regarding intelligence (e.g., that it is fixed and cannot be developed over time), they would also hold the "entity" naïve theory regarding morality. Similarly, if a person holds the "incremental" naïve theory, they would assume malleability across a wide range of important human traits. This idea of coherence is important because it has been shown that people use this idea of coherence in generating inferences from observations. For example, the "entity" vs. "incremental" naïve theory has a direct impact on inferences since someone who holds the "entity" (compared to those that hold the "incremental") naïve theory will tend to form stronger inferences based on the behaviour of other people (Chiu et al., 1997; Hong, Chiu, Dweck, & Sacks, 1997). From a consumer behaviour perspective, consider how someone draws inferences about a celebrity endorser. A consumer sees a celebrity strongly endorsing a specific product. Someone who holds the "entity" naïve theory (versus "incremental") may be more likely to infer that the celebrity always uses that brand and is loyal to that brand, which may then influence his or her attitudes or behaviours towards the brand.

Naïve theories are typically adopted and held without being scientifically tested and are often rooted in common sense or even myth or misinformation (Osberg, 2002). However, they may overlap with scientific theories (Furnham, 1988). Further, despite the principle of coherence, research into naïve theories as explanations for phenomena has been ambiguous and inconsistent. But the main discrepancy between naïve and scientific theories is that the former do not control for cause and effect (Furnham, 1988). Naïve theories emerge from a lot of different influences, including myths, folklore, direct experience and repeated observations of co-occurrences as the basis of lay inferencing (Kelley & Thibaut, 1969). Translating this idea into a consumer behaviour context, advertising tag lines can create naïve theories that last.

For example, the diamond engagement ring has its roots in the fifteenth century, but it did not become popular for the average consumer until DeBeers Diamond Company started using the tag line "A Diamond is Forever" in 1948 to connect the diamond with the solid stability that one desires in a marriage (Bruno, 2010). The connection took hold and by 1965, over 80 per cent of all new brides received a diamond engagement ring with their proposal (American Gem Society, 2015). The DeBeers Company invested in a campaign that not only generated an enduring tagline; it also instilled the naïve theory that the diamond symbolizes the depth of man's commitment into cultures across the world. Similarly, the repeated observations of a co-occurrence can cement expectations and establish an inference or heuristic rule. For example, long before meteorologists had elaborate models to try and predict the weather, people used everyday observation of the sky and nature to make weather forecasts. Such observations and lay inferencing have been summarized and passed down generations with proverbs such as "clear Moon, frost soon," or "red sky at night, sailor's delight". Similarly, the tag line "the best part of waking up is Folger's in your cup" summarizes the connection between the caffeine in the coffee and the transition between sleep and alertness. Kelley and Thibaut's framework assumes that the observer is objective, but even while objectivity is attempted, it is possible that Selective hypothesis testing and confirmation bias, (i.e., the tendency to interpret information in a way that confirms our prior beliefs) (Sanbonmatsu et al., 1998), are at play and contribute to the solidification of the naïve theory with time and repeated experiences. However, even with the repeated co-occurrence, naïve theories can generate invalid assumptions and biased decision making.

How naïve theories can lead to bias

As an illustration of the various ways naïve theories can play in biasing consumer information processing, Wyer (2008) considers their crucial role in knowledge accessibility and memory. The role of memory in consumers' information processing and decision making is crucial since consumers have to retrieve relevant and applicable knowledge in a given situation in order to evaluate a product. When an initial experience occurs people likely do not pay attention to all the details uniformly and the experience may not be especially noteworthy as part of all the daily experiences. Later, if people are called upon to remember the experience, they could reconstruct it using naïve theories "without searching memory for a representation of the experience itself" (Wyer, 2008). Wyer goes on to illustrate his point with the work of Bem and McConnell (1970), which suggests the role of naïve theories in reconstructing memory. In their experiment, a participant's attitude towards a certain position was assessed in an early experimental session. Later, they were asked to argue against their previously stated position either by their own choice (they were given the choice to argue for or against the original issue and they voluntarily chose the opposite position) or at the request of the experimenter (they were instructed to argue against their original position). At the end of the task they were asked to recall the attitude they had originally reported. Participants who had generated counter-arguments voluntarily reported their earlier attitude to be closer to the revised attitude that they had just reported. Conversely, participants who had generated counter arguments reluctantly (at the experimenter's request) reported their earlier attitude more accurately. Participants seemed to have used their most recent behaviour to infer what their attitude had been previously without consulting their memory for the attitude they had actually reported. From a naïve theory perspective, it appears that participants are using the naïve theory that "people who advocate a position voluntarily are likely to advocate it personally" in assessing their own previously reported attitude. This is one example that demonstrates that naïve theories play a pivotal role in potential bias, and this occurs during consumer information processing. Of central importance to our topic, naïve theories are used as inference rules and heuristics by consumers to make all sorts of judgements, evaluations and choices.

Naïve theories and consumer inference

Naïve theories are generally applicable to a wide array of judgements, situations and domains, but are also inherently tied to memory-based information processing and inference formation (Kardes, Posavac, & Cronley, 2004). Looking across these various applications, the influence of naïve theories on the inference process can be grouped into three broad consumer inference categories: inter-attribute correlations, categorical groupings and accessibility of experiences (Kardes, Posavac, Cronley, & Herr, 2008).

Inter-attribute correlations

First, consumers often hold naïve theories about how product attributes relate to one another, and often make judgements and inferences about products based on these assumed attribute relationships. For example, product quality is generally perceived to be positively and strongly correlated with price, warranty, packaging etc. (e.g., the price–quality heuristic rule of "you get what you pay for"). Thus in this situation, when presented with limited attribute information, consumers can infer other information about the product based on the naïve theory that the unknown attribute information (e.g., product quality) about a product is consistent with the known attributes (e.g., price information). Cronley, Posavac, Meyer, Kardes and Kellaris (2005) illustrated how crucial the role of naïve theories was in drawing inferences in a judgement task where the actual data presented to the participant did not overtly support the pre-existing naïve theory. In one experiment, the pre-existing naïve theory about the price–quality relationship was measured by asking participants to indicate their assumptions about the strength of the relationship. Next, participants were presented with information about 10 brands of wine, including price and quality ratings purportedly generated by wine experts (i.e., the learning phase). The data portrayed a very weak correlation ($r = .27$) between price and quality; thus, a truly objective learner should mitigate the perceived strength of the price–quality relationship in light of the low correlation in the data. As the data was presented, the lack of price–quality correlation was either made salient by providing a randomly displayed list of the expert ratings or it remained inconspicuous by providing a rank-ordered list of ratings. In addition, the participant was explicitly asked to focus on the data or given no process instruction. Subsequently, the strength of the perceived relationship between price and quality was measured a second time. The results showed that when participants were shown data that was strongly inconsistent with their pre-existing naïve theory (i.e., lack of correlation between price and quality was made salient by presenting the data in a random order), the participant reported both a higher task difficulty and a significantly greater reduction in strength of the price–quality relationship. Conversely, when the data was presented such that the low correlation was inconspicuous, the task was reported to be less difficult and the reduction in strength of price-quality relationship was minimal. This was true regardless of the inclusion (or not) of the instruction to focus on the presented data. These results suggest that only when disconfirming evidence is made highly salient do people make a significant revision to their pre-existing naïve theory.

These results are consistent with the selective hypothesis testing framework suggested by Sanbonmatsu et al. (1998). In this case, the pre-existing naïve theory serves as the select hypothesis. When data is then presented that is inconsistent with that initial belief, it carries minimal influence unless the inconsistency is made clearly salient. Specifically, consumers overestimate the strength of the relationship between two variables when they are linked by an existing naïve theory (e.g., positive correlation between quality and price) and disconfirming evidence has to be salient in order for naïve theories to change. Further, the stronger the belief in the pre-existing naïve theory, the more it will play a role in evaluation and decision making, even in the face of disconfirming information. This effect can also be further exacerbated when a person has a dispositional proclivity towards selective hypothesis testing, as in the case of individuals with high need for cognitive closure (Kruglanski & Webster, 1996). Research has suggested similar results for naïve theories that infer correlations between quality and various product attributes such as advertising costs (Kirmani, 1990), company reputation or warranty length (Purohit & Srivastava, 2001).

Another area where naïve theory provides an inference between product attributes is in the contexts of the relationship between healthiness of food and how good the food tastes (Raghunathan, Naylor, & Hoyer, 2006). Specifically, the naïve theory links higher healthiness of food items with poor taste expectations. Raghunathan and colleagues successfully show that the healthier food items are perceived to be lower in inferred tastiness. Again, this naïve theory stems from an intuition or expectation. There is no scientific evidence that tastiness and healthiness are indeed negatively correlated. The authors propose that the source of this naïve theory is related to both internal and external sources and finds its origin in a more general causal association that "unwholesome things must be more fun". In addition, the data show that this naïve theory had clear implications for both judgement and consumption of the food. In one experiment, Raghunathan et al. (2006) had participants at a party taste a *mango lassi* and portrayed it either as a healthy item ("made out of real mango pulp and milk; generally considered very healthy"), or an unhealthy item ("made out of real mango pulp and milk; generally considered unhealthy"). Participants in the trial in which the food item was portrayed as being unhealthy reported significantly higher enjoyment of the food compared to participants in the trial in which the food was portrayed as being healthy. Across the authors' four experiments, their results show that the less healthy a product is portrayed, the tastier it is inferred to be, the more it is enjoyed during actual consumption and the more it is chosen when a hedonic goal is made salient. Thus, situational factors are important in activating a pre-existing naïve theory, however, the category to which the item belongs, discussed in the next section, may also help to define the naïve theory activated.

Categorical grouping

Consumers also draw naïve theory inferences on the basis of the category to which a product is assigned (Broniarczyk & Alba 1994). If a product belongs to a category it is expected to share core features with other products in that category, but, categories are quite complex. For example, when it comes to a category based on a product type such as "restaurant" all exemplars may not elicit the same naïve theories. "Fast-food restaurant" may generate one set of expectations; "sit-down restaurant" may elicit a different set of expectations; "Buffet" may generate a third set; etc. Cho and Schwarz (2008) have shown that participants will evaluate the same product differently depending on the naïve theory that was primed prior to the evaluation. Thus, it is highly likely that the evaluation of a particular restaurant could be vastly different depending on the subcategory to which the consumer assumes the restaurant belongs. Extending Cho and Schwarz's findings into the consumption arena, it would be expected that people may evoke a prototype or an abstract mental representation of a "typical" product in the category or subcategory and then evaluate the focal exemplar based on the naïve theory generated by the prototype. Thus, the category to which a product is assigned will evoke a corresponding naïve theory that will allow the consumer to infer many attributes about the product (Dick et al., 1990; Kardes et al., 2004; Berger & Heath, 2007). For example, a "fast-casual restaurant" may be categorized as a fast-food restaurant leading consumers to draw inferences about the menu, the quality of the food, the price or the speed of service, however, if that same restaurant were assumed to be a "sit-down restaurant" the expectations for each of these attributes may differ significantly. Thus the delivered service may be perceived to be superior or inferior to the expected service and the product evaluation would differ accordingly.

Thus, depending on the situation and which attributes of a product are most evident, the categorization protocols may group the item into different subcategories based on the prevalent features such as the country of origin, the brand, relative quality of the firm's products or the relative success of the firm selling a product – all of these can be used by consumers to generate naïve theories and build inferences (Hong & Wyer, 1989, 1990; Loureiro & Umberger, 2007). To continue with the restaurant example, consumers will draw inferences about a restaurant if they know it is French or if they know that it is a restaurant associated with a nationally recognized chef. Further, these inferences are likely to be very different from the inferences drawn for a restaurant grouped into the fast food category. This process becomes interesting when a particular product can be classified into two different categories with very different expectations (Deval et al., 2013). For example, the restaurant Au Bon Pain could be classified as "fast food" or "French" and the inferences that are generated would create vastly different expectations and could change the perception of the resulting experience of eating in that restaurant.

In order for category-based inferences to occur, consumers have to engage in causal reasoning (if X, then Y) (Gelman & Noles, 2011). That is, if a product belongs to a particular category, the product is expected to have features and properties similar to those of other products in the category to which the product has been classified. But consumers often neglect to consider other categories into which the product could be classified and thus neglect attributes that are inconsistent with the evoked category in favour of the attributes that are consistent with that category. For example, if Au Bon Pain is considered a "fast food restaurant," the food is likely to be assumed to be fast, cheap and mediocre. However, if Au Bon Pain is categorized as "French," then the food is likely to be assumed to be high calorie, rich and tasty. Depending on the goals of the restaurant selection, the category to which the restaurant is classified could determine if it is selected as the meal destination.

For this reason, it is important to understand when consumers are likely to engage in categorical reasoning and thus when they will resort to category-based inferences. Personal and situational influences, such as high vs. low involvement or consumer product expertise, have been shown to influence the likelihood that categorical-based inferences will be used. Brewer (1988) underlined the crucial role of involvement in this process and concluded that when involvement is low, consumers attempt to assign a product to a category and use category-based inference. Conversely, when involvement is high, consumers attempt to evaluate the product as a unique entity and use effortful piecemeal or attribute-based inference. Sujan (1985; Sujan & Dekleva, 1987) showed that the level of expertise has a direct impact on the ability of consumers to draw effective category-based inferences. Novice consumers tend to have less category knowledge and thus use general category associations rather than specific attributes associated with the product to reach a conclusion about the target product. Conversely, experts tend to use more precise subcategory classifications to draw category-based inferences and revert to the more effortful, attribute-based inference process when the specified attributes of the product do not adequately conform to the available subcategories. The expert is more likely to use a piecemeal approach to evaluation when it would be more appropriate, but the novice is more likely to use superordinate category classification and category-based naïve theories even when they realize that the category to which they have classified the brand is inadequate.

One type of categorical reasoning that has been studied quite extensively in the literature is the idea of country of origin. Specifically, the naïve theories relevant to country of origin have been shown to play both direct and indirect roles (Hong & Wyer, 1989, 1990) on product evaluations. However, the impact of country of origin is quite complex – the naïve theory activated differs based on both product category and country of origin. For some countries, the generalizations are fairly robust (e.g., "Japanese products are high quality", "Chinese products are cheap") and are generally applicable to a large number of product categories. However, for other countries, the activated naïve theory is very dependent on the product category. That is, for most products, the fact that the product comes from Canada may not generate strong associations, but for other products, like maple syrup, ice skates or lobsters, the fact that the product comes from Canada becomes quite relevant. It has been shown that when the associations are identified, these stereotypes are used by consumers to draw inferences about products. Hong and Wyer (1989; 1990) showed that the country of origin (e.g., Mexico or Japan) did have a direct impact on evaluation when the participant was asked to either evaluate a product or assess how easy given information was to understand. However, if participants were asked to process the information carefully regardless of the country of origin, they tended to process the information at the attribute level, but country of origin still had an indirect effect on evaluation by causing the participant to think more extensively about certain product attributes. Additionally, they showed that the timing of presentation of the information plays is crucial in determining how the country of origin is used by consumers to draw inferences. Specifically, when country of origin was presented 24 hours before the rest of the information about the product it became a guiding principle in processing the rest of the information. When presented just before, after or simultaneously with other attribute information it was only considered as part of the attribute set (Hong & Wyer, 1990). The country of origin also has been shown to impact the perceived valence of ambiguous attributes and appears to be important in forming inferences when limited information about a product is available (Li & Wyer, 1994). Cross-cultural studies and international research has revealed some interesting differences in country-of-origin-based inferences (e.g., Balabanis & Diamantopoulos, 2004). For example, Gürhan-Canli and Maheswara (2000) investigated country-of-origin effects on product evaluations in two countries: in Japan versus the United States. A mountain bike made in either Japan or the United States was described as either superior or inferior to competition. Japanese participants evaluated the product that originated in their home country more favourably regardless of product superiority while American participants evaluated the product that originated in the home country more favourably only when the product was superior to competition. Such results underline that naïve theories may not always be generalizable across international contexts.

The naïve theories associated with categorical reasoning are important to understanding brand-based inferences associated with brand extensions. An extensive stream of literature concludes that when a new, unfamiliar product is linked to a familiar brand via a brand extension (i.e., a shared brand name), the new product is generally assigned the naïve theory that it has properties typical of the parent brand and of the general product category (e.g., Aaker & Keller, 1990; Boush & Loken, 1991; Bridges, Keller, & Sood, 2000; Broniarczyk & Alba, 1994; Chakravarti, MacInnis, & Nakamoto, 1990; Farquhar, Herr, & Fazio, 1990; Keller, 1993; Keller & Aaker, 1992; Yorkston, Nunes, & Matta, 2010). Among other things, several different matching procedures (e.g., similarity, fit, typicality, relatedness) have been investigated and the results show that when the match between the line extension and the parent brand is high, brand category-based inferences are likely and the brand extension is more effective (Aaker & Keller, 1990; Yorkston et al., 2010).

More recently, individual differences have been investigated to understand how more distant brand extensions could be perceived as acceptable in certain circumstances. Yorkston et al. (2010) investigate how the naïve theory relating to one's own personal trait malleability (entity theory vs. incremental theory) could be imposed on brand extension evaluations. In three experiments, the authors demonstrate that a person's perception about the malleability of his/her own personal traits can be extrapolated and imposed on the evaluation of a brand extension. That is, those that subscribe to the idea that traits are malleable (incremental theorists) are more accepting of distant brand extensions, and more likely to perceive the new brand as fitting with the parent brand compared to consumers who believe that traits are fixed (entity theorists). Further, the authors demonstrated that the entity vs. incremental naïve theory could be situationally primed, suggesting that marketers could provide context to their distant brand extension in an attempt to generate the appropriate naïve theory that will most adventitiously influence product evaluations of a brand extension, which is not closely related to the parent.

Naïve theories can also be used to understand and leverage the marketing mix variables (pricing, promotion etc.) to make products more attractive and competitive. For example, Posavac, Herzenstein, Kardes and Sundaram (2010), showed that consumers tend to use a firm's profitability as an inferential basis to generate an attitude about the firm according to the naïve theory that companies belonging to the "financially successful" category will possess a constellation of favourable traits leading to greater perceived advertisement credibility, more positive brand attitudes and increased purchase intention. Their results have direct implications for enhancing the effectiveness of advertisements. For example, making firm profitability salient in advertisements is likely to initiate multiple favourable inferences and result in positive feelings and positive behaviours towards the advertisement, the product and the firm. Firms can overtly solicit associations such as these through advertising. Similarly, favourable naïve theories can sometimes be primed in memory, impacting how consumers will be influenced by the information that is recalled from memory.

Accessibility experiences

While many naïve theories are generated from the environment through observation, some are dependent on metacognition or the characteristics of memory – particularly the ease with which certain elements are recalled. For example, if it were more difficult for us to recall a personal example of a certain trait being exhibited, then the likely naïve theory would assume that we do not often exhibit that trait. In a classic study, people were asked to recall either 6 or 12 examples of their own assertive or unassertive behaviour (Schwarz et al., 1991). Consistent with the hypothesis, participants appear to use the ease of recall to infer the strength of the personal trait. That is, participants rated themselves as more assertive when it was easier to recall examples of assertive behaviour (e.g., they recalled only 6 occasions) and less assertive when the set of examples was more difficult to recall (e.g., they tried to recall as many as 12 examples of assertive behaviour). Similarly, they also rated themselves as more *un*assertive when they recalled few (6) rather than many (12) examples of unassertive behaviour. Because it is easier to recall few rather than many examples of a particular type of behaviour, the naïve theory would predict that more extreme trait inferences will be formed when few rather than many examples are recalled.

In some circumstances, the implications of ease of processing may be tempered by external stimuli. Briñol, Petty and Tormala (2006) exposed participants to one of two naïve theories implying opposing interpretations of ease with which a mental task is completed. One group read a description that equated a feeling of ease when thinking with a lack of intelligence and a feeling of difficulty when thinking with intelligence (i.e., ease is bad/difficulty is good). The other group read a description that presented the opposite conclusions (i.e., ease is good/ difficulty is bad). The two groups were then asked to evaluate a personally relevant issue either by generating a few (easy task) or many (difficult task) arguments for or against the issue. The results show that the attitude reported was dependent on both the ease of the argument retrieval task and the valence of the prime (e.g., ease of thought is good vs. ease of thought is bad). That is, the ease experienced during the thought generation task signalled validity of those thoughts for the participants who had been presented with positive implications associated with ease of thought, but the same ease signalled invalidity when negative implications were offered before the thought generation task.

Similarly, when people are primed to focus on the details and the process (low construal level) rather than on the outcomes and the benefits (high construal level), the naïve theory associated with effort of fluency will have different interpretations. Several studies showed the importance of the level of construal in generating naïve theories to interpret a variety of situations (Tsai & McGill, 2011; Trope & Liberman, 2003). Subjective fluency experiences can be interpreted in terms of effort or ability depending on whether consumers are focused, respectively, on the desirability (typically associated with higher levels of construals) or the feasibility of the event (usually tied to lower levels of construals). Further, fluency can increase or decrease confidence depending on the applicable naïve theory that serves as the inference rule. Tsai and McGill (2011) use the following example: processing difficulty experienced in studying for an exam could lead to a feeling of high confidence, providing this difficulty is interpreted as effort put forth to ensure a good grade. Alternatively, the same difficulty of processing could lead to feeling uncertain about one's performance if interpreted as inability to process the study materials. Thus, naïve theories can help people interpret the world, but they are contingent on the ease with which information is recalled from memory and the social and situational factors that provide context to the perception of that processing ease.

Also, considering the processing style is crucial to understanding the role of ease of processing and the impact of accessibility experiences. Deval and Kardes (2015) showed that the feeling of ease can play different roles in attitude formation depending on whether a judgement task is memory-based or stimulus-based. Similarly, Schwarz (e.g., 2004) proposes that accessibility experiences operate as heuristic cues, suggesting that the effect should be attenuated under high elaboration conditions. In contrast, Petty and colleagues (e.g., 2007) find stronger effects when people attend to their own thoughts and try to assess their validity (the self-validation hypothesis), implying that accessibility experiences require greater thinking to be included as input for judgement. Deval and Kardes (2015) show that ease can indeed play the role of a heuristic cue when judgements are memory-based, but contributes to a self-validation process when judgements are stimulus-based. They illustrate that when a judgement is stimulus-based and does not require actively searching memory for relevant thoughts, the impact of ease on attitude formation is mediated by the level of confidence they have in their own thoughts. That is, those who are more confident that their thoughts are correct are more likely to have a favourable attitude when the stimulus-based evaluation is easy. Such a process is only possible under high elaboration conditions when people have both the motivation and ability to attend their thoughts carefully. Even while memory-based category knowledge can help to generate naïve theories, the variability of attributes within the category can also generate effective naïve theories.

Perceived variability, halo and inference

Consumers also possess naïve theories about the extent to which the possible values of different attributes are likely to vary. Some attributes are assumed to have a wide range of possible values, whereas others are assumed to have a relatively narrow range of possible values. For example, the prevalence of low-fat and reduced-fat products in the marketplace have encouraged consumers to expect that calories can vary dramatically across brands in a given product category. Other attributes, such as the flavour enhancer, monosodium glutamate, are assumed to vary less across brands in a given product category. Research on perceived attribute variability has shown that uncertainty is higher for high variability attributes than for low variability attributes, and consequently, consumers form more conservative and more moderate inferences about the values of missing attributes associated with high variability (Meyer, 1981). However, this effect is reduced when the product has a halo label that is viewed favourably and changes the way consumers think about the product, such as "organic", "locally produced", "low cholesterol", "low fat", "low sodium", "gluten free" or "fair trade". Labels such as these produce a health halo effect and lead to more favourable inferences about the values of missing attributes (Schuldt & Schwarz, 2010; Schuldt, Muller, & Schwarz, 2010; Sundar & Kardes, 2015). These effects were observed for different attributes that differ in perceived variability and for the same attribute when perceived variability was manipulated via priming (Sundar & Kardes, 2015).

Importantly, recent research has shown that the influence of attribute variability is reversed when consumers have direct experience with a product and when a halo label is present (Sundar & Kardes, 2015). This occurs because the halo-triggering label influences the interpretation of ambiguous product consumption experiences (Ha & Hoch, 1989; Hoch & Ha, 1986). In the Sundar and Kardes (2015) Experiment 4, the halo label "fair trade" was used, and this label lead to more favourable nutritional inferences even though the label provided absolutely no nutritional information. Moreover, subjects actually consumed more chocolate when the product was labelled as a "fair trade" product and when perceived variability was high. The results suggest that naïve theories about perceived variability and halo labels have important implications for understanding how consumer expectations about nutrition influence food consumption rates. In these cases, the expectations were based on an attribute that is present in the product, but it can also be effective when the attribute is just implied – creating a marketing placebo effect.

The marketing placebo effect

Research has shown that when consumers assume that an attribute or relationship is present even when it is not (the marketing placebo effect) the resulting naïve theories still influence expectations about the effectiveness of products which then influences behavioural performance when these products are consumed (Shiv, Carmon, & Ariely, 2005). For example, participants were told that the price of an energy drink was either $1.89 or $0.89. Subjects believed that the more expensive drink was more effective and they completed more intellectual puzzles after consuming the more expensive drink. Wright, Hernandez, Sundar, Dinsmore and Kardes (2013) replicated this study with a Brazilian energy drink and Brazilian subjects. They also demonstrated that several variables other than price can also produce a marketing placebo effect.

For instance, consumers frequently believe that products that contain a large number of ingredients (i.e., six) are more effective than products that contain a small number of ingredients (i.e., two). Consequently, subjects correctly solve a greater number of intellectual puzzles after consuming a beverage purported to have a large (vs. small) number of ingredients. Wright et al.

(2013) also demonstrated that consumers frequently expect scarce products to be more effective than widely available products. Scarcity was manipulated via shelf space (e.g., the target product had as much shelf space or half as much as its competitor). Subjects solved more puzzles after consuming a scarce beverage rather than a common beverage.

Consumers also frequently believe that bad-tasting beverages are more effective than good-tasting beverages. Consequently, subjects performed better on a memory task after consuming a bad-tasting beverage rather than a good-tasting beverage (Wright et al., 2013). These findings have significant implication for marketers. A wide range of marketing activities could potentially influence consumers' expectations and consumers' actual behaviour performance after consuming a product. Thus, the marketer can look to the research on naïve theories to construct a better marketing strategy for their products.

When naïve theories are useful

While many studies focus on proving the existence of a naïve theory, it is not enough to simply prove the existence to understand how naïve theories are used as an inference rule. As seen in the context of ease of mental processing, two competing naïve theories may be applicable and the chosen naïve theory will depend of the external stimuli within which the situation is presented. More specifically, situational factors that may bias the use or interpretation of a given naïve theory are many: time constraints, the desire to evaluate and think about the information, situational expertise, cognitive stress, attitude relevance and many more.

In many situations, more than one naïve theory might be relevant and the situational influences will highlight one naïve theory over another and create malleability in the response reported (Briñol et al., 2006; Tsai & McGill, 2011). Deval, Mantel, Kardes, & Posavac (2013) illustrate that in situations where two competing naïve theories are possible, situational influences will activate one of those options and the resulting evaluation will be reported in light of the activated naïve theory. There are a vast number of contradictory naïve theories associated with the marketing mix variables. For example, when a consumer encounters a product that is on sale, they may conclude, "if the product is on sale, then the store must be overstocked – the product must not be desirable". Conversely, they may conclude, "if the product is on sale, it must be a great deal". Therefore, the likelihood of purchasing a product that is on sale may depend on which of these naïve theories is active during the store visit.

While marketers have control over the messaging in an advertisement or a packaging design, they may have less control over which naïve theory is activated at the time that the brand is encountered. For example, some marketers rely on social influence techniques to increase the effectiveness of their persuasive attempts. Some may use a "bandwagon" type of appeal ("everybody loves this"), others may use a scarcity appeal ("only certain consumers will get this") and both have been proven efficient techniques of influence (Deval et al. 2013). While these two techniques are not mutually exclusive, the same product description may create very different perceptions depending on which naïve theory is activated. If a product is portrayed as one that a large proportion of people prefer, or have bought, the product may be viewed as "very good" by those with the bandwagon naïve theory activated and "very bad" for those that subscribe to the scarcity naïve theory. That is, with regard to scarcity, perceived value is increased precisely by the fact that only a limited number of people have access to the product. Thus, learning that a product is widely available may serve as a cue that it is not exclusive or serve as a cue of its popularity and high utility. Deval et al. (2013) show that a subtle priming manipulation can activate one or the other naïve theory and lead to opposite conclusions about a product. That is, they presented participants with an ad for a bottle of wine containing either a social validation appeal – "More than 200,000 cases sold" – or a scarcity appeal – "Less than 2,000 cases available". Participants who were primed with the concept of popularity, formed more favourable evaluations about the wine when a social validation appeal was used, than when a scarcity appeal was used. The opposite pattern was observed for participants who were primed with the concept of exclusivity. The conclusions of the four experiments suggest that either appeal can be successful and either appeal can be unsuccessful. The defining factor is the extent to which the activated naïve theory matches the consumption-related stimulus (e.g., an advertisement or a product attribute). When the activated naïve theory matches the stimulus message, then consumers' product perceptions tend to be more favourable compared to the situation where the naïve theory and the stimulus are mismatched.

All in all, naïve theories serve the consumers by simplifying the decision situation and sometimes even serve a role in bias correction. Naïve theories play a role in spontaneous inferences that happen without consumers' intention, awareness or effort. They also have an impact on the way judgement and attitudes change (e.g., Petty & Briñol, 2012); however, naïve theories may also have direct implications for bias correction (Wegener & Petty, 1995, 1997). When people identity potentially biasing factors, they often attempt to remove that bias from their judgements and evaluations. In doing so, people may turn to naïve theories to assess how biasing factors might possibly influence or have already influenced their evaluation of an object. In a succession of experiments, Wegener and Petty (1995) evaluated the way people consider how context influences target perception. They documented that people correct in opposite ways for the same context if they hold opposing theories about the way context impacted their judgement. Even so, these corrections sometimes result in overcorrection (experiment 3) because the corrections are made for the "perceived" bias rather than the actual bias. In their last study, Wegener and Petty (1995) show that individual perceptions of the bias generated by the naïve theories predict the direction and magnitude of corrections observed.

Individual naïve theories about persuasion itself are therefore likely to lead people to correct for persuasion attempts. Briñol, Rucker and Petty (2015) show that naïve theories about persuasion (beyond advertising scepticism) can affect information processing. Their results illustrate that consumers who have negative, as opposed to positive, views of persuasion are more likely to attend to, examine and analyze the arguments presented to them. Yet the observed increased elaboration may not be completely objective and could itself contain bias, depending on the inherent nature of naïve theory being used. Thus, this increased elaboration carries no guarantee of accuracy of judgement, despite the fact that consumers believe they are more objective and their judgements and inferences are more accurate. Because of this, marketers must be wary of taking a simplistic view of naïve theories. Depending on the situation, various naïve theories may be activated by different consumers generating vastly different product evaluations. Thus, marketers must actively control the brand associations so that consumers are more likely to evaluate the product from the context of a favourably interpreted naïve theory.

Summary

Consumers hold naïve theories about the relationships of a wide range of marketing and consumption-related variables, and these naive theories influence a broad range of inferences, judgements, decisions and behaviours. Consumers develop expectations regarding accessibility experiences, brand names, country of origin, price, scarcity, taste, packaging, promotions and the use of jargon in product descriptions. These expectations guide external information search and memory search in a manner that supports or bolsters the original expectations. These updated expectations then drive inferences about missing or unknown attributes and benefits, as well as judgements of attributes and benefits that were included in a product description. These inferences and judgements drive choice, consumption and post-consumption behavioural performance.

Our review also shows that consumers hold so many naïve theories about marketing and consumption that some of these naïve theories are likely to contradict one another. Surprisingly, consumers tend to be unaware of these contradictions, and subtle priming manipulations can be used to activate one naïve theory over another. The more accessible naïve theory then guides inference formation and choice. Moreover, research on the marketing placebo effect shows that these inferences can subsequently influence behavioural performance following product consumption.

Naïve theories also guide judgement adjustment or correction when consumers suspect that their judgements may be unduly influenced by an irrelevant piece of information. The direction of the adjustment and the amount of adjustment depends on the judgemental implications of the naïve theory and on the naïve theory's assumptions about the magnitude of the bias that was produced.

Future research should investigate naïve theories about additional marketing activities, such as loyalty programmes, advertising appeals and claims, and interactions with salespersons. In some situations, several different types of marketing activities are likely to seem like gimmicks, and this should undermine their effectiveness. In other situations, several different types of marketing activities may seem to add value to the consumer. Naïve theories about comparative advertising may be particularly interesting, for example, because in some situations the claims seem dubious or unfair, whereas in others the claims seem legitimate. The comparison brand (e.g., an abstract leading brand or a concrete, specifically named leading brand), the type of comparison (e.g., attribute or benefit) and the degree of alignability of the points of comparison (Zhang, Kardes, & Cronley, 2002) could potentially influence which specific naïve theory about comparison advertising is activated, which could influence comparison advertising effectiveness.

Further, how naïve theories compare across cultural contexts is an area for additional research. As mentioned earlier certain naïve theories resulting from a given type of categorising or stereotyping, like country of origin naïve theories, may not be cross-culturally applicable. The use of categories themselves is different when observed cross-culturally. For example, analytic cultures tend to pay more attention to categories and rules when holistic cultures consider a larger field to assign causality (Nisbett 2001). One can speculate that any naïve theory has a limited scope of application. Even when different naïve theories coexist one may dominate the other depending on stable individual characteristics (Deval et al., 2013). From such results it seems reasonable to venture that different cultures have different naïve theories driving inference processes. Given the current state of research there is no reason to believe that the process itself would be different because of international differences. The generic if-then linkage should be robust across different cultures. It seems likely however, that different naïve theories may be used by people of different cultures. So if the inference process is potentially universal, the actual inference may be very distinct. Because of the way naïve theories are developed, the relevant variables to their construction may be distinct from one context to another. For example, lay thinking about the economy (Bastounis, Leiser, & Levy, 2004) or folk biological reasoning (Medin & Scott, 2004) have been shown to be culturally distinct. It is therefore capital for researchers and marketers alike to understand the frame of reference of consumers before assuming that a certain naïve theory will be used to interpret and infer from a given piece of information. Some naïve theories do seem more likely to be widely generalizable across cultures than others depending how domain specific they are.

Understanding consumers' naïve theories is crucial for understanding consumer inference processes, and for predicting the conditions under which marketing tactics are likely to be effective versus ineffective. When marketing tactics and consumers' naïve theories match, the tactics are likely to be quite successful. However, when marketing tactics mismatch consumers' naïve theories, the tactics are likely to backfire. Future research should identify additional naïve theories and additional factors that influence which naïve theory is likely to be activated in a particular consumer setting.

References

Aaker, D. A., & Keller, K. L. (1990). Consumer evaluations of brand extensions. *Journal of Marketing*, *54*(1), 27–41. doi: 10.2307/1252171

American Gem Society. (2015, July 14). The history of the diamond as an engagement ring. Retrieved from www.americangemsociety.org/the-history-of-the-diamond-as-an-engagement-ring

Balabanis, G., & Diamantopoulos, A. (2004). Domestic country bias, country-of-origin effects, and consumer ethnocentrism: A multidimensional unfolding approach. *Journal of the Academy of Marketing Science*, *32*(1), 80–95. doi: 10.1177/0092070303257644

Bastounis, M., Leiser, D., & Roland-Lévy, C. (2004). Psychosocial variables involved in the construction of lay thinking about the economy: Results of a cross-national survey. *Journal of Economic Psychology*, *25*(2), 263–278. doi: 10.1016/S0167-4870(02)00198-8

Bem, D. J., & McConnell, H. K. (1970). Testing the self-perception explanation of dissonance phenomena: On the salience of premanipulation attitudes. *Journal of Personality and Social Psychology*, *14*(1), 23–31. doi: 10.1037/h0020916

Berger, J., & Heath, C. (2007). Where consumers diverge from others: Identity signaling and product domains. *Journal of Consumer Research*, *34*(2), 121–134.

Blackwell, L. S., Trzesniewski, K. H., & Dweck, C. S. (2007). Implicit theories of intelligence predict achievement across an adolescent transition: A longitudinal study and an intervention. *Child Development*, *78*(1), 246–263. doi: 10.1111/j.1467-8624.2007.00995.x

Boush, D. M., & Loken, B. (1991). A process-tracing study of brand extension evaluation. *Journal of Marketing Research*, *28*(1), 16–28. doi: 10.2307/3172723

Brewer, M. B. (1988). A dual process model of impression formation. In T. K. Srull & R. S. Wyer Jr (Eds.), *Advances in social cognition* (Vol. 1, pp. 1–36). Hillsdale, NJ: Lawrence Erlbaum Associates, Inc.

Bridges, S., Keller, K. L., & Sood, S. (2000). Communication strategies for brand extensions: Enhancing perceived fit by establishing explanatory links. *Journal of Advertising*, *29*(4), 1–11. doi: 10.2307/4189157

Briñol, P., Petty, R. E., & Tormala, Z. L. (2006). The malleable meaning of subjective ease. *Psychological Science*, *17*(3), 200–206.

Briñol, P., Rucker, D., & Petty, R. (2015). Naïve theories about persuasion: Implications for information processing and consumer attitude change. *International Journal of Advertising* (ahead-of-print), 1–22.

Broniarczyk, S. M., & Alba, J. W. (1994). The importance of the brand in brand extension. *Journal of Marketing Research*, *31*(2), 214–228. doi: 10.2307/3152195

Bruno, Ken (2010, April 29). Best-Ever Advertising Taglines. Forbes.com. Retrieved from www.forbes.com/2010/05/28/nike-bmw-amex-apple-cmo-network-best-advertising-taglines.html

Carey, S. (1985). *Conceptual change in childhood*. Cambridge, MA: MIT Press.

Chakravarti, D., MacInnis, D. J., & Nakamoto, K. (1990). Product category perceptions, elaborative processing and brand name extension strategies. *Advances in Consumer Research*, *17*(1), 910–916.

Chen, S., & Chaiken, S. (1999). The heuristic-systematic model in its broader context. In S. Chaiken & Y. Trope (Eds.), *Dual-process theories in social psychology*. (pp. 73–96). New York, NY: Guilford Press.

Chisnall, P. M. (1974). Aluminium household foil in the common market: research for an effective brand name. *Journal of Management Studies*, *11*(3), 246–255. doi: 10.1111/j.1467-6486.1974.tb00697.x

Chiu, C.-y., Hong, Y.-y., & Dweck, C. S. (1997). Lay dispositionism and implicit theories of personality. *Journal of Personality and Social Psychology*, *73*(1), 19–30. doi: 10.1037/0022-3514.73.1.19

Cho, H, & Schwarz N. (2008). Of great art and untalented artists: Effort information and the flexible construction of judgmental heuristics. *Journal of Consumer Psychology*, *18*, 205–211.

Cronley, M. L., Posavac, S. S., Meyer, T., Kardes, F. R., & Kellaris, J. J. (2005). A selective hypothesis testing perspective on price–quality inference and inference-based choice. *Journal of Consumer Psychology, 15*(2), 159–169.

Deval, H., Mantel, S. P., Kardes, F. R., & Posavac, S. S. (2013). How naïve theories drive opposing inferences from the same information. *Journal of Consumer Research, 39*(6), 1185–1201. doi: 10.1086/668086

Deval, H., & Kardes, F. R. (2015). The role of accessibility experiences in attitude formation: Effects of stimlus-based versus memory-based processing, Working paper, Dalhousie University.

Dick, A., Chakravarti, D., & Biehal, G. (1990). Memory-based inferences during consumer choice. *The Journal of Consumer Research, 17*(1), 82–93.

Dweck, C. S., Chiu, C.-y., & Hong, Y.-y. (1995). Implicit theories and their role in judgments and reactions: A world from two perspectives. *Psychological Inquiry, 6*(4), 267–285. doi: 10.2307/1448940

Farquhar, P. H., Herr, P. M., & Fazio, R. H. (1990). A relational model for category extensions of brands. *Advances in Consumer Research, 17*(1), 856–860.

Furnham, A. (1988). *Lay theories: Everyday understanding of problems in the social sciences*. Elmsford, NY: Pergamon Press.

Gelman, S. A., & Noles, N. S. (2011). Domains and naïve theories. *Wiley Interdisciplinary Reviews: Cognitive Science, 2*(5), 490–502. doi: 10.1002/wcs.124

Gunasti, K., & Ross, W. T. (2009). How inferences about missing attributes cecrease the tendency to defer choice and increase purchase probability. *Journal of Consumer Research, 35*(5), 823–837. doi: 10.1086/593684

Gürhan-Canli, Z., & Maheswaran, D. (2000). Cultural variations in country of origin effects. *Journal of Marketing Research, 37*(3), 309–317. doi: 10.1509/jmkr.37.3.309.18778

Ha, Y., & Hoch, S. J. (1989). Ambiguity, processing strategy, and advertising-evidence interactions. *Journal of Consumer Research, 16*, 354–360.

Hoch, S. J., & Ha, Y. (1986). Consumer learning: Advertising and the ambiguity of product experience. *Journal of Consumer Research, 13*, 221–233.

Hong, Y.-Y., Chiu, C.-Y., Dweck, C. S., & Sacks, R. (1997). Implicit theories and evaluative processes in person cognition. *Journal of Experimental Social Psychology, 33*(3), 296–323. doi: 10.1006/jesp.1996.1324

Hong, S. T., & Wyer, R. S. (1989). Effects of country-of-origin and product-attribute information on product evaluation: An information-processing perspective. *Journal of Consumer Research, 16*(2), 175–187. doi: 10.1086/209206

Hong, S. T., & Wyer, R. S. (1990). Determinants of product evaluation: Effects of the time interval between knowledge of a product's country of origin and information about its specific attributes. *Journal of Consumer Research, 17*(3), 277–288. doi: 10.1086/208557

Kardes, F. R., Posavac, S. S., & Cronley, M. L. (2004). Consumer inference: A review of processes, bases, and judgment contexts. *Journal of Consumer Psychology, 14*(3), 230–256.

Kardes, F. R., Posavac, S. S., Cronley, M. L., & Herr, P. M. (2008). Consumer inference. In C. P. Haugtvedt, P. M. Herr & F. R. Kardes (Eds.), *Handbook of consumer psychology* (pp. 165–191). New York, NY: Taylor & Francis Group/Lawrence Erlbaum Associates.

Kardes, F. R., & Wyer Jr, R. S. (2013). Consumer information processing. In D. Carlston (Ed.), *The Oxford handbook of social cognition* (pp. 806–828). Oxford, UK: Oxford University Press.

Keller, K. L. (1993). Conceptualizing, measuring, and managing customer-based brand equity. *Journal of Marketing, 57*(1), 1–22. doi: 10.2307/1252054

Keller, K. L., & Aaker, D. A. (1992). The effects of sequential introduction of brand extensions. *Journal of Marketing Research, 29*(1), 35–50. doi: 10.2307/3172491

Kelley, H. H., & Thibaut, J. W. (1969). Group problem solving. In G. Lindzey & E. Aronson (Eds.), *The handbook of social psychology*. Reading, MA: Addison-Wesley.

Kirmani, A. (1990). The effect of perceived advertising costs on brand perceptions. *Journal of Consumer Research, 17*(2), 160–171. doi: 10.2307/2626808

Kruglanski, A., & Webster, D. M. (1996). Motivated closing of the mind: "Seizing" and "freezing". *Psychological Review, 103*, 263–283.

Li, W.-K., & Wyer Jr, R. S. (1994). The role of country of origin in product evaluations: Informational and standard-of-comparison effects. *Journal of Consumer Psychology, 3*(2), 187–212. doi: 10.1016/S1057-7408(08)80004-6

Loureiro, M. L., & Umberger, W. J. (2007). A choice experiment model for beef: What US Consumer responses tell us about relative preferences for food safety, country-of-origin labeling and traceability. *Food Policy, 32*, 496–514.

Maheswaran, D., Mackie, D. M., & Chaiken, S. (1992). Brand name as a heuristic cue: The effects of task importance and expectancy confirmation on consumer judgments. *Journal of Consumer Psychology, 1*(4), 317–336.

Medin, D. L., & Atran, S. (2004). The native mind: Biological categorization and reasoning in development and across cultures. *Psychological Review, 111*(4), 960–983. doi: 10.1037/0033-295x.111.4.960

Meyer, R. J. (1981). A model of multiattribute judgments under attribute uncertainty and informational constraint. *Journal of Marketing Research, 18*, 428–441.

Nisbett, R. E., Peng, K., Choi, I., & Norenzayan, A. (2001). Culture and systems of thought: Holistic versus analytic cognition. *Psychological Review, 108*(2), 291–310. doi: 10.1037/0033-295x.108.2.291

Osberg, T. M. (2002). Psychology is not just common sense: An introductory psychology demonstration. In R. A. Griggs (Ed.), *Handbook for teaching introductory psychology* (Vol. 3, pp. 180–181). Mahwah, NJ: Erlbaum.

Petty, R. E., & Briñol, P. (2012). The elaboration likelihood model. In P. A. M. Van Lange, A. Kruglanski & E. T. Higgins (Eds.), *Handbook of theories of social psychology* (Vol. 1, pp. 224–245). Thousands Oaks, CA: Sage.

Petty, R. E., Briñol, P., & DeMarree, K. G. (2007). The meta-cognitive model (MCM) of attitudes: Implications for attitude measurement, change, and strength, *Social Cognition, 25*(5), 657–686.

Petty, R. E., Cacioppo, J. T., & Schumann, D. (1983). Central and peripheral routes to advertising effectiveness: The moderating role of involvement. *Journal of Consumer Research, 10*, 135–146.

Petty, R. E., & Wegener, D. T. (1999). The elaboration likelihood model: Current status and controversies. In S. Chaiken & Y. Trope (Eds.), *Dual-process theories in social psychology* (pp. 37–72). New York, NY: Guilford Press.

Posavac, S. S., Herzenstein, M., Kardes, F. R., & Sundaram, S. (2010). Profits and halos: The role of firm profitability information in consumer inference. *Journal of Consumer Psychology, 20*(3), 327–337.

Purohit, D., & Srivastava, J. (2001). Effect of manufacturer reputation, retailer reputation, and product warranty on consumer judgments of product quality: A cue diagnosticity framework. *Journal of Consumer Psychology, 10*(3), 123–134. doi: 10.1207/s15327663jcp1003_1

Raghunathan, R., Naylor, R. W., & Hoyer, W. D. (2006). The unhealthy = tasty intuition and its effects on taste inferences, enjoyment, and choice of food products. *Journal of Marketing, 70*(4), 170–184.

Ratneshwar, S., & Chaiken, S. (1991). Comprehension's role in persuasion: The case of its moderating effect on the persuasive impact of source cues. *Journal of Consumer Research, 18*, 52–62.

Sanbonmatsu, D., Posavac, S., Kardes, F., & Mantel, S. (1998). Selective hypothesis testing. *Psychonomic Bulletin and Review*, 5(2), 197–220.

Schuldt, J. P., Muller, D., & Schwarz, N. (2012). The "fair trade" effect: Health halos from social ethics claims. *Social Psychological and Personality Science, 3*, 581–589.

Schuldt, J. P., & Schwarz, N. (2010). The "organic" path to obesity? Organic claims influence calorie judgments and exercise recommendations. *Judgment and Decision Making, 5*, 144–150.

Schwarz, N. (2004). Metacognitive experiences in consumer judgment and decision making, *Journal of Consumer Psychology, 14*(4), 332–348.

Schwarz, N., Strack, F., Bless, H., Klumpp, G., Rittenauer-Schatka, H., & Simons, A. (1991). Ease of retrieval as information: Another look at the availability heuristic. *Journal of Personality and Social Psychology, 61*(2), 195–202.

Shah, A. K., & Oppenheimer, D. M. (2008). Heuristics made easy: An effort-reduction framework. *Psychological Bulletin, 134*(2), 207–222. doi: 10.1037/0033-2909.134.2.207

Shiv, B., Carmon, Z., & Ariely, D. (2005). Placebo effects of marketing actions: Consumers may get what they pay for. *Journal of Marketing Research, 42*, 383–393.

Sujan, M. (1985). Consumer knowledge: Effects on evaluation strategies mediating consumer judgments. *Journal of Consumer Research, 12*(1), 31–46. doi: 10.1086/209033

Sujan, M., & Dekleva, C. (1987). Product categorization and inference making: Some implications for comparative advertising. *Journal of Consumer Research, 14*(3), 372–378. doi: 10.1086/209120

Sundar, A., & Kardes, F. R. (2015). The role of perceived variability and the health halo effect in nutritional inference and consumption. *Psychology and Marketing, 32*(5), 512–521.

Trope, Y., & Liberman, N. (2003). Temporal construal. *Psychological Review, 110*(3), 403–421. doi: 10.1037/0033-295x.110.3.403

Tsai, C. I., & McGill, A. L. (2011). No pain, no gain? How fluency and construal level affect consumer confidence. *Journal of Consumer Research, 37*(5), 807–821.

Wegener, D. T., & Petty, R. E. (1995). Flexible correction processes in social judgment: The role of naïve theories in corrections for perceived bias. *Journal of Personality and Social Psychology, 68*(1), 36–51. doi: 10.1037/0022-3514.68.1.36

Wegener, D. T., & Petty, R. E. (1997). The flexible correction model: The role of naïve theories of bias in bias correction. In P. Z. Mark (Ed.), *Advances in experimental social psychology* (Vol. 29, pp. 141–208). Waltham, MA: Academic Press.

Wheeler, S. C., Petty, R. E., & Bizer, G. Y. (2005). Self-schema matching and attitude change: Situational and dispositional determinants of message elaboration. *Journal of Consumer Research, 31*, 787–797.

Wright, S. A., Hernandez, J. M., Sundar, A., Dinsmore, J., & Kardes, F. R. (2013). If it tastes bad it must be good: Consumer naïve theories and the marketing placebo effect. *International Journal of Research in Marketing, 30*, 197–198.

Wyer, R. S., Jr. (2008). The role of knowledge accessibility in cognition and behaviour: Implications for consumer information processing. In C. P. Haugtvedt, P. M. Herr & F. R. Kardes (Eds.), *Handbook of consumer psychology* (pp. 31–76). New York, NY: Taylor & Francis Group/Lawrence Erlbaum Associates.

Yorkston, E. A., Nunes, J. C., & Matta, S. (2010). The malleable brand: The role of implicit theories in evaluating brand extensions. *Journal of Marketing, 74*(1), 80–93.

Zhang, S., Kardes, F. R., & Cronley, M. L. (2002). Comparative advertising: Effects of structural alignability on target brand evaluation. *Journal of Consumer Psychology, 12*(4), 303–312.

24

What makes tomorrow's gain worth today's pain?

Cognitive, motivational and affective influences in consumers' self-control dilemmas

Aparna A. Labroo and Anastasiya Pocheptsova

Consumers pursuing long-term goals often face choices that trade off immediate pleasure for long-term benefits. For example, consumers on a diet may have to choose between indulgent foods and healthier options, those on a budget between splurging and saving for more essential items and those committed to social welfare between work to improve society and fun. While the domains of these choices vary widely, they all have one thing in common: Consumers have to override the temptation to choose a momentarily alluring alternative in favour of an immediately less alluring one that instead facilitates pursuit of their long-term goals of health, financial stability or social welfare. All these choices thus pose a self-control dilemma for consumers engaged in the pursuit of long-term goals.

In this chapter, we review research on such choices that involve tradeoffs between short-term desires and long-term benefits and pose a self-control dilemma for consumers engaged in pursuit of long-term goals. We review existing theories of self-control in the context of consumer decision making, including early views that self-control is a dispositional trait and more recent ones that view self-control as a state variable affected by situational factors. Next, we examine the cognitive, motivational and affective influences on consumers' resolution of self-control dilemmas. We conclude with important directions for future research.

What is self-control?

The benefits of exerting self-control have been widely documented (see de Ridder, Lensvelt-Mulders, Finkenauer, Stok, & Baumeister, 2012, for a meta-analysis and Baumeister & Vohs, 2004, for a review). Exerting self-control is known to lead to better life outcomes, such as improved long-term well-being, better health and savings, improved personal relationships and professional achievements (Baumeister & Vohs, 2004; Tangley, Baumeister, & Boone, 2004). By contrast, low self-control is associated with a number of negative outcomes, such as substance abuse, criminal behaviour and obesity (Baumeister & Heatherton, 1996; de Ridder et al., 2012). Among consumers, a low level of self-control has been linked to impulsive buying (Vohs & Feber, 2007), choice of vice products over virtue products (Wang, Novemsky, Dhar, & Baumeister, 2010; Wertenbroch, 1998) and overconsumption of indulgent foods

(Vohs & Heatherton, 2000). Although the negative consequences of low self-control are clear, a considerable debate still wages regarding what self-control exactly is (Duckworth & Kern, 2011), and particularly the role inherent ability vs. situational influences play in one's ability to exert self-control (Vohs, Baumesiter, & Schmeichel, 2013).

Early views proposed self-control as a dispositional trait that is stable across different contexts and over time for each individual. Therefore, people with higher levels of self-control are better than low self-control individuals at controlling impulses and achieving long-term goals. For example, in a classic study of dispositional self-control by Mischel, Shoda and Peake (1988), children with lower self-control (measured as the ability to delay gratification) performed significantly worse academically ten years later than children who exhibited high self-control in their pre-school years. Further, in a study conducted by Hoffman, Baumeister, Förster and Vohs (2012a), consumers with higher levels of trait self-control reported experiencing less intense desires towards temptations and, consequently, less conflict between desires and long-term goals. Other research similarly suggests that consumers with high self-control manage their money better than other consumers, saving more for the future and spending less on indulgences (Baumiester, 2002; Romal & Kaplan, 1995).

In contrast to this view that self-control is a trait, more recent theories recognize that a person's ability to exert self-control varies significantly over time and across contexts (Baumiester, 2002). Different cognitive, motivational and affective factors can all influence the extent of self-control a consumer exerts in a given situation. The same consumer can exhibit high versus low self-control under different conditions and the exact same choice may pose a self-control dilemma in some contexts but not others for a consumer based on her goals, affective states and the manner in which she construes her choice options.

So when does a choice pose a self-control dilemma and when does it not? The fundamental determinant of whether a choice involves a self-control dilemma for a consumer is whether the choice forces the consumer to trade off something she desires in the long term against something that is also momentarily desirable. For example, choosing whether to consume a healthy or an indulgent afternoon snack involves a self-control dilemma for a consumer on a diet who is pursuing a goal to become healthier but who also enjoys high-calorie indulgent foods. If a consumer is not on diet and is not pursuing a health goal, or a consumer does not particularly enjoy consuming high-caloric indulgent foods, or both, then this exact same choice between a healthy and indulgent snack does not pose a self-control dilemma. For a choice to involve self-control dilemma for a consumer, the consumer must value both the long-term and the short-term outcome equally. Her choice must involve a tradeoff between an outcome valued more in the long-term, but involving immediate effort to accomplish, and an outcome damaging pursuit of the long-term goal but offering immediate pleasure. While many health, savings or social welfare choices involve such tradeoffs for many consumers in many contexts, other such choices may not involve tradeoff for some consumers or in some contexts.

Faced with choices that involve tradeoffs between the pursuit of long-term goals and immediate desires, consumers have to exert willpower to reign in their immediate impulses and desires and instead nudge action towards long-term goals. But overriding these immediate desires can be effortful and depleting for consumers, resulting in giving in to the momentary indulgence. To demonstrate the breadth of self-control dilemmas people face every day, Hoffman and colleagues (Hoffman et al., 2012a, Hoffman, Vohs, & Baumeister, 2012b) conducted a large descriptive study of human desires and conflicts between such desires, in which they asked participants to report daily the self-control conflicts they experienced. The authors identified that desire for perceived temptations, such as leisure, sleep and media use, most often elicited a conflict with consumers' long-term goals, and such conflict often led to self-control failure, with participants choosing temptations over actions consistent with long-term pursuits. The rate of self-control failure was relatively high, reaching 42 per cent in the case of desire to engage in media activities (short-term temptation) instead of focusing on work (long-term benefit). Importantly, the strength of the desire for temptations, the level of conflict experienced between desires and goals and ultimately the rate of self-control failure varied substantially between individuals and between contexts for a given individual, suggesting that a magnitude of factors influence the human ability to exert self-control. In what follows, we describe several prominent research streams that explicate three distinct factors affecting consumer self-control: cognitive, motivational and emotional.

Cognitive influences on self-control

Self-control as a limited cognitive resource

One of the most prominent theories of self-control, self-regulatory resource theory, posits that exerting self-control is similar to exercising a muscle. Consumers have a "pool" of self-regulation resources (Baumeister & Heatherton, 1996; Baumeister et al., 1998). Exerting self-control can deplete this pool of self-regulatory resources. Depletion of regulatory resources negatively affects the likelihood of successfully resisting future temptations. Thus, the longer a person tries to engage in self-control, the more likely she is to fail at self-control because her regulatory resources will become depleted. Also, all self-control tasks draw on the same pool of self-regulation resources. Therefore, the depletion of these regulatory resources increases the likelihood of failure on subsequent tasks requiring self-control, including deliberate, cognitively effortful decision making (Pocheptsova, Amir, Dhar, & Baumeister, 2009).

The negative effects of depleted regulatory resources on consumption behaviour have been observed in various self-control domains. For example, Vohs and Heatherton (2000) demonstrated that dieters who first resisted eating tempting snacks, and thus depleted their self-regulatory resource, later ate more ice cream, a tempting alternative, than did dieters who did not face the original temptation. Further, Bruyneel, Dewitte, Vohs and Warlop, (2006) and Wang et al. (2010), using different manipulations to deplete self-regulatory resources, provided converging evidence that resource depletion increases the choice of immediately tempting vices over virtues that hold long-term benefits (e.g., chocolates and granola bars). Milkman (2012) further demonstrated that consumers who had to cope with uncertainty (e.g., not knowing what they would consume for dinner) also experienced depletion of their self-regulatory resources. They were then more likely to choose a temptation (brownie) over a healthy option (fresh fruit). In the financial domain, heterosexual men who were exposed to sexy female undergarments, and had to therefore self-regulate arousing thoughts, were found to become more impatient and prefer smaller, sooner monetary rewards as a result (Van den Bergh, Dewitte & Warlop, 2008). Finally, Vohs and Faber (2007) established the relationship between exhausted self-regulatory resources and impulsive (unplanned) buying. In a series of studies, the authors found that depleted consumers were willing to spend more money and purchase more impulsive goods. These studies provide convergent evidence that when prior self-regulatory tasks or other executive function activities deplete self-regulatory resources, consumers are more likely to resolve self-control dilemmas in favour of immediate temptations.

Beliefs about self-control ability

In contrast to the view that self-control is bounded by limited self-regulatory resources, as described in the preceding section, other researchers proposed that the likelihood of self-control success is contingent on consumers' lay beliefs about their ability to exercise self-control (Mukhopadhyay & Johar, 2005). These authors propose that people differ in their beliefs regarding the extent to which self-control abilities are malleable and can be improved through effort or are fixed qualities that remain stable. Consumers' beliefs about whether willpower is an unlimited or limited resource can moderate the previously reported depletion effects on performance in self-control tasks. Specifically, Mukhopadhyay and Johar (2005) found that consumer beliefs about how much self-control they have ranges from very limited to almost unlimited. They also found that depletion effects are only observed among people who believe self-regulatory resources are fixed because these consumers wish to conserve resources after they have engaged in self-control. Instead, consumers who believe self-control is unlimited do not experience depletion effects. For example, consumers, who believed self-control is an unlimited resource, set more goals and persisted longer on their New Year's resolutions than consumers who believed self-control is a limited resource, regardless of the amount of self-control they actually possessed. The authors observed this effect both when lay beliefs were measured and when they were temporarily activated. Job, Dweck and Walton (2010) recently reported similar findings. They found that college students who believed willpower is unlimited exhibited more self-control and made healthier food choices during stressful exam periods when they were depleted. In sum, consumers' lay theories about willpower can impact their pursuit of long-term goals and consumption decisions.

Follow-up work by Mukhopadhyay and Yeung (2010) revealed that the perceived amount of self-control also affects how consumers select products for their children's consumption. Consistent with their own perceptions of their self-control ability, unlimited-malleable theorists are more likely to choose less virtuous options for children (e.g., fast-food meals or TV watching), in contrast to limited-malleable theorists, who want to help children develop self-control, and therefore are more likely to steer children towards more virtuous choices. Finally, McFerran and Mukhopadhyay (2013) demonstrated the role of self-control beliefs in the health domain. They found that consumers who believed self-control failure in the domain of food consumption caused obesity were less likely to be overweight and were more successful in controlling their food intake than consumers who believed self-control failure in the domain of exercising caused obesity. These studies suggest consumers' beliefs about their ability to exert self-control can influence the resolution of self-control dilemmas and that this effect holds even when consumers' self-regulatory pool has been depleted. Importantly, Vohs, Baumeister and Schmechel (2012) found that the effect of lay beliefs in reducing depletion is limited only to tasks that do not severely deplete self-regulatory resources. In fact, lay theories that self-control is an unlimited pool do not benefit self-regulation activities among participants who complete multiple self-control tasks and become severely depleted. Therefore, consumer beliefs regarding self-control might help them resist a temptation once, but they could have a limited effect when consumers are faced with multiple purchase decisions requiring tradeoffs between immediate indulgences and long-term gains.

Cognitive strategies to reduce self-control conflict

Consumers can employ cognitive strategies to increase success at pursuing their long-term goals when faced with temptation (Metcalfe & Mischel, 1999). Some of these strategies are targeted at reducing self-control conflicts by decreasing the salience and the availability of indulgences (Hoch & Loewenstein, 1991). For example, Wertenbroch (1998) found that consumers tempted by fast foods and cigarettes forgo quantity discounts in order to limit their stock of temptations and indulgences. As a result, these consumers are willing to pay more per unit of consumption for temptations, "paying a price premium to enhance their ability to engage in self-control" (p.317). Other research has found that consumers often recategorize tempting products as inconsistent with long-term goals rather than as indulgences. For example, Haws and Poynor (2008) found that product categorization could help consumers resist temptations. They reported that consumers high on the trait of self-control are more likely than consumers low in self-control to categorize products as inconsistent with their high-order goals, thus creating a larger set of temptations to avoid. Redden and Haws (2012) additionally found that consumers control indulgent consumption by altering their perceived rate of satiation to products. These authors reported that consumers with high-trait self-control satiate on unhealthy tempting foods faster than on healthy foods, resulting in lower overall consumption of unhealthy foods because consumers tell themselves faster that they have consumed enough indulgent foods.

Other studies suggest that consumers can increase their self-control by focusing on and increasing salience or importance of their self-control goals. For instance, Muraven and Slessareva (2003) increased importance of the self-control goal by framing it as beneficial to other people. This framing increased depleted participants' performance on the task to the same level as that of non-depleted participants. Similarly, Schmeichel and Vohs (2009) asked depleted participants to elaborate on important personal values prior to completing a self-control task. This self-affirmation exercise negated the effect of depletion on self-regulation. The authors suggest that self-affirmation increases the level of abstraction at which a person construes self-control. Higher abstraction promotes self-control by making the benefits of long-term goals come to mind more easily, a point we will turn to next.

Psychological distance and self-control

Construal level theory (Trope & Liberman, 2003) has proposed that stimuli that are psychologically distant are mentally represented or construed at an abstract high level and stimuli that are psychologically close are perceived at a concrete low level. Psychological distance can take a form of temporal distance, spatial distance or even social distance (Trope et al., 2007). The level of mental representation of the stimuli has implications for their evaluation and consumers' behaviour towards them (Dhar & Kim, 2007; Trope et al., 2007). Specific to self-control conflicts, research has shown that focus on the distant future increases commitment to high-order goals and the likelihood of virtuous behaviour (Dhar & Kim, 2007; Fishbach, Dhar, & Zhang, 2006; Fujita, Henderson, Eng, Trope, & Liberman, 2006; Rogers & Bazerman, 2008). Construing a self-control dilemma more abstractly can increase consumer focus on desirability rather than feasibility of engaging in action. The shift in focus from feasibility to desirability can increase self-control (Fujita et al., 2006; Schmeichel & Vohs, 2009; Trope & Liberman, 2003). For example, in a study by Fujita et al. (2006), participants evaluated temptations, such as partying, drinking and playing video games, that could distract them from their higher-level goal of studying. The temptations were evaluated less favourably when participants were first primed to think about the temptations at a high vs. low level of abstraction. Read, Loewenstein and Kalyanaraman (1999) additionally showed that participants were more likely to pick lowbrow movies when making a series of sequential choices of which movie to watch that day as compared to when participants were making simultaneous selections of movies for future viewing, with the latter increasing the level of abstraction with which consumers consider their choice options. Similarly, Rogers and Bazerman (2008) found that participants were more likely to choose "should" options (e.g., making a charitable donation instead of keeping money for themselves) when implementation of these choices was scheduled in the distant (one week from now) as opposed to the near future (today). Finally, Milkman,

Rogers and Bazerman (2009, 2010) replicated this pattern using online grocery purchase data and video rental data. They found that consumers bought more healthy products (e.g., vegetables) and fewer unhealthy products (e.g., ice cream) when the delivery was further in the future. Consumers also were likely to keep rented highbrow movies for a longer period of time, whereas they returned lowbrow movies sooner. This pattern is consistent with the view that virtues may seem more attractive when one is thinking about the future because the future cues thoughts about desirability and benefits, but vices become more appealing during present consumption because focus shifts to feasibility.

Exerting self-control can also affect construal level. Wan and Agrawal (2011) demonstrated that depletion of self-regulatory resources via prior self-control acts results in low-level construal. To illustrate this point, the authors examined the preference for low- versus high-level construal features of the products, such as feasibility and desirability, for depleted vs. control participants. They found that relative to non-depleted participants, depleted consumers were more likely to prefer products dominant in the features consistent with low-level construal, for example, a restaurant with mediocre food but a great view. This effect was attenuated when depleted participants were primed to think at higher-level construal. Thus, depletion can result in low-level construal and reminding people who are depleted or with low-level construal to think more abstractly can increase self-control and shift focus back to desirability rather than feasibility of engaging in long-term goals, consistent with the research reviewed earlier.

The papers reviewed so far suggest that creating distance between consumers and self-control tasks activates higher-level construal of the tasks and thereby leads consumers to resolve self-control conflicts in favour of higher-order goals, by devaluing temptations and increasing commitment to the goals. By contrast, a smaller distance and a correspondingly low-level construal of the situation are associated with lower self-control. Correspondingly, exerting and depleting self-control leads consumers to adopt a lower-level construal.

While all the findings reviewed thus far offer suggestions to consumers on cognitive strategies they can employ to act according to long-term goals when faced with immediate temptations that deter from goal pursuit, another stream of research looks at people who over-engage in self-control. Consumers who over-engage in self-control over indulgences can feel regret not having indulged enough in the past. These kinds of consumers need to engage in self-regulation of self-control, so to speak, and curb their overwhelming inclination to choose long-term options over immediate indulgences. For example, Kivetz and colleagues (Keinan & Kivetz, 2006, 2008; Kivetz & Simonson, 2002) found that some consumers exhibit hyperopia – they possess too much self-control, which prevents them from engaging in indulgent experiences. This literature shows that for such consumers, guilt dominates decision making when they are considering immediate consumption. These feelings of guilt diminish with an increase in temporal distance. Additionally, feelings of missing out on pleasures in life increase over time (Kivetz and Keinan, 2006). These two forces increase the rate of consumption of indulgences as the temporal distance increases. For example, in one study, students that were evaluating their winter breaks from a one-year versus one-week distance expressed less guilt over indulgent activities they had committed (e.g., spending money or travelling). In another study, when participants were asked to think about regretting their current choice in 10 years (vs. one day), they were more likely to pick an indulgent alternative when approaching a choice from a longer temporal perspective. Mehta, Zhu and Meyers-Levy (2014) suggested that there are two types of indulgence: a deliberate indulgence that comes from a realization of consumers' overall hyperopic tendency, and an impulsive indulgence that happens in response to a consumption context without self-retrospection. Self-focus can increase guilt and the need for deliberate indulgence.

Overall, the findings on hyperopia are consistent with those on construal. Both sets of findings show that considering outcomes at a distance helps consumers engage in whatever goal they find effortful to engage in. The former set of findings on construal pertains to most consumers who find self-control and the pursuit of long-term goals effortful and find "spontaneous" indulgence a temptation. The latter findings on hyperopia pertain to the few consumers for whom indulgence is effortful and who instead engage "spontaneously" in self-regulation. Both sets of findings show that considering things that are effortful – whether it is self-control or indulgence – at a distance can increase choice of the effortful outcome and help overcome whatever is tempting in the moment – "spontaneous" indulgence as with most consumers or self-regulation as with hyperopic consumers.

Connectedness in self-control decisions

Building on the ideas pertaining to level of construal and self-control, some authors have suggested that viewing choices more broadly as part of a larger set of decisions or even increasing the perceived connectedness between the future self and current choices can increase consumer self-control (Bartels & Urminsky, 2011). Indeed, consideration of sets of choices more broadly or a consideration of the future self should increase the level of abstraction a consumer considers choice with (Trope & Liberman, 2003). This level of abstraction should increase a focus on desirability of the future and one's future goals and link current choices to those broader goals, as the literature on construal level has proposed. Consider, for example, a typical health-related self-control dilemma: a person with a diet goal who is facing a choice between a chocolate cake and a fruit salad. Thinking about this conflict as a single-shot self-control choice versus a series of similar repeated choices unfolding over time is likely to affect how much a consumer is focused on the present versus the future and how damaging one will see this yielding to temptation. Evaluating a self-control dilemma within a context of other related self-control choices can potentially help consumers identify patterns of self-control behaviour and appreciate the overall costs of repeatedly yielding to temptation. In one study illustrating this phenomenon, Myrseth and Fishbach (2009) asked participants to choose between carrots and chocolates from a food stand on campus, and either framed the decision as a single-shot choice (labelling their food stand as "April 12th food stand") or as a part of a broader number of choices (labelling the same food stand as "Spring food stand"). When the self-control choice was seen as part of a broader set of choices, participants presumably developed a more abstract style of thinking and as a result consumed more healthful foods (carrots) and fewer indulgent foods (chocolates). Similar work by Bartels and Urminsky (2011) demonstrated that when consumers perceive a stronger connection between their current and their future self, thus increasing the frame in which to view their self-control decisions, they are more likely to behave less impatiently and more in line with their long-term goals than their short-term gains.

Whereas the papers reviewed above predominantly demonstrate positive effects of adopting a broader view of self-control decisions and increasing connectedness between multiple self-control choices, several other studies have identified potential negative effects of seeing self-control decisions as interconnected. For example, Khan and Dhar (2007) found that if consumers were told they would be making multiple self-control choices (vs. a single choice), they believed they would select a more virtuous option in the future. Such an optimistic view of future self-control ability licenses consumers to pick a vice option now. For example, in one study, participants were asked to choose between a cookie and a fat-free yogurt. The choice was framed either as a single choice or as part of a series of repeated choices that would take place in the future. As predicted, the choice share of a vice (cookie) was significantly higher in a repeated-choice frame than in a single-choice frame, suggesting that in the presence of future choices, self-control conflicts are resolved toward tempting immediate alternatives. Importantly, though, when the authors offered participants the option to actually execute their future choices, the choice share of a virtuous option did not differ from that of participants in the single-shot condition, suggesting consumers' optimism about future self-control was unwarranted.

Mukhopadhyay, Sengupta and Ramanathan (2008) examined a similar pattern of behaviour, but instead of asking consumers to think about future similar choices between vices and virtues, they asked consumers to recall how they had resolved self-control conflicts in the past. Interestingly, they found that recalled past resolution of self-control conflicts (resisting vs. yielding) had different effects on impulsive versus non-impulsive individuals. Impulsive individuals who recalled prior acts of succumbing to or resisting temptation (e.g., unhealthy food) exhibited a switching pattern, consistent with Khan and Dhar (2007): If they had resisted temptation in the past, they were more likely to indulge in the present (e.g., eat cookies). By contrast, if they had chosen an indulgent item in the past, participants were more likely to show restraint in the present. This temporal pattern of switching between resisting temptation and yielding to it is consistent with a strong competition for impulsive individuals between the desire to indulge and the desire to resist the temptation. The authors suggested that non-impulsive individuals experience substantially less self-control conflict when they face a choice between indulging and restraining, and therefore are less likely to exhibit a switching pattern. These papers suggest that framing choice more broadly as part of a set of other choices can increase indulgence.

The influence of framing choices broadly therefore appears to depend on whether there is an effect of abstract construal on increasing self-control or of beliefs about future or past actions on increasing indulgence. On the one hand, framing choices broadly, for example, as a part of a larger set of choices or as connected with those a future-self would desire, can increase abstract construal and result in more self-control by bringing to mind the desirability of engaging in self-control. On the other hand, beliefs about what a person can do in the future or thoughts about what one already did in the past can license indulgence if a consumer believes she can exert control in the future or already did so adequately in the past. Cognitive strategies that increase abstract thinking can increase self-control, but contexts that encourage justification of indulgence (such as potential to engage in self-control some other time) can reduce self-control.

Motivational influences on self-control

Goal-theoretic perspective on self-control

A large body of research examines self-control dilemmas from a goal-theoretic perspective. In this view, consumers simultaneously hold two competing goals: a long-term goal with delayed benefits and a short-term goal with an immediate appeal but adverse long-term consequences. Consumers try to balance between the two goals because making progress towards one goal takes away from the progress made towards the other goal (Fishbach & Zhang, 2008; Myrseth, Fishbach, & Trope, 2009). For example, pursuing an indulgence goal and consuming a calorie-rich dessert comes at the expense of the pursuit of a higher-order health goal. At the same time, foregoing the dessert to satisfy the health goal hurts the pursuit of the indulgence goal.

In this multiple-goal view of self-control conflict, exercising self-control means an increase in motivational strength towards the long-term goal in order to override temptation, or a weakening of the motivation towards the temptation goal, thus increasing long-term goal adherence. For example, when a consumer with a savings goal encounters a tempting purchase, she experiences a conflict between a goal to save and a goal to indulge. Either increasing her motivation to adhere to the savings goal or decreasing the attractiveness of the tempting purchase will result in exercising self-control. Research has demonstrated several pathways by which such a motivational shift between goals can occur when multiple goals compete for consumers' resources (Fishbach & Dhar, 2005; Shah, Friedman, & Kruglanski, 2002; Shah & Kruglanski, 2002). Next, we will review how these principles of multiple-goal pursuit apply specifically to the resolution of self-control conflict.

Counteractive control

Counteractive control theory (Trope and Fishbach, 2000) proposes that when facing a temptation, people pursuing higher-order goals tend to boost their motivation towards those goals. Fishbach and Trope (2000) explicate three factors that moderate this effect: value of the long-term goal (more valuable goals tend to elicit more counteractive self-control); the valence of the temptation (as the valence of temptation increases, so does counteractive self-control, but only up to the point at which temptation is too attractive to pass); and timing (counteractive self-control is engaged before the self-control decision is made but not after, when one of the goals has already been chosen). For example, in one study, the authors demonstrated that the perceived value of the cognitive functioning test (action consistent with long-term goal) increased when the testing time was scheduled at a very inconvenient time (12:30am) as opposed to a somewhat inconvenient time (9:30pm). Interestingly, this counteractive self-control effect disappeared when the test was conducted at an extremely inconvenient time (3:30am) and the attractiveness of the temptation (sleep) was very high. Similarly, in another study, participants rated the usefulness of a glucose intake test higher when they were asked to abstain from glucose-containing food for a longer rather than a shorter time period in preparation for the test. Finally, the authors show that these effects only occur prior to participants taking an action and not after.

In a follow-up work, Myrseth, Fishbach and Trope (2009) focused on the other side of counteractive control – the devaluation of temptation when the long-term goal is active. In one study, they approached consumers entering a gym (with an active health goal) and asked for their valuation of longer-goal-consistent items (health bars) versus temptations (chocolate bars). They found that consumers significantly devalued temptations in the presence of an active long-term health goal, but only prior to making a decision to consume these foods. Further, when the self-control conflict was between a goal of studying and a goal of leisure, participants devalued leisure time, particularly when they judged studying as interesting.

Similar effects were observed in studies that used subtle cues to prime conflicting self-control goals instead of explicit activation of these goals. Fishbach, Zhang and Trope (2010), for example, reveal that priming dieters with unhealthy foods (temptation) leads them to perceive healthy foods as more positive and unhealthy foods as more negative compared to control participants who did not receive a prime. The authors argue this effect occurs because temptation is automatically seen as a threat to achievement of the long-term goal of dieting; therefore, priming leads to implicit activation of counteractive self-control.

These studies convincingly argue that an activation of a tempting alternative in the presence of a long-term goal leads consumers to strategically boost the value of the long-term goal and to devalue the temptation. The resulting gap in motivation between the long-term goal and the temptation increases the likelihood of a successful resolution of the self-control conflict. Further, these asymmetric changes in the evaluation of temptations and means of reaching long-term goals can occur outside consumers' conscious awareness.

An interesting follow-up work by Zhang and Fishbach (2010) on the effect they have labelled "counteractive optimism" expands the view of counteractive self-control to include consumers' predictions about future goal attainment. Building on the literature that demonstrates that optimistic views of future events increase motivation to achieve them, the authors claim that people strategically increase their perceptions of the likelihood of success of long-term goals when they encounter temptations or obstacles to their goal pursuit. For example, in one study, the authors examined students' time allocation for a long-term goal (studying) and manipulated the perceptions of the obstacle to goal pursuit (leisure). The authors found that when an obstacle for goal pursuit was salient and students were experiencing self-control conflict between the long-term goal of studying and the short-term goal of leisure, they predicted they would spend more time studying and less time on leisure, consistent with an optimistic view of the future goal attainment. Similarly, Nikolova, Lamberton and Haws (2015) demonstrated that consumers were more likely to engage in self-control when they recalled instances of successful self-control easily rather than with effort. Presumably, recalling past instances of self-control with difficulty can make consumers feel bad because they infer that they are not good at self-control which then licenses them to indulge.

Balancing between short-term and long-term goals

Dhar and Simonson (1999) proposed the idea that when consumers hold multiple goals they may highlight or balance their goals over time, suggesting that self-regulation should be viewed as a dynamic phenomenon. In the view of this stream of research, a person can pursue multiple conflicting goals in a sequential fashion, one goal at a time. In this context, a consumer can either decide to balance the pursuit of the active goals, alternating between them, or to highlight the pursuit of one goal over others and consistently prefer that goal in subsequent actions. For example, in a typical self-control dilemma, a consumer can choose to go to a gym first and then indulge in a calorie-rich lunch (balancing goal pursuit), or she can go to the gym and then eat a salad (highlighting goal pursuit). Dhar and colleagues (Fishbach & Dhar 2005; Fishbach et al., 2006; Zhang, Fishbach, & Dhar, 2007) followed up on the ideas initially proposed by Dhar and Simonson (1999) and extended them to examine factors that would lead consumers to exhibit the pattern of highlighting one goal over the other or a pattern of alternating between the goals.

Although research generally finds that consumers are more likely to use a balancing strategy when their goals are in direct conflict, such as in self-control dilemmas (Dhar & Simonson, 1999), follow-up work suggests several ways in which consumers' goal-pursuit strategies can be altered. For example, a series of papers has examined how the different ways in which consumers interpret goal-related actions affect the subsequent exercise of self-control via a balancing or highlighting strategy of goal pursuit. When one performs a goal-consistent action, for example, going for a run when the goal is good health, one can see that action as a sign of progress made towards that goal or as a sign of expressed commitment to the goal (Fishbach & Dhar, 2005). The distinction is critical: progress towards the goal elicits feelings of goal accomplishment and suggests that less effort is required to accomplish the goal, whereas commitment to the goal increases the feelings of how valuable the goal is and the likelihood of goal attainment. Correspondingly, perceived progress towards the goal is more likely to lead to balancing dynamics, and perceived commitment to the goal is more likely to lead to highlighting dynamics.

In the key paper on the topic, Fishbach and Dhar (2005) demonstrate that perceiving goal progress hinders subsequent goal pursuit by increasing the rate of goal switching. A study on dieters illustrates this point: when dieters felt they had made progress towards their health goals, they were significantly more likely to indulge by picking chocolate over apples. This effect was observed even when consumers had not in fact made any progress towards the goal, but instead were "borrowing" from their future goal progress. In this study, participants approached prior to entering gym held optimistic expectations of the amount of progress they would make towards their exercising goals, and were more likely to pick less healthy dinner options. In a follow-up work, Zhang et al. (2007) similarly demonstrated that framing both the future and past goal-congruent activities as progress (vs. commitment) leads to the adoption of balancing (vs. highlighting) dynamics. Interestingly, the effect of past goal-congruent actions was weaker than the effect of future actions.

Can choice context spontaneously direct consumers to interpret their goal-consistent actions as goal progress or goal commitment and consequently affect how self-control conflict is resolved? Consistent with the literature on time construal reviewed earlier, Fishbach et al. (2006) find that temporal distance affects whether consumers interpret their goal-related actions as a sign of making progress towards the goal or as commitment to a higher-level goal of being healthy. At a longer temporal distance, consumers interpreted their actions as a sign of commitment, whereas at a shorter temporal distance, the same action was seen as a sign of goal progress.

Affective influences on self-control

Hot affect vs. cold reason

Loewenstein (1996; see also Metcalfe & Mitchel, 1999) suggest that the self-control dilemma arises from a competition between "cold" forces or consumers' rational self-interest and "hot" forces or "visceral factors" such as moods, emotions and basic drive states (hunger, thirst, sex, physical pain). "Hot" forces are impulsive and reflexive, and consumers who are under the influence of such forces are seen as stimuli driven. These visceral factors are proposed to have a disproportionally large effect on consumer behaviour as compared to the influence of long-term goals promoting one's self-interest. Exercising self-control, in this view, means behaving in accordance with rational self-interest and suppressing visceral influences. For example, choosing to ignore feelings of hunger and the lure of a calorie-rich dessert (i.e., visceral factors) and instead selecting a fruit salad would be consistent with exercising self-control.

Further, impulsive behaviour (preference for short-term rewards over long-term gains) occurs because people disproportionally overweight the visceral factors in the current decision and systematically underweight the effect of visceral factors in the future (Lowenstein, 1996). For example, a consumer deciding to spend money, on a lavish meal today, because of the strong emotional appeal of the meal, instead of saving the money, effectively underweights the feeling of hunger he will experience tomorrow. Similarly to underweighting impact of visceral factors on future behaviour, consumers underestimate how much influence these factors had on their past choices, decreasing consumer's ability to use retrospection to better inform their current self-control decisions.

Other researchers (Isen & Labroo, 2003; Labroo & Patrick, 2009; Lazarus, 1982; Trope & Liberman, 2003), however, have suggested that affect and thinking need not be as distinct as Lowenstein (1996) suggested. For example, Lazarus (1982) proposed that thinking gives rise to and intensifies affect, so all affect is not instinctive and intense, but in fact thinking causes affect. In his view, fruit salad could evoke positive affect when thinking about it in the long-term frame. Even in the short-term, fruit salad is delicious and fresh and can be associated with positive affect, but with less intense affect than a chocolate cake. Indeed, Williams, Stein and

Galguera (2014) showed that while thoughts about the future correspond with less intense affect, they also correspond with more positive affect. Researchers should therefore consider valence and arousal of emotions as orthogonal constructs (Cacioppo, Petty, Losch, & Kim, 1986; Mano & Oliver, 1993; Posner, Russell, & Peterson, 2005). Some emotions can be hot (i.e., arousing, such as passion, anger) while others can be relatively cold (i.e., low arousing, such as sadness, happiness); similarly, some thoughts, such as those that pertain to hostility and aggression, may be hot and others may be cold. Arousal, rather than affect valence, leads to a narrowing of attention and increase in instinctual actions, including myopic, short-term consumer choices. Positive affect does not lead to myopic choices, and in fact, it can broaden thinking (Frederickson, 2001) and result in actions that promote accomplishment of long-term goals (Aspinwall, 1998; Labroo & Patrick, 2009).

Also, arousal may not always result in instinctual choice. The effect of arousal on goal pursuit, self-control and self-regulation is likely to be moderated by the kinds of goals the emotion itself is associated with (Cacioppo & Berntson, 1994). High-arousal emotions such as anger, for example, can result in people becoming more goal-directed and engaging more in long-term goal pursuit (Tamir, Mitchell, & Gross, 2008). The reason is that anger is associated with approach goals and these goals intensify goal-pursuit. The implication of this finding is that consumers with a self-regulation goal may engage in more self-control when angry than when not in an emotional state. Similarly, cold (low arousal) emotions like sadness can increase a desire for mood repair and therefore increase consumers' preference for indulgences (Fishbach & Labroo, 2007). Based on this body of literature, the previously proposed hot–cold distinction may be combining several constructs: instinctual vs. deliberative, intense vs. mild, affective vs. cognitive etc., and the effect of affect rather than cognition on self-control is more complex than previously assumed. The distinction between the two views may also be that the former set of hot–cold studies may be focused more on integral affect or affect immediately evoked by a stimulus characteristic. The latter are focused more on incidental affect, the feelings evoked within an individual and their interactions with other thoughts and motivations that consumers might have at the moment.

This multidimensional view of the effect of emotions on self-control implies that the same emotion may sometimes increase and at other times reduce self-control via different psychological mechanisms. For example, a positive mood can result in more positive thoughts, including positive thoughts about long-term goals (Labroo & Patrick, 2009), and feeling energized and that one has resources to engage in self-control (Aspinwall, 1998). But a positive mood can also increase heuristic processing (Schwarz & Clore, 1983) or evoke mood maintenance goals (Clark & Isen, 1982), and these factors could increase indulgence and reduce self-control. Moreover, a positive mood, when associated with arousal, can also increase indulgence (Fedorikhin & Patrick, 2010). In sum, rather than separating emotions as hot and cognitions as cold, and suggesting that hot emotions disrupt self-control whereas cold cognitions enhance it, a fruitful direction for investigation may be to understand when and whether cognition and emotion can be made truly independent, and even when independent, whether the same cognition or the same emotion could impact different psychological processes based on the context in which choice is presented to a consumer and thereby differentially impact self-control.

Temptations and affect regulation

A different interpretation of self-control failure is that it arises from consumers' mood-regulation goals. Consumers chose temptations over long-term goals in service of momentary mood improvement (Baumeister, Heatherton & Tice, 1994, Tice, Bratslavsky & Baumesiter, 2001).

Note that unlike visceral forces view of self-control conflict described above that is agnostic regarding the valence of visceral factors (for example, a visceral factor could be a negative emotion of pain or a positive emotion of receiving hedonic reward), mood repair view of self-control conflict focuses on current negative affect as reducing self-control choices. This view of self-control states that when people are experiencing negative mood they are more likely to choose options that would deliver immediate rewards and mood enhancement over options that could deliver delayed benefits. For example, a consumer who is upset is more likely to buy on impulse or consume calorie rich foods that a consumer who is happy.

Consistent with this proposition, in a study conducted by Tice et al. (2001) participants who were induced to feel distress ate more snack foods (such as chocolates) than did participants who did not experience distress, whereas people in a good mood engaged in self-control. Importantly, this effect was moderated by whether the participants believed indulgence could improve their mood. When participants were made to believe that indulgence cannot repair their mood, they became less indulgent. Similarly, in a study conducted by Andrade (2005), participants who associated eating chocolates with mood lifting were more likely to express desire to consume the chocolates when they were experiencing negative rather than neutral affect. Similar effects were found by numerous other papers and across several self-control areas, such as smoking (Ashton & Stepny, 1982), drinking (Sayette, 1993) and impulsive shopping (O'Guinn & Faber, 1987).

Labroo and Mukhopadhyay (2009) additionally reported that beliefs about the malleability of emotion could also influence self-control. They found that consumers generally believe their current emotion is somewhat lasting, and as a result people in a good mood engage in self-control because they feel they have the mood resource to expend towards engaging in self-control. By contrast, consumers in negative mood indulge, because they infer that unless they do something to repair their mood, they will continue to feel bad. However, people's beliefs about emotion malleability are malleable in themselves, thus people can be made to consider instead that emotion is transient. When consumers are primed with the belief that emotions are transient, those in a good mood are more likely to indulge, because they believe they must do so to maintain their mood. By contrast, consumers in a negative mood become less likely to indulge, because they instead believe bad mood will pass on its own and so the cost of engaging in self-control is low. Importantly, while there is ample evidence that consumers resolve self-control conflicts in favour of mood regulation by choosing temptations over long-term goals, other research has noted that the belief that temptations improve mood are not well grounded and consumption of temptations frequently leads to the spiralling effect into further negative affect, when a person reflects upon their self-control failure (Tice et al., 2001).

Another line of inquiry suggests that consumers might avoid rather than approach temptations in an attempt to regulate affect. This line of research argues that indulgent consumption is tainted by feelings of guilt because consumers recognize that yielding to temptation has only short-term benefits but large long-term costs (Goldsmith, Cho, and Dhar, 2012; Khan and Dhar, 2006, 2010; Kivetz and Zheng, 2006; Okada, 2005). In fact, consumers frequently experience mixed emotions when consuming indulgent products and the feelings of guilt and pleasure are closely linked in consumers' affective system (Goldsmith et al., 2012). These feelings of guilt can arise in anticipation of self-control choice and thus affect consumer decisions. Because consumers are motivated to avoid feelings of guilt they might avoid indulgent consumption as a mood maintenance strategy. This desire to avoid temptations because of associated negative affect due to self-control failure is particularly strong for individuals in positive mood (Andrade, 2005; Fedorikhin & Patrick, 2010). Affect regulation dynamic suggests that anticipating negative feelings in the future (due to succumbing to temptation) would drive consumers in a positive mood to avoid temptation to preserve their positive affective state.

Consistent with these theoretical propositions, several papers demonstrate that actions that mitigate anticipated guilt increase consumption of indulgent products. For example, offering price discounts for hedonic products in a hedonic-utilitarian bundle increases likelihood of purchase (Khan & Dhar, 2010) or making donations to charity just prior to consumers' self-control choice licenses consumers to buy indulgent goods and services without guilt (Khan & Dhar, 2006). Including virtuous choices in an assortment increases likelihood of yielding to temptation through vicarious goal fulfilment (Wilcox, Vallen, Block, & Fitzsimons, 2009). Finally, consumers prefer mixed bundles of vices and virtues to the pure consumption of vices to mitigate the guilt of self-control failure (Liu et al., 2014).

Positive mood and self-control

Early views on mood proposed a computer metaphor to understand human cognition (Simon, 1967). According to this model, any emotion, but especially positive mood, was viewed as a disruption to the cognitive system (Forgas, 1995), causing the system to overload and result in a person engaging in actions that reflected little thought. A positive mood was proposed to take up cognitive capacity (Mackie & Worth, 1989). If positive mood uses cognitive capacity, it would follow that it causes depletion and because depletion reduces self-control, a positive mood should reduce self-control.

Follow up work, however, demonstrated that positive mood reduces motivation to process information rather than cognitive capacity (Bodenhausen, Kramer, & Susser, 1994). The idea was that a positive mood can signal to a person that her environment is benign, and therefore there is little need to expend cognitive resources (Schwarz & Clore, 1983). In contrast, a negative mood signals danger in the environment and a need to attend carefully to the situation at hand. It follows from this view that a positive mood can result in heuristic processing and a negative mood in systematic processing (Bless, Bohner, Schwarz, & Strack 1990; Clore, Schwarz, & Conway, 1994; Schwarz & Clore, 1983). In contrast to the previous capacity view of mood, the implication of this view is that people in a positive mood will engage in self-control when they have an adequate motivation to do so, or when they are alerted to expend cognitive resources to consider the negatives of indulgence over restraint. This account is consistent with a mood management view that suggests that happy consumers avoid activities that can hurt their positive mood (Clark & Isen, 1982), and a cognitive accessibility view that happy consumers are more likely to spontaneously consider positive outcomes (Isen, Shalker, Clark, & Carp, 1978). All of these views predict that consumers in a positive mood will be more indulgent, because a positive mood takes up cognitive capacity so they are more likely to spontaneously consider positive outcomes. They maintain a goal of mood maintenance, and they consider the environment benign and therefore lack motivation to expend cognitive resources.

However, ample evidence now shows instead that a positive mood can have beneficial effects on long-term goal pursuit (Aspinwall, 1998; Isen & Labroo, 2003). A positive mood facilitates self-regulation by serving as a resource that can be traded for effortful self-control (Aspinwall, 1998; Fredrickson, 1998; Raghunathan & Trope, 2002). Rather than signal a need to disengage from the environment because it is benign, a positive mood allows consumers to instead psychologically distance themselves from the situation (Labroo & Patrick, 2009). As a result, consumers become more abstract and more likely to consider the distant future and long-term goals. For example, Labroo and Patrick (2007) found that consumers in a positive mood were more likely than those in a negative mood to describe activities, such as painting a room, abstractly (e.g., beautifying one's environment) rather than concretely (e.g., choosing a paint colour). In fact, merely adding smiley rather than frowny bullet points next to the activity that had to be described (painting a room) resulted in consumers in a neutral mood becoming more likely to describe the activity abstractly rather than concretely. As a result, happy consumers were more likely to consider activities in their long-term interests compared to unhappy consumers, because such activities are consistent with abstract thinking. Interestingly, this result was reversed when experimenters framed future goals concretely. For example, happy rather than unhappy participants were motivated to work longer on a cognitive test when they considered abstract reasons why studying is important. They also valued products with long-term health benefits more. Instead, unhappy rather than happy participants were motivated to work longer on a cognitive test when they considered concrete reasons why studying is important. Also, they valued products with immediate health benefits more. The implication of this research showing that happy consumers value outcomes that provide long-term benefits is that they may be better at engaging in self-control than unhappy consumers.

Fishbach and Labroo (2007) further demonstrated a beneficial effect that being in a positive mood can have on self-control. They proposed that happy consumers see goals as opportunities to be engaged in and so a positive mood promotes adoption of any accessible goals. When the accessible goal is the one of self-improvement, happy individuals exercise more self-control. But if the accessible goal is mood maintenance, happy participants also adopt this goal more readily and therefore exert less self-control. In one of the studies, Fishbach and Labroo (2007) measured participants' persistence on a physically draining task, a task that required self-control and was consistent with a long term goal of maintaining health. The participants were primed with either a health goal or a mood maintenance goal and with either a positive or a neutral mood prior to completing the task. Consistent with the expectations, participants, for whom the health goal was accessible, performed better on the self-control task if they experienced positive mood. By contrast, participants with an accessible mood maintenance goal did not perform better than their neutral mood counterparts on the self-control task. Similar effects were observed in other self-control domains, such as charitable donations and academic performance.

Other work indicates that positive affect does not have a uniform effect on self-control and the level of arousal associated with positive affect changes the nature of the relationship between positive affect and self-control (Fedorikhin & Patrick, 2010). In several studies, the authors replicate previous findings, showing greater resistance to temptation under positive mood, while demonstrating that elevated arousal diminishes this effect. The argument for this moderation is based on the more heuristic processing under high arousal and therefore a shift in motivation towards immediate pleasure and short-term rewards. In one of the studies reported in the paper, participants in positive mood with low arousal were less likely to choose a temptation (M&M's) over a healthy option (grapes) and were less likely to consume tempting snacks. However, being in a positive mood with elevated arousal eliminated these effects. It is possible that because arousal narrows attention and because concrete thinking is associated with narrow attention and also with less self-control (Fujita et al., 2006), arousal led positive affect consumers to become less abstract in their thinking and also to exhibit less self-control.

In sum, these studies propose that in general positive affect should increase consumers' ability to exercise self-control. They also note nudges and conditions under which a positive mood can instead increase indulgence and a negative mood can increase self-control.

Conclusions

Consumers often face tradeoffs between immediate pleasure and long-term gain when deciding between indulgent and healthy foods, relaxation and exercise, fun and work, spending and saving, among other choices. Self-control conflicts are omnipresent. While domains of these choices are quite different they similarly evoke conflict between long-term and short-term goals and similar forces influence the final choices that consumers make. These forces range from how consumers frame their choice and which aspects are more salient at the time of choice, to how much cognitive resources consumers have available to expend, to their beliefs about their self-control ability or to the psychological distance they can put between themselves and the conflict. Consumers' motivations and their past choices as well as their affective states also affect their present self-control decisions. In this chapter, we described current understanding of how consumers make such tradeoffs and these forces in detail. This understanding can be important for advancing theoretical research among academics and developing policy applications that nudge consumers towards decisions beneficial to them (and the society) in the long term.

Future research should identify other sources of influence on the resolution of self-control dilemmas. Some promising avenues for research may include interactions between the three influences we identified – cognition, motivation and affect. For example, how might affect change consumers' naïve theories or the weights they put on different aspects of their choice? How might their affective state impact accessibility of thoughts regarding past episodes of indulgence vs. self-control, or their justification and valuation of future indulgences and self-control? How might consumers' motivation impact the way they frame self-control choice, and how might framing change their level of motivation as they attempt to engage in self-control? Future research could also develop nudges that make self-control easier for consumers. For example, labelling indulgences as indulgences clearly can increase healthy choice among consumers and their tendency to pick more nutritious produce in the grocery store (Nikolova & Inman, 2015). Our hope is that this integrative review will foster new ideas among researchers and policy makers to advance new theory but also to develop a comprehensive toolbox of nudges to steer consumers away from short-sighted choices and towards decisions consistent with their long-term goals.

Another avenue for research may be to understand cross-cultural differences among consumers in their self-control decisions. In this context, it is important to remember that our basic principles regarding cognitive, motivational and affective influences are likely to be the same. For example, cross-culturally, a self-control dilemma is still defined as a conflict between short-term and long-term goals. This conflict is likely to result in the depletion effects we noted. Cognitive factors such as an abstract construal is likely to facilitate self-control (Fujita et al. 2006), regardless of cultural background of a person. Similarly, across cultures, motivational strength is likely to increase among people committed to their goal and who face a difficult self-control dilemma (Labroo & Kim, 2009), and a positive mood that is without high levels of arousal is likely to benefit self-control as long as populations do not hold a goal to indulge (Fishbach & Labroo, 2007; Labroo & Patrick, 2009). But because of the distinct situational and social influences that vary across populations in different cultures, different types of cognitions, motivations and affective states might be more accessible among different consumers. For example, eastern cultures tend to be more interdependent and define their identities in relation to others compared to western populations that are more independent (Gardner, Gabriel, & Lee, 1999). If people are brought up to consider the self in the context of others and relationships are important to such people, it is possible that food choices may remind them of shared consumption experiences. Reminders of shared consumption experiences might reduce self-control dilemmas by making the temptation seem less pleasing if consumed individually, thereby reducing strength of the temptation. Similarly, eastern cultures tend to be motivated by prevention concerns or vigilance towards potential losses compared to western cultures that are more motivated by advancement, enjoyment and growth (Aaker & Lee, 2001; Lee & Aaker, 2004). One possible consequence of these differences in motivation is that people in different cultures may spontaneously employ different self-control strategies – for example those in eastern cultures may be vigilant towards losing sight of their self-control goal whereas western cultures may seek to advance past the lure of the temptation (Koo, Labroo, & Lee, 2015). These strategies may be differentially effective. Similarly, eastern cultures may experience different kinds of emotions – calmness rather than happiness – or may experience emotions that are less arousing. These variations in emotional experience could impact self-control differently. In sum, many interesting theoretical issues and practical nudges to guide choices pertaining to self-control remain to be explored in a cross-cultural domain.

Yet, the best-intentioned actions can backfire. Consumer researchers and practitioners should therefore be careful when attempting to change consumer behaviour. For example, in the future, as consumers look back on their actions, they may experience regret for having not indulged occasionally or having not indulged enough. Researchers and policy makers are advised to consider whether the nudges they design, while changing consumer behaviours towards long-term benefits, do not increase retrospective regret in the future. To enhance usefulness in the nudges they create, researchers should link self-control decisions to long-term consumer well-being, an area with little systematic research to date. Doing so will increase chances that when consumers look back at today's pain they find it is indeed worth tomorrow's gain.

References

Aaker, J. L., & Lee, A. Y. (2001). I seek pleasures and we avoid pains: The role of self-regulatory goals in information processing and persuasion. *Journal of Consumer Research*, *28*(June), 33–49

Andrade, E. B. (2005). Behavioural consequences of affect: Combining evaluative and regulatory mechanisms. *Journal of Consumer Research*, *32*(3), 355–362.

Ashton, H., & Stepney, R. (1982). *Smoking: Psychology and pharmacology* (Vol. 244). London: Taylor & Francis.

Aspinwall, L. G. (1998). Rethinking the role of positive affect in self-regulation. *Motivation and Emotion*, *22*(1), 1–32.

Bartels, D. M., & Urminsky, O. (2011). On inter-temporal selfishness: How the perceived instability of identity underlies impatient consumption. *Journal of Consumer Research*, *38*(1), 182–198.

Baumiester, R. F. (2002). Yielding to temptation: Self-control failure, impulsive purchasing, and consumer behaviour. *Journal of Consumer Research*, *28*, 670–676.

Baumeister, R. F., Bratslavsky, E., Muraven, M., & Tice, D. M. (1998). Ego depletion: Is the active self a limited resource? *Journal of Personality and Social Psychology*, *74*, 1252–1265.

Baumeister, R. F., & Heatherton, T. F. (1996). Self-regulation failure: An overview. *Psychological Inquiry*, *7*(1), 1–15.

Baumeister, R. F., Heatherton, T. F., & Tice, D. M. (1994). *Losing control: How and why people fail at self-regulation*. San Diego, CA: Academic Press.

Baumeister, R. F., & Vohs, K. D. (2004). Sexual economics: Sex as female resource for social exchange in heterosexual interactions. *Personality and Social Psychology Review*, *8*, 339–363.

Bless, H., Bohner, G., Schwarz, N., & Strack, F. (1990). Mood and persuasion: A cognitive response model. *Personality and Social Psychology Bulletin*, *16*, 331–345.

Bodenhausen, G. V., Kramer, G. P., & Susser, K. (1994). Happiness and stereotypic thinking on social judgment. *Journal of Personality and Social Psychology*, *66*, 621–632.

Bruyneel, S. D., Dewitte, S., Vohs, K. D., & Warlop, L. (2006). Repeated choosing increases susceptibility to affective product features. *International Journal of Research in Marketing*, *23*, 215–225.

Cacioppo, J. T., & Berntson, G. G. (1994). Relationship between attitudes and evaluative space: A critical review, with emphasis on the separability of positive and negative substrates. *Psychological Bulletin*, *115*, 401–423.

Cacioppo, J. T., Petty, R. E., Losch, M. E., & Kim, H. S. (1986). Electromyographic activity over facial muscle regions can differentiate the valence and intensity of affective reactions. *Journal of Personality and Social Psychology*, *50*, 260–268.

Clark, M. S., & Isen, A. M. (1982). Toward understanding the relationship between feeling states and social behaviour. In A. H. Hastorf & A. M. Isen (Eds.), *Cognitive social psychology* (pp. 73–108). New York. NY: Elsevier/North-Holland.

Clore, G. L., Schwarz, N., & Conway M. (1994). Affective causes and consequences of social information processing. In R. S. Wyer & T. K. Srull (Eds.), *Handbook of social cognition*, (pp. 323–417). Hillsdale, NJ: Erlbaum.

de Ridder, D. T., Lensvelt-Mulders, G., Finkenauer, C., Stok, F. M., & Baumeister, R. F. (2012). Taking stock of self-control: A meta-analysis of how trait self-control relates to a wide range of behaviours. *Personality and Social Psychology Review*, *16*(1), 76–99.

Dhar, R., & Kim, E. Y. (2007). Seeing the forest or the trees: Implications of construal level theory for consumer choice. *Journal of Consumer Psychology*, *17*(2), 96–100.

Dhar, R., & Simonson, I. (1999). Making complementary choices in consumption episodes: Highlighting versus balancing. *Journal of Marketing Research*, *36*(1), 29–44.

Duckworth, A. L., & Kern, M. L. (2011). A meta-analysis of the convergent validity of self-control measures. *Journal of Research in Personality*, *45*(3), 259–268.

Fedorikhin, A., & Patrick, V. M. (2010). Positive mood and resistance to temptation: The interfering influence of elevated arousal. *Journal of Consumer Research*, *37*(4), 698–711.

Fishbach, A., & Dhar, R. (2005). Goals as excuses or guides: The liberating effect of perceived goal progress on choice. *Journal of Consumer Research*, *32*(3), 370–377.

Fishbach, A., Dhar, R., & Zhang, Y. (2006). Subgoals as substitutes or complements: The role of goal accessibility. *Journal of Personality and Social Psychology*, *91*(2), 232.

Fishbach, A., & Labroo, A. A. (2007). Be better or be merry: How mood affects self-control. *Journal of Personality and Social Psychology*, *93*(2), 158.

Fishbach, A., & Zhang, Y. (2008). Together or apart: When goals and temptations complement versus compete. *Journal of Personality and Social Psychology*, *94*, 547–559. Retrieved from http://faculty.chicagobooth.edu/ayelet.fishbach/research/FZ_jpsp08.pdf

Forgas, J. P. (1995). Mood and judgments: The affect infusion model. *Psychological Bulletin*, *117*(1), 39–66.

Fredrickson, B. L. (1998). What good are positive emotions? *Review of General Psychology*, *2*, 300–319.

Fredrickson, B. L. (2001). The role of positive emotions in positive psychology: The broaden-and-build theory of positive emotions. *American Psychologist*, *56*, 218–226. Retrieved from www.unc.edu/peplab/publications/Fredrickson_AmPsych_2001.pdf

Fujita, K., Henderson, M., Eng, J., Trope, Y., & Liberman, N. (2006). Spatial distance and mental construal of social events. *Psychological Science*, *17*, 278–282.

Gardner, W. L., Gabriel, S., & Lee, A. Y. (1999). "I" value freedom, but "We" value relationships: Self-construal priming mirrors cultural differences in judgment. *Psychological Science*, *10*(4), 321–326.

Goldsmith, K., Cho, E. K., & Dhar, R. (2012). When guilt begets pleasure: The positive effect of a negative emotion. *Journal of Marketing Research*, *49*(6), 872–881.

Hoch, S. J., & Loewenstein, G. F. (1991). Time-inconsistent preferences and consumer self-control. *Journal of Consumer Research*, *17*(March), 492–507.

Hofmann, W., Baumeister, R. F., Förster, G., & Vohs, K. D. (2012). Everyday temptations: An experience sampling study of desire, conflict, and self-control. *Journal of Personality and Social Psychology*, *102*(6), 1318.

Hofmann, W., Vohs, K. D., & Baumeister, R. F. (2012). What people desire, feel conflicted about, and try to resist in everyday life. *Psychological Science*, *23*(6), 582–588.

Isen, A. M., & Labroo, A. A. (2003). Some ways in which positive affect facilitates decision making and judgment. In S. Schneider & J. Shanteau (Eds.), *Emerging perspectives on judgment and decision research* (pp. 365–393). Cambridge: Cambridge University Press.

Isen, A. M., Shalker, T. E., Clark, M., & Karp, L. (1978). Affect, accessibility of material in memory, and behaviour: A cognitive loop? *Journal of Personality and Social Psychology*, *36*(1), 1–12.

Job, V., Dweck, C. S., & Walton, G. M. (2010). Ego depletion—Is it all in your head? Implicit theories about willpower affect self-regulation. *Psychological Science*, *21*(11), 1686–1693.

Khan, U., & Dhar, R. (2006). Licensing effect in consumer choice. *Journal of Marketing Research*, *43*(2), 259–266.

Khan, U., & Dhar, R. (2007). Where there is a way, is there a will? The effect of future choices on self-control. *Journal of Experimental Psychology: General*, *136*(2), 277.

Khan, U., & Dhar, R. (2010). Price-framing effects on the purchase of hedonic and utilitarian bundles. *Journal of Marketing Research*, *47*(6), 1090–1099.

Kivetz, R., & Keinan, A. (2008). Remedying hyperopia: The effects of self-control regret on consumer behaviour. *Journal of Marketing Research*, *45*(6), 676–689.

Kivetz, R., & Simonson, I. (2002). Self-control for the righteous: Toward a theory of pre-commitment to indulge. *Journal of Consumer Research*, *29*(3), 199–217.

Kivetz, R., & Zheng, Y. (2006). Determinants of justification and self-control. *Journal of Experimental Psychology: General*, *135*(4), 572–587.

Koo, M., Labroo, A. A., & Lee, A. Y. (2016). *The role of goal vigilance in self-control: The winning strategy of prevention orientation*. Working Paper, Northwestern University.
Labroo, A. A., & Kim, S. (2009). The "instrumentality" heuristic: Why metacognitive difficulty is desirable during goal pursuit. *Psychological Science, 20*(1), 127–134.
Labroo, A. A., & Mukhopadhyay, M. (2009). Lay theories of emotion transience and the search for happiness: A fresh perspective on affect regulation. *Journal of Consumer Research, 36*, 242–254.
Labroo, A. A., & Patrick, V. M. (2009). Psychological distancing: Why happiness helps you see the big picture. *Journal of Consumer Research, 35*, 800–809.
Lazarus, R. S. (1982). Thoughts on the relations between emotion and cognition. *American Psychologist, 37*, 1019–1024.
Lee, A. Y., & Aaker, J. L. (2004). Bringing the frame into focus: The influence of regulatory fit on processing fluency and persuasion. *Journal of Personality and Social Psychology, 86*, 205–218.
Liu, P. J., Haws, K. L., Lamberton, C., Campbell, T. H., & Fitzsimons, G. J. (2015). Vice-virtue bundles. *Management Science, 61*(1), 204–228.
Loewenstein, G. (1996). Out of control: Visceral influences on behaviour. *Organizational Behaviour and Human Decision Processes, 65*(3), 272–292.
Mackie, D. M., & Worth, L. T. (1989). Processing deficits and the mediation of positive affect in persuasion. *Journal of Personality and Social Psychology, 57*(1), 27–40.
Mano, H., & Oliver, R. (1993). Assessing the dimensionality and structure of the consumption experience: Evaluation, feeling, and satisfaction. *Journal of Consumer Research, 20*(3), 451–466.
McFerran, B., & Mukhopadhyay, A. (2013). Lay theories of obesity predict actual body mass. *Psychological Science. 24*(8), 1428–1436.
Mehta, R., Zhu, R. J., & Meyers-Levy, J. (2014). When does a higher construal level increase or decrease indulgence? Resolving the myopia versus hyperopia puzzle. *Journal of Consumer Research, 41*, 475–488.
Metcalfe, J., & Mischel, W. (1999). A hot/cool system analysis of delay of gratification: Dynamics of willpower. *Psychological Review, 106*(1), 3–19.
Milkman, K. L. (2012). Unsure what the future will bring? You may overindulge: Uncertainty increases the appeal of wants over shoulds. *Organizational Behaviour and Human Decision Processes, 119*(2), 163–176.
Milkman, K. L., Rogers, T., & Bazerman, M. H. (2009). Highbrow films gather dust: Time-inconsistent preferences and online DVD rentals. *Management Science, 55*(6), 1047–1059.
Milkman, K. L., Rogers, T., & Bazerman, M. H. (2010). I'll have the ice cream soon and the vegetables later: A study of online grocery purchases and order lead time. *Marketing Letters, 21*(1), 17–36.
Mischel, W., Shoda, Y., & Peake, P. K. (1988). The nature of adolescent competencies predicted by preschool delay of gratification. *Journal of Personality and Social Psychology, 54*(4), 687.
Mukhopadhyay, A., & Johar, G. V. (2005). Where there is a will, is there a way? Effects of lay theories of self-control on setting and keeping resolutions. *Journal of Consumer Research, 31*(4), 779–786.
Mukhopadhyay, A., Sengupta, J., & Ramanathan, S. (2008). Recalling past temptations: An information processing perspective on the dynamics of self-control. *Journal of Consumer Research, 35*(4), 586–599.
Mukhopadhyay, A., & Yeung, C. W. (2010). Building character: Effects of lay theories of self-control on the selection of products for children. *Journal of Marketing Research, 47*(2), 240–250.
Muraven, M., & Slessareva, E. (2003). Mechanisms of self-control failure: Motivation and limited resources. *Personality and Social Psychology Bulletin, 29*(7), 894–906.
Myrseth, K., & Fishbach, A. (2009). Self-control a function of knowing when and how to exercise restraint. *Current Directions in Psychological Science, 18*(4), 247–252.
Myrseth, K., Fishbach, A., & Trope, Y. (2009). Counteractive self-control when making temptation available makes temptation less tempting. *Psychological Science, 20*(2), 159–163.
Nikolova, H., & Inman, J. J. (2015). Healthy choice: The effect of simplified POS nutritional information on consumer food choice behaviour. *Journal of Marketing Research, 52*(6), 817–835.
Nikolova, H., Lamberton, C., & Haws, K. (2015). Haunts or helps from the past: How does recalling past self-controls acts affects current self-control? *Journal of Consumer Psychology, 26*(2), 245–256.
O'Guinn, T. C., & Faber, R. J. (1987). Mass mediated consumer socialization: Non-utilitarian and dysfunctional outcomes. *Advances in Consumer Research, 14*(1), 473–477.
Okada, E. M. (2005). Justification effects on consumer choice of hedonic and utilitarian goods. *Journal of Marketing Research, 42*(1), 43–53.
Pocheptsova, A., Amir, O., Dhar, R., & Baumeister, R. F. (2009). Deciding without resources: Resource depletion and choice in context. *Journal of Marketing Research, 46*(3), 344–355.

Posner, J., Russell, J. A., & Peterson, B. S. (2005). The circumplex model of affect: An integrative approach to affective neuroscience, cognitive development, and psychopathology. *Development and Psychopathology*, *17*, 715–734.

Raghunathan, R., & Trope, Y. (2002). Walking the tightrope between feeling good and being accurate: Mood as a resource in processing persuasive messages. *Journal of Personality and Social Psychology*, *83*, 510–525.

Read, D., Loewenstein, G. F., & Kalyanaraman, S. (1999). Mixing virtue and vice: Combining the immediacy effect and the diversification heuristic. *Journal of Behavioural Decision Making*, *12*, 257–273.

Redden, J. P., & Haws, K. L. (2013). Healthy satiation: The role of decreasing desire in effective self-control. *Journal of Consumer Research*, *39*(5), 1100–1114.

Rogers, T., & Bazerman, M. H. (2008). Future lock-in: Future implementation increases selection of "should" choices. *Organizational Behaviour and Human Decision Processes*, *106*, 1–20.

Romal, J. B., & Kaplan, B. J. (1995). Difference in self-control among spenders and savers. *Psychology: A Quarterly Journal of Human Behaviour*, *32*, 8–17.

Sayette, M. A. (1993). An appraisal-disruption model of alcohol's effects on stress responses in social drinkers. *Psychological Bulletin*, *114*(3), 459.

Schmeichel, B. J., & Vohs, K. (2009). Self-affirmation and self-control: Affirming core values counteracts ego depletion. *Journal of Personality and Social Psychology*, *96*(4), 770–782.

Schwarz, N., & Clore, G. L. (1983). Mood, misattribution, and judgments of well-being: Informative and directive functions of affective states. *Journal of Personality and Social Psychology*, *45*(3), 513–523.

Shah, J. Y., Friedman, R., & Kruglanski, A. W. (2002). Forgetting all else: On the antecedents and consequences of goal shielding. *Journal of Personality and Social Psychology*, *83*(6), 1261–1280.

Shah, J. Y., & Kruglanski, A. W. (2002). Priming against your will: How accessible alternatives affect goal pursuit. *Journal of Experimental Social Psychology*, *38*(4), 368–383.

Simon, H. A. (1967). Motivational and emotional controls of cognition. *Psychological Review*, *74*, 29–39.

Tamir, M., Mitchell, C., & Gross, J. J. (2008). Hedonic and instrumental motives in anger regulation. *Psychological Science*, *19*, 324–328.

Tangney, J. P., Baumeister, R. F., & Boone, A. L. (2004). High self-control predicts good adjustment, less pathology, better grades, and interpersonal success. *Journal of Personality*, *72*(2), 271–324.

Tice, D. M., Bratslavsky, E., & Baumeister, R. F. (2001). Emotional distress regulation takes precedence over impulse control: If you feel bad, do it! *Journal of Personality and Social Psychology*, *80*, 53–67.

Trope, Y., & Liberman, N. (2003). Temporal construal. *Psychological Review*, *110*(3), 403–421.

Trope, Y., Liberman, N., & Wakslak, C. (2007). Construal levels and psychological distance: Effects on representation, prediction, evaluation, and behaviour. *Journal of Consumer Psychology*, *17*, 83–95. Retrieved from http://psych.nyu.edu/tropelab/publications/Tropeetal2007.pdf

Van den Bergh, B., Dewitte, S., & Warlop, L. (2008). Bikinis instigate generalized impatience in intertemporal choice. *Journal of Consumer Research*, *35*, 85–97.

Vohs, K. D., Baumeister, R. F., & Schmeichel, B. J. (2012). Motivation, personal beliefs, and limited resources all contribute to self-control. *Journal of Experimental Social Psychology*, *48*(4), 943–947.

Vohs, K. D., Baumeister, R. F., & Schmeichel, B. J. (2013). Motivation, personal beliefs, and limited resources all contribute to self-control, *Journal of Experimental Social Psychology*, *49*, 184–188.

Vohs, K. D., & Faber, R. J. (2007). Spent resources: Self-regulatory resource availability affects impulse buying. *Journal of Consumer Research*, *33*(4), 537–547.

Vohs, K. D., & Heatherton, T. F. (2000). Self-regulatory failure: A resource-depletion approach. *Psychological Science*, *11*(3), 249–254.

Wan, E. W., & Agrawal, N. (2011). Carryover effects of self-control on decision making: A construal-level perspective. *Journal of Consumer Research*, *38*(1), 199–214.

Wang, J., Novemsky, N., Dhar, R., & Baumeister, R. F. (2010). Tradeoffs and depletion in choice. *Journal of Marketing Research*, *47*(5), 910–919.

Wertenbroch, K. (1998). Consumption self-control by rationing purchase quantities of virtue and vice. *Marketing Science*, *17*(4), 317–337.

Wilcox, K., Vallen, B., Block, L., & Fitzsimons, G. J. (2009). Vicarious goal fulfillment: When the mere presence of a healthy option leads to an ironically indulgent decision. *Journal of Consumer Research*, *36*(3), 380–393.

Williams, L. E., Stein, R., & Galguera, L. (2014). The distinct affective consequences of psychological distance and construal level. *Journal of Consumer Research*, *40*, 1123–1138.

Zhang, Y., & Fishbach, A. (2010). Counteracting obstacles with optimistic predictions. *Journal of Experimental Psychology: General*, *139*(1), 16–31.

Zhang, Y., Fishbach, A., & Dhar, R. (2007). When thinking beats doing: The role of optimistic expectations in goal-based choice. *Journal of Consumer Research*, *34*(4), 567–578.

25

Sex drive and consumer decision making

Rui Chen and Maggie Wenjing Liu

The sex drive, probably the most basic and powerful motive experienced by humans or other living creatures, has fundamental impact on various decisions and behaviours (Darwin, 1871; Miller, 1999, 2000; Trivers, 1972). In this chapter, we review four areas in previous research on sex drive theories and their effects on consumer decision making, namely: (1) mating motives in evolutionary psychology, (2) ovulation as an adaptive mating motive, (3) sex as rewards, and (4) sexual appeal and persuasion.

First, we review mating motives in evolutionary psychology, which suggests that, in order to impress and attract potential mates, an individual needs to display their desirable mating qualities that contribute to the survival of offspring, such as good genes and wealth (Cronin, 1991; Gangestad, 1993; Miller, 1999). Many studies have offered empirical evidence for this theory, suggesting that mating motives induce men to engage in conspicuous consumption (Sundie et al., 2011), saving less but borrowing more (Griskevicius, Tybur, Ackerman, Delton, & Robertson, 2012), as well as women showing benevolence and helping behaviour (Griskevicius et al., 2007). Previous research has also explored gender differences and different mating strategies, both short- and long-term (Cantú et al., 2014; Griskevicius, Cialdini, & Kenrick, 2006).

Second, we summarize research on ovulation and menstrual phases as an adaptive mating motive. The ovulatory shift hypothesis proposes that women at peak fertility should have more pronounced preferences for potential sex partners who demonstrate classic biological indicators of male genetic fitness (e.g., symmetry, masculinity and intelligence (Gangestad & Thornhill, 2008). Researchers have found that ovulation as an adaptive mating motive also has an enormous effect on female behaviour, including choosing sexy clothing (Durante, Griskevicius, Hill, Perilloux, & Li, 2011), wearing red (Beall & Tracy, 2013) and the decreased consumption of food but increased consumption of clothes (Saad & Stenstrom, 2012).

Third, neuroimaging findings have demonstrated that reward circuitry is commonly involved when people process a variety of rewarding stimuli, including primary rewards, such as palatable food, drugs and sex and secondary rewards, such as money (Aharon et al., 2001; Camerer, Loewenstein, & Prelec, 2005; Stark et al., 2005). Therefore, sexual stimuli would induce people to crave monetary and food rewards (Van den Bergh, Dewitte, & Warlop, 2008). In addition, gender differences and underlying mechanisms have been discussed (Festjens, Bruyneel, & Dewitte, 2014; Kim & Zauberman, 2013).

Fourth, we review the more established literature on sexual appeal and persuasion in consumer psychology. Sexual appeal has been widely employed in advertisement persuasion, even if the product has little relevance to sex (Peterson & Kerin, 1977). Prior research investigated the effects of sexual appeal on attention capturing in advertisement (Alexander & Judd, 1978; Steadman, 1969), brand evaluation and purchasing intention (Dahl, Sengupta, & Vohs, 2009; Sengupta & Dahl, 2008; Vohs, Sengupta, & Dhal, 2014), cross-culture difference (Mofrad & Fah, 2015) and ethical issues (LaTour & Henthome, 1994).

Table 25.1 summaries key reference and take-aways from the four streams of research in sex drive's effect on consumer decision making. Finally, we discuss the interplay and connection between different streams and the gender differences in sex drive's effects on consumer decisions, and propose some future research directions.

Mating motives in evolutionary psychology

The motivation to seek a mate is a fundamental motive of humans and other creatures (Darwin, 1871). Evolution theory suggests the reason that people seek a mate is because of intersexual selection, which is defined as the tendency of members of one sex to preferentially choose certain members of the opposite sex as mates (Miller, 1999, 2000; Trivers, 1972). In order to impress and attract potential mates, individuals have to display their desirable mating qualities that contribute to the survival of offspring, such as good genes and wealth (Cronin, 1991; Gangestad, 1993; Miller, 1999). Examples of such behaviour include choosing conspicuous products, wearing sexy dresses and getting tanned, giving gifts to romantic partners, saving less but borrowing more (Durante et al., 2011; Griskevicius et al., 2007; Griskevicius, Tybur, Ackerman, Delton, & Robertson, 2012; Saad & Gill, 2003; Saad & Peng, 2006; Sundie et al., 2011).

Previous research has also explored gender differences and short- and long-term mating strategies. The difference between genders is mainly driven by intersexual selection and different roles in giving birth and rearing offspring (Darwin, 1871; Miller, 1999; Saad, 2013). Intersexual selection is often called female selection, suggesting that females have more rights in selecting a mate because they often invest more in bearing and nurturing offspring (Kokko, 2001; Trivers, 1972). Moreover, mating strategies cause different mate preferences (Buss & Barnes, 1986, Buss & Schmitt, 1993). When a female pursues a short-term mate, she values heritable fitness, which results in greater genetic benefits to offspring. However, if a female aims to seek a long-term mate, she prefers a male who is willing and able to provide sufficient economic resources. Indeed, several investigators (e.g., Buss & Schmitt, 1993; Li & Kenrick, 2006) have demonstrated that women's mate preferences systematically differ in long-term versus short-term mating contexts. In many cultures, for example, women place relatively greater emphasis on the physical attractiveness and muscularity of men when evaluating them as short-term mates and less weight on attributes that signal the quality of paternal care and investment (e.g., conscientiousness, loyalty and good parenting qualities) in short-term contexts (see Buss & Schmitt, 1993; Schmitt, 2005).

Mating motives and showing off desirable mate qualities

A numbers of studies have demonstrated that the mating motive has induced many showing off behaviours. Male participants report more wealth and higher status and indicate themselves as more extroversive after viewing pictures of attractive women (Roney, 2003), because showing off these desirable qualities and personality traits can attract females (Miller, 1999). Females

Table 25.1 Sex drive and decision making

Effect of sex drive	*Sample references*	*Main take-away*
Showing off behaviours	Ackerman, Delton and Robertson, (2012); Griskevicius, Cialdini and Kenrick (2006); Griskevicius, Tybur, Sundie, Cialdini, Miller and Kenrick (2007); Griskevicius, Tybur, Monga and Gürhan-Canli (2012); Huang and Bargh (2008); Sundie, Kenrick, Griskevicius, Tybur, Vohs and Beal (2011)	Mating motive affects enormous consumption behaviours due to the motivation to show off qualities as a desirable mate, such as conspicuous consumption, economic decisions and dressing behaviours. External social factors can trigger individuals' mating motive, which in turn affects showing-off behaviour. The mating mindset can cause some sex-unrelated behaviour.
Menstrual cycle	Beall and Tracy (2013); Cantú, Simpson, Griskevicius, Weisberg, Durante and Beal (2014); Durante, Griskevicius, Hill, Perilloux and Li (2011); Miller, Tybur and Jordan (2007); Puts (2005); Saad and Stenstrom (2012)	Females in the ovulation phase have a stronger sexual desire, preference for good genes and stronger motivation for showing off. These preferences and motivation affect economic, dressing and shopping behaviours.
Reward seeking	Festjens, Bruyneel and Dewitte (2013); Gal (2012); Kim and Zauberman (2013); Van den Bergh, Dewitte and Warlop (2008)	Sexual stimuli can activate the general reward circuitry, which leads to more impatience towards rewards in females. Males even salivate while anticipating the reward after viewing attractive females' pictures. Touching sexual stimuli can activate females' reward circuitry.
Persuasion	Alexander and Judd (1978); Dahl, Sengupta and Vohs (2009); LaTour and Henthorne (1994); Peterson and Kerin (1977); Vohs, Sengupta and Dahl (2014)	Sexual appeal on the advertisement can capture males' attention, but it has little or negative effect on brand evaluation and purchase intent. In addition, males respond more favourably to sexual advertisements than females. Recent studies suggest that when sex is used as a commitment cue or relating to high price/value, the effect could be positive on females.

are also inclined to show off their desirable qualities when they are induced into the mating motive. However, due to the different roles of bearing and rearing offspring (Kokko, 2001; Trivers, 1972), there is a gender difference of what qualities to show off, e.g., wealth, heroism and dominance for males and benevolence for females (Griskevicius et al., 2007). Since these behaviours are of mating motive, they disappear when other people cannot observe the showing off behaviours. Conspicuous consumption is a form of economic behaviour in which self-presentational concerns override desires to obtain goods at bargain prices (Veblen, 1899);

therefore, conspicuous spending may be a social signal directed at potential mates (Saad, 2007; Sundie et al. 2011). Sundie et al. (2011) investigated such conspicuous signals and showed that males, rather than females, resort to conspicuous consumption to attract mates. Besides, males tend to prefer short-term and uncommitted sexual relationships, so there is generally more competitive intensity among men when they seek short-term relationships than when they pursue long-term partners (Buss & Schmitt, 1993). Accordingly, males' conspicuous consumption behaviours are more significant when they are triggered by short-term (vs. long-term) mating motives. Interestingly, females can detect that males employing conspicuous consumption bear short-term mating motives (Sundie et al., 2011). In addition to attracting mates, another function of conspicuous consumption is mate guarding (Wang & Griskevicius, 2014). Buss (1988) suggested an effective mate-guarding tactic for a woman is to convey to other women that her partner cares for her deeply and is committed to the relationship. Luxury products can deliver such signals because they require considerable economic resources (Belk, Bahn, & Mayer, 1982). Wang and Griskevicius (2014) tested the above argument by showing that activating the motive to guard one's mate triggered women to seek and display lavish possessions in order to signal their romantic partners' devotion. Relatedly, Saad and Gill (2003) showed men were more frequently giving gifts to romantic partners than women, and women were aware of men's tactical motive of gift giving.

In addition, creative abilities are presumed to evolve for human beings since creativity can enhance the likelihood of our ancestors' survival without adding unnecessary metabolic costs (e.g., Byrne, 1995; Gibson & Ingold, 1993; Kingdon, 1993). Thus, it is reasonable to predict that courtship might stimulate creative displays. Consistent with this reasoning, men and women express relatively equal preferences for creativity in a mate (Li, Bailey, Kenrick, & Linsenmeier, 2002). Deeper research revealed that even without other incentives to be creative, romantic motives enhanced creativity on subjective and objective measures. For men, any cue designed to activate a short-term or a long-term mating goal increased creative displays; however, women displayed more creativity only when primed to attract a high-quality long-term mate (Griskevicius et al., 2006). Aggression is related to status in many social cultures (Cohen, Nisbett, Bowdle, & Schwarz, 1996; McCarthy, 1994). For example, many societies offer great respect to individuals who fight for their honour (Cohen et al., 1996). Meanwhile, status is a very valuable trait to attract a romantic partner and attain success in the same-sex competition (Li & Kenrick, 2006; Maner, DeWall, & Gailliot, 2008). Accordingly, Griskevicius et al. (2009) found that men's aggression was boosted by mating motives, but only when observers were other men. In contrast, mating motives did not increase women's aggression directly unless when they were motivated to compete for scarce resources.

Economic and environmental factors can also prime mating motives and lead to economic and consumption behaviours. Economic recession and sex ratios have demonstrated such magical effects (Hill, Rodeheffer, Griskevicius, Durante, & White, 2012; Griskevicius et al., 2012). Economic recession causes insufficient resource and poverty and sends cues of environmental harshness. Prior research suggested that individuals living in harsh environments tend to allocate effort towards more immediate reproduction than those living in more financially secure environments (Belsky, Schlomer, & Ellis, 2012; Ellis, Figueredo, Brumbach, & Schlomer, 2009). It is reasonable that females would invest more effort and financial resources to attract males and then facilitate reproduction. The results of historical spending data and rigorous experiments supported the prediction, such that recessionary cues – whether naturally occurring or experimentally primed – decreased desire for most products (e.g., electronics and household items), but increased women's desire for products that increase attractiveness to mates; this effect is driven by the desire of women to attract mates with resources (Hill et al., 2012).

Intrasexual competition in humans is associated with the population sex ratio (Balshine-Earn, 1996). The relationship between competition and the population sex ratio in humans parallels findings in the animal literature and suggests that men may amplify mating efforts when women are scarce (Barber, 2003; Hudson & Den Boer, 2002). Specifically, an overabundance of men appears to lead men to allocate more resources and effort towards mating (Griskevicius et al., 2012). Specifically, a scarcity of women leads men to spend more money during courtship (e.g., by paying more for engagement rings), to choose immediate smaller rewards rather than delayed larger rewards and to save less and borrow more.

Moreover, mating motives also influence cognition style and cognitive performance; these influences may powerfully affect consumer decision making. Förster, Epstude and Özelsel (2009) showed that short-term mating motives induce analytic thinking, but that long-term mating motives induce holistic thinking. Whether information processing is analytic or holistic directly relates to brand extension (Monga & Jhon, 2007), and advertisement message persuasiveness evaluation (Mehta & Zhu, 2009). Karremans, Verwijmeren, Pronk and Reitsma (2009) found that men's (but not women's) cognitive performance declined following a mixed-sex encounter; sex appeal advertisement strategies should therefore consider sex appeal's effects on advertisement and brand recollection.

Mating mindset and nonsexual behaviour

Although extant research has documented numerous types of sex-related "showing-off" behaviour in situations in which mating motivation is primed, it has also been suggested that mating motives can affect nonsexual behaviour (Huang & Bargh, 2008; Monga & Gürhan-Canli, 2012). The effects of mating motive on nonsexual behaviour may be driven by joint information processing styles for humans and other living things (Huang & Bargh, 2008) or some extension of motivations leading to showing off (Monga & Gürhan-Canli, 2012). Huang and Bargh (2008) found that mating motivation activates related adaptive mechanisms, including a general sensitivity to cues of growth and decay associated with determining mate value in human courtship, which sequentially increases people's preferences for "ripe" fruits and "newly blossomed" flowers. Monga and Gürhan-Canli (2012) showed that a mating mindset increases male (but not female) consumers' fit perceptions and evaluations for moderately dissimilar brand extensions, as the mating motive causes men to engage in relational processing. Consistent with the principles of differential parental investment and sexual selection, men generally demonstrate greater desire for short-term mates than women, leading men to behave in ways that maximize such opportunities (Buss & Schmitt, 1993; Wilson & Daly, 1985), suggesting that men are likely to downplay typical concerns about potential losses when mating opportunities are salient. Li, Kenrick, Griskevicius and Neuberg (2011) found that mating motives remove loss aversion in men but not in women; specifically, that activating mating motives causes men to spend less in avoiding some potential losses (e.g., disease and physical danger).

Ovulation as an adaptive mating motive

The female reproductive system is based on a cyclical pattern averaging 28 days in length. Within this cycle, women may only conceive during a short fertile period (Carlson, 2001; Nelson, 2005; Wilcox, Dunson, & Baird, 2000). The ovulatory shift hypothesis proposes that natural selection has shaped aspects of women's mating psychology to shift during the menstrual cycle's fertile period (Gangestad & Thornhill, 2008). This hypothesis predicts that women at peak fertility should have significantly increased reproductive motivation, inducing stronger sexual desire and preference for potential sex partners with good genetic fitness, and should engage in self-ornamentation behaviour in order to attract desirable partners (Adams, Gold, & Burt, 1978; Gangestad & Thornhill, 1998; Haselton & Gangestad, 2006; Penton-Voak & Perrett, 2000; Röder, Brewer, & Fink, 2009). The ovulatory shift hypothesis further proposes that these fundamental motives powerfully affect consumer decision making in such domains as dressing, spending on status products and variety seeking, and may affect such outcomes as lap dancers' tips earnings (Beall & Tracy, 2013; Durante, Griskevicius, Cantú, Simpson, 2014; Faraji-Rad, Moeini-Jazani, & Warlop 2013; Miller, Tybur, & Jordan, 2007).

Ovulation and sexual desire

Women are only able conceive during the ovulation phase (Carlson, 2001; Wilcox et al., 2000); they consequently exhibit peaks of sexual activity at ovulation, in order to maximize the chance of conception. These peaks are statistically significant for female-initiated behaviour, including both autosexual and female-initiated heterosexual behaviour, but are not present in male-initiated behaviour (Adams, Gold, & Burt, 1978). Prior research has found that women are more interested in non-primary partners and are more likely to engage in extra-pair sexual activities, when they are closer to the ovulation stage (Bellis & Baker, 1990; Birkhead & Møller, 1995; Gangestad, Thornhill, & Garver-Apgar, 2005).

Durante and Arsena (2015) argued that women's increased desire for sex-partner variety during the ovulation phase may activate a general variety-seeking mindset, causing women to seek greater product variety, but that ovulation's effect on women's variety-seeking in product consumption would diminish if ovulating women were primed with loyalty. By contrast, Faraji-Rad et al. (2013) proposed that the underlying mechanism of ovulation's effect on variety seeking in product consumption is the reward circuitry that is activated by increased sexual desire during ovulation. Additionally, sexual desire (as greater openness to short-term sexual relationships) is associated with lower religiosity (Weeden, Cohen, & Kenrick, 2008) and more liberal political attitudes (Kurzban, Dukes, & Weeden, 2010). Durante, Rae and Griskevicius (2013) thus propose that ovulation may affect women's attitudes towards liberalism and political orientation, but argue that these effects may be moderated by romantic relationships. They found that, during the ovulation rather than the luteal phase, single women become more liberal and more likely to vote for the Democratic Party, but that, during the same phase, women in committed relationships become more conservative and more likely vote for the Republican Party.

Ovulation and the mate selection motive

Prior research has found that women at peak fertility prefer male partners exhibiting indicators of genetic fitness, and have argued that this effect reflects the fact that good genes facilitate the survival of offspring (e.g., Penton-Voak et al., 1999; Thornhill & Gangestad, 2008). For example, masculine facial features and lower-pitched voices are more preferred by women who are close to ovulation (Penton-Voak & Perrett, 2000; Puts, 2005). Similarly, Durante, Griskevicius, Simpson, Cantú and Li (2012) found that women evaluate charismatic and physically attractive men more positively when ovulating. These findings suggest that women prefer attractive male celebrity actors and male singers with lower-pitched voices more when ovulating, and that attractive male sellers may more easily promote products to women who are close to ovulation.

Further, Lens, Driesmans, Pandelaere and Janssens (2012) argued that women close to ovulation should also prefer men of higher social status, since these men are able to offer greater stability, economic resources and protection to women and their offspring, and that women may therefore be more attracted by status products during ovulation. They showed that women close to ovulation remembered status products, but not functional products, better than women in the menstrual and luteal phases.

Ovulation and mate attraction

Although humans differ from many other primates in the apparent absence of obvious indicators of fertility within the ovulatory cycle (Benshoof & Thornhill, 1979; Burley, 1979), recent studies indicate that human ovulation may be marked by observable changes in overt behaviour (Beall & Tracy, 2013; Durante et al., 2011; Haselton, Mortezaie, Pillsworth, Bleske-Rechek, & Frederick, 2007). Haselton et al. (2007) found that females dressed more attractively and showed more skin during the ovulation phase than during the luteal phase. Similarly, Schwarz and Hassebrauck (2008) conducted a longitudinal diary study through one complete menstrual cycle and analyzed women's reported clothing style and self-perceived attractiveness. Their results indicated that women perceived themselves, and were perceived by men, to be dressed more provocatively during the fertile phase of their menstrual cycle, compared to the luteal phase.

Durante et al. (2011) also found that at peak fertility, women unconsciously choose products that enhance appearance (e.g., choosing provocative rather than conservative clothing); however, they noted that this hormonally regulated effect appears to be driven by desire to outdo attractive rival women rather than desire to attract potential mates. They further demonstrated that minimizing the salience of potential rival women suppresses the ovulatory effect on women's product choice. Since men are sexually attracted to women wearing or surrounded by red (e.g., Elliot & Pazda, 2012; Greenfield, 2005), Beall and Tracy (2013) argued that females tend to wear reddish clothing more when at peak fertility, but that conception chance has no effect on the prevalence of any other clothing colour. Due to the influence of ovulation on mating motivation, females allocate resources to food and clothes in a cyclic way over the course of the menstrual cycle (Saad & Stenstrom, 2012). The results indicated that food-related desire, money expenditure on food, and food consumption were greater during the luteal (non-fertile) phase, whereas appearance-related desire, money expenditure on appearance and beautification behaviours increased during the fertile phase. However, money spent on products unrelated to food or beautification was not significantly influenced by the menstrual cycle.

Interestingly, Miller et al. (2007) found professional lap dancers earned more tips during their ovulation phase than during their luteal phase, but this effect disappeared for females who used hormonal contraception. Cantú et al. (2014) suggested the ovulatory cycle's effects on tip earnings may be driven by women maintaining a more attractive appearance or engaging in more flirting behaviour during the ovulation phase. Cantú et al. monitored the behaviour of women talking to potential mating partners. Their results showed that women in the ovulatory phase reported greater interest in men who showed markers of genetic fitness as short-term mates, but not as long-term mates. Furthermore, behavioural ratings of the observed interactions indicated that women displayed more flirting behaviour when they were at high rather than low fertility. Importantly, fertile women only flirted more when interacting with men who showed signs of genetic fitness, and not with other men.

Sex as reward

Craving for reward caused by sexual stimuli

Wilson and Daly (2004) first found that sex stimuli increase men's (but not women's) craving of rewards (e.g., money). Their results demonstrated that after viewing attractive female images (vs. unattractive female images), male participants were more likely to choose smaller immediate monetary rewards instead of larger delayed monetary rewards, but there was no difference for females who viewed attractive male images. They argued that these findings were caused by different "mating opportunity" mindsets held by males and females. Because men have always had some chance of gaining fitness from short-term expenditures of mating effort, whereas successful reproduction typically requires greater prolonged parental investment by women, men should have evolved to more strongly discount the future than women do (Wilson & Daly, 2004). Relatedly, Van den Bergh and Dewitte (2006) showed that males were even willing to accept unfairly small rewards after exposure to sexual stimuli (viewing sexual female pictures and touching a bra) in ultimatum games. This effect was stronger for low 2D:4D ratios males because the ratio between the length of the index finger (2D) and the ring finger (4D) reflects the degree to which humans are exposed to pre-natal androgen, such that lower digit ratios are associated with greater sensitivity to testosterone (Manning, Bundred, Newton, & Flanagan 2003) and higher circulating testosterone levels (Manning, Scutt, Wilson, & Lewis-Jones, 1998). These findings suggest that marketers may increase male consumers' preference for reward products, such as pleasure foods and luxury goods (e.g., chocolate cake and sports cars), through sex appeal, and that certain physiological traits (e.g., digit ratios) may be considered market segment variables.

Activated reward circuitry as the mechanism

Although the above research verifies that sexual stimuli cause males to be more shortsighted and seek immediate rewards, there is neither comprehensive theory nor sufficient evidence that elaborates on the mechanism underlying this effect. Building on neuroscientific research, reward circuitry has been proposed to explain these findings (Berger & Shiv, 2011; Van den Bergh et al., 2008). Rewards are a central component for driving incentive-based learning, appropriate responses to stimuli and the development of goal-directed behaviours (Berridge & Robinson, 1998). Rewarding goods have three distinct basic functions (Schultz, 2002; Berridge & Robinson, 1998). Their first function is to reward and elicit approach and consummatory behaviour. This is due to the objects being labelled with appetitive value through innate mechanisms or, in most cases, learning. In their second function, rewards increase the frequency and intensity of behaviour leading to such objects (learning), and they maintain learned behaviour by preventing extinction. The third function of rewards is to serve as positive reinforcers of behaviour in classical and instrumental conditioning procedures.

Neuroscientific studies have demonstrated that sexual cues, such as pictures of attractive opposite-gender individuals or a romantic interaction, can activate the reward circuitry in the brain (Aharon et al., 2001; Aron et al., 2005), which consequently increases sensitivity to sex-related rewards. Interestingly, this reward circuitry is commonly involved when people process a variety of rewarding stimuli, for example, food, sex and money. (Aharon et al., 2001; Camerer et al., 2005; Montague, King-Casas, & Cohen, 2006; Stark et al., 2005).

Building on the general reward circuitry logic, Van den Bergh et al. (2008) proposed that activation of the general reward circuitry, by exposure to "hot stimuli" (sexual cues), leads to general, nonspecific effects in reward processing. They revealed that exposure to sexual cues increased the preference for a smaller and immediate monetary (or food) reward over a larger but delayed monetary (or food) reward. They also demonstrated that the extent of sensitivity to rewards moderated the effects of sexual cues on intertemporal discounting of monetary rewards. In particular, sexual stimuli would more easily activate the reward circuitry of males who are more sensitive to rewards, and thus cause steeper delay discounting of monetary (food) rewards (Van den Bergh et al., 2008).

Physiological phenomenon was also implicated in the effect of sexual stimuli on reward seeking. Gal (2012) found "salivation" was not only for food, but also for other material rewards, such as money and luxury sports cars. His results indicate that men salivate in response to sports cars when primed with a mating goal but not in a control condition. Berger and Shiv (2011) argued that distinctiveness also possesses motivational reward characteristics, so exposure to sexual stimuli can influence preferences for more unique options. They further found that the positive effect of sex on uniqueness seeking was erased when participants received a food reward, which can satiate the reward craving, before making uniqueness choices.

The above studies consistently demonstrated the positive effect of sexual stimuli on reward seeking for males; however, few studies tested the effect for females or observed a gender difference (Wilson & Daly, 2004). Festjens, Sabrina and Dewitte (2014) argued that women's previously documented unresponsiveness to sexual primes when making economic decisions may be a consequence of the specific types of primes that have been used (i.e., visual primes). They demonstrated that women are susceptible to tactile sexual primes. Similar to the effect found in men, their results demonstrated that touching a pair of boxer shorts leads to a craving for monetary (or food) rewards in women.

Previous research has emphasized the reward effect of sex, but Kim and Zauberman (2013) proposed a different psychological mechanism to explain this effect: Sexual cues induce impatience through their ability to lengthen the perceived temporal distance to delayed rewards and this process is due to the arousing nature of sexual cues. That is, sexual cues make the temporal delay seem subjectively longer, resulting in greater impatience for monetary rewards. Their results demonstrated that males in the sexual cues condition perceived the same future durations to be longer and were more impatient when making inter-temporal monetary tradeoffs, choosing smaller immediate amounts over larger delayed amounts, than did those in the control condition.

Sexual appeal and persuasion

Attention and memory of sexual advertisements

Attention has been referred to as the scarcest resource in today's business (Adler & Firestone, 1997; Davenport & Beek, 2001). The failure to capture consumers' attention (i.e., to attract and retain it) reduces the effectiveness of advertisements, which make it an increasingly important aim of advertising. Pictorial illustrations are commonly supposed to be the chief element in capturing consumers' attention (Assael, Kofron, & Burgi, 1967; Poffenberger, 1925; Singh, Lessig, & Kim, 2000), and sex is one of the most effective pictorial stimuli. Thus, sexual illustrations are widely utilized in advertisements to capture consumer's attention. Some findings also indicated that sexual pictures have a high attention-getting value, and that sex, as an element in advertisements, will arouse the immediate interest of both men and women (Baker, 1961). However, an advertisement has three key elements: brand, pictorial illustration and text (Alexander & Judd, 1978; Steadman, 1969). Therefore, sexual illustrations in advertisements may attract a great deal of attention, but may not develop an association with the brand and product information. Thus, due to the incongruence between sexual appeal and the type of product, sexual advertisements may not be effective in projecting their message. For example, sexual advertisements are not effective for household products, but it would be better for underclothes and deodorants, which are logically associated with sex (Steadman, 1969).

Steadman (1969) investigated 60 male undergraduates' ability to recall brand names accompanying sexual or non-sexual illustrations, and the moderation effect of time delay.

Findings revealed no differences in correct brand recall in 24 hours, but after seven days, the correct brand recall was lower for sexual advertisements than non-sexual ones. This indicates that sex appeal may attract attention to an advertisement, but does not enhance brand recollection. In addition, the more favourable the attitude to the sexual advertisement, the more correct was the recall of the brand name accompanying sexual illustrations. Alexander and Judd (1978) replicated the above findings with a more general sample of 141 male participants, and showed that the number of brand names recalled will significantly decrease as the amount of nudity depicted in the advertisement increases. Interestingly, married men recalled more brand names than single men, indicating that marital status may affect sex appeal's effect on advertisements. Besides brand recall, some other studies examined the effect of sexual advertisement on copy points and product information recall (Severn, Belch & Belch, 1990). They used sexual advertisement (vs. non-sexual advertisement) and different number of copy points (three vs. seven) to test their interaction effect, as well as brand and copy points recall. The results showed that the brand name recall did not differ significantly as a function of the presence or absence of a sexual appeal, but sexual advertisements decreased copy points recall, suggesting that sexual appeal inhibits consumers' attention to product information.

Sexual advertisements and brand attitudes

Before employing sexual advertisements, practitioners should be first clear about the various uses of sexual appeal, and make sure that their objectives match with the use of sexual appeal. In order to provide some guidance, Richmond and Hartman (1982) developed a theoretical framework concerning the uses of sexual appeal in advertising, which included five dimensions: functional, fantasy, symbolism, inappropriate and male/female orientations. The functional dimension suggests that sexual advertisements are used to introduce the function of the product, such as the considerable array of products – e.g., undergarments and personal hygiene – that could be presented in a straightforward sexual presentation. The "Fantasy" dimension means that the sexual advertisement can induce or fulfil some sexual fantasies. "Symbolism", for instance, may be illustrated through use of words such as silk to represent feminine, and wool tweed to represent masculine traits. The "Inappropriate" dimension argues that the use of sexual appeal is primarily an attention device – typically exploiting the female body, degrading the feminine role and insulting propriety. Sexual advertisements can also be used for product or brand position. For example, sexual pictures in a watch advertisement aim to position it for men with high status.

When sexual appeal is employed in advertisements, the illustration and copy may predominantly address a male or female audience. Richmond and Hartman (1982) also provided empirical evidence for their theoretical framework by asking 50 adult males and females to evaluate a collection of several hundred advertisements, each with varying types of sexual appeals. They advised that a manager should have enough knowledge about how various subgroups of the population respond to different aspects of a "sexy" advertisement. Morrison and Sherman (1972) asked 615 undergraduates to rate 300 advertisements and then analyzed their response by Q-analysis and a heuristic clustering method. The heuristic clustering method effectively classifies consumers into groups and generates a variety of interpretable dimensions. Their analysis suggested that the suggestiveness of advertising copy was the most consequential variable in sex advertisements targeting women, but that men were divided into groups that differed in their response to sexual advertisements. Generally, men reported low perception of nudity in sex advertisement.

To observe the effect of sexual appeal on brand attitude in detail, Peterson and Kerin (1977) designed advertisements with various levels of female nudity (product only, female demure model, seductive model, nude model), with two types of products (body oil, ratchet set). Body oil is a sexual cue, while the ratchet set is not. Across products and respondents, the advertisement containing a nude model was consistently perceived as the least appealing, and the associated product and producing company were perceived as possessing the lowest quality and being the least reputable, respectively. In addition, there was a consistently significant product-by-advertisement type interaction effect. Specially, the seductive model/body oil combination was simultaneously perceived as the most appealing advertisement, containing the highest quality product, produced by the most reputable company. These results suggested that nudity is considered bad, and sexual appeal should be relevant to the product.

Reidenbach and McCleary (1983) designed a similar experiment investigating consumers' responses to advertisements with nude males. A men's cologne represented the sexually-oriented product, while a frying pan was chosen as the non-sexually oriented product. They found significant gender differences such that females reacted to the advertisement more negatively than did the male. However, Simpson, Horton and Brown (1996) revealed a controversial result; that is, female respondents reacted much more favourably to advertisements containing male models in various dress levels than did the male respondents, especially with reference to mood, attitude towards the advertiser and attitude towards the advertisement. Further, female attitudes towards the advertisement were enhanced by increasing levels of nudity, but declined with the suggestion of full nudity (Simpson et al., 1996). This inconsistency among results may be due to differences in the products chosen; that is, Simpson et al. (1996)'s product (body oil) is often bought by women for men, and this may have caused a sexually suggestive image of a man to have positive effects (Dahl et al., 2009). LaTour (1990) argued that arousal is an important factor that causes gender differences in attitudes to sexual appeal in advertisements. In their study, women were found to generate more tension and negative feelings towards explicit female nudity in print advertisements than were men. Further, men were more energized and positive about such advertisements. Although most of the above research, which indicates that sex advertisement is ineffective, was conducted more than two decades ago, recent research continues to support these findings, and explore additional moderators.

Some studies attempted to reveal some moderating conditions in which sexual appeal would have a positive effect on brand evaluation and persuasion. Reichert, Heckler and Jackson (2001) argued that if sexual advertisements employed sexual appeal appropriately (e.g., the appeal should be crafted to be relevant and free of sexism, and to appeal to both genders), it could stimulate more positive execution-related thoughts than would advertisements without sexual appeal. Further, it would stimulate fewer cognitive responses towards the message, finally resulting in a greater level of agreement with the advocated position for social marketing messages. This is because sexual information may inhibit elaboration in two ways: First, processing of the sexual information limits the resources available for elaboration; second, positive responses to sexual information may decrease motivation to engage in effortful elaboration (Reichert et al., 2001). They incorporated sexual appeal into a social marketing message (e.g., HIV, public library, skin cancer etc.) and tested the above argument. Putrevu (2008) found that sexual appeal led to better memory and superior attitudes and purchase intent among low-involvement consumers, whereas high-involvement consumers processed both sexual and non-sexual advertisements more thoroughly, and exhibited superior attitudes and purchase intent towards advertisements without sexual appeal. Similarly, female consumers with low need for cognition (NFC) favoured sexual appeal when there was a strong fit between the advertisement and brand, but not when the fit was weak. In contrast, men responded favourably to sexual appeal irrespective of the level of fit. Based on a similar logic, Sengupta and Dahl (2008) investigated the differences and similarities between men and women in their spontaneous reactions to gratuitous sexual appeal in advertising. They hypothesized and found that, under constrained processing conditions that allowed the elicitation of spontaneous, gut-level reactions, men generally exhibited a more positive attitudinal response to gratuitous sexual appeal than did women. Further, they revealed that women with more liberal attitudes to sex, per se, reacted in a manner very similar to men, i.e., they reported liking preference for a sexual advertisement than a nonsexual one. Mittal and Lassar (2000) showed that while the advertisement with high sexual content was uniformly judged to be ethically more unjust (as compared to advertisements with low sexual content), the adverse effect on attitude towards the advertisement was not observed in consumers who were more sexually liberal. The above findings suggested that the individuals' preference for sexual appeals would manifest with rational social norm inhibited by cognitive load or with a liberal attitude to sex (Putrevu, 2008; Mittal & Lassar, 2000).

More deeply, studies have suggested that people's deep-seated preferences about how sex should be used and understood contribute to how consumers respond to sexual advertisements. For instance, Dahl et al. (2009) contended that the differences between men and women's attitudes about sex, either as an end in itself (men) or as inextricably linked to relationship commitment (women), are key factors in understanding attitudes towards the gratuitous use of sex in advertising. In line with these predictions, the results showed that women's spontaneous dislike of sexual advertisements softened when the advertisement could be interpreted in terms of commitment-related resources being offered by men to women. In contrast, men's positive attitudes towards sexual advertisements were relatively unaffected by the salience of relationship commitment cues. Vohs et al. (2014) reasoned that this outlook would translate to women tolerating sexual images more when those images are linked to high worth as opposed to low worth. They showed that women's negative attitude was softened when the advertised product is expensive, because the high value represents a sign that sex is precise for women.

Additionally, significant cultural differences exist among consumers' attitudes towards sex advertisements. Khraim (2012) suggested that Muslim consumers would not react positively to sex advertisement, due to more conservative attitudes towards sex. He found that Jordanian male consumers reported negative attitudes towards advertisements depicting sexually attractive women, and that the "culture factor" (i.e., the perception that depicting Jordanian women in an indecent manner in advertising conveys a negative impression of Jordanian culture and religion) significantly affected participants' attitudes. Mofrad and Fah (2015) found that collectivist consumers disliked sex appeal marketing more than individualist consumers; they proposed that collectivists' inclination to think and feel about others may cause this effect by promoting feelings of shame in response to sexualized advertisements.

Sexual advertisements and ethical issues

Besides some studies that examined the effectiveness of sexual advertisement, Gould (1994) suggested pursuing the other deontological research stream, which addressed the morality of using sexual appeals apart from their effects. Such research should examine how different sociocultural groups and value segments of people (i.e., liberals, anti-sexual-appeal feminists, and religious and other conservatives) viewed such appeals, as well as how they came to do so. LaTour and Henthome (1994) found that regardless of the respondent's gender, the use of a strong overt sexual appeal in a print advertisement was not well received because these advertisements resulted in significantly less favourable responses in moral, philosophical and ethical dimensions. Consequently, advertisers need to rethink the use of strong overt sexual appeal, especially given the controversial issues surrounding such advertising stimuli, and their popular use to break through media clutter. Bongiorno, Bain and Haslam (2013) explored the issue of sex appeal in promoting ethical causes. They found that pro-social intentions towards ethical causes decreased after viewing sexualized advertisements, and suggested that participants' perception that sexually suggestive advertisements dehumanize women caused this response.

Discussion and conclusions

Interplay of the four streams

A deep understanding of sex has shaped the four streams of sex-drive-related research. The persuasion, sex as rewards and evolutionary psychology streams actually elaborated different impacts of sex, namely attention attraction, reward craving and motivation to show off. The attention attracting effect is simple and well-documented (Dahl et al., 2009). However, the reward craving and showing off motivation effects have been focused on and investigated by many scholars only recently, and they have established different theories on their effects (e.g., the reward circuitry view, Aharon et al., 2001; Aron et al., 2005; the evolutionary causes, Cronin, 1991; Gangestad, 1993; Miller, 1998). The reward craving effect is proposed to be based on neuroscientific studies, which have demonstrated that it was a general reward circuitry that processed various rewards, including sex, food, heroin and money (Aharon et al., 2001; Camerer, et al., 2005; Montague et al., 2006; Stark et al., 2005). The effect of showing off desirable mating qualities is elaborated by the evolutionary theory (Colarelli & Dettman, 2003; Griskevicius et al., 2009; Miller, 2009; Saad, 2004, 2006).

There are some differences between the reward craving effect and the showing off effect. First, the experimental material is different. Reward craving is often induced by sexual stimuli (e.g., sexual female images, sexual pictures, bras etc.) (Berger & Shiv, 2011; Festjens et al., 2014; Van den Bergh et al., 2008), but showing off behaviours are generally employed in dating scenarios (Griskevicius et al., 2006, 2007; Sundie et al., 2011; Hill et al., 2012). Moreover, the key difference is that sexual stimuli are often in line with short-term mating motives (Förster et al., 2009), while showing off desirable mating qualities focuses on both short-term and long-term mating motives (Griskevicius et al., 2006, 2007). Second, the effect of reward craving is more limited as compared with the effect of showing off desirable mating qualities, because the reward craving effect is only limited to sex, food, money and other hedonic rewards (Berger & Shiv, 2011). Third, there is a conflict between the general reward circuitry theory and the concept of "domain-specific rule sticking" suggested by the evolutionary theory, which assumes that the evolved algorithm used to evaluate prospective mates is distinct from the one employed to judge prospective food patches (Barrett & Kurzban, 2006; Cosmides & Tooby, 1992; Fiddick, Cosmides, & Tooby, 2000; Saad, 2013).

Finally, the ovulation cycle is adapted like a kind of internal mating motive (Gangestad & Thornhill, 1998, 2008), so the mating motive findings can also apply to the ovulation cycle research. However, besides mating motive (like approach motivation), during the ovulation phase, females have the "avoidance motivation", because there are high levels of parental investment for bearing and rearing offspring (Trivers, 1972), so females should show heightened sensitivity towards potentially costly sexual behaviours, such as sexual insult and inbreeding (Chavanne & Gallup, 1998; Lieberman, Elizabeth, Pillsworth, & Haselton, 2011). In particularly, Chavanne & Gallup (1998) investigated females' risk taking behaviour (e.g., low risk: stay at home, go to class; high risk: go to bar, walk in dimly lit area) and found females took less risk activities and more safe activities during the ovulation phase compared to the luteal phase. Interestingly, Lieberman et al. (2011) showed that the female has less phone contact with her father when she is in her fertile phase than non-fertile phase, because she is unconsciously preventing the chance of inbreeding. Future research can invest to the "avoidance motivation" shaped by ovulation and explore the effects on consumer decision making.

Gender differences in sex drive

Gender differences are an important factor in the literature on sex drive. First, sex generally has a stronger effect on males than females. For example, a sexual advertisement is favoured more by males than females (Alexander & Judd, 1978; Dahl et al., 2009; Steadman, 1969), reward craving literature rarely includes females in the studies (Wilson & Daly, 2004; Roney, 2003; Van de Bergh et al., 2008) and short mating motives can increase males' creativity rather than that of females (Griskevicius et al., 2006). The second reason for sex having a stronger effect on males is that they prefer short-term mating strategies that can maximize their reproduction opportunities by increasing the number of partners, while females often pursue long-term partners because it can offer them stable external resources that are secure for themselves and their children (Buss & Barnes, 1986; Buss & Schmitt, 1993). There is also a gender difference in showing off desirable mating qualities. For example, males show off their wealth, status and heroic quality, while females display benevolence when they have the mating motive (Griskevicius et al., 2007).

Future research

Griskevicius and Kenrick (2013), Kenrick, Saad and Griskevicius (2013) and Saad (2013) proposed the concept of evolutionary consumption, and encouraged marketing scholars to explore consumers' behaviour from the perspective of the ultimate evolutionary motivation. Besides displaying motive, another important component accompanying mating motive is mating strategy (Buss & Barnes, 1986; Buss & Schmitt, 1993). However, the mating strategy has often been considered as an interference moderating the effect of mating motive on various behaviours, but little research has discussed whether the mating strategy can independently induce any motivation or any mindset. Förster et al. (2009) provided some enlightenment by showing that low construal level was induced by short-term mating strategy, because short-term mating strategy makes people overvalue the present benefits. On the other hand, high construal level was activated by long-term mating strategy, because long-term mating strategy causes people to pursue the future benefits. Future research needs to explore if other aspects have extensive influence on consumer behaviour along with mating strategy, such as males' low commitment in short-term strategy (Buss & Schmitt, 1993).

Previous studies have identified sex ratio and economic recession as important external factors that influence individuals' mating motives and then affect their economic decision (Griskevicius et al., 2012) and dressing behaviour (Hill et al., 2011). This aspect needs more research attention to explore any other social and economic factors that could trigger mating motives and lead to related consumption behaviour.

Additionally, some research has examined cultural differences in responses to sexual advertisement (Khraim, 2012; Mofrad & Fah, 2015); however, these studies are limited to the examination of openness to sex. Deeper elaboration of cultural differences regarding sex and romantic relationships would facilitate understanding of sex drive's effect on consumer decision making. For example, Seepersada, Choib and Shin (2008) found that western people desire romantic relationships more strongly than eastern people. This implies that the mating motive may affect western and eastern consumers' decision making differently.

Acknowledgements

This research is supported by funds from National Natural Science Foundation of China (Grant No. 71102008 and 71472105) and the Beijing Youth Elite Plan (No.YETP0136).

References

Adams, D. B., Gold, A. R., & Burt, A. D. (1978). Rise in female-initiated sexual activity at ovulation and its suppression by oral contraceptives. *New England Journal of Medicine, 299*, 1145–1150.

Adler, R. P., & Firestone, C. M. (1997). *The future of advertising: New approaches to the attention economy*. Washington, DC: Aspen Institute.

Aharon, I., Etcoff, N., Ariely, D., Chabris, C. F., O'Connor, E., & Breiter, H. C. (2001). Beautiful faces have variable reward value: fMRI and behavioural evidence. *Neuron, 32*, 537–551.

Alexander, M. W., & Judd, B. (1978). Do nudes in ads enhance brand recall? *Journal of Advertising Research, 18*(1), 47–50.

Aron, A., Fisher, H., Mashek, D. J., Strong, G., Li, H., & Brown, L. L. (2005). Reward, motivation, and emotion systems associated with early-stage intense romantic love. *Journal of Neurophysiology, 94*(1), 327–337.

Assael, H., Kofron, J. H., & Burgi, W. (1967). Advertising performance as a function of print ad characteristics. *Journal of Advertising Research*, 7(2), 20–26.

Baker, S. (1961). *Visual persuasion*. New York, NY: McGraw-Hill.

Balshine-Earn, S. (1996). Reproductive rates, operational sex ratios and mate choice in St. Peter's fish. *Behavioural Ecology and Sociobiology, 39*, 107–116.

Barber, N. (2003). The sex ratio and female marital opportunity as historical predictors of violent crime in England, Scotland, and the United States. *Cross-Cultural Research, 37*, 373–392.

Barrett, H. C., & Kurzban, R. (2006). Modularity in cognition: Framing the debate. *Psychological Review, 113*, 628–647.

Beall, A. T., & Tracy, J. L. (2013). Women are more likely to wear red or pink at peak fertility. *Psychological Science, 24*(9), 1837–1841.

Belk, R. W., Bahn, K. D., & Mayer, R. N. (1982). Developmental recognition of consumption symbolism, *Journal of Consumer Research, 9*, 4–17.

Bellis, M. A., & Baker, R. R. (1990). Do females promote sperm competition? *Animal Behaviour, 40*, 997–999.

Belsky, J., Schlomer, G. L., & Ellis, B. J. (2012). Beyond cumulative risk: Distinguishing harshness and unpredictability as determinants of parenting and early life history strategy. *Developmental Psychology, 48*(3), 662–673.

Benshoof, L., & Thornhill, R. (1979). The evolution of monogamy and concealed ovulation in humans. *Journal of Social and Biological Structures, 2*, 95–106.

Berger, J., & Shiv, B. (2011). Food, sex and the hunger for distinction. *Journal of Consumer Psychology, 21*, 464–472.

Berridge, K. C., & Robinson, T. B. (1998). What is the role of dopamine in reward: Hedonic impact, reward learning, or incentive salience? *Brain Research Reviews, 28*(3), 309–369.

Birkhead, T. R., & Møller, A. P. (1995). Extra-pair copulation and extra-pair paternity in birds. *Animal Behaviours, 49*, 843–848.

Bongiorno, R., Bain, P. G., & Haslam, N. (2013). When sex doesn't sell: Using sexualized images of women reduces support for ethical campaigns. *PLoS ONE, 8*(12), e8311.

Burley, N. (1979). The evolution of concealed ovulation. *American Nature, 114*, 835–858.

Buss, D. M. (1988). From vigilance to violence: Tactics of mate retention in American undergraduates. *Ethnology and Sociobiology, 9*(5), 291–317.

Buss, D. M., & Barnes, M. (1986). Preferences in human mate selection. *Journal of Personality and Social Psychology, 50*, 559–570.

Buss, D. M., & Schmitt, D. P. (1993). Sexual strategies theory: An evolutionary perspective on human mating. *Psychological Review, 100*, 204–232.

Byrne, R. (1995). *The thinking ape: Evolutionary origins of intelligence*. Oxford, UK: Oxford University Press.

Camerer, C., Loewenstein, G., & Prelec, D. (2005). Neuroeconomics: How neuroscience can inform economics. *Journal of Economic Literature, 43*, 1, 9–64.

Cantú, S. M., Simpson, J. A., Griskevicius, V., Weisberg, Y. J., Durante, K. M., & Beal, D. J. (2014). Fertile and selectively flirty: Women's behaviour toward men changes across the ovulatory cycle. *Psychological Science, 25*, 431–438.

Carlson, N. R. (2001). *Physiology of behaviour* (7th ed.). Boston, MA: Allyn and Bacon.

Chavanne, T. J., & Gallup, G. G. (1998). Variation in risk taking behaviour among female college students as a function of the menstrual cycle. *Evolution and Human Behaviour, 19*, 27–32.

Cohen, D., Nisbett, R. E., Bowdle, B. F., & Schwarz, N. (1996). Insult, aggression, and the southern culture of honor: An "experimental ethnography". *Journal of Personality and Social Psychology, 70*(5), 945–960.

Colarelli, S. M., & Dettman, J. R. (2003). Intuitive evolutionary perspectives in marketing practices. *Psychology and Marketing, 20*, 837–865.

Cosmides, L., & Tooby, J. (1992). Cognitive adaptations for social exchange. In J. H. Barkow, L. Cosmides & J. Tooby (Eds.), *The adapted mind: Evolutionary psychology and the generation of culture* (pp. 163–228). New York, NY: Oxford University Press.

Cronin, H. (1991). *The ant and the peacock*. Cambridge: Cambridge University Press.

Dahl, D. W., Sengupta, J., & Vohs, K. D. (2009). Sex in advertising: Gender differences and the role of relationship commitment. *Journal of Consumer Research, 36*, 215–231.

Darwin, C. (1871). *The descent of man and selection in relation to sex*. London: Murray.

Davenport, T. H., & Beek, J. C. (2001). *The attention economy: Understanding the currency of business*. Boston, MA: Harvard Business School Press.

Durante, K. M., & Arsena, A. R. (2015). Playing the field: The effect of fertility on women's desire for variety. *Journal of Consumer Research, 41*, 1372–1391.

Durante, K. M., Griskevicius, V., Cantú, S. M., & Simpson, J. A. (2014). Money, status, and the ovulatory cycle. *Journal of Marketing Research, 51*(1), 27–39.

Durante, K. M., Griskevicius, V., Hill, S. E., Perilloux, C., & Li, N. P. (2011). Ovulation, competition, and product choice: Hormonal influences on consumer behaviour. *Journal of Consumer Research, 37*, 921–934.

Durante, K. M., Griskevicius, V., Simpson, J. A., Cantú, S. M., & Li, N. P. (2012). Ovulation leads women to perceive sexy cads as good dads. *Journal of Personality and Social Psychology, 103*, 292–305.

Durante, K. M., Rae, A., & Griskevicius, V. (2013). The fluctuating female vote: Politics, religion, and the ovulatory cycle. *Psychological Science, 24*(6), 1007–1016.

Elliot, A. J., & Pazda, A. D. (2012). Dressed for sex: Red as a female sexual signal in humans. *PLoS ONE, 7*(4), e34607.

Ellis, B. J., Figueredo, A. J., Brumbach, B. H., & Schlomer, G. L. (2009). Fundamental dimensions of environmental risk: The impact of harsh versus unpredictable environments on the evolution and development of life history strategies. *Human Nature, 20*, 204–268.

Faraji-Rad, A., Moeini-Jazani, M., & Warlop, L. (2013). Women seek more variety in rewards when closer to ovulation. *Journal of Consumer Psychology, 23*(4), 503–508.

Festjens, A., Bruyneel, S., & Dewitte, S. (2014). What a feeling! Touching sexually laden stimuli makes women seek rewards. *Journal of Consumer Psychology, 24*(3), 387–393.

Fiddick, L., Cosmides, L., & Tooby, J. (2000). No interpretation without representation: The role of domain-specific representations and inferences in the Wason selection task. *Cognition, 77*, 1–79.

Förster, J., Epstude, K., & Özelsel, A. (2009). Why love has wings and sex has not: How reminders of love and sex influence creative and analytic. *Personality and Social Psychology, 35*(11), 1479–1491.

Gal, D. (2012). A mouth-watering prospect: Salivation to material reward. *Journal of Consumer Research, 38*(6), 1022–1030.

Gangestad, S. W. (1993). Sexual selection and physical attractiveness: Implications for mating dynamics. *Human Nature, 4*, 205–235.

Gangestad, S. W., & Thornhill, R. (1998). Menstrual cycle variation in women's preferences for the scent of symmetrical men. *Proceedings of the Royal Society of London B, 265*, 927–933.

Gangestad, S. W., & Thornhill, R. (2008). Human oestrus. *Proceedings of the Royal of Society B*, 275, 991–1000.

Gangestad, S. W., Thornhill, R., & Garver-Apgar, C. E. (2005). Women's sexual interests across the ovulatory cycle depend on primary partner developmental instability. *Proceedings of the Royal of Society B, 272*, 2023–2027.

Gibson, K. R., & Ingold, T. (1993). *Tools, language, and cognition in human evolution*. Cambridge, UK: Cambridge University Press.

Gould, S. J. (1994). Sexuality and ethics in advertising: A research agenda and policy guideline perspective. *Journal of Advertising, 23*(3), 73–80.
Greenfield, A. B. (2005). *A perfect red: Empire, espionage, and the quest for the color of desire*. New York, NY: HarperCollins.
Griskevicius, V., Cialdini, R. B., & Kenrick, D. T. (2006). Peacocks, Picasso, and parental investment: The effects of romantic motives on creativity. *Journal of Personality and Social Psychology, 91*, 63–76.
Griskevicius, V., & Kenrick, D. T. (2013). Fundamental motives: How evolutionary needs influence consumer behaviour. *Journal of Consumer Psychology, 23*(3), 372–386.
Griskevicius, V., Tybur, J. M., Ackerman, J. M., Delton, A. W., & Robertson, T. E. (2012). The financial consequences of too many men: Sex ratio effects on saving, borrowing, and spending. *Journal of Personality and Social Psychology, 102*(1), 69–80.
Griskevicius, V., Tybur, J. M., Gangestad, S. W., Perea, E. F., Shapiro, J. R., & Kenrick, D. T. (2009). Aggress to impress: Hostility as an evolved context-dependent strategy. *Journal of Personality and Social Psychology, 96*, 980–994.
Griskevicius, V., Tybur, J. M., Sundie, J. M., Cialdini, R. B., Miller, G. F., & Kenrick, D. T. (2007). Blatant benevolence and conspicuous consumption: When romantic motives elicit strategic costly signals. *Journal of Personality and Social Psychology, 93*, 85–102.
Haselton, M., & Gangestad, S. W. (2006). Conditional expression of women's desires and men's mate guarding across the ovulatory cycle. *Hormones and Behaviour, 49*, 509–518.
Haselton, M. G., Mortezaie, M., Pillsworth, E. G., Bleske-Rechek, A., & Frederick, D. A. (2007). Ovulatory shifts in human female ornamentation: Near ovulation, women dress to impress. *Hormones and Behaviour, 51*, 40–45.
Hill, S. E., Rodeheffer, C. D., Griskevicius, V., Durante, K., & White, A. E. (2012). Boosting beauty in an economic decline: Mating, spending, and the lipstick effect. *Journal of Personality and Social Psychology, 103*(2), 275–287.
Huang, J. Y., & Bargh, J. A. (2008). Peak of desire: Activating the mating goal changes life-stage preferences across living kinds. *Psychological Science, 19*, 573–579.
Hudson, V., & Den Boer, A. (2002). A surplus of men, a deficit of peace: Security and sex ratios in Asia's largest states. *International Security, 26*, 5–38.
Karremans, J. C., Verwijmeren, T., Pronk, T. M., & Reitsma, M. (2009). Interacting with women can impair men's cognitive functioning. *Journal of Experimental Social Psychology, 45*, 1041–1044.
Kenrick, D. T., Saad, G., & Griskevicius, V. (2013). Evolutionary consumer psychology: Ask not what you can do for biology, but... *Journal of Consumer Psychology, 23*(3), 404–409.
Khraim, H. S. (2012). Jordanian male consumers' attitude towards using women in advertisement. *International Journal of Business and Social Science, 3*(2), 182–192.
Kim, B. K., & Zauberman, G. (2013). Can Victoria's secret change the future? A subjective time perception account of sexual cue effects on impatience. *Journal of Experimental Psychology: General, 142*(2), 328–335.
Kingdon, J. (1993). *Self-made man and his undoing*. New York, NY: Simon & Schuster.
Kokko, H. (2001). Fisherian and "good genes" benefits of mate choice: How (not) to distinguish between them. *Ecology Letters, 4*, 322–326.
Kurzban, R., Dukes, A., & Weeden, J. (2010). Sex, drugs, and moral goals: Reproductive strategies and views about recreational drugs. *Proceedings of the Royal Society B: Biological Sciences, 277*, 3501–3508.
LaTour, M. S. (1990). Female nudity in print advertising: An analysis of gender differences in arousal and ad response. *Psychology and Marketing*, 7(1), 65–81.
LaTour, M. S., & Henthome, T. L. (1994). Ethical judgments of sexual appeals in print advertising. *Journal of Advertising, 23*(3), 81–90.
Lens, I., Driesmans, K., Pandelaere, M., & Janssens, K. (2012). Would male conspicuous consumption capture the female eye? Menstrual cycle effects on women's attention to status products. *Journal of Experimental Social Psychology, 48*, 346–349.
Li, N. P., Bailey, J. M., Kenrick, D. T., & Linsenmeier, J. A. (2002). The necessities and luxuries of mate preferences: Testing the trade-offs. *Journal of Personality and Social Psychology, 82*, 947–955.
Li, N. P., & Kenrick, D. T. (2006). Sex similarities and differences in preferences for short-term mates: What, whether, and why. *Journal of Personality and Social Psychology, 90*, 468–489.
Li, Y. J., Kenrick, T. D., Griskevicius, V., & Neuberg, S. L. (2012). Economic decision biases and fundamental motivations: How mating and self-protection alter loss aversion. *Journal of Personality and Social Psychology, 102*, 550–561.

Lieberman, D., Pillsworth, E. G., & Haselton, M. G. (2011). Kin affiliation across the ovulatory cycle: Females avoid fathers when fertile. *Psychological Science, 22*(1), 13–18.

Maner, J. K., DeWall, C. N., & Gailliot, M. T. (2008). Selective attention to signs of success: Social dominance and early stage interpersonal perception. *Personality and Social Psychology Bulletin, 34*, 488–501.

Manning, J. T., Bundred, P. E., Newton, D. J., & Flanagan, B. F. (2003). The 2nd to 4th digit ratio and variation in the androgen receptor gene. *Evolution of Human Behaviour, 24*, 399–405.

Manning, J. T., Scutt, D., Wilson, J., & Lewis-Jones, D. I. (1998). The ratio of 2nd to 4th digit length: A predictor of sperm numbers and concentrations of testosterone, luteinizing hormone and oestrogen. *Human Reproduction, 13*, 3000–3004.

McCarthy, B. (1994). Warrior values: A socio-historical survey. In J. Archer (Ed.), *Male violence* (pp. 105–120). New York, NY: Routledge.

Mehta, R., & Zhu, R. (2009). Blue or red? Exploring the effect of color on cognitive task performances. *Science, 323*(5918), 1226–1229.

Miller, E. M. (1999). The pheromone androstenol: Evolutionary considerations. *Mankind Quarterly, 39*, 455–466.

Miller, G. F. (1998). How mate choice shaped human nature: A review of sexual selection and human evolution. In C. Crawford & D. Krebs (Eds.), *Handbook of evolutionary psychology: Ideas, issues, and applications* (pp. 87–130). Lawrence Erlbaum.

Miller, G. (2009). *Spent: Sex, evolution, and consumer behaviour*. New York, NY: Viking Adult.

Miller, G. F. (2000). *The Mating Mind*. London: Heinemann.

Miller, G., Tybur, J. M., & Jordan, B. D. (2007). Ovulatory cycle effects on tip earnings by lap dancers: Economic evidence or human estrus? *Evolution and Human Behaviour, 28*, 375–381.

Mittal, B., & Lassar, W. M. (2000). Sexual liberalism as a determinant of consumer response to sex in advertising. *Journal of Business and Psychology, 15*(1), 111–127.

Mofrad, H. E., & Fah, B. C. Y. (2015). Any correlation between sex appeal marketing with individual's temperaments and cultural orientations? *European Academic Research, 2*(11), 14257–14262.

Monga, A. B., & Gürhan-Canli, Z. (2012). The influence of mating mind-sets on brand extension evaluation. *Journal of Marketing Research, 49*, 581–593.

Monga, A. B., & John, D. R. (2007). Cultural differences in brand extension evaluation: The influence of analytic versus holistic thinking. *Journal of Consumer Research, 33*(4), 529–536.

Montague, P. R., King-Casas, B., & Cohen, J. D. (2006). Imaging valuation models in human choice. *Annual Review of Neuroscience, 29*, 417–448.

Morrison, B. J., & Sherman, R. C. (1972). Who responds to sex in advertising? *Journal of Advertising Research, 12*, 15–19.

Nelson, R. J. (2005). *An introduction to behavioural endocrinology* (3rd ed.). Sunderland, MA: Sinauer.

Penton-Voak, I. S., & Perrett, D. I. (2000). Female preference for male faces changes cyclically: Further evidence. *Evolution and Human Behaviour, 21*, 39–48.

Penton-Voak, I. S., Perrett, D. I., Castles, D. L., Kobayashi, T., Burt, D. M., Murray, L. K., et al. (1999). Menstrual cycle alters face preference. *Nature, 399*, 741–742.

Peterson, R. A., & Kerin, R. A. (1977). The female role in advertisements: Some experimental evidence. *Journal of M*arketing, *41*(4), 59–63.

Poffenberger, A. T. (1925). *Psychology in advertising*. Chicago, IL: A.W. Shaw Company.

Putrevu, S. (2008). Consumer response toward sexual and nonsexual appeals: The influence of involvement, NFC and gender. *Journal of Advertising, 37*, 57–69.

Puts, D. A. (2005). Mating context and menstrual phase affect women's preferences for male voice pitch. *Evolutionary of Human Behaviour, 26*, 388–397.

Reichert, T., Heckler, S. E., & Jackson, S. (2001). The effects of sexual social marketing appeals on cognitive processing and persuasion. *Journal of Advertising, 30*(1), 13–27.

Reidenbach, R. E., & McCleary, K. W. (1983). Advertising and male nudity: An experimental investigation. *Journal of the Academy of Marketing Science, 11*(4), 444–454.

Richmond, D., & Hartman, T. P. (1982). Sex appeal in advertising. *Journal of Advertising Research, 22*, 53–61.

Röder, S., Brewer, G., & Fink, B. (2009). Menstrual cycle shifts in women's self-perception and motivation: A daily report method. *Personality and Individual Differences, 47*, 616–619.

Roney, J. R. (2003). Effects of visual exposure to the opposite sex: Cognitive aspects of mate attraction in human males. *Personality and Social Psychology Bulletin, 29*(3), 393–404.

Saad, G. (2004). Applying evolutionary psychology in understanding the representation of women in advertisements. *Psychology and Marketing, 21*, 593–612.

Saad, G. (2006). Applying evolutionary psychology in understanding the Darwinian roots of consumption phenomena. *Managerial and Decision Economics, 27*, 189–201.

Saad, G. (2007). *The evolutionary bases of consumption*. Mahwah, NJ: Erlbaum.

Saad, G. (2013). Evolutionary consumption. *Journal of Consumer Psychology, 23*, 351–371.

Saad, G., & Gill, T. (2003). An evolutionary psychology perspective on gift giving among young adults. *Psychology and Marketing, 20*, 765–784.

Saad, G., & Peng, A. (2006). Applying Darwinian principles in designing effective intervention strategies: The case of sun tanning. *Psychology and Marketing, 23*, 617–638.

Saad, G., & Stenstrom, E. (2012). Calories, beauty, and ovulation: The effects of the menstrual cycle on food and appearance-related consumption. *Journal of Consumer Psychology, 22*, 102–113.

Schmitt, D. P. (2005). Is short-term mating caused by insecure romantic attachment? A test of competing evolutionary theories. *Personality and Social Psychology Bulletin, 31*(6), 747–768.

Schultz, W. (2002). Getting formal with dopamine and reward. *Neuron, 36*(2), 241–263.

Schwarz, S., & Hassebrauck, M. (2008). Self-perceived and observed variations in women's attractiveness throughout the menstrual cycle: A diary study. *Evolution and Human Behaviour, 29*, 282–288.

Seepersad, S., Choi, M., & Shin, N. (2008). How does culture influence the degree of romantic loneliness and closeness? *Journal of Psychology, 142*(2), 209–216.

Sengupta, J., & Dahl, D. W. (2008). Gender-related reactions to gratuitous sex appeals in advertising. *Journal of Consumer Psychology, 18*, 62–78.

Severn, J., Belch, G. E., & Belch, M. A. (1990). The effects of sexual and nonsexual advertising appeals and information level on cognitive processing and communication effectiveness. *Journal of Advertising, 19*(1), 14–22.

Simpson, P. M., Horton, S., & Brown, G. (1996). Male nudity in advertisements: A modified replication and extension of gender and product effects. *Journal of the Academy of Marketing Science, 24*(3), 257–262.

Singh, S. N., Lessig, V. P., & Kim, D. (2000). Does your ad have too many pictures? *Journal of Advertising Research, 40*, 11–27.

Stark, R., Schienle, A., Girod, C., Walter, B., Kirsch, P., Blecker, C., et al. (2005). Erotic and disgust-inducing pictures-differences in the hemodynamic responses of the brain. *Biological Psychology, 70*, 19–29.

Steadman, M. (1969). How sexy illustrations affect brand recall. *Journal of Advertising, 9*(1), 15–19.

Sundie, J. M., Kenrick, D. T., Griskevicius, V., Tybur, J., Vohs, K., & Beal, D. J. (2011). Peacocks, Porsches, and Thorsten Veblen: Conspicuous consumption as a sexual signaling system. *Journal of Personality and Social Psychology, 100*, 664–680.

Thornhill, R., & Gangestad, S. W. (2008). *The evolutionary biology of human female sexuality*. New York, NY: Oxford University Press.

Trivers, R. L. (1972). *Parental investment and sexual selection*. In B. Campbell (Ed.), *Sexual selection and the descent of man, 1871–1971* (pp. 136–179). Chicago, IL: Aldine.

Van den Bergh, B., & Dewitte, S. (2006). Digit ratio (2D:4D) moderates the impact of sexual cues on men's decisions in ultimatum games. *Proceedings of the Royal Society, 273*, 2091–2095.

Van den Bergh, B., Dewitte, S., & Warlop, L. (2008). Bikinis instigate generalized impatience in intertemporal Choice. *Journal of Consumer Research, 35*(1), 85–97.

Veblen, T. (1899). *The theory of the leisure class*. New York, NY: Macmillan.

Vohs, K. D., Sengupta, J., & Dahl, D. W. (2014). The price had better be right: Women's reactions to sexual stimuli vary with market factors. *Psychological Science, 25*(1), 278–283.

Wang, Y., & Griskevicius, V. (2014). Conspicuous consumption, relationships, and rivals: Women's luxury products as signals to other women. *Journal of Consumer Research, 40*, 834–854.

Weeden, J., Cohen, A. B., & Kenrick, D. T. (2008). Religious participation and reproductive strategies. *Evolution and Human Behaviour, 29*, 327–334.

Wilcox, A. J., Dunson, D, & Baird, D. D. (2000). The timing of the "fertile window" in the menstrual cycle: Day-specific estimates from a prospective study. *British Medical Journal, 32*, 1259–1262.

Wilson, M., & Daly, M. (1985). Competitiveness, risk-taking, and violence: The young male syndrome. *Ethology and Sociobiology, 6*, 59–73.

Wilson, M., & Daly, M. (2004). Do pretty women inspire men to discount the future? *Proceedings of the Royal Society London B, 271*(4, supplement), S177–S179.

26

Ageing and consumer behaviour

Challenges and opportunities

Stephanie M. Carpenter and Carolyn Yoon

The population of older consumers in developed countries is ever growing. This shift in demographic makeup can be seen, for example, in the United States (Kalache, Barreto, & Keller, 2005) and underscores the importance of understanding the effects of ageing on consumer behaviour. The purpose of this chapter is to describe extant research on older adults' consumer behaviour and to explore promising directions for future research.

Although research on consumer behaviour across the adult lifespan is limited, prior research has investigated the effects that cognitive ageing, decision processing, life events, environmental context and affect have on consumer choices and behaviours. The sections in this chapter outline how these different factors influence the consumer behaviour of older adults. We review evidence of age-related changes in a variety of cognitive processes and behaviours that are important to our understanding of consumer behaviour across the adult lifespan.

The first section discusses how cognitive ageing influences memory and information search processes, and the implications this has for consumer behaviour. We follow this with a discussion of how human decision making changes across the adult lifespan, from decision competence to strategy use. Also reviewed is evidence suggesting that important domains within the realm of health and financial decision making are affected as consumers' age. Our next section describes how cohort effects and critical life events importantly influence older consumer behaviour. Other environmental effects on ageing consumers, including time pressure, distraction, human factors and culture are also discussed. We then move to a review of extant literature on how affective processing changes across the adult lifespan, and how a tendency to self-report greater satisfaction with products, as well as greater product experience and expertise, has the potential to buffer some of the challenges faced by consumers. The time of day in which an older adult is asked to perform a task or decision and the use of mental imagery are reviewed as other conditions that may also buffer consumers against age-related decrements.

Cognitive ageing and consumer behaviour

Memory processes

Cognitive declines associated with normal ageing have been well documented within the literature (Mather, 2006; Park et al., 2002). These declines can be seen across a variety of cognitive processes, including memory and general executive functioning. Tasks that rely primarily on working memory processes show the greatest age-related performance declines (Moscovitch & Winocur, 1995; see Yoon, Cole, & Lee, 2009, for a review), suggesting that working memory is more sensitive to cognitive decline than long-term memory.

Diminished working memory may be especially problematic when older adults need to make decisions among a number of alternatives (Roedder & Cole, 1986; Cole & Houston, 1987). This is because information about each of the alternatives needs to be held in mind, and declines in working memory mean that less information can be effectively held in mind during the decision process. Working memory is but one in a larger group of general executive functioning processes, which include the ability to shift between task goals, update the contents of working memory and inhibit irrelevant information (Roedder & Cole, 1986; Hasher, Lustig, & Zacks, 2007). Thus, age-related impairments on these measures of general executive functioning have been well documented, and navigating noisy or busy environments and complex settings can be particularly difficult for older consumers (Hedden & Yoon, 2006; West, 1996).

Explicit memory processes (i.e., memory for information that people consciously intend to recollect, such as information recall) are also more negatively affected by cognitive declines than are implicit (i.e., non-conscious) memory processes (Hess, 2005; Yoon et al., 2009). More specifically, the declines in explicit memory observed across the lifespan (Fleischmann et al., 2004) include worse memory for source (e.g., for physical setting, specific context, speaker) (McIntyre & Craik, 1987; Spencer & Raz, 1995) and greater difficulty with locating relevant information in complex environments (Cole & Gaeth, 1990).

Implicit memory does not rely on conscious processing or the reconstruction of recent memories, but rather on non-conscious processes that improve behaviour like reaction times towards non-consciously activated information (Fleischmann et al., 2004). Fleischmann and colleagues (2004) conducted both a meta-analysis and longitudinal research by collecting multiple measures of explicit and implicit memory from older adults across four annual data-collection waves. Findings from both procedures revealed that while explicit memory declined significantly, implicit memory generated through priming remained mostly intact. This suggests that implicit memory and priming effects are fairly stable across the lifespan, whereas explicit memory shows significant declines from young to older adulthood. The authors thus posit the view that implicit and explicit types of memory processes are dissociable across the lifespan.

All types of explicit memory, however, may not be as strongly affected by cognitive ageing. In particular, explicit memory decrements observed across the adult lifespan are particularly linked to episodic memory, or memory for specific experiences or events (Fleischman et al., 2004). Long-term semantic memory, which is associated with general knowledge rather than episodic events, has been found to be relatively resistant to the effects of ageing (Yoon et al., 2009).

Information search and decision processes

Information search tends to be cognitively taxing for older adults. When making consumption decisions, older adults exhibit a "shrinkage effect" in their information search, whereby they spend less time searching, construct smaller consideration sets and consider fewer options than younger adults (Lambert-Pandraud et al., 2005; Lambert-Pandraud et al., 2010). These smaller consideration sets are associated with a tendency for older adults to engage in repeat purchase behaviour, and to also exhibit a preference for purchasing long-established brands (Lambert-Pandraud et al., 2005). This affinity for long-established brands, as opposed to new brands, is due to such factors as older adults' experience with brands, attachment to brands, nostalgia, habit and an aversion to change (Lambert-Pandraud et al., 2010).

Research on information search has also shown that when given specific instructions about what nutritional information to seek out, older adults are not as intensely engaged as younger adults, and are somewhat less likely to select the product that is best on the given informational criteria (Cole & Balasubramanian, 1993). However, when able to write down the nutritional information, age differences between younger and older adults are eliminated. This indicates that holding complicated information in memory during information search tasks may present a significant challenge to individuals as they age; being able to write down this information allows older adults to effectively process the necessary information during complex search tasks.

Further, the research on how older adults navigate complicated decision-making problems is mixed. Some research shows that when comparing relatively complex options involving many kinds of information, such as decisions related to apartments, health-care plans or cars, older adults are more feature-oriented, while younger adults are more option-oriented (Mather et al., 2005). In this case, older adults reduce options and the cognitive effort involved in a decision, which may translate into a greater focus on the experiential benefits offered by the features. Other research, however, has not shown this effect consistently, and indicates that the motivation of the older adult changes the way in which a decision is made (cf. Hess, Queen, & Ennis, 2013). For example, older adults with a high motivation to search for information will not show differences in their search behaviour compared to younger adults. This is important because it indicates that information search processes may be preserved when the choice is within a domain that is especially relevant or important to the older consumer. Additional research is needed to explore how information search varies with age across product domains and with different levels of consumer involvement or motivation.

Decision processing across the consumer lifespan

Decision competence

Research suggests that age-related declines in one's decision competency (i.e., decision skills correlated with good life-decision outcomes) is closely tied to age-related declines in working memory and episodic memory (Del Missier et al., 2013), but not all measures of decision competency decline into older adulthood. Working memory is implicated in more cognitively demanding decision tasks including resistance to framing, applying decision rules, and exhibiting under/overconfidence, whereas episodic memory appears to be involved in performing experience-based tasks. Performance decrements on a variety of tasks are thus mediated by declines in working memory and episodic memory. Semantic memory capability, on the other hand, has been found to be positively associated with performance on knowledge-based decision tasks including consistency in risk perception and resistance to sunk costs (Del Missier et al., 2013).

Similarly, performance on the decision competency measures of resistance to framing and applying decision rules have been shown to decrease with age due to declines in fluid intelligence, whereas risk perceptions and recognizing age-group social norms remain consistent across the adult lifespan (Bruine de Bruin, Parker, & Fischhoff, 2012). Under/overconfidence and resistance to sunk costs, however, have in some cases actually shown improvements across older adulthood (Bruine de Bruin et al., 2012). These findings suggest that performance on decision tasks relying on fluid intelligence, rather than crystallized intelligence, may be more susceptible to decrements.

Other work by Li and colleagues posits a "complementary capabilities" hypothesis, whereby improvements in crystallized intelligence among older adults provide an alternate, complementary pathway to good decision making in the face of declining fluid intelligence (Li, Baldassi, Johnson, & Weber, 2012). In particular, older adults' crystallized intelligence leads to similar or better performance than younger adults on temporal discounting, financial literacy and debt literacy tasks. Loss aversion also remains similar across the lifespan, although it was not related to crystallized intelligence (Li et al., 2012). These findings are of exceptional importance, as financial literacy (as well as health literacy) is associated with the use of diverse resources, including executive functioning, episodic memory and education (Boyle, et al., 2012), and with better decision making (James, Boyle, Bennett, & Bennett, 2012) among older adults. The described evidence, taken together, suggests that while some age-related decrements do exist in decision making, many important skills may be preserved across the adult lifespan as a result of improvements in experience-based memory and intelligence.

Systematic and heuristic decision-making strategies

A more complete understanding of consumer decision making requires an attention towards the use of decision strategies that vary from thoughtful and systematic to more biased and heuristic (Tversky & Kahneman, 1974). Older adults have been shown to use heuristic or biased strategies in their decision making to a greater extent than younger adults (Kim, Goldstein, Hasher, & Zacks, 2005). Framing effects are a phenomenon whereby the language used to describe a decision problem importantly influences what choice is made (Kim et al., 2005). Although older adults spontaneously rely on heuristic processing and are thus susceptible to framing effects, the susceptibility is reduced when they are prompted to provide a justification prior to making a choice. This suggests that older adults use heuristic processing as a way to easily manage the decision process without expending too many cognitive resources.

Satisficing is a heuristic, non-compensatory processing strategy that aims at adequate, rather than maximal, decision making (Schwartz et al., 2002). Research has shown that older adults tend to examine option information only until they determine that the amount of acquired information is sufficient and acceptable, relative to younger adults who tend to use more systematic, maximizing strategies when making decisions (Chen & Sun, 2003; Yoon et al., 2010; Peters, 2010). Satisficing is thus often construed as a decision strategy that older adults adopt in order to decrease the amount of effort required during potentially cognitively taxing forms of decision making, such as those inherent in making choices in busy or complex consumer environments.

Heuristic processing can have both positive and negative consequences for consumer decision making in older adulthood. For example, a greater reliance on cognitive biases in older age allows for quick and effective decisions (Yates & Patalano, 1999) when making choices in simple or mundane domains (e.g., shopping for groceries or household items). People are, however, often faced with much more consequential choices. Older consumers must make important choices about health care, retirement and financial planning, all of which typically involve a large amount of complicated information that the consumer must navigate in order to arrive at an effective decision. It is in these more complicated domains that is potentially problematic the increased use of cognitive biases and heuristic processing. Identifying decision domains in which older adults use heuristic vs. systematic processing strategies will provide a better understanding of when heuristic strategies are actually beneficial to older adults' decision making, and when they are detrimental. Researchers can then begin to develop decision aids and other strategies, such as choice justification, to help buffer decision making in those contexts where older adults are likely to face poor decision outcomes.

Financial and health decisions

Two complicated consumer domains that older adults routinely face are that of financial and health decision making. For example, research has begun to examine how one's experience in the financial domain interacts with ageing to influence older adults' investment decisions (Korniotis & Kumar, 2009). Older and more experienced financial investors have been found to use experience-based "rule of thumb" strategies that can seemingly overcome the negative effects of ageing. However, the more general population of older adults who are not especially experienced in the financial domain are generally less able to apply their knowledge and experience when faced with actual investment decisions. Thus, ageing has been found to have negative effects that are not offset by experience for these groups of older adults.

Predictable declines also occur in the domain of older adults' borrowing and credit card usage decisions. Agarwal and colleagues (2009; 2010) have shown that "financial sophistication" (i.e., the tendency to borrow at lower interest rates and pay fewer fees), increases across the lifespan from younger to middle-aged adulthood, and peaks at approximately age 53. Beyond this age, however, one's financial sophistication has been shown to decline.

When useful supplementary financial information (e.g., presented in a simple format, provision of expected value information) is given to older adults during the decision process, their risky financial decisions have been found to improve, and may even to reach performance levels similar to that of younger adults (Samanez-Larkin et al., 2011). Although experience can bolster some decisions in the financial realm, there appears to be significant negative influences of age on general financial decision ability. Providing useful information during the decision-making process, however, can improve performance, again suggesting that financial decision aids might be especially helpful for older adults.

Within the domain of health decision making, older adults are often faced with an overwhelming amount of information, multiple options, risk and uncertainty, changing technologies and innovations, and outcomes that can strongly influence their well-being. While decision making research might suggest that older adult consumers are prone to making poor decisions because of the cognitive and financial factors that can hinder their ability to navigate complex choices and search for information, existing literature casts a more positive outlook on their medical decision making. For example, older consumers report wanting an active, agentic role in their medical decisions, and desire access to greater amounts of information when making complex decisions (Chang et al., 2008). Older consumers have also been shown to rely more than younger adults on both marketer-supplied and informal information sources (Boscarino, 1982; Lumpkin and Festervand, 1988). Future research should seek to understand in what medical contexts older adults actually seek out and prefer more information, and when they do not. Hess, Queen, and Ennis (2013) suggested that consumer motivation strongly influences information search, and the medical domain is likely to be one in which the older consumer is highly motivated.

In fact, older consumers who have greater expertise in the medical domain, or whose motivational goals are activated, are more likely to engage in information search and exhibit preserved memory for information that is indistinguishable from that of younger adults (Löckenhoff & Carstensen, 2007). This again suggests the importance of experience and motivational goals in maintaining performance across the consumer lifespan.

Cohort effects and life events

One important consideration when studying the consumer behaviour of older adults is birth cohort effects. These cohort effects reflect cultural and socio-demographic shifts that occur across time and influence the way different cohorts of people perceive and interact with their environments. A recent examination of cohort effects on consumer behaviour used data from the Health and Retirement Study (HRS, 2012) to document a number of interesting cohort differences in adults aged 50 and over (Webster et al., 2014). The HRS is a longitudinal panel study of more than 26,000 nationally representative adults, aged 50 and older, in the United States, who are interviewed every two years. Using this database, Webster and colleagues found that as compared to younger birth cohorts, older cohorts generally consume less. Among the products they do consume, however, older cohorts spend more money than younger adults on donations and gifts. They spend less money on food, transportation, vacations and durable goods, and a similar amount of money on health-care related expenses. The latter finding, that both younger and older cohorts spend similar amounts on health-care expenses, is counterintuitive because one might think that as people grow older their health will decline and they will need to spend more money on health-care expenses. Webster et al. (2014) provide the plausible explanation that the lack of observed differences might actually reflect a cohort difference in people's health, such that younger cohorts in the U.S. may be relatively unhealthy compared to older cohorts. It is also possible that younger adults have a lower threshold for what conditions they deem necessary to seek medical care. Notwithstanding these findings based on the HRS, older adults tend to experience more chronic illness than any other age group, and thus they need to remember a great deal of complex health information such as diet and medication guidelines (Brown & Park, 2003).

It is also interesting that older adults spend relatively more money on donations and gifts, expenses one might consider to be "other-focused", and less money on expenses that may be considered more "self-focused" (e.g., transportation, food, vacations, durable goods). While the causes of these effects are likely multi-determined, one possibility is that the other-focused nature of older adults' spending may be partly explained by increases in the importance of social connections with ageing that has been documented (Charles & Carstensen, 2009). Another possibility is that older adults are more likely to perceive that they already have the products they need, and thus want to provide gifts and donations to others who may be more in need. Yet another possibility is that younger cohorts place more emphasis on self-focused endeavours in general than older cohorts due to the socio-cultural factors that have shaped them. These and other potential explanations should be explored in future investigations on this topic.

Research has also sought to understand how critical events experienced over the lifespan are associated with changes in consumer behaviour. Mathur, Moschis and Lee (2003) suggest that when consumers experience (or even anticipate) major life events that signify a change or transition into a new life role, this generates stress. The stress created from these life transitions is associated with changes in brand preferences, which the authors argue allows the consumers to adapt to their new life situations. It is also suggested that if a brand reminds an individual of a stressful life event, then that brand may be avoided. For example, if a person goes through a divorce, he/she may avoid brands that were favoured by their ex-spouse, causing the individual to generate new brand preferences (Mathur et al., 2003). One explanation given for these preference shifts is that products and brands often become associated with one's self-concept, and major life transitions that change the self-concept alter the kinds of products and brands one prefers.

While it is an important examination of how preferences are constructed and can shift across the lifespan, the work by Mathur and colleagues (2003) was based on descriptive survey research. Thus factors other than stress and the avoidance of bad memories may also contribute to changes in preferences during these major life transitions. Future research is needed to further elucidate what factors influence these preference changes.

The reviewed findings are important in their indication of how spending and preferences change across older consumer cohorts and important life transitions. Understanding what types of products and services older adults are particularly likely to prefer and spend money on can allow marketers to better meet their consumption needs and improve satisfaction with the purchased products.

Environmental factors and consumer behaviour

Time pressure

Time pressure is an environmental factor that has a large influence on the decision-making ability of consumers across the adult lifespan (Earles et al., 2004; Park et al., 1989). Consumers under time pressure, particularly in an unfamiliar environment, become less able to locate their preferred brands and as a result end up purchasing brands they did not intend to purchase (Park et al., 1989). This outcome has the potential to lead to lower satisfaction and negative outcomes for older consumers. Time pressure has also been shown to magnify decrements in information recall by older adults, as compared to younger adults. In addition, time pressure is believed to increase anxiety by activating negative stereotypes associated with ageing, which is one plausible explanation for the link between inhibited information recall and time pressure (Earles et al., 2004).

Distraction

Another important predictor of consumer decision ineffectiveness is distraction. Prior findings have documented robust age-related increases in vulnerability to distraction across a variety of cognitive tasks (McDowd, 1997). For example, older adults exposed to environmental distractors report more difficulty with locating a specific object in a cluttered visual field (Kosnik et al., 1988), exhibit slower response times and commit more errors during search tasks (Madden, 1983; Plude & Hoyer, 1986). Divided attention has also been shown to exacerbate the effects of age on dual-task performance, especially when components of the task are more difficult.

Older adults are especially susceptible to the disruptive effects of distraction from task-irrelevant sources, which can include events that occurred in the past (Hasher, Lustig, & Zacks, 2007). These effects reflect the inability of older adults to inhibit irrelevant environmental primes, and indicate that irrelevant information remains active in memory and carries over to influence subsequent, unrelated tasks. These inhibitory deficits can diminish both older adults' immediate task performance and their downstream performance for up to 15–20 minutes after being exposed to the distraction (Hasher et al., 2007).

Interestingly, while most accounts of distraction effects on older adults' performance highlight the negative influence of diminished inhibitory control, older adults' greater sustained activation of irrelevant past information may also have positive consequences for subsequent tasks. For example, Kim, Hasher and Zacks (2007) reported superior performance of older adults, compared to younger adults, on a Remote Associates Task (RAT) after exposure to distracting information on a preceding task (Mednick, 1968). Samanez-Larkin, Wagner and Knutson (2011) also found that distractions have less of an influence on older adults when the critical information (e.g., expected value information in a financial domain) is presented in a simplified format.

Human factors

Older consumers are often faced with changing technologies, which can be especially intimidating and frustrating. Research on human factors has examined the importance of product design to assist older adults in the successful use of a variety of products. This research becomes especially important within the technological realm, including the use of computers and the Internet (Czaja et al., 2006; Rogers & Fisk, 2000). The proper use of technology has been associated with greater functional independence and well-being in older adult populations, and thus it is important for research to focus on ways to improve older adults' comfort levels and abilities when it comes to technology. Improvements are especially needed in the system design usability of such technologies, as well as in training programmes that will improve older adults' use of computers and other technologies.

In focusing on user-friendly design, a technology should be such that it places little demand on the cognitive resources of the consumer (Czaja, et al., 2006), or else it may create frustration and lead consumers to altogether stop using the technology (Rogers & Fisk, 2000). User-friendly technologies should be designed with an understanding of how cognitive functioning and information processing change across the lifespan. Doing so will allow for the production of technologies that appeal to a wider range of consumers. Training programmes should also be readily available to provide consumers of all ages with the skills necessarily to easily and effectively interface with technologies. s

This interest in improving consumer interactions with technology has become especially critical in a time when technologies are ever-changing. Learning how to use a technology today does not guarantee that this technology will be the same in a few years, and the dynamic nature of this consumption domain is likely to be especially challenging for older consumers. Future research should seek to expand upon the existing literature on human factors and ageing to further understand how to improve older consumers' feelings of efficacy and competence in the face of ever-changing technologies.

Culture

One environmental factor that critically influences patterns of behaviour is culture. Kitayama (2000) described culture as a collection of meanings embodied in behavioural routines, conventions, social institutions, political systems and icons. As age-related cognitive decline occurs predictably, it is likely that culture interacts with cognition to influence behavioural outcomes. Extant research on culture and ageing has suggested that while many cognitive processes do decline at a similar rate across cultures, suggesting the universality of cognitive ageing, other processes appear to be modulated by culture (see Park & Gutchess, 2006, for a review). For example, across the lifespan, East Asians tend to process background information to a greater extent than Westerners, who tend to show greater attention to the foreground objects in a scene (Chua, Boland, & Nisbett, 2005). Consequently, research has shown that older Singaporeans show less activation in object-processing neural structures (i.e., the lateral occipital complex) than do older Americans who show differences in background processing structures (i.e., the hippocampus). These findings suggest that the cultural biases in information processing observed across the lifespan have implications for not only structural changes in the brain (Chee et al., 2006), but downstream consequences in terms of behaviour. Future research should continue to explore how these cultural biases in information processing influence consumer behaviour across the lifespan.

Cultural differences have also been observed with respect to a construct known as ideal affect. Ideal affect refers to how people ideally want to feel, and may have important implications for consumer behaviour (Tsai, Chim, & Sims, 2015). Models of ideal affect argue that Westerners tend to value higher-arousal positive (HAP) affective states and Easterners tend to value lower-arousal positive (LAP) affective states. These cultural differences in ideal affect have important implications for how products should be advertised to consumers, and likely have interesting and unexplored consequences across the lifespan given that affective processes also change as people age (see Charles & Carstensen, 2009, for a review).

The existing cross-cultural literature on ageing is sparse. Thus this is an exciting area for future research. Due to differences in how Eastern and Western individuals process information across the lifespan, we might expect cultural differences in how cognitive ageing occurs in a cultural context. Cultural differences observed in younger adults may be more pronounced in older adults if the basis of the difference is primarily culture-specific world knowledge. Plausible differences in outcomes that may occur as a function of age and culture suggest that consumer information directed towards Eastern and Western individuals should be represented differently depending on context. However, it is also possible that in some decision domains that require effortful, controlled processing, cultural differences in older adults may be minimized because neurobiological declines with age are a universal phenomenon that act to minimize cultural differences. Future research should seek to further disentangle how differences in message processing affect older and younger consumers across cultures.

Affective information and older consumers

Affective modes of processing

In light of predictable age-related declines in deliberative processing, affective information becomes more influential to decision making as people age (see Peters et al., 2007, for a review). While a shift towards the use of affective information may seem like a negative consequence of ageing, a greater attention to and use of affective information is likely also due to age-related motivational changes. Thus, despite declines in deliberative processing, older adults are able to rely on several strategies to maintain high levels of decision quality (Peters et al., 2007).

One such strategy is a shift in focus from deliberative to affective modes of processing that occurs across the adult lifespan. Specifically, older age brings about a shift in attention from more deliberative-focused to more emotion-focused goals. The socio-emotional selectivity theory of ageing posits that older adults focus on regulation strategies that enhance positive emotion goals by directing their attention away from negative stimuli (e.g., image of a snake), and towards positive stimuli (e.g., image of a butterfly) (Carstensen, 1992; Carstensen et al., 1999; Mather & Carstensen, 2005). This bias towards positive information, however, is unlikely to occur in situations where older adults feel threatened or do not have the time to act consistently with motivational goals (Charles & Carstensen, 2009).

One prominent explanation for the change in emotion goals across the adult lifespan is a change in one's awareness of the temporal horizon (Carstensen, 1992). Carstensen (1992) demonstrated that individuals unconsciously evaluate time as either limited or expansive, and this orientation has important consequences for goals. When the time horizon is viewed as limited (as with older adults), people tend to become present-oriented and find satisfaction in the moment. People with a limited time perspective also have a tendency to focus more on connectedness, feeling states and the emotional meaning derived from experiences. Conversely, when time is perceived to be expansive (as with younger adults), people tend to become future-oriented and pay greater attention to planning, analytical thinking and the pursuit of knowledge. This orientation allows people with an expansive time horizon to plan and be prepared for future challenges.

These changes in emotion goals and time perspective predictably influence behaviour and have important implications for older consumers. For example, temporal horizon and emotion goals have been investigated in studies on information-processing responses to advertising across the adult lifespan. In this research, older adults focused more on emotionally meaningful information and goals (Fung & Carstensen, 2003) and subsequently responded more positively to advertising appeals containing affective information than did younger cohorts (Williams & Drolet, 2005). Emotional advertisements also increased older adults' liking for and recall of information, and a limited time horizon perspective was found to drive the observed age-related differences. Also in line with socio-emotional selectivity theory, advertisements that focused on avoiding negative emotions were liked and recalled more among younger consumers induced to have a limited time horizon perspective. These findings suggest that one's temporal horizon perspective can alter the positivity and negativity biases typically exhibited by older and younger adults, respectively.

Simply presenting information in an emotion-focused manner may also benefit older consumers' decision making. Mikels and colleagues (2010) suggested that older adults have higher decision quality when given emotion-focused instructions than when given information-focused instructions that require a reliance on memory for details or deliberative processing. This has important implications for how message information should be displayed to consumers. Future research should further examine both the positive and negative consequences of a greater reliance on affective processing for consumer decision making across the lifespan.

Buffering older consumers' challenges

Increased consumer satisfaction

Yoon, Feinberg and Schwarz (2010) recently discussed cross-sectional findings based on data from the American Consumer Satisfaction Index (ACSI; Fornell et al., 1996). Their analysis revealed a phenomenon referred to as the "older-and-more satisfied" effect. The ACSI is a large-scale database that contains information on consumer satisfaction with products and services across the adult lifespan. More than 200 companies in 45 industries and some government agencies are represented in the ACSI. In their paper, Yoon et al. (2010) revealed that older adults (aged 65 and above) reported higher satisfaction across a variety of product and service categories. Why this robust phenomenon occurs is not well understood and is likely to be multi-causal. The authors proposed several potential explanations, including older consumers' greater experience with products and services; a lower sensitivity to and knowledge about the "latest and greatest" products; and a greater tendency than younger consumers to satisfice given that the product or service meets their basic requirements. This increased product satisfaction may, in effect, contribute to greater happiness and less choice regret among older adults, which may have positive consequences for older consumers' health and well-being.

Experience effects

Experience effects have been found to buffer or perhaps even enhance older consumers' abilities. For example, due to their more extensive experience and familiarity with grocery store contexts, older consumers are able to remember grocery prices just as well as younger consumers (Castel, 2005). These types of experience effects can aid older consumers in making more successful and satisfying consumption choices.

Experience effects also allow older adults to rely on affective information and in some cases actually make better decisions (Peters et al., 2007) because they presumably have higher levels of comfort with the decision domain. Having experience with a decision context may further allow older consumers to feel more efficacious about the decisions that they make. Not having experience with a domain, however, may lead to worse decisions (Peters et al., 2007), and this is an important question for future inquiry. Finding ways to promote decision quality by highlighting older consumers' experience with a domain may serve to increase consumer well-being and choice satisfaction.

Adaptive decision strategies

Older consumers often use adaptive decision strategies to facilitate good decision making and choices despite age-related cognitive decline. Mata et al. (2007) found that although older adults both sought out less financial information and took longer to process acquired information, they utilized simpler and less cognitively demanding information processing strategies. This consequently led to higher monetary payoffs for older adults.

Using in-depth surveys to collect responses from subjects across the adult lifespan (i.e., ages 18–74), Kirmani and Campbell (2004) indicated that older adults self-reported a wider range of strategies for dealing with persuasion attempts, as compared to younger adults. This finding suggests that such strategies are used by older adults, despite cognitive and performance declines. Older adults' greater exposure to and experience with persuasive messages may make them relatively less resistant to deceptive appeals. Future research should further explore this possibility.

Expertise effects

Consumer expertise is typically described as a function of both familiarity (i.e., repeated experience) with a decision domain and greater objective knowledge or skill (Alba & Hutchinson, 1987). In general, expertise is thought of as a positive consequence of ageing that can help bolster older adults' performance and improve consumer decision outcomes. Domain expertise is often accompanied by more confidence about their ability to make choices and find information, and this confidence may foster older consumers' self-efficacy and lead to greater action and more decisiveness (Bandura, 1976). Increased expertise also leads to more effective decision making by increasing efficiency in information search and learning (Brucks, 1985; Johnson & Russo, 1984).

Expertise can, however, also have negative consequences for older consumers (Camerer & Johnson, 1991; Shanteau, 1992; Wood & Lynch, 2002). Numerous studies have demonstrated that repetition of the same information reliably increases its perceived truth (Begg et al., 1992; Hasher et al., 1977). Older adults have been found to be particularly sensitive to this "illusion of truth" effect (Law et al., 1998), and the reliance on familiarity to infer truth can lead to misjudgements and other negative consequences. For instance, being repeatedly exposed to a false health claim increases the likelihood of later misremembering the same false claims as true (Skurnik et al., 2005). Within health-related fields, misremembering false information as true can be extremely detrimental to one's health and general well-being. Falsely believing that information is true could also influence how decisions are made within a consumer domain, and lead to ineffective choices and reduced consumer satisfaction among older consumers. Thus, future research should seek to examine in what contexts expertise promotes high-quality decisions, and when it instead hinders them.

Time of day

There are conditions that seem to improve older adults' ability to process information in a detailed manner, at levels that are equivalent to those of younger adults. One such example is the time of day in which the older, versus younger, consumer processes information, completes tasks and makes decisions. Both older and younger consumers are able to engage more effectively in detailed information processing tasks during their respective peak times of day (Yoon, 1997). What qualifies as a peak time of day is determined by differences in circadian arousal patterns that influence cognitive abilities and decision-making performance across the lifespan (Yoon, 1997; May, Hasher, & Stoltzfus, 1993). The peak circadian arousal for older and younger adults tends to occur at different times of day. Older adults tend to reach this peak level of circadian arousal in the morning, whereas younger adults tend to reach their peak level of circadian arousal in the afternoon or evening (Yoon, 1997; May, Hasher, & Stoltzfus, 1993; Yoon et al., 2007; Anderson, et al., 2014). This suggests that it is more adaptive for older adults to engage in complex tasks that require more detailed or elaborate information processing earlier in the day. It also importantly indicates that comparisons of task performance between younger and older adult populations should account for time of day effects; older adults should complete such tasks in the morning, and younger adults in the afternoon or evening.

Mental imagery

Task performance across the adult lifespan can also be maintained by engaging in mental imagery. Engaging in mental imagery by imagining some claim or object allows for the encoding of information in a manner that improves memory for details in older adults (Law et al., 1998). The negative effects of cognitive ageing are thus reduced in decision contexts where older consumers are encouraged to elaborate on the task at hand by using mental imagery. For example, older adults who formed a mental image of brand claims were better able to process information in detail (Law et al., 1998), and their memory performance was equivalent to that of younger adults.

These processing boosts from mental imagery yield outcomes that go above and beyond simply instructing older consumers to justify their decisions (Kim et al., 2005) or to think deeply about information before making decisions (Cole & Houston, 1987). Thus, providing older consumers with cues that facilitate engagement in imagery may effectively induce more systematic processing and better memory for details in decision situations that require careful deliberation.

Conclusions

In the present chapter, we review research on older adults that consumer behaviour that sheds light the effects of ageing on consumer behaviour. Examining age-related changes in a variety of cognitive processes and behaviours will contribute to a better understanding of how consumer behaviour changes across the adult lifespan. The extant literature on this topic reveals that although age-related decrements in cognitive processing, information search, and decision making do exist, there are decision strategies and environmental conditions that can buffer these challenges that accompany ageing.

One important consideration for future research is identifying what tasks and contexts are the most meaningful and relevant to consumers across the adult lifespan. This is important because tasks and decisions that are actually meaningful and relevant lead to insights that can inform the most influential outcomes for consumers of all ages. Similarly, it is critical that future research begins to uncover the contexts that promote positive and negative outcomes for older consumers. This would enhance our knowledge of when older adults may struggle the most with decisions or tasks, and thus allow us to better predict when older consumers benefit the most from environmental supports like the use of mental imagery. Answering these questions will potentially yield insights that ultimately enhance older consumers' well-being. Future research should also determine what mechanisms underlie the observed "older-and-more-satisfied" effect, as this phenomenon may meaningfully contribute to positive consumer outcomes.

Given the burgeoning number of older consumers worldwide, it is crucial that we are able to anticipate and understand age-related changes in consumer behaviour. However, it is clear that there are still many gaps in our understanding of older consumers, and many opportunities for the advancement of knowledge exist. We hope that this chapter will both inform and encourage future research to fill in the gaps.

References

Agarwal, S., Driscoll, J. C., Gabaix, X., & Laibson, D. (2009). The age of reason: Decisions over the life-span with implications for regulation. *Brookings Papers on Economic Activity*, *2*, 51–117. Washington D.C.: Brookings Institution Press.

Agarwal, S., Driscoll, J. C., Gabaix, X., & Laibson, D. (2010). What is the age of reason? *Center for Retirement Research at Boston College*, 1–7.

Alba, J. W., & Hutchinson, J. W. (1987). Dimensions of consumer expertise. *Journal of Consumer Research*, *13*, 411–454.

Anderson, J. A., Campbell, K. L., Amer, T., Grady, C. L., & Hasher, L. (2014). Timing is everything: Age differences in the cognitive control network are modulated by time of day. *Psychology and Aging*, *29*, 648–657.

Bandura, A. (1976). Self-reinforcement: Theoretical and methodological considerations. *Behaviourism*, *4*, 135–155.

Begg, I. M., Anas, A., & Farinacci, S. (1992). Dissociation of processes in belief: Source recollection, statement familiarity, and the illusion of truth. *Journal of Experimental Psychology: General*, *12*, 446–458.

Boscarino, J., & Steiber, S. R. (1982). Hospital shopping and consumer choice. *Journal of Health Care Marketing*, *2*, 15–23.

Boyle, P. A., Yu, L., Wilson, R. S., Gamble, K., Buchman, A. S., & Bennett, D. A. (2012). Poor decision making is a consequence of cognitive decline among older persons without alzheimer's disease or mild cognitive impairment. *PLoS ONE*, 7(8), e43647. doi:10.1371/journal.pone.0043647

Brown, S. C., & Park, D. C. (2003). Theoretical models of cognitive aging and implications for translational research in medicine. *Gerontologist*, *43*(suppl 1), 57–67.

Brucks, M. (1985). The effects of product class knowledge on information search behaviour. *Journal of Consumer Research*, *12*, 1–16.

Bruine de Bruin, W., Parker, A. M., & Fischhoff, B. (2012). Explaining adult age differences in decision-making competence. *Journal of Behavioural Decision Making*, *25*, 352–360.

Camerer, C. F., & Johnson, E. J. (1991). The process-performance paradox in expert judgment: How can experts know so much and predict so badly? In K. Anders Ericsson & J. Smith (Eds.), *Toward a general theory of expertise: Prospects and limits*, (pp. 195–217). New York, NY: Cambridge University Press.

Carstensen, L. L. (1992). Social and emotional patterns in adulthood: Support for socioemotional selectivity theory. *Psychology and Aging*, 7, 331–338.

Carstensen, L. L., Isaacowitz, D. M., & Charles, S. T. (1999). Taking time seriously: A theory of socioemotional selectivity. *American Psychologist*, *54*, 165–181.

Castel, A. D. (2005). Memory for grocery prices in younger and older adults: The role of schematic support. *Psychology and Aging, Special Issue: Emotion-Cognition Interactions and the Aging Mind*, 718–721.

Chang, C. (2008). Chronological age versus cognitive age for younger consumers: Implications for advertising persuasion. *Journal of Advertising*, *37*, 19–32.

Charles, S. T., & Carstensen, L. L. (2009). Social and emotional aging. *Annual Review of Psychology*, *61*, 383–409.

Chee, M. W., Goh, J. O., Venkatraman, V., Tan, J. C., Gutchess, A., Sutton, B., ... & Park, D. (2006). Age-related changes in object processing and contextual binding revealed using fMR adaptation. *Journal of Cognitive Neuroscience*, *18*(4), 495–507.

Chen, Y., & Sun, Y. (2003). Age differences in financial decision-making: Using simple heuristics. *Educational Gerontology*, *29*(7), 627–635.

Chua, H. F., Boland, J. E., & Nisbett, R. E. (2005). Cultural variation in eye movements during scene perception. *Proceedings of the National Academy of Sciences of the United States of America, 102*(35), 12629–12633.

Cole, C. A., & Balasubramanian, S. K. (1993). Age differences in consumers' search for information: Public policy implications. *Journal of Consumer Research, 20*, 157–169.

Cole, C. A., & Gaeth, G. J. (1990). Cognitive and age-related differences in the ability to use nutritional information in a complex environment. *Journal of Marketing Research, 27*, 175–184.

Cole, C. A., & Houston, M. J. (1987). Encoding and media effects on consumer learning deficiencies in the elderly. *Journal of Marketing Research, 11*, 551–563.

Czaja, S. J., Charness, N., Fisk, A. D., Hertzog, C., Nair, S. N., Rogers, W. A., & Sharit, J. (2006). Factors predicting the use of technology: Findings from the Center for Research and Education on Aging and Technology Enhancement (CREATE). *Psychology and Aging, 21*, 333–352.

Del Missier, F., Mäntylä, T., Hansson, P., Bruine de Bruin, W., Parker, A. M., & Nilsson, L. G. (2013). The multifold relationship between memory and decision making: An individual-differences study. *Journal of Experimental Psychology: Learning, Memory, and Cognition, 39*(5), 1344–1364.

Earles, J. L., Kersten, A. W., Mas, B. B., & Miccio, D. M. (2004). Aging and memory for self-performed tasks: Effects of task difficulty and time pressure. *Journal of Gerontology: Psychological Sciences, 59B*, 285–293.

Fleischmann, D. A., Wilson, R. S., Gabrieli, J. D. E., Bienias, J. L., & Bennett, D. A. (2004). A longitudinal study of implicit and explicit memory in old persons. *Psychology and Aging, 19*, 617–625.

Fornell, C., Johnson, M. D., Anderson, E. W., Cha, J., & Bryant, B. E. (1996). The American Consumer Satisfaction Index: Nature, purpose, and findings. *Journal of Marketing, 60*, 7–18.

Fung, H. H., & Carstensen, L. L. (2003). Sending memorable messages to the old: Age differences in preferences and memory for advertisements. *Journal of Personality and Social Psychology, 85*, 163–178.

Hasher, L., Goldstein, D., & Toppino, T. (1977). Frequency and the conference of referential validity. *Journal of Verbal Learning and Verbal Behaviour, 16*, 107–112.

Hasher, L., Lustig, C., & Zacks, R. (2007). In A. Miyake, A. R. A. Conway, C. Jarrold, M. J. Kane & J. N. Towse (Eds.), *Variation in working memory* (pp. 227–249). New York, NY: Oxford University Press.

Health and Retirement Study. (2012). About the Health and Retirement Study. Retrieved December 18, 2012, from http://hrsonline.isr.umich.edu/index.php

Hedden, T., & Yoon, C. (2006). Individual differences in executive processing predicts susceptibility to interference in verbal working memory. *Neuropsychology, 20*, 511–528.

Hess, T. M. (2005). Memory and aging in context. *Psychological Bulletin, 13*, 383–406.

Hess, T. M., Queen, T. L., & Ennis, G. E. (2013). Age and self-relevance effects on information search during decision making. *Journal of Gerontology Series B: Psychological Sciences and Social Sciences, 68*, 703–711.

James, B. D., Boyle, P. A., Bennett, J. S., & Bennett, D. A. (2012). The impact of health and financial literacy on decision making in community-based older adults. *Gerontology, 58*, 531–539.

Johnson, E. J., & Russo, J. E. (1984). Product familiarity and learning new information. *Journal of Consumer Research, 11*, 542–550.

Kalache, A., Barreto, S. M., & Keller, I. (2005). Global ageing: The demographic revolution in all cultures and societies. In M. L. Johnson (Ed.), *Cambridge Handbook of Ageing*. Cambridge: Cambridge University Press.

Kim, S., Goldstein, D., Hasher, L., & Zacks, R. T. (2005). Framing effects in younger and older adults. *Journal of Gerontology: Series B: Psychological Science and Social Sciences, 60B*, 215–218.

Kim, S., Hasher, L., & Zacks, R. T. (2007). Aging and benefit of distractibility. *Psychonomic Bulletin and Review, 14*, 301–305.

Kirmani, A., & Campbell, M. C. (2004). Goal seeker and persuasion sentry: How consumer targets respond to interpersonal marketing persuasion. *Journal of Consumer Research, 31*, 573–582.

Kitayama, S. (2000). Cultural variations in cognition: Implications for aging research. In *The aging mind: Opportunities in cognitive research* (pp. 218–237). Washington, DC: National Academy Press.

Korniotis, G. M., & Kumar, A. (2009). Do older investors make better investment decisions? *Review of Economics and Statistics, 93*, 244–265.

Kosnik, W., Winslow, L., Rasinski, K., & Sekuler, R. (1988). Visual changes in daily life throughout adulthood. *Journal of Gerontology: Psychological Sciences, 43*, P63–P70.

Lambert-Pandraud, R., & Laurent, G. (2010). Impact of age on brand choice. In A. Drolet, N. Schwarz & C. Yoon (Eds.), *The aging consumer: Perspectives from psychology and economics* (pp. 191–208). London: Taylor & Francis.

Lambert-Pandraud, R., Laurent, G., & Lapersonne, E. (2005). Repeat purchasing of new automobiles by older consumers: Empirical evidence and interpretations. *Journal of Marketing*, *69*, 97–103.

Law, S., Hawkins, S. A., & Craik, F. I. M. (1998). Repetition-induced belief in the elderly: Rehabilitating age-related memory deficits. *Journal of Consumer Research*, *25*, 91–107.

Li, Y., Baldassi, M., Johnson, E. J., & Weber, E. U. (2012). Compensating cognitive capabilities, decision performance and aging. *Working Paper.*

Löckenhoff, C. E., & Carstensen, L. L. (2007). Aging, emotion, and health-related decision strategies: Motivational manipulations can reduce age differences. *Psychology and Aging*, *22*, 134–146.

Lumpkin, J. R., & Festervand, T. A. (1988). Purchase information-sources of the elderly. *Journal of Advertising Research*, *27*(6), 31–44.

Madden, D. J. (1983). Aging and distraction by highly familiar stimuli during visual search. *Developmental Psychology*, *19*, 499–507.

Mata, R., Schooler, L. J., & Rieskamp, J. (2007). The aging decision maker: Cognitive aging and the adaptive selection of decision strategies. *Psychology and Aging*, *22*, 796–810.

Mather, M. (2006). A review of decision making processes: Weighing the risks and benefits of aging. In L. L. Carstensen & C. R. Hartel (Eds.), *When I'm 64* (pp. 145–173). Washington, DC: National Academic Press.

Mather, M., & Carstensen, L. L. (2005). Aging and motivated cognition: The positivity effect in attention and memory. *Trends in Cognitive Sciences*, *9*, 496–502.

Mather, M., Knight, M., & McCaffrey, M. (2005). The allure of the alignable: Younger and older adults' false memories of choice features. *Journal of Experimental Psychology: General*, *134*, 38–51.

Mathur, A., Moschis, G. P., & Lee, E. (2003). Life events and brand preference changes. *Journal of Consumer Behaviour*, *3*, 129–141.

May, C. P., Hasher, L., & Stoltzfus, E. R. (1993). Optimal time of day and the magnitude of age differences in memory. *Psychological Science*, *4*, 326–330.

McDowd, J. M. (1997). Inhibition in attention and memory. *Journal of Gerentology: Psychological Sciences*, *528*, 265–273.

McIntyre, J. S., & Craik, F. I. M. (1987). Age differences in memory for item and source information. *Canadian Journal of Psychology*, *41*, 175–192.

Mednick, S. A. (1968). The remote associates task. *Journal of Creative Behaviour*, *2*, 213–214.

Mikels, J. A., Löckenhoff, C. E., Maglio, S. J., Carstensen, L. L, Goldstein, M. K., & Garber, A. (2010). Following your heart or your head: Focusing on emotions versus information differentially influences the decision of younger and older adults. *Journal of Experimental Psychology: Applied*, *16*, 87–95.

Moscovitch, M., & Winocur, G. (1995). Frontal lobes, memory, and aging. *Annals of the New York Academy of Sciences*, *789*, 119–150.

Park, D., & Gutchess, A. (2006). The cognitive neuroscience of aging and culture. *Current Directions in Psychological Science*, *15*(3), 105–108.

Park, C. W., Iyer, E. S., & Smith, D. C. (1989). The effects of situational factors on in-store grocery shopping behaviour: The role of store environment and time available for shopping. *Journal of Consumer Research*, *15*, 422–433.

Park, D. C., Lautenschlager, G., Hedden, T., Davidson, N. S., & Smith, A. D. (2002). Models of visuospatial and verbal memory across the adult life span. *Psychology and Aging*, *17*, 299–320.

Peters, E. (2010). Aging-related changes in decision making. In A. Drolet, N. Schwarz & C. Yoon (Eds.), *The aging consumer: Perspectives from psychology and economics* (pp. 75–101). New York, NY: Taylor & Francis.

Peters, E., Hess, T. M., Västfjäll, D., & Auman, C. (2007). Adult age differences in dual information processes. *Perspectives on Psychological Science*, *2*, 1–23.

Plude, D. J., & Hoyer, W. J. (1986). Age and the selectivity of visual information processing. *Psychology and Aging*, *1*, 4–10.

Roedder John, D., & Cole, C. A. (1986). Age differences in information processing: Understanding deficits in young and elderly consumers. *Journal of Consumer Research*, *13*, 297–315.

Rogers, W. A., & Fisk, A. D. (2000). Human factors, applied cognition, and aging, In F. I. M. Craik & T. A. Salthouse (Eds.), *The handbook of aging and cognition* (Vol. 2, pp. 559–591).

Samanez-Larkin, G. R., Wagner, A. D., & Knutson, B. (2011). Expected value information improves financial risk taking across the adult life span. *Social Cognitive and Affective Neuroscience*, *6*, 207–217.

Schwartz, B., Ward, A., Monterosso, J., Lyubomirsky, S., White, K., & Lehman, D. R. (2002). Maximizing versus satisficing: Happiness is a matter of choice. *Journal of Personality and Social Psychology*, *83*(5), 1178–1197.

Shanteau, J. (1992). Competence in experts: The role of task characteristics. *Organizational Behavioural and Human Decision Processes, 53*, 252–266.

Skurnik, I., Yoon, C., Park, D. C., & Schwarz, N. (2005). How warnings about false claims become recommendations. *Journal of Consumer Research, 31*, 713–723.

Spencer, W. D., & Raz, N. (1995). Differential effects of aging on memory for content and context: A meta-analysis. *Psychology and Aging, 10*, 527–539.

Tsai, J. L., Chim, L., & Sims, T. (2015). Consumer behaviour, culture, and emotion. In S. Ng & A. Y. Lee (Eds.), *Handbook of culture and consumer behaviour* (pp. 68–86).

Tversky, A., & Kahneman, D. (1974). Judgment under uncertainty: Heuristics and biases. *Science, 185*, 1124–1131.

Webster, N. J., Antonucci, T. C., Yoon, C., McCullough, W. R., Fin, D. N., & Hartsell, D. L. (2014). Older adults as consumers: An examination of differences by birth cohort. In S. D. Preston, M. L. Kringelbach & B. Knutson (Eds.), *The interdisciplinary science of consumption* (pp. 281–298).

West, R. L. (1996). An application of prefrontal cortex function theory to cognitive aging. *Psychological Bulletin, 120*, 272–292.

Williams, P., & Drolet, A. (2005). Age-related differences in responses to emotional advertisements. *Journal of Consumer Research, 32*, 343–354.

Wood, S. L., & Lynch, J. G. (2002). Prior knowledge and complacency in new product learning. *Journal of Consumer Research, 29*, 416–426.

Yates, J. F., & Patalano, A. L. (1999). Decision making and aging. In D. Park, R. Morrell & K. Khifren (Eds.), *Processing of medical information in aging patients: Cognitive and human factors perspectives* (pp. 31–54). Mahwah, NJ: Erlbaum.

Yoon, C. (1997). Age differences in consumers' processing strategies: An investigation of moderating influences. *Journal of Consumer Research, 24*, 329–342.

Yoon, C., Cole, C. A., & Lee, M. P. (2009). Consumer decision making and aging: Current knowledge and future directions. *Journal of Consumer Psychology, 19*, 2–16.

Yoon, C., Feinberg, F., & Schwarz, N. (2010). Older consumers and satisfaction. In A. Drolet, N. Schwarz & C. Yoon (Eds.), *The aging consumer: Perspectives from psychology and economics*. London: Taylor & Francis.

Yoon, C., Lee, M. P., & Dazinger, S. (2007). The effects of optimal time of day on persuasion processes in older adults.

Part VI

Products, branding preferences and sustainability

27

Sustainability and consumer psychology

Eda Gurel-Atay, Lynn R. Kahle and Elizabeth A. Minton

According to the U.S. Environmental Protection Agency (2014), global greenhouse gas emissions from human activities increased by 35 per cent from 1990 to 2010. The National Research Council (2010) report states that the Earth is 1.4° F warmer compared to the last century and additional warming of 2.0 to 11.5° F (1.1 to 6.4° C) is expected over the 21st century. These changes in the physical environment (e.g., climate change, decreases in non-renewable resources) have prompted many scholars and practitioners to realize that we cannot continue to use the world's resources without considering the consequences (Ottman, 1998; Wasik, 1996). This increase in environmental awareness have led businesses to engage in sustainable business practices more (e.g., decreasing emissions, increasing recycling or repurposing practices, using energy-efficient transportation systems), making the green economy one of the world's new economic engines (e.g., Hawken, Lovins, & Lovins, 1999). However, although firms adopt more and more sustainable business practices every day, many consumers do not follow suit (Schafer, Jeager-Erben, & Santos, 2011; Thøgersen & Crompton, 2009). Accordingly, when consumers do not "reward" the companies that use sustainable business practices with their sustainable consumption practices (e.g., buying green products), companies may lose the motivation to invest in those expensive practices. In other words, businesses need to see a return on investment for their sustainable initiatives. Therefore, it is important for researchers and practitioners to identify the factors that keep customers from engaging in environmentally sustainable consumption (e.g., knowledge, motivation or access to necessary resources) and find ways to deal with those factors. Consumer psychology has the potential to be both the cause of and/or the solution to many of these factors.

In this chapter, we first provide a definition of environmental sustainability and discuss the importance of it to consumer psychology research. Then, we discuss consumer psychology theories that can be used to understand sustainable consumption. Among the theories we examine are social adaptation, means–end chains, Theory of Planned Behaviour, functional theory and learning theory. Finally, we look at the past research on sustainability and consumer psychology and provide ideas for future research.

Overview of sustainability research

Defining environmental sustainability

Although some researchers think that settling on a single definition of sustainable consumption is not helpful for sustainability research (Peattie & Collins, 2009), others have provided their own definitions in order to minimize confusion for consumers, researchers, practitioners and policy makers (Kolandai-Matchett, 2009). The official definition by the Organization of Economic Cooperation and Development of sustainable consumption is "the use of goods and related products which respond to basic needs and bring a better quality of life, while minimizing the use of natural resources and toxic materials as well as the emissions of waste and pollutants over the life cycle, so as not to jeopardize the needs of future generations" (OECD, 2002). Luchs et al. (2011, p. 2) simplified this official definition by describing sustainable consumption as "consumption that simultaneously optimizes the environmental, social and economic consequences of consumption in order to meet the needs of both current and future generations". Similarly, Thompson, Anderson, Hansen and Kahle (2010, p. 320) defined it as the "the consumption of goods and services that satisfy the needs of the present generations without compromising the needs of future ones". Kahle and Gurel-Atay (2013, p. 9) suggested that sustainable consumption is engaging in consumer behaviours that contribute to environmental sustainability, which can be described as "the use of resources in a manner that can continue indefinitely". Examples of these consumer behaviours are buying green products, shopping at green retailers, supporting companies that adopt sustainable practices, recycling products at the end of their life cycles, purchasing organic food, and using energy resources that are based on renewable resources (e.g., solar energy).

Importance of environmentally sustainable consumption to consumer psychology

Some researchers view sustainable consumption as oxymoronic because consuming, using or destroying something is the opposite of sustaining, keeping or holding something (Peattie & Collins, 2009). Indeed, private consumption has been considered as one of the most important causes of environmental degradation and resource depletion (e.g., European Environment Agency, 2005; Schrader & Thøgersen, 2011; Tanner & Kast, 2003), leading to anti-consumption movements in which consumers avoid consumption to live sustainable lives. However, because avoiding consumption completely is not possible, it is important to make consumption practices as environmentally friendly as possible. Accordingly, many researchers (e.g., Kahle & Gurel-Atay, 2013; Schafer, Jeager-Erben, & Santos, 2011; Schrader & Thøgersen, 2011) from various disciplines worldwide have been working on topics related to sustainable consumption (e.g., the meaning of sustainable consumption, factors that encourage/discourage sustainable consumption) since the discussion of sustainable consumption in the Agenda 21 (United Nations' non-binding action plan for sustainable development) at the Rio Conference in 1992 (Schrader & Thøgersen, 2011).

Indeed, as the global population, industrialization and national economies keep growing, environmental degradation and resource depletion will become one of the most important issues in the world, making sustainable consumption (and research related to it) even more critical. Such importance can be seen in the active agenda of politicians around the world discussing sustainability-related issues as well as businesses around the world seeking to incorporate sustainable practices into business operations. At the core of acceptance of sustainable policy or spending on sustainable products is the consumer's sustainable practices. Consumer psychology, therefore, is an essential part of efforts to increase sustainable consumption because consumer psychology theories can be used to understand what sustainability means to consumers, which socio-demographic and psychographic variables are more important to encourage sustainable consumption, how consumers can be persuaded to devote themselves to sustainable consumption and more.

Using consumer psychology theories to understand sustainable consumption

Although there are consumers who are aware of the importance of environmental sustainability and want to minimize their impact on earth by adopting environmentally friendly consumer behaviours, the majority of consumers are still reluctant to engage in those behaviours (Schafer, Jeager-Erben, & Santos, 2011). In this section, we discuss consumer psychology theories to understand some of the major factors affecting the participation in environmentally sustainable consumption.

Social adaptation theory

Social adaptation theory, developed by Kahle (1984) based on Piaget's (1952) work on cognitive development, suggests that consumers' cognitive life facilitates their functioning in their social environments. Adaptation is defined as the "equilibration with the environment" (Kahle, 1984, p. 42), which implies an interaction between the self and the environment that changes both. According to this theory, communication is most effective when connections to a person's values, attitudes and lifestyles are emphasized (Homer & Kahle, 1988; Kahle, 1996; Kahle & Beatty, 1987b). In other words, the impact of any information depends on the adaptive significance of the information to the consumers' lives. Consumers will process the information as long as that information provides usefulness for adaptation, or facilitates adaptation. New information has the greatest impact if it is integrated into the recipient's lifestyle (Kahle & Valette-Florence, 2012).

One of the most important factors in engaging in sustainable consumption is environmental awareness. People who have the appropriate knowledge and information about sustainable consumption tend to understand the importance of sustainable consumption and engage in sustainable consumption more (Thøgersen, 2005; Valor, 2008). Accordingly, it is important to increase "environmental awareness" among consumers through public policy and social marketing efforts. However, research shows that some consumers may still not engage in sustainable consumption, although they are knowledgeable about it, thereby creating a "knowledge-to-action gap" (Markkula & Moisander, 2012). One reason for this gap is that consumers are bombarded with excessive amounts of information. Too much, and sometimes contradictory, information about sustainable consumption may lead consumers to get confused when processing this information and trying to understand what they can personally do to help the environment (Moisander, 2007). Social adaptation theory suggests that, in order to close this gap between knowledge and action, the information about sustainable consumption should focus on the adaptive and lifestyle significance of that information for consumers. In other words, the information should clearly explain why engaging in sustainable consumption is personally relevant and important to a particular consumer segment.

Another factor that may affect engaging in sustainable consumption is a consumer's everyday consumption routine. Everyday routines are used to "minimize the effort of organizing daily life" and tend to be well-adapted to social demands, personal needs and financial and time resources of consumers (Schäfer, Jaeger-Erben, & Bamberg, 2012, p. 2). These routines, or habits, however, may prevent people from adopting new consumption practices that are sustainably oriented (Beatty & Kahle, 1988). One approach to deal with this problem is to focus on people who are experiencing life-course transitions, such as graduating from college, getting married, moving to a new house, moving to another city or giving birth (Schäfer, Jaeger-Erben, & Bamberg, 2012, p. 2). Because these people are already in need of changing their everyday routines, they may adopt more sustainable alternatives (e.g., having solar panels at the new house, shopping at green retailers in the new city or buying organic food for the new baby). The behaviour intervening programmes for these people must address lifestyle changes and effectively communicate how sustainable consumption may be integrated in their new lifestyles by emphasizing the adaptive significance of sustainable consumption (Kahle & Valette-Florence, 2012).

Means–end chains

One other factor that might affect engaging in sustainable consumption is the congruency between consumers' self-identity and the identity that sustainable products or brands represent. Research has shown that consumers have values, personalities and self-images that determine how they respond to brands and products (e.g., Batra, Homer, & Kahle, 2001; Homer & Kahle, 1986; Kahle & Valette-Florence, 2012; Reynolds & Olson, 2001). Similarly, brands and products possess values and personalities that shape their perceived images (Aaker, 1997; De Chernatony, Drury, & Segal-Horn, 2004), and those perceived images influence how consumers respond to the brand or product (Da Silva & Syed Alwi, 2006). In general, consumers form stronger relations with brands and products when there is congruence between consumers' self-identity (i.e., values, personalities and self-images) and the identity represented by the product or brand (i.e., values, personalities and perceived images) (Fournier, 1998; McAlexander, Schouten, & Koenig, 2002). The research on the means–end chain theory provides strong support for this congruence effect. The means–end chain theory suggests that "consumers use a cognitive chain for buying decisions that relates product attributes to benefits, which in turn contribute to fulfil personal values" (Huber, Beckmann, & Herrmann, 2004, p. 715). In other words, the end goal of consumers to buy certain products/brands is to define their identities by fulfilling their own core values. This logic applies to sustainable consumption as well as it applies to other types of consumption.

Consider purchasing green products (e.g., products that are made of recycled materials). In spite of some important challenges (e.g., high price of green products, the lack of green product alternatives), purchasing green products has benefits to consumers. Some of these benefits include saving the environment, participation in a movement, saving resources, showing off to others and making a difference in the world. Some of the core values to which these attributes might link include self-respect, sense of accomplishment, security and warm relationships with others (Kahle, 1996). For the person who values self-respect, the most important attribute of green products might be making a difference in the world. The key attribute might be conspicuous consumption for the person who values sense of accomplishment. If a person values security, saving the environment and/or saving resources might be considered as important benefits. The opportunity to bond with other green product users may be critical if a person values warm relationships with others. Accordingly, it is important for change agents to understand the end goals of consumers when it comes to sustainable consumption and design change programmes that will foster those end goals.

Theory of planned behaviour

The Theory of Planned Behaviour suggests that attitude towards a behaviour, subjective norms and perceived behavioural control are the key determinants of behavioural intentions, which, in turn, are a key determinant of actual behaviours (Ajzen, 1985). Consumers who have positive feelings/thoughts about sustainable consumption may be more motivated to engage in sustainable consumption. Minton, Lee, Orth, Kim and Kahle (2012), for instance, showed that three attitude-commitment factors (responsibility, involvement and internalization) had significant effects on sustainable consumption behaviours. More specifically, responsible attitudes lead to organic food purchase, while involvement and internalization attitudes lead to increased green transportation use, among many other factors.

If social pressure to engage in sustainable consumption exists, consumers may be more likely to comply with others. Goldstein, Cialdini and Griskevicius (2008), for instance, found that persuasive appeals that are based on social norms (e.g., "the majority of guests in this room reuse their towels") have been more effective in generating sustainable consumption behaviours than traditional appeals that focus only on the protection of the environment. Salazar, Oerlemans and Stroe-Biezen (2013) showed that people are more likely to prefer sustainable products (e.g., chocolate) when they receive information about other people's choices on sustainable products. Rettie, Burchell and Barnham (2014) suggested that if green consumption behaviours are repositioned as normal, meaning that those behaviours have been employed by many other consumers, those behaviours can be adopted more easily by mainstream consumers.

Consumers may also be more inclined to engage in sustainable consumption if they know that they are making a difference. According to the Theory of Planned Behaviour (Ajzen, 1985), if people think that their own actions will not change the world (or reverse the environmental changes), they may be less willing to engage in green consumption. Accordingly, public policy and social marketing efforts should communicate the message that even a single person and/or action can make a difference.

To test the overall validity of the Theory of Planned Behaviour (Ajzen, 1985) to improve sustainable consumption, Vermeir and Verbeke (2007) conducted a survey with Belgium young adults. Their findings indeed supported the Theory of Planned Behaviour: Attitudes towards sustainable food products, social norms and perceived behavioural control (measured through perceived consumer effectiveness and perceived product availability) had positive and significant effects on sustainable food consumption intentions.

Functional theory

The functional theory of attitudes (e.g., Katz, 1960; Kelman, 1958) holds that attitudes and behaviours may serve different psychological functions. Indeed, the functional approach was proposed as an "attempt to understand the reasons people hold the attitudes they do" (Katz, 1960, p. 170) and assumes that different attitudes are based on different motives.

Katz (1960), based on different major psychological approaches, focused on four functions. The utilitarian function, grounded in behaviourism, tries to maximize external rewards and minimize punishment. For instance, some people may think that using energy-efficient lightbulbs will save them money in the long run (a reward) or not using energy-efficient lightbulbs will increase their electricity expenses in the long run (a punishment). The ego-defensive function, built on psychoanalysis, focuses on internal processes and protects people from internal conflicts and external threats. For instance, energy-efficient lightbulbs may be used to prove to oneself and/or others that the person is a good homemaker. The value-expressive function, based on humanism, is used to enhance self-concept, maintain self-identity and express central values. Some consumers, for instance, may believe that using energy-efficient bulbs will let them help save the environment, which, in turn, will lead them to achieve higher-order values, such as a world of beauty (Rokeach, 1973) or universalism (Schwartz, 1994). This view is similar to the means–end approach. Finally, knowledge function, rooted in cognitive psychology, conveys structure and meaning. It satisfies the need for order and understanding. Some people may, for example, believe that using energy-efficient bulbs makes their life more predictable as those bulbs are more durable and do not require replacement as often as traditional lightbulbs.

Kelman (1958) also worked on functions of attitudes and behaviours, but his focus was on the social relations that took place in social influence situations. Specifically, Kelman (1958) identified three functions: compliance, identification and internalization. Compliance, similar to the utilitarian function of Katz (1960), is based on rewards and punishment and requires complying with requests from others (e.g., law force, people who are at the higher ranks such as boss or teacher). Identification refers to holding attitudes and/or participating in activities that may advance interpersonal goals, such as following a social leader to become a part of a group. Internalization, on the other hand, does not require any external motivation to hold an attitude and/or participate in an activity. Instead, similar to the value-expressive function of Katz (1960), internalization requires self-definition, and fitting into existing values and beliefs. Each of these functions can be effective in increasing participation in sustainable consumption. For instance, people may use energy-efficient lightbulbs to comply with a law (compliance function) or to be part of an environmental group (identification function). Alternatively, people may believe that using energy-efficient bulbs would fit into their existing pro-environmental attitudes and start using them as a result. These functions are similar to the Katz approach in that each function relies on one body of psychological theory: compliance reflects behaviourism, identification is rooted in psychoanalysis and internalization is tied to humanism. Kelman (1958) would say that all human activity is related to understanding the world, the knowledge function based on cognitive theory.

Overall, the above discussion on attitude functions suggests that engaging in sustainable consumption may be the result of different attitudinal and/or behavioural functions (Minton, Lee, Orth, Kim, & Kahle, 2012). Accordingly, in order to reach consumers effectively with sustainable consumption-related change programmes, functions of sustainable attitudes and behaviours should be uncovered first. The functional approach implies that different theories will have optimal applicability in different psychological contexts and that each theory has some utility.

Positive psychology

Positive psychology, "the science and practice of improving well-being" (Lomas, Hefferon, & Ivtzan, 2014, p. ix), focuses on practices that help people live happy lives. Research on positive psychology (e.g., Peterson, 2006) has shown that happiness does not always come from obtaining more things. Perhaps consumers would experience more happiness if they enjoyed what they have rather than obtaining ever more products; hence, to become more sustainable, consumers may need to be convinced to consume less but to savour what they have. Although this idea seems contrary to the ideals of marketing, which generally follow an economic model regarding consumption where more is better, a reduction in consumption is aligned with the ideals of improving well-being of consumers (Kotler, 2011). One way of conceptualizing this idea is with mindful consumption, where consumers commit to more finite materialism (Sheth, Sethia, & Srinivas, 2011). Indeed, some consumers follow the voluntary simplicity movement to improve their quality of life (Prothero et al., 2011). Etzioni (1998) described three variations of voluntary simplicity: downshifting (voluntarily giving up luxuries by people who can afford them), strong simplification (voluntarily giving up high-paying jobs to have simpler lives and less consumption) and holistic simplification (voluntarily adjusting the entire lifestyle around the philosophy of voluntary simplicity). Each of these movements can be used to encourage consumers to improve their quality of life by consuming less. Another perspective to improve consumers' well-being is to shift from the marketing concept, that companies should give consumers what they want, to the societal marketing concept, that companies should give consumers what is good for them in a societal sense (Crittenden, Crittenden, Ferrell, Ferrell, & Pinney, 2011; Hult, 2011). At the very least, this shift would somewhat decrease marketing's contribution to unsustainability and perhaps simultaneously result in greater subjective satisfaction among consumers.

Learning theory

Learning theories in marketing focus on the ways consumption-related attitudes and behaviours develop. One such theory is the persuasion knowledge model (PKM) (Friestad & Wright, 1994). The PKM states that consumers develop knowledge related to an agent (e.g., companies promoting sustainable products) and topic (e.g., sustainable consumption), as well as general persuasion knowledge (e.g., the use of ads to promote sustainable products). Such knowledge about the motives and tactics in persuasion attempts is gained through consumers' experiences. Related to the PKM, one factor that prevents consumers from engaging in sustainable consumption is the lack of trust of sustainability claims that come from businesses. Greenwashing attempts, which are exaggerated claims about sustainability (Martin & Schouten, 2012), shape consumers' agent, topic and/or persuasion knowledge and contribute to the lack of trust of sustainability claims. To overcome this problem, companies should be encouraged to be transparent with their business practices and avoid deceiving consumers as much as possible. Eco-seals, "environmentally oriented assurance or certification cues" developed by companies (Bickart & Ruth, 2012, p. 51; Thompson, Anderson, Hansen, & Kahle, 2010) can also be used to increase the trust in sustainable claims. Indeed, Bickart and Ruth showed that consumers with high environmental concern tend to have more positive brand attitudes and higher purchase intentions when the eco-seal is used by familiar brands.

Social learning theory (Bandura, 1971) is another learning theory that can be used to understand and promote sustainable consumption. According to social learning theory, consumers, in addition to their own past experiences, learn attitudes and behaviours by observing people around them (Bandura, 1971). The majority of sustainable consumption practices can be observed by others. The purchase of organic and green products can be observed at grocery stores, the use of solar panels can be observed at the top of roofs or the use of recycling bins can be observed when they are put in front of houses for pick-up by waste management trucks. Moreover, community-based activities (e.g., a farmer's market, recycling events) and celebrities can be used to encourage sustainable consumption among consumers. Such a partnership could be beneficial because celebrities are often mimicked (Kahle & Homer, 1985), and thus consumers can "learn" sustainable behaviours from these often-watched personality figures.

Salazar, Oerlemans and Stroe-Biezen (2013), for instance, showed that people who received information about other people's choices on sustainable consumption were more likely to engage in sustainable consumption than people who did not receive such information. Moreover, these authors provided support for a biased social learning effect. Specifically, they found that specific social groups that have a higher social proximity to consumers (such as family and friends) are more effective in sustainable consumption decision-making process than more general social groups, suggesting that "individuals have specific reference groups and that they do not follow randomly other individuals or groups" (Salazar, Oerlemans, & Stroe-Biezen, 2013, p. 178). The majority of the research on social learning and reference groups showed that people tend to imitate behaviours of aspirational reference groups and avoid behaviours of non-aspirational reference groups (e.g., Berger & Heath 2007; White & Dahl 2006). However, White, Simpson and Argo (2014) showed that when a consumer learns that a non-aspirational group performs well on a positively viewed public behaviour (e.g., composting, recycling, conserving water), the consumer is more likely to engage in that same behaviour because the consumer wants to present his/her own group in a positive light too. These studies also suggest that social learning theory can be used effectively to increase sustainable consumption.

Past research on sustainability and consumer psychology

Understanding the psychology of consumers is critical to increasing sustainable consumption and growing the green economy. By using psychology, advertising and marketing theories discussed above, consumers can be convinced to engage in green consumption. The literature on using these theories to increase sustainable behaviour is small but growing (e.g., Kahle & Valette-Florence, 2012; Kaufmann-Hayoz et al., 2012; Matthies, Kastner, Kleese, & Wagner, 2011; Steg & Norland, 2012; Stern, 2000). In this section, we will review past research on sustainability and consumer psychology.

Research on the meaning of sustainability to consumers

Encouraging consumers to engage in sustainable consumption is closely related to what it means to a consumer to be sustainable. However, as a result of abundant and sometimes contradictory information on sustainable consumption provided to consumers, consumers may get confused and feel lost about being sustainable and/or participating in sustainable consumption (Black & Cherrier, 2010; Heiskanen & Pantzar, 1997; Markkula & Moisander, 2012). For some people, sustainable consumption is equivalent to the consumption of greener products, while for others, it is "broader and includes rethinking the social and cultural function of material consumption and affluence" (Black & Cherrier, 2010, p. 439). Accordingly, several research articles have sought to clarify the meanings of sustainability and sustainable consumption to consumers.

Markkula and Moisander (2012, p. 106) stated that "the meaning of 'sustainable consumption' is socioculturally constructed, premised upon, and supported by particular discourses of sustainable development, which have both material and linguistic, interconnected dimensions and have different effects". The existence of multiple meanings of sustainable consumption leads to struggle over meanings and discursive confusion among consumers. To illustrate their arguments empirically, Markkula and Moisander (2012) conducted interviews about the meanings of sustainable consumption in the fashion and clothing industry in Finland. These interviews provided support for the notion that discursive confusion over the meanings of sustainable consumption can indeed discourage consumers from engaging in sustainable behaviours.

Parsons, Soo and Berth (2013) used two theoretical developments, the Greenness Matrix and the meaning transfer model, to understand what sustainability means to both consumers and businesses. Based on studies conducted in New Zealand, the authors identified five greenness factors that can help manufacturers and buyers to place a business into one of the quadrants (i.e., green washer, sustainable superiority, honest, nongreen and missed opportunity/strategic choice) of the Greenness Matrix. Parsons, Soo and Berth (2013) also examined the symbolic meanings of sustainable products to understand why consumers choose them and uncovered symbolic meanings of virtue, personal and collective values, health and trust.

Research on factors that affect sustainable consumption

Many individual and situational factors may affect consumers' participation in sustainable consumption. In this section, we will review research on the impact of personal values, religion, thinking type (analytic vs. holistic), socio-demographic variables, personality, culture and social media on sustainable consumption.

Values have been considered as one of the most important constructs in social science by researchers (Kahle, 1996; Rokeach, 1973) because values are central to people's lives (Kahle & Timmer, 1983), define who people are, help people differentiate themselves from other people (Rokeach, 1973) and convey what is most important in life (Steenhaut & Kenhove, 2006). Values also motivate and guide behaviours and judgements across specific situations (Rokeach, 1973; Kahle & Timmer, 1983), including sustainable consumption behaviours (Stern, Dietz, & Kalof 1993; Thøgersen & Grunert-Beckmann 1997). Pinto, Nique, Añaña and Herter (2011) found that social-oriented values (e.g., conformity, self-direction, universalism) result in more environmentally responsible consumption than person-oriented values (e.g., exiting life, ideal world). Based on a survey with Belgian young adults, Vermeir and Verbeke (2007) found that consumers who hold traditional values (e.g., being humble, respecting traditions, holding no extreme ideas or feelings) are more inclined to buy sustainable products than consumers who hold power-related values (e.g., being influential, preserving image, having authority). Şaner and Hazer (2008) showed that, for Turkish women, there are significant positive correlations between universalism and benevolence values and sustainable consumption behaviours (e.g., turning the lights off when they are not used, recycling). Similarly, Karp (1996) found that people who value self-transcendence/openness to change are more likely to engage in sustainable consumption behaviours (e.g., recycling, buying green products, reducing the amount of plastic products purchased).

Although religion has not been one of the main variables used to understand consumer behaviour, some studies showed that religion does affect different aspects of consumer behaviour (e.g., Bailey & Sood, 1993; Essoo & Dibb, 2004; Minton, 2015), including sustainable consumption. Minton (2013) treats religious affiliation and degree of religiosity as individual difference variables and investigates their impact on sustainable consumption practices (both attitudes and behaviours). By focusing on Christian denominations and non-religious respondents, Minton (2013) shows that non-religious consumers are more likely to engage in sustainable consumption practices than religious consumers. Among religious consumers, those people belonging to denominations that support an inerrant view of scripture are less likely to engage in sustainable consumption than those people belonging to denominations that support human interpretation of scripture in light of cultural changes. Similarly, Kalamas, Cleveland and Laroche (2014) found that if consumers attribute environmental changes (e.g., global warming) to powerful others (e.g., a God or divine being), as opposed to chance or fate, they are more likely to participate in sustainable behaviours. More recently, Minton, Kahle and Kim (2015) showed that the relation between religion and sustainability differs based on whether a consumer is part of a minority religion or majority religion. Following inoculation theory, consumers of minority religions (e.g., a Buddhist in the United States or a Christian in South Korea) held more strongly to their religious values than consumers of majority religions, in order not to get their beliefs inoculated by the majority. Specifically, Eastern religious followers were more sustainable than their Western religious counterparts, likely due to the fact that most Eastern religious followers believe in a pantheistic view that God is in and through all elements of nature (James, 1902). In other words, destroying an element of nature destroys an element of God.

Another personal factor influencing sustainability is thinking type. Differences in cognitive processes of holistic and analytic thinkers tend to affect people's reactions towards the social and ethical issues, including sustainability issues (e.g., Lee, Youn, & Nayakankuppam, 2011). Lee, Youn and Nayakankuppam (2013) focused on the differences in cognitive processes of holistic and analytic thinkers, and proposed a framework to stimulate sustainable behaviour as a function of holistic thinking. Indeed, it was found that holistic thinking, as opposed to analytic thinking, is associated with increased perceived importance of social values related to sustainability. This increased perceived importance, in turn, leads to greater willingness to enhance sustainability.

Gender differences on sustainable consumption have also been identified by researchers. For instance, it has been found that women put more importance on responsible consumption (Berenguer et al., 2005) and engage in consumption practices aligned with environmental concerns (Diamantopoulos et al., 2003; Roberts, 1996; Steel, 1996). Zelezny, Chua and Aldrich (2000), based on a review of 13 studies and primary data, reported that women have more positive environmental attitudes, and their concern for the environment starts at an earlier age than men's. Luchs and Mooradian (2012) showed that the personality trait of agreeableness mediates the influence of gender on sustainable consumer behaviours, such that women reported higher agreeableness and that this personality trait resulted in higher sustainable consumption behaviours.

Other socio-demographic characteristics of consumers also affect participation in sustainable consumption. Abeliotis, Koniari and Sardianou (2010) showed with a Greek sample that age and income are the most important predictors of 3R (reduce, reuse, recycle) activities. Engaging in 3R activities becomes more frequent as consumers get older. Also, as income increases, participation in 3R activities decreases. In fact, age has been found as an important predictor of sustainable behaviours by many researchers, such that consumers' level of participation in sustainable consumer behaviours increases as they get older (e.g., Diamantopoulos et al., 2003; Gilg et al., 2005; Ngo et al., 2009; Smallbone, 2005). Findings on income, however, have been mixed. Some researchers found that income has a positive impact on sustainable consumption (Gilg et al., 2005; Schultz et al., 1995; Smallbone, 2005), probably because people with high income have more resources to devote to sustainable consumption practices. Other researchers, however, revealed opposite results, suggesting that people with high income are less likely to engage in sustainable consumption (Iyer & Kashyap, 2007; Ngo et al., 2009). Education has a positive impact on sustainable consumption as well because highly educated people tend to be more concerned with environmental issues (Diamantopoulos et al., 2003; Schultz et al., 1995; Steel, 1996; Tilikidou & Delistavrou, 2008).

Because populations with different social and cultural characteristics may have different attitudes, knowledge and behaviours regarding environmental issues (e.g., Johnson, Bowker, & Cordell, 2004), it is important to understand how various cultural groups approach environmental issues. Segev (2013) compared sustainable behaviours (e.g., green purchase intentions, actual green purchasing and conservation behaviours) and the drivers influencing them for non-Hispanic (i.e., native-born) consumers and Hispanic immigrant consumers. Four acculturation segments were examined (assimilation, integration, separation and marginalization), revealing differences among each of these segments. For instance, the Hispanic integration group scored significantly higher on several green behaviours than non-Hispanics and other Hispanics acculturation groups. Minton et al. (2012) examined sustainable behaviours and motivation patterns for such sustainable behaviours among participants from the United States, South Korea and Germany. Respondents from South Korea were found to engage in organic food purchase and the use of green transportation more than the respondents from the United States or Germany, while German respondents were the most frequent recyclers. Significant differences were also found in the motivation patterns for sustainable consumption behaviours. For instance, involvement attitudes led to recycling and green transportation use in all countries but led to organic food purchase in only the US and Germany. On the other hand, internalization attitudes led to green transportation use in the US and Germany, and organic food purchase in South Korea.

The discussion in the previous section shows that consumers' participation in sustainable consumption can be affected by others through such actions as observing and identification. One possible context for consumers to get interaction with other consumers is social media. Indeed, with the increasing adoption of social media, new opportunities are available for researching the impact of online conversation in environmental issues on sustainable consumption. In an attempt to show the feasibility of social media to detect awareness, describe attitudes and infer influence about sustainability communication campaigns, Russell et al. (2013) examined online conversations about energy efficiency behaviour by using the data collected on Twitter through the analysis of the messages, users and content hash tags in Tweets over four months. Results indicate that studying Twitter communications can be an important tool to assess engagement, identify influencers and identify word-of-mouth communities that can accelerate change in energy efficiency behaviours and other sustainable behaviours.

Research on approaches to increase sustainable consumption

Because many consumers are still reluctant to engage in sustainable consumption, it is important to develop theories, frameworks and change programmes that can be used to convince consumers to engage in sustainable consumption. In this section, we review some of the frameworks and change programmes developed for this purpose.

Xie, Cavallero and Cheng (2013) connect two streams of research – green advertising and persuasion knowledge – to understand the mechanisms responsible for consumer resistance against green advertising and other messages about increased participation in sustainable consumption. Specifically, Xie, Cavallero and Cheng (2013) first suggest that in terms of information processing, the integration of the green persuasion knowledge with dual and/or tri-process models can enhance the effectiveness of the study of persuasion knowledge. Second, green persuasion knowledge studies and construal level studies should be integrated so that the types and frames of green claims can interact with the construal level when consumers assess those green claims. Lastly, the perceptions of self-efficacy (i.e., how green tactics influence oneself) and other-efficacy (i.e., how green tactics influence other people) may be important factors when studying green persuasion knowledge.

Message framing strategies have been found to influence the effectiveness of persuasive communication in previous consumer psychology studies (e.g., Smith & Petty, 1996). Accordingly, message framing has been proposed by many researchers as one of the approaches to increase sustainable consumption. Su Han, Yu and Teng (2013) proposed a model of message framing to address the communication problems related to promoting the low-carbon policy (LCP) to the public. Based on a hierarchical order of promotional goals from awareness to action (awareness → memory → attitude → intention → action), this model considers the impact of various moderators (i.e., target audience's self-regulation, subjective knowledge, culture, the level of involvement and prior advertising messages) on the relationship between message framing and LCP promotional goals. Kolandai-Matchett (2009) used several message framing strategies (e.g., local relevance, emotional appeals) to implement a campaign in a real-world setting. More specifically, several articles written by using message-framing strategies were published in a free non-profit community newsletter in New Zealand as a part of a quasi-experiment. Exposure to these articles resulted in significant increases in understanding of sustainable consumption. Obermiller (1995) compared sick baby appeals (appeals that focus on the problem and its severity) and well baby appeals (appeals that focus on the actions to take to solve the problem) in different sustainable consumption settings. The results revealed that when the environmental problem is perceived as unimportant or has low awareness (e.g., energy conservation, solid waste reduction), sick baby appeals work better. However, when the environmental problem is perceived as important or already has high awareness (e.g., water conservation, recycling), well baby appeals work better. Thus, message framing tactics and different ad appeals have been shown to be useful for increasing knowledge of sustainable consumption both in academic studies as well as field tests.

Consumers' regulatory focus can also be used to increase participation in sustainable consumption. Regulatory focus theory (Higgins, 1997) suggests that consumers' consumption behaviours (including sustainable consumption) are shaped by either promotion or prevention focus. Promotion focus is about attainment of positive outcomes (e.g., achievement) whereas prevention focus is about the avoidance of negative outcomes (e.g., failure). Ku, Kuo, Wu and Wu (2012) showed that promotion-focused consumers are more likely to purchase green products if they are advertised through product-related nongreen appeals, but prevention-focused consumers are more likely to purchase green products if they are advertised through product-related green appeals. Kareklas, Carlson and Muehling (2012) combined the regulatory focus and self-construal research in a sustainable consumption context and examined the impact of the interaction between these two variables on attitudes towards green brands. The results indicated that consumers who were primed to have an independent self-construal (i.e., focus on one's self) had more favourable attitudes towards green brands when they were advertised through prevention-focused environmental appeals. In contrast, consumers who were primed to have an interdependent self-construal (i.e., focus on others) had more favourable attitudes towards green brands when they were advertised through promotion-focused environmental appeals.

Yang, Bublitz, Wang and Peracchio (2013) integrated the research on environmental sustainability and creativity to discuss how consumer creativity can encourage sustainable consumption. More specifically, Yang et al. (2013) suggested that various factors (e.g., forcing consumers to adopt a creative mindset, encouraging consumers to think at an abstract level, inducing a visual processing style among consumers), can be used to shift consumers towards innovations in sustainable consumption. For instance, it is suggested that creative ads are more likely to activate a creative mindset among consumers, which will, in turn, help consumers find new and creative ways to engage in sustainable consumption.

Jones, Owen and Kahle (2013) examined Germany's Green Dot (GD) Programme and its impact on the progress towards sustainable development in Germany and Europe. The GD programme is a change program that requires manufacturers to take back the post-consumer packaging waste from the products that they produce to recycle it. In order to evaluate the applicability of this programme to other countries, Jones, Owen and Kahle (2013) discussed both the criticisms (e.g., not giving enough attention to avoid waste in the first place, not promoting refillable bottles, misleading the public with the GD symbol and being perceived as a barrier to trade) and the successes of the GD Programme in detail. Then, the authors identified several factors (e.g., resistance from municipal and state governments, industry cooperation in the venture, consumer attitudes towards recycling and recycling capacities and technologies currently available) that might affect the success of the programme in the US and elsewhere.

Germany has also been working to become a low-carbon society by reducing greenhouse gas (GHG) emissions (Paetz, Dütschke, & Fichtner, 2012). Reducing GHG emissions and increasing energy efficiency in households require new, innovative solutions based on information and communication technologies (ICT). In order to understand if these ICTs would encourage consumers to engage in sustainable consumption more and learn possible reactions of consumers to these smart homes, Paetz, Dütschke and Fichtner (2012) conducted focus groups in Germany. The results showed that the reactions of consumers to smart homes were generally positive. More importantly, this study revealed that the main barrier to the ICTs is the cognitive effort needed to change daily routines and behavioural patterns. Once this barrier is overcome (through smart appliances or home automation systems, for instance), consumers are more likely to increase their participation in sustainable consumption.

Another piece of sustainable legislation, the Oregon Bottle Bill (OBB), is a bottle return system that encourages participation from consumers and beverage companies to increase sustainable behaviours (Kahle and Beatty, 1987a). Initial research showed that offering a small incentive (5 US cents) increases the rate of bottle return. Due to insufficient justification, as in the early cognitive dissonance experiments, it also improves the attitudes towards environmentalism. The logic is that people return bottles because it is a social norm, and when they observe themselves returning bottles they justify the activity based on their support for environmentalism because the 5 cents by itself cannot explain why a middle-class family would exert the effort to return bottles. This approach results in significant energy saving because recycles containers require less energy consumption than manufacturing containers from virgin materials.

Moscowitz and Kahle (2013) examined the potential consequences and problems of revisions made to OBB (including all glass, metal and plastic containers; opening privately operated redemption centres; and raising the current 5-cent deposit to 10 cents per container if participation rates fall below 80 per cent) from a comprehensive, marketing-based business perspective. Based on interviews and comparisons with other similar change programmes, Moscowitz and Kahle (2013) identified ways to improve the OBB, such as rebranding the programme, to encourage consumers to participate in this change programme more vigorously.

Other research has focused on how to increase sustainable consumption among the working and middle classes of developing countries. For instance, Schäfer, Jeager-Erben and Santos (2011) conducted a survey to see if previously developed sustainable communication strategies could be adopted in Southern Brazil and concluded that leapfrogging of consumers would not work well in Southern Brazil as there are already developed tendencies towards a resource-intensive lifestyle. Instead, Schäfer et al. (2011) suggested that differentiated sustainability communication strategies should be used to reach five different consumer segments (the home-centred traditionals, the indifferent, the up-to-date privileged, the wannabe materialists and the quality of life-oriented post-materialists). For instance, trendy bikes, community service for sharing products and messages about the social and ecological implications of production would work well for the quality-of-life oriented post-materialists, but second-hand electronic devices and sustainable consumption patterns that reflect the lifestyles of the high-income class would work better for the wannabe materialists.

Educating consumers about the expanded options at different stages of consumption (i.e., acquisition, usage and disposition) was offered as another way to convince consumers to engage in sustainable consumption (Luchs et al., 2011). The authors suggested that if consumers know that they have many choices available to them at different consumption stages, they can make more informed decisions that would benefit both consumers as well as the society/environment at large. For instance, at the acquisition stage, consumers can buy sustainable products to support sustainable businesses; buy used products to extend the life of existing products; rent, lease, share or borrow products to increase the use of products; or postpone or cancel purchasing some products. At the usage stage, consumers can use products more efficiently to slow down consumption, they can take advantage of repairing or refurbishing products or they can repurpose products by finding other uses for products that are not used for original purposes any more. There are many options at the final stage, including disposition, too. Recycling is one of the most established methods for a sustainable disposition. Consumers also have options to sell, barter, gift and donate a product at this disposition stage.

Future research

As the problems with the environment (e.g., climate change, environmental degradation and resource depletion) continue to exist, sustainable consumption will remain central to environment protection efforts. Accordingly, research on sustainable consumption will become one of the mainstream research areas in consumer psychology. Although the literature on sustainable consumption has been growing, there are still areas future research could and should emphasize.

The majority of the empirical research on sustainable consumption has been conducted in industrialized countries, such as the United States and Germany; however, research in developing countries is also necessary. Because education levels tend to be lower in those countries, it is possible that environmental awareness is also low. In that case, future research attempts should focus on increasing awareness and clarifying the meaning of sustainable consumption. Current research is mostly national based. Cross-cultural comparisons would also benefit researchers, practitioners and policy makers. If, for instance, future research finds that a certain type of appeal works well in both the developed and developing countries, universal messages can be used to increase sustainable consumption. Such findings would be beneficial for marketers and policy makers alike.

Although there has been some research on the relations between personal values and sustainable consumption, research on cultural values is lacking. Future research should examine how the meaning of sustainable consumption differs based on cultural values (e.g., uncertainty avoidance) and how that difference affects participation in sustainable consumption behaviours. Further research on other socio-demographic characteristics as predictors of sustainable behaviours would also be beneficial. Such characteristics could provide clues as to which consumers to target with sustainable products or messaging. For example, the characteristic of religion is underresearched, with most research only examining the relations between Western religious affiliation and sustainability. Future research would benefit from exploring religious beliefs from around the world, including Eastern religious affiliations (Hinduism, Islam, Buddhism, Taoism and Confucianism) as well as tribal or Native American spiritual beliefs on sustainable consumption practices.

In general, further research is needed to examine sustainability more holistically. Many of the studies reviewed in this chapter examine one small component of sustainability, such as the socio-demographic characteristics of consumers just discussed, a message framing technique or different promotional programmes. To fully understand how sustainability can be encouraged, more complex models need to be developed that more accurately reflect actual consumption experiences. For example, consumers are often faced with a state of cognitive load when making any decision in the marketplace given the vast number of choice options as well as continual distracters (e.g., other consumers, family members, messages over a store loudspeaker and constant reminders from smartphone). Research should examine how sustainable consumption practices differ when cognitive load and other less-explored factors are taken into consideration. Similarly, most research on sustainability focuses on one stage of consumption cycle only, such as buying green products or recycling. Studies that examine multiple stages of the consumption cycle (e.g., initial buying decision, product usage and disposal) are needed to encourage consumers in participating in sustainable consumption at each stage.

References

Aaker, J. (1997). Dimensions of brand personality. *Journal of Marketing Research, 34*(August), 347–357.

Abeliotis, K., Koniari, C., & Sardianou, E. (2010). The profile of the green consumer in Greece. *International Journal of Consumer Studies, 34*(2), 153–160.

Ajzen, I. (1991). The theory of planned behaviour. *Organizational Behaviour and Human Decision Processes, 50*(2), 179–211.

Bailey, J., & Sood, J. (1993). The effects of religious affiliation on consumer behaviour: A preliminary investigation. *Journal of Managerial Issues, 5*(3), 328–352.

Bandura, A. (1971). *Social learning theory*. New York, NY: General Learning Press.

Batra, R., Homer, P. M., & Kahle, L. R. (2001). Values, susceptibility to normative influence, and attribute importance weights: A nomological analysis. *Journal of Consumer Psychology, 11*(2), 115–128.

Beatty, S. E., & Kahle, L. R. (1988). Alternative hierarchies of the attitude-behaviour relationship: The impact of brand commitment and habit. *Journal of the Academy of Marketing Science, 16*(Summer), 1–10.

Berenguer, J., Corraliza, J. A., & Martín, R. (2005). Rural-urban differences in environmental concern, attitudes, and actions. *European Journal of Psychological Assessment, 21*(2), 128–138.

Bickart, B. A., & Ruth, J. A. (2012). Green eco-seals and advertising persuasion. *Journal of Advertising, 41*(4), 51–67.

Black, I. R., & Cherrier, H. (2010). Anti-consumption as part of living a sustainable lifestyle: Daily practices, contextual motivations and subjective values. *Journal of Consumer Behaviour, 9*, 437–453.

Crittenden, V. L., Crittenden, W. F., Ferrell, L. K., Ferrell, O. C., & Pinney, C. C. (2011). Market oriented sustainability: A conceptual framework and propositions. *Journal of the Academy of Marketing Science, 39*, 71–85.

Da Silva, R. V., & Syed Alwi, S. F. (2006). Cognitive, affective attributes and conative, behavioural responses in retail corporate branding. *Journal of Product and Brand Management, 15*(5), 293–305.

De Chernatony, L., Drury, S., & Segal-Horn, S. (2004). Identifying and sustaining services brands' values. *Journal of Marketing Communications, 10*(2), 73–93.

Diamantopoulos, A., Schlegelmilch, B. B., Sinkovics, R. R., & Bohlen, G. M. (2003). Can sociodemographics still play a role in profiling green consumers? A review of the evidence and an empirical investigation. *Journal of Business Research, 56*, 465–480.

Essoo, N., & Dibb, S. (2004). Religious influences on shopping behaviour: An exploratory study. *Journal of Marketing Management, 20*(7), 683–712.

European Environment Agency. (2005). *Household consumption and the environment*. Copenhagen: European Environment Agency.

Fournier, S. (1998). Consumers and their brands: Developing relationship theory in consumer research. *Journal of Consumer Research, 24*(4), 343–373.

Friestad, M., & Wright, P. (1994). The Persuasion Knowledge Model: How people cope with persuasion attempts. *Journal of Consumer Research, 21*(1), 1–31.

Gilg, A., Barr, S., & Ford, N. (2005). Green consumption or sustainable lifestyles? Identifying the sustainable consumer. *Futures, 37*, 481–504.

Goldstein, N. J., Cialdini, R. B., & Griskevicius, V. (2008). A room with a viewpoint: Using social norms to motivate environmental conservation in hotels. *Journal of Consumer Research, 35*, 472–482.

Han, S. S., Yu, Y., & Teng, L. (2013). Promoting low-carbon policy to the public: Message framing matters. In L. R. Kahle & E. Gurel-Atay (Eds.), *Communicating sustainability for the green economy* (pp. 3–21). Armonk, NY: M. E. Sharpe.

Hawken, P., Lovins, A., & Lovins, L. H. (1999). *Natural capitalism: Creating the next industrial revolution*. Boston, MA: Little, Brown.

Heiskanen, E., & Pantzar, M. (1997). Toward sustainable consumption: Two new perspectives. *Journal of Consumer Policy, 20*(4), 409–442.

Higgins, E. T. (1997). Beyond pleasure and pain. *American Psychologist, 52*, 1280–1300.

Homer, P. M., & Kahle, L. R. (1988). A structural equation test of the value-attitude-behaviour hierarchy. *Journal of Personality and Social Psychology, 54*(April), 638–646.

Huber, F., Beckmann, S. C., & Herrmann, A. (2004). Means–end analysis: Does the affective state influence information processing style? *Psychology and Marketing, 21*, 715–737.

Hult, G. T. M. (2011). Market-focused sustainability: Market orientation plus! *Journal of the Academy of Marketing Science, 39*, 1–6.

Iyer, E. S., & Kashyap, R. K. (2007). Consumer recycling: Role of incentives, information, and social class. *Journal of Consumer Behaviour, 6*, 32–47.

James, W. (1902). *The varieties of religious experience*. New York, NY: Touchstone.

Johnson, C. Y., Bowker, J. M., & Cordell, H. K. (2004). Ethnic variation in environmental belief and behaviour: An examination of the new ecological paradigm in a social psychological context. *Environment and Behaviour, 36*(2), 157–186.

Jones, L., Owen, S., & Kahle, L. R. (2013). Consequences of legislating packaging behaviour: Germany's green dot program and its communications. In L. R. Kahle & E. Gurel-Atay (Eds.), *Communicating sustainability for the green economy* (pp. 104–121). Armonk, NY: M.E. Sharpe.

Kahle, L. R. (1984). *Attitudes and social adaptation: A person- situation interaction approach*. Oxford, UK: Pergamon Press.

Kahle, L. R. (1996). Social values and consumer behaviour: Research from the list of values. In C. Seligman, J. M. Olson & M. P. Zanna (Eds.), *The psychology of values: The Ontario symposium* (pp. 135–152). Mahwah, NJ: Lawrence Erlbaum Associates.

Kahle, L. R., & Beatty, S. E. (1987a). Cognitive consequences of legislating post-purchase behaviour: Growing up with the bottle bill. *Journal of Applied Social Psychology, 17*, 826–840.

Kahle, L. R., & Beatty, S. E. (1987b). The task situation and habit in the attitude-behaviour relationship: A social adaptation view. *Journal of Social Behaviour and Personality, 2*(1), 219–232.

Kahle, L. R., Beatty, S. E., & Homer, P. M. (1986). Alternative measurement approaches to consumer values: The list of values (LOV) and the values and life style (VALS). *Journal of Consumer Research, 13*(4), 405–409.

Kahle, L. R., & Gurel-Atay, E. (2013). Introduction to the psychology of communicating sustainability. In L. R. Kahle & E. Gurel-Atay (Eds.), *Communicating sustainability for the green economy* (pp. 3–21). Armonk, NY: M. E. Sharpe.

Kahle, L. R., & Homer, P. M. (1985). Physical attractiveness of the celebrity endorser: A social adaptation perspective. *Journal of Consumer Research, 11*(March), 954–961.

Kahle, L. R., & Timmer, S. G. (1983). A theory and a method for studying values. In L. R. Kahle (Ed.), *Social values and social change: Adaptation to life in America*. New York, NY: Praeger.

Kahle, L. R., & Valette-Florence, P. (2012). *Marketplace lifestyles in an age of social media: Theory and method*. Armonk, NY: M. E. Sharpe.

Kalamas, M., Cleveland, M., & Laroche, M. (2014). Pro-environmental behaviours for thee but not for me: Green giants, green gods, and external environmental locus of control. *Journal of Business Research, 67*(2), 12–22.

Kareklas, I., Carlson, J. R., & Muehling, D. D. (2012). The role of regulatory focus and self-view in "green" advertising message framing. *Journal of Advertising, 41*(4), 25–39.

Karp, D. G. (1996). Values and their effect on pro-environmental behaviour. *Environment and Behaviour, 28*, 111–133.

Katz, D. (1960). The functional approach to the study of attitudes. *Public Opinion Quarterly, 24*, 163–204.

Kaufmann-Hayoz, R., Brohmann, B., Defila, R., Di Giulio, A., Dunkleberg, E., Erdmann, L., et al. (2012). Theoretical perspectives on consumer behaviour: Attempt at establishing an order to the theories. In R. Defila, A. Di Giulio & R. Kaufmann-Hayoz (Eds.), *The nature of sustainable consumption and how to achieve it* (pp. 81–112). Munich, Germany: oekom verlag.

Kelman, H. C. (1958). Compliance, identification, and internalization: Three processes of attitude change. *Journal of Conflict Resolution, 2*(1), 51–60.

Kolandai-Matchett, K. (2009). Mediated communication of "sustainable consumption" in the alternative media: A case study exploring a message framing strategy. *International Journal of Consumer Studies, 33*, 113–125.

Kotler, P. (2011). Reinventing marketing to manage the environmental imperative. *Journal of Marketing, 75*, 132–135.

Ku, H. H., Kuo, C. C., Wu, C. L., & Wu, C. Y. (2012). Communicating green marketing appeals effectively: The role of consumers' motivational orientation to promotion versus prevention. *Journal of Advertising, 41*(4), 41–50.

Lee, Y., Youn, N., & Nayakankuppam, D. (2011). The content of a brand scandal moderating the effect of thinking styles on the scandal's spillover. In R. Ahluwalia, T. L. Chartrand & R. K. Ratner (Eds.), *Advances in consumer research* (Vol. 39). Duluth, MN: Association for Consumer Research.

Lee, Y., Youn, N., & Nayakankuppam, D. (2013). Sustainable behaviour and holistic thinking. In L. R. Kahle & E. Gurel-Atay (Eds.), *Communicating sustainability for the green economy* (pp. 88–103). Armonk, NY: M.E. Sharpe.

Lomas, T., Hefferon, K., & Ivtzan, I. (2014). The LIFE model: A meta-theoretical conceptual map for applied positive psychology. *Journal of Happiness Studies, 15*(4).

Luchs, M. G., & Mooradian, T. A. (2012). Sex, personality, and sustainable consumer behaviour: Elucidating the gender effect. *Journal of Consumer Policy, 35*, 127–144.

Luchs, M., Naylor, R. W., Rose, R. L., Catlin, J. R., Gau, R., Kapitan, S., et al. (2011). Toward a sustainable marketplace: Expanding options and benefits for consumers. *Journal of Research for Consumers, 19*, 1–12.

Markkula, A., & Moisander, J. (2012). Discursive confusion over sustainable consumption: A discursive perspective on the perplexity of marketplace knowledge. *Journal of Consumer Policy, 35*, 105–125.

Martin, D., & Schouten, J. (2012). *Sustainable marketing*. Boston, MA: Prentice Hall.

Matthies, E., Kastner, I., Kleese, A., & Wagner, H. J. (2011). High reduction potentials for energy user behaviour in public buildings: How much can psychology-based interventions achieve? *Journal of Environmental Studies and Sciences, 1*(3), 241–255.

McAlexander, J., Schouten, J., & Koenig, H. (2002). Building brand community. *Journal of Marketing, 66*(1), 38–54.

Minton, E. A. (2013). Religion and religiosity's influence on sustainable consumption behaviours. In L. R. Kahle & E. Gurel-Atay (Eds.), *Communicating sustainability for the green economy* (pp. 73–87). Armonk, NY: M. E. Sharpe.

Minton, E. A. (2015). In advertising we trust: Religiosity's influence on marketplace and relational trust. *Journal of Advertising, 44*(4), 1–12.

Minton, E. A., Kahle, L., & Kim, C. H. (2015). Religion and motives for sustainable behaviours: A cross-cultural comparison and contrast. *Journal of Business Research, 68*(9), 1937–1944.

Minton, E., Lee, C., Orth, U., Kim, C. H., & Kahle, L. R. (2012). Sustainable marketing and social media: A cross-country analysis of motives for sustainable behaviours. *Journal of Advertising, 41*(4), 69–84.

Moisander, J. (2007). Motivational complexity of green consumerism. *International Journal of Consumer Studies, 31*, 404–409.

Moscowitz, E., & Kahle, L. R. (2013). Oregon's iconic bottle bill. In L. R. Kahle & E. Gurel-Atay (Eds.), *Communicating sustainability for the green economy* (pp. 242–257). Armonk, NY: M.E. Sharpe.

National Research Council. (2010). *Advancing the science of climate change*. Washington, DC: National Academies Press.

Ngo, A. T., West, G. E., & Calkins, P. H. (2009). Determinants of environmentally responsible behaviours for greenhouse gas reduction. *International Journal of Consumer Studies, 33*, 151–161.

Obermiller, C. (1995). The baby is sick/the baby is well: A test of environmental communication appeals. *Journal of Advertising, 24*(2), 55–70.

OECD. (2002). *Towards sustainable household consumption? Trends and policies in OECD countries*. Paris: Organisation for Economic Co-Operation and Development.

Ottman, J. A. (1998). *Green marketing: Opportunity for innovation*. Lincolnwood, IL: NTC Business Books.

Paetz, A.-G., Dütschke, E., & Fichtner, W. (2012). Smart homes as a means to sustainable energy consumption: A study of consumer perceptions. *Journal of Consumer Policy, 35*(1), 23–41.

Parsons, A. G., Soo, S., & Berth, N. (2013). Sustainability: Is perception as good as reality. In L. R. Kahle & E. Gurel-Atay (Eds.), *Communicating sustainability for the green economy* (pp. 23–42). Armonk, NY: M.E. Sharpe.

Peattie, K., & Collins, A. (2009). Guest editorial: Perspectives on sustainable consumption. *International Journal of Consumer Studies, 33*, 107–112.

Peterson, C. (2006). *A primer in positive psychology*. New York, NY: Oxford University Press.

Piaget, J. (1952). *The origins of intelligence in children*. New York, NY: International Universities Press.

Pinto, D. C., Nique, W. M., Añaña, E. D. S., & Herter, M. M. (2011). Green consumer values: How do personal values influence environmentally responsible water consumption? *International Journal of Consumer Studies, 35*, 122–131.

Prothero, A. Dobscha, S., Freund, J., Kilbourne, W. E., Luchs, M. G., Ozanne, L. K., et al. (2011). Sustainable consumption: Opportunities for consumer research and public policy. *Journal of Public Policy and Marketing, 30*(1), 31–38.

Rettie, R., Burchell, K., & Barnham, C. (2014). Social normalisation: Using marketing to make green normal. *Journal of Consumer Behaviour, 13*, 9–17.

Reynolds, T. J., & Olson, J. C. (2001). *Understanding consumer decision making: The means-end approach to marketing and advertising strategy*. Mahwah, NJ: Lawrence Erlbaum Associates.

Roberts, J. A. (1996). Green consumers in the 1990s: Profile and implications for advertising. *Journal of Business Research, 36*(3), 217–231.

Rokeach, M. (1973). The nature of human values. In J. W. Berry, M. H. Segall & Ç. Kağıtçıbaşı (Eds.), *Handbook of cross-cultural psychology*. Boston, MA: Allyn and Bacon.

Russell, M. G., Flora, J., Strohmaier, M., Pöschko, J., Perez, R., Yu, J., et al. (2013). Semantic analysis of energy-related conversations in social media: A twitter case study. In L. R. Kahle & E. Gurel-Atay (Eds.), *Communicating sustainability for the green economy* (pp. 223–241). Armonk, NY: M.E. Sharpe.

Schäfer M., Jaeger-Erben, M., & Bamberg, S. (2012). Life events as windows of opportunity for changing towards sustainable consumption patterns? Results from an intervention study. *Journal of Consumer Policy, 35*, 65–84.

Schäfer, M., Jaeger-Erben, M., & Santos, A. (2011). Leapfrogging to sustainable consumption? An explorative survey of consumption habits and orientations in Southern Brazil. *Journal of Consumer Policy, 34*(1), 175–196.

Schrader, U., & Thøgersen, J. (2011). Putting sustainable consumption into practice. Editorial. *Journal of Consumer Policy, 34*, 3–8.

Schultz, W. P., Oskamp, S., & Mainieri, T. (1995). Who recycles and when? A review of personal and situational factors. *Journal of Environmental Psychology, 15*, 105–121.

Schwartz, S. H. (1994). Are there universal aspects in the content and structure of values? *Journal of Social Issues, 50*, 19–45.

Segev, S. (2013). Green advertising and behaviour: Non-Hispanics vs. acculturating Hispanics. In L. R. Kahle & E. Gurel-Atay (Eds.), *Communicating sustainability for the green economy* (pp. 104–121). Armonk, NY: M.E. Sharpe.

Sener, A., & Hazer, O. (2008). Values and sustainable consumption behaviour of women: A Turkish sample. *Sustainable Development, 16*, 291–300.

Sheth, J. N., Sethia, N. K., & Srinivas, S. (2011). Mindful consumption: A customer-centric approach to sustainability. *Journal of the Academy of Marketing Science, 39*, 21–39.

Smallbone, T. (2005). How can domestic households become part of the solution to England's recycling problems? *Business Strategy and the Environment, 14*, 110–122.

Smith, S. M., & Petty, R. E. (1996). Message framing and persuasion: A message processing analysis. *Personality and Social Psychology Bulletin, 22*, 257–268.

Steel, B. S. (1996). Thinking globally and acting locally? Environmental attitudes, behaviour and activism. *Journal of Environmental Management, 47*, 27–36.

Steenhaut, S., & Kenhove, V. P. (2006). An empirical investigation of the relationships among a consumer's personal values, ethical ideology and ethical beliefs. *Journal of Business Ethics, 64*(2), 137–155.

Steg, L., & Norland, A. (2013). Models to explain environmental behaviour. In L. Steg, A. E. van den Berg & J. I. M. de Groot (Eds.), *Environmental psychology: An introduction* (pp. 185–196). Chichester, West Sussex, UK: Wiley-Blackwell.

Stern, P. C. (2000). Toward a coherent theory of environmentally significant behaviour. *Journal of Social Issues, 56*, 407–424.

Stern, P. C., Dietz, T., & Kalof, L. (1993). Value orientations, gender, and environmental concern. *Environment and Behaviour, 25*, 322–348.

Tanner, C., & Kast, S. W. (2003). Promoting sustainable consumption: Determinants of green purchases by Swiss consumers. *Psychology and Marketing, 20*, 883–902.

Thøgersen, J. (2005). How may consumer policy empower consumers for sustainable lifestyles? *Journal of Consumer Policy, 28*, 143–178.

Thøgersen, J., & Crompton, T. (2009). Simple and painless? The limitations of spillover in environmental campaigning. *Journal of Consumer Policy, 32*, 141–163.

Thøgersen, J., & Grunert-Beckmann, S. C. (1997). Values and attitude formation towards emerging attitude objects: From recycling to general, waste minimizing behaviour. In D. MacInnis & M. Brucks (Eds.), *Advances in consumer research* (pp. 182–189). Provo, UT: Association for Consumer Research.

Thompson, D. W., Anderson, R. C., Hansen, E. N., & Kahle, L. R. (2010). Green segmentation and environmental certification: Insights from forest products. *Business Strategy and the Environment, 19*, 319–334.

Tilikidou, I., & Delistavrou, A. (2008). Types and influential factors of consumers' non-purchasing ecological behaviours. *Business Strategy and the Environment, 18*, 61–76.

U.S. Environmental Protection Agency. (2014). *Climate change indicators in the United States, 2014*. EPA 430-R-14-004. Retrieved from www.epa.gov/climatechange/indicators.

Valor, C. (2008). Can consumers buy responsibly? Analysis and solutions for market failures. *Journal of Consumer Policy*, *31*, 315–326.

Wasik, J. F. (1996). *Green marketing and management: A global perspective*. Cambridge, MA: Blackwell.

Xie, G. X., Cavallero, A., & Cheng, M. (2013). Reluctant for a reason? A persuasion knowledge perspective on green advertising. In L. R. Kahle & E. Gurel-Atay (Eds.), *Communicating sustainability for the green economy* (pp. 141–157). Armonk, NY: M.E. Sharpe.

Yang, X., Bublitz, M. G., Wang, K. Y., & Peracchio, L. A. (2013). Consumer creativity and its implications for sustainability marketing. In L. R. Kahle & E. Gurel-Atay (Eds.), *Communicating sustainability for the green economy* (pp. 174–190). Armonk, NY: M.E. Sharpe.

Zelezny, L. C., Chua, P., & Aldrich, C. (2000). Elaborating on gender differences in environmentalism. *Journal of Social Issues*, *56*(3), 443–458.

28

Moving towards sustainable consumption

A psychological perspective on improvement of public transport

Margareta Friman and Tommy Gärling

Fast motorized transportation of people and cargo is instrumental for consumption in contemporary societies with their specialization of functions at different locations. Cargo needs to be transported between different units in the manufacturing process as well as from manufacturers to retailers. In urban areas of developed countries, private motorized travel contributes to well-being by increasing opportunities for residents to purchase wide assortments of goods, patronize restaurants, visit recreational places and attend entertaining and cultural events (Leyden, Goldberg, & Michelbach, 2011; Reardon & Abdallah, 2013). In sparsely populated rural areas, private motorized travel is essential for sustenance. Private motorized travel is sometimes in itself enjoyable consumption (Moktharian & Salomon, 2001). Driving a new luxury car on a recreational journey is an example of this. The downside is that the unprecedented increase in private motorized travel is primarily responsible for a number of local, global and societal consequences that threaten people's well-being.

In this chapter, we argue that there is a unanimous requirement that current private motorized travel be changed such that daily travel becomes environmentally sustainable without compromising social and economic sustainability. The main focus of the chapter is on how public transport would fulfil the need for daily travel such that automobile use is importantly reduced. In the next section, we briefly describe the rise of the private automobile to emerge as the most popular travel mode and the negative effects on environmental sustainability that mass motorization of travel to some extent already has and is expected to increasingly have in the future. This section is followed by a review of current and future public transport. A third section discusses different measures for increasing choice of public transport.

Rise and fall of the automobile

Few other human inventions have so drastically altered the development of the world like the automobile. In developed countries, and now in developing countries, its versatility strongly contributes to why it is the preferred mode of urban, suburban and rural travel (Jakobsson, 2007). Instrumental motives, however, do not alone explain its choice. The automobile is also attractive because it is fun to drive and ride, provides privacy and security and signals social status (Gatersleben, 2014).

Even though cars were available at the beginning of the twentieth century, it was only in the years after World War II with the subsequent spread of affluence and the acceleration of automobile mass production that ownership was brought within the reach of the majority of households in the industrialized world. Car ownership is related to household socio-economic characteristics (e.g., income, household composition, employment status), the characteristics of the transportation system (e.g., car purchase costs, available road infrastructure, non-access to public transport) and the attributes of the built environment (e.g., population density, access to services and amenities) (Giuliano & Dargay, 2006).

Car ownership in the United Kingdom has risen from 19 million in 1971 to over 31 million in 2007 (average growth rate of 3 per cent per annum) and 34 million people have a valid driving license (Leibling, 2008). In the United States, over 211 million people (about two-thirds of all inhabitants) had driver's licenses in 2010 and the total number of registered vehicles rose by 14 million between 2001 and 2011 (Puentes, 2012). Such a growth in car ownership is not limited to these Anglo-Saxon countries, to which Australia and Canada can be added, with increases in average annual growth rate in total number of vehicles (millions) for the period 1960–2002 from 0.5 to 5.1 and from 5.2 to 18.2, respectively (Dargay, Gately, & Sommer, 2007). Similar trends have been observed for other industrialized countries, including several in the European Union. According to Eurostat (2012) the automobile accounts for more than 80 per cent of the total daily distance of passenger travel. Furthermore, sharply increasing automobile ownership and use are observed in countries only beginning the industrialization process or that are, to some extent, industrialized, such that citizens are beginning to experience income growth and the spread of affluence (Kitamura & Mohamad, 2009). Sperling and Claussen (2004) note that the fastest growth has been observed in Latin America and Asia, with vehicle sales in China, for instance, having increased annually by more than 50 per cent in recent years (from 700,000 in 2001 to 1.1 million in 2002, and about 1.7 million in 2003).

The downside is that the unprecedented increase in motorized travel is primarily responsible for a number of negative effects (van Wee, 2014). Locally, urban environments are made less liveable due to accident risks, particle emissions, noise and road infrastructure's infringement on land that negates other valuable uses as well as destroying historical and cultural values. Global long-term effects include increases in global warming due to emissions of greenhouse gases from motorized traffic. These emissions are substantial and increasing. Another global long-term effect is road infrastructure construction resulting in a dearth of land to produce food for an increasing world population. Shortage of material and fossil energy due to the production and use of motorized gasoline-powered vehicles is still another global long-term effect. Constructing road infrastructure, controlling noise (e.g. replacing old road surfaces with new quiet ones; building protective walls along roads), preventing and mitigating damages from traffic accidents, medical treatments of accident victims and loss of work hours due to injuries are societal costs accrued to tax payers, insurance companies and directly and indirectly to road users. The time loss due to congestion is also considered a societal cost.

Recent evidence suggests an interrupted increase in private automobile travel. Referred to as peak car use, stagnation or even decrease has been observed in eight developed countries (Australia, Canada, France, Germany, Japan, Sweden, the United Kingdom and the United States). Different explanations are offered. Millard-Ball and Schipper (2011) propose that increasing fuel prices accounts for peak car use. Litman (2012) highlights a number of additional determinants: automobile saturation, wealth effects, ageing populations, increased urbanization, improved alternative travel options and incentives, changing consumer preferences and increased concerns for health and environment. Goodwin (2012) argues that peak car use should be considered a turning point followed by decline. However, this remains speculation until any or more of the proposed explanations are corroborated. Current levels of automobile use are still not sustainable.

The fact is that the world has not yet seen a fall in automobile use. What conditions need to exist for this to happen? Gärling and Friman (2012, 2015) review several propositions. Prominent among them are, in the longer term, new infrastructure that increases accessibility without motorized travel, and in the shorter term, improved public transport. It is still unlikely that the private automobile will not play any future role. Alternatives are not equally feasible everywhere, for instance in rural compared to urban areas or in developing compared to developed countries. Therefore, it is essential in the shorter term that the number of fuel-efficient automobiles increases, and in the longer term that automobiles running on clean fuel penetrate the market.

Current and future public transport

Europe

Historically, public transport (railways, buses and tramways) originated in Europe primarily in connection with nineteenth century industrialization, urbanization and separation of residences from workplaces. Industrialization both increased demand for fast mass transportation at a large scale of both people and goods as well as provided the means for building railways, trains and buses meeting that demand. The market share of public transport grew steadily until the depression in the 1930s. After World War II, the market again started to grow, partly due to the expansion of high-speed trains (e.g., in France, Germany and the United Kingdom). However, the steep rise in popularity of the private automobile during the 1950s caused sharp declines in public transport use. A continuous modernization of public transport services has, despite this negative development, contributed to a relatively high market share in EU member states. European cities generally offer public transport services that are reliable, accessible, comfortable, safe and flexible (Mees, 2010; Newman & Kenworthy, 1999; Pucher & Kurth, 1996). Furthermore, several reviews (e.g., Albalate & Bel, 2010; Buehler & Pucher, 2012) suggest that other success factors include economic (e.g., low employment, high taxes, high automobile costs and public transport subsidies), demographic (population growth) and environmental (high-density cities).

In 2012, local public transport in the EU carried 57 billion passengers (The mobility in cities database, 2012). The majority of journeys (56 per cent) were undertaken by bus. The shares for each mode in the member states vary with five countries (Austria, Croatia, Czech Republic, France and Germany) having a higher share of urban rail than buses. Where metro networks exist (in 16 of the 28 member states), these attract a significant share of the number of public transport journeys. In Austria, France and Spain, for instance, metro journeys make up over one quarter.

Public transport has had an annual growth in Europe between 2000 and 2012 with a small decrease in 2009 (the year of the economic crisis). A more important question is whether use has increased relative to other modes. Eurostat (2012) estimates that current public transport services account for 16–17 per cent of the total daily distance of passenger travel. In Figure 28.1, we have compiled statistics from the EU countries as well as some other European countries (Iceland, Turkey, Switzerland, Republic of Macedonia and Norway) showing changes in percentage distance of passenger travel by public transport from 2003 to 2012. As may be seen, the variation between countries is large, whereas the within-country variation over years is

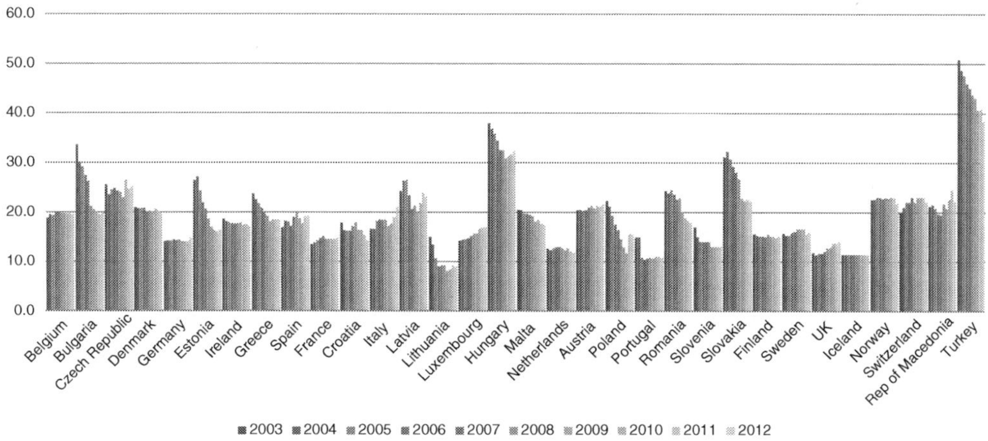

Figure 28.1 Per cent distance of passenger travel in Europe by bus and train from 2003 to 2012.
Source: Eurostat, 2012.

smaller. Since total daily mobility has increased, the figures indicate a stable development in a minority of countries (Belgium, Denmark, The Netherlands, Iceland and Finland), and a weak-to-medium–large relative increase in another minority (Austria, France, Germany, Italy, Latvia, Luxembourg, Republic of Macedonia, Spain, Sweden, Switzerland and the United Kingdom). In a few other countries (Bulgaria, Estonia, Greece and Turkey), a relative decrease is evident. A likely explanation is increases in automobile ownership. In the remaining countries, no clear development is discernible.

Women, students and households without access to cars tend to dominate public transport ridership (Eurobarometer, 2011). A slight increase has been noted among young men in recent years (Buehler & Pucher, 2012; Davis & Dutzik, 2012), at the same time as a downward trend in car use is observed (Aretun & Nordbakke 2014, Sivak & Schoettle, 2012). In some European countries (e.g., Germany), public transport use by people with access to cars has been increasing (Buehler & Pucher, 2012).

Several studies both in Europe and other countries have attempted to identify attributes of public transport services that increase user satisfaction (e.g., Barabino, Deiana, & Tilocca, 2012; Beirão & Sarsfield Cabral, 2007; Cantwell, Caulfield, & O'Mahony, 2009; Eboli & Mazzulla, 2009; Fellesson & Friman, 2008; Hensher, Mulley, & Yahya, 2010). A recent review (Redman, Friman, Gärling, & Hartig, 2013) concludes that there are two types of quality attributes in public transport (Table 28.1). *Perceived attributes* directly refer to users' experience and are measured by observing user responses. If, for instance, new seats or improved lighting are implemented in vehicles to increase comfort, this is frequently assessed by means of on-board interviews. In contrast, *physical attributes* are measured without involvement of users. A change in timetable is one example where measures of time keeping (e.g., before and after a change) are used to infer how the users perceive the reliability of the service.

Redman et al. (2013) argue that for improving public transport services it is essential to know the effects of physical attributes on users. For example, explanations of why travellers feel negative towards unreliable services include the impact it has (e.g., being late to important meetings) or the stress that the uncertainty creates in itself. Little is still known about how travellers perceive variability in travel times and how their perceptions differ from the objective variability

Table 28.1 Definition of quality attributes in public transport

Category	*Attribute*	*Definition*
Perceived	Comfort	How comfortable the journey is regarding access to seating, noise levels, driver handling and air conditioning
	Safety/Security	How safe from traffic accidents passengers feel during the journey as well as personal safety
	Convenience	How simple the service is to use and how much it adds to ease of mobility
	Aesthetics	Aesthetic appeal of vehicles, stations and wait areas
Physical	Reliability	How closely the actual service matches the route timetable
	Frequency	How frequently the service operates during different hours
	Speed	The time spent travelling from origin to destination
	Accessibility	The degree to which the service is available to as many as possible
	Price	The monetary cost of travel
	Ease of transfers/ interchanges	How simple transport connections include wait times
	Vehicle conditions	The physical and mechanical conditions of vehicles, including frequency of breakdowns
	Information provision	How accurate the information is about routes and interchanges

Source: Redman et al. (2013)

(Bates, Polak, Jones, & Cook, 2001). People obviously want to feel confident that they can reach their destination on time. It is thus known that delays will have consequences for both satisfaction (Friman, Edvardsson, & Gärling, 2001) and intentions to reuse the service (Carrel, Halvorsen, & Walker, 2013). Friman (2010) found that wait times elicit negative emotions with stronger emotions associated with wait times while being in the vehicle (e.g., delays) than wait times before entering the vehicle. A study conducted in The Netherlands (Reitveld, Bruinsma, & Vuuren, 2001) showed that the average delay of public transport was about 6 minutes on a 1-hour trip. It was also not unusual for buses to depart earlier than the scheduled time. Both delays and early departures are major concerns in particular if they result in missed connections.

The bulk of previous research has investigated commuters of public transport. The results are therefore not easily generalized to automobile commuters. Travel time and unreliability are common reasons stated by car users for why they do not choose public transport (e.g., Beirão & Sarsfield Cabral, 2007; Eurobarometer, 2011). Yet, travel time with public transport is often overestimated by car users (Fujii, Gärling, & Kitamura, 2001). Pedersen, Friman and Kristensson (2011) found that reliability and security are perceived as less satisfactory by automobile commuters, but after having switched to public transport, these attributes tend to be relatively more positively evaluated. In some large-scale studies (Brög, Erl, Ker, Ryle, & Wall, 2009), the number of people judging the public transport service to have a higher quality after than before switching from automobile commuting has been observed to increase despite no improvements in public transport services. Their difficulty in making accurate predictions may also explain why some car users fail to set goals to switch to public transport as the main commuting mode (Taniguchi, Gräås, & Friman, 2014).

Based on surveys asking automobile commuters to state what improvements of public transport services would make them switch (Eriksson, Friman, & Gärling, 2008), some tentative suggestions are apparent. Short travel times, few exchanges, reliability and frequency of service are basic requirements but probably not sufficient. Accessibility and price are other important attributes. People may also demand mobility experiences that are enjoyable and social, not only convenient and efficient. In order to attract car users, it is thus important to develop a public transport service that offers value in addition to performance efficiency. Surveys or interviews are needed to identify additional context-specific aspects. For instance, the opportunity to work while traveling may be important for some, while social interactions may be important for others.

Several innovations in European public transport have emerged in the past few years. Provision of integrated door-to-door services in Amsterdam, The Netherlands (e.g., bicycle parking areas outside suburban railway stations) and other Dutch cities has generally been successful and has resulted in increases in bicycle use, bus use as well as larger market shares (Martens, 2006). In Sweden, the municipalities of Lund and Göteborg have integrated payment for a bike-sharing system with payment for public transport. Thus, a season pass or a three-day pass on public transport includes free access to the bike-sharing system.

Other innovations include integration of public transport by means of multimodal terminals (e.g., Zürich, Switzerland and London airports), development of new information systems (e.g., real-time applications for journey planning in several cities in Sweden), better coordination of timetables (e.g., Schaffhausen Transportation, Switzerland) and combined ticketing and tariff systems (e.g., network cards in Germany). In London, a transport smart card (the Oyster card) has been implemented that facilitates fast and easy service and reduced queues.

Improvements during recent years have transformed the Oyster card into a contactless payment card possible to use on local bus, metro and tram services as well as national rail services. The card automatically provides travellers with the cheapest fare and accounts can be managed online. Due to this innovative payment system, the number of people paying cash has, since its introduction in 2003, dropped dramatically to less than 1 per cent. The popularity of the card (Lewis, 2010) generates data which enables, for instance, real-time changes and real-time information to passengers.

An additional challenge is to provide high-quality public transport in sparsely populated rural areas. An example is a county in Sweden (Värmland) with only 311,225 residents (3 per cent of the country's population). In this county, all bus services involving about 40 contractors are procured and coordinated by a transport authority. Due to improved interchanges, improved infrastructure and shorter travel times, the market share has increased during recent years from 7 per cent to 12.3 per cent. This is still far below 50.4 per cent in the more densely populated capital of Stockholm. If occupancy on the busses is low, public transport is not more sustainable than car travel. Yet provision is necessary to meet the travel needs of people lacking access to cars. A variety of other innovative rural transport services have therefore been developed in recent years. Well-synchronized timetables are connecting different public transport services in rural areas of Germany, Denmark, The Netherlands and Switzerland. Fares are also integrated. As an example, in rural areas close to Copenhagen, travellers buy a ticket for the whole journey. In Sweden, a number of transport companies have collaborated in developing a ticketing system that connects more than 3,500 locations in both rural and urban areas. All transport modes are included such that the travellers purchase a ticket for the whole journey, regardless of how they choose to travel.

In some rural areas, public transport has successfully been supplemented by car-sharing schemes and car clubs. Villagecarshare.com in England is one example of an online journey-matching service that allows people to find others who are making similar journeys. Similar innovative solutions with a broad range of flexible transport services have been enabled by the development of transport telematics/Intelligent Transport Systems (Brake, Mulley, Nelson, & Wright, 2007; Mulley & Nelson, 2009). One outcome is Demand-Responsive-Transport

(DRT) systems that either provide feeder links, additional service during off-peaks, service to special locations (e.g., large workplaces) or fully substitute traditional public transport (Enoch, Potter, Parkhurst, & Smith, 2004). Due to its flexibility, DRT has the potential to become an alternative public transport system in rural areas or for different market segments. A high-quality DRT system should include integrated timetables with connecting services, guarantees to reach connections on time and comfortable vehicles. DRT systems are found in England (InterConnect), in Germany (RUF-BUS) and in France (TaxiTub).

Other continents

In the United States, people are less likely to use public transport than people in Europe. The total market share is only 5 per cent (data from 2006–2010 American Community Survey, Rapino & Field, 2012) and has been relatively constant since the 1970s (Millard-Ball & Lee Schipper, 2011). In 2013, Americans still made 10.7 billion trips with public transport, which is the highest annual ridership in over 50 years (American Public Transportation Association, 2013). Cities with developed rail systems are, for example, Los Angeles, New York and Cleveland. Large bus systems are running in Washington DC, Houston, Cincinnati and Seattle. Public transport use in the US is dominated by work commutes. Women, low-income people and ethnic minorities use public transport more than other groups (Buehler & Pucher, 2012; Bullard, 2003).

"Transit agencies" and their partners are currently in the US proactively creating new markets for public transport by targeting growth in and around bus and rail stations (Transportation Research Board, 2004). Several joint innovative development projects are taking place with the aim to increase ridership. Joint developments often occur at rail stations surrounded by a mix of office, commercial and institutional land-uses. In the San Francisco Bay Area, one such example is that an improved railway station led to more passengers and a positive economic development in the local district (Transportation Research Board, 2004).

A bus rapid transit (BRT) system is another innovative solution that is implemented in some cities in the US and in many other cities around the world. A BRT system is a high-quality bus-based public transport service, which complies with an objective quality standard (Institute for Transportation and Development Policy, 2014). The quality criteria (in total 29) include off-board payment, segregated bus lanes, platform-level boarding, integration with bicycle-sharing systems and minimal bus emissions. BRT systems are ranked as Gold, Silver or Bronze Standard (e.g., Hensher, Mulley, & Li, 2014) depending on the number of quality criteria that are fulfilled. Implementing BRT systems may increase ridership by between 5 per cent and 25 per cent (Hensher, 2007). Some US examples of significant ridership increases include Boston's Silver Line (85 per cent), the Metro Rapid Wiltshire Corridor (42 per cent) and Ventura Corridor (27 per cent) (Federal Transport Administration, 2004). Travel time savings, reliability and an easily identified brand are proposed explanations of the increases.

An issue that has been debated in many countries is whether to invest in tramways or BRT systems. Politicians seem to prefer tramways referred to as Light Rail (Mulley, Hensher, & Rose, 2014) despite it being more expensive. Research also shows that mode of public transport (bus vs. rail) does not have a significant ridership effect, measured as the number of boardings per vehicle kilometre (Currie & Delbrosc, 2013). Other factors (e.g., frequency and reliability) have larger impact on ridership and ridership potential (Currie & Wallis, 2008; Hensher & Li, 2012).

Growing Asian cities have experienced rapid economic development and urbanization since the latter half of last century, which has resulted in a highly automobile-dependent mobility of people and goods (Hayashi, Doi, Yagishita, & Kuwata, 2004). Severe congestions are the outcome of the Asian trend with increases in road transport demand in conjunction with a lack of road supply and public transport. Current public transport in Asia is dependent on buses and intermediate public transport modes rather than on rail. Their market share varies widely. For instance, the use of public transport is low in Indonesian cities (2 per cent), while it is high in other Asian cities such as Hong Kong (90 per cent) and Singapore (60 per cent). Within individual countries, the variation in ridership is large. Pucher, Korattyswaroopam and Ittyerah (2004) showed that in India the percentage of use is high in some parts (e.g., 60 per cent in Mumbai), while it is low in other areas (e.g., 5 per cent in Kolkata). During recent years China has aggressively implemented several BRT systems in more than ten cities (Cervero, 2013), including Beijing, Hangzhou, Xiamen, Jinan and Guangzhou. There are many other cities in Asia that also strive to expand public transport to encourage mode switch. In Japan, public transport operators own rail infrastructure and rail stations. This has contributed to an interest in developing connected residential areas, department stores and shopping centres (Beuthe, Himanen, Reggiani, & Zamparini, 2003). Close relationships between private and public actors have furthermore been a driving force for innovation and some consider this involvement as a success factor (Van de Velde, 1999). The argument is that the transport service and real estate developments strengthen each other. If the public transport operator performs poorly, the value of the real estate falls, and if the real estate is poorly managed, there will be fewer passengers on rail and buses.

Bus and train represents less than 10 per cent of all urban passenger transport in Australia. Approximately 35 per cent of bus journeys in Greater Metropolitan Sydney are made by a person from a low-income household (Hensher, 2000). Younger people (11–20 year olds), students, people with no driving licenses and people with no motor vehicles in the household use public transport more than others. This is confirmed in a recent study showing that Australian "baby boomers" switched to public transport during the global financial crisis (Kamruzzaman, Yigitcanlar, Washington, Currie, & Turrell, 2014). Lack of access to a car is associated with lower car use and higher public transport use (Corpuz, McCabe, & Ryszawa, 2006). This is an indication that automobile ownership tends to exclude use of other modes.

Several countries in Africa (e.g., Sierra Leone, Niger and Liberia) are expected to grow faster than China during the coming years. Considerable investments are needed in infrastructure to meet this development. Currently approximately 8 per cent of the population uses public transport to travel to and from work (Households National Travel Survey, 2013). Important policy implementations have been delayed for many years (Walters, 2013). A recent introduction of BRT systems (e.g., the Rea Vaya system in Johannesburg and MyCiTi in Cape Town) has, however, been successful. Africa has furthermore developed its own innovative bus system ("BRT-Lite") implemented in Lagos. This system does not require infrastructure investments to physically segregate bus lanes but is instead monitored by the police. The modal shift from private transport (car and taxi) was 6 per cent when the system was implemented (Mobereola, 2009). The same report shows that many users (including former public transport users) changed travel mode and that their quality of life was enhanced. An innovative approach that contributed to the success was to integrate multiple modes of transport. It thus became possible to offer a public transport service that is supplemented with an extensive bicycle route network and that all motorized travel modes (e.g., bus, taxi and rail) are linked to achieve seamless travel.

Cities in Latin America have experienced explosive growth in recent decades. The need to solve congestion and pollution problems has driven public transport development, and Latin America is today world leader in implementing BRT systems. This change in provision of public transport services has been very successful with increased quality and performance. Main achievements are travel-time reductions and increased safety and reliability. Surveys from large cities show that buses have market shares of 50–60 per cent and metro and rail an additional 10 per cent (Schipper, Ng, Gould, & Deakin, 2010). The system in Curitiba, Brazil, has been named Latin America's first BRT system. It was initially set up in 1972 as part of a broader town planning policy. A number of projects in Brazil have followed, for instance in São Paulo where separate bus lanes have been combined with an integrated fare structure between bus and metro. Mexico City has implemented a bus system (the Metrobus) as a complement to the existing metro network. An attractive public transport system is found in the city of Medellin, Colombia. This is a wide network of buses combined with a metro system. Medellin implemented the world's first cable car system in 2004 with the aim to connect poorer inhabitants living in remote rural communities.

Summary

What factors trigger a switch from automobile travel to use of public transport? Some factors are general and concern the community at large. Demographic and economic factors are examples. An ageing population and rising car-use costs (e.g., higher fuel prices) tend to increase demand for walking, cycling, ridesharing and public transport (Litman, 2011). Another factor is urban structure with Europe having the advantage of small and dense cities compared to the big and spread-out American cities. In denser cities, it is easier to provide public transport with high frequency and reliability. Also important are policies known to influence public transport use: (1) more and better public transport services; (2) attractive fares and convenient ticketing; (3) full multimodal and regional integration; (4) high taxation of and restrictions on car use, and (5) land use that promotes compact, mixed-use developments. Integration of such supportive policies may explain why public transport successfully competes with the automobile in, for instance, Germany compared to the US (Buehler & Pucher, 2012).

Innovations in public transport can be observed in Europe as well as in the rest of the world. Active collaboration between different actors, high-quality bus systems, visual and distinct brands, and integration of travel modes are some success factors. Furthermore, innovation projects characterized by high commitment among transport providers, management and governance, and a service development based on the needs and involvements of potential users are additional key factors. Although many of these projects have been evaluated at an aggregated level with respect to increases in ridership, research is still lacking that shows how car use is affected. It is recognized that travel mode choices are frequently the result of habits (Gärling & Axhausen, 2003), which innovations of public transport may fail to break. Measures that we discuss in the next section are therefore still needed to influence people's travel mode choice.

Influencing choice of travel mode

In Sweden, the nation-wide organization of public transport providers has recently agreed on setting the goal of doubling public transport ridership in 2020 than in 2006. A similar goal has been set in Europe by the International Association of Public Transport. However, such a goal does not guarantee that daily travel becomes more sustainable unless resulting in a switch of mode from car to public transport for a substantial number of journeys. As some previous research shows (e.g., De Witte et al., 2006), an increase in public transport ridership obtained by, for instance, offering free tickets, does not result in that a large number of car users switching to public transport. The set goal must be to reduce car use. Yet sustainable alternatives need to be available for car journeys, and public transport is frequently the only sustainable alternative.

Prohibition or charges are common transport policy measures for reducing car use. Examples of charges include vehicle purchase and fuel taxes, kilometre taxes, road and cordon tolls, and parking fees. Frequently, prohibition, road or cordon tolls are implemented in conjunction with improvement of public transport and infrastructure for walking and cycling.

The effectiveness of prohibition depends on what exemptions are made for certain types of traffic (e.g., delivery and emergency vehicles) and its spatial and temporal scale. A GIS-based feasibility study in a Swedish municipality (population appr. 500,000) using national travel diary data (Loukopolulos, Gärling, & Vilhelmson, 2005) demonstrated that prohibiting car traffic in the central business district may reduce total automobile travel even when restricted to peak hours during weekdays. It is still possible that some of the suppressed car journeys would be substituted by car journeys to more distant (e.g., shopping) destinations. This may possibly be counteracted if prohibition is combined with increased accessibility by public transport. However, no attempt was made to estimate the potential number of switches to public transport. Positive effects would still be observed of reduced local emissions of particles, reduced traffic noise and more liveable streets that are attractive and safe for walking.

Independent lines of research show that, at least in the short term, vehicle purchases and fuel taxes are associated with low price elasticities (Goodwin, Dargay, & Hanly, 2004). Jakobsson (2004) summarizes the mainly negative outcomes of a limited number of field experiments evaluating the effectiveness of kilometre charges. It is believed that differentiated charges are more effective by influencing when and where automobile users drive. A reason for a generally less than expected effectiveness is that differentiated charges are implemented without applying knowledge of how motivation and cognitive capacity influence car users' processing of the price information (Bonsall, Shires, Matthews, Maule, & Beale, 2007). In line with this finding, Jakobsson, Fujii and Gärling (2002) found that to have an impact, differentiated charges would need to be supplemented by customized information about travel alternatives.

In recent years, several European cities have implemented cordon tolls following the early example of Singapore. In London, cordon tolls were introduced in 2003. An unexpectedly high 30 per cent reduction of congestion was initially observed, attributed to both switches to public transport and to drivers not crossing the cordon (Transport for London, 2008). Another example is Stockholm for which the effects have been broadly assessed (Eliasson, Hultkrantz, Nerhagen, & Smidfelt Rosqvist, 2009). An average 20 per cent reduction of cordon crossings appears to be sustained after 5 years (Börjesson, Eliasson, Hugosson, & Brundell-Freij, 2012). Initially a 14 per cent reduction of carbon-dioxide emissions was observed within the cordon area corresponding to a 2–3 per cent reduction in the metropolitan area at large. Other positive effects within the cordon area included reductions of particle emissions, increased accessibility by walking and cycling, increased liveability and reduction of traffic accidents. Reduced private automobile travel to the inner city due to improvements of public transport services before the implementation probably played some role in the outcome (Kottenhoff & Brundell Freij, 2009). A small increase from 72.1 per cent to 75.9 per cent in commuting by bus in direct corridors was shown in travel surveys. In on-board interviews, close to 4 per cent of the bus passengers stated that they used to commute by car 6 months before.

Pricing measures are theoretically grounded in neoclassical economics. Consumption is regulated by supply and demand such that if the price of the product (transportation) increases, its demand will decrease, and vice versa (Emmerink, Nijkamp, & Rietveld, 1995; Rothengatter, 2003). Psychology offers the complementary view that people acquire information from different sources about what to think, how to judge and evaluate, and how to act or react (Loukopoulos, Gärling, Jakobsson, & Fujii, 2008). The information is acquired in advance (referred to as feedforward), after having acted (feedback or knowledge of results) or both. Effectiveness of pricing measures therefore also depends on how authorities inform citizens. A good example from the European Union is "Do The Right Mix" (www.youtube.com/watch?v=55yhNqMtdxA). Yet many have argued that information is more effective if it is customized (Kreuter, Strecher, & Glassman, 1999; Lorenzoni, Nicholson-Cole, & Whitmarsh, 2007). This has led to an upsurge of studies of what may be referred to as individualized information measures.

The general aim of individualized information measures targeting automobile users is to increase awareness of more sustainable alternatives to their current car use and to empower them to switch to these alternatives (Ampt, 2004). Although the main evaluation criterion is reduced negative consequences of current car use, the potential changes car users may choose to achieve this goal are several: suppressing car journeys (possibly instead using telecommunication), choosing more sustainable travel modes (e.g., walking or cycling instead of driving short distances or public transport for longer distances), driving to closer destinations (e.g., local stores instead of distant shopping malls), combining more errands on the same car journeys and sharing car journeys with other household members or acquaintances.

In Australia, Germany, Japan and the United Kingdom, car users have voluntarily participated in large-scale programs targeting car-use reduction (Brög et al., 2009; Cairns et al., 2008; Fujii & Taniguchi, 2006; Taylor, 2007). Participants are recruited in residential areas, at work places or in schools. In order to increase motivation to participate, several techniques have been used including persuasive messages stressing personal, societal and environmental benefits (Friman, Larhult, & Gärling, 2013), information promoting positive attitudes towards public transport (Brög et al., 2009), and economic incentives (Thøgersen, 2014). Participants then obtain customized (feedforward) information about sustainable alternatives to car use. Meta-analyses show that while a maximum of 30–40 per cent of car users participate in the programs, for the total number in a targeted area (including also non-particants) relatively stable 5–20 per cent car-use reductions are attained (Fujii, Bamberg, Friman, & Gärling, 2009; Möser & Bamberg, 2008). Cost-effectiveness is claimed to be high (Brög et al., 2009). There are still several remaining gaps of knowledge (Richter, Friman, & Gärling, 2010, 2011).

In order to increase effectiveness of information measures, they need to be combined with prohibition and pricing measures (sometimes referred to as "hard" measures in contrast to the "soft" information measures) (Fujii & Taniguchi, 2014). The measures may also need to include persuasion techniques (Bamberg, Fujii, Friman, & Gärling, 2011). In order to achieve this, it is essential to understand the process of reducing car use.

A majority of all personal travel is motivated by desires, needs and obligations to participate in out-of-home activities (e.g., Axhausen & Gärling, 1992). Therefore, as has been proposed (Gärling et al., 2002), car-use reduction should be viewed broadly as an adaptation by car users that potentially has consequences for their engagement in different activities and their satisfaction from this engagement (Jakobsson Bergstad et al., 2012). Figure 28.2 illustrates a conceptualization of how information measures influence car-use reduction. More elaborate, similar models have been proposed by Bamberg (2012) and Jones and Sloman (2006). The process starts with the car user setting a car-use reduction goal forced on them by, for instance, some changes in the transportation system (e.g., increased car-use costs due to the implementation of pricing measures), strengthened by persuasive messages and customized information. Information is also provided by public transport companies, the Internet (e.g., Google Maps) or word-of-mouth. Setting a high and specific reduction goal followed by requests to form a plan for how to attain the goal has been found to be particularly effective (Fujii et al., 2009). Knowledge of the change outcome (e.g., feedback about travel times, costs, carbon dioxide emissions) is customized such that participants are able to improve their plan.

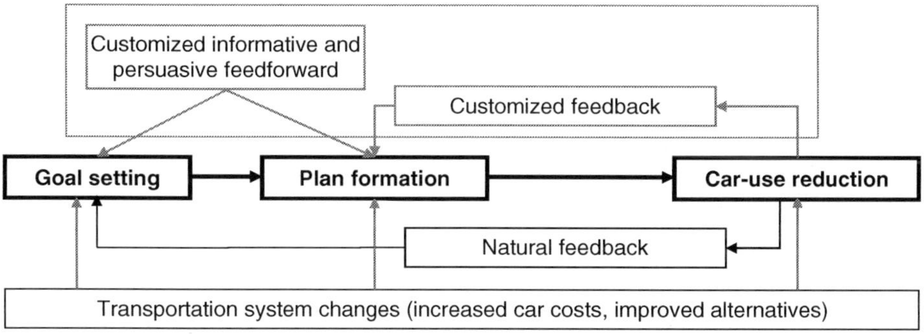

Figure 28.2 A model of the effects on car-use reduction of information measures when the transportation system is changed.

If the goal is to reduce car use through increasing public transport ridership, how should an individualized information measure be designed to achieve this? It may first be noted that some programs aimed at reducing car use have been found to be more effective if implemented accompanied by improvements to public transport services ranging from minor increases in frequency to extension of a subway line to the target area (Brög et al., 2009). This speaks to the feasibility of approaching car users in connection with a planned change in public transport services.

In the first stage, car users that would benefit from the improved service should be identified. Second, they would need to be contacted personally to be made aware of how they would benefit from the new service. Persuasive techniques may be implemented such as offering a free monthly pass, explaining the societal and environmental benefits from many using public transport or several others based on research in social psychology (Bamberg, 2014). Some studies have systematically evaluated the effects of providing a free monthly pass on switching to public transport (e.g., Fujii & Kitamura, 2003; Thøgersen, 2009; Thøgersen & Møller, 2008). These studies tend to show that car users' choice of public transport increases only as long as the fare is free. Another approach has been to provide customized timetables. This has proven to be ineffective even in the short run when distributed to randomly assigned drivers (Thøgersen & Møller, 2008). General appeals (Hutton & Ahtola, 1991) as well as information about the societal/environmental benefits of using alternative options have also proven to be ineffective (Staats, Wit, & Midden, 1996). Some more successful cases are reported by Thøgersen (2014), referred to as social marketing (Donovan & Henley, 2010), where free tickets have been offered in conjunction with a change in the public transport service.

In an intervention study (Pedersen et al., 2011) shedding light on why a free monthly pass may be ineffective, a sample of car users received a free monthly bus pass if they signed a contract to use the bus as their primary mode of travel to and from work for one month. A follow-up questionnaire two years after the intervention revealed that the car users' remembered satisfaction with public transport was significantly lower than their previously reported online experienced satisfaction. Furthermore, when choices were made as to whether or not to use public transport as their primary travel mode, remembered satisfaction had more impact on the choice than the reported online satisfaction. Thus, even though satisfaction with the alternative is high, the degree of satisfaction may not be remembered after some time, hence increasing the likelihood of switching back to the private car. It is however not possible to refute the alternative explanation that, when the free ticket expires, satisfaction with public transport is not high enough to motivate continued use compared to driving the private car.

Yet another intervention study (Taniguchi et al., 2014) demonstrated the importance of requiring car users to set a goal to switch to public transport. Those recruited to the study faced a minimum switching goal when agreeing to participate. Many adopted this goal while about 30 per cent set higher switching goals. The results showed that close to half of the total sample achieved or exceeded their goal of switching to public transport.

A promising high-tech approach, not yet fully evaluated, is the UbiGo system developed in Göteborg, Sweden during 2013. Households are asked to subscribe to a customized travel service with access to a pool of cars, public transport, taxis and bikes. Subscribers pay for their monthly need of public transport (number of days in one or more zones) and car rental (number of hours). They receive bonus points for sustainable choices of travel that can be used as payment in movie theatres and museums. Results show no drop-outs and a very high satisfaction with the service (Sochor, Strömberg, & Karlsson, 2015). Convenience and control over travel expenditures are stated to be advantages, whereas the online feature of the service has resulted in some complaints.

Summary

In the preceding section, we noted the need to break the habitual use of private car use. In this section, we have reviewed measures, and evaluations of such measures, with this aim. Prohibition, charges and information are measures that have been relatively successful in reducing automobile use in urban areas by as much as 20–30 per cent. However, few studies (e.g., Gärling, A. Gärling, & Johansson, 2000) have attempted to reveal how car users manage to reduce driving, nor to document the process in households (goal setting, planning, monitoring) leading to the car-use reduction. For this reason, there is still uncertainty about what is the best ways of implementing reduction measures (Bamberg et al., 2011).

Another shortcoming is the scarcity of studies on how to successfully influence car users to switch to public transport. We believe such influences are more successful if habitual car users in some way are forced to use public transport for some time such that they develop a new habit (Fujii & Gärling, 2003). A necessary condition is thus that public transport services are not worse than expected such that use is discontinued for this reason. This may seem feasible since, as has been noted, habitual car users tend to have biased negative expectations, which appears to be one reason why they do not spontaneously choose public transport. These are however speculations until confirmed by additional studies.

Conclusions

The choice of how to travel plays a crucial role for the future of an increasingly crowded urbanized planet. The car is often preferred due to its flexibility, convenience and comfort. Yet the increasing car use is not sustainable. A more frequent choice of alternative travel modes would yield significant sustainability benefits. Against this backdrop, innovations in public transport services should be implemented to improve its attractiveness to increase car users' switching.

The chapter exemplified public transport innovations that have been implemented in Europe and the rest of the world. It is concluded from evaluations that improvements lead to increased public transport ridership, but to what extent car use is suppressed still remains an open question. Peak car use observed in some countries may be the consequence of improvements in public transport and infrastructure for cycling and walking in conjunction with increased travel costs for purchasing, owning and driving a car. However, there is still a lack of firm scientific evidence for peak car use. Additional research is needed to settle the issue. A major challenge is also to provide sustainable travel alternatives in rural areas. Innovative integrations between different travel modes seem to be a promising way to go but need to be further developed and evaluated.

We argue that innovations in public transport are necessary although not sufficient if the goal is to reduce car use such that sustainability of daily travel increases. Car-use habits are difficult to break. The implementation of car-use reduction measures is required in addition to the provision of high-quality, innovative public transport services. Car-use reduction should be viewed broadly as an adaptation by households including several different changes in travel with potential consequences for their engagement in desirable activities. The process starts with setting a car-use reduction goal, frequently motivated by some changes in the transportation system, strengthened by persuasive messages and customized information. Our conclusion is therefore that hard and soft policy measures should be combined. Soft information measures such as campaigns or individualized social marketing techniques including persuasion are thus not likely to have massive effects unless car use is made worse (through prohibition and/or increased costs) and the sustainable alternatives are made better. The same is likely to be true of prohibition or increased costs implemented without the complement of information measures and improvement of alternatives.

Acknowledgements

Preparation of this chapter was financially supported by grant (#2011-03424) from the Swedish Governmental Agency for Innovation Systems (VINNOVA) to the SAMOT research group at Karlstad University.

References

Albalate, D., & Bel, G. (2010). What shapes local public transportation in Europe? Economics, mobility, institutions, and geography. *Transportation Research Part E*, *46*, 775–790.

American Public Transportation Association. (2013). APTA 2013 ridership report. Retrieved from www.apta.com/resources/statistics/Documents/2013-q4-ridership-APTA.pdf. Retrieved 15 October, 2014.

Ampt, E. S. (2004). Understanding voluntary travel behaviour change. *Transport Engineering in Australia*, *9*, 53–66.

Aretun, Å., & Nordbakke, S. (2014). *Developments in driver's licence holding among young people: Potential explanations, implications and trends*. Linköping, Sweden: VTI.

Axhausen, K. W., & Gärling, T. (1992). Activity-based approaches to travel analysis: Conceptual frameworks, models, and research problems. *Transport Reviews*, *12*, 323–341.

Bamberg, S. (2012). Changing environmentally harmful behaviours: A stage model of self-regulated behavioural change. *Journal of Environmental Psychology*, *34*, 151–159.

Bamberg, S. (2014). Psychological contributions to the development of car use reduction interventions. In T. Gärling, D. Ettema & M. Friman (Eds.), *Handbook of sustainable travel* (pp. 131–151). Dordrecht, The Netherlands: Springer Science.

Bamberg, S., Fujii, S., Friman, M., & Gärling, T. (2011). Behaviour theory and soft transport policy measures. *Transport Policy*, *18*, 228–235.

Barabino, B., Deiana, E., & Tilocca, P. (2012). Measuring service quality in urban bus transport: A modified SERVQUAL approach. *International Journal of Quality and Service Sciences*, *4*, 238–252.

Bates, J., Polak, J., Jones, P., & Cook, A. (2001). The valuation of reliability for personal travel. *Transportation Research Part E*, *37*, 191–229.

Beirão, G., & Sarsfield Cabral, J. A. (2007). Understanding attitudes towards public transport and private car: A qualitative study. *Transport Policy*, *14*, 478–489.

Beuthe, M., Himanen, V., Reggiani, A., & Zamparini, L. (2003). *Transport developments and innovations in an evolving world*. Berlin, Germany: Springer.

Bonsall, P. W., Shires, J. D., Matthews, B., Maule, J., & Beale, J. (2007). Responses to complex pricing signals: Theories, evidence and implications for road pricing. *Transportation Research Part A*, *41*, 672–683.

Börjesson, M., Eliasson, J., Hugosson, M. B., & Brundell-Freij, K. (2012). The Stockholm congestion charges – 5 years on: Effects, acceptability and lessons learnt. *Transport Policy, 20*, 1–12.
Brake, J. F., Mulley, C, Nelson, J. D., & Wright, S. D. (2007). Key lessons learned from recent experience with Flexible Transport Services. *Transport Policy, 14*, 458–466.
Brög, W., Erl, E., Ker, I., Ryle, J., & Wall, R. (2009). Evaluation of voluntary travel behaviour change: Experiences from three continents. *Transport Policy, 16*, 281–292.
Buehler, R., & Pucher, J. (2012). Demand for public transport in Germany and the USA: An analysis of rider characteristics. *Transport Reviews, 32*, 541–567.
Bullard, D. R. (2003). Addressing urban transportation equity in the United States. *Fordham Urban Law Journal, 31*, 1183–1209.
Cairns, S., Sloman, L., Newson, C., Anable, J., Kirkbride, A., & Goodwin, P. (2008). Smarter choices: Assessing the potential to achieve traffic reduction using "soft measures". *Transport Reviews, 28*, 593–618.
Cantwell, M., Caulfield, B., & O'Mahony, M. (2009). Examining the factors that impact public transport commuting satisfaction. *Journal of Public Transportation, 12*, 1–21.
Carrel, A., Halvorsen, A., & Walker, J. L. (2013). Passengers' perception of and behavioural adaptation to unreliability in public transportation. *Transportation Research Record: Journal of the Transportation Research Board, 2351*, 153–162.
Cervero, R. (2013). *Suburban gridlock.* New Brunswick, NJ: Transaction Publishers.
Corpuz, G., McCabe, M., & Ryszawa, K. (2006). *The development of a Sydney VKT regression model.* Paper presented at the 29th Australian Transport Research Forum 29 Gold Coast: ATRF.
Currie, G., & Delbrosc, A. (2013). Exploring comparative ridership drivers of bus rapid transit and light rail transit routes. *Journal of Public Transportation, 16*, 47–65.
Currie, G., & Wallis, I. (2008). Effective ways to grow urban bus markets: A synthesis of evidence. *Journal of Transport Geography, 16*, 419–429.
Dargay, J., Gately, D., & Sommer, M. (2007). Vehicle ownership and income growth, worldwide: 1960–2030. *Energy Journal, 28*, 143–170.
Davis, B., & Dutzik, T. (2012). *Transportation and the new generation: Why young people are driving less and what it means for transportation policy.* Boston, MA: Frontier Group.
De Witte, A., Macharis, C., Lannoy, P., Polain, C., Steenberghen, T., & Van de Walle, S. (2006). The impact of "free" public transport: The case of Brussels. *Transportation Research Part A, 40*, 671–689.
Donovan, R. J., & Henley, N. (2010). *Principles and practice of social marketing: An international perspective.* Cambridge: Cambridge University Press.
Eboli, L., & Mazzulla, G. (2009). A new customer satisfaction index for evaluating transit service quality *Journal of Public Transportation, 12*, 21–37.
Eliasson, J., Hultkrantz, L., Nerhagen, L., & Smidfelt Rosqvist, L. (2009). The Stockholm congestion charging trial 2006: Overview of effects. *Transportation Research Part A, 43*, 240–250.
Emmerink, R. H. M., Nijkamp, P., & Rietveld, P. (1995). Is congestion pricing a first-best strategy in transport policy? A critical review of arguments. *Environment and Planning B, 22*, 581–602.
Enoch, M., Potter, S., Parkhurst, G., & Smith, M. (2004). *INTERMODE: Innovations in demand responsive transport.* Loughborough University, UK: Department for Transport and Greater Manchester Passenger Transport Executive.
Eriksson, L., Friman, M., & Gärling, T. (2008). Stated reasons for reducing work-commute by car. *Transportation Research Part F: Traffic Psychology and Behaviour, 11*, 427–433.
Eurobarometer. (2011). *Future of transport. Analytical report.* Flash EB Series #312. Hungary: Gallup Organisation.
Eurostat. (2012). *Themes/Transport*, Retrieved 15 October, 2013, from http://epp.eurostat.cec.eu.int.
Federal Transport Administration. (2004). *Characteristics of bus rapid transit for decision-making.* Springfield, Virginia: Office of Research, Demonstration and Innovation.
Fellesson, M., & Friman, M. (2008). Perceived satisfaction with public transport services in nine European cities. *Journal of Transportation Research Forum, 47*, 93–103.
Friman, M. (2010). Affective dimensions of the waiting experience. *Transportation Research Part F: Traffic Psychology and Behaviour, 13*, 197–205.
Friman, M., Edvardsson, B., & Gärling, T. (2001). Frequency of negative critical incidents and satisfaction with Public Transport Services. *Journal of Retailing and Consumer Services, 8*, 95–104.
Friman, M., Larhult L., & Gärling, T. (2013). An analysis of soft transport policy measures implemented in Sweden to reduce private car use. *Transportation, 40*, 109–129.
Fujii, S., Bamberg, S., Friman, M., & Gärling, T. (2009). Are effects of travel feedback programs correctly assessed? *Transportmetrika, 5*, 43–57.

Fujii, S., & Gärling, T. (2003). Development of script-based travel mode choice after forced change. *Transportation Research Part F*, *6*, 117–124.

Fujii, S., Gärling, T., & Kitamura, R. (2001). Changes in drivers' perceptions and use of public transport during a freeway closure: Effects of temporary structural change on cooperation in a real-life social dilemma. *Environment and Behaviour*, *33*, 796–808.

Fujii, S., & Kitamura, R. (2003). What does a one-month free bus ticket do to habitual drivers? An experimental analysis of habit and attitude change. *Transportation*, *30*, 81–95.

Fujii, S. & Taniguchi, A. (2006). Determinants of the effectiveness of travel feedback programs: A review of communicative mobility management measures for changing travel behaviour in Japan. *Transport Policy*, *13*, 339–348.

Fujii, S., & Taniguchi, A. (2014). Theoretical understanding of practical strategies of changing travel behaviour. In T. Gärling, D. Ettema & M. Friman (Eds.), *Handbook of sustainable travel* (pp. 151–162). Dordrecht, The Netherlands: Springer Science.

Gärling, T., & Axhausen, K. W. (2003). Introduction: Habitual travel choice. *Transportation*, *30*, 1–11.

Gärling, T., Eek, D., Loukopoulos, P., Fujii, S., Johansson-Stenman, O., Kitamura, R., &Vilhelmson, B. (2002). A conceptual analysis of the impact of travel demand management on private car use. *Transport Policy*, *9*, 59–70.

Gärling, T., & Friman, M. (2012). A behavioural perspective on voluntary reduction of private car use. In B. Van Wee (Ed.), *Keep moving, towards sustainable mobility* (pp. 109–134). Hague, The Netherlands: Eleven International Publishing.

Gärling, T., & Friman, M. (2015). Unsustainable travel becoming (more) sustainable. In L. Reisch & J. Thøgersen (Eds.), *Handbook of research on sustainable consumption*. London: Edward Elgar.

Gärling, T., Gärling, A., & Johansson, A. (2000). Household choices of car-use reduction measures. *Transportation Research Part A*, *34*, 309–320.

Gatersleben, B. (2014) Psychological motives for car use. In T. Gärling, D. Ettema & M. Friman (Eds.), *Handbook of sustainable travel* (pp. 85–94). Dordrecht, The Netherlands: Springer Science.

Giuliano, G., & Dargay, J. (2006). Car ownership, travel and land use: A comparison of the US and Great Britain. *Transportation Research Part A*, *40*, 106–124.

Goodwin, P. (2012). Three views on peak car. *World Transport Policy and Practice*, *17*, 8–18.

Goodwin, P. B., Dargay, J., & Hanly, M. (2004). Elasticities of road traffic and fuel consumption with respect to price and income: A review. *Transport Reviews*, *24*, 275–292.

Hayashi, Y., Doi, K., Yagishita, M., & Kuwata, M. (2004). Urban transport sustainability: Asian trends, problems and policy practices. *European Journal of Transport and Infrastructure Research*, *4*, 27–45.

Hensher, D. A. (2000). Urban public transport challenges. *The Drawing Board. An Australian Review of Public Affairs*, *1*, 47–62.

Hensher, D. A. (2007). Some insights into the key influences on trip-chaining activity and public transport use of seniors and the elderly. *International Journal of Sustainable Transportation*, *1*, 53–68.

Hensher D. A., & Li, Z. (2012). Ridership drivers of bus rapid transit systems. *Transportation*, *39*, 1209–1221.

Hensher, D. A., Mulley, C., & Li, Z. (2014). High quality public transport: Gaining acceptance of bus rapid transit systems. In T. Gärling, M. Friman & D. Ettema (Eds.), *Handbook of sustainable travel* (pp. 257–276). Dordrecht, The Netherlands: Springer Science.

Hensher, D. A., Mulley, C., & Yahya, N. (2010). Passenger experience with quality-enhanced bus service: The tyne and wear "superoute" services. *Transportation*, *37*, 239–256.

Housholds National Travel Survey. (2013). *Statistics South Africa*. P0320. Pretoria: South Africa.

Hutton, R. B., & Ahtola, O. T. (1991). Consumer response to a five-year campaign to combat air pollution. *Journal of Public Policy and Marketing*, *10*, 242–256.

Institute for Transportation and Development Policy (ITDP). (2014). The Bus Rapid Transit Standard. ITDP. Retrieved 22 September, 2014.

Jakobsson Bergstad, C., Gamble, A., Hagman, O., Polk, M., Gärling, T., Ettema, D., et al. (2012). Influences on subjective well-being of affect associated with routine out-of-home activities. *Applied Research in Quality of Life*, *7*, 49–62.

Jakobsson, C. (2004). *Motivational and volitional control of private automobile use: The effectiveness of transport policies*. Doctoral dissertation. Göteborg, Sweden: Göteborg University, Department of Psychology.

Jakobsson, C. (2007). Instrumental motives for private car use. In T. Gärling & L. Steg (Eds.), *Threats from car traffic to the quality of urban life: Problems, causes, and solutions* (pp. 205–217). Oxford, UK: Elsevier.

Jakobsson, C., Fujii, S., & Gärling, T. (2002). Effects of economic disincentives on private car use. *Transportation*, *29*, 349–370.

Jones, P., & Sloman, L. (2006). Encouraging behavioural change through marketing and management: What can be achieved? In K. W. Axhausen (Ed.), *Moving through nets: The physical and social dimensions of travel* (pp. 189–218). Oxford, UK: Elsevier.

Kamruzzaman, Md., Yigitcanlar, T., Washington, S., Currie, G., & Turrell, G. (2014). Australian baby boomers switched to more environment friendly modes of transport during the global financial crisis. *International Journal of Environmental Science and Technology*, *11*, 2133–2144.

Kitamura, R., & Mohamad, J. (2009). Rapid motorization in Asian cities: Urban transport infrastructure, spatial development and travel behaviour. *Transportation*, *36*, 269–274.

Kottenhoff, K., & Brundell Freij, K. (2009). The role of public transport for feasibility and acceptability of congestion charging: The case of Stockholm. *Transportation Research Part A*, *43*, 297–305.

Kreuter, M. W., Strecher, V. J., & Glassman, B. (1999). One size does not fit all: The case for tailoring print materials. *Annals of Behavioural Medicine*, *21*, 276–283.

Leibling, D. (2008). *Carownership in Great Britain*. London, UK: The Royal Automobile Club Foundation for Motoring.

Lewis, P. (2010). *London's Oyster card revolution to evolution*. Paper presented at the MasterCard Europe Debit & Prepaid (PREPAID) Conference. Budapest, Hungary.

Leyden, K. M., Goldberg, A., & Michelbach, P. (2011). Understanding the pursuit of happiness in ten major cities. *Urban Affairs Review*, *47*, 861–888.

Litman, T. (2011). *London congestion pricing. Implications for other cities*. Canada: Victoria Transport Policy Institute.

Litman, T. (2012). Current mobility trends: Implications for sustainability. In B. van Wee (Ed.), *Keep moving, towards sustainable mobility* (pp. 23–44). The Hague: Eleven International Publishing.

Lorenzoni, I., Nicholson-Cole, S., & Whitmarsh, L. (2007). Barriers perceived to engaging with climate change among the UK public and their policy implications. *Global Environmental Change*, *17*, 445–459.

Loukopoulos, P., Gärling, T., Jakobsson, C., & Fujii, S. (2008). A cost-minimization principle of adaptation of private car use in response to road pricing schemes. In C. Jensen-Butler, M. Larsen, B. Madsen, O. A. Nielsen & B. Sloth, B. (Eds.), *Road pricing, the economy, and the environment* (pp. 331–349). Oxford, UK: Elsevier.

Loukopoulos, P., Gärling, T., & Vilhelmson, B. (2005). Mapping the potential consequences of car-use reduction in urban areas. *Journal of Transport Geography*, *13*, 135–150.

Martens, K. (2006). The bicycle as a feedering mode: Experiences from three European countries. *Transportation Research Part D*, *9*, 281–294.

Mees, P. (2010). *Transport for Suburbia: Beyond the automobile age*. London: Earthscan.

Millard-Ball, A., & Schipper, L. (2011). Are we reaching peak travel? Trends in passenger transport in eight industrialized countries. *Transport Reviews: A Transnational Transdisciplinary Journal*, *31*, 357–378.

Mobereola, D. (2009). Africa's first bus rapid transit scheme. The lagos BRT-lite system, Sub-Saharan Africa Transport Policy Program. SSATP Discussion Paper No. 9. Urban Transport Series.

Moktharian, P. L., & Salomon, I. (2001). How derived is the demand for travel? Some conceptual and measurement considerations. *Transportation Research Part A*, *31*, 35–50.

Möser, G., & Bamberg, S. (2008). The effectiveness of soft transport policy measures: A critical assessment and meta-analysis of empirical evidence. *Journal of Environmental Psychology*, *28*, 10–26.

Mulley, C., Hensher, D. A., & Rose, J. M. (2014). Do preferences for BRT and LRT vary across geographical jurisdictions? A comparative assessment of six Australian capital cities. *Case Studies on Transport Policy*, *2*, 1–9.

Mulley, C., & Nelson, J. D. (2009). Flexible transport services: A new market opportunity for public transport. *Research in Transportation Economics*, *25*, 39–45.

Newman, P., & Kenworthy, J. (1999). *Sustainability and cities: Overcoming automobile dependence*. Washington, DC: Island Press.

Pedersen, T., Friman, M., & Kristensson, P. (2011). The role of predicted, on-line experienced and remembered satisfaction in current choice to use public transport services. *Journal of Retailing and Consumer Services*, *18*, 471–475.

Pucher, J., Korattyswaroopam, N., & Ittyerah, N. (2004). The crisis of public transport in India: Overwhelming needs but limited resources. *Journal of Public Transportation*, *7*, 1–20.

Pucher, J., & Kurth, C. (1996). Verkehrsverbund: The success of regional public transport in Germany, Austria and Switzerland. *Transport Policy*, *2*, 279–291.

Puentes, R. (2012). *Have Americans hit peak travel? A discussion of the changes in US driving habits*. Discussion Paper No. 2012-14 at the International Transport Forum. The Brookings Institution, Washington, DC.

Rapino, M. A., & Field, A. K. (2012). Mega commuting in the U.S. time and distance in defining long commutes using the 2006–2010 American Community Survey. Poster presented at the Presented at the Association for Public Policy Analysis and Management (APPAM) Fall Conference, Baltimore, MD, 8–10 November, 2012.

Reardon, L., & Abdallah, S. (2013). Well-being and transport: Taking stock and looking forward. *Transport Reviews: A Transnational Transdisciplinary Journal, 33*, 634–657.

Redman, L., Friman, M., Gärling, T., & Hartig, T. (2013). Quality attributes of public transport that attract car users. *Transport Policy, 25*, 119–127.

Reitveld, P., Bruinsma, F. R., & van Vuuren, D. J. (2001). Coping with unreliability in public transport chains: A case study for Netherlands. *Transportation Research Part A: Policy and Practice, 35*, 539–559.

Richter, J., Friman, M., & Gärling, T. (2010). Review of implementations of soft transport policy measures. *Transportation: Theory and Application, 2*, 5–18.

Richter, J., Friman, M., & Gärling, T. (2011). Soft transport policy measures: Gaps of knowledge. *International Journal of Sustainable Transportation, 5*, 199–215.

Rothengatter, W. (2003). How good is first best? Marginal cost and other pricing principles for user charging in transport. *Transport Policy, 10*, 121–130.

Schipper, L., Ng, W.-S., Gould, B., & Deakin, E. (2010). *Carbon in Motion 2050 for North America and Latin America*. Berkeley, CA: University of California, Global Metropolitan Studies.

Sivak, M., & Schoettle, B. (2012). Percentage of young persons with a driver's license continues to drop. *Traffic Injury Prevention, 13*, 341.

Sochor, J., Strömberg, H., & Karlsson, I. C. M. (2015). *Challenges in integrating user, commercial, and societal perspectives in an innovative mobility service*. TRB 94th Annual Meeting Compendium of Papers, Report 15-0360. Washington, DC.

Sperling, D., & Claussen, E. (2004). Motorizing the developing world. *Access, 24*, 10–15.

Staats, H. J., Wit, A. P., & Midden, C. Y. H. (1996). Communicating the greenhouse effect to the public: Evaluation of a mass media campaign from a social dilemma perspective. *Journal of Environmental Management, 45*, 189–203.

Taniguchi, A., Grääs, C., & Friman, M. (2014). Satisfaction with travel, goal achievement, and voluntarily behavioural change. *Transportation Research Part F: Traffic Psychology and Behaviour, 26*, 10–17.

Taylor, M. (2007). Voluntary travel behaviour change programs in Australia: The carrot rather than the stick in travel demand management. *International Journal of Sustainable Transportation, 1*, 173–192.

The mobility in cities database (2012). International Association of Public Transport (UITP), Brussels, Belgium.

Thøgersen, J. (2009). Promoting public transport as a subscription service: Effects of a free month travel card. *Transport Policy, 16*, 335–343.

Thøgersen, J. (2014). Social marketing in travel demand management. In T. Gärling, D. Ettema & M. Friman (Eds.), *Handbook of sustainable travel* (pp. 113–131). Dordrecht, The Netherlands: Springer Science.

Thøgersen, J., & Møller, B. (2008). Breaking car-use habits: The effectiveness of a free month travel card. *Transportation, 35*, 329–345.

Transport for London (2008). *Central London congestion charging. Impacts monitoring. Sixth Annual Report*. Retrieved from www.tfl.gov.uk/assets/downloads/sixth-annual-impacts-monitoring-report-2008-07.pdf

Transportation Research Board. (2004). *Transit-oriented development in the United States: Experiences, challenges, and prospects*. Washington, DC: TRB.

van de Velde, D. (1999). Organisational forms and entrepreneurship in public transport: Classifying organisational forms. *Transport Policy, 6*, 147–157.

van Wee, B. (2014). The unsustainability of car use. In T. Gärling, D. Ettema & M. Friman (Eds.), *Handbook of sustainable travel* (pp. 69–83). Dordrecht, The Netherlands: Springer Science.

Walters, J. (2013). Overview of public transport policy developments in South Africa. *Research in Transportation Economics, 39*, 34–45.

29
The psychology of branding

Arnd Florack and Johanna Palcu

The monetary value of brands is impressive. In a ranking from 2014, the consulting agency Interbrand, for instance, estimated the brand equity of Apple to be more than $118 billion USD. In many cases, the monetary value of a brand even exceeds the monetary value of all other assets of a company. Whilst part of the monetary value of the world's leading brands can unarguably be attributed to the high quality or innovativeness of their products and services, much of the benefit of brands is based on psychological effects. Take the brand "Stradivarius" as an example. Stradivari was a traditional Italian crafter who built string instruments with a leading quality more than 200 years ago. The instruments are still played by professionals today and are sold for record prices at auctions, sometimes for more than $2 million USD for a single instrument. The most fascinating fact about this, however, is not that antique instruments receive high bids at auctions or that professionals are willing to pay large amounts of money to play such an exceptional instrument, but that, in blind tests, professionals cannot distinguish the sound of a Stradivarius violin from that of other prominent violins that cost only $10,000 USD – a small fraction of the price of a Stradivarius (Fritz, Curtin, Poitevineau, Morrel-Samuels, & Tao, 2010). Hence, an instrument made by Stradivari obviously provides a utility that goes beyond the functional benefit of producing an excellent acoustic experience. Instead, research suggests that the value of the brand Stradivarius depends on a unique bundle of brand associations and benefits that "work in concert" to create a distinctive brand perception.

Park, Jaworski and MacInnis (1986) argue that strategic brand management has to take into account at least three different benefits of brands: a functional benefit, a symbolic benefit and an experiential benefit. A functional benefit is related to solving a current problem or preventing a potential problem. A detergent, for instance, can possess the functional benefit of cleaning clothes. Park et al. (1986) define a functional benefit as one that is related to externally generated needs. Functional benefits can regard needs to improve a current status (e.g., dirty clothes need to be washed) or secure a current status (e.g., a new car needs an insurance; Florack & Scarabis, 2006; Florack, Scarabis, & Gosejohann, 2005). By contrast, a brand with a symbolic benefit is a brand that fulfils internally generated psychological needs for self-enhancement, self-verification or affiliation with a group. For example, a consumer can use a brand to increase his or her status (self-enhancement), to act in line with his or her values and express these values (self-verification) or to signal that he or she belongs to a specific social group (affiliation).

Finally, brands with an experiential benefit can satisfy needs that arise from seeking pleasant sensory experiences, stimulation or variety. A brand of coffeehouse, for example, could be associated with a relaxing atmosphere and the particular smells and tastes of its coffee and pastries.

The different brand benefits often occur in a mixed form, but in many cases, one benefit is predominant. For brand management activities, it is important to identify which kind of benefit is predominant in consumers' responses in a given situation in order to be able to direct product development, positioning, communication, and distribution and, thus, to nurture long-term consumer behaviour.

To understand how different brand benefits work and interact to shape consumers' brand perceptions and behaviour, it is important to bear in mind that brand benefits address different, yet often interrelated psychological processes. On the one hand, functional benefits are predominantly related to the cold cognitive processing of information. In this sense, brands can be understood as (consciously or unconsciously) accumulated sets of brand-related information stored in memory that directly or indirectly influence consumer judgements (Alba & Hutchinson, 1987, 2000; Krishnan, 1996). In the aforementioned example of Stradivarius, this might include, for instance, brand associations such as tradition, quality or excellence, which translate into the amount musicians are willing to pay for a Stradivarius violin. Symbolic benefits, on the other hand, are related to processes of self-expression and identity management (Escalas & Bettman, 2005). In other words, brands contain the ability to communicate relevant information about the person who is using them and his or her role in the social group of relevance. A violinist who is playing a Stradivarius might, for instance, be perceived by others as one of the best of his or her kind. Finally, experiential benefits include a diversity of emotional and sensory brand experiences that go beyond the cognitive appraisal of the functional attributes of the brand, such as the warmth of the wooden surface of a violin or its unique sound. In this chapter, we illustrate how these different groups of psychological processes work together to influence the perception and choice of brands and how they can be successfully implemented for brand management purposes. We base our illustration on the extensive amount of research on the psychological effects of brands across different cultural contexts and discuss unresolved issues and challenges for future research. Also, we provide examples of brand effects to show that the cultural context of brand use has to be taken into account. Because of the relevance and the large spectrum of symbolic aspects of brand management, we further distinguish between benefits that are related to the symbolic expression of the self and those that are related to the consumer-brand relationship, thus providing individuals with a feeling of belonging. We use the term *relational benefit* for this particular kind of symbolic benefit (Strebinger, 2004).

Brands as schemata and categories

A very basic conception of a brand understands a brand as a schema (Sujan & Bettman, 1989). A brand schema is a cognitive knowledge structure that includes all associations with a brand (Krishnan, 1996). The brand schemata of strong brands are characterized by a large number of mostly positive associations that are prototypical for a specific product category yet unique in comparison with the associations of weaker competitors (Aaker, 1997; Krishnan, 1996).

Brand schemata can influence information processing by directing attention (Pieters & Warlop, 1999; Pieters & Wedel, 2004; Russo & Leclerc, 1994), the selective processing of information (Dawar & Pillutla, 2000; Posavac, Sanbonmatsu, Kardes, & Fitzsimons, 2004) or the differential activation of information in memory (Morrin, 1999) as well as by guiding interpretation (Monga & John, 2008). In other words, before consumers actually choose a product, they have to attend to the range of available products, form a set to be considered with relevant alternatives, draw inferences about the different alternatives and form a final opinion about which product best meets their prevailing needs. An available brand schema can influence the final outcome of such a situation at every link of the aforementioned chain of processes. A strong brand can attract attention (Russo & Leclerc, 1994), activate positive attributes in memory (Alba & Hutchinson, 1987), influence consumers' inferences about the brand product in relation to the other available alternatives (Meyers-Levy & Tybout, 1989) and, finally, shift the choice outcome in favour of the brand product (Alison & Uhl, 1964; Hoyer & Brown, 1990). The fact that brands, even more than the product attributes at hand, serve as the decisive factor in consumer judgements has repeatedly been shown in studies in which consumers are either requested to compare correctly labelled products or to judge products with incorrect brand labels or no brand information at all. In an early study, Alison and Uhl (1964) asked consumers to rate several beer brands and found that consumers tended to judge their preferred beer brand better when it was correctly labelled than when they were not able to identify the brand. Hoyer and Brown (1990) conducted a study with different peanut butter brands. They found that the awareness of a familiar brand in a set led individuals to explore fewer brands. Moreover, consumers falsely judged a low-quality product to be of high quality when it was labelled with a familiar brand label, and they mistook a high-quality brand for a low-quality brand when it was tagged with an unfamiliar brand label.

Importantly, studies have shown that brand associations often involve an implicit and automatic low-level processing of information that happens directly upon exposure to brands and can take place outside of consumers' conscious awareness (Chartrand & Fitzsimons, 2011). Fitzsimons, Chartrand and Fitzsimons (2008), for instance, found that the perception of a brand logo without conscious awareness can evoke behaviour that is consistent with the brand schema. Neuroscientific evidence for the implicit or automatic nature of brand effects was found in a recent study that reported that consumers' neural responses to brands predicted their later brand preference even when they did not actively attend to the brand information (Tusche, Bode, & Haynes, 2010). Deppe, Schwindt, Kugel, Plassmann and Kenning (2005) observed particularly strong changes in brain activity when a favourite brand was present in choice options. Hence, favourite brands already have immediate effects on the level of brain processes, resembling a "winner takes all" heuristic. In concert, the multifaceted processes, including automatic neural responses to brands, the direction of attention and the selective processing of information, contribute to the strong influence of brands on behaviour (Plassmann, Ramsøy, & Milosavljevic, 2012) revealed, for example, in the studies by Alison and Uhl (1964), Hoyer and Brown (1990) and Fitzsimons et al. (2008).

Moderators of brand schema effects

The studies described above have led to the conclusion that brand schemata are a commonly used heuristic in consumer decisions as they allow consumers to make rapid and effortless inferences about the quality and performance of a brand product (Dawar & Parker, 1994; Deppe et al., 2005). As such, their effect is particularly pronounced when consumers lack the knowledge, opportunity or motivation to thoroughly process relevant product information (Fazio & Towles-Schwen, 1999).

Maheswaran, Mackie and Chaiken (1992), for example, reported that brands had less of an effect on judgements when participants judged a product they thought would be available to them soon, compared with when they judged a product they did not expect to get anytime soon. The researchers supposed that the availability of a product would induce the motivation to process information about the product in a more elaborated fashion. In a different study,

Fazio, Powell, and Williams (1989) showed that brands have a choice advantage when the attitude towards the brand is positive and highly accessible in memory and when the choice is made spontaneously. Similar results were obtained with regard to implicit brand evaluations: Researchers found higher correlations between implicit brand associations and brand choice when consumers made a quick choice or one based on a more affective response (Friese, Wänke, & Plessner, 2006; Scarabis, Florack, & Gosejohann, 2006).

With regard to the influence of consumers' previous knowledge or expertise, for example, Maheswaran (1994) studied the influence of a country schema (similar to a brand schema) when consumers judged products from a particular country of origin. They found that the country of origin influenced the product evaluations of novices more than those of experts. Interestingly, however, when the product attributes were ambiguous, country of origin affected the evaluations of novices and experts equally. On the basis of these findings, the researchers concluded that novices used the country of origin to interpret the product attributes, whereas experts recalled information from memory that was congruent with the image of the country of origin.

In addition to motivational or resource-based influences on brand schemata effects, researchers have recently suggested that some consumers are more predisposed than others to process product information according to their existing brand schemata. According to Puligadda, Ross and Grewal (2012), brand-schematic consumers show a higher preoccupation with brands and a higher likelihood of relying on their brand schemata when making sense of their consumption environment, whereas brand-aschematic consumers use available product attributes or higher-order schemata (e.g., technology) to evaluate a product. In this sense, high-brand schematicity can be understood as a chronically high motivation to engage in the processing of brand information, which might indeed result in more stable brand schemata that can be readily accessed and employed in consumption settings.

The above-mentioned studies reveal that the effects of a brand schema vary with the motivation, expertise and personality of the brand users. However, it is important to consider that not only can consumers differ in their reliance on a brand schema in judgement and decision making, but they can also change their brand schema when exposed to information that is inconsistent with the existing schema. But the important question is: What are the factors that are most likely to result in a change in schema?

Brand schemata: Stability and change

In 2005, the German car magazine AutoBild published an article with the title "Does love make you blind?" (Czajka, 2005) referring to the fact that – despite the disappointing and disenchanting results of several test runs – the brand Mini, owned and produced by the high-end car manufacturer BMW, remained on its course to success. One explanation for consumers' reluctance to react to shortfalls in quality with a refusal to purchase the brand is that brand schemata are very stable constructs that are often resistant to schema-inconsistent information (Diamantopoulos, Smith, & Grime, 2005). For the BMW example that was just described, this means that the more firmly the association of quality is anchored in consumers' brand schema of the manufacturer BMW, the more likely they are to ignore or reappraise new information that is not in line with their overall brand perception. Thus, immunizing brands against negative information by consistently developing a very positive and strong brand image over a long period of time is highly important for companies if they want to avoid having consumers react to brand failures by switching to a competing brand.

Consumers' tendency to ignore negative aspects of brands can be explained with selective hypothesis testing (Sanbonmatsu, Posavac, Kardes, & Mantel, 1998). In general, individuals tend to search for information that supports their hypotheses. Brand schemata directly imply hypotheses about a brand's attributes. For brands with a positive brand schema, this can result in a positive evaluation that is biased in such a way that consumers neglect negative attributes. In other words, this means that consumers attend to information that is consistent with the brand schema, recall consistent information from memory, and interpret ambiguous information in a schema-consistent way. Moreover, research has shown that selective hypothesis testing leads to a brand positivity effect, that is, if alternatives are not specified or involvement is low, consumers focus their attention on one brand, amplifying their evaluation of that brand in comparison with the average of the other brands in the same category (Kardes, Sanbonmatsu, Cronley, & Houghton, 2002; Posavac et al., 2004). However, when involvement is high or consumers are asked to compare a focal brand with other brands, the positivity effect is often reduced (Kapoor & Heslop, 2009; Posavac et al., 2004). In other words, if consumers are not particularly motivated and a focal brand is strong, consumers are less likely to include several brands in the set of brands they will consider. The reduced set of alternatives means fewer comparisons, and, hence, a more positive evaluation of the focal brand.

Despite the fact that a positive brand schema can often mitigate consumers' responses to negative brand experiences, research on social cognition demonstrates that, in the long run, the adaptation of schemata is possible (Dolderer, Mummendey, & Rothermund, 2009). Indeed, consumers should be likely to change a positive brand schema (a) when negative incidents such as product failures occur repeatedly with products that are typical for a brand (e.g., Dawar & Lei, 2009; Lei, Dawar, & Gürhan-Canli, 2012; Loken & John, 1993) and (b) when those incidents are unambiguous and relevant for the brand schema (e.g., Aggarwal, 2004). In addition, change in a positive brand schema is likely when individuals have the goal of finding schema-inconsistent information and when they cannot plausibly explain why information deviates from their expectations (cf. Alison, Mackie, Muller, & Worth, 1993). However, if consumers regard negative brand experiences as rare or atypical for a brand, they are likely to exclude such experiences from their brand representation. For instance, Dawar and Lei (2009) found that consumers familiar with a brand responded more negatively when negative information about the brand in a news story was relevant to the brand than when it was not relevant. Consumers who were not familiar with the brand evaluated the brand more negatively after reading the news story irrespective of whether the negative information was related to the brand or not. The conditions under which a brand schema changes are particularly relevant for managers who plan to extend a successful brand. Indeed, a brand extension has the potential to increase sales by transferring the brand image to a new product, but it is also associated with the risk that an unsuccessful brand extension might dilute the brand image.

Brand schemata and brand extensions

Studies on brand extensions suggest that unsuccessful brand extensions will not necessary result in negative effects on parent brands (Batra, Lenk, & Wedel, 2010; Michel & Donthu, 2014; Romeo, 1991). Romeo (1991) showed that an unsuccessful extension of a brand into a new product category did not harm the brand as much as an unsuccessful extension into the brand-typical product category. In a similar vein, Michel and Donthu (2014) recently found that brand extensions were evaluated in reference to the parent brand only when they shared central brand associations (i.e., associations that constitute the brand core) but not when they shared peripheral brand associations. Thus, when considering brand extensions, an important question that firms need to address is how to successfully include (or in some cases exclude) a new brand extension in (or from) the parent brand category.

Whether the object is included in or excluded from a category has a strong impact on the judgement of this object (Bodenhausen, Macrae, & Shermann, 1999; Fiske & Neuberg, 1990) as well as for the representation of the category (Hewstone, 1994; Kunda & Oleson, 1995). Several theories provide predictions about possible categorization effects and formulate assumptions about the processes that underlie these effects (Bless, Schwarz, & Wänke, 2003; Higgins, Rhodes, & Jones, 1977; Herr, Sherman, & Fazio, 1983; Schwarz & Bless, 1992). The different theories share the idea that including an object in a category leads to assimilation. For example, a new product might be perceived as more similar to other brand products when the brand logo is depicted on the product or when the product name indicates that it belongs to the brand category (Wänke, Bless, & Schwarz, 1998). The assimilation of a brand extension is important when the aim is to leverage favourable parent brand associations.

Importantly, including a new product in the brand category is facilitated when the fit between the product and the benefit of the brand is high (Buil, de Chernatony, & Hem, 2009). A perception of fit is likely when the product is viewed as a substitute for previous products or when the competence that is required to develop or manufacture the typical brand products is perceived as important for the new product (Aaker & Keller, 1990; Voelckner & Sattler, 2006). However, fit is also perceived when the brand extensions share highly relevant brand-specific associations, that is, associations that are unique to the parent brand as opposed to its competitors (Broniarczyk & Alba, 1994) or when the product name or packaging signals similarities between typical brand products and the new product (Wänke et al., 1998). Moreover, a perception of fit is more likely when the brand offers a large number of diverse products with different benefits, which increases brand reliability (Del Vecchio, 2000), or when the fit is supported by advertising (Lane, 2000).

Less obvious than assimilation is the possibility of contrast effects. In a sophisticated model of assimilation and contrast effects, Bless, Schwarz and Wänke (2003) proposed that an object that is not considered representative of a category can be viewed as a standard of comparison for the entire category or its members. Hence, if consumers react to an incongruity between the new product and the brand category (e.g., different logo or different product name) by excluding the product from the category, they might accentuate the differences between the new product and other brand products when evaluating the new product in comparison to the brand category. Contrast effects can be desirable in brand management if a product is intended to be positioned in a new category or customer segment to which a transfer of brand associations is not desired. For example, Mercedes does not use its traditional naming and logo for the Smart, which is presented in a completely different way than typical Mercedes cars. In this case, contrast effects are actually an anticipated means by which to emphasize the divergence in positioning between the brand extension and the parent brand. In addition to extending a single product to a new or typical product category, brand managers can reduce the risk of negative feedback effects by relying on sub-brands. Using a sub-brand can facilitate the perception of a product as atypical of a brand category, and this in turn can mitigate negative effects on the evaluation of the brand if a sub-brand fails as a whole or is associated with product failures (Milberg, Park, & McCarthy, 1997). Recent evidence that sub-branding results in less category-based processing of the sub-branded product was found in a study by Sood and Keller (2012). The authors showed that category similarity positively affected brand extension evaluations by minimizing the speed with which participants made these evaluations when the brand extensions directly referred to the parent brand but not for sub-branded extensions.

In other cases, however, contrast effects can be related to undesirable consequences. For instance, Wänke, Bless and Igou (2001) demonstrated that excluding brand extensions from the parent brand category can bear an evident risk for consumer brand perception. If excellent brand extensions are excluded from representing the brand, the overall brand image might not benefit from the positive attributes of such products. Moreover, given that contrast effects highlight differences rather than similarities between the excluded brand extension and the parent brand category, the image of the other brand products can decline in comparison with the excellent extension. As this example shows, categorization effects have an impact on the categorized brand product as well as on the other brand products and the overall brand schema.

Above, we described how categorization affects assessments of the attributes of brands and their extensions. However, brand schemata are not only used to assess the attributes of products; they are also relevant to the consumers' self-concept.

Brands and self-concept

In 2004, the beauty brand Dove launched its "real beauty" campaign with an attempt to redefine the concept of beauty by accounting for the natural variations in beauty that occur in real life. What this campaign did was to add symbolic meaning to the brand image of Dove. Specifically, by consuming the Dove brand, women had the opportunity to communicate to their social environment that they shared Dove's notion that our current society's beauty values need to be reconsidered and reformulated. As this example shows, a brand is not only a schema or category that directs attention and information processing, but it responds to identity-based motives in that it communicates consumers' characteristics, values and attitudes to their social environment (Oyserman, 2009; Shavitt, Torelli, & Wong, 2009). For example, a consumer can use a brand to express the opinion that the pursuit of a sustainable and healthy lifestyle is important. Consequently, when a consumer observes another person using a brand that is associated with identity-relevant attributes, such as a healthy lifestyle, he or she may make similar inferences about the characteristics, values, and attitudes of the brand user (Belk, Bahn, & Mayer, 1982). In the introduction to this chapter, we used the term *symbolic benefit* to describe the social-signalling and identity-communicating functions of brands. Because brands provide consumers with a way to express their identity and socially categorize themselves, it is reasonable for consumers to prefer brands that are consistent with their self-concept (Sirgy, 1982).

The idea that individuals are motivated to perceive themselves as consistent in their values, attitudes and behaviour is a central tenet of early theories in social psychology, such as consistency theory (Heider, 1944) or dissonance theory (Festinger, 1957). In line with these and more recent approaches (Swann, 1990), several studies have demonstrated that individuals invest resources such as effort, time and money to appear consistent and thereby verify their self-concept (*self-verification*).

Swann, Rentfrow and Guinn (2003) proposed that a consistent and stable self-view enables individuals to classify and organize their experiences and to guide their behaviour. In addition, consistent behaviour increases predictability by others, which promotes a coherent environment for social interactions. A consumer holding values of sustainability might, for instance, actively avoid driving a car brand that is linked to power (and gas consumption) and might instead choose a brand that is known for its low gas consumption. By choosing this brand, the consumer provides a small window into his or her personality that others can "peek into" to predict his or her future behaviour, which in turn influences their responses to the consumer and makes the environment more predictable for the consumer as well.

The self-concept that drives consumer behaviour is to some degree flexible. It depends on which aspects of the self are accessible in a given context (Higgins, 1987). The accessibility of self-concept components is higher if the components have been repeatedly activated in the past and if they have been made salient more recently. Also, it is not necessarily the case that the self-concept has to be conscious in order for it to influence consumer behaviour (Oyserman, 2009).

A self-concept can represent a consumer's own viewpoint (how a consumer sees him- or herself) or the viewpoint of significant others (how the consumer thinks others see him or her) (Higgins, 1987). As a consequence of this dichotomy, consumers may perceive discrepancies between their own self-views and the way others perceive them, and in line with the consistency theories that were just mentioned, they should be motivated to reduce such discrepancies. Using brands with a symbolic benefit helps to resolve this conflict because such brands allow consumers to publicly display who they are, bringing other individuals' representations closer to an individual's representation of his or her self. A consumer who possesses the self-perception that he or she is a creative person but thinks that others do not share this self-view may, for instance, (consciously or unconsciously) use brands associated with creativity to signal his or her creativity to others.

The best-known example of a brand application with the intention to influence others' views of one's identity is the application of brands as status symbols. At first glance, it seems irrational that individuals would buy expensive brands that fulfil the same utilitarian functions as cheaper brands. However, the fact that a consumer can afford to buy expensive brands symbolizes his or her possession of resources, such as money or power. In evolutionary psychology, the use of status symbols is described as a costly form of signalling that men might apply in order to appear attractive to females (Griskevicius & Kenrick, 2013). Indeed, studies have found that men are more interested in purchasing conspicuous luxury goods that signal wealth when mating goals are primed compared with when such goals are not primed (Griskevicius et al., 2007). However, research has also shown that this is a short-term mating strategy that is also perceived as such by women (Sundie, et al., 2011). An interesting finding is that the social-signalling function of brands is not limited to luxury brands. Green products such as hybrid cars can similarly be regarded as status symbols (Griskevicius, Tybur, & Van den Bergh, 2010), but only when it is transparent that these products are more expensive than comparable nongreen products.

Importantly, not only might symbolic brand benefits communicate a person's actual self-view, but they also provide consumers with an opportunity to express their personality as they would ideally like it to be and to reduce a possible conflict between their actual and ideal self. This idea can be derived from self-discrepancy theory (Higgins, 1987). It implies that consumers can use brands for symbolic *self-completion* and *self-enhancement* (cf. Wicklund & Gollwitzer, 1981) and that brands can become part of the self (Belk, 1988, 2013). Interestingly, a reduction in self-discrepancies is related not only to the ideal aspects of the self but also to the aspects that a consumer thinks he or she should possess (the ought self) (cf. Higgins, 1987). For example, a consumer might think that it is his or her duty to take care of the environment, but he or she might sometimes also feel that he or she does not fully live up to this responsibility (discrepancy with the ought self). Consumers can use brands to reduce this discrepancy, as well. They could, for instance, purchase products from a supermarket associated with sustainability such as Whole Foods.

Similarly, the *feeling of uncertainty about one's self-concept* can motivate brand use. The feeling of uncertainty about one's self-concept is supposed to yield the motivation to reaffirm the self (Baumgartner, 1990; Gao, Wheeler, & Shiv, 2009; Steele, 1988). In one study, Gao et al. (2009) showed that participants were more likely to choose a product consistent with an activated self-view (competence or excitement) when participants felt uncertain about their self-view.

Relationships between brands and consumers

Not only is consumers' self-concept related to their personal identity, but it also includes their social identity as constituted by their memberships in social groups (Brewer & Gardner, 1996).

As a brand can be used as a symbol for individual aspects of the self, it can also be used as a symbol for one's membership in social groups (Muniz & O'Guinn, 2001). Fournier (2009) argues that consumers are often more interested in the social links to other consumers that are provided by the brand than in the brand itself. Indeed, research has found that consumers are more likely to include brands in their self-concept when members of relevant reference groups use the brands (Escalas & Bettman, 2003). Also, it has been found that self-enhancement motives amplify this effect for groups to which consumers aspire to belong, and self-verification motives amplify this effect for groups to which consumers actually belong (Escalas & Bettman, 2003). Importantly, not all brands can be used as symbols of group membership (Escalas & Bettman, 2005). Brand use can only be diagnostic of membership in a particular group when the brand is used to some degree exclusively by this group and not by groups from which consumers would like to be distinct.

Communal and exchange relationships

Going one step further than simply viewing brands as symbols of various groups, consumers can actually form relationships with brands similar to how they form relationships with humans or groups (Fournier, 1998). Fournier (2009) states that such relationships evolve because they are a means for symbolic benefits, but importantly, also because of functional benefits.

Similar to Fournier (2009), Aggarwal (2004) also suggests that consumers can form relationships with brands. The researcher distinguishes between exchange and communal relationships. *Exchange relationships* are those in which self-interest is the key driver. In these relationships, consumers focus on the outcome they get in return for how much they invested, similar to what business partners usually do. For example, if an online bank brand offers low fees, this provides a monetary benefit for the consumer. *Communal relationships* are those in which the relationship partners take care of each other's needs and are motivated to ensure the well-being of the interaction partners. In such relationships, a cost-benefit comparison is not the focus. For example, the company Henkel used the slogan "Henkel – a brand like a friend" to emphasize this kind of relationship.

Aggarwal and Law (2005) argue that the type of relationship between a consumer and a brand influences the level of abstractness on which information is processed. On the basis of the ideas that individuals often keep track of concrete inputs and outcomes in exchange relationships and that abstract concepts such as friendship are more important in communal relationships, the researchers hypothesized that consumers process information in exchange relationships on a lower level of abstraction than they do in communal relationships. In line with their hypothesis, Aggarwal and Law found that, compared with activated exchange relationship norms, activated communal relationship norms led consumers to evaluate a brand extension in a more abstract manner, to recognize abstract brand information better and to describe a brand product in a more abstract manner. If brand managers take this research into account, they could rely more on abstract information (e.g., the brand is the best in the category) when advertising for brands with communal relationships and more on concrete information when advertising for brands with exchange relationships (e.g., the brand is superior on a specific attribute). A further implication of the research on communal and exchange relationships is that brands with communal relationships are less likely to be threatened by concrete negative incidents such as product failures or information about single negative attributes. In line with this reasoning, Pham and Muthukrishnan (2002) found that brands with an abstract positioning were revised less after consumers were exposed to negative information than brands with a concrete positioning on attributes.

The above-mentioned research implies that communal relationships—which, according to the relationship definition, are abstract—are more immune to being damaged by concrete negative information or single negative incidents. However, it has to be noted that this immunizing effect has limits. Concrete information can harm brands with a communal relationship when the concrete information threatens the core promises of the relationship. For instance, Aggarwal (2004) found that, in communal relationships, consumers are very sensitive to being charged additional fees by the brand for only a small amount of help. In one study, the researcher studied consumers' relationships with a fictitious brand of bank. The researcher asked participants to imagine having a communal relationship or an exchange relationship with a bank. Participants were then asked how they would respond to being charged a fee for help with a problem that occurred in a financial transaction. Participants who were told to imagine having a communal relationship with the bank were less likely to regard the fee as a good business practice than participants who were told to imagine having an exchange relationship with the bank.

Perceiving brands as intentional agents

One characteristic of positive communal relationships is plausibly that the interaction partners regard each other as friendly and warm. One characteristic of exchange relationships is likely to be that the competence of the interaction partner in delivering the promised outcomes is relevant. Hence, it is reasonable to consider not only the relationship type but also the agents in the consumer–brand relationship and, in particular, the perception of the brand as warm and competent in this relationship (Fournier & Alvarez, 2012). Kervyn, Fiske and Malone (2012) posited that warmth (intention) and competence (ability) are important dimensions of the perception of brands (see also Ivens, Leischnig, Muller, & Valta, 2015). Kervyn et al. formulated a model of brand perception. They argued that consumers often ascribe mental states to brands and perceive brands as intentional agents with good or bad intentions. In this view, consumers can regard brands as intentional agents in the very same way in which they regard humans as intentional agents. The researchers suggested that consumers "perceive, feel, and behave towards brands in ways that closely mirror those towards other people and social groups" (Kervyn et al., 2012) and distinguished brands on the basis of warmth (intention) and competence (ability). According to this framework, the competence or ability to provide the promised outcomes is one important dimension, and the perception of brands as more or less well-intentioned is a second important dimension individuals rely on to judge a brand. For instance, consumers might perceive a bank as providing a good service to its customers, but at the same time, they might also perceive the bank as focused on its own profits and as not having good intentions towards its customers or society in general.

The distinction between warmth and competence represents a fundamental dimension in social perception, and these constructs are sometimes termed the "Big Two" (Abele & Bruckmüller, 2011; Cuddy, Fiske, & Glick, 2007; Fiske, Cuddy, Glick, & Xu, 2002). For instance, Diamantopoulos, Florack and Serfas (2014) studied whether the perceived warmth and competence of the people from a country could influence how the brands that come from this country are perceived. For many real brands from different countries, they found, in particular, that the competence stereotypes consumers hold about the people from a country influence people's intentions to purchase brands from that country.

The concept of brands as intentional agents suggested by Kervyn et al. (2012) means that consumers perceive not only the people in a country but their brands as having good or bad intentions towards consumers and society in general. Also, these authors suggested that consumers hold stereotypes about the abilities and competence of a brand. Such brand stereotypes can be based on consumers' past experiences or information that is provided. For example, polluting the environment or using child labour during production is not compatible with a perception of warmth and might lead to the perception that a brand is cold. However, consumers often do not have information about such practices by the brand and might fill in their gaps in knowledge with the help of an implicit theory (Schneider, 1973). On the one hand, consumers might be more likely to infer that a brand shows sustainable behaviour and responsibility for the environment and workers in production when they perceive that the brand is warm and well intentioned. On the other hand, they might also be more likely to infer that specific brand products are of high quality if they hold the stereotype that the brand is competent. Kervyn et al.'s (2012) approach implies that consumers rely on their immediate perception of a brand as warm and competent to make inferences, to respond to the brand and finally, to choose or reject the brand. Most importantly, the authors argue that warmth (intentions) and competence (ability) independently contribute to consumers' intentions to purchase the brand.

Whereas there is an agreement that perceptions of brands show similarities to perceptions of humans, it has to be taken into account that there are also differences in perceptions of brands and the processing of information about brands compared with perceptions of humans and the processing of information about humans. People's perceptions of other humans were already important early in the evolution of the human species. The development of specialized areas in the brain for perceiving and processing information about humans was the consequence. Interestingly, information about brands and information about humans are not processed equally in the same areas of the brain (Yoon, Gutchess, Feinberg, & Polk, 2006). Hence, even if brands are often perceived to be like humans, they are also specific. The difference becomes more apparent in the lexical approach to finding dimensions in descriptions of brands and humans. A lexical approach first asks participants to rate a person or a brand on many different attributes and then uses factor analysis to reduce the ratings to basic dimensions (Aaker, 1997; Goldberg, 1990). If this approach is applied to humans, the result is often five dimensions that are termed the Big Five (Goldberg, 1990). These dimensions include, for instance, extraversion and neuroticism. If this approach is applied to brands, sometimes five dimensions result (sincerity, excitement, competence, sophistication, ruggedness (Aaker, 1997). But these dimensions differ between different product categories (Caprara, Barbaranelli, & Guido, 2001), and most importantly, they differ at least in part from the Big Five found for describing humans. For example, the neuroticism dimension is not used to describe brands, whereas the human personality dimension of extraversion corresponds to the brand personality dimension of excitement.

Even if brand personality is not identical to human personality, the concept of brand personality is useful in brand management to form a brand that has meaning to consumers. Also, despite the differences between brand personality and human personality, there are similarities such as the dimension of extraversion, which is relevant for perceptions of brands and the (self-) perceptions of humans. Consumers can complete or self-verify their own extraversion by using a brand with the corresponding brand personality as we described above.

Brand experiences

Every year, the US company IBM announces their "5 in 5" – 5 innovations that are predicted to change the lives of consumers in the following 5 years. In 2012, this announcement was dedicated to the five human senses. By enabling consumers to, for instance, "feel the satin or silk of the gown, or the lace on the veil, all from the surface of the screen" (IBM, 2012), IBM is picturing itself as a brand of technology that, among other things, provides consumers with a rich and versatile brand experience. IBM's attempt to build a brand image that refers to human senses is not unique, as can be seen in recent marketing campaigns of brands such as Unilever's "Magnum" ice cream, with their "Five Senses" product line, or Wrigley's "5 gums".

What all these endeavours have in common is that they respond to a fundamental consumer need that has largely been neglected by classical marketing approaches: the need for sensory and affective experiences and stimulation. On the basis of the assumption that consumers are driven by intentions other than problem solving or price-quality comparisons, the concept of experiential brand benefits or brand experiences has been introduced into the marketing literature (e.g., Holbrook & Hirschman, 1982; Park et al., 1986; Schmitt, 1999). According to Schmitt (2009), the concept of brand experiences "captures the very essence of branding much more than analytically and cognitively oriented brand concepts" because it accounts for consumers' basic search for a brand that "engages their senses and touches their hearts" (p. 417) in times when the functionality of products is usually taken for granted. Moreover, in addition to the long-term oriented goals of self-expression and self-enhancement addressed by symbolic brand benefits, experiential brand benefits take into account consumers' desire for immediate hedonic experience and gratification (Holbrook & Hirschman, 1982).

Conceptually, brand experiences are commonly understood as sensory, affective, intellectual and behavioural brand–consumer interactions that take place when consumers search for, purchase or consume brand goods or services (Brakus, Schmitt, & Zarantonello, 2009; Schmitt, 1999). Out of these dimensions, the affective and multisensory responses elicited by brands have attracted the largest amounts of academic interest (cf. Brakus, Schmitt, & Zhang, 2014). We already addressed affective responses to brands in the context of brand–consumer relationships. In the following, we will therefore limit our discussion to the sensory dimensions of brand experiences as well as their underlying psychological processes and consequences for consumer behaviour. Moreover, we will take a closer look at the consequences of experiential brand dimensions for brand extension considerations.

Multisensory dimensions of brand experiences

The idea that consumption is fundamentally sensual in nature has only recently been introduced into the academic literature with the emergence of the sensory marketing perspective (e.g., Hultén, 2011; Krishna, 2012; Lindstroem, 2005). According to the sensory marketing account, consumption is inextricably linked to a variety of visual, olfactory, auditory, gustatory and tactile experiences that may appear as part of a store's physical environment (Spence, Pucinelli, Grewal, & Roggeveen, 2014) or a brand's design and identity (e.g., packaging, communication) (Spence, 2012).

Previous literature has recognized two main functions of sensory brand characteristics that are relevant for brand management purposes: First, as consumers naturally enjoy the mere occurrence of positive sensory experiences, they are more likely to engage in brand-related behaviour when this behaviour, or the environment in which it takes place, provides sensory pleasure (Krishna, 2012; Spence et al., 2014). For instance, prior studies have demonstrated that consumers spend more time and money in a store environment that provides positive olfactory or auditory experiences (Spangenberg, Crowley, & Henderson, 1996; Chebat & Michon, 2003) or they evaluate products more positively if they are allowed to touch these products (Peck & Wiggins, 2006). Spence and colleagues (2014) argue that pleasurable sensory experiences produce a positive affective response in the form of a general and unspecific positivity and stimulation that is consequently transferred to the evaluation of the shopping environment and the brand products that are evaluated in this environment. This assumption is in line with social psychology's feeling-as-information perspective (Schwarz, 1990; Schwarz & Clore,

1983), which posits that individuals use their immediate affective responses to a situation or an object as an evaluative standard for that situation or object. Importantly, the theory predicts that, if consumers' attention is called to the source of their positive affective responses, their feelings should no longer influence their brand evaluations in the same context (Schwarz & Clore, 1983). Thus, marketers need to be careful about the intensity of the sensory experiences they provide.

Second, sensory brand dimensions offer perceptual symbols that facilitate consumers' identification and understanding of the brand product and, if identification and interaction are achieved, increase their confidence in their brand evaluations as well as their engagement in current and future brand interactions (Elder et al., 2011; Krishna, 2012; Krishna & Schwarz, 2014). In other words, by seeing, touching, smelling, hearing and tasting a brand product, consumers establish an internal representation of what a brand product is like, what it can do, and how it can respond to their prevailing consumption needs. The role of sensory information in enhancing (or impeding) how people understand products has impressively been shown in prior studies that have examined the consequences of altering the sensory characteristics of a brand product for consumer behaviour and consumer brand evaluations. Zampini and Spence (2004), for instance, asked participants to rate the crispiness and freshness of chips while participants' received auditory feedback on their biting action via headphones. Importantly, for some participants, the volume and frequency of their sensory feedback during consumption was amplified. The results demonstrated that amplified auditory feedback led to higher perceptions of freshness and crispiness. Similarly, Krishna and Morrin (2008) found that the haptic characteristics of a product container affected the taste of the product in the container, and Hoegg and Alba (2007) showed that consumers made inferences about the sweetness of orange juice on the basis of only its colour saturation. These results strikingly show that consumers use sensory (in these cases haptic, auditory and visual) experiences to inform their judgements about the characteristics of a product or brand.

The notion that brands provide perceptual experiences as symbols for identification and interaction is widely shared among researchers who study embodied cognition (e.g., Barsalou, 2008; Niedenthal, Barsalou, Winkielman, Krauth-Gruber, & Ric, 2005; Wilson, 2002). In contrast to computational accounts of information processing that have postulated that experiences are stored in memory as abstract symbols (or representations) that guide high-level cognition (e.g., categorization, memory or inference), embodied cognition accounts assume that mental processes are grounded in sensory experiences with the environment. In other words, when individuals originally interact with their environment (e.g., drinking a Coke), all perceptual, motor and introspective experiences acquired during this interaction are stored as a multimodal representation in memory (e.g., the look and texture of the can, the motor action of grasping the can, the touch of the cold can, the sugary smell of the contents, introspections of freshness and relaxation). Moreover, perceptual symbols that are encountered in a consumption situation may trigger mental simulations of these prior product- or brand-related experiences and actions (Barsalou, 2008). For example, seeing a Coke on a supermarket shelf may lead consumers to mentally simulate or re-enact their previous brand experiences.

Importantly, whether these mental simulations of prior experiences lead consumers to approach a specific brand product depends on the degree to which the perceptual symbols that are provided by the brand facilitate or hinder the person's mentally simulated interaction with the product. Elder and Krishna (2012) found, for instance, that orienting the handle of a mug towards participants' dominant (vs. non-dominant) hand increased their intention to purchase the brand associated with the mug, even in the absence of actual interactions with the object.

Brand extensions of experiential brands

Brand experiences are described as holistic and highly idiosyncratic (Schmitt, 1999; Verhoef et al., 2009). This allows unique predictions to be made about the extension of brands with an experiential brand identity dimension as compared with a brand extension with functional or symbolic brand benefits. More specifically, brand extensions have the potential to (a) add an experiential dimension to an otherwise less experiential parent brand, (b) enhance the overall experiential identity of the parent brand and increase the intensity of the brand experience, or (c) add an additional dimension to the experiential brand image, thus creating an even more holistic brand experience (Schmitt, 1999).

However, two things need to be held in mind when thinking about extending brands with experiential brand benefits: First, creating an experiential brand dimension by adding an experiential brand shifts the comparison standard of the parent brand and its competitors to a more holistic comparison category. Specifically, a brand is no longer compared only along the functional dimension that it shares with its product category but also along an experiential dimension that is shared by all other brands that might provide a similar brand experience independent of the category they belong to (Schmitt, 1999).

Second, as sensory experiences are highly idiosyncratic and culture-specific, extending experiential brands to a global market might entail some special challenges. Whereas some colours, for instance, are perceived similarly by different countries and cultures, other colours show less cross-cultural consistency (Jacobs, Keown, Worthley, & Ghymn, 1991). Similarly, consumers differ in their preferences for taste or scent intensities (Hultén, Broweus, & Dijk, 2009), factors that need to be accounted for when sensory experiences are intended to be similarly pleasing in different countries. However, the culture-specific meaning of brands is not limited to sensory experiences; it concerns the processing of brand-related information as well as brand users' self-concept and consumer–brand relationships. Because cross-cultural differences are highly important in a time when global branding strategies are necessary to sell products in global markets (Aaker & Joachimsthaler, 1999), we discuss cross-cultural research through the psychological processes that underlie the perception of brands in the following section of this chapter.

Cultural differences in brand perception

The relation between the meaning of a brand and the consumers' cultural context can already be seen in the analysis of brand personality in different cultures (Aaker, Benet-Martínez, & Garolera, 2001; Sung & Tinkham, 2005). For instance, Aaker et al. (2001) found that brand personality dimensions in Japan and Spain, two cultures with strong harmony-oriented values, included peacefulness, whereas this dimension did not play a role in the US. Furthermore, the authors observed additional culture-specific dimensions such as passion in Spain. Sung and Tinkham (2005) observed passive likeableness and ascendency as culture-specific factors in Korea. The cultural differences between brand personality dimensions support the view that brands are symbols that carry cultural meaning and that cross-cultural differences are relevant to the perception of brands (Aaker et al., 2001; Sung & Tinkham, 2005).

Cross-cultural researchers have a long tradition in the study of cross-cultural differences in the construction of personality (Markus & Kitayama, 1998; Triandis, 1989) and thinking (Nisbett, Peng, Choi, & Norenzayan, 2001; Oyserman, & Lee, 2008). A basic implication of this research is that the self and thereby also the symbols used to describe the self are influenced by the social and cultural systems people live in (Markus & Kitayama, 2010). Hence, consumers rely on different symbols, including brands, in different cultures, but they also differ in how they process information (Mooij &Hofstede, 2011; Shavitt, Lee, & Johnson, 2008).

One basic difference between cultures involves the distinction between individualism and collectivism (Triandis, 1989). Individuals in individualistic cultures are assumed to give higher priority to their individual goals, whereas collective goals are assumed to be more important or equal to individual goals in collectivistic cultures (Triandis, 1989). The differences between individualistic and collectivistic cultures are rich, but two aspects of this differentiation are particularly relevant to the understanding of differences in the perception and use of brands. One aspect involves people's social orientation as emphasized by independence versus interdependence in individualistic and collectivistic cultures, respectively. The other aspect is the difference in the dominance of an analytical versus a holistic processing of information (Nisbett & Miyamoto, 2005).

A study by Eisingrich and Rubera (2010) examined the drivers of brand commitment by comparing consumers from the United Kingdom, an individualistic culture, and China, a collectivistic culture. In line with the assumption that the differences in social orientations between these cultures can also be seen in the perception of brands, the researchers found that the self-relevance of brands was a more important driver of brand commitment in the individualistic culture than in the collectivistic culture, whereas social responsibility was more important in the collectivistic culture. Interestingly, differences between individualistic and collectivistic cultures were also revealed in differences in the content of advertising in the different cultures (Shavitt et al., 2008). A content analysis of television commercials indicated that commercials in the United States, an individualistic culture, more frequently featured a person as unique or emphasized benefits for individuals than commercials in Korea, a collectivistic culture (Cho, Kwon, Gentry, Jun, & Kropp, 1999).

Research on the analytical and holistic processing of information in individualistic and collectivistic cultures implies, for example, that people in individualistic cultures attend more to focal objects in a scene, whereas individuals in collectivistic cultures are more likely to perceive scenes holistically (Nisbett & Miyamoto, 2005). We do not know of research that has directly measured differences in attention to brands between consumers from individualistic and collectivistic countries. However, it is interesting that advertising in individualistic countries seems to emphasize information that fits analytical thinking (e.g., product attributes or price) more than advertising in collectivistic countries (Javalgi, Cutler, & Malhotra, 1995; Shavitt et al., 2008).

A consequence of holistic thinking is that individuals are more likely to see similarities rather than differences or contradictions between objects, statements or concepts (Peng & Nisbett, 1999). Because this means that consumers should be able to see more relationships between products and tolerate differences, Monga and John (2007) formulated the hypothesis that consumers from collectivistic cultures are more likely to perceive fit between a parent brand and an extension. The researchers tested their hypothesis with American and Indian students and different brands. As expected, the Indian students (collectivistic culture) provided more favourable evaluations of the brand extension than the American students (individualistic culture).

The research we discussed above implies that marketing managers should consider cross-cultural differences in the perception of brands when developing global branding strategies. However, considering cultural differences does not mean that local brands are more successful than global brands. Indeed, research has reliably shown that global brands can create value for companies (Davvetas, Sichtmann, & Diamantopoulos, in press; Steenkamp, Batra, & Alden, 2003). The potential of global brands is not that they disregard cultural differences but that perceived globalness is a heuristic cue indicating quality and resulting in an increased willingness to pay (Davvetas et al., in press). Also, it has to be noted that even global brands are often assessed on the basis of the country from which they originated (Sichtmann & Diamantopoulos, 2013). Hence, global brands are often related to their country of origin, which might influence the perception of brands on the basic dimensions of warmth and competence we described above (Diamantopoulos et al., 2014).

Implications for marketing: Management of brand architectures

In this chapter, we discussed the ideas that brands are key categories in information processing, are perceived as relationship partners and are relevant for consumers' self-concept and that brands can drive consumers' experiences. Also, we stressed the idea that brands can serve different consumer needs and provide functional, symbolic, relational and experiential benefits. While explaining the different processes by which brands shape perceptions and behaviour, we already mentioned many marketing implications. To conclude this chapter, we will complete our discussion of these marketing implications with an example from the management of brand architectures that relies on the whole set of different functions and benefits of brands we described above (cf. Strebinger, 2004). Brand managers often have to make the difficult decision of how to integrate the different brands owned by a company. Companies such as Procter & Gamble, Nestle, or Unilever, for instance, own many different brands that are connected in many different ways. Some brands are positioned as single brands (product brands) with no connection to the other brands in the portfolio at all. Other brands are more closely related within a family of brands (family brands). Finally, sometimes a corporate brand is used for all products with only slight differentiations (corporate brand). If marketing managers take the different functions and benefits of brands into account, they are able to make a deliberate decision about how to structure their brand architecture. For example, if the predominant brand benefit is functional (e.g., high-quality product solutions) and if the brand relationship is a communal relationship that is built on serving functional needs, corporate brands can be used to signal the reliability and quality of all products of the brand very well. In such a case, the brand is perceived like a friend helping out in many situations. The brand meaning is very abstract and can easily be transferred to products in different product categories. However, the brand architecture has to be completely different if it includes brands that are used to verify, enhance or complete the consumer's self. In this case, a corporate brand that is targeted towards many different users is completely unable to serve the symbolic function of self-expression because it will not be diagnostic of a specific group or specific values to either the brand user or to other consumers who observe the use of the brand. The symbolic function of self-expression requires that brands be targeted towards a specific group. Hence, marketing managers should use target brands, which might include family brands, that are linked to the symbolic meaning of the brand but are targeted towards a specific target group. In this sense, the family brand can also be used across product categories as long as the brand is advertised for a specific target group and is used by this group. Finally, the predominant benefit of a brand might be a specific experience such as a specific taste. In this case, the benefit of the brand is concrete, and the extension to other categories is difficult because the specific experience is automatically activated by the brand. A positioning of such a brand as a single product brand or a distinct sub-brand might provide more of an advantage by offering integration into a larger brand family without explicit differentiation. Hence, the different benefits and functions of brands can be the basis for decisions about how to build a brand architecture, which, of course, is a more complex task than what we described here.

Conclusions and future research

In this chapter, we reviewed the research on the psychological processes that underlie effects of brands. We distinguished between effects that are related to functional, symbolic, relational and experiential benefits of brands. We linked these benefits to processes on the level of information processing, the self-concept, the formation of consumer–brand relations and multisensory brand experiences. Whereas the research on these processes is already extensive and evolving quickly, many gaps in research remain. In particular, there is often an imbalance between the study of the processes in basic areas of psychology and the transfer to the field of consumer psychology. To illustrate this point, we refer to the application of the stereotype content model in consumer psychology.

Although research in social psychology on the stereotype content model and warmth and competence as basic dimensions of impression formation of human targets is substantial (Cuddy et al., 2007), research on the importance of these dimensions in the consumer psychology of brands and research on the related *brands as intentional agents framework* (BAIF; Kervyn et al., 2012) is not yet comprehensive. Therefore, we would like to stress four starting points for the further study of these models in psychological brand research. First, further research is needed to examine whether the dimensions of warmth and competence are used to judge brand products or whether these dimensions influence the perception of the people associated with the brand products. At present, research cannot rule out the possibility that warmth and competence are more linked to the people representing the product (e.g., the CEO, the service personnel or the people of the country from which the brand originates) than to the brand products. Second, it is not clear whether the same mechanisms apply to the influence of warmth and competence with regard to brands and humans. From an evolutionary perspective, a primacy of warmth compared with competence is reasonable in impression formation for human targets (Cuddy et al., 2007). Individuals have to judge quickly whether a target has good or bad intentions before the individual can assess whether the target might implement such good or bad intentions. It is possible that a primacy of warmth exists in the perception of brands. However, it might also be the case that the competence of a brand is more important to consumers when brands are assessed in a context where functional brand benefits are important (see e.g., Maher & Carter, 2011 and Zawisza's chapter in this Handbook). Third, it is currently not clear whether the concepts of warmth and competence operate at an implicit level of information processing, whether consumers deliberately use these dimensions to judge brands, and what the conditions that amplify the relevance of these concepts are. If the mechanisms linked to the assessment of warmth and competence operate at an implicit level, the effects of warmth and competence might be less obvious in well-conceived consumer behaviour. Fourth, research should study whether the basic dimensions of the stereotype content model and the BIAF can be linked to consumer–brand relationships. Fournier (2012) previously formulated this research gap and wrote "that the most interesting research pertinent to the BIAF lies in the intersection of theories concerning social perception and people's relationships with brands" (p. 183).

We referred to the application of the stereotype content model in the area of consumer psychology as an example that shows that an application of basic psychological models in the consumer psychology of brands is very fruitful but that additional conditions have to be tested to see how far the transfer of these models can go. The application of the stereotype content model, however, is just one example. Another example is the study of cultural differences. More than 10 years ago, Maheswaran and Shavitt (2000) concluded that cross-cultural research is still in its infancy. Since then, considerable attempts have been made to take cross-cultural differences into account (for an overview, see Shavitt et al., 2008). However, the fields in which cross-cultural differences have been studied remain limited, and even though the research in this area may have left the stage of infancy, it is still in its youth. For example, as we pointed out, research on analytical and holistic processing in individualistic and collectivistic cultures (Nisbett & Miyamoto, 2005) allows the formulation of hypotheses about how individuals in these cultures form an impression of a brand or a brand advertisement, but we are not aware of research that has applied state-of-the-art methods (e.g., eye tracking) to study such differences in the perception of brand advertisements. Moreover, knowledge about whether these differences can already be observed at the level of brain activation is scarce. It would be an effortful but also promising endeavour to study such cross-cultural differences in consumer research in behaviour and with regard to brain processes, attention, and information processing.

References

Aaker, J. L. (1997). Dimensions of brand personality. *Journal of Marketing Research, 34*(3) 347–356.

Aaker, J. L., Benet-Martínez, V., & Garolera, J. (2001). Consumption symbols as carriers of culture: A study of Japanese and Spanish brand personality constructs. *Journal of Personality and Social Psychology, 81*(3), 492–508.

Aaker, D., & Joachimsthaler, E. (1999). The lure of global branding. *Harvard Business Review*, 77(6), 137–144.

Aaker, D. A., & Keller, K. L. (1990). Consumer evaluations of brand extensions. *Journal of Marketing, 54*(1), 27–41.

Abele, A. E., & Bruckmüller, S. (2011). The bigger one of the "Big Two"? Preferential processing of communal information. *Journal of Experimental Social Psychology, 47*(5), 935–948.

Aggarwal, P. (2004). The effects of brand relationship norms on consumer attitudes and behaviour. *Journal of Consumer Research, 31*(1), 87–101.

Aggarwal, P., & Law, S. (2005). Role of relationship norms in processing brand information. *Journal of Consumer Research, 32*(3), 453–464.

Alba, J. W., & Hutchinson, J. W. (1987). Dimensions of consumer expertise. *Journal of Consumer Research, 13*(4), 411–454.

Alba, J. W., & Hutchinson, J. W. (2000). Knowledge calibration: What consumers know and what they think they know. *Journal of Consumer Research, 27*(2), 123–156.

Allison, S. T., MacKie, D. M., Muller, M. M., & Worth, L. T. (1993). Sequential correspondence biases and perceptions of change: The Castro studies revisited. *Personality and Social Psychology Bulletin, 19*(2), 151–157.

Allison, R. I., & Uhl, K. P. (1964). Influence of beer brand identification on taste perception. *Journal of Marketing Research, 1*(3), 36–39.

Barsalou, L. W. (2008). Grounded cognition. *Annual Review of Psychology, 59*, 617–645.

Batra, R., Lenk, P., & Wedel, M. (2010). Brand extension strategy planning: Empirical estimation of brand–category personality fit and atypicality. *Journal of Marketing Research, 47*(2), 335–347.

Baumgardner, A. H. (1990). To know oneself is to like oneself: Self-certainty and self-affect. *Journal of Personality and Social Psychology, 58*(6), 1062–1072.

Belk, R. W. (1988). Possessions and the extended self. *Journal of Consumer Research, 15*(2), 139–168.

Belk, R. W. (2013). Extended self in a digital world. *Journal of Consumer Research, 40*(3), 477–500.

Belk, R. W., Bahn, K. D., & Mayer, R. N. (1982). Developmental recognition of consumption symbolism. *Journal of Consumer Research, 9*(1), 4–17.

Bless, H., Schwarz, N., & Wänke, M. (2003). The size of context effects in social judgment. In J. P. Forgas, K. D. Williams & W. von Hippel (Eds.), *Social judgments* (pp. 180–197). Cambridge: Cambridge University Press.

Bodenhausen, G. V., Macrae, N. C., & Sherman, J. S. (1999). On the dialectics of discrimination: Dual processes in social stereotyping. In S. Chaiken & Y. Trope (Eds.), *Dual-process theories in social psychology* (pp. 271–290). New York, NY: Guilford Press.

Brakus, J. J., Schmitt, B. H., & Zarantonello, L. (2009). Brand experience: What is it? How is it measured? Does it affect loyalty? *Journal of Marketing, 73*(3), 52–68.

Brakus, J., Schmitt, B. H., & Zhang, S. (2014). Experiential product attributes and preferences for new products: The role of processing fluency. *Journal of Business Research, 67*(11), 2291–2298.

Brewer, M. B., & Gardner, W. (1996). Who is this "we"? Levels of collective identity and self representations. *Journal of Personality and Social Psychology, 71*, 83–93.
Broniarczyk, S. M., & Alba, J. W. (1994). The importance of the brand in brand extension. *Journal of Marketing Research, 31*(2), 214–228.
Buil, I., de Chernatony, L., & Hem, L. (2009). Brand extension strategies: Perceived fit, brand type, and culture influence. *European Journal of Marketing, 43*(11/12), 1300–1324.
Bussey, K., & Bandura, A. (1999). Social cognitive theory of gender development and differentiation. *Psychological Review, 106*, 676–713.
Caprara, G. V., Barbaranelli, C., & Guido, G. (2001). Brand personality: How to make the metaphor fit? *Journal of Economic Psychology, 22*(3), 377–395.
Chartrand, T. L., & Fitzsimons, G. J. (2011). Nonconscious consumer psychology. *Journal of Consumer Psychology, 21*(1), 1–3.
Cho, B., Kwon, U., Gentry, J. W., Jun, S., & Kropp, F. (1999). Cultural values reflected in theme and execution: A comparative study of U.S. and Korean television commercials. *Journal of Advertising, 28*(4), 59–73.
Cuddy, A. J. C., Fiske, S. T., & Glick, P. (2007). The BIAS map: Behaviours from intergroup affect and stereotypes. *Journal of Personality and Social Psychology, 92*(4), 631–648. Retrieved from http://doi.org/10.1037/0022-3514.92.4.631
Czajka, G. (2005). Macht Liebe blind? [Does love make you blind?] Retrieved from www.autobild.de/artikel/dauertest-mini-cooper-52898.html
Dawar, N., & Lei, J. (2009). Brand crises: The roles of brand familiarity and crisis relevance in determining the impact on brand evaluations. *Journal of Business Research, 62*(4), 509–516.
Dawar, N., & Parker, P. (1994). Marketing universals: Consumers' use of brand name, price, physical appearance, and retailer reputation as signals of product quality. *Journal of Marketing, 58*(2), 81–95.
Davvetas, V., Sichtmann, C., & Diamantopoulos, A. (in press). The impact of perceived brand globalness on consumers' willingness to pay. *International Journal of Research in Marketing.*
Dawar, N., & Pillutla, M. M. (2000). Impact of product-harm crises on brand equity: The moderating role of consumer expectations. *Journal of Marketing Research, 37*(2), 215–226.
Del Vecchio, D. (2000). Moving beyond fit: The role of brand portfolio characteristics in consumer evaluations of brand reliability. *Journal of Product and Brand Management, 9*(7), 457–471.
Deppe, M., Schwindt, W., Kugel, H., Plassmann, H., & Kenning, P. (2005). Non-linear responses within the medial prefrontal cortex reveal when specific implicit information influences economic decision-making. *Journal of Neuroimaging, 15*, 171–182.
Diamantopoulos, A., Florack, A., & Serfas, B. (2014). The stereotype content model applied to country-of-origin stereotypes: Model validation and prediction of purchase intentions. *Advances in Consumer Research, 42*, 782–782.
Diamantopoulos, A., Smith, G., & Grime, I. (2005). The impact of brand extensions on brand personality: Experimental evidence. *European Journal of Marketing, 39*(1/2), 129–149.
Dolderer, M., Mummendey, A., & Rothermund, K. (2009). And yet they move: The impact of direction of deviance on stereotype change. *Personality and Social Psychology Bulletin, 35*(10), 1368–1381.
Elder, R. S., Aydinoglu, N. Z., Barger, V., Caldara, C., Chun, H., Lee, C. J., ... & Stamatogiannakis, A. (2011). A sense of things to come. In A. Krishna (Ed.), *Sensory marketing: Research on the sensuality of products.* New York, NY: Routledge.
Elder, R. S., & Krishna, A. (2012). The "visual depiction effect" in advertising: Facilitating embodied mental simulation through product orientation. *Journal of Consumer Research, 38*(6), 988–1003.
Escalas, J. E., & Bettman, J. R. (2003). You are what they eat: The influence of reference groups on consumers' connections to brands. *Journal of Consumer Psychology, 13*(3), 339–348.
Escalas, J. E., & Bettman, J. R. (2005). Self-construal, reference groups, and brand meaning. *Journal of Consumer Research, 32*(3), 378–389.
Fazio, R. H., Powell, M. C., & Williams, C. J. (1989). The role of attitude accessibility in the attitude-to-behaviour process. *Journal of Consumer Research, 16*(3), 280–288.
Fazio, R. H., & Towles-Schwen, T. (1999). The MODE model of attitude-behaviour processes. In S. Chaiken & Y. Trope (Eds.), *Dual-process theories in social psychology* (pp. 97–116). New York, NY: Guilford Press.
Festinger, L. (1957). *A theory of cognitive dissonance.* Stanford, CA: Stanford University Press.
Fiske, S. T., Cuddy, J., Glick, P., & Xu, J. (2002). A model of (often mixed) stereotype content: Competence and warmth respectively follow from perceived status and competition. *Journal of Personality and Social Psychology, 82*(6), 878–902.

Fiske, S. T., & Neuberg, S. L. (1990). A continuum of impression formation from category-based to individuating processing: Influences of information and motivation on attention and interpretation. In M. P. Zanna (Ed.), *Advances in Experimental Social Psychology*, *23*, 1–74.

Fitzsimons, G. M., Chartrand, T. L., & Fitzsimons, G. J. (2008). Automatic effects of brand exposure on motivated behaviour: How Apple makes you "think different". *Journal of Consumer Research*, *35*(1), 21–35.

Florack, A., & Scarabis, M. (2006). How advertising claims affect brand preferences and category–brand associations: The role of regulatory fit. *Psychology and Marketing*, *23*(9), 741–755.

Florack, A., Scarabis, M., & Gosejohann, S. (2005). Regulatory focus and consumer information processing. In F. R. Kardes, P. M. Herr & J. Nantel (Eds.), *Applying social cognition to consumer-focused strategy* (pp. 235–263). Mahwah, NJ: Lawrence Erlbaum Associates.

Fournier, S. (1998). Consumers and their brands: Developing relationship theory in consumer research. *Journal of Consumer Research*, *24*(4), 343–373.

Fournier, S. (2009). Lessons learned about consumers' relationships with their brands. In D. J. MacInnis, C. W. Park & J. R. Priester (Eds.), *Handbook of brand relationships* (pp. 5–23). Armonk, NY: M E Sharpe.

Fournier, S., & Alvarez, C. (2012). Brands as relationship partners: Warmth, competence, and in-between. *Journal of Consumer Psychology*, *22*(2), 177–185.

Friese, M., Wänke, M., & Plessner, H. (2006). Implicit consumer preferences and their influence on product choice. *Psychology and Marketing*, *23*(9), 727–740.

Fritz, C., Curtin, J., Poitevineau, J., Morrel-Samuels, P., & Tao, F.-C. (2012). Player preferences among new and old violins. *Proceedings of the National Academy of Sciences of the United States of America*, *109*(3), 760–763.

Gao, L., Wheeler, S. C., & Shiv, B. (2009). The "shaken self": Product choices as a means of restoring self-view confidence. *Journal of Consumer Research*, *36*(1), 29–38.

Gerbner, G. (1999). The stories we tell. *Peace Review*, *11*(1), 9–15. doi.org/10.1080/10402659908426225

Goldberg, L. R. (1990). An alternative "description of personality": The Big-Five factor structure. *Journal of Personality and Social Psychology*, *59*(6), 1216–1229.

Griskevicius, V., & Kenrick, D. T. (2013). Fundamental motives: How evolutionary needs influence consumer behaviour. *Journal of Consumer Psychology*, *23*(3), 372–386.

Griskevicius, V., Tybur, J. M., Sundie, J. M., Cialdini, R. B., Miller, G. F., & Kenrick, D. T. (2007). Blatant benevolence and conspicuous consumption: When romantic motives elicit strategic costly signals. *Journal of Personality and Social Psychology*, *93*(1), 85.

Griskevicius, V., Tybur, J. M., & Van den Bergh, B. (2010). Going green to be seen: Status, reputation, and conspicuous conservation. *Journal of Personality and Social Psychology*, *98*(3), 392–404.

Heider, F. (1944). Social perception and phenomenal causality. *Psychological Review*, *51*(6), 358–374.

Herr, P. M., Sherman, S. J., & Fazio, R. H. (1983). On the consequences of priming: Assimilation and contrast effects. *Journal of Experimental Social Psychology*, *19*, 323–340.

Higgins, E. T. (1987). Self-discrepancy: A theory relating self and affect. *Psychological Review*, *94*(3), 319–340.

Higgins, E. T., Rholes, W. S., & Jones, C. R. (1977). Category accessibility and impression formation. *Journal of Experimental Social Psychology*, *13*, 141–154.

Hoegg, J., & Alba, J. W. (2007). Taste perception: More than meets the tongue. *Journal of Consumer Research*, *33*(4), 490–498.

Holbrook, M. B., & Hirschman, E. C. (1982). The experiential aspects of consumption: Consumer fantasies, feelings, and fun. *Journal of Consumer Research*, *9*(2), 132–140.

Hoyer, W. D., & Brown, S. P. (1990). Effects of brand awareness on choice for a common, repeat-purchase product. *Journal of Consumer Research*, *17*(2), 141–148.

Hultén, B. (2011). Sensory marketing: The multi-sensory brand experience concept. *European Business Review*, *23*(3), 256–273.

Hultén, B., Broweus, N., & Van Dijk, M. (2009). *Sensory marketing*. New York, NY: Palgrave Macmillan.

IBM. (2012). *News release (Dec 17, 2012): IBM reveals five innovations that will change our lives within five years*. Retrieved from http://www-03.ibm.com/press/us/en/pressrelease/39685.wss

Ivens, B. S., Leischnig, A., Muller, B., & Valta, K. (2015). On the role of brand stereotypes in shaping consumer response toward brands: An empirical examination of direct and mediating effects of warmth and competence. *Psychology and Marketing*, *32*(8), 808–820.

Jacobs, L., Keown, C., Worthley, R., & Ghymn, K.-I. (1991). Cross-cultural colour comparisons: Global marketers beware! *International Marketing Review*, *8*(3), 21–30.

Javalgi, R. G., Cutler, B. D., & Malhotra, N. K. (1995). Print advertising at the component level: A cross-cultural comparison of the United States and Japan. *Journal of Business Research, 34*(2), 117–124.
Kapoor, H., & Heslop, L. A. (2009). Brand positivity and competitive effects on the evaluation of brand extensions. *International Journal of Research in Marketing, 26*(3), 228–237.
Kardes, F. R., Sanbonmatsu, D. M., Cronley, M. L., & Houghton, D. C. (2002). Consideration set overvaluation: When impossibly favorable ratings of a set of brands are observed. *Journal of Consumer Psychology, 12*(4), 353–361.
Kervyn, N., Fiske, S. T., & Malone, C. (2012). Brands as intentional agents framework: How perceived intentions and ability can map brand perception. *Journal of Consumer Psychology, 22*(2), 166–176.
Krishna, A. (2012). An integrative review of sensory marketing: Engaging the senses to affect perception, judgment and behaviour. *Journal of Consumer Psychology, 22*(3), 332–351.
Krishna, A., & Morrin, M. (2008). Does touch affect taste? The perceptual transfer of product container haptic cues. *Journal of Consumer Research, 34*(6), 807–818.
Krishna, A., & Schwarz, N. (2014). Sensory marketing, embodiment, and grounded cognition: A review and introduction. *Journal of Consumer Psychology, 24*(2), 159–168.
Krishnan, H. S. (1996). Characteristics of memory associations: A consumer-based brand equity perspective. *International Journal of Research in Marketing, 13*(4), 389–405.
Kunda, Z., & Oleson, K. C. (1995). Maintaining stereotypes in the face of disconfirmation: Constructing grounds for subtyping. *Journal of Personality and Social Psychology, 68*, 565–579.
Lei, J., Dawar, N., & Gürhan-Canli, Z. (2012). Base-rate information in consumer attributions of product-harm crises. *Journal of Marketing Research, 49*(3), 336–348.
Lindström, M. (2005). Broad sensory branding. *Journal of Product and Brand management, 14*, 84–87.
Loken, B., & John, D. R. (1993). Diluting brand beliefs: When do brand extensions have a negative impact? *Journal of Marketing, 57*(3), 71–84.
Maher, A. A., & Carter, L. L. (2011). The affective and cognitive components of country image: Perceptions of American products in Kuwait. *International Marketing Review, 28*(6), 559–580.
Maheswaran, D. (1994). Country of origin as a stereotype: Effects of consumer expertise and attribute strength on product evaluations. *Journal of Consumer Research, 21*(2), 354–365.
Maheswaran, D., Mackie, D. M., & Chaiken, S. (1992). Brand name as a heuristic cue: The effects of task importance and expectancy confirmation on consumer judgments. *Journal of Consumer Psychology, 1*(4), 317–336.
Maheswaran, D., & Shavitt, S. (2000). Issues and new directions in global consumer psychology. *Journal of Consumer Psychology, 9*(2), 59–66.
Markus, H. R., & Kitayama, S. (1998). The cultural psychology of personality. *Journal of Cross-Cultural Psychology, 29*(1), 63–87.
Markus, H. R., & Kitayama, S. (2010). Cultures and selves a cycle of mutual constitution. *Perspectives on Psychological Science, 5*(4), 420–430.
Meyers-Levy, J., & Tybout, A. M. (1989). Schema congruity as a basis for product evaluation. *Journal of Consumer Research, 16*(1), 39–54.
Michel, G., & Donthu, N. (2014). Why negative brand extension evaluations do not always negatively affect the brand: The role of central and peripheral brand associations. *Journal of Business Research, 67*(12), 2611–2619.
Milberg, S. J., Whan Park, C., & McCarthy, M. S. (1997). Managing negative feedback effects associated with brand extensions: The impact of alternative branding strategies. *Journal of Consumer Psychology, 6*(2), 119–140.
Monga, A. B., & John, D. R. (2007). Cultural differences in brand extension evaluation: The influence of analytic versus holistic thinking. *Journal of Consumer Research, 33*(4), 529–536.
Monga, A. B., & John, D. R. (2008). When does negative brand publicity hurt? The moderating influence of analytic versus holistic thinking. *Journal of Consumer Psychology, 18*(4), 320–332.
Mooij, M. de, & Hofstede, G. (2011). Cross-cultural consumer behaviour: A review of research findings. *Journal of International Consumer Marketing, 23*(3/4), 181–192.
Morrin, M. (1999). The impact of brand extensions on parent brand memory structures and retrieval processes. *Journal of Marketing Research, 36*(4), 517–525.
Muniz, J., & O'Guinn, T. C. (2001). Brand community. *Journal of Consumer Research, 27*(4), 412–432.
Niedenthal, P. M., Barsalou, L. W., Winkielman, P., Krauth-Gruber, S., & Ric, F. (2005). Embodiment in attitudes, social perception, and emotion. *Personality and Social Psychology Review, 9*(3), 184–211.
Nisbett, R. E., & Miyamoto, Y. (2005). The influence of culture: Holistic versus analytic perception. *Trends in Cognitive Sciences, 9*(10), 467–473.

Nisbett, R. E., Peng, K., Choi, I., & Norenzayan, A. (2001). Culture and systems of thought: Holistic versus analytic cognition. *Psychological Review, 108*(2), 291–310.
Oyserman, D. (2009). Identity-based motivation and consumer behaviour. *Journal of Consumer Psychology, 19*(3), 276–279.
Oyserman, D., & Lee, S. W. (2008). Does culture influence what and how we think? Effects of priming individualism and collectivism. *Psychological Bulletin, 134*(2), 311.
Park, C. W., Jaworski, B. J., & MacInnis, D. J. (1986). Strategic brand concept-image management. *Journal of Marketing, 50*, 135–145.
Peck, J., & Wiggins, J. (2006). It just feels good: Customers' affective response to touch and its influence on persuasion. *Journal of Marketing, 70*(4), 56–69.
Peng, K., & Nisbett, R. E. (1999). Culture, dialectics, and reasoning about contradiction. *American Psychologist, 54*(9), 741–754.
Pieters, R., & Warlop, L. (1999). Visual attention during brand choice: The impact of time pressure and task motivation. *International Journal of Research in Marketing, 16*(1), 1–16.
Pieters, R., & Wedel, M. (2004). Attention capture and transfer in advertising: Brand, pictorial, and text-size effects. *Journal of Marketing, 68*(2), 36–50.
Pham, M. T., & Muthukrishnan, A. V. (2002). Search and alignment in judgment revision: Implications for brand positioning. *Journal of Marketing Research, 39*(1), 18–30.
Plassmann, H., Ramsøy, T. Z., & Milosavljevic, M. (2012). Branding the brain: A critical review and outlook. *Journal of Consumer Psychology, 22*(1), 18–36.
Posavac, S. S., Sanbonmatsu, D. M., Kardes, F. R., & Fitzsimons, G. J. (2004). The brand positivity effect: When evaluation confers preference. *Journal of Consumer Research, 31*(3), 643–651.
Puligadda, S., Ross Jr., W. T., & Grewal, R. (2012). Individual differences in brand schematicity. *Journal of Marketing Research, 49*(1), 115–130.
Romeo, J. B. (1991). The effect of negative information on the evaluations of brand extensions and the family brand. *Advances in Consumer Research, 18*, 399–406.
Russo, J. E., & Leclerc, F. (1994). An eye-fixation analysis of choice processes for consumer nondurables. *Journal of Consumer Research, 21*(2), 274–290.
Sanbonmatsu, D. M., Posavac, S. S., Kardes, F. R., & Mantel, S. P. (1998). Selective hypothesis testing. *Psychonomic Bulletin and Review, 5*(2), 197–220.
Scarabis, M., Florack, A., & Gosejohann, S. (2006). When consumers follow their feelings: The impact of affective or cognitive focus on the basis of consumers' choice. *Psychology & Marketing, 23*(12), 1015–1034.
Schmitt, B. (1999). Experiential marketing. *Journal of Marketing Management, 15*(1–3), 53–67.
Schmitt, B. (2009). The concept of brand experience. *Journal of Brand Management, 16*(7), 417–419.
Schneider, D. J. (1973). Implicit personality theory: A review. *Psychological Bulletin, 79*(5), 294–309.
Schwarz, N., & Bless, H. (1992). Scandals and the public's trust in politicians: Assimilation and contrast effects. *Personality and Social Psychology Bulletin, 18*, 574–579.
Schwarz, N., & Clore, G. L. (1983). Mood, misattribution, and judgments of well-being: Informative and directive functions of affective states. *Journal of Personality and Social Psychology, 45*(3), 513–523.
Shavitt, S., Lee, A., & Johnson, T. P. (2008). Cross-cultural consumer psychology. In C. P. Haugtvedt, P. Herr & F. Kardes (Eds.), *Handbook of consumer psychology* (pp. 1103–1131). New York, NY: Lawrence Erlbaum Associates.
Shavitt, S., Torelli, C. J., & Wong, J. (2009). Identity-based motivation: Constraints and opportunities in consumer research. *Journal of Consumer Psychology, 19*(3), 261–266.
Sichtmann, C., & Diamantopoulos, A. (2013). The impact of perceived brand globalness, brand origin image, and brand origin–extension fit on brand extension success. *Journal of the Academy of Marketing Science, 41*(5), 567–585.
Sirgy, M. J. (1982). Self-concept in consumer behaviour: A critical review. *Journal of Consumer Research, 9*(3), 287–300.
Sood, S., & Keller, K. L. (2012). The effects of brand name structure on brand extension evaluations and parent brand dilution. *Journal of Marketing Research, 49*(3), 373–382.
Spangenberg, E. R., Crowley, A. E., & Henderson, P. W. (1996). Improving the store environment: Do olfactory cues affect evaluations and behaviours? *Journal of Marketing, 60*(2), 67–80.
Spence, C. (2012). Managing sensory expectations concerning products and brands: Capitalizing on the potential of sound and shape symbolism. *Journal of Consumer Psychology, 22*(1), 37–54.
Spence, C., Puccinelli, N. M., Grewal, D., & Roggeveen, A. L. (2014). Store atmospherics: A multisensory perspective. *Psychology and Marketing, 31*(7), 472–488.

Steele, C. M. (1988). The psychology of self-affirmation: Sustaining the integrity of the self. *Advances in Experimental Social Psychology, 21,* 261–302.

Steenkamp, J.-B. E. M., Batra, R., & Alden, D. L. (2003). How perceived brand globalness creates brand value. *Journal of International Business Studies, 34*(1), 53–65.

Strebinger, A. (2004). Strategic brand concept and brand architecture strategy-a proposed model. *Advances in Consumer Research, 31*(1), 656–661.

Sujan, M., & Bettman, J. R. (1989). The effects of brand positioning strategies on consumers' brand and category perceptions: Some insights from schema research. *Journal of Marketing Research, 26*(4), 454–467.

Sundie, J. M., Kenrick, D. T., Griskevicius, V., Tybur, J. M., Vohs, K. D., & Beal, D. J. (2011). Peacocks, Porsches, and Thorstein Veblen: Conspicuous consumption as a sexual signaling system. *Journal of Personality and Social Psychology, 100*(4), 664–680.

Sung, Y., & Tinkham, S. F. (2005). Brand personality structures in the United States and Korea: Common and culture-specific factors. *Journal of Consumer Psychology, 15*(4), 334–350.

Swann Jr., W. B. (1990). To be adored or to be known? The interplay of self-enhancement and self-verification. In E. T. Higgins & R. M. Sorrentino (Eds.), *Handbook of motivation and cognition: Foundations of social behaviour, Vol. 2* (pp. 408–448). New York, NY: Guilford Press.

Swann Jr., W. B., Rentfrow, P. J., & Guinn, J. S. (2003). Self-verification: The search for coherence. In M. R. Leary & J. P. Tangney (Eds.), *Handbook of self and identity* (pp. 367–383). New York, NY: Guilford Press.

Triandis, H. C. (1989). The self and social behaviour in differing cultural contexts. *Psychological Review, 96*(3), 506–520.

Tusche, A., Bode, S., & Haynes, J. D. (2010). Neural responses to unattended products predict later consumer choices. *Journal of Neuroscience, 30*(23), 8024–8031.

Verhoef, P. C., Lemon, K. N., Parasuraman, A., Roggeveen, A., Tsiros, M., & Schlesinger, L. A. (2009). Customer experience creation: Determinants, dynamics and management strategies. *Journal of Retailing, 85*(1), 31–41.

Völckner, F., & Sattler, H. (2006). Drivers of brand extension success. *Journal of Marketing, 70*(2), 18–34.

Wänke, M., Bless, H., & Igou, E. R. (2001). Next to a star: Paling, shining, or both? Turning interexemplar contrast into interexemplar assimilation. *Personality and Social Psychology Bulletin, 27*(1), 14–29.

Wänke, M., Bless, H., & Schwarz, N. (1998). Context effects in product line extensions: Context is not destiny. *Journal of Consumer Psychology*, 7(4), 299–322.

Wicklund, R. A., & Gollwitzer, P. M. (1981). Symbolic self-completion, attempted influence, and self-deprecation. *Basic and Applied Social Psychology, 2*(2), 89–114.

Wilson, M. (2002). Six views of embodied cognition. *Psychonomic Bulletin and Review, 9*(4), 625–636.

Yoon, C., Gutchess, A. H., Feinberg, F., & Polk, T. A. (2006). A functional magnetic resonance imaging study of neural dissociations between brand and person judgments. *Journal of Consumer Research, 33*(1), 31–40.

Zampini, M., & Spence, C. (2004). The role of auditory cues in modulating the perceived crispness and staleness of potato chips. *Journal of Sensory Studies, 19*(5), 347–363.

30

Aesthetics

Antecedents, underlying processes and behavioural consequences

Martin Reimann and C. Clark Cao

Ever since Gustav Theodor Fechner first empirically investigated the aesthetic properties of different rectangles in his seminal work *Vorschule der Ästhetik* more than 130 years ago (Fechner, 1876), psychologists have been fascinated with the experimental study of aesthetics – in spite of the intricacy of the subject. In this chapter, we ask and methodically review what has happened since Fechner's very early attempt to empirically understand aesthetics in both general psychology and its applied domain, consumer psychology. We also attempt to categorize the existing empirical literature on aesthetics to see which aspects of aesthetics have received the most attention from researchers and which may be understudied.

Our chapter contributes a systematic review and comprehensive overview of the subject of empirical aesthetics to the extant literature. Specifically, our review shows that Fechner's effort to empirically understand aesthetics (which was published in the form of two-volume book in 1876) was indeed the preschool (*Vorschule*) of aesthetics, as it would be another 45 years before empirical aesthetics research first emerged in journals; the first journal publication on aesthetics that our review identified dates back to 1921 (Perrin, 1921). Our review of all volumes of some of the most traditional journals in psychology (e.g., the *Journal of Experimental Psychology*) also documents that, over the decades, investigations of aesthetics have evolved from an interest in understanding the aesthetics of objects (e.g., the beauty of different ratios in rectangles, as studied by Thompson 1946; Shipley et al. 1947) and the aesthetics of subjects (e.g., the physical attractiveness of humans, as studied by Milord, 1978) to social factors (Eysenck, 1939) and cultural variables (Cunningham, Roberts, Barbee, Druen, & Wu, 1995) that influence aesthetics. Undeniably, Fechner's initial studies set the stage for what has become a fruitful field of discovery; in total, our review identified 77 articles dealing empirically with aesthetics, 55 of which have been published in general psychology outlets.

In more recent decades, work on aesthetics has also appeared in consumer psychology. The first paper identified in consumer research journals (i.e., the *Journal of Consumer Psychology*, the *Journal of Consumer Research* and the *Journal of Marketing Research*) was published in 1977 (Baker & Churchill, 1977). The fact that it took more than half a century for aesthetics research to impact our understanding of consumer psychology is interesting, given the former's many potential applications to product and package design, advertising and other aspects of marketing. While product and package designers, ad and web designers and related creative professionals have developed a wealth of tacit knowledge on what makes things and beings beautiful, systematic empirical research has surprisingly only emerged in consumer psychology journals in recent years. It was a 2010 special issue published in the *Journal of Consumer Psychology* that propelled interest in the topic by curating a collection of empirical investigations of aesthetics (Patrick & Peracchio, 2010). However, there are still few publications (out of all marketing journals reviewed in this chapter, only 14 papers on consumer aesthetics were identified). This observation has, in many respects, changed little since the first seminal review on aesthetics in consumer psychology by Hoegg and Alba (2008) in the *Handbook of Consumer Psychology*, which commented that aesthetics "has been largely ignored by consumer psychologists" (p. 748).

In the following sections of this chapter, we will report and discuss a systematic review of extant aesthetics research, which are categorized into five major areas: (1) aesthetic judgements based on sensory, referring to the questions of how and why individuals perceive and judge beauty based on their sensations (e.g., Perrin, 1921; Steck & Machotka, 1975); (2) aesthetic judgements based on ease of processing, referring to the questions of how and why individuals perceive and judge beauty based on the ease of processing the stimuli that they encounter (e.g., Martindale & Moore, 1988; Veryzer & Hutchinson, 1998); (3) aesthetic affect, referring to the question of which emotions, feelings and moods result from perceptions of beauty (e.g., Strube, Turner, Patrick, & Perrillo, 1983); (4) responses to aesthetics, referring to the question of what behaviours are triggered by beauty (e.g., Dion, Berscheid, & Walster, 1972; Peracchio & Meyers-Levy, 1994); and (5) individual and culture difference in aesthetics (Gordon, 1923; Yang, Zhang, & Peracchio, 2010). We also review the methodological approaches that have been applied most often in empirical studies of aesthetics. Researchers have contrived a broad spectrum of ways to manipulate aesthetics, ranging from visual stimuli (e.g., product designs, human faces) to auditory stimuli (e.g., music). Most prior research, however, has focused on manipulating visual aesthetics, leaving aesthetics related to the other four senses (i.e., audition, olfaction, haptics and taste) largely understudied.

Through the aforementioned discussions, this chapter aims to (1) achieve clarity on the key conceptual and methodological issues in empirical aesthetics research, (2) develop an integrative view of aesthetics for both general psychology and consumer psychology, and (3) discuss ideas and directions for further research on the subject of aesthetics.

Literature review

In our literature review, we deliberately focused on empirical studies of aesthetics published in leading journals in psychology and consumer research, including the *Journal of Consumer Psychology*, the *Journal of Consumer Research*, the *Journal of Experimental Psychology* (*JEP: General, JEP: Applied* and *JEP: Human Perception and Performance*), the *Journal of Marketing Research*, the *Journal of Personality and Social Psychology* and *Psychological Science*.

Our literature search started with the first issues of each journal, up to and including the last issue of the 2014 volume. The first relevant article was published in 1921. The keywords *aesthetic, aesthetics, beauty* and *beautiful* served to identify relevant articles by their titles, abstracts and lists of keywords. We acknowledge that many more published articles are related to the idea of aesthetics. However, we did not include in our literature review articles that (1) did not explicitly include the terms *aesthetic, aesthetics, beauty* and *beautiful* in their titles, abstracts and/or lists of keywords (e.g., Cho & Schwarz, 2010; Madzharov & Block, 2010); (2) did not contain empirical work (e.g., Park, 2012); (3) reported qualitative work (Joy & Sherry, 2003; Venkatesh, Joy, Sherry, & Deschenes, 2010); and/or (4) appeared in other journals (e.g., *Psychology of Aesthetics, Creativity, and the Arts*). In total, 196 empirical studies in 77 relevant articles (note that many articles reported multiple studies) were identified. Table 30.1 summarizes

Table 30.1 Literature review

Author(s) (year)	*Discipline*	*Focal topic*	*N*	*Core finding(s)*	*Journal*	*Category*
Perrin (1921)	General psychology	How do physical traits affect the perception of attractiveness?	Only partially reported (29 for the second investigation, seven judges in the third investigation, etc.)	Physical characteristics associated with sexual appeals positively correlate with the perception of attractiveness.	*JEP*	Aesthetic judgements (sense perception: visual); physical attractiveness
Gordon (1923)	General psychology	Do aesthetic judgements have external standards?	207	Individual judgements on pictures of oriental rugs show great diversity in aesthetic judgements. However, individual preferences are consistent over time. Moreover, the agreement between group judgements is high and increases with the size of groups.	*JEP*	Aesthetic judgements (sense perception: visual); Individual differences
Eysenck (1939)	General psychology	How does the number of judges influence the validity of aesthetic judgements?	900	As the number of judges becomes larger, the validity of aesthetic judgements increases.	*JEP*	Aesthetic judgements (sense perception: visual)
Campbell (1941)	General psychology	How do "natural" characteristics influence the perception of designs?	Part I: 15; Part II: 25 for Presentation 1, 9 for Presentation 2, 23 for Presentation 3; Part III: 18; Part IV: 21	Principles of natural sensory organization, experience or meaning are determinants of visual aesthetic perceptions.	*JEP*	Aesthetic judgements (sense perception: visual)

(*Continued*)

Table 30.1 (Continued)

Author(s) (year)	*Discipline*	*Focal topic*	*N*	*Core finding(s)*	*Journal*	*Category*
Thompson (1946)	General psychology	How do the aesthetic preferences for rectangles of different proportions vary across age groups?	100	College students prefer rectangles with width-length ratios from 0.55 to 0.65. Preschool children, however, show no consistent preferences.	*JEP*	Aesthetic judgements (sense perception: visual); rectangles; individual differences
Shipley et al. (1947)	General psychology	How do children and adults differ in their preference for rectangles?	200	Children prefer larger rectangles, whereas adults prefer more medium-sized rectangles for any given width-length ratio.	*JEP*	Aesthetic judgements (sense perception: visual); rectangles; individual differences
Guilford and Holley (1949)	General psychology	What are determinants of aesthetic judgements?	12	Four theme factors and one special design variable emerge as determinants of aesthetic judgements on playing card designs.	*JEP*	Aesthetic judgements (sense perception: visual); individual differences
Crandall (1967)	General psychology	How does familiarity influence stimuli preference?	Preliminary Study: 30; Study 1: 30; Study 2: 16; Study 3: 35	Foreign words and consonant-vowel-consonant syllables at intermediate levels of familiarity are rated more favourably than unfamiliar or very familiar ones.	*JEP*	Aesthetic judgements (sense perception: visual)
Child and Iwao (1968)	General psychology	What is the relationship between aesthetic sensitivity and cognitive independence/ openness?	Study 1: 72 (final sample); Study 2: 131	There is a positive relationship between aesthetic sensitivity and cognitive independence/ openness in both American secondary-school students and male Japanese college students.	*JPSP*	Individual differences

Bryson and Driver (1972)	General psychology	How does introversion/ extroversion influence the preference for complexity?	40	Extraverts prefer moderate levels of complexity in stimuli. However, introverts with greater cognitive complexity (i.e., those assumed to prefer more complex stimuli) prefer the simplest stimuli, while introverts low in cognitive complexity (i.e., those assumed to prefer less complex stimuli) prefer the most complex stimuli.	*JPSP*	Aesthetic judgements (sense perception: visual); individual differences
Dion et al. (1972)	General psychology	Are physically attractive individuals assumed to possess more socially favourable traits and to live better lives than physically unattractive individuals?	60	Attractive individuals are indeed perceived to possess more favourable traits and to live better lives.	*JPSP*	Responses to aesthetics; physical attractiveness
Wilson et al. (1973)	General psychology	How do liberalism and conservatism influence the preference for paintings?	30	Conservative individuals prefer paintings that are simple representations and dislike complex and abstract paintings, whereas liberal individuals show a preference for more complex and abstract artworks.	*JPSP*	Aesthetic judgements (sense perception: visual); artwork; individual differences
Sigall and Landy (1973)	General psychology	How can having a physically attractive romantic partner influence one's perceived physical attractiveness?	Study 1: 56; Study 2: 40	A male is evaluated more favourably when he is associated with an attractive female and less favourably when associated with an unattractive female.	*JPSP*	Aesthetic judgements (sense perception: visual); physical attractiveness; responses to aesthetics

(*Continued*)

Table 30.1 (Continued)

Author(s) (year)	*Discipline*	*Focal topic*	*N*	*Core finding(s)*	*Journal*	*Category*
Landy and Sigall (1974)	General psychology	How can task performance evaluation be influenced by the performers' physical attractiveness?	60	Individuals evaluate a writer and his/her work most favourably when the writer is attractive, least favourably when the writer is unattractive and intermediately when her appearance is unknown.	*JPSP*	Responses to aesthetics; physical attractiveness
Aitken (1974)	General psychology	How does complexity influence the preference for polygons?	30	As complexity increases, group judgements of pleasingness and interestingness also go up, whereas individual judgements of pleasingness decrease with complexity.	*JEP*	Aesthetic judgements (sense perception: visual)
Moskowitz et al. (1974)	General psychology	How does odour intensity influence odour pleasantness?	33	In the case of butanol, pleasantness and intensity correlate inversely for individual judgement but not group judgement.	*JEP*	Aesthetic judgements (sense perception: olfactory)
Sigall and Ostrove (1975)	General psychology	How does physical attractiveness of a criminal defendant work for or against his or her punishment?	120	When a crime is unrelated to attractiveness (e.g., burglary), individuals will assign more lenient sentences to an attractive defendant than to an unattractive defendant; however, when the crime relates to physical attractiveness (e.g., swindling), harsher punishment will be meted out to an attractive defendant.	*JPSP*	Responses to aesthetics; physical attractiveness

Dermer and Thiel (1975)	General psychology	Do individuals perceive physically attractive females as having more favourable traits?	Study 1: 40; Study 2: 354	Physically attractive females are perceived to have some positive traits (e.g., more sociable or more professionally successful). However, they are also perceived to have negative traits (e.g., more likely to engage in adultery or more bourgeois).	*JPSP*	Responses to aesthetics; physical attractiveness
Steck and Machotka (1975)	General psychology	Do individuals have absolute preference for the complexity of music (specifically, how many different tones make up a piece of music), or is this preference influenced by contextual factors (e.g., the range of complexity to which the subject adapts)?	60	The range of complexity to which the subject adapts partially determines the preference for complexity, suggesting that the complexity preference for music is to a large extent relative rather than absolute.	*JEP: Human Perception and Performance*	Aesthetic judgements (sense perception: auditory); music
Baker and Churchill (1977)	Consumer psychology	How does the physical attractiveness of male and female models influence evaluations of ads?	96	Individuals will more highly evaluate an ad showing a model of the opposite sex than an ad showing a model of their own sex. Physical attractiveness of the model positively influences the rating.	*JMR*	Aesthetic judgements (sense perception: visual); responses to aesthetics; physical attractiveness
Milord (1978)	General psychology	How do individuals build face perceptions?	Study 1A: 10; Study 1B: 12; Study 1C: 16; Study 1D: 32	People build face perceptions on dimensions such as beauty, race, and features/expression.	*JPSP*	Aesthetic judgements (sense perception: visual); physical attractiveness

(*Continued*)

Table 30.1 (Continued)

Author(s) (year)	*Discipline*	*Focal topic*	*N*	*Core finding(s)*	*Journal*	*Category*
Kenrick and Gutierres (1980)	General psychology	How can judgements of average females' attractiveness or dating desirability be adversely affected by exposing judges to extremely attractive prior stimuli?	Study 1: 81; Study 2: 48; Study 3: 98	A contrast effect was found. Specifically, subjects' previous exposure to extremely beautiful females decreases average females' attractiveness and dating desirability.	*JPSP*	Aesthetic judgements (sense perception: visual); physical attractiveness
Reis, Nezlek and Wheeler (1980)	General psychology	How does physical attractiveness influence social interaction?	71	For males, attractiveness correlates strongly with the quantity of social interaction (positively with the opposite sex and negatively with the same sex). There is no specific pattern for females. Attractiveness also influences the satisfaction and form (e.g., conversation or activity) of social interaction.	*JPSP*	Responses to aesthetics; physical attractiveness
Maddux and Rogers (1980)	General psychology	Will the expertness and attractiveness of the source influence the effect of persuasion?	106	Expertness positively influences the effect of persuasion. Attractiveness, however, does not show this influence.	*JPSP*	Responses to aesthetics; physical attractiveness
Machotka (1982)	General psychology	What are some personality categories in aesthetic judgements?	35	Participants are tested on aesthetic judgement under two different instructions: subjective preference and objective judgement. The two instructions yield four personality categories: "warm" judges (high scorers under the preference	*JPSP*	Aesthetic judgements; aesthetic affect; individual differences

				instructions) who are open to emotional experience; "cool" judges (high scorers under the judgement instructions) who believe in evaluative standards; "aesthetic" subjects (high scorers under both instructions) who are emotionally open to art and guided by standards; and "non-artistic" subjects (low scorers under both instructions) who do not believe in standards and are emotionally constricted.		
Reis et al. (1982)	General psychology	What is the relationship between physical attractiveness and social interaction?	116	Physical attractiveness is a predictor of the quantity of socializing but only for males. Physical attractiveness also influences assertiveness, fear of rejection etc.	*JPSP*	Responses to aesthetics; physical attractiveness
Strube et al. (1983)	General psychology	How do simple and predictable aesthetic stimuli (e.g., simplex melodies) influence task performance for Type A (coronary prone) and Type B (non-coronary prone) personalities?	62	Simple, predictable, aesthetic stimuli mitigate negative affect and increase task performance of a frustrating cognitive task for Type B individuals. Type A individuals, however, do not exhibit these effects.	*JPSP*	Aesthetic affect; responses to aesthetics; individual differences
Sussman, Mueser, Grau and Yarnold (1983)	General psychology	Is female facial attractiveness relatively persistent during childhood?	96	Physical attractiveness shows some stability over time.	*JPSP*	Aesthetic judgements (sense perception: visual); physical attractiveness

(*Continued*)

Table 30.1 (Continued)

Author(s) (year)	*Discipline*	*Focal topic*	*N*	*Core finding(s)*	*Journal*	*Category*
Cunningham (1986)	General psychology	What is the relationship between specific female facial features and the attraction of adult males?	Study 1: 75; Study 2: 82	Neonate features (e.g., large eyes, small nose, and small chin); maturity features (e.g., prominent cheekbones and narrow cheeks); and expressive features (e.g., high eyebrows, large pupils, and large smile) are positively correlated with female attractiveness ratings.	*JPSP*	Aesthetic judgements (sense perception: visual); physical attractiveness
Martindale and Moore (1988)	General psychology	How does preference for colours relate to mental representations of colour?	Study 1: 17; Study 2: 48; Study 3: 31; Study 4: 51; Study 5: 89	More typical colours are marked by greater mental representations and are thus more preferred.	*JEP: Human Perception and Performance*	Aesthetic judgements (sense perception: visual); colour; aesthetic judgements (ease of processing)
Langlois and Roggman (1990)	General psychology	What makes a face beautiful?	297	A face is deemed beautiful if it presents the average value (i.e., the "average" or "prototypical" face) of the population. This is because average faces are more evolutionarily adaptive (evolutionary pressure works against extreme characteristics) and thus cognitively preferred.	*PS*	Aesthetic judgements (sense perception: visual); physical attractiveness; aesthetic judgements (ease of processing)
Graziano, Jensen-Campbell, Shebilske and Lundgren (1993)	General psychology	How do peer evaluations influence ratings on physical attractiveness?	Study 1: 138; Study 2: 105; Study 3: 265; Study 4: 203	When evaluating physical attractiveness, females are more influenced by peer evaluations than are males.	*JPSP*	Aesthetic judgements (sense perception: visual); physical attractiveness

Holbrook and Schindler (1994)	Consumer psychology	How do consumers' aesthetic tastes change over their lifetimes, and what are some predictors of this taste?	237	This research supported the previous finding that individuals usually form stable preference in a sensitive period in their lives. Age, sex and attitude towards the past are major predictors of this tendency.	*JMR*	Aesthetic affect; individual differences
Peracchio and Meyers-Levy (1994)	Consumer psychology	Does severe cropping of persons and/ or objects in advertisements (e.g., only showing a leg or an arm) influence individuals' product evaluations?	493	If individuals are motivated to complete the cropped objects, and if the attempt to verify the ad claims is not impeded by the cropped person/object, cropped ad stimuli will enhance product evaluations.	*JCR*	Responses to aesthetics
Diener, Wolsic and Fujita (1995)	General psychology	How does physical attractiveness relate to subjective well-being?	Study 1: 221; Study 2: 131; Study 3: 155	The positive correlation between physical attractiveness and subjective well-being drops when appearance enhancers (e.g., hair, clothing, and jewellery) are covered or removed.	*JPSP*	Responses to aesthetics; physical attractiveness
Cunningham et al. (1995)	General psychology	Are physical attractiveness ratings consistent across cultures?	Study 1: 45; Study 2: 33; Study 3: 63	The rating of physical attractiveness towards Asian, Hispanic, Black and White photographed women are highly consistent across cultures, with some difference in ratings of certain features (e.g., sexual maturity, expressive features).	*JPSP*	Aesthetic judgements (sense perception: visual); physical attractiveness; individual differences

(*Continued*)

Table 30.1 (Continued)

Author(s) (year)	*Discipline*	*Focal topic*	*N*	*Core finding(s)*	*Journal*	*Category*
Schlosser (1998)	Consumer psychology	Can an aesthetically pleasing shopping atmosphere serve a social identity function?	Study 1: 88; Study 2: 70	An aesthetically pleasing shopping atmosphere can serve as a social identity appeal, having a positive influence on perceived quality of social identity products (e.g., products used for social communication) but not utilitarian products.	*JCP*	Responses to aesthetics
Veryzer and Hutchinson (1998)	Consumer psychology	How do unity and prototypically affect aesthetic responses?	Study 1: 50; Study 2: 197; Study 3: 240; Study 4: 257	Unity and prototypically positively affect aesthetic responses to new product designs.	*JCR*	Aesthetic judgements (sense perception: visual); aesthetic judgements (ease of processing)
Page and Herr (2002)	Consumer psychology	How does product design, characterized as product aesthetics and function, interact with brand strength to moderate consumers' liking for and quality evaluation of the product?	Study 1: 80; Study 2: 200	Product design (i.e., product aesthetics and function) positively impacts liking and quality evaluation. Brand strength does not influence liking, but it does influence quality evaluation when product aesthetics and product function are in conflict, or when product aesthetics and brand strength are in conflict.	*JCP*	Responses to aesthetics
Bloch, Brunel and Arnold (2003)	Consumer psychology	When determining consumers' relationship with products, how is the importance of visual aesthetics to a certain consumer to be measured?	Study 1: 4; Study 2: 318; Study 3: 136; Study 4: 108; Study 5: 53; Study 6: 62; Study 7: 190	The authors proposed and tested a centrality of visual product aesthetics (CVPA) scale to measure individual difference in the significance of visual product aesthetics.	*JCR*	Aesthetic judgements (sense perception: visual); responses to aesthetics; individual difference

Maner et al. (2003)	General psychology	What role does selective processing (i.e., allocating limited cognitive resources in a way that is most beneficial for surviving and proliferation) play in the perception of physical attractiveness?	Study 1: 149; Study 2: 108; Study 3: 256; Study 4: 151; Study 5: 205	Mating-related motives may guide the selective processing of attractive males and females.	*JPSP*	Aesthetic judgements (sense perception: visual); physical attractiveness
Koole and Van den Berg (2005)	General psychology	When is wilderness perceived to be beautiful and when it is not?	Study 1: 90; Study 2: 48; Study 3: 60; Study 4: 48; Study 5: 115	Salience of the concept of death reduces the perceived beauty of wilderness, whereas action orientation increases the perceived beauty of wilderness.	*JPSP*	Aesthetic judgements (sense perception: visual); individual differences
Landau et al. (2006)	General psychology	How does mortality salience (e.g., being reminded of death) influence the evaluation of apparently meaningless art?	Study 1: 25; Study 2: 62; Study 3: 95; Study 4: 92	Mortality salience decreases liking for apparently meaningless art.	*JPSP*	Aesthetic judgements (sense perception: visual); artwork
Winkielman et al. (2006)	General psychology	Why do people prefer prototypical stimuli?	Study 1: 68; Study 2: 66; Study 3: 21	Prototypical stimuli are fluent to processing and are thus more favoured.	*PS*	Aesthetic judgements (sense perception: visual); aesthetic judgements (ease of processing); aesthetic affect

(*Continued*)

Table 30.1 (Continued)

Author(s) (year)	*Discipline*	*Focal topic*	*N*	*Core finding(s)*	*Journal*	*Category*
Hönekopp (2006)	General psychology	Are facial attractiveness judgement standards private or shared?	Study 1: 31; Study 2: 31; Study 3: 100	Private taste is approximately as powerful as shared taste regarding facial attractiveness.	*JEP: Human Perception and Performance*	Aesthetic judgements (sense perception: visual); physical attractiveness; individual differences
Häfner and Trampe (2009)	Consumer psychology	How do round and thin models influence the effectiveness of advertisements?	Study 1: 72; Study 2: 34; Study 3: 55; Study 4: 76	For impulsive product evaluations, thin models produce more favourable implicit responses than round models; whereas for reflective product evaluations, this pattern is reversed.	*JCP*	Responses to aesthetics; physical attractiveness
Eidelman, Crandall and Pattershall (2009)	General psychology	Is the mere existence of something evidence of its goodness?	Study 1: 69; Study 2: 42; Study 3: 60; Study 4: 62; Study 5: 88	The more a form is described as prevalent, the more aesthetically attractive that form will be perceived to be.	*JPSP*	Aesthetic judgements (sense perception: visual)
Falk, Falk and Ayton (2009)	General psychology	How do aesthetic values influence individuals' behavioural patterns when the individuals are asked to generate random responses?	Study 1: 1676; Study 2: 386; Study 3: 966	Aesthetic value shapes individuals' responses in a way that is consistent with individuals' aesthetic preferences.	*JEP: Human Perception and Performance*	Responses to aesthetics
Deng, Hui and Hutchinson (2010)	Consumer psychology	What are some rules of the preference for colour combinations in product designs?	142	In a self-design task of the colour combination of sneakers, participants emphasize a colour's hue and saturation more than its lightness. Given this emphasis, individuals tend to combine similar colours and use a relatively small total	*JCP*	Aesthetic judgements (sense perception: visual); colour

Pandelaere, Millet, and den Bergh (2010)	Consumer psychology	How does exposure order influence consumer attitudes and preference?	Study 1: 1364; Study 2a: 78; Study 2b: 114	Stimuli to which individuals are first exposed are more preferred than similar stimuli presented later.	*JCP*	Aesthetic judgements (sense perception: visual, auditory); music
Kumar and Garg (2010)	Consumer psychology	What is the relationship between aesthetic principles and the subconscious cognitive appraisals associated with emotions?	Pre-test 1: 35; Pre-test 2: 35; Pre-test 3: 38; Main Study: 56	When a design can balance the levels of both attentional resources needed and pleasantness in visually evaluating the design, the design will be more preferred.	*JCP*	Aesthetic judgements (sense perception: visual); aesthetic affect
Hoegg, Alba and Dahl (2010)	Consumer psychology	How does aesthetic design influence product evaluation?	Study 1: 196; Study 2: 45; Study 3: 99	Individuals will rate a functional product feature more positively if the feature is paired with an unattractive product design than if it is not paired with an unattractive design. However, this effect only happens when individuals encounter a conflict between design and functionality.	*JCP*	Responses to aesthetics
Reimann et al. (2010)	Consumer psychology; consumer neuroscience	What are the behavioural, neural and psychological properties of package design?	Study 1A: 326; Study 1B: 82; Study 2: 176; Study 3 (fMRI study): 17	Aesthetic packages: significantly increase the reaction time of consumers' choice responses; are chosen over products with well-known brands in standardized packages, despite higher prices; and result in increased activation in the nucleus accumbens and the ventromedial prefrontal cortex, suggesting that reward value plays an important role in aesthetic product experiences.	*JCP*	Responses to aesthetics; aesthetic affect

(*Continued*)

Table 30.1 (Continued)

Author(s) (year)	*Discipline*	*Focal topic*	*N*	*Core finding(s)*	*Journal*	*Category*
Meyers-Levy and Zhu (2010)	Consumer psychology	Of the two meanings music can convey (i.e., referential meanings that consist of descriptive associations and the embodied meaning that is purely hedonic), which will individuals use when forming product perceptions?	Study 1: 98; Study 2: 133	Males with high (low) Need for Cognition (NFC) are sensitive to only referential (embodied) meaning. Females, however, use both meanings regardless of the level of NFC.	*JCP*	Aesthetic judgements (sense perception: auditory); music; individual differences
Townsend and Shu (2010)	Consumer psychology	Can aesthetic design influence consumer financial decision making?	Study 1: 255; Study 2: 379; Study 3: 55	In hypothetical investment decisions, the aesthetics of a financial document (e.g., an annual report) can influence both stock valuation and financial decision making under certain circumstances.	*JCP*	Responses to aesthetics
Krishna et al. (2010)	Consumer psychology	How does smell influence touch?	Study 1: 73; Study 2: 116	When the semantic associations of the smell and touch of a stimulus are congruent, this congruence can enhance haptic perception and product evaluation.	*JCP*	Aesthetic judgements (sense perception: olfactory and haptic)
Yang et al. (2010)	Consumer psychology	How do stylistic properties of visual images (e.g., camera angle) impact the	Study 1: 115; Study 2: 63; Study 3: 171	When a product is depicted employing an upward-looking camera angle, individuals with an ought-self (i.e., those	*JCP*	Responses to aesthetics; individual differences

		product evaluation of individuals with different self-concepts (i.e., ought-self or ideal-self)?		who are motivated by duties and obligations) evaluate the product more favourably than do individuals with an ideal-self (those who are motivated by hopes and aspirations). When a downward-looking angle is employed, the reversed pattern occurs.		
Lorenzo, Biesanz and Human (2010)	General psychology	Are more attractive individuals viewed more accurately than less attractive individuals?	73	More physically attractive individuals are perceived both more positively and more accurately by others.	*PS*	Responses to aesthetics; physical attractiveness
Topolinski (2010)	General psychology	Can motor processes (e.g., eye movements) influence aesthetic perceptions?	Study 1: 26; Study 2: 76; Study 3: 30	After training the eyes to follow the movement of a certain stimulus, preferences for trained stimulus movements increase compared to untrained stimulus movements.	*PS*	Aesthetic judgements (sense perception: visual); aesthetic judgements (ease of processing)
Elliot et al. (2010)	General psychology	How does the colour red influence women's romantic attraction to men?	Study 1: 21; Study 2: 57; Study 3: 33; Study 4: 55; Study 5a: 20; Study 5b: 20; Study 6a: 37; Study 6b: 38; Study 7: 27	When seen on a red background or in red clothing, males are regarded by females as more attractive and more sexually desirable. This effect appears to be the result of status perceptions and seems to be specific to women's romantic attraction to men.	*JEP: General*	Aesthetic judgements (sense perception: visual); colour; physical attractiveness

(*Continued*)

Table 30.1 (Continued)

Author(s) (year)	*Discipline*	*Focal topic*	*N*	*Core finding(s)*	*Journal*	*Category*
Patrick and Hagtvedt (2011)	Consumer psychology	Why and how do individuals resolve aesthetic incongruity (i.e., inconsistency that arises from a mismatch between an object and its environment)?	Pilot Study: 125; Study 1: 56; Study 2: 65; Study 3: 65	Incongruity gives rise to regret and thus needs to be solved. Nevertheless, for high (low) design-salience products, the incongruity also creates a higher (lower) level of frustration than regret. This effect gives rise to a higher (lower) likelihood of accommodating the product in the environment by buying more.	*JMR*	Aesthetic affect; responses to aesthetics
Hawley-Dolan and Winner (2011)	General psychology	Do abstract expressionist paintings really differ from children's scribbles in terms of viewers' perception and evaluation?	72	Individuals prefer professional paintings and judge them more positively than nonprofessional paintings, even when professional paintings are labelled as children's works and children's works are labelled as professional paintings.	*PS*	Aesthetic judgements (sense perception: visual); artwork
Townsend and Sood (2012)	Consumer psychology	Do aesthetic products serve as a form of self-affirmation?	Study 1: 159; Study 2: 275; Study 3: 326	Aesthetic products enhance self-affirmation.	*JCR*	Responses to aesthetics
Saad and Stenstrom (2012)	Consumer psychology	How are female consumers influenced by their own menstrual cycles in their consumer behaviour?	470	A 35-day survey shows that appearance-related behaviour (desire, dollars spent and beatification) increases during women's fertile phase, whereas food-related behaviour increases during women's non-fertile phase.	*JCP*	Responses to aesthetics; physical attractiveness

Hill, Rodeheffer, Griskevicius, Durante and White (2012)	General psychology	Why does economic recession increase women's spending on beauty products?	Study 2: 154; Study 3: 76; Study 4: 64; Study 5: 72	Women's desire to be more attractive to mates drives this effect.	*JPSP*	Responses to aesthetics; physical attractiveness
Leder et al. (2012)	General psychology	Can aesthetic pleasure in art appreciation stem from body resonances (of the perceiver's body) with the movements that the artist made when producing the artwork?	114	While viewing artwork, if individuals execute hand movements similar to the movements the artist made while producing the artwork, the work will be more highly evaluated compared to when the same movement is executed before viewing the artwork.	*PS*	Aesthetic judgements (sense perception: visual); artwork; aesthetic affect
Segal-Caspi, Roccas and Sagiv (2012)	General psychology	Do physically attractive females have particularly positive inner traits?	118	Physical attractiveness correlates positively with conformity values rather than independence values and with self-enhancement values rather than universalism values.	*PS*	Responses to aesthetics; physical attractiveness
Wöllner et al. (2012)	General psychology	Are prototypical motions perceived as more aesthetically favourable than non-prototypical motions?	24	Prototypical human motion in task-related actions (e.g., a professional conductor conducting an orchestra) is judged more favourably than non-prototypical motion (e.g., that of novice conductors).	*JEP: Human Perception and Performance*	Aesthetic judgements (sense perception: visual); aesthetic judgements (ease of processing)
Sammartino and Palmer (2012)	General psychology	When a picture features the vertical placement of a single object, how does the vertical composition of the picture influence individuals' preference for the pictures?	Study 1: 12; Study 2: 15; Study 3: 17; Study 4: 24	The object's position in relation to the observer's viewpoint and to the centre of the frame influences the perceived aesthetics of the picture.	*JEP: Human Perception and Performance*	Aesthetic judgements (sense perception: visual)

(Continued)

Table 30.1 (Continued)

Author(s) (year)	*Discipline*	*Focal topic*	*N*	*Core finding(s)*	*Journal*	*Category*
Newman and Bloom (2012)	General psychology	Why are original artworks regarded as more valuable than their identical duplicates?	Study 1: 33; Study 2: 115; Study 3: 150; Study 4: 180; Study 5: 256	The special value of original artwork lies in the assessment of the art object as a unique creative act and the degree of physical contact with the original artist.	*JEP: General*	Aesthetic judgements (sense perception: visual); artwork
Lee et al. (2013)	Consumer psychology	When individuals are in a negative mood, why do they sometimes prefer mood-congruent (i.e., negative) aesthetic stimuli (e.g., sad music) even when positive alternatives (e.g., cheerful music) are available?	Study 1: 233; Study 2: 76; Study 3: 111	Emotional distress from failed/broken interpersonal relationships (but not non-interpersonal issues) increases preference for mood-congruent aesthetic/emotional stimuli.	*JCR*	Aesthetic judgements (sense perception: auditory); music; aesthetic affect
White, Kenrick and Neuberg (2013)	General psychology	Why are physically attractive political candidates more likely to win elections?	Study 2: 123; Study 3: 210; Study 4: 66	Leadership preferences are related to disease-avoidance mechanisms, in which physical attractiveness is a cue to health. Activating concerns related to disease leads individuals to prefer physically attractive leaders.	*PS*	Responses to aesthetics; physical attractiveness

Halberstadt, Pecher, Zeelenberg, Wai and Winkielman (2013)	General psychology	Does the recognizability of faces influence the attractiveness ratings of blended faces compared to unblended faces?	112	When constituent faces are unrecognizable, a blend (i.e., morph) of two faces is perceived to be more attractive than the individual faces; however, when the constituent faces are recognizable (e.g., Barack Obama and George W. Bush), the blended face is perceived to be less attractive the individual faces.	*PS*	Aesthetic judgements (sense perception: visual); physical attractiveness; aesthetic judgements (ease of processing)
Cogan et al. (2013)	General psychology	How do extreme context stimuli (e.g., extremely beautiful faces) influence the hedonic contrast effect (i.e., seeing a beautiful face decreases the perceived attractiveness of subsequently presented faces) on perceived facial attractiveness?	Study 1: 28; Study 2: 23; Study 3: 23	Exposure to moderately attractive faces makes subsequently viewed moderately unattractive faces more unattractive. If the order of presentation is reversed, the moderately attractive faces will be perceived as more attractive. Moreover, when the moderately attractive faces are replaced with extremely attractive faces, this contrast effect diminishes.	*JEP: Human Perception and Performance*	Aesthetic judgements (sense perception: visual); physical attractiveness; responses to aesthetics
Taylor et al. (2013)	General psychology	Are colour preferences and the mechanisms that govern those preferences universal?	Colour preferences: 80; object description: 90; object valence: 62	Patterns of colour preference vary across individuals and cultural groups. Moreover, the underlying mechanisms and dimensions of colour preference also vary across individuals and cultures.	*JEP: General*	Aesthetic judgements (sense perception: visual); colour; individual differences

(*Continued*)

Table 30.1 (Continued)

Author(s) (year)	*Discipline*	*Focal topic*	*N*	*Core finding(s)*	*Journal*	*Category*
Fisher and Ma (2014)	Consumer psychology	Does the physical attractiveness of children in need reduce empathy and help from others?	Study 1: 152; Study 2: 138; Study 3: 227; Study 4: 192	Physical attractiveness of children in need reduces empathy evoked and thus the help they receive from unrelated individuals, so long as the need is not severe.	*JCR*	Responses to aesthetics; physical attractiveness
Shu and Townsend (2014)	General psychology	Can individuals' affiliation with high aesthetics affirm their sense of self and thus encourage their openness to arguments advocating the selection of one option over another?	Study 1: 52; Study 2: 362; Study 3: 370	Affiliating individuals with high (vs. low) aesthetics assists self-affirmation. Therefore, individuals are more likely to select the advocated option regardless of whether or not it is the riskier option.	*JEP: Applied*	Responses to aesthetics

all identified articles, sorted chronologically and displaying authors' name(s), year of publication, discipline, focal topic, sample size, core findings, journal name and category. Because we initially categorized studies into specific topics (e.g., judgements of aesthetics), we calculated the percentage of each topic from the total number of identified articles. Note that some articles fell into, and were thus categorized into, more than one category.

Aesthetic judgements based on sense perception

Because aesthetic judgements have previously been linked to the psychology of sense perception (cf. Gregor, 1983; Osborne, 1979), we categorized articles according to the sense through which a stimulus was perceived. It was found that 61% of the total number of identified studies dealt with *aesthetic judgements based on sense perception*, which were defined as weighing whether a specific stimulus is aesthetically appealing based on specific characteristics. Of the studies on sense perception, 89 per cent investigated visual aesthetics (i.e., the aesthetics of rectangles, colours, visual artwork and the physical attractiveness of humans), 9 per cent investigated auditory aesthetics (i.e., the aesthetics of music) and only 4 per cent investigated olfactory and/or somatosensory aesthetics (i.e., aesthetics associated with smelling and touching objects). Note that the percentages add up more than 100 per cent because some of the articles concerned more than one sense. Within the studies dealing with aesthetic judgements, none investigated gustatory aesthetics (i.e., the aesthetics of taste).

Visual aesthetics

Forty-two identified articles investigated aesthetic judgements of visual stimuli, indicating that this subfield strongly dominates articles on aesthetic judgements based on sense perception (42 out of all 47 identified articles). Physical attractiveness represents the largest proportion of this subfield, with 16 identified articles, ranging from the earliest journal article identified by our review, regarding how physical traits affect perceived body attractiveness (Perrin, 1921), to a recent article (Cogan, Parker, & Zellner, 2013). Some of the physical attractiveness studies focus on how specific facial features contribute to physical attractiveness. For instance, Cunningham (1986) found that neonate features (e.g., large eyes, small nose and small chin), maturity features (e.g., prominent cheekbones and narrow cheeks) and the expressive features (e.g., high eyebrows, large pupils and large smile) were positively correlated with female attractiveness ratings. The author argued that such facial features can serve as cues of sexual arousal, health, maturity for mating, fertility and friendliness and sociability. Together, these factors of perceived facial attractiveness to a large extent reflect the individual's adaptive desirability for mating. This argument is also supported by other studies reviewed. For instance, Elliot et al. (2010) demonstrated that females found images of males on red backgrounds or in red clothes more attractive because red colour increases females' perceptions the male's social status – another signal for mating desirability (but also see criticisms of this research by Francis, 2013). Moreover, Langlois and Roggman (1990) maintained that "average" faces are more aesthetically favourable, partially because evolution does not favour extreme characteristics. Therefore, our review summarizes that adaptive factors such as survival, mating and reproducing play a crucial role in physical aesthetics.

Some other studies in the subfield of visual aesthetics concern topics such as what proportion makes a rectangle more attractive. For instance, Thompson (1946) showed that college students prefer rectangles with width-to-length ratios from 0.55 to 0.65 (note that this ratio is close to the multiplicative inverse of the golden ratio 1.618). Preschool children, however, showed no consistent preferences. Moreover, Shipley, Dattman and Steele (1947) discovered that children prefer larger rectangles, whereas adults prefer more medium-sized rectangles for any given width–length ratio.

Colour is another issue that has drawn the attention of prior investigators. For example, Martindale and Moore (1988) discovered that more "typical" colours (e.g., primary colours such as primary yellow) were more preferred among participants than "atypical colors". Moreover, Deng, Hui and Hutchinson (2010) showed that participants designing the colour combination of sneakers put more emphasis on a colour's hue and saturation than on its lightness.

Artwork appreciation also constitutes a topic of interest in the subfield of visual aesthetics. Hawley-Dolan and Winner (2011) demonstrated that abstract expressionist paintings are considered superior to children's scribbles by their viewers. Landau, Greenberg, Solomon, Pyszczynski and Martens (2006), on the other hand, showed that the positive evaluation of an apparently meaningless artwork decreased when human mortality was made salient compared to when it was not made salient. This is because, according to terror management theory (Greenberg et al., 1990; Rosenblatt, Greenberg, Solomon, Pyszczynski, & Lyon, 1989), maintaining a meaningful view of reality is fundamental in managing the fear and anxiety caused by the thought of death. Meaningless artworks appear to suggest no meaning at all; thus, they are deemed objectionable by a reviewer who is thinking of death.

Auditory aesthetics

Articles concerning auditory aesthetics make up about 9 per cent of all the reviewed articles on aesthetic judgements (4 out of 47 articles). All articles in this area focused on a specific type of auditory stimuli, namely music. For example, Steck and Machotka (1975) studied the preference for complexity in music (e.g., how many different tones made up a piece of music) and found that the preference for complexity in music was, to a large extent, relative rather than absolute. That is, there is no degree of complexity that individuals will naturally and unconditionally prefer. Instead, the preference for complexity is determined by the range of complexity being judged. Moreover, Lee, Andrade and Palmer (2013) answered the intriguing question of why individuals experiencing negative moods sometimes choose to listen to cheerful music and other times prefer sad music. The authors argued that emotional distress from failed/broken interpersonal relationships increases preference for mood-congruent aesthetic/emotional stimuli (i.e., sad music), whereas distress from non-interpersonal issues enhances the preference for more positive music.

Olfactory and somatosensory aesthetics

Only two articles in the area of aesthetics judgements studied non-visual and non-auditory aesthetics. Specifically, Moskowitz, Dravnieks and Gerbers (1974) studied how odour intensity influences odour pleasantness and found that pleasantness from smelling butanol correlates inversely with the intensity of the chemical in the case of individual judgements but not group judgements. Further, Krishna, Elder and Caldara (2010) discovered that congruence between the semantic associations of the smell and the touch of a stimulus can enhance haptic perceptions and product evaluations. For instance, if a piece of paper smelled "masculine" (e.g., the smell of men's fragrances), participants rated it more positive when it also felt rough, because "masculine" and "rough" are semantically congruent. Similarly, a piece of paper that smelled feminine (e.g., the smell of women's fragrances) was rated more favourably if it also felt smooth.

Aesthetic judgements based on ease of processing

Nine per cent of the total number of identified studies (7 out of 77) dealt with *aesthetic judgements based on ease of processing*, which we defined as how easy or difficult it is for a stimulus to be psychologically processed. This domain primarily concerns how and why prototypical stimuli are more preferred.

Psychologists have long noticed that prototypicality (sometimes also referred to as typicality) can increase aesthetic responses. For example, Martindale and Moore (1988) found that more typical colours are characterized by more mental representations and are thus more preferred. Further, in their seminal study, Langlois and Roggman (1990) demonstrated that an "average face" (i.e., a face whose "facial configuration is close to the mean configuration of a population of faces", Langlois, Roggman, & Musselman, 1994, p. 214) is consistently considered attractive. Moreover, in consumer psychology, Veryzer and Hutchinson (1998) showed that prototypicality affects aesthetic response to new product designs such that the design will be less aesthetically favourable the more it is distorted from the prototype. Furthermore, Wöllner, Deconinck, Parkinson, Hove and Keller (2012) observed that more typical human motions (e.g., the conducting of a professional conductor) are more highly evaluated and perceived to be more aesthetic than atypical motions (e.g., the conducting of an amateur conductor).

The identified papers on ease of processing in our review echo a comprehensive review paper by Reber, Schwarz and Winkielman (2004). In this review, the authors effectively summarized a great number of studies on aesthetics to argue that the more fluently an object can be processed by a perceiver, the more aesthetic the object will be regarded to be. This argument reveals an important underlying mechanism of perceived beauty: often, beauty is related to ease of processing. Specifically, Reber et al. (2004) argued that symmetrical objects, stimuli to which individuals are repeatedly exposed, and prototypical forms are aesthetically preferred because they can be more easily processed than their asymmetrical, novel or non-prototypical counterparts. The authors further argued that fluent processing gives rise to positive affective responses, which in turn can produce more positive aesthetic judgements. The basic argument from this review paper – that prototypical stimuli are fluent to processing and are thus more favoured – was empirically tested and supported by Winkielman, Halberstadt, Fazendeiro and Catty (2006), who tested directly the effect of prototypicality on attractiveness mediated by fluency and found that fluency indeed accounts for the preference for prototypicality.

Aesthetic affect

Out of all articles identified, 12 per cent of them (9 out of 77) dealt with *aesthetic affect*, especially in terms of how affective states play a role in aesthetic experiences. Affective states such as aesthetic pleasure (e.g., Leder, Bär, & Topolinski, 2012) often serve as the medium through which aesthetic experiences exert an impact upon downstream processes and behaviours such as additional judgements, decisions, choices and task performance. For example, Strube et al. (1983) demonstrated that aesthetic stimuli can improve task performance by reducing negative affect. Specifically, the authors found that simple, predictable aesthetic melodies had a soothing effect that caused a decrease in negative emotions such as frustration, which in turn could benefit performance in the following tasks. Further, Reimann, Zaichkowsky, Neuhaus, Bender and Weber (2010) observed that individuals are more affectively involved in an object when its appearance is more aesthetic. This research also found that, when experiencing aesthetic object, individuals engage a brain area – the striatum, specifically the nucleus accumbens – that has been linked to the release of the neurochemical dopamine. This finding suggests that affective states such as desiring and yearning for the aesthetic object play an important role in aesthetic experiences and may even trigger downstream aesthetic decision making. Furthermore, Patrick and Hagtvedt (2011) showed that aesthetic incongruity (i.e., inconsistency that arises from a mismatch between an object and its environment, such as a beautiful object placed in ugly surroundings) could give rise to regret. Finally, the aesthetic value of prototypicality also partially arises from the positive affect that prototypical stimuli elicit (Winkielman et al., 2006).

Responses to aesthetics

In addition to the aforementioned categories, we found that 40 per cent of the total number of identified studies (31 out of 77) dealt with *responses to aesthetics*, defined as studies in which an aesthetic stimulus triggered either judgements on other variables, the choice of the aesthetic object over another object or decision or performance in unrelated tasks. A great number of studies investigate how perceived physical attractiveness can influence judgement towards the individual on variables other than attractiveness. For example, an early study done by Dion et al. (1972) shows that attractive individuals are also perceived as possessing more favourable traits. Moreover, Sigall and Ostrove (1975) examined how perceived physical attractiveness of criminal defendants will influence the sentence assigned to them. The authors discovered that, when the crime was unrelated to attractiveness (e.g., burglary), individuals would assign more lenient sentences to an attractive defendant than to an unattractive defendant; however, when the crime was related to physical attractiveness (e.g., swindling), harsher punishment would be meted out to an attractive defendant.

Works in this category also examine the influence aesthetics exerts on other factors. For instance, Strube et al. (1983) found that simple, predictable aesthetic stimuli increased performance of a frustrating cognitive task for people with Type B personalities (i.e., individuals who live at a generally low stress level) but not for people with Type A personalities (individuals that are more ambitious, impatient, sensitive and prone to coronary heart disease). Moreover, Townsend and Sood (2012) demonstrated that products with high aesthetic value can enhance self-affirmation.

The idea that aesthetics can influence judgements on other variables and decision making has important implications, especially for consumer research. In fact, a large number of identified consumer psychology studies fall into this category. For example, the earliest consumer psychology article in our review (Baker and Churchill, 1977) shows that the attractiveness of the model in an advertisement positively influences the evaluation of the advertisement. More recently, Townsend and Shu (2010) provided evidence that the aesthetics of a financial document (e.g., an annual report) might influence both stock valuation and financial decision making. Further, in our own work, we have demonstrated that products in aesthetic packages were chosen over well-known branded products in standardized packages even when the aesthetic packages had higher prices (Reimann et al., 2010).

Individual and cultural differences in aesthetics

Due to the subjective, idiosyncratic nature of the aesthetic experience, one can expect that individual differences play an important role in aesthetics. 21 per cent of the total number of identified studies (16 out of 77) dealt with *individual differences in aesthetics*, defined as differences in aesthetic judgements based on personality traits. In as early as the second decade of the twentieth century, Gordon (1923) noted the highly divergent opinions in aesthetic judgements of pictures of oriental rugs, which showed great diversity between individuals. Such variation in aesthetic judgements was also found by recent studies on facial attractiveness (Hönekopp, 2006). More specific individual differences were identified over time. For instance, Bryson and Driver (1972) demonstrated that introversion and extraversion could influence the aesthetic preference for complex designs. Further, Wilson, Ausman and Mathews (1973) argued that liberalism and conservatism influence preferences for paintings: Conservative individuals preferred paintings with simple representations and disliked complex and abstract paintings, whereas liberal individuals showed the opposite pattern in their preference.

Apart from the individual level of differences, aesthetic appreciation also varies at a cultural level. Admittedly, a number of identified papers reveal that there exist universal patterns in certain types of aesthetic appreciation. For instance, Child and Iwao (1968) reported that the positive relationship between aesthetic sensitivity and cognitive independence/openness they found with American students were also observed with Japanese students. Also, Cunningham et al. (1995) found that ratings of physical attractiveness towards Asian, Hispanic, Black and White photographed women are to a large extent consistent across cultures. This universality of certain aesthetic experience is not surprising, because we are, after all, *homo sapiens* sharing similar if not identical physiological structures and evolutionary drives. Therefore, if a certain type of aesthetic experience depends greatly on a certain cognitive structure (e.g., the activation of specific brain areas in face of certain aesthetic stimuli) or serves evolutionary adaptive purpose (e.g., the evolutionary psychological basis of physical attractiveness addressed above), it is possible to observe universal patterns across cultures.

That being said, humans are also cultural beings dwelling in their particular sociocultural environments. These distinct environments can influence or even define what is epistemologically, morally or aesthetically good and what is bad, often in very different ways. Since aesthetics judgements and preferences can be rooted in cross-cultural differences and shaped by cultural meanings, one can reasonably expect cultural differences in aesthetic judgements. For instance, not only did Cunningham et al. (1995) report the universal patterns in the physical attractiveness of females; they also discovered some differences in some aspects of ratings which the authors attributed to cultural factors. For instance, the authors hypothesized that Asians appreciated female sexual maturity and expressive features less than their Western counterparts because of the cultural emphasis on female submissiveness in Asia. Sometimes the cultural differences can be great. In a recent study, Taylor, Clifford and Franklin (2013) examined the colour preferences of 42 British participants and 38 participants from the Himba tribe in northern Namibia and discovered totally different patterns in the colour preferences of the two groups, especially in the chroma (i.e., perceived intensity) and lightness of the colour. According to the authors, chroma and lightness accounted for virtually none of the colour preferences of the British participants (0 per cent for males and 2 per cent for females) but explained a huge proportion of variance in the colour preferences of the Himba participants (57 per cent for males and 47 per cent for females).

Towards a unifying framework of aesthetics

This chapter provided an overview of some antecedents, mechanisms and consequences of aesthetics from several decades of empirical research in mostly general psychology but more recently also consumer psychology. Figure 30.1 illustrates a framework based on the article categorization in our review.

In summary, our identified aesthetics studies fall into five major categories. In our review, a substantial number of articles examined the question of what makes a specific stimulus aesthetic; these articles constitute two of our major categories related to aesthetic judgements. The first category, namely aesthetic judgements based on sense perception, investigates how individuals regard visual, auditory, olfactory and haptic stimuli as aesthetic or unaesthetic. Visual aesthetics studies dominate this category and extend to subfields such as physical attractiveness, ratios in rectangles and colours. Notably in physical attractiveness, evolutionarily adaptive features signalling the advantages of survival, fertility and social status are also aesthetically preferred, suggesting that the

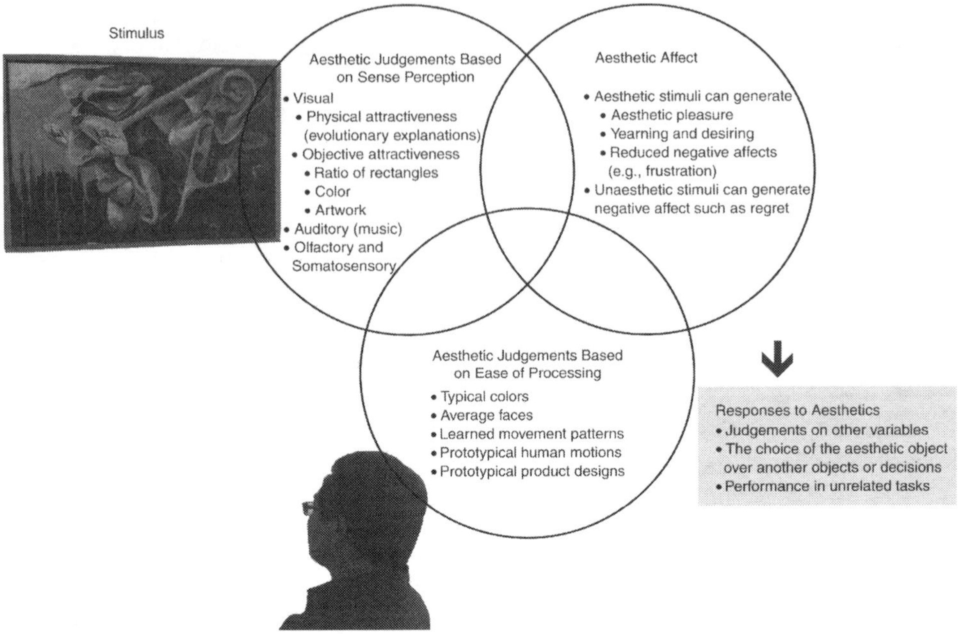

Figure 30.1 Framework of aesthetics.

nature of aesthetics lies partially in our biological features. Another category of aesthetic judgements, namely aesthetic judgements based on ease of processing, demonstrates another important aspect of aesthetics. A large body of research shows that prototypical stimuli (e.g., face, colour, geometrical shape, motion, etc.) are aesthetically favourable, and it has been argued (e.g., Reber et al., 2004; Winkielman et al., 2006) that this effect is due to the fluency of processing associated with prototypes. The basic idea here is that the more fluent a stimulus is to process, the more aesthetic it is regarded to be. In other words, beauty also lies in the ease of processing. Our third category, aesthetic affect, refers to the fact that aesthetic perception can give rise to emotional responses. Aesthetic stimuli engage individuals in affective states such as yearning and desiring (Reimann et al., 2010) or aesthetic pleasure (Leder et al., 2012). Aesthetic experience also helps to mitigate negative affect such as frustration (Strube et al., 1983). Moreover, a lack of aesthetic congruency (i.e., a mismatch between an object and its environment, such as a beautiful object placed in ugly surroundings) can also result in a negative affect, such as regret (Patrick & Hagtvedt, 2011). The fourth category, namely responses to aesthetics, investigates the consequences of perceived aesthetics. Reviewed studies show that aesthetic stimuli exert an influence and cause biases subsequently following decision-making processes and in the performance of unrelated tasks. Lastly, due to the subjective nature of aesthetic perception, aesthetic judgement and decision making are subject to individual differences, such as individual tastes, personality traits, genders, political stances and cultural factors, which can influence aesthetics in many different ways. Our review has led to a few follow-up questions that future research could attempt to answer.

Has prior work "over-focused" on visual aesthetics?

Baumgarten coined the word *aesthetics* in 1735 on the basis of the Greek word *aisthēsis*—that is, the perception from the senses, feeling, hearing and seeing. Based on this understanding of aesthetics, Baumgarten subsequently refined the definition of aesthetics by referring to the *perfection of sensate cognition* (cf. Osborne, 1979). Our literature review shows that, while important groundwork to understand "sensual perfection" has been conducted, prior research has excessively focused on the visual sense – that is, how we judge the beauty of visual stimuli. Based on the existing empirical work alone, one could therefore strip down the definition of aesthetics to the visual sense alone, as most researchers seem to do. One reason for this excessive focus on visual aesthetics could be rooted in the early philosophical conception of aesthetics, especially the Kantian notion that vision and audition are the more interesting, "higher" senses, while smell, taste and touch are less relevant, "lower" senses (Osborne, 1977). Arguably, however, aesthetics is much broader than this idea suggests. Undeniably, smell, taste and touch all have aesthetic qualities. Also, because humans tend to holistically view stimuli in their environments (e.g., Eysenck, 1942), a visual stimulus may be perceived to be more beautiful if it is embedded in a context that also speaks to the other senses (compared to when viewed alone). For example, imagine the visit to the lobby of a grand hotel such as the Waldorf Astoria in New York City. Experiencing the lobby not only "perfects" the visual sense through beautiful architecture, artworks on walls and fluently arranged seating area but also speaks to the auditory sense through appealing music from a live piano player, the wonderful smell of flowers that were arranged in the center of the lobby and the touch of leather, wood and marble throughout the room. It is often such combinations and related spillover effects between senses that trigger a *holistic* perfection of sensate cognition, and an overall feeling of awe upon perception. When viewed alone, each stimulus (e.g., the flower centrepiece, the painting on the wall) may be appealing but in combination they are *perfect* (to borrow Baumgartner's terminology). Indeed, with closed eyes and covered nose, Mozart's *Eine Kleine Nachtmusik* is still beautiful, but viewing a pianist perform this piece on a Steinway grand piano at the philharmonic in Salzburg elevates more than just one sense towards such holistic sensual perfection. Similarly, classic oil paintings from the old masters are often perceived to be more beautiful than abstract paintings, possibly because they speak to more than one sense; for example, the realistic style in Joseph Mallord William Turner's landscape paintings (see an example in Figure 30.2) attracts mainly the visual sense but may also stimulate the other senses, as one can "hear" the river flowing through the meadows, "feel" the warm autumn sun on one's skin and "smell" the grasses and trees. Is it because abstract art speaks only to the visual sense that that many individuals perceive abstract paintings to be less appealing than realistic artworks?

In an example from the marketing context, retailers such as Abercrombie and Fitch stimulate consumers through more than one sensual dimension to achieve such perfection: Its stores not only feature appealing fashion complemented by physically attractive human models on walls but also create an environment that speaks to the olfactory sense (refreshing perfume), auditory

Figure 30.2 Joseph Mallord William Turner: Bolton Abbey, Yorkshire (1809).

sense (invigorating music) and haptic sense (rich materials and an elk over the register). Such multisensory stimulation obviously triggers behavioural effort in consumers, which are often willing to wait in line, pay a price premium and/or drive a substantial distance to get to the next store. Some firms, however, do not achieve such sensual perfection: Microsoft's flagship stores, for example, do not feature the same rich materials that Apple stores do (e.g., thick wooden tables, glass and concrete storefront); moreover, the lighting of Microsoft stores and the staging of products is different (e.g., price information and product description right next to tablets and phones) compared to Apple stores (e.g., focus on the product). As such, a better understanding of the interaction between aesthetic judgements, emotions, fluency and the different senses should be the goal of future marketers and psychologist.

Is there a dark side to aesthetics?

Arguably, there is much that is positive to say about aesthetics. Humans like to be stimulated by beauty in their environment: We desire a physically attractive partner, we visit and soak in the beauty of our natural environment and we seek, purchase and treasure aesthetically appealing products to reward ourselves. However, aesthetics may have a dark side, in that a focus on aesthetics can possibly lead to discrimination and manipulation. For example, an overemphasis on slim and symmetrical human models in advertising can lead to stereotyping and discrimination against individuals who do not resemble the advertised physique or do not meet the "aesthetic standard". Further, aesthetics can lead to manipulation: a technically bad product in an aesthetically appealing package is still a bad product; however, the aesthetic package suggests otherwise because of the notion that "beauty is good". For example, can a firm in financial distress look better to its investors simply by enhancing the aesthetics of its financial report? Or, along the same line of thought, can a technologically obsolete product survive longer in the marketplace because its package is aesthetically pleasing? The answer to these questions, in some cases, is yes.

Do investments in aesthetics pay off?

For practitioners, one question may be whether investments in aesthetics pay off. Aesthetic principles can be applied in many different areas, from store environments to the design of aesthetically appealing products and packages. Clearly, aesthetics are highly relevant to consumer psychology; the design of products has been acknowledged as a key success factor in marketing and sales, because aesthetic appeal has been shown to effectively differentiate a firm and its products from its competitors (Bloch, 1995; Patrick & Peracchio, 2010; Schmitt & Simonson, 1997). However, not every product may be suited to be "aesthetics-enhanced". Of course, there are obvious product categories in which such enhancement is likely not a good fit because it stands in the way of practicality and technical goodness, such as trying to make a Caterpillar Backhoe Loader look aesthetically appealing. Yet even for product categories for which aesthetics seems appropriate, bad investment decisions can be made. For example, Apple – known for its design capability – tries to position its Apple wristwatch as a direct competitor to Swiss luxury wristwatches by manufacturing a version of the watch with precious materials such as gold and offering it for a price of up to $17,000. However, like all technological devices, the Apple Watch will become obsolete in the near future, and being technologically obsolete will arguably decrease the aesthetic properties of the Apple Watch as well as its value. If a 1999 flip phone, for example, were made of gold, today it would likely be melted down and sold for the value of the gold. On the other hand, Swiss watches, if properly maintained, will last many decades and maintain their aesthetic value because they do not become technologically obsolete. In sum, investments in aesthetics will have to be analyzed in terms of product category fit and cost.

References

Aitken, P. P. (1974). Judgments of pleasingness and interestingness as functions of visual complexity. *Journal of Experimental Psychology, 103*(2), 240–244. doi: 10.1037/h0036787

Baker, M. J., & Churchill, G. A. (1977). The impact of physically attractive models on advertising evaluations. *Journal of Marketing Research, 14*(4), 538–555.

Bloch, P. H. (1995). Seeking the ideal form: Product design and consumer response. *Journal of Marketing, 59*(3), 16–29. doi: 10.2307/1252116

Bloch, P. H., Brunel, F. F., & Arnold, T. J. (2003). Individual differences in the centrality of visual product aesthetics: Concept and measurement. *Journal of Consumer Research, 29*(4), 551–565. doi: 10.1086/346250

Bryson, J. B., & Driver, M. J. (1972). Cognitive complexity, introversion, and preference for complexity. *Journal of Personality and Social Psychology, 23*(3), 320–327. doi: 10.1037/h0033121

Campbell, I. G. (1941). Factors which work toward unity or coherence in visual design. *Journal of Experimental Psychology, 28*(2), 145–162. doi: 10.1037/h0056758

Child, I. L., & Iwao, S. (1968). Personality and esthetic sensitivity: Extension of findings to younger age and to different culture. *Journal of Personality and Social Psychology, 8*(3, Pt.1), 308–312. doi: 10.1037/h0025599

Cho, H., & Schwarz, N. (2010). I like those glasses on you, but not in the mirror: Fluency, preference, and virtual mirrors. *Journal of Consumer Psychology, 20*(4), 471–475. doi: 10.1016/j.jcps.2010.07.004

Cogan, E., Parker, S., & Zellner, D. A. (2013). Beauty beyond compare: Effects of context extremity and categorization on hedonic contrast. *Journal of Experimental Psychology: Human Perception and Performance, 39*(1), 16–22. doi: 10.1037/a0031020

Crandall, J. E. (1967). Familiarity, preference, and expectancy arousal. *Journal of Experimental Psychology, 73*(3), 374–381. doi: 10.1037/h0024279

Cunningham, M. R. (1986). Measuring the physical in physical attractiveness: Quasi-experiments on the sociobiology of female facial beauty. *Journal of Personality and Social Psychology, 50*(5), 925–935. doi: 10.1037/0022-3514.50.5.925

Cunningham, M. R., Roberts, A. R., Barbee, A. P., Druen, P. B., & Wu, C. H. (1995). "Their ideas of beauty are, on the whole, the same as ours": Consistency and variability in the cross-cultural perception of female physical attractiveness. *Journal of Personality and Social Psychology, 68*(2), 261–279. doi: 10.1037/0022-3514.68.2.261

Deng, X., Hui, S. K., & Hutchinson, J. W. (2010). Consumer preferences for color combinations: An empirical analysis of similarity-based color relationships. *Journal of Consumer Psychology, 20*(4), 476–484. doi: 10.1016/j.jcps.2010.07.005

Dermer, M., & Thiel, D. L. (1975). When beauty may fail. *Journal of Personality and Social Psychology, 31*(6), 1168–1176. doi: 10.1037/h0077085

Diener, E., Wolsic, B., & Fujita, F. (1995). Physical attractiveness and subjective well-being. *Journal of Personality and Social Psychology, 69*(1), 120–129. doi: 10.1037/0022-3514.69.1.120

Dion, K., Berscheid, E., & Walster, E. (1972). What is beautiful is good. *Journal of Personality and Social Psychology, 24*(3), 285–290. doi: 10.1037/h0033731

Eidelman, S., Crandall, C. S., & Pattershall, J. (2009). The existence bias. *Journal of Personality and Social Psychology, 97*(5), 765–775. doi: 10.1037/a0017058

Elliot, A. J., Niesta Kayser, D., Greitemeyer, T., Lichtenfeld, S., Gramzow, R. H., Maier, M. A., & Liu, H. (2010). Red, rank, and romance in women viewing men. *Journal of Experimental Psychology: General, 139*(3), 399–417. doi: 10.1037/a0019689

Eysenck, H. J. (1939). The validity of judgments as a function of the number of judges. *Journal of Experimental Psychology, 25*(6), 650–654. doi: 10.1037/h0058754

Eysenck, H. J. (1942). The experimental study of the "good Gestalt": A new approach. *Psychological Review, 49*(4), 344–364. doi: 10.1037/h0057013

Falk, R., Falk, R., & Ayton, P. (2009). Subjective patterns of randomness and choice: Some consequences of collective responses. *Journal of Experimental Psychology: Human Perception and Performance, 35*(1), 203–224. doi: 10.1037/0096-1523.35.1.203

Fechner, G. T. (1876). *Vorschule der Ästhetik*. Leipzig: Breitkopf & Härtel.
Francis, G. (2013). Publication bias in "Red, rank, and romance in women viewing men," by Elliot et al. (2010). *Journal of Experimental Psychology: General, 142*(1), 292–296. doi: 10.1037/a0027923
Fisher, R. J., & Ma, Y. (2014). The price of being beautiful: Negative effects of attractiveness on empathy for children in need. *Journal of Consumer Research, 41*(2), 436–450. doi: 10.1086/676967
Gordon, K. (1923). A study of esthetic judgments. *Journal of Experimental Psychology, 6*(1), 36–43. doi: 10.1037/h0071285
Greenberg, J., Pyszczynski, T., Solomon, S., Rosenblatt, A., Veeder, M., Kirkland, S., & Lyon, D. (1990). Evidence for terror management theory II: The effects of mortality salience on reactions to those who threaten or bolster the cultural worldview. *Journal of Personality and Social Psychology, 58*(2), 308–318. doi: 10.1037/0022-3514.58.2.308
Graziano, W. G., Jensen-Campbell, L. A., Shebilske, L. J., & Lundgren, S. R. (1993). Social influence, sex differences, and judgments of beauty: Putting the interpersonal back in interpersonal attraction. *Journal of Personality and Social Psychology, 65*(3), 522–531. doi: 10.1037/0022-3514.65.3.522
Gregor, M. J. (1983). Baumgarten's "Aesthetica". *Review of Metaphysics, 37*(2), 357–385. doi: 10.2307/20128010
Guilford, J. P., & Holley, J. W. (1949). A factorial approach to the analysis of variances in esthetic judgments. *Journal of Experimental Psychology, 39*(2), 208–218. doi: 10.1037/h0054864
Häfner, M., & Trampe, D. (2009). When thinking is beneficial and when it is not: The effects of thin and round advertising models. *Journal of Consumer Psychology, 19*(4), 619–628. doi: 10.1016/j.jcps.2009.06.004
Halberstadt, J., Pecher, D., Zeelenberg, R., Wai, L. I., & Winkielman, P. (2013). Two faces of attractiveness making beauty in averageness appear and reverse. *Psychological Science, 24*(11), 2343–2346. doi: 10.1177/0956797613491969
Hawley-Dolan, A., & Winner, E. (2011). Seeing the mind behind the art: People can distinguish abstract expressionist paintings from highly similar paintings by children, chimps, monkeys, and elephants. *Psychological Science, 22*(4), 435–441. doi: 10.1177/0956797611400915
Hill, S. E., Rodeheffer, C. D., Griskevicius, V., Durante, K., & White, A. E. (2012). Boosting beauty in an economic decline: Mating, spending, and the lipstick effect. *Journal of Personality and Social Psychology, 103*(2), 275–291. doi: 10.1037/a0028657
Hoegg, J., Alba, J. W., & Dahl, D. W. (2010). The good, the bad, and the ugly: Influence of aesthetics on product feature judgments. *Journal of Consumer Psychology, 20*(4), 419–430. doi: 10.1016/j.jcps.2010.07.002
Holbrook, M. B., & Schindler, R. M. (1994). Age, sex, and attitude toward the past as predictors of consumers' aesthetic tastes for cultural products. *Journal of Marketing Research, 31*(3), 412–422.
Hönekopp, J. (2006). Once more: Is beauty in the eye of the beholder? Relative contributions of private and shared taste to judgments of facial attractiveness. *Journal of Experimental Psychology: Human Perception and Performance, 32*(2), 199–209. doi: 10.1037/0096-1523.32.2.199
Joy, A., & Sherry, J. F., Jr. (2003). Speaking of art as embodied imagination: A multisensory approach to understanding aesthetic experience. *Journal of Consumer Research, 30*(2), 259–282. doi: 10.1086/376802
Kenrick, D. T. & Gutierres, S. E. (1980). Contrast effects and judgments of physical attractiveness: When beauty becomes a social problem. *Journal of Personality and Social Psychology, 38*(1), 131–140. doi: 10.1037/0022-3514.38.1.131
Koole, S. L. & Van den Berg, A. E. (2005). Lost in the wilderness: Terror management, action orientation, and nature evaluation. *Journal of Personality and Social Psychology, 88*(6), 1014–1028. doi: 10.1037/0022-3514.88.6.1014
Krishna, A., Elder, R. S., & Caldara, C. (2010). Feminine to smell but masculine to touch? Multisensory congruence and its effect on the aesthetic experience. *Journal of Consumer Psychology, 20*(4), 410–418. doi: 10.1016/j.jcps.2010.06.010
Kumar, M. & Garg, N. (2010). Aesthetic principles and cognitive emotion appraisals: How much of the beauty lies in the eye of the beholder? *Journal of Consumer Psychology, 20*(4), 485–494. doi: 10.1016/j.jcps.2010.06.015
Landau, M. J., Greenberg, J., Solomon, S., Pyszczynski, T., & Martens, A. (2006). Windows into nothingness: Terror management, meaninglessness, and negative reactions to modern art. *Journal of Personality and Social Psychology, 90*(6), 879–892. doi: 10.1037/0022-3514.90.6.879
Landy, D. & Sigall, H. (1974). Beauty is talent: Task evaluation as a function of the performer's physical attractiveness. *Journal of Personality and Social Psychology, 29*(3), 299–304. doi: 10.1037/h0036018

Langlois, J. H., & Roggman, L. A. (1990). Attractive faces are only average. *Psychological Science, 1*(2), 115–121. doi: 10.2307/40062595

Langlois, J. H., Roggman, L. A., & Musselman, L. (1994). What is average and what is not average about attractive faces? *Psychological Science, 5*(4), 214–220. doi: 10.2307/40063104

Leder, H., Bär, S., & Topolinski, S. (2012). Covert painting simulations influence aesthetic appreciation of artworks. *Psychological Science, 23*(12), 1479–1481. doi: 10.1177/0956797612452866

Lee, C. J., Andrade, E. B., & Palmer, S. E. (2013). Interpersonal relationships and preferences for mood-congruency in aesthetic experiences. *Journal of Consumer Research, 40*(2), 382–391. doi: 10.1086/670609

Lorenzo, G. L., Biesanz, J. C., & Human, L. J. (2010). What is beautiful is good and more accurately understood: Physical attractiveness and accuracy in first impressions of personality. *Psychological Science, 21*(12), 1777–1782. doi: 10.1177/0956797610388048

Machotka, P. (1982). Esthetic judgment warm and cool: Cognitive and affective determinants. *Journal of Personality and Social Psychology, 42*(1), 100–107. doi: 10.1037/0022-3514.42.1.100

Maddux, J. E., & Rogers, R. W. (1980). Effects of source expertness, physical attractiveness, and supporting arguments on persuasion: A case of brains over beauty. *Journal of Personality and Social Psychology, 39*(2), 235–244. doi: 10.1037/0022-3514.39.2.235

Madzharov, A. V., & Block, L. G. (2010). Effects of product unit image on consumption of snack foods. *Journal of Consumer Psychology, 20*(4), 398–409. doi: 10.1016/j.jcps.2010.06.007

Maner, J. K., Kenrick, D. T., Becker, D. V., Delton, A. W., Hofer, B., Wilbur, C. J., & Neuberg, S. L. (2003). Sexually selective cognition: Beauty captures the mind of the beholder. *Journal of Personality and Social Psychology, 85*(6), 1107–1120. doi: 10.1037/0022-3514.85.6.1107

Martindale, C., & Moore, K. (1988). Priming, prototypicality, and preference. *Journal of Experimental Psychology: Human Perception and Performance, 14*(4), 661–670. doi: 10.1037/0096-1523.14.4.661

Meyers-Levy, J., & Zhu, R. (2010). Gender differences in the meanings consumers infer from music and other aesthetic stimuli. *Journal of Consumer Psychology, 20*(4), 495–507. doi: 10.1016/j.jcps.2010.06.006

Milord, J. T. (1978). Aesthetic aspects of faces: A (somewhat) phenomenological analysis using multidimensional scaling methods. *Journal of Personality and Social Psychology, 36*(2), 205–216. doi: 10.1037/0022-3514.36.2.205

Moskowitz, H. R., Dravnieks, A., & Gerbers, C. (1974). Odor intensity and pleasantness of butanol. *Journal of Experimental Psychology, 103*(2), 216–223. doi: 10.1037/h0036793

Newman, G. E., & Bloom, P. (2012). Art and authenticity: The importance of originals in judgments of value. *Journal of Experimental Psychology: General, 141*(3), 558–569. doi: 10.1037/a0026035

Osborne, H. (1977). Odours and appreciation. *British Journal of Aesthetics, 17*(1), 37–48. doi: 10.1093/bjaesthetics/17.1.37

Osborne, H. (1979). Some theories of aesthetic judgment. *Journal of Aesthetics and Art Criticism, 38*(2), 135–144.

Page, C., & Herr, P. M. (2002). An investigation of the processes by which product design and brand strength interact to determine initial affect and quality judgments. *Journal of Consumer Psychology, 12*(2), 133–147. doi: 10.1207/S15327663JCP1202_06

Pandelaere, M., Millet, K., & den Bergh, B. V. (2010). Madonna or Don McLean? The effect of order of exposure on relative liking. *Journal of Consumer Psychology, 20*(4), 442–451. doi: 10.1016/j.jcps.2010.07.003

Park, C. W. (2012). Two types of attractive research: Cute research and beautiful research. *Journal of Consumer Psychology, 22*(3), 299–302. doi: 10.1016/j.jcps.2012.05.005

Patrick, V. M., & Hagtvedt, H. (2011). Aesthetic incongruity resolution. *Journal of Marketing Research, 48*(2), 393–402. doi: 10.1509/jmkr.48.2.393

Patrick, V. M., & Peracchio, L. A. (2010). "Curating" the JCP special issue on aesthetics in consumer psychology: An introduction to the aesthetics issue. *Journal of Consumer Psychology, 20*(4), 393–397. doi: 10.1016/j.jcps.2010.08.003

Peracchio, L. A., & Meyers-Levy, J. (1994). How ambiguous cropped objects in ad photos can affect product evaluations. *Journal of Consumer Research, 21*(1), 190–204. doi: 10.2307/2489750

Perrin, F. A. C. (1921). Physical attractiveness and repulsiveness. *Journal of Experimental Psychology, 4*(3), 203–217. doi: 10.1037/h0071949

Reber, R., Schwarz, N., & Winkielman, P. (2004). Processing fluency and aesthetic pleasure: Is beauty in the perceiver's processing experience? *Personality and Social Psychology Review, 8*(4), 364–382. doi: 10.1207/s15327957pspr0804_3

Reimann, M., Zaichkowsky, J., Neuhaus, C., Bender, T., & Weber, B. (2010). Aesthetic package design: A behavioural, neural, and psychological investigation. *Journal of Consumer Psychology, 20*(4), 431–441. doi: 10.1016/j.jcps.2010.06.009

Reis, H. T., Nezlek, J., & Wheeler, L. (1980). Physical attractiveness in social interaction. *Journal of Personality and Social Psychology, 38*(4), 604–617. doi: 10.1037/0022-3514.38.4.604

Reis, H. T., Wheeler, L., Spiegel, N., Kernis, M. H., Nezlek, J., & Perri, M. (1982). Physical attractiveness in social interaction: II. Why does appearance affect social experience? *Journal of Personality and Social Psychology, 43*(5), 979–996. doi: 10.1037/0022-3514.43.5.979

Rosenblatt, A., Greenberg, J., Solomon, S., Pyszczynski, T., & Lyon, D. (1989). Evidence for terror management theory: I. The effects of mortality salience on reactions to those who violate or uphold cultural values. *Journal of Personality and Social Psychology, 57*(4), 681–690. doi: 10.1037/0022-3514.57.4.681

Saad, G., & Stenstrom, E. (2012). Calories, beauty, and ovulation: The effects of the menstrual cycle on food and appearance-related consumption. *Journal of Consumer Psychology, 22*(1), 102–113. doi: 10.1016/j.jcps.2011.10.001

Sammartino, J., & Palmer, S. E. (2012). Aesthetic issues in spatial composition: Effects of vertical position and perspective on framing single objects. *Journal of Experimental Psychology: Human Perception and Performance, 38*(4), 865–879. doi: 10.1037/a0027736

Schlosser, A. E. (1998). Applying the functional theory of attitudes to understanding the influence of store atmosphere on store inferences. *Journal of Consumer Psychology*, 7(4), 345–369. doi: 10.1207/s15327663jcp0704_03

Schmitt, B., & Simonson, A. (1997). *Marketing aesthetics*. New York, NY: Free Press.

Segal-Caspi, L., Roccas, S., & Sagiv, L. (2012). Don't judge a book by its cover, revisited: Perceived and reported traits and values of attractive women. *Psychological Science, 23*(10), 1112–1116. doi: 10.1177/0956797612446349

Shipley, W. C., Dattman, P. E., & Steele, B. A. (1947). The influence of size on preferences for rectangular proportion in children and adults. *Journal of Experimental Psychology, 37*(4), 333–336. doi: 10.1037/h0059356

Shu, S. B., & Townsend, C. (2014). Using aesthetics and self-affirmation to encourage openness to risky (and safe) choices. *Journal of Experimental Psychology: Applied, 20*(1), 22–39. doi: 10.1037/xap0000003

Sigall, H., & Landy, D. (1973). Radiating beauty: Effects of having a physically attractive partner on person perception. *Journal of Personality and Social Psychology, 28*(2), 218–224. doi: 10.1037/h0035740

Sigall, H., & Ostrove, N. (1975). Beautiful but dangerous: Effects of offender attractiveness and nature of the crime on juridic judgment. *Journal of Personality and Social Psychology, 31*(3), 410–414. doi: 10.1037/h0076472

Steck, L., & Machotka, P. (1975). Preference for musical complexity: Effects of context. *Journal of Experimental Psychology: Human Perception and Performance, 1*(2), 170–174. doi: 10.1037/0096-1523.1.2.170

Strube, M. J., Turner, C. W., Patrick, S., & Perrillo, R. (1983). Type A and Type B attentional responses to aesthetic stimuli: Effects on mood and performance. *Journal of Personality and Social Psychology, 45*(6), 1369–1379. doi: 10.1037/0022-3514.45.6.1369

Sussman, S., Mueser, K. T., Grau, B. W., & Yarnold, P. R. (1983). Stability of females' facial attractiveness during childhood. *Journal of Personality and Social Psychology, 44*(6), 1231–1233. doi: 10.1037/0022-3514.44.6.123

Taylor, C., Clifford, A., & Franklin, A. (2013). Color preferences are not universal. *Journal of Experimental Psychology: General, 142*(4), 1015–1027. doi: 10.1037/a0030273.supp (Supplemental)

Thompson, G. G. (1946). The effect of chronological age on aesthetic preferences for rectangles of different proportions. *Journal of Experimental Psychology, 36*(1), 50–58. doi: 10.1037/h0054675

Townsend, C., & Shu, S. B. (2010). When and how aesthetics influences financial decisions. *Journal of Consumer Psychology, 20*(4), 452–458. doi: 10.1016/j.jcps.2010.06.013

Topolinski, S. (2010). Moving the eye of the beholder: Motor components in vision determine aesthetic preference. *Psychological Science, 21*(9), 1220–1224. doi: 10.1177/0956797610378308

Townsend, C., & Sood, S. (2012). Self-affirmation through the choice of highly aesthetic products. *Journal of Consumer Research, 39*(2), 415–428. doi: 10.1086/663775

Venkatesh, A., Joy, A., Sherry, J. F., Jr., & Deschenes, J. (2010). The aesthetics of luxury fashion, body and identify formation. *Journal of Consumer Psychology, 20*(4), 459–470. doi: 10.1016/j.jcps.2010.06.011

Veryzer, R. W., Jr., & Hutchinson, J. W. (1998). The influence of unity and prototypicality on aesthetic responses to new product designs. *Journal of Consumer Research, 24*(4), 374–385. doi: 10.1086/209516

White, A. E., Kenrick, D. T., & Neuberg, S. L. (2013). Beauty at the ballot box: Disease threats predict preferences for physically attractive leaders. *Psychological Science, 24*(12), 2429–2436. doi: 10.1177/0956797613493642

Wilson, G. D., Ausman, J., & Mathews, T. R. (1973). Conservatism and art preferences. *Journal of Personality and Social Psychology, 25*(2), 286–288. doi: 10.1037/h0033972

Winkielman, P., Halberstadt, J., Fazendeiro, T., & Catty, S. (2006). Prototypes are attractive because they are easy on the mind. *Psychological Science, 17*(9), 799–806. doi: 10.2307/40064456

Wöllner, C., Deconinck, F. J. A., Parkinson, J., Hove, M. J., & Keller, P. E. (2012). The perception of prototypical motion: Synchronization is enhanced with quantitatively morphed gestures of musical conductors. *Journal of Experimental Psychology: Human Perception and Performance, 38*(6), 1390–1403. doi: 10.1037/a0028130

Yang, X., Zhang, J., & Peracchio, L. A. (2010). Understanding the impact of self-concept on the stylistic properties of images. *Journal of Consumer Psychology, 20*(4), 508–520. doi: 10.1016/j.jcps.2010.06.012

31
Anthropomorphism

Pankaj Aggarwal and Ann L. McGill

Anthropomorphism, or endowing human traits to non-human entities, is commonplace in modern-day life, in part due to the numerous ways in which marketers encourage consumers to see their products and brands in human terms (e.g., Aaker, 1997; Biel, 2000). Anthropomorphism is also pervasive due to the motivational and cognitive factors that promote the interpretation of stimuli through a human lens (e.g., Epley, Waytz, & Cacioppo, 2007). Marketers often endow products with physical traits that resemble human characteristics (e.g., giving the Coke bottle the shape of a human figure; designing the fronts of cars so that they appear to have faces). Marketers also anthropomorphize their brands by giving them humanlike names (e.g., Mr. Clean) or associating them with characters that seem to be living beings (e.g., The Michelin Man).

Although marketers may believe that associating products and brands with humanlike traits will make them more endearing and desirable, recent research has revealed that anthropomorphizing may produce complex patterns of results, sometimes serving as an effective tactic and sometimes being counterproductive. In this chapter, we will briefly summarize prior research on anthropomorphism from diverse fields such as psychology, religion and robotics. Next, we will review the growing work in marketing that has studied this fascinating phenomenon to identify the main findings that emerge – primarily in terms of the antecedents, processes and consequences of product and brand anthropomorphism. Subsequently, we will suggest some key directions for future research in the area.

Origins of anthropomorphism

Research on anthropomorphism in marketing has become an active area of investigation within the last two decades although the concept of anthropomorphism dates back many centuries. Throughout history, people have been versatile in anthropomorphizing various entities such as gods, demons, natural phenomena, fictional and imaginary characters, aliens, animals and even man-made objects and artefacts (Guthrie, 1993). The word *anthropomorphism* originates from the Greek words "*anthropos*" (human) and "*morphe*" (shape or form (Epley et al., 2007); that is, anthropomorphism is the phenomenon by which non-human entities are given human shape or form. Epley et al. (2007) noted that anthropomorphism is the "tendency to imbue the real or imagined behaviour of non-human agents with humanlike characteristics, motivations, intentions or emotions". Anthropomorphism pervades human judgement and is prevalent in almost all cultures and aspects of human life, especially religion, art and storytelling. It is not surprising then that anthropologists like Guthrie (1993) suggest that anthropomorphism is a phenomenon that comes very naturally and easily to humans, and that the human brain has an innate tendency to see "human" in natural phenomena and events.

Anthropomorphism in literature and art

One of the earliest pieces of evidence of anthropomorphism is an ancient sculpture from over 30,000 years ago, showing a human body with the head of a lion – a clear case of imbuing a non-human entity with human attributes. Anthropomorphism also pervades literature across diverse cultures appearing in ancient pieces of work such as the Indian *Panchatantra* and the Greek *Aesop's Fables* – both of which are collections of stories about anthropomorphized animals that highlight useful everyday principles of life. Poets and writers have used anthropomorphism and personification to make their writings more evocative and alive. From Shakespeare to Wordsworth, from T. S. Eliot to James Joyce, classical authors have anthropomorphized diverse elements like clouds, rain, crabs, islands, garden, tulips, fish, mountains, death and imagination. More recent works, such as *Alice in Wonderland* and *The Jungle Book*, and the popularity of movies like *The Lion King* highlight the pervasiveness of anthropomorphism in literature and art. Of course, commercial art such as advertisements, television commercials and other tools used by marketers frequently employ product and brand anthropomorphism to better relate to the consumers, which is seen as an effective way to sell in the marketplace.

Anthropomorphizing animals

Relatedly, anthropomorphizing animals has been a common context in which people tend to see the human in the animals around them, especially the pets that they own. Research has shown that people perceive animals to be similar to themselves and that the extent to which humanness is attributed to different animals is in the following order: invertebrates, fish, amphibians, reptiles, birds, mammals (Eddy, Gallup, & Povinelli, 1993). Although not readily anthropomorphized, it has been noted that amphibians and reptiles show many traits common with birds and mammals such as sophisticated communication, problem solving, parental care and complex sociality, and hence do show traits that encourage anthropomorphism (Burghardt, 2013). Further, when it comes to pets (e.g., cats and dogs), there is a marked increase in perceived similarity of the animal to self, and in our ability to ascribe more complex humanlike cognitive ability to it (Eddy et al., 1993). It has been noted that four distinct types of social interactions recur in dog–human play: directed responses by one player to the other; indications of intent; mutual behaviours; and contingent activity – all behaviours that point to reasons why we anthropomorphize dogs (Horowitz & Bekoff, 2007). In fact, research also indicates that we use appearance to judge and perceive pets, especially domestic dogs, in much the same way that we use stereotypes to assess people (Kwan, Gosling, & John, 2008). Importantly, anthropomorphism, attachment and level of empathy towards pets seem to significantly affect human–animal interactions (Ellingsen et al., 2010).

Other work has noted that pet owners tend to anthropomorphize their animals as a means of social support and to reduce their level of stress (Antonacooulos and Pychyl, 2008). Pets provide people with the much needed social connection that they may be missing in their lives such that the pets often fulfil the needs that other humans do not. Interestingly and quite surprisingly, it has been noted that pet owners who think that their pets are capable of complex emotions such as guilt, may end up punishing their pets for perceived transgressions, which may then result in lowered welfare of these animals (Bradshaw and Casey, 2007). On the other hand, research on animal welfare suggests that taking an integrative and "whole animal" approach to view animal behaviour is important so that we fully appreciate them as sentient beings, and can take proper measures to improve their quality of life (Wemelsfelder, 2007; Wemelsfelder, Hunter, Mandl, & Lawrence, 2001). Further, animal well-being depends not just on fully understanding animal needs and perspective but also factors such as human, social and individual values that come with anthropomorphizing these animals (Clark, Rager, & Calpin, 1997).

Anthropomorphism in religion

One other context that employs anthropomorphism that is common across most cultures and is a part of people's everyday lives is the manner in which people relate to, and represent religious deities and gods. With the exception of a few notable religions such as Islam and Judaism, most religions tend to reflect human form in the images of gods, goddesses and other divine entities. Guthrie (1993) suggests that religion may best be understood as systematic anthropomorphism, that is, "religion consists of seeing the world as humanlike" (p. 4). Historically, the development of God concepts has been explained anthropomorphically with God being seen, especially by children, as a big superhuman who lives in the sky above the earth (Barret & Richert, 2003). In fact, very young children (pre-schoolers) attribute humanlike capacities to special entities like God (Lane, Wellman & Evans, 2010) and are able to conceptualize these representational properties held by Godlike entities even before they achieve representational understanding of the human mind (Makris & Pnevmatikos, 2007).

Believers tend to think that gods and humans are much alike, even continuous. In many religions, gods eat, drink, make war and love, have offspring, much like humans. Divine beings that are represented as intentional agents are subject to the cognitive intuitions that govern all intentional agents (Barrett, 1998). In some cultures, ancestors are seen as a kind of god, and are continuous with living people. Groups that are based on clans and lineages give ancestors a prominent role in religion. Importantly, gods are humanlike in that people are able to communicate with them. Gods speak to humans through lightning, thunder, rainbows, traffic accidents, natural calamities, death and destruction. Humans too are able to speak to god either directly or through religious leaders and priests. The Greek philosopher Xenophanes famously said that if horses and cattle could depict their gods, their gods too would look like horses and cattle, respectively. Recent research has noted that although humanness is associated with having both agency and conscious experience, Gods are seen as possessing agency but not experience. God is seen as the ultimate moral agent, the entity people blame and praise for negative and positive outcomes (Gray & Wegner, 2010). In fact, an interesting article by Werblowsky (1987) on anthropomorphism in religion concludes with the simple question: Can one pray to a non-anthropomorphic deity?

Anthropomorphism in robotics and computer interactions

Evidence from the field of computers and robotics shows that people interact with computers as if they are social beings, and employ social rules in their interactions with computers (Nass, Steuer, & Tauber, 1994). It has been suggested that social robots – or robots working as social partners in our everyday lives is the next bit stage for robotic research. In fact, robots are likely to be more acceptable to us humans if these robots are built in our own image – the human form (Duffy, 2003). Others agree with this idea, suggesting that robots whose appearance and movements are very humanlike are likely to be able to interact naturally with people (Ishiguro, 2006). Further, it has been shown that anthropomorphism of computers is often mindless and unconscious (Y. Kim & Sundar, 2012). Importantly, the more anthropomorphic is the representation of a computer agent or an avatar, the greater is the degree of social responses that it receives from computer users (Li, 2008). Further, aspects of computer–human interaction such as utility and feeling are associated with increases in anthropomorphic features of the computer interface (Burgoon et al., 2000). Similarly, research on computer–human interface and the consequences on increasing human likeness to virtual characters and avatars suggests a variety of positive outcomes and strengthening of social connection between the consumer and the computer (Green et al., 2008).

Interestingly, it has been suggested that people's evaluations of robots that look increasingly human will not be linear. According to this view, as the appearance of a robot becomes more humanlike, people's emotional response to the robot will initially be increasingly positive until a point is reached beyond which the response is that of strong revulsion. However, as the robot's appearance becomes indistinguishable from that of a human, the emotional response becomes positive once again and approaches human-to-human empathy levels. This area of repulsive response aroused by a robot with an appearance between a "barely human" and "fully human" entity is called the "uncanny valley" (Mori, MacDorman, & Kageki, 2012). The name uncanny valley suggests that an almost human-looking robot will seem overly "strange" to some people, will produce a feeling of uncanniness and will thus fail to evoke the empathic response required for productive human–robot interaction.

The uncanny valley has been explained by the activation of conflicting cognitive stimuli. If an entity looks sufficiently non-human, its human characteristics will be noticeable, generating empathy. However, if the entity looks almost human, it will elicit people's model of a human other rather than that of a robot, and its associated normative expectations. However, because the non-human characteristics will still be noticeable, the human viewer will get a sense of strangeness. In other words, a robot stuck inside the uncanny valley is no longer being judged by the standards of a robot doing a passable job at pretending to be human, but is instead being judged by the standards of a human doing a terrible job at acting like a normal person. This dissonance experienced due to perceptual tension occurring from conflicting cues to category membership leads to psychological "eeriness" or negative perception.

One of the key reasons why technology, especially computers, is so readily anthropomorphized seems to be due to the agentic properties associated with these machines. Computers seem to do things on their own, have a mind and are able to think often even faster and better than human minds. This ability of computers to do things at will allow us so readily to anthropomorphize them. Further, technical devices that are seen as helpers or friends – a very anthropomorphic relationship – were also seen as less unfriendly compared to technical devices that were seen as merely tools (Luczak, Roetting, & Schmidt, 2003). In fact, it has been argued that one approach to get people to naturally interact with robots is to build androids whose appearance and movements are very humanlike; consequently, conscious and subconscious human recognition of androids is a fundamental area of focus in android science (Ishiguro, 2006).

Why anthropomorphize?

Why is it that people are able to so readily ascribe humanlike characteristics to non-human entities? Three explanations have been offered for people's tendency to anthropomorphize (see Guthrie [1993] for a review). One explanation is that doing so comforts people by providing relationships or companionship. This view sees anthropomorphism as following on from wishful thinking: People who wish to have more relationships in their everyday lives use products and other entities to meet that need. A second explanation relates to the idea that we anthropomorphize to make sense of the world around us. People use what they are familiar with – their knowledge of themselves – and ascribe humanlike characteristics to events or entities to better account for outcomes and things that they know less about. Being humans, we know ourselves best, and use the same lens to see things around us, especially things that are novel, different or uncertain. Anthropomorphism is our way to make the unfamiliar familiar. Finally, Guthrie (1993) suggests that anthropomorphizing might be seen as a cognitive and perceptual strategy akin to making a bet that the world is humanlike: a bet that has more upside than downside risk. From an evolutionary perspective, making this bet may have developed as a mechanism to help people identify potential predators (Guthrie, 1993). While this mechanism may yield false positive results such as identifying a tree with humanlike limbs as an enemy, the upside is that it would also lead to correctly identifying predators if and when they are around in the environment. Such an adaptive mechanism is something that is crucial for survival, and in fact may be hard-wired in us. In addition, the tendency to anthropomorphize may be a developmental trait, where young children learn about human interactions and relationships, and then overgeneralize them to interactions with non-humans (Guthrie, 1993).

Antecedents of anthropomorphism: Motivational and cognitive

Building upon the propositions by Guthrie (1993), Epley et al. (2007) proposed a three-factor model to explain why people anthropomorphize. The antecedent factors proposed by Epley et al. (2007) are, in fact, quite similar to those suggested by Guthrie (1993). Two of these factors are motivational, specifically, sociality motivation and effectance motivation, while the third factor is cognitive and relates to knowledge activation.

Much like Guthrie (1993), Epley et al. (2007) also suggest that humans have a strong and universal need for affiliation and belongingness (Baumeister &Leary, 1995), and when this need is activated (i.e., people feel lonely or isolated), people feel eager to seek out and form social connections. Being in isolation or cut off from other humans is a punishment that is seen as being equivalent to death. Those experiencing distress from a lack of social connection seek out ways to form connections with other people. Consequently, there will be an increased likelihood that they will anthropomorphize non-human objects. Consistent with this view, Epley et al. (2008) demonstrate that people who are lonely compensate for their lack of social connections through anthropomorphizing animals, and even gadgets, thereby creating a sense of connection with these non-humans. One reason why children's stories, movies and other literature are full of anthropomorphic characters might be because children have a very high need to make friends, so these media portray human characteristics to young children in a way that is both non-threatening and endearing (Barker, 1996).

The second factor – effectance motivation – arises from individuals' needs to understand and predict their environment, and to reduce their level of uncertainty much like Guthrie's (1993) suggestion that people like to make sense of the world around them. Similar to making inferences about other people's behaviour by using the self as a reference point, individuals anthropomorphize non-humans in order to comprehend and predict the behaviour of objects (Dawes & Mulford, 1996). By using a familiar reference point (i.e., human behaviour), individuals feel that they have more control over their environment, are better able to explain ambiguous elements in their surroundings and make better predictions about how the future might unfold (Burger & Cooper, 1979). Epley et al. (2007) suggest that anthropomorphism is influenced by the human motivation to resolve uncertainty, seek meaning and feel efficacious. This general motivation to interact effectively with one's environment is therefore called the effectance motivation, and it suggests that humans are driven to master their environments by increasing the environment's predictability and apparent controllability. Furthermore, Guthrie (1993) notes that anthropomorphic propensity increases during times of uncertainty and rapid technological change, which likely explains why complex products like computers are ascribed humanlke traits and are treated as similar to humans (Nass & Moon, 2000; Nass, Fogg, & Moon, 1996).

The third factor proposed by Epley et al. (2007) as an antecedent of why we anthropomorphize is cognitive in nature and refers to the accessibility and applicability of anthropocentric knowledge that people might already have. Humans have direct and immediate access to the experience of being a human. A person's own knowledge and experience are so accessible and richly organized that they continue to serve as an automatic base and guide when reasoning about other humans (egocentrism), and as a guide when reasoning about non-human agents (anthropomorphism). In other words, when reasoning about the mental states of non-human agents, people use themselves as a guide and only correct that egocentric simulation when they have the motivation, capacity and the requisite non-egocentric information to do so.

From a cognitive perspective, when people view objects that have humanlike traits (e.g., physical shape of things, movement, voice, other behaviour, etc.), the human schema becomes more readily accessible in the mind, which in turn increases the likelihood that the object itself will be anthropomorphized by the observer. In other words, when primed with human category knowledge, people tend to engage with the environment around them by applying this knowledge to the stimulus itself. Thus, past research has shown that the similarity of a non-human object's movement to human movement leads observers to perceive the object as being alive (Tremoulet & Feldman, 2000), which is why an insect is not humanized (it is seen as moving too randomly) nor is a growing plant humanized (it is seen as moving too slowly); in addition, if the speed of the object is more in line with natural human speed, then the object is more likely to be perceived as being humanlike (Morewedge, Preston, & Wegner, 2004), as might be the case with Roomba, the robotic vacuum cleaner.

Consistent with this explanation, marketers often take advantage of human schema activation by employing brand characters and mascots. Brown (2010) finds that marketers are most likely to use stylized human beings as brand characters or mascots, followed by domesticated animals. Further, the popularity of the brand animal is directly correlated with the species' physiological (shape) and psychological (presence of mind) distance from humankind. Even when the object is completely inanimate – that is, the object is without a conscious mind and without movement – observers are still able to detect humanlike features. When faced with a row of soft drink bottles of varying sizes, consumers prefer to see them as a "family" of products rather than a "line" of products (Aggarwal & McGill, 2007).

In sum, the human tendency to anthropomorphize non-human entities is driven by a need to connect with others, a need to make sense of the world around them, and when features of the object activate the human schema. These factors are likely rooted in evolution and manifest in early childhood – powerful bases for anthropomorphism by consumers.

Antecedents of anthropomorphism: Individual differences

Although the motivational and cognitive factors noted above often depend upon the specific context and particular situation facing a person, there are also individual level differences that result in an increased likelihood to anthropomorphize. Some people are more likely than others to feel lonely, and such chronically lonely people are more likely to anthropomorphize compared to others (Epley et al., 2008). In addition, there are some people who have a greater need for control than others, and this difference will lead these people to anthropomorphize more so compared to those who are chronically low on need for control (Epley et al., 2008). The greater the individual's need to be in control of things, the greater their likelihood to anthropomorphize since they desire to explain others' behaviour often by focusing on anthropomorphic concepts such as intentions and desires (Burger & Hemans, 1988). Furthermore, it has also been suggested that another individual level difference – the need for closure – is likely to lead to a greater degree of anthropomorphism: The greater the need for closure, the greater is the individual's need to avoid uncertainty and make sense of the world around them – an individual difference that is consistent with the effectance motivation (Epley et al., 2007). Finally, it has been argued that the need for cognition is likely to result in a reduced likelihood to anthropomorphize. Those individuals high in need for cognition tend to enjoy engaging in effortful thinking, and this effortful thinking is likely to help them overcome the easily accessible knowledge that may get applied – the one related to humanness – in contexts that do not relate to human interaction. Thus, those high in need for cognition may show lowered effect of knowledge activation – the starting point when anthropomorphic inference gets applied to non-human entities due to sheer accessibility.

In addition, recent work by Waytz, Cacioppo and Epley (2010) has proposed a scale that taps into stable individual level differences that can predict people's likelihood to anthropomorphize. This questionnaire-based scale examines people's tendency to anthropomorphize three different classes of entities – non-human animals, natural phenomena and technological devices by asking the extent to which these entities seem durable, useful, good-looking, active and lethargic. The scale further asks people the extent to which a stimulus has a mind of its own, free will, intentions, emotions and consciousness. Subsequent research has found that this scale is able to successfully predict individual level differences in people's likelihood to anthropomorphize (Caruso, Waytz, & Epley, 2010; Neave et al., 2015).

Anthropomorphism and consumer research

A review of prior research on anthropomorphism in the diverse fields of literature, religion, animal welfare and robotics suggests that this phenomenon is widespread and commonplace. Marketing practitioners have built upon this prevalent human tendency to imbue humanness with inanimate objects or non-human concepts. By endowing their products with physical traits that resemble those of people, or their brands with personality traits, marketers have attempted to enhance consumer evaluations, to build relationships between brands and consumers in ways that might foster loyalty and to encourage consumer responses that follow social conventions rather than cold, commercial utility assessments. Interestingly, however, academic research on this topic in marketing has only recently seen significant progress. The literature at this stage documents a variety of individually important and interesting effects but an overarching theory of anthropomorphism in consumer behaviour and a complete picture of its potential influence have yet to emerge, an issue we address later in this chapter.

In the next section, we summarize consumer research on anthropomorphism, looking first at the substantial number of papers that have examined the effect of product-based anthropomorphism. That is, we focus on papers that endow the product with physical characteristics like those of people or otherwise ask people to see the physical product in human terms. The majority of these papers have centred on differences in evaluations for anthropomorphized and non-anthropomorphized products. Subsequently, we review research that has delved further into the consequences of anthropomorphism, primarily looking at brand rather than product anthropomorphism. The issues examined by these studies include enabling rich characterization of brand imagery that parallels human personality traits, fostering emotional connection to products and brands, supporting the development of relationships some of which showcase power perceptions and risk-taking behaviour and even encouraging pro-social behaviour. Within this latter set of papers, we note those that have employed distinctive means of manipulating anthropomorphism.

Product anthropomorphism

Evaluations of products

A substantial portion of the literature on anthropomorphism in marketing has considered the effects of giving physical products characteristics that resemble those of people. For example, an early paper on the consequences of product anthropomorphism by the authors of the present chapter examined the role of schema congruity in the evaluation of anthropomorphized products (Aggarwal & McGill, 2007; see also Mandler, 1982). These authors focused in particular on the effects of marketers' efforts to encourage the consumer to view the product in human terms and they uncovered a complex relationship between anthropomorphism and evaluations. In particular, when the product was presented with humanlike traits, and when these traits were consistent with the features of the schema that the anthropomorphized product brought to mind, then the evaluation of the product was more positive. For example, when the car was presented as a spokesperson (a type of human schema), and the car had a smiling front face, which was consistent with the schema of a spokesperson, the evaluation of the car was positive. However, if the car's front face was frowning rather than smiling and hence had features that were inconsistent with the schema of a spokesperson, the evaluation of the car was negative. The authors observed that the positive influence of anthropomorphism was limited to schemas that evoke positive affect, just the sort marketers would typically choose for their products.

Aggarwal and McGill (2007) thus propose a non-conscious application of schema as the mechanism that drives the effects of anthropomorphism, noting that when marketers encourage consumers to anthropomorphize a product through giving their product characteristics that are typical of a human being, consumers bring to mind their schema for the type of person suggested by these characteristics, and the product is evaluated in part by how well its features fit that schema of the person being brought to mind. Some objects may be more readily seen as human than others, for example, objects that resemble human form and shape (e.g., bottles) or that have features like a human face (e.g., the front of a car or a clock). Depending on the characteristics of the object, therefore, consumers may or may not be able to see the analogy suggested by the marketer to anthropomorphize products successfully. This perceived schema congruity or lack of it then drives consumers' ability and likelihood to anthropomorphize a product as well as the extent to which such anthropomorphized products will be evaluated positively. This conceptual framework was further explored by van den Hende and Mugge (2014) who examined the specific case of gender anthropomorphism and proposed a gender-schema congruity effect.

In a related vein, Landwehr, McGill and Hermann (2011) show that people are able to detect emotional expressions from the "faces" of products such as cars and cell phones. For example, with respect to cars, this research finds that design elements such as the grille and headlights may be perceived as corresponding to eyes and a mouth, respectively, of a human face. Furthermore, based on the particular shape and angle of these two design elements (grille and headlights), people are able to make judgements about the friendliness and aggressiveness of the expression conveyed following the same rules applied to the interpretation of human expressions. Interestingly, a particular combination of headlights and grille shapes on cars – aggressive-looking eyes and a friendly-looking grille – results in a positive affective state of high pleasure and high arousal – which leads to a preference for these cars. Furthermore, humans cannot produce this exact expression, that is, by making their eyes look angry while simultaneously smiling. Nevertheless, the basic premise is somewhat similar to the one put forward by Aggarwal and McGill (2007) – that when elements of the product stimuli cue the human schema, the product itself is assessed as a human would be assessed. Extending this stream of work, Keaveney et al. (2012), find an interesting effect of product form anthropomorphism on how consumers evaluate brand extensions. This research explores consumer reactions when line extensions become too visually similar to the original brand. Using the context of automobiles and employing changes to the car's "eyes" (headlights) and the car's "mouth" (grille), the results show that visual similarity of line extensions, especially by anthropomorphizing car faces, leads to a negative attitude not only for the brand extension but also for the parent brand.

Similarly, Miesler, Leder and Hermann (2011) suggest that car faces that incorporate the baby schema were seen as cute and resulted in greater positive affect compared to control conditions, thus replicating the finding that car faces might be judged like human faces. However, unlike the prior work just noted, these authors prefer an evolutionary account for the effect of anthropomorphism. From an evolutionary perspective, the need for nurturing and caretaking of babies is an important human behaviour. The baby schema with its typical physical characteristics of a round face, large eyes, a small nose and a high forehead, serves as a visual stimulus to trigger positive affect in people. Miesler et al. (2011) manipulated car fronts in accordance with the baby schema (e.g., by enlarging the headlights/eyes), and used facial electromyography to find that participants showed more positive affective responses to the baby-faced car fronts than to the original stimuli. These authors thus argue that consumers' rapid affective response to visual product designs that could be detected by facial EMG (Electromyography, or the technique used for recording the activity of skeletal muscles) are really driven by evolutionary factors rather than cognitive processes such as those related to schema congruity.

Humans' proneness to see faces even in inanimate structures such as cars has also been examined by Windhager et al. (2010). Eye movement patterns indicated a predominance of headlights in attracting and guiding people's gaze irrespective of the feature they were asked to compare – equivalent to the role of the eyes during face perception, an effect that is explained as being evolutionary. Others like Veer (2013) look to understand why anthropomorphic images are so overused by marketers to attract very young consumers. He too draws on theories from evolutionary biology and evolutionary psychology to argue that anthropomorphism acts as a catalyst for kin recognition and encourages attachment and liking.

Although there is evidence supporting an innate preference towards designs mimicking human shape, Miesler (2012) identified a moderator of the positive effect of anthropomorphism on consumer evaluations. According to this research, which exposed participants to different types of consumption scenarios, it was found that anthropomorphic forms have a positive effect when the product serves a consumption goal that is emotional but not when it is functional in nature. These results thus show the limits of biologically determined preferences, and emphasize the impact of anticipating future interactions on present design preferences.

Other research by Hart, Jones and Royne (2013) compared the degree of anthropomorphism of different products varying on the level of complexity. In particular, this research compared a toothbrush, a USB drive, a cellphone and a laptop on the extent to which people readily anthropomorphize them. Participants in the study were requested to think of each product and asked to respond to questions about the product's price, frequency of use, method of acquisition and personal value. The respondents then answered questions assessing their anthropomorphism of the product. Results suggest that after marketplace variables were considered, anthropomorphism had a positive and significant influence on personal value for the four products. Additionally, the magnitude of anthropomorphism is related to product complexity, suggesting that the effectiveness of product managers to prime or otherwise influence consumer anthropomorphism may depend upon what product is being anthropomorphized.

Emotional connections to products

The forgoing research reveals that asking consumers to view products in human terms may change the bases of their evaluations to align with those used to judge people and, as a consequence, change their assessments. Other work has considered consequences beyond evaluations and has found that seeing products as people may lead consumers to change their responses and actions towards these products in ways that parallel interpersonal interactions. For example, research by Chandler and Schwarz (2010) shows that when consumers are induced to think of their car in anthropomorphic terms, they are less willing to replace the car, and give less weight to its quality when making replacement decisions compared to when the car is not anthropomorphized. Thinking of the product as a person appears to cause consumers to see it in more emotional rather than rational terms and to use social norms of interpersonal interaction when pondering product replacement decisions, such that replacing an old friend (who might be frail or sick) is not seen as appropriate behaviour.

Timpano and Shaw (2013) mirror the results noted by Chandler and Schwarz (2010) by finding a significant positive correlation between people's tendencies, their emotional attachment to products and their hoarding behaviour. Hoarding is characterized by a persistent and extreme difficulty with discarding one's possessions primarily due to strong emotional attachment to possessions, often resulting in cluttered living spaces. Anthropomorphism is one mechanism that contributes to this emotional attachment. The current research shows that anthropomorphic tendencies were significantly associated with greater saving behaviours and the acquisition of free things.

Nenkov and Scott (2014) examine the effect of anthropomorphism on people's consumption behaviour in the domain of cute looking products to find that consumers become more indulgent in their behaviour after exposure to such products. This research argues that since cute products are associated with fun and frivolity, an exposure to cute products primes a mental representation of fun, increasing consumers' focus on approaching self-rewards and making consumers more likely to choose indulgent options.

Brand anthropomorphism

Consistent with the findings noted above, physical products might readily be seen in human terms, for example, as a cute little family of bottles, or a menacing looking car, simply by adding features that look like those of people. Interestingly, people may also anthropomorphize brands and abstract concepts. Consequently, brand associations, meaning and imagery may figure in the perception of a brand personality with traits akin to those of people. Foundational to this line of research, Aaker (1997) developed a reliable and generalizable scale to measure brand personality dimensions, and suggested that consumers tend to perceive brands on five distinct personality dimensions: excitement, sincerity, competence, ruggedness and sophistication. Given that human personality research has identified the "Big Five" dimensions, this research is interesting in that three of the five brand personality dimensions (excitement, sincerity and competence) seem to map on very closely to three of the five human personality dimensions, thereby underscoring the merit of using the framework of brand anthropomorphism.

Evaluations of brands

Much like anthropomorphizing a product, anthropomorphizing a brand may affect its evaluation. For example, Puzakova, Kwak and Rocerto (2013) examine the issue in the context of brand wrongdoing. These authors suggest that when a brand faces negative publicity caused by brand wrongdoing, people who are entity theorists (i.e., those who believe that human personality traits do not change over time), view anthropomorphized brands less positively compared to non-anthropomorphized brands. In contrast, consumers who are incremental theorists (i.e., those who believe that human personality traits are malleable over time) are less likely to devalue the anthropomorphized brand compared to the non-anthropomorphized brand. Furthermore, when trying to combat the negative effect of anthropomorphized brands, entity theorists are less receptive to brand responses such as denial, apology or compensation relative to incremental theorists.

In the same vein, Delbaere, Mcquarrie and Phillips (2011) examine how anthropomorphism can influence brand personality perceptions and consumer brand preferences. These authors posit that advertising often employs anthropomorphism in the form of spokes characters, mascots and brand animals, and by metaphorically representing a product as being engaged in some kind of human behaviour. These different forms of personification lead to consumers making an emotional connection with the brand, and imbuing it with a unique brand personality. With brand emotions and personality elicited, the liking for the brand also shifts upwards.

Other work by Lloyd and Woodside (2013) suggests that the use of animal symbols in brand communication that is implicitly or explicitly anthropomorphic, activates cultural schema that the brand represents, thereby strengthening the brand's equity and effectiveness of its message. Puzakova, Rocerto and Kwak (2013), on the other hand, find that the effect of an anthropomorphized recommendation agent on attitude towards a brand message is predominantly negative when the recommendation itself requires that the customer reveal personally sensitive information, thereby highlighting an interesting and an important boundary condition for the potential benefits of brand anthropomorphism.

Consumer relationships with brands

Beyond its influence on evaluations, anthropomorphism also affects emotional connections to brands as it did with products and provides the basis for, and interpretation of experiences with the brand over time. A very influential paper by Fournier (1998) argued that consumers form relationships with brands much like their relationships with other people in a social context. People think of brands as social partners and interact with them in a number of ways, forming complex relationships such as flings, committed partnerships, arranged marriages, best friendships and even enslavements. Thus, Fournier (1998) suggested that consumers anthropomorphize brands as being akin to real people, and that these relationships are real lived experiences that give meaning to their lives.

Building on this work, Aggarwal (2004) proposed that consumers often apply norms of interpersonal relationships in their interactions with brands, and that these norms guide people's behaviour as well as their evaluations of the brands. Specifically, Aggarwal (2004) used the framework of communal relationships in which people are motivated by mutual care and concern and exchange relationships in which people are motivated by a need for quid pro quo.

He found that how the brand and its actions will be evaluated by the consumers depends on whether the particular relationship norms are upheld or violated.

Recent work by Aggarwal and McGill (2012) further explored the effect of brand anthropomorphism on consumers' actions. Drawing on prior research on the behaviour of people when primed with social groups (e.g., the elderly; Cesario, Plaks, & Higgins, 2006), the central finding of this research is that anthropomorphized brands trigger people's goals for a successful social interaction, resulting in behaviour that is assimilative or contrastive to the brand's image depending on what might best achieve the social goal. Three studies show that consumers are more likely to assimilate behaviour associated with anthropomorphized partner brands that they like, consistent with the goal of drawing in the liked co-producer, and servant brands that they dislike, consistent with the goal of pushing the disliked would-be helper away by signalling self-sufficiency. Results also show a contrastive behaviour when primed with disliked partner brands and liked servant brands. No effects of liking or image (partner or servant) were observed for brands that were not anthropomorphized, supporting the view that anthropomorphism leads consumers to interact with brands as they would with other people in a social context. Findings of this research also reveal that anthropomorphized brands may influence consumer behaviour outside the brand context, not just in direct interaction with the brand. These findings lead to the intriguing possibility that perceived similarities between people and their chosen brands may not reflect consumers' selecting brands that seem to suit their identities but instead may reflect people acting like the brands they have selected (for other reasons). Interestingly, this surprising consumer behaviour was observed in diverse decision domains such as fitness, risk taking and academic performance.

Rauschnabel and Ahuvia (2014) find another interesting effect of brand anthropomorphism: an increase in brand love which in turn predicts greater brand loyalty. Their research suggests that anthropomorphic thinking leads to stronger consumer–brand relationships, which in turn leads to greater integration of the brand into the consumer's self-identity. This research identifies five theoretical mechanisms through which anthropomorphism could influence brand love: category-level evaluation, cognitive fluency, cognitive consistency, self extension and self-congruence.

Extensions: Power, risk, patience and pro-social behaviour

Consumer researchers have recently extended the investigation of anthropomorphism to other entities than products and brands, such as diseases and time, and in so doing have considered other kinds of judgements and behaviour such as risk perception, patience and pro-social behaviour. This research also introduces other moderating factors to the influence of anthropomorphism such as social power or the perception of an entity and moral agent or patient.

Power and control

Kim and McGill (2011) studied how people's feelings of power might influence their beliefs about risk-bearing entities such as gambling devices and diseases. In this research, the slot machine was anthropomorphized through design elements that resembled a face and the disease was anthropomorphized by describing it as part of a criminal family. These researchers found that risk perceptions are systematically influenced by product anthropomorphism, and that these effects are moderated by individual's feelings of social power. In particular, consumers who felt themselves to have a high level of social power thought they were more likely to win while playing a slot machine and were less likely to get skin cancer when these items were anthropomorphized, presumably because high-power consumers believed they could control the humanized entity. The reverse effects, albeit somewhat weaker for the disease study, were observed for low-power participants, who presumably thought the anthropomorphized entity could dominate them in a harmful way. Hence, people judged riskiness by applying their expectations for a social interaction when the entity was anthropomorphized, instead of considering mechanical processes of the machine or biological processes of the disease.

Kim and McGill (2011) also noted that people's willingness to anthropomorphize depended on whether the entity appeared to have conformed to social rules. In a third study, high-power people who won frequently saw an ambiguous slot machine as more human than those who lost while the reverse was true for low-power people. These findings align with the those of Puzakova, Kwak and Rocertao (2009) who posited that having high need for control would induce consumers to explain brands' behaviours through anthropomorphic representations (e.g., intentions, desires) of the brand.

Research by May and Monga (2014), who also examine the effect of perceived power and anthropomorphism but in the context of humanizing time, shows that time anthropomorphism reduces patience for low-power (but not high-power) individuals because anthropomorphism makes the aversive force of wait time seem more potent (i.e., more aversive) to those who feel less potent themselves (i.e., low-power individuals). These authors verify the effect on patience and confirm the process via both mediation (i.e., the effect is mediated by how aversively time is perceived) and moderation (i.e., the effect reverses when time is made to seem beneficent). Thus, they introduce time as a consequential anthropomorphic entity, and present novel effects on intertemporal preferences.

Kim and Kramer (2015) took a different tack in the investigation of power and anthropomorphism by studying the type of power observed in hierarchical social structures. This research incorporated perceptions of brands as partners and brands as servants as studied by Aggarwal and McGill (2012) and found different preferences depending on the degree of materialism among consumers. Materialism was viewed in this work as a value system that emphasizes possession and ownership as a route to happiness. Because this value system facilitates a master–servant hierarchical relationship, more materialistic consumers preferred a servant brand to a partner brand when the brands were anthropomorphized, and they responded more favourably to the anthropomorphized servant brand than did less materialistic consumers. This line of research further showcases the importance of looking beyond the effects of anthropomorphizing brands and products to the nature of the relationships consumers anticipate with these anthropomorphized entities.

Pro-social behaviour

The extent to which the anthropomorphized entity can affect people's pro-social behaviour is highlighted in recent work by Ahn, Kim and Aggarwal (2014) and Tam, Lee and Chao (2013). Tam et al. (2013) examine the context of people's concern for the environment and suggest that anthropomorphizing the environment (e.g., Mr Nature or Mother Earth), makes people more connected to the cause, and hence more likely to comply with it. Thus, this research finds that anthropomorphism of nature was associated with connectedness to nature, which in turn led to conservation behaviour. These findings held across different operationalizations of anthropomorphism of nature and multiple measures of conservation behaviour.

Ahn et al. (2014), on the other hand, extend this idea to examine multiple types of pro-social issues such as those related to environment, energy and recycling, and found that when an anthropomorphized pro-social cause such as "Save electricity" delivered an emotional appeal showing a humanized lightbulb red hot with heat saying, "I am burning. Please turn me off!" individuals were more likely to comply with the request compared to when the same bulb appealed in a non-anthropomorphized manner (This bulb is burning. Please turn it off!). These authors suggest that anthropomorphizing a social cause results in an intrinsic incentive for the people to comply with the pro-social cause – the need to avoid aversive feelings of guilt that emanate from harming or not helping another person (in this case, the anthropomorphized social cause) through one's action or inaction. In other words, a request for help from an anthropomorphized entity leads to the activation of anticipatory guilt for not helping it, which is an unpleasant emotional state which then makes people more likely to help.

Looking back and looking forward

Consumer research has examined anthropomorphism of myriad entities including products, brands, diseases, time and the environment revealing important effects on evaluations, emotional connections, attributions, risk perceptions, relationships and behaviour, including actions towards the anthropomorphized entity, pro-social actions and behaviour outside the brand context. Despite this broad array of effects, we provide two somewhat contradictory summary characterizations of this body of work. First, nearly all the papers reviewed support the same broad hypothesis: If consumers think of something as human they evaluate it and respond to it as they would to people. Second, the body of work, beyond this reductionist characterization, does not reveal clear patterns or subareas of investigation. The research appears to reflect "one-off" interests and insights of research teams and while these are individually valuable, for the area to mature, to constitute something other than a list of effects, we encourage two areas for future research. First, we advocate greater investigation of the factors that are distinct to consumers and consumption contexts that promote anthropomorphism. Now that we know anthropomorphism leads to responses akin to those for people, the field should document when we are most likely to see those effects, particularly around unifying principles. Second, we advocate further investigation into differences in the nature of anthropomorphism, degree of anthropomorphism and its form.

With respect to the nature of anthropomorphism, we note that prior research appears to reveal three types. One type is metaphorical such that people apply human terms and schema but know full well that the entity is not human – the human metaphor is handy for the organization and communication of information. Research on brand personality (Aaker, 1997) and schema congruity (Aggarwal & McGill, 2007) appears to fall into this category. A second type reflects non-conscious processes in which anthropomorphism primes knowledge and goals related to human interactions, which guide people's responses. In this case, the consumer is acting *as if* the entity were really a person but would likely desist if that were pointed out to them. Research on power and control (May & Monga, 2014; S. Kim & McGill, 2011; H. C. Kim and Kramer 2015) and priming of behaviour that is assimilative or contrastive of the brand's image might all into this category. A third type, and one that is possibly rare, occurs when the consumer actually believes the entity possesses at least some real human traits going beyond superficial features such as the appearance of a face or body shape to the ability to think and feel. Research on the environment (Tam et al., 2013) might have tapped this form of anthropomorphism. As products grow in technical complexity, drawing further on the fields of artificial intelligence and robotics, this form of anthropomorphism may grow more common. As research on the different types of anthropomorphism progresses, researchers may uncover the differential influence of the manipulations used to date, from giving the entity the look of a person to asking people to think of the entity as a person, to showing the entity engaged in speech.

With respect to the degree and form of anthropomorphism, we advocate moving beyond studies that have looked at anthropomorphism as present or absent to those that manipulate extent of anthropomorphism – a little human, somewhat human, very human – to determine if consumer responses depend on these differences and, perhaps, interact with the nature of anthropomorphism discussed above. As researchers consider partial anthropomorphism further, they might begin a programmatic investigation of the human features afforded non-human entities. Prior research on dehumanization has noted that people can be degraded robotically (as having complex thought but no feelings) or animalistically (as having feelings but not complex thought – Haslam 2006) and that people might be seen as moral agents (acting towards others) or moral patients (being acted upon by others – see Ahn et al., 2014 for further discussion). In the same vein, it would be interesting to see how might objects and concepts be given some human traits but not others under different circumstances and with differential implications.

Consistent with this idea, Touré-Tillery and McGill (2015) report that anthropomorphized entities may be perceived as more credible than actual people at least among some consumers. Specifically, these authors found that advertisements in which anthropomorphized entities (e.g., "talking" lamps) serve as spokespeople and are more persuasive than those in which real people deliver the product claims but only among consumers who are low in interpersonal trust. This finding thereby supports the possibility that anthropomorphized entities might be seen as better than real people at least sometimes and opens the door to considerations of when they might sometimes be seen as worse. It further supports the importance of investigating the degree to which a brand or object is anthropomorphized because the core effect is anchored in the partial humanity of the anthropomorphized objects. Specifically, the anthropomorphized entities were given enough humanity to convey an advertising message but, apparently, not enough humanity to trigger the natural wariness that consumers who are low in interpersonal trust commonly apply to commercial messages.

In sum research on anthropomorphism has just begun with the research summarized in this chapter laying the base for a deeper, more programmatic investigation of this fascinating topic. As the field moves from documenting effects to building conceptual frameworks, we anticipate an enriched understanding of consumers' relationships to the brands, products and concepts that comprise central and meaningful aspects of their lives.

References

Aaker, J. (1997). Dimensions of brand personality. *Journal of Marketing Research, 34*(3), 347–356.

Aggarwal, P. (2004). The effects of brand relationship norms on consumer attitudes and behaviour. *Journal of Consumer Research, 31*(1), 87–101.

Aggarwal, P., & McGill, A. L. (2007). Is that car smiling at me? Schema congruity as a basis for evaluating anthropomorphized products. *Journal of Consumer Research, 34*(4), 468–479.

Aggarwal, P., & McGill, A. L. (2012). When brands seem human, do humans act like brands? Automatic behavioural priming effects of brand anthropomorphism. *Journal of Consumer Research, 39*(2), 307–323.

Ahn, H. K., Kim, H. J., & Aggarwal, P. (2014). Helping fellow beings: Anthropomorphized social causes and the role of anticipatory guilt. *Psychological Science, 25*(1), 224–229.

Antonacopoulos, N. M. D., & Pychyl, T. A. (2008). An examination of the relations between social support, anthropomorphism and stress among dog owners. *Anthrozoös, 21*(2), 139–152.

Barker, K. (1996). *Animal stories* (pp. 282–94). New York, NY: Routledge.

Barrett, J. L. (1998). Cognitive constraints on Hindu concepts of the divine. *Journal for the Scientific Study of Religion, 37*(4), 608–619.

Barrett, J. L., & Richert, R. A. (2003). Anthropomorphism or preparedness? Exploring children's god concepts. *Review of Religious Research, 44*(3), 300–312.

Baumeister, R. F., & Leary. M. R. (1995). The need to belong: Desire for interpersonal attachments as a fundamental human-motivation. *Psychological Bulletin, 117*(3), 497–529.

Biel, A. L. (2000). Converting image into equity. In D. A. Aaker & A. L. Biel (Eds.), *Brand equity and advertising: Advertisings role in building strong brands* (pp. 67–82). Hillsdale, NJ: Lawrence Erlbaum Associates.
Bradshaw, J., & Casey, R. (2007). Anthropomorphism and anthropocentrism as influences in the quality of life of companion animals. *Animal Welfare, 16*, 149–154.
Brown, S. (2010). Where the wild brands are: Some thoughts on anthropomorphic marketing. *Marketing Review, 10*(3), 209–224.
Burger, J. M., & Cooper, H. M. (1979). The desirability of control. *Motivation and Emotion, 3*(4), 381–393.
Burger, J. M., & Hemans, L. T. (1988). Desire for control and the use of attribution processes. *Journal of Personality, 56*(3), 531–546.
Burghardt, G. M. (2013). Environmental enrichment and cognitive complexity in reptiles and amphibians: Concepts, review, and implications for captive populations. *Applied Animal Behaviour Science, 147*(3/4), 286–298.
Burgoon, J. K., Bonito, J. A., Bengtsson, B., Cederberg, C., Lundeberg, M., & Allspach, L. (2000). Interactivity in human–computer interaction: A study of credibility, understanding, and influence. *Computers in Human Behaviour, 16*(6), 553–574.
Caruso, E. M., Waytz, A., & Epley, N. (2010). The intentional mind and the hot hand: Perceiving intentions makes streaks seem likely to continue. *Cognition, 116*(1), 149–153.
Cesario, J., Plaks, J. E., & Higgins, E. T. (2006). Automatic social behaviour as motivated preparation to interact. *Journal of Personality and Social Psychology, 90*(6), 893–910.
Chandler, J., & Schwarz, N. (2010). Use does not wear ragged the fabric of friendship: Thinking of objects as alive makes people less willing to replace them. *Journal of Consumer Psychology, 20*(2), 138–145.
Clark, J. D., Rager, D. R., & Calpin, J. P. (1997). Animal well-being. II. Stress and distress. *Laboratory Science, 47*(6), 571–579.
Dawes, R. M., & Mulford, M. (1996). The false consensus effect and overconfidence: Flaws in judgment or flaws in how we study judgment. *Organizational Behaviour and Human Decision Processes, 65*(3), 201–211.
Delbaere, M., McQuarrie, E. F., & Phillips, B. J. (2011). Personification in advertising: Using a visual metaphor to trigger anthropomorphism. *Journal of Advertising, 40*(1), 121–130.
Duffy, B. R. (2003). Anthropomorphism and the social robot. *Robotics and Autonomous, 42*(3/4), 177–190.
Eddy, T. J., Gallup, G. G., & Povinelli, D. J. (1993). Attribution of cognitive states to animals: Anthropomorphism in comparative perspective. *Journal of Social Issues, 49*(1), 87–101.
Ellingsen, K., Zanella, A. J., Bjerkås, E., & Indrebø, A. (2010). The relationship between empathy, perception of pain and attitudes toward pets among Norwegian dog owners. *Anthrozoös, 23*(3), 231–243.
Epley, N., Akalis, S., Waytz, A., & Cacioppo, J. T. (2008). Creating social connection through inferential reproduction: Loneliness and perceived agency in gadgets, gods, and greyhounds. *Psychological Science, 19*(2), 114–120.
Epley, N., Waytz, A., & Cacioppo, J. T. (2007). On seeing human: A three-factor theory of anthropomorphism. *Psychological Review, 114*(4), 864–886.
Fournier, S. (1998). Consumers and their brands: Developing relationship theory in consumer research. *Journal of Consumer Research, 24*(4), 343–373.
Gray, K., & Wegner, D. M. (2010). Blaming god for our pain: Human suffering and the divine mind. *Personality and Social Psychology Review, 14*(1), 7–16.
Green, R. D., MacDorman, K. F., Ho, C. C., & Vasudevan, S. (2008). Sensitivity to the proportions of faces that vary in human likeness. *Computers in Human Behaviour, 24*(5), 2456–2474.
Guthrie, S. (1993). *Faces in the clouds: A new theory of religion*. New York, NY: Oxford University Press.
Hart, P. M., Jones, S. R., & Royne, M. B. (2013). The human lens: How anthropomorphic reasoning varies by product complexity and enhances personal value. *Journal of Marketing Management, 29*(1/2), 105–121.
Haslam, N. (2006). Dehumanization: An integrative review. *Personality and Social Psychology Review, 10*(3), 252–264.
Horowitz, A. C., & Bekoff, M. (2007). Naturalizing anthropomorphism: Behavioural prompts to our humanizing of animals. *Anthrozoös, 20*(1), 23–35.
Ishiguro, H. (2006). Android science: Conscious and subconscious recognition. *Connection Science, 18*(4), 319–332.
Keaveney, S. M., Herrmann, A., Befurt, R., & Landwehr, J. R. (2012). The eyes have it: How a car's face influences consumer categorization and evaluation of product line extensions. *Psychology and Marketing, 29*(1), 36–51.

Kim, H. C., & Kramer, T. (2015). Do materialists prefer the "brand-as-servant"? The interactive effect of anthropomorphized brand roles and materialism on consumer responses. *Journal of Consumer Research, 42*(1), 284–299.

Kim, S., & McGill, A. L. (2011). "Gaming with Mr. Slot or gaming the slot machine? Power, anthropomorphism, and risk perception. *Journal of Consumer Research, 38*(1), 94–107.

Kim, Y., & Sundar, S. S. (2012). Anthropomorphism of computers: Is it mindful or mindless? *Computers in Human Behaviour, 28*(1), 241–250.

Kwan, V. S.Y., Gosling, S. D., & John, O. P. (2008). Anthropomorphism as a special case of social perception: A cross-species social relations model analysis of humans and dogs. *Social Cognition, 26*(2), 129–142.

Landwehr, J. R., McGill, A. L., & Herrmann, A. (2011). It's got the look: The effect of friendly and aggressive "facial" expressions on product liking and sales. *Journal of Marketing, 75*(3), 132–146.

Lane, J. D., Wellman, H. M., & Evans, E. M. (2010). Children's understanding of ordinary and extraordinary minds. *Child Development, 81*(5), 1475–1489.

Li, G. (2008). How social is social responses to computers? The function of the degree of anthropomorphism in computer representations. *Computers in Human Behaviour, 24*(4), 1494–1509.

Lloyd, S., & Woodside, A. G. (2013). Animals, archetypes, and advertising (A3): The theory and the practice of customer brand symbolism. *Journal of Marketing Management, 29*(1/2), 5–25.

Luczak, H., Roetting, M., & Schmidt, L. (2003). Let's talk: Anthropomorphization as means to cope with stress of interacting with technical devices. *Ergonomics, 46*(13/14), 1361–1374.

Makris, N., & Pnevmatikos, D. (2007). Children's understanding of human and super-natural mind. *Cognitive Development, 22*(3), 365–375.

Mandler, G. (1982). The structure of value: Accounting for taste. In M. S. Clark & S. T. Fiske (Eds.), *Affect and cognition: The 17th annual carnegie symposium* (pp. 3–36). Hillsdale, NJ: Lawrence Erlbaum Associates.

May, F., & Monga, A. (2014). When time has a will of its own, the powerless don't have the will to wait: Anthropomorphism of time can decrease patience. *Journal of Consumer Research, 40*(5), 924–942.

Miesler, L. (2012). Product choice and anthropomorphic designs: Do consumption goals shape innate preferences for human-like forms? *Design Journal, 15*(3), 373–392.

Miesler, L., Leder, H., & Herrmann, A. (2011). Isn't it cute: An evolutionary perspective of baby-schema effects in visual product designs. *International Journal of Design, 5*(3), 17–30.

Morewedge, C. K., Preston, J., & Wegner, D. M. (2007). Timescale bias in the attribution of mind. *Journal of Personality and Social Psychology, 93*(1), 1–11.

Mori, M., MacDorman, K. F., & Kageki, N. (2012). The uncanny valley [from the field]. *Robotics and Automation Magazine, 19*(2), 98–100.

Nass, C., Fogg, B. J., & Moon, Y. (1996). Can computers be teammates? *International Journal of Human-Computers Studies, 45*(6), 669–678.

Nass, C, & Moon, Y. (2000). Machines and mindlessness: Social responses to computers. *Journal of Social Issues, 56*(1), 81–103.

Nass, C., Steuer, J., & Tauber, E. R. (1994). Computers are social actors. *Human factors in computing systems, chi '94 conference proceedings – celebrating interdependence*, 72–78.

Neave, N., Jackson, R., Saxton, T., & Hönekopp, J. (2015). The influence of anthropomorphic tendencies on human hoarding behaviours. *Personality and Individual Differences, 72*, 214–219.

Nenkov, G. Y., & Scott, M. L. (2014). "So cute I could eat it up": Priming effects of cute products on indulgent consumption. *Journal of Consumer Research, 41*(2), 326–341.

Puzakova, M., Kwak, H., & Rocereto, J. F. (2009). Pushing the envelope of brand and personality: Antecedents and moderators of anthropomorphized brands. *Advances in Consumer Research, 36*, 413–420.

Puzakova, M., Kwak, H., & Rocereto, J. F. (2013). When humanizing brands goes wrong: The detrimental effect of brand anthropomorphization amid product wrongdoings. *Journal of Marketing*, 77(3), 81–100.

Puzakova, M., Rocereto, J. F., & Kwak, H. (2013). Ads are watching me: A view from the interplay between anthropomorphism and customization. *International Journal of Advertising: The Quarterly Review of Marketing Communications, 32*(4), 513–538.

Rauschnabel, P. A., & Ahuvia, A. C. (2014). You're so lovable: Anthropomorphism and brand love. *Journal of Brand Management, 21*(5), 372–395.

Tam, K. P., Lee, S. L., & Chao, M. M. (2013). Saving Mr. Nature: Anthropomorphism enhances connectedness to and protectiveness toward nature. *Journal of Experimental Social Psychology, 49*(3), 514–521.

Timpano, K. R., & Shaw, A. M. (2013). Conferring humanness: The role of anthropomorphism in hoarding. *Personality and Individual Differences, 54*(3), 383–388.

Touré-Tillery, M., & McGill, A. L. (2015). Who or what to believe: Interpersonal trust and the differential persuasiveness of anthropomorphized and human agents. *Journal of Marketing, 79*(July), 94–110.

Tremoulet, P. D., & Feldman, J. (2000). Perception of animacy from the motion of a single object. *Perception –London, 29*(8), 943–952.

Van den Hende, E. A., & Mugge, R. (2014). Investigating gender-schema congruity effects on consumers' evaluation of anthropomorphized products. *Psychology and Marketing, 31*(4), 264–277.

Veer, E. (2013). Made with real crocodiles: The use of anthropomorphism to promote product kinship in our youngest consumers. *Journal of Marketing Management, 29*(1/2), 195–206.

Waytz, A., Cacioppo, J. T., & Epley, N. (2010). Who sees humans? The stability and importance of individual differences in anthropomorphism. *Perspectives on Psychological Science, 5*(3), 219–232.

Wemelsfelder, F. (2007). How animals communicate quality of life: The qualitative assessment of animal behaviour. *Animal Welfare, 16*(S), 25–31.

Wemelsfelder, F., Hunter, T. E. A., Mendl, M. T., & Lawrence, A. B. (2001). Assessing the "whole animal": A free choice profiling approach. *Animal Behaviour, 62*(2), 209–220.

Werblowsky, R. J. Z. (1987). Anthropomorphism. *Encyclopedia of Religion, 1*, 316–320.

Windhager, S., Hutzler, F., Carbon, C. C., Oberzaucher, E., Schaefer, K., Thorstensen, T., et al. (2010). Laying eyes on highlights: Eye movements suggest facial features in cars. *Collegium Antropologicum, 34*(3), 1075–1080.

Part VII
Internet and electronic media

32

Novel phenomena, evolving frameworks

Exploring social influence in the online world

Rebecca Walker Reczek and Cait Lamberton

Only connect! That was the whole of her sermon.
Only connect the prose and the passion, and both will be exalted,
And human love will be seen at its height.
Live in fragments no longer.
Only connect...

E.M. Forster (2013 [1910], p. 172)

Despite the enormous volume of research exploring the behaviours of consumers as isolated actors, it is obvious that we can have profound influences on one another. The presence of others has been shown to affect the way we process and recall information (Geen, 1971, 1973, 1974, 1979), learn (Burwitz & Newell, 1972; Martens, 1969), allocate resources in couples (Dzhogleva & Lamberton, 2014) and even when we laugh (Chapman, 1973). Further, over the course of the lifespan, observing and interacting with other individuals and groups can prompt compliance (Brock, 1965; Brown & Reingen, 1987; Naylor, Lamberton, & Norton, 2011; Simons, Berkowitz, & Moyer, 1970), conformity (Asch, 1951; Gerard, Wilhelmy, & Conolley, 1968; Naylor, Lamberton, & West, 2012; Rosenberg, 1961) or differentiation (Chan, Berger, & Van Boven, 2012; Tian, Bearden, & Hunter, 2001). For example, observing others similar to the self supporting a brand will lead to greater affinity for the brand (Escalas & Bettman, 2003), while observing dissimilar others supporting a brand can lead consumers to avoid the brand (Berger & Heath, 2007; White & Dahl, 2006, 2007). The vast majority of research aimed at understanding how social influence affects consumers has focused on offline, in-person connections, previously considered the primary source of social influence. However, the volume of influence to which consumers now expose themselves and exert on others in online settings may approach or eclipse in-person influence opportunities. 82 per cent of adults worldwide now use social networking sites, totalling 1.2 billion users (Pring, 2012), highlighting the fact that connections may occur within and between diverse geographies, across cultures, among both online and offline friends, and with strangers known only in the virtual world. And while approximately 40 per cent of all users regularly search for products using Twitter, implying that consumers are interested in interacting with brands online, 73 per cent of consumers are skeptical that firms are using social media for anything but advertising – suggesting that consumers may also be less influenced by firms than they are by other consumers in online settings (Forrester, 2012). Supporting the importance of consumer-to-consumer communication about products online, in a survey conducted in 2013, approximately two-thirds of respondents reported reading online reviews, with Facebook the most common source for positive product reviews and online review sites the most common source for negative reviews (Gesenhues, 2013). Combined, these and related statistics suggest that social influence online is both sought and experienced as an everyday component in consumers' lives.

As such, understanding social influence online is critical if we want to understand the vast majority of consumers' behaviour in their present lived experience. In the first section of the chapter, we discuss the evolution of social influence research as it has moved from offline to online settings. We then introduce four key areas where social influence research or popular press observation has begun to uncover phenomena distinct to this modality of influence, highlighting recent research that offers preliminary frameworks for study and noting areas that remain in need of rigorous exploration and theoretical development.

From social impact theory to mere virtual presence

We never know which lives we influence, or when, or why.

Stephen King (2011, p, 454)

Beginning with Allport (1920), modern psychologists have recognized that the people around us can exert strong influences on our behaviour. Arguably the most fundamental contemporary framework for understanding social influence was presented by Bibb Latané, who along with John Darley, developed Social Impact Theory (Latané, 1981).

In his ground-breaking paper, Latané draws on research conducted across a wide range of in-person contexts, including judging line lengths (Asch, 1951, 1952, 1956), gawking at a window (Milgram, Bickman, & Berkowitz, 1969), stuttering (Porter, 1939) and tipping (Freeman et al., 1975), in order to develop a meta-theory of influence based on the hard sciences' understanding of psychophysical impacts. In Social Impact Theory (SIT), the influence of one person on another is dependent on the strength of the source of the interpersonal influence, the immediacy of the source and the number of sources sending a message. Social influence is at its strongest when the influence is provided by important or powerful sources, the sources are in close physical proximity to the target and the source individuals are present in large numbers.

Consumer research has provided important qualifications to SIT. For example, consumer behaviour work has showed that the *mere presence* of others (see Chapman, 1974; Markus, 1978) influences buyer behaviour in ways unique to retail settings. For example, consumers are more likely to buy name brand products, spend less time making decisions and are less likely to physically touch products when even a single other person, who they do not know, is present in an aisle with them. Mere presence effects are exhibited when simply having others in one's environment alters one's behaviour, even though they do not interact with a given target individual and are typically strangers lacking source strength (Argo, Dahl, & Manchanda, 2005; Dahl, Manchanda, & Argo, 2001).

Recent work suggests that understanding online social influence requires yet further deviations from SIT. In an online environment, the requirements outlined in SIT for social influence to be exerted are not present. Our actions both online and offline (i.e., the products we choose to buy, the causes we choose to support, etc.) may be significantly influenced by those we encounter online, even though we may never share physical proximity with them or even know their true identity (given that consumers may post and review under pseudonyms or anonymously).

Departing from SIT as well as the mere presence framework, research on *mere virtual presence* (MVP) has shown that brand attitudes and purchase behaviour can be altered through the simple depiction of other brand supporters via thumbnail-size profile pictures shown on Facebook or other social networking sites (Naylor et al., 2012). In this work, a target individual's response to the depiction of others as supporters of a brand depends on their similarity or dissimilarity to the pictured consumers – similar others prompt conformity with brand support, whereas dissimilar others squelch positive brand attitudes. Importantly, differences in influence are observed even when the size of the influencing group is small (usually six people in Naylor et al.'s 2012 studies), they are unknown to the target and have no specific reason to have high-source strength and they are in potentially enormous physical distance from the target consumer.

Thus, as we have moved from every day to retail to online settings, the basic frameworks for understanding social influence appear to have shifted. We anticipate further shifts, as new online contexts and ways of interacting with others continue to evolve. In the sections that follow, we highlight some unique phenomena that have sparked preliminary understandings of social influence in the online world and offer fertile ground for new work. We focus specifically on four key areas for understanding online social influence: (1) the desire to "share," (2) the impact of hidden versus revealed identities, (3) social shopping and consumption and (4) the intersection and relative potential of the online and offline worlds to shape behaviour.

The drive to share

> *You are what you share.*
>
> C.W. Leadbeater (2008, p. 1)

Seminal work in marketing identifies some consumers – called "market mavens", as primary sources of social influence, possessing an inherent drive to share marketplace information and experiences with others (Feick & Price, 1987). Research in both marketing and psychology has also focused on identifying specific individuals as trusted opinion leaders (Flynn, Goldsmith, & Eastman, 1996; Katz, 1957; Merton, 1968), who consume and interpret media or other information (e.g., information about new products) and then share their opinions with other less-informed or able consumers.

It is important to note that much of the work on market mavenism and opinion leadership was conducted before the advent of social media. While market mavens and opinion leaders no doubt exist in an online world (and are probably more likely to engage in influential activities like writing blogs or having their own YouTube channel than the average consumer), in an online world, anyone with an Internet connection can access vast amounts of information as well as share their opinions on it. In fact, given social media's penetration, it does not appear that the *desire* to share is restricted to only a certain subset of consumers. Rather, it may be assumed that the vast majority of social media users all display, to varying degrees, a fundamental desire to share, though the forums they use, the types of content they share and their motivation for doing so may vary. Further, the consequences of sharing may differ across sharing platforms, types of content and individuals. We now discuss the way this desire to share is manifest in online settings.

Where, what and why are consumers sharing

In 2013, Facebook held sway as the most popular social networking site in the world, followed by YouTube. Recent trends in "where" consumers choose to share include the rise of non-US based platforms (e.g., the China-only site Qzone), as well as incredible growth in messaging-only platforms, such as WhatsApp, and increasing focus on the visual, as seen by the growth in primarily pictorial platforms like Tumblr, Instagram and Pinterest (Moritz, 2013; Smith, 2013).

Where consumers choose to share information appears to be both a function of demographics, including where consumers live (as some sites are restricted to a single country) (Smith, 2013), gender (e.g., Pinterest is more popular with women than with men, and LinkedIn is more popular with men than with women) (MarketingCharts, 2014) and age (e.g., Instagram is more popular with those 18–29 than those 30–49) (Marketing Charts, 2014). However, which social networking site a consumer chooses can shift rapidly and can be difficult to predict, as new competitors can quickly supplant older networks (as Facebook did to MySpace). What is perhaps more enduring than where consumers choose to share is what they choose to share and why they choose to share it.

Typology of shared content

Content shared in social media contexts can be broadly grouped into three main types: (1) personal content, (2) experiential content and (3) commercial content. Personal content refers to daily experiences, hobbies and opinions that consumers may be driven to share with others. While this may include references to consumption, this type of communication is not expressly intended to persuade others about specific brands or products, but rather, to facilitate interpersonal connection and affiliation. Examples of this type of content include status updates or Tweets about what the consumer is doing that day, opinions about news events, family photos, etc. Research shows that, as may be expected given platform differences, such self-disclosure information is generally most common on Twitter and Facebook, and that consumers tend to focus on positive information rather than negative information about their own lives (Bronner & deHoog, 2014).

Experiential content allows social media users to literally share the same experience with others online – not perhaps simultaneously, but by posting and allowing others to access the associated media. Examples of this type of sharing include sharing a link to a funny viral video or an emotion-provoking advertisement on Facebook, posting a recipe on Pinterest, tweeting a link to a news story etc.

Commercial content is the deliberate transmission of information intended to persuade or inform about particular brands or products. This type of content includes online reviews or comments on a brand's Facebook or Twitter account and is also referred to as "nontraditional word of mouth" (Chen & Xie, 2008; Das & Chen, 2007; Godes et al., 2005). Like traditional word-of-mouth, such content "influences consumers' product trial and adoption (Arndt, 1967; Sheth, 1971), switching behaviour (Wangenheim & Bayon, 2004) and attitudes (Bone, 1995), which in turn influence firms' sales and revenues (Chevalier & Mayzlin, 2006; Dellarocas, Zhang, & Awad, 2007)" (Moore, 2012, p. 1140).

As this framework suggests, many different types of content can be shared online. Some work has begun to explore the precise nature of the most "sharable" content. For example, Berger & Milkman's (2012) analysis suggest that more practically useful, surprising, interesting, positive and emotionally arousing news articles are more likely to be transmitted by email. However, much remains to be learned about the relationship between type of content and the platform on which it is shared. Further, as Berger and Iyengar (2013) show, people share different content online as opposed to in person. Specifically, these authors found that consumers tend to discuss more "interesting" products and brands online than they do offline. Continuing this line of inquiry is an important avenue for future research for both consumers and firms: How does what is shared online differ from what is shared offline? Does this differ cross-culturally, such that consumers from collectivist cultures with more interdependent self-construals (Markus & Kitayama, 1991; Oyserman, Coon, & Kemmelmeier, 2002) are more likely to share information that helps them affiliate with relevant social others (e.g., sharing experiential content they think will be enjoyed by those in their social network) while those with more individualist self-construals are more likely to share information designed to create or affirm an individual online persona (e.g., personal content designed to display their uniqueness to others)? Why, and among which consumers, does the mode of sharing alter content, in tone, extremity or valence? And, at the most fundamental level, why do consumers decide to share content online and how do these motives differ across types of content and platform?

Motives for sharing in the social media environment

One obvious motivation for sharing online, as it is offline, is to accumulate social capital. Differing from an offline setting, however, online forums allow even "ordinary people" to obtain "megaphones" – thereby amassing substantial audiences without any professional intermediary (McQuarrie, Miller, & Phillips, 2013). The presence of an enormous potential audience, or of a small but important audience, raises the probability that online sharing will be used as a means of managing one's self-presentation. Depending on the self that one wishes to present to the world, we may expect that different individuals will choose different platforms and content to share. For example, a consumer who wishes to build a large public following, and become a perceived expert in a particular domain (e.g., fashion, cooking, sports), may choose to start a blog on Tumblr or to create a YouTube channel, while a consumer who wishes to share details of his or her daily life only with friends and family may opt to use Facebook for status updates and posting family pictures.

Classic work in the offline world shows that self-presentation may include both real and fraudulent signals (e.g., Goffman, 1951), making it difficult to understand the real nature of those around us. The same is perhaps even more obviously challenging in the online world, both as perpetrated by consumers and firms. In recent years, "catfishing," or presenting a fake profile in an online dating site, has gained widespread attention. Indeed, academic research shows that much information presented in online dating sites may be false, but that individuals balance their desire to falsify against the possibility of future interaction (Toma, Hancock, & Ellison, 2008). Further, firms' use of guerrilla marketing tactics, such as the use of paid spokespeople disguised as ordinary consumers to post positive reviews, has gained both legal and popular press attention, with some commentators arguing that it is even more damaging than traditional false advertising (Streitfield, 2013). However, work providing a framework for consumers' detection of and responses to false signals online remains nascent and thus offers fertile ground for future work. Researchers could fruitfully explore both consumers' perceptions of others' motives for posting on social media and how these perceptions affect their response to a given post. For example, if consumers believe a given post is motivated solely by the desire to persuade, their persuasion knowledge (Friestad & Wright, 1994) may be activated, resulting in reactance (Campbell & Kirmani, 2000). Future research could also explore the cues consumers use to detect different motives for sharing (e.g., to persuade, inform or entertain others for their own enjoyment or to enhance their own image) by both brands and other consumers.

Such research may be particularly important, as recent research suggests that consumers' general motivation for sharing content on social media may shift over time as social media users become more experienced. Toubia and Stephen (2013) build on prior pro-social behaviour research (e.g. Glazer & Konrad, 1996; Bénabou & Tirole, 2006; Ariely, Bracha, & Meier,

2009) and online survey research (e.g. Bughin, 2007; Hennig-Turau et al., 2004) that makes the distinction between intrinsic and image-related utility of sharing to understand this shift. In an online context, intrinsic utility is provided simply via enjoyment of the activity of sharing, as described in psychological work discussing intrinsic motivation. By contrast, sharing provides image-related utility inasmuch as it confers status or prestige on the sharer. Through a clever experiment, Toubia and Stephen (2013) are able to show that most non-commercial users evolve in their motivation to use social media, beginning with intrinsic utility when they have a small audience and progressing to image-related utility as their follower group grows. Additional research may explore transitions in other motivations to share, as social media and its users mature and evolve.

Consequences of sharing

Regardless of consumers' motivations to share, recent research also suggests that some surprising and perhaps unwanted consequences can emerge from online sharing.

Self-revelation. As Belk notes (2013) in his discussion of the extended self in the digital world, online sharing can be thought of as including two major facets: self-revelation and loss of control. The first, self-revelation, offers numerous opportunities for research, as the online context offers different possibilities for sharing personal content and norms about doing so compared to the offline world. As an example, sharing a photo of one's meal on Facebook or Instagram would not be considered out of the ordinary, but the same behaviour in person (e.g., showing colleagues the same photograph at work the next day) would be considered odd and potentially inappropriate. Thus, what constitutes "oversharing" in the online world may be different than in the offline environment. Recent research suggests that context plays an important role in determining the extent to which individuals engage in self-revelation, such that consumers are relatively insensitive to cues about the risks of self-disclosure in online settings (John, Acquisti, & Loewenstein, 2011). Clinical psychologists have argued that excessive or indiscriminate sharing online may serve the purpose of allowing us to connect to others. However, anecdotal evidence suggests that oversharing can lead to what has been referred to as the "post-conversation cringe", (Bernstein, 2013), a common offline phenomenon.

Further, while first amendment rights protect individuals' rights to disclose at will in the offline world, the courts have repeatedly upheld decisions to terminate employment based on individuals' online sharing (Simpson, 2009). Posting about personal behaviours that might be accepted by some friends can turn into a disaster when social media facilitates a wider audience, with the blame going to the posting individual (Giacobbe, 2013). Such instances suggest that we lack a comprehensive framework for defining oversharing in the online world, as well as an understanding of its prevalence – when is it most likely to occur? Among whom? On which platforms? And do the consequences of oversharing differ based on the way these questions are answered?

Other work suggests that sharing even positive word-of-mouth, usually associated with positive affect, may decrease consumers' happiness. Specifically, Cheema and Kaikati (2010) find that if individuals high in need for uniqueness recommend publicly-consumed items to others, those objects lose their ability to distinguish them from the crowd. That is, high-need-for-uniqueness individuals neither want nor seek a bandwagon; should their own information sharing create one, these individuals will no longer be interested in a previously appreciated good. More specifically, it is increasingly noted that it is not just whether one shares that determines its consequences, but *what* one shares. That is, the nature of shared content may have negative effects, both on readers and authors. Recognizing the effect of content type on readers, in February 2012, Tumblr made the policy to ban blogs that advocated suicide, self-harming behaviours and eating disorders. In a novel exploration, Moore (2012) shows that effects can also accrue to the sharer – depending on the way that one discusses his or her experience. In her work, Moore shows that when online social media users employ "explaining language", that is, language that lays out the causality behind one's actions or opinions, they are able to make sense of their experiences to a greater extent than when they share via storytelling. However, the use of explaining language dampens evaluations of and purchase intentions towards hedonic experiences, dimming the pleasure associated with them. In addition, sharing via explaining language polarizes attitudes towards utilitarian experiences in ways that may or may not reflect good decision making.

Finally, when one considers self-revelation in light of SIT, consumers may be surprised at the amount of influence they may have by sharing online. As consumers are more accustomed to offline social influence, in which they primarily influence only those with whom they share geographic proximity, they may be surprised when something they post is read by another consumer on the other side of the world, shaping his or her attitudes and behaviour. Similarly, when posting anonymous messages, a consumer may be surprised that these messages can still have an impact on others when not backed by a disclosed identity. Educating consumers about the potential influence of what they choose to share (essentially explaining that the tenets of SIT do not always hold online) is extremely important in combating issues like cyber-bullying. Younger consumers, in particular, may not understand the potential impact of what they share online and that it can be as impactful as information shared in offline, face-to-face contexts.

Loss of control

The second facet of sharing, "loss of control" over one's information and behavioural record, raises the thorny question of privacy. While the discussion of regulation lies outside the scope of the current chapter, it can be noted that consumers' desire to influence or be influenced online can lend itself to a number of psychological and practical dangers. Researchers argue that social media creates a sense of "psychological privacy", which may or may not equate to "informational privacy" (Walther, Trepte, & Reinecke, 2011). While consumers may seek to build social capital by sharing large amounts of information, they simultaneously increase the amount of privacy risk they face, as such information may be easily re-posted or shared either by other consumers or by firms (unless the consumer assiduously monitors privacy controls). Future work should explore the inferences that consumers make about the degree of privacy they have when undertaking social interactions online, as well as their willingness to sacrifice privacy in order to satisfy their many motivations for social sharing.

Relatedly, exposure to social influence online may lead to offline losses of control. Wilcox and Stephen's work (2013) was paraphrased by some popular press outlets as suggesting that Facebook makes you "fat and poor" (Mielach, 2012). The research underlying this contention argues that focusing on one's close friends on Facebook raises one's self-esteem. In turn, heightened self-esteem reduces self-control. In addition to a number of experiments establishing causality, the authors report data showing that as Facebook use increases among people with strong ties to their social network, so does body mass index (BMI) and credit card debt.

It may also be the case that virtually experiencing pleasures in the online world can diminish your enjoyment offline. For example, if your friends tend to post pictures of your favourite foods online, recent findings imply that your enjoyment may be decreased (Larson, Redden, & Elder, 2014). As the media has suggested, this may mean that Instagram could, in fact, ruin your meal (Dockterman, 2013).

Even actions that one would expect would bolster one's good behaviour in the offline world may, in fact, be counterproductive. For example, sharing one's beliefs online may dilute one's propensity to act in the offline world. Termed "slacktivism", this effect exists when one's online support of a cause or pro-social behaviour reduces subsequent drive to extend more costly support to the same cause in the offline world (Kristofferson, White, & Peloza, 2014).

Thus, though the motivation to engage in online sharing may be to provide information, obtain a low-cost source of self-affirmation, or build relationships that may enrich our lives, future work should continue to explore the cases when online social influence may expose people, as well as companies, to more negative than positive consequences.

Hiding and revealing identity online

On the internet, no one knows you're a dog.

Cartoonist Peter Steiner, *New Yorker* cartoon, July 5, 1993, as quoted in Belk (2013, p. 481)

Once we have decided to lend our voice to the vast amount of social influence occurring online, we have decisions to make about doing so that do not exist in the offline world. Chief among these is the decision to reveal or conceal our identities as a source of influence. A large part of social media's disruptive power may lie in its ability to promote or eliminate transparency. In 2011, the online entity, "Anonymous", gained widespread media attention for its ability to carry out protests, hacks and pranks against large and powerful entities. Though "Anonymous" members have never desired identification, wearing Guy Fawkes masks when appearing in the offline world, it was acknowledged that, perhaps precisely because they had not revealed a single identity in the online world, the group wielded considerable social influence (Coleman, 2013). Indeed, there may be some advantages to remaining unidentified online. When someone chooses to remain anonymous, they are shielded against discrimination on demographic bases, they can adopt any desired form or personality and they cannot be countered by *ad hominem* arguments.

In fact, whether one reveals or displays one's identity in online social forums may have a strong effect on the type of influence they wield. However, we are still learning about the way identification shapes social influence online. For example, Naylor et al. (2011) demonstrated that consumers are as likely to comply with an online product recommendation from an unidentified (i.e., ambiguous) reviewer as they are with a reviewer who has revealed his or her demographic characteristics to be similar to the target. Naylor et al. (2011) show that in cooperative contexts like review websites where consumers share commercial content online, anonymous others are inferred to be similar to the self. The authors argue that this occurs through a process called egocentric anchoring, where, in the absence of any information about anonymous others, individuals are inferred to be like the self in the sense that they share a similar preference structure. This finding presents a challenge to SIT, which would predict that anonymous consumer reviews would not be particularly persuasive, since an anonymous other lacks clear source strength without the assumption of egocentric anchoring, which SIT does not predict. Future research on egocentric anchoring online could fruitfully explore how far egocentrically-anchored inferences reach. While Naylor et al. (2011) demonstrated that consumers infer anonymous others to have similar preference structures, future research could explore whether they are also inferred to have similar levels of expertise and a similar geographic location, etc. Moreover, research could also investigate whether the tendency to egocentrically anchor is reduced in individuals from cultures that are less self-focused, that is, cultures characterized by more interdependent than independent self-construals (Markus & Kitayama, 1991).

Recent research has also demonstrated that consumers do not make egocentric inferences of anonymous others in all online contexts; in competitive contexts (e.g., online auctions), Norton, Lamberton and Naylor (2013) show that anonymous others are instead inferred to be dissimilar to the self, making it easier for the target to compete aggressively against them. Given that this type of anonymous social influence was not particularly common before the advent of online communication (meaning that it was not a possible field of generalization for SIT researchers), anonymous online social communication has created a unique opportunity for researchers to understand how consumers respond to social influence by unidentified sources.

Just as the potential for anonymity online creates a unique research opportunity, so does the choice to reveal one's identity online. For example, Norton, Frost and Ariely (2007) explored the consequences of moving from relative anonymity to identification in the context of online dating. Similar to Naylor et al.'s (2011) work showing the potential positive impact of ambiguity online, Norton et al. (2007) demonstrated that potential dating partners like each other more the less they know about each other, as revealing more information results in more opportunities to discover dissimilarities.

So how do consumers make the decision to identify versus reveal their own identity? This question remains largely unanswered and is in need of further exploration. Some work in the use of avatars suggests that even these fictional selves are often constructed in ways that bear some resemblance to the actual self (Bryant & Akerman, 2009; Meadows, 2008; Zhao, Grasmuck & Martin, 2008, as discussed in Belk, 2013). However, are such tendencies context dependent, in the same way that inferences about unidentified others are? Are they dependent on our situational goal or our self-image? These are important avenues for future research.

Future work should also explore how online behaviour differs when one's identity is revealed vs. concealed. Some of this work has already begun. As one example, Chen and Berger (2013) demonstrated that anonymity on an online discussion board affects people's willingness to discuss controversial topics; when people do not have to reveal their identity, moderate controversy increases their likelihood of posting. Controversy fails to increase interest in posting when people must reveal their identities because it makes potential posters feel uncomfortable. Anecdotal evidence from the comments section of various websites (e.g., YouTube) suggests that the ability to post information anonymously can also bring out the worst in individual commenters, as discourse can become remarkably uncivil in anonymous forums. Future research should explore how being identified versus anonymous constrains or liberates our online behaviour and how that changes the influence we have on others and they on us.

Just as consumers can choose whether they wish to hide or reveal their identity online, brands must also make decisions about how identified they want their consumers to be with one another. Naylor et al. (2012) demonstrate that consumers like brands whose supporters remain anonymous as much as they like brands whose supporters are identified as being demographically similar to the self and significantly more than brands with dissimilar supporters. These findings suggest that firms may wish to leave supporters' identities ambiguous when expanding to new target markets where potential customers are likely to encounter demographically dissimilar others among brand supporters. Thus, a brand's choice to hide or reveal supporters is an important strategic decision. This choice may also influence whether consumers decide to affiliate with a brand on a social networking site. Image-related concerns may lead consumers to be reluctant to publicly affiliate with a brand (e.g., liking it on Facebook) that they actually do like and use offline more privately. Similarly, consumers may "like" brands online that they would never actually buy or use offline (e.g., because they cannot afford them) if doing so enhances their status by being displaying publicly to friends on a social networking site. Consumers may therefore choose whether to affiliate with a brand online based on whether their identity will be revealed if they do so. Future research should explore the drivers of the choice to publicly or privately affiliate with brands online.

Future research should also explore how the choice to self-identify or remain anonymous affects other robust effects established in the literature. For example, we might ask how important the identified voice of an individual or firm may be in driving social proof effects (Cialdini, 2009). In offline settings, a great deal of work has established the importance of social norms in prompting conformity (see Goldstein, Cialdini, & Griskevicius, 2008). Some work has also suggested that when consumers are aware of the aggregate demand for products – with no identification of the buyers' characteristics – markets tend to concentrate more than normal: consumers show herd behaviour (Maecker et al., 2013; Salganik et al., 2006; Tucker & Zhang, 2011). Thus, it may be that in the online world, social proof effects are stronger than in the offline world.

Further, we are only beginning to understand the power of online platforms to facilitate activities that are both inherently social and, in many cases, productive – but which online settings allow with a low degree of face-to-face identification. Intriguing findings suggest that online ideation may initially be more productive when individuals collaborate with others, but that this collaboration may limit creativity on subsequent attempts (Bayus, 2013). However, other work taking a networks perspective qualifies this finding, showing that interdependent ideation decreases in innovativeness when one's partners become increasingly connected (Stephen, Zubcsek, & Goldenberg, 2014), as a highly connected set of partners tend to increase the redundancy of ideas. This research has obvious implications for understanding the effectiveness of online crowdsourcing to solve a variety of problems (Rosenberg, 2011), as well as for research aimed at understanding how to best leverage consumers for co-creation of new product ideas (Hoffman, Kopalle, & Novak, 2010).

It also remains to be understood if social phenomena that are commonly experienced offline are similar in structure or experience online. For example, do people feel "crowding" at any point in an online social experience? Are there ways to offset the diffusion of responsibility in online settings – perhaps through varying the extent to which consumers are identified to one another – that do not exist in offline settings? When are privacy concerns triggered in online settings as opposed to offline settings, given the nature of mere virtual presence as opposed to real-world presence?

Future research should explore these and other issues created by the unique ability to interact and influence others anonymously online. In the next section, we explore consumers choosing to interact in online groups formed around a specific interest: shopping.

Social shopping

> *A tribe is a group of people connected to one another, connected to a leader, and connected to an idea. For millions of years, human beings have been part of one tribe or another. A group needs only two things to be a tribe: a shared interest and a way to communicate.*
>
> Seth Godin (2008, p. 1)

Social shopping is a type of e-commerce where other consumers are an integral part of the online buying experience. Although definitions and typologies for the scope of social shopping vary as this technology emerges, its primary distinguishing attribute is its ability for consumers to make purchases while connected to others. In such contexts, shoppers create ad hoc buying "tribes", which may vary in their composition and temporal stability: The shared interest that connects them is their interest in purchasing a similar offering. This situation is notably different from a traditional e-commerce scenario, where a single consumer goes to a website and buys a product without the involvement of others. Although some practitioners consider making purchases from a site like Amazon.com to be social shopping, where a consumer has access to product reviews and recommendations from others, we focus on two types of social shopping where the connection to others is more direct.

One popular form of social shopping is social buying, purchasing "deals" on group buying sites (e.g., Groupon, LivingSocial), where large groups of people buy together at steep discounts. Social media's ability to connect consumers allows individual consumers to obtain economies of scale in a way previously reserved for corporate or government buyers. Group buying sites create temporary cooperatives of buyers, all interested in obtaining a low price on a certain product. Most academic work in this domain has focused on the profitability of social couponing programmes for firms (Bertini et al., 2012; Kumar & Rajan, 2012a; Kumar & Rajan, 2012b; but see Kuan, Zhong, & Chau, 2014 for an exception). This avenue for research will no doubt remain fruitful, but interesting future research perspectives could investigate the impact of purchasing these deals on consumers, including how purchasing a Groupon or similar deal impacts satisfaction, repurchase intentions and self-brand connections.

The second type of social shopping we explore, shopping community websites, seeks to replicate the offline experience of going shopping with a group of friends. Online shopping communities, which are particularly common in the fashion industry, are sites where a shopper curates images of products they are interested in purchasing or simply that they like and admire. One popular site, particularly among young, female consumers, is the fast-growing fashion-focused WaNeLo (which stands for "want, need, love;" Marikar, 2014; Lieber, 2013), where the content that an individual consumer sees when logging in is dictated by the content that his or her friends have posted. A second example is the community-powered social commerce website Polyvore, created in 2006, which boasted over 15 million unique monthly visitors by 2012 (Taylor, 2012). While similar to other fashion sites or a social networking site like Pinterest where users curate images, what distinguishes such sites is the ability to make a relatively seamless transition from the shopping community to purchase. Consumers experience near-simultaneous access to the broad store assortment on the Internet, as clothing and accessories from any online site can appear on a shopping community site like WaNeLo. Here, consumers effectively act as smart agents for one another, lowering search costs and, optimally, raising consideration set quality.

Brands are starting to take notice of this new form of shopping; Urban Outfitters has more followers on WaNeLo than it does on Twitter (Lieber, 2013), and venture capitalists are increasingly investing in such platforms (Miller, 2012). Reflecting commercial interest, some work has begun to explore specific aspects of these sites, such as consumer-generated tags and high store ratings, that prompt "click-out" – following a link to a participating online shop (Olbrich & Holsing, 2012). While such insights provide helpful prescriptions for web developers, as researchers we lack a framework for understanding the specifics of how consumers influence each other and interact with brands in online shopping communities. Thus, this type of social shopping offers a virtually untapped research area, with huge potential for deepening our understanding of social influence.

More broadly, though, consumer researchers need to consider the psychology that underlies social shopping and how it is different from a bandwagon-based purchase, if at all. One major difference is that social shopping is particularly notable in its ability to identify a participant as part of a group, regardless of whether they make any purchases. Classic marketing work shows that brand choice within groups will converge when groups are highly cohesive and members are very knowledgeable about one another (Witt, 1969). By adopting the same choice as others in their group, an individual maintains their well-being and belongingness in that community. Participation in social shopping forums – with virtual strangers - may be a way of affiliating with an in-group of knowledgeable fashionistas, but it is questionable whether such affiliation will lead to convergence or lead to a desire to differentiate oneself within that group. At the same time, in both social buying contexts and within shopping communities, participation may be driven by primarily economic rather than relationship-related motivations, although this may be moderated by cross-cultural differences, with relationship-related goals more important in collectivist cultures and economic motives more important in individualistic cultures (Oyserman et al., 2002). Little is known about the balancing points between relational capital development and economic rationality in social shopping situations and how this balancing act may differ across cultures.

In addition, social shopping may include dangers that should be carefully considered by researchers before recommending wholesale adoption. First, a high degree of mere virtual presence chasing the same goods or vying to be most influential in the community may shift the tacit relationship among community members from cooperation to competition. Knowing that a large community of shoppers may be interested in a scarce deal or an exclusive product, social shopping participants may experience a high sense of either reputation or product risk. Such a competitive "sharing" environment may not lend itself to strong social bonds or the best use of scarce resources (Lamberton & Rose, 2012). Another potential down-side of social shopping relates to classic work on mere presence effects (Markus, 1978). Such work shows that the presence of others can help us perform familiar tasks but can hinder performance on novel tasks, via social facilitation and social interference, respectively. Will social shopping therefore be detrimental to the choice quality of newer or less experienced shoppers, who may be joining a shopping community for the express purpose of improving their knowledge or decision ability? At the same time, might social shopping provide even greater advantages for those who are already fluent in the marketplace? Will the momentum of the buying tribe justify the purchase of novel goods and experiences, even when one would not ordinarily make such an individual purchase?

Finally, and from a broader perspective, an observation of online social shopping communities suggests that they may be more suited for certain types of content but not for others. For example, posters on WaNeLo can include personal information with photos of products they endorse (e.g., "I wore this to my brother's wedding, and it was fabulous!"). They can also often explicitly endorse firms, such that the shopping community is easily used for commercial information about products. However, it is unclear whether shopping communities work well to create shared experiences, making it difficult to exert influence about more experiential purchases like sporting events, vacations or dining. Further, it appears that a high proportion of social shopping sites and daily deal platforms focus on discretionary products: items like beauty products, lifestyle-based interior design and fashion. Why is this the case? Can social shopping extend its reach to necessities, where the power of group buying may allow consumers to build their own economies of scale and obtain needed resources at lower prices than solo purchasing? If social shopping allows broad groups of consumers to purchase necessities (e.g., health-related products like vitamins or over-the-counter medications) at more affordable prices, social shopping may be usable as a tool to increase overall well-being across a wide range of the population and at different points in the consumer's life cycle.

The intersection and relative potential of the online and offline worlds to shape behaviour

A final area of research that consumer psychologists should address with respect to online social influence is the intersection of the online and offline worlds. Although consumers may have the drive to share personal, experiential and commercial content online, how do they respond when information that they have posted online is brought up in a face-to-face conversation? Depending on the type of content and the relationship with the offline communicator, reactions could vary from pleasure that the other person noticed and cared about one's online post enough to discuss it in person to discomfort or embarrassment that a quick online comment posted with little thought has now become a topic for in-depth discussion in a face-to-face conversation. Similarly, content shared on a social shopping site may be information that a consumer is comfortable sharing within a shopping community (e.g., a photo of the new Louboutin heels she is coveting) but that she would not consider an appropriate offline conversation in many contexts.

Although part of the power of online social influence lies in the fact that we can be influenced by virtual strangers from around the globe, many times the people a consumer interacts with online are not strangers, but others with whom we also interact offline (e.g., some of one's Facebook friends). Future research needs to explore the impact of taking an online conversation offline not only on the consumer but also on his or her relationship with the online and offline relationship partner. An important potential moderator to explore in understanding how such movement from the online to the offline world may affect relationships more broadly are cross-cultural differences, as maintaining harmonious relationships with others in both online and offline spaces is a more important goal in collectivist versus individualistic cultures (Oyserman et al., 2002). The potential for this spread of information from online to offline conversations could also influence the consumer's decision to identity him or herself when posting online content, so future research should explore this angle, as well as other issues related to the desire for privacy when a consumer wishes to insulate his or her online conversations from their offline relationships.

At a more general level, consumers are increasingly integrating their online experience into every aspect of their lives, as mobile applications allow them to bridge the real world – their location, the location of friends, real-time information about nearby consumption opportunities etc. – with the online world, where they can easily interact with others whose proximity may vary. The integration of the "so-lo-mo" (social-local-mobile) marketing platforms with one another will lend itself to a vast amount of research that not only informs effective use of these converging technologies, but that also allows us more insight into the psychology of social influence across the consumption process. Recognizing such potential, major industry and academic coalitions, such as the Marketing Science Institute, have made exploration of the comprehensive consumer decision journey, involving both online and offline components, a priority. In addition, policy makers are increasingly seeking to bridge technologically mediated forms of social influence and offline interventions to create behavioural change. For example, Castleman, Page and Schooley (2014) used a set of carefully developed text messages to reduce "summer melt" – the phenomenon observed when students admitted to college fail to attend in the fall. Generating creative interventions like this may yield positive long-lasting consequences, both for participants and for society as a whole.

Thus, while a burgeoning area of research in marketing and consumer psychology has begun to examine the negative consequences of social media use and social influence online, we should not forget that online social influence also has the potential to positively impact not only the marketplace (e.g., by increasing product information flow to consumers from unbiased sources) but also consumer well-being more broadly. For example, could interacting with others online generate and amplify the experience of online "flow" (Novak, Hoffman, & Duhachek, 2003)? Could social networking reduce feelings of loneliness and isolation in individuals who have difficulty interacting with others in face-to-face settings or who are unable to do so because of mobility restrictions? Future research should explore these and other topics in order to understand how interacting with others online can positively impact consumer well-being in unique ways relative to offline interactions.

Finally, from the highest-level perspective, there are several "big picture" questions remaining about online social influence. For example, is social influence stronger or weaker in online vs. offline settings in terms of its potential to shape behaviour? On what factors does the answer to this question depend? Does the answer and do the moderating factors depend on the behaviour that one is trying to shape (e.g., encouraging purchase of a specific product or brand versus encouraging behaviours designed to improve consumer welfare, like healthy eating or quitting smoking)? These large questions are likely being addressed across a variety of fields, but consumer psychologists can and should be part of this important conversation.

References

Allport, F. H. (1920). The influence of the group upon association and thought. *Journal of Experimental Psychology, 3*, 159–182.

Argo, J. J., Dahl, D. W., & Manchanda, R. V. (2005). The influence of a mere social presence in a retail context. *Journal of Consumer Research, 32*(2), 207–212.

Ariely, D., Bracha, A., & Meier, S. (2009). Doing good or doing well? Image motivation and monetary incentives in behaving prosocially. *American Economic Review, 99*(1), 544–555.

Arndt, J. (1967). Role of product-related conversations in the diffusion of a new product. *Journal of Marketing Research, 4*(3), 291–295.

Asch, S. E. (1952). *Social psychology*. Englewood Cliffs, NJ: Prentice Hall.

Asch, S. E. (1956). Studies of independence and conformity: A minority of one against a unanimous majority. *Psychological Monographs*, 70, (Whole no. 416).

Asch, S. E. (1951). Effects of group pressure upon the modification and distortion of judgments. *Groups, Leadership, and Men*. Pittsburgh, PA: Carnegie Press.

Bayus, B. L. (2013). Crowdsourcing new product ideas over time: An analysis of the dell ideastorm community. *Management Science, 59*(1), 226–244.

Belk, R. W. (2013). Extended self in a digital world. *Journal of Consumer Research, 40*(3), 477–500.

Bénabou, R., & Tirole, J. (2006). Incentives and prosocial behaviour. *American Economic Review, 96*(5), 1652–1678.

Berger, J., & Heath, C. (2007). Where consumers diverge from others: Identity signaling and product domains. *Journal of Consumer Research, 34*(2), 121–134.

Berger, J., & Iyengar, R. (2013). Communication channels and word of mouth: How the medium shapes the message. *Journal of Consumer Research, 40*(3), 567–579.

Berger, J., & Milkman, K. L. (2012). What makes online content viral? *Journal of Marketing Research, 49*(2), 192–205.

Bernstein, E. (2013). Thank you for not sharing. Retrieved from http://online.wsj.com/article/SB10001424127887323826804578466831263674230.html

Bertini, M., Wathieu, L., Sigman, B. P., & Norton, M. I. (2012). Do social deal sites really work? *Harvard Business Review, 90*, 139–143. Retrieved from http://blogs.hbr.org/2012/02/do-social-deal-sites-really-wo/

Bone, P. F. (1995). Word-of-mouth effects on short-term and long-term product judgments. *Journal of Business Research, 32*(3), 213–223.

Brock, T. C. (1965). Communicator-recipient similarity and decision change. *Journal of Personality and Social Psychology, 1*, 650–654.

Bronner, F., & de Hoog, R. (2014). Social media and consumer choice. *International Journal of Market Research, 56*, 51–71.

Brown, J. J., & Reingen, P. H. (1987). Social ties and word-of-mouth referral behaviour. *Journal of Consumer Research, 14*(3), 350–362.

Bryant, J. A., & Akerman, A. (2009). Finding mii: Virtual social identity and the young consumer. In N. T. Wood & M. R. Solomon (Eds.), *Virtual Social Identity and Consumer Behaviour* (pp. 127–140). Armonk, NY: M. E. Sharpe.

Bughin, J. R. (2007). How companies can make the most of user generated content. *McKinsey Quarterly*, (August), 1–4.

Burwitz, L., & Newell, K. M. (1972). The effects of the mere presence of coactors on learning a motor skill. *Journal of Motor Behaviour, 4*, 99–102.

Campbell, M., & Kirmani, A. (2000). Consumers' use of persuasion knowledge: The effects of accessibility and cognitive capacity on perceptions of an influence agent. *Journal of Consumer Research, 27*(1), 69–83.

Castleman, B. L., Page, L. C., & Schooley, K. (2014). The forgotten summer: Does the offer of college counseling after high school mitigate summer melt among college-intending, low-income high school graduates? *Journal of Policy Analysis and Management, 32*, 320–344.

Chan, C., Berger, J., & van Boven, L. (2012). Identifiable but not identical: Combining social identity and uniqueness motives in choice. *Journal of Consumer Research, 39*(3), 561–563.

Chapman, A. J. (1973). Social facilitation of laughter in children. *Journal of Experimental Social Psychology, 9*, 528–541.

Chapman, A. J. (1974). An electromyographic study of social facilitation: A test of the "mere presence" hypothesis. *British Journal of Psychology, 65*, 123–128.

Cheema, A., & Kaikati, A. (2010). The effect of need for uniqueness on word of mouth. *Journal of Marketing Research, 47*(3), 553–563.

Chen, Z., & Berger, J. (2013). When, why, and how controversy causes conversation. *Journal of Consumer Research, 40*(3), 580–593.

Chen, Y., & Xie, J. (2008). Online consumer review: Word-of-mouth as a new element of marketing communication mix. *Management Science, 54*(3), 477–491.

Chevalier, J. A., & Mayzlin, D. (2006). The effect of word of mouth on sales: Online book reviews. *Journal of Marketing Research, 43*(3), 345–354.

Cialdini, R. B. (2009). *Influence: Science and practice* (5th ed.). Boston, MA: Pearson.

Coleman, G. (2013). Anonymous in context: The politics and power behind the mask. *Internet Governance Series*, Centre for International Governance Innovation. Retrieved from www.cigionline.org/publications/2013/9/anonymous-context-politics-and-power-behind-mask

Dahl, D. W., Manchanda, R. V., & Argo, J. J. (2001). Embarrassment in consumer purchase: The roles of social presence and purchase familiarity. *Journal of Consumer Research, 28*(3), 473–481.

Das, S., & Chen, M. (2007). Yahoo! for Amazon: Sentiment extraction from small talk on the web. *Management Science, 53*(9), 1375–1388.

Dellarocas, C., Zhang, X., & Awad, N. F. (2007). Exploring the value of online product reviews in forecasting sales: The case of motion pictures. *Journal of Interactive Marketing, 21*(4), 23–45.

Dockterman, E. (2013). Instagram-will-ruin-your-meal. Retrieved from http://newsfeed.time.com/2013/10/06/instagram-will-ruin-your-meal/

Dzhogleva, H., & Lamberton, C. (2014). Should birds of a feather flock together? Understanding self-control decisions in dyads. forthcoming at the *Journal of Consumer Research.*

Escalas, J. E., & Bettman, J. R. (2003). You are what they eat: The influence of reference groups on consumers' connections to brands. *Journal of Consumer Psychology, 13*(3), 339–348.

Feick, L. F., & Price, L. L. (1987). The market maven: A diffuser of marketplace information. *Journal of Marketing, 51*(1), 83–97.

Flynn, L. R., Goldsmith, R. E., & Eastman, J. K. (1996). Opinion leaders and opinion seekers: Two new measurement scales. *Journal of the Academy of Marketing Science, 24*(2), 137–147.

Forrester. (2012). Forrester research world online population forecast, 2012–2017. Retrieved from www.forrester.com/Forrester+Research+World+Online+Population+Forecast+2012+To+2017+Global/fulltext/-/E-RES81381?intcmp=blog:forrlink

Forster, E. M. (2013/1910). *Howards end.* New Jersey: J. P. Piper Books.

Freeman, S., Walker, M. R., Borden, R., & Latane, B. (1975). Diffusion of innovation and restaurant tipping: Cheaper by the bunch. *Personality and Social Psychology Bulletin, 1975*(1), 584–587.

Friestad, M., & Wright, P. (1994). The persuasion knowledge model: How people cope with persuasion attempts. *Journal of Consumer Research, 21*(1), 1–31.

Geen, R. G. (1971). Social facilitation of long-term recall. *Psychonomic Science, 24*, 89–90.

Geen, R. G. (1973). Effects of being observed on short- and long-term recall. *Journal of Experimental Psychology, 100*, 395–398.

Geen, R. G. (1974). Effects of evaluation apprehension on memory over intervals of varying length. *Journal of Experimental Psychology, 102*, 908–910.

Geen, R. G. (1979). Effects of being observed on learning following success and failure experiences. *Motivation and Emotion, 3*, 355–371.

Gerard, H. B., Wilhelmy, R. A., & Conolley, E. S. (1968). Conformity and group size. *Journal of Personality and Social Psychology, 8*(1), 79.

Gesenhues, A. (2013). Survey: 90% of customers say buying decisions are influenced by online reviews. Retrieved from http://marketingland.com/survey-customers-more-frustrated-by-how-long-it-takes-to-resolve-a-customer-service-issue-than-the-resolution-38756

Giacobbe, A. (2013). 6 ways social media can ruin your life. Retrieved from www.bostonglobe.com/magazine/2014/05/21/ways-social-media-can-ruin-your-life/St8vHIdqCLk7eRsvME3k5K/story.html

Glazer, A., & Konrad, K. A. (1996). A signaling explanation for charity. *American Economic Review, 86*(4), 1019–1028.

Godes, D., Mayzlin D., Yubo, C., Das, S., Dellarocas, C., Pfeiffer B., et al. (2005). The firm's management of social interactions. *Marketing Letters, 16*(3/4), 415–428.

Godin, S. (2008). *Tribes: We need you to lead us*. New York, NY: Penguin Group.

Goffman, E. (1951). Symbols of class status. *British Journal of Sociology, 2*(4), 294–304.

Goldstein, N. J., Cialdini, R. B., & Griskevicius, V. (2008). A room with a viewpoint: Using social norms to motivate environmental conservation in hotels. *Journal of Consumer Research, 35*(3), 472–482.

Hennig-Thurau, T., Gwinner, K. P., Walsh, G., & Gremler, D. D. (2004). Electronic word-of-mouth via consumer-opinion platforms: What motivates consumers to articulate themselves on the Internet? *Journal of Interactive Marketing, 18*(1), 38–52.

Hoffman, D., Kopalle, P., & Novak, T. (2010). The "right" consumers for better concepts: Identifying consumers high in emergent nature to develop new product concepts. *Journal of Marketing Research, 47*(5), 854–865.

John, L. K., Acquisti, A., & Loewenstein, G. (2011). Strangers on a plane: Context-dependent willingness to divulge sensitive information. *Journal of Consumer Research, 37*(5), 858–873.

Katz, E. (1957). The two-step flow of communication: An up-to-date report on a hypothesis. *Public Opinion Quarterly, 21*(1), 61–78.

King, S. (2011). *11/22/63*. New York, NY: Scribner.

Kristofferson, K., White, K., & Peloza, J. (2014). The nature of slacktivism: How the social observability of an initial act of token support affects subsequent prosocial action. *Journal of Consumer Research, 40*(6), 1149–1166.

Kuan, K. K. Y., Zhong, Y., & Chau, P. Y. K. (2014). Informational and normative social influence in group-buying: Evidence from self-reported and EEG data. *Journal of Management Information Systems, 30*(4), 151–178.

Kumar, V., & Rajan, B. (2012a). The perils of social coupon campaigns. *MIT Sloan Management Review, 53*(4), 15–16.

Kumar, V., & Rajan, B. (2012b). Social coupons as a marketing strategy: A multifaceted perspective. *Journal of the Academy of Marketing Science, 40*(1), 120–136.

Lamberton, C. P., & Rose, R. (2012). Yours, mine and ours: An investigation of consumers' propensity to participate in commercial sharing systems. *Journal of Marketing, 76*(4), 109–125.

Latané, B. (1981). The psychology of social impact. *American Psychologist, 36*(4), 343–356.

Leadbetter, C. W. (2008). *We-Think: Mass innovation, not mass production*. London, UK: Profile Books.

Lieber, C. (2013). Wanelo wants to crush the category of social shopping. Retrieved from http://racked.com/archives/2013/12/05/a-new-social-shopping-tool-for-the-holidays.php

Maecker, O., Grabennstroer, N. S., Clement, M., & Heitmann, M. (2013). Charts and demand: Empirical generalizations on social influence. *International Journal of Research in Marketing, 30*(4), 429–431.

Marikar, S. (2014). Like mall browsing, with a click. Retrieved from www.nytimes.com/2014/05/08/fashion/Wanelo-Social-Media-Shopping-Site-Deena-Varshavskaya-ecommerce.html

Marketing Charts. (2014). User demographic highlights from 5 major – and growing – social networks. Retrieved from www.marketingcharts.com/wp/online/user-demographic-highlights-from-5-major-and-growing-social-networks-38939/

Markus, H. (1978). The effect of mere presence on social facilitation: An unobtrustive test. *Journal of Experimental Social Psychology, 14*(4), 389–397.

Markus, H., & Kitayama, S. (1991). Culture and the self: Implications for cognition, emotion, and motivation. *Psychological Review, 98*, 224–253.

Martens, R. (1969). Effect of an audience on learning and performance of a complex motor skill. *Journal of Personality and Social Psychology, 12*, 252–260.

McQuarrie, E. F., Miller, J., & Phillips, B. J. (2013). The megaphone effect: Taste and audience in fashion blogging. *Journal of Consumer Research, 40*(1), 136–158.

Meadows, M. (2008). *I, avatar: The cultures and consequences of having a second life*. Berkeley, CA: New Riders.

Merton, T. K. (1968). *Social theory and social structure*. New York, NY: Free Press.

Mielach, D. (2012). Can Facebook make you fat and poor? Retrieved from www.businessnewsdaily.com/3574-facebook-fat-poor.html

Milgram, S., Bickman, L., & Berkowitz, L. (1969). Notes on the drawing power of crowds of different size. *Journal of Personality and Social Psychology, 13*, 79–82.

Miller, C. C. (2012). Polyvore, the fashion site, gets more money and a new C.E.O. Retrieved from http://bits.blogs.nytimes.com/2012/01/23/polyvore-the-fashion-site-gets-more-money-and-a-new-c-e-o/?_php=true&_type=blogs&_r=0

Moore, S. G. (2012). Some things are better left unsaid: How word of mouth influences the storyteller. *Journal of Consumer Research, 38*(6), 1140–1154.

Moritz, D. (2013). As social media becomes more visual, a tool for analyzing image engagement. Retrieved from www.entrepreneur.com/article/227789

Naylor, R. W., Lamberton, C. P, & Norton, D. A. (2011). Seeing ourselves in others: Reviewer ambiguity, egocentric anchoring, and persuasion. *Journal of Marketing Research, 48*(3), 617–631.

Naylor, R. W., Lamberton, C. P., & West, P. M. (2012). Beyond the "like" button: Exploring the effects of mere virtual presence on brand evaluations and purchase intentions in social media settings. *Journal of Marketing, 76*, 105–120.

Norton, M. I., Frost, J. H., & Ariely, D. (2007). Less is more: The lure of ambiguity, or why familiarity breeds contempt. *Journal of Personality and Social Psychology, 92*, 97–105.

Norton, D. A., Lamberton, C. P., & Naylor, R. W. (2013). The devil you (don't) know: Interpersonal ambiguity and inference making in competitive contexts. *Journal of Consumer Research, 40*(2), 239–254.

Novak, T. P., Hoffman, D. L., & Duhachek, A. (2003). The influence of goal-directed and experiential activities on online flow experiences. *Journal of Consumer Psychology, 13*(1/2), 3-16.

Olbrich, R., & Holsing, C. (2012). Effect of user-generated content on website stickiness: The case of social shopping communities. *Proceedings of the 14th Annual International Conference on Electronic Commerce*, 301–308.

Oyserman, D., Coon, H., & Kemmelmeier, M. (2002). Rethinking individualism and collectivism: Evaluation of theoretical assumptions and meta-analyses. *Psychological Bulletin, 128*, 3–73.

Porter, H. (1939). Studies in the psychology of stuttering: XIV. Stuttering phenomena in relation to size and personnel of audience. *Journal of Speech Disorders*, 4, 323–333.

Pring, C. (2012). 99 new social media stats for 2012. Retrieved from http://thesocialskinny.com/99-new-social-media-stats-for-2012/

Rosenberg, L. A. (1961). Group size, prior experience, and conformity. *Journal of Abnormal and Social Psychology, 63*, 436–437.

Rosenberg, T. (2011). Crowdsourcing a better world. Retrieved from http://opinionator.blogs.nytimes.com/2011/03/28/crowdsourcing-a-better-world/

Salganik, M. J., Dodds, P. S., & Watts, D. J. (2006). Experimental study of inequality and unpredictability in an artificial cultural market. *Science, 311*, 854–856.

Sheth, J. N. (1971). Word-of-mouth in low-risk innovations. *Journal of Advertising Research, 11*(3), 15–18.

Simons, H. W., Berkowitz, N. N., & Moyer, J. R. (1970). Similarity, credibility and attitude change: A review and a theory. *Psychological Bulletin, 73*, 1–16.

Simpson, M. (2009). Social networking nightmares. Retrieved from www.nea.org/home/38324.htm

Smith, C. (2013). The planet's 24 largest social media sites, and where their next wave of growth will come from. Retrieved from www.businessinsider.com/a-global-social-media-census-2013-10

Stephen, A. T., Zubcsek, P. P., & Goldenberg, J. (2014). Lower connectivity is better: The effects of network structure on customer innovativeness in interdependent ideation tasks. *Columbia Business School Working Paper 13-13*. New York, NY: Columbia University.

Streitfeld, D. (2013). Give yourself 5 stars? Online, it might cost you. Retrieved from www.nytimes.com/2013/09/23/technology/give-yourself-4-stars-online-it-might-cost-you.html

Taylor, C. (2012). Polyvore hits 15M monthly uniques by embracing the Pinterest effect. Retrieved from http://techcrunch.com/2012/03/06/polyvore-hits-15m-monthly-uniques-by-embracing-the-pinterest-effect/

Tian, K. T., Bearden, W. O., & Hunter, G. L. (2001). Consumers' need for uniqueness: Scale development and validation. *Journal of Consumer Research, 28*(1), 50–66.

Toma, C. L., Hancock, J. T., & Ellison, N. B. (2008). Separating fact from fiction: An examination of deceptive self-presentation in online dating profiles. *Personality and Social Psychology Bulletin, 34*(8), 1023–1036.

Toubia, O., & Stephen, A. T. (2013). Intrinsic vs. image-related utility in social media: Why do people contribute content to Twitter? *Marketing Science, 32*(3), 368–392.

Tucker, C., & Zhang, J. (2011). How does popularity information affect choices? A field experiment. *Management Science, 57*(5), 828–842.

Walther, J. B., Trepte, S., & Reinecke, L. (Eds.) (2011). Introduction to privacy online. *Privacy Online: Perspectives on privacy and disclosure in the social web, 3–8.* Springer-Verlag, Berlin Heidelberg.

Wangenheim, F., & Bayon, T. (2004). Satisfaction, loyalty and word of mouth within the customer base of a utility provider: Differences between stayers, switchers and referral switchers. *Journal of Consumer Behaviour, 3*(3), 211–220.

White, K., & Dahl, D. W. (2006). To be or not be? The influence of dissociative reference groups on consumer preferences. *Journal of Consumer Psychology, 16*(4), 404–414.

White, K., & Dahl, D. W. (2007). Are all out-groups created equal? Consumer identity and dissociative influence. *Journal of Consumer Research, 34*(4), 525–536.

Wilcox, K., & Stephen, A. T. (2013). Are close friends the enemy? Online social networks, self-esteem, and self-control. *Journal of Consumer Research, 40*(1), 90–103.

Witt, R. (1969). Informal social group influence on consumer brand choice. *Journal of Marketing Research, 6*(4), 473–476.

Zhao, S., Grasmuck, S., & Martin, J. (2008). Identity construction on Facebook: Digital empowerment in anchored relationships. *Computers in Human Behaviour, 24*(5), 18–16.

33

Representations of race, gender and sexual orientation in gaming content

Melody A. Stotler and Karen E. Dill-Shackleford

Gaming research has become increasingly important over the last few years. Universities are giving scholarships to skilled eSports (aka electronic sports) players (Tassi, 2015). Major League Gaming (aka MLG) is a professional sports market in the United States and across the globe via the Internet ("Major League Gaming," 2015). Businesses and schools are using principles associated with gaming (e.g., leadership, economics and time management) to create more positive user experiences, overcome learning disabilities and solve financial crises, to name a few (Annetta, 2010; Dennis & O'Toole, 2014). Understanding how and why games are played, who plays them as well as how globally diverse groups of players may differ from one another, allows developers to make increasingly marketable games, provides a basis for understanding intergroup dynamics between gamers and non-gamers and allows researchers to understand the increasingly complex way in which people continue to experience entertainment. Where once much of the research revolved around gaming and resulting behaviours, researchers now seek to understand cultural and individual aspects of gamers, gaming as a subculture and how game content affects the gaming experience. Personality and motivations for game choices, subculture norms and content diversity represent only a few of the gaming aspects currently examined in psychological research.

This chapter explores the representation of social groups, including race – where it has been explored – both inside games and within the gaming community. We will discuss how identity contributes to the gaming experience, including the effects of avatar use. As such, the first section of this chapter reviews representations of gender and race by game developers. The second section provides a summary of existing research on LGBT game content and LGBT gamers. The third section discusses player demographics as they are currently understood via research. The fourth section shifts gears slightly to consider avatar representations of and by players. Finally, we discuss avenues for future research on portrayals in gaming.

Portrayals of gender and race in video games

Theorists such as Bandura (Social Learning Theory) (e.g., Bussey & Bandura, 1999) and Gerbner (Cultivation Theory) (e.g., Gerbner, 1999) explained how the role models for social categories that we see in the media, expose viewers to expectations for members of their social category, as well as the consequences of their behaviour. This is important because it insinuates that the stories we tell in games contribute to social construction and social action out of the gaming environment. Furthermore, media may demonstrate that some social groups are hegemonic, have social power and approval or may be viewed as normative, while other groups are marginalized. Understanding of the portrayals of social groups in video games emerges from content analyses which use a variety of sources including video game magazines (Burgess, Dill, Stermer, Burgess, & Brown, 2011a; Dill & Thill, 2007; Miller & Summers, 2007; Scharrer, 2004), game covers (Burgess et al., 2011a; Burgess, Stermer, & Burgess, 2007; Near, 2013), online game reviews (Ivory, 2009), screenshots (Martins, Williams, Harrison, & Ratan, 2009) and live or recorded gameplay (Burgess et al., 2011a; Dietz, 1998; Dill, Gentile, Richter, & Dill, 2005; Downs & Smith, 2010; Sisler, 2008).

This section will present an overview of existing research on portrayals of gender and race in game content as created by game developers, rather than created by players. Based on social learning theory and cultivation theory, understanding what is being communicated in media will help us understand behaviours outside media.

Gender representation in games

Gender differences in game representation seem irrational. Research shows that the ratio of women to men in gaming does not reflect reality (Williams, Martins, Consalvo, & Ivory, 2009). For example, Williams and colleagues (2009) conducted a demographic-focused content analysis of video game characters considering 150 games available from nine game systems, including handheld devices. They weighed the frequency of characters by game sales as a measure of exposure, calling their analysis a "virtual census". They calculated that the world of popular video games includes a population that is roughly 85 per cent male and 15 per cent female as compared with the roughly 49/51 ratio of males to females according to census statistics. Though game development seems to have included more female protagonists and character options, representation research is yet to reflect that change (e.g., Massive Online Battle Arenas aka MOBAS).

Game content research has also found discrepancies in gender portrayals. In a seminal study, Dietz (1998) analyzed the content of video games that were popular in the mid-1990s. This analysis revealed a game landscape where a primary theme of aggression was about twice as common (at 80 per cent) as the presence of women in games (at 41 per cent). Sex-role stereotypes that were noted as common at the time included women as damsels in distress (e.g., Princess Peach of the *Super Mario* series), and the female as a vision of beauty. More currently, there have been continued reports that female characters were objectified and sexualized (Behm-Morawitz, 2014; Burgess et al., 2007; Dill & Thill, 2007; Downs & Smith, 2010; Miller & Summers, 2007). Studies revealed that females were represented as conforming to the thin beauty ideal (Behm-Morawitz, 2014; Downs & Smith, 2010; Martins et al., 2009) and as being busty (Burgess et al., 2007; Dill et al., 2005; Dill & Thill, 2007; Downs & Smith, 2010). In addition, females were also more likely to be portrayed as naïve, while a number of investigations found that male characters were portrayed as aggressive, muscular and powerful (Dill & Thill, 2007; Miller & Summers, 2007; Scharrer, 2004).

There is evidence that adolescents are aware of the gender stereotypes present in video games. Dill and Thill (2007) asked college freshmen to describe typical male and typical female video game characters. These young people (median and modal age was 18) described typical male video game characters as powerful, aggressive, possessing a hostile attitude, athletic and thuggish. They described female video game characters as provocatively dressed with sexy, thin figures and aggressive behavioural tendencies. These characterizations mirrored a content analysis by the same authors (Dill & Thill, 2007, Study 1) that revealed that the common trope of female video game characters identified in earlier research (Dietz, 1998) as damsel in distress, had been supplanted by a view of female game characters as sexual and aggressive (e.g., the original Lara Croft).

Readily visible representations and portrayals, such as game box art, may contribute to these stereotypes. Dill and colleagues (2005) also found that 70 per cent of the main characters in the top-selling games were male and 68 per cent were White. Similarly, Near (2013) found that on video game box art of the bestselling games, about 42 per cent featured a males-only cast, while only 7 per cent featured only females. Furthermore, about 26 per cent of the box art depicted sexualized, supporting female characters and 36 per cent depicted a sexualized protagonist female character.

Gaming researchers have called for the inclusion of more proportionate gender ratios in game content (van Reijmersdal, Jansz, Peters, & van Noort, 2013). Near (2013) offered an explanation for why video game sellers may be hesitant to respond to repeated calls for change in the nature of video game characters they utilize. Near's approach was to link game sales to the representation of social groups on video game box art. He contended that some gamers prefer to have a protected straight-white-male-dominated space, where women are subordinate and sexualized, and traditional men are the heroes. Near (p. 255) referred to Kimmel's (2008) book *Guyland* when making his argument. Specifically, he wrote:

> According to Kimmel (2008), it is in part because video games are usually gendered as a masculine-only space that they are attractive to males. Video games are one of the few spaces in which it is still conventional to overtly privilege males and assume a specifically masculine perspective. Thus, the absence of female characters or their depiction as sexualized and powerless help to maintain this gendered space, both by preserving an association between masculinity and privilege and by deterring "invasion" of the space by female players.

Near posits that it is in the gaming industry's best financial interest to condone this desired hegemony. In his investigation, he found that video game box art that depicts males as central, and females as peripheral, are positively associated with game sales. On the other hand, game art that depicts women as central, and women who are present but not central, is negatively associated with video game sales. While this is correlational, the conclusion that Near drew was that preserving the masculine-only space of male privilege is in the best financial interest of the game sellers.

Adrienne Shaw (2012), however, notes that it may not be the game content that keeps potential new gamers from playing games. She points out that the stigmatization of the gaming community is more likely to stop someone from becoming a gamer than the game content itself. In her research on LGBT gamers (Shaw, 2012), which will be expounded on in a later section, she notes that the community – not the game content – is more important to gamers in their identification with the subculture. For this reason, the exposure that the larger non-gaming society has to the gaming subculture must be primarily positive if there is to be increased consumerism.

It stands to reason, however, that negative perceptions of the gaming culture are due to availability heuristics. In other words, it is easy to make out-group judgements based on negative events made public. For example, it may seem as though when women decry the depiction of their gender in the game world, men in the gaming space rebuke them. This example has played itself out on the public stage in the case of Anita Sarkeesian, and her part in the scandal known as Gamer Gate. Sarkeesian's blog site hosts videos where she critiques the role of women in gaming. Opponents of her opinions participated in "doxing" her – revealing her address and other personal information. Many people threatened to kill her and/or rape her, and sent her drawings of herself being raped by video game characters. Though there is little evidence of who participated in these threats, many assumed male gamer involvement. However, many gamers devoted time and resources to uncovering her attackers, and the attackers of others involved in the scandal.

Gaming research may also serve as a source of stigmatization fodder. For example, one study showed that, compared to controls, those men exposed to sexualized portrayals of women in video games had a greater tolerance for sexual harassment of women, but women did not show the same increase in tolerance after exposure (Dill, Brown, & Collins, 2008). Similarly, in another study (Yao, Mahood, & Linz, 2010), men exposed to objectified women in a video game showed greater levels of sexual objectification of women. Though these portrayals and representations are alarming, research also suggests that people purchase and play games for escapism from real world distress (Yee, 2006). This transportation effect has been seen in storytelling research for years (Green, Brock, & Kaufman, 2004). It suggests that individuals immerse themselves in fictional environments for vicarious experiences, implying distinction between real life and game worlds.

Representation of race in gaming

In terms of racial representation, Williams and colleagues (2009) report that, when compared to the proportions of race within out-of-game society, Whites are about 7 per cent over-represented, while Asians are about 25 per cent over-represented. Meanwhile, Blacks are under-represented by about 13 per cent, Latinos by about 78 per cent and Native Americans by about 90 per cent.

The patterns of under-representation and differential treatment by race extended to popular video game covers as well. For example, men of colour were disproportionally likely to be depicted as street criminals. In an experiment (Burgess, Dill, Stermer, Burgess, & Brown, 2011b, Study 3), White participants were exposed to game play with either a White or a Black male character. Exposure to the Black, but not the White, male characters primed the category of violent weapons, as measured by a relative decrease in reaction time to the violent stimuli. The latter findings indicate that stereotypes of Black – but not White – men as violent criminals were primed by the game content. That being said, research on box art depictions of race may not include all game genres. Some genres, such as sports games, are more likely to feature minority characters in non-violent situations as opposed to genres such as first person shooters (aka FPSs).

Dill and colleagues (2005) studied race in terms of the perpetrators and targets of violence in games, and found an over-representation of Middle Eastern characters as targets of violence (20 per cent). This issue was explored in a related paper by Unkelbach, Forgas and Denson (2008) who reported the results of an experiment which demonstrated what they called the "turban effect". In this study, non-Muslim participants were more likely to shoot at targets wearing turbans than at those without turbans. These results are related to the finding discussed earlier that Black game characters primed faster responses to weapons than did White game characters (Burgess et al., 2011b). Again, these results were likely constrained to a specific genre of games, and not representative of all game genres, specifically as new genres of games have emerged.

Intersections of gender and race in gaming

Content analyses have also indicated the commonality of misrepresentation at the intersection of gender and race. If women are underrepresented in general, women of colour are even more underrepresented. For instance, one study found 2.8 per cent of female characters were Black, compared with 12 per cent of the American population (Burgess and colleagues, 2011b, p. 289). The authors called this under-representation a virtual absence. In addition to being under-represented, men of colour were also misrepresented.

In an important study on the intersection of race and gender, Behm-Morawitz's (2014) work revealed that White characters were more likely than Black or Latino characters to be depicted as sexualized. Delving deeper, these findings revealed that White females were more likely to be depicted as sexualized than Black females or Latinas. Additionally, Behm-Morawitz (2014) demonstrated that while White, female characters were commonly presented as attractive, female characters of colour were less likely to be represented as attractive. That being said, differences in the ways female game characters are designed may introduce confounding variables in attractiveness. Characteristics used, as well as art style, may factor into attractiveness, and should be taken into consideration during research.

A recent study of the intersection of race and gender in video game advertisements (Behm-Morawitz, 2014) uncovered the continuing reliance on tropes in games such as the Black male criminal, the sexy and submissive female, the Asian martial artist and the White male hero. Behm-Morawitz argued that a reliance on stereotypes results in a missed opportunity for the video game industry to appeal to a growing population of customers. She cites the auto-racing industry as a successful example of a business where marketers adjusted to appeal to a racial minority group.

Representations and portrayals of genders and races in game may have a variety of causes. Most research analyses some aspect of game content (e.g., game covers and magazine articles). While these analyses allow us to understand the proportionate accuracy of this content, it does not tell us much about the cause of the disproportion. It is useful, as well, to keep in mind that games are a source of escapism for many who play them, and as such may not be meant to accurately represent a larger society.

LGBT gamers and game content

Diversity in gaming has become a hot topic in recent years, and with the proliferation of the LGBT movement, orientation research in gaming is starting to appear. Though there is very little research as of yet on LGBT content and LGBT gamers (aka gaymers), this section will cover existing research from both academia and LGBT gaming communities, as it pertains to gaymers and LGBT game content.

In a series of interviews, Shaw (2012) discussed identity, community and queer game content with gaymers. What she found was that gaymers prioritized accepting gaming communities, and the freedom of true self-expression, over queer game content. Gaymers often feel aggressed against by both the LGBT community (for being gamers), and the gaming community (for being LGBT) (MidBoss, 2015; Shaw, 2012). This intersectional marginalization contributes to gaymers seeking gayming communities in which they feel more comfortable being themselves. Though some may also appreciate communities for their increased ability to promote social change in gaming, some simply wish to enjoy games with like-minded individuals.

Creating the freedom to express orientation, without restraint or judgement, is a positive stride in inclusive game content (Macdonald, 2012). This is one of the goals of the GaymerX convention. GaymerX is an annual convention – currently approaching its third year – that welcomes gaymers and allies in a culturally rich and accepting environment. GaymerX includes panels, gaming areas and speakers that range from game developers to iconic community leaders and celebrities.

Relatable LGBT characters are just as necessary for gaymers as they are to any gamer (Macdonald, 2012). Characters that the player can relate to open the doors for increased enjoyment, can affect self-esteem and identity, and allow more – and deeper – social connections (Klimmt et al., 2010; Trepte & Reinecke, 2010). "Gaming in Colour" is a documentary on gaming and the LGBT community that highlights queer content, LGBT game developers and the gaymer community (MidBoss, 2015). Queer content includes gender-neutral characters, themes, and/or gameplay (MidBoss, 2015). Inclusive content may consist of options such as relationship choices (e.g., Mass Effect or Dragon Age) or LGBT characters written into games (e.g., Gone Home) (MidBoss, 2015). Some game developers have made consistently larger strides in inclusive content (e.g., BioWare and Bethesda). Interestingly, these companies are among the most popular, their games consistently bringing in the most revenue (Macdonald, 2012).

Surprisingly, when asked about queer content, gaymer responses were mixed (Shaw, 2012). Consistent with expectations, some gaymers advocated for increased queer content in games. However, some gaymers argued that inclusion must be done in a way that is natural to the flow of the game, and not simply in response to societal pressures or expectations. They contend that escaping into the game, and away from political struggles and real-life worries, remains the priority for immersion and positive gaming experiences. In truth, creating acceptable queer content for games is a complex undertaking (Shaw, 2009). Developers must take into consideration a very diverse group of community members, so as to not promote stereotypes or stigmas. They must also consider who is buying games and why, how they are depicting the group, how that depiction will be received by gamers and non-gamers alike and who will publish the games. Solutions such as leaving the content to members of the community or independent developers do not solve the problem, but rather put it in a displaced corner of the gaming market; which is not helpful to normalization (Shaw, 2009).

Normalization is the process of accepting a stigmatized group as part of the major social group such that it is no longer a separate group (Nadal, 2013). Rather, it becomes part of the major social group. When a group is no longer considered different or stigmatized, marginalization also discontinues. However, normalization is not likely to happen without also considering how individuals are affected by media. In the first section of this chapter, we looked at how developers represent various groups in game universes. That being said, it is useful to understand who plays games, and who creates games, as this may help us come closer to an understanding of why game content is created.

Demographics

This section considers demographic information about not only players, but developers as well. Understanding who the audience is, and who the storytellers are, helps us shed some light on what their motivations in content may be. Some of the "why" in the inclusion of story or game play components may be found in studies on group dynamics.

It is instructive to relate the stories we tell about social groups in video games to the theoretical work of Fiske, Glick, Rudman and Cuddy (2007). These authors study stereotypes and how they relate to prejudice and discrimination. For example, the BIAS Map (Cuddy, Fiske, & Glick, 2007) shows how we classify social groups according to two central factors – warmth and competence. Warmth is akin to likability while competence relates to competitiveness – if one is competent, they may compete with others successfully for limited resources. Not only can these stereotyping concepts apply to assumptions by non-gamers about gamers, but they can also apply to assumptions by developers about players, and even players about other players, as we will see in our section about avatar use.

These studies can also be applied to the previously discussed topic of gender and race portrayals in gaming. For example, ambivalent sexism theory (Glick & Fiske, 1996) posits that the sexes can have mixed attitudes towards each other. Women in traditional society are construed as "wonderful but weak", whereas men are "bad but bold" (Fiske, Xu, Cuddy, & Glick, 1999; Glick et al., 2004; Glick & Fiske, 1996; Lee, Fiske, & Glick, 2010). As social roles shift, there is a change in perspective on gender relations. If, for instance, some men come to see some women as cold and competent (e.g., some men's feelings towards successful working women), then that will tend to evoke discrimination in order to thwart potential competitors. These stereotypes and attitudes may be held by developers and translated into game components, even without any explicit intention of doing so.

Player's demographics

The Pew Internet and American Life project reports that almost all teenagers (97 per cent) say they play video games. Boys play more often than girls, and play for longer. Younger teens play more often than older teens. The games teens play tend to be diverse, with most teens reporting that they play a number of different genres of games. Of those who say they are daily gamers, 65 per cent are male and 35 per cent are female. Young, male teens are the most likely to play and older female teens report the least enthusiasm for video games (Lenhart et al., 2008). The Pew Internet and American Life project found that while gaming online, about half of teens reported seeing or hearing "people being hateful, racist or sexist". The teens also said that it was common for gamers to discourage those behaviours at least some of the time.

According to a report by the Entertainment Software Association, there is no stereotypical age group of gamers any more. They report that the average gamer is 31 and that 52 per cent of gamers are male and 48 per cent are female. According to Williams and colleagues (Williams, Yee, & Caplan, 2008), 40 per cent of adults and 83 per cent of teens play games. Women are a larger segment of the world of gaming than teen boys (Near, 2013). We must note that teenagers in general are a minority of the entire population. It is estimated that only 7 per cent of the US population are teenagers as compared with 60 per cent who are adults (as differentiated from children, young adults, and older adults). With only 7 per cent of the population being teenaged, even though 97 per cent of teens play video games, it would be numerically unlikely for them to make up the largest group of gamers. These numbers show us that previously held beliefs about who plays are now moot.

The stereotype of the typical gamer depicts a male teen or young adult (Williams et al., 2008). In reality, many adult women are gamers, though they may be less likely to classify themselves as such. This may be for a variety of reasons. For example, it may be because the term *gamer* is associated with a more "hardcore" approach to gaming, such as playing action/first person shooter games. And, according to Near (2013), women tend to prefer casual games. It may also be because *gamer* is a stigmatized identity. Due to research findings that consumers may see as negative (Huesmann, 2010), inaccurate stereotypes about gamers such as low-income, uneducated or social ineptitude (Williams et al., 2008), and newsworthy incidents such as Gamer Gate, as mentioned above (Richard, 2015), individuals may choose to not associate with the gamer identity for fear of marginalization (Shaw, 2012).

Ultimately, gamer demographics are defined in a variety of ways. It is informative to consider whether research reflects people who identify as gamers or people who play games.

Developer's demographics

According to a recent report by the International Game Developers Association (Edwards, Weststar, & Meloni, 2014), game developers are young (69 per cent are between 25 and 39 years old), White (79 per cent), male (76 per cent) and heterosexual (86 per cent). 75 per cent of respondents reported having a disability. Mental illness was classified in this survey as being a disability, and, as such, it was the most common disability listed. When asked whether they felt that there was equal treatment and opportunities for all in the gaming industry, the largest group (47 per cent) responded in the negative. These statistics are useful in that they describe for us who is telling the stories that are depicted in video games with regard to race and gender and other demographics. When the storytellers are from a limited and/or privileged group of the population, this suggests that the stories about those outside that dominant group are being told by the dominant group. While telling stories about others is not, in and of itself, wrong – it would enhance the storytelling ability of developers to include those who have experienced those identities first-hand.

The first part of this chapter has discussed portrayals of gender, race and sexual orientation in games, as well as both player and developer demographics. While player and developer demographics only provide peripheral data, they give us a foundation for understanding the consumer base for this prolific and profitable industry. Though demographic data does not confirm causality of gaming research phenomena, understanding who buys games and who develops them allows us a jumping off point from which to further delve into the field of gaming research. The next section of this chapter takes a deeper look at how individuals represent *themselves* within game universes.

Avatar use in gaming

Avatars, in the context of gaming, are virtual representations of the player using them (Dietrich, 2013; Trepte & Reinecke, 2010; You, Kim, & Lee, 2015). An avatar embodies the attributes chosen, and is used, by the player to navigate the game or virtual world (aka VW) (Castronova, 2004). These attributes could mean performance-based characteristics such as health and ability statistics, or a virtual stand-in that puts a face with the player's name into cyberspace. Avatars may also represent personality choices of the player, whether they are similar or dissimilar to the actual players themselves.

Research on avatar use in virtual spaces has been conceptualized in both binary and quaternary terms (Carter, Gibbs, & Arnold, 2012). In a binary concept, users and players are interchangeable, as are avatars and characters. Here, the users are the individuals creating and controlling the virtual representations, while the avatar is the virtual representation of the self. In the quaternary concept, players, users, avatars and characters all represent specific, and different, identities in virtual world participation. Here, differentiations are made between physical and mental representations. Namely, the player and the character represent the mental, or identity, aspect of the offline and online representations, respectively, whereas the user and the avatar denote the physical aspects of the offline and online representations, respectively (Carter et al., 2012).

Avatars can be used, not only in games, but in any online space that allows for a consistent visual representation of the user (e.g., hovercards, profile pictures etc.) (Dietrich, 2013; Taylor,

2002). Additionally, these avatars may be created by the player or by the game developer, and from first-person or third-person perspectives. That being said, immersion is not necessarily dependent on the perspective from which the player controls the avatar (Newman, 2009). Avatar use tends to fit into two categories of use: physical representations and representations of identity. This section of the chapter will cover these representations, how they are implemented and discuss future avenues for avatar research in video game play.

Physical representations

Players use avatars as cyberspace representations of their physical selves, but they do not always make them accurate to their actual appearance. Ducheneaut, Wen, Yee and Wadley (2009) explain that age and gender cause a shift in focus during avatar creation and customization. These preferences also correlate with various game worlds. For example, Second Life players tended to be older than in the other two games included in the study. They note that "This demographic segment cares about projecting an 'idealized self'" (p. 1159). In World of Warcraft, they found that players tended to be male, and were more interested in creating extreme visual traits in their characters. As such, it behoves game developers to either create a wider variety of customization options for a wider variety of play styles, or options that are geared more specifically to the game's typical player base and their play style (Ducheneaut et al., 2009). That being said, very interesting research has shown trends in the physical appearance of avatars, as well as how well they represent players, regardless of how much they depend on the customization kits offered via game developers.

Subtle differences exist between males and females in avatar use. Gender-bending is not uncommon in avatar choice. However, it is far more common in men (Coulson, Barnett, Ferguson, & Gould, 2012) and is positively correlated with age in men (Yee, Ducheneaut, Yao, & Nelson, 2011). It may be that males choose female avatars in order to offset the proliferation of male characters in gaming, as well as to create avatars that they find attractive. But this gender-bending may have other, less obvious, side-effects. Yee and Bailenson (2007) found that when provided with avatars that were controlled for various physical attributes (i.e., created by researchers and not by participants), individuals took on behaviours related to the perceived identities of their characters (e.g., more willing to make intimate connections with other players while they were playing an attractive avatar). Martey, Stromer-Galley, Banks, Wu and Consalvo (2014) found that males who play female characters are more likely to exhibit behaviours similar to those of females playing female characters. However, males did not completely match female movement patterns. These researchers suggest the possibility that gender-bending males chose more stereotypical attributes of attractiveness, but more sustained behaviours tended to be only subtly conforming to gender roles (Martey et al., 2014).

Interestingly, when players created their own avatars, they were more likely to experiment with avatar physical appearance than personality choices (i.e., the avatar is likely to have the same personality as the user, but different physical appearances) (Sung, Moon, Lin et al., 2011). In truth, some games may not offer or require sought-after customization options in personality. That is not to say that enough options are available for physical customization, though. Among massive multi-player role-playing games (MMORPGs), few avatar creation processes provide sufficient racial variations, especially for non-white female character creation. Researchers note that games that do include these options, tend to be among the best-selling MMORPGs available (Dietrich, 2013). Other research supports the need for inclusive customization options, noting that hair style and colour were the most highly valued options in avatar creation (Ducheneaut et al., 2009). Hair may be the most important aspect of customization because not only is it among the most well-seen aspect of a character, but it is also something that holds contextual meaning in real life. Additionally, hair is one of the few physical features in real life that can be changed according to an individual's preferences. That being said, participants in this research felt that options provided in the three games studied (i.e., World of Warcraft, Second Life and Maple Story) were insufficient (Ducheneaut et al., 2009).

Though the need for more variety in customization seems apparent, players are not always looking to replicate themselves using their avatars. In fact, researchers have found an order of likely discrepancies between online and offline selves. When people create avatars, occupations are least likely to remain consistent with offline self, followed by age, ethnicity and gender (Sung, Moon, & Lin, 2011). When there are discrepancies between real self and online self, players are more likely to make virtual improvements (i.e., avatars will be made more attractive than the offline self) (Sung et al., 2011).

These perceived improvements make sense for several reasons. Social norms that exist in offline society tend to transfer to virtual societies (Yee, Bailenson, Urbanek, Chang, & Merget, 2007). For instance, research suggests that attractive avatars are preferred social partners in both adults and children (Principe & Langlois, 2013). This may create situations where attractiveness is used as a manipulative tool in virtual spaces between players, (e.g., for gain in social capital) (Principe & Langlois, 2013) or situations where players form emotional bonds with non-player characters (Coulson et al., 2012).

Representations of identity

An avatar opens a variety of ways in which the user can better understand themselves and others (Dunn & Guadagno, 2012). Identity theory explains that people have notions of what various identities mean – identity standards – and compare behaviours and experiences to those standards to determine how well they fit into those standards (Burke & Stets, 2009). This is how we adopt identities. But adopting the identities of avatars takes this to a whole new level. A growing body of research has sought to understand how identification with avatars can change our behaviours and how we identify in our offline lives. For example, identification with game characters in females mirrored identification with game characters in males, with regards to motivations for gameplay (van Reijmersdal et al., 2013). Researchers found that identification with game characters intensified the motivations for playing the games. This suggests that the more someone identifies with a character in-game, the more gameplay will satisfy the motivation for playing (van Reijmersdal et al., 2013).

People may also enjoy the game more if they identify more with the avatar (Trepte & Reinecke, 2010). There are some caveats to that, however. If the avatar closely resembles the player in appearance, the way in which that avatar is represented is likely to have an effect on the player. For example, Fox, Bailenson and Tricase (2013) found that women who had embodied sexualized characters that looked like virtual versions of themselves had more body-related thoughts and began to think of themselves in more sexualized ways than those who had embodied sexualized characters that looked like a stranger. In this case, identifying physically with the avatar had negative consequences.

That is not to say that avatars that represent us closely always have negative effects, but it illustrates that avatars seem to have consequences in offline behaviours and experiences (Fox et al., 2013). Avatar appearance may actually reflect self-esteem. Individuals with higher self-esteem tend to create characters that more accurately look more like them (You et al., 2015). Those with lower self-esteem, or who are more introverted, tend to create avatars that are consistently more attractive than the players themselves, and people who judge their avatars to be better than themselves tend to have low self-esteem (Bessière, Seay, & Kiesler, 2007). However, some people play more for true self-expression than ideal self-creation (Williams, Kennedy, & Moore, 2011).

Players of MMORPGs that are younger tend to spend more time playing, and higher score is dissociation as a motivation for playing. This may be because younger players likely have not established an identity and are able to more freely do so through role-play (Fuster, Carbonell, Chamarro, & Oberst, 2013). Similarly, research suggests that age is negatively correlated with character identification in females who play "pink games" (i.e., games whose content is targeted specifically at females) (van Reijmersdal et al., 2013). This also lends itself to the conclusion that players, in attempting to understand and come to terms with who they are, may identify more with game characters via role-play. Indeed, Taylor (2003) notes that females who play MMOs tend to be motivated by aspects of gaming typically associated with male gender roles, and therefore prefer gender-neutral games. Taylor also notes that one of the pleasures females derive from game play is identity exploration. Williams, Consalvo, Caplan and Yee (2009) note that females who play MMOs tend to be older than males. Considered together, it stands to reason that as female gamers get older, and have less salient identities, they tend to prefer games which allow them to go outside the bounds of typical gender roles.

It is not just young players that use avatars and virtual worlds to solidify identity. Players use avatars to explore, fix and verify identities (Bargh, McKenna, & Fitzsimons, 2002). For example, someone who is struggling to come out as LGBT, may first come out in a virtual environment where perceived anonymity can give them a shield from possible consequences (Cabiria, 2008). In fact, role-players tend to consist more of stigmatized/marginalized groups (e.g., females, racial minorities, younger players etc.), and use games/avatars to overcome or escape stigmatism (Williams et al., 2011). Escapism/dissociation is one of the most common motivations for gameplay (Fuster et al., 2013; Jeng & Teng, 2008; N. Yee, 2006).

Identification with the avatar a player is using also facilitates stronger social connections in-game (van Reijmersdal et al., 2013). People may also experience stronger connections to online friends when experiencing those friendships through avatar facilitated interactions (Bargh et al., 2002). Games also teach, and utilize already developed social skills. This, in turn, provides social capital which may also translate into offline relationships (Taylor, 2003). On the other hand, the anonymity of being online allows people the relative freedom of disinhibition. That is, people may feel above reproach/punishment when using avatars and thus may behave in ways that would otherwise be socially unacceptable (Joinson, 2007). This includes "trolling", a behaviour in which people try to bait others into embarrassing themselves or becoming angry (Fragoso, 2014).

Conclusion and directions for future research

In this chapter, we have discussed portrayals of gender, race and orientation in games and gaming communities. Because gaming is such a dynamic entertainment industry, future research on portrayals in gaming must be consistently updated to include current games and downloadable content. Additionally, it is important that gaming researchers consider a wide variety of genres in research, as much of the current research focuses on MMORPGs and first-person shooters (FPSs). For example, research in female portrayals may not include the diverse range of characters from massive online battle arenas (MOBAs) or flash games (e.g., Wolf Among Us). As these game genres are relatively new, exclusions are not likely due to oversight by researchers, but rather due to their non-existence at the time of the research. This also applies to queer content in gaming, including prominent LGBT characters, path options and diversity in avatar creation.

Similarly, further developments are needed in the realm of cross-cultural research. Cultural differences in gaming, and not just representation, have been examined to some extent. Research on Brazilian gamers has shown trolling behaviour – the harassment of other players – to be a typical bonding experience for Brazilian players (Fragoso, 2014). Calls and responses are used to seek out fellow Brazilian gamers, then behaviours such as griefing, spamming and intentional feeding are used to upset other players, particularly players from the United States. Fragoso also points out that online connectivity seems to allow Brazilian gamers to stray from cultural norms, such as politeness.

Cultural game play differences are also visible in other ways. For example, Taiwanese and American students asked to play a board game exhibited culturally motivated, yet spontaneously applied, implicit rules during gameplay (Hofstede & Murff, 2011). They found that cultural norms, such as individualism versus collectivism, lead to socially motivated interpretations of rules and acceptable behaviours. In this case, cultural norms carried over into gameplay, whereas online connectivity may have yielded different results due to disinhibition, as it seemed to with the Brazilian online gamers.

Disinhibition and cyberbullying in gaming tends to be targeted at sub-cultural minorities such as females, ethnic minorities and LGBT gaymers (Richard, 2015). This may be more of a contributing factor than misrepresentation when considering why individuals do not identify as gamers (Richard, 2015; Shaw, 2012).

Moving forward it will be important to continue to focus on the stories we tell about social groups – questions of who are soldiers and who are targets, for instance, and what effects these portrayals have on related behaviours need to be considered. If, as posited in social learning theory and cultivation theory, social and individual cues are taken from game content, it would be useful to research the specifics of those affects. Additionally, this should be done on both the group and individual levels, as affects may be specific to one or the other. Age range should also be taken into account in such studies. Questions regarding perception of gamers and game content should be asked of all ages, in addition to races, genders and sexual orientations. Research in gaming has typically only involved college-aged students. Including a variety of participants more representative of the gamer demographic would be beneficial in looking for effects caused by factors such as cognitive development, a matured understanding of social norms and expectations as well as a more robust exposure to game culture (for those who identify as gamers).

Furthermore, there has been a focus on negative outcomes in general across the discipline of media psychology. Future research should focus more on positive outcomes. In the context of this chapter, this could mean building on some work that has demonstrated that positive portrayals lead to positive outcomes (Dill & Burgess, 2012). Future studies might focus on exposure to countertypes – or counter-stereotypical prototypes, especially repeated exposure to such countertypes over periods of developmental growth (e.g., Gone Home). If particularly powerful counter-stereotypical game characters emerge in the market, exposure to those characters and subsequent positive outcomes should be studied. We would particularly like to see: 1) non-sexualized, smart, strong female characters in main character roles (e.g., Ellie from The Last of Us, Johanna from Heroes of the Storm, and Shephard from Mass Effect 3); and 2) Black male characters who counter criminal stereotypes (e.g., Lucian from League of Legends and Coltrane from Gears of War) and who are protagonists (e.g., Franklin from Grand Theft Auto V).

This chapter also discusses player demographics. Though these demographics have shown some consistency, future research should take care in defining gamers, because it is important to note that people who play games are not necessarily the same as those who identify as gamers (Shaw, 2012). Research is currently being done by one of the current authors (Stotler) on the application of identity theories to gamers. Consistent measures must be used to identify gamers if researchers seek to understand gaming identities and subcultures. Research operationally defines "gamer" in a variety of ways that are often inconsistent. For example, some research uses the number of hours played to determine whether a participant is a "gamer", while others may simply consider anyone who has played a video game via an online connection in the last 12 months to be a "gamer". However, it should be noted that playing games does not make someone a gamer any more than knowing how to knit makes someone a knitter (Schubert, 2010). The differences between operational definitions could transform the findings in many areas of gaming research.

Additionally, researchers investigating developer demographics should be careful to include assistants, consultants and other developer team members, as developers' perspectives are not necessarily inherent in demographic descriptions alone. Though correlations may exist which link products and perspectives to developers, these correlations may be due to confounding factors such as the perspectives of team members or other external pressures. For example, while some members of non-gaming society call for the inclusion of additional/different marginalized groups, gamers from those same groups may claim that content made simply to fill a perceived void is more off-putting than content that supports hegemony, but makes more sense for the storyline. And, as mentioned above, if developers are looking to remain relevant in their market, they are more likely to follow the desires of the gamers rather than non-gamers.

Finally, we presented a concise presentation of avatar studies in gaming research. Though avatar research has covered a large variety of users and purposes, confounding variables should be consistently controlled for. For example, in measuring self-esteem, enjoyment or escapism with avatar use, researchers should keep in mind that behaviours may be the result of external factors such as hardships in the home, distress or pre-existing health conditions.

In terms of representation by individuals, game developers should keep in mind that more developed options for customization (e.g., providing more control over every aspect of appearance) will be better received by both marginalized and normalized groups. This allows players to choose their experience in terms of identification and socialization, but also in terms of escapism and enjoyment. In other words, when you allow the player to choose who and what they want to be, you also allow them to choose how they will experience the game. This allows for replay-ability (i.e., the degree to which a game, once completed, is enjoyable when played repeatedly), the inherent inclusion of marginalized groups and allows for increased immersion.

Larger and more diverse pools of participants, online and offline game play and a more inclusive list of genres researched will add depth to avatar research, as well as gaming research in general. Research including a variety of cultural studies can help us understand differences in how games are played, the level of gamer stigmatization across or within cultures and differences in subculture definitions of "gamer". Cross-cultural research may also include differences in socially mediated gaming behaviours both online and offline. Variations in players from a variety of cultures may help us understand disinhibition within and across cultures, how social norms mediate competition (e.g., Major League Gaming) and how these variations may help or hinder socialization in gamer cultures. This will also allow us to better understand implications for social and personal development via online environments in our increasingly digital societies.

References

Annetta, L. A. (2010). The "I's" have it: A framework for serious educational game design. *Review of General Psychology*, *14*(2), 105–112. Retrieved from http://doi.org/10.1037/a0018985

Bargh, J. A., McKenna, K. Y., & Fitzsimons, G. M. (2002). Can you see the real me? Activation and expression of the "true self" on the Internet. *Journal of Social Issues*, *58*(1), 33–48.

Behm-Morawitz, E. (2014). Examining the intersection of race and gender in video game advertising, Journal of Marketing Communications, (June 2015), 37–41. Retrieved from http://doi.org/10.1080/13527266.2014.914562

Bessière, K., Seay, A. F., & Kiesler, S. (2007). The ideal elf: Identity exploration in World of Warcraft. *CyberPsychology & Behaviour, 10*(4), 530–535. Retrieved from http://doi.org/10.1089/cpb.2007.9994

Burgess, M. C., Dill, K. E., Stermer, S. P., Burgess, S. R., & Brown, B. P. (2011a). Playing with prejudice: The prevalence and consequences of racial stereotypes in video games. *Media Psychology, 14*(3), 289–311. Retrieved from http://doi.org/10.1080/15213269.2011.596467

Burgess, M. C., Dill, K. E., Stermer, S. P., Burgess, S. R., & Brown, B. P. (2011b). Playing with prejudice: The prevalence and consequences of racial stereotypes in video games. *Media Psychology, 14*(3), 289–311. http://doi.org/10.1080/15213269.2011.596467

Burgess, M. C., Stermer, S. P., & Burgess, S. R. (2007). Sex, lies, and video games: The portrayal of male and female characters on video game covers. *Sex Roles, 57*(5–6), 419–433. Retrieved from http://doi.org/10.1007/s11199-007-9250-0

Burke, P., & Stets, J. E. (2009). *Identity theory*. New York, NY: Oxford University Press. Retrieved from http://site.ebrary.com/id/10329671

Carter, M., Gibbs, M., & Arnold, M. (2012). Avatars, characters, players and users: Multiple identities at/in play. In *Proceedings of the 24th Australian Computer-Human Interaction Conference* (pp. 68–71). ACM. Retrieved from http://dl.acm.org/citation.cfm?id=2414547

Castronova, E. (2004). The price of bodies: A hedonic pricing model of avatar attributes in a synthetic world. *KYKLOS, 57*, 173–196.

Coulson, M., Barnett, J., Ferguson, C. J., & Gould, R. L. (2012). Real feelings for virtual people: Emotional attachments and interpersonal attraction in video games. *Psychology of Popular Media Culture, 1*(3), 176–184. Retrieved from http://doi.org/10.1037/a0028192

Cuddy, A. J. C., Fiske, S. T., & Glick, P. (2007). The BIAS map: Behaviours from intergroup affect and stereotypes. *Journal of Personality and Social Psychology, 92*(4), 631–648. Retrieved from http://doi.org/10.1037/0022-3514.92.4.631

Dennis, T. A., & O'Toole, L. J. (2014). Mental health on the go effects of a gamified attention-bias modification mobile application in trait-anxious adults. *Clinical Psychological Science, 2*(5), 576–590.

Dietrich, D. R. (2013). Avatars of whiteness: Racial expression in video game characters. *Sociological Inquiry, 83*(1), 82–105. Retrieved from http://doi.org/10.1111/soin.12001

Dietz, T. L. (1998). An examination of violence and gender role portrayals in video games. *Sex Rolesx, 38*(5–6), 425–442.

Dill, K. E., Brown, B. P., & Collins, M. a. (2008). Effects of exposure to sex-stereotyped video game characters on tolerance of sexual harassment. *Journal of Experimental Social Psychology, 44*(5), 1402–1408. Retrieved from http://doi.org/10.1016/j.jesp.2008.06.002

Dill, K. E., & Burgess, M. C. (2012). Influence of black masculinity: Game exemplars on social judgments. *Simulation & Gaming, 44*(4), 562–585. Retrieved from http://doi.org/10.1177/1046878112449958

Dill, K. E., Gentile, D. A., Richter, W. A., & Dill, J. C. (2005). Violence, sex, race and age in popular video games: A content analysis. In A. P. Association (Ed.), *Featuring females: Feminist analyses of the media* (pp. 115–130). New York.

Dill, K. E., & Thill, K. P. (2007). Video game characters and the socialization of gender roles: Young people's perceptions mirror sexist media depictions. *Sex Roles, 57*(11-12), 851–864. Retrieved from http://doi.org/10.1007/s11199-007-9278-1

Downs, E., & Smith, S. L. (2010). Keeping abreast of hypersexuality: A video game character content analysis. *Sex Roles, 62*(11), 721–733. Retrieved from http://doi.org/10.1007/s11199-009-9637-1

Ducheneaut, N., Wen, M.-H., Yee, N., & Wadley, G. (2009). Body and mind: A study of avatar personalization in three virtual worlds. In *Proceedings of the SIGCHI Conference on Human Factors in Computing Systems* (pp. 1151–1160). ACM. Retrieved from http://dl.acm.org/citation.cfm?id=1518877

Dunn, R. A., & Guadagno, R. E. (2012). My avatar and me: Gender and personality predictors of avatar-self discrepancy. *Computers in Human Behaviour, 28*(1), 97–106. Retrieved from http://doi.org/10.1016/j.chb.2011.08.015

Edwards, K., Weststar, J., & Meloni, W. (2014). *IGDA Developer Satisfaction Survey 2014*.

Fiske, S. T., Xu, J., Cuddy, A., & Glick, P. (1999). (Dis)respecting versus (dis)liking: Status and interdependence predict ambivalent stereotypes of competence and warmth. *Journal of Social Issues, 55*, 473–489.

Fox, J., Bailenson, J. N., & Tricase, L. (2013). The embodiment of sexualized virtual selves: The Proteus effect and experiences of self-objectification via avatars. *Computers in Human Behaviour, 29*(3), 930–938. Retrieved from http://doi.org/10.1016/j.chb.2012.12.027

Fragoso, S. (2014). "HUEHUEHUE" "BR?BR?": The carnivalesque griefing behaviour of Brazilian online gamers. In M. Strano, H. Hrachovec, S. Fragoso, C. Ess & M. van der Velden (Eds.), *9th International Conference in Culture, Technology, Communication: Celebration, Transformation, New Directions* (pp. 167–185). Oslo, Norway: Culture, Technology, and Communication.

Fuster, H., Carbonell, X., Chamarro, A., & Oberst, U. (2013). Interaction with the game and motivation among players of massively multiplayer online role-playing games. *The Spanish Journal of Psychology, 16*. Retrieved from http://doi.org/10.1017/sjp.2013.54

Glick, P., & Fiske, S. T. (1996). The ambivalent sexism lnventory: Differentiating hostile and benevolent sexism. *Journal of Personality and Social Psychology, 70*(3), 491–512. Retrieved from http://doi.org/10.1037/0022-3514.70.3.491

Glick, P., Lameiras, M., Fiske, S. T., Eckes, T., Masser, B., Volpato, C., ... Glick, P. (2004). Bad but bold: Ambivalent attitudes toward men predict gender inequality in 16 nations. *Journal of Personality and Social Psychology, 86*(5), 713–728. Retrieved from http://doi.org/10.1037/0022-3514.86.5.713

Green, M., Brock, T. C., & Kaufman, G. (2004). Understanding media enjoyment: The role of transportation into narrative worlds. *Communication Theory, 14*(4), 311–327.

Hofstede, G. J., & Murff, E. (2011). Repurposing an old game for an international world. *Simulation & Gaming, 43*(1), 34–50.

Huesmann, L. R. (2010). Nailing the coffin shut on doubts that violent video games stimulate aggression: Comment on Anderson et al. (2010). *Psychological Bulletin, 136*(2), 179–181. Retrieved from http://doi.org/10.1037/a0018567

Ivory, J. D. (2009). Still a man's game: Gender representation in online reviews of video games. *Mass Communication and Society, 9*(1), 103–114. Retrieved from http://doi.org/10.1207/s15327825mcs0901_6

Jeng, S.-P., & Teng, C.-I. (2008). Personality and motivations for playing online games. *Social Behaviour and Personality: An International Journal, 36*(8), 1053–1060. Retrieved from http://doi.org/10.2224/sbp.2008.36.8.1053

Joinson, A. (2007). Disinhibition and the internet. In J. Gackenbach (Ed.), *Psychology and the internet: Intrapersonal, interpersonal, and transpersonal implications* (pp. 75–92). Amsterdam: Elsevier/Academic Press.

Klimmt, C., Hefner, D., Vorderer, P., Roth, C., & Blake, C. (2010). Identification with video game characters as automatic shift of self-perceptions. *Media Psychology, 13*(4), 323–338. Retrieved from http://doi.org/10.1080/15213269.2010.524911

Lee, T. L., Fiske, S. T., & Glick, P. (2010). Next gen ambivalent sexism: Converging correlates, causality in context, and converse causality. *Sex Roles, 62*(7-8), 395–404. Retrieved from http://doi.org/10.1007/s11199-010-9747-9

Lenhart, A., Kahne, J., Middaugh, E., Macgill, A. R., Evans, C., & Vitak, J. (2008). *Teens, video games and civics*. Washington, DC: American Psychological Association. Retrieved from http://www.pewinternet.org/files/old-media/Files/Reports/2008/PIP_Teens_Games_and_Civics_Report_FINAL.pdf.pdf

Macdonald, K. (2012, January). A gay history of gaming. Retrieved from www.ign.com/articles/2012/01/25/a-gay-history-of-gaming

Major League Gaming. (2015). Retrieved from www.majorleaguegaming.com/

Martey, R. M., Stromer-Galley, J., Banks, J., Wu, J., & Consalvo, M. (2014). The strategic female: gender-switching and player behaviour in online games. *Information, Communication & Society, 17*(3), 286–300. Retrieved from doi.org/10.1080/1369118X.2013.874493

Martins, N., Williams, D. C., Harrison, K., & Ratan, R. A. (2009). A content analyisis of female body imagery in video games. *Sex Roles, 61*, 824–836. Retrieved from http://doi.org/10.1007/s11199-009-9682-9

MidBoss. (2015). Gaming in color. Retrieved from http://gamingincolor.tv/

Miller, M. K., & Summers, A. (2007). Gender differences in video game characters' roles, appearances, and attire as portrayed in video game magazines. *Sex Roles, 57*(9–10), 733–742. Retrieved from http://doi.org/10.1007/s11199-007-9307-0

Near, C. E. (2013). Selling gender: Associations of box art representation of female characters with sales for teen- and mature-rated video games. *Sex Roles, 68*(3–4), 252–269. Retrieved from http://doi.org/10.1007/s11199-012-0231-6

Newman, J. (2009). Playing the system: Videogames/players/characters. *Semiotica, 173*. Retrieved from http://doi.org/10.1515/SEMI.2009.024

Principe, C. P., & Langlois, J. H. (2013). Children and adults use attractiveness as a social cue in real people and avatars. *Journal of Experimental Child Psychology, 115*(3), 590–597. Retrieved from doi.org/10.1016/j.jecp.2012.12.002*Real Life + Virtual Life = One life by Dr. Jonathan Cabiria.* (2008). Retrieved from www.youtube.com/watch?v=N3qwdQLSt2I

Richard, G. T. (2015). Intersecting vulnerabilities in game culture: The effects of inequities and stereotype threat on player confidence, identification and persistence across gender and race. In *Proceedings of DiGRA 2015: Diversity of play: Games – Cultures – Identities.* Digital Games Research Association. Retrieved from www.researchgate.net/profile/Gabriela_Richard/publication/275771792_Identities_Intersecting_Vulnerabilities_in_Game_Culture_The_Effects_of_Inequities_and_Stereotype_Threat_on_Player_Confidence_Identification_and_Persistence_Across_Gender_and_Race/links/5546da700cf234bdb21dae11.pdf

Scharrer, E. (2004). Virtual violence: Gender and aggression in video game advertisements. *Mass Communication and Society,* 7(4), 393–412. Retrieved from http://doi.org/10.1207/s15327825mcs0704

Schubert, D. (2010). DESIGN: The casual/hardcore continuum. *Game Developer, 17*(8), 44.

Shaw, A. (2009). Putting the gay in games: Cultural production and LGBT content in video games. *Games and Culture, 4*(3), 228–253. Retrieved from http://doi.org/10.1177/1555412009339729

Shaw, A. (2012). Do you identify as a gamer? Gender, race, sexuality, and gamer identity. *New Media & Society, 14*(1), 28–44. Retrieved from http://doi.org/10.1177/1461444811410394

Shaw, A. (2012). Talking to gaymers: Questioning identity, community and media representation. *Westminster Papers in Communication and Culture, 9*(1), 67–89.

Sisler, V. (2008). Digital Arabs: Representation in video games. *European Journal of Cultural Studies, 11*(2), 203–219.

Sung, Y., Moon, J. H., Lin, J.-S., & others. (2011). Actual self vs. avatar self: The effect of online social situation on self-expression. *Journal for Virtual Worlds Research, 4*(1). Retrieved from https://jvwr-ojs-utexas.tdl.org/jvwr/index.php/jvwr/article/view/1927

Tassi, P. (2015, January). Second US college now offering "League of Legends" scholarship. Retrieved from www.forbes.com/sites/insertcoin/2015/01/08/second-us-college-now-offering-league-of-legends-scholarship/

Taylor, T. L. (2003). Multiple pleasures women and online gaming. *Convergence: The International Journal of Research into New Media Technologies, 9*(1), 21–46.

Trepte, S., & Reinecke, L. (2010). Avatar creation and video game enjoyment: Effects of life-Satisfaction, game competitiveness, and identification with the avatar. *Journal of Media Psychology: Theories, Methods, and Applications, 22*(4), 171–184. Retrieved from http://doi.org/10.1027/1864-1105/a000022

Unkelbach, C., Forgas, J. P., & Denson, T. F. (2008). The turban effect: The influence of Muslim headgear and induced affect on aggressive responses in the shooter bias paradigm. *Journal of Experimental Social Psychology, 44*(5), 1409–1413. Retrieved from http://doi.org/10.1016/j.jesp.2008.04.003

van Reijmersdal, E. A., Jansz, J., Peters, O., & van Noort, G. (2013). Why girls go pink: Game character identification and game-players' motivations. *Computers in Human Behaviour, 29*(6), 2640–2649. Retrieved from http://doi.org/10.1016/j.chb.2013.06.046

Williams, D., Consalvo, M., Caplan, S., & Yee, N. (2009). Looking for gender: Gender roles and behaviours among online gamers. *Journal of Communication, 59*(4), 700–725. Retrieved from http://doi.org/10.1111/j.1460-2466.2009.01453.x

Williams, D., Kennedy, T. L. M., & Moore, R. J. (2011). Behind the avatar: The patterns, practices, and functions of role playing in MMOS. *Games and Culture, 6*(2), 171–200. Retrieved from http://doi.org/10.1177/1555412010364983

Williams, D., Martins, N., Consalvo, M., & Ivory, J. D. (2009). The virtual census: representations of gender, race and age in video games. *New Media & Society, 11*(5), 815–834. Retrieved from http://doi.org/10.1177/1461444809105354

Williams, D., Yee, N., & Caplan, S. E. (2008). Who plays, how much, and why? Debunking the stereotypical gamer profile. *Journal of Computer-Mediated Communication, 13*(4), 993–1018. Retrieved from http://doi.org/10.1111/j.1083-6101.2008.00428.x

Yao, M. Z., Mahood, C., & Linz, D. (2010). Sexual Priming, gender stereotyping, and likelihood to sexually harass: Examining the cognitive effects of playing a sexually-explicit video game. *Sex Roles, 62*(1–2), 77–88. Retrieved from http://doi.org/10.1007/s11199-009-9695-4

Yee, N. (2006). Motivations for play in online games. *CyberPsychology & Behaviour, 9*(6), 772–775.

Yee, N., & Bailenson, J. N. (2009). The difference between being and seeing: The relative contribution of self-perception and priming to behavioural changes via digital self-representation. *Media Psychology, 12*(2), 195–209. Retrieved from http://doi.org/10.1080/15213260902849943

Yee, N., Bailenson, J. N., Urbanek, M., Chang, F., & Merget, D. (2007). The unbearable likeness of being digital: The persistence of nonverbal social norms in online virtual environments. *CyberPsychology & Behaviour, 10*(1), 115–121. Retrieved from http://doi.org/10.1089/cpb.2006.9984

Yee, N., Ducheneaut, N., Yao, M., & Nelson, L. (2011). Do men heal more when in drag?: Conflicting identity cues between user and avatar (p. 773). ACM Press. Retrieved from http://doi.org/10.1145/1978942.1979054

You, S., Kim, E., & Lee, D. (2015). Virtually real: Exploring avatar identification in game addiction among massively multiplayer online role-playing games (MMORPG) players. *Games and Culture*, 1–16. Retrieved from http://doi.org/10.1177/1555412015581087

34

Personality-customized advertising in the digital environment

Sandra Matz

By the end of 2014, global business-to-consumer (B2C) e-commerce sales hit $1.5 trillion, with a predicted growth of about 20 per cent yearly (Emarketers, 2015). More than 80 per cent of the 1.3 billion Internet users worldwide have shopped online and more than 50 per cent have done so more than once (CPC Strategy, 2015). This rapid migration of traditional B2C commerce to the digital environment has changed the way in which consumers search for and purchase products dramatically. While only 20 years ago, most consumers were limited by the assortment of local suppliers, the Internet makes it possible to access products and services from all around the world. Today, consumers order their books on Amazon, search for a new watch on Ebay and have their smartphone delivered from Best Buy. They compare products and prices across countries, platforms and providers and have their purchases shipped to them from around the globe at very low cost. Although the migration of e-commerce to the digital environment certainly offers tremendous opportunities for both businesses and consumers, it also poses considerable challenges.

From a business perspective, the Internet has become a global-market arena in which businesses find themselves in a constant struggle to secure and expand their market positions. Whereas a retail shop in the past was competing against other shops in the area, it is now competing against innumerable online retail stores around the world, many of which may benefit from cheaper labour costs or more liberal taxation laws. This growing competition has made a sophisticated and effective marketing strategy even more indispensable than before. In order to gain advantage over competitors, businesses need to understand how they can best exploit the unique opportunities offered by digital advertising. They need to find the right audience for their products and communicate their unique selling proposition in the most compelling fashion possible.

From a consumer perspective, the unprecedented wealth of products and services renders the digital shopping environment increasingly difficult to navigate and comprehend. On March 5, 2015, for example, ebay.com listed more than 1.2 million entries for the search query "watch" and Amazon.com offered its customers more than 5 million products under the category "mobile phone". While having access to such a vast range of products and services might at first sight appear to be a blessing, it can easily turn into an "agony of choice". Whereas picking the "right" watch from a small local store was relatively simple and straightforward, the choice of thousands of different models in the online retail environment can be overwhelming. In fact, research summarized under the heading of *The Paradox of Choice* has shown that an overabundance of options can significantly decrease peoples well-being (Schwartz & Ward, 2004). While most of us value increased freedom, autonomy and self-determination and often follow a philosophy of "the more choice the better", Schwartz and Ward argue that there is a cost to having an overabundance of choice. As the number of options grows, the more negative aspects begin to appear "until, ultimately, choice no longer liberates, but debilitates" (Schwartz & Ward, 2004, p. 87).

Customized advertising constitutes a valuable tool to tackle these challenges by (a) boosting the effectiveness of advertising for businesses and (b) preselecting the most relevant information and products for consumers. The idea behind customization concepts is to personalise consumers' shopping experience in a way that addresses their individual preferences and needs (Sheth, Sisodia, & Sharma, 2000; Montaner, Lopez, & de la Rosa, 2003; Liang, Lai, & Ku, 2006). By targeting only those consumers most likely to buy or engage with the product, and simultaneously connecting with them on a personal level, businesses can decrease their advertising costs significantly while at the same time increasing conversion rates and turnover. Likewise, a sophisticated customization mechanism can help improve user experience by finding the right piece of content for a user and by making it personally relevant and engaging. The Amazon recommendation system "People who bought X also bought Y" enables users to navigate through the vast assortment of goods and suggests additional products that might be relevant to them. While a large proportion of current advertising is perceived as irrelevant spam, such customization mechanisms are often highly valued by users and considered helpful information (Liang et. al., 2006).Taken together, there is hence a demand for sophisticated customization mechanisms from both business and consumer sides.

Although the term "customized advertising" might be new to some of the readers, the vast majority of us have experienced the underlying concept in one way or another before. Think about a typical salesperson in an apparel store, for example. If she knows her business, she will try to form an impression of what the customer opposite of her is like: How much will he be willing to spend? How much does he care about his appearance? Does he prefer expressive or conservative clothes? Does he care about brands that highlight his status? Answers to those questions help her to anticipate and predict the preferences and wishes of her customer and to adapt her communication in a way that convincingly highlights the benefits of buying the products. Regrettably, most communication with consumers in the digital environment is highly generic and impersonal. Customized advertising therefore provides not only a tool to overcome the aforementioned challenges, but a chance to bring back the "personal element" to online shopping.

Scope of this chapter

This chapter will discuss how a combination of psychological theory and innovative psychometric assessment methods can be used to make advertising more personal than ever before. Drawing on the law of interpersonal attraction (Byrne, 1961), we will first introduce the two fit-based customization approaches of *Product-Targeting* and *Message-Tailoring* and provide empirical evidence for their effectiveness. Following up on the question of why these approaches have barely been used in advertising practice, we introduce an innovative way of predicting consumers' psychological traits from digital footprints, such as Facebook profile information. We then link back to digital advertising and show that these predictions offer an unprecedented opportunity to put psychological theory into practice. Taking account of the personalization mechanisms that are already in place (e.g., Amazon recommendation system) we discuss the idiosyncratic advantages of personality-based customization mechanisms. Finally, we will investigate and critically evaluate major ethical challenges related to personality-based advertisement customization.

A psychological perspective on customized advertising

The rationale of customized advertising is simple: to make advertisements more effective by offering products to consumers that meet their current needs and are personally relevant to them. Although there are different ways to achieve this goal (see Section 5, "Comparison to other customization approaches"), psychological theory offers valuable insights into how the wealth of information available on individuals online can be condensed and interpreted in a meaningful way.

The concept of "similarity" is deeply rooted in theories of social psychology and consumer behaviour (e.g., law of attraction by Byrne & Nelson, 1965). It suggests that our attitudes, emotions and behaviours towards other persons or entities are more positive when those entities share our characteristics (Byrne, 1961). Translated to the context of marketing research, similarity has been studied as the fit between (a) product and consumer characteristics (*product-person fit*) or (b) message and consumer characteristics (*message-person fit*). In both cases, consumers were found to show a more favourable response to products and advertisements corresponding to their own characteristics (e.g., Aaker, 1999; Hirsh, Kang, & Bodenhausen, 2012). In order to increase product-person or message-person fit, two types of customization approaches have been suggested that are directed at either (a) selecting the right audience for a product or (b) adapting the advertisement content to the characteristics of a given audience. We refer to the first case as *Product-Targeting* and the second as *Message-tailoring*. A skydiving company, for instance, might decide to target young and extroverted users and make the message even more persuasive by tailoring the content to the target groups characteristics (e.g., "Looking for excitement and fun? Benefit from our latest offer!"). Taking account of their shared objective, namely to create a fit between a consumer and a product or brand, we suggest summarizing the two approaches under the heading of *fit-based advertisement customization*. While other approaches have predominantly been developed by computer scientists and are mainly data-driven, fit-based advertisement customization is deeply rooted in social psychological theory. Figure 34.1 illustrates the idea of fit-based customization.

Fit-based advertisement customization is nothing new and by no means unique to digital advertising. Indeed, businesses have long started to use demographic variables such as age, gender or geographic location to target different user segments and to design their messages accordingly. A beauty retailer, for example, might decide to target young women and emphasize the affordability and trendiness of their styling products, while another might choose to target women aged 50+ and highlight the high quality of their anti-aging products. What is indeed new and unique to the digital environment is the breadth of information that can be used to create fit. While demographic variables might be an effective first step in defining one's target group (by excluding all consumers for which the product is not relevant) they very quickly reach their limits of discriminating between consumers in a meaningful way. For example, women can differ as much in their tastes from other women as they do from men. Considering that the aim of customized advertising is to make consumers feel understood on an individual level, addressing them generically as a woman of a certain age would appear to be rather superficial. Compared to traditional advertising contexts, the Internet provides marketers with consumer information that reaches far beyond simple demographics and allows them

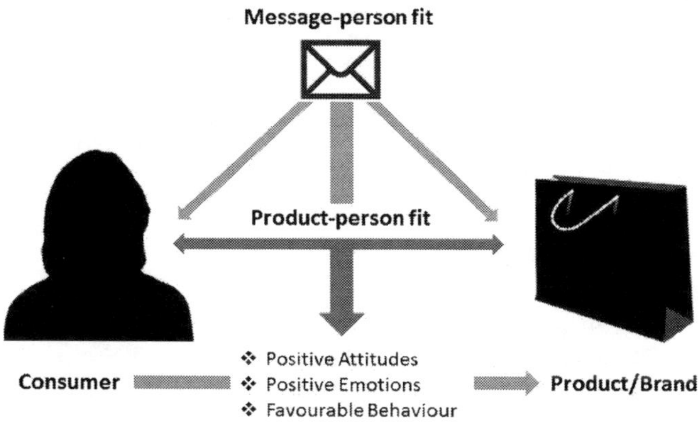

Figure 34.1 Fit-based customisation mechanisms. Product-person fit directly results from the match between consumer and product characteristics. It can therefore be conceptualized as a "true" fit. Message-person fit, on the other hand, does not necessarily require a true fit between product and consumer (although it can also be used to support a true fit), it somewhat artificially creates a fit by presenting it in a way that implies certain characteristics. Both customisation mechanisms lead to more positive attitudes, emotions and behaviours of the consumer towards the product.

to tap into the "psychology" of consumers. For example, knowing that one is advertising to a young woman with a strong social motive and an extraverted character will make it easier for marketers to select their products and design their messages in a way that gets to the heart of the consumers' needs. Generally speaking, the more unique an informative the information that is gathered on consumers, the more effective customized advertising should become. And indeed, there is a substantial body of scientific research supporting the usefulness of psychological traits in advertisement customization. The next two sections will briefly outline research supporting the effectiveness of product–person and message–person fit for eliciting desired consumer outcomes, such as favourable attitudes and emotions, purchase intentions or consumer satisfaction.

Product-person fit

The idea that the fit between a product's personality and the self-concept of its targeted consumers plays an important role in eliciting favourable consumer responses has a long-standing tradition in consumer research. It is based on the assumption that people consume products for both functional value and symbolic meaning: People purchase products not only for what they can do, but also for what they mean (Levy, 1959). While some spending is necessary to fulfil basic needs like food and shelter, most is about buying that reflects who we are as individuals. According to the self-congruity theory (also self-image congruence), consumers choose and evaluate products based on how well their associated characteristics reflect their own identity (Aaker, 1997; Sirgy, 1986). Motivated by the need to express themselves in a way that is consistent with their self-perception (self-consistency motive, Lecky, 1945) consumers are more likely to favour brands or products that express their own selves (Sirgy, 1985). A person who perceives herself to be creative and open to new experiences, for example, is likely to buy products that help her highlight her artistic and open-minded side. Supported by meta-analytical evidence (Aguirre-Rodriguez, Bosnjak, & Sirgy, 2012) the self-congruity effect has been linked to different outcome variables such as brand attitudes and purchase intentions (Aaker, 1999, Sirgy, 1986), product choice (Malhorta, 1988), consumer satisfaction (Back, 2005) or brand loyalty (Kressmann et al., 2006). Aaker (1999), for example, investigated the role of product–person congruence by focusing on the match between the personality of two apparel/two fragrance brands and the personality of participants. The personality of brands was established with the help of the five dimensions of brand personality developed by Aaker (1997). 20 participants rated a set of brands in each product category on the five dimensions of Excitement, Ruggedness, Sincerity, Competence and Sophistication. Brands with the highest and respectively lowest scores on the target traits of Excitement and Ruggedness and constant scores on the remaining three dimensions were selected for the experiment. Those were: Bennetton and CKOne fragrance for Excitement as well as Patagonia apparel and Polo fragrance for Ruggedness. In the main experiment, 93 participants were asked to report their own personality characteristics and to rate their preferences for the four brands as well as the likelihood of using them in a certain situation. The results confirm that participants indeed report more favourable attitudes towards brands that match their personality – both for Excitement and Ruggedness.

Message–person fit

Evidence for the concept of message–person fit comes from research related to the value-from-fit hypothesis (Higgins, 2000) and message–person congruence (Hirsh et al., 2012). Both theories suggest that the persuasiveness of a message increases alongside its fit with the characteristics of its recipients. The value-from-fit hypothesis stipulates that a match between the dominant motivational orientation of individuals (promotion- vs. prevention-oriented) and the means they deploy to achieve certain goals (eager vs. vigilant strategic means) leads to a more positive evaluation of the action. With regard to persuasive communication, the value-from-fit hypothesis has been used to influence the way in which individuals experience the messages they receive. There is robust empirical evidence supporting the value-from-fit hypothesis in the context of persuasive communication, ranging from health behaviour (Cesario, Grant, & Higgins, 2004; Spiegel, Grant-Pillow, & Higgins, 2004), to volunteerism (Koenig, Cesario, Molden, Kosloff, & Higgins, 2009) and social policy issues (Cesario et al., 2004), to advertising and consumer behaviour (e.g., Avnet & Higgins, 2006; Higgins, Idson, Freitas, Spiegel, & Molden, 2003). By framing the persuasive message according to the dominant motivational orientation of its recipients, researchers have been able to manipulate their emotional, cognitive as well as behavioural responses towards the message. Whereas the persuasive impact of eager-framed messages was found to be greater for promotion- than prevention-oriented individuals, the opposite is true for messages framed in a vigilant way (e.g., Cesario et al., 2004). Taking account of the fact that the motivational orientation of promotion vs. prevention-oriented goals constitutes a rather narrow psychological trait, Hirsh et al. (2012) investigated the message-tailoring mechanism within the framework of the Big Five personality traits (Costa & McCrae, 1985; Goldberg, 1992). Following the general descriptions of the traits, they designed five different advertisement messages for a mobile phone, each of which reflected the unique characteristics of one of the traits. While the message for Extraversion, for example, included references to "excitement", "life of the party" and "being in the spotlight", the message for Openness highlighted "innovation", "intelligent and sophisticated design", and "imagination". 324 participants were asked to (a) rate the messages according to their effectiveness and personal preference as well as to (b) complete a personality questionnaire. Similar to the results reported for the value-from-fit hypothesis, Hirsh et al. (2012) found that tailoring a message for a phone advertisement to consumers' dominant Big Five personality traits (Costa & McCrae, 1985;

Goldberg, 1992) resulted in significantly higher ratings of effectiveness. Taken together, the findings obtained from research on the value-from-fit hypothesis as well as message–person congruence demonstrate the effectiveness of personality tailored advertisements.

The lack of psychology in applied advertisement customization

Considering the outlined benefits of using psychological insights for fit-based advertisement customization, it seems rather surprising that most businesses still rely on simple user demographics to define and target different consumer segments (Moon, 2002). One possible explanation for this slow adaptation is that psychological characteristics are not as easily available as demographic variables, such as age or gender. As a matter of fact, ever since its introduction in the early 1920s, psychological assessment has been largely dependent upon questionnaire measures. Whereas it is easy for researchers to include questionnaires in laboratory settings, marketing practitioners can hardly expect their potential customers to fill in a questionnaire before showing the most appropriate advertisement to them. Consequently, in order to make psychological traits a viable alternative to demographic variables in customized advertising, businesses need mechanisms to establish psychological characteristics of consumers without relying on self-report measures.

Whereas marketers in traditional advertising settings had very little information about individual consumers, the Internet offers an unprecedented wealth of users' digital footprints. Whether it is their browsing history, their playlist on Spotify or their public Facebook profile, these digital footprints create extensive records of consumers' habits, preferences, motivations and more. Taken together, such records offer a unique opportunity to make inferences about consumers' psychological traits and therefore to understand their individual needs much better than ever before. The question that arises is: "How can we translate personal user information into psychological profiles?" Indeed, despite the wealth of information available on individual consumers the translation of such data into valid psychological profiles is far from trivial. Marketers who are familiar with personality frameworks such as the Big Five might be tempted to make intuitive assumptions about the relationships between certain digital footprints and psychological traits. Knowing that Extraverts tend to actively seek out social environments and stimulation, for example, it seems reasonable to assume that Extraverts have a larger social network and post about social events more frequently than Introverts. Although such an "intuition-driven approach" might lead to the discovery of valid relationships that prove valuable in attracting consumers, they also pose a considerable risk of following false assumptions and stereotypes. This might not only lead to financial losses for businesses but also alienate and frustrate consumers. Furthermore, the more information one has available on consumers the more difficult it becomes to integrate the individual pieces of information into one coherent user profile. Rather than relying on their intuitions, marketers should therefore base their customization decision on actual data and validated empirical links between digital footprints and psychological traits ("insight-driven approach"). The following section therefore reviews some of the established relationships that have been reported in the psychological literature.

Using digital footprints to predict consumers' psychology

The Internet has become an integral part of the lives of almost 3 billion people around the globe. On average, Internet user spend 16 hours per month online (almost 32 hours per month for US users; Go Gulf, 2015), leaving digital footprints that provide researchers and marketers with a valuable source of information about their personal habits and preferences. Indeed, consumers' personality has been successfully predicted from personal websites (Marcus, Machilek, &

Schütz, 2006), browsing logs (Kosinski, Stillwell, Kohli, Bachrach, & Graepel, 2012) or Twitter messages (Quercia, Kosinski, Stillwell, & Crowcroft, 2011; Golbeck, Robles, Edmondson, & Turner, 2011). One of the most extensive sources of personal user information, however, can be found in Online Social Networks (OSNs). Although nomenclature, appearance and additional functionality of web-based services may vary from site to site, the possibility to create a public or semi-public profile is a fundamental component of every OSN (Boyd & Ellison, 2007). Individual profile information is voluntarily provided by each member and usually includes highly personal data such as the user's birthday, hometown or relationship status, information about favourite interests, activities, books, quotes and movies as well as shared pictures, videos and wall entries.

Facebook is the most popular OSN. With 1.3 billion users, more than one-third of the Internet population uses Facebook, sharing over 4 billion pieces of content per day (Wilson, Gosling & Graham, 2012). While there have been doubts as to whether one can trust the information provided by Facebook users, there is now substantial empirical evidence that Facebook profiles provide fairly accurate description of user's offline characteristics (*extended real-life hypothesis*) rather than idealized presentations of themselves (*idealized virtual identity hypothesis*) (e.g., Back et al., 2009). We therefore take Facebook as an example to illustrate how OSNs can be used to predict psychological traits from profile information (for a more comprehensive overview see Kosinski, Matz, Gosling, Popov & Stillwell, 2015). Although some studies have investigated psychological traits in a broader sense, most of this research focuses on the Big Five personality traits (Costa & McCrae, 1985; Goldberg, 1992). The Big Five model is the most widely accepted research model of personality today. It posits the five personality traits of Openness to Experience, Conscientiousness, Extraversion, Agreeableness and Neuroticism. Since the remaining sections of this chapter will focus on research related to the Big Five, we advise readers who are not familiar with the Big Five model to consult Cervone and Pervin (2013) for a detailed description of the traits.

Predicting personality from Facebook profiles

The information that can be used to make inferences about the personality of Facebook users falls into two categories: Identity Claims and Behavioural Residue (Gosling, Ko, Manarelli & Morris, 2002). Identity claims refer to symbolic statements – both subtle and explicit – that are deliberately made by individuals with the objective of expressing themselves. Liking "Green Peace", for example, is a very explicit expression of political commitment or social responsibility. Behavioural residue, on the other hand, relate to clues that are inadvertently conveyed as a result of one's activity within a given context. Having a large number of friends and wall posts, for example, is an indicator of a rather sociable and extraverted personality. Table 34.1 presents an overview of the Facebook information available in both categories.

Table 34.1 Examples of behavioural residue and identity claims on Facebook

Behavioural residue	*Identity claims*
• Self/other generated wall entries (status updates)	• Activities and interests
• Number of Likes	• Favourite music
• Number of pictures	• Favourite books
• Number of picture albums	• Favourite movies/TV shows
• Number of friends	• Favourite games
• Number of joined Facebook groups	• "About me" section

The following sections provide an overview of empirical findings on the links between various types of Facebook information and the Big Five personality traits. While early research in this domain has largely focused on the frequencies of certain behaviours, later research has adopted machine-learning techniques to investigate the content of profile information.

Frequencies of behavioural residue

Several studies have related the frequency of behavioural residue outlined in Table 34.1 to the Big Five personality traits (e.g., Amichai-Hamburger & Vinitzky, 2010; Bachrach, Kosinski, Graepel, Kohli & Stillwell, 2012; Gosling et al., 2011). The number of friends, wall posts, groups, photos and Likes, for example, have been consistently related to the trait of Extraversion. Likewise, the trait of Openness has been linked to the number of wall posts and groups as well as the number of friends and Likes. Neuroticism and Conscientiousness, on the contrary, were found to be negatively related to the number of friends and the number of groups joined respectively. Taken together, behavioural residues found on Facebook profiles have been shown to be significantly associated with psychological traits such as the Big Five. Indeed, Bachrach et al. (2011) showed that up to 33 per cent of variance in Extraversion and 26 per cent variance in Neuroticism can be explained when predicting the Big Five with the frequency of behavioural residue.

Language (status updates)

Status updates are a Facebook feature that allows users to share their thoughts, whereabouts and other information with friends, providing very rich information about users preferences as well as the way they articulate them. Analyzing the data of 66,732 Facebook users, Park et al. (2014) showed that the content of status updates can be used to accurately predict the Big Five with the help of natural language analysis. With correlations between 0.38 for Conscientiousness and 0.46 for Openness to experience, the language based predictions of the Big Five show a similar accuracy as short personality tests (see Figure 34.2 for all traits). While highly extraverted

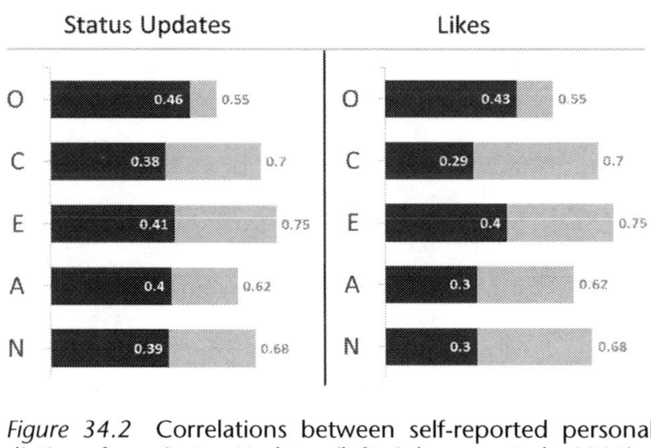

Figure 34.2 Correlations between self-reported personality and computer-based predictions from Status Updates (left, Schwartz et al., 2014) and Likes (right, Kosinski et al., 2012). The light grey bars indicate the baseline accuracy of the questionnaire, expressed as its test-retest reliability.

users, for example, most frequently use words like "party", " amazing" or "exciting", highly introverted users most frequently use words like "computer", "Internet" or "read".

Facebook Likes

Facebook Likes are particularly useful types of identity claims as they summarize most of the individual preferences outlines in Table 34.1 (e.g., favourite books, movies or political parties) and are publicly available by default. Furthermore, most preferences expressed via Likes are merely a mirror of preferences in the offline world. Liking "Lady Gaga" on Facebook, for example, can be interpreted as an expression of a general preference for the singer and her music rather than a preference that is unique to Facebook. Likes therefore constitute highly informative and generalizable pieces of user information. Using the Likes of 58,000 Facebook users, Kosinski, Stillwell and Graepel (2013) were able to accurately predict the Big Five traits. Figure 34.2 displays the correlations between the predicted and actual scores on each of the traits. Prediction accuracy was highest for Extraversion and Openness. In a follow-up paper, Wu, Kosinski and Stillwell (2015) further underlined the power of computer-based predictions by showing that the predictions made by computers were in fact more accurate than those made by co-workers, friends or even spouses. Only 10 Likes were needed to be more accurate than someone's co-workers, 70 to be more accurate than someone's friends, 150 to be more accurate than family members, and 300 to be more accurate than someone's spouse.

Taken together, personality predictions from digital footprints on Facebook reach an astonishingly high accuracy. Such predictions are not only fast and cheap, but also do not require consumers to complete tedious questionnaires. Hence, they provide marketers with a unique opportunity to learn more about the "psychology" of their consumers.

Transforming digital footprints into audience insights: Group-level and individual-level approaches

> *The goal is to turn data into information, and information into insight.*
>
> Carly Fiorina, former CEO of Hewlett-Packard

As Carly Fiorina has highlighted, large amounts of data on consumers alone are rather useless; what counts are the insights about consumers that we can gain from them. However, turning available data into useful consumer insights is far from trivial. In the following sections we present two different approaches that can be used for personality-customized advertising. First, we discuss how available information can be used to gain insights on the group level (group-level approach). Second, we outline how insights can be made more fine-grained by analyzing consumers on the level of the individual (individual-level approach). As we will discuss in Section 6, "Ethical considerations", the approaches differ with regard to their intrusiveness and amount of information that is made available on the individual user. The approaches outlined in the following sections can be applied to any type of digital footprints as well as any type of psychological data. This chapter illustrates the two approaches with the help of the myPersonality database, which is open-source for researchers. myPersonality was set up as a Facebook application in 2007 to establish large-scale empirical links between personality traits and Facebook profile information, including users' individual "Likes". Mostly free of charge, myPersonality offers users the possibility to take more than 25 psychometric tests such as the IPIP proxy for the NEO-PI-R inventory, Diener's Satisfaction with Life Scale and a computer-adaptive proxy of Ravens Standard Progressive Matrices. In return, users were encouraged to grant the application access to their personal profile and social network data, resulting in a database of more than 6,000,000 test results and information from over 4,000,000 user profiles (myPersonality Wiki, 2015). As test results from the psychometric questionnaires can easily be combined with users Facebook profile information, connections between psychological traits and certain profile features (e.g., Likes or status updates) can be established for an extremely large and heterogeneous sample.

Group-level insights

Based on more than 36,000,000 user-like pairs available in the myPersonality database, detailed psychological profiles can be extracted for each Facebook Like. Figure 34.3 illustrates the Big Five brand profiles of Maltesers and M&M's, which were gained from the average personality profiles of users who like their official Facebook pages. The question that remains is: How can these insights be leveraged for personality-customized advertising? Although group-level insights can be used to increase the effectiveness of offline campaigns – e.g., by tailoring the generic brand communication to the psychological profiles of customers – the possibilities of using such insights in the online environment are by far greater. For example, the insights on M&M's from above could be used to target users of a similar personality. All that is required for such an approach is to extract Likes with a similar personality profile as the one of "M&M's" from the myPersonality database and use them as Target-Likes in the "Interest" section within the Facebook advertising platform (see Section 4 for a case study using a similar approach).

Individual-level insights

Given that the accuracy of personality predictions increases with the amount of information available, insights about consumers' personal preferences and needs can be further enhanced by accessing their full Facebook profile and making predictions on the level of the individual user. Instead of targeting a group of users that is defined by only one Target-Like per person,

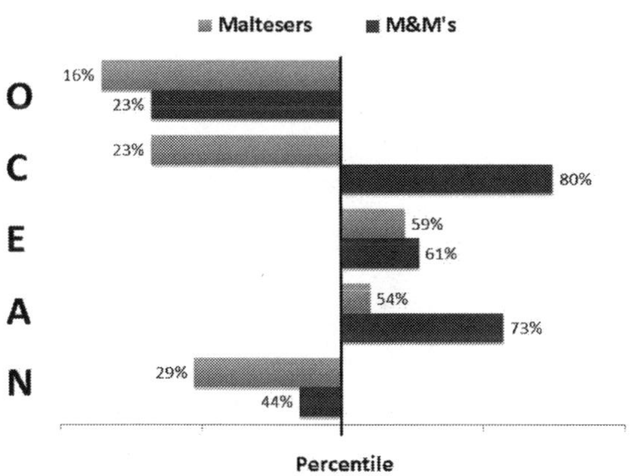

Figure 34.3 Big Five personality profiles for Maltesers and M&M's as extracted from the myPersonality database.

one could use adaptive prediction engines to estimate individuals' psychological profiles on the fly (for example, the University of Psychometrics Centre has developed the applymagicsauce.com API which is based on the models presented in Kosinski et al. [2012] and translates Facebook Likes and status updates into estimates of personality, intelligence, satisfaction with life, gender, age, political and religious views, and a number of other traits). Such an approach would not only make the manual set up of different Facebook ads redundant but would also provide much more detailed information about the individual user. Every time a user is registered by the engine, his or her psychological profile would be established automatically. This profile could then be used to display the most appealing content for each consumer. The more a consumer feels that his or her individual needs are understood and actively taken care of, the more likely he/she is to have a positive and enjoyable experience. This should in turn result in a higher likelihood of purchasing a product, being satisfied with the decision and feeling affiliated with the product/brand. In order to give users the opportunity to learn more about what their Facebook Likes say about their personality and other psychological traits, the University of Cambridge Psychometrics Centre has set up a website where users can log in with their Facebook account and access their predicted profile (applymagicsauce.com/you.html). As will be outlined in more detail in Section 5, individual-level approaches are more intrusive to users' privacy rights. Hence, although they have considerable advantages with regard to information quality they are also associated with a number of ethical challenges that need to be considered before implementing them.

Case studies

Given that the prediction of psychological traits from digital footprints is a highly innovative and very recent development, there are as of yet very few studies that demonstrate its value for fit-based advertising in the digital environment. This section therefore presents two case studies by the author and her colleagues which set out to answer the following questions: Can we increase the effectiveness of marketing campaigns on Facebook by targeting users based on their personality? Can we make the advertising even more effective by tailoring message content according to the dominant trait of the target audience?

Case study 1: Insurance company

Case study 1 was aimed at increasing the effectiveness of marketing campaigns for an insurance company by identifying the desired psychological profile of customers and subsequently targeting people of this profile in a real-life advertising campaign on Facebook. Together with the insurance company we first identified the characteristics of customers who add the biggest value to the company: people who (a) are willing to plan ahead and are concerned about potential future risks and who (b) are unlikely to claim their insurance. The Big Five Trait of Conscientiousness corresponds well to both of the criteria; it refers to the extent to which people prefer an organized or a flexible approach in life, and is thus concerned with the way in which we control, regulate and direct our impulses. People scoring high on Conscientiousness can be described as organized, reliable, perfectionist and efficient, while people scoring low on this trait are generally characterized as spontaneous, impulsive, careless, absentminded or disorganized (McCrae & John, 1992). Conscientious people are thus not only likely to be more interested in buying insurance but are also less likely to claim their insurance due to accidents.

Based on group-level insights from the myPersonality database (see section 3.1), we subsequently identified three different target Likes to define a "conscientious audience" on

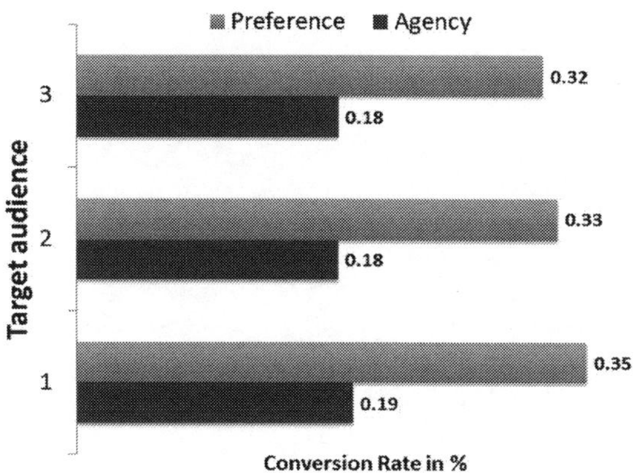

Figure 34.4 Comparison of psychological targeting (preference) against agency benchmark for three different Target Likes.

Facebook. We used Facebook targeting mechanisms to implement an A/B test where half of the company's budget was spent on our personality-based targeting aimed at conscientious people while the other half was spent on the benchmark targeting of the insurance company. Advertisements were sent to 16–17 year olds living in the UK over the course of a week. Overall, the campaigns resulted in more than 60 million views. The evaluation criterion "Conversion Rate" corresponded to the proportion of people entering their contact details after having clicked through to the website. As Figure 34.4 shows, all three personality-based target groups preference outperformed the three benchmark-target groups (agency), indicating that personality-based targeting is able to significantly increase the effectiveness of real-life advertising campaigns.

Case study 2: Crossword app

Following up on the findings of the first case study, Case study 2 was aimed at investigating the joint effects of product targeting and message tailoring. We promoted a crossword app that was known to be associated with Introversion and created two different advertisements reflecting introverted vs. extraverted message characteristics (Figure 34.5).

According to the description of extraverted people as being "active, assertive, energetic, enthusiastic, outgoing and talkative" (McCrae & John, 1992), the picture for the extraverted advertisement showed three young adults (two women, one man) laughing and playing the App on a tablet. The advertisement text of "Looking for excitement and fun? Play with friends and become a crossword champion" took account of extraverts' preference for other peoples' company, for excitement and novelty as well as for being in the centre of attention. For the introverted advertisement we chose a picture that showed only the hands of a person holding a tablet displaying the crossword app, together with the advertisement text of "Take some time for yourself! Sit down, relax and get immersed in the world of word puzzles". The advertisement design corresponded to the description of introverts as being "quiet, reserved, retiring, shy, silent, and withdrawn" (McCrae & John, 1992).

Both ads were advertised to extraverted and introverted users on Facebook (defined with the help of Target Likes, see Section 3.1). A total of 54,572 Facebook users saw at least one of the two ads. Figure 34.6 displays the results of the campaigns.

Figure 34.5 Extraverted (left) and introverted (right) advertisements used in Case study 2.

Conforming to the assumptions of product–person fit, we found that introverted Facebook users whose personality corresponded with that of the cross-word app clicked on the advertisement about 20 per cent more often than extraverted users. This effect becomes even more meaningful when considering that extraverts usually engage more in social networks than

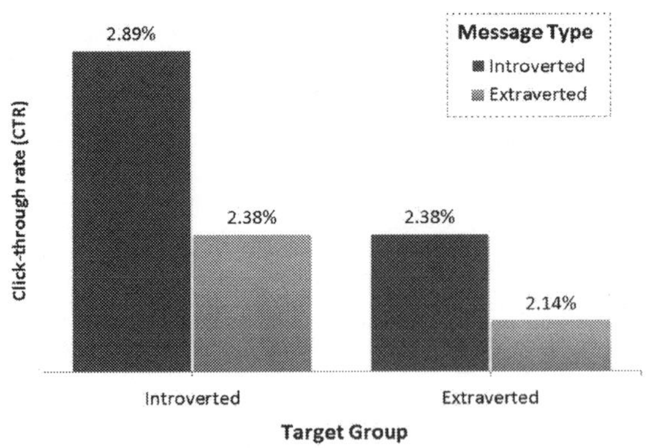

Figure 34.6 Click-through rate (CTR) for introverted vs. extraverted users (Target Group) and introverted vs. extraverted advertisements (Message Type).

introverts (Gosling et al., 2011). Contrary to the assumptions of message–person fit, there was no significant interaction between the advertisement characteristics and the personality of users. Even though introverted users showed a significant preference for the introverted advertisement, the expected preference for the extraverted advertisement was not confirmed for extraverted users. Although not significant, extraverted users in fact demonstrated a slight preference for the introverted rather than extraverted advertisement. This finding might indicate that message tailoring only works, if the message content does not contradict the inherent characteristics of the product itself. Indeed, messages that match consumers' personality but contradict that of the product run the risk of rendering advertising content too implausible for the positive effects of message–person congruence to show.

The aforementioned results clearly generate optimism for using personality-customized advertising in real-life online marketing. While the practical implications of previous studies were considerably limited by their laboratory-based nature and their use of self-report measures of personality, the case studies show that personality predictions from digital footprints make it possible to implement personality-based advertisement customisation in the real world.

Comparison to other customization approaches

Up to this point, we have referred to customized advertising as an approach that tries to increase the fit between a consumer and the products that are suggested to him/her or the marketing messages that are used to promote these products. However, there are other customization approaches that have been suggested and implemented in order to increase advertisement effectiveness. Most of them are data-driven recommendation models. Advocates of such approaches legitimately argue that in order to suggest the best products to consumers, one does not necessarily need to understand them on the level of their psychological characteristics. Instead, they use the vast number of digital footprints to recommend products on the basis of either consumers' past behaviour (e.g., using their search queries, unfinished check-out baskets or previously visited websites to retarget the same or a related product on a different platform) (Montaner et al., 2003) or the preferences of other consumers (e.g., the Amazon recommendation system "People who like X also like Y"). Although both approaches are known to increase the effectiveness of advertisements, they have a number of inherent limitations that can be overcome with fit-based approaches.

First, both approaches are restricted with regard to *what* they will suggest to consumers. While the first approach faces the problem that a consumer who has just bought a camera and equipment is highly unlikely to buy another one, the second approach is somehow constrained by the range of products that will be suggested. If a consumer has been searching for a book on "The art of cocktail mixing", for example, the products that will be recommended to him or her will all be related to cocktails. Following a fit-based approach, however, the fact that a person shows an interest in cocktail mixing could also be taken as an indicator of a strong social motive and a rather extraverted personality. Based on this information, other products could be suggested that match the same characteristics and satisfy the same needs – and are thus more likely to be of interest to the person – but do not directly relate to cocktails.

Second, neither of the two approaches provides any recommendations as to *how* to best communicate with consumers. The message they send is the same for all consumers, regardless of whether a consumer is male or female, old or young, introverted or extraverted. While using several hundreds or even thousands of dimensions to predict a consumer's future preference are likely to result in better targeting, the complexity of such purely data-driven approaches makes it almost impossible for marketers to grasp the "human element" of a consumer. This lack of understanding prevents them from tailoring their marketing messages in a way that appeals to the individual needs of consumers. By contrast, fit-based approaches offer theory-driven recommendations as to how to communicate with consumers in a way that appeals most to them. Indeed, the Big Five model of personality can easily be understood and exploited by marketers and their creative workforce in order to design highly personalised and engaging advertising content.

Third, none of the data-driven approaches enable marketers to reach out to audiences that are genuinely new while at the same time equally likely to purchase. The Facebook Look-Alike approach, for instance, suggest a list of target Likes of products that are similar to the product being promoted. Such an approach might be able to identify users that are more likely than average to show an interest in the product, but it also leads to users being swamped with advertisements for the same product category. As a consequence, businesses have to compete against all of their competitors in attracting the attention of a very restricted audience, which inflates the average price per impression and reduces the effectiveness of advertisements. Fit-based approaches avoid this problem by suggesting Likes that are independent of the specific product.

Ethical considerations

The use of personality predictions from digital footprints in applied marketing contexts raises an important ethical question: Is it legitimate to infer and use personal user characteristics from publicly available profile information without gaining individual consent? In fact, there is an on-going discussion among scientists as to whether the collection of publicly available data falls within the regulatory definition of Human Subject Research (HSR; Economic and Social Research Council, 2012), and therefore requires participants' consent and IRB approval (Kosinski, Matz, Gosling, Popov, & Stillwell, in press; Schultze & Mason, 2012; Solberg, 2010; Bruckman, 2002).

Taking account of the differences in the amount of information that is gathered on the individual user, we suggest separate guidelines for approaches that make predictions on the level of the group (group-level approach) and those that infer a psychological profile on the level of the individual (individual-level approach). In fact, the group-level approaches applied in the case studies presented in Section 4 are 100 per cent anonymous on the individual level. At no point in time is it possible to identify or track individual consumers. The only information that is made available is the overall performance of the target group or one of its subgroups (e.g., age bands or gender). Since, in this particular case, no personal information on users is collected, we suggest that no consent is required.

Researchers as well as marketers should be required to obtain informed consent, however, when they decide to collect and store personal user information. As only a fraction of users will agree to donate their data, individual-level approaches are more likely to be implemented as optional add-ons rather than fixed components of customization systems. However, we believe that researchers as well as businesses can influence the likelihood of users sharing their data by making user experience the primary goal of customization efforts. Indeed, as we have outlined at the beginning of this chapter, a sophisticated personalization mechanism does not only help businesses to maximise their profits but can also be used to increase consumer satisfaction by transforming advertisements into helpful information rather than irrelevant spam. Considering that we live in a world in which we are confronted with an abundance of information and choices every day, customized advertising can help us to reduce this complexity by pre-selecting a range of products and services that are most likely to satisfy our needs. For example, businesses could offer their customers an option to further improve and personalize their existing recommendation system by receiving access to their

Facebook profiles. Although at first glance such an approach might seem to benefit consumers more than researchers or businesses, a responsible and diligent implementation of customization mechanisms is of vital importance to maintain customers' trust and loyalty. Rather than running the risk of damaging one's reputation by secretly gathering and using highly personal information about consumers behind their backs, the outlined framework establishes a mutual agreement of "giving and taking" that is beneficial for both sides.

Summary

The Internet offers an unprecedented wealth of highly personal user information. Together with insights from psychological theories, this information can be used to make advertising more personal and relevant than ever before. Whereas marketers in traditional advertising contexts knew very little about the people they were advertising to, innovative prediction mechanisms make it possible to infer consumers' psychological traits from digital footprints such as Facebook data, browsing histories or Twitter feeds. The use of such insights within fit-based frameworks of customized advertising offers tremendous opportunities. On the one hand, businesses can gain a competitive advantage by making their advertising campaigns more effective. On the other, consumers can benefit from a better preselection of relevant information that reduces the abundance of information to a manageable level while at the same time making it more engaging and personal. To make the most of the opportunities offered by personality-based advertising customization, however, it will be necessary to establish ethical guidelines that respect consumers' privacy rights and highlight a value exchange that is mutually beneficial.

References

Aaker, J. L. (1997). Dimensions of brand personality. *Journal of Marketing Research, 34*(3), 347–356. doi: 10.2307/3151897

Aaker, J. L. (1999). The malleable self: The role of self-expression in persuasion. *Journal of Marketing Research, 36*(2), 45–57.

Aguirre-Rodriguez, A., Bosnjak, M., & Sirgy, M. J. (2012). Moderators of the self-congruity effect on consumer decision-making: A meta-analysis. *Journal of Business Research, 65*, 1179–1188. doi: 10.1016/j.jbusres.2011.07.031

Amichai-Hamburger, Y., & Vinitzky, G. (2010). Social network use and personality. *Computers in Human Behaviour, 26*, 1289–1295.

Avnet, T., & Higgins, E. T. (2006). How regulatory fit affects value in consumer choices and opinions. *Journal of Marketing Research, 43*, 1–10. doi: 10.1509/jmkr.43.1.1

Bachrach, Y., Kosinski, M., Graepel, T., Kohli, P., & Stillwell, D. (2012, June). Personality and patterns of Facebook usage. In *Proceedings of the 4th Annual ACM Web Science Conference* (pp. 24–32). ACM.

Back, K. J. (2005). The effects of image congruence on hotel customers' brand loyalty. *Journal of Hospitality and Tourism Research, 28*(4), 448–467.

Back, M. D., Stopfer, J. M., Vazire, S., Gaddis, S., Schmukle, S. C., Egloff, B., & Gosling, S. D. (2009). Facebook profiles reflect actual personality, not self-idealization. *Psychological Science, 21*(3), 372–374. doi: 10.1177/0956797609360756

Boyd, D. M., & Ellison, N. B. (2007). Social network sites: Definition, history and scholarship. *Journal of Computer-Mediated Communication, 13*, 210–230.

Bruckman, A. (2002). Studying the amateur artist: A perspective on disguising data collected in human subjects research on the Internet. *Ethics and Information Technology, 4*(3), 217–231.

Byrne, D. (1961). Interpersonal attraction and attitude similarity. *Journal of Abnormal and Social Psychology, 62*, 713–715. doi: 10.1037/h0044721

Byrne, D., & Nelson, D. (1965). Attraction as a linear function of proportion of positive reinforcement. *Journal of Personality and Social Psychology, 1*, 659–663. doi: 10.1037/h0022073

Cervone, D., & Pervin, L. A. (2013). *Personality: Theory and research* (12th Edition). Hoboken, NJ: Wiley.

Cesario, J., Grant, H., & Higgins, E. T. (2004). Regulatory fit and persuasion: Transfer from "feeling right". *Journal of Personality and Social Psychology, 86*, 388–404.

Costa Jr., P. T., & McCrae, R. R. (1985). *The NEO personality inventory manual*. Odessa, FL: Psychological Assessment Resources.

CPC Strategy. (2015, March 6). *How many people shop online?* Retrieved from www.cpcstrategy.com/blog/2013/08/ecommerce-infographic/

Economic and Social Research Council. (2012). *ESRC framework for research ethics 2010* (revised September 2012).

Emarketers. (2015, March 10). *Global B2C ecommerce sales to hit $1.5 trillion this year driven by growth in emerging markets*. Retrieved from www.emarketer.com/Article/Global-B2C-Ecommerce-Sales-Hit-15-Trillion-This-Year-Driven-by-Growth-Emerging-Markets/1010575

Go Gulf. (2015, March 10). *How people spend their time online*. Retrieved from www.go-gulf.com/blog/online-time/

Golbeck, J., Robles, C., Edmondson, M., & Turner, K. (2011). Predicting personality from twitter. In *Proceedings of the International Conference on Privacy, Security, Risk and Trust and IEEE International Conference on Social Computing* (pp. 149–156).

Goldberg, L. R. (1992). The development of markers for the Big-Five factor structure. *Psychological Assessment, 4*(1), 26–42.

Gosling, S. D., Augustine, A. A., Vazire, S., Holtzman, N., & Gaddis, S. (2011). Manifestations of personality in online social networks: Self-reported Facebook-related behaviours and observable profile information. *Cyberpsychology, Behaviour, and Social Networking, 14*(9), 483–488. doi: 10.1089/cyber.2010.0087

Gosling, S. D., Ko, S., Mannarelli, T., & Morris, M. E. (2002). A room with a cue: Personality judgments based on offices and bedrooms. *Journal of Personality and Social Psychology (JPSP), 82*(3), 379–398.

Higgins, E. T. (2000). Making a good decision: Value from fit. *American Psychologist, 5*, 1217–1230. doi: 10.1037/0003-066X.55.11.1217

Higgins, E. T., Idson, L. C., Freitas, A. L., Spiegel, S., & Molden, D. C. (2003). Transfer of value from fit. *Journal of Personality and Social Psychology, 84*, 1140–1153. doi: 10.1037/0022-3514.84.6.1140

Hirsh, J. B., Kang, S. K., & Bodenhausen, G. V. (2012). Personalized persuasion: Tailoring persuasive appeals to recipient"s personality traits. *Psychological Science, 23*(6), 578–581. doi: 10.1177/0956797611436349

Koenig, A. M., Cesario, J., Molden, D. C., Kosloff, S., & Higgins, E. T. (2009). Experiences of incidental regulatory fit and the depth of processing of persuasive appeals. *Personality and Social Psychology Bulletin, 35*, 1342–1355. doi:10.1177/0146167209339076

Kosinski, M., Matz, S. C., Gosling, S., Popov, V., & Stillwell, D. (2015). Facebook as a social science research tool: Opportunities, challenges, ethical considerations and practical guidelines. *American Psychologist, 70*(6), 543–556.

Kosinski, M., Stillwell, D. J., & Graepel, T. (2013). Private traits and attributes are predictable from digital records of human behaviour. *Proceedings of the National Academy of Sciences of the United States of America, 110*(15), 5802–5805.

Kosinski, M., Bachrach, Y., Kohli, P., Stillwell, D., & Graepel, T. (2014). Manifestations of user personality in website choice and behaviour on online social networks. *Machine learning, 95*(3), 357–380.

Kressmann, F., Sirgy, M. J., Herrmann, A., Huber, F., Huber, S., & Lee, D.-J. (2006). Direct and indirect effects of self-image congruence on brand loyalty. *Journal of Business Research, 59*, 955–964. doi: 10.1016/j.jbusres.2006.06.001

Lecky, P. (1945). *Self-consistency: A theory of personality*. New York, NY: Island Press.

Lee, A. Y., & Aaker, J. L. (2004). Bringing the frame into focus: The influence of regulatory fit on processing fluency and persuasion. *Journal of Personality and Social Psychology, 86*, 205–218. doi: 10.1037/0022-3514.86.2.205

Levy. S. J. (1959). Symbols for sale. *Harvard Business Review, 37*(4), 117–124.

Liang, T.-P., Lai, H.-J., & Ku Y.-C. (2006). Personalized content recommendation and user satisfaction: Theoretical synthesis and empirical findings. *Journal of Management Information Systems, 23*(3), 45–70.

Malhotra, N. K. (1988). Self-concept and product choice: An integrated perspective. *Journal of Economic Psychology, 9*, 1–28. doi: 10.1016/0167-4870(88)90029-3

Marcus, B., Machilek, F., & Schütz, A. (2006). Personality in cyberspace: Personal web sites as media for personality expressions and impressions. *Journal of Personality and Social Psychology (JPSP), 90*(6), 1014–1031.

McCrae, R. R., & John, O. P. (1992). An introduction to the five-factor model and its applications. *Journal of Personality, 60*(2), 175–215. doi: 10.1111/j.1467-6494.1992.tb00970.x

Montaner, M., Lopez, B., & de la Rosa, J. L. (2003). A taxonomy of recommender agents on the Internet. *Artificial Intelligence Review, 19*, 285–330.

Moon, Y. (2002). Personalization and personality: Some effects of customizing message style based on consumer personality. *Journal of Consumer Psychology, 12*(4), 313–326. doi: 10.1207/15327660260382351

MyPersonality Wiki. (2015). Some Stats about myPersonality. Retrieved March 2, 2012 from http://mypersonality.org/wiki/doku.php

Park, G., Kosinski, M., Stillwell, D., Eichstaedt, J., Schwartz, A., Kern, P., & Seligman, M. (2014). Automatic personality assessment through social media language. *Journal of Personality and Social Psychology (JPSP), 108*(6), 934–952.

Quercia, D., Kosinski, M., Stillwell, D. J., & Crowcroft, J. (2011). Our Twitter profiles, our selves: Predicting personality with Twitter. *IEEE International Conference on Social Computing: Proceedings of the 2011 IEEE International Conference on Privacy, Security, Risk, and Trust, and IEEE International Conference on Social Computing*, pp 180–185.

Schultze, U., & Mason, R. O. (2012). Studying cyborgs: Re-examining Internet studies as human subjects research. *Journal of Internet Technology, 27*(4), 301–312.

Schwartz, H. A., Eichstaedt, J. C., Kern, M. L., Dziurzynski, L., Ramones, S. M., Agrawal, M., & Ungar, L. H. (2013). Personality, gender, and age in the language of social media: The open-vocabulary approach. *PLoS ONE, 8*(9).

Schwartz, B., & Ward, A. (2004). Doing better but feeling worse: The paradox of choice. In P. A. Linley & S. Joseph (Eds.), *Positive psychology in practice*. Hoboken, NJ: Wiley. doi: 10.1002/9780470939338.ch6

Sheth, J. N., Sisodia, R. S., & Sharma, A. (2000). The antecedents and consequences of customer-centric marketing. *Journal of the Academy of Marketing Science*, 28(1), 55–66.

Sirgy, M. J. (1985). Self-image/product image congruity and consumer decision making. *International Journal of Management, 2*(4), 49–63.

Sirgy, M. J. (1986). Using self-congruity and ideal congruity to predict purchase motivation. *Journal of Business Research, 13*(1), 195–206.

Solberg, L. (2010). Data mining on facebook: A free space for researchers or an irb nightmare? *University of Illinois Journal of Law, Technology and Policy, 2*, 311–343.

Spiegel, S., Grant-Pillow, H., & Higgins, E. T. (2004). How regulatory fit enhances motivational strength during goal pursuit. *European Journal of Social Psychology, 39*, 39–54.

Wilson, R. E., Gosling, S. D., & Graham, L. T. (2012). A review of Facebook research in the social sciences. *Perspectives on Psychological Science*, 7(3), 203–220. doi: 10.1177/1745691612442904

Wu, Y., Kosinski, M., & Stillwell, D. (2015). Computer-based personality judgments are more accurate than those made by humans. *Proceedings of the National Academy of Sciences of the USA (PNAS)*.

Author index

Subject index

Made in the USA
Monee, IL
13 September 2026

62977682R10411